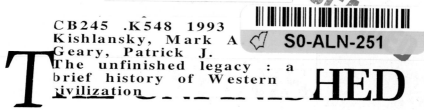

THE UNFINISHED

LEGACY

A Brief History of
Western Civilization

MARK KISHLANSKY
Harvard University

PATRICK GEARY
University of Florida

PATRICIA O'BRIEN
University of California, Irvine

■ HarperCollins*CollegePublishers*

Executive Editor: Bruce Borland
Developmental Editor: Marisa L. L'Heureux
Project Coordination, Text and Cover Design: York Production Services
Cover Illustration/Photo: The Bodleian Library, Oxford, Ms.Bodl.264 fol.218r
Photo Researcher: Sandy Schneider
Production/Manufacturing: Michael Weinstein/Paula Keller
Compositor: York Production Services
Printer and Binder: R.R. Donnelley & Sons Company
Cover Printer: The Lehigh Press, Inc.

The Unfinished Legacy: A Brief History of Western
Civilization

Library of Congress Cataloging-in-Publication Data

Kishlansky, Mark A.
    The unfinished legacy : a brief history of western civilization / Mark
Kishlansky, Patrick Geary, Patricia O'Brien.
        p.   cm.
    Includes bibliographical and index.
    ISBN 0-673-46604-3
    1. Civilization, Western—History.   I. Geary, Patrick J., 1948–
    II. O'Brien, Patricia, 1945–   .   III. Title.
CB245.K548   1993
909'.09812—dc20   93-37246
                                                                   CIP

92 93 94 95 9 8 7 6 5 4 3 2 1

Brief Contents

Detailed Contents

5 Imperial Rome and the Changing Classical World 146

6 The Classical Legacy in the East: Byzantium and Islam 190

17 *Industrial Europe* 618

18 *Revolutions and Reforms, 1815–1871* 656

21 Searching for Stability: Europe, 1920–1932 776

22 Crisis and Global Conflict, 1933–1945 812

Maps, Timelines, and Dynastic Charts

Maps

Timelines

Dynastic Charts

Preface

When we set out to write *Civilization in the West*, we tried to write, first of all, a book that students would *want* to read. Throughout many years of planning, writing, revising, rewriting, and numerous meetings together, this was our constant overriding concern. Would the text work across the variety of Western Civilization courses, with the different levels and formats that make up this fundamental course? It was not easy to keep this concern in the forefront through the long months of composition, but it was easy to receive the reaction of scores of reviewers to this single question: "Would students *want* to read these chapters?" Whenever we received a resounding "No!" we began again—not just rewriting, but rethinking how to present material that might be complex in argument or detail or that might simply seem too remote to engage the contemporary student. Though all three of us were putting in long hours in front of word processors, we quickly learned that we were engaged in a teaching rather than a writing exercise. And though the work was demanding, it was not unrewarding. We enjoyed writing this book, and we wanted students to enjoy reading it.

The result of our efforts was a book that successfully accomplished our objectives. It stimulated student interest and motivated students to read about and enjoy the study of European history. With its flair, its eloquence, and its literary merit, *Civilization in the West* was successful beyond our expectations.

The text has been so well received, in fact, that we have decided to publish this alternative version. *The Unfinished Legacy: A Brief History of Western Civilization* is briefer than the original text and is published in a different format. It is designed for students, as our 1991 edition was, but *The Unfinished Legacy* is also designed for the general reader interested in a history of European civilization.

There is no doubt that there is great value in the standard Western civilization textbook, with its fully detailed narrative, pedagogical features, and learning aids. But, in an era of rapidly changed educational materials, there should be alternative formats and models available. We believe that students and general readers alike will enjoy a conveniently sized book that offers them a coherent, well-told story in single-column format.

pproach

The approach used in *The Unfinished Legacy: A Brief History of Western Civilization* upholds and confirms a number of decisions made early in the writing of *Civilization in the West*. First, this brief, alternative version is, like the full-length text, a mainstream text in which most energies have been placed in developing a solid, readable narrative of Western civilization that integrates coverage of women and minorities into the discussion. We highlight personalities while identifying trends. We spotlight social history, both in sections of chapters and in separate chapters, while maintaining a firm grip on political developments.

Neither *The Unfinished Legacy: A Brief History of Western Civilization* nor *Civilization in the West* is meant to be an encyclopedia of Western civilization. Information is not included in a chapter unless it fits within the themes of that chapter. In both the full-length and brief versions of this text, we are committed to integrating the history of ordinary men and women into our narrative. We believe that isolated sections placed at the end of chapters that deal with the experiences of women or minority groups in a particular era profoundly distort historical experience. We call this technique *caboosing*, and whenever we found ourselves segregating women or families or the masses, we stepped back and asked how we might recast our treatment of historical events to account for a diversity of actors. How did ordinary men, women, and children affect the course of world historical events? How did world historical events affect the fabric of daily life for men, women, and children from all walks of life? We tried to rethink critical historical problems of civilization as gendered phenomena.

We take the same approach to the coverage of central and eastern Europe that we did to women and minorities. Even before the epochal events of the late 1980s and early 1990s that returned this region to the forefront of international attention, we realized that in many textbooks the Slavic world was treated as "marginal" to the history of Western civilization. Thus, we worked to integrate more of the history of eastern Europe into our text than is found in most others, and to do so in a way that presented these regions, their cultures, and their institutions as integral rather than peripheral to Western civilization.

*F*eatures

We wanted to reuse in *The Unfinished Legacy: A Brief History of Western Civilization* those features that had the most immediate and positive impact on our readers and fulfilled our goal of involving students in learning. Thus, *The Unfinished Legacy* features pictorial chapter openers in which an illustration—a painting, a photograph, an artifact, an edifice—appears at the beginning of each chapter, accompanied by text through which we explore the picture, guiding students across a canvas or helping them see in an artifact or a piece of architecture details that are not immediately apparent. It is the direct combination of text and image that allows us to achieve this effect, to "unfold" both an illustration and a theme. All of the opening images have been chosen to illustrate a dominant theme within the chapter, and the dramatic and lingering impression they make helps reinforce that theme.

The Unfinished Legacy continues the image-based approach to the presentation of geography used in *Civilization in the West*. When teachers of Western civilization courses are surveyed, no single area of need is cited more often than geographical knowledge. Students simply have no mental image of Europe, no familiarity with those geophysical features that are a fundamental part of the geopolitical realities of Western history. Maps, carefully planned and skillfully executed, are an important component of our text. In addition to the standard map program, several times throughout the text, we pause in the narrative to take a tour of Europe. Sometimes we follow an emperor as he tours his realm; sometimes we examine the impact of a peace treaty; sometimes we follow the travels of a merchant. The number of maps throughout the text, the tour-of-Europe geographical feature, and the ancillary program of map transparencies and workbook exercises combine to provide the strongest possible program for teaching historical geography.

There are several reasons why the time is now right for a new survey of Western civilization , appropriate for both students and general readers. The sudden, dramatic political and social changes that have taken place in Europe have resulted in a surge of new interest in European history. In addition, there has been in the last decade a tremendous amount of new historical research on such topics as social history and gender. What historians study, the issues they are interested in, and what they have learned have changed significantly. The moment is now for a new survey of European history that both presents this new information and integrates it effectively into the familiar story.

*A*cknowledgments

We want to thank the many conscientious historians who reviewed our manuscript and gave generously of their time and knowledge. Their valuable critiques and suggestions have contributed greatly to the final product. We are grateful to the following:

Frank Lee Earley, *Arapahoe Community College*
Gary L. Johnson, *University of Southern Maine*
John M. McCulloh, *Kansas State University*
Martha G. Newman, *University of Texas at Austin*
Steven G. Reinhardt, *University of Texas at Arlington*
Maryloy Ruud, *University of West Florida*
Jose M. Sanchez, *St. Louis University*
Erwin Sicher, *Southwestern Adventist College*
John E. Weakland, *Ball State University*

We also acknowledge the assistance of the many reviewers of *Civilization in the West* whose comments have been invaluable in the development of *The Unfinished Legacy*.

Meredith L. Adams, *Southwest Missouri State University*
John W. Barker, *University of Wisconsin*
William H. Beik, *Emory University*
Lenard R. Berlanstein, *University of Virginia*
Raymond Birn, *University of Oregon*
Donna Bohanan, *Auburn University*
Werner Braatz, *University of Wisconsin at Oshkosh*
Thomas A. Brady, Jr., *University of California at Berkeley*
Anthony M. Brescia, *Nassau Community College*
Elaine G. Breslaw, *Morgan State University*
Daniel Patrick Brown, *Moorpark College*
Ronald A. Brown, *Charles County Community College*
Edward J. Champlin, *Princeton University*
Stephanie Evans Christelow, *Western Washington University*
Gary B. Cohen, *University of Oklahoma*
John J. Contreni, *Purdue University*
Samuel E. Dicks, *Emporia State University*
Frederick Dumin, *Washington State University*
Margot C. Finn, *Emory University*
Allan W. Fletcher, *Boise State University*
Elizabeth L. Furdell, *University of North Florida*
Thomas W. Gallant, *University of Florida*
Joseph J. Godson, *Hudson Valley Community College*
Eric Haines, *Bellevue Community College*
David A. Harnett, *University of San Francisco*
Paul B. Harvey, Jr., *Pennsylvania State University*
Daniel W. Hollis, *Jacksonville State University*
Kenneth G. Holum, *University of Maryland*
Charles Ingrao, *Purdue University*
George F. Jewsbury, *Oklahoma State University*
Donald G. Jones, *University of Central Arkansas*
William R. Jones, *University of New Hampshire*
Richard W. Kaeuper, *University of Rochester*
David Kaiser, *Carnegie-Mellon University*
William R. Keylor, *Boston University*
Joseph Kicklighter, *Auburn University*
Charles L. Killinger, III, *Valencia Community College*
David C. Large, *Montana State University*

Roberta T. Manning, *Boston College*
Lyle McAlister, *University of Florida*
Therese M. McBride, *College of the Holy Cross*
Robert Moeller, *University of California at Irvine*
Pierce C. Mullen, *Montana State University*
Thomas F. X. Noble, *University of Virginia*
Dennis H. O'Brien, *West Virginia University*
Peter E. Piccillo, *Rhode Island College*
Marlette Rebhorn, *Austin Community College*
John P. Ryan, *Kansas City Kansas Community College*
Steven Schroeder, *Indiana University of Pennsylvania*
Bonnie Smith, *Rutgers University*
Peter N. Stearns, *Carnegie-Mellon University*
Darryl R. Sycher, *Columbus State Community College*
Steven Vincent, *North Carolina State University*
Richard A. Voeltz, *Cameron University*
Eric Weissman, *Golden West College*

Each author also received invaluable assistance and encouragement from many colleagues, friends, and family members over the years of research, reflection, writing, and revising that went into the making of this text.

Mark Kishlansky wishes to thank Ann Adams, Robert Bartlett, Ray Birn, David Buisseret, Ted Cook, Frank Conaway, Constantine Fasolt, Katherine Haskins, Richard Hellie, Matthew Kishlansky, Donna Marder, Mary Beth Rose, Jeanne Thiel, the staff of the Joseph Regenstein Library, and the Newberry Library.

Patrick Geary wishes to thank Mary Geary, Catherine Geary, and Anne Geary for their patience, support, and encouragement, as well as Anne Picard and Dale Schofield for their able assistance throughout the project.

Patricia O'Brien thanks Jon Jacobson for his constant support and for sharing his specialized knowledge and his historical sense. She also wishes to thank Elizabeth Bryant for her encouragement and enthusiasm throughout the project; Robert Moeller for his keen eye for organization and his suggestions for writing a gendered history; and Katherine Turley for her unflagging assistance with bibliographic issues.

All the authors would also like to thank, though words are but a poor expression of our gratitude, Bruce Borland, Betty Slack, Susan Ritchey, and Marisa L'Heureux. If ever authors have had more felicitous experiences with their editors than we have had with ours, they have been lucky indeed. The authors also extend sincere appreciation to Michael Weinstein, Paula Cousin, and Sandy Schneider, who contributed their skills and expertise to the editorial, production, and photo research, processes involved in this book.

upplements

For instructors:

Instructor's Resource Manual   Margot C. Finn, *Emory University*

This thorough instructor's manual contains an introductory essay on "Teaching Western Civilization" and a bibliographic essay on the use of primary sources for class discussion and analytical thinking. For each text chapter it provides a brief summary, list of key terms, and several discussion or examination questions.

Discovering Western Civilization Through Maps and Views
Gerald Danzer, *University of Illinois, Chicago*

Created by the recipient of the AHA's 1989 James Harvey Robinson Award for his work in the development of map transparencies, this set of 140 four-color acetates is a unique instructional tool. It contains an introduction on teaching history through maps and a detailed commentary on each transparency. The collection includes cartographic and pictoral maps, views and photos, urban plans, building diagrams and works of art.

Test Bank   John Paul Bischoff, *Oklahoma State University*
Daniel Patrick Brown, *Moorpark College*

Approximately 50 multiple-choice and essay questions per chapter. Multiple-choice items are referenced by topic, text page number, and type (factual or interpretive).

TestMaster Computerized Testing System

This flexible, easy-to-master computer test bank includes all the test items in the printed Test Bank. The TestMaster software allows you to edit existing questions and add your own items. Tests can be printed in several different formats and can include figures such as graphs and tables. Available for IBM and Macintosh computers.

Grades

A grade-keeping and classroom management software program that maintains data for up to 200 students.

Visual Enhancements

There are further visual enhancements to accompany HarperCollins Western civilization texts. Instructor's who are interested should discuss these with their college sales representative.

For students:

Study Guide   Steven Schroeder, *Indiana University of Pennsylvania*
Werner Braatz, *University of Wisconsin, Oshkosh*

Available in one volume, this guide offers for each text chapter a summary, glossary list, and self-quiz items, including identification, multiple-choice, and essay questions.

SuperShell Computerized Tutorial   Ken Weatherbie,
Delmar College

This interactive program for IBM computers helps students learn the major facts and concepts through drill and practice exercises and diagnostic feedback. SuperShell provides immediate correct answers and the text page number on which the material is discussed. Missed questions appear with greater frequency; a running score of the student's performance is maintained on the screen throughout the session.

Mapping Western Civilization: Student Activities   Gerald Danzer,
University of Illinois, Chicago

A free map workbook for students featuring exercises designed to teach students to interpret and analyze cartographic materials as historical documents. The instructor is entitled to a free copy of the workbook for each copy of the text purchased from HarperCollins.

TimeLink Computer Atlas of Western Civilization   William Hamblin,
Brigham Young University

An introductory software tutorial and textbook companion. This Macintosh program covers material on European developments from 400 to 1500 AD. Students can watch animated maps display geopolitical changes and study special topics including the Anglo-Saxon migration to Britain and the Hundred Years War.

Mark Kishlansky
Patrick Geary
Patricia O'Brien

About the Authors

Mark Kishlansky

Recently appointed Professor of History at Harvard University, Mark Kishlansky is among today's leading young scholars. Professor Kishlansky received his Ph.D. from Brown University and is a member of the Harvard University faculty. A Fellow of the Royal Historical Society, his primary area of expertise is seventeenth-century English political history. Among his main publications are *Parliamentary Selection: Social and Political Choice in Early Modern England* and *The Rise of the New Model Army*. He is the editor of the *Journal of British Studies* and the recipient of the 1989 Most Distinguished Alumnus Award from SUNY Stony Brook.

Patrick Geary

Holding a Ph.D. in Medieval Studies from Yale University, Patrick Geary is both a noted scholar and teacher. Named outstanding undergraduate history teacher for the 1986–87 year at the University of Florida, where he currently teaches, Professor Geary has also held academic positions at the École des hautes études en sciences sociales, Paris; the Universitat Wien; and Princeton University. His many publications include *Readings in Medieval History; Before France and Germany: The Creation* and *Transformation of the Merovingian World; Aristocracy in Provence: The Rhone Basin at the Dawn of the Carolingian Age;* and *Furta Sacra: Thefts of Relics in the Central Middle Ages.*

Patricia O'Brien

Professor O'Brien teaches at the University of California, Irvine, and is Associate Vice Chancellor in the Office of Research and Graduate Studies, Professor O'Brien holds a Ph.D. from Columbia University in modern European history. Among her many publications are *The Promise of Punishment: Prisons in 19th Century France; "l'Embastillement de Paris: The Fortification of Paris During the July Monarchy";* and *"Crime and Punishment as Historical Problems."*

THE UNFINISHED

LEGACY

*A Brief History of
Western Civilization*

1

The First Civilizations

The Idea of Civilization

The West is an idea. It is not visible from space. An astronaut viewing the blue-and-white terrestrial sphere can make out the forms of Africa, bounded by the Atlantic, the Indian Ocean, the Red Sea, and the Mediterranean. Australia, the Americas, and even Antarctica are distinct patches of blue-green in the darker waters that surround them. But nothing comparable separates Europe from Asia, East from West. Viewed from 100 miles up, the West itself is invisible. Although astronauts can see the great Eurasian landmass curving around the Northern Hemisphere, the Ural Mountains, the theoretical boundary between East and West, appear but faintly from space. Certainly they are less impressive than the towering Himalaya, the Alps, or even the Caucasus. People, not geology, determined that the Urals should be the arbitrary boundary between Europe and Asia.

Even this determination took centuries. Originally, Europe was a name that referred only to central Greece. Gradually, Greeks extended it to include the whole Greek mainland and then the landmass to the north. Later, Roman explorers and soldiers carried Europe north and west to its modern boundaries. Asia, too, grew with time. Initially, Asia was only that small portion of what is today Turkey inland from the Aegean Sea. Gradually, as Greek explorers came to know of lands farther east, north, and south, they expanded their understanding of Asia to include everything east of the Don River to the north and the Red Sea to the south.

Western civilization is as much an idea as the West itself. Under the right conditions, astronauts can see the Great Wall of China snaking its way from the edge of the Himalaya to the Yellow Sea. No comparable physical legacy of the

2

West is so massive that its details can be discerned from space. Nor are Western achievements rooted forever in one corner of the world. What we call Western civilization belongs to no particular place. Its location has changed since the origins of civilization, that is, the cultural and social traditions characteristic of the *civitas*, or city. "Western" cities appeared first outside the "West," in the Tigris and Euphrates river basins in present-day Iraq and Iran, a region we today term the Middle East. These areas have never lost their urban traditions, but in time other cities in North Africa, Greece, and Italy adapted and expanded this heritage.

Until the sixteenth century after Jesus, the western end of the Eurasian landmass, what we think of as western Europe, was the crucible in which disparate cultural and intellectual traditions of the Near East, the Mediterranean, and the North were smelted into a new and powerful alloy. Then the "West" expanded beyond the confines of Europe, carried by the ships of merchants and adventurers to India, Africa, China, and the Americas.

Western technology for harnessing nature, Western forms of economic and political organization, Western styles of art and music are—for good or ill—dominant influences in world civilization. Japan is a leading power in the Western traditions of capitalist commerce and technology. China, the most populous country in the world, adheres to Marxist socialist principles—a European political tradition. Millions of people in Africa, Asia, and the Americas follow the religions of Islam and Christianity. Both are monotheistic faiths that developed from Judaism in the cradle of Western civilization.

3

Many of today's most pressing problems are also part of the legacy of the Western tradition. The remnants of European colonialism have left deep hostilities around the globe. The integration of developing nations into the world economy keeps much of humanity in a seemingly hopeless cycle of poverty as the wealth of poor countries goes to pay interest on loans from Europe and America. Western material goods lure millions of people from their traditional worlds into the sprawl of third-world cities. The West itself faces a crisis. Impoverished citizens of former colonies flock to Europe and North America seeking a better life but often finding instead poverty, hostility, and racism. Finally, the advances of Western civilization endanger our very existence. Technology pollutes the world's air, water, and soil, and nuclear arms threaten the destruction of all civilization. And yet these are the same advances that allow us to lengthen life expectancy, harness the forces of nature, and conquer disease. It is the same technology that allows us to view our world from outer space.

How did we get here? In this book we attempt to answer this question. This history of Western civilization is not simply the triumphal story of progress, the creation of a better world. Even in areas in which we can see development, such as technology, communications, and social complexity, change is not always for the better. However, it would be equally inaccurate to view Western civilization as a progressive decline from a mythical golden age of the human race. The roughly three hundred generations since the origins of civilization have bequeathed a rich and contradictory legacy to the present. Inherited political and social institutions, cultural forms, and religious and philosophical traditions form the framework within which the future must be created. The past does not determine the future, but it is the raw material from which the future will be made. To use this legacy properly, we must first understand it, not because the past is the key to the future, but because understanding yesterday frees us to create tomorrow.

$\mathcal{B}$efore Civilization

The human race was already ancient by the time civilization first appeared around 3500 years before the traditional date of the birth of Jesus. (Such dates are abbreviated B.C. for "before Christ"; A.D., the abbreviation of the Latin for "in the year of the Lord," is used to refer to dates after the birth of Jesus.) The first humanlike creatures whose remains have been discovered date from as long as five million years ago. One of the best known finds, nicknamed "Lucy" by the scientist who discovered her skeleton in 1974, stood

4

only about four feet tall and lived on the edge of a lake in what is now Ethiopia. Lucy and her band did not have brains that were as well developed as those of modern humans. They did, however, use simple tools such as sticks, bone clubs, and perhaps chipped rocks. Although small and relatively weak compared with other animals, Lucy's species of creatures—neither fully apes nor human—survived for over four million years.

Varieties of the modern species of humans, *Homo sapiens* (thinking human), appeared well over one hundred thousand years ago and spread across the Eurasian landmass and Africa. The earliest *Homo sapiens* in Europe, the *Neanderthal,* differed little from us today. Although the term *Neanderthal* has gained a negative image in the popular imagination, these early humans were roughly the same size and had the same cranial capacity as we. They spread throughout much of Africa, Europe, and Asia during the last great ice age. To survive in the harsh tundra landscape, they developed a cultural system that enabled them to modify their environment. Customs such as the burial of their dead with food offerings indicate that Neanderthals may have developed a belief in an afterlife. Thus they apparently had the capacity for carrying on intellectual activities such as abstract and symbolic thought.

No one knows why or how the Neanderthals were replaced by our subspecies, *Homo sapiens sapiens* (thinking thinking human), around forty thousand years ago. Whatever the reason and whatever the process—extinction, evolution, interbreeding, or extermination—this last arrival on the human scene was universally successful. All humans today, whether blond, blue-eyed Scandinavians, Australian aborigines, Africans, Japanese, or Amerindians, belong to this same subspecies. Differences in skin color, type of hair, or build are minor variations on the same theme. The identification of races, while selectively based on some of these physical variations, is, like civilization itself, a fact not of biology but of culture.

Early *Homo sapiens sapiens* lived in small kin groups of 20 or 30, following game and seeking shelter in tents, lean-tos, and caves. People of the Paleolithic era or Old Stone Age (ca. 600,000–10,000 B.C.) worked together for hunting and defense and apparently formed emotional bonds based on more than sex or economic necessity. The skeleton of a man found a few years ago in Iran, for example, suggests that although he was born with one arm and was crippled further by arthritis, the rest of his community supported him and he lived to adulthood. Clearly his value to his society lay in something more than his ability to make a material contribution to its collective life.

During the upper or late Paleolithic era (ca. 35,000–10,000 B.C.), *culture,* meaning everything about humans not inherited biologically, was increasingly determinant in human life. Paleolithic people were not on an endless and all-consuming quest to provide for the necessities of life. They spent less time on such things than we do today. Thus they found time to develop speech, religion, and artistic expression. Wall paintings, small clay and stone figurines of female figures (which may reflect concerns about fertility), and finely decorated stone and bone tools indicate not just artistic ability but also abstract and symbolic thought.

The arid wastes of Africa's Sahara Desert may seem an unlikely place to find a continuous record of the civilizing of the West. Yet at the end of the last ice age, around 10,000 B.C., much of North Africa enjoyed a mild, damp climate and supported a diverse population of animals and humans. At Tassili-n-Ajjer in modern Algeria, succeeding generations of inhabitants have left over four thousand paintings on cliff and cave walls that date from ca. 6000 B.C. until the time of Jesus. Like a pictorial time line, these paintings show the gradual transformations of human culture.

The earliest cave paintings were produced by people who, like the inhabitants of Europe and the Near East, lived by hunting game and gathering edible plants, nuts, and fruit. Through this long period, humans perfected the making of stone tools, learned to work bone, antler, and ivory into weapons and utensils, and organized an increasingly complex society.

Sometime around 5000 B.C., the artists at Tassili-n-Ajjer began to include in their paintings images of domesticated cattle and harnesslike equipment. Such depictions give evidence of the arrival in North Africa of two of the most profound transformations in human history, sedentarization, that is, the adoption of a fixed dwelling place, and the agricultural revolution. These fundamental changes in human culture began independently around the world and continued for roughly five thousand years. They appeared first around 10,000 B.C. in the Near East, then elsewhere in Asia around 8000 B.C. By 5000 B.C., the domestication of plants and animals was under way in Africa and what is today Mexico.

Around 10,000 B.C., many hunter-gatherers living along the coastal plains of what is today Syria and Israel and in the valleys and the hill country near the Zagros Mountains between modern Iran and Iraq began to develop specialized strategies that led, by accident, to a transformation in human culture. Rather than constantly traveling in search of food, people living near the Mediterranean coast stayed put and exploited the various seasonal sources of food, fish,

In this cave painting at Tassili in northern Africa, animal magic evokes help from the spirit world in ensuring the prosperity of the cattle herd. A similar ceremony is still performed by members of the Fulani tribes in the Sahel, on the southern fringe of the Sahara.

wild grains, fruits, and game. In communities such as Jericho, people built and rebuilt their mud brick and stone huts over generations rather than moving on as had their ancestors. In the Zagros region, sedentary communities focused on single abundant sources of food at specific seasons, such as wild sheep and goats in the mountains during summer and pigs and cattle in the lower elevations in winter. These people also harvested the wild forms of wheat and barley that grew in upland valleys.

No one really knows why settlement led to agriculture, which is, after all, a riskier venture than hunting and gathering. Specialization in only a few species of plants or animals could spell starvation if severe weather caused that crop to fail or if disease destroyed herds. Some scholars speculate that the push to take nature in hand came from population growth and the development of a political hierarchy that reduced the natural breaking away of groups when clans or tribes became too large for the natural resources of an area to support. In settled communities, infant mortality decreased and life expectancy rose. In part, these changes occurred because life in a fixed location was less exhausting than constant wandering for the very young and the very old.

As population growth put pressure on the local food supply, gathering activities demanded more formal coordination and organization and led to the development of political leadership. This leadership and the perception of safety in numbers may have prevented the traditional breaking away to form other similar communities in the next valley, as had happened when population growth pressured earlier groups. In any case, people no longer simply looked for favored species of plants and animals where they occurred naturally. Now they introduced them into other locations and favored them at the expense of plant and animal species not deemed useful. Agriculture had begun.

The ability to domesticate goats, sheep, pigs, and cattle and to cultivate barley, wheat, and vegetables changed human communities from passive harvesters of nature to active partners with it. These peoples of the Neolithic, or New Stone Age, approximately 8000–6500 B.C., organized sizable villages. Jericho, which had been settled before the agricultural revolution, grew into a fortified town complete with ditch, stone walls, and towers and sheltered perhaps two thousand inhabitants. Catal Hüyük in southern Turkey may have been even larger.

The really revolutionary aspect of agriculture was not simply that it ensured settled communities a food supply. The true innovation was that agriculture was portable. For the first time, rather than looking for a place that provided them with the necessities of life, humans could carry with them what they needed to make a site inhabitable. This portability also meant the rapid spread of agriculture throughout the region.

Agricultural societies brought changes in the form and organization of formal religious cults. Elaborate sanctuary rooms decorated with frescoes, bulls' horns, and sculptures of heads of bulls and bears indicate that structured religious rites were important to the inhabitants of Catal Hüyük. At Jericho, human skulls covered with clay, presumably in an attempt to make them look

Sculptured skulls found at Jericho date from between 7000 and 6000 B.C. They are actual human skulls whose faces have been reconstituted with molded and tinted plaster. Pieces of seashells represented the eyes.

as they had in life, suggest that these early settlers practiced ancestor worship. In these larger communities the bonds of kinship that had united small hunter-gatherer bands were being supplemented by religious organization, which helped control and regulate social behavior. The nature of this religion is a matter of speculation. Images of a female deity, interpreted as a guardian of animals, suggest the religious importance of fertility and women's role in it.

Around 1500 B.C., a new theme appears on the cliff walls at Tassili-n-Ajjer. Now men herd horses and drive horse-drawn chariots. These innovations had only gradually reached the arid world of North Africa. They had developed over fifteen hundred years before in Mesopotamia (a name that means "between the rivers"), that featureless desert plain stretching to the marshes near the mouths of the Tigris and Euphrates rivers. Chariots symbolized a new, dynamic, and expansive phase in Western culture. Constructed of wood and bronze and used for transport and especially for aggressive warfare, they are symbolic of the culture of early river civilizations, the first civilizations in western Eurasia.

Before Civilization

ca. 100,000 B.C.	*Homo sapiens*
ca. 40,000 B.C.	*Homo sapiens sapiens*
ca. 35,000–10,000 B.C.	*Late Paleolithic era (Old Stone Age)*
ca. 8000–6500 B.C.	*Neolithic era (New Stone Age)*
ca. 3500 B.C.	*Civilization begins*

$\mathcal{B}$etween the Two Rivers

Need drove the inhabitants of Mesopotamia to create a civilization; nature itself offered little for human comfort or prosperity. The upland regions of the north receive most of the rainfall, but the soil is thin and poor. In the south, the soil is fertile but rainfall is almost nonexistent. There the twin rivers provide life-giving water, but also bring destructive floods that normally arrive at harvesttime. Thus agriculture is impossible without irrigation. But irrigation systems, if not properly maintained, deposit harsh alkaline chemicals on the soil, gradually reducing its fertility. In addition, Mesopotamia's only natural resource is clay. It has no metals, no workable stone, no valuable minerals of use to ancient people. These very obstacles pressed the people to cooperative, innovative, and organized measures for survival. Survival in the region required planning and the mobilization of manpower possible only through centralization.

Until around 3500 B.C., the inhabitants of the lower Tigris and Euphrates lived in scattered villages and small towns. Then the population of the region, known as Sumer, began to increase rapidly. Small settlements became increasingly common; then towns such as Eridu and Uruk in modern Iraq began to grow rapidly. These towns developed in part because of the need to concentrate and organize population who could carry on the extensive irrigation systems necessary for supporting Mesopotamian agriculture. In most cases, the earlier role of particular villages as important religious centers favored their growth into towns. These towns soon spread their control out to the surrounding cultivated areas, incorporating the small towns and villages of the region. They also fortified themselves against the hostile intentions of their neighbors.

Nomadic peoples inhabited the arid steppes of Mesopotamia, constantly trading with and occasionally threatening settled villages and towns. Their menace was as ever present in Near Eastern history as drought and flood. But nomads were a minor threat compared with the dangers posed by settled neighbors. As population growth increased pressure on the region's food supply, cities supplemented their resources by raiding their more prosperous neighbors. Victims sought protection within the ramparts of the settlements that had grown up around religious centers. As a result, the population of the towns rose along with their towering temples, largely at the expense of the countryside. Between ca. 3500 and 3000 B.C., the population of Uruk quadrupled, from 10,000 to 40,000. Other Mesopotamian cities, notably Umma, Eridu, Lagash, and Ur, developed along the same general lines as they concentrated water supplies within their districts with artificial canals and dikes. At the same time, the number of smaller towns and villages in the vicinity decreased rapidly. The city had become the dominant force in the organization of economy and society, and the growth of the Sumerian cities established a precedent that would continue throughout history.

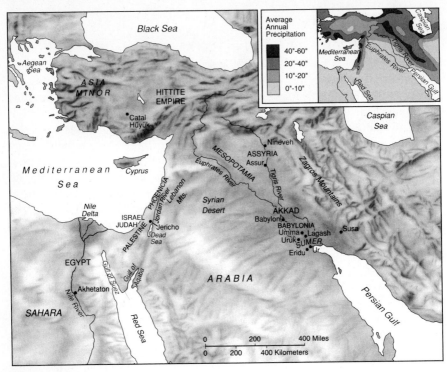

The Ancient World

The Ramparts of Uruk

Cities did more than simply concentrate population. Within the walls of the city, men and women developed new technologies and new social and political structures. They created cultural traditions such as writing and literature. The pride of the first city dwellers is captured in a passage from the *Epic of Gilgamesh*, the first great heroic poem, which was composed sometime before 2000 B.C. In the poem, the hero Gilgamesh boasts of the mighty walls he had built to encircle his city, Uruk:

> Go up and walk on the ramparts of Uruk
> Inspect the base terrace, examine the brickwork:
> Is not its brickwork of burnt brick?
> Did not the Seven Sages lay its foundations?

Gilgamesh was justly proud of his city. In his day (ca. 2700 B.C.) these walls were marvels of military engineering, and even now their ruins remain a tribute to his age. Archaeologists have uncovered the remains of the ramparts of Uruk, which stretched over five miles and were protected by some nine hundred semicircular towers. These protective walls enclosed about two square miles of houses, palaces, workshops, and temples. For the first time, a true urban environment had appeared in the West, and Uruk was the first city. Within

Uruk's walls, the peculiar circumstances of urban life changed the traditional social structure of Mesopotamia. In Neolithic times, social and economic differences within society had been minimal. Urban immigration increased the power, wealth, and status of two groups. In the first group were the religious authorities responsible for the temples. The second consisted of the emerging military and administrative elites, represented by Gilgamesh, who were responsible for the construction and protection of the cities. These two groups probably encouraged much of the migration to the cities.

Whether they lived inside the city or on the farmland it controlled, Mesopotamians formed a highly stratified society that shared unequally in the benefits of civilization. Slaves, who did most of the unskilled labor within the city, were the primary victims of civilization. Most were prisoners of war, but some were people forced by debt to sell themselves or their children. Most of the remaining rural people were peasants who were little better than slaves. Better off were soldiers, merchants, and workers and artisans who served the temple or palace. At the next level were landowning free persons. Above all of these were the priests responsible for temple services and the rulers. Rulers included the *ensi*, or city ruler, and the *lugal*, or king, the earthly representative of the gods. Kings were powerful and feared.

Urban life also redefined the role and status of women, who in the Neolithic period had enjoyed roughly the same roles and status as men. In cities, women tended to exercise private authority over children and servants within the household, while men controlled the household and dealt in the wider world. This change in roles resulted in part from the economic basis of the first civilization. Southern Mesopotamia has no sources of metal or stone. To acquire these precious commodities, trade networks were extended into Syria, the Arabian Peninsula, and even India. The primary commodities that Mesopotamians produced for trade were textiles, and these were largely produced by women captured in wars with neighboring city-states. Some historians suggest that the disproportionate numbers of low-status women in Mesopotamian cities affected the status of women in general. Although women could own property and even appear as heads of households, by roughly 1500 B.C. the pattern of patriarchal households predominated. Throughout Western history, while individual women might at times exercise great power, they did so largely in the private sphere.

Changes in society brought changes in technology. The need to feed, clothe, protect, and govern growing urban populations led to major technological and conceptual discoveries. Canals and systems of dikes partially harnessed water supplies. Farmers began to work their fields with improved plows and to haul their produce to town, first on sleds and ultimately on carts. These land-transport devices, along with sailing ships, made it possible not only to produce greater agricultural surplus but also to move this surplus to distant markets. Craft workers used a refined potter's wheel to produce ceramic vessels of great beauty. Government officials and private individuals began to use cylinder seals, small stone cylinders engraved with a pattern, to mark ownership. Metalworkers fashioned gold and silver into valuable items of adornment and prestige. They also began to cast bronze, an alloy of copper and tin, which came into use for tools and weapons about 3000 B.C.

Perhaps the greatest invention of early cities was writing. As early as 7000 B.C., small clay or stone tokens with distinctive shapes or markings were being used to keep track of animals, goods, and fruits in inventories and bartering. By 3500 B.C., government and temple administrators were using simplified drawings, today termed *pictograms*, which were derived from these tokens, to assist them in keeping records of their transactions. Scribes used sharp reeds to impress the pictograms on clay tablets. Thousands of these tablets have survived in the ruins of Mesopotamian cities.

The first tablets were written in Sumerian, a language related to no other known tongue. Each pictogram represented a single sound, which corresponded to a single object or idea. In time, these pictograms developed into a true system of writing, called *cuneiform* (from the Latin *cuneus*, wedge) after the wedge shape of the characters. Finally, scribes took a radical step. Rather than simply using pictograms to indicate single objects, they began to use cuneiform characters to represent concepts. For example, the pictogram for "foot" could also mean "to stand." Ultimately, pictograms came to represent sounds divorced from any particular meaning.

The implications of the development of cuneiform writing were revolutionary. Since symbols were liberated from meaning, they could be used to record any language. Over the next thousand years, scribes used these same symbols to write not only in Sumerian but also in the other languages of Mesopotamia, such as Akkadian, Babylonian, and Persian. Writing soon allowed those who had mastered it to achieve greater centralization and control of government, to communicate over enormous distances, to preserve and transmit information, and to express religious and cultural beliefs. Writing reinforced memory, consolidating and expanding the achievements of the first civilization and transmitting them to the future. Writing was power, and for much of subsequent history a small minority of merchants and elites and the scribes in their employ wielded this power. In Mesopotamia, this power served to increase the strength of the king, the servant of the gods.

Gods and Mortals in Mesopotamia

Uruk had begun as a village like any other. Its rise to importance resulted from its significance as a religious site. A world of many cities, Mesopotamia was also a world of many gods, and Mesopotamian cities bore the imprint of the cult of their gods.

The gods were like the people who worshiped them. They lived in a replica of human society, and each god had a particular responsibility. Every object and element from the sky to the brick or the plow had its own active god. The gods had the physical appearance and personalities of humans as well as human virtues and vices. Greater gods like Nanna and Ufu were the protectors of Ur and Sippar. Others, such as Inanna, or Ishtar, the goddess of love, fertility, and wars, and her husband Dumuzi, were worshiped throughout Mesopotamia. Finally, at the top of the pantheon were the gods of the sky, the air, and the rivers.

Mesopotamians believed that the role of mortals was to serve the gods and to feed them through sacrifice. Towns had first developed around the gods' temples for this purpose. By around 2500 B.C., although military lords and kings had gained political power at the expense of the temple priests, the temples still controlled a major portion of economic resources. They owned vast estates where peasants cultivated wheat and barley as well as vegetable gardens, vineyards, flocks of sheep, and herds of cattle and pigs. The produce from temple lands and flocks supported the priests, scribes, craft workers, laborers, farmers, teamsters, smiths, and weavers who operated these complex religious centers. At Lagash, for example, the temple of the goddess Bau owned over eleven thousand acres of land. The king held a quarter of this land for his own use. The priests divided the remainder into individual plots of about thirty-five acres, each to be cultivated for the support of the temple workers or rented out to free peasants. At a time when the total population was approximately forty thousand, the temple employed more than twelve hundred workers of various sorts, supervised by an administrator and an inspector appointed by the priests. The temple of Bau was only one of twenty temples in Lagash—and not the largest or most wealthy among them.

By around 2000 B.C., a ziggurat, or tiered tower, dedicated to the god, stood near many temples. The great Ziggurat of Ur, for example, measured nearly two thousand square feet at its base and originally stood more than 120 feet high. It is easy to see why people of a later age thought the people who had built the ziggurats wanted a tower that would reach to heaven—the origin of the biblical story of the Tower of Babel.

Although Mesopotamians looked to hundreds of personal divinities for assistance, they did not attempt to establish personal relationships with their great gods. However, since they assumed the gods lived in a structured world that operated rationally, they believed mortals could deal with them and enlist

Ziggurats were constructed of mud bricks, covered with baked bricks set in bitumen, and were often ornamented with elaborate multicolored mosaics. Today the weathered remains are small hills rising unexpectedly from the Iraqi plain.

their aid by following the right rituals. Rites centered on the veneration of idols. The most important care was feeding. At the temple of Uruk, the idols of the gods were offered two meals a day, each consisting of two courses served in regal quantity and style.

Through the proper rituals, a person could buy the god's protection and favor. Still, mortal life was harsh and the gods offered little solace to the great issues of human existence. This attitude is powerfully presented in the *Epic of Gilgamesh* which, while not an accurate picture of Mesopotamian religion, still conveys much of the values of this civilization. In this popular legend Gilgamesh, king of Uruk, civilizes the wild man Enkidu, who had been sent by the gods to temper the king's harshness. Gilgamesh and Enkidu become friends and undertake a series of adventures. However, even their great feats cannot overcome death. Enkidu displeases the gods and dies. Gilgamesh then sets out to find the magic plant of eternal life with which to return his friend from the somber underworld. On his journey he meets Ut-napishtim, the Mesopotamian Noah, who recounts the story of the Great Flood and tells him where to find the plant. Gilgamesh follows Ut-napishtim's advice and is successful but loses the plant on his journey home. The message is that only the gods are immortal, and the human afterlife is at best a shadowy and mournful existence.

Sargon and Mesopotamian Expansion

The temple was one center of the city; the palace was the other. As representative of the city's god, the king was the ruler and highest judge. He was responsible for the construction and upkeep of religious buildings and the complex system of canals that maintained the precarious balance between swamp and arid steppe. Finally, he commanded the army, defending his community against its neighbors and leading his forces against rival cities.

The cultural and economic developments of early Mesopotamia occurred within the context of almost constant warfare. From around 3000 B.C. until 2300 B.C., the rulers of Ur, Lagash, Uruk, and Umma fought among themselves for control of Sumer, their name for the southern region of Mesopotamia. The population was a mixture of Sumerians and Semites, peoples speaking Semitic languages related to modern Arabic or Hebrew, all jealously protective of their cities and gods and eager to extend their domination over their weaker neighbors.

The extraordinary developments in this small corner of the Middle East might have remained isolated phenomena were it not for Sargon (ca. 2334–2279 B.C.), king of Akkad and the most important figure in Mesopotamian history. During his long reign of 55 years, Sargon built on the conquests and confederacies of the past to unite, transform, and expand Mesopotamian civilization. Born in obscurity, after his death he was worshiped as a god. Sargon was the son of a priestess and an unknown father. In his youth he was the cupbearer to the king of Kish. Later, he overthrew his master and conquered Uruk, Ur, Lagash, and Umma. This made him lord of Sumer. Such glory had satisfied his predecessors, but not Sargon. Instead he extended his military operations east across the Tigris, west along the Euphrates, and north into modern Syria, thus creating the Akkadian state—the first great multi-ethnic empire state in the West—so named by contemporary historians for Sargon's capital at Akkad.

Sargon attempted to rule a vast and heterogeneous collection of city-states and territories by transforming the traditions of royal government. Rather than eradicating the traditions of conquered cities, he allowed them to maintain their own institutions, but replaced many of their autonomous ruling aristocracies with his own functionaries. He also reduced the economic power of local temples in favor of his supporters. At the same time, however, he tried to win the loyalty of the ancient cities of Sumer by naming his daughter high priestess of the moon-god Nanna at Ur. He was thus the first in a long tradition of Near Eastern rulers who sought to unite his disparate conquests into a true state.

Sargon did more than just conquer cities. Although a Semite, he spread the achievements of Sumerian civilization throughout his vast state. Akkadian scribes used cuneiform to write the Semitic Akkadian language. So important did Sargon's successors deem his accomplishments that they ordered him worshiped as a god.

The Akkadian nation-state proved as ephemeral as Sargon's accomplishments were lasting. All Mesopotamian states tended to undergo a cycle of rapid rise under a gifted military commander, then begin to crumble under the internal stresses of dynastic disputes and regional assertions of autonomy. Thus weakened, they could then be conquered by other expanding states. First Ur, under its Sumerian king and first law codifier, Shulgi (2094–2047 B.C.), and then Amoritic Babylonia, under its great ruler, Hammurabi (1792–1750 B.C.), assumed dominance in the land between the rivers. From about 2000 B.C. on, the political and economic centers of Mesopotamia were in Babylonia and in Assyria, the region to the north at the foot of the Zagros Mountains.

Hammurabi and the Old Babylonian Empire

In the tradition of Sargon, Hammurabi expanded his state through arms and diplomacy. He expanded his power south as far as Uruk and north to Assyria. In the tradition of Shulgi, he promulgated an important body of law, known as the Code of Hammurabi. In the words of its prologue, this code sought

> To cause justice to prevail in the country
> To destroy the wicked and the evil,
> That the strong may not oppress the weak.

As the favored agent of the gods, the king held responsibility for regulating all aspects of Babylonian life, including dowries and contracts, agricultural prices

A 7-foot-high diorite stele dating from about 1750 B.C. is inscribed with the law code of Hammurabi. The relief at the top shows Hammurabi standing at left in the presence of the sun god, perhaps explaining his code of laws.

and wages, commerce and money lending, and even professional standards for physicians, veterinarians, and architects. Hammurabi's code thus offers a view of many aspects of Babylonian life, although always from the perspective of the royal law. This law lists offenses and prescribes penalties, which vary according to the social status of the victim and the perpetrator. The code creates a picture of a prosperous society composed of three legally defined social strata: a well-to-do elite, the mass of the population, and slaves. Each group had its own rights and obligations in proportion to its status. Even slaves enjoyed some legal rights and protection, could marry free persons, and might eventually obtain freedom.

Much of the code sought to protect women and children from arbitrary and unfair treatment. Husbands ruled their households, but they did not have unlimited authority over their wives. Women could initiate their own court cases, practice various trades, and even hold public positions. Upon marriage, husbands gave their fathers-in-law a payment in silver or in furnishings. The father of the wife gave her a dowry over which she had full control. Some elite women personally controlled great wealth.

The Code of Hammurabi was less a royal attempt to restructure Babylonian society than an effort to reorganize, consolidate, and preserve previous laws in order to maintain the established social and economic order. What innovation it did show was in the extent of such punitive measures as death or mutilation. Penalties in earlier codes had been primarily compensation in silver or valuables.

Law was not the only area in which the Old Babylonian kingdom began an important tradition. In order to handle the economics of business and government administration, Babylonians developed the most sophisticated mathematical system known prior to the fifteenth century A.D. Babylonian mathematics was based on the number 60 (we still divide hours and minutes into 60 units today). Babylonian mathematicians devised multiplication tables and tables of reciprocals. They also devised tables of squares and square roots, cubes and cube roots, and other calculations needed for computing such important figures as compound interest. Although Babylonian mathematicians were not primarily interested in theoretical problems and were seldom given to abstraction, their technical proficiency indicates the advanced level of sophistication with which Hammurabi's contemporaries could tackle the problems of living in a complex society.

For all its successes, Hammurabi's state was no more successful than those of his predecessors at defending itself against internal conflicts or external enemies. Despite his efforts, the traditional organization inherited from his Sumerian and Akkadian predecessors could not ensure orderly administration of a far-flung collection of cities. Hammurabi's son lost over half of his father's kingdom to internal revolts. Weakened by internal dissension, the kingdom fell to a new and potent force in Western history, the Hittites.

From their capital of Hattushash (modern Bogazköy in Turkey), the Hittites established a centralized state based on agriculture and trade in the metals mined from the ore-rich mountains of Anatolia and exported to Mesopotamia. Perfecting the light horse-drawn war chariot, the Hittites expanded into northern Mesopotamia and along the Syrian coast. They were

Between the Two Rivers

ca. 3500 B.C.	Pictograms appear
ca. 3000–2316 B.C.	War for control of Sumer
ca. 2700 B.C.	Gilgamesh
ca. 2334–2279 B.C.	Sargon
1792–1750 B.C.	Hammurabi
ca. 1600 B.C.	Hittites destroy Old Babylonian state
ca. 1286 B.C.	Battle of Kadesh

able to destroy the Babylonian state around 1600 B.C. Unlike the Sumerians, the Semitic nomads, the Akkadians, and the Babylonians, the Hittites were an Indo-European people, speaking a language that was part of a linguistic family which includes most modern European languages as well as Persian, Greek, Latin, and Sanskrit. The Hittites' gradual expansion south along the coast was checked at the battle of Kadesh around 1300 B.C., when they encountered the army of an even greater and more ancient power—the Egypt of Ramses II.

*T*he Gift of the Nile

Like that of the Tigris and Euphrates valleys, the rich soil of the Nile Valley can support a dense population. There, however, the similarities end. Unlike the Mesopotamian, the Nile floodplain required little effort to make the land productive. Each year the river flooded at exactly the right moment to irrigate crops and to deposit a layer of rich, fertile silt. South of the last falls or cataracts, the fertile region called Upper Egypt is about eight miles wide and is flanked by high desert plateaus. Near the Mediterranean in Lower Egypt, the Nile spreads across a lush marshy delta more than a hundred miles wide. Egypt knew only two environments, the fertile Nile Valley and the vast wastes of the Sahara Desert surrounding it. This inhospitable and largely uninhabitable region limited Egypt's contact with outside influences. Thus while trade, communication, and violent conquest characterized Mesopotamian civilization, Egypt knew self-sufficiency, an inward focus in culture and society, and stability. In its art, political structure, society, and religion, the Egyptian universe was static. Nothing was ever to change.

The earliest sedentary communities in the Nile Valley appeared on the western margin of the Delta around 4000 B.C. In villages such as Merimda, which had a population of over ten thousand, huts constructed of poles and adobe bricks huddled together near *wadis*, fertile riverbeds that were dry except during the rainy season. Farther south, in Upper Egypt, similar communities developed somewhat later but achieved an earlier political unity and a higher level of culture. By around 3200 B.C., Upper Egypt was in contact with Mesopotamia and had apparently borrowed something of that region's artistic and architectural traditions. During the same period, Upper Egypt developed a pictographic script.

These cultural achievements coincided with the political centralization of Upper Egypt under a series of kings. Probably around 3150 B.C., King Narmer or one of his predecessors in Upper Egypt expanded control over the fragmented south, uniting Upper and Lower Egypt and establishing a capital at Memphis on the border between these two regions. For over twenty-five hundred years, the Nile Valley, from the first cataract to the Mediterranean, enjoyed the most stable civilization the Western world has ever known.

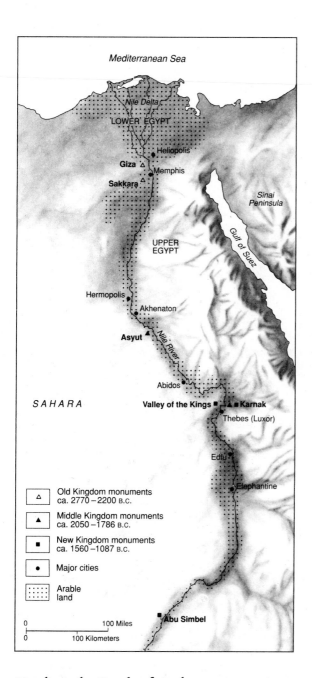

Ancient Egypt

Tending the Cattle of God

Historians divide the vast sweep of Egyptian history into 31 dynasties, regrouped in turn into 4 periods of political centralization: pre- and early dynastic Egypt (ca. 3150–2770 B.C.), the Old Kingdom (ca. 2770–2200 B.C.), the Middle Kingdom (ca. 2050–1786 B.C.), and the New Kingdom (ca. 1560–1087

B.C.). The time gaps between kingdoms were periods of disruption and political confusion termed intermediate periods. While minor changes in social, political, and cultural life certainly occurred during these centuries, the changes were less significant than the astonishing stability and continuity of the civilization that developed along the banks of the Nile.

Divine kingship was the cornerstone of Egyptian life. The king lived in the royal city of Memphis in the splendor of a *Per-ao*, or "great house," from which comes the word *pharaoh*, the Hebrew term for the Egyptian king. Initially, the king was the incarnation of Horus, a sky and falcon god. Later, the king was identified with the sun-god Ra (subsequently known as Amen-Re, the great god), as well as with Osiris, the god of the dead. As divine incarnation, the king was obliged above all to care for his people. It was he who assured the annual flooding of the Nile, which brought water to the parched land. His commands preserved *maat*, the ideal state of the universe and society, a condition of harmony and justice. In the poetry of the Old Kingdom, the king was the divine herdsman; the people were the cattle of god:

> Well tended are men, the cattle of god.
> He made heaven and earth according to their desire
> and repelled the demon of the waters . . .
> He made for them rulers (even) in the egg,
> a supporter to support the back of the disabled.

Unlike the rulers in Mesopotamia, the kings of the Old Kingdom were not warriors but divine administrators. Protected by the Sahara Desert, Egypt had few external enemies and no standing army. A vast bureaucracy of literate court officials and provincial administrators assisted the god-king. They wielded wide authority as religious leaders, judicial officers, and, when necessary, military leaders. A host of subordinate overseers, scribes, metalworkers, stonemasons, artisans, and tax collectors rounded out the royal administration. At the local level, governors administered provinces called *nomes*, the basic units of Egyptian local government.

Women of ancient Egypt were more independent and involved in public life than those of Mesopotamia. Egyptian women owned property, conducted their own business, entered legal contracts, and brought lawsuits. They shared in the economic and professional life of the country at every level except one. Women were apparently excluded from formal education. The professional bureaucracy was open only to those who could read and write. As a result, the primary route to public power was closed to women, and the bureaucratic machinery remained firmly in the hands of men. The role of this bureaucracy was to administer estates, collect taxes, and channel revenues and labor toward vast public works projects. These construction projects focused on the king.

During the Old and Middle kingdoms, great pyramid temple-tomb complexes were built for the kings. Within the temples priests and servants performed rituals to serve the dead kings just as they had served the kings when they were alive. Even death did not disrupt the continuity so vital to

Egyptian civilization. The cults of dead kings reinforced the monarchy, since veneration of past rulers meant veneration of the kings' ancestors. The founder of the Old Kingdom, King Zoser, who was an approximate contemporary of Gilgamesh, built the first pyramid-temple, the Step Pyramid at Saqqara.

Building and equipping the pyramids focused and transformed Egypt's material and human resources. Artists and craft workers had to be trained, engineering and transportation problems solved, quarrying and stoneworking techniques perfected, and laborers recruited. In the Old Kingdom, whose population has been estimated at perhaps 1.5 million, more than seventy thousand workers at a time were employed in building these great temple-tombs. No smaller work force could have built such a massive structure as the Great Pyramid of Khufu (ca. 2600 B.C.), which stood 481 feet high and contained almost six million tons of stone. In comparison, the great Ziggurat of Ur rose only some 120 feet above the Mesopotamian plain. The pyramids were constructed by peasants working when the Nile was in flood and they could not till the soil. Although actual construction was seasonal, the work was unending. No sooner was one complex completed than the next was begun.

Feeding the masses of laborers absorbed most of the country's agricultural surplus. Equipping the temples and pyramids provided a constant demand for the highest quality luxury goods, since royal tombs and temples were furnished as luxuriously as palaces. Thus the construction and maintenance of these vast complexes focused the organization and production of Egypt's economy and government.

The pyramids at Giza, near modern Cairo. In the center rises the Great Pyramid, the royal tomb of the pharaoh Khufu.

Democratization of the Afterlife

In the Old Kingdom, future life was available only to the king or through the king. The graves of thousands of his attendants and servants surrounded his temple. All the wealth, labor, and expertise of the kingdom thus flowed into these temples, reinforcing the position of the king. Like the tip of a pyramid, the king was the summit, supported by all of society.

Gradually, however, the absolute power of the king declined. The increasing demands for consumption by the court and the cults forced agricultural expansion into areas where returns were poor, thus decreasing the flow of wealth. As bureaucrats increased their efforts to supply the voracious needs of living and dead kings and their attendants, they neglected the maintenance of the economic system that supplied these needs. The royal government was not protecting society; the "cattle of god" were not being well tended. Finally, tax-exempt religious foundations, established to ensure the perpetual cult of the dead, received donations of vast amounts of property and came to rival the power of the king. This removed an ever greater amount of the country's wealth from the control of the king and his agents. Thus the wealth and power of the kings declined at roughly the time that Sargon was expanding his Akkadian state in Mesopotamia. By around 2200 B.C., Egyptian royal authority collapsed entirely, leaving political and religious power in the hands of provincial governors.

After almost two hundred years of fragmentation, the governors of Thebes in Upper Egypt reestablished centralized royal traditions, but with a difference. Kings continued to build vast temples, but they did not resume the tremendous investments in pyramid complexes on the scale of the Old Kingdom. The bureaucracy was opened to all men, even sons of peasants, who could master the complex pictographic writing. Private temple-tombs proliferated and with them new pious foundations. These promised eternal care by which anyone with sufficient wealth could enjoy a comfortable afterlife.

The memory of the shortcomings of the Old Kingdom introduced a new ethical perspective expressed in the literature written by the elite. For the first time, the elite voiced the concern that justice might not always be served and that the innocent might suffer at the hands of royal agents. In the story of Sinuhe, a popular tale from around 1900 B.C., an official of Amenemhet I (d. 1962 B.C.) flees Egypt after the death of his king. He fears that through false reports of his actions he will incur the wrath of Amenemhet's son, Senusert I. Only in his old age, after years in Syria and Palestine, does Sinuhe dare to return to his beloved Egypt. There, through the intercession of the royal children, Senusert receives him honorably and grants him the ultimate favor, his own pyramid-tomb. The moral is clear: The state system at times failed in its responsibility to safeguard *maat*.

The greater access to power and privilege in the Middle Kingdom benefited foreigners as well as Egyptians. Assimilated Semites from Palestine rose to important administrative positions. By around 1600 B.C., when the Hittite armies were destroying the state of Hammurabi's successors, large bands of

Palestinians had settled in the eastern Delta, setting the stage for the first foreign conquest of Egypt. A series of kings referred to by Egyptian sources as "rulers of foreign lands," or *Hyksos*, overran the country and ruled the Nile Valley as far south as Memphis. These foreigners adopted the traditions of Egyptian kingship and continued the tradition of divine rule.

The Hyksos kings introduced their military technology and organization into Egypt. In particular, they brought with them the light horse-drawn war chariot. This mobile fighting platform, manned by warriors armed with bows, bronze swords of a type previously unknown in Egypt, and lances, transformed Egyptian military tactics. These innovations remained even after the Hyksos were expelled by Ahmose I (1552–1527 B.C.), the Theban founder of the Eighteenth Dynasty, with whose reign the New Kingdom began.

The Egyptian Empire

Ahmose did not stop with the liberation of Egypt. He forged an empire. He and his successors used their newfound military might to extend the frontiers of Egypt south up the Nile beyond the fourth cataract and well into Nubia. To the east they absorbed the caravan routes to the Red Sea, from which they were able to send ships to Punt (probably modern Somalia), the source of the myrrh and frankincense needed for funeral and religious rituals. Most important was the Egyptian expansion into Canaanite Palestine and Syria. Here Egyptian chariots crushed their foes as kings pressed on as far as the Euphrates. Thutmose I (1506–1494 B.C.) proclaimed, "I have made the boundaries of Egypt as far as that which the sun encircles."

Thutmose's immediate successors were his children, Thutmose II (1494–1490 B.C.) and Hatshepsut (1490–1468 B.C.), who married her brother. Such brother-sister marriages, although not unknown in polygamous Egyptian society, were rare. After the death of Thutmose II, Hatshepsut ruled both as regent for her stepson Thutmose III (1490–1436 B.C.) and as co-ruler. She was by all accounts a capable ruler, preserving stability and even personally leading the army on several occasions to protect the empire.

In spite of the efforts of Hatshepsut and her successors, the Egyptian empire was never as grand as its kings proclaimed. Many of the northern expeditions were raids rather than conquests. Still, the expanded political frontiers meant increased trade and unprecedented interaction with the rest of the ancient world. The cargo excavated from the wreck of a ship that sank off the coast of modern Turkey around 1350 B.C. vividly portrays the breadth of international exchange in the New Kingdom. The nationality of the ship, its origins, and its destination are unknown, but it carried a cargo of priceless and exotic merchandise from around the Mediterranean world. The lost ship was probably not a merchant vessel in the modern sense; private merchants were virtually unknown in the Egyptian empire. Instead, most precious commodities circulated through royal ventures or as gifts and tribute.

*Painted limestone head of Hatshep-
sut. The traditions of male leadership
were such that she had herself portrayed in the formal rigid pose and
dress of a king, including a false
beard.*

Religion was both the heart of royal power and its only limiting force. Though the king was the embodiment of the religious tradition, he was also bound by that tradition, as it was interpreted by an ancient and powerful system of priesthoods, pious foundations, and cults. The intimate relationship between royal absolutism and religious cult culminated in the reign of Amenhotep IV (1364–1347 B.C.), the most controversial and enigmatic ruler of the New Kingdom, who challenged the very basis of royal religious control. In a calculated break with over a thousand years of Egyptian religious custom, Amenhotep attempted to abolish the cult of Amen-Re along with all of the other traditional gods, their priesthoods, and their festivals. In their place he promoted a new divinity, the sun-disk god Aten. Amenhotep moved his capital from Thebes to a new temple city, modern Tell al- 'Amarna, and changed his own name to Akhenaten ("It pleases Aten").

Akhenaten has been called the first monotheist, a reformer who sought to revitalize a religion that had decayed into superstition and magic. Yet his monotheism was not complete. The god Aten shared divine status with Akhenaten himself. Akhenaten attacked other cults, especially that of Amen-Re, to consolidate royal power and to replace the old priesthoods with his own family members and supporters.

In attempting to reestablish royal divinity, Akhenaten temporarily transformed the aesthetics of Egyptian court life. Traditional archaic language gave way to the everyday speech of the fourteenth century B.C. Wall paintings and statues showed people in the clothing that they actually wore rather than in stylized parade dress. This new naturalism rendered the king at once more human and more divine. It differentiated him from the long line of preceding kings, emphasizing his uniqueness and his royal power.

The strength of royal power was so great that during his reign Akhenaten could command acceptance of his radical break with Egyptian stability. However, his ambitious plan did not long survive his death. His innovations annoyed the Egyptian elite, while his abolition of traditional festivals alienated the masses. His son-in-law, Tutankhamen (1347–1337 B.C.), the son of Akhenaten's predecessor, was a child when he became king upon Akhenaten's death. Under the influence of his court advisers, probably inherited from his father's reign, he restored the ancient religious traditions and abandoned the new capital of Amarna for his father's palace at Thebes.

Return to the old ways meant return to the old problems. Powerful pious foundations controlled fully 10 percent of the population. Dynastic continuity ended after Tutankhamen and a new military dynasty seized the throne. These internal problems provided an opportunity for the Hittite state in Asia Minor to expand south at the expense of Egypt. Ramses II (1289–1224 B.C.) checked the Hittite expansion at the battle of Kadesh, but the battle was actually a draw. Eventually, Ramses and the Hittite king Hattusilis III signed a peace treaty whose terms included nonaggression and mutual defense. The agreement marked the failure of both states to unify the Fertile Crescent, the region

The Gift of the Nile

ca. 3150–2770 B.C.	Predynastic and early dynastic Egypt
ca. 2770–2200 B.C.	Old Kingdom
ca. 2600 B.C.	Pyramid of Khufu
ca. 2050–1786 B.C.	Middle Kingdom
ca. 1560–1087 B.C.	New Kingdom
1552–1527 B.C.	Ahmose I
1506–1494 B.C.	Thutmose I
1494–1490 B.C.	Thutmose II
1490–1468 B.C.	Hatshepsut
1364–1347 B.C.	Amenhotep IV (Akhenaten)
1347–1337 B.C.	Tutankhamen
1289–1224 B.C.	Ramses II

stretching from the Persian Gulf northwest through Mesopotamia and down the Mediterranean coast to Egypt.

The mutual standoff at Kadesh did not long precede the disintegration of both Egypt and the Hittite state. Within a century, states large and small along the Mediterranean coast from Anatolia to the Delta and from the Aegean Sea in the west to the Zagros Mountains in the east collapsed or were destroyed in what seems to have been a general crisis of the civilized world. The various raiders, sometimes erroneously called the "Sea Peoples," who struck Egypt, Syria, the Hittite state, and elsewhere were not the primary cause of the crisis. It was rather internal political, economic, and social strains within both of these great states that provided the opportunity for various groups—including Anatolians, Greeks, Israelites, and others—to raid the ancient centers of civilization. In the ensuing confusion, the small Semitic kingdoms in Syria and Palestine developed a precarious independence in the shadow of the great powers.

$\mathcal{B}$etween Two Worlds

Civilization was an endangered species throughout antiquity. Just beyond the well-tilled fields of Mesopotamia and the fertile delta of the Nile lay the world of anticivilization—that of the Semitic tribes of seminomadic shepherds and traders. Of course, not all Semites were uncivilized. Many had formed part of the heterogeneous population of the Sumerian world. Sargon's Semitic Akkadians and Hammurabi's Amorites created great Mesopotamian nation-states, adopting the ancient Sumerian cultural traditions. Along the coast of Palestine, other Semitic groups established towns modeled on those of Mesopotamia, which were involved in the trade between Egypt and the north. But the majority of Semitic peoples continued to live a life radically different from that of the floodplain civilizations. From these, one small group, the Hebrews, emerged to establish a religious and cultural tradition unique in antiquity.

A Wandering Aramaean Was My Father

Sometime after 2000 B.C., small Semitic bands under the leadership of patriarchal chieftains spread into what is today Syria and Palestine. These bands crisscrossed the Fertile Crescent, searching for pasture for their flocks. Occasionally they participated in the trade uniting Mesopotamia and the towns of the Mediterranean coast. For the most part, however, they pitched their tents on the outskirts of towns only briefly, moving on when their sheep and goats had exhausted the supply of pasturage. Semitic Aramaeans and Chaldeans brought with them not only their flocks and families, but Mesopotamian culture as well. Hebrew history records such Mesopotamian traditions as the story of the flood (Gen. 6–10), legal traditions strongly reminiscent of those of Hammurabi, and the worship of the gods on high places. Stories such as that of the Tower of Babel (Gen. 11) and the garden of Eden (Gen. 2–4) likewise have a Mesopotamian flavor, but with a difference. For these wandering shepherds, civilization was a curse. In the Hebrew Bible (the Christian Old Testament), the first city was built by Cain, the first murderer. The Tower of Babel, probably a ziggurat, was a symbol not of human achievement but of human pride.

At least some of these wandering Aramaeans, among them the biblical patriarch Abraham, rejected the gods of Mesopotamia. Religion among these nomadic groups focused on the specific divinity of the clan. In the case of Abraham, this was the god El. Abraham and his successors were not monotheists. They did not deny the existence of other gods. They simply believed that they had a personal pact with their own god.

In its social organization and cultural traditions, Abraham's clan was no different from its neighbors. These independent clans were ruled by a senior male (hence the Greek term *patriarch*—rule by the father). Women, whether wives, concubines, or slaves, were treated as distinctly inferior, virtually as property.

Some of Abraham's descendants must have joined the steady migration from Palestine into Egypt that took place during the Middle Kingdom and the Hyksos period. Although initially well treated, after the expulsion of the Hyksos in the sixteenth century B.C., many of the Semitic settlers in Egypt were reduced to slavery. Around the thirteenth century B.C., a small band of Semitic slaves numbering possibly less than a thousand left Egypt for Sinai and Palestine under the leadership of Moses. The memory of this departure, known as the Exodus, became the formative experience of the descendants of those

The Kingdoms of Israel and Judah

who had taken part and those who later joined them. Moses, a Semite who carried an Egyptian name and who, according to tradition, had been raised in the royal court, was the founder of the Israelite people.

During the years that they spent wandering in the desert and then slowly conquering Palestine, the Israelites forged a new identity and a new faith. From the Midianites of the Sinai Peninsula, they adopted the god Yahweh as their own. Although composed of various Semitic and even Egyptian groups, the Israelites adopted the oral traditions of the clan of Abraham as their common ancestor and identified his god, El, with Yahweh. They interpreted their extraordinary escape from Egypt as evidence of a covenant with this god, a treaty similar to those concluded between the Hittite kings and their dependents. Yahweh was to be the Israelites' exclusive god; they were to make no alliances with any others. They were to preserve peace among themselves, and they were obligated to serve Yahweh with arms. This covenant was embodied in the law of Moses, a series of terse absolute commands ("Thou shall not . . .") quite unlike the conditional laws of Hammurabi. Inspired by their new identity and their new religion, the Israelites swept into Palestine. Taking advantage of the vacuum of power left by the Hittite-Egyptian standoff following the battle of Kadesh, they destroyed or captured the cities of the region.

A King Like All the Nations

During its first centuries, Israel was a loosely organized confederation of tribes whose only focal point was the religious shrine at Shiloh. This shrine, in contrast with the temples of other ancient peoples, housed no idols, but only a chest, known as the Ark of the Covenant, which contained the law of Moses and mementos of the Exodus. At times of danger temporary leaders would lead united tribal armies. The power of these leaders, called judges in the Hebrew Bible, rested solely on their personal leadership qualities. This "charisma" indicated that the spirit of Yahweh was with the leader. Yahweh alone was the ruler of the people.

By the eleventh century B.C., this disorganized political tradition placed the Israelites at a disadvantage in fighting their neighbors. The Philistines, who dominated the Palestinian seacoast and had expanded inland, posed the greatest threat. By 1050 B.C., the Philistines had defeated the Israelites, captured the Ark of the Covenant, and occupied most of their territory. Many Israelites clamored for "a king like all the nations" to lead them to victory. To consolidate their forces, the Israelite religious leaders reluctantly established a kingdom. Its first king was Saul and its second was David.

David (ca.1000–962 B.C.) and his son and successor, Solomon (ca. 961–922 B.C.), brought the kingdom of Israel to its peak of power, prestige, and territorial expansion. David defeated and expelled the Philistines, subdued Israel's other enemies, and created a united state that included all of Palestine from the desert to the sea. He established Jerusalem as the political and religious capital. Solomon went still further, building a magnificent temple complex to house the Ark of the Covenant and to serve as Israel's national shrine. David and Solomon restructured Israel from a tribal to a monarchical society. The old tribal structure remained only as a religious tradition. Solomon centralized land divisions, raised taxes, and increased military service in order to strengthen the monarchy.

The cost of this transformation was high. The kingdom under David and especially under Solomon grew more tyrannical as it grew more powerful. Solomon behaved like any other king of his time. He contracted marriage alliances with neighboring princes and allowed his wives to practice their own cults. He demanded extraordinary taxes and services from his people to pay for his lavish building projects. When he was unable to pay his Phoenician creditors for supplies and craft workers, he deported Israelites to work as slaves in Phoenician mines. Not surprisingly, the united kingdom did not survive Solomon's death. The northern region broke off to become the Kingdom of Israel with its capital in Shechem. The south, the Kingdom of Judah, continued the tradition of David from his capital of Jerusalem.

Beginning in the ninth century B.C., a new Mesopotamian power, the Assyrians, began a campaign of conquest and unprecedented brutality throughout the Near East. The Hebrew kingdoms were among their many victims. In 722 B.C., the Assyrians destroyed the Kingdom of Israel and deported thousands of its people to upper Mesopotamia. In 586 B.C., the Kingdom of Judah was conquered by Assyria's destroyers, the New Babylonian empire under King Nebuchadnezzar II (604–562 B.C.). The temple of Solomon was destroyed, Jerusalem was burned, and Judah's elite were deported to Babylon. This Babylonian captivity ended some fifty years later when the Persians, who

In this gypsum bas-relief panel, Israelite refugees are seen sadly departing their home city of Lachish after its subjugation by the Assyrians in 701 B.C. The sculpture was commissioned by King Sennacherib to commemorate his victory.

had conquered Babylonia, allowed the people of Judah to return to their homeland.

The Law and the Prophets

The religious significance of the people of Israel is as great as their political significance is small. The faith of the Israelites is the direct source of the three great Western religions: Judaism, Christianity, and Islam. Gradually, the relationship between Yahweh and the people of Israel was transformed from one of simple exclusivity to monotheism. Particularly after the Babylonian captivity, Yahweh was not simply one god among many but rather the one universal god, creator and ruler of the universe. Yahweh was so beyond human understanding that he could not be depicted in any image.

Although beyond all earthly powers, Yahweh intervened in human history to accomplish his goals. He formed a covenant with Abraham and renewed it with Moses. The covenant promised that Israel would be Yahweh's special people, but in return for this favor he demanded not simply sacrifices but righteousness. Thus ethics was a central aspect of Israel's religion.

Religious leaders, termed *prophets*, constantly explained historical events in terms of the faithfulness of the Israelite or, later, Jewish people (the term *Jew* means a descendant of those who occupied the Kingdom of Judah) to their covenant with Yahweh. The prophets were independent of royal control and spoke out constantly against any ruler whose immorality compromised the terms of the convenant. They called upon rulers and people to reform their lives and to return to Yahweh. The prophet Jeremiah (ca. 650–570 B.C.) boldly accused King Jehoiakim (ca. 609–598 B.C.) of Judah of reviving the cult of Ishtar and practicing child sacrifice and warned that Yahweh would send Babylon to destroy him. In Egypt or Mesopotamia, such dissenters would have been liquidated. Even in Israel and Judah, prophets often met with persecution. Some prophets were killed. Still they persisted, establishing a tradition of religious opposition to royal absolutism, a tradition that, like monotheism itself, is an enduring legacy.

Between Two Worlds

ca. 1050 B.C.	Philistines defeat the Israelites
ca. 1000–961 B.C.	David, king of Israel
ca. 961–922 B.C.	Solomon, king of Israel
722 B.C.	Assyrians destroy Kingdom of Israel
604–562 B.C.	Nebuchadnezzar II
586 B.C.	Nebuchadnezzar II conquers Kingdom of Judah

Nineveh and Babylon

The Assyrian state that destroyed Israel accomplished what no other power had ever achieved. It tied together the floodplain civilizations of Mesopotamia and Egypt. But the Assyrian state was not just larger than the nation-states that had preceded it; it differed in nature as well as in size. The nation-states of Akkadia, Babylonia, the Hittites, and even the Egyptian empire were essentially diverse collections of city-states. Each preserved its own institutions and cultural traditions while diverting its economic resources to the capital. The Assyrian empire was an integrated state in which conquered regions were reorganized and remade along the model of the central government. By the middle of the seventh century B.C., the Assyrian empire stretched from the headwaters of the Tigris and Euphrates rivers to the Persian Gulf, along the coast from Syria to beyond the Delta, and up the Nile to Thebes.

The Assyrian plain north of Babylonia had long been a small Mesopotamian state threatened by seminomads and great powers such as the Babylonians and later the Hittites. When King Assur-dan II mounted the throne in 934 B.C., his country was, as he himself later said, exhausted. Gradually he and his successors began to strengthen the state against its enemies and to allow its population to rebuild its agricultural and commercial base. The Assyrian army, forged by constant warfare into a formidable military machine, began to extend the frontiers of the kingdom both toward the Mediterranean and down the twin rivers toward the Persian Gulf. However, like its predecessors, within a century this empire seemed destined for collapse.

Rapid growth and unprecedented wealth had created a new class of noble warriors who were resented and mistrusted by the petty nobility of the old heartland of the Assyrian kingdom. The old nobility demanded a greater share in the imperial wealth and a more direct role in the administration of the empire. When the emperors ignored their demands, they began a long and bitter revolt that lasted from 827 B.C. until 750 B.C. This internal crisis put Assyria at the mercy of its external enemies, who seemed on the verge of destroying the Assyrian state. Instead, the revolt paved the way for the ascension of Tiglath-pileser III (746–727 B.C.), the greatest empire builder of Mesopotamia since Sargon. Tiglath-pileser and his successors transformed the structure of the Assyrian state and expanded its empire. They created a model for an empire that would later be copied by Persia, Macedonia, and Rome. In the sense that the Assyrians not only conquered but created an administrative system by which to rule, theirs was the first true empire.

From his palace at Nineveh, Tiglath-pileser combined all of the traditional elements of Mesopotamian statecraft with a new religious ideology and social system to create the framework for a lasting multiethnic imperial system. This sytem rested on five bases: a transformed army, a new religious military ideology, a novel administrative system, a social policy involving large-scale population movements, and the calculated use of massive terror.

The heart of Tiglath-pileser's program was the most modern army the world had ever seen. In place of traditional armies of peasants and slaves supplied by great aristocrats, he raised professional armies from the conquered lands of the empire, commanded by Assyrian generals. The Assyrian army was also the first to use iron weapons on a massive scale. Assyrian armies were well balanced, including not only infantry, cavalry, and chariots, but also engineering units for constructing the siege equipment needed to capture towns. Warfare had become a science.

In addition to the professional army, Tiglath-pileser created the most developed military-religious ideology of any ancient people. Kings had long been agents of the gods, but Ashur, the god of the Assyrians, had but one command: Enlarge the empire! Thus warfare was the mission and duty of all, a sacred command paralleled through the centuries in the cries of "God wills it" of the Christian crusaders and the "God is great" of Muslims.

Tiglath-pileser restructured his empire, both at home in Assyria and abroad, so that revolts of the sort that had nearly destroyed it would be less possible. Within Assyria, he increased the number of administrative districts, thus decreasing the strength of each. This reduced the likelihood of successful rebellions launched by dissatisfied governors. Outside Assyria proper, whenever possible the king liquidated traditional leaders and appointed Assyrian governors, or at least assigned loyal overseers to protect his interests. Even then he did not allow governors and overseers unlimited authority or discretion; instead, he kept close contact with local administrators through a system of royal messengers.

In order to shatter regional identities, which could lead to separatist movements, Tiglath-pileser deported and resettled conquered peoples on a massive scale. He transported the Hebrews to Babylon, sent 30,000 Syrians to the Zagros Mountains, and moved 18,000 Aramaeans from the Tigris to Syria. The resettled peoples, cut off from their homelands by hundreds of miles and surrounded by people speaking different languages and practicing different religions, posed no threat to the stability of the empire.

Finally, in the tradition of his Assyrian predecessors, Tiglath-pileser and his successors maintained control of conquered peoples through a policy of unprecedented cruelty and brutality. One, for example, boasted of once having flayed an enemy's chiefs and using their skins to cover a great pillar he erected at their city gate and on which he impaled his victims.

Ironically, while the imperial military and administrative system created by the Assyrians became in time the blueprint for future empires, its very ferocity led to its downfall. The hatred inspired by such brutality led to the destruction of the Assyrian empire at the hands of a coalition of its subjects. In what is today Iran, Indo-European tribes coalesced around the Median dynasty. Egypt shook off its Assyrian lords under the leadership of the pharaoh Psamtik I (664–610 B.C.). In Babylon, which had always proven difficult for the Assyrians to control, a new Aramaean dynasty began to oppose Assyrian rule. In 612 B.C., the Medes and Babylonians joined forces to attack and destroy

Nineveh and Babylon

827–750 b.c. Revolt of Assyrian petty nobility
746–727 b.c. Tiglath-pileser III
612 b.c. Medes and Babylonians take Nineveh
539 b.c. Cyrus II of Persia takes the city of Babylon

Nineveh. Once more, the pattern begun by Sargon, of imperial expansion, consolidation, decay, and destruction, was repeated.

However, the lessons the Assyrians taught the world were not forgotten by the Babylonians, who modeled their imperial system on that of their predecessors. Administration of the New Babylonian empire, which extended roughly over the length of the Tigris and extended west into Syria and Palestine, owed much to Assyrian tradition. The Code of Hammurabi once more formed the fundamental basis for justice. Babylonian kings restored and enriched temples to the Babylonian gods, and temple lands, administered by priests appointed by the king, played an important role in Babylonian economy and culture. Babylonian priests, using the mathematical methods developed during the Old Kingdom, made important advances in mathematical astronomy.

Under King Nebuchadnezzar II, the city of Babylon reached its zenith, covering some five hundred acres and containing a population of over one hundred thousand, over twice the population of Uruk at its height. The city walls, counted among the seven wonders of the world by the later Greeks, were so wide that two chariots could ride abreast on them. And yet this magnificent fortification was never tested. In 539 b.c., a Persian army under King Cyrus II (ca. 585–ca. 529 b.c.), who had ousted the Median dynasty in 550 b.c., slipped into the city through the Euphrates riverbed at low water and took the city by surprise.

The legacy of the first 3000 years of civilization is more than a tradition of imperial conquest, exploitation, and cruelty. It goes beyond a mere catalog of discoveries, inventions, and achievements, impressive as they are. The legacy includes the basic structure of Western civilization. The floodplain civilizations and their neighbors provided the first solutions to problems of social and political organization and complex government. They built what we now recognize to have been the first cities, city-states, nation-states, and finally multinational empires. They attacked the problems of uneven distribution of natural resources through irrigation, long-distance trade, and communication. Their religious traditions, from polytheism to monotheism, provided patterns for subsequent Western religious traditions. Mesopotamian astronomy and mathematics and Egyptian engineering and building were fundamental for future civilizations. The immediate successors of these civilizations, however, would be to the west of the great river valleys, in the mountainous peninsulas and scattered islands of southern Europe.

Suggestions for Further Reading

General Reading

Cambridge Ancient History, Vol. 1, Part 1 (Cambridge: Cambridge University Press, 1970). Contains essays on every aspect of ancient civilizations.

*A. Bernard Knapp, *The History and Culture of Ancient Western Asia and Egypt* (Chicago: Dorsey Press, 1987). A good general survey of the entire period.

*Gerda Lerner, *The Creation of Patriarchy* (New York: Oxford University Press, 1986). A study of gender and politics in antiquity by a leading feminist historian.

*Barbara Lesko, "Women of Egypt and the Ancient Near East" in Renate Bridenthal, Claudia Koonz, and Susan Stuart, eds., *Becoming Visible*, 2nd ed. (Boston: Houghton Mifflin, 1987). A general survey of women in ancient civilizations.

Before Civilization

*Lewis R. Binford, *In Pursuit of the Past* (New York: Thames & Hudson, 1988). A general introduction to prehistoric archaeology, intended for a general audience by an expert.

Peter Ucko and G. W. Dimbleby, *The Domestication and Exploitation of Plants and Animals* (Chicago: Aldine, 1969). Technical essays on the origins of domestication.

Between the Two Rivers

*O. Neugebauer, *The Exact Sciences in Antiquity* (New York: Dover, 1970). A series of technical essays on ancient mathematics and astronomy.

Hans J. Nissen, *The Early History of the Ancient Near East 9000–2000 B.C.* (Chicago: University of Chicago Press, 1988). An up-to-date survey of early Mesopotamia.

*A. L. Oppenheim, *Ancient Mesopotamia*, 2nd ed. (Chicago: University of Chicago Press, 1977). Another general introduction by an expert.

*Georges Roux, *Ancient Iraq* (New York: Penguin Books, 1980). A very readable general introduction intended for a broad audience.

Morris Silver, *Economic Structures of the Ancient Near East* (New York: B&N Imports, 1985). A controversial analysis of ancient Near Eastern economy.

The Gift of the Nile

H. Frankfort, *Ancient Egyptian Religion* (New York: Harper & Row, 1961). A classic study of Egyptian religion.

---

*Indicates paperback edition available.

*B. B. G. Trigger et al., *Ancient Egypt: A Social History* (Cambridge: Cambridge University Press, 1983). A current survey of ancient Egyptian social history by a group of experts.

Between Two Worlds

John Bright, *A History of Israel*, 3rd ed. (Louisville, KY: Westminster John Knox Press, 1981). A standard history of the Israelites until the middle of the second century B.C.

A. T. Olmstead, *History of Assyria* (Chicago: University of Chicago Press, 1975). The fundamental survey of the Assyrian empire.

H. W. F. Saggs, *Everyday Life in Babylonia and Assyria* (New York: Putnam, 1965). A readable account of Babylonian and Assyrian society.

2

Early Greece

Hecuba and Achilles

The wrath of the great warrior Achilles is the subject of Homer's *Iliad*, the first and greatest epic poem of the West, written shortly after 750 B.C. Angered by a perceived slight to his honor, Achilles sulks in his tent while the other Achaeans, or Greeks, fight a desperate and losing battle against their enemies, the defenders of the city of Troy. Only after his friend Patroclus is slain by the Trojan Prince Hector does Achilles return to the battle to avenge his fallen comrade and propel the Achaeans to victory. Near the end of the epic, after he has slain Hector in hand-to-hand combat, Achilles ties his foe's body to the back of his chariot and drags it three times around Patroclus's tomb to appease his friend's spirit. The gods are horrified at this demeaning treatment of the body of one who had always been faithful in his sacrifices. Zeus, the chief god, sends his messenger Iris to Hector's mourning parents, his father, Priam, king of Troy, and his mother, Hecuba. Iris urges them to ransom their son's body from Achilles. Moved by the message, Priam goes to Achilles's tent to plead for Hector's body. Achilles, moved by pity and grief for his own father and for Patroclus, grants the old king his request, and Priam returns in sorrow to Troy bearing the body of his son for burial.

The first portions of this episode are brilliantly rendered on the side of the sixth-century B.C. *hydria*, or water pitcher, shown here. At the center, Achilles leaps into his chariot. The naked body of Hector stretches below him and the chariot rushes around the tumulus, or burial mound, of Achilles's friend, represented by the white hill to the right. Above it, the small winged spirit of Patroclus watches. In death he is a pale reflection, a shade of his former self, still attired in the clothing and arms of a warrior. But even as Achilles carries

36

out his deed of vengeance, Iris, the winged messenger of Zeus, rushes to Hector's parents, who are shown under a columned portico, which represents Troy. Typically, the artist has taken some liberty with the story. It is not the grieving father the artist has chosen to feature but rather Hecuba, Hector's disconsolate mother. In a vivid manner, totally alien to previous artistic traditions, the Greek artist, like the Greek poet, has captured the essentials of human tragedy.

For all its violent action, the *Iliad* is concerned less with what people do than with how they face the great moments of their life, their time of suffering, their time of death. Hector had died well and in so doing won immortal fame from his enemies, the Greeks. Achilles eventually acted well, and in his encounter with Priam faced the universal elements of human destiny: life, love, suffering, endurance, death. Such sentiments, expressed by Homer, became an enduring heritage of Greek civilization and, through it, the civilization of the West. In the small, fragile, and violent communities of Greek speakers spread across the Mediterranean, citizen soldiers first struggled with these and other fundamental issues that have set the agenda for the West to the present day.

*G*reece in the Bronze Age

Early in the *Iliad* Homer pauses to list the captains and ships of the besieging forces. The roll call of heroes and their homelands is more than a literary device. It is the distant echo of a vanished world, the world of "the goodly citadel of Athens, wealthy Corinth, Knossos and Gortys of the great walls, and the established fortress of Mycenae." The poet lived in an age of illiterate warrior herdsmen, of impoverished, scattered, and sparsely populated villages. Still, in the depths of this "Dark Age," roughly from 1200 to 700 B.C., the distant memory of a time of rich palaces, teeming cities, and powerful kings lived on. Homer and his contemporaries could not know that these confused memories were of the last great Bronze Age (ca. 3500–1200 B.C.) civilization of the Mediterranean. Still less could they have imagined they were preparing the foundations of a far greater and lasting civilization, that of classical Greece.

Unlike the rich floodplains of Mesopotamia and Egypt, Greece is a stark world of mountains and sea. The rugged terrain of Greece, only 10 percent of which is flat, and the scores of islands that dot the Aegean and Ionian seas

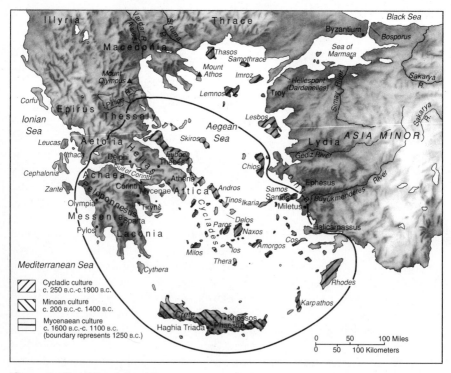

Greece in the Bronze Age

favor the development of small self-contained agricultural societies. The Greek climate is uncertain, constantly threatening Greek farmers with failure. Rainfall varies enormously from year to year, and arid summers alternate with cool, wet winters. Greek farmers struggled to produce the Mediterranean triad of grains, olives, and wine, which first began to dominate agriculture around 3000 B.C. Wheat, barley, and beans were the staples of Greek life. Constant fluctuations in climate and weather from region to region helped break down the geographical isolation by forcing insular communities to build contacts with a wider world in order to survive.

Islands of Peace

To Homer, the Greeks were all Achaeans no matter whether they came from the Greek mainland, the islands in the Aegean Sea, or the coast of Asia Minor. Since the late nineteenth century, archaeologists have discerned three fairly distinct late Bronze Age cultures—the Cycladic, the Minoan, and the Mycenaean—that flourished in the Mediterranean prior to the end of the twelfth century B.C.

The first culture appeared on the Cyclades, the rugged islands strewn across the bottom of the Aegean from the Greek mainland to the coast of Asia Minor. As early as 2500 B.C., craft workers in small settlements on the islands of Naxos and Melos developed a high level of metallurgical and artistic skill.

Cycladic society was not concentrated into towns, nor apparently was it particularly warlike. Many of the largest Cycladic settlements were unfortified. Cycladic religion, to judge from fragments of large clay statues of female figures found in a temple on the island of Ceos, focused on female deities, perhaps fertility goddesses.

This early Bronze Age society faded slowly and imperceptibly, but not before influencing its neighbors, especially Crete, the large Mediterranean island to the south. There, beginning around 2500 B.C., developed a remarkably sophisticated centralized civilization termed *Minoan* after the legendary King Minos of Crete.

Knowledge of Minoan civilization burst upon the modern world suddenly in 1899. In that year the English archaeologist Sir Arthur Evans made the first of a series of extraordinary archaeological discoveries at Knossos, the legendary palace of Minos. Crete's location between the civilizations of the Fertile Crescent and the barbarian worlds of the north and west made the island a natural point of exchange and amalgamation of cultures. Still, during the golden age of Crete, roughly between 2000 and 1550 B.C., the island developed its unique traditions.

Great palace complexes were constructed at Knossos, Phaistos, Hagia Triada, and elsewhere on the island. They appear as a maze of storerooms, workrooms, and living quarters clustered around a central square. Larger public rooms may have existed at an upper level, but all traces of them have

Marble statue of a seated harp player from the Cyclades Islands, dating from the third millennium B.C. The statue is executed in great detail despite the primitive tools at the sculptor's disposal.

disappeared. Palace bureaucrats, using a unique form of syllabic writing known as Linear A, controlled agricultural production and distribution as well as the work of skilled artisans in their surrounding areas. Towns with well-organized street plans, drainage systems, and clear hierarchies of elite and lesser homes dotted the landscape.

Like other ancient civilizations, Minoan Crete was a strongly stratified system in which the vast peasantry paid a heavy tribute in olive oil and other produce. Tribute or taxes flowed to local and regional palaces and ultimately to Knossos, which stood at the pinnacle of a four-tier network uniting the island. To some extent, the palace elites redistributed this wealth back down the system through their patterns of consumption.

Though the system may have been exploitative, it was not militaristic. None of the palaces or towns of Crete was fortified. Nor was the cult of the ruler particularly emphasized. Monumental architecture and sculpture designed to exalt the ruler and to overwhelm the commoner is entirely absent from Crete. A key to this unique social tone may be Cretan religion and, with it, the unusually high status of women. Although male gods received veneration, Cretans particularly worshiped female deities. Bulls and bull horns as well as the double-headed ax, or *labris*, played an important if today mysterious role

Faience statuette of a priestess, or perhaps a deity, from the Palace of Minos, holding two squirming snakes. The stiff, flounced skirt and bare breasts are typical of female figures found in Cretan frescoes and on gold signet rings.

in the worship of the gods. Chief among the female deities was the mother goddess, who was the source of good and evil. One must however be careful not to paint too idyllic an image of Cretan religion. Children's bones found in excavations of the palace of Knossos show traces of butchering and the removal of slices of flesh.

Although evidence such as the frequent appearance of women participating in or watching public ceremonies and the widespread worship of female deities cannot lead to the conclusion that Minoan society was a form of matriarchy, it does suggest that Minoan civilization differed considerably from the floodplain civilizations of the Near East and the societies developing on the mainland. At least until the fourteenth century B.C., Cretan society was truly unique. Both men and women seem to have shared important roles in religious and public life and together built a structured society without the need for vast armies or warrior kings.

Around 1450 B.C., a wave of destruction engulfed all of the Cretan cities except Knossos, which finally met destruction around 1375 B.C. The causes of this catastrophe continue to inspire historical debate. Some argue that a natural disaster such as an earthquake or the eruption of a powerful volcano on Thera was responsible for the destruction. More likely, given the martial traditions of the continent and their total absence on Crete, the destruction was the work of mainland Greeks taking control of Knossos and other Minoan centers. An Egyptian tomb painting from the fifteenth century B.C. graphically illustrates the transition. An ambassador in Cretan dress was overpainted by one wearing a kilt characteristic of that worn by mainland Greeks. Around this same time, true warrior graves equipped with weapons and armor begin to appear on Crete and at Knossos for the first time. Following this violent conquest, only Knossos and Phaistos were rebuilt, presumably by Greek lords who had eliminated the other political centers on the island. A final destruction hit Knossos around 1200 B.C.

Mainland of War

Around 1600 B.C., a new and powerful warrior civilization arose on the Peloponnesus at Mycenae. The only remains of the first phase of this civilization are 30 graves found at the bottom of deep shafts arranged in two circles. The swords, axes, and armor that fill the graves emphasize the warrior lives of their occupants. By 1500 B.C., mainland Greeks were using huge *tholoi*, or beehive-shaped tombs, for royal burials. These structures were magnificent achievements of architecture and masonry, far beyond anything seen previously in Europe. Over fifty such tombs have been found on the Greek mainland, as have the remains of over five hundred villages and great palaces at Mycenae, Tiryns, Athens, Thebes, Gla, and Pylos. This entire civilization, which encompassed not only the mainland but also parts of the coast of Asia Minor, is called Mycenaean, although there is no evidence that the city of Mycenae actually ruled all of Greece.

The Mycenaeans quickly adopted artisanal and architectural techniques from neighboring cultures, especially from the Hittites and from Crete. However, the Mycenaeans incorporated these techniques into a distinctive tradition of their own. Unlike the open Cretan palaces and towns, Mycenaean palaces were strongly walled fortresses. From these palaces Mycenaean kings, aided by a small military elite, organized and controlled the collection of taxes and tribute from subordinate towns and rural districts. Their palace administrators adopted the Linear A script of Crete, transforming it to write their own language, a Greek dialect, in a writing known as Linear B, which appears to have been used almost exclusively for record keeping in palaces. Mycenaean domination did not last for long. Around 1200 B.C., many of the mainland and island fortresses and cities were sacked and totally destroyed. In some areas, such as Pylos, the population fell to roughly 10 percent of what it had been previously. Centralized government, literacy, urban life, civilization itself disappeared from Greece for over four hundred years. Why and how this happened is one of the great mysteries of world history.

In later centuries the Greeks believed that following the Trojan War, new peoples, especially the Dorians, had migrated into Greece, destroying Mycenae and most of the other Achaean cities. More recently, some historians have argued that catastrophic climatic changes, volcanic eruptions, or some other natural disaster wrecked the cities and brought famine and tremendous social unrest in its wake. Neither theory is accurate. Mycenaean Greece was destroyed neither by barbarian invaders nor by acts of God. It self-destructed. Its disintegration was part of the widespread crisis affecting the eastern Mediterranean in the twelfth century B.C. (see Chapter 1, p. 31). The pyramid of Mycenaean lordship, built by small military elites commanding maritime commerical networks, was always threatened with collapse. Overpopulation, the fragility of the agrarian base, the risks of overspecialization in cash crops such as grain in Messenia and in sheep raising in Crete, and rivalry among states—all made Mycenaean culture vulnerable. The disintegration of the Hittite empire and the near collapse of the Egyptian disrupted Mediterranean commerce, exacerbating hostilities among Greek states. As internal warfare raged, the delicate structures of elite lordship disappeared in the mutual sackings and destructions of the palace fortresses. The Dark Age poet Hesiod (ca. 800 B.C.), although writing about his own time, probably got it about right:

> Father will have no common bond with son
> Neither will guest with host, nor friend with friend
> The brother-love of past days will be gone . . .
> Men will destroy the towns of other men.

The Dark Age

With the collapse of the administrative and political system on which Mycenaean civilization was built, the tiny elite that had ruled it vanished as well. Some of these rulers probably migrated to the islands, especially Cyprus, and the eastern Mediterranean. Others took to piracy. What later Greeks remembered as the Trojan War may have been a cloudy recollection of the last raids of freebooters along the edge of the collapsing Hittite empire. From roughly 1200 until 800 B.C., the Aegean world entered what is generally termed the Dark Age, a confused and little known period during which Greece returned to a more primitive level of culture and society.

In the wake of the Mycenaean collapse, bands of northerners moved slowly into the Peloponnesus while other Greeks migrated out from the mainland to the islands and the coast of Asia Minor. As these tribal groups merged with the indigenous populations they gave certain regions distinctive dialectic and cultural characteristics. Thus the Dorians settled in much of the Peloponnesus, Crete, and southwest Asia Minor. Ionians made Attica, Euboea, and the Aegean islands their home; a mixed group called Aeolians began to migrate to central and northwest Asia Minor. As a result, from the eleventh century B.C., both shores of the Aegean became part of a Greek-speaking world. Still later, Greeks established colonies in what is today southern Ukraine, Italy, North Africa, Spain, and France. Throughout its history, Greece was less a geographical than a cultural designation.

Everywhere in this world, between roughly 1100 and 1000 B.C., architecture, urban traditions, even writing disappeared along with the elites for whose exclusive benefit these achievements had served. The Greece of this Dark Age was much poorer, more rural, and more simply organized. It was also a society of ironworkers. Iron began to replace bronze as the most common metal for ornaments, tools, and weapons. At first this was a simple necessity. The collapse of long-distance trade deprived Greeks of access to tin and copper, the essential ingredients of bronze. Gradually, however, the quality of iron tools and weapons began to improve as smiths learned to work hot iron into a primitive steel.

What little is known of this period must be gleaned from archaeology and from two great epic poems written down around 750 B.C., near the end of the Dark Age. The archaeological record is bleak. Pictorial representation of humans and animals almost disappears. Luxury goods and most imports are gone from tombs. Pottery made at the beginning of the Dark Age shows little innovation, crudely imitating forms of Mycenaean production.

Gradually, beginning in the eleventh century B.C., things began to change a bit. New geometric forms of decoration begin to appear on pottery. New types of iron pins, weapons, and decorations appeared, which owe little or nothing to the Mycenaean tradition. Cultural changes accompanied these material changes. Around the middle of the eleventh century B.C., Greeks in some locations stopped burying their dead and began to practice cremation. Whatever the meaning of these changes, they signaled something new on the shores of the Aegean.

The two epic poems, the *Iliad* and the *Odyssey*, hint at this something new. The *Iliad* is the older poem, dating probably to the second half of the eighth century B.C. The *Odyssey* dates from perhaps fifty years later. Traditionally ascribed to Homer, these epics were actually the work of oral bards or performers who composed as they chanted. The world in which the action of the Homeric epics takes place was already passing away when the poems were composed, but the world described is not really that of the late Bronze Age. Although the poems explicitly harken back to the Mycenaean age, much of the description of life, society, and culture actually reflects Dark Age conditions.

Homer's heroes were petty kings, chieftains, and nobles, whose position rested on their wealth, measured in land and flocks, on personal prowess, on networks of kin and allies, and on military followings. The Homeric hero Odysseus is typical of these Dark Age chieftains. In the *Iliad* and the *Odyssey* he is king of Ithaca, a small island on the west coast of Greece. To the Homeric poets he was "goodly Odysseus" as well as "the man of wiles" and "the waster of cities." He retained command of his men only as long as he could lead them to victory in the raids against their neighbors, which formed the most honorable source of wealth. Odysseus describes his departure for home after the fall of Troy with pride:

The wind that bore me from Ilios brought me . . . to Ismarus,
whereupon I sacked their city and slew the people. And from the

city we took their wives and much goods, and divided them among
us, that none through me might go lacking his proper share.

Present, the king was judge, gift giver, lawgiver, and commander. Absent, no legal or governmental institutions preserved his authority. Instead the nobility, lesser warriors who were constantly at odds with the king, sought to take his place. In the *Odyssey* only their mutual rivalry saves Odysseus's wife, Penelope, from being forced to marry one of these haughty aristocrats eager to replace the king.

These nobles, warriors wealthy enough to possess horses and weapons, lived to prove their strength and honor in combat against their equals, the one true test of social value. The existence of chieftains such as Odysseus was a threat to their honor, and by the eighth century B.C., the aristocracy had eliminated kings in most places. Ranking beneath these proud warriors was the populace. Some of this group were slaves, but most were shepherds or farmers too mired down in the laborious work of subsistence agriculture to participate in the heroic lifestyle of their social betters. Still, even the populace were not entirely excluded from public life. Odysseus's son Telemachus summoned the assembly of the people, the *demos*, to listen to his complaints against the noble suitors of his mother. This does not mean that the assembly was particularly effective. They listened to both sides and did nothing. Still, a time was coming when changes in society would give a new and hitherto unimagined power to the silent farmers and herdsmen of the Dark Age.

*A*rchaic Greece

Between roughly 800 and 500 B.C., extraordinary changes took place in the Greek world. The descendants of the farmers and herdsmen of Homer's Dark Age brought about a revolution in political organization, artistic traditions, intellectual values, and social structures. In a burst of creativity forged in conflict and competition, they invented politics, invented abstract thought, invented the individual. Greeks of the Archaic Age (ca. 700–500 B.C.) set the agenda for the rest of Western history.

The first sign of radical change in Greece was a major increase in population in the eighth century B.C. In Attica for example, between 780 and 720 B.C., the population increased perhaps sevenfold. The reasons for this extraordinary increase are obscure, but it may have resulted from a shift from herding to agriculture. In any case the consequences were enormous. First, population increase meant more villages and towns, greater communication among them, and thus the more rapid circulation of ideas and skills. Second, the rising population placed impossible demands on the agricultural system of much of Greece. Third, it led to greater division of labor and, with an increasingly diverse population, to fundamental changes in political systems.

The old structure of loosely organized tribes and chieftains became inadequate to deal with the more complex nature of the new society.

The multiplicity of political and social forms developing in the Archaic Age set the framework in which developed the first flowering of Greek culture. Economic and political transformations laid the basis for intellectual advance by creating a broad class with the prosperity to enjoy sufficient leisure for thought and creative activity. Finally, maritime relations brought people and ideas from around the Greek world together, cross-fertilizing artists and intellectuals in a way never before seen in the West.

Ethnos and Polis

In general, two forms of political organization developed in response to the population explosion of the eighth century B.C. On the mainland and in much of the western Peloponnesus, people continued to live in large territorial units called *ethnē* (sing. *ethnos*). In each ethnos people lived in villages and small towns scattered across a wide region. Common customs and a common religion focusing on a central religious sanctuary united them. The ethnos was govered by an elite, or *oligarchy*, meaning "rule by the few," made up of major landowners who met from time to time in one or another town within the region. This form of government, which had its roots in the Dark Ages, continued to exist throughout the classical period.

A much more innovative form of political organization, which developed on the shores of the Aegean and on the islands, was the *polis* (pl. *poleis*), or city-state. Initially, *polis* meant simply "citadel." Villages clustered around these fortifications, which were both protective structures and cult centers for specific deities. These high fortified sites—*acropolis* means "high citadel"—were sacred to specific gods: in Athens and Sparta, to Athena; in Argos and Samos, to Hera; at Corinth and Thermon, to Apollo. In addition to protection, the polis offered a marketplace, or *agora*, where farmers and artisans could trade and conduct business. The rapid population growth of the eighth century B.C. led to the fusion of these villages and the formation of real towns. Each town was independent, each was ruled by a monarch or an oligarchy, and each controlled the surrounding region, the inhabitants of which were on an equal footing with the townspeople. At times of political or military crisis, the rulers might summon an assembly of the free males of the community to the agora to participate in or to witness the decision-making process. In the following centuries, these city-states became the center for that most dramatic Greek experiment in government—democracy.

The general model of the polis may have been borrowed from the eastern Mediterranean Phoenicians, the merchant society responsible for much of the contact Greeks of the eighth century B.C. had with the surrounding world. The Phoenicians were certainly the source of an equally important innovation that appeared in Greece at the same time: the reintroduction of writing. The Linear

B script had entirely disappeared, along with the complex palace systems that it had served. Sometime in the eighth century B.C., Greeks adopted the Phoenician writing system. But this time the purpose was not primarily central administrative record keeping. From the start this writing system was intended for private, personal use and was available to virtually anyone. The Greeks radically transformed the Phoenician system, making its Semitic characters stand for arbitrary sounds and adding vowel notation in order to record poetry. Soon this writing system was used to indicate ownership of objects, to record religious and secular vows, and even to entertain.

Within the polis, political power was not the monopoly of the aristocracy. The gradual expansion of the politically active population resulted largely from the demands of warfare. In the Dark Age, warfare had been dominated by heavily armed, mounted aristocrats who engaged their equals in single combat. In the Archaic Age, such individual combat between aristocratic warriors gave way to battles decided by the use of well-disciplined ranks of infantrymen called *phalange* (sing. *phalanx*). While few Greeks could afford costly weapons, armor, and horses, between 25 and 40 percent of the landowners could provide the shields, lances, and bronze armor needed by the infantryman, or *hoplites*.

The democratization of war led gradually to the democratization of political life. Those who brought victory in the phalanx were unwilling to accept total domination by the aristocracy in the agora. The rapid growth of the urban population, the increasing impoverishment of the rural peasantry, and the rise of a new class of wealthy merchant commoners were all challenges that traditional forms of government failed to meet. Everywhere

A Greek hoplite

traditional aristocratic rule was being undermined, and cities searched for ways to resolve this social conflict. No one solution emerged, and one of the outstanding achievements of archaic Greece was the almost limitless variety of political forms elaborated in its city-states.

Colonists and Tyrants

Colonization and tyranny were two intertwined results of the political and social turmoil of the seventh century B.C. Population growth, changes in economy, and opposition to aristocratic power led Greeks to seek change externally through emigration and internally through political restructuring.

Already late in the eleventh century B.C., Greeks began to migrate to new homes on the islands and along the coast of Asia Minor, in search of commercial advantages or a better life. By the eighth century B.C., Greeks had pushed east as far as Al Mina in northern Syria and Tarsus in eastern Asia Minor.

Beginning around 750 B.C., a new form of colonization began in the western Mediterranean. The impetus for this expansion was not primarily trade, but rather the need to reduce population pressure at home. The first noteworthy colony, Cumae near Naples, was founded by emigrants from Euboea. Soon other cities sent colonists to southern Italy and Sicily. Around 700 B.C., similar colonies appeared in the northeast in Thrace, on the shores of the Black Sea, and as far as the mouth of the Don River.

Colonists were not always volunteers. At Thera, for example, young men were chosen by lot to colonize Cyrene. The penalty for refusing to participate was death and confiscation of property. Usually colonists included only single

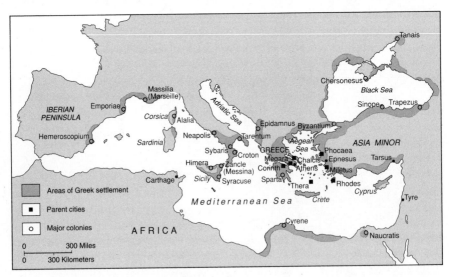

Greek cities and colonies of the Archaic Age

males, the most volatile portion of the community. Colonies were thus a safety valve to release the pressures of population growth and political friction. Although colonies remained attached culturally to their mother cities, they were politically independent. The men who settled them were warriors as well as farmers or traders and carved out their new cities at the expense of the local population.

Colonization relieved some of the population pressure on Greek communities, but it did not solve the problem of political conflict. As opposition to entrenched aristocracies grew, first in Argos, then at Corinth, Sicyon, Elis, Mytilene, and elsewhere, individuals supported by those opposed to aristocratic rule seized power. These rulers were known as *tyrants*, a term that originally meant the same as *king*. In the course of the later sixth century B.C., *tyrant* came to designate those who had achieved supreme power without benefit of official position. Often, this rise to power came through popularity with hoplite armies. However, the term *tyrant* did not carry the negative connotation associated with it today. Early tyrants were generally welcomed by their fellow citizens and played a crucial role in the destruction of aristocratic government and the creation of civic traditions.

Generally, tyrants were motivated not so much by great civic spirit as they were by the desire to win and maintain power. Still, to this end they weakened the power of entrenched aristocratic groups, promoted the prosperity of their supporters by protecting farmers and encouraging trade, undertook public works projects, founded colonies, and entered marriage alliances with rulers of other cities, which provided some external peace. Although they stood outside the traditional organs of government, tyrants were frequently content to govern through them, leaving magistracies and offices intact but ensuring that through elections these offices were filled with the tyrant's supporters. Thus at Corinth, Mytilene, Athens, and elsewhere, tyrants preserved and even strengthened constitutional structures as a hedge against the return to power of aristocratic factions.

Greece in the Bronze Age

ca. 2500 B.C.	Beginning of Minoan civilization in Crete
ca.2000–1500 B.C.	Golden Age of Crete
ca. 1600 B.C.	Beginning of Mycenaean civilization in Greece
ca. 1450 B.C.	Cretan cities, except Knossos, destroyed
ca. 1375 B.C.	Knossos destroyed
ca. 1200–700 B.C.	Greek Dark Age
ca. 1200 B.C.	Mycenaean sites in Greece destroyed; Knossos destroyed again
ca. 1100–1000 B.C.	Writing disappears from Greece

The great weakness of tyrannies was that they depended for their success on the individual qualities of the ruler. Tyrants tended to pass their powers on to their sons and, as tyrannies became hereditary, cities came to resent incompetent or excessively harsh heirs' arbitrary control of government. As popular tyranny gave way to harsh and arbitrary rule, opposition brought on civil war and the deposition or abdication of the tyrant. Gradually tyranny acquired the meaning it bears today, and new forms of government emerged. Still, in spite of the bitter memory Greek tyranny left in people's minds, in many cities tyrants had for a time solved the crisis of political order and had cleared the way for broader participation in public life than had ever before been known.

Gender and Power

Military, political, and cultural life in the city-states became more democratic, but this democratization did not extend to women. Greek attitudes toward gender roles and sexuality were rigid. Except in a few cities, and in certain religious cults, women played no public role in the life of the community. They remained firmly under male control throughout their lives, passing from the authority of their fathers to that of their husbands. For the most part friendship existed only between members of the same sex, and this friendship was often intensely sexual. Thus bisexuality was the norm in Greek society, although neither Greek homosexuality nor heterosexuality were the same as they are in modern society. Rather, both coexisted and formed a part of a sexuality of domination by those considered superior in age, rank, or sex over others. Mature men took young boys as their lovers, helped to educate them, and inspired them by word and deed to grow into ideal warriors and citizens. We know less about such practices among women, but teachers such as Sappho of Lesbos (ca. 610–ca. 580 B.C.) formed similar bonds with their pupils, even while preparing them for marriage.

Those women who were in public life were mostly slaves, frequently prostitutes. These ranged from impoverished streetwalkers to *hetairai*, educated, sophisticated courtesans who entertained men at *symposia* (sing. *symposion*), or male banquets, which were the centers of cultural and social life. Greek society did not condemn or even question infanticide, prostitution, and sexual exploitation of women and slave boys. These practices formed part of the complex and varied social systems of the developing city-states.

Gods and Mortals

Greeks and their gods enjoyed an ambivalent, peculiar, almost irreverent relationship. On the one hand, Greeks made regular offerings to the gods, pleaded with them for help, and gave them thanks for assistance. On the other, the gods were thoroughly human, sharing in an exaggerated manner not only human strengths and virtues but also weaknesses and vices.

Greeks offered sacrifices to the gods on alters, which were raised everywhere—in homes, in fields, in sacred groves. No group had the sort of monopoly on the cult of the gods enjoyed by Mesopotamian and Egyptian priests. Unlike the temples of other societies, Greek temples were houses of the gods, not centers of ritual. The so-called Doric temple, which housed a statue of the god, consisted of an oblong or rectangular room covered by a pitched roof and circled by columns. These temples reflected the wealth and patriotism of the city. They stood as monuments to the human community rather than to the divine.

On special occasions, festivals celebrated at sanctuaries honored the gods of the city with processions, athletic contests, and feasts. Some of these celebrations drew participants from all of the Greek world. The two greatest pan-Hellenic (meaning "all Greek," from *Hellas*, the Greek word for Greece) sanctuaries were Olympia and Delphi. Because both were remote from centers of political power, they were insulated from interstate rivalry and provided neutral ground on which hostile neighbors could meet in peace.

Beginning in 776 B.C., every four years, wars and conflicts were temporarily suspended while athletes from the whole Greek world met at Olympia to participate in contests in honor of Zeus. The religious nature of the contests lowered neither their heated interstate rivalry nor the violence with which they were pursued. Wrestling in particular could be deadly, since matches continued until one participant signaled that he had had enough. Many wrestlers chose death rather than defeat. Victors were seen as ideal humans, the perfect triumph of body and soul, and Olympic victors were treated as national heroes.

Delphi, the site of the shrine of Apollo, god of music, archery, medicine, and prophecy, was the second pan-Hellenic cult center. Like Olympia, Delphi drew athletes from the whole Greek world to its athletic contests. However, Delphi's real fame lay in its oracle, or spokeswoman for the god Apollo. From the eighth century B.C., before undertaking any important decision such as establishing a colony, beginning a war, or even contracting a marriage, individuals and representatives of distant cities traveled to Delphi to ask Apollo's advice or to seek purification from the guilt attached to shedding others' blood and reconciliation with their fellow citizens. For a stiff fee, visitors were allowed to address questions to the god through a female medium. She entered a trance state and uttered a reply, which lay priests at the shrine then put into verse form and transmitted to the petitioner. The ambiguity of the Delphic replies was legendary.

Though gods were petitioned, placated, and pampered, they were not privileged or protected. Unlike the awe-inspiring gods of the Mesopotamians and Egyptians, the traditional Greek gods, inherited from the Dark Age, were represented in ways that showed them as all too human, vicious, and frequently ridiculous. Zeus was infamous for his frequent rapes of boys and girls. His lust was matched only by the fury of his jealous wife, Hera. The Greek gods were immortal, superhuman in strength, and able to interfere in human affairs. But in all things, they reflected the values and weaknesses of the Greek mortals, who could bargain with them, placate them, and even trick them.

Religious cults were not under the exclusive control of any priesthood or political group. Thus there were no official versions of stories of gods and goddesses. This is evident both from Greek poetry, which often presents contradictory stories of the gods, and from pottery, which bears pictorial versions of myths that differ greatly from written ones. No one group or sacred site enjoyed a monopoly on access to the gods. Like literacy and government, the gods belonged to all.

Myth and Reason

The glue holding together the individual and frequently hostile Greek poleis and ethnē scattered throughout the Mediterranean was their common stock of myths and a common fascination with the Homeric legends. Stories of gods and heroes, told and retold, were fashioned into *mythoi* (myths, literally, "formulated speech"), which explained and described the world both as it was and as it should be. Myths were told about every city, shrine, river, mountain, and island. Myths explained the origins of cities, festivals, the world itself. What is the place of humans in the cosmos? They stand between beasts and gods because Prometheus tricked Zeus and gave men fire with which they cook their food and offer the bones and fat of sacrificial animals to the gods. Whey is there evil and misfortune? Because, Greek men explained, in revenge for Prometheus's trickery, Zeus offered man Pandora (the name means "all gifts"), the first woman, whose beauty hid her evil nature. By accepting this gift, humans brought evil and misfortune on themselves. Such stories were more than simply fanciful explanations of how things came to be. Myths sanctioned and supported the authority of social, political, and religious traditions. They presented how things had come to be in a manner that prescribed how they were to remain. In the process of revising and retelling, myths became a powerful and dynamic tool for reasoning about the world.

Archaic Greeks showed a similar combination of veneration and liberty in dealing with the Homeric legends. Thoughtful Greeks approached the heroic ideals of these epics with a sense of detachment and criticism. Some mothers might tell their sons as they marched off to war, "Return with your shield or on it," that is, victorious or dead. But Archilochus, a seventh-century B.C. lyric poet, could take a very different view of shields and honor:

> A perfect shield bedecks some Thracian now;
>   I had no choice, I left it in a wood.
> Ah, well, I saved my skin, so let it go!
>   A new one's just as good.

The new open examination of traditional values extended into all areas of investigation. By the sixth century B.C., a number of Ionian Greeks began to investigate the origins and nature of the universe, not in terms of myth or religion, but by observation and rational thought. Living on the coast of Asia Minor, these Ionians were in contact with the ancient civilizations of Mesopotamia and learned much from the Babylonian traditions of astronomy, mathematics, and science. However, their primary interest went beyond observing and recording to speculating. They were the first philosophers, intellectuals who sought natural explanations for the world around them.

Thales of Miletus (ca. 625–ca. 547 B.C.) regarded water as the fundamental substance of the universe. For Anaximander (610–ca. 527 B.C.) the primary substance was matter—eternal and indestructible. It was Anaximenes of Miletus (fl. ca. 545 B.C.) who regarded air as the primary substance of the universe. Heraclitus of Ephesus (ca. 540–ca. 480 B.C.) saw the universe not as one unchanging substance but rather as change itself. For him, the universe is constantly in flux, changing like a flickering fire. Thus all is constantly in a state of becoming, not in a static state of being. And yet this constant change is not random. The cosmic tension between stability and flux is regulated by laws that human reason can determine. The universe is rational.

The significance of such speculative thought was not in the conclusions reached, but rather in the method employed. The Ionian philosophers no longer spoke in myth but rather in plain language. They reached their conclusions through observation and rational thought in which religion and the gods played no direct role. As significant as their original speculations was the manner in which these philosophers were received. Although as late as the fourth century B.C., intellectuals still occasionally fell prey to persecution, by the sixth century B.C., much of Greek society was ready to tolerate such nonreligious rational teaching, which in other times and places would have been thought scandalous or atheistic.

Art and the Individual

Archaic Greeks borrowed from everywhere and transformed all that they borrowed. Just as they adopted and adapted the Phoenician alphabet and Mesopotamian science, they took Near Eastern and Egyptian painting and sculpture and made them their own. During the Dark Age, the Mycenaean traditions of art had entirely disappeared. Pottery showed only geometric decorations; sculpture was unknown. Gradually, from the ninth century B.C., stylized human and animal figures, lions, griffins, and other strange beasts began to appear within the tightly composed geometric patterns. But by the eighth century B.C., such exotic subjects had given way to the Greek passion for human images taken from their own myths and legends. The preferred technique was the so-called black figure style developed first at Corinth. Subjects were painted in black silhouette on red clay and then details were cut with a sharp point so that the background could show through. As the popularity of these mythic and heroic scenes increased, so, too, did the artists'

The François Vase, a wine vessel from the Greek colonies of Sicily, 570 B.C. Sixth-century B.C. potters experimented with techniques of portraying long and complicated narratives on individual vases.

technical competence. Greek artists competed with one another to overcome technical problems of perspective and foreshortening. From the sixth century B.C., many of the finest examples were signed. Such masterpieces celebrated not only the heroes of the past but also the artist as individual and as the interpreter of culture no less original than the poet.

Greek sculpture underwent a similar dramatic development. The earliest and most common subject of archaic sculpture was the standing male nude, or *kouros* figure, which was in wide demand as a grave monument, dedication to a god, or even cult statue of male deity. In Egypt, seventh-century B.C. Greeks had seen colossal statues and had learned to work stone. They brought these techniques home, improved on them by using iron tools (the Egyptians knew only bronze ones), and began to create their own human images. The rigidly formulaic position of the kouros—standing, arms by the sides, looking straight ahead, left foot extended—followed Egyptian tradition and left little room for originality. Thus sculptors sought to give their statues originality and individuality, not as representations of individuals, but as the creations of the individual sculptor. To this end, they experimented with increasingly natural molding of limbs and body and began signing their works. Thus, as in vase painting, Greek sculpture reflected the importance of the individual, not in its subject matter, but in its creator. The female counterparts of the kouros figures, called *korai*, followed similarly rigid traditions to which sculptors added female attributes.

The real challenges in sculpture came in the portrayal of narrative in decorations on monuments, primarily temples. Unlike kouroi, which were usually private commissions intended to adorn the tombs of aristocrats, these public buildings were constructed as expressions of civic pride and were accessible to everyone. Here the creativity and dynamism of Greek cities could be paralleled in stone. Figures such as the Calf-Bearer (ca. 590) from the Athenian acropolis are daring in the complexity of composition and the

Female korē and male kouros figures from the Greek Archaic period, seventh century B.C. Egyptian influence can be seen in the stiff formal poses, the broad square shoulders, and the rigid symmetry of the design.

The Calf-Bearer

delicacy of execution. These are statues that tell stories. In the Calf-Bearer, a master farmer carries a calf to be sacrificed to Athena. The two gentle heads and the cross formed by the farmer's hands and the calf's legs are individual traits without precedent in ancient art. Although formally intended for religious purposes, these figures serve not only the gods and the aristocratic elite, but the whole community.

A Tale of Three Cities

The political, social, and cultural transformations that occurred in the Archaic Age took different forms across the Greek world. No community or city-state was typical of Greece. The best way to understand the diversity of Archaic Greece is to examine three very different cities which, by the end of the sixth century B.C., had become leading centers of Greek civilization. Corinth, Sparta, and Athens present something of the spectrum of political, cultural, and social models of the Hellenic world. Corinth, like many cities, developed into a commercial center in which the assembly of citizens was dominated by an oligarchy. Sparta developed into a state in which citizenship was radically egalitarian but restricted to a small military elite. In Athens, the Archaic Age saw the foundations of an equally radical democracy.

Wealthy Corinth

Corinth owed its prosperity to its privileged site, dominating both a rich coastal plain and the narrow isthmus connecting the Peloponnesus to the mainland. In the eighth century B.C., as Greeks turned their attention to the west, Corinthians led the way. Corinthian pottery appeared throughout western Greece and southern Italy. Corinthian trade led to colonization, and settlers from Corinth founded Syracuse and other cities in Sicily and Italy, which served as markets for Corinthian products. Even more important to Corinthian prosperity was its role in the transport of other cities' products from east to west. By carrying goods across the isthmus and loading them onto other ships, merchants could avoid the long and dangerous passage around the Peloponnesus.

The precise details of early Corinthian government are uncertain. Still, it appears that in Corinth as in many other cities, a tyranny replaced a ruling clan and in time this tyranny ended with an oligarchic government. Until the middle of the seventh century B.C., Corinth and its wealth were ruled in typical Dark Age fashion by an aristocratic clan known as the Bacchiads. Corinth began its rise under this aristocratic rule, and individual Bacchiads led colonizing expeditions to Italy and Sicily. However, the increasing pressures of population growth, rapidly expanding wealth, and dramatic changes in the economy produced social tensions that the traditional aristocratic rulers were unable to handle. As in cities throughout the Greek world, these tensions led to the creation of a new order.

The early history of Corinth is obscure, but apparently around 650 B.C. a revolution led by a dissident Bacchiad named Cypselus (ca. 657–627 B.C.) and supported by non-Bacchiad aristocrats and other Corinthians broke the Bacchiads' grip on the city. The revolution led to the establishment of Cypselus as tyrant. Cypselus and his son Periander (ca. 627–586 B.C.) seem to have been generally popular with most Corinthians.

In Corinth, as in many other cities, the tyrants restructured taxes, relying primarily on customs duties, which were less of a burden on the peasantry. Around 600 B.C., Periander began construction of a causeway across the isthmus on which ships could be hauled from the Aegean to the western Mediterranean. This causeway eventually became a major source of Corinth's wealth. Periander attacked conspicuous consumption on the part of the aristocracy. He introduced laws against idleness and put thousands of Corinthians to work in extensive building programs. He erected temples and sent colonists to Italy. Under his leadership the Corinthian fleet developed into the most powerful naval force in the Adriatic and Aegean seas. Under its tyrants, Corinth led the Greek world in the production of black figure pottery, which spread throughout the Mediterranean.

The tyrants also laid the foundation for broader political participation. Cypselus divided the population into eight tribes, based not on traditional ethnic divisions, but on arbitrary groupings by region. All of Corinth was divided into three large regions. The population of each region was distributed among each of the eight tribes. This assignment prevented the emergence of political factions based on regional disputes. Ten representatives from each tribe formed a council of 80 men. Under the tyrants, this council was largely advisory and provided a connection between the autocratic rulers and the citizens.

In Corinth as elsewhere, the strength or weakness of tyranny rested on the abilities and personality of individual tyrants. Cypselus had been a beloved liberator. His son Periander, in spite of his accomplishments, was remembered for his cruelty and violence. Shortly after Periander's death in 586 B.C., a revolt killed his successor, and tyranny in Corinth ended.

The new government continued the tribal and council system established by Cypselus. From the sixth century B.C. until its conquest by Macedonia in 338 B.C., Corinth was ruled by an oligarchy. Although an assembly of the *demos*, or adult males, met occasionally, actual government was in the hands of 8 deliberators, or *probouloi*, and 9 other men from each tribe who together formed the council of 80. The oligarchs who made up the council avoided the kind of exclusive and arbitrary tendencies that had destroyed both the Bacchiads and the tyrants. They were remarkably successful in maintaining popular support among the citizens and provided a reliable and effective government.

Thus Corinth flourished, a city more open to commerce and wealth than most, moderate in its political institutions and eager for stability. As one fourth-century B.C. poet wrote:

> (There) lawfulness dwells, and her sister,
> Safe foundation of cities,
> Justice, and Peace, who was bred with her;
> They dispense wealth to men.

Martial Sparta

At the beginning of the eighth century B.C., the Peloponnesus around Sparta and Laconia faced circumstances similar to those of Corinth and other Greek communities. Population growth, increasing disparity between rich and poor, and an expanding economy created powerful tensions. However, while Corinthian society developed into a complex mix of aristocrats, merchants, artisans, and peasants, ruled by an oligarchy, the Spartan solution presented a rigid two-tiered social structure. By the end of the Archaic Age, a small homogeneous class of warriors called *homoioi*, or equals, ruled a vast population of state serfs, or *helots*. The two classes lived in mutual fear and mistrust. Spartans controlled the helots through terror and ritual murder. The helots in turn were "an enemy constantly waiting for the disasters of the Spartans." And yet, throughout antiquity the Spartans were the Greeks most praised for their courage, simplicity of life, and service to the state.

War was the center of Spartan life, and war lay at the origin of the Spartans' extraordinary social and political organization. In the eighth century B.C., the Spartans conquered the fertile region of Messenia and compelled the vanquished Messenians to turn over one-half of their harvests. The spoils were not divided equally, but went to increase the wealth of the aristocracy, thus creating resentment among the less privileged. Early in the seventh century B.C., the Spartans attempted a simlar campaign to take the plain of Thyreatis from the city of Argos. This time they were not so fortunate; they were defeated, and resentment of the ordinary warriors toward their aristocratic leaders flared into open conflict. The Messenians seized upon this time as a moment to revolt, and for a time Sparta was forced to fight at home and abroad for its very existence. In many cities, such crises gave rise to tyrants. In Sparta, the crisis led to radical political and social reforms that transformed the polis into a unique military system.

The Spartans attributed these reforms to the legendary lawgiver Lycurgus (seventh century B.C.). Whether or not Lycurgus ever existed and was responsible for all of the reforms, they saved the city and ended its internal tensions at the expense of abandoning the mainstream of Greek development. Traditionally, Greeks had placed personal honor above communal concerns. During the crisis of the second Messenian war, Spartans of all social ranks were urged to look not to individual interest but to *eunomia*, good order and obedience to the laws, which alone could unite Spartans and bring victory. United, the

---

Archaic Greece

ca. 780–720 B.C.	Population increase in Greece
776 B.C.	First Olympic Games held
ca. 750–700 B.C.	Greeks develop writing system based on Phoenician model; Greeks begin colonizing western Mediterranean
ca. 700–500 B.C.	Archaic Age of Greece
ca. 700 B.C.	First stone temples appear in Greece
ca. 650 B.C.	Cypselus breaks rule of Bacchaids in Corinth; rules city as tyrant
594 B.C.	Solon elected chief archon of Athens; institutes social and political reforms
586 B.C.	Death of Periander ends tyrants' rule in Corinth
499 B.C.	Ionian cities revolt

Spartans crushed the Messenians. In return for obedience, poor citizens received equality before the law and benefited from a land distribution that relieved their poverty. Conquered land, especially that in Messenia, was divided and distributed to Spartan warriors. However, the Spartan warriors were not expected to work the land themselves. Instead, the state reduced the defeated Messenians to the status of helots and assigned them to individual Spartans. While this system did not erase all economic inequalities among the Spartans (aristocrats continued to hold more land than others), it did decrease some of the disparity. It also provided a minimum source of wealth for all Spartan citizens and allowed them to devote themselves to full-time military service.

This land reform was coupled with a political reform that incorporated elements of monarchy, oligarchy, and democracy. The state was governed by two hereditary kings and a council of elders, the *gerousia*. In peacetime, the authority of the two royal families was limited to familial and religious affairs. In war, they commanded the army and held the power of life and death.

In theory at least, the central institution of Spartan government was the gerousia, which was composed of 30 men at least 60 years of age and included the two kings. The gerousia directed all political activity, especially foreign affairs, and served as high court. Members were elected for life by the assembly, or *apella*, which was composed of all equals over the age of 30 and which approved decisions of the gerousia. However, this approval, made by acclamation, could easily be manipulated, as could the course of debate within the gerousia itself. Wealth, cunning, and patronage were more important in the direction of the Spartan state than its formal structures.

Actual administration was in the hands of five magistrates termed *ephors*. Their powers were extremely broad. They presided over joint sessions of the gerousia and apella. They held supreme authority over the kin during war-time and acted as judges for noncitizens. Finally, the ephors controlled the *krypteia*, or secret police, a band of youths who practiced state terrorism as part of their rite of passage to the status of equal. On the orders of the ephors, the krypteia assassinated, intrigued, arrested powerful people, and terrorized helots. Service in this corps was considered a necessary part of a youth's education.

The key to the success of Sparta's political reform was an even more radical social reform that placed everyone under the direct supervision and service of the state from birth until death. Although admiring aristocratic visitors often exaggerated their accounts of Spartan life, the main outlines are clear enough. *Eunomia* was the sole guiding principle, and service to the state came before family, social class, and every other duty or occupation.

Spartan equals were made, not born. True, only a man born of free Spartan parents could hope to become an equal, but birth alone was no guarantee of admission to this select body, or even of the right to live. Public officials examined infants and decided whether they were sufficiently strong to be allowed to live or should be exposed on a hillside to die. From birth until age 7, a boy lived with his mother, but then he entered the state education system, or *agoge*, living in barracks with his contemporaries and enduring 13 years of rigorous military training. At age 12, training with swords and spears became more intense, as did the rigors of the lifestyle. Boys were given only a single cloak to wear and slept on thin rush mats. They were encouraged to supple-ment their meager diet by stealing food, although if caught they were severely whipped, not for the theft but for the failure. All of this they were expected to endure in silence.

Much of the actual education of the youths was entrusted to older accomplished warriors who selected boys as their homosexual lovers. Not only did the lover serve as tutor and role model, but in time the two became a fighting team, each inspiring the other to show the utmost valor. At age 20, Spartan youths were enrolled in the krypteia. Each was sent out into the countryside with nothing but a cloak and a knife and forbidden to return until he had killed a helot.

If a youth survived the rigors of his training until age 30, he could at last be incorporated into the rank of equals, provided he could pass the last obstacle. He had to be able to furnish a sufficient amount of food from his own lands for the communal dining group to which he would be assigned. This food might come from inherited property or, if he had proved himself an outstanding warrior, from the state. Those who passed this final qualification became full members of the assembly, but they continued to live with the other warriors. Men could marry at age 20, but family life in the usual sense was nonexistent. A man could not live with his wife until age 30 because he was bound to the barracks.

Although their training was not as rigorous as that of males, Spartan women were given an education and allowed a sphere of activity unknown elsewhere in Greece. Girls, like boys, were trained in athletic competition and, again like them, competed naked in wrestling, footraces, and spear throwing. This training was based not on a belief in the equality of the sexes but simply on the desire to improve the physical stamina and childbearing abilities of Spartan women. Women were able to own land and to participate widely in business and agricultural affairs, the reason being that since men were entirely involved in military pursuits, women were expected to look after economic and household affairs.

Few Lacedaemonians (as Spartans were also called) ever became equals. Not only were there far more helots than Spartans, but many inhabitants of the region, termed *perioikoi*, or peripherals, although they were free citizens of their local communities, were not allowed into the agoge. Others were washed out, unable to endure the harsh life, and still others lacked the property qualifications to supply their share of the communal meals. Thus for all the trappings of egalitarianism, equality in Sparta was the privilege of a tiny minority.

The total dedication to military life was reinforced by a deliberate rejection of other activities. From the time of the second Messenian war, Sparta withdrew from the mainstream of Greek civilization. Equals could not engage in crafts, trade, or any other forms of economic activity. Because Sparta banned silver and gold coinage, it could not participate in the growing commercial network of the Greek world. Although a group of free citizens of subject towns could engage in such activities, the role of Sparta in the economic, architectural, and cultural life of Greece was negligible after the seventh century B.C. Militarily, Sparta cast a long shadow across the Peloponnesus and beyond, but the number of equals was always too small to allow Sparta both to create a vast empire and to maintain control over the helots at home. Instead, Sparta created a network of alliances and nonaggression pacts with oligarchic neighbors. In time this network came to be known as the Peloponnesian League.

Democratic Athens

Athens did not enjoy the advantages of a strategic site such as that of Corinth, nor was it surrounded by rich plains like Sparta. However, the "goodly citadel of Athens" was one of the few Mycenaean cities to have escaped destruction at the start of the Dark Age. Gradually Athens united the whole surrounding region of Attica into a single polis, by far the largest in the Greek world. Well into the seventh century B.C., Athens followed the general pattern of the polis seen in Corinth and Sparta. Like other Dark Age communities, Athens was ruled by aristocratic clans, particularly the Alcmaeonids. Only the members of these clans could participate in the *areopagus*, or council, which they entered after serving a year as one of the nine *archons*, or magistrates, elected yearly. Until the seventh century B.C., Athens escaped the social pressures brought on by population growth and economic prosperity that led to civil strife, colonialism, and tyranny elsewhere. This was due largely to its relative abundance of arable land and its commercial prosperity based on the export of grain.

By the late seventh century B.C., however, Athens began to suffer from the same class conflict that had shaken other cities. Sometime around 630 B.C., an aristocrat named Cylon attempted to seize power as tyrant. His attempt failed, but when he was murdered by one of the Alcmaeonids, popular revulsion drove the Alcmaeonids from the city. A decade of strife ensued as aristocratic clans, wealthy merchants, and farmers fought for control of the city. Violence between groups and families threatened to tear the community apart. In 621 B.C., the Athenians granted a judge, Draco, extraordinary powers to revise and systematize traditional laws concerning vengeance and homicide. His restructuring of procedures for limiting vengeance and preventing bloodshed were harsh enough to add the term *Draconian* to Western legal vocabulary. When asked why death was the most common penalty he imposed, Draco explained that minor offenses merited death and he knew of no more severe penalty for major ones. Still, these measures did nothing to solve the central problems of political control. Finally in 594 B.C., Solon (ca. 630–ca. 560 B.C.), an aristocratic merchant, was elected chief archon and charged with restructuring the city's government. Solon based his reform on the ideal of eunomia as had the Spartans, but he followed a very different path to secure good order.

In Sparta, Lycurgus had begun with a radical redistribution of land. In Athens, Solon began with the less extreme measure of eliminating debt bondage. Athenians who had been forced into slavery or into sharecropping because of their debts were restored to freedom. A law forbade mortgaging free men and women as security for debts. Athenians might be poor, but they would be free. This free peasantry formed the basis of Athenian society throughout its history.

Solon also reorganized the rest of the social hierarchy and broke the aristocracy's exclusive control of the areopagus by dividing the society into four classes based on wealth rather than birth and opening the archonship to the top two classes. He further weakened the areopagus by establishing a council of 400 members drawn from all four classes to which citizens could appeal decisions of the magistrates.

Although Solon's reforms established the framework for a resolution of Athens's social tensions, they did not entirely succeed. Solon himself did not consider his new constitution perfect, only practical. Resistance from the still powerful aristocracy prompted some Athenians to urge Solon to assume the powers of a tyrant in order to force through his reforms. He refused, but after his death, Peisistratus (d. 527 B.C.), an aristocrat strongly supported by the peasants against his own class, hired a mercenary force to seize control of the city. After two abortive attempts, Peisistratus ruled as tyrant from 545 B.C. until his death.

Peisistratus might have governed the city, for a while at least, as an absolute tyrant. Instead, he and later his son Hippias (d. 490 B.C.), who succeeded him until 510 B.C., continued to rule through Solon's constitution but simply ensured that the archons elected each year were their agents.

Peisistratus and Hippias drew their support from the demos, or people at large, rather than from an aristocratic faction. They claimed divine justification for their rule and made a great show of devotion to the Athenian gods. Peisistratus promoted annual festivals, and in so doing began the great tradition of Athenian literature. At the festival of Athena, professional reciters of *rhapsoidiai* (epic poetry) recited large portions of the *Iliad* and the *Odyssey*. During a festival in honor of Dionysus, actors performed the first tragedies and comedies. The tyrants also directed a series of popular nationalistic public works programs that beautified the city, increased national pride, and provided work for the poor. They rebuilt the temple of Athena on the acropolis, for which the statue of the Calf-Bearer was commissioned. These internal measures were accompanied by support for commerce and export, particularly of grain. Soon, Athens was challenging Corinth as the leading commercial power and trading in grain as far away as the Black Sea.

Peisistratus was firm. His son Hippias was harsh. Still, even Hippias enjoyed the support of the majority of the citizens of both popular and aristocratic factions. Only after the assassination of his younger brother did Hippias become sufficiently oppressive to drive his opponents into exile. Some of these exiles obtained the assistance of Sparta and returned to overthrow Hippias in 510 B.C. Hippias's defeat ended the tyrants' rule in Athens and won for Sparta an undeserved reputation as the opponent of all tyranny.

Following the expulsion of Hippias, some aristocrats attempted to return to the "good old days" of aristocratic rule. However, for more than eighty years, Athenians had been accustomed to Solon's constitution and were unwilling to give it up. Moreover, the tyrants had created a fierce sense of nationalistic pride among all ranks of Athenians, and few were willing to turn over

Bronze statue of a Greek warrior from the sixth century B.C. The figure is slightly less than six inches high and stands on a base of red marble. The warrior is draped in a cloak and wears a helmet of the Corinthian type, covering the head and face.

government to the hands of only a few. Thus, when the aristocrats made their bid to recover power, their primary opponent, Cleisthenes (ca. 570–ca. 507 B.C.), "made the demos his faction" and pushed through a final constitutional reform that became the basis for Athenian democracy.

The essence of Cleisthenes's reform lay in his reorganization of the major political units by which members of the council were selected. Previously, each citizen had belonged to one of four tribes, further broken down into 12 brotherhoods, or *phratries*, which were administrative and religious units. In a manner similar to that of Cypselus in Corinth, Cleisthenes reshuffled these phratries into 30 territorial units, or *demes*, comprising urban, inland, or coastal regions. These 30 units in turn were grouped into 10 tribes, each consisting of one unit from each of the urban, inland, and coastal regions. The tribes elected the members of the council, military commanders, jurors, and magistrates. As in Corinth, this reorganization destroyed the traditional kin-based social and political pattern and integrated people of differing social, economic, and regional backgrounds. Aristocrats, merchants, and poor farmers had to work together to find common ground for political action, both regionally and nationally. With this new integrated democracy and its strong sense of nationalism, Athens emerged from the Archaic Age as the leading city of the Hellenic world.

$\mathcal{T}$he Fragility of the Archaic Creation

By the end of the sixth century B.C., the products of Greek experimentation were evident throughout the Mediterranean. Greek city-states had resolved the crises of class conflict. Greek merchants and artisans had found ways to flourish despite poor soil and uncertain climate. Greek philosophers, poets, and artists had begun to celebrate the human form and the human spirit. Still, these achievements were the product of small, independent, and relatively weak communities on the fringe of the civilized world.

In the second half of the sixth century B.C., this changed. The Persian empire, under its dynamic king Cyrus II, began a process of conquest and expansion west into Asia Minor, absorbing the kingdom of Lydia and conquering Ionia on the coast of Asia Minor. The Persians put tyrants loyal to Cyrus to rule over these Greek communities and for a few decades these centers of Greek culture and thought accepted foreign control. In 499 B.C., the passion for democracy, which had swept much of mainland Greece, reached Ionia. Cities such as Miletus, Ephesus, Chios, and Samos revolted, expelled their Persian-appointed tyrants, established democracies, and sent ambassadors to the mainland to seek assistance. Eretria and Athens, two mainland cities with Ionian roots, responded, sending ships and men to aid the Ionian rebels. Athenian interests were more than simple solidarity with their Ionian cousins. Athens depended on grain from the Black Sea region and felt its direct

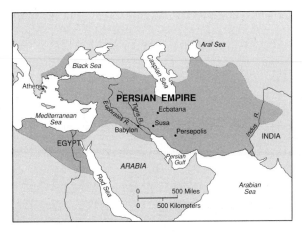

The Persian Empire, ca. 500 B.C.

interests to lie with the area. The success of the revolt was short lived. The puny Greek cities were dealing with the largest empire the West had yet known. By 500 B.C., the Persian empire included Asia Minor, Mesopotamia, Palestine, and Egypt, uniting all peoples from the Caucasus to the Sudan.

The giant Persian empire responded slowly, but with force, to the Greek revolt. King Darius I (522–486 B.C.) gathered a vast international force from throughout his empire and set about to recapture the rebellious cities. The war lasted five years and ended in a Persian victory. By 494 B.C., the Persians had retaken the cities of the coast and nearby islands. In the cities deemed most responsible for the revolt, the population was herded together, the boys were castrated and made into royal eunuchs, the girls sent to Darius's court, the remainder of the population sold into slavery, and the towns burned to the ground. Once the rebels had been disposed of, Darius set out to punish their supporters on the mainland, Eretria and Athens. With the same meticulous planning and deliberate pace, the Persian king turned his vast armies toward the Greek mainland.

Civilization developed much later in the Mediterranean world than it had in the floodplains of the Near East. The earliest Bronze Age societies of Greece and the neighboring islands, while influenced by contact with the great civilizations of Mesopotamia and Egypt, developed distinctive societies and cultures tied closely to the sea around them. Still, they too were caught up in the general cataclysm of the twelfth century B.C. Out of the ruins emerged a society much less centralized, wealthy, or powerful, but possessing an extraordinary dynamism.

The Archaic Age was an age of experimentation. Greeks, propelled by demographic and political pressures and inspired by the legends of vanished heroes, began in the eighth century B.C. to recast traditions and techniques acquired from their ancient neighbors into new forms. The multiplicity of

independent communities, their relative isolation, and their differing traditions created a wide spectrum of political forms, social structures, and cultural
values. And yet from Sicily to Asia Minor, Greeks felt themselves united by a
common language, a common cultural heritage, and a common commitment to
individual freedom within the community, whether that freedom was protected within a monarchy, a tyranny, an oligarchy, or a democracy. That
commitment to freedom, fostered in the hoplite ranks, protected in the
assembly, and increasingly expressed in poetry and sculpture, hung in the
balance as Darius and the Persians marched west.

Suggestions for Further Reading

General Reading

John Boardman, Jasper Griffin, and Oswyn Murray, *Greece and the Hellenistic
World* (Oxford: Oxford University Press, 1988). An excellent collection of essays on
Greek civilization by British scholars.

Cambridge Ancient History, Vol. 4. Contains more detailed essays on all aspects of
early Greek history.

Greece in the Bronze Age

*M. I. Finley, *The World of Odysseus*, 2nd rev. ed. (New York: Penguin, 1979). A
brilliant analysis of the Dark Age through the Homeric epics.

*M. I. Finley, *Early Greece: The Bronze and Archaic Ages*, 2nd ed. (New York: W. W.
Norton, 1982). A very readable overview by a leading Greek historian.

J. T. Hooker, *Mycenaean Greece* (New York: Routledge, Chapman & Hall, 1976).
The best introduction to Mycenaean history.

O. Krzyszkowska and L. Nixon, eds., *Minoan Society* (Bristol: Bristol Classical
Press, 1983). Excellent collection of essays on early Crete.

*N. K. Sandars, *The Sea Peoples* (New York: Thames & Hudson, 1985). A recent
survey of the controversy over the crisis of the twelfth century B.C.

*Emily Vermeule, *Greece in the Bronze Age* (Chicago: University of Chicago Press,
1964). A standard though somewhat dated study, particularly for the early material.

Archaic Greece

A. Andrewes, *The Greek Tyrants* (Atlantic Highlands, NJ: Humanities Press
International, 1956). Standard survey of Greek tyranny.

*John Boardman, *Preclassical Style and Civilization* (Harmondsworth: Penguin,
1967). A study of early Greek art by a leading archaeologist.

*John Boardman, *The Greeks Overseas* (New York: Thames & Hudson, 1982).
Description of varieties of Greek involvement abroad and their effects on Greece.

John Boardman, *Greek Sculpture: Archaic Period* (New York: Thames & Hudson,
1985). A well-illustrated survey of early Greek sculpture.

---

*Indicates paperback edition available.

*Walter Burkert, *Structure and History in Greek Mythology and Ritual* (Berkeley: University of California Press, 1980). Relates myth and religion to society and history.

R. M. Cook, *Greek Painted Pottery*, 2nd ed. (New York: Routledge, Chapman & Hall, 1972). The basic handbook of Greek vase painting.

W. B. Dinsmoor, *The Architecture of Ancient Greece* (New York: W. W. Norton, 1952). An old but still valuable survey.

W. G. Forrest, *The Emergence of Greek Democracy* (New York: McGraw-Hill, 1966). Covers the politics of the Archaic period.

*A. J. Graham, *Colony and Mother City in Ancient Greece* (Chicago: Ares, 1983). A synthetic look at Greek colonies.

E. Hussey, *The Presocratics* (New York: Scribner's, 1972). Standard study of early Greek philosophers.

Eva C. Keuls, *The Reign of the Phallus: Sexual Politics in Ancient Athens* (New York: Harper & Row, 1985). Controversial study of sexual politics.

G. E. R. Lloyd, *Magic, Reason and Experience* (New York: Cambridge University Press, 1979). Enlightening analysis of early Greek thought and culture.

*S. B. Pomeroy, *Goddesses, Whores, Wives, and Slaves: Women in Classical Antiquity* (New York: Schocken, 1975). Pioneering study of gender in antiquity.

Anthony Snodgrass, *Archaic Greece: The Age of Experiment* (Totowa, NJ: Biblio Distribution Center, 1980). Excellent survey of the creative achievements of the Archaic period.

T. B. L. Webster, *Everyday Life in Classical Athens* (New York: Putnam, 1969). A general look at ordinary life but concentrating on the classical period.

A Tale of Three Cities

Paul Cartledge, *Sparta and Lakonia: A Regional History 1300–362 B.C.* (New York: Routledge, Chapman & Hall, 1978). The best survey of Spartan history.

J. R. Salmon, *Wealthy Corinth: A History of the City to 338 B.C.* (New York: Oxford University Press, 1984). A comprehensive history of early Corinth.

David Whitehead, *The Demes of Attica (ca. 508–250 B.C.)* (Princeton, NJ: Princeton University Press, 1986). An excellent study of Athenian politics and society.

3

Classical Greece

Alexander at Issus

War with Persia opened and closed the centuries of Greek glory. The invasion of the Greek mainland by Darius I in 490 B.C. pitted the greatest empire the West had ever known against a few small, mutually suspicious states. His failure created among the Greeks a new belief in the superiority of the Greek world over the barbarian and of free men over Eastern despots. Darius III (336–330 B.C.) suffered a far more devastating defeat than his ancestor at the hands of Alexander the Great (336–323 B.C.) and a combined Greek army 157 years later. Darius I had lost his pride. Darius III lost his empire and, shortly afterward, his life.

Alexander had announced his expedition as a campaign to punish the Persians for their invasion of Greece over a century and a half earlier. Greeks rightly viewed Alexander's victory at Issus in 333 B.C. as the beginning of the end for the Persians, and it was long celebrated by Greek poets and artists. The most famous of these was Philoxenus of Eretria, whose paintings marked the high point of Greek pictorial art. His masterpiece, like all other Greek paintings executed on wood, is long vanished. However sometime in the first century B.C., a wealthy Roman commissioned a mosaic copy of the painting for his villa at Pompeii in southern Italy. The mosaic, measuring some sixteen feet by eight feet and containing a million and a half stones, each the size of a grain of rice, is itself a masterpiece. It is also a faithful copy of Philoxenus's painting, which a Roman critic had characterized as "surpassed by none."

Alexander, with reckless disregard for his own safety, had led his right wing across a small stream at a gallop and routed the Persians' left flank. At the same time the Persian center, which consisted of Greek mercenaries, managed

68

to push Alexander's center back into the stream. Finally, Alexander and his right wing swung left, cutting Darius's Greeks to pieces, scattering his Persian guard, and forcing Darius to flee for his life.

In muted tones of red, brown, black, and yellow, Philoxenus brings all the skills developed through two centuries of Greek art to capture this most dramatic moment of the battle. The action takes place on a dusty and barren plain. The only landscape features are a lone dead tree and a forest of spears. Bold foreshortening, first used in the previous century, renders the rear of the horse in the center almost three dimensional as it runs in blind fury toward Darius's chariot. Although the entire scene is wildly chaotic, each man and each mount is portrayed as an individual, with his own expression of emotion and his own part to play in the violent action.

The young Alexander, his hair blowing free and his eye fixed not on Darius but on his greater destiny, exudes the reckless courage and violence for which he was so famous. And yet he is not the center of the composition. That place of honor goes to Darius, whose kindly, tortured face looks back as his horses pull his chariot to safety. His hand stretches out in helpless sympathy toward the young Persian who has thrown himself between his king and Alexander, taking through his chest the spear that the Greek king had intended for the Persian ruler.

The effect of the painting is at once heroic and disconcerting. Who is the hero of the battle? Is it the wild-eyed Alexander in his moment of victory, or is it the aged Persian monarch, whose infinite sadness at his moment of defeat is not for himself but for his young aide, who had given his life so that Darius might live? The picture here is no simple juxtaposition of civilization against barbarity. Greeks fought on both sides at Issus, just as they had in the Persian wars of the fifth century B.C. Nor did Alexander's warriors despise their Persian enemies. Alexander told Darius's mother, captured after the battle, that he felt no personal bitterness toward her son. By the fourth century B.C., Greeks had learned that right and wrong, good and evil, civilized and barbarian were not simple issues. In the past century and a half, they had seen many wars, many leaders, and many defeats. Greek intellectuals had explored the complexity of human existence, agreeing with the philosopher Socrates that the unexplored life was not worth living. Greek dramatists had taught that suffering brought wisdom. Philoxenus's depictions of Darius and Alexander reflect the same complexity. Who is the hero here? Who is the man of wisdom?

Learning to ask these questions was a painful education for Greeks of the fifth and fourth centuries. The victories over the Persian forces of Darius and his successors brought an unprecedented period of political and cultural freedom and creativity, but also deadly rivalry between Athens and Sparta, the leaders of the victorious Greeks. Democratic Athens transformed its wartime alliance into an empire, and only a generation after Athenian and Spartan troops had faced the Persians, they fought each other in a long and futile war, which left the Greek world exhausted and easy prey for the ambitious Macedonian dynasty.

*W*ar and Politics in the Fifth Century

The vast Persian army moving west in 490 B.C. threatened the fruits of three centuries of Greek political, social, and cultural experimentation. The shared ideal of freedom within community and the common bond of language and culture seemed no basis on which to build an effective resistance to the great Persian Empire. Moreover, Darius I was not marching against the Greeks as such. Few Greek states other than Athens had supported the Ionians against their Persian conquerors. Many Greeks saw the Persians as potential allies or even rulers preferable to their more powerful Greek neighbors and rivals within their own states. Separated by political traditions, intercity rivalries, and cultural differences, the Greeks did not feel any sense of national or ethnic unity. Particular interest, rather than patriotism or love of freedom, determined which cities opposed the Persian march. In the end, only Eretria, a badly divided Athens, and the small town of Plataea were prepared to refuse the Persian king's demand for gifts of earth and water, the traditional symbols of submission.

The Persian Wars

Initially, the Persian campaign followed the pattern established in Ionia. In the autumn of 490 B.C., Darius quickly destroyed the city of Eretria and carried off its population in captivity. The victorious Persian forces, numbering perhaps twenty thousand infantrymen and mounted archers, then landed at the Bay of Marathon. Even with around six hundred Plataeans, the total Athenian force was no more than half that of its enemies, but the Greeks were better armed and commanded the hills facing the Marathon plain on which the Persian troops had massed. The Athenians also benefited from the leadership of Miltiades (ca. 544–489 B.C.), an experienced soldier who had served Darius and who knew the Persian's strengths and weaknesses. For over a week the two armies faced each other in a battle of nerves. Growing dissension in the Athenian ranks finally led the Greek generals to make a desperate and unexpected move. Abandoning the high ground, the Athenian hoplites rushed in disciplined phalanxes over almost a mile of open fields and then attacked the amazed Persian forces at a run. Although the Persians broke through the center of the Greek lines, the Athenians routed the Persian flanks and then turned in, enveloping the invaders in a deadly trap. In a few hours it was all over. Six thousand Persians lay dead, while fewer than two hundred Athenians were buried in the heroes' grave that still marks the Marathon plain. The Persians retreated to their ships and sailed for the Bay of Phalerum near Athens, hoping to attack the city itself before its victorious troops could return. However, the Athenians, though exhausted from the battle, rushed the 23 miles home in under eight hours, beating the Persian fleet. When the Persians learned that they had lost the race, they turned their ships for Asia.

The almost miraculous victory at Marathon had three enormous consequences for Athens and for Greece in general. First, it established the superiority of the hoplite phalanx as the finest infantry formation in the Mediterranean world. Second, Greeks expanded this belief in military superiority to a faith in the general superiority of Greeks over the "barbarians" (those who spoke other languages). Finally, by proving the value of the citizen army, the victory of the Athenians solidified and enhanced the democratic reforms of Cleisthenes.

Common citizens were determined that the victory won by the hoplite phalanx at Marathon should not be lost to an aristocratic faction at home. To guard against this danger, the Athenian assembly began to practice *ostracism*, ten-year exile without loss of property, imposed on those who threatened to undermine the constitution of Cleisthenes. Each year every Athenian citizen had the opportunity to write on a potsherd (in Greek, *ostrakon*) the name of the man he most wished to leave Attica. If at least six thousand citizens voted, the state sent the individual receiving the most votes into temporary exile. No charges or accusations had to be made, much less proven. Anyone who had offended the Athenians or who, by his prominence, seemed a threat to democracy, could be ostracized. At the same time, Athenians also began to select their chief officers not simply by direct election but by lot. This practice prevented any individual from rising to power by creating a powerful faction.

Occupied by problems elsewhere in their vast empire and the unexpected death of Darius I in 486 B.C., Persia paid little attention to Greece for six years. After Darius's death, his son Xerxes (486–465 B.C.) began to amass foodstuffs, weapons, and armies for a land assault on his Greek enemies. In response to these preparations, Greek cities began to attempt to close ranks against the invaders. Still, however, many Greek communities saw their neighbors as

This ostrakon was found in the Athenian agora. It was used to cast a vote to choose a person who would be ostracized—banished from Athens for a period of ten years. The name on the first line is Themistocles.

greater threats than the Persians. Some states, including Thebes, Argos, and Thessaly, more or less willingly allied with the Persians against Athens or Sparta. North of the Peloponnesus only Athens, Plataea, and a few other small states were willing to fight the Persians. Sparta was prepared to defend itself and its league but was not interested in campaigns far from home. Finally, in 481 B.C., when the Persian invasion was imminent, representatives of what a contemporary called "the Greeks who had the best thoughts for Greece" met in Sparta to plan resistance. The allies agreed that the Spartans would take command of the combined land and sea forces, which probably totaled roughly 35,000 helots, 5,000 hoplites, and 378 ships.

Although larger than those mustered by Athens against Darius, the Greek forces were puny compared with Xerxes's estimated two hundred thousand infantry and one thousand light and highly maneuverable Ionian and Phoenician ships. The Spartan commanders sought a strategic point at which the numerical superiority of the Persian forces would be neutralized. The choice fell on the narrow pass of Thermopylae and the adjacent Euboean strait. While a select force of hoplites held the pass, the Greek fleet, following a strategy devised by Themistocles, harried the larger Persian one. Neither action produced a Greek victory, but none could have been expected.

At Thermopylae, the Greeks held firm for days against wave after wave of assaulting troops. Finally, Greek allies of the Persians showed them a narrow mountain track by which they were able to attack the Greek position from the rear. Seeing that all was lost, the Spartan king Leonidas (490–480 B.C.) sent most of his allies home. Then he and his 300 Spartan equals faced certain death with a causal disdain characterized by the comment made by one Spartan equal. Told that when the Persians shot their arrows, they were so numerous that they hid the sun, the Spartan replied, "Good. If the Persians hide the sun, we shall have our battle in the shade." The epitaph raised later by the Spartan state to Leonidas and his men read simply, "Go tell the Spartans, you who read: we took their orders, and are dead."

While the Persian troops were blocked at Thermopylae, their fleet was being battered by fierce storms in the Euboean straits and harassed by the heavier Greek ships. Here the Greeks learned that in close quarters, they could stand up to Xerxes's Phoenician navy. This lesson proved vital a short time later. While the Persian army burned Athens and occupied Attica, Themistocles lured the fleet into the narrow strait between Salamis and the mainland.

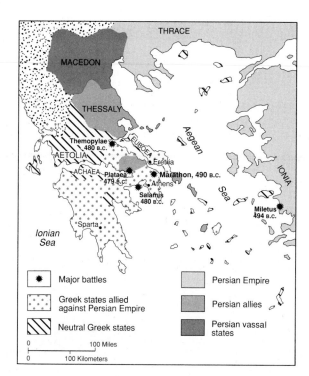

The Persian Wars

There the slower Greek vessels bottled up the larger and vastly more numerous enemy ships and cut them to pieces.

After Salamis, Xerxes lost his appetite for fighting Greeks. Without his fleet, he could not supply a vast army far from home in hostile territory. Leaving a force to do what damage it could, he led the bulk of his forces back to Persia. At Athenian urging, the Greek allies under Leonidas's kinsman Pausanias (d. ca. 470 B.C.) met the Persians at Plataea in 479 B.C. Once again hoplite discipline and Greek determination meant more than numerical superiority. That night the Spartan king dined in the splendor of the captured tent of the defeated Persian commander. Athenian sea power and Spartan infantry had proven invincible. Soon the Athenians were taking the offensive, liberating the Ionian cities of Asia Minor and, in the process, laying the foundations of an Athenian empire every bit as threatening to their neighbors as that of Xerxes.

The Athenian Empire

Sparta, not Athens, should have emerged as the leader of the Greek world after 479 B.C. However, the constant threat of a helot revolt and the desire of the members of Sparta's Peloponnesian League to go their separate ways left Sparta too preoccupied with internal problems to fill the power vacuum left by the Persian defeat.

Athens, on the other hand, was only too ready to take the lead in bringing the war home to the Persians. With Sparta out of the picture, the Athenian fleet was the best hope of liberating the Aegean from Persians and pirates. Athens accepted control in 478 B.C. of what historians have come to call the Delian League, after the island of Delos, a religious center that housed the league's treasury. Athens and some of the states with navies provided ships; others contributed annual payments to the league. Initially, the league pursued the war against the Persians, driving them back along the Aegean and the Black seas. At the same time, Athens hurriedly rebuilt its defensive fortifications, a move correctly interpreted by Sparta and other states as directed more against them than against the Persians.

Athens's domination of the Delian League assured its prosperity. Attica, with its fragile agriculture, depended on Black Sea wheat, and the league kept these regions under Athenian control. Since Athens received not only cash "contributions" from league members but also one-half of the spoils taken in battle, the state's public coffers were filled. The new riches made possible the reconstruction of the city that was burned by the Persians into the most magnificent city of Greece.

The league was too vital to Athenian prosperity to stand and fall with the Persian threat. The drive against the Persian Empire began to falter after a league expedition to Egypt in 454 B.C. ended in total defeat. Discouraged by this and other setbacks, the Athenian Callias, acting for the league, apparently concluded a treaty of peace with Persia in 449 B.C., making the alliance no longer necessary. For a brief moment it appeared that the Delian League might disband. But it was too late. The league had become an empire and Athens's allies were its subjects.

The Athenian empire was an economic, judicial, religious, and political union held together by military might. Athens controlled the flow of grain through the Hellespont to the Aegean, ensuring its own supply and heavily taxing cargoes to other cities. Athens controlled the law courts of member cities and used them to repress anti-Athenian groups. Rich and poor Athenian citizens alike acquired territory throughout the empire. The rich took over vast estates confiscated from local opponents of Athenian dominance, while the poor replaced hostile populations in the colonies. Control over this empire depended on the Athenian fleet to enforce cooperation. Athenian garrisons were established in each city and "democratic" puppet governments ruled according to the wishes of the garrison commanders. Revolt, resignation from the league, or refusal to pay the annual tribute resulted in brutal suppression. Persian tyranny had hardly been worse than Athenian imperialism.

Private and Public Life in Athens

During the second half of the fifth century B.C., Athens, enriched by tribute from its over 150 subject states, was a vital, crowded capital drawing merchants, artisans, and laborers from throughout the Greek world. At its height, the total population of Athens and surrounding Attica numbered perhaps 350,000, although probably fewer than 60,000 were citizens, that is, adult males qualified to own land and participate in Athenian politics. Over one-quarter of the total population were slaves. Great landowners, unable to force ordinary freemen to work their estates, had turned to slave labor. Slaves were also vital in mining and other forms of craft and industrial work.

Greek slaves were not distinguished by race, ethnicity, or physical appearance. Anyone could become a slave. Prisoners of war, foreigners who failed to pay taxes, victims of pirate raids, could all end up on the auction blocks of the ancient world. Slaves were as much the property of their owners as their land, houses, cattle, and sheep. Many masters treated their slaves well, but beatings, tattooing, starvation, and shackling were all too common as a means of enforcing obedience.

Roughly half of Athens's free population were foreigners—*metoikoi*, or metics. These were primarily Greek citizens of the tributary states of the empire, but they might also be peoples from Africa or from Asia Minor, such as Lydians. The number of metics increased after the middle of the fifth century B.C. both because of the flood of foreigners into the empire's capital and because Athenian citizenship was restricted to persons with two parents who were of citizen families. Metics could not own land in Attica nor could they participate directly in politics. They were required to have a citizen protector and to pay a small annual tax. Otherwise, they were free to engage in every form of activity. The highest concentration of metics was found in the port of Piraeus, where they participated in commerce, manufacturing, banking, and skilled crafts.

More than half of those born into citizen families were entirely excluded from public life. These were the women, who controlled and directed the vital sphere of the Athenian home, but who were considered citizens only for purposes of marriage, transfer of property, and procreation. From birth to death, every female citizen lived under the protection of a male guardian, either a close relative such as father or brother, or a husband or son. Women spent almost their entire lives in the inner recesses of the home. Fathers arranged marriages, the purposes of which are abundantly clear from the ritualized exchange of words sealing the betrothal:

I give this woman for the procreation of legitimate children.
I accept.
And (I give a certain amount as) dowry.
I am content.

A wife had no control over her dowry, which passed to her son. In the event of divorce or the death of her husband, the woman and her dowry returned to her father. An honorable Athenian woman stayed at home and managed her husband's household. Only the poorest citizens sent their wives and daughters to work in the marketplace or the fields. Even the most casual contact with other men without permission was strictly forbidden, although men were expected to engage in various sorts of extramarital affairs. In the words of one

Athenian male, "Hetairai we have for our pleasure, mistresses for the refreshment of our bodies, but wives to bear us legitimate children and to look after the house faithfully." The household, as Athenians never tired of repeating, was the foundation of all society. Thus the role of women was indeed important, even though the public sphere was entirely closed to them.

Male control over women may have resulted in part from fear. Women were identified with the forces of nature, which included both positive forces such as fertility and life and negative forces such as chaotic irrationality, which threatened civilization. These two poles were epitomized by the cult of Dionysus. He was the god of wine, lifeblood, and fertility, but he was also the deity whose female devotees, the *maenads*, were portrayed as worshiping him in a state of frenzied savagery that could include tearing children and animals limb from limb.

The male citizens of fifth-century B.C. Athens were free to an extent previously unknown in the world. But Athenian freedom was freedom in community, not freedom from community. The essence of their freedom lay in their participation in public life, especially self-government, which was their passion. This participation was always within a complex network of familial, social, and religious connections and obligations. Each person belonged to a number of groups: a deme, a tribe, a family, various religious associations, and occupational groups. Each of these communities placed different and even contradictory demands on its members. The impossibility of satisfying all of these demands, of responding to the special interests of each, forced citizens to make hard choices, to set priorities, and to balance conflicting obligations. This process of selection was the essence of Athenian freedom, a freedom which, unlike that of the modern world, was based not on individualism but on a multitude of collectivities. The sum of these overlapping groupings was Athenian society, in which friends and opponents alike were united.

Unity did not imply equality. Even in fifth-century B.C. Athens, not all Athenians were socially or economically equal. Most were farmers who looked to military service as a means of increasing their meager income. Others engaged in trade or industry, although metics, with their commercial contacts in their cities of origin, dominated much of these activities in Athens. However, the aristocracy was still strong, and most of the popular leaders of the century came from the ranks of old wealth and influence. Still, sovereignty lay not with these aristocrats but with the demos, the people.

In theory the adult male citizens of Athens were Athens's sovereigns. Since the time of Solon, they had formed the *ekklesia*, or assembly. On particularly solemn occasions, as many as six thousand citizens might convene in the *pnyx*, the meeting place of the assembly. They also made up the large juries, always composed of several hundred citizens, who decided legal cases less on law than on the political merits of the case and the quality of the orators who pleaded for each side. Such large bodies were too unwieldy to deal with the daily tasks of government. Thus control of these tasks fell to the council, or *boule*, composed of five hundred members selected by lot by the tribes; the magistrates, who were also chosen by lot; and ten military commanders or generals, the only major officeholders elected rather than chosen at random.

Paradoxically, the resolute determination of Athenian democrats to prevent individuals from acquiring too much power helped to create a series of extraconstitutional power brokers. Since most offices were filled by lot and turned over frequently, real political leadership came not from officeholders but from generals and from popular leaders. These so-called demagogues, while at times holding high office, exercised their power through their speaking skills, informal networks, and knowledge of how to get things done. They acquired this knowledge through their willingness to serve for long periods in various capacities on committees, as unpaid government workers, and in minor elected offices. Demagogues tended to be wealthy aristocrats who could afford to put in the time demanded by these largely voluntary services. Governing an empire demanded skill, energy, and experience, but Athenian democracy was formally run by amateurs. Small wonder that the city's public life was dominated by these popular leaders.

Although many demagogues competed for power and attracted the support of the people, the Athenian demos was not kind to its heroes. Ten years after the Greek victory at Salamis in 480 B.C., Athens ostracized Themistocles, whose leadership there had saved Athens. Mistrusted by many of his co-citizens, he ended his days ironically in the service of the Persian king. Cimon (ca. 510–451 B.C.), the son of the Marathon hero Miltiades, helped destroy Themistocles and succeeded him as the most influential leader of the city. As long as Cimon lavished his wealth on the populace and led Athenian armies to victory against the Persians, he remained popular. But in 462 B.C., Cimon led an army to assist Sparta in suppressing a revolt of its helots. The Spartans, fearing that he was actually planning to plot with the helots against them, sent him and his army home in disgrace. This disgrace was fatal, and Athens ostracized Cimon upon his return.

For the next 30 years, one individual dominated Athenian public life, the general Pericles (ca. 495–429 B.C.). Although not an original thinker, he was a great orator and a successful military commander, who proved to be the man most able to win the confidence of Athens and to lead it during the decades of its greatest glory. Athens's system of radical democracy reached its zenith under the leadership of Pericles, even while its imperial program drew it into a long and fatal war against Sparta, the only state powerful enough to resist it.

Pericles and Athens

Pericles was descended from the greatest aristocratic families of Athens. Nevertheless, as one ancient author put it, he "took his side, not with the rich and the few, but with the many and the poor." Pericles acquired intimate knowledge of government through long service on various public works projects, projects that provided lucrative income to poorer citizens. Pericles was also president of the commission responsible for constructing the great ivory and gold statue of Athena that stood in the Parthenon, the main temple in Athens. He served on the commission that built the Lyceum, or city exercise center, and the Parthenon itself. These enormous projects won him a great popular following while giving him an intimate knowledge of public finance and the details of Athenian government. He enhanced his position further through his great powers of persuasion.

Pericles never ruled Athens. As a general he could only carry out the orders of the ekklesia and the boule, and as a citizen he could only attempt to persuade his fellows. Still he was largely responsible for the extension of Athenian democracy to all free citizens. Under his influence Athens abolished the last property requirements for officeholding. He convinced the state to pay those who served on juries, thus making it possible for even the poorest citizens to participate in this important part of Athenian government. But he was also responsible for a restriction of citizenship to those whose mothers and fathers had been Athenians. Such a law would have denied citizenship to many of the most illustrious Athenians of the sixth century B.C., including his own ancestors. The law also prevented citizens of Athens's subject states from developing a real stake in the fate of the empire.

Pericles had been an opponent of the aristocratically oriented Cimon at home and disputed Cimon's foreign policy, which saw Athens and Sparta as "yoke mates" against Persia. Pericles had little fear of Persia, but shared Cimon's view that the Athenian empire had to be preserved at all costs. This policy ultimately drew Athens into deadly conflict with Sparta. The first clash between the two great powers came around 460 B.C. Megara, which lay between the Peloponnesus and Attica, withdrew from the Spartan alliance and sought Athens's assistance against nearby Corinth in a border dispute. The Athenians, eager to add Megara to their empire, went to their assistance. Soon Sparta and Aegina entered the fray, but Athens emerged victorious, checking Sparta and absorbing Megara, Aegina, and Boeotia. However, in 446 B.C., after the Athenian defeat in Egypt, Megara and Boeotia rebelled and Sparta invaded the disputed region. Unable to face this new threat at home after the disastrous loss abroad, in 445 B.C. the Athenians, under the leadership of Pericles, concluded a peace treaty with Sparta whereby Athens abandoned all of its continental possessions. The treaty was meant to last for 30 years. It held for 14.

The two great powers were eager to preserve the peace, but the whole Greek world was a tinderbox ready to burst into flame. The spark came from an unexpected direction. In 435 B.C., Corinth and its colony Corcyra on the Adriatic Sea came to blows and Corcyra sought the assistance of Athens. Athens did not want the Corinthian fleet, vital to the Spartan alliance, augmented by absorbing the ships of Corcyra. Therefore the Athenians agreed to a defensive alliance with Corcyra and assisted it in defeating its enemy. This assistance infuriated Corinth, an ally of Sparta, and in 432 B.C., the Corinthians convinced the Spartans that Athenian imperial ambitions were insatiable. In the words of the great historian of the war, Thucydides (d. ca. 401 B.C.), "What made war inevitable was the growth of Athenian power and the fear which this caused in Sparta." The next year, Sparta invaded Attica. The Peloponnesian War, which would destroy both great powers, had begun.

The Peloponnesian War

The Peloponnesian War was actually a series of war and rebellions. Athens and Sparta waged two devastating ten-year wars, from 431 B.C. to 421 B.C. and then again from 414 B.C. to 404 B.C. At the same time, cities in each alliance took advantage of the wars to revolt against the great powers, eliciting terrible vengeance from both Athens and Sparta. Within many of the Greek city-states, oligarchs and democrats waged bloody civil wars for control of their governments. Moreover, between 415 and 413 B.C., Athens attempted to expand its empire in Sicily, an attempt that ended in disaster. Before it was over, the Peloponnesian War had become an international war, with Persia entering the fray on the side of Sparta. In the end, there were no real victors, only victims.

Initially, Sparta and Athens both hoped for quick victory. Sparta's strength was its army, and its strategy was to invade Attica, devastate the countryside, and force the Athenians into an open battle. Pericles urged Athens to a strategy of conserving its hoplite forces while exploiting its naval strength. Athens was

The Delian League and the Peloponnesian War

a naval power and, with its empire and control of Black Sea grain, could hold out for years behind its fortifications, the great walls linking Athens to its port of Piraeus. At the same time, the Athenian fleet could launch raids along the coast of the Peloponnesus, thus bringing the war home to the Spartans. Pericles hoped in this way to outlast the Spartans. In describing the war, Thucydides uses the same word for "survive" and "win."

The first phase of the war, called the Archidamian War after the Spartan king Archidamus (431–427 B.C.), was indecisive. Sparta pillaged Attica but could not breach the great wall nor starve Athens. In 430 B.C., the Spartans received unexpected help in the form of plague, which ravaged Athens for five years. By the time it ended in 426 B.C., as much as a third of the Athenian population had died, including Pericles. Still Athens held out, establishing bases encircling the Peloponnesus and urging Spartan helots and allies to revolt. At Pylos in 425 B.C., the Athenian generals Cleon and Demosthenes captured a major force of Spartan equals. The Spartans offset this defeat by capturing the city of Amphipolis on the northern Aegean. The defeated Athenian commander, Thucydides, was exiled for his failure and retired to Spartan territory to write his great history of the war. Exhausted by a decade of death and destruction, the two sides contracted peace in 421 B.C. Although Athens was victorious in that its empire was intact, the peace changed nothing and tensions festered for five years.

After the peace of 421 B.C., Pericles's kinsman Alcibiades (ca. 450–404 B.C.) came to dominate the demos. Well spoken, handsome, and brave, but also vain, dissolute, and ambitious, Alcibiades led the city into disaster. Although a demagogue who courted popular support, he despised the people and schemed to overturn the democracy. In 415 B.C., he urged Athens to expand its empire west by attacking Syracuse, the most prosperous Greek city of Sicily, which had largely escaped the devastation of the Archidamian War. The expedition went poorly and Alcibiades, accused at home of having profaned one of the most important Athenian religious cults, was ordered home. Instead, he fled to Sparta, where he began to assist the Spartans against Athens. The Sicilian expedition ended in disaster. Athens lost over two hundred ships and fifty thousand men. At the same time, Sparta resumed the war, this time with naval support provided by Persia.

Suddenly Athens was fighting for its life. Alcibiades soon abandoned Sparta for Persia and convinced the Athenians that if they would abandon their democracy for an oligarchy, Persia would withdraw its support of Sparta. In 411 B.C., the desperate Athenian assembly established a brutal oligarchy controlled by a small faction of antidemocratic conspirators. Alcibiades's promise proved hollow and the war continued. Athens reestablished its democracy, but the brief oligarchy left the city bitterly divided. The Persian king renewed his support for Sparta, sending his son Cyrus (ca. 424–401 B.C.) to coordinate the war against Athens. Under the Spartan general Lysander (d. 395 B.C.), Sparta and its allies finally closed in on Athens. Lysander captured the Athenian fleet in the Hellespont, destroyed it, and severed Athens's vital grain supply. Within months Athens was entirely cut off from the outside world and starving. In 404 B.C., Sparta accepted Athens's unconditional surrender. Athens's fortifications came down, its empire vanished, and its fleet, except for a mere 12 ships, dissolved.

Athenian Culture

Throughout the fifth century B.C., the turbulent issues of democracy and oligarchy, war and peace, hard choices and conflicting obligations found expression in Athenian culture even as the glory of the Athenian empire was manifested in art and architecture. During this century, Athens transformed Greek and indeed Western civilization. Most of what we today call Greek is actually Athenian: the great dramatists Aeschylus, Sophocles, and Euripides were Athenian, as were the sculptor Phidias, the Parthenon architects Ictinus and Callicrates, the philosophers Socrates and Plato. To Athens came writers, thinkers, and artists from throughout the Greek world.

The Examined Life

A primary characteristic of Athenian culture was its critical and rational nature. In heated discussions in the assembly and the agora, the courtroom and the private symposium, Athenians and foreigners drawn to the city no longer looked to the myths and religion of the past for guidance. Secure in their identity and protected by the openness of their radical democracy, they began to examine past and present and to question the foundations of traditional values. From this climate of inquiry emerged the traditions of moral philosophy and its cousin, history.

The Ionian interest in natural philosophy, the explanation of the universe in rational terms, continued throughout the fifth century B.C. But philosophers began also to turn their attention to the human world, in particular to the powers and limitations of the individual's mind and the individual's relationship with society. By the end of his life, the philosopher Heraclitus (see Chapter 2, p. 53) had become intrigued with the examination of the rational faculties themselves rather than what one could know with them. In part, this meant a search for personal inner understanding that would lead to proper action within society, in other words, to the search for ethics based in reason. In part, too, such an inquiry led to a study of how to formulate arguments and persuade others through logic. In the political world of fifth-century B.C. Athens, rhetoric, the art of persuasion, was particularly important, because it was the key to political influence. Teachers, called *sophists* ("wise people"), traveled throughout Greece offering to provide an advanced education for a fee. Although the sophistic tradition later gained a negative reputation, teachers such as Gorgias (ca. 485–ca. 380 B.C.) and Protagoras (ca. 490–421 B.C.) trained young men not only in the art of rhetoric but also in logic. By exercising their students' minds with logical puzzles and paradoxical statements, the sophists taught a generation of wealthy Greeks the powers and complexities of human reason.

Socrates (ca. 470–399 B.C.) was considered by many of his contemporaries as but one more sophist, but he himself reacted against what he saw as the amoral and superficial nature of sophistic education. Although as a young man he had been interested in natural philosophy, he abandoned this tradition in favor of the search for moral self-enlightenment urged by Heraclitus. "Know thyself" was Socrates's plea. An unexamined life, he argued, was not worth living. Socrates refused any pay for his teaching, arguing that he had nothing to teach. He knew nothing, he said, and was superior to the sophists only because he recognized his ignorance while they professed wisdom.

Socrates's method infuriated his contemporaries. He would approach persons with reputations for wisdom or skill and then, through a series of disarmingly simple questions, force them to defend their beliefs. The inevitable result was that in their own words the outstanding sophists, politicians, and poets of the day demonstrated the inadequacy of the foundations of their beliefs.

Since Socrates refused to commit any of his teaching to writing, we have no direct knowledge of the content of his instruction. We know of him only from the conflicting reports of his former students and opponents. One thing is certain, however. While demanding that every aspect of life be investigated, Socrates never doubted the moral legitimacy of the Athenian state. Condemned to death in 399 B.C. on the trumped-up charges of corrupting the morals of the Athenian youth and introducing strange gods, he rejected the opportunity to escape into exile. Rather than reject Athens and its laws, he drank the fatal potion of hemlock given him by the executioner.

The philosophical interest in human choices and social constraints found echo in the historical writing of the age. Herodotus (ca. 484–420 B.C.), the first historian, was one of the many foreigners who found in Athens the intellectual climate and audience he needed to write an account of the Persian wars of the preceding generation. His book of inquiries, or *historia*, into the origins and events of the conflict between Greeks and Persians is the first true history. Herodotus had traveled widely in the eastern Mediterranean, collecting local stories and visiting famous temples, palaces, and cities. In his study he presents a great panorama of the civilized world at the end of the sixth century B.C. Herodotus does not hesitate to report myths, legends, and outrageous tales. His faith in the gods is strong and he believes that the gods intervene in human affairs. Still, he is more than just a good storyteller or a chronicler of legends. Often, after reporting conflicting accounts he will conclude, "Both stories are told and the reader may take his choice between them." In other cases, after recounting a particularly farfetched account heard from local informants, he comments, "Personally, I think this story is nonsense."

As he explains in his introduction, Herodotus's purpose in writing was twofold. First, he sought to preserve the memory of the past by recording the achievements of both Greeks and non-Greeks. Second, he set out to show how the two came into conflict. It was this concern to explain, to go beyond mere storytelling, that earned Herodotus the designation of the "father of history." Herodotus is less interested in the mythic dimensions of the conflict than in the human, and his primary concern is the action of individuals under the press of circumstances. Ultimately, the Persian wars become for Herodotus the conflict between freedom and despotism, and he described with passion how different Greek states chose between the two.

The story of the Peloponnesian War was recorded by a different sort of historian, one who focused more narrowly on the Greek world and on political power. Thucydides had been an Athenian general and a major actor in the first part of the Peloponnesian War until his exile in 425 B.C. He began his account at the very outbreak of the conflict, thus writing a contemporary record of the war rather than a history of it. As Herodotus is called the father of history, Thucydides might be called the first social scientist.

Not myth, nor religion, nor morality takes center stage in Thucydides's account of what he saw. For him, the central subject is human society in action. Thucydides views the Greek states acting out of rational self-interest. His favorite device for showing the development of such policies is the political set speech in which two opposing leaders attempt to persuade their fellow citizens on the proper course of action. Thucydides was seldom actually present at the events he describes. Even when he was, he could not have transcribed the speakers' exact words. Rather he attempted to put into the mouths of the speakers "whatever seemed most appropriate to me for each speaker to say in the particular circumstances." Although fictitious by modern standards, these speeches penetrate to the heart of the tough political choices facing the opposing forces. This hard-nosed approach to political decisions continues to serve as a model to historians and practitioners of power politics.

Still, morality is always just below the surface of Thucydides's narrative. Even as he unflinchingly chronicles the collapse of morality and social order in the face of political expediency, he recognizes that this process will destroy his beloved Athens. The consequences of political self-interest, devoid of other considerations, follow their own natural course to disaster and ruin. In the later, unfinished chapters (Thucydides died shortly after Athens's final defeat), the Peloponnesian War takes on the characteristics of a tragedy. Here Thucydides, the ultimate political historian, shows the deep influence of the dominant literary tradition of his day, Greek drama.

Athenian Drama

Since the time of its introduction by Peisistratus in the middle of the sixth century B.C., drama had become popular, not only in Athens, but throughout the Greek world. Plays formed part of the annual feast of Dionysus and dealt with mythic subject matter largely taken from the *Iliad* and the *Odyssey*. Three types of plays honored the Dionysian festival. Tragedies dealt with great men who failed because of flaws in their natures. Their purpose was, in the words of the philosopher Aristotle, to effect "through pity and terror the correction and refinement of passions." Comedies were more directly topical and political. They parodied real Athenians, often by name, and amused even while making serious points in defense of democracy. Somewhere between tragedies and comedies, satyr plays remained closest to the Dionysian cult. In them lecherous drunken satyrs, mythical half-man, half-goat creatures, interact with gods and men as they roam in search of Dionysus.

Only a handful of the hundreds of Greek plays written in the fifth century B.C. survive. The first of the great Athenian tragedians whose plays we know is Aeschylus (525–456 B.C.), a veteran of Marathon and an eyewitness of the battle of Salamis. His one surviving trilogy, the *Oresteia*, traces the fate of the family of Agamemnon, the Greek commander at Troy. The three plays of the trilogy explore the conflicting obligations of filial respect and vengeance, which ultimately must be settled by rational yet divinely sanctioned law. Upon his return from Troy, the victorious Agamemnon is murdered by his unfaithful wife Clytemnestra. Orestes, his son, avenges his father's murder by murdering Clytemnestra, but in so doing incurs the wrath of the Furies, avenging spirits who pursue him for killing his mother. The conflict of duties and loyalties cannot be resolved by human means. Finally, Orestes arrives at the shrine of Apollo at Delphi, where the god purifies him from the pollution of the killing. Then at Athens, Athena rescues Orestes, creating the Athenian law court and transforming the Furies into the Eumenides, the kindly guardian spirits of Athens.

In his mature plays, Aeschylus's younger contemporary Sophocles (496–406 B.C.) sought to express human character. He shows how humans make decisions and carry them out, constrained by their pasts, their weaknesses, and their vices, but free nonetheless. Sophocles's message is endurance, acceptance of human responsibility and, at the same time, of the ways of the gods, who overrule people's plans. The heroine of *Antigone* is the sister of Polyneices, exiled son of King Oedipus of Thebes. Polyneices has died fighting his city, and Creon, its new ruler, commands under penalty of death that Polyneices's body be left unburied. This would mean that his soul would never find rest, the ultimate punishment for a Greek. Antigone, with a determination and courage equal to her love for her brother, buries Polyneices and is entombed alive for her crime. Here the conflict between the state, which claims the total obedience of its people, and the claims of familial love and religious piety meet in tragic conflict. Creon, warned by a prophet that he is offending heaven, orders Antigone's release, but it is too late. Rather than wait for death, she has already hanged herself.

Euripides (485–406 B.C.) was far more original and daring in his subject matter and treatment of human emotions. Unlike the stately dramas of Aeschylus and the deliberate progressions of Sophocles, Euripides's plays abound in plot twists and unexpected, violent outbursts of passion. His characters are less reconciled to their fates and less ready to accept the traditional gods:

> *Does someone say that there are gods in heaven?*
> *There are not, there are not—unless one chooses to follow old*
> *tradition like a fool.*

Neither passion nor reason, but politics rules the world of Greek comedy. Rather than the timelessness of the human condition, Athenian comic playwrights focused their biting satire on the political and social issues of the moment. Particularly the comic genius Aristophanes (ca. 450–ca. 388 B.C.) used wit, imagination, vulgarity, and great poetic sensitivity to attack everything that offended him in his city. In his plays he mocks and ridicules statesmen, philosophers, rival playwrights, and even the gods. His comedies are full of outrageous twists of plot, talking animals, obscene jokes and puns, and mocking asides. And yet Aristophanes was a deeply patriotic Athenian, dedicated to the democratic system and equally dedicated to the cause of peace. In his now-lost *Babylonians*, written around 426 B.C., as Athenians struggled to recover from the plague and Cleon continued to pursue the bloody war against Sparta, he mocks Cleon and the Athenian demagogues while portraying the cities of the Delian League as slaves forced to grind grain at a mill. In *Lysistrata*, written in 411 B.C., after Athens had once more renewed the war, the women of Greece force their men to make peace by conspiring to refuse them sex as long as war continues. Through the sharp satire and absurd plots of his plays, Aristophanes communicates his sympathy for ordinary people, who must match wits with the charlatans and pompous frauds who attempt to dominate Athens's public life.

The Human Image

The humanity in Greek drama found its parallel in art. In the late sixth century B.C., a reversal of the traditional black figure technique had revolutionized vase painting. Artists had begun to outline scenes on unfired clay and then fill in the background with black or brown glaze. The interior details of the figures were also added in black. The result was a much more lifelike art, a lighter, more natural coloring, and the possibility of more perspective, depth, and molding. Sculpture reflected the same development toward balance and realism contained within an ideal of human form. The finest bronzes and marbles of the fifth century B.C. show freestanding figures whose natural vigor and force, even when engaged in strenuous exertion, are balanced by the placidity of their faces and their lack of emotion. The tradition established by the Athenian sculptor Phidias (ca. 500–ca. 430 B.C.) sought a naturalism in the portrayal of the human figure, which remained ideal rather than individual.

The greatest sculptural program of the fifth century B.C. was that produced for the Athenian acropolis, the greatest complex of buildings in the ancient

Drinking cup signed by Douris, one of the finest fifth-century B.C. vase painters. The two figures interact and balance each other, exactly filling the circular space of the cup's interior.

world. One entered the acropolis complex through the monumental *Propylaea*, or gateway, a T-shaped structure approached by a flight of steps. From the top of the steps, one could glimpse both Phidias's great bronze statue of Athena Promachos in the center of the acropolis and, to the right, the Parthenon. As visitors entered the acropolis itself, they passed on the right the small temple of Athena as Victory. Continuing on the Sacred Way, one saw on the left the delicate Erechtheum, which housed the oldest Athenian cults. On the right, visitors were overawed by the Parthenon, a monument as much to Athens as to Athena. Even today, the ruined temple seems a rectangular embodiment of order, proportion, and balance, an effect achieved through irregularity, illusion, and variation. Every surface, from the floor to the columns to the horizontal beams, curves slightly. The spacing of the columns varies and each leans slightly inward. Those at the rear are larger than those at the front to compensate for the effect of viewing them from a greater distance.

An illusion, too, was the sense of overwhelming Athenian superiority and grandeur the acropolis was intended to convey. By the time the Erechtheum was completed in 406 B.C., the Athenian empire was all but destroyed, the city's population devastated, and its democracy imperiled. Two years later Athens surrendered unconditionally to Sparta.

The Parthenon

*F*rom City-States to Macedonian Empire

The Peloponnesian War touched every aspect of Greek life. The war brought changes to the social and political structures of Greece by creating an enduring bitterness between elites and populace and a distrust of both democracy and traditional oligarchy. The mutual exhaustion of Athens and Sparta left a vacuum of power in the Aegean. Finally, the war raised fundamental questions about the nature of politics and society throughout the Greek world.

Politics After the Peloponnesian War

Over the decades-long struggle, the conduct of war and the nature of politics had changed, bringing new problems for victor and vanquished alike. Lightly armed professional mercenaries willing to fight for anyone able to pay gradually replaced hoplite citizen soldiers as the backbone of the fighting forces. The rise of mercenary armies meant trouble for democracies such as Athens as well as for Sparta with its class of equals.

Victory left Sparta no more capable of assuming leadership in 404 B.C. than it had been in 478 B.C. Years of war had reduced the population of equals to less than three thousand. The Spartans proved extremely unpopular imperialists. As reward for Persian assistance, Sparta returned the Ionian cities to Persian control. Elsewhere it established hated oligarchies to rule in a way favorable to Sparta's interests. In Athens, a brutal tyranny of 30 men took control in 404 B.C. With Spartan support, they executed 1500 democratic leaders and forced 5000 more into exile. The Thirty Tyrants evoked enormous hatred and opposition. Within a year the exiles recaptured the city, restored democracy, and killed or expelled the tyrants.

Similar opposition to Spartan rule emerged throughout the Greek world, shattering the fragile peace created by Athens's defeat. For over seventy years the Greek world boiled in constant warfare. Mutual distrust, fear of any city that seemed about to establish a position of clear superiority, and the machinations of the Persian Empire to keep Greeks fighting each other produced a constantly shifting series of alliances.

Persia turned against its former ally when in 401 B.C. Sparta supported an unsuccessful attempt by Cyrus to unseat his brother Artaxerxes II. Soon the unlikely and unstable alliance of Athens, Corinth, Argos, Thebes, and Euboea, financed by Persia, entered a series of vicious wars against Sparta. The first round ended in Spartan victory, due to the shifting role of Persia, whose primary interest was the continued disunity of the Greeks. By 377 B.C., however, Athens had reorganized its league and with Thebes as ally was able to break Spartan sea power. The decline of Sparta left a power vacuum soon filled by Thebes. Athens, concerned by this new threat, shifted alliances, making peace with its old enemy. However, Spartan military fortunes had so declined that when Sparta attacked Thebes in 371 B.C., its armies were destroyed and Spartan power broken. The next year Thebes invaded the Peloponnesus and freed Messenia, the foundation of Sparta's economic prosperity. Sparta never recovered. Deprived of its economic base, its body of equals reduced to a mere 800, and its fleet gone, Sparta never regained its historic importance. Theban hegemony was short lived. Before long the same process of greed, envy, and distrust that had devastated the other Greek powers destroyed Thebes. Athens's reconstituted league disintegrated as members opposed Athenian attempts once more to convert a free association of states into an empire. By the 330s, all of the Greek states had proven themselves incapable of creating stable political units larger than their immediate polis.

Philosophy and the Polis

The failure of Greek political forms, oligarchy and democracy alike, profoundly affected Athenian philosophers. Plato (ca. 428–347 B.C.), an aristocratic student of Socrates, grew up during the Peloponnesian War and had witnessed the collapse of the empire, the brutality of the Thirty Tyrants, the execution of

Socrates, and the revival of the democracy and its imperialistic ambitions. From these experiences he developed a hatred for Athenian democracy and a profound distrust of ordinary people's ability to tell right from wrong. Disgusted with public life, Plato left Attica for a time and traveled in Sicily and Italy, where he encountered different forms of government and different philosophical schools. Around 387 B.C., he returned to Athens and opened the Academy, a school to provide Athenian youth with what he considered to be knowledge of what was true and good for the individual and the state.

Plato chose a most unlikely literary form for transmitting his teachings. He used the dialogue, in the form of discussions between his teacher, Socrates, and a variety of students and opponents, to develop his ideas. While Plato shared with his mentor the conviction that human actions had to be grounded in self-knowledge, Plato's philosophy extended much further. His arguments about the inadequacy of all existing forms of government and the need to create a new form of government through the proper education of elite philosopher rulers were part of a complex understanding of the universe and the individual's place in it.

Plato argued that true knowledge is impossible as long as it focuses on the constantly changing, imperfect world of everyday experience. Real knowledge can only be of that which is eternal, perfect, and beyond the experience of the senses, the realm of what Plato calls the Forms. When we judge that individuals or actions are true or good or beautiful, we do so not because these particular persons or events are truly virtuous, but because we recognize that they participate in some way in the Idea or Form of truth or goodness or beauty.

The evils of the world and in particular the vices and failures of government and society result from ignorance of the truth. Most people live as though chained in a cave in which all they can see are the shadows cast by a fire on the walls. In their ignorance, they mistake these flickering, imperfect images for reality. Their proper ruler must be a philosopher, one who is not deceived by the shadows. The philosopher's task is to break their chains and turn them toward the source of the light so that they can see the world as it really is.

Plato's idealist view (in the sense of the Ideas or Forms) of knowledge dominated much of ancient philosophy. His greatest student, Aristotle (384–322 B.C.), however, rejected this view in favor of a philosophy rooted in the natural world. Aristotle came from a medical family of northern Greece and, although a student in Plato's Academy for almost twenty years, he never abandoned observation for speculation. Systematic investigation and explanation characterize Aristotle's vast work, and his interests ranged from biology to statecraft to the most abstract philosophy. In each field, he employed essentially the same method. He observed as many individual examples of the topic as possible and from these specific observations extracted general theories. His theories, whether on the nature of matter, the species of animals, the working of the human mind, ethics, or the proper form of the state, are distinguished by clarity of logical thinking, precision in the use of terminology, and respect for the world of experience.

Aristotle brought this approach to the question of life in society. He defined humans as "political animals," that is, animals particularly characterized by life in the polis. Unlike Plato, he did not regard any particular form of government as ideal. Rather, he concluded that the type of government ultimately mattered less than the balance between narrow oligarchy and radical democracy. And yet, during the very years that Aristotle was teaching, the vacuum created by the failure of the Greek city-states was being filled by the dynamic growth of the Macedonian monarchy that finally ended a century of Greek warfare and with it, the independence of the Greek city-states.

The Rise of Macedon

The polis had never been the only form of the Greek state. Alongside the city-states of Athens, Corinth, Syracuse, and Sparta were more decentralized ethne ruled by traditional hereditary chieftains and monarchs. Macedonia, in the northeast of the mainland, was one such ethnos. Its kings, chosen by the army from within a royal family, ruled in cooperation with nobles and clan leaders. The Macedonian people spoke a Greek dialect, and Macedonian kings and elite identified with Greek culture and tradition. Macedonia had long served as a buffer between the barbarians to the north and the Greek mainland, and its tough farmers and pastoralists were geared to constant warfare. As Athens, Sparta, and Thebes fought each other to mutual exhaustion, Macedonia under King Philip II (359–336 B.C.) moved into the resulting power vacuum. Philip showed a particular genius for rapidly organizing and leading armies and for conducting complex multiple campaigns each year. He secured his borders against northern barbarians and captured the northern coast of the Aegean, including the gold and silver mines of Mount Pangaeus, which gave him a ready source of money for his campaigns. Then he turned his attention to the south.

In 346 B.C., Philip intervened in the war between Thebes and Phocis, ending that conflict but forcing himself into the center of Greek affairs. From then on he was relentless in his efforts to swallow up one Greek state after another. The Greek states resisted uniting against Philip, and one by one they fell. In 338 B.C., Philip achieved a final victory at Chaeronea and established a new league, the League of Corinth. However, unlike all those that had preceded it, this league was no confederation of sovereign states. It was an empire ruled by a king and supported by wealthy citizens whose cooperation Philip rewarded well. This new model of government, a monarchy drawing its support from a wealthy elite, became a fixture of the Mediterranean world for over two thousand years.

Philip's success was based on his powerful military machine, which combined both Macedonian military tradition and the new mercenary forces that had emerged over the past century in Greece. The heart of his army was the infantry trained in the use of pikes some fourteen feet long, four feet longer than those of the Greek hoplites. Macedonian phalanxes moved forward in disciplined ranks, pushing back their foes, whose shorter lances could not reach the Macedonians. When the enemy were contained, the Macedonian cavalry charged from the flank and cut them to pieces. The cavalry, known as the Royal Companions, were the elite of Macedon and the greatest beneficiaries of Philip's conquests.

No sooner had Philip subdued Greece than he announced a campaign against Persia. He intended to lead a combined Greek force in a war of revenge and conquest to punish the great empire for its invasion of Greece 150 years earlier and its subsequent involvement in the Greek world. Before he could begin, however, he met the fate of his predecessors. At the age of 46 he was cut down by an assassin's knife, leaving his 20-year-old son, Alexander (336–323 B.C.), to lead the expedition. Within thirteen years Alexander conquered the world.

The Empire of Alexander the Great

Alexander was less affected by his teacher, the philosopher Aristotle, than he was by the poet Homer. Envisioning himself a new Achilles, Alexander sought to imitate and surpass that legendary warrior and hero of the *Iliad*. Alexander's military genius, dedication to his troops, reckless disregard for his own safety, and ability to move both men and supplies across vast distances at great speed inspired the war machine developed by Philip and led it on an odyssey of conquest that stretched from Asia Minor to India. In 334 B.C., the first year of his campaign, Alexander captured the Greek cities of Asia Minor. Then he continued east. At Gordium, according to legend, he confronted an ancient puzzle, a complex knot tied to the chariot of the ancient king of that city. Whoever could loosen the knot, the legend said, would become master of Asia. Alexander solved that puzzle, as he did all of his others, with his sword. Two months later he defeated the Persian king Darius III at Issus and then headed south toward the Mediterranean coast and Egypt. After his victories there, he turned again to the north and entered Mesopotamia. At Gaugamela in 331 B.C., he defeated Darius a second, decisive time. Shortly after, Darius was murdered by the remnants of his followers. Alexander captured the Persian capital of Persepolis with its vast treasure and became the undisputed ruler of the vast empire.

The conquest of Persia was not enough. Alexander pushed on, intending to conquer the whole world. His armies marched east, subduing the rebellious Asian provinces of Bactria and Sogdiana. He negotiated the Khyber Pass from modern Afghanistan into the Punjab, crossed the Indus River, and defeated the local Indian king. Everywhere he went he reorganized or founded cities, entrusting them to loyal Macedonians and other Greeks, settling there veterans of his campaigns, and then pushed on toward the unknown. On the banks of the Hyphasis River in modern Pakistan, his Macedonian warriors finally

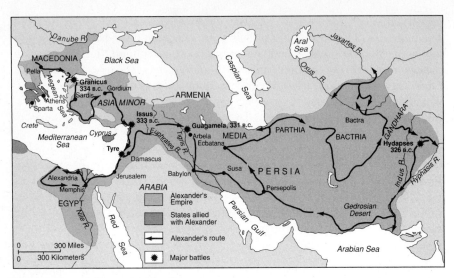

The Empire of Alexander the Great

halted. Worn out by years of bloody conquest and exhausting travel, they refused to go further, and Alexander led his troops back to Persepolis in 324 B.C. No mortal had ever before accomplished such a feat. Even in his own lifetime, Alexander was venerated as a god.

Alexander is remembered as a greater conqueror than ruler, but his plans for his reign, had he lived to complete them, might have won him equal fame. Unlike his Macedonian followers who were interested mainly in booty and power, he recognized that only by merging local and Greek peoples and traditions could he forge a lasting empire. Thus, even while founding cities on the Greek model throughout his empire, he carefully respected the local social and cultural traditions of the conquered peoples. Whether his program of cultural and social amalgamation could have succeeded is a moot point. In 323 B.C., less than two years after his return from India, he died at Babylon at the age of 32.

The empire did not outlive the emperor. Vicious fighting soon broke out among his generals and his kin. Alexander's wife Roxane and son Alexander IV (323–317 B.C.) were killed, as were all other members of the royal family. The various units of the empire broke apart into separate kingdoms and autonomous cities in which each ruler attempted to continue the political and cultural tradition of Alexander in a smaller sphere. Alexander's empire became a shifting kaleidoscope of states, kingdoms, and cities, dominated by priest-kings, native princelings, and territorial rulers, all vying to enhance their positions while preserving a relative balance of power. By 275 B.C., three large kingdoms dominated Alexander's former domain. The most stable was Egypt, which Ptolemy I (323–285 B.C.), one of Alexander's closest followers, acquired upon Alexander's death and which he and his descendants ruled until Cleopatra VII (51–30 B.C.) was defeated by the Roman Octavian in 31 B.C. In the east, the Macedonian general Seleucus (246–226 B.C.) captured Babylon in 312 B.C., and he and his descendants ruled a vast kingdom reaching from what is today western Turkey to Afghanistan. Whittled away in the east by both the Greek kingdom of Bactria and the non-Greek Parthians and in the west by the Greek Attalids in Pergamum, the Seleucid kingdom gradually shrank to a small region of northern Syria before it fell to Rome in 64 B.C. After 50 years of conflict, Antigonus Gonatas (276–239 B.C.), the grandson of another of Alexander's commanders, secured Macedon and Greece. His Antigonid successors ruled the kingdom until it fell to the Romans in 168 B.C.

$\mathcal{T}$ he Hellenistic World

Although vastly different in geography, language, and custom, the Hellenistic kingdoms (so called to distinguish them from the Hellenic civilization of the fifth and early fourth centuries B.C.) shared two common traditions. First, great portions of the Hellenistic world, from Asia Minor to Bactria and south to Egypt, had been united at various times by the Assyrian and Persian empires. During these periods they had absorbed much of Mesopotamian civilization and in particular the administrative traditions begun by the Assyrian Tiglath-pileser. Thus the Hellenistic kings ruled kingdoms already accustomed to centralized government and could rely on the already existing machinery of tax collection and administration to control the countryside. For the most part, however, these kings had little interest in the native populations of their kingdoms beyond the amount of wealth that they could extract from them. Hellenistic monarchs remained Greek and lavished their attentions on the newly created Greek cities, which absorbed vast amounts of the kingdom's wealth.

These cities and their particular form of Greek culture were the second unifying factor in the Hellenistic world. In the tradition of Alexander himself, the Ptolemys, Seleucids, and Antigonids cultivated Greek urban culture and recruited Greeks for their most important positions of responsibility. Alexander had founded over thirty-five cities during his conquests. The Seleucids established almost twice as many throughout their vast domain, even replacing the ancient city of Babylon with their capital, Seleucia, on the Tigris. In Egypt the Ptolemys replaced the ancient capital of Memphis with the new city of Alexandria. These cities became the centers of political control, economic consumption, and cultural diffusion throughout the Hellenistic world.

Urban Life and Culture

The Hellenistic kingdoms lived in a perpetual state of warfare with one another. Kings needed Greek soldiers, merchants, and administrators and competed with their rivals in offering Greeks all the comforts of home. Hellenistic cities were Greek in physical organization, constitution, and language. Each had an agora, or marketplace, that would not have been out of place in Attica. They boasted temples to the Greek gods and goddesses, theaters, baths, and most importantly, a *gymnasion*, or combination sports center and school. In the gymnasion young men competed in Greek sports and absorbed Greek poetry and philosophy just as did their cousins on the Peloponnesus. Sophocles's tragedies played to enthusiastic audiences in an enormous Greek theater in what is today Ai Khanoum on the Oxus River in Afghanistan, and the rites of Dionysus were celebrated in third-century B.C. Egypt with processions of satyrs, maenads, free wine for all, and a golden phallus 180 feet long. These Greeks were drawn from throughout the Greek-speaking world, and in time a universal Greek dialect, *koine*, became the common language of culture and business.

For all their Greek culture, Hellenistic cities differed fundamentally from Greek cities and colonies of the past. Not only were they far larger than any earlier Greek cities, but their government and culture were different from other cities or colonies. Colonies had been largely independent poleis. The Hellenistic cities were never politically sovereign. The regional kings maintained firm control over the cities, even while working to attract Greeks from the mainland and the islands to them. This policy weakened the political significance of Greek life and culture. While these cities were in theory democracies, kings firmly controlled city government, and participation in the city councils and magistracies became the affair of the wealthy.

In the new cities of the east, Greeks from all over were welcomed as soldiers and administrators regardless of their city of origin. By the second century B.C., Greeks no longer identified themselves by their city of origin but as "Hellenes," that is, Greeks. The great social and geographical mobility possible in the new cities extended to women as well as men. No longer important simply as transmitters of citizenship, women began to assume a greater role in the family, in the economy, and in public life. Marriage contracts, particularly in Ptolemaic Egypt, emphasized the theoretical equality of husband and wife. In one such contract, the husband and wife were enjoined to take no concubines or male or female lovers. The penalty for the husband was loss of the wife's dowry; for the wife, the punishment was divorce.

Since women could control their own property, many engaged in business and some became wealthy. Wealth translated into civic influence and power. Phyle, a woman of the first century B.C. from Priene in Asia Minor, spent vast sums on a reservoir and aqueducts to bring water to her city. She was rewarded with high political office, as was a female archon in Histria on the Black Sea in the second century B.C.

The most powerful women in Hellenistic society were queens, especially in Egypt, where the Ptolemys adopted the Egyptian tradition of royal marriages between brothers and sisters. Arsinoë II (ca. 316–270 B.C.) ruled as an equal with her brother-husband Ptolemy II (286–246 B.C.) She inaugurated a tradition of powerful female monarchs that ended only with Cleopatra VII, the last independent ruler of Egypt, who successfully manipulated the Roman generals Julius Caesar (100–44 B.C.) and Mark Antony (81–30 B.C.) to maintain Egyptian autonomy.

Just as monarchs competed with one another in creating Greek cities, they vied in making their cities centers of Greek culture. Socially ambitious and newly wealthy citizens supported poets, philosophers, and artists and endowed gymnasia and libraries. The largest library was in Alexandria in Egypt. In time the library housed half a million book-rolls, including all of the great classics of Greek literature. Generations of poet-scholars edited and commented on the classics, in the process inventing literary criticism and preserving much of what is known about classical authors.

Hellenistic writers were not simply book collectors or critics. They developed new forms of literature, including the romance, which often recounted imaginary adventures of Alexander the Great, and the pastoral poem, which the Sicilian Theocritus (ca. 310–250 B.C.) developed out of popular shepherd songs.

Political rivalry also encouraged architectural and artistic rivalry, as kings competed for the most magnificent Hellenistic cities. Temples, porticoes, and public buildings grew in size and ornamentation. Hellenistic architects not only developed more elaborate and monumental buildings, they also combined these buildings in harmonious urban ensembles. In cities such as Rhodes and Pergamum, planners incorporated their constructions into the terrain, using natural hills and slopes to create elegant terraced vistas.

Freestanding statues and magnificent murals and mosaics adorned the public squares, temples, and private homes of Hellenistic cities. While artists continued the traditions of the Hellenic age, they displayed more freedom in portraying tension and restlessness as well as individuality in the human form. Sculptors demonstrated their skill in the portrayal of drapery tightly folded or falling naturally across the human form. The Nike (Victory) from Samothrace (ca. 200 B.C.) and the Aphrodite from Melos, known more commonly as the Venus de Milo (ca. 120 B.C.), are supreme examples of Hellenistic sculptural achievement.

Hellenistic Philosophy

Philosophy, too, flourished in the Hellenistic world, but in directions different from those initiated by Plato and Aristotle, who were both deeply committed to political involvement in the free polis. Instead, Cynics, Epicureans, and Stoics turned inward, advocating types of morality less directly tied to the state and society. These philosophies appealed to the rootless Greeks of the Hellenistic east no longer tied by bonds of religion or patriotism to any community. Each philosophy was as much a way of life as a way of thought and offered different answers to the question of how the individual, cut loose from the security of traditional social and political networks, should deal with the whims of fate.

The Cynic tradition, established by Antisthenes (ca. 450–ca. 350 B.C.), a pupil of Socrates, and Diogenes of Sinope (d. ca. 320 B.C.), taught that excessive attachment to the things of this world was the source of evil and unhappiness. Individual freedom comes through renunciation of material things, society, and pleasures. The more one has, the more one is vulnerable to the whims of fortune. The Cynics's goal was to reduce their possessions, connections, and pleasures to the absolute minimum. "I would rather go mad than enjoy myself," Antisthenes said.

Like the Cynics, the Epicureans sought freedom, but from pain rather than from the conventions of ordinary life. Epicurus (341–270 B.C.) and his disciples have often been attacked for their emphasis on pleasure ("You need only possess perception and be made of flesh, and you will see that pleasure is good," Epicurus wrote), but this search for pleasure was not a call to sensual indulgence. Pleasure must be pursued rationally. Today's pleasure can mean tomorrow's suffering. The real goal is to reduce desires to that which are simple and attainable. Thus Epicureans urged retirement from politics, retreat from public competition, and concentration instead on friendship and private enjoyment. For Epicurus, reason properly applied illuminates how best to pursue pleasure. The traditional image of the Epicurean as an indulgent sensualist is a gross caricature. As Epicurus advised one follower, an Epicurean "revels in the pleasure of the body—on a diet of bread and water."

The Stoics also followed nature, but rather than leading them to retire from public life, it led them to greater participation in it. Just as the universe is a system in which stars and planets move according to fixed laws, so too is human society ordered and unified. As the founder of Stoicism, Zeno (ca. 335–ca. 263 B.C.), expressed it, "All men should regard themselves as members of one city and people, having one life and order." Every person has a role in the divinely ordered universe, and all roles are of equal value. True happiness consists in freely accepting one's role, whatever it may be, while unhappiness and evil result from attempting to reject one's place in the divine plan. Stoic virtue consists in applying reason to one's life in such a way that one knowingly lives in conformity to nature. Worldly pleasures, like worldly pain, have no particular value. Both are to be accepted and endured.

All three philosophical traditions emphasized the importance of reason and the proper understanding of nature. Hellenistic understanding of nature was one area in which Greek thinkers were influenced by the ancient Oriental traditions brought to them through the conquests of Alexander. Particularly for mathematics, astronomy, and engineering, the Hellenistic period was a golden age.

Mathematics and Science

Ptolemaic Egypt became the center of mathematical studies. Euclid (ca. 300 B.C.), whose *Elements* was the fundamental textbook of geometry until the twentieth century, worked there, as did his student Apollonius of Perga (ca.

262–ca. 190 B.C.), whose work on conic sections is one of the greatest monuments of geometry. Both Apollonius and his teacher were as influential for their method as for their conclusions. Their treatises follow rigorous logical proofs of mathematical theorems, which established the form of mathematical reasoning to the present day. Archimedes of Syracuse (ca. 287–212 B.C.) corresponded with the Egyptian mathematicians and made additional contributions to geometry, such as the calculation of the approximate value of pi, as well as to mechanics, arithmetic, and engineering. Archimedes was famous for his practical application of engineering, particularly to warfare, and legends quickly grew up about his marvelous machines with which he helped Syracuse defend itself against Rome.

Many mathematicians, such as Archimedes and Apollonius, were also mathematical astronomers, and the application of their mathematical skills to the exact data collected by earlier Babylonian and Egyptian empirical astronomers greatly increased the understanding of the heavens and earth. Archimedes devised a means of measuring the diameter of the sun, and Eratosthenes of Cyrene (ca. 276–194 B.C.) calculated the circumference of the earth to within two hundred miles. Aristarchus of Samos (ca. 270 B.C.) theorized that the sun and fixed stars were motionless and that the earth moves around the sun. His theory, unsupported by mathematical evidence and not taking into account the elliptical nature of planetary orbits or their nonuniform speeds, was rejected by contemporaries.

Like astronomy, Hellenistic medicine combined theory and observation. In Alexandria, Herophilus of Chalcedon (ca. 270 B.C.) and Erasistratus of Ceos (ca. 260 B.C.) conducted important studies in human anatomy. The Ptolemaic kings provided them with condemned prisoners whom they dissected alive and thus were able to observe the functioning of the organs of the body. The terrible agonies inflicted on their experimental subjects were considered to be justified by the argument that there was no cruelty in causing pain to guilty men to seek remedies for the innocent.

For all of the vitality of the Hellenistic civilization, these cities remained parasites on the local societies. No real efforts were made to merge the two and to develop a new civilization. Some ambitious members of the indigenous elites tried to adopt the customs of the Greeks, while others plotted insurrection. The clearest example of these conflicting tensions was that of the Jewish community. Early in the second century B.C., a powerful Jewish faction, which included the High Priest of Yahweh, supported Hellenization. With the assistance of the Seleucid king, this faction set up a gymnasion in Jerusalem where Jewish youths and even priests began to study Greek and participate in Greek culture. Some even underwent painful surgery to reverse the effects of circumcision so that they could pass for Greeks in naked athletic contests. This rejection of tradition infuriated a large portion of the Jewish population. When the Seleucids finally attempted to introduce pagan cults into the temple in 167 B.C., open rebellion broke out and continued intermittently until the Jews gained independence in 141 B.C.

This violent opposition was repeated elsewhere from time to time,

Classical Greece

525–456 B.C.	Aeschylus
ca. 500–ca. 430 B.C.	Phidias
496–406 B.C.	Sophocles
490 B.C.	Battle of Marathon
485–406 B.C.	Euripides
ca. 484–ca. 420 B.C.	Herodotus
480 B.C.	Battles of Thermopylae and Salamis
478 B.C.	Athens assumes control of Delian League
ca. 470–399 B.C.	Socrates
ca. 460–430 B.C.	Pericles dominates Athens
ca. 450–ca. 388 B.C.	Aristophanes
431–421; 414–404 B.C.	Peloponnesian War
ca. 428–347 B.C.	Plato
384–322 B.C.	Aristotle
338 B.C.	Philip of Macedon defeats Athens
336–323 B.C.	Reign of Alexander the Great

especially in Egypt and Persia, where, as in Judea, old traditions of religion and monarchy provided rallying points against the transplanted Greeks. In time the Hellenistic kingdoms' inability to bridge the gap between Greek and indigenous populations proved fatal. In the East, the non-Greek kingdom of Parthia replaced the Seleucids in much of the old Persian Empire. In the West, continuing hostility between kingdoms and within kingdoms prepared the way for their progressive absorption by the new power to the west: Rome.

In the fifth century B.C., the rugged slopes, fertile plains, and islands of the Greek world developed characteristic forms of social, political, and cultural organization that have reappeared in varying forms wherever Western civilization has taken root. In Athens, which emerged from the ruins of the Persian invasion as the most powerful and dynamic state in the Hellenic world, the give-and-take of a direct democracy challenged men to raise fundamental questions about the relationship between individual and society, freedom and absolutism, gods and mortals. At the same time, this society of free males excluded the majority of its inhabitants—women, foreigners, and slaves—from participation in government and fought a long and ultimately futile war to hold together an exploitative empire.

The interminable wars among Greek states ultimately left the Greek world open to conquest by a powerful semi-Greek monarchy that went on to spread Athenian culture throughout the known world. Freed from the particularism of individual city-states, Hellenistic culture became a universal tradition emphasizing the individual rather than the community of family, tribe, or religious association. And yet, this universal Hellenistic cultural tradition remained a thin veneer, hardly assimilated into the masses of the ancient world. Its proponents, except for Alexander the Great, never sought a real synthesis of Greek and barbarian tradition. Such a synthesis would only begin with the coming of Rome.

Suggestions for Further Reading

General Reading

*Michel M. Austin and Pierre Vidal-Naquet, *Economic and Social History of Ancient Greece* (Berkeley: University of California Press, 1977). An excellent survey of Greek society.

John Boardman, Jasper Griffin, and Oswyn Murray, *Greece and the Hellenistic World* (New York: Oxford University Press, 1988). An excellent up-to-date survey of Greek history by a series of experts.   *Cambridge Ancient History*, 2nd ed., Vols. 5 (1989) and 7 (1984). Contains essays on most aspects of Greek history.

*Simon Hornblower, *The Greek World, 479–323 B.C.* (New York: Routledge, Chapman & Hall, 1983). An up-to-date survey concentrating on political history.

War and Politics in the Fifth Century

*Renate Bridenthal and Claudia Koonz, eds., *Becoming Visible: Women in European History*, 2nd ed. (Boston: Houghton Mifflin, 1988). Includes essays on women in classical Greece.

John Manuel Cook, *The Persian Empire* (New York: Schocken, 1983). The standard history of Persia from the perspective of history and archaeology.

*M. I. Finley, *Democracy Ancient and Modern*, 2nd ed. (New Brunswick, NJ: Rutgers University Press, 1985). A valuable essay on Athenian democracy by a leading historian of antiquity.

---

*Indicates paperback edition available.

*Yvon Garlan, *Slavery in Ancient Greece* (Ithaca, NY: Cornell University Press, 1988). A recent study of Greek slavery.

A. W. Gomme, *Historical Commentary on Thucydides*, 5 vols. (New York: Oxford University Press, 1945–80). The fundamental study of the sources.

*A. H. M. Jones, *Athenian Democracy* (Baltimore, MD: Johns Hopkins University Press, 1957). A collection of essays by a major traditional historian.

*W. K. Lacey, *The Family in Classical Greece* (Ithaca, NY: Cornell University Press, 1984). Ordinary life in the Greek world.

R. Meiggs, *The Athenian Empire* (New York: Oxford University Press, 1979). The standard account.

W. R. O'Connor, *The New Politicians of Fifth-Century Athens* (Princeton, NJ: Princeton University Press, 1971). Reappraises the demagogues within the context of Athenian political life.

P. J. Rhodes, *The Athenian Empire* (1985). A short summary.

*David M. Schaps, *Economic Rights of Women in Ancient Greece* (New York: Columbia University Press, 1979). An examination of the roles of women in Greek society, focusing on property rights.

G. E. M. de St. Croix, *The Origins of the Peloponnesian War* (Ithaca, NY: Cornell University Press, 1972). An interpretation of the Peloponnesian War broader than the title indicates.

Athenian Culture

*J. Boardman, *Greek Art*, 3rd ed. (New York: Thames & Hudson, 1985). A handbook introduction by period.

W. Burkert, *Greek Religion* (Cambridge, MA: Harvard University Press, 1985). General survey of the topic.

I. Crombie, *An Examination of Plato's Doctrines*, 2 vols. (Atlantic Highlands, NJ: Humanities Press International, 1963). A safe guide into works on Plato.

*Simon Goldhill, *Reading Greek Tragedy* (New York: Cambridge University Press, 1986). A general introduction to Athenian tragedy.

*W. K. C. Guthrie, *History of Greek Philosophy*, Vol. 3. (New York: Cambridge University Press, 1971). Covers the Sophists.

*G. E. R Lloyd, *Aristotle: The Growth and Structure of His Thought* (New York: Cambridge University Press, 1968). A developmental approach to Aristotle.

From City-States to Macedonian Empire

*A. B. Bosworth, *Conquest and Empire* (New York: Cambridge University Press, 1988). A scholarly but readable account of Alexander the Great.

G. Cawkwell, *Philip of Macedon* (Boston: Faber & Faber, 1978). A political biography of the Macedonian king.

The Hellenistic World

J. Barnes et al., *Science and Speculation* (New York: Cambridge University Press, 1982). A collection of papers on Hellenistic science.

A. A. Long, *Hellenistic Philosophy* (Wolfeboro, NH: Longman, 1974). On Hellenistic thought.

*J. J. Pollitt, *Art in the Hellenistic Age* (New York: Cambridge University Press, 1986). A recent survey.

*R. W. Walbank, *The Hellenistic World* (Cambridge, MA: Harvard University Press, 1981). General overview.

4

Early Rome and the Roman Republic

Eternal Rome

Five miles from its mouth, the Tiber River snakes in a lazy S around the first highlands that rise from the marshes of central Italy. These weathered cliffs, separated by tributary streams, look down on the river valley that broadens to over a mile and a half wide, the first and only natural ford for many miles. Only three promontories, the Capitol, Palatine, and Aventine, are separate hills. The others, the Quirinal, Viminal, Caelian, Oppian, and Esquiline, are actually spurs of the distant Apennines. Gradually the pastoral villages founded on these hills spread down to the valleys between them, united, and grew to a city whose name for over two thousand years was synonymous with empire.

Rome wasn't built in a day. The earliest Roman villages were found on the Palatine, from whose heights the picture was taken and which remained throughout Rome's history the favored residential area. Here first Latin shepherds erected their crude huts and then republican senators built their homes. Later, emperors built on its slopes their increasingly splendid residences until the term *palace* became synonymous with the seat of royalty. The Capitol with its steep cliffs, which begin at the extreme left of the photograph, served as an acropolis, the religious center of the community. Here were found not only temples but also the state archives and the city mint beside the temple of Juno the Admonisher *Juno Moneta*, hence our word for money. The Capitol, so the Romans thought, was indestructible and became a symbol of the eternal city. As Romans established colonies across Italy and throughout the Mediterranean, the colonies too had their hill temples, their so-called capitols.

The area shown in the center of the photograph between the Palatine and Capitol was originally a low, marshy burial ground. In the seventh century B.C.,

102

Etruscan kings drained the marshes, making it possible to pave the area between and turn it into a public meeting place, or forum. The Forum became the heart of the city. Through it ran the Sacred Way, the road that cuts diagonally from left to right in the photograph. At the south end, to the right of the photograph, was the marketplace, which bustled with shops and businesses. To the north, where the domed church of Saints Luca and Magartina now stands, was the *Comitium*, the meeting place of the citizens' assembly. Here the king and, in republican times, the popular assembly conducted political business. Just below it still stands the *Curia*, the meeting place of the Roman Senate, which survives because it was converted into a Christian church in the seventh century A.D.

Here too temples and monuments rose to meet religious and public needs. Perhaps the most ancient structure was the circular temple of Vesta, the hearth goddess, the surviving columns of which can be seen in the lower center of the photograph. In this temple consecrated virgins, the most honored women of Rome, tended the sacred fire, the symbol of the life of Rome. The ruins of the virgins' magnificent residence fill the lower right of the photograph. Just above it stood the royal residence, the *Regia*, which during the republic came to be the quarters of one of Rome's chief priests, the *pontifex maximus*. To the lower right stood the temple to the twin gods, Castor and Pollux, who were credited with bringing victory in the early days of the republic against Rome's Latin neighbors. In time, still other temples joined these, for honoring the gods and honoring Rome were one.

As Rome grew from a simple city to an empire, the Forum reflected these changes. Simple Etruscan architecture gave way to the Greek style of building. Marble replaced brick and stucco. Near the Curia, the golden milestone marked the point from which all distances were measured and to which all roads of the empire led. The turmoil of the last years of the republic also left its mark. In the center of the picture the semicircular brown stone ruin is all that remains of the temple of the Divine Julius, erected on the spot where Julius Caesar's remains were cremated after his murder on the Ides of March. After his death, Caesar received divine honors, the first Roman to be so treated by his city. Next to the temple stands all that remains of the monumental arch of Caesar's adopted son, Octavian, known to history as Augustus, the first and greatest of the Roman emperors.

By the time of Caesar and Augustus, Rome had replaced its Forum, just as it had replaced its republican constitution. Caesar had begun and Augustus completed new forums, known collectively as the Forum of the Caesars, which lay beyond the trees at the top of the picture. Their successor Trajan (A.D. 98–117) would build a still greater one just beyond it. Still, for centuries of Romans and for the Western societies that succeeded them, the narrow space encompassing the Capitoline, Palatine, and the Forum was the epicenter of the city and the world.

*T*he Western Mediterranean

Civilization came late to the western Mediterranean, carried in the ships of Greeks and Phoenicians. While the great floodplain civilizations of Mesopotamia and Egypt and the Greek communities of the eastern Mediterranean were developing sophisticated systems of urban life and political organization, western Europe and Africa knew only the scattered villages of simple farmers and pastoralists. These populations, such as the Ligurians of northern Italy, were the descendants of Neolithic peoples only remotely touched by the developments in the East. The West was, however, rich in metals, and an indigenous Bronze Age culture developed slowly between 1500 and 1000 B.C., spreading widely north of the Alps and south into Italy and Spain. By the twelfth century B.C., workshops in northern Italy were producing bronze spearheads, swords, and axes both for local use and for export to Crete, Naxos, Corfu, and Mycenae. At the same time, southern Italians were importing bronze knives and ornaments from Greece. In addition to finished weapons and other objects, the eastern cities sought in Italy and Spain unworked bronze, silver bullion, tin, and iron.

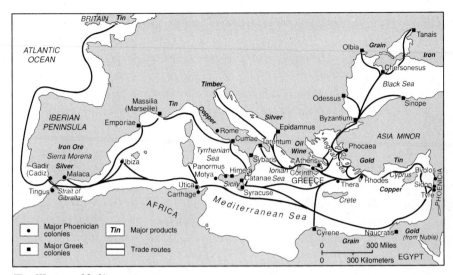

The Western Mediterranean

The western shores of the Mediterranean did not escape the widespread crisis of the twelfth century B.C., which transformed so profoundly the established civilizations of Mycenae and the Near East, but its exact effects on the West are unknown. Sometime around the year 1000 B.C., a new, distinctive iron-using civilization first appeared in northern Italy. These Villanovans, so called for a major archaeological discovery of this civilization at Villanova near Bologna, differed from earlier Italian peoples in their use of iron, in the practice of cremating their dead and burying their ashes in large urns, and in the greater size and complexity of their settlements.

No one knows whether the Villanovans were new arrivals in Italy or simply the descendants of previous inhabitants. However, around this same time small groups of peoples did begin to infiltrate Italy from the east and the north, occupying the mountainous terrain of the Apennines and pushing the indige-nous society west. These new arrivals shared no common organization or identity, but all spoke related Indo-European languages we call Italic, includ-ing Latin. These newcomers were warriors. Like the Dark Age Greeks, they soon developed the art of making iron weapons, which gave them a decided advantage over the older inhabitants of the peninsula. By 800 B.C., they were in firm control of the mountainous region of central Italy and threatened the coastal societies of the west and south.

Merchants of Baal

Also around 800 B.C., Phoenicians arrived in the West, first as traders and then as colonists. Setting out in warships from the regions of Tyre, Sidon, and

Byblos, they ventured beyond the Straits of Gibraltar in search of supplies of silver and tin. They established a trading post at Cádiz (Gadir, "walled place" in Phoenician) at which they could trade with the local inhabitants for silver from the Sierra Morena and for tin, which the Spanish (Iberians) obtained from distant Britain and Ireland. The Phoenicians established a series of bases along the route to and from Spain on the coast and on the islands of Corsica, Sicily, Ibiza, and Motya in the Mediterranean and at Utica and Carthage on the coast of North Africa. Carthage was initially no more than a small anchorage for ships. Gradually, its population grew as overcrowding forced emigration from Tyre. When, in the sixth century B.C., Tyre was conquered by Nebuchadnezzar and incorporated into the Babylonian empire, Carthage became an independent city and soon established itself as the center of an expanding Phoenician presence in the western Mediterranean.

The city was perfectly situated to profit both from the land and the sea. Its excellent double harbor, which had attracted the Phoenicians initially, made it an ideal port. Here ships could lie at rest, protected from storms as well as from enemies by a narrow 70-foot entrance to the sea that could be closed with iron chains. The city was equally protected on land, situated on a narrow isthmus and surrounded by massive walls. As long as Carthage controlled the sea, its commercial center was secure from any enemies. The wealth of Punic (from *Puni* or *Poeni*, the Roman name for the Carthaginians) commerce was supplemented by the agricultural riches of the surrounding region, which produced grain and fruits for export in abundance, while inland the subject native population engaged in cattle raising and sheep herding for their masters.

By the middle of the sixth century B.C., Carthage was the center of a real empire. But in contrast with the Athenian empire of the following century, that of Carthage was much more successful at integrating other cities and peoples into its military and thus sharing the burden of warfare. Carthaginian mercenary armies consisted of Libyan light infantry, Numidian cavalry, Spanish hill people, Balearic sling throwers, Gallic infantry, Italians, and often Greeks. Only the fleet was composed primarily of Carthaginians. This multiethnic empire proved far more stable than any of those created by the Greeks, succeeding in victory and withstanding defeat to endure for over three centuries.

Carthage was governed by a mixed constitution that combined elements of monarchical, aristocratic, and popular rule. The assembly of citizens annually elected the heads of state. In spite of the role of the free citizenry in their selection, however, these officials consistently came from among the wealthy and powerful merchant aristocracy. They presided over the popular assembly and the smaller, aristocratic senate, and dispensed justice. In their governmental tasks these officials were assisted by "judges," actually a select body of magistrates chosen from the senate, who had broad judicial and administrative responsibility.

As a society of merchants, Carthaginians mistrusted military leaders and carefully separated military authority from civil. Generals were elected and served open-ended terms. Because almost all of Carthage's wars were conducted far from home, using mercenaries or citizens of subject cities, selection of commanders was often based more on the aristocracy's concern to avoid giving too much power to ambitious, capable leaders than to select the best soldiers.

Although superficially similar to many Greek cities, the Punic state differed profoundly in the relationship between citizen and state. Compared with that of the Greek states, Punic popular politics has been termed essentially apolitical. In spite of the formal role of the assembly, ordinary citizens had little involvement and, apparently, little interest in government. According to Aristotle, the aristocracy treated the rest of the population generously, sharing with it profits in the exploitation of its commercial and imperial wealth. Thus the class pressures that created the Greek tyrants never emerged in Carthage.

This traditional, conservative perspective of Carthaginian government was also evident in Carthaginian religion. The gods of Carthage were local variations of the Phoenician gods, especially Baal Hammon, the supreme god El of the Semitic world, and the goddess Tanit, a version of the Near Eastern goddess Asherat. Baal Hammon was an awesome figure. The Greeks equated him not with Zeus but with the more ancient supreme god, Kronos, a cruel tyrant who devoured his children. Tanit, goddess of fertility, assumed an importance equal to that of Baal Hammon, probably under the influence of the indigenous Libyan society.

According to hostile Greek and Roman sources, all Carthaginian citizens were obligated to sacrifice their firstborn sons. The sacrifice of children constituted the most important and, to their Greek and barbarian neighbors, the most repulsive aspect of Punic culture. The basic reliability of these reports was dramatically confirmed in 1922, when archaeologists excavated the sanctuary of Tanit at Salammbo. It was found to contain urns filled with the remains of hundreds of children. Other similar sacred sites have since been found. While some scholars have suggested that these are simply infant burial sites, the appearance of animal bones mixed in with those of children in levels from the fourth century B.C. and then, in the level from the third century, the appearance of only animal remains, indicates that child sacrifice did indeed take place, only gradually disappearing toward the end of Carthaginian history.

Stable, prosperous, and devout, Carthage was the master of the western Mediterranean. But its dominion was not undisputed. From the sixth century B.C., the Punic empire felt the pressure of ambitious Greek cities eager to gain a share of the West's riches.

The Western Greeks

The Greek arrival in the west was the result of a much more complex process than the trading policy of the Phoenicians. As we saw in Chapter 2, toward the end of the Dark Age, commerce, overpopulation, and civic tension sent Greek colonists out in all directions. In the eighth century B.C., Crete, Rhodes, Corinth,

Argos, Chalcis, Eretria, and Naxos all established colonies in Sicily and southern Italy.

In the seventh century B.C., Syracuse became the greatest city of Sicily and one of the most prosperous cities of the Greek world. Greek colonies spread slowly up the boot of Italy, known as Greater Greece, in pursuit of trade and arable land. By the last quarter of the seventh century B.C., the autonomous Greek colonies began to encroach on the Carthaginian empire's sphere of influence. Around 631 B.C., Greeks from Thera founded a colony at Cyrene in North Africa. The Greek city of Phocaea in Asia Minor established a colony at Marseilles around 600 B.C.

Both commercial rivalry and open warfare characterized the relationship between Greeks and Phoenicians in the western Mediterranean. In the course of the sixth century B.C., Greeks in Sicily attempted to expel the Phoenicians from the island. In the fifth century B.C., Syracuse, under its tyrant Gelon (ca. 540–478 B.C.), threatened both Punic and Greek cities on the island. In an attempt to defend its colonies, in 480 B.C. Carthage launched an enormous force to support Gelon's Greek enemies. The attack took place, probably not coincidentally, at the same moment that Xerxes invaded Greece. At the battle of Himera, fought, we are told, on the same day as the battle of Salamis, the Syracusans soundly defeated the Carthaginians.

Gelon's victory at Himera ushered in a period of prosperity and cultural achievement in Sicily only slightly less extraordinary than that which followed the battles of Marathon and Salamis in Greece. The tyrants of Syracuse, enriched with the spoils of victory, created a court whose magnificence, wealth, and generosity won admiration throughout the Greek world. This prosperity continued after the elimination of the tyranny in mid-century, and in 415 B.C., Syracuse was able to withstand Athens's attempt at conquest (see Chapter 3, p. 80).

A far more serious threat appeared in 410 B.C., when a new Carthaginian army arrived in Sicily seeking revenge. The Carthaginians rapidly captured and destroyed Himera, extending the boundaries of Punic Sicily. This invasion initiated a century of inconclusive conflict between Syracuse and Carthage.

Early on in their struggle with the Sicilian Greeks, the Carthaginians found allies in the third major civilization of the West. These were the Etruscans, who in the seventh century B.C. dominated the western part of central Italy known as Etruria.

Italy's First Civilization

Etruscan civilization was the first great civilization to emerge in Italy. The Etruscans have long been regarded as a people whose origins, language, and customs are shrouded in mystery. Actually, the mystery is more apparent than real. The Greek historian Herodotus thought that the Etruscans had emigrated from Lydia in Asia Minor, and many historians, noting similarities between Etruscan and Eastern traditions, have subsequently accepted the thesis of eastern origins. A second ancient tradition, reported by the Greek scholar Dionysius of Halicarnassus, is that the Etruscans did not emigrate from anywhere but rather had always been in western Italy. In recent years, archaeologists have demonstrated that this latter thesis is likely correct. Probably, just as in the Aegean, an indigenous cultural tradition was overwhelmed by the chaos of the twelfth-century B.C. crisis and the migration of Indo-Europeans from the north. This tradition shares much with Eastern civilizations, such as fertility cults and the high status of women. Some scholars even speak of a common Mediterranean civilization submerged for a time but reemerging transformed centuries later.

Etruscan language is commonly seen as the second great mystery. Unlike the early Minoan writing, which was found to be early Greek written in an unknown script, Etruscan is written in an alphabet derived from that of Greece. Still, despite the derivation of the alphabet, the Etruscan language appears unrelated to any other language and even today some of the extant Etruscan texts remain incompletely deciphered.

Etruscan civilization coalesced slowly in Etruria over the course of the seventh century B.C. from diverse regional and political groups sharing a similar cultural and linguistic tradition. In the mid sixth century B.C., in the face of Greek pressure from the south, 12 of these groups united in a religious and military confederation. Over the next 100 years, the confederation expanded north into the Po Valley and south to Campania. Cities, each initially ruled by a king, were the centers of Etruscan civilization, and everywhere the Etruscans spread they either improved upon existing towns or founded new ones. Towns in the north included Bologna, Parma, Modena, Ravenna, Milan, and Mantua; in the south, there were Nola, Nuceria, Pompeii, Sorrento, and Salerno. The Etruscan confederation never developed into a centralized empire. Etruscan kings assumed power in conquered towns, but between the sixth and fifth centuries B.C., Etruscan kingship gave way to oligarchic governments, much as Greek monarchies did a bit earlier. In the place of kings, aristocratic assemblies selected magistrates, often paired together or combined into "colleges" to prevent individuals from seizing power. These republican institutions provided the foundation for later Roman republican government.

The remnants of an ancient civilization, the Etruscans retained throughout their history social and cultural traditions long since vanished elsewhere in the Mediterranean. Society divided sharply into two classes, lords and servants. The lords' wealth was based on the rich agricultural regions of Etruria where grain grew in abundance and on the equally rich deposits of copper and iron. The vast majority of the population were actual slaves, working the lands and mines of the aristocracy.

The aristocrats developed hydraulic systems for draining marshes, established a wine production famous throughout the Mediterranean, and put their slaves to work in mines and in smelting. They were largely absentee landlords, spending much of their time in the towns that characterized Etruscan civilization. These cities, with their massive walls, enclosed populations of as many as twenty thousand. Their extensive cemeteries have preserved a vivid image of

Etruscan life. Tombs were furnished with the wares of everyday life, including benches, beds, ornaments, utensils, and vessels and platters of Etruscan and Corinthian manufacture.

The most striking aspect of Etruscan life to Greek contemporaries and to later Romans was the elevated status of Etruscan women. The decorations and furnishings of tombs, inscriptions, and reports by contemporaries indicate that, as in the much earlier Minoan civilization, women played an active, public role in society. Unlike honorable Greek women, Etruscan women took part in banquets. They attended and even occasionally presided over dances, concerts, and sporting events. Women, as wives and mothers, were also active in political life. When a king died, his successor had to be designated and consecrated by the Etruscan queen to establish his legitimacy. Greeks such as Aristotle regarded the public behavior of Etruscan women as lewd. The great philosopher accused them of lying under the same cloak with men at banquets. To later Romans, the political role of women such as Tullia, wife of King Lucius Tarquinius Superbus (Tarquin the Proud), the Etruscan king of Rome, was equally shocking. The Roman historian Livy (59 B.C.–A.D. 17) pretends that when Tullia was the first person to acknowledge her husband as the rightful king, he was so shocked that he sent her home. In truth, he was surely grateful.

While the Etruscans were consolidating their hegemony in western Italy, they were at the same time establishing their maritime power. From the

On the Etruscan sarcophagus of Larthia Scianti, a matron reclines as at a banquet. Much of our knowledge of this first Italian civilization comes from the elaborate paintings and statuary found in Etruscan cemeteries.

seventh to the fifth centuries B.C., Etruscans controlled the Italian coast of the Tyrrhenian Sea as well as Sardinia, from which their ships could reach the coast of what is today France and Spain. Attempts to extend farther south into Greek southern Italy and toward the Greek colonies on the modern French coast brought the Etruscans and the Greeks into inevitable conflict. Etruscan cities fought sporadic sea battles against Greek cities in the waters of Sicily as well as off the coasts of Corsica and Etruria. Common hostility toward the Greeks as well as complementary economic interests soon brought the Etruscans into alliances with Carthage. Toward the end of the sixth century B.C., Etruscan cities including Rome signed a series of pacts with Carthage that created military alliances against the Phocaeans and Syracuse. Etruscan fleets were victorious over the Phocaeans, driving them from Corsica, but they were no match for Syracuse. In 474 B.C., shortly after the battle of Himera, the Syracusan fleet destroyed that of the Etruscans off Cumae. Cumae marked the beginning of Etruscan decline. Through the fifth century B.C., Etruscan cities lost control of the sea to the Greeks. Around the same time, Celts from north of the Alps invaded and conquered the Po Valley. And to the south, Etruscans saw their inland territories progressively slipping into the hands of their former subjects, the Romans.

ℱrom City to Empire

What manner of people were these who, from obscure origins, came to rule an empire? Their own answer would have been simple: They were farmers and soldiers, simple people accustomed to simple, straightforward actions. Throughout their long history, Romans liked to refer to the clearcut models provided by their semilegendary predecessors: Cincinnatus, the farmer, called away to the supreme office of dictator in time of danger, then returning to his plow; Horatius Cocles, the valiant warrior who held back an Etruscan army on the Tiber bridge until it could be demolished and then, despite his wounds, swam across the river to safety; Lucretia, the wife who chose death after dishonor. These were myths, but they were important myths to Romans, who preferred concrete models to abstract principles.

Later Romans liked to imagine the history of their city as one predestined by the gods for greatness. Some liked to trace the origins of Rome to Romulus and Remus, twin sons of the war god Mars and a Latin princess. According to legend, the children were raised by a she-wolf. Other Romans, having absorbed the Homeric traditions of Greece, taught that the founder of Rome was Aeneas, son of the goddess of love Aphrodite and the Trojan Anchises, who had wandered west after the fall of Troy. All agreed that Rome had been ruled by kings, who underwent a steady decline in ability and morals until the last, Tarquin the Proud, was expelled by outraged Latins. These legends tell much about the attitudes and values of later Romans. They tell nothing about the origins of the city, its place in the Latin and Etruscan worlds, and its rise to greatness.

Latin Rome

Civilization in Italy meant Etruria to the north and Greater Greece to the south. In between lay Latium, a marshy region punctured by hills on which a sparse population could find protection from disease and enemies. This population was an amalgam of aboriginal Ligurians and the more recently arrived Latins and Sabines who lived a pastoral life in small scattered villages.

The Alban Hills south of the Tiber were a center of Latin population. Sometime in the eighth century B.C., roughly forty Latin villages formed a loose confederation, the Alban League, for military and religious purposes. Not long after, in the face of an expanding Etruscan confederation from the north and Sabine penetration from the east, the Albans established a village on the steep Palatine hill to the north. The Palatine was one of several hills overlooking a natural ford on the Tiber. This Alban village, called Roma Quadrata, was soon joined by other Latin and Sabine settlements on nearby hills. By the end of the eighth century B.C., seven Latin villages along the route from the Tiber to Alba had formed a league for mutual defense and shared religious cults.

Early Roman society was composed of households; clans, or *gentes;* and village councils, or *curiae* (sing. *curia*). The male head of each household, the *paterfamilias*, had power of life and death over its members and was responsible for the proper worship of the spirits of the family's ancestors, on whom continued prosperity depended. Within some villages, these families were grouped into gentes, which claimed descent from a semimythical ancestor.

Male members of village families formed councils, which were essentially religious organizations but also provided a forum for public discussion. These curiae tended to be dominated by gentes, but all males could participate, including *plebeians* (those who belonged to the *plebs*, that is, families not organized into gentes). Later, the leaders of the gentes called themselves *patricians* ("descendants of fathers") and claimed superiority to the plebs.

Important plebeian and patrician families increased their power through a system of *clientage*, which remained a fundamental aspect of social and political organization throughout Roman history. Clients were free men who depended on the protection of a more powerful individual or family and who owed various services, including political support, in return for this protection.

Villages themselves grouped together for military and voting purposes into ethnic tribes, each composed of a number of curiae. Each curia supplied a contingent of infantry and each tribe cooperated to supply a unit of horsemen to the Roman army.

Assemblies of all members of the curiae expressed approval of major decisions, especially declaration of war and the selection of new kings, and thus played a real if limited political role. More powerful although less formal was the role of the *senate* (assembly of elders), which was composed of heads of families. The senate's power derived from the individual importance of its members and from its role in selecting a candidate for king, who was then presented to the assembly of the curiae for approval.

Kings served as religious leaders, the primary means of communication between gods and men. Through the early Latin period royal power remained fundamentally religious and limited by the senate, curiae, gentes, and families.

The seven villages that made up primitive Rome developed independently of their Etruscan and Greek neighbors. Initially, Romans lived in thatched huts, tended their flocks on the hillsides, and maintained their separate village identities. By the seventh century B.C., they had begun fortifications and other structures indicating the beginnings of a dynamic civic life. This independent course of development changed in the middle of the seventh century B.C., when the Etruscans overwhelmed Latium and absorbed it into their civilization. Under its Etruscan kings, Rome first entered civilization.

Etruscan Rome

The Etruscans introduced in Latium and especially in Rome their political, religious, and economic traditions. Etruscan kings and magistrates ruled Latin towns, increasing the power of traditional Latin kingship. The kings were not only religious leaders, directing the cults of their humanlike gods, but also led the army, served as judges, and held supreme political power. As Latium became an integral part of the Etruscan world, the Tiber became an important commercial route. For the first time, Rome began to enter the wider orbit of Mediterranean civilization. The town's population swelled with the arrival of merchants and craftworkers.

As Rome's importance grew, so did its size. Surrounding villages were added to the original seven, as were the Sabine colonies on the Quirinal and Capitoline hills. Etruscan engineers drained the marshes into a great canal flowing to the Tiber, thus opening the lowlands between the hills to settlement. This in turn allowed them to create and pave the Forum. The Etruscans were also builders, constructing a series of vast fortifications encircling the town. Under Etruscan influence, the fortified Capitoline hill, which served much like a Greek acropolis, became the cult center with the erection of the temple to Jupiter, the supreme god; Juno, his consort; and Minerva, an Etruscan goddess of craftwork similar to Athena. In its architecture, religion, commerce, and culture, Latin Rome was deeply indebted to its Etruscan conquerors.

As important as the physical and cultural changes brought by the Etruscans was their reorganization of the society. As in Greece, this restructuring was tied to changes in the military. The Etruscans had learned from the Greeks the importance of hoplite tactics, and King Servius Tullius (578–534 B.C.) introduced this system of warfare into Rome. This led to the abolition of the earlier curia-based military and political system in favor of one based only on property holding. The king divided Roman society into two groups. Those landowners wealthy enough to provide armed military service were organized into five *classes* (from which the word *class* is derived), ranked according to the quality of their arms and hence their wealth. Each class was further divided into military units called centuries. Members of these centuries constituted the centuriate assembly, which replaced the older curial assemblies for such vital decisions as the election of magistrates and the declaration of war.

The constitution and operation of this centuriate assembly ensured control by the most conservative forces within the society. Small centuries of wealthy well-armed cavalrymen and fully armed warriors outnumbered the more modestly equipped but numerically greater centuries. Likewise, men over the age of 47, although in a minority, controlled over half of the centuries in each class. Since votes were counted not by individuals but by centuries, this ensured within the assembly the domination of the rich over the poor, the elder over the younger. The rest of the society was *infra classem* (literally "under class"). Owning no property, they were excluded from military and political activity.

With this military and political reorganization came a reconstruction of the tribal system. Servius Tullius abolished the old tribal organization in favor of geographically organized tribes into which newcomers could easily be incorporated. Henceforth, while the family remained powerful, involvement in public life was based on property and geography. Latins, Sabines, Ligurians, and Etruscans could all be active citizens of the growing city.

While the old tribal units and curiae declined, divisions between the patricians and the plebeians grew more distinct. During the monarchy the patricians came to compose an upper stratum of wealthy nobles. They forbade marriage outside their own circle, forming a closed, self-perpetuating group that monopolized the senate, religious rites, and magisterial offices. Although partially protected by the kings, the plebeians, whether rich or poor, were pressed into a second-class status and denied access to political power.

In less than two centuries, the Etruscans transformed Rome into a prosperous, unified urban center that played an important role in the economic and political life of central Italy. They laid the foundations of a free citizenry, incorporating Greek models of military and social organization. The transformations brought about by the Etruscan kings became an enduring part of Rome. The Etruscans themselves did not. Just as the hoplite revolution in Greece saw the end of most Hellenic monarchies, around the traditionally reported date of 509 B.C. the Roman patricians expelled the last king, Tarquin the Proud, and established a republic (from the Latin *res publica*, public property, as opposed to *res privata*, private property of the king).

Rome and Italy

Always the moralizers, later Roman historians made the expulsion of King Tarquin the dramatic result of his son's lust. According to legend, Sextus, the son of Tarquin, raped Lucretia, a virtuous Roman matron. She told her husband of the crime and then took her own life. Outraged, the Roman patricians were said to have driven the king and his family from the city. Actually, monarchy was giving way to oligarchic republics across Etruria in the sixth century B.C. Rome was hardly exceptional. However, the establishment of the Roman republic coincided roughly with the beginning of the Etruscan decline, allowing Rome to assert itself and to develop its Latin and Etruscan traditions in unique ways.

The patrician oligarchy had engineered the end of the monarchy, and patricians dominated the offices and institutions of the new republic at the expense of the plebs who, in losing the king, lost their only defender. Governmental institutions of the early republic developed within this context of patrician supremacy.

Characteristic of republican institutions was that at every level, power was shared by two or more equals elected for fixed terms. This practice of shared power was intended to ensure that magistrates would consult with each other before making decisions and that no individual could achieve supreme power at any level. Replacing the king were the two *consuls*, each elected by the assembly for a one-year term. Initially only the consuls held the *imperium*, the supreme power to command, to execute the law, and to impose the death penalty. Only in moments of grave crisis might a consul, with the approval of the senate, name a single *dictator* with extraordinary absolute power for a very brief period, never more than six months. In time other magistracies developed to perform specialized functions. *Praetors*, who in time also exercised the imperium, administered justice and defended the city in the absence of the consuls. *Quaestors* controlled finances. *Censors* assigned individuals their places in society, determined the amount of their taxes, filled vacancies in the senate, and negotiated contracts for public construction projects. A variety of military commanders directed wars against neighboring cities and peoples under the imperium of the consuls. In all their actions these officeholders consulted with each other and with the senate, which was composed of roughly three hundred powerful former magistrates. The centuriate assembly functioned as the legislative organ of the state, but it continued to be dominated by the eldest and wealthiest members of society.

During the early republic, wealthy patricians, aided by their clients, monopolized the senate and the magistracies. Successful magistrates rose through a series of increasingly important offices, which came to be known as the *cursus honorum*, to the position of consul. Censors selected from among former magistrates in appointing new senators, thus ensuring that the senate would be dominated by the patrician elite. Patricians also controlled the system of priesthoods, which they held for life. With political and religious power came economic power. The poorer plebs in particular found themselves sinking into debt to wealthy patricians, losing their property, and with it the basis for military service and political participation. In the courtroom, in the temple, in the assembly, and in the marketplace, plebeians found themselves subjected to the whims of an elite from which they were excluded.

The plebs began to organize in response to patrician control. On several occasions in the first half of the fifth century B.C., the whole plebeian order withdrew a short distance from the city, refusing to return or to serve in the military until conflicts with the patricians were resolved. In time the plebs created their own assembly, the Council of the Plebs, which enacted laws binding on all plebeians. This council founded its own temples and elected magistrates called *tribunes*, whose persons were declared sacred to the gods. The tribunes protected the plebs from arbitrary patrician power. Anyone harming the tribunes, whether patrician or plebeian, could be killed by the plebs without trial. With their own assembly, magistracies, and religious cults, the plebeians were well on the way to creating a separate republic. This conflict between the plebeians and the patricians, known as the Struggle of Orders, threatened to tear the Roman society apart just as pressure from hostile neighbors placed Rome on the defensive. Roman preeminence in Latium had ended with the expulsion of the last king. The Etruscan town of Veii just north of the Tiber began periodic attacks against Rome. To the south, the Volscians had begun to expand north into the Litis and Trerus valleys.

This military pressure, and the inability of the patricians to meet it alone, ultimately forced them to a compromise with the plebeians. One of the first victories won by the plebs around 450 B.C. was the codification of basic Roman law, the Law of the Twelve Tables, which recognized the basic rights of all free citizens. Around the same time, the state began to absorb the plebeian political and religious organizations intact. Gradually, priesthoods, magistracies, and thus the senate were opened to plebeians. The consulship was the last prize finally won by the plebs in 367 B.C. In 287 B.C., as the result of a final secession of the plebs, the decisions of the plebeian assembly became binding on all citizens, patrician and plebeian alike.

Bitter differences at home did not prevent patricians and plebs from presenting a united front against their enemies abroad. External conquest deflected internal hostility and profited both orders. By the beginning of the fourth century B.C., the united patrician-plebeian state was expanding its rule both north and south. Roman legions, commanded by patricians but formed of the whole spectrum of property-owning Romans, reestablished Roman preeminence in Latium and then began a series of wars that brought most of Italy under Roman control. In 396 B.C., Roman forces captured and destroyed Veii and shortly after conquered the rest of southern Etruria. In the south, Roman and Latin forces turned back the Volscians. In 390 B.C., Rome suffered a temporary setback at the hands of the Gauls, or Celts, of northern Italy, who raided south and sacked much of the city before being bought off with a large tribute payment. Even this event had a silver lining. The damage to Rome was short lived, but the Gauls had dealt a deathblow to the Etruscan cities of the north, clearing the way for later Roman conquest. By 295 B.C., Rome had secured its rule as far north as the Po Valley. In the south, Roman infantry and persistence proved the equal of professional Greek armies. Rome won a war of attrition against a series of Hellenistic commanders, the last of whom was the Greek king Pyrrhus of Epirus (319–272 B.C.). Pyrrhus, regarded as the greatest tactician of his day, won a number of victories that proved more costly to him than to his Roman opponents. In 275 B.C., after losing two-thirds of his troops in these "Pyrrhic victories," he withdrew to Sicily. By 265 B.C., Rome had absorbed the Hellenistic cities of the south.

The Roman conquest benefited patrician and plebeian alike. While the patricians acquired wealth and power, the plebeians received a prize of equal value: land. After the capture of Veii, for example, the poor of Rome received shares of the conquered land. Since landowning was a prerequisite for military service, this distribution created still more peasant soldiers for further expeditions. Still, while the constant supply of new land did much to diffuse the tensions between orders, it did not actually resolve them. Into the late third century B.C., debt and landlessness remained major problems creating tensions in Roman society. Probably not more than one-half of the citizen population owned land by 200 B.C.

The Roman manner of treating conquered populations, radically different from anything seen before, also contributed to Rome's success. In war, no one could match the Roman legions for ruthless, thorough destruction. Yet no conquerors had ever shown themselves so generous in victory. After the crushing of the Latin revolt of 338 B.C., virtually all of the Latins were incorporated into the Roman citizenry. Later colonies founded outside of Latium were given the same status as Latin cities. Other more distant conquered peoples were considered allies and required to provide troops but no tribute to Rome. In time, they too might become citizens.

The implications of these measures were revolutionary. By extending citizenship to conquered neighbors and by offering the future possibility to allies, Rome tied their fate to its own. Rather than potentially subversive subjects, conquered populations became strong supporters. Thus, in contrast to the Hellenistic cities of the east where Greeks jealously guarded their status from the indigenous population, Rome's colonies acted as magnets, drawing local populations into the Roman cultural and political orbit. Greeks were scandalized by the Roman tradition of giving citizenship even to freed slaves. By the end of the fourth century B.C., some of the sons of these freedmen were finding a place in the senate. Finally, in all of its wars of conquest, Rome claimed a moral mandate. Romans went to great lengths to demonstrate that theirs were just wars, basing their claims on alleged acts of aggression by their enemies, on the appeal to Rome by its allies, and, increasingly, by presenting themselves as the preservers and defenders of Greek traditions of freedom. Both these political and propagandistic measures proved successful. Between 265 B.C. and 91 B.C., few serious revolts shook the peace and security of Italy south of the Po.

Benevolent treatment of the conquered spurred further conquest. Since subject cities and peoples did not pay tribute, the only way for Rome to benefit from its conquests or to exercise its authority was to demand and use troops. By 264 B.C., all of Italy was united under Roman hegemony. Roman expansion finally brought Rome into conflict with the great Mediterranean power of the west, Carthage.

Rome and the Mediterranean

Since its earliest days, Rome had allied itself with Carthage against the Greek cities of Italy. The zones of interest of the two cities had been quite separate. Carthage was a sea empire, whereas Rome was a land-based power without a navy. The Greeks, aspiring to power on land and sea, posed a common threat to both Rome and Carthage. However, once Rome had conquered the Greek cities to the south, it became enmeshed in the affairs of neighboring Sicily, a region with well-established Carthaginian interests. There, in 265 B.C., a group of Italian mercenary pirates in Messina, threatened by Syracuse, requested Roman assistance. The senate refused but the plebeian assembly, eager for booty, exercised its newly won right to legislate for the republic and accepted. Shortly afterward the Romans invaded Sicily, and Syracuse turned to its old enemy, Carthage, for assistance. The First Punic War had begun.

The First Punic War, which lasted from 265 to 241 B.C., was a costly, brutal, and drawn-out affair that Rome won by dint of persistence and methodical calculation rather than strategic brilliance. Rome invaded and concluded an alliance with Syracuse in 263 B.C. The war rapidly became a sea war. Rome had little previous naval experience but quickly learned the rules of the game and then rewrote them to its own advantage. Taking a wrecked Carthaginian ship as a model, Roman builders constructed 20 fast ships propelled by roughly two hundred oarsmen to ram and sink opposing ships. Rome also built 100 larger ships with crews of 300, manned by Roman allies. Unaccustomed to fighting at sea, Roman engineers turned sea battles into land battles by placing on their

Relief of a Roman war galley. The deck is crowded with infantrymen. Galleys were usually rowed by slaves while the soldiers remained fresh for the task of subduing enemy ships.

ships heavy gangplanks that could be dropped onto enemy ships. The gang-planks were equipped with a heavy iron spike to secure them to the enemy's deck. This allowed a contingent of legionnaires to march onto the enemy ship and fight as though on dry land.

With these innovations, the Romans won impressive initial victories but still could not deliver a knockout blow either in Sicily or North Africa for over twenty years. Finally, in 241 B.C., Rome forced the Carthaginian commander, Hamilcar Barca (ca. 270–229 B.C.), to surrender simply because the Romans could afford to build one more fleet than he. Carthage paid a huge indemnity and abandoned Sicily. Syracuse and Messina became allies of Rome. In a break with tradition, Rome obligated the rest of Sicily to pay a true tribute in the form of a tithe (one-tenth) of their crops. Shortly after that, Rome helped itself to Sardinia as well, from which it again demanded tribute, not simply troops. Rome had established an empire.

During the next two decades Roman legions defeated the Ligurians on the northwest coast, the Celtic Gauls south of the Alps, and the Illyrians along the Adriatic coast. At the same time, Carthage fought a bitter battle against its own mercenary armies, which it had been unable to pay off after its defeat. Carthage then began the systematic creation of an empire in Spain. Trade between Carthage and Rome reached the highest level in history, but trade did not create friendship. On both sides, powerful leaders saw the treaty of 241 B.C. as just a pause in a fight to the death. Hamilcar Barca had his 9-year-old son Hannibal swear to be Rome's eternal enemy. Fearful and greedy Romans insisted that Carthage had to be destroyed for the security of Rome. They were particularly disturbed by the growth of Carthage's Spanish empire, even though Hamilcar Barca assured the senate that he was simply trying to raise funds to pay off Carthage's indemnity.

Carthaginian successes in Spain, led after Hamilcar's death by his son-in-law Hasdrubal (d. 221 B.C.) and his son Hannibal (247–183 B.C.), finally provoked Rome to war in 218 B.C. As soon as this Second Punic War had begun, Hannibal began an epic march north out of Spain, along the Mediterranean coast, and across the Alps. In spite of great hardships, he was able to transport over twenty-three thousand troops and approximately eighteen war elephants into the plains of northern Italy. Hannibal's brilliant generalship brought victory after victory to the Carthaginian forces. In the first engagement on the Trebia River in the Po Valley the Romans lost 20,000 men, two-thirds of their army. Carthaginian success encouraged the Gauls to join the fight against the Romans. Initially, Italian, Etruscan, and Greek allies remained loyal, but after Rome's catastrophic defeats at Lake Trasimene in Etruria in 217 B.C. and especially at Cannae in 216 B.C., a number of Italian colonies and allies, especially the cities of Capua and Syracuse, went over to the enemy. In the east, Philip V of Macedon (238–179 B.C.) made a treaty with Carthage in the hope of taking Illyria from a defeated Rome.

As commanders chosen by the patrician-dominated senate failed to stop the enemy, the Roman plebs became increasingly dissatisfied with the way the oligarchy was conducting the war. In 217 B.C., following the battle of Lake

Trasimene, the senate named the capable general Quintus Fabius Maximus (d. ca. 203 B.C.) dictator. He used delaying tactics successfully to slow the Carthaginians. The popular assembly, impatient for a decisive victory, elected a second dictator, thus effectively canceling the position of Quintus Fabius Maximus. The next year popular pressure forced the election of Gaius Terentius Varro as consul. Varro quickly led the army to the greatest defeat in Roman history at Cannae. There Hannibal surrounded and annihilated Varro's numerically superior army.

Three things saved the Roman state. First, while some important allies and colonies defected, the majority held firm. Rome's traditions of sharing the fruits of victory with its allies, extending the rights of Roman citizenship, and protecting central and southern Italy against its enemies proved stronger than the appeals of Hannibal. Although victorious time and again, without local support Hannibal could not hold the terrain and cities he won. New allies such as Syracuse, which fell in 212 B.C., were forcibly returned to the Roman camp. Fabius resumed his delaying tactics and gradually Hannibal's victories slipped from his hands.

The second reason for Rome's survival was the tremendous social solidarity all classes and factions of its population showed during these desperate years. In spite of the internal tensions between particians and plebeians, their ultimate dedication to Rome never faltered. Much of this loyalty was due to the

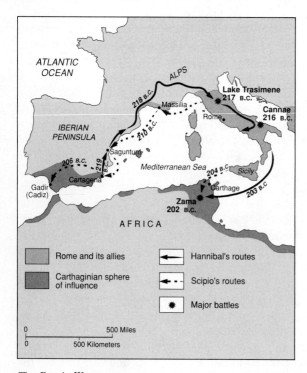

The Punic Wars

The Roman Republic

509 B.C.	Expulsion of the last Etruscan king; beginning of Roman republic
ca. 450 B.C.	Law of Twelve Tables
396 B.C.	Rome conquers southern Etruria
295 B.C.	Rome extends rule north to Po Valley
265–241 B.C.	First Punic War
264 B.C.	All of Italy under Roman control
218–202 B.C.	Second Punic War
149–146 B.C.	Third Punic War; Carthage is destroyed

Roman system of strong family and patronage ties. Kinsmen and clients answered the call of their patriarchs and patrons to bounce back repeatedly from defeat. Roman farmer-soldiers stood firm.

The final reason for Rome's ultimate success was Publius Cornelius Scipio (236–184 B.C.), also known as Scipio the Elder, a commander able to force Hannibal from Italy. Scipio, who earned the title Africanus for his victory, accomplished this not by attacking Hannibal directly, but by taking the war home to the enemy, first in Spain and then in Africa. In 210 B.C. Scipio arrived in Spain and rapidly captured the city of Cartagena (New Carthage). Within four years he destroyed Punic power in Spain. Riding the crest of popular enthusiasm at home, he raised a new army and in 204 B.C. sailed for Africa. His victories there drew Hannibal home, where at Zama in 202 B.C. the Roman commander destroyed the Carthaginian army. Zama put an end to both the Second Punic War and Carthaginian political power. Saddled with a huge indemnity and forced to abandon all of its territories and colonies to Rome, reduced to a small portion of the North African coast, Carthage had become in effect a Roman subject.

But still this humiliating defeat was not enough for Rome. While some Roman senators favored allowing Carthage to survive as a means of keeping the Roman plebs under senatorial control, others demanded destruction. Chief among them was the censor Marcus Porcius Cato, known as Cato the Elder (234–149 B.C.), who ended every speech with *Delenda est Carthago*, "Carthage must be destroyed." Ultimately trumped-up reasons were found to renew the war in 149 B.C. In contrast to the desperate, hard-fought campaigns of the Second Punic War, the Third was an unevenly matched slaughter. In 146 B.C. Scipio Aemilianus (184–129 B.C.), or Scipio the Younger, the adopted grandson of Scipio the Elder, overwhelmed Carthage and sold its few survivors into slavery. As a symbolic act of final destruction, he then had the site razed, plowed, and cursed. Carthage's fertile hinterland became the property of wealthy Roman senators.

In the same year that Carthage was destroyed, Roman armies destroyed Corinth, a second great center of Mediterranean commerce. This victory marked the culmination of Roman imperialist expansion east into the Greek and Hellenistic world, which had begun with the conquest of Illyria. This expansion was not simply the result of Roman imperialist ambitions. The Hellenistic states, in their constant warring and bickering, had drawn Rome into their conflicts against their neighbors. Greek states asked the Roman senate to arbitrate their disputes. Pergamum requested military assistance against Macedonia. Appealing to Rome's claims as "liberator," cities pressed the senate to preserve their freedom in the face of aggressive expansion by their more powerful neighbors. In a series of intermittent, uncoordinated, and sporadic engagements, Rome did intervene, although its real focus was on its life-and-death struggle with Carthage. Roman intentions may not have been conquest, but Roman intervention upset the balance of power in the Hellenistic world. The price of Roman arbitration, intervention, and protection was loss of independence. Gradually the Roman shadow fell over the eastern Mediterranean.

The treaty Philip V of Macedon concluded with Carthage during the Second Punic War provided an initial excuse for war, one seized upon more eagerly by the plebeian assembly than by the senate. Shortly after its victory at Zama, Rome provoked Philip to war and then easily defeated him in 197 B.C., proclaiming the freedom of the Greek cities and withdrawing from Greece. In 189 B.C., the Seleucid Antiochus III (223–187 B.C.) of Syria suffered the same fate, and Rome declared the Greek cities in Asia Minor he had controlled free. The Greeks venerated the Roman commander, Titus Quinctius Flamininus (228–174 B.C.), as a god—the first Roman to be accorded this Eastern honor. In reality, the control of the cities lay in the hands of local oligarchs favorable to Rome. In 179 B.C., Philip's son Perseus (179–168 B.C.) attempted to stir up democratic opposition to Rome within the cities. This time Rome responded more forcefully. The Macedonian kingdom was divided into four republics governed by their own senates and magistrates selected from among the local aristocrats. In Epirus, 70 cities were destroyed and 150,000 people sold into slavery. This harsh punishment prompted other Greek cities to react with panic even to the mere threat of Roman retribution. When the citizens of Rhodes heard that the senate was contemplating declaring war on them, they quickly executed all of their anti-Roman fellows.

The final episode of Rome's expansionist drama unfolded during the Third Punic War. When Rome resumed its war with Carthage in 149 B.C., several Greek cities attempted once more to assert their autonomy from the hated oligarchies established by Rome. Retribution was swift. Roman legions crushed the rebel forces and, as an example to all, Corinth was razed as thoroughly as Carthage. In the west, in northern Italy, Spain, and Africa, Roman conquest had been direct and complete. Tribal structures had been replaced with Roman provinces governed by former magistrates or proconsuls. In the east, Rome preferred to work through the existing political hierarchies. Still, Rome cultivated its image as protector of Greek liberties against the Macedonian and Seleucid monarchies and preferred indirect control to annexation. Its power was no less real for being indirect.

By 146 B.C., the Roman republic controlled the whole rim of the Mediterranean from Rhodes in the east across Greece, Dalmatia, Italy, southern Gaul, Spain, and North Africa. Even Syria and Egypt, although nominally independent, had to bow before Roman will. This subjugation had been graphically demonstrated in 168 B.C., when the Seleucid Antiochus IV (175–164 B.C.) invaded the kingdom of the Egyptian ruler Ptolemy VI (180–145 B.C.) and besieged Alexandria. The Ptolemys had long before made a treaty with Rome, and the senate sent an envoy to Antiochus with written instructions to withdraw immediately from Egypt. The king replied that he would like to consult before making a decision. The Roman envoy immediately drew a circle around Antiochus, ordering him to give an answer before he stepped out of the ring. Such directness was unknown in the world of Hellenistic diplomacy. After a moment's hesitation, the deeply shocked Antiochus replied that he would do whatever the Romans demanded. Roman perseverance and determination had brought Rome from obscurity to the greatest power the West had ever known. The republic had endured great adversity. It would not survive prosperity.

Republican Civilization

Territorial conquest, the influx of unprecedented riches, and exposure to sophisticated Hellenistic civilization ultimately overwhelmed earlier Roman civilization. This civilization had been created by stubborn farmers and soldiers who valued above all else authority, simplicity, and piety. This unique culture was the source of strength that led Rome to greatness, but its limitations prevented the republic from resolving its internal social tensions and the external problems caused by the burden of empire.

Farmers and Soldiers

The ideal Roman farmer was not the great estate owner of the Greek world, but the smallholder, the dirt farmer of central Italy. The most important crop of Roman farms was citizens. "From farmers come the bravest men and the sturdiest soldiers," wrote Cato the Elder. Nor was the ideal Roman soldier the gallant cavalryman but rather the solid foot soldier. Cavalry, composed of wealthy citizens who made up the elite equestrian order (from the Latin *equus*, horse), and especially allies, provided reconnaissance and protected Roman flanks. However, the main fighting force was the infantry. Sometime in the early republic the Greek phalanx was transformed into the Roman legion, a flexible unit composed of 30 companies of 120 men each.

Constant training, careful preparation, and painstaking execution characterized every aspect of Roman military expeditions. Wars were won as much by engineering feats as by feats of arms. Engineers constructed bridges, siege machines, and catapults. By the time of the late republic, Roman armies on the march could construct identical camps each night, quickly building a strong square fort 2150 feet on a side. Within the camp, every unit had exactly the same location for its quarters, as did the commander and paymaster. The chain of command was rigidly maintained from the commander, a Roman consul, through military tribunes and centurions, two of whom commanded each company of 120 men.

These solid, methodical troops, the backbone of the republican armies that conquered the Mediterranean, were among the victims of that conquest. The pressures of constant international warfare were destroying the farmer-soldiers whom the traditionalists loved to praise. When the Roman sphere of interest had been confined to central Italy, farmers could do their planting in spring, serve in the army during the summer months, and return home to care for their farms in time for harvest. When Rome's wars became international expeditions lasting for years, many soldiers, unable to work their lands while doing military service, had to mortgage their farms in order to support their families. When they returned they often found that during their prolonged absences they had lost their farms to wealthy aristocratic moneylenders. While aristocrats amassed vast landed estates worked by imported slaves, ordinary Romans and Italians lacked even a family farm capable of supporting themselves and their families. Without land, they and their sons were excluded from further military service and sank into the growing mass of desperately poor, disenfranchised citizens.

The Roman Family

In Roman tradition, the *paterfamilias* was the master of the family, which in theory included his wife, children, and slaves, over whom he exercised the power of life and death. This authority lasted as long as he lived. Only at his death did his sons, even if long grown and married, achieve legal and financial independence. The family was the basic unit of society, of the state.

Although not kept in seclusion as in Greece, Roman women theoretically never exercised independent power in this male-dominated world. Before marriage, a Roman girl was subject to the authority of her father. When she married, her father traditionally transferred legal guardianship to her husband, thus severing her bonds to her paternal family. A husband could divorce his wife at will, returning her and her dowry to her father. Wives did exercise real though informal authority within the family. Part of this authority came from their role in the moral education of their children and the direction of the household. Part also came from their control over their dowries. Widows might exercise even greater authority in the raising of their children.

Paternal authority over children was absolute. Not all children born into a marriage became members of the family. The Law of the Twelve Tables allowed defective children to be killed for the good of the family. Newborn infants were laid on the ground before the father, who decided whether the child should be raised. By picking up a son, he accepted the child into the family. Ordering that a daughter be nursed similarly signified acceptance. If there were too many mouths to feed or the child was simply unwanted, the father could command that the infant be killed or abandoned. Abandoned children might be adopted by childless couples.

Nor were all sons born into Roman families. Romans made use of adoption for many purposes. Families without heirs could adopt children. Powerful political and military figures might adopt promising young men as their political heirs. These adopted sons held the same legal rights as the natural offspring of the father and thus were integral members of his family.

Slaves, too, were members of the family. On the one hand, slaves were property without personal rights. On the other, they might live and work alongside the free members of the family, worship the family gods, and enjoy the protection and endure the authority of the paterfamilias. In fact, the authority of the paterfamilias was roughly the same over slave and free members of the family. If he desired, he could sell the free members of the family into slavery.

The center of everyday life for the Roman family was the *domus*, the family house whose architectural style had developed from Etruscan traditions. Visitors entered through the front door into the *atrium*, a central courtyard containing a collecting pool into which rainwater for household use flowed from the roof through terra-cotta drains. In niches or on shelves stood wax or terra-cotta busts of ancestors and statues of the household gods. Around the atrium, openings gave on to workrooms, storerooms, bedrooms, offices, and small dining rooms.

In the wake of imperial conquests, the Roman family and its environment began to change in ways disturbing to many of the oligarchy. Some women, perhaps in imitation of their more liberated Hellenistic sisters, began to take a more active role in public life. One example is Cornelia, a daughter of Scipio Africanus. After her husband's death in 154 B.C., she refused to remarry, devoting herself instead to raising her children, administering their inheritance, and directing their political careers.

Some married women, too, escaped the authority of their husbands. Fewer and fewer fathers transferred authority over their daughters to their husbands. Instead, daughters remained under their father's authority as long as he lived. This meant that upon the father's death, they became independent persons, able to manage their own affairs without the consent of or interference by their

The atrium of the House of the Silver Wedding in Pompeii. The pool in the floor caught the rainwater that entered through the opening in the high roof.

husbands. Although some historians believe that sentimental bonds of affection may have increased between many husbands and wives and parents and children as legal bonds loosened, it also meant that the wife's relationship to her children was weakened. Roman mothers had never been legally related to their children. Wives and mothers were not fully part of their husband's families. Thus their brother's families, not their own children, were their natural heirs. Just as adoption created political bonds, marriage to daughters sealed alliances between men. However, when these alliances fell apart or more advantageous ones presented themselves, fathers could force their daughters to divorce their husbands and to marry someone else. Divorce became increasingly common in the second century B.C. More and more, wives were temporary visitors in their husband's homes.

Not every Roman family could afford its own *domus*, and in the aftermath of the imperial expansion, housing problems for the poor became acute. In Rome and other towns of Italy, shopkeepers lived in small houses attached to their shops or in rooms behind their workplaces. Peasants forced off their land and crowded into cities found shelter in multistory apartment buildings, an increasingly common sight in the cities of the empire. In these cramped structures, families crowded into small low rooms about ten feet square. In Roman towns throughout Italy, simple dwellings, luxurious mansions, shops, and apartment buildings existed side by side. The rich and the poor rubbed shoulders every day, producing a friction that threatened to burst into flame.

Roman Religion

Romans worshiped many gods, the more the better. Every aspect of daily life and work was the responsibility of individual powers, or *numina*. Every man had his *genius* or personal *numen*, just as every woman had her *juno*. Each family had its household powers, the *lares* familiares, whose proper worship was the responsibility of the paterfamilias. The *Vesta* was the spirit of the hearth fire. The *lares* were the deities of farmland, the *domus*, and the guardians of roads and travelers. The *penates* guarded the family larder or storage cupboard. These family spirits exercised a binding power, a *religio*, upon the Romans, and the pious Roman householder recognized these claims and undertook the *officia*, or duties, to which the spirits were entitled. These basic attitudes of religion, piety, and office lay at the heart of Roman reverence for order and authority. They extended to other traditional Roman and Latin gods such as Jupiter, the supreme god; Juno, his wife; Mars, the god of war; and the two-faced Janus, spirit of gates and new beginnings.

Bronze statuette of a Lar, a Roman household god representing an ancestral spirit. In some houses, such statuettes were placed in miniature shrines fashioned after Roman temples. At mealtimes bits of food were burned as offerings to the ancestors.

Outside the household, worship of the gods and the reading of the future in the entrails of sacrificed animals, the flight of birds, or changes in weather were the responsibilities of colleges of priests. Roman priests did not, as did those in the Near East, form a special caste but rather were important members of the elite who held priesthoods in addition to other public offices. Religion was less a matter of personal relationship with the gods than a public, civic activity binding society together. State-supported cults with their colleges of priests, Etruscan- and Greek-style temples, and elaborate ceremonies were integral parts of the Roman state and society. The world of the gods reflected that of mortals. As the Roman mortal world expanded, so did the divine. Romans were quick to identify foreign gods with their own. Thus Zeus became Jupiter, Hera became Juno, and Aphrodite became Venus.

Still, the elasticity of Roman religion could stretch just so far. With the empire came not only the cults of Zeus, Apollo, and Aphrodite to Rome but that of Dionysus as well. Unlike the formal public cults of the other Greek deities, which were firmly in the control of authorities, that of Dionysus was largely outside state control. Women, in the tradition of the maenads, controlled much of the ecstatic and overtly sexual rituals associated with the god. Following the Second Punic War, the cult of Dionysus, known in Latin as Bacchus, spread rapidly in Italy. At its secret rites, or *Bacchanalia*, men and women were rumored to engage in every kind of sexual act.

In 186 B.C., the senate decreed the cult of Bacchus a conspiracy and ordered an inquiry. The consul Spurius Postumius Albinus, acting on the spurious testimony of a former prostitute, began a brutal persecution. Rituals were banned, priests and adherents arrested, and rewards offered to informants who provided lurid and fanciful accounts of what had taken place at the Bacchanalia. Hundreds of people were imprisoned and greater numbers were executed. The senate ordered all shrines to Bacchus destroyed and Bacchanalia banned throughout Italy. Perhaps more than any other episode, the suppression of the Bacchic cult showed the oligarchy's fear about the changes sweeping Roman civilization.

Republican Letters

As Rome absorbed foreign gods, it also absorbed foreign letters. From the Etruscans the Romans adopted and adapted the alphabet, the one in which most Western languages are written to this day. Early Latin inscriptions are largely funeral monuments and some public notices such as the Law of the Twelve Tables. The Roman high priest responsible for maintaining the calendar of annual feasts also prepared and updated annals, short accounts of important religious and secular events of each year. However, prior to the third century B.C., apart from extravagant funerary eulogies carefully preserved within families, Romans had no apparent interest in writing or literature as such. The birth of Latin letters began with Rome's exposure to Greek civilization.

Early in the third century B.C., Greek authors had begun to pay attention to expanding Rome. The first serious Greek historian to focus on this new Western power was Timaeus (ca. 356–ca. 260 B.C.), who spent most of his productive life in Athens. There he wrote a history of Rome up to the Pyrrhic war, interviewing Roman and Greek witnesses in order to gain an understanding of this Italian city that had defeated a Hellenistic army. Polybius (ca. 200–ca. 118 B.C.), the greatest of the Greek historians to record Rome's rise to power, gathered his information firsthand. As one of a thousand eminent Greeks deported to Rome for political investigation, he became a close friend of Scipio Aemilianus and accompanied him on his Spanish and African campaigns. Polybius's history is both the culmination of the traditions of Greek historiography and its transformation, since it centers on the rise of a non-Greek power to rule "almost the whole inhabited world."

At the same time that Greeks began to take Rome seriously, Romans themselves became interested in Greece and in particular in the international Hellenistic culture of the eastern Mediterranean. The earliest Latin literary works were clearly adaptations if not translations of Hellenistic genres and texts. Already in 240 B.C., plays in the Greek tradition were said to have been performed in Rome. The earliest extant literary works, ironically for the sober image of the Roman farmer-soldier, are the plays of Plautus (ca. 254–184 B.C.) and Terence (186–159 B.C.), lightly adapted translations of Hellenistic comedies.

Scheming servants, mistaken identities, bedroom farces, young lovers, and lecherous elders make up the plots of the Roman plays. The authors of these comedies experimented with and transformed Greek literature. Plautus in particular, while maintaining superficially the Greek settings of his plays, actually creates a world more Roman than Greek. References to Roman laws, magistrates, clients, and social situations abound, as do humorous derogatory comments on Greek mores. Terence, although remaining closer to Greek models, Romanized his material through the creation of an elegant, natural style. His plays rapidly became classics, influencing subsequent generations of Latin authors who worked to create a literary language separate from but equal to Greek.

*T*he Burden of Empire

The effects of Rome's rise to world power within less than a century profoundly affected every aspect of republican life. Magistrates operating far from senatorial control in conquered provinces exercised power and found opportunities for enrichment never before seen. Successful commanders, honored and even deified by eastern cities, felt the temptation to ignore the strict requirements of senatorial accountability. During the time of a provincial command, it was said, one had to make three fortunes: the first to pay off the bribes it took to get the office, the second to pay off the jury that would investigate corruption after the command had expired, and a third to live on for the rest of one's life. Thus provincial commanders enriched themselves through extortion, collusion with dishonest government contractors and tax collectors, and wholesale bribe taking. Ordinary citizens, aware of such abuses, felt increasingly threatened by the wealthy and powerful. The old traditions of the farmer-soldier, the paterfamilias, the pious venerator of the gods, and the plain-speaking Latin dissolved before the vast new horizons, previously unimagined wealth, alien culture, and unprecedented opportunities of empire.

In the second century B.C., Romans found themselves in a dilemma as the old and the new exerted equal pressures. These tensions led to almost a century of bitter civil strife and ultimately to the disintegration of the republic. The complex interaction of these tensions can best be seen in the life of one man, Marcus Porcius Cato.

Cato the Elder is often presented as the preserver of the old traditions, in contrast to Scipio Aemilianus, destroyer of Carthage and proponent of Hellenism in the Roman world. True, as censor fighting against conspicuous consumption and as self-conscious defender of the past, Cato cast himself in the mold of the traditional Roman. And Scipio, with his love of Hellenism and his political career defined more by personal achievement than traditional magistracies, represented a new type of Roman. But if the division between old and new, between Cato and Scipio, had been so clear cut, the dilemma of republican Rome would not have been so great. As it was, Cato reflected in himself this contradictory clash of values. Like the two-faced god Janus whom he invoked in all his undertakings, Cato was the stern censor, the guardian and proponent of traditional Roman virtue, as well as the new Roman of shrewd business acumen, influence, and power unimaginable to the simple farmers he professed to admire.

Cato was born in the Latin town of Tusculum in 234 B.C. and grew to maturity on a family estate in Sabine territory. He came of age just at the start of the Second Punic War and distinguished himself in campaigns against Hannibal in Italy and Syracuse in Sicily. In between campaigns he became even more famous for his eloquence in pleading legal cases. His talents, matched by his drive and energy, brought him to the attention of a number of powerful members of the senatorial aristocracy, under whose patronage he came to Rome. There he began to rise through the offices of military tribune, quaestor, and ultimately consul and censor.

This first-generation senator became the spokesman for the traditional values of Rome, for severity and simplicity, for honesty and frugality in private and public life. Cato glorified his simple farm life and the care he took in the management of his estates and of his extended *familia* and working his fields side by side with his slaves. He ridiculed Greek philosophy and education, warning his son that the Romans would be destroyed once they were infected with Greek learning. Cato presented himself as the epitome of the old Roman farmer-soldier, a man of simplicity and traditional values.

Actually, Cato, as much as anyone else, was deeply involved in the rapid changes brought about by the empire. He may have worked along with his slaves and shared their table, but as soon as they grew old he sold them to the state to avoid having to support them, something no conscientious paterfamilias would ever have done. Although he led the battle to prevent senators from participating in commerce, he was perhaps the first of that body to diversify his holdings and investments. He bought up land, hot baths, and mineral deposits. Although he avoided conspicuous consumption himself, as consul and censor he was responsible for many of the sumptuous building projects in Rome through which ordinary Romans first experienced the luxuries of the Hellenistic world. While scorning Greek culture, he worked bits of Greek authors even into his attacks on Greek civilization.

Cato was neither duplicitous nor hypocritical. He was simply typical. Many senators agreed with him that the old values were slipping away and with them the foundation of the republic. Many feared that personal ambition was undermining the power of the oligarchy. And yet these same people could not resist exploiting the changed circumstances for their own benefit.

The Price of Empire

Roman victory defeated the republic. Roman conquest of the Mediterranean world and the establishment of the Roman Empire spelled the end of the republican system. Roman society could not withstand the tensions caused by the enrichment of the few, the impoverishment of the many, and the demands of the excluded populations of the empire to share in its benefits. Traditional Roman culture could not survive the attraction of Hellenistic civilization with its wealth, luxuries, and individualistic values. Finally, Roman government could not restrain the ambitions of its oligarchs or protect the interests of its ordinary citizens. The creation of a Mediterranean empire brought in its wake a century of revolutionary change before new, stable social, cultural, and political forms emerged in the Roman world.

Winners and Losers

Rome had emerged victorious in the Punic and Macedonian wars against Carthage and Macedon, but the real winners were the members of the oligarchy, the *optimates* or the "best," as they called themselves, whose wealth and power had grown beyond all imagining. These optimates included roughly three hundred senators and magistrates, most of whom had inherited wealth, political connections, and long-established clientages. Since military command and government of the empire were entrusted to magistrates who were answerable only to the senate of which they were members, the empire was essentially their private domain.

But new circumstances created new opportunities for many others. Italian merchants, slave traders, entrepreneurs, and bankers, many of lowly origin, poured into the cities of the east in the wake of the Roman legions. These newly enriched Romans constituted a second elite and formed themselves into a separate order, that of the *equites*, or equestrians, distinguished by their wealth and honorific military service on horseback, but connected with the old military elite. Since the senate did not create a government bureaucracy to administer the empire, equestrian tax farmers became essential to provincial government. Companies of these publicans, or tax collectors, purchased the right to collect rents on public land, tribute, and customs duties from provincials. Whatever they collected beyond the amount contracted for by Roman officials was theirs to keep. Publicans regularly bribed governors and commanders to allow them to gouge the local populations with impunity and on occasion even obtained Roman troops to help them make their collections. Gradually, some of these "new men," their money "laundered" through investments in land, manged to achieve lower magistracies and even move into the senatorial order. Still, the upper reaches of office were closed to all but a tiny minority. By the end of the Punic wars, only some twenty-five families could hope to produce consuls.

The losers in the wars included the vanquished who were sold into slavery by the tens of thousands, the provincials who bore the Roman yoke, the Italian allies who had done so much for the Romans, and even the citizen farmers, small shopkeepers, and free craftworkers of the republic. All four groups suffered from the effects of empire, and over the next century all resorted to violence against the optimates.

The slaves revolted first. Thousands of them, captured in battle or taken after victory, flooded the Italian and Sicilian estates of the wealthy. Estimates vary, but in the first century B.C., the slave population of Italy was probably around two million, fully one-third of the total population. These millions of slaves could not be integrated into the traditional role of slaves within the traditional role of slaves within the Roman *familia*. Rural slaves on absentee

Roman slaves sifting grain. Roman victories in the Punic and Macedonian wars brought in a huge influx of slaves from the conquered lands. Slaves were pressed into service on the estates and plantations of wealthy landowners.

estates enjoyed none of the protections afforded traditional Roman servants. Cato sold off his slaves who reached old age; others simply worked them to death. Many slaves, born free citizens of Hellenistic states, found such treatment unbearable.

The most serious slave revolt occurred in Italy between 74 and 71 B.C. Gladiators, professional slave fighters trained for Roman amusement, revolted in Capua. Under the competent leadership of the Thracian gladiator Spartacus, over a hundred thousand slaves took up arms against Rome. Ultimately eight legions, more troops than had met Hannibal at Zama, were needed to put down the revolt. Retribution was terrible. After the defeat of Spartacus, crucified rebels lined the road from Rome to Naples.

Revolts profoundly disturbed the Roman state, all the more because it was not just slaves who revolted. In many cases poor free peasants and disgruntled provincials rose up against Rome. The most significant provincial revolt was that of Aristonicus, the illegitimate half brother of Attalus III (ca. 138–133 B.C.) of Pergamum, a Roman client state. Attalus had left his kingdom to Rome at his death. In an attempt to assert his right to the kingdom, Aristonicus armed slaves and peasants and attacked the Roman garrisons. The Hellenized cities of Asia Minor remained loyal to Rome, but this provincial uprising, the first of many over the centuries, lasted more than three years, from 133 to 130 B.C.

Revolts by slaves and provincials were disturbing enough. Revolts by Rome's Italian allies were much more serious. After the Second Punic War, these allies, on whose loyalty Rome had depended for survival, found themselves badly treated and exploited. Government officials used state power to undermine the position of the Italian elites. At the same time Roman aristocrats used their economic power to drive the Italic peasants from their land, replacing them with slaves. Some reform-minded Romans attempted to diffuse tensions by extending citizenship to the allies, but failure of this effort led to a revolt at Fregellae south of Rome in 125 B.C. A broader and more serious revolt took place between 91 and 89 B.C. after the senate blocked an attempt to extend citizenship to the allies. During this so-called Social War (from *socii*, the Latin word for *allies*), almost all the Italian allies rose against Rome. These revolts differed from those in the provinces in that the Italian elites as well as the masses aligned themselves against the Roman oligarchy. Even some ordinary Roman citizens joined the rebel forces against the powerful elite.

Optimates and Populares

The despair that could lead ordinary Roman citizens to armed rebellion grew from the social and economic consequences of conquests. While aristocrats amassed vast landed estates worked by cheap slaves, ordinary Romans often lacked even a family farm capable of supporting themselves and their families. Many found their way to Rome, where they swelled the ranks of the unemployed, huddled into shoddily constructed tenements and living off the public subsidies.

While many senators bemoaned the demise of the Roman farmer-soldier, few were willing to compromise their own privileged position to help. In the face of the oligarchy's unwillingness to deal with the problem, the tribune Tiberius Gracchus (ca. 163–133 B.C.) in 133 B.C. attempted to introduce a land-reform program that would return citizens to agriculture. Gracchus was the first of the *populares*, political leaders appealing to the masses. His motives were probably a mixture of compassion for the poor, concern over the falling numbers of citizens who had the minimum land to qualify for military service, and personal ambition. Over the previous century, great amounts of public land had illegally come into private hands. With the support of reform-minded aristocrats and commoners, Gracchus proposed a law that would limit the amount of public land an individual could hold to about 312 acres. He also proposed a commission to distribute to landless peasants the land recovered by the state as a result of the law. Because many senators who illegally held vast amounts of public land strongly opposed the measure, it faced certain failure in the senate. Gracchus therefore took it to the plebeian assembly. Since 287 B.C., assembly measures had been binding on all society and only the ten elected tribunes could veto its decisions. Here Gracchus's proposal was assured of support by the rural poor who flocked to Rome to vote for it. When optimates, aristocratic opponents hoping to preserve their position, influenced one of the other nine tribunes to oppose the law, Gracchus had him deposed by the assembly. Senators, bound by custom and tradition, found Gracchus's maneuver to avoid the senate and his unprecedented deposition of a tribune novel and deeply disturbing. The law passed and a three-person commission to distribute land was established. However, Gracchus's maneuvering lost him many of his aristocratic supporters, who feared that a popular democracy led by a demagogue was replacing the senatorial oligarchy.

Also in 133 B.C., Gracchus introduced another bill which provided that the royal treasury of the kingdom of Pergamum bequeathed to Rome by Attalus III be used to help citizens receiving land purchase livestock and equipment. These laws, which challenged the senate's traditional control over finance and foreign affairs, deeply disturbed the conservative elite, but as long as Gracchus held office, he was protected from any sort of attack by the traditional immunity accorded tribunes. It was no secret, however, that the senate planned to prosecute him as soon as his one-year term expired. To escape this fate, he appealed to the assembly to reelect him for an unprecedented second consecutive term. To his opponents, this appeal smacked of an attempt to make himself sole ruler, a democratic tyrant on the Greek model. A group of senators and their clients, led by one of Gracchus's own cousins, broke into the assembly meeting at which the election was to take place and murdered the tribune and 300 of his supporters.

The optimates in the senate could eliminate Tiberius Gracchus, but they could not so easily eliminate the movement he had led. In 123 B.C., his younger brother, Gaius Gracchus (153–121 B.C.), became tribune and during his two one-year terms initiated an even broader and more radical reform program. Tiberius had been concerned only about poor citizens. Gaius attempted to broaden the citizenry and to shift the balance of power away from the senate. Alarmed by the revolt at Fregellae, he attempted to extend citizenship to all Latins and improve the status of Italian allies by extending to them the right to vote in the assembly. In order to check the power of senatorial magistrates in the provinces, he transferred to the equestrians the right to investigate provincial corruption. This move brought the wealthy equestrian order into politics as a counterbalance to the senate. Gaius also improved the supply and distribution of grain in Rome and other Italian cities to benefit the urban poor. He reestablished his brother's land distribution project, extended participation to Latins and Italians, and encouraged colonization as a means to provide citizens with land. Finally, in order to protect himself and his party from the anticipated reaction of the senate and to prepare to avenge his brother's death, he pushed through a law stipulating that only the people could condemn a citizen to death.

Gaius's program was extraordinary for several reasons. In the first place, it was exactly that, a program, the first comprehensive attempt to deal with the problems facing Roman society. Secondly, it proposed a basic shift of power, drawing the equestrian order for the first time into the political arena opposite the senate and making the assembly rather than the senate the initiator of legislation. Finally, it offered a solution to the problem of the allies which, although rejected at the time, was finally adopted some twenty years later. In the short run, however, Gaius's program was a failure. In 121 B.C., he failed to be reelected for a third term and thus lost the immunity of the tribunate. Recalling the fate of his brother, he armed his supporters. Once more the senate acted, ordering the consul to take whatever measures he deemed necessary. Gaius and some three thousand of his supporters died.

The deaths of Tiberius and Gaius Gracchus marked a new beginning in Roman politics. Not since the end of the monarchy had a political conflict been decided with personal violence. The whole episode provided a model for future attempts at reform. Reformers would look not to the senate or the aristocracy but to the people, from whom they would draw their political power. The experience of the Gracchi also provided a model for repression of other reform programs: violence.

The End of the Republic

With the Gracchi dead and the core of their reforms dismantled, the senate appeared victorious against all challengers. At home, the masses of ordinary Roman citizens and their political leadership were in disarray. The conquered lands of North Africa and the Near East filled the public coffers as well as the private accounts of Roman senators and publicans.

In reality, Rome had solved neither the problem of internal conflict between rich and poor nor that of how to govern its enormous empire. The apparent calm ended when revolts in Africa and Italy exposed the fragility of the senate's control and ushered in an ever increasing spiral of violence and civil war.

The Crisis of Government

In 112 B.C., the senate declared war against Jugurtha (ca. 160–104 B.C.), the king of a North African client state who, in his war against a rival, had killed some Roman merchants in the Numidian city of Cirta. The war dragged on for five years amid accusations of corruption, incompetence, and treason. Finally in 107 B.C.), the people elected as consul Gaius Marius (157–86 B.C.), a "new man" who had risen through the tribunate, and entrusted him with the conduct of the war. In order to raise an army, Marius ignored property qualifications and enlisted many impoverished Romans and armed them at public expense. Although recruiting of landless citizens had probably taken place before, no one had done it in such an overt and massive manner. Senators looked on Marius's measure with great suspicion, but the poor citizen recruits, who had despaired of benefiting from the land reforms proposed by the Gracchi, looked forward to receiving a grant of land at the end of their military service.

Marius quickly defeated Jugurtha in 106 B.C. In the next year Celtic and Germanic barbarians crossed the Alps into Italy and, although technically disqualified from further terms, Marius was elected consul five times between 104 and 100 B.C. to meet the threat. During this period he continued to recruit soldiers from among the poor and on his own authority extended citizenship to allies. To his impoverished soldiers, Marius promised land but, after his victory in 101 B.C., the senate refused to provide veterans with farms. As a result, Marius's armies naturally shifted their allegiance away from the Roman state and to their popular commander. Soon this pattern of loyalty became the norm. Politicians forged close bonds with the soldiers of their armies. Individual commanders, not the state or the senate, ensured that their recruits received their pay, shared in the spoils of victory, and obtained land upon their retirement. In turn, the soldiers became fanatically devoted to their commanders. Republican armies had become personal armies, potent tools in the hands of ambitious politicians.

The outbreak of the Social War in 91 B.C. marked the first use of these armies in civil war. Both Marius and the consul Lucius Cornelius Sulla (138–78 B.C.) raised armies to fight the Italians, who were only pacified after Roman citizenship was extended to all Italians in 89 B.C. The next year Mithridates VI (120–63 B.C.), the king of Pontus, took advantage of the Roman preoccupation in Italy to invade the province of Asia. As soon as the Italian threat receded, Sulla, as the representative of the optimates, raised an army to fight Mithridates. Marius, as leader of the populares who favored reform, attempted to have Sulla relieved of command. Sulla marched on Rome, initiating a bloody civil war. In the course of this war Rome was occupied three times, once by Marius, twice by Sulla. Each commander ordered mass executions of his opponents and confiscated their property, which he then distributed to his supporters.

Ultimately Sulla emerged victorious and ruled as dictator from 82 to 79 B.C., using this time to shore up senatorial power. He doubled the size of the senate to 600, filling the new positions with men drawn from the *equites*. He reduced the authority of tribunes and returned jury courts from the equites to the senators. In order to weaken the military power of magistrates, he abolished the practice of assigning military commands to praetors and consuls. Rather, they were to be held by proconsuls, or former magistrates, who would serve for one year as provincial governors.

In 79 B.C., his reforms in place, Sulla stepped down to allow a return to oligarchic republican rule. Although his changes bought a decade of peace, they did not solve the fundamental problems dividing optimates and populares. If anything, his rule had proven that the only real political option was a dictatorship by a powerful individual with his own army. During the last generation of the republic, idealists continued their hopeless struggle to prop up the dying republican system while more forward-thinking generals fought among themselves for absolute power.

The Civil Wars

Marcus Tullius Cicero (106–43 B.C.) reflected the strengths and weaknesses of the republican tradition in the first century B.C. Although cultivated, humane, and dedicated to the republican constitution, he was also ambitious, blind to the failings of the optimates, a poor judge of character, and out of touch with the political realities of his time. Like Cato in an earlier age, he was a "new man," the son of a wealthy equestrian who provided his children with the best possible education both in Rome and in Athens and Rhodes. In Greece, Cicero developed a lifelong attachment to Stoic philosophy and developed the oratory skills necessary for a young Roman destined for public life. After returning to Rome he quickly earned a reputation for his skills as a courtroom orator. At the same time he began his climb up the political ladder by championing popular causes while protecting the interests of the wealthy and soliciting the assistance of young optimates. Cicero identified firmly with the elite, hoping that the republic could be saved through the harmonious cooperation of the equestrian and senatorial orders. Neither group was interested in following his program, but most considered him a safer figure than military strongmen like Sulla, who sought high office. In 63 B.C. Cicero was elected consul, the first "new man" to hold the office in over thirty years. The real threat to the existence of the republic was posed by the ambitions of powerful military commanders—Pompey (106–48 B.C.), Crassus (ca. 115–53 B.C.), and Julius Caesar (100–44 B.C.).

Pompey and Crassus, both protégés of Sulla, rose rapidly and unconstitutionally through a series of special proconsular commands by judicious use of fraud, violence, and corruption. Pompey first won public acclaim by commanding a victorious army in Africa and Spain. Upon his return to Rome in 70 B.C., he united with Crassus, who had won popularity for suppressing the Spartacus rebellion. Together they worked to dismantle the Sullan constitution to the benefit of the populares. In return, Pompey received an extraordinary command over all of the coasts of the Mediterranean, in theory to suppress piracy but actually to give him control over all of the provinces of the empire. When in 66 B.C., King Mithridates of Pontus again attacked Greece, Pompey assumed command of the provinces of Asia. His army not only destroyed Mithridates but continued on, conquering Armenia, Syria, and Palestine, acquiring an impressive retinue of client kings and increasing the income from the provinces by some 70 percent.

While Pompey was extending the frontiers of the empire to the Euphrates, Crassus, whose wealth was legendary—"no one should be called rich," he once observed, "who is not able to maintain an army on his income"—was consolidating his power. He allied himself with Julius Caesar, a young, well-connected orator from one of Rome's most ancient patrician families, who nevertheless promoted the cause of the populares. The senate feared the ambitious and ruthless Crassus, and it was to block the election of Crassus's candidate Catiline (Lucius Sergius Catilina, ca. 108–62 B.C.) to the consulate in 63 B.C. that the senate elected Cicero instead. Catiline soon joined a conspiracy of Sullan veterans and populares, but Cicero quickly uncovered and suppressed the conspiracy and ordered Catiline's execution.

When Pompey returned from Asia in triumph in 62 B.C., he expected to find Italy convulsed with the Catiline revolt and in need of a military savior in the tradition of Sulla. Instead, thanks to Cicero's quick action, all was in order. Although he never forgave Cicero for stealing his glory, Pompey disbanded his army and returned to private life, asking only that the senate approve his organization of the territories he had conquered and grant land to his veterans. The senate refused. In response Pompey formed an uneasy alliance with Crassus and Caesar. This alliance was known as the first triumvirate, from the Latin for *three men*. Caesar was elected consul in 59 B.C. and the following year received command of the province of Cisalpine Gaul in northern Italy.

Pompey and Crassus may have thought that this command would remove the ambitious young man from the political spotlight. Instead, Caesar, who has been called with only some exaggeration "the sole creative genius ever produced by Rome," used his province as a staging ground for the conquest of a vast area of western Europe to the mouth of the Rhine. His brilliant military skills beyond the Alps and his dedication to his troops made him immensely popular with his legions. His ability for self-promotion ensured that this popularity was matched at home, where the populares eagerly received news of his Gallic wars. In 53 B.C. Crassus died leading an army in Syria, leaving Pompey and the popular young Caesar to dispute supreme power. As word of Caesar's military successes increased his popularity at Rome, they also increased Pompey's suspicion of his younger associate. Finally, in 49 B.C., Pompey's supporters in the senate relieved Caesar of his command and ordered him to return to Italy.

Return he did, but not as commanded. Rather than leave his army on the far side of the Rubicon River, which marked the boundary between his province of Cisalpine Gaul and Italy, as ordered, he marched on Rome at the head of his legions. This meant civil war, a vicious bloodletting that convulsed the whole Mediterranean world. In 48 B.C., Caesar defeated Pompey in northern Greece, and Pompey was assassinated shortly after in Egypt. Still the wars went on between Pompey's supporters and Caesar until 45 B.C., when with all his enemies defeated, Caesar returned to Rome. There, unlike Sulla, he showed his opponents clemency as he sought to heal the wounds of war and to undertake an unprecedented series of reforms. He enlarged the senate to 900 and widened its representation, appointing soldiers, freedmen, provincials, and above all wealthy men from the Italian towns. He increased the number of magistracies to broaden participation in government, founded colonies at Carthage and Corinth, and settled veterans in colonies elsewhere in Italy, Greece, Asia, Africa, Spain, and Gaul. Still, he made no pretense of returning Rome to republican government. In early 44 B.C., although serving that year as consul together with his general Mark Antony (ca. 81–30 B.C.), Caesar had himself declared perpetual dictator. This move was finally too much for some sixty diehard republican senators. On March 15, a group led by two enemies whom Caesar had pardoned, Cassius Longinus and Marcus Junius Brutus, assassinated him as he entered the senate chamber.

Cicero rejoiced when he heard of the assassination, clear evidence of his political naïveté. The republic was dead long before Caesar died, and the assassination simply returned Rome to civil war, a civil war that destroyed Cicero himself. Antony, Marcus Lepidus (d. 12 B.C.), another of Caesar's generals, and Caesar's grandnephew and adopted son Octavian (63 B.C.–A.D. 14),

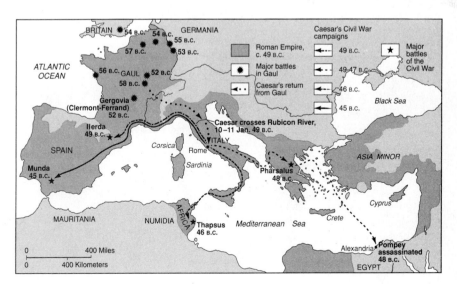

The career of Julius Caesar

This silver coin was struck to commemorate the assassination of Julius Caesar. Two daggers flank a cap symbolizing liberty. The legend reads, "the Ides of March." On the other side is a profile of Brutus.

who took the name of his great uncle, soon formed a second triumvirate to destroy Caesar's enemies. After a bloody purge of senatorial and equestrian opponents including Cicero, Antony and Octavian set out after Cassius and Brutus, who had fled into Macedonia. At Philippi in 42 B.C. Octavian and Antony defeated the armies of the two assassins (or, as they called themselves, liberators) who preferred suicide to capture.

After the defeat of the last republicans at Philippi, the members of the second triumvirate began to look suspiciously at one another. Antony took

The End of the Republic

135–81 B.C.	Revolts against the republic
133–121 B.C.	Gracchi reform programs
107 B.C.	Gaius Marius elected consul
91–82 B.C.	Social War and civil war (Marius vs. Sulla)
82–79 B.C.	Sulla rules as dictator
79–27 B.C.	Era of civil wars
63 B.C.	Cicero elected consul First Triumvirate (Pompey, Crassus, Caesar)
59 B.C.	Caesar elected consul
45 B.C.	Caesar defeats Pompey's forces
44 B.C.	Caesar assassinated Second Triumvirate (Mark Antony, Lepidus, Octavian)
42 B.C.	Octavian and Mark Antony defeat Cassius and Brutus at Philippi
31 B.C.	Octavian defeats Mark Antony and Cleopatra at Actium
27 B.C.	Octavian is declared Augustus

command of the east, protecting the provinces of Asia Minor and the Levant from the Parthians and bleeding them dry in the process. Lepidus received Africa, and Octavian was left to deal with the problems of Italy and the west.

Initially Octavian had cut a weak and unimposing figure. He was only 18 when he was named adopted son and heir in Caesar's will. He had no military or political experience and was frequently in poor health. Still, he had the magic of Caesar's name with which to inspire the army, he had a visceral instinct for politics and publicity, and he combined these with an absolute determination to succeed at all costs. Aided by more competent and experienced commanders, notably Marcus Agrippa (ca. 63–12 B.C.), and Gaius Maecenas (ca. 70–8 B.C.), he began to consolidate his power at the expense of his two colleagues. Lepidus attempted to gain a greater share in the empire but found that his troops would not fight against Octavian. He was forced out of his position and allowed to retire in obscurity, retaining only the honorific title of *pontifex maximus*.

Antony, to meet his ever growing demand for cash, became dependent on the Ptolemaic ruler of Egypt, the clever and competent Cleopatra. For her part, Cleopatra manipulated Antony in order to maintain the integrity and independence of her kingdom. Octavian seized the opportunity to portray Antony as a traitor to Rome, a weakling controlled by an Oriental woman who planned to move the capital of the empire to Alexandria. Antony's supporters replied with propaganda of their own, pointing to Octavian's humble parentage and his lack of military ability. The final break came in 32 B.C. Antony, for all his military might, could not attack Italy as long as the despised Cleopatra was with him. Nor could he abandon her without losing her essential financial support. Instead, he tried to lure Octavian to a showdown in Greece. His plan misfired. Agrippa forced him into a naval battle off Actium in 31 B.C. in which Antony was soundly defeated. He and his Egyptian queen committed suicide and Octavian ruled supreme in the Roman empire.

The Good Life

Mere survival was a difficult and elusive goal through the last decades of the republic. Still, some members of the elite sought more. They tried to make sense of the turmoil around them and formulate a philosophy of life to provide themselves with a model of personal conduct. By now Rome's elite were in full command of Greek literature and philosophy, and they naturally turned to the Greek tradition to find their answers. However, they created from it a distinctive Latin cultural tradition. The most prominent figure in the late republic is Cicero, who combined his active life as lawyer and politician with an abiding devotion to Stoic philosophy. In stoicism's belief in divine providence, morality, and duty to one's allotted role in the universe, he found a rational basis for his deeply committed public life. In a series of written dialogues, Cicero presented Stoic values in a form that created a Latin philosophical language freed from slavish imitation of Greek. He also wrote a number of works of political philosophy, particularly *The Republic* and *The Laws*, in conscious imitation of Plato's concern for the proper order of society. For Cicero, humans and gods are bound together in a world governed not simply by might but by justice. The universe, while perhaps not fully intelligible, is nonetheless rational, and reason must be the basis for society and its laws.

These same concerns for virtue are evident in the writings of the great historians of the late republic, Sallust (86–ca. 34 B.C.) and Livy (59 B.C.–A.D. 17). Sallust was a supporter of Julius Caesar, who had written his own stylistically powerful histories of the Gallic and Civil wars. For him as well as for his younger contemporary Livy, the chaos of civil war was the direct result of moral corruption and decline that followed the successes of the empire. For Sallust, the moral failing was largely that of the senate and its members, who trampled the plebs in their quest for power and personal glory. Livy, who was much more conservative, condemned plebeian demagogues as well as power-hungry senators. Only those aristocratic conservatives who, like Cato, had stood for the ancient Roman traditions merited praise. In the second century B.C. the Greek historian Polybius had been fascinated with the rise of the Roman republic to world supremacy. A century later the Roman historians were even more fascinated with its decline.

A different kind of morality dominated the work of Lucretius (ca. 100–55 B.C.), the greatest poet of the late republic. Just as Cicero had molded stoicism into a Roman civic philosophy, Lucretius presented Epicurean materialist philosophy as a Roman alternative to the hunger for power, wealth, and glory. In his great poem, *On the Nature of Things*, Lucretius presents the Epicurean's thoroughly physical understanding of the universe. He describes its atomic composition, the evolution of man from brutish beginnings to civilization, and the evil effects not only of greed and ambition but also of religion. All that exists is material reality. Religion, whether the state-supported cults of ancient Rome or the exotic cults introduced from the East, plays on mortal fear of death, a fear that is irrational and groundless. "Death is nothing to us," Lucretius writes. "It is only the natural fulfillment of life. A rational, proportional enjoyment of life is all that matters. Sorrow and anxiety come from but an ignorant emotionalism."

Emotion was precisely the goal of another poetic tradition of the late republic, that of the "neoteric" or new-style poets, especially Catullus (ca. 84–ca. 54 B.C.). Avoiding politics or moralistic philosophy, these poets created short, striking lyric poems which, although inspired by Hellenistic poetry, combine polished craftsmanship with a direct realism that is without precedent. One of the most striking differences between this Latin poetry and its Greek antecedents is the reality and individuality of the persons and relationships expressed.

The same interest in the individual affected the way artists of the late republic borrowed from Greek art. Since Etruscan times, Romans had commemorated their ancestors in wax or wooden busts displayed in the atria of their homes. Hellenistic artists concentrated on the ideal, but Romans cherished the individual. The result was a portraiture that caught the personality of the individual's face, even while portraying him or her as one of a type. Statues of the ideal nude, the armored warrior, or the citizen in his simple toga followed the proportions and conventions of Hellenistic sculpture. The heads, however, created in hard, dry style, are as unique and personal as the characters who live in Catullus's lyric poems. We see in them the strengths and weaknesses, the stresses and the privileges, that marked the last generation of the Roman republic.

Rome had come a long way since its origin as an outpost of the Alban League. At first overshadowed by its more civilized neighbors to the north and south, it had slowly and tenaciously achieved independence from and then domination over its more ancient neighbors. It is difficult to point to particular Roman ideas, institutions, or techniques that made this possible. Virtually all of these were absorbed or adapted from the Etruscans, Greeks, and others with whom Rome came into contact. Rome's great success was largely due to Roman authoritarianism as well as to its genius for creative adaptation, flexibility, and thoroughness, and its willingness to give those it conquered a stake in Roman victory. Until the middle of the second century B.C., this formula had served the republic well. After the final destruction of Carthage, however, an isolated and fearful oligarchy appeared unwilling or unable to broaden the base of those participating in the Roman achievement. The result was a century and a half of intermittent violence and civil war before a new political and social order headed by an absolute monarch established a new equilibrium.

Suggestions for Further Reading

Primary Sources

Much of the works of Polybius, Livy, Cato, Caesar, Cicero, and other Roman authors are available in English translation from Penguin Books. The first volume by Naphtali Lewis and Meyer Reinhold, *Roman Civilization Selected Readings Vol. I: The Republic* (1951) contains a wide selection of documents with useful introductions.

The Western Mediterranean

Massimo Pallottino, *The Etruscans* (Bloomington: Indiana University Press, 1975). A general introduction to Etruscan history, language, and civilization.

---

*Indicates paperback edition available.

B. H. Warmington, *Carthage*, rev. ed. (New York: F. A. Praeger, 1969). A basic introduction.

From City to Empire

*Mary Beard and Michael Crawford, *Rome in the Late Republic* (Ithaca, NY: Cornell University Press, 1985). A short interpretative essay on the crisis of the late republic.

John Boardman, Jasper Griffin, and Oswyn Murray, *The Roman World* (New York: Oxford University Press, 1988). A balanced collection of essays on all aspects of Roman history and civilization.

*P. A. Brunt, *Social Conflicts in the Roman Republic* (New York: W. W. Norton, 1971). Analyzes the continuing struggle between patricians and plebeians until the end of the republic.

Michael Crawford, *The Roman Republic* (Cambridge, MA: Harvard University Press, 1978). A modern survey of the Republican period, emphasizing political history.

Leon Homo, *Primitive Italy and the Beginnings of Roman Imperialism* (Philadelphia: Century Bookbindery, 1968). Classic introduction to early Italian history.

Keith Hopkins, *Conquerors and Slaves* (New York: Cambridge University Press, 1978). A sociological study of the effects of slavery on imperial society and government.

Republican Civilization

Géza Alfoldy, *The Social History of Rome* (Berlin: Walter de Gruyter, 1988). A survey of Rome that emphasizes the relationship between social structure and politics.

Suzanne Dixon, *The Roman Mother* (Norman: University of Oklahoma Press, 1988). A balanced view of Roman mothers in law and in society.

*Erich S. Gruen, *The Hellenistic World and the Coming of Rome*, 2 vols. (Berkeley: University of California Press, 1984). A detailed history of the Hellenistic world, presenting Rome's gradual and unintended rise to dominance in it.

The Burden of Empire

Alan E. Astin, *Cato the Censor* (New York: Oxford University Press, 1978). An excellent biography of Cato that also analyzes his writings.

The Price of Empire

*E. Badian, *Roman Imperialism in the Late Republic* (Ithaca, NY: Cornell University Press, 1968). A study of the contradictory forces leading to the development of the empire.

*Mary Beard and Michael Crawford, *Rome in the Late Republic* (Ithaca, NY: Cornell University Press, 1985). An analysis of the political processes of the last republic as part of the development of Roman society, not simply the decay of the republic.

The End of the Republic

E. S. Gruen, *The Last Generation of the Roman Republic* (Berkeley: University of California Press, 1973). A recent and controversial analysis of the politics of the late republic.

D. Stockton, *Cicero: A Political Biography* (London: Oxford University Press, 1971). A biography of the great orator in the context of the end of the republic.

5

Imperial Rome and the Changing Classical World

Coin of the Realm

The magnificent medallion shown here depicts on one side likenesses of the imperial brothers Valentinian I and Valens, who jointly ruled the Roman Empire from 364 to 375. On the obverse is pictured a mounted emperor, surrounded by a nimbus, the symbol of divinity, and the gods Tellus (earth) and Fortuna (good fortune). The inscription reads, "The glory of the Romans," and the AN indicates that the medallion was struck at the imperial mint at Antioch. Beneath these facts about the medallion, however, lies a much broader story. It is the story of the transformation of the Roman Empire in late antiquity.

The medallion fairly bristles with apparent contradictions and incongruities. Now two emperors instead of one rule the empire. The emperors are Christian, yet they are surrounded with pagan symbols and appear to be equated with the gods. Finally, the inscription on the face, "King of the Romans," reveals the medallion for what it is: a counterfeit. The Romans never called their emperors kings, but that was the term the barbarian Goths, who did not have kings themselves, used for the Roman emperors. Although the medallion is counterfeit, it is not worthless. Its gold is of higher purity than many genuine Roman coins of the period.

By the last quarter of the fourth century, the barbarian and Roman worlds were inextricably connected, like the two sides of the coin itself. The Goths had struck the coin to show their esteem for the Roman Empire and its rulers. Yet, only a few years after this coin had been struck, the Emperor Valens and his army were destroyed by the very Goths who had produced it in his honor. This counterfeit medallion demonstrates the considerable extent to which the Goths had absorbed and imitated Roman cultural and political traditions. At

the same time it reflects the radical transformations of Roman and barbarian culture, society, and institutions that took place in the two centuries following the death of Marcus Aurelius in 180.

By the end of the second century, most of the Mediterranean world had been part of the Roman Empire for more than two centuries—a longer period than the 50 states have been part of the United States. It was, however, the empire's success in expanding its frontiers and in incorporating greatly diverse peoples that was the cause of its radical change during late antiquity. Even while the provinces were becoming Romanized, the meaning of *Roman* was being altered. Accelerating this process of change and transformation was the combination of events collectively referred to as the crisis of the third century.

*T*he Augustan Age

It took Octavian two years following his victory at Actium in 31 B.C. to eliminate remaining pockets of resistance and to work out a system to reconcile his rule with Roman constitutional traditions and yet not surrender any of his power. That power rested on three factors: his immense wealth, which he used to secure support; his vast following among the surviving elites as well as among the populares; and his total command of the army. It also rested on the exhaustion of the Roman people, who were eager, after decades of civil strife, to return to peace and stability. Remembering the fate of Julius Caesar, however, Octavian had no intention of rekindling opposition by establishing an overt monarchy. Instead, in 27 B.C., he returned the republic from his own charge to the senate and the people of Rome. In turn the senate decreed him the title of *Augustus*, meaning "exalted."

What this meant was that Augustus, as he was now called, continued to rule no less strongly than before, but he did so not through any autocratic office or title—he preferred to be called simply the "first citizen," or *princeps*—but by preserving the form of the traditional Roman magistracies. For four years he rested his authority on consecutive terms as consul, and after 23 B.C., held a life position as tribune. The senate granted him proconsular command of the provinces of Gaul, Spain, Syria, and Egypt, the major sources of imperial wealth and the locations of more than three-quarters of the Roman army. Later the senate declared his command *imperium* of these "imperial" provinces superior to that of any governors of other provinces. Thus Augustus, through the power of the plebeian office of tribune, stood as the permanent protector of the Roman people. As simultaneously either consul or proconsul,

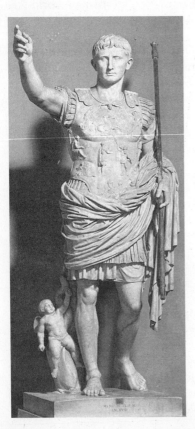

An idealized marble portrait statue of the emperor Augustus addressing his army. Augustus ruled without benefit of any aristocratic office or title. He preferred to be called simply the "first citizen," or princeps.

he held the imperium, the command of the army, the basis of the ancient patrician authority. He was the first and greatest emperor.

These formalities deceived no one. Augustus's power was absolute. However, by choosing not to exercise it in an absolutist manner, he forged a new constitutional system that worked well for himself and his successors. By the end of his reign, few living could remember the days of the republic and fewer still mourned its passing. Under Augustus and his successors the empire enjoyed two centuries of stability and peace, the *pax Romana*.

The Empire Renewed

Cicero had sought in vain a concord of the orders, a settlement of the social and political frictions of the empire through the voluntary efforts of a public-minded oligarchy. What could not happen voluntarily, Augustus imposed from above, reforming the Roman state, society, and culture.

Key to Augustus's program of renewal was the senate, which he made, if not a partner, then a useful subordinate in his reform. He gradually reduced the number of senators, which had grown to over a thousand, back down to 600. In the process he eliminated the unfit and incompetent as well as the impoverished and those who failed to show the appropriate reverence toward the *princeps*, the emperor. At the same time he made membership hereditary, although he continued to appoint individuals of personal integrity, ability, and wealth to the body. Most conspicuous among the "new men" to enter the senate under Augustus were the wealthy leaders of Italian cities and colonies. These small-town notables formed the core of Augustus's supporters and worked most closely with him to renew the Roman elite.

Augustus also shared with the senate the governance of the empire, although again not on an equal footing. The senate named governors to the peaceful provinces, while Augustus named commanders to those frontier "imperial" provinces where the bulk of the legions were stationed. Senators themselves served as provincial governors and military commanders. The senate also functioned as a court of law in important cases. Still in all, the senate remained a creature of the emperor, seldom asserting itself even when asked to do so by Augustus or his successors and competing within its own ranks to see who could be first to do the emperor's bidding.

Augustus undertook an even more fundamental reform of the equites, those wealthy businessmen, bankers, and tax collectors who had vied with the senatorial aristocracy since the reforms of Tiberius Gracchus. After Actium many equites found themselves proscribed—sentenced to death or banishment—and had their property confiscated. Augustus began to rebuild their ranks by enrolling a new generation of successful merchants and speculators, who became the foundation of his administration. Equestrians formed the backbone of the officer corps of the army, of the treasury, and of the greatly expanded imperial administration. The equestrian order was open at both ends. Freedmen and soldiers who acquired sufficient wealth moved into the order, and the most successful and accomplished equestrians were promoted into the senate. Still, the price for a renewed equestrian order was its removal from the political arena. No longer was provincial tax collection farmed out to companies of equestrian publicans nor were they allowed a role in executive or judicial deliberations. For most, these changes were a small price to pay for security, standing, and avenues to lucrative employment. Small wonder that emperors often had difficulty persuading the most successful equites to give up their positions for the more public but less certain life of a senator.

The land crisis had provoked much of the unrest in the late republic, and after Actium, Augustus had to satisfy the needs of the loyal soldiers of his 60 legions. Drawing on his immense wealth, acquired largely from the estates of his proscripted enemies, he pensioned off 32 legions, sending them to colonies he purchased for them throughout the empire. The remaining 28 legions became a permanent professional army stationed in imperial provinces. In time the normal period of enlistment became fixed at 20 years, after which time Augustus provided the legionnaires with land and enough cash to settle in among the notables of their colonies. After A.D. 5 the state assumed the payment of this retirement bonus. Augustus established a small elite unit, the praetorian guard, in and around Rome as his personal military force. Initially, the praetorians protected the emperors. In later reigns, they would make them.

These measures created a permanent solution to the problem of the citizen-soldier of the later republic. Veteran colonies, all built as model Roman towns with their central forum, baths, temples, arenas, and theaters as well as their outlying villas and farms, helped Romanize the far provinces of the empire. These colonies, unlike the independent colonies of Greece in an earlier age, remained an integral part of the Roman state. Thus Romanization and political integration went hand in hand, uniting through peaceful means an empire first acquired by arms. Likewise, ambitious provincials, through service as auxiliaries and later as citizens, acquired a stake in the destiny of Rome.

Not every citizen, of course, could find prosperity in military service and a comfortable retirement. The problems of urban poverty in Rome continued to grow. By the time of Augustus, the capital city had reached a population of perhaps six hundred thousand people. A tiny minority relaxed in the comfortable homes built on the Palatine. Tens of thousands more crammed into wooden and brick tenements and jostled each other in the crowded, noisy streets. Employment was hard to find, since free labor had difficulty competing against slaves. The emperors, their power as tribunes making them protectors of the poor, provided over 150,000 resident citizens with a basic dole of wheat brought from Egypt. They also built aqueducts to provide water to the city. In addition, they constructed vast public recreation centers. These included both the sumptuous baths, which were combination bathing facilities, health clubs, and brothels; and arenas such as the Colosseum, where 50,000 spectators could watch gladiatorial displays, and the Circus Maximus, where a quarter of the city's population could gather at once to watch chariot races. Such mass gatherings replaced the plebeian assemblies of the republic as the occasions on which the populace could express its will. Few emperors were foolish enough to ignore the wishes of the crowd roared out in the Circus.

Divine Augustus

Augustus's renewal of Rome rested on a religious reform. In 17 B.C. he celebrated three days of sacrifices, processions, sacred games, and theater performances, known as the secular games. After the death of Lepidus in 12 B.C., he assumed the office of *pontifex maximus* and used it to direct a reinvigoration of Roman religion. He restored numerous temples and revived ancient Roman cults. He established a series of public religious festivals, reformed priesthoods, and encouraged citizens to participate in the traditional cults of Rome. His goals in all these religious reforms were twofold. After decades of public authority controlled by violence and naked aggression, he was determined to restore the traditions of Roman piety, morality, sacred order, and faith in relationship between the gods and Roman destiny. An equally important goal was Augustus's promotion of his own cult. His adoptive father, Julius Caesar, had been deified after his death, and Augustus benefited from this association with a divine ancestor. His own *genius*, or guiding spirit, received special devotion in temples throughout the West dedicated to "Rome and Augustus." In the East he was worshiped as a living god. In this manner the emperor became identical with the state, and the state religion closely akin to emperor worship. After his death Augustus and virtually all of the emperors after him were worshiped as official deities in Rome itself.

Closely related to his fostering of traditional cults was Augustus's attempt to restore traditional Roman virtues, especially within the family. Like the reformers of the late republic, he believed the declining power of the paterfamilias was at the root of much that was wrong with Rome. To reverse the trend and to restore the declining population of free Italians, Augustus encouraged marriage, procreation, and the firm control of husbands over wives. He imposed penalties for those who chose not to marry and bestowed rewards on those who produced large families. He enacted laws to prevent women from having extramarital affairs and even exiled his own daughter and granddaughter for promiscuity.

Augustus actively patronized those writers who shared his conservative religious and ethical values and who might be expected to glorify the *princeps*, and he used his power to censor and silence writers he considered immoral. Chief among the favored were the poets Virgil (70 B.C.–19 B.C.) and Horace (65 B.C.–8 B.C.). Both came from provincial and fairly modest origins, although both received excellent educations. Each lost his property in the proscriptions and confiscations during the civil wars, but their poetry eventually won them the favor of Augustus. In time Horace received a comfortable estate at Licenza east of Rome. Virgil's family estates were returned and he received a villa at Nola and houses in Rome and Naples. In return, through their poetry in praise of the emperor, Horace and Virgil conferred immortality on Augustus.

Horace celebrated Augustus's victory at Actium, his reform of the empire, and reestablishment of the ancient cults that had brought Rome divine favor. In Horace's poems, Augustus is almost a god. His deeds are compared to those of the great heroes of Roman legend and judged superior. Interspersed with the poems praising Augustus are poems of great beauty praising the love of both boys and girls and the enjoyment of wine and music. To Horace, the glories of the new age inaugurated by Augustus with the secular games of 17 B.C. included not only the splendor of empire but also the enjoyment of privileged leisure.

Virgil began his poetic career with pastoral poems celebrating the joys of rural life and the bitterness of the loss of lands in the civil wars. By 40 B.C. he was turning to greater themes. In his fourth *Eclogue*, he announced the birth of a child, a child who would usher in a new golden age. Later, under the patronage of Maecenas and Augustus, Virgil turned directly to glorifying Augustus and the new age. The ultimate expression of this effort was the *Aeneid*, an epic consciously intended to serve for the Roman world the role of the Homeric poems in the Greek.

As he reworked the legend of Aeneas, a Trojan hero who escaped the destruction of the the city, wandered throughout the Mediterranean, and ultimately came to Latium, Virgil presented a panoramic history of Rome and its destiny. Unlike the Homeric heroes, Achilles and Odysseus, who were driven by their own search for glory, Aeneas is driven by his piety, that is, his duty toward the gods and his devotion to his father. Aeneas must follow his destiny, which is the destiny of Rome, to rule the world in harmony and justice. In the midst of his wanderings, Aeneas (like Odysseus before him) enters the underworld to speak with his dead father. Here he sees a vision of Rome's greatness to come. He sees the great heroes of Rome, including Augustus, "son of a god," and he is told of the particular mission of Rome:

> Let others fashion in bronze more lifelike, breathing images
> Let others (as I believe they will) draw living faces from marble
> Others shall plead cases better and others will better
> Track the course of the heavens and announce the rising stars.
> Remember, Romans, your task is to rule the peoples
> This will be your art: to teach the habit of peace
> To spare the defeated and to subdue the haughty.

The finest of the poets who felt the heavy hand of Augustus's disfavor was Ovid (43 B.C.–A.D. 17), the great Latin poet of erotic love. In *Art of Love* and *Amores*, he cheerfully preaches the art of seduction and adultery. He delights in poking irreverent fun at everything from the sanctity of Roman marriage to the serious business of warfare. In his great *Metamorphoses*, a series of artfully told myths, he parodies the heroic epic, mocking with grotesque humor the very material Virgil used to create the *Aeneid*. By A.D. 8 Augustus had had enough. He exiled the witty poet to Tomis, a miserable frontier post on the

Black Sea. There Ovid spent the last nine years of his life, suffering from the harsh climate, the danger of nomadic attacks and, most of all, the pain of exile from the center of the civilization he loved.

Augustus's Successors

Horace and Virgil may have made Augustus's fame immortal. His flesh was not. The problem of succession occupied him throughout much of his long reign and was never satisfactorily solved. Since the princeps was not a specific office, but a combination of offices and honors held together by military might and religious aura, formal dynastic succession was impossible. Instead Augustus attempted to select a blood relative as successor, include him in his reign, and have him voted the various offices and dignities that constituted his own position.

Unfortunately, Augustus outlived all of his first choices. His nephew and adopted son Marcellus, to whom he married his only child Julia, died in 23 B.C. He then married Julia to his old associate Agrippa and began to groom him for the position, but Agrippa died in 12 B.C. Lucius and Gaius, the sons of Julia and Agrippa, also died young. Augustus's final choice, his stepson Tiberius (A.D. 14–37), proved to be a gloomy and unpopular successor but nevertheless a competent ruler under whom the machinery of the empire functioned smoothly. The continued orderly functioning of the empire even under the subsequent members of Augustus's family—the mad Gaius, also known as Caligula (37–41), the bookish but competent Claudius (41–54), and initially under Nero (54–68)—is a tribute to the soundness of Augustus's constitutional changes and the vested interest that the descendants of Augustus's military and aristocratic supporters had in them.

Nero was, however, more than even they could bear. Profligate, vicious, and paranoid, Nero divided his time between murdering his relatives and associates, including his mother, his aunt, his wife, his tutors, and eventually his most capable generals, and squandering his vast wealth on mad attempts to gain recognition as a great poet, actor, singer, and athlete. (When he competed in games, other contestants wisely lost.) Finally in A.D. 68, the exasperated commanders in Gaul, Spain, and Africa revolted. Once more war swept the empire. Nero slit his own throat, and in the next year, the "Year of the Four Emperors," four men in quick succession won the office only to lose their lives just as quickly. Finally, in 70 Vespasian (A.D. 69–79), the son of a "new man," who had risen through the ranks to the command in Egypt, secured the principate and restored order.

The first emperors had rounded off the frontiers of the empire, transforming the client states of Cappadocia, Thrace, Commagene, and Judaea in the east and Mauritania in North Africa into provinces. Claudius (A.D. 41–54) presided over the conquest of Britain in A.D. 43. These emperors introduced efficient means of governing and protecting the empire, and tied together its inhabitants, roughly fifty million in the time of Augustus, in networks of mutual

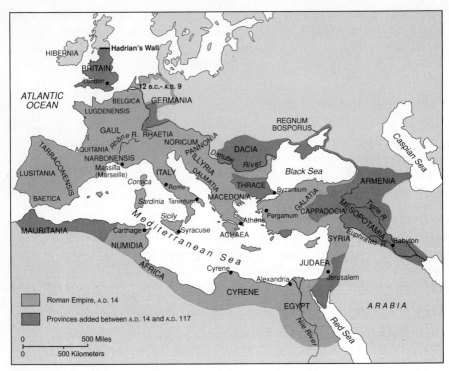

The Roman Empire, A.D. *14 and 117*

dependence and common interest. Augustus established peaceful relations with the Parthian empire, which permitted unhampered trade between China, India, and Rome. In the west, after a disastrous attempt to expand the empire to the Elbe ended in the loss of three legions in A.D. 9, the frontier was fixed at the Rhine. In the east, the northern border stopped at the Danube. The deserts of Africa, Nubia, and southern Arabia formed what in the first century A.D. many saw as the "natural" southern boundaries of the empire.

When Vespasian's troops fought their way into Rome in vicious hand-to-hand street fighting, the populace watched with idle fascination. The violence of A.D. 69, unlike that of the previous century, involved mostly professional legions and their commanders. The rest of the empire sat back to watch. In a few restive regions of the empire some Gauls, the Batavians along the Rhine, and diehard Jewish rebels tried to use the momentary confusion to revolt, but by and large the empire remained stable. This stability was the greatest achievement of Augustus and his immediate successors.

The emperors of the Flavian dynasty, Vespasian and his sons and successors Titus (79–81) and Domitian (81–96), were stern and unpretentious provincials who restored the authority and dignity of their office, although they also did away with much of the trappings of republican legitimacy that

Augustus and his immediate successors had used. They solidified the administrative system, returned the legions to their fairly permanent posts, and opened the highest reaches of power as never before to provincial elites. After the Flavian emperors, the Antonines (96–193), especially Trajan (98–117), Hadrian (117–138), and Antoninus Pius (138–161), ruled for what has been termed "the period in the history of the world during which the human race was most happy and prosperous."

$\mathcal{T}$he Pax Romana

Not all was peaceful during this period. Trajan initiated a new and final expansion of the imperial frontiers. Between 101 and 106 he conquered Dacia (modern Romania). He resumed war with the Parthians, conquering the provinces of Armenia and Mesopotamia by 116. During the second century, the Palestinian Jews revolted in 115–117 and again in 132–135. The emperor Hadrian put down this second revolt and expelled the surviving Jews from Judaea. Along both the eastern and western frontiers legions had to contend with sporadic border incidents.

Administering the Empire

The imperial government of this vast empire was as oppressive as it was primitive. Taxes, rents, forced labor service, military levies and requisitions, and outright extortion weighed heavily on its subjects. To a considerable extent, the inhabitants of the empire continued to be governed by the indigenous elites whose cooperation Rome won by giving them broad autonomy. Thus Hellenistic cities continued to manage their own affairs under the supervision of essentially amateur Roman governors. Local town councils in Gaul, Germany, and Spain supervised the collection of taxes, maintained public works projects, and kept the peace. In return for their participation in Roman rule, these elites received Roman citizenship, a prize that carried prestige, legal protection, and the promise of further advancement in the Roman world.

In those imperial provinces controlled directly by the emperor, the army was much more in evidence, and the professional legions were the ultimate argument of imperial tax collectors and imperial representatives, or *procurators*. Moreover, as the turmoil of the Year of the Four Emperors amply demonstrated, the military was the ultimate foundation of imperial rule itself. Still, soldiers were as much farmers as fighters. Legions usually remained in the same location for years, and around military camps veterans' colonies sprang up.

Finally, much of the governing of the empire was done by the vast households of the Roman elite, particularly that of the princeps. Freedman and slaves from the emperor's household often governed vast regions, oversaw imperial estates, and managed imperial factories and mines. The descendants of the old Roman nobility might look down their noses at imperial freedmen, but they obeyed their orders.

The empire worked because it rewarded those who worked with it and left alone those who paid their taxes and kept quiet. Local elites, auxiliary soldiers, and freedmen could aspire to rise to the highest ranks of the power elite. As provincials were drawn into the Roman system, they were also drawn into the world of Roman culture. Proper education in Latin and Greek, the ability to hold one's own in philosophical discussion, the absorption of Roman styles of dress, recreation, and religious cults, all were essential for ambitious provincials. Thus, in the course of the first century A.D., the disparate portions of the empire competed, not to free themselves from the Roman yoke, but to become Roman themselves.

Eastern Religions

The same openness that permitted the spread of Latin letters and Roman baths to distant Gaul and the shores of the Black Sea provided paths of dissemination for other distinctly un-Roman religious traditions. For many in the empire, the traditional rituals offered to the household gods and the state cults of Jupiter, Mars, and the other official deities were insufficient foci of religious devotion.

As discussed in Chapter 4, already in the second century B.C. the Roman world had been caught up in the emotional cult of Dionysus, an ecstatic, personal, and liberating religion entirely unlike the official Roman cults. Again in the first century A.D., so-called mystery cults, that is, religions promising immediate personal contact with a deity that would bring immortality, spread throughout the empire. Some were officially introduced into Rome as part of its open polytheism. These included the Anatolian Cybele or great mother-goddess cult, which was present in Rome from the late third century B.C. Devotees underwent a ritual in which they were bathed in the blood of a bull or a ram, thereby obtaining immortality. From Persia came the cult of Mithras, the ancient Indo-Iranian god of light and truth who, as bringer of victory, found special favor with Roman soldiers and merchants eager for success in this life and immortality beyond the grave. Generally Rome tolerated these alien cults as long as they could be assimilated or at least reconciled in some way into the cult of the Roman gods and the genius of the emperor.

With one religious group this assimilation was impossible. The Jews of Palestine had long refused any accommodation with the polytheistic cults of the Hellenistic kingdoms or with Rome. Roman conquerors and emperors, aware of the problems of their Hellenistic predecessors, went to considerable lengths to avoid antagonizing this small and unusual group of people. When

Pompey seized Jerusalem in 63 B.C., he was careful not to interfere in Jewish religion and even left Judaea under the control of the Jewish high priest. Later, Judaea was made into a client kingdom under the puppet Herod. Jews were allowed to maintain their monotheistic cult and were excused from making sacrifices to the Roman gods.

Still, the Jewish community remained deeply divided about its relationship with the wider world and with Rome. At one end of the spectrum were the Sadducees, a party composed largely of members of priestly families who enjoyed considerable influence with their foreign rulers. They were staunch defenders of the ancient Jewish law, or Torah, but not to the exclusion of other later religious and legal traditions. They were willing to work with Rome and even adopt some elements of Hellenism, as long as the services in the temple could continue.

At the other end of the spectrum were the Hasidim, those who rejected all compromise with Hellenistic culture and collaboration with foreign powers. Many expected the arrival of a messiah, a liberator who would destroy the Romans and reestablish the kingdom of David. One party within the Hasidim were the Pharisees, who practiced strict dietary rules and rituals to maintain the separation of Jews and Gentiles (literally, "the peoples," that is, all non-Jews). The Pharisees accepted the writings of the Hebrew prophets along with the Torah and abided by a still larger body of orally transmitted law, the "tradition of the elders." The most prominent figure in this movement was Hillel (ca. 30 B.C.–A.D. 10), a Jewish scholar from Babylon who came to Jerusalem as a teacher of the law. He began a tradition of legal and scriptural interpretation which, in an expanded version centuries later, became the

Spoils from the Temple in Jerusalem, *a marble relief from the Arch of Titus. The arch was begun by Titus's father, the emperor Vespasian, to commemorate Titus's victory over the Jews in A.D. 78.*

Talmud. Hillel was also a moral teacher who taught peace and love, not revolt. "Whatever is hateful to you, do not to your fellow man: this is the whole Law; the rest is mere commentary," he taught.

For all their insistence on purity and separation from other peoples, the Pharisees did not advocate violent revolt against Rome. They preferred to await divine intervention. Another group of Hasidim, the Zealots, were less willing to wait. After A.D. 6, when Judaea, Samaria, and Idumaea were annexed and combined into the province of Judaea administered by imperial procurators, the Zealots began to organize sporadic armed resistance to Roman rule. As ever, armed resistance was met with violent suppression. Through the first century A.D., clashes between Roman troops and Zealot revolutionaries grew more frequent and more widespread.

The already complex landscape of the Jewish religious world became further complicated by the brief career of Joshua ben Joseph (ca. 6 B.C.–A.D. 30), known to history as Jesus of Nazareth and to his followers as Jesus the Messiah or the Christ. Jesus came from Galilee, an area known as a Zealot stronghold. However, while Jesus preached the imminent coming of the kingdom, he did so in an entirely nonpolitical manner. He was, like many popular religious leaders, a miracle worker. When people flocked around him to see his wonders, he preached a message of peace and love of God and neighbor. His teachings were entirely within the Jewish tradition and closely resembled those of Hillel—with one major exception. While many contemporary religious leaders announced the imminent coming of the messiah, Jesus informed his closest followers, the apostles and disciples, that he himself was the messiah.

For roughly three years Jesus preached in Judaea and Galilee, drawing large excited crowds. Many of his followers pressed him to lead a revolt against Roman authority and reestablish the kingdom of David, even though he insisted that the kingdom he would establish was not of this world. Other Jews saw his claims as blasphemy and his assertion that he was the king of Jews, even if a heavenly one, as a threat to the status quo. Jesus became more and more a figure of controversy, a catalyst for violence. Ultimately the Roman procurator, Pontius Pilate, decided that he posed a threat to law and order. Pilate, like other Roman magistrates, had no interest in the internal religious affairs of the Jews. However, he was troubled by anyone who had the potential for causing political disturbances, no matter how unintentionally. Pilate ordered Jesus scourged and put to death by crucifixion, a common Roman form of execution for slaves, pirates, thieves, and noncitizen troublemakers.

The cruel death of this gentle man ended the popular agitation he had stirred up, but it did not deter his closest followers. They soon announced that three days after his death he had risen and had appeared to them numerous times over the next weeks. They took this resurrection as proof of his claims to be the messiah and confirmation of his promise of eternal life to those who believed in him. Soon a small group of his followers, led by Peter (d. ca. A.D. 64), formed another Jewish sect, preaching and praying daily in the temple. New members were initiated into this sect, soon known as Christianity, through baptism, a purification rite in which the initiate was submerged briefly in flowing water. They also shared a ritual meal in which bread and wine were distributed to members. Otherwise, they remained entirely within the Jewish religious and cultural tradition, and Hellenized Jews and pagans who wished to join the sect had to observe strict Jewish law and custom.

Christianity spread beyond its origin as a Jewish sect because of the work of one man, Paul of Tarsus (ca. A.D. 5–ca. 67). Although Paul was an observant Jew, he was part of the wider cosmopolitan world of the empire and from birth enjoyed the privileges of Roman citizenship. He saw Christianity as a separate tradition, completing and perfecting Judaism but intended for the whole world.

Paul set out to spread his message, crisscrossing Asia Minor, Greece, and even traveling to Rome. Wherever he went, Paul won converts and established churches, called *ecclesiae*, or assemblies. Everywhere Paul and the other disciples went they worked wonders, cast out demons, cured illnesses, and preached. Paul's teachings, while firmly rooted in the Jewish historical tradition, were radically new. God had created the human race, he taught, in the image of God and destined it for eternal life. However, by deliberate sin of the first humans, Adam and Eve, humans had lost eternal life and introduced evil and death into the world. Even then God did not abandon his people but began, through the Jews, to prepare for their eventual redemption. That salvation was accomplished by Jesus, the son of God, through his faith, a free and unmerited gift of God to his elect. Through faith, the Christian ritual of baptism, and participation in the church, men and women can share in the salvation offered by God.

The Early Roman Empire

Julio-Claudian Period	Augustus (27 B.C.–A.D. 14)
	Tiberius (A.D. 14–37)
	Caligula (37–41)
	Claudius (41–54)
	Nero (54–68)
Year of the Four Emperors A.D. 69	
Flavian Period A.D. 69–96	Vespasian (69–79)
	Titus (79–81)
	Domitian (81–96)
Antonine Period 96–193	Trajan (98–117)
	Hadrian (117–138)
	Marcus Aurelius (161–180)
	Commodus (180–192)

How many conversions resulted from Paul's theological message and how many resulted from the miracles he and the other disciples worked will never be known, but another factor certainly played a part in the success of conversions. That was the courage Christians showed in the face of persecution.

Even the tolerance and elasticity of Rome for new religions could be stretched only to a point. The Christians' belief in the divinity of their founder was no problem. Their offer of salvation to those who participated in their mysteries was only normal. But their stubborn refusal to acknowledge the existence of the other gods and to participate in the cult of the genius of the emperor was intolerable. Christianity was an aggressive and successful cult, attracting followers throughout the empire. This was not religion, it was subversion. Beginning during Nero's reign, Roman officials sporadically rounded up Christians, destroyed their sacred scriptures, and executed those who refused to sacrifice to the imperial genius. But instead of decreasing the cult's appeal, persecution only aided it. For those who believed that death was birth into a new and better life, martyrdom was a reward, not a penalty.

$\mathcal{A}$ Tour of the Empire

Each town in the sprawling empire, from York in the north of Britain to Dura Europus on the Euphrates, was a center of *Romanitas* in provinces still closely tied to local provincial traditions. Each boasted a forum where locals conducted business and government affairs. Each had an arena for gladiatorial games, baths, a racetrack, and a theater where Greek and Latin plays entertained the populace. Temples to the Capitoline Jupiter and to the deified emperors adorned the cities. Aqueducts brought fresh water from distant springs into the heart of the cities.

Connecting these towns was a network of well-maintained roads frequented by imperial administrators, merchants, the idle rich, and soldiers. Beginning in 120 the roads of the empire saw a most unusual traveler: the emperor Hadrian, who traveled them to conduct an extraordinary inspection of the length and breadth of his empire. Hadrian, the adopted son and heir of Trajan, had received an excellent Greek education and was an accomplished writer, poet, connoisseur, and critic. Still, he had spent most of his early career as a successful field commander and administrator in Dacia and the lower Danube. Years of military experience had made Hadrian very aware of the potential weaknesses of the vast Roman borders, and his primary interest was to inspect those military commands most critical for imperial stability.

Thus he set out west, traveling first through the provinces of Gaul, prosperous and pacific regions long integrated into the Roman world. Gaul was known for its good food, its pottery manufacture, and its comfortable if culturally slightly backward local elites. Much of Gaul's prosperity came from

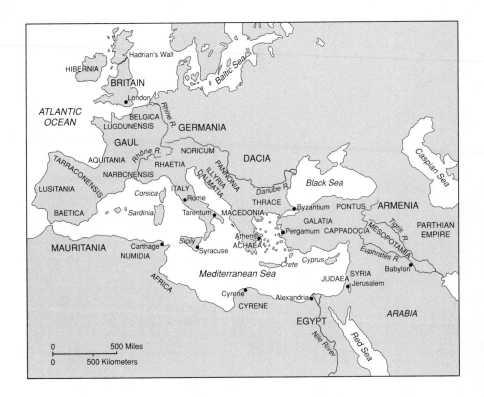

supplying the legions guarding the Rhine-Danube frontier, and it was across the Rhine toward Germany, where the legions faced the barbarians of "Free Germany," that Hadrian was headed. Legions stationed at Xanten, Cologne, and Trier were far removed from the Mediterranean world that formed the heart of the empire. The dark forests, cold winters, and crude life made Germany a hardship post. Hadrian threw himself into the harsh camp life of Germany in order to bolster discipline and combat readiness. He shared rough field rations, long marches, and simple conditions with his troops.

From Germany, Hadrian traveled down the Rhine through what is today Holland and then crossed over to Britain. Here, too, defense was utmost on his mind. Celts from the northern unconquered portion of the island had been harassing the Romanized society to the south. The emperor ordered the erection of a great wall over fifty miles long across Britain from coast to coast. South of the wall, Roman Britain was studded with hundreds of Roman villas, ranging from simple country farmhouses to vast mansions with over sixty rooms. Over a hundred towns and villages were large enough to boast walls, ranging from London with a population of roughly thirty thousand to numerous settlements of between two thousand and ten thousand.

No sooner had he put things straight in Britain than Hadrian returned to Gaul, paused in Nîmes in the south, and then headed south toward his native

Spain. By the second century A.D., Spain was even more thoroughly Romanized than most of Gaul, having been an integral part of the empire since the Second Punic War. It was also far richer. Spanish mines yielded gold, iron, and tin, and Spanish estates produced grain and cattle. Since the reign of Vespasian, the residents of Spanish communities had been given some of the rights of Roman citizens, thus making them eligible for military service, a value even greater to the empire than Spain's mineral wealth. Problems with military service brought Hadrian to Spain. The populace was becoming increasingly resistant to conscription, a universal phenomenon, and Hadrian's presence strengthened the efforts of recruiters.

Hadrian soon set sail for the provinces of Asia. Here he was in the heart of the Hellenistic world so central to the empire's prosperity. Its great cities were centers of manufacture and its ports the vital links in Mediterranean trade. As in Hellenistic times, these cities were the organizing principle of the region, with local senates largely self-governing and rivalries among cities preventing the creation of any sort of provincial identities. Thus in Asia Hadrian worked with individual communities, showering honors and privileges on the most cooperative and founding new communities in the Anatolian hinterland. The last activity was particularly important because, for all of the civilized glory of urban Asia, the rural areas remained strongly tied to traditions that neither Greeks nor Romans had managed to weaken. The empire remained two worlds: one urban, Hellenized, mercantile, and collaborationist; the other rural, traditional, exploited, and potentially separatist.

In 125, Hadrian left Asia for Greece, where he participated in traditional religious cults. Greek culture continued to be vital for Rome, and by participating in the rituals of Achaia and Athens the emperor placed himself in the traditions of the legendary Heracles and Philip of Macedon. Finally, in 127 Hadrian returned to Rome via Sicily, a prosperous amalgam of Greek and Latin cultures dominated by vast senatorial estates, or *latifundia*.

This restless emperor spent less than twelve months in Rome before setting out again, this time for Africa. There, as in Germany, his concern was the discipline and preparedness of the troops guarding the rich agricultural areas and thriving commercial centers of the coast from the marauding nomads on the edges of the desert. Shortly after that, he was again in Athens to dedicate public works projects he had undertaken as well as an altar to himself. From Greece he headed east, again crossing Asia and this time moving into Cappadocia and Syria. His concerns here were again defense, but against a powerful civilized Parthian empire, not barbarian tribes.

Moving south, Hadrian stopped in Jerusalem, where he dedicated a shrine to Jupiter Capitolinus on the site of the destroyed Jewish temple before heading to Egypt for an inspection trip up the Nile. Egypt remained the wealthiest Roman province and the most exploited. Since Augustus, Egypt had been governed directly by the imperial household, its agricultural wealth from the Nile Delta going to feed the Roman masses. At the same time Alexandria continued to be one of the greatest cultural centers of the Roman world. This culture, however, was a fusion of Greek and Egyptian traditions, constantly threatening to form the basis for a nationalist opposition to Roman adminis-trators and tax collectors. Hadrian sought to defuse this powder keg by disciplining administrators and by founding a new city, Antinopolis, which he hoped would create a center of loyalty to Rome.

Hadrian finally returned to the imperial residence on the Palatine in 131. He had spent over ten years on the road and had no doubt done much to strengthen and preserve the *pax Romana,* or Roman peace. Still, to the careful observer the weaknesses of the empire were as evident as its strengths. The frontiers were vast and constantly tested by a profusion of hostile tribes and peoples. Roman citizens from Italy, Gaul, and Spain were increasingly unwill-ing to serve in such far-flung regions. As a result, the legions were manned by progressively less Romanized soldiers, and their battle readiness and disci-pline, poorly enforced by homesick officers, declined dangerously. In the more civilized eastern provinces, corrupt local elites, imperial governors, and officials siphoned off imperial revenues destined for the army to build their personal fortunes. Also, in spite of centuries of Hellenization and Roman administration, city and countryside remained culturally and politically sepa-rated. Early in the second century, such problems were small clouds on the horizon, but in the following century they would grow into a storm that would threaten the very existence of the empire.

The Culture of Antonine Rome

Annius Florus, a poet friend of Hadrian, commenting on the emperor's exhausting journeys, wrote:

> I do not want to be Caesar,
> To walk about among the Britons,
> To endure the Scythian hoar-frosts.

To which Hadrian replied:

> I do not want to be Florus,
> To walk about among taverns,
> To lurk about among cook-shops.

Like the other members of his dynasty, Hadrian enjoyed an easy familiarity with men of letters, and like other men of letters of the period, Florus was a provincial, an African drawn from the provincial world to the great capital. Another provincial, Rome's greatest historian, Cornelius Tacitus (ca. 56–ca. 120), recorded the history of the first century of the empire. Tacitus wrote to instruct and to edify his generation and did so in a style characterized by irony and a sharp sense of the differences between public propaganda and the realities of power politics. His picture of Germanic and British societies served as a warning to Rome against excessive self-confidence and laxity.

Tacitus's contemporaries, Plutarch (ca. 46–after A.D. 119) and Suetonius (ca. 69–after A.D. 122), were biographers rather than historians. Plutarch, who wrote in Greek, composed *Parallel Lives*, a series of character studies in which he compared an eminent Greek with an eminent Roman. Suetonius also wrote biographies, using anecdotes to portray character. Suetonius's biographies of the emperors fall short of the literary and philosophical qualities of Plutarch's character studies and far short of Tacitus's histories. Suetonius delighted in the rumors of private scandals that surrounded the emperors and used personal vice to explain public failings.

In the later second century, Romans in general preferred the study and writing of philosophy, particularly stoicism, over history. The most influential Stoic philosopher of the century was Epictetus (ca. A.D. 55–135), a former slave who taught that man could be free by the control of his will and the cultivation of inner peace. Like the early Stoics, Epictetus taught the universal brotherhood of humankind and the identity of nature and divine providence. He urged his pupils to recognize that dependence on external things was the cause of unhappiness and therefore they should free themselves from reliance on material possessions, public esteem, and all other things prized by the worldly.

The slave's philosophy found its most eager pupil in an emperor. Marcus Aurelius (A.D. 161–180) reigned during a period when the stresses glimpsed by Hadrian were beginning to show in a much more alarming manner. Once more the Parthians attacked the eastern frontier, while in Britain and Germany barbarians struck across the borders. In 166 a confederation of barbarians known as the Marcomanni crossed the Danube and raided as far south as northern Italy. A plague, brought west by troops returning from the Parthian front, ravaged the whole empire. Like his predecessor Hadrian, Aurelius felt bound to endure the Scythian hoar-frosts rather than luxuriate in the taverns of Rome. He spent virtually the whole of his reign on the Danubian frontier, repelling the barbarians and shoring up the empire's defenses.

Throughout his reign Aurelius found consolation in the Stoic philosophy of Epictetus. In his soldier's tent at night he composed his *Meditations*, a volume of philosophical musings. Like the slave, the emperor sought freedom from the burden of his office in his will and in the proper understanding of his role in the divine order. He called himself to introspection, to a constant awareness, under the glories and honors heaped upon him by his entourage, of his true human nature: "A poor soul burdened with a corpse."

Aurelius's Stoic philosophy did not serve the empire well. For all his emphasis on understanding, Aurelius badly misjudged his son Commodus (A.D. 180–192), who succeeded him. Commodus, whose chief interest was in being a gladiator, saw himself the incarnation of Heracles and appeared in public clad as a gladiator and as consul. As Commodus sank into insanity, Rome was once more convulsed with purges and proscriptions. Commodus's assassination in 192 did not end the violence. The pax Romana was over.

*T*he Crisis of the Third Century

From the reign of Septimius Severus (193–211) to the time of Diocletian (284–305), both internal and external challenges shook the Roman Empire. The empire survived, but its social, political, and economic structures were radically transformed.

Sheer size was a fundamental problem for the empire. Haphazard expansion in many regions—to the north and west, for instance—overextended the frontiers. The manpower and resources needed to maintain this vast territory strained the economic system of the empire. Like a thread stretched to the breaking point, the thin line of border garrisons and forts was ready to snap.

The economic system itself was part of the reason for this strain on resources. For all of its commercial networks, the economy of the empire remained tied to agriculture. To the aristocrats of the ancient world, agriculture was the only honorable source of wealth. The goal of the successful merchant was to liquidate his commercial assets, buy estates, and rise into the leisured land-holding elite. As a result, liquid capital either for investment or taxation was always scarce.

The lack of sophistication in commercial and industrial business practice characterized the financial system of the empire as well. Government had always been conducted on the cheap. The tax system of the empire had never been very efficient at tapping into the real wealth of the aristocracy. Each individual city made its own collective assessments. Individuals eager to win the gratitude of their local communities were expected to provide essential services from their own pockets. Even with the vast wealth of the empire at its disposal, the government never developed a system of public debt—that is, a policy of borrowing against future revenues. As a result, the only way to solve short-term cash-flow problems was to debase the coinage by using more copper and less silver. This practice became epidemic in the third century, when the price of a bushel of wheat rose over 200 percent.

The failure of the empire to develop a stable political base complicated its economic problems. In times of emergency, imperial control relied on the personal presence and command of the emperor. As the empire grew, it became impossible for this presence to be felt everywhere. Moreover, the empire never developed either a regular system of imperial succession or an adequate power base. Control of the army, which was the ultimate source of imperial power, was possible only as long as the emperor was able to lead his armies to victory.

Enrich the Army and Scorn the Rest

Through much of the late second and third centuries, emperors failed dismally to lead their armies to victory. The barely Romanized provincials in the military bore the brunt of these attacks. When the emperors selected by the distant Roman Senate failed to win victory, front-line armies unhesitatingly raised their own commanders to the imperial office. These commanders set about restructuring the empire in favor of the army. They opened important administrative posts to soldiers, expanded the army's size, raised military pay, initiated expensive building programs in frontier settlements, and in general introduced authoritarian military discipline throughout society. To finance these costly measures, the new military government confiscated senatorial wealth, introduced new forms of taxation, and increasingly debased the coinage.

With their first rise in real income, soldiers in the provinces could improve their standard of living while in service and buy their way into provincial elites upon retirement. Free-spending soldiers and imperial extravagance helped the bleak settlements on the edges of military camps grow into prosperous cities with all the comforts of the older parts of the empire.

For the first time capable soldiers could hope to rise to the highest levels of public power regardless of their birth. One extraordinarily successful soldier was Publius Helvius Pertinax. Born the son of a freed slave in the north of Italy (Liguria) in 126, he abandoned a career as a schoolteacher to enter the military. By the time he was 50, his success as a military commander won for him the office of consul. He then held a series of military, civil, and proconsular positions in Syria, Britain, Italy, and Africa before returning to Rome. When the Emperor Commodus was murdered in 192, the palace guard proclaimed Pertinax emperor—the first emperor who had not come from the privileged senatorial class.

Soon, however, the military control of the empire turned into a nightmare even for the provinces and their armies. Exercising their newly discovered power, armies raised and then destroyed pretender after pretender, offering support to whichever imperial candidate promised them the greatest riches. Pertinax, the first of these soldier-emperors, was murdered by his soldiers less than three months after becoming emperor. The army's incessant demands for higher pay led emperors to lower the amount of silver in the coins with which the soldiers were paid. But the less the coins were worth, the more of them were necessary to purchase goods. And the more goods cost, the less valuable was the salary of the soldiers. Such drastic inflation wrecked the economic stability of the empire and spurred the army on to greater and more impossible demands for raises. Emperors who could not meet the demands were killed by their troops. In fact, the army was much more effective at killing emperors than enemies. Between 235 and 284, 17 of the 20 more or less legitimate emperors were assassinated or killed in civil war.

The crisis of the third century did not result only from economic and political instability within the empire. Rome's internal crises coincided with an increase of attacks from outside the empire. In Africa, Berber tribes harassed the frontiers. The Sassanid dynasty in Persia threatened Rome's eastern frontier. When the Emperor Valerian (253–260) attempted to prevent the

Persian king of kings Shapur I from seizing Roman Mesopotamia and Armenia, he was captured and held prisoner for the rest of his life.

The greatest danger to Rome came not from the south or east, but rather from the west. There, along the Rhine, various Germanic tribes known collectively as the Franks and the Alemanni began raiding expeditions into the empire. Along the lower Danube and in southern Ukraine, the Gothic confederation raided the Balkans and harassed Roman shipping on the Black Sea.

An Empire on the Defensive

The central administration of the empire simply could not deal effectively with the numerous barbarian attacks. Left on their own, regional provincial commanders at times even headed separatist movements. Provincial aristocrats who despaired of receiving any help from distant Rome often supported these pretenders. One such commander was Postumus, whom the armies of Spain, Britain, and Gaul proclaimed emperor. His nine-year separatist reign (ca. 258–268) was the longest and most stable of that of any emperor, legitimate or otherwise, throughout this whole troubled period.

Political and military instability had devastating effects on the lives of ordinary people. Citizenship had been extended to virtually all free inhabitants of the empire in 212, but that right was a formality given simply to enlarge the tax base, since only citizens paid inheritance taxes. Society became sharply divided into the privileged *honestiores*—senators, municipal gentry, and the military—and the increasingly burdened *humiliores*—everyone else. The humiliores suffered the most from the tax increases because unlike the honestiores they could neither bribe their way out of them nor intimidate tax collectors with private armies. They were also frequent targets of extortion by the military and of violence perpetrated by bandits.

Slave and peasant bandits, rustlers, and even pirates played an ambivalent role in society. Often they terrorized the countryside, descending from the hills to attack villages or travelers. However, at times they also protected peasants from greedy tax collectors and military commanders. In Gaul and Spain,

This cameo was made to the order of Shapur I after the capture of Valerian during the great battle near Antioch in A.D. 260. The symbolic scene has Shapur seizing Valerian simply by grasping his hand.

peasants and local leaders organized armed resistance movements, termed *Bacaudae*, to withstand the exorbitant demands of tax collectors. In the first centuries of the empire bandits operated primarily in peripheral areas recently and poorly subjugated to Roman rule. In the late second and third centuries they became an increasing problem in Italy itself.

The Barbarian World

Compounding the internal violence that threatened to destroy the Roman Empire were the external attacks of the Germanic barbarians. These attacks reflected changes within the Germanic world as profound as those within the empire. Between the second and fifth centuries the Germanic world was transformed from a mosaic of small decentralized, agricultural tribes into a number of powerful military tribal confederations capable of challenging Rome itself. We cannot understand the impact of the barbarians on the empire without understanding the social and political organization and the transformation of these people living beyond the frontier.

The Germanic peoples typically inhabited small villages organized into patriarchal households, integrated into clans, which in turn composed tribes. For the most part, clans governed themselves, and except in war tribal leaders had little authority over their followers. In the second century many tribes had kings, but they were religious rather than political leaders.

Germanic communities lived by farming, but cattle raising and especially warfare carried the highest social prestige. Men measured their status by the number of cattle they owned and by their martial ability. Women took care of agricultural chores and household duties. Like the number of cattle, the number of wives showed a man's social position. Polygyny was common among chiefs.

Warfare defined social groupings, and warriors dominated public life. Only within the clan was fighting inappropriate. But rival clans within the same tribe dealt with one another brutally. Conflict took the form of the feud, and each act of aggression was repaid in kind. If an individual within a clan had a grievance with an individual within another clan, all his kinsmen were obliged to assist him. Thus a single incident could result in a continuous escalation of acts of revenge.

Clans in other tribes were fair game for raiding, looting, and conquering. Individuals, clans, and tribes built their wealth and reputations on warfare. The more successful a tribe was in warfare, the more clans it attracted and the greater its position became in the barbarian world.

The practice of feuding, especially within the tribe, had enormous costs. Families were decimated and strong warriors who were needed to defend the tribe from outside attack faced constant danger from members of their own tribe. Thus tribal leaders attempted to reduce hostilities by establishing payments called *wergeld* in place of the blood vengeance demanded in reparation for crimes. Such *wergeld*, normally paid in cattle or slaves, was voluntary, since the right of vengeance was generally recognized, and the unity of the tribe remained precarious.

Tribes also attempted to reinforce unity through religious cults involving shared myths of common ancestry and rituals intended to underline group cohesion. Drinking was the most important of these rituals. When not fighting, Germanic warriors spent much of their time drinking beer together at the table of their war leader. Because it provided the most ready means of preserving grain, beer was a staple of Germanic diet. Communal beer drinking was also a way of uniting potentially hostile neighbors. Not surprisingly, it could also lead to drunken brawls that reopened the very feuds drinking bouts were intended to end. These feuds could in turn lead to the hiving off of irreconcilable factions, which might in time form their own tribes.

In contrast to the familial structure of barbarian society stood another warrior group that cut across kindred and even tribal units. This was the warrior band, called in Latin the *comitatus*. Some young warriors formed personal bonds with particularly able leaders and pledged them absolute loyalty. In return the leaders were obligated to lead their warriors to victory and to share with them the spoils of war. These warrior societies, far from being the basic units of a larger tribal military force, were organized for their own plunder and fighting. While they might be a valuable aid in intertribal warfare, they could also shatter the fragile peace by conducting raids on neighbors, thus bringing whole tribes into internal conflict. Successful warrior leaders might draw sufficient numbers of followers and conquer so many other groups that in time the band would become a new tribe.

This intratribal and intertribal violence produced a rough equilibrium of power and wealth as long as small Germanic tribes lived in isolation. The presence of the Roman Empire, felt both directly and indirectly in the barbarian world, upset this equilibrium. Unintentionally, Rome itself helped transform the Germanic tribes into the major threat to the imperial system.

The direct presence of Roman merchants extended only about a hundred miles beyond the frontiers into "free Germany." However, the attraction of Roman luxury goods and the Romans' efforts to establish friendly Germanic buffer zones along the borders drew even distant tribes into the Roman imperial system. Across the barbarian world, tribal leaders and comitatus leaders sought the prestige that Roman goods brought them. Roman provincial commanders encouraged these leaders to enter into commercial arrangements with the Romans. In exchange for their cattle, which the Romans needed for their troops, the Germanic leaders received gold and grain. This outside source of wealth greatly increased economic disparity within Germanic society. In addition, some leaders made treaties with Rome, thus receiving the advantage of Roman support, which other tribal leaders lacked. In return for payments of gold and foodstuffs, chieftains of these "federated" tribes agreed to oppose tribes hostile to Rome and to prevent young hotheads of their own tribes from raiding across the frontier. Some chiefs supplied warriors for the Roman army. Others even led their comitatus into Roman service. By the late third century the Roman army included Franks, Goths, and

Saxons serving as far away from their homes as Egypt. Such "imperial Germans" moved back and forth between the Roman and barbarian worlds, using each as a foundation for increased power in the other and obscuring the cultural and political differences between the two.

The effects of contact between barbarians and Romans reached far and wide throughout the empire and beyond the frontier. Along the Rhine and Danube, the result was the so-called West Germanic Revolution. In order to survive in a time of constant warfare, tribes had to become armies. The armies needed a united and effective leadership. Among most of the western Germanic peoples, the tradition of the older tribal king was abandoned. A new kind of nonroyal chieftain emerged as the war leader of the people and as the representative of the war god Woden. In the later second and third centuries the turmoil resulted in the formation of new tribes and tribal confederations—the Marcomanni, the Alemanni, and the Franks. By the end of the second century this internal barbarian transformation spilled over into the empire in the form of the Marcomannian wars and the Saxon, Frankish, and Alemannic incursions into the western provinces.

Around the same time, along the Oder and Vistula rivers to the north, a group later known as the Goths began their slow consolidation around a royal family. The Goths were unique in that their kings exercised more military authority than was usual for a Germanic tribe. These kings formed the nucleus of a constantly changing barbarian group. A Goth was not necessarily a biological descendant of the small second-century tribe living along the shore of the Baltic. Anyone who fought alongside the Gothic king was a Goth.

Between the second and fourth centuries, the bearers of this Gothic royal tradition began to filter to the south and east, ultimately transferring their model of barbarian organization to the area of present-day Kiev in southern Ukraine. This move was not so much a physical migration of thousands of people across Europe as the gradual confederation under Gothic leadership of various Germanic, Slavic, and Scythian peoples living around the Black Sea. By the early third century this Gothic confederation was strong enough to challenge Roman supremacy in the region. These first Gothic wars in the east were even more devastating than the later wars in the west.

$\mathcal{T}$he Empire Restored

By the last decades of the third century, the empire seemed in danger of crumbling under combined internal and external pressure. That it did not was largely due to the efforts of the soldier-emperor Aurelian (270–275), who was able to repulse the barbarians, restore the unity of the empire, and then set about stabilizing the internal imperial structure.

Diocletian the God-Emperor

Diocletian (284–305), a Dalmatian soldier who had risen through the ranks to become emperor, completed the process of stabilization and reorganization of the imperial system begun by Aurelian. The result was a regime that in some ways increased imperial power and in other ways simply did away with the pretenses that had previously masked the emperor's true position.

No longer was the emperor *princeps*, or "first citizen." Now he was *dominus*, or "lord," the term of respect used by slaves in addressing their masters. He also assumed the title of *Iovius*, or Jupiter, thus claiming divine status, and demanded adoration as a living god. Diocletian recognized that the empire was too large and complex for one man to rule. To solve the problem, he divided the empire into eastern and western parts, each part to be ruled by both an augustus and a junior emperor, or caesar. Diocletian was augustus in the east, supported by his caesar, Galerian. In the west the rulers were the augustus Maximian and his caesar, Constantius.

In theory this tetrarchy, or rule by four, provided for regular succession. The caesars, who were married to daughters of the augusti, were to succeed them. Although from time to time subsequent emperors would rule alone, Diocletian's innovation proved successful and enduring. The empire was divided administratively into eastern and western parts until the death of Julius Nepos, the last legitimate emperor in the west, in 480.

In addition to this constitutional reform, Diocletian enacted or consolidated a series of measures to improve the functioning of the imperial

The tetrarchy was an attempt to regulate the succession. Here, the emperors Diocletian and Maximian are depicted with their caesars, Constantius of the West and Galerius of the East, who were their respective sons-in-law.

administration. He reorganized and expanded the army, approximately doubled the number of provinces, separated their military and civil administration, and greatly increased the number of bureaucrats to administer them. He attempted to stem runaway inflation by increasing the amount of silver in coins and fixing maximum prices and wages throughout the empire. He restructured the imperial tax system, basing it on payments in goods and produce in order to distribute the burden more equitably on all citizens and to avoid problems of currency debasement.

The pillar of Diocletian's success was his victorious military machine. He was effective because, like the barbarian chieftains who had turned their tribes into armies, he militarized society and led this military society to victory. Like Diocletian himself, his soldiers were drawn from provincial marginal regions. They showed tremendous devotion to their god-emperor. By the time of Diocletian's reign, a career such as that of Pertinax (p. 166) had become the rule for emperors rather than the exception.

Some aspects of Diocletian's program, such as the improvement of the civil administration and the military, were successful. Others, such as the reform of silver currency and wage and price controls, were dismal failures. One effect of the fiscal reforms was to bind *colons*, or hereditary tenant farmers, to their lands, since they were forbidden to leave the villages where they were registered to pay their taxes. In this practice lay the origins of European serfdom. Another effect was the gradual destruction of the local city councils, since their members, the *decurions*, were held personally responsible for the payment of local assessments whether or not they could be collected from the other inhabitants. In time this led to the dissolution of local civil government.

All of these measures were designed to marshal the entire population in the monumental task of preserving *Romanitas*. Central to this task was the proper reverential attitude toward the divine emperors who directed it. One group seemed stubbornly opposed to this heroic effort: the Christians. In 298 an incident occurred that seemed to confirm their subversive attitude. At a sacrifice in the presence of Diocletian, the Roman priests were unable to obtain the desired favorable omens, and they attributed their failure to the presence of Christians, who were crossing themselves to ward off demons. Such blasphemous conduct—it might be compared, for instance, to desecrating the flag at a public assembly—led to the beginning of the Great Persecution, which formally began in 303 and lasted sporadically until 313. It resulted in the death of hundreds of Christians who refused to sacrifice to the pagan gods.

Constantine the Emperor of God

In 305, in the midst of the Great Persecution, Diocletian and his co-augustus Maximian took the extraordinary step of abdicating in favor of their caesars, Galerius and Constantius. This abdication was intended to provide for an orderly succession. Instead, the sons of Constantius and Maximian, Constantine (306–337) and Maxentius (306–312), drawing on the prejudice of the increasingly barbarian armies toward hereditary succession, set about wrecking the tetrarchy. In so doing they plunged the empire once more into civil war as they fought over the western half of the empire.

Victory in the west came to Constantine in 312, when he defeated and killed Maxentius in a battle at the Mulvian Bridge outside Rome. Constantine attributed his victory to a vision telling him to paint a ⳨ on the shields of his soldiers. For pagans this symbol indicated the solar emblem of the cult of the Unconquered Sun. For Christians it was the Chi-Rho, ☧, formed from the first two letters of the Greek word for Christ. The next year in Milan Constantine rescinded the persecution of Christians and granted Christian clergy the same privileges enjoyed by pagan priests. Constantine himself was not baptized until near death, a common practice in antiquity. However, during his reign Christianity grew from a persecuted minority to the most favored cult in the empire.

Almost as important as Constantine's conversion to Christianity was his decision to establish his capital in Byzantium, a city founded by Greek colonists on the narrow neck of water connecting the Black Sea to the Mediterranean. He transformed and enriched this small town, calling it the New Rome. Later it was known as Constantinople, the city of Constantine. For the next 11 centuries Constantinople served as the heart of the Roman and then the Byzantine world. From his new city, Constantine began to transform the empire into a Christian state and Christianity into a Roman state religion.

The effects of Constantine's conversion on the empire and on Christianity were obvious and enormous. Constantine himself continued to maintain cordial relations with representatives of all cults and to use ambiguous language that would offend no one when talking about "the deity." His successors were less broad-minded. They quickly reversed the positions of Christianity and paganism. In 341 pagan sacrifice was banned, and by 355 the temples had been closed and the death penalty for sacrificing to the gods had been decreed, although not enforced.

While paganism was being disestablished, Christianity was rapidly becoming the established religion. Constantine made enormous financial contributions to Christian communities to repay them for their losses during persecutions. He erected rich churches on the model of Roman basilicas, or administrative buildings, and converted temples into Christian places of worship. He gave bishops the authority to act as magistrates within the Christian community. Once the particular objects of persecution, bishops became favored courtiers. Constantine attempted to make himself the de facto head of the Church. He even presided at the Council of Nicaea in 325, at which the assembled bishops condemned the Arian teaching that Jesus as Son of God was not equal to God the Father. Constantine and his successors, with the exception of his nephew Julian (361–363), who attempted unsuccessfully both to reestablish paganism and to promote traditional Hellenism, sought to use the cult of the one God to strengthen their control over the empire.

Although imperial support was essential to the spread of Christianity in the fourth century, other factors encouraged conversion as well. Christian miracles, particularly that of exorcism, or casting out of demons, won many converts. The ancient world was filled with *daimons*, supernatural creatures whose power for good or ill no one doubted. Wandering Christian preachers seemed more competent than others to deal with these tormentors, proving that their God was more powerful than the spirits and that their message was worthy of a hearing. Over the course of the fourth century, the number of Christians rose from 5 to 30 million. Imperial support, miracles, and preaching could not, by themselves, account for this phenomenal growth. Physical coercion played a large part. The story was told that in one town, upon imperial command, all of the local temples were destroyed and "a great number" of leading pagans who refused conversion were tortured to death. The remaining pagan population converted. Whether or not the story is true, it illustrates the essential role that naked force often played in the process of conversion. Conversion—by whatever method—also suited the emperors, who saw a unified cult as an essential means of bolstering their position.

A Parting of the Ways

The emperors and the empire needed bolstering in 376 when the Huns, a nomadic horse people from central Asia, swept into the Black Sea region and threw the entire barbarian world once more into chaos. The Huns quickly destroyed the Gothic confederation and absorbed many of the peoples who had constituted the Goths. Others sought protection in the empire. The Visigoths, as they came to be known, were the largest of these groups, and their fate illustrated how precarious existence could be for all the occupants of the imperial frontier. Driven from their lands and thus from their food supply, the Visigoths turned to the empire for assistance. But the Roman authorities treated them as brutally as had the Huns, forcing some to sell their children into slavery in return for morsels of dog flesh. In despair the Visigoths rose up against the Romans, and against all odds their desperate rebellion succeeded. They annihilated an imperial army at Adrianople in 378, and the emperor Valens himself was killed. His successor, Theodosius (379–395), was forced to allow the Visigoths to settle along the Danube and to be governed by their own leaders despite the fact that they lived within the boundaries of the empire.

Theodosius's treaty with the Visigoths set an ominous precedent. Never before had a barbarian people been allowed to settle as a political unit within the empire. Within a few years, the Visigoths were again on the move, traveling across the Balkans into Italy under the command of their chieftain Alaric (ca. 370–410). In 410 they captured Rome and sacked it for three days, an event that sent shock waves throughout the entire empire. The symbolic effect of the Visigoths' victory far exceeded the amount of real damage, which was

The Later Roman Empire

Septimius Severus	193–211
Valerian	253–260
Aurelian	270–275
(West) Maximian	286–305
(East) Diocletian	284–305
(West) Maxentius	306–312
Constantine	306–337
Julian	361–363
(West) Valentinian I	364–375
(East) Valens	364–378
Theodosius	379–395

relatively light. Only after Alaric's death did the Visigoths leave Italy, ultimately settling in Spain and southern Gaul with the approval of the emperor.

The Barbarization of the West

Rome did not fall. It was transformed. Romans participated in and even encouraged this transformation. Roman accommodation with the Visigoths set the pattern for subsequent settlement of barbarians in the western half of the empire. By this time, barbarians made up the bulk of the imperial army, and commanders were frequently themselves barbarians. Indeed, these so-called imperial Germans had often proven even more loyal to Rome than the Roman provincial populations they were to protect. In the late fourth and fifth centuries, emperors accepted whole barbarian peoples as integral parts of the Roman army and settled them within the empire.

The Visigothic kingdom in southern Gaul and Spain was typical in this respect. Alaric's successor, Ataulf, was extremely eager to win the approval of the emperor. He married Galla Placidia, the daughter of the Emperor Theodosius and the sister of Emperor Honorius, in a Roman ceremony in Narbonne in 414. Soon afterward he established a government at Bordeaux directed by Gallo-Roman aristocrats. Although his opponents soon assassinated him, his successors concluded a treaty with Constantinople in which the Visigoths were recognized as a legitimate, established political presence within the empire.

The Visigoths were not the only powerful barbarian people to challenge the empire. The Vandals, who had entered the empire in 406, crossed over into

Africa, the richest region of the western empire, and quickly conquered it. In 455 they sacked Rome much more thoroughly than had the Goths 45 years earlier.

Another threat appeared in the 430s, when the Huns, formerly Roman allies, invaded the empire under their charismatic leader Attila (ca. 406–453). Although defeated in Gaul by a combined army of barbarians under the command of the Roman general Flavius Aëtius in 451, they turned toward Italy and penetrated as far as Rome. There they were stopped not by the rapidly disintegrating imperial forces but by the bishop of Rome, Pope Leo I, who met Attila before the city's gates. What transpired between the two is not known, but Attila's subsequent withdrawal from Italy vastly increased the prestige of the papacy. Now not only were popes successors of Saint Peter and bishops of the principal city of the west, but they were replacing the emperor as protector of the city. The foundations of the political power of the papacy were established.

The confederation of the Huns collapsed after the death of Attila in 453, but imperial power did not revive in Italy. A series of incompetent emperors were pushed aside by barbarian generals who assumed power in the peninsula and sought recognition from Zeno, the emperor in the east. However, after the death of the last legitimate western emperor, Julius Nepos, in 480, Zeno conferred the title of patrician on the Ostrogothic king Theodoric. In 489 Theodoric invaded Italy with imperial blessing and established himself as ruler. Imperial presence had ceased to exist in Italy.

In Gaul, between the Seine and the Loire, the Roman general Flavius Aëtius and, after his death, the general Syagrius continued to represent some imperial presence. But the armies that Aëtius and Syagrius commanded consisted entirely of barbarians, particularly of Visigoths and Franks, and they represented the interests of local aristocratic factions rather than those of Constantinople. So thoroughly barbarized had these last Roman commanders become in their military command and political control that the barbarians referred to Syagrius as "king of the Romans." Ultimately in 486 Syagrius was defeated and replaced by the Frank Clovis, son of his military commander Childeric, probably with the blessing of the emperor.

Britain met a similar fate. Abandoned by Roman legions around 407, the Romano-Celtic population in this province concluded a treaty with bands of Saxons and Angles to protect Britain from other barbarian raiders. As had happened elsewhere in the empire, the barbarians came as federated troops and stayed as rulers. Gradually, during the fifth century, Germanic warrior groups conquered much of the island. The Anglo-Saxons pushed the native inhabitants to the west and the north. There, as the Cornish and the Welsh, they preserved the Christian religion but largely lost their other Roman traditions.

The establishment of barbarian kingdoms within the Roman world meant the end of the western empire as a political entity. However, the emperors east and west continued to pretend that all these barbarian peoples, with the exception of the Vandals, were Roman troops commanded by loyal Roman officers who happened to be of barbarian origin. Occasionally emperors granted them portions of abandoned lands or existing estates. Local Roman elites considered these leaders rude and uncultured barbarians who neverthe-less could be made to serve these elites' own interests more easily than better educated imperial bureaucrats.

As a result, the aristocracy of the west, the *maiores*, viewed the decay of the civil government without dismay. This decay was due largely to the poverty of the imperial treasury. In the fifth century the entire public revenues of the west amounted to little more than the annual incomes of a few wealthy private aristocrats. Managing to escape both taxation and the jurisdiction of public officials, these individuals carved out for themselves vast estates, which they and their families controlled with private armies and which they governed as virtually autonomous lordships. Ordinary freemen, pressed by the remnants of imperial taxation and by barbarians, were forced into accepting the protection and hence control offered by aristocrats, who thereby came to control whole villages and districts.

The primary source of friction between barbarians and provincial elites was religion. Many Goths had converted to Christianity around the time that the Huns had destroyed the Gothic confederation. However, they had chosen the Arian form of Christianity in order to appease the Arian emperors Constantius and Valens. But the Goths and most other barbarian peoples held to their Arian form of faith long after it had been abandoned in the empire. Thus, wherever the barbarians settled, they were met with distrust and hostility from the orthodox clergy. In southern Gaul and Italy this hostility created serious difficulties because during the fifth century bishops had assumed many of the traditional duties and powers held by provincial Roman administrators.

In Gaul, bishops were regularly selected from members of the greatest Gallo-Roman senatorial families, establishing veritable episcopal dynasties. In Italy and Spain too, bishops were drawn from the landed aristocracy. These bishops, most of whom were elected after long years of outstanding secular leadership, served as the primary protectors and administrators of their communities, filling the vacuum left by the erosion of other civil offices.

Barbarian military leaders needed local ties by which to govern the large indigenous populations over whom they ruled. They found cooperation with these aristocrats both necessary and advantageous. Thus while individual landowners might have suffered in the transition from Roman to barbarian rule, for the most part this transition took place with less disturbance of the local social or political scene than was once thought. During the fifth century the imperial presence simply faded away as barbarian kings came to rule in the name of the emperor. After 480, the emperor resided exclusively in the east. The last western emperors disappeared without serious opposition either from western aristocrats or from their eastern colleagues.

The Hellenization of the East

The eastern half of the empire, in contrast to the west, managed to survive and even to prosper in the fifth and sixth centuries. In the east, beginning in 400, the trends toward militarization and barbarization of the administration were reversed, the strength of the imperial government was reaffirmed, and the vitality and integrity of the empire were restored.

Several reasons account for the contrast between east and west. First, the east had always been more urbanized and civilized than the west. It had an old tradition of civil control that antedated the Roman Empire itself. When the decay of Roman traditions allowed regionalism and tribalism to arise in the west, the same decay brought in the east a return to Hellenistic traditions. Second, the east had never developed the tradition of public poverty and private wealth characteristic of the west. In the east, tax revenues continued to support an administrative apparatus, which remained in the hands of civilians rather than barbarian military commanders. Moreover, the local aristocracies in the eastern provinces never achieved the wealth and independence of their western counterparts. Finally, Christian bishops, frequently divided over doctrinal issues, never managed to monopolize either sacred power, which was shared by itinerant holy men and monks, or secular power, which was wielded by imperial agents. Thus under the firm direction of its emperors, especially Theodosius and later Zeno, the eastern empire not only survived but prepared for a new expansionist phase under the emperor Justinian.

Everywhere, the patina of Latin culture began to wear thin as provincials began to rise to positions of prominence and power. In the east, this meant the reemergence of regional cultures and especially of Hellenistic traditions. It also meant that Christian and pagan thinkers would use these traditions to interpret the crises of their world.

*T*he Crisis of Elite Culture

The transformation of the classical world from a pagan empire, secure in its mastery over the civilized world, to a fragmented Christian one was as profoundly felt in the cultural sphere as it was in the political and social spheres. Crisis forces choice, and in the third through fifth centuries the choices faced by intellectuals were as profound as those faced by emperors. Where should one look for peace—within or without? Ought Christians to reject the intellectual tradition of the Greco-Roman world or recast it in Christian form? Finally, was the Roman political system in which Christianity had become so deeply embedded essential to its survival?

Three very different figures—Plotinus, Origen, and Augustine—exemplify this transformation and set the stage for future European cultural developments. During the crisis of the third century, Hellenistic culture reached its zenith in the life and work of the pagan Egyptian philosopher Plotinus (205–270), who recast Platonism into the form that was the foundation of Christian, Islamic, and Jewish thought through the Middle Ages. His contemporary and compatriot Origen (185–254) began to intellectualize the meaning of the Christian Scriptures and transformed pagan philosophy into a Christian intellectual tradition. As a result of his work Christian intellectuals could no longer be dismissed as "wool seekers, cobblers, laundry workers, and the most illiterate and rustic yokels." In the following century Augustine of Hippo (354–430) faced a new, internal challenge. Victory over paganism was quickly followed by serious disagreements over the proper relationship between the Christian community and the Christian empire. In the early period of Christianity the question was whether to be a Christian meant to be a Jew. Now Augustine had to decide whether to be a Christian meant to be a Roman.

Living in Harmony with the Universe

Plotinus exemplified the vital Hellenistic high culture of late antiquity. He was born in a small provincial town in Upper Egypt, but his restless intellect led him first to dabble in Gnosticism and then to travel to Mesopotamia in the hope of studying Persian and Indian philosophy. The crucial event in his life was his introduction to Platonic philosophy as a student in Alexandria in his late twenties. The new, or Neoplatonic tradition, which he studied and of which he became the principal spokesperson, was by the third century much more than a philosophy. It was a virtual religion, combining Platonic and Stoic thought and demanding withdrawal from the world and full-time dedication to the pursuit of wisdom.

Plotinus and his fellow Neoplatonists believed that through rational contemplation it was possible to see beyond material existence and to recognize the intimate connection between the invisible God and the visible world. This intimate connection was made through an unbroken chain of

Relief from the tomb of a Roman man of letters, thought to be Plotinus (late third to fourth century). As he studies a scroll, he is surrounded by sages and disciples. A bundle of books reposes at his feet.

intermediate beings linking God, who was beyond all knowing, to creatures and especially to man. The most important link in this chain was the World Soul, and this link between the universe and God was reflected in the relationship between the body and the soul. Material and spiritual reality were thus intimately and properly associated.

Plotinus thus molded the major philosophical traditions of antiquity into a way of life and an understanding of the universe in which man and God were intimately interconnected. For those too ignorant or superstitious to see the beauty of this harmony, especially Christians, Plotinus and his followers had nothing but scorn. And yet the same Alexandrian teacher who instructed Plotinus had another, even more influential student. He also taught Origen, who would reconcile Christianity and classical philosophy.

Inventing the Christian Intellectual

Origen was born into a Christian family in Alexandria, then the most cultivated city of the Hellenistic world, and grew up with an acute sense of the challenge of being a Christian. When Origen was 17 his father was executed for his faith and his property was confiscated. To support his mother and six younger brothers, Origen began to teach rhetoric, that is, traditional pagan learning. Later he headed the Christian education program of Alexandria. While still a layman, his reputation spread throughout the empire. Important Christians and pagans sought his advice. However, his brilliant career and his bold teachings infuriated his jealous bishop in Alexandria, who attacked him for personal and heretical improprieties. The pope ultimately confirmed these charges, but this judgment was never recognized in much of the east. Origen followed in his father's footsteps and died a martyr in 254.

Origen invented a new sort of Christian, the Christian intellectual. Intellectuals like Plotinus had condemned Christians as superstitious ignoramuses because they sought truth in Scripture rather than in philosophical reason. Origen moved Christian teaching from a literal to a symbolic understanding of Scripture and gave it a sound philosophical foundation by synthesizing the Neoplatonic tradition, represented by Plotinus, with Christianity.

Initially Origen had accepted the literal sense of Scripture. But eventually he rejected such a literal and destructive meaning of Scripture as he came to realize the importance of symbolism. He applied to Scripture the same sort of symbolic analysis pagan scholars had used to understand the classics of the Greek and Roman traditions. For Origen the Scriptures became a symbol of God's eternal teaching—incomprehensible to those who sought a literal meaning but apparent to those who looked for the hidden spiritual message. This allegorical tradition would dominate Christian biblical studies for over a thousand years.

Against the charge of anti-intellectualism leveled at Christianity, Origen replied that since God endowed humans with reason, he must have intended that they reach true wisdom through reason. Only because people failed at the task did God give them revelation. "It is far better to accept doctrines with reason and wisdom," he wrote, "than with mere faith." Origen's insistence that there was no contradiction between faith and reason established an intellectual basis for Christianity that continued through Western history.

Finding the City of God

Origen was the father of Christian philosophy. Augustine was the father of Christian political science. Born into a well-off North African family in the town of Tagaste, he was quickly drawn into the good life and upward mobility open to bright young provincials in the fourth century. In his *Confessions*, the first psychological autobiography, Augustine describes how his skills in rhetoric took him to the provincial capital of Carthage and then on to Rome and finally Milan, the western imperial residence, where he gained fame as one of the foremost rhetoricians of the empire.

Connections as well as talent contributed to his rise to fame. Although his mother was a Christian, he was not baptized at birth, and while in Carthage he joined the Manichees, a materialist dualist sect which taught that good and evil were caused by two different ultimate principles and which rejected the notion of spiritual reality. As protégé of the Manichees, Augustine gained introductions to the leading pagan aristocrats of his day.

While in Milan, Augustine came into contact with kinds of people he had never encountered in Africa, particularly with Neoplatonists and Christians. The most important of these was Ambrose, bishop of Milan. The encounter with a spiritual philosophy and a Christianity compatible with it profoundly changed the young professor. After a period of agonized searching, Augustine converted to the new religion. Abandoning his Italian life, he returned to the North African town of Hippo to found a monastery where he could devote himself to reading the Scriptures. However, his neighbors were determined to harness the intellectual talents of their brilliant native son. When their bishop died, they forcibly seized Augustine and made him their bishop.

Augustine spent the remainder of his life as bishop of this small provincial town, but his reputation as spokesperson for the Christian tradition spread throughout the empire. Much of his episcopal career was spent in debates with enemies within and without the Church. Chief among the former were the Donatists, a North African sect, and the Pelagians, who taught that humans were responsible for their own salvation. Enemies outside the Church were the defenders of the pagan Roman tradition.

All three of these groups represented sincere responses to the challenges of the new Christian empire. The Donatists had developed in North Africa as a response to the political conversions of the early fourth century. During the last persecutions many Christians and even bishops had collaborated with Roman authorities, handing over sacred Scriptures to be burned. Disturbed by the ease with which these traitors (our word *traitor* comes from the Latin verb *tradere* "to hand over") had returned to positions of power in the Church under

Constantine and by the growth of political conversions, the Donatists insisted that the Church had to be pure and its ministers blameless. Thus they argued that baptisms and ordinations performed by these traitors were invalid.

The Pelagians also held themselves to a higher standard than that of ordinary Christians, who accepted sin as an inevitable part of human life. Pelagians believed rather that human nature had been so created that people could achieve perfection in this life. They believed that members of the true Church were those who perfected themselves by the force of their own wills, thus making a radical break with the compromising world in which they lived.

These appeals to heroic virtue were paralleled in the attacks launched against Christianity by the remaining adherents to the cult of the old Roman gods. The disasters of recent history and in particular the sack of Rome had occurred, they argued, because the west had abandoned the gods and the traditions of Roman virtue and justice that had made Rome great.

In responding to these attacks, Augustine elaborated a new Christian understanding of human society and the individual's relationship to God, which dominated Western thought for the next 15 centuries. He argued that the true members of God's elect necessarily coexisted in the world with sinners. No earthly community, not even the empire or the Church, was the true "city of God." Earthly society participated in the true "city of God" through the sacraments and did so quite apart from the individual worthiness of the recipients or even of the ministers of these rites. Salvation came through the Church, but the saved were not identified solely with any particular group of Christians. In this way, Augustine argued for a distinction between the visible Christian empire and the Christian community. Earlier, Paul, the pharisaic Jew, had determined that Christianity would survive Judaism even as the latter was being persecuted by Rome. Now Augustine, the Roman rhetorician, determined that Christianity would survive the disappearance of the Roman Empire just as it was disintegrating into barbarian kingdoms. Even as Augustine lay dying in Hippo, the city was under siege by the Vandals.

*T*he Transformation of Popular Culture

The responses of Plotinus, Origen, and Augustine to the choices of late antiquity were fundamental for the subsequent intellectual development of Western civilization. On a more popular level a different sort of Christian had an equally profound influence on the future. This was the hermit, monk, or recluse, who taught less by his or her words than by his or her life, a life often so unusual that even the most ignorant and worldly citizen of the late empire could recognize in it the power of God. Beneath the apparent eccentricity, however, lay a fundamental principle: the radical rejection of society's values in favor of absolute dedication to God's.

While Plotinus was teaching in the serenity of his Roman villa, and shortly after Origen had died fighting for the integrity of the Christian intellectual tradition, another Egyptian was undertaking a different path to enduring fame. Anthony (ca. 250–355), a well-to-do peasant, heard the same biblical text that later converted Augustine, "Go, sell all you have and give to the poor and follow me." Anthony was uneducated; it was said that he had been too shy as a boy to attend school. This straightforward peasant did exactly what the text commanded. He disposed of all his goods and left his village for the Egyptian desert. There, for the next 70 years, he sought to follow Christ in a life of constant self-mortification and prayer.

This dropout from civilization deeply touched his fellow Christians, many of whom were disturbed by the abrupt transformation of their religion from persecuted minority to privileged majority. By the time of his death this monk—the word comes from the Greek *monos*, alone—found himself the head of a large loosely knit community of like-minded persons who looked to him as spiritual father, or abbot. Over the next centuries thousands rejected the worldliness of civilization and the easy life of the average Christian to lead a monastic life in the wildernesses of the empire.

Monastic Communities

Monasticism took two forms, communal organization or solitary life. Pachomius (ca. 290–346) and Basil the Great (ca. 329–379) in the east and Benedict of Nursia (ca. 480–547) in the west perfected the communal life. Faced with the impossibility of surviving in a harsh environment without cooperation, Egyptian monks banded together into small monastic towns. In these monasteries lived as many as two thousand monks. They placed themselves under the control of the abbot, who served as spiritual guide and administrator of the community. These men and women sought spiritual perfection through physical self-mortification and through the subordination of their own wills to that of the abbot. Monks drank no wine, ate no meat, used no oil. They spent their days in prayer, either communal or individual. During the fourth century this monastic tradition spread east to Bethlehem, Jerusalem, Caesarea, and Constantinople and west to Rome, Milan, Trier, Marseille, and Tours. In the following centuries it reached beyond the borders of the empire when Egyptian-style monasticism was introduced into Ireland.

Intellectuals as well as peasants heard the call of monastic life. Chief among the intellectuals was Jerome (ca. 347–420), the greatest linguist of antiquity, who was so impressed by a visit to the monastic communities of the east that he became a priest and founded a monastery in Bethlehem. There he translated the Bible into Latin. This Latin translation, known as the Vulgate, became the standard version of Christian Scripture in the west until the Reformation and, in Roman Catholic countries, until the twentieth century.

In the Greek-speaking world, the definitive form of the monastic community was provided by Basil the Great. Basil had visited the monasteries of

Egypt, Palestine, and Syria before founding his own monastery at Pontus near his family estate at Annesi in present-day Turkey. Although he did not write a specific rule for the governance of his monastery, his collection of commentaries and spiritual advice to his followers outlined a form of monastic life in which a day of agriculture, craft work, and care for the sick and the poor was organized within an ordered progression of liturgical prayer. His emphasis on communal life rather than on heroic acts of individual asceticism provided the model for eastern monasticism from his day to the present.

Unlike Anthony of Egypt, Basil was a brilliant and well-educated intellectual who frequently left his monastery to throw himself into the ecclesiastical politics of the empire. By the end of his life Basil had become bishop of Caesarea. Eastern monastic communities continued this active involvement in political and secular affairs. Monasteries provided the early religious training for most religious leaders. Monks and abbots often involved themselves wholeheartedly in the politics of the empire. Monks rioting in the streets of Constantinople over political issues was a familiar sight for over a thousand years.

In the west, Benedict of Nursia was as influential in structuring communal religious life as Basil in the east. In time Benedict became abbot of a small community of monks at Monte Cassino, between Rome and Naples. The rule that he drafted for the governance of his community, while drawn largely from earlier monastic rules circulating in Italy, became the definitive statement of western monasticism. Benedict's rule encouraged moderation and flexibility while emphasizing a life of poverty, chastity, and obedience to an elected abbot. Monks were required to perform some physical labor, and the monastery was intended to be a self-sufficient community. However, the real task of the monk was the continuous praise of God. This consisted of gathering at regular intervals through the day and night for communal prayer. Although Benedict lived and died in obscurity, within two and a half centuries his rule became the universal rule for western monasticism.

Western monasteries, too, provided their share of bishops, but unlike those in the east, western monks remained more isolated from population centers and from direct involvement in public affairs. Western monasteries were not, however, peripheral to western society and religion. Rather, these rustic communities were centers of religious and economic activity as well as education and learning in the largely rural west. They remained under the authority of the local bishops who were usually drawn from the lay aristocracy of the empire in the west. Also, western monasteries depended on the political and economic support that they received from lay patrons.

Solitaries and Hermits

Although Anthony had begun as a hermit, he and most Egyptian monks eventually settled into communal lives. Elsewhere, particularly in the desert of

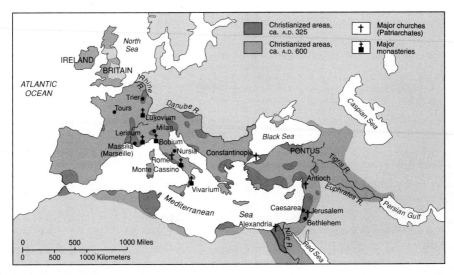

The spread of Christianity

Syria, the model of the monk remained the individual hermit. The Syrian desert, unlike that of Egypt, was particularly suitable for such an ascetic life. Here the desert was milder, an individual could find food in wild roots and water in rain pools, and villages were never too far off. Moreover, the life of the wandering hermit was closely connected to traditional seminomadic lifestyles in the Fertile Crescent. But the Christian hermits who appeared across Syria in late antiquity were unlikely to be mistaken for the familiar Bedouin nomads. The Christian hermits were wild men and women who came down from the mountainsides and galvanized the attention of their contemporaries by their lifestyles. The most famous of the hermits, Simeon Stylites (ca. 390–459), spent 36 years perched at the top of a pillar 50 feet high.

Their lack of ties to human society made such people of God the perfect arbitrators in the constant disputes that threatened to disrupt village life. They were "individuals of power," whose proven ability to cast out demons and work miracles made them ideal community patrons at a time when traditional power brokers of the village were being lured away to imperial service or provincial cities. The greatest of these holy people, like Simeon Stylites, received as visitors not only local peasants but also emperors and empresses, who eagerly sought their advice.

Unlike the eastern monks, the Syrian hermits of the fourth and fifth centuries had few parallels in the west. Hermits did inhabit the caves and forests of Italy and Gaul, but these westerners did not establish themselves either as independent sources of religious power or as political power brokers.

In the west, in spite of the creation of the barbarian kingdoms, cultural and political leadership remained firmly in the hands of the aristocracy. Aristo-

Gold plaque from a sixth-century Syrian reliquary. The subject is Simeon Stylites on his pillar. The snake represents the vanquished devil. Clients could consult the holy man by climbing up the ladder on the left.

cratic bishops, rather than hermits, monopolized the role of mediators of divine power just as their lay brothers, in cooperation with barbarian rulers, monopolized the role of mediators of secular power.

During the first and second centuries, a deeply Hellenized Roman civilization tied together the vast empire by incorporating the wealthy and powerful of the Western world into its fluid power structure while brutally crushing those who would not or could not conform. The binding force of the Roman Empire was great and survived the political crises of the third century, which were as serious as those that had brought down the republic 300 years before.

Thereafter, the fundamental differences between east and west led to a divergent transformation of the two halves of the Roman Empire at the close of late antiquity. The east remained more firmly attached not only to Roman traditions of government but also to the much more ancient traditions of social complexity, urban life, and religious culture that stretched back to the dawn of civilization.

The west experienced a transformation even more profound than that of the east. The triple heritage of late Roman political and military forms, barbarian society, and Christian culture coalesced into a new civilization that was perhaps less the direct heir of antiquity than that of the east, but the more dynamic for its distinctiveness. In culture, politics, and patterns of urban and rural life, the west and the east had gone separate ways, and their paths diverged ever more in the centuries ahead.

Suggestions for Further Reading

Primary Sources

Major selections of the works of Tacitus, Plutarch, Suetonius, and Marcus Aurelius are available in English translation from Penguin Books. The second volume, *Naphtali Lewis and Meyer Reinhold, *Roman Civilization Selected Readings Vol. II: The Empire* (1951), contains a wide selection of documents with useful introductions.

The Augustan Age

G. W. Bowersock, *Augustus and the Greek World* (New York: Oxford University Press, 1965). A cultural history of the Augustan Age.

J. B. Campbell, *The Emperor and the Roman Army* (New York: Oxford University Press, 1984). Essential for understanding the military's role in the Roman Empire.

Richard Duncan-Jones, *The Economy of the Roman Empire*, 2nd ed. (New York: Cambridge University Press, 1982). A series of technical studies on Roman wealth and its economic context and social applications.

Ronald Syme, *The Roman Revolution*, 2nd ed. (New York: Oxford University Press, 1960). A classic study of the social groups who made up the party of Augustus.

D. A. West and A. J. Woodman, *Poetry and Politics in the Age of Augustus* (New York: Cambridge University Press, 1984). The cultural program of Augustus.

The Pax Romana

Philippe Ariès and Georges Duby, eds., *History of Private Life Vol. 1: From Pagan Rome to Byzantium* (Cambridge, MA: Harvard University Press, 1986). Essays on the interior private life of Romans and Greeks by leading French and British historians.

Edward Champlin, *Fronto and Antonine Rome* (Cambridge, MA: Harvard University Press, 1980). A cultural history of Antonine court life through the letters of the second century's greatest rhetorician.

*Joseph Jay Deiss, *Herculaneum: Italy's Buried Treasure* (New York: Harper & Row, 1985). A vividly written and well-illustrated introduction to Herculaneum for a general audience.

Jane E. Gardner, *Women in Roman Law and Society* (Bloomington: Indiana University Press, 1986). A study of the extent of freedom and power over property enjoyed by Roman women.

Peter Garnsey and Richard Saller, *The Roman Empire: Economy, Society, and Culture* (Berkeley: University of California Press, 1987). A topical study of imperial administration, economy, religion, and society, arguing the coercive and exploitative nature of Roman civilization on the agricultural societies of the Mediterranean world.

---

*Indicates paperback edition available.

*Judith P. Hallett, *Fathers and Daughters in Roman Society & the Elite Family* (Princeton, NJ: Princeton University Press, 1984). A study of indirect power exercised by elite women in the Roman world as daughters, mothers, and sisters.

*Ramsay MacMullen, *Paganism in the Roman Empire* (New Haven, CT: Yale University Press, 1981). A description of the varieties and levels of pagan religion in the Roman world.

Fergus Millar, *The Emperor in the Roman World* (Ithaca, NY: Cornell University Press, 1977). A study of emperors, stressing their essential passivity, responding to initiatives from below.

Fergus Millar, *The Roman Empire and Its Neighbors*, 2nd ed. (New York: Holmes & Meier, 1981). A collection of essays surveying the diversity of the empire.

The Crisis of the Third Century

*Peter Brown, *The World of Late Antiquity*, A.D. *150–750* (New York: Harcourt Brace Jovanovich, 1971). A brilliant essay on the cultural transformation of the ancient world.

*A. H. M. Jones, *The Later Roman Empire, 284–602: A Social, Economic and Administrative Survey*, 2 vols. (Baltimore, MD: Johns Hopkins University Press, 1986). The standard detailed survey of late antiquity by an administrative historian.

E. A. Thompson, *The Early Germans* (Oxford: Oxford University Press, 1965). An important social and economic view of Germanic society.

The Empire Restored

T. D. Barnes, *The New Empire of Diocletian and Constantine* (Cambridge, MA: Harvard University Press, 1982). A current examination of the transformations brought about under these two great emperors.

*Ramsay MacMullen, *Paganism in the Roman Empire* (New Haven, CT: Yale University Press, 1981). A sensible introduction to the varieties of Roman religion in the imperial period.

A Parting of the Ways

*Patrick J. Geary, *Before France and Germany* (New York: Oxford University Press, 1988). On the origins of the barbarian West.

Herwig Wolfram, *History of the Goths* (Berkeley: University of California Press, 1988). An ethnologically sensitive history of the formation of the Gothic peoples.

The Crisis of Elite Culture

*Judith Herrin, *The Formation of Christendom* (Princeton, NJ: Princeton University Press, 1987). A history of early Christianity from the perspective of a noted Byzantinist.

*Ramsay MacMullen, *Christianizing the Roman Empire (100–400)* (New Haven, CT: Yale University Press, 1984). A view of Christianity's spread from the perspective of Roman history.

*Karl E. Morrison, ed., *The Church in the Roman Empire* (Chicago: University of Chicago Press, 1986). Major documents of early Christianity.

The Transformation of Popular Culture

Peter Brown, *Society and the Holy in Late Antiquity* (Berkeley: University of California Press, 1982). Imaginative essays on religion and society, emphasizing the role of saints.

*David Knowles, *Christian Monasticism* (New York: McGraw-Hill, 1969). A very readable introduction by a great historian of monastic history.

6

The Classical Legacy in the East: Byzantium and Islam

From Temple to Mosque

First a temple dedicated to the Syriac god Hadad and then to the Roman Jupiter, later the Christian church of St. John, and finally a mosque, the Great Mosque of Damascus in Syria bears testimony to the great civilizations that have followed one another in the Near East. Like the successive houses of worship, each civilization rose upon the ruins of its predecessor, incorporating and transforming the rich legacy of the past into a new culture. Little of the pagan and Christian structures is visible, although the mosque owes much to both, as does the civilization it represents.

Nothing remains of the pre-Roman structure. In the first century the Romans rebuilt the temple to include an outer enclosure 1233 by 1000 feet with four monumental gateways. In the interior was a porticoed court marked by four corner towers. Monumental portals, or gateways, in the east and west with triple doorways provided access to this inner court, in the center of which stood a structure housing the statue of Jupiter.

Around the time of Constantine, the temple was converted into a Christian church dedicated to Saint John the Baptist. Apparently a portion of the interior porticoed court, which measured roughly 517 by 318 feet, was enclosed to provide a space for worshipers. Two of the four towers were raised to serve as bell towers. For a time after Damascus fell to the Arabs in 635, Christians and Muslims shared the church. Initially, there were only a few Muslims, who required no more than a small place in the exterior courtyard.

However, the Muslim population of the city grew rapidly, and by 705 Damascus was the capital of a vast, expanding Muslim empire, which would soon stretch from the Pyrenees to the Indus River. The caliph al-Walid

(705–715) wanted a place of prayer befitting his capital's glory. He invited the Christian community to choose a site for another church. When they refused, he expelled them and hired Greek architects to adapt the structure to Muslim worship. They demolished the interior walls of the church, leaving only the ancient walls of the porticoed court and the tower at each of the four corners. These four Christian towers became the first minarets, towers from which Muslim religious leaders call the faithful to prayer five times each day. Within the ancient walls, the courtyard was surrounded by porticoes on three sides and by the facade of the sanctuary on the fourth.

Al-Walid wanted his mosque to be the most magnificent in his empire, and he wished to employ the finest artists in the world to cover its walls with mosaics. The supreme center of mosaic art was Constantinople, capital of the Byzantine, or eastern Roman, Empire. Although the caliphate and the Byzantine Empire were bitter enemies, the Christian emperor loaned the caliph Byzantine artists for the task. Even today, the surviving Barada mosaics show Damascus as it appeared to al-Walid's Byzantine artists: a rich, verdant valley of palaces and houses.

The Christian antecedents of the mosque did not entirely disappear. During the preliminary work, an underground chapel was said to have been found, containing a chest with a human head. On the chest was written, "This is the head of John, son of Zacharias." Al-Walid had the sacred relic placed under one of the pillars and a monument erected over it. To this day the shrine survives in the mosque, a symbol of the continuity among Judaism, Christianity, and Islam.

This moment of artistic and religious cooperation was brief. Only a few years later, in 717, al-Walid's successor subjected Constantinople to the most fearful siege it would endure for 500 years. Still, the continuity of religious worship and the common taste for classical art show how deeply both the caliphate and the empire were bound together in the common heritage of late antiquity, of which both were the true heirs.

The Byzantines

At the end of the fifth century, the eastern empire of Theodosius and Zeno had escaped the fate that its western counterpart had suffered at the hands of the Germanic peoples. Wealthier and more urbanized than the west, its population had also been accustomed to centralized government for more

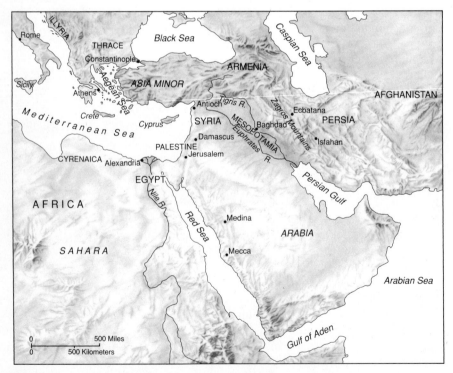

The Eastern Mediterranean

than a thousand years. Still, the long-term survival of the eastern empire seemed far from certain. Little unified the empire of Constantinople. The population of the capital split into rival political factions, whose violent conflicts often threatened the stability of the government. These rival groups, organized militarily and politically, controlled the Circus, or Hippodrome, where the games and chariot races that were the obsession of the city's population took place. These factions took their names, the Greens and the Blues, from their circus colors. When these two factions joined forces with the army, they were powerful enough to create or destroy emperors. Beyond Constantinople, the empire's population consisted of the more or less Hellenized peoples of Asia Minor, Armenians, Slavs, Arabs, Syrians, Egyptian Copts, and others. Unlike western Europe, the east was still a world of cities, which were centers of commerce, industry, and Hellenistic culture. But the importance of these urban centers began to decline in favor of the rural peasant world, which not only fed the empire and was the source of its great wealth but also provided the generations of tough soldiers necessary to protect it from its enemies.

Finally, the eastern empire was more divided than unified by its Christianity. Rivalry among the great cities of Antioch, Alexandria, Jerusalem, Rome, and Constantinople was expressed in the competition among their bishops, or patriarchs. The official "right teaching," or orthodox, faith of Constantinople and its patriarch was bitterly opposed by "deviant," or heterodox, bishops of other religious traditions, around which developed separatist ethnic political movements. By the time of Justinian (527–565), emperors were obsessed with maintaining absolute authority and imposing uniformity on their empire.

Justinian and the Creation of the Byzantine State

Strong-willed, restless, and ambitious, Justinian is remembered as "the emperor who never slept." Although his goals were essentially conservative, he transformed the very foundations of the imperial state, its institutions, and its culture. He hoped to restore the territory, power, and prestige of the ancient Roman Empire, but his attempts to return to the past created a new world. With the assistance of his dynamic wife Theodora, his great generals Belisarius and Narses, his brilliant jurist Thibonian, his scientists Anthemius of Tralles and Isidorus of Miletus, and his brutally efficient administrator and tax collector John of Cappadocia, he remade the empire.

Spurred on by the ambitious Theodora, in 532 Justinian checked the power of the circus factions by brutally suppressing a riot that left 30,000 dead in the capital city. Belisarius and Narses recaptured North Africa from the Vandals, Italy from the Ostrogoths, and part of Spain from the Visigoths, restoring for one last moment some of the geographical unity of the empire of Augustus and Constantine. Tribonian revised and organized the existing codes of Roman law into the *Justinian Code*, a great monument of western jurisprudence that

The interior of Hagia Sophia. The building was converted into a mosque after the Ottoman conquest of 1453. The magnificent mosaics were painted over to conform to Islamic religious dictates against representing human figures.

remains today the foundation of most of Europe's legal systems. Anthemius and Isidorus combined their knowledge of mathematics, geometry, kinetics, and physics to build the Church of the Holy Wisdom (Hagia Sophia) in Constantinople, one of the largest and most innovative churches ever constructed. This structure was as radical as it was simple. In essence it is a huge rectangle, 230 by 250 feet, above which a vast dome 100 feet in diameter rises to a height of 180 feet and seems to float, suspended in air. As spectacular but not as well appreciated were the achievements of John of Cappadocia, who was able to squeeze the empire's population for the taxes to pay for these conquests, reforms, and building projects. Justinian may have been referring to more than just his new church when, upon entering it for the first time, he compared himself to the biblical builder of the first temple in Jerusalem, declaring, "Solomon, I have vanquished thee!"

Ultimately, Justinian's spectacular achievements came at too high a price. He left his successors an empire virtually bankrupt by the costs of his wars and his building projects, bitterly divided by his attempts to settle religious controversies, and poorly protected on its eastern border, where the Sassanid Empire was a constant threat. Most of Italy and Spain soon returned to barbarian control. In 602 the Sassanid emperor Chosroes II (d. 628) invaded the empire, capturing Egypt, Palestine, and Syria, and threatening Constantinople itself. In a series of desperate campaigns, the emperor Heraclius (610–641) turned back the tide and crushed the Sassanids, but it was too late. A new power, Islam, had emerged in the deserts of Arabia. This new power was to challenge and ultimately absorb both the Sassanids and much of the eastern

Roman Empire. As a result, the east became increasingly less Roman and more Greek or, specifically, more *Byzantine*, a term derived from the original name of Constantinople, Byzantium.

For over seven hundred years the Byzantine Empire played a major role in Western history. From the seventh through tenth centuries, when most of Europe was too weak and disorganized to defend itself against the expansion of Islam, the Byzantines stood as the bulwark of Christianity. When organized government had virtually disappeared in the west, the Byzantine Empire provided a model of a centralized bureaucratic state ruled according to principles of Roman law. When, beginning in the fourteenth century, western Europeans began once more to appreciate the heritage of Greek and Roman art and literature, they turned to Constantinople. There the manuscripts of Greek writers such as Plato and Homer were available to contribute to a rebirth of classical culture in the west. When the Slavic north, caught between the Latin Christians and the Muslims, sought its cultural and religious orientation, it looked to the liturgical culture of Byzantine orthodoxy. Perhaps most importantly, when urban civilization had all but disappeared from the rest of Europe, Greeks and Latins could still look "to The City," *eis ten polin*, or as the Turks pronounced it, *Istanbul.*

Emperors and Individuals

The classic age of Byzantine society, roughly from the eighth through the tenth centuries, has been described as "individualism without freedom." The Byzantine world was intensely individualistic, but Byzantine individualism did not lead to a great amount of individual initiative or creativity. Still less did it imply individual freedom of action within the political sphere. Instead Byzantine individualism meant that individuals and small family groups stood as isolated units in a society characterized, until the mid eleventh century, by the direct relationship between an all-powerful emperor and citizens of all ranks.

In part this individualism resulted from the Byzantine form of government. The Byzantine state was in theory and often in fact an autocracy. Since the time of Diocletian, all members of society were subjects of the emperor, who alone was the source of law. How a person became emperor remained, as it had been in the Roman Empire, more a question of military power than constitutional succession. Although in theory the emperor was elected by the senate, army, and people of Constantinople, generally emperors selected their own successors and had them crowned in their own lifetime.

As long as the empire remained a civilian autocracy, it was even possible for a woman to rule, either as regent for a minor son or as sovereign. Thus Irene (780–802), widow of Leo IV (725–780), ruled first as regent for her son Constantine VI (780–797) and then as emperor herself. In the eleventh century the empire was ruled at times by two sisters, Zoe (1028–1034) and Theodora (1042–1056).

The Empress Irene, widow of Leo IV, was the only woman to rule the Byzantine Empire in her own right. As regent during the minority of her son, she summoned a council that confirmed the worship of icons. In 802 Irene was dethroned and exiled to Lesbos.

Male or female, emperors were above and beyond their subjects, often quite literally. In the tenth century, a mechanical throne was installed in the main audience room. The throne would suddenly lift the emperor high above the heads of astonished visitors. Like God the Father, with whom he was closely identified in imperial propaganda, the emperor was separated from the people by an unbridgeable gulf.

Thus the traditional corporate bodies of the Roman Empire wasted away or became window dressing for the imperial cult. The senate, which had received the rights and privileges of the Roman Senate in 359, gradually ceased to play any autonomous role. Senators were present when important foreign ambassadors were received. Senatorial acclamation of new emperors was always a part of the imperial coronation ceremony. But such roles were simply part of an elaborate ritual emphasizing the dignity and power of the emperor. The Senate's powers were officially abolished in the ninth century.

The circus factions, which in the sixth century had the power to make or break emperors, met the same fate. From autonomous political groups, they too gradually became no more than participants in imperial ceremonies. By the tenth century, the Greens and the Blues were simply officially constituted groups whose role was to praise the emperor by mouthing traditional formulas on solemn occasions.

While the emperor was the source of all authority, the actual administration of the empire was carried out by a vast bureaucracy composed of military and civilian officers. The empire was divided into roughly twenty-five provinces, or themes. The soldiers in each theme were also farmers, rather than full-time warriors. Each soldier received a small farm by which to support himself and his family. Soldiers held their farms as long as they served in the army. When a soldier retired or died, his farm and his military obligation passed to his eldest son. These farmer-soldiers were the backbone of both the imperial military and the economic system. They not only formed a regular, native, locally based army, but they also kept much of Byzantine agriculture in the hands of small free peasants rather than great aristocrats. The themes were governed by military commanders, or *strategoi*, who presided over both civilian and military bureaucrats.

In contrast to the military command of the themes, the central administration, which focused on the emperor and the imperial family, was wholly civil. The most important positions at court were occupied by eunuchs, castrated men who offered a number of advantages to imperial administration. Eunuchs often directed imperial finance, served as prime ministers, directed the vast bureaucracy, and even undertook military commands. Because they could not have descendants, there was no danger that they would attempt to turn their offices into hereditary positions or that they would plot and scheme on behalf of their children. Moreover, since the sacred nature of the emperor required physical perfection, eunuchs could not aspire to replace their masters on the throne. Finally, although at times their influence with the emperor made them immensely powerful, eunuchs were at once feared and despised by the general population. Thus they had little likelihood of building autonomous power bases outside of imperial favor. One Byzantine historian described the powerful eunuch John the Orphanotrophos (mid eleventh century) by saying that "nothing at all escaped his notice nor did anyone even try to do so, for everyone feared him and all dreaded his vigilance." The extensive use of eunuchs was one of the keys to the survival of absolutist authority in the empire. They preserved imperial authority at a time when both Islamic and Latin states were experiencing a progressive erosion of central power to the benefit of ambitious aristocratic families.

A godlike emperor and a centralized bureaucracy left little room for the development of the hierarchies of private patronage, lordship, and group action that were characteristic of western Europe. In the Byzantine Empire, aristocrat and peasant were equal in their political powerlessness. Against the emperor and the bureaucracy, no extended kin group or local political unit offered security or comfort. Thus Byzantine society tended to be organized at the lowest level, that of the nuclear family. Daily life focused on the protective enclosure of the private home, which served as both shelter and workplace. Professional and craft associations continued to exist as they had in antiquity. However, like everything else in Byzantium, these were not autonomous professional groups intended to protect the interests of their members. Instead, they were fostered and controlled by imperial officials to regulate and tax urban industry.

The countryside, which was the backbone of Byzantine prosperity into the eleventh century, was also a world with limited horizontal and vertical social bonds. Villages were the basic elements in the imperial system. The village court handled local affairs and tax assessments, but it in turn dealt directly with the imperial bureaucracy. Occasionally, villages might unite against imperial tax collectors, but normally villagers dealt with each other and with outside powers as wary individuals. This attitude was an outgrowth of agricultural techniques practiced in Greece and Asia Minor, where a peasant's prosperity depended not on teamwork but rather on individual effort. Most peasants, whether they were landowners, peasant soldiers, or renters on great estates, survived on the labor of their own family and perhaps one or two slaves. Large cooperative undertakings as in Islamic lands or the use of communal equipment as became the rule in the west was unknown. Individual families worked their own fields, which were usually enclosed with protective stone or brick walls. Byzantine peasants would have agreed with the saying in the poem by New Englander Robert Frost: "Good fences make good neighbors."

Like the villages, Byzantine towns were isolated in location and activities. The mountainous terrain of Greece and Asia Minor contributed to this isolation, cutting off ready overland communication among communities and forcing them to turn to the sea. In this respect Constantinople was ideally situated to develop into the greatest commercial center of the West, at its height boasting a population of over one million. Because of Constantinople's strategic location on the Bosporus, that slim ribbon of water uniting the Black and Mediterranean seas, all of the products of the empire and those of the Slavic, Latin, and Islamic worlds, as well as Oriental goods arriving overland from central Asia, had to pass through the city. Silks, spices, and precious metals were loaded onto ships at Trebizond and then transported south to Constantinople. Baltic amber, slaves, and furs from the Slavic world were carried down the Dnepr River to the Black Sea and then to the capital. There, all goods passing north or south had to be unloaded, assessed, and subjected to a flat import-export tariff of 10 percent.

The empire's cities were centers for the manufacture of luxury goods in demand throughout the Islamic and Christian worlds. Imperial workshops in Constantinople and closely regulated workshops in Corinth and Thebes produced fine silks, brocades, carpets, and other luxury products marketed throughout the Mediterranean, again subject to the state's customary 10 percent tax.

As vital as maritime commerce was to the empire, most Byzantines despised the sea. They feared it as a source of constant danger from Muslim and Christian pirates. They dreaded its sudden storms and hidden dangers. Moreover, particularly among the elite, commerce was considered demeaning. Never great mariners, Byzantines were largely content to allow others—first Syrians and Slavs and later Italians—to monopolize the empire's commerce.

A Foretaste of Heaven

The cultural cement that bound emperor and subjects together was Orthodox Christianity. The Islamic capture of Alexandria, Jerusalem, and Antioch had removed the centers of regional religious particularism from the empire. The barbarian domination of Italy had isolated Rome and reduced its influence. These two processes left Constantinople as the only remaining patriarchate in the empire and thus the undisputed center of Orthodox Christianity. However, like virtually every other aspect of Byzantine society and culture, the patriarch and the Orthodox faith he led were subordinated to the emperor. Although in theory patriarchs were elected, in reality emperors appointed them. Patriarchs in turn controlled the various levels of the Church hierarchy, which included metropolitans, bishops, and the local clergy. This ecclesiastical structure reflected the organization of the state bureaucracy, which it reinforced. Local priests were drawn from the peasant society of which they were a part. They were expected to be married and to live much like their neighbors. Bishops, metropolitans, and patriarchs were recruited from monasteries and remained celibate. They were, so to speak, spiritual eunuchs who represented the emperor.

The essence of Orthodox religion was the liturgy, or ceremonies, of the Church, which provided, it was said, a foretaste of heaven. Adoration of God and veneration of the emperor went hand in hand as the cornerstone of imperial propaganda. Ecclesiastical and court processions assured that everything and everyone was in the proper place, that order and stability reigned in this world as a reflection of the eternal order of the next. This confirmation, in churches and in court, of stability and permanence in the face of possible crisis and disruption calmed and reassured the liturgically oriented society. The effects of Byzantine ceremonial reached far beyond the Byzantines themselves. According to Russian sources, the prince of Kiev sent observers to report on the manners of worship in Islamic, Latin, and Greek societies. So strong was the impression made by the rituals of the Byzantine liturgy that the prince decided to invite Byzantine clergy to instruct his people.

The one aspect of religious life not entirely under imperial control was monasticism. Since the time of the desert fathers, monastic communities had been an essential part of Christianity. From the sixth century, numerous monastic communities were founded throughout the empire, and by the eleventh century there were at least three hundred monasteries within the walls of Constantinople alone. Monasteries were often wealthy and powerful. Moreover, their religious appeal, often based on the possession of miracle-working religious images, or icons, posed an independent source of religious authority at odds with the imperial centralization of all aspects of Byzantine life. To the faithful, icons were not simply representations or reminders of Jesus and the saints. They had a real if intermediary relationship with the person represented, and as such themselves merited veneration and, some argued, adoration.

Beginning with Emperor Leo III, the Isaurian (717–741), the military emperors who had driven back Islam sought to curtail the independence of monastic culture and particularly the cult of icons that was an integral part of it. These emperors and their supporters, termed *iconoclasts* (literally, "breakers of images"), objected to the mediating role of sacred images in worship. While the iconoclasts may have been influenced by Jewish and Islamic prohibitions of images, they were also fighting the sort of decentralization in religion that the imperial bureaucracy prevented in government. Monasteries, with their miracle-working icons, became the particular object of imperial persecution. Monasteries were closed and their estates confiscated. Monks, termed by one emperor "idolaters and lovers of darkness," were forced to marry. Everywhere imperial agents destroyed icons, statues, and illustrated manuscripts, and painted over frescoes in churches. The defenders of icons, *iconodules*, or image venerators, were imprisoned, tortured, and even executed. Most bishops, the army, and much of the non-European population of the empire supported the iconoclast emperors, but monks, the lesser clergy, and the majority of the populace, particularly women, violently resisted the destruction of their beloved images. For over a century, the iconoclast dispute threatened to tear the empire apart. Finally, in 843, the Empress Theodora (842–858), who ruled during the minority of her son, ended the persecution and restored image worship. Monasteries reopened and regained much of their former wealth and prestige. Images were brought out of hiding or new ones created, and they resumed their role in the eastern Christian church. The longest lasting effect of the iconoclastic struggle was in Byzantium's relations with the west. Christians in western Europe and particularly the popes of Rome never accepted the iconoclast position. The popes considered the iconoclast emperors heretics and looked increasingly to the Frankish Carolingian family for support against them and the Lombards of Italy. In this manner the Franks first entered Italian politics and began, with papal support, to establish themselves as a rival imperial power in the west, which culminated in the coronation of Charlemagne in 800.

*T*he Rise of Islam

> Recite: in the name of your Lord,
> The Creator Who created man from clots of blood!
> Recite: Your Lord is the Most Bounteous One,
> Who taught by the pen,
> Taught mankind things they did not know.

This command to recite, to reveal God's will, communicated directly by God, launched an obscure merchant in the Arabian city of Mecca on a career that would transform the world. Through faith, Abu al-Qasim Muhammad ibn 'Abd Allah ibn 'Abd al-Muttalib ibn Hashim (ca. 570–632), or more simply Muhammad, united the tribes of the Arabian Peninsula and propelled them on an unprecedented mission of conquest. Within a century of Muhammad's death, the world of *Islam*—a word that means "submission to the will of God"— included all of the ancient Near East and extended from the Syr Darya River in Asia, south into the Indian subcontinent, west across the African coast to the Atlantic, north through Spain, and along the Mediterranean coast to the Rhone River. Just as their faith combined elements of traditional Arab worship with Christianity and Judaism, the Arabian conquerors and their subject populations created a vital civilization from a mix of Arabian, Roman, Hellenistic, and Sassanid traditions.

Arabia Before the Prophet

Although Arabs did not appear in written sources as such before the ninth century B.C., their ancestors had played an important if supporting role in Near Eastern history for thousands of years. Already in the Egyptian Old Kingdom, the incense trees of southern Arabia had drawn Egyptians to the region, then known as the land of Punt. Trade routes between the Fertile Crescent and Egypt had crossed northern Arabia for just as long. By the sixth century A.D., Arabic-speaking peoples from the Arabian Peninsula had spread through the Syrian Desert as far north as the Euphrates.

Those who lived on the fringes of the Byzantine and Sassanid empires had been largely absorbed into the cultural and political spheres of these two great powers. The northern borders of Arabia along the Red Sea formed Roman provinces that even produced an emperor, Philip the Arab (244–249). Hira, to the south of the Euphrates, became a Sassanid puppet principality that, although largely Christian, often provided the Persians with auxiliaries. Within both empires, the distinction between Arab and non-Arab populations was blurred. Except for a common language and a hazy idea of common kinship, nothing differentiated Arabs from their neighbors.

Southern Arabia, with a relatively abundant rainfall and fertile soils, was an agricultural region long governed by monarchs. Here was the kingdom of Saba, the Sheba of the Bible, which had existed since the tenth century B.C. During the fifth century A.D. the kings of the Yemen had extended their influence north over the Bedouin tribes of central Arabia in order to control and protect the caravan trade between north and south. However, in the late sixth century Ethiopian and then Persian conquerors destroyed the Arabian kingdom of the Yemen and absorbed it into their empires. The result was a power vacuum that left central Arabia and its trade routes across the deserts in confusion.

The interior of the Arabian Peninsula was much less directly affected by the great empires to the north or the Arabian kingdoms to the south. Waterless steppes and seas of shifting sand dunes had long defeated Roman and Persian or Sassanid efforts to control the Arabic Bedouin. These nomads roamed the peninsula in search of pasturage for their flocks. Theirs was a life of independence, simplicity, and danger.

Although they acknowledged membership in various tribes, the Bedouin's real allegiance was to much more narrow circles of lineages and tenting groups. As in the Germanic tribes of Europe, kin relationships rather than formal governmental systems protected individuals through the obligation for vengeance and blood feud. In the words of a pre-Islamic poet, "Blood for blood—wiped out were the wounds, and those who had gained a start in the race profited not by their advantage." Tribal chieftains, called sheikhs, chosen from ruling families, had no coercive power, either to right wrongs or to limit feuds. They served only as arbitrators and executors of tribal consensus. The patriarch of each family held final say over his kin. He could ignore the sheikh and go his own way.

The individual was unimportant in Bedouin society. Private land ownership was unknown, and flocks and herds were often held in common by kindreds. The pastoral economy of the Bedouin provided meat, cheese, and wool. Weapons, ornaments, women, and livestock could be acquired through exchange at the market towns around desert oases. More commonly, these goods were taken in raids against other tribes, caravans, and settlements or by exacting payments from weaker neighbors in return for protection. Raids, however, yielded much more than mere booty. Often launched in defense of family honor, they were the means of increasing prestige and glory in this warrior society. Prizes won in battle were lightly given away as signs of generosity and marks of social importance.

Some of the Arabs of the more settled south, as well as inhabitants of towns along caravan routes, were Christian or Jewish. As farmers or merchants, these groups were looked down upon by the nomadic Bedouin, most of whom remained pagan. Although they recognized some important gods and even a high god usually called Allah, Bedouin worshiped local tribal deities often thought of as inhabiting a sacred stone or spring. Worship involved gifts and offerings and played only a small part in nomadic life. Far more important was commitment to the tribe, expressed through loyalty to the tribal cult and through unity of action against rival tribes.

Rivalry and feuding among tribes could be set aside at a mutually accepted neutral site, which might grow up around a religious sanctuary. A sanctuary, or *haram*, which was often on the border between tribal areas, was founded by a holy man not unlike the Christian holy men of the Syrian Desert. The holy man declared the site and surrounding area neutral ground on which no violence could take place. Here enemies could meet under truce to settle differences under the direction of the holy man or his descendants. Merchant communities sprang up within the safety of these sites, since the sanctuary gave them and their goods protection from their neighbors.

Mecca was just such a sanctuary, around whose sacred black rock, of *Ka'bah*, a holy man named Qusayy established himself and his tribe, the Quraysh, as its guardians sometime early in the sixth century. In the next century Mecca grew into an important center under the patronage of the Quraysh, who made it the center of a commercial network. Through religious, diplomatic, and military means, they organized camel caravans, which could safely cross the desert from the Yemen in the south to Iran and Syria in the north. During the early seventh century, when increased hostilities between the Byzantine and Sassanid empires severed the direct trading links between the empires, the Quraysh network became the leading commercial organization in northern Arabia. Still, its effectiveness remained tied to the religious importance of Mecca and the Ka'bah. When Muhammad, a descendant of Qusayy, began to recite the monotheistic message of Allah, his preaching was seen as a threat to the survival of his tribe and his city.

Muhammad, Prophet of God

More is known about Muhammad's life than about that of Moses, Jesus, Buddha, or any of the other great religious reformers of history. Still, Muhammad's early years were quickly wrapped in a protective cloak of pious stories by his adherents, making it difficult to discern truth from legend. A member of a lesser branch of the Quraysh, Muhammad was an orphan raised by relatives. At about age twenty he became the business manager for Khadijah, a wealthy widow whom he later married. This marriage gave him financial security among the middle ranks of Meccan merchants. During this time he may have traveled to Syria on business and heard the preaching of Christian monks. He certainly became familiar with Judaism through contact with Jewish traders. In his thirties, he began to devote an increasing amount of time to meditation, retiring to the barren, arid mountains outside the city. There, in the month of Ramadan in the year 610, he reported a vision of a man, his feet astride the horizon. The figure commanded: "O Muhammad! Thou art the Messenger of God. Recite!"

Khadijah, to whom he confided his revelation in fear and confusion, became his first convert. Within a year he began preaching openly. His early teachings stressed the absolute unity of God, the evils of idolatry, and the threat of divine judgment. Further revelations to Muhammad were copied word for word in what came to be the *Qur'an*, or Koran. These messages offered Arabs a faith founded on a book. In their eyes, this faith was both within the tradition of and superior to the Christianity and Judaism of their neighbors. The *Qur'an* was the final revelation and Muhammad the last and greatest prophet. To Muslims—the term means "true believers"—Muhammad is simply the Prophet.

Allah's revelation emphasized above all his power and transcendence. The duty of humans is worship. The prayers of Islam, in contrast with those of Christianity and Judaism, are essentially prayers of praise, seldom prayers of petition. This reverential attitude places little premium on scriptural interpretation or theological speculation. Muslims regard the whole *Qur'an* as the exact and complete revelation of God, literally true, and forming a unified whole, though revelations contained in it came at various times throughout the Prophet's life. It is the complete guide for secular and religious life, the fundamental law of conduct for Islamic society. The Prophet emphasized constantly that he was simply God's messenger and merited no special veneration or worship. For this reason Muslims have always rejected the label Muhammadan, which nonbelievers often apply to them. Muslims are not followers of Muhammad but of the God of Abraham and Jesus, who chose to

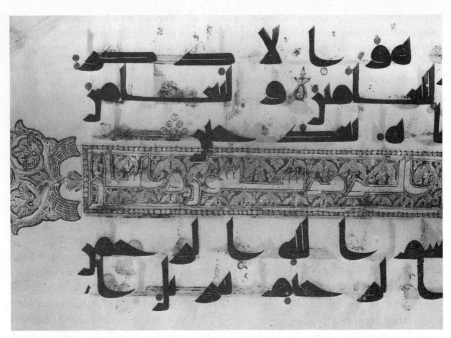

Arabic manuscripts were decorated with intricate geometric designs. This page from an eighth- or ninth-century copy of the Qur'an illustrates the elegance and formality of the Kufic form of Arabic calligraphy. Vowel marks appear as dots of various colors.

make the final and complete revelation of his power and his judgment through the Prophet.

Initially, such revelations of divine power and judgment neither greatly bothered nor influenced Mecca's merchant elite. Muhammad's earliest adherents, such as his cousin 'Ali ibn Abi (ca. 600–661), came from his own clan and from among the moderately successful members of the Meccan community, the "nearly haves" rather than the "have-nots," as one scholar put it. Elite clans such as the Umayya, who controlled the larger Quraysh tribe, saw little to attract them to the upstart. But soon Muhammad began to insist that those who did not accept Allah as the only God were damned, as were those who continued to venerate the sorts of idols on which Mecca's prosperity was founded. With this proclamation, toleration gave way to hostility. Muhammad and his followers were ostracized and even persecuted.

Around 620, some residents of Medina, a smaller trading community populated by rival pagan, Jewish, and Islamic clans and racked by internal political dissension, approached the Prophet and invited him to govern the community in order to end the factional squabbles. Rejected at home, he answered their call. On 24 September 622, Muhammad and one supporter secretly made their way from Mecca to Medina. This short journey of less than three hundred miles, known as the *Hijra*, was destined to change the world.

The Hijra marks the beginning of the Islamic dating system in the way that the birth of Jesus begins the Christian. The Hijra was the Prophet's first step—or steps—in the shift from preaching to action. He organized his followers from Mecca and Medina into the *Umma*, a community that transcended the old bonds of tribe and clan. He set about turning Medina into a haram like Mecca, with himself as founding holy man and the Umma as his new family. But this was not to be a haram nor indeed a family like any other. Muhammad was not merely a sheikh whose authority rested on consensus. He was God's messenger, and his authority was absolute. His goal was to extend this authority far beyond his adopted town of Medina to Mecca and ultimately to the whole Arab world.

First, he gained firm control of Medina at the expense of its Jewish clans. He had expected these monotheists to embrace his teachings. Instead, they rejected the unlettered Arab's attempt to transform Judaic and Christian traditions into an Arab faith. Rejection was their undoing. The Prophet expelled them in the name of political and religious unity. Those not expelled were executed.

Muhammad then used this unified community to attack the Quraysh where they were most vulnerable—in their protection of camel caravans. Inability to destroy the upstarts or protect its trading network cost the Quraysh tribe much of its prestige. More and more members of Meccan families and local tribes converted to Islam. In 629 Muhammad and 10,000 warriors marched on Mecca and captured the city in a swift and largely bloodless campaign.

During the three years between Muhammad's triumphant return to Mecca and his death, Islam moved steadily toward becoming the major force in the Arabian Peninsula. The divine revelations increasingly took on legal and practical dimensions as Muhammad was forced to serve, not just as Prophet, but as political leader of a major political and economic power. The Umma had become a sort of supertribe, open to all individuals who would accept Allah and his Prophet. The invitation extended to women as well as to men.

Islam brought a transformation of the rights of women in Arabian society. This did not mean that they achieved equality with men any more than they did in any premodern civilization east or west. Men continued to dominate Islamic society in which military prowess and male honor were so valued. Women remained firmly subordinate to men, who could have up to four wives, could divorce them at will, and often kept women segregated from other men. When in public, Islamic women in many regions adopted the Syriac Christian practice of wearing a veil that covers all of the face but the eyes. Islam did, however, forbid female infanticide, a common practice in pre-Islamic society. Brides, and not their fathers or other male relatives, received the dowry from their husbands, thus making marriage more a partnership than a sale. All wives had to be treated equally. If a man was unable to do so, he had to limit himself to a single wife. Islamic women acquired inheritance and property rights, and protection against mistreatment in marriage. Although they remained second-class in status, at least women had a status, recognized and protected within the Umma.

The rapid spread of Islam within the Arab world can be explained by a number of religious and material factors. Perhaps most attractive, though actually least important, was the sensuous vision of the after life promised to believers. Paradise is presented as a world of refreshing streams and leafy bowers, where redeemed men lie upon divans, eat exotic foods served by handsome youths, and are entertained by beautiful virgins called *Houris*, created especially for them by Allah. Probably more compelling than the description of heaven was the promise of the torments awaiting nonbelievers on the day of judgment.

"For the wrong-doers we have prepared a fire which will encompass them like the walls of a pavilion. When they cry out for a drink they shall be showered with water as hot as melted brass, which will scald their faces. Evil shall be their drink, dismal their resting-place."

But as central as these otherworldly considerations were, the concrete attractions of Islam in this world were equally important. These included both economic prosperity and the opportunity to continue a lifestyle of raiding and warfare in the name of Allah.

The seven-tiered heaven of Islam. The Bedouin, in their harsh dry land under the implacable sun, conceived of paradise as a cool shaded garden full of lush fruiting plants and washed by the waters of murmuring fountains.

Muhammad won over the leaders of the Quraysh by making Mecca the sacred city of Islam and by retaining the Ka'bah, cleansed of idols, as the center of Islamic pilgrimage. Not unlike the Roman courtiers of Constantine's day who rapidly adopted Christianity, the once disdainful elite now rushed to convert and reestablish their preeminent position within the community. The rapid rehabilitation of old families such as the Umayyads greatly disturbed many of Muhammad's earliest followers, especially those from Medina whose timely invitation had been essential in launching the Prophet's career.

Muhammad's message spread to other tribes through diplomatic and, occasionally, military means. The divisive nature of Bedouin society contributed to his success. Frequently factions within other tribes turned to Muhammad for mediation and support against their rivals. In return for his assistance, petitioners accepted his religious message. Since the *Qur'an* commanded Muslims to destroy idol worship, conversion provided the occasion for holy wars (*jihads*) of conquest and profitable raids against their still-pagan neighbors. Converts showed their piety by sending part of their spoils as alms to Medina. The *Qur'an* permitted Christians and Jews living under the authority of Islamic communities to continue to practice their faith, but they were forced to pay a head tax shared among members of the Umma.

The Spread of Islam

Muhammad died in the summer of 632 after a short illness, leaving no successor and no directions concerning the leadership of the Umma. Immediately his closest and most influential followers selected Abu Bakr (632–634), the fourth convert to Islam, to be caliph, or successor of the Prophet. Abu Bakr and, after his death two years later, the caliph 'Umar (634–644) faced formidable obstacles. Within the Umma, tensions between the early Medina followers of the Prophet and the Meccan elite were beginning to surface. A more critical problem was that the tribes which had accepted the Prophet's leadership believed his death freed them from their treaty obligations. Now they attempted to go their own ways. Some sent emissaries to announce that while they would remain Muslims, they would no longer pay alms. Others attempted to abandon Islam altogether.

To prevent the collapse of the Umma, Abu Bakr launched a war of reconversion. Purely by chance, this war developed into wars of conquest that reached far beyond the Arab world. Commanded by Khalid ibn al-Walid (d. 642), the greatest early Islamic general, Muslim forces defeated tribe after tribe and brought them back into the Umma. But long-term survival demanded expansion. Since Muslims were forbidden to raid fellow believers, and raids were an integral part of Bedouin life, the only way to keep recently converted Bedouin in line was to lead them on military expeditions against non-Muslims. Khalid and his armies were people of the desert and they used this sea of sand as the British Empire would later use the oceans in the nineteenth century.

Arab armies could move men and supplies quickly across the arid wastes, crush their enemies, and then retreat back into the desert, beyond the reach of Byzantine and Sassanid forces. Under Abu Bakr, Muslim expansion covered all of Arabia. Under 'Umar, Islam conquered Iran, Iraq, Syria, and Egypt.

The swift and total collapse of the Sassanid Empire and the major portion of the Byzantine Empire astounded contemporaries, not least the Muslims themselves. Their success seemed to be irrefutable proof that Muhammad's message was from God. By 650 Islam stretched from Egypt to Asia Minor, from the Mediterranean to the Indus River.

The Islamic Conquest

Of course, there were other factors that contributed to the Muslims' phenomenal success. Protracted wars between the Byzantine and Sassanid empires as well as internal divisions within the Byzantine world helped. For over two decades (ca. 602–628) Egypt, Palestine, and Syria had been under Persian control. Although eventually reconquered by the Byzantine emperor Heraclius, these provinces had not yet recovered from the decades of warfare, and within them a whole generation had grown up with no experience of Byzantine government.

In addition, the reimposed Byzantine yoke was widely resented because of profound cultural differences between Greeks and the inhabitants of Syria, Iraq, and Egypt. Many looked on the Byzantines not as the liberators but as the enemy. Syria and Egypt had always been different from the rest of the Roman world. Although their great cities of Antioch and Alexandria had long been

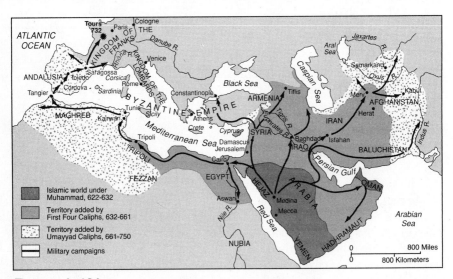

The spread of Islam

centers of Hellenistic learning and culture, the hinterlands of each enjoyed ancient cultural traditions totally alien to those of their urban neighbors. In Syria, this rural society was Aramaic and Arabic speaking. In Egypt, it was Coptic. With the steady decay of urban life and the rising demands on the rural economy, these local differences rose to greater prominence. Eventually these peculiarities coalesced around religious traditions sustained by liturgies in the vernacular and sharply at odds with the Orthodox Christianity of Constantinople.

These profound cultural, ethnic, and social antagonisms were largely fought out in the sphere of doctrine, particularly over the nature of Jesus Christ. The form of Christianity that the emperors sought to impose, defined at the Council of Chalcedon in 451, insisted that Jesus was only one person but had two complete natures, one fully human, the other entirely divine. Such a distinction rested less on the language of the New Testament than on the Greek philosophical tradition. To the Syrian and Egyptian communities, this position was heresy. "Anathema to the unclean Synod of Chalcedon!" wrote one Egyptian monk. Closer to the Jewish tradition of the transcendence of God, the Syriac and Egyptian Monophysite (meaning "one nature") Christians insisted that Christ had but a single nature and it was divine.

The two groups vented their intense hatred of each other in riots, murders, and vicious persecutions directed by zealous emperors. As a result, for many Christians of the Near East, the arrival of the Muslims, whose beliefs about the unity and transcendence of God were close to their own and who promised religious toleration and an end to persecution, was seen initially as a divine blessing.

Many Christians and Jews in Syria, Palestine, Egypt, and North Africa shared this view of the Muslim conquest as liberation rather than enslavement. Jews and Christians may have been second-class citizens in the Islamic world, but at least they had a defined place. Conquered populations were allowed to practice their religion in peace. Their only obligation was to pay a head tax to their conquerors, a burden considerably less onerous than the exactions of the Byzantine tax collectors.

The Byzantines' defeat of the Sassanids indirectly facilitated the Muslims' conquest of Iraq. When the Bedouin realized that the Persians were too weakened to protect their empire against raiders, they intensified their attacks. Soon, recent converts to Islam, too late to profit from the conquests of Syria and Egypt, were spearheading the conquest. By 650 the great Sassanid Empire had disappeared and the Byzantine Empire had lost Egypt, Syria, Mesopotamia, Palestine, portions of Asia Minor, and much of North Africa. During the reigns of Constantine IV (668–685) and Leo III (717–741), Constantinople itself fought for its own survival against besieging Muslim fleets. Each time it survived only through the use of a secret weapon, so-called Greek fire, an explosive liquid that burst into flame when sprayed by siphons onto enemy ships. Although the city itself survived, the Muslim conquests left the once vast empire a small state reduced to little more than Greece, western Asia Minor, southern Italy, and the Balkans.

Authority and Government in Islam

Conquering the world for Islam proved easier than governing it. What had begun as a religious movement within Arabian society had created a vast multinational empire in which Arabs were a tiny minority. Nothing in the *Qur'an*, nothing in Arabian experience, provided a blueprint for empire. Thus the Muslims' ability to consolidate their conquests is even more remarkable than the conquests themselves. Within the first decades following the death of the Prophet, two models of governance emerged, models that continue to dominate Islamic politics to the present.

The first model was that of pre-Islamic tribal authority. The Umma could be considered a supertribe, governed by leaders whose authority came from their secular power as leaders of the superior military and economic elements within the community. This model appealed particularly to Quraysh and local tribal leaders who had exercised authority before Muhammad. The second model was that of the authority exercised by the Prophet. In this model, the Umma was more than a supertribe, and its unity and purity had to be preserved by a religiously sanctioned rule exercised by a member of the Prophet's own family. This model was preferred by many of the more recent converts to Islam, especially the poor. Governance under each of the two models was attempted successively in the seventh and eighth centuries.

Regardless of their disagreements on the basis of political authority, both groups adopted the administrative systems of their conquered lands. Byzantine and Sassanid bureaucracy and government, only slighly adjusted, became the models for government in the Islamic world until the twentieth century. In Syria and Egypt, Byzantine officials and even churchmen were incorporated into the government, much as had been the case in Europe following the Germanic conquests. John of Damascus (ca. 676–ca. 754), a Christian theologian venerated as a saint, for example, served as the caliph's chief councillor. His faithfulness to the Islamic government and opposition to Byzantine imperial iconoclasm earned him the title of "cursed favorer of Saracens (Muslims)" from the Byzantine emperor.

Likewise, the Muslims left intact the social structures and economic systems of the empires they conquered. Lands remained in the hands of their previous owners. Only state property or, in the Sassanid Empire, that of the Zoroastrian priesthood, became common property of the Muslim community. The monastery of Saint Catherine on Mount Sinai, founded by the emperor Justinian around 540, for example, survived without serious harm and still shelters Orthodox monks today.

The division of the spoils of conquest badly divided the Umma and precipitated the first crises in the caliphate. Under 'Umar, two groups received most of the spoils of the conquests. First were the earliest followers of the Prophet, who received a disproportionate share of revenues. Second were the conquerors themselves, who were often recent converts from tribes on the fringes of Arabia. After 'Umar's death, his successor 'Uthman (d. 656), a member of the powerful Umayya clan of Mecca, attempted to consolidate control over Islam by Quraysh elite. He began to reduce the privileges of early converts in favor of the old Meccan elite. At the same time, he demanded that revenue from the provinces be sent to Medina. The result was rebellion, both within Arabia and in Egypt. 'Uthman's only firm support lay in distant Syria, ruled by members of his own clan. Abandoned at home and abroad, he was finally murdered as he sat reading the *Qur'an* in his home.

In spite of 'Uthman's unpopularity, his murder sent shock waves throughout the Umma. The fate of his successor, Muhammad's beloved son-in-law and nephew 'Ali (656–661), had an even more serious effect on the future of Islam. Although chosen as fourth caliph, 'Ali was immediately charged with complicity in 'Uthman's murder and strongly opposed by the Umayyad commander of Syria. To protect himself, 'Ali moved the caliphate from Arabia to Iraq. There he sought the support of underprivileged recent converts by stressing the equality of all believers and the religious role of the caliph, who was to be less governor and tax collector than spiritual guide of Islam.

'Ali's spiritual appeal could not make up for his political weakness. At home and abroad his support gradually crumbled as the Quraysh and their Syrian supporters gained the upper hand. In 661 'Ali was murdered by supporters of his Umayyad rivals. Still, the memory of the "last orthodox caliph" remained alive in the Islamic world, especially in Iraq and Iran. Centuries later, a tradition developed in Baghdad that legitimate leadership of Islam could come only from the house of 'Ali. Adherents of this belief developed into a political and religious sect known as Shi'ism. Although frequently persecuted as heretical by the majority of Muslims, Shi'ism remains a potent minority movement within the Islamic world today.

The immediate effect of 'Ali's death, however, was the triumph of the old Quraysh and in particular the Umayyads, who established at Damascus in Syria a caliphate that lasted a century. The Umayyads made no attempt to base their rule on spiritual authority. Instead, they ruled as secular leaders, attempting to unite the Islamic empire through an appeal to Arab unity. Profits from this state went entirely to the Quraysh and members of Arabian tribes who formed the backbone of the early Umayyad army, monopolized high administration, and acquired rich estates throughout the empire.

The Umayyads extended the Islamic empire to its farthest reaches. In the north, armies from Syria marched into Anatolia and were only stopped in 677 by the Byzantine fleet before Constantinople itself. In the east, Umayyad armies pressed as far as the Syr Darya River on the edge of the Chinese Tang empire. In the south and southwest, Umayyad progress was even more successful. After the conquest of the Mediterranean coast of Africa, the general Tariq ibn Ziyad (d. ca. 720) in 711 crossed the strait separating Morocco from Spain near the Rock of Gibraltar (the name comes from the Arabic *jabal Tariq*, "Tariq's mountain") and quickly conquered virtually the entire peninsula. Soon raiding parties had ventured as far north as the Loire Valley of what is today France. There they were halted by the Frankish commander Charles Martel in 732. Much of Spain, however, remained part of the *Dar al-Harab* (the House of Islam) until 1492.

The Umayyad caliphate's external success in conquering failed to extend to its dealings with the internal tensions of the Umma. The Umayyads could not build a stable empire on the twin foundations of a tiny Arabian elite and a purely secular government taken over from their Byzantine predecessors. Arabs as well as Jews, Zoroastrians, and Christians converted in great numbers. Not all Muslim commanders looked favorably on such conversions. Far from practicing "conversion by the sword," as was often the case in Christian missionary activity, Muslim leaders at times even discouraged the spread of Islam among the non-Arabs they had conquered. The reason was simple. Christians and Jews had to pay the head tax imposed upon them. If they converted, they no longer paid the tax. In time, this growing population of non-Arab Muslims began to demand a share in the empire's wealth.

Not only were the numbers of Muslims increasing, so also was their fervor. Growing numbers of devout Muslims—Arabs and non-Arabs alike—were convinced that leadership had to be primarily spiritual, and that this spiritual mandate was the exclusive right of the family of the Prophet. Ultimately, a coalition of dissatisfied Persian Muslims and Arabian religious reformers united under the black banners of the descendants of Muhammad's paternal uncle, 'Abbas (566–ca. 653). In 750 this group overthrew the Umayyads everywhere but in Spain and established a new caliphate in favor of the 'Abbasids.

With the fall of the Umayyad caliphate, Arabs lost control of Islam forever. The 'Abbasids attempted to govern the empire according to religious principles. These were found in the *Qur'an* and in the *sunnah*, or practices established by the Prophet and preserved first orally and then in the *hadith*, or traditions, which were somewhat comparable to the Christian Gospels. This new empire was to be a universal Muslim commonwealth in which Arabs had no privileged position. "Whoever speaks Arabic is an Arab," ran a popular saying. The 'Abbasids had risen to power as "the group of the saved," and they hoped to make the moral community of Islam the cornerstone of their government, with obedience to 'Abbasid authority an integral part of Islamic belief.

The institutional foundations of the new caliphate, however, like those of the Umayyads, remained firmly in the ancient empires they had conquered. The great caliph Mansur (754–775) moved the capital from Damascus to Baghdad, an acknowledgment of the crucial role of Iraqi and Iranian military and economic strength. The city, a few miles from the ruins of Ctesiphon on the Tigris, was largely constructed from building stones hauled by slaves from the old city to the new. In the same manner, the 'Abbasids constructed an autocratic imperial system on the model of their Persian predecessors. With their claims to divine sanction as members of the "holy family" and their firm control of the military, increasingly composed of slave armies known as Mamluks, the 'Abbasids governed the Islamic empire at its zenith.

Ultimately, however, the 'Abbasids were no more successful than the Umayyads in maintaining authority over the whole Muslim world. By the tenth century, local military commanders, termed *emirs*, took control of provincial governments in many areas while preserving the fiction that they were appointed by the 'Abbasid caliphs. The caliphs maintained the symbolic unity of Islam while the emirs went their separate ways. The majority of Muslims accepted this situation as a necessary compromise. In contrast to the Shi'ites, who continued to look for a leader from the family of 'Ali, the Sunnis, as they came to be known, remain to the present the majority group of Muslims. The Sunnis had no fixed theory of government or succession to the caliphate. Instead, they accepted the events of history in a practical manner, secure in the truth of the hadith, "My umma will never agree upon an error."

In the west the 'Abbasids could not maintain even a facade of unity. Supporters of 'Ali's family had never accepted the 'Abbasid claims to be the legitimate spiritual leaders of the Islamic community. These Shi'ites launched sporadic revolts and separatist movements. The most successful was that of 'Ubayd Allah the Fatimid (d. 934), who claimed to be the descendant of 'Ali and rightful leader of Islam. In 909, with the support of North African seminomadic Berbers, he declared himself caliph in defiance of the 'Abbasids at Baghdad. In 969 'Ubayd's Fatimid successors conquered Egypt and established a new city, Cairo, as the capital of their rival caliphate. By the middle of the eleventh century, the Fatimid caliphate controlled all of North Africa, Sicily, Syria, and western Arabia.

In Umayyad Spain, although the Muslim population remained firmly Sunni, the powerful emir 'Abd ar-Rahman III (891–961) took a similar step. In 929 he exchanged his title for that of caliph, thus making his position religious as well as secular. Everywhere the political and religious unity of Islam was being torn apart.

The arrival in all three caliphates of Muslim peoples not yet integrated into the civilization of the Mediterranean world accelerated this disintegration. From the east, Seljuq Turks, long used as slave troops, entered Iraq and in 1055 conquered Baghdad. Within a decade they had conquered Iran, Syria, and Palestine as well. Around the same time Moroccan Berbers conquered much of North Africa and Spain, while Bedouin raided freely in what are today Libya and Tunisia. These invasions by Muslims from the fringes of the Islamic commonwealth had catastrophic effects on the Islamic world. The Turks, unaccustomed to commerce and to the administrative traditions of the caliphate, divided their empire among their war leaders, displacing traditional landowners and disrupting commerce. The North African Berbers and Bedouin destroyed the agricultural and commercial systems that had survived successive Vandal, Byzantine, and Arabian invasions.

Islamic Civilization

The Islamic conquest of the seventh century brought peace to Iraq and Iran after generations of struggle and set the stage for a major agricultural recovery. In the tradition of their Persian predecessors, the caliphs organized vast irrigation systems, which made Mesopotamia the richest agricultural region west of China. Peasants and slaves raised dates and olives in addition to wheat, barley, and rice. Sophisticated hydraulics and scientific agriculture brought great regions of Mesopotamia and the Mediterranean coast into cultivation for the first time in centuries.

By uniting the Mediterranean world with Arabia and India, the 'Abbasid empire created the greatest trade network that had ever been seen. Muslim merchants met in bustling ports on the Persian Gulf and the Red Sea. There they traded silks, paper, spices, and horses from China for silver and cotton from India. Gold from the Sudan was exchanged for iron from Persia. Carpets from Armenia and Tabaristan, what is today Iran, were traded; from western Europe came slaves. Much of these luxury goods found their way to Baghdad, known as the markeplace for the world.

The marketplace for ideas was as active as that for merchandise. Within a few generations, descendants of Bedouin established themselves in the great cities of the ancient Near East and absorbed the traditions of Persian, Roman, and Hellenistic civilization. However, unlike the Germanic peoples of western Europe, who quickly adopted the Latin language and Roman Christianity, the Muslims recast Persian and Hellenistic culture in an Arabic form. Even in Iran, where Farsi, or Persian, survived as the majority language, Arabic vocabulary and structure transformed the traditional language. While 'Abassid political unity was falling apart, this new civilization was reaching its first great synthesis.

As desert conquerors, the Arabs might have been expected to destroy or ignore the heritage of Persian and Hellenistic culture. Instead, they became its protectors and preservers. As early as the eighth century, caliphs collected Persian, Greek, and Syriac scientific and philosophical works and had them translated into Arabic. Legal scholars concerned with the authenticity of hadith used Greek rationalist methods to distinguish genuine from spurious traditions. Religious mystics called *Sufis* blended Neoplatonic and Muslim traditions to create new forms of religious devotion. The medical writings of Hippocrates and Galen circulated widely in the Islamic world, and Muslim physicians were by far the most competent and respected in the West through the fifteenth century. Mathematics and astronomy were both practical and theoretical fields. Muslim intellectuals introduced the so-called Arabic numerals from India and by the tenth century had perfected the use of the decimal, fractions, and algebra. Although theoretical astronomy was limited to reforming rather than recasting Ptolemaic theory, Muslim astronomers absorbed and continued the highly accurate traditions of Mesopotamian planetary observation. The tables they compiled were more accurate than those known in the Byzantine and Latin worlds.

Although most Islamic scientists were professional physicians, astronomers, or lawyers, they were also deeply concerned with abstract philosophical questions, particularly those raised by the works of Plato and Aristotle, which had been translated into Arabic. Many sought to reconcile Islam with this

This engraved brass astrolabe was made by the Yemeni sultan al-Ashraf in 1291. Astrolabes such as this were used by seafarers from ancient times to measure the angles of celestial bodies above the horizon.

philosophical heritage in the same manner that Origen and Augustine had done for Christianity. Ya'qub al-Kindi (d. 873), the first Arab philosopher, noted that "The truth . . . must be taken wherever it is to be found, whether it be in the past or among strange peoples." The Persian physician Ibn Sina (980–1037), known in the west as Avicenna, wrote over a hundred works on all aspects of science and philosophy. He compiled a vast encyclopedia of knowledge in which he attempted to synthesize Aristotelian thought into a Neoplatonic view of the universe. In the next century the Cordoban philosopher Ibn Rushd (1126–1198), called Averroës in the west, went still further, teaching an authentic Aristotelian philosophy stripped of Neoplatonic mystical trappings. His commentaries on Aristotle were enormously influential even outside the Islamic world. For Christian philosophers of the thirteenth century, Averroës was known simply as "the Commentator."

At the same time that Muslim thought and culture was at its most creative, Islam faced invasion from a new and unaccustomed quarter: Constantinople. In the tenth and early eleventh centuries, the Byzantines pressed the local rulers of northern Syria and Iraq in a series of raids, which reached as far as the border of Palestine. At the end of the eleventh century western Europeans, encouraged and supported by the Byzantines, captured Jerusalem and established a western-style kingdom in Palestine that survived for over a century. Once more, Constantinople was a power in the Mediterranean world.

*T*he Byzantine Apogee

During the tenth and eleventh centuries, Byzantium dominated the Mediterranean world for the last time. Imperial armies under the Macedonian dynasty (867–1059) began to recover some lands lost to Islam during the previous two centuries. Antioch was retaken in 969, and for over a century Byzantine armies operated in Syria and pushed to the border of Palestine. By the middle of the eleventh century Armenia and Georgia, which had formed independent principalities, had been reintegrated into the empire. To the west Sicily remained in Muslim hands, but southern Italy, which had been subject to Muslim raids and western barbarian occupation, was secured once more. Byzantine fleets recaptured Crete, cleared the Aegean of Muslim pirates, and reopened the vital commercial sea routes. To the north, missionaries spread not only the Christian religion but also Byzantine culture among the Slavic peoples beyond the frontiers of the empire. The most important missionaries were the brothers Cyril (ca. 827–869) and Methodius (ca. 827–885), who preached to the Khazars and the Moravians. They also invented the Cyrillic alphabet, which they used to translate the Bible and other Christian writings into Slavic. Their missionary activities laid the foundation for the conversion of Serbia, Bulgaria, and Russia. In 1018 Basil II (976–1025) destroyed the Bulgarian kingdom and brought peace to the Balkan Peninsula.

The conquests of the Macedonian dynasty laid the foundation for a short-lived economic prosperity and cultural renaissance. Conquered lands, particularly Anatolia, brought new agricultural wealth. Security of the sea fostered a resurgence of commerce, and customs duties enriched the imperial treasury. New wealth financed the flourishing of Byzantine art and literature. However, just as in the spheres of Byzantine liturgy and court ceremonial, the goal of Byzantine art was not to reflect the transient "reality" of this world but rather the permanent classical values inherited from the past. Thus rarely in Byzantine art, literature, or religion was innovation appreciated or cultivated. The language, style, and themes of classical Greek literature, philosophy, and history completely dominated Byzantine culture. Only in rare works such as the popular epic *Digenis Akrites* does something of the flavor of popular Byzantine life appear. The title of the work means roughly "the border defender born of two peoples," for the hero, Basil, was the son of a Muslim father and a Christian Greek mother. The epic consists of two parts, one describing the exploits of the father, a Muslim emir or general, and the other those of of Digenis Akrites himself, fighting against both Muslims and bandits. The descriptions of his battles, his encounters with wild beasts and dragons, and his heroic death, as well as those of his intelligence, learning, and magnificent palace, are at once part of the western epic tradition and a reflection of life on the edge of the empire. *Digenis Akrites* is unique for its close relation to popular oral traditions of Byzantine society.

Another picture of Byzantine life was created by cultivated authors who were able to master completely their ancient models and to fashion within these inherited forms of literature compelling works of enduring value. One such author was the historian and imperial courtier Michael Psellus (1018–ca. 1078). His firsthand descriptions of rampaging mobs in Constantinople, hounding their enemies "like wild beasts," his acute analyses of imperial politics, and his descriptions of the inner workings of court intrigues bring to life Byzantine society at its height.

The Disintegration of the Empire

In all domains, however, the successes of the Macedonian emperors set the stage for serious problems. Rapid military expansion and economic growth allowed new elites to establish themselves as autonomous powers and to position themselves between the imperial administration and the people. The constant demand for troops always exceeded the supply of traditional salaried soldiers. In the eleventh century, emperors began to grant imperial estates to great magnates in return for military service. These grants, termed *pronoia*, often included immunity from imperial taxation and the right to certain administrative activities traditionally carried out by the central government. The practice created in effect a largely independent, landed military aristoc-racy that stood between the peasantry and the imperial government. This policy weakened the centralized state and reduced its income from taxes.

As generals became dissatisfied with the civilian central administration, they began to turn their armies against the emperors, launching over thirty revolts in as many years. To defend itself against both the Muslims without and the generals within, the central government, composed of intellectuals, eu-nuchs, and urban aristocrats, had to spend vast sums on mercenary armies. These armies, composed largely of Armenians, Germans, and Normans, soon began to plunder the empire they were hired to protect. Further danger came from other, independent Normans who, under their commander Robert Guiscard (ca. 1015–1085), conquered Byzantine Bari and southern Italy and then Muslim Sicily. Soon Guiscard was threatening the empire itself. The hostility between aristocracy and imperial administration largely destroyed the tradition of civilian government. "Do not wish to be a bureaucrat," one general advised his son. "It is not possible to be both a general and a comedian."

Under increasing pressure from local magnates on the one hand and desperate imperial tax collectors on the other, villages began to make deals with powerful patrons who would represent them in return for the surrender of their independence. Through the eleventh and twelfth centuries, the Byzantine peasantry passed from the condition of individualism without freedom to collectivism without freedom. Through the same process landlords and patrons acquired the means to exercise a political role, which ended the state's monopoly on public power.

At the same time that civil war and external pressure were destroying the provincial administration, Byzantine disdain for commerce was weakening the empire's ability to control its income from customs duties. Initially the willingness to turn over commerce to Italians and others posed few problems. Those engaged in actual commerce were for the most part citizens of the empire and were in any case subject to the 10 percent tariffs. However, in the tenth and eleventh centuries, merchants of Amalfi, Bari, and then Venice came to dominate Byzantine commerce. Venetian merchant fleets could double as a powerful navy in times of need, and by the eleventh century the Venetians were the permanent military and commercial power in the Mediterranean. When Robert Guiscard and his Normans threatened the empire, the emperors had to turn to the Venetians for protection and were forced to cede them major economic privileges. The Venetians acquired the right to maintain important self-governing communities in major ports throughout the empire and were allowed to pay lower tariffs than the Byzantines themselves.

In 1071, the year that Robert Guiscard captured the last Byzantine city in Italy, the empire suffered an even more disastrous defeat in the east. At Manzikert in Anatolia the emperor Romanus IV (1067–1071) and his unreliable mercenary army fell to the Seljuq Turks, who captured Romanus himself. Manzikert sealed the fate of the empire. Anatolia was lost, and the gradual erosion of the empire both west and east had begun.

The Conquests of Constantinople and Baghdad

At the end of the eleventh century the Comnenian dynasty (1081–1185) briefly halted the political and economic chaos of the empire. Rather than fighting the tendency of the centralized state to devolve into a decentralized aristrocratic one, Alexius I Comnenus (1081–1118) tied the aristocracy to his family, thus making it an instrument of imperial government. In the short run the process was successful. He expanded the use of pronoia to strengthen loyal aristocrats and granted them offices in the central administration that had been tradition-ally reserved for eunuchs. He stabilized Byzantine currency, which was the international exchange medium in the Islamic and Christian worlds and had been dangerously devalued by his predecessors. Still, by the late twelfth century, the empire was a vulnerable second-rate power caught between Latin Europe and Islam.

Initially, the Christian west was a more deadly threat than the Islamic east. In the eleventh century, after more than five hundred years of economic and political weakness, western Europe was beginning to reach parity with Byzantium. Robert Guiscard and his Normans, who had conquered Sicily and southern Italy, were typical examples of the powerful militaristic aristocracy developing in the remains of the old western empire. This military threat from the west was paralleled by a religious one. In the centuries that Rome had been largely cut off from Constantinople, western Christianity had developed a number of rituals and beliefs differing from Orthodox practice. This parting of the ways had already appeared during the iconoclastic controversies of the eighth and ninth centuries. In the eleventh, it was directed by an independent and self-assertive papacy in Rome, which claimed supreme authority through-out Christendom. Disagreements between the patriarchs of Constantinople and the popes of Rome prevented cooperation between the two Christian worlds and led to further deterioration of relationships between Greeks and Latins. These disagreements came to a head in 1054, when the papal represen-tative, or legate, Cardinal Humbert (ca. 1000–1061) met with the patriarch of Constantinople, Michael Cerularius (ca. 1000–1059), to negotiate ecclesiastical control over southern Italy and Sicily. Humbert was arrogant and demanding, Michael Cerularius haughty and uncompromising. Acting beyond his author-ity, Humbert excommunicated the patriarch and all his followers. The patri-arch responded in kind, excommunicating Humbert and all connected with him. This formal excommunication was lifted in the 1960s, but the schism, or split, between the churches of Rome and Constantinople continues to the present.

Excommunication was probably the least of the dangers the Byzantines faced from the west. The full fury of this often ignorant, greedy, and violent western society reached the empire when, after the defeat at Manzikert, the emperor Alexius called on western Christians for support against the Muslims. To his horror, adventurers of every sort eager to conquer land and wealth in the name of the cross of Jesus flooded the empire. In the penetrating and often cynical biography of her father, Alexius's daughter Anna (ca. 1093–1148) describes how, as quickly as possible, Alexius hurried these crusaders (from the Latin *cruciata*, "marked with a cross") on to Palestine before they could

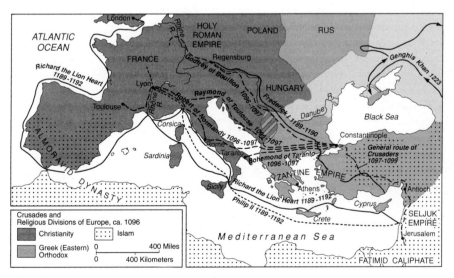

The Crusades

turn their violence against his empire. Even while recognizing that the crusaders were uncouth and barbarous, the Byzantines had to admit that the Latins were effective. Despite enormous hardships, the First Crusade was able to take advantage of division in the Muslim world to conquer Palestine and establish a Latin kingdom in Jerusalem in 1099.

The crusaders' initial victories and the growth of Latin wealth and power created in Constantinople a temporary enthusiam for western European styles and customs. The Byzantines soon realized, however, that the Latin kingdom posed a threat not only to Islam but to them as well. While crusaders threatened Byzantine territories, Venetian merchants imposed a stranglehold on Byzantine trade. When emperors granted other Italian towns concessions equal to those of the Venetians, they found that they had simply amplified their problems. Anti-Latin sentiment reached the boiling point in 1183. In the riots that broke out in that year Italians and other westerners in Constantinople were murdered and their goods seized. Just 21 years later, in 1204, a wayward crusade, egged on by Venice, turned aside from its planned expedition to Palestine to capture a bigger prize: Constantinople. After pillaging the city for three days—the Byzantine survivors commented that even the Saracens would have been less cruel—the westerners established one of their own as emperor and installed a Venetian as patriarch.

The Byzantine Empire and the Rise of Islam

527–565	Reign of Justinian
610	Muhammed's vision
622	The Hijra, Muhammad's journey from Mecca to Medina
726	Iconoclast dispute begins
732	Muslim advance halted by Franks
750	'Abbasids overthrow Umayyads; take control of Muslim world
843	Empress Theodora ends iconoclast persecution; restores image worship
867–1059	Macedonian dynasty rules Byzantine Empire; begins recovering lands from Muslims
1054	Schism splits churches of Rome and Constantinople
1071	Robert Guiscard captures southern Italy and Sicily; Battle of Manzikert; Seljuq Turks defeat Byzantines
1099	First Crusade establishes Latin kingdom in Jerusalem
1221	Ghengis Khan leads Mongol army into Persia
1453	Constantinople falls to Ottomans

The Byzantines did manage to hold on to a portion of their empire centering on Nicaea, and before long the Latins fell to bickering among themselves. In 1261 the ruler of Nicaea, Michael Palaeologus (ca. 1224–1282), recaptured Constantinople with the assistance of the Genoese and had himself crowned emperor in the Hagia Sophia. Still, the empire was fatally shattered, its disintegration into autonomous lordships complete. The restored empire consisted of little more than the district around Constantinople, Thessalonica, and the Peloponneseus. Bulgarians and Serbs had expanded far into the Greek mainland. Most of the rich Anatolian regions had been lost to the Turks, and commercial revenues were in the hands of the Genoese allies. The restored empire's survival for almost two hundred years was due less to its own prerogative than to the internal problems of the Islamic world.

The caliphs of Baghdad, like the emperors of Constantinople, succumbed to invaders from the barbarous fringes of their empire. In 1221 the Mongol prince Temujin (ca. 1162–1227), better known to history as Genghis Khan (Universal Ruler), led his conquering army into Persia from central Asia. From there, a portion of the Mongols went north, invading Russia in 1237 and dividing it into small principalities ruled by Slavic princes under Mongol control. In 1258 a Mongol army captured Baghdad and executed the last 'Abbasid caliph, ending a 500-year tradition. The Mongol armies then moved west, shattering the Seljuq principalities in Iraq, Anatolia, and Syria and turning back only before the fierce resistance of the Egyptian Mamluks.

From the ruins of the Seljuq kingdom arose a variety of small Turkish principalities, or emirates. After the collapse of the Mongol empire, one of these, the Ottoman, began to expand at the expense of both the weakened Byzantine and the Mongol-Seljuq empires. In the next centuries the Ottomans expanded east, south and west. Around 1350, they crossed into the Balkans as Byzantine allies but soon took over the region for themselves. By 1450 the Ottoman stranglehold on Constantinople was complete. The final scene of the conquest, long delayed but inevitable, occurred three years later.

For Greeks and for Italian intellectuals of the Renaissance, the conquest of Constantinople by the Ottomans was the end of an imperial tradition that

The Ottoman Empire, ca. 1450

reached back to Augustus. But Mehmed the Conqueror (1452–1481) could as easily be seen as its restorer. True, the city was plundered by the victorious army. But this was simply the way of war in the fifteenth century. The city, its palaces, and its religious edifices fared better under the Turks than they had under its previous, Christian conquerors. The Latins had placed a prostitute on the Patriarch's throne in the Hagia Sophia. Mehmed, after purging the church of its Christian trappings, rededicated it to the worship of the one God. Once more Constantinople, for centuries a capital without a country, was the center of a great Mediterranean empire. In the following centuries, Ottoman rule stretched from the gates of Vienna to the Caspian Sea and from the Persian Gulf to the Strait of Gibraltar. The legacy of absolutism, of imperial government, and of cultural pluralism, inherited from Sassanid Persia and imperial Rome, survived until the beginning of the twentieth century.

Although often deadly enemies, the Byzantine and Islamic worlds were both genuine heirs of the great eastern empires of antiquity. The traditions of the Assyrian, Alexandrian, Persian, and Roman empires lived on in their cities, their bureaucracies, their agricultural and commercial systems. Both also shared the monotheistic religious tradition that had emerged from Judaism. In their schools and libraries, they preserved and transmitted the literary and scientific heritage of antiquity. Through Islam, the legacy of the West reached the Far East. Through Byzantium, the peoples of the Slavic world became heirs of the caesars. The inhabitants of western Europe long viewed these two great civilizations with hostility, incomprehension, and fear. Still, in the areas of culture, government, religion, and commerce, the West learned much from its eastern neighbors.

Suggestions for Further Reading

The Byzantines

*J. W. Barker, *Justinian and the Later Roman Empire* (Madison: University of Wisconsin Press, 1975). A survey of Justinian's reign intended for a general public.

Joan M. Hussey, *The Orthodox Church in the Byzantine Empire* (New York: Oxford University Press, 1986). An introduction to Orthodox Christianity.

Alexander Kazhdan and Giles Constable, *People and Power in Byzantium* (Washington, DC: Dumbarton Oaks, 1982). An imaginative and controversial analysis of Byzantine culture by a Russian Byzantinist and a western medievalist.

Cyril Mango, *Byzantium: The Empire of New Rome* (New York: Scribner's, 1980). An imaginative and provocative reevaluation of the Byzantine world.

*Dimitri Obolensky, *The Byzantine Commonwealth: Eastern Europe 500–1453*

---

*Indicates paperback edition available

(Crestwood, NY: St. Vladimir's Seminary Press, 1983). Relates Byzantium to the Slavic world.

George Ostrogorsky, *History of the Byzantine State* (New Brunswick, NJ: Rutgers University Press, 1969). The standard one-volume history of Byzantium.

A. A. Vasiliev, *History of the Byzantine Empire* (Madison: University of Wisconsin Press, 1952). A classic survey of Byzantine history by a great Russian scholar.

Speros Vryonis, Jr., *Byzantium and Europe* (New York: Harcourt Brace Jovanovich, 1967). A survey of the relationship between Byzantium and the West.

The Rise of Islam

Aziz Al-Azmeh, *Arabic Thought and Islamic Societies* (London: Routledge, Chapman & Hall, 1986). A demanding but valuable introduction to Islamic intellectual history.

*John L. Esposito, *Women in Muslim Family Law* (Syracuuse, NY: Syracuse University Press, 1982). A general introduction to the topic, with historical material in the first two chapters.

*Hugh Kennedy, *The Prophet and the Age of the Caliphates* (White Plains, NY: Longman, 1986). A valuable summary of the early political history of Islam.

*Bernard Lewis, *The Arabs in History* (New York: Harper & Row, 1966). A well-written general introduction by an authority.

*Bernard Lewis, *The Muslim Discovery of Europe* (New York: W. W. Norton, 1985). Views of the West by Muslim travelers.

*Bernard Lewis, ed., *Islam and the Arab World* (New York: Knopf, 1976). An illustrated collection of essays on Islamic history and culture.

Roy P. Mottahedeh, *Loyalty and Leadership in an Early Islamic Society* (Princeton, NJ: Princeton University Press, 1980). An important introduction to the social values and structures of western Iran and southern Iraq in the tenth and eleventh centuries.

G. E. Von Grunebaum, *Classical Islam: A History 600–1258* (Chicago: Aldine, 1970). A general introduction to early Islamic history.

The Byzantine Apogee

*Michael Agold, *The Byzantine Empire 1025–1204* (White Plains, NY: Longman, 1985). A solid recent survey of the Byzantine Empire prior to the capture of Constantinople by the Latins.

*P. M. Holt, *The Age of the Crusades: The Near East from the Eleventh Century to 1517* (White Plains, NY: Longman, 1986). An excellent up-to-date survey of the political history of the Near East in the later Middle Ages.

7

The West and the Birth of a New Europe

The Chapel at the Waters

The Palatine Chapel in Aachen, now a small German city near the Belgian border, brings together a fascination with the traditions of the Roman past with the creativity of a new epoch. These two strands describe Europe during the Middle Ages, generally the period between 500 and 1000. Aachen was a favorite residence of the Frankish king Charles the Great, or Charlemagne (768–814), who often came there to enjoy its natural hot springs. In time it came to be his primary residence, the capital of his vast kingdom, which stretched from central Italy to the mouth of the Rhine River. Around 792 Charlemagne, a descendant of barbarian warriors, commissioned an architect to design a palace complex as his residence, one that would rival the great Roman and Byzantine buildings of Italy and Constantinople.

Royal agents scoured Europe for Roman ruins from which columns, precious marble, and ornaments could be salvaged and reused. From these ancient stones masons raised a complex of audience rooms, royal apartments, baths, and quarters for court officials. The whole ensemble was intentionally reminiscent of the Lateran Palace in Rome, which had been the residence of the emperors before being given to the popes.

The central building of Charlemagne's palace complex was the chapel, a symmetrical octagon 300 feet on its principal axes, modeled on San Vitale in Ravenna. The choice of model was significant. Ravenna had been the former capital of Roman Italy and of Theodoric the Great, the Ostrogothic king whom Charlemagne greatly admired. But although modeled on Roman buildings, the Palatine Chapel was admirably suited to the glorification of Charlemagne.

The building was divided into three tiers. The first tier on the ground floor

held the sanctuary, where priest and people met for worship. The topmost tier, supported by ancient Roman pillars shipped to Aachen from Rome and Ravenna, represented the heavens. Between the two was a gallery connected by a passage to the royal residence. On this gallery sat the king's throne. From his seat, Charlemagne could look down upon the religious services being conducted below. Looking up to where he sat, worshipers were constantly reminded of the king's intermediary position between ordinary mortals and God. This architectural design boldly asserted that Charlemagne was more than a barbarian king. By 805 when the chapel was dedicated, he had made good this assertion. As a contemporary chronicler wrote, while in Rome in the year 800,

> *On the most holy day of Christmas, when the king rose from prayer in front of the shrine of the blessed apostle Peter to take part in the Mass, Pope Leo placed a crown on his head and he was hailed by the whole Roman people. . . . He was now called Emperor and Augustus.*

Thus, to Charlemagne and to his supporters, this coronation ceremony revived the Roman Empire in the west. Charlemagne, with his vast empire and his imperial palace, was a true successor of the ancient Roman emperors. Like his chapel in Aachen (long after known as Aix-la-Chapelle, the chapel at the waters), this empire was built on the remains of Roman traditions grafted onto a vigorous tradition of Germanic kinship and society. According to the Byzantines, who looked on Charlemagne and his imperial coronation with alarm, the western empire could not be revived because it had never really ended. According to them, the death of the last western emperor Julius Nepos in 480 had ended the division of the empire. Since then, the Byzantine emperors had pretended that they ruled both east and west. Charlemagne's claims, made through the ceremony in Rome and more subtly in the imperial architecture of his palace, represented to them not a revival of the empire but a threat to its existence.

*T*he Making of the Barbarian Kingdoms

The existence of a united empire had long been but a dream. In the year 500, Emperor Anastasius I (491–518) could delude himself that he ruled the whole empire of Augustus, Diocletian, and Constantine, both east and west. Never mind that in the east war against the Persians dragged on. Never mind that along the northern border of the empire the Bulgarians, a new multiethnic barbarian confederation, had begun to raid into the Balkans. Neither of these conflicts, Anastasius contended, threatened the stability of the empire. In the west, the governor who ruled Italy had sworn that he "rejoiced to live under Roman law, which we are prepared to defend by arms." The king of the once troublesome Vandals had concluded a marriage alliance with the Italian governor and seemed ready to accept Roman statecraft.

Beyond the Alps a Roman officer called a *patrician* ruled the regions of the upper Rhone, and a consul controlled Gaul. In Aquitaine and Spain, legitimate, recognized officers of the empire ruled both Romans and barbarians. What need was there to speak of the end of the empire in the west?

This imperial unity was more apparent than real. The Italian governor was the Ostrogothic king Theodoric the Great (493–526), whose Roman title meant less than his Ostrogothic army. The patrician was the Burgundian king Gondebaud (480–516). The Roman officer in Aquitaine and Spain was the Visigothic king Alaric II (485–507), and the Gallic consul was the Frankish king Clovis (482–511). Each of these rulers courted imperial titles and recognition, but none regarded Anastasius as his soverign.

The Goths: From Success to Extinction

In the early sixth century all of the Germanic peoples settled within the old Roman Empire acknowledged the Goths as the most successful of the "blond-haired peoples," as the Romans called the barbarians. The Ostrogoths had created an Italian kingdom in which Romans and barbarians lived side by side. The Visigoths ruled Spain and southern Gaul by combining traditions of Roman law and barbarian military might. Yet neither Gothic kingdom endured more than two centuries.

Theodoric the Ostrogoth was the most cultivated, capable, and sophisticated barbarian ruler. He was also the most powerful. Burgundians, Visigoths, and Alemanni looked to him for leadership and protection. Even Clovis, the ambitious Frankish king, usually bowed to his wishes. Theodoric had spent his teenage years as a pampered hostage in Constantinople. There he had learned to understand and admire Roman ways. Later, after he had conquered Italy at the head of his Gothic army, he established a dual government, which respected both the remains of Roman civil administration and Gothic military organization.

Religion as well as government divided Italy's population. The Ostrogoths were Arians; the majority of the Romans were orthodox Christians. Initially, Theodoric made no effort to interfere with the religion of his subjects, stating, "We cannot command the religion of our subjects, since no one can be forced to believe against his will." This religious toleration attracted into his government outstanding Roman intellectuals and statesmen. Boethius (480–524), while serving in Theodoric's government, was also trying to synthesize the philosophical traditions of Plato and Aristotle. Cassiodorus (ca. 490–ca. 585), a cultivated Roman senator, served as Theodoric's secretary and held important positions in his government before retiring to found monasteries, where he and his monks worked to preserve the literary and philosophical traditions of Rome. Following Theodoric's death in 526, internal conflict over the succession paved the way for a protracted and devastating invasion, which destroyed not only the Ostrogothic kingdom but also much of what remained of Roman

Italy. These new invaders were not another barbarian tribe but the civilized Byzantines.

Italy was simply too close to Constantinople and too important for the ambitious Emperor Justinian I (527–565) to ignore. Encouraged by his easy victory over the Vandals, he sent an army into Italy, where he anticipated an easy reconquest of the peninsula (see p. 194). He got instead almost twenty years of vicious warfare. Not only were the Goths more formidable foes than he had expected, but when Roman tax collectors arrived with the Roman armies, Justinian found that the Italian people did not greet their "liberators" with open arms. In addition, in the midst of the reconquest a new and terrible disease appeared throughout the Mediterranean world. The plague cut down as much as one-third of Europe's population in the next two centuries.

The destruction of Italy by war and disease paved the way for its conquest by the Lombards. As allies in Justinian's army, some members of this Germanic tribe from along the Danube had learned of the riches of Italy firsthand. In 568 the whole Lombard people left the Carpathian basin to their neighbors, the Avars, and invaded the exhausted and war-torn Italian peninsula. By the end of the sixth century the Ostrogoths had disappeared, and the Byzantines retained only the heel and toe of the boot of Italy and a narrow strip stretching from Ravenna to Rome. The Byzantine presence in Rome was weak, and by default the popes, especially Gregory the Great (590–604), became the defenders and governors of the city. Gregory organized the resistance to the Lombards, fed the population during famines, and comforted them through the dark years of plague and warfare. A vigorous political as well as spiritual leader, he laid the foundations of the medieval papacy.

The Lombards largely eliminated the Roman tax system under which Italians had long suffered. They were less concerned with preserving their own cultural traditions than were the Ostrogoths, even in the sphere of religion. Initially many of the Lombards were Arians, but in the early seventh century the Lombard kings and their followers accepted orthodox Christianity. This conversion paved the way for the unification of the society.

Rather than accepting a divided society as did the Ostrogoths or merging into an orthodox Roman culture as did the Lombards, the Visigoths of Gaul and Spain sought to unify the indigenous population of their kingdom through law and religion. Roman law deeply influenced Visigothic law codes and formed an enduring legal heritage to the West. Religious unity was a more difficult goal. The king's repeated attempts to force conversion to Arianism failed and created tension and mistrust. This mistrust proved fatal. In 507 Gallo-Roman aristocrats supported the Frankish king Clovis in his successful conquest of the Visigothic kingdom of Toulouse. Defeat drove the Visigoths deeper into Spain, where they gradually forged a unified kingdom based on Roman administrative tradition and Visigothic kingship.

The long-sought-after religious unity was finally achieved when King Recared (586–601) and, along with him, the Gothic aristocracy embraced orthodox Christianity. This conversion further blurred the differences between Visigoths and Roman provincials in the kingdom. It also initiated an unprecedented use of the Church and its ideology to strengthen the monarchy. Visigothic kings modeled themselves after the Byzantine emperors, proclaimed themselves new Constantines, and used Church councils, held regularly at Toledo, as governing assemblies.

Still, Visigothic distrust directed toward anyone who was different continued. It focused especially on the considerable Jewish population, which had lived in Spain since the Diaspora, or dispersion, in the first century of the Roman Empire. Almost immediately after Recared's conversion, he and his successors began to enact a series of anti-Jewish measures, culminating in 613 with the command that all Jews accept baptism or leave the kingdom. Although this mandate was never fully carried out, the virulence of the persecution of the Jews grew through the seventh century. At the same time rivalry within the aristocracy weakened the kingdom and left it vulnerable to attack from without. In 711 Muslims from North Africa invaded and quickly conquered the Visigothic kingdom. While some remnants of the Visigoths held on in small kingdoms in the northwest, most of the population quickly came to terms with their new masters. Jews rejoiced in the religious toleration brought by Islam, and many members of the Christian elite converted to Islam and retained their positions of authority under the new regime.

The Anglo-Saxons: From Pagan Conquerors to Christian Missionaries

The motley collection of Saxons, Angles, Jutes, Frisians, Suebians, and others who came to Britain as federated troops and stayed on as rulers did not coalesce into a united kingdom until amost the eleventh century. Instead, these Germanic warriors carved out small kingdoms for themselves, enslaving the Romanized Britons or driving them into Wales. Although independent, these little kingdoms (their number varied from five to as many as eleven at different times) maintained some sort of identity as a group. The king of the dominant kingdom enjoyed some deference from his fellow rulers. Other kings looked to him as first among equals and sought his advice and influence in their dealings with one another. Unlike the Goths, none of these peoples had previously been integrated into the Roman world. Thus rather than fusing Roman and Germanic traditions, they eradicated the former. Urban life disappeared and with it the Roman traditions of administration, taxation, and culture.

In their place developed a world whose central values were honor and glory, whose primary occupation was fighting, and whose economic system was based on plunder and the open-handed distribution of riches. In many ways this Anglo-Saxon world resembled the heroic age of ancient Greece. This was a society dominated by petty kings and their aristocratic war leaders. These invaders were not, like the Goths, just a military elite. They also included free farmers who replaced the Romanized British peasantry, introducing their language, agricultural techniques, social organization, and folkloric traditions to the southeastern part of the island. These ordinary settlers, much more than the kings and aristocrats, were responsible for the gradual transformation of Britain into England, the land of the Angles.

The Anglo-Saxons were pagans, and although Christianity survived, the relationship between conquered and conquerors did not provide a climate conducive to conversion. Christianity came instead from without. The conversion of England resulted from a two-part effort. The first originated in Ireland, the most western society of Europe and the one in which Celtic traditions had survived little changed for over a thousand years. Ireland had never formed part of the Roman Empire and thus had never adapted the forms of urban life and centralized hierarchal government or religion characteristic of Britain and the continent. In the fifth century merchants and missionaries introduced an eastern monastic form of Christianity to Ireland, which adapted easily to the rural tribal organization of Irish society. Although Irish Christianity was entirely orthodox in its beliefs, the isolation of Ireland led to the development of numerous practices at odds with those common to Constantinople and Rome. Thus, although Ireland had important bishops, the most influential churchmen were powerful abbots of strict ascetic monasteries, closely connected with tribal chieftains, who directed the religious life of their regions. Around 565 the Irish monk Columba (521–597) established a monastery on the island of Iona off the coast of Scotland. From there wandering Irish monks began to convert northern Britain.

The second effort at Christianizing Britain began with Pope Gregory the Great. In 596 he sent the missionary Augustine (known as Augustine of Canterbury to distinguish him from the bishop of Hippo) to attempt to convert the English. Augustine laid the foundations for a hierarchal bishop-centered church based on the Roman model. In time the pagan king Ethelbert and much of his southwest kingdom of Kent accepted Christianity, and Augustine was named archbishop of Canterbury by the pope.

As Irish missionaries spread south from Iona and Roman missionaries moved north from Canterbury, their efforts created in England two opposing forms of orthodox Christianity. One was Roman, episcopal, and hierarchical. The other was Celtic, monastic, and decentralized. The Roman and Celtic churches agreed on basic doctrines. However, each had its own calendar of religious feasts and its own rituals. King Oswy of Northumbria (d. 670) called an episcopal meeting, or *synod*, in 664 at Whitby to settle the issue. After hearing arguments from both sides, Oswy accepted the customs of the Roman Church, thus allying himself and ultimately all of Anglo-Saxon England with the centralized, hierarchical form of Christianity, which could be used to strengthen his monarchy.

During the century and a half following the Synod of Whitby, Anglo-Saxon Christian civilization blossomed. Contact with the Continent and especially with Rome increased. The monasteries of Monkwearmouth and Jarrow became centers of learning, culminating in the writings of Bede (673–735), the greatest scholar of his century. His history of the English church and people is the finest historical work of the early Middle Ages.

A portrait of Bede, known as The Venerable. This illustration is from a manuscript of his Vita Sancti Cuthberti. Bede's *Ecclesiastical History of the English Nation earned him the title Father of English History.*

The Franks: An Enduring Legacy

In the fourth century various small Germanic tribes along the Rhine coalesced into a loose confederation known as the Franks. A significant group of them, the Salians, made the mistake of attacking Roman garrisons and were totally defeated. The Romans resettled the Salians in a largely abandoned region of what is now Belgium and Holland. There they formed a buffer to protect Roman colonists from other Germanic tribes and provided a ready supply of recruits for the Roman army. During the fourth and fifth centuries, these Salian Franks and their neighbors assumed an increasingly important role in the military defense of Gaul and began to spread out of their "reservation" into more settled parts of the province. Although many high-ranking Roman officers of the fourth century were Franks, most were neither conquerors nor members of the military elite. They were rather soldier-farmers who settled beside the local Roman peoples they protected.

In 486 Clovis, leader of the Salian Franks and commander of the barbarized Roman army, staged a successful coup (possibly with the approval of the Byzantine emperor), defeating and killing Syagrius, the last Roman commander in the west. Although Clovis ruled the Franks as king, he worked closely with the existing Gallo-Roman aristocracy as he consolidated his control over various Frankish factions and over portions of Gaul and Germany held by other barbarian kingdoms. Clovis's early conversion to orthodox Christianity helped ensure the effectiveness of this Gallo-Roman cooperation.

Clovis converted hoping that God would give him victory over his enemies and that his new faith would win the support of the Roman aristocracy in Gaul. The king's baptism convinced many of his subjects to convert as well and paved the way for assimilation of Franks and Romans into a new society. This Frankish society became the model for European social and political organization for over a thousand years.

The mix of Frankish warriors and Roman aristocrats spread rapidly across western Europe. Clovis and his successors absorbed the Visigothic kingdom of Toulouse, the Thuringians, and the kingdom of the Burgundians, and expanded Frankish hegemony through modern Bavaria and south of the Alps into northern Italy. Unlike other barbarian kingdoms such as those of the Huns or Ostrogoths, which evaporated almost as soon as their great founders died, the Frankish synthesis was enduring. Although the dynasty established by Clovis, called the Merovingian after a legendary ancestor, lasted only until the mid eighth century, the Frankish kingdom was the direct ancestor of both France and Germany.

After Clovis's death in 511, his kingdom was divided among his four sons. For the next 200 years the heart of the Frankish kingdom, the region between the Rhine and Loire rivers, was often divided into the kingdoms of Neustria, Burgundy, and Austrasia, each ruled by a Merovingian king. The outlying regions of Aquitaine and Provence to the south and Alemania, Thuringia, and Bavaria to the east were governed by Frankish dukes appointed by the kings. Still, the Frankish world was never as divided as Anglo-Saxon England. In the early eighth century a unified Frankish kingdom reemerged as the dominant force in Europe.

L iving in the New Europe

The substitution of Germanic kings for imperial officials made few obvious differences in the lives of most inhabitants of Italy, Gaul, and Spain. The vast majority of Europeans were poor farmers whose lives centered on their villages and fields. For them the seasons in the agricultural year, the burdens of rent and taxation, and the frequent poor harvest, food shortages, famines, and epidemics were more important than empires and kingdoms. Nevertheless, fundamental if imperceptible changes were transforming ordinary life. These changes took place at every level of society. The slaves and semifree peasants of Rome gradually began to form new kinds of social groups and to practice new forms of agriculture as they merged with the Germanic warrior-peasants. Elite Gallo-Roman landowners came to terms with their Frankish conquerors, and these two groups began to coalesce into a single unified aristocracy. In the same way that Germanic and Roman society began to merge, Germanic and Roman traditions of governance united between the sixth and eighth centuries to create a powerful new kind of medieval kingdom.

Creating the European Peasantry

Three fundamental changes transformed rural society during the early Middle Ages. First, Roman slavery virtually disappeared. Next, the household emerged as the primary unit of social and economic organization. Finally, Christianity spread throughout the rural world. Economics, not ethics, destroyed Roman slavery. In the kind of slavery typical of the Roman world, large gangs of slaves were housed in dormitories and directed in large-scale operations by overseers. This form of slavery demanded a highly organized form of estate management and could be quite costly, since slaves had to be fed and housed year round. Since slaves did not always reproduce at a rate sufficient to replace themselves, the supply had to be replenished from without. However, as the empire ceased to expand, the supply of fresh captives dwindled. As cities shrank, many markets for agricultural produce disappeared, making market-oriented large-scale agriculture less profitable. Furthermore, the Germanic societies that settled in the west had no tradition of gang slavery.

As a result, from the sixth through the ninth centuries, owners abandoned the practice of keeping gang slaves in favor of the less complicated practice of establishing slave families on individual plots of land. The slaves and their descendants cultivated these plots, made annual payments to their owners, and also cultivated the undivided portions of the estate, the fruits of which went directly to the owner. Thus slaves became something akin to sharecroppers. Gradually they began to intermarry with colons and others who, though nominally free, found themselves in an economic situation much like that of slaves. By the ninth century, the distinction between slaves who had acquired traditional rights to their farms, or manses, and free peasants who held and worked manses belonging to others was blurred. By the tenth and eleventh centuries, peasant farmers throughout much of Europe were subject to the private justice of their landlords, no matter whether their ancestors had been slave or free. Although not slaves in the classical sense, the peasantry had fused into a homogeneous unfree population.

The division of estates into separate peasant holdings contributed to the second fundamental transformation of European peasant society: the formation of the household. Neither the Roman tradition of slave agriculture nor the Germanic tradition of clan organization had encouraged the household as the basic unit of society. Now individual slaves and their spouses were placed on manses, which they and their children were expected to cultivate. The household had become the basic unit of Western economy.

The household was, however, more than an economic unit. It was also the first level of government. The head of the household, whether slave or free, male or female—women, particularly widows, were often heads of households—exercised authority over its other members. This authority made the householder a link in the chain of the social order, which stretched from the peasant hovel to the royal court. Households became the basic form of peasant life, but not all peasants could expect to establish their own household. The number of manses was limited, a factor that condemned many men and women to life within the household of a more fortunate relative or neighbor.

Peasant life centered on the house, the village, and the field. Peasant houses often consisted simply of two or three rooms in which dwelt both the human and animal members of the household. The rhythm of peasant life was tied to the agricultural cycle, which had changed little since antiquity. Although women and men worked together on the harvest, normally peasants divided labor into male and female tasks. Husbands and sons worked in the fields. Wives and daughters tended chickens, prepared the dark bread that was the staple of their diet, spun, and wove.

Peasant culture, like peasant society, experienced a fundamental transformation during the early Middle Ages. During this period the peasantry became Christian. In antiquity Christianity had been an urban phenomenon. The term for the rural population had been synonymous with "unbelievers." They were called pagans, that is, the inhabitants of the countryside, or *pagus*. The spread of Christianity throughout the rural world began in earnest in the sixth century, when bishops and monks began to replace the peasant's traditional agrarian cults with Christian feasts, rituals, and beliefs.

Christianity penetrated more deeply into rural society with the systematic establishment of parishes, or rural churches. By the ninth century this parish system began to cover Europe. Bishops founded parish churches in the villages of large estates, and owners were obligated to set aside one-tenth of the produce of their estates for the maintenance of the parish church. The priests who staffed these churches came from the local peasantry and received a basic education in Latin and in Christian ritual from their predecessors and from their bishops. The continuing presence of priests in each village had a profound effect on the daily lives of Europe's peasants.

"The labors of the months" was a popular motif in medieval art. This illustration from the Astronomical Notices *was found in Salzburg. The annual round of agricultural tasks, such as sowing, reaping, and threshing, vine dressing and grape picking, and the autumn slaughter of pigs are depicted along with scenes of hunting and hawking.*

Creating the European Aristocracy

At the same time that a homogeneous peasantry was emerging from the blend of slaves and free farmers, a homogeneous aristocracy was evolving out of the mix of Germanic and Roman traditions. In Germanic society, the elite had owed its position to a combination of inherited status and wealth, perpetuated through military command. Families who produced great military commanders were thought to have a special war-luck granted by the gods. The war-luck bestowed on men and women of these families a near-sacred legitimacy. This legitimacy made the aristocrats largely independent of their kings. In times of war kings might command, but otherwise the extent to which they could be said to govern aristocrats was minimal.

The Roman aristocracy was also based on inheritance, but of land rather than leadership. During the third and fourth centuries, Roman aristocrats' control of land extended over the persons who worked that land. At the same time, great landowners were able to free themselves from provincial government. Like their Germanic counterparts, Roman aristocrats acquired a sacred legitimacy, but within the Christian tradition. They monopolized the office of bishop and became identified with the sacred and political traditions associated with the Church.

In Spain and Italy, the religious differences separating Arians and orthodox Christians impeded the fusion of the Germanic and Roman aristocracies. In Gaul, the conversion of Clovis and his people facilitated the rapid blending of the two worlds. North of the Loire River, where the bulk of the Franks had settled, Roman aristocrats soon became Franks. By the mid sixth century the descendants of Bishop Remigius of Reims, who had baptized Clovis, had Frankish names and considered themselves Franks. Still, the Roman aristocratic tradition of great landholders became an integral part of the identity of the Frankish elite.

In the late sixth century, this northern Frankish aristocracy found its own religious identity and legitimacy in the Irish monasticism introduced by Saint Columbanus (543–615) and other wandering monks. At home in Ireland, these monks had been accustomed to working not with kings but with leaders of clans. In Gaul they worked closely with the Frankish aristocrats, who encouraged them to build monasteries on their estates. Eventually these monasteries amassed huge landholdings and became major economic and political centers headed by aristocrats who abandoned secular life for the cloister.

South of the Loire, conditions were decidedly different. Here Irish monasticism was less important than episcopal office. The few Frankish and Gothic families who had settled in the south were rapidly absorbed into the Gallo-Roman aristocracy, which drew its prestige from control of local religious and secular power. Latin speech and Roman culture distinguished these "Romans," regardless of their ancestry.

Aristocratic life was similar whether north or south of the Loire, in Anglo-Saxon England, Visigothic Spain, or Lombard Italy. Aristocratic family structures were loosely knit clans that traced descent from important ancestors through either the male or the female line. Clans jealously guarded their autonomy against rival clans and from royal authority.

The aristocratic lifestyle focused on feasting, on hospitality, and on the male activities of hunting and warfare. In southern Europe, great nobles lived in spacious villas, often surrounded by solid stone fortifications, an inheritance of Roman traditions. In the north, Frankish and Anglo-Saxon nobles lived in great wooden halls, richly decorated but lacking fortifications. During the fall and winter, aristocratic men spent much of their time hunting deer and wild boar in their forests. Hunting was not merely sport. Essentially it was preparation for war, the activity of the summer months. In March, as soon as the snows of winter had begun to melt and roads had become passable, aristocrats gathered their retainers, who had enjoyed their winter hospitality, and marched to war. The enemy varied. It might be rival families with whom feuds were nursed for generations. It might be raiding parties from a neighboring region. Or the warriors might join a royal expedition led by the king and directed against a rival kingdom. Whoever the enemy, warfare brought the promise of booty and, as important, glory.

Within this aristocratic society women played a wider and more active role than had been the case in either Roman or barbarian antiquity. In part, women's new role was due to the influence of Christianity, which recognized the distinct—though always inferior—rights of women, fought against the barbarian tradition of allowing chieftains numerous wives, and acknowledged women's right to lead a cloistered religious life. In addition, the combination of Germanic and Roman familial traditions permitted women to participate in court proceedings, to inherit and dispose of property, and, if widowed, to serve as tutors and guardians for their minor children. Finally, the long absence of men at the hunt, at the royal court, or on military expeditions left wives in charge of the domestic scene for months or years at a time. The religious life in particular opened to aristocratic women possibilities of autonomy and authority previously unknown in the West. Saint Hilda of Whitby (614–680), an Anglo-Saxon princess, for example, established and ruled a religious community that included both women and men. It was in Hilda's community that the Synod of Whitby took place, and Hilda played an active role advising the king and assembled bishops.

Governing Europe

The combination in the early Middle Ages of the extremes of centralized Roman power and fragmented barbarian organization produced a wide variety of governmental systems. At one end of the spectrum were the politically fragmented Celtic and Slavic societies. At the other end were the Frankish kingdoms, in which descendants of Clovis, drawing on the twin heritages of Roman institutions and Frankish tradition, attempted not simply to reign but to rule.

Rulers and aristocrats both needed and feared each other. Kings had emerged out of the Germanic aristocracy and could rule only in cooperation with aristocrats. Aristocrats were primarily concerned with maintaining and expanding their own spheres of control and independence. They perceived royal authority over them or their dependents as a threat. Still, they needed kings. Strong kings brought victory against external foes and thus maintained the flow of booty to the aristocracy. Aristocrats in turn redistributed the spoils of war among their followers to preserve the bonds of warrior society. Thus under capable kings aristocrats were ready to cooperate, not as subjects but as partners.

As the successors of Germanic war leaders and late Roman generals, kings were primarily military commanders. During campaigns and at the annual "March-field," when the free warriors assembled, the king was all-powerful. At those times he could cut down his enemies with impunity. At other times, the king's role was strictly limited. His direct authority extended only over the members of his household and his personal warrior band.

The king's role in administering justice was similarly ambivalent. He was not the source of law, which was held to be simply the customs of the past, nor was he responsible for enforcing this customary law. Enforcement was the duty of individuals and families. Only if they wished did they bring their grievances to the king or his agents for arbitration or judgment. However, even though they could not formally legislate, kings effectively molded law and legal procedure by collecting, selecting, clarifying, and publishing customary laws. Clovis presents a model for such legislative activity in the compilation of Salic law made during his reign. Visigothic and Anglo-Saxon kings of the seventh through tenth centuries did the same.

As heirs of Roman governmental tradition, kings sought to incorporate these traditions into their roles. By absorbing the remains of local administration and taxation, kings acquired nascent governmental systems. Through the use of written documents, Roman scribes expanded royal authority beyond the king's household and personal following. Tax collectors continued to fill royal coffers with duties collected in markets and ports.

Finally, by assuming the role of protector of the Church, kings acquired the support of educated and experienced ecclesiastical advisers and the right to intervene in disputes involving clergy and laity. Further, as defenders of the Church, kings could claim a responsibility for the preservation of peace and the administration of justice—two fundamental Christian (but also Roman) tasks.

Early medieval kings had no fixed capitals from which they governed. Instead they were constantly on the move, supervising their kingdoms and consuming the produce of their estates. Since kings could not be everywhere at once, they were represented locally by aristocrats who enjoyed royal favor. In the Frankish world these favorites were called *counts* and their districts, *counties*. In England royal representatives were termed *ealdormen* and their regions were known as *shires*. Whether counts or ealdormen, these representatives were military commanders and judicial officers drawn from aristocratic families close to the king. Under competent and effective kings, partnership with these aristocratic families worked well. Under less competent rulers and during the reigns of minors, these families often managed to turn their districts into hereditary, almost autonomous regions.

The Carolingian Achievement

The Merovingian dynasty initiated by Clovis presided over the synthesis of Roman and Germanic society. It was left to the Carolingians who followed to forge a new Europe. In the seventh century, members of the new aristocracy were able to take advantage of royal minorities and dynastic rivalries to make themselves into virtual rulers of their small territories. By the end of the century the kings had become little more than symbolic figures in the Frankish kingdoms. The real power was held by regional strongmen called *dukes*. The most successful of these aristocratic factions was that led by Charles Martel (ca. 688–741) and his heirs, known as the Carolingians.

This family had risen to prominence in the seventh century by controlling the office of mayor of the palace in Austrasia, the highest court official who advised the king as spokesman for the aristocracy. The Carolingians increased their influence by marrying their sons to daughters of other aristocratic families. In the late seventh century they extended their control to include Neustria and Burgundy as well as Austrasia. By the second quarter of the eighth century Charles Martel, while not king, was the acknowledged ruler of the Frankish kingdom.

Charles Martel was ruthless, ambitious, and successful. He crushed rivals in his own family, subdued competing dukes, and united the Frankish realm. He was successful in part because he molded the Frankish cavalry into the most effective military force of the time. His mounted, heavily armored warriors were extremely effective but very costly. He financed them with property confiscated from his enemies. In return for oaths of absolute fidelity he gave his followers, or vassals, estates, which they held as long as they served him faithfully. With this new army he practiced a scorched earth policy against his opponents that left vast areas of Provence and Aquitaine desolate for decades.

Charles Martel looked beyond military power to the control of religious and cultural institutions. He supported Anglo-Saxon missionaries such as Boniface (ca. 680–755), who were trying to introduce on the Continent the Roman form of Christianity they knew in England. This hierarchal style of Christianity served Carolingian interests in centralization, especially since Charles appointed his loyal supporters as bishops and abbots. Missionaries and Frankish armies worked hand in hand to consolidate Carolingian rule.

The ecclesiastical policy that proved most crucial to later Carolingians was Charles's support of the Roman papacy. Charles caught the attention of Pope Gregory III (731–741) in 732, when he defeated a Muslim raiding party near Tours, which had appeared to threaten the northward expansion of Islam. A few years later, when the pope needed protection from the Lombards to maintain his central Italian territories, he sought and obtained help from the Frankish leader.

The alliance with the papacy solidified during the lifetime of Charles's son Pippin (ca. 714–768). Pippin inherited his father's power. However, since he was not of the royal Merovingian family, he had no more right to supreme authority than any other powerful aristocrat. Pippin needed more than the power of a king: He needed the title. No Frankish tradition provided a precedent by which a rival family might displace the Merovingians. Pippin turned instead to the pope. Building on his increasingly close relationship with the papacy and the Frankish church dominated by his supporters, Pippin sought legitimacy in religious authority. In a carefully orchestrated exchange between Pippin and Pope Zacharias (741–752), the latter declared that the individual who exercised the power of king ought also to have the title. Following this declaration the last Merovingian was deposed, and in 751 a representative of the pope anointed Pippin king of the Franks. The alliance between the new dynasty and the papacy marked the first union of royal legitimacy and ecclesiastical sanction in European history. Frankish, Gothic, and Anglo-Saxon kings had been selected on secular criteria. Kings combined royal descent with military power. Now the office of king required the active participation of the Church.

Charlemagne and the Renewal of the West

Pippin's son Charlemagne was the heir of the political, religious, and social revolutions begun by his grandfather and father. He was a large man, over six feet tall, with piercing eyes, a robust physique, and a restless spirit. To his intimates he was a generous lord constantly surrounded by friends. To his enemies he was the man of iron—the grim and invincible warrior clad head to foot in steel, sweeping all before him. He was a conqueror, but he was also a religious reformer, a state builder, and a patron of the arts. As the leader of a powerful, united Frankish kingdom for over forty years, Charlemagne changed the West more profoundly than anyone since Augustus.

Almost every spring Charlemagne assembled his Frankish armies and led them against internal or external enemies. He subdued the Aquitainians and Bavarians, conquered the kingdom of the Lombards and assumed the title of king of the Lombards, crushed the Saxons, annexed the Spanish region of Catalonia, and destroyed the vast Pannonian kingdom of the Avars. In wars of aggression, his armies were invincible. Not only were they better armed and mounted, but their ability to transport men and matériel great distances was unmatched.

War booty fueled Charlemagne's renewal of European culture. As a Christian king he considered it his duty to reform the spiritual life of his kingdom and to bring it into line with his concept of the divinely willed order. To achieve this goal, he needed a dedicated and educated clergy. Most of the native clergy were poorly educated and indifferent in their observance of the rules of religious life. Creating a reformed, educated clergy was an effort as complex and demanding as organizing the army.

Charlemagne recruited leading intellectuals from England, Spain, Ireland, and Italy to the royal court to lead a thorough educational program. The architect of his cultural reform, Alcuin of York (ca. 732–804), directed a school for young lay and ecclesiastical aristocrats in the king's palace and encouraged the king to finance a wide variety of educational programs. Charlemagne supported schools in great monasteries such as Fulda and St. Gall for the training of young clerics and laymen. Schools needed books. Charlemagne's educational reformers scoured Italy for fading copies of works by Virgil, Horace, and Tacitus with the same determination that his builders hunted antique marbles and columns for his chapel. Caroline minuscule, the new style of handwriting developed to preserve these texts, was so clear and readable that during the Renaissance, humanists adopted it as their standard script.

The reformers of this era laid the necessary foundation for what has been called the Carolingian renaissance. Their successors in the ninth century built on this foundation to make creative contributions in theology, philosophy, and historiography, and to some extent in literature. The pursuit of learning was not a purely clerical affair. In the later ninth century, great aristocrats were highly literate and collected their own personal libraries. Count Everard of Friuli, who died in 866, left an estate that included over fifty books, among them works by Augustine, histories, saints' lives, and seven law books. Elite women participated fully in the Carolingian renaissance. One example is the noblewoman Dhuoda, who composed a manual of instruction for her son.

Educational reform went hand in hand with reform of ecclesiastical institutions. Charlemagne and his son Louis the Pious (814–840) worked to establish the Benedictine rule as the norm for monastic life and to reform the parish clergy. The goal was a purified and organized clergy performing its essential role of celebrating Christian ritual and praying for the Frankish king. At the same time, the monasteries were to provide competent clerics to serve the royal administration at every level. These reforms were expensive. The fiscal reorganization of ecclesiastical institutions was as far-reaching as their cultural reform. For the first time, Frankish synods or councils made tithing mandatory, specifying that one-tenth of all agricultural harvests were to go to the Church. Reform took on new life in 909 with the foundation of the monastery of Cluny in eastern France. Inspired by the monastic program of the previous century and granted immunity from secular interference, Cluny became the center of the expansion of Benedictine monasticism throughout the West.

Carolingian Government

Charlemagne recognized that conquest alone could not unify his enormous kingdom with its vast differences in languages, laws, customs, and peoples. The glue that held it together was loyalty to him and to the Roman Church. He appointed as counts throughout Europe members of the great Frankish families who had been loyal to his family for generations. Thus he created what might be termed an "imperial aristocracy" truly international in scope. In addition to supervising the royal estates in their counties, each spring these counts led the local military contingent, which included all the free men of the county. Counts also presided over local courts, which exercised jurisdiction over the free persons of the county. The king maintained his control over the counts by sending teams of emissaries, or *missi dominici*, composed of bishops and counts to examine the state of each county.

Charlemagne recognized that while his representatives might be drawn from Frankish families, he could not impose Frankish legal and cultural traditions on all his subjects. The only universal system that might unify the kingdom was Roman Christianity. Unity of religious practices, directed by the reformed and educated clergy, would provide spiritual unity. Furthermore, since the clergy could also participate in the administration of the kingdom, they could guarantee administrative unity as well. Carolingian monarchs did not intend the enriched and reformed Church to be independent of royal authority; it was rather to be an integral part of the Carolingian system of government. However, at least some of the educated clerics and lay aristocrats who participated in the system formed a clear political ideology based on Augustinian concepts of Christian government. They attempted to educate Charlemagne and his successors to the duties of a king: maintaining peace and providing justice.

Carolingian government was no modern bureaucracy or state system. The laymen and clerics who served the king were tied to him by personal oaths of loyalty rather than by any sense of dedication to a state or nation. Still, the attempts at governmental organization were far more sophisticated than anything that the West had seen for four centuries or would see again for another four. The system of counts and missi provided the most effective system of government prior to the thirteenth century and served as the model for subsequent medieval rulers.

The size of Charlemagne's empire approached that of the old Roman Empire in the west. Only Britain, southern Italy, and parts of Spain remained outside Frankish control. With the reunification of most of the West and the creative adaptation of Roman traditions of culture and government, it is not surprising that Charlemagne's advisers began to compare his empire to that of Constantine. This comparison was accentuated by Charlemagne's conquest of Lombard Italy and his protection of Pope Leo III—a role traditionally played by the Byzantine emperors. By the end of the eighth century the throne in Constantinople was held by a woman. Irene (752–802) was powerful and capable, but Western male leaders considered her unfit by reason of her sex for

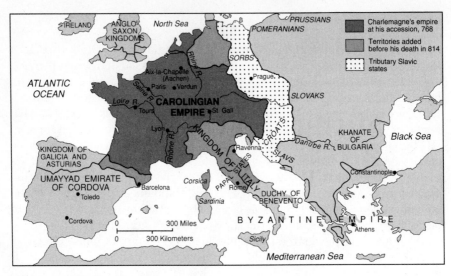

Charlemagne's Empire, 814

such an office. All these factors finally converged in one of the most momentous events in Western political history: Charlemagne's imperial coronation on Christmas Day in the year 800.

Historians debate the precise meaning of this event, particularly since Charlemagne was said to have remarked afterward that he would never have entered St. Peter's Basilica in Rome had he known what was going to happen. Presumably he meant that he wished to be proclaimed emperor by his Frankish people rather than by the pope, since this is how he had his son Louis the Pious acclaimed emperor in 813. Nevertheless, the imperial coronation of 800 subsequently took on great significance. Louis attempted to make his imperial title the sole basis for his rule, and for the next thousand years Germanic kings traveled to Rome to receive the imperial diadem and title from the pope. In so doing they inadvertently strengthened papal claims to enthrone—and at times to dethrone—emperors.

Carolingian Art

The same creative adaptation of the classical heritage that gave birth to a new Western empire produced a new Western art. The artistic traditions of the barbarian world consisted almost entirely of the decoration of small portable objects such as weapons, jewelry, and, after conversion, manuscripts. Barbarian art was essentially nonrepresentational and consisted primarily of elaborate interlaced geometric forms of great sophistication.

For Charlemagne and his reformers, such abstract art was doubly inappropriate. Not only was it too distant from the Roman heritage that they were

A page from the Book of Kells, *which dates from around 800. It was the work of scribes in Columba's monastery at Kells, Ireland. In this magnificent manuscript, human and animal motifs are transformed into intricate patterns of decoration.*

trying to emulate, but neither could it be used for instruction or propaganda. Thus Charlemagne invited Italian and Byzantine artists and artisans to his kingdom to teach a form of representational art that would decorate as well as educate. However, these southern traditions were no more slavishly followed by northern artists than were Roman political traditions wholly taken over by Charlemagne's government. The synthesis of Mediterranean and northern artistic traditions produced a dynamic plastic style of representation in which figures seem intensely alive and active. These figures, which appear in manuscript illuminations, ivories, and bas-reliefs, are often arranged in narrative cycles that engage the mind as well as the eye.

Tour of Europe in the Ninth Century

The Carolingian empire stretched from the Baltic Sea to the Adriatic and linked, through a network of commerce and exchange, the Germanic and Slavic worlds of the north, the Islamic world of Spain and the Near East, and the Mediterranean world of Byzantium. Carolingian kings rebuilt roads, bridges, and ports to facilitate trade. Charlemagne also reformed Western currency, abandoning gold coinage in favor of the more easily obtainable and liquid silver.

Silver was the medium of exchange at the northern ports of Durstede near the mouth of the Rhine and Quentovic near modern Étaples, where Frankish

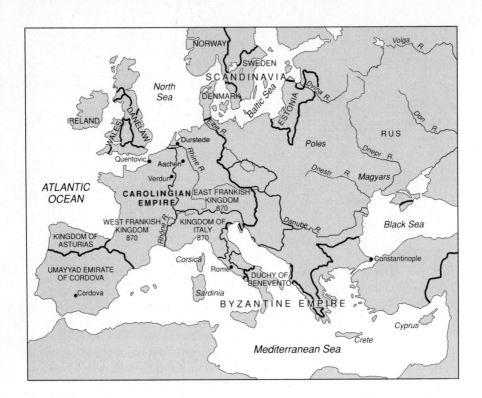

merchants haggled with Anglo-Saxon and Danish traders over cloth, furs, and amber from the Baltic. Merchants along the Slavic frontier and down the Danube dealt primarily in human commodities. Great slave trains passed from these regions into the Rhine region. Jewish and Greek merchants supplied the Frankish church and aristocracy with luxury goods from Constantinople and the East. The travels of such a merchant in the early ninth century might begin with a short trip from Quentovic to the English coast and then continue clockwise around the Frankish world.

England

A continental visitor in England would be well treated. In 796 Charlemagne had written to King Offa of Mercia (757–796), offering English merchants protection in his kingdom. Offa, the only king Charlemagne referred to as "brother," ruled a prosperous southeast England. Charlemagne's letter indicates that Mercia's prosperity owed much to trading, in which Anglo-Saxon woolens and silver were exchanged for wine, oil, and other products of the Continent.

Mercian supremacy did not long survive Offa. In the constant warfare among Anglo-Saxon kingdoms during the first half of the ninth century, Mercia fell to Wessex. The cycle of rise and fall of little kingdoms might have continued had the Vikings not come onto the scene. These Scandinavian raiders had been harassing the coast since 786. They did not pose a serious threat to England, however, until 865, when a great Viking army interested not in raiding but in conquest landed north of the Humber River. All but one of the Anglo-Saxon kingdoms were destroyed.

The surviving king, Alfred of Wessex (870–899), reorganized his army, established a network of fortifications, created a navy, and thus temporarily halted the Viking conquest. Still, he realized that his military achievement could be consolidated only by the transformation of his political base. Few of Alfred's contemporaries saw him as the savior of England. He had first to win the loyalty of people in his own kingdom and then attract that of Anglo-Saxons outside it.

He won support by reforming the legal and cultural foundations of his kingdom. Alfred's legal reforms aimed to reassure subjects of the various Anglo-Saxon kingdoms of equal treatment. At the same time they emphasized the importance of oaths of loyalty and the gravity of treason. Finally, Alfred inaugurated a religious and cultural program to extend literacy and learning so that his people might better understand and follow God's word. Because by this time Latin was almost entirely unknown in England, Alfred and his reformers used the vernacular Anglo-Saxon. Alfred encouraged the translation of the greatest books of the Christian tradition into Anglo-Saxon, even translating some of them himself. By the time Alfred died in 899, southern England was united under Wessex leadership. The north, from the Thames to Chester, was occupied and colonized by Danes. In this region, known as the Danelaw, the Vikings settled down as farmers and slowly merged with the local population.

Scandinavia

Scandinavians in England were mechants as well as raiders. They sold furs, amber, and fish for English silver and cloth. A merchant interested in the northern trade might depart England from York and travel down the Ouse and the Humber to the North Sea. To make this passage, he might sail with a Scandinavian merchant-Viking in his longboat, that supreme expression of Viking culture. These magnificent ships, over seventy feet long, were fast, flexible, and easily maneuverable. A merchant's journey would begin with passage across the Channel, followed by a two-day sail north along the coast of Jutland to the mouth of the Eider. From here travelers could cross the peninsula to Hedeby at the head of the Slie Fjord on the Baltic. After a few days a serious trader would press on, passing the Swedish archipelago, out past Öland and Gotland, through the narrow straits where Stockholm now stands, to Birka, the greatest port of Scandinavia. Here Danes, Swedes, Franks, Frisians, Anglo-Saxons, Balts, Greeks, and Arabs met to trade furs, ivory, and amber for weapons, fine English cloth, silver, and gold. Like England, Scandinavia had long been an area of Frankish commercial and political interest. The Saxons had previously formed a buffer between the Scandinavians and the Frankish world, but Charlemagne's conquests had brought the two societies into direct contact.

Scandinavian society resembled Germanic society of the first century. It was composed of three social classes. At the top were wealthy chiefs or *jarlar* (earls) who had numerous servants, slaves, and free retainers. At the bottom were thralls, or bondsmen. In between were peasant freeholders, who formed the bulk of the population. In this society women enjoyed considerable freedom and authority that shocked more "civilized" observers. But in the ninth century internal developments began to threaten the traditional independence of men and women alike, contributing to the Scandinavian expansion into the rest of Europe.

Scandinavian kings were traditionally selected by groups of earls and exercised a position more as first among equals than as ruler. However, around the end of the eighth century, Scandinavian kings began to consolidate power at home and to look to the wealthy Anglo-Saxon and Frankish worlds as sources of booty and glory. Earls and royal pretenders, threatened or displaced by the kings, also began to go "viking"—that is, raiding—in order to replace abroad what they had lost at home. The directions in which Northmen went viking depended on the region of Scandinavia from which they came. Swedes looked east, trading with the Slavic world and Byzantium. Norwegians looked to Ireland and Scotland and later to Greenland, Iceland, and North America. The Danes tended to focus on England and the Frankish empire.

Swedish merchant-Vikings, known as the *Rus'*, traveled down the Volga, Dvina, and Dnepr rivers as far as the Black and Caspian seas in search of furs and slaves. There they met the trading routes of the Byzantine Empire and the caliphate of Baghdad. Rus'-fortified trading settlements at Novgorod, Smolensk, and Kiev became the nuclei of a Slavic-Scandinavian political unit to which they eventually gave their name: Russia.

Norwegians began their viking in the western islands in the late eighth century. Ireland, until then undisturbed either by Roman or Germanic invaders, was the first victim. Other Norwegians raided south along the coast of the Frankish kingdom, Spain, and even into the Mediterranean, where they raided Provence, North Africa, and Italy. The political consolidation in Norway under Harold Finehair (860–933), which culminated in 872, led more Norwegians to go viking as earls who objected to Harold's consolidation went abroad to maintain their freedom. Some settled in the Faroe Islands; others colonized Iceland.

The southernmost Scandinavians, the Danes, were most intimately familiar with the Frankish and Anglo-Saxon realms. Some of these Vikings, led by Danish kings, colonized whole areas such as Northumbria and the region of the mouth of the Seine. It was this area that later became Normandy—land of the Northmen.

The Slavic World

A merchant in Scandinavia might join an expedition of Swedish Rus' to cross the Baltic Sea and enter the Slavic world in search of ermine and slaves. Here too the Carolingians' effects were felt, both in merchant activity and in the presence of imperialist armies and missionaries. The Slavic world of the ninth century was a rapidly changing amalgam of Germanic and Slavic peoples whose ultimate orientation—north to Scandinavia, east to Constantinople, or west to Aachen—was an open question.

The development of Slavic society and culture was quite similar to that of the Germans. In the sixth century, Slavic tribes had begun to filter west. In the seventh century, a Frank named Samo (d. ca. 660) organized a brief but powerful confederation of Slavs in the area between the Sudeten Mountains and the eastern Alps.

In the following century the Great Moravian Empire developed out of Slavic tribes along the March River. Both the Byzantine and Carolingian empires sought to bring Moravia into their spheres of influence. In the middle of the ninth century Frankish, Italian, and Greek missionaries began to compete to organize a Christian church in this Slavic empire. In 852 a Slavic prince, particularly suspicious of the Franks, turned to the Greeks. He encouraged the missionary efforts of Cyril and Methodius, who enjoyed the encouragement of both the Byzantines and the papacy.

The promising beginning made by the two brothers was short lived, as the Franks feared an independent Slavic church. In 864 the Carolingian king Louis the German (843–876) conquered Moravia. Methodius, who had been appointed archbishop of Moravia and Pannonia by the pope, was imprisoned in a German monastery. The Frankish hegemony lasted only a few decades. In 895 a new steppe people, the Magyars, or Hungarians, swept into Pannonia as had the Huns and Avars before them. These new invaders destroyed the Franks' puppet Moravian empire and split the Slavic world in two. The Magyar kingdom proved a greater threat to the Franks than the Slavs or Avars. The Magyars not only conquered Pannonia as far as the Enns River, but they raided deep into the Carolingian empire.

Muslim Spain

The Slavic world was not only in contact with the Christian societies of Byzantium and the West. Muslim merchants used Arab gold to buy furs and slaves from Rus' traders at settlements along the Dnepr. A Spanish merchant might depart from Kiev and, to avoid the Magyars, travel down the Dnepr to the Black Sea, past Constantinople, and then across the length of the Mediterranean to Al-Andalus, as the Muslims called Spain.

After the disintegration of the Umayyad caliphate (see pp. 211–213), the last Umayyad, 'Abd ar-Rahman I (731–788), made his way to Spain, where in 756 he established an independent emirate. Under the centralized control of the Umayyad emirs, the economic and cultural life of urban Spain, which had stagnated under the Visigoths, experienced a renaissance as vital as that taking place across the Pyrenees in the Frankish empire. To secure the emirate, 'Abd ar-Rahman and his successors had to overcome internal division and external aggression. The Spanish population included an elite minority of Arabs, recently arrived Syrians, North African Berbers, converted Spaniards, Christian Spaniards, and Jews. In addition, Frankish aggression and Scandinavian Vikings continually harassed Al-Andalus.

In the short run, 'Abd ar-Rahman secured control by brute force. Relying on a professional army composed mainly of slaves, the emirs crushed revolts mounted by various Muslim factions. They strengthened a series of semiautonomous districts, or marches, commanded by military governors as buffers against the Frankish kingdom to the north. Finally, they established a line of guard posts along the coast to protect themselves against the Northmen. In the long run, the emirs sought stability in religion and law. They presented themselves as the champions and protectors of Islam, thus building a religious foundation for their rule. Likewise, they cultivated the study and application of Islamic law as a source of justice and social order.

The economic prosperity of Al-Andalus was based on an enlightened system of agriculture, which included the introduction of oranges, rice, sugarcane, and cotton from the eastern Mediterranean. Complementing agriculture was a renewed urban life bolstered by vigorous trade to the north, east, and south. In the ninth and tenth centuries, Spain was the most prosperous region of Europe and one of the wealthiest areas of the Muslim world.

In this climate of security and prosperity developed the most sophisticated and refined culture in the West. Arabic poetry and art developed in a manner exactly the opposite of that in the Carolingian world. Poetry, visual art, and architecture deemphasized physical forms and encouraged abstraction and meditation. Such abstract contemplative art did not develop in Western Christendom for centuries.

Alien, dynamic, and potentially threatening neighbors surrounded the Carolingian kingdom. To the west was Anglo-Saxon England, to the east were the Slavic and Byzantine worlds. Scandinavia lay to the north, and Al-Andalus threatened to the south. In the later ninth and tenth centuries, the Frankish kingdom collapsed, due in part to the actions of these neighbors, but primarily to its own internal weaknesses.

After the Carolingians: From Empire to Lordships

Charlemagne, despite his imperial title, had remained dependent on his traditional power base, the Frankish aristocracy. For them, learned concepts of imperial renovation meant little. They wanted wealth and power.

Under Charlemagne, the empire's prosperity and relative internal peace had resulted largely from continued successful expansion at the expense of neighbors. Its economy had been based on the redistribution of war booty among the aristocracy and wealthy churches. As wars of conquest under Charlemagne gave place to defensive actions against Magyars, Vikings, and Saracens, the supply of wealth dried up. Aristocratic supporters were rewarded with estates within the empire and thus became enormously wealthy and powerful.

Competition among Charlemagne's descendants as well as grants to the aristocracy weakened central authority. By fate rather than by design, Charlemagne had bequeathed a united empire to his son Louis the Pious (814–840). Charlemagne had intended to follow Frankish custom and divide his estate among all his sons but only Louis survived him. Louis's three sons, in contrast, fought one another over their inheritance, and in 843 they divided the empire among them. The eldest son, Lothair (840–855), who inherited his father's imperial title, received an unwieldy middle portion that stretched from the Rhine south through Italy. Louis the German (840–876) received the eastern portions of the empire. The youngest son, Charles the Bald (840–877), was allotted the western portions. In time the western kingdom became France, and the eastern kingdom became the core of Germany. The middle kingdom, which included modern Holland, Belgium, Luxembourg, Lorraine (or Lotha-

The division of Charlemagne's Empire

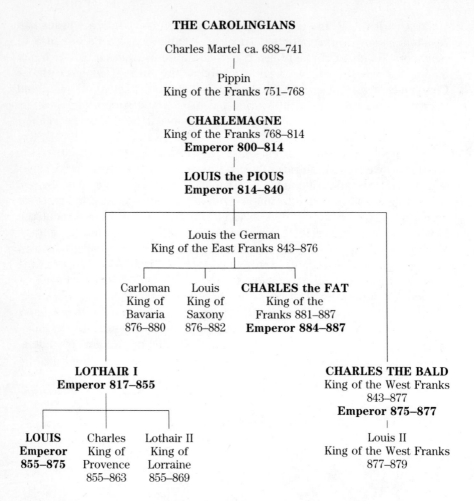

THE CAROLINGIANS

Charles Martel ca. 688–741

Pippin
King of the Franks 751–768

CHARLEMAGNE
King of the Franks 768–814
Emperor 800–814

LOUIS the PIOUS
Emperor 814–840

Louis the German
King of the East Franks 843–876

Carloman
King of
Bavaria
876–880

Louis
King of
Saxony
876–882

CHARLES the FAT
King of the
Franks 881–887
Emperor 884–887

LOTHAIR I
Emperor 817–855

CHARLES THE BALD
King of the West Franks
843–877
Emperor 875–877

LOUIS
Emperor
855–875

Charles
King of
Provence
855–863

Lothair II
King of
Lorraine
855–869

Louis II
King of the West Franks
877–879

ringia, from *Lothair*), Switzerland, and northern Italy, remained a disputed region into the twentieth century.

The disintegration of the empire meant much more than its division among Charlemagne's heirs. In no region were his successors able to provide the degree of peace and public control that he had established. The Frankish armies, designed for wars of aggression, were too clumsy and slow to deal with the lightning raids of Northmen, Magyars, and Saracens. The constant need to please aristocratic supporters made it impossible for kings to prevent aristocrats from absorbing free peasants and churches into their economic and political spheres. Increasingly, these magnates were able to transform the offices of count and bishop into inherited familial positions. They also determined who would reign in their kingdoms and sought kings who posed no threat to themselves.

Most aristocrats saw this greater autonomy as their just due. Only dukes, counts, and other local lords could organize resistance to internal and external foes at the local level. They needed both economic means and political authority to provide protection and maintain peace. These resources could be acquired only at the expense of royal power. Thus during the late ninth and tenth centuries, much of Europe found its equilibrium at the local level as public powers, judicial courts, and military authority became the private possession of wealthy families.

Ultimately, new royal families emerged from among these local leaders. The family of the counts of Paris, for example, gained enormous prestige from the fact that they had led the successful defense of the city against the Vikings in 885–886. For a time they alternated with Carolingians as kings of the West Franks. After the ascension of Hugh Capet in 987, they entirely replaced the Carolingians.

In a similar manner, the eastern German kingdom, which was divided into five great duchies, began to elect non-Carolingians as kings. In 919 the dukes of this region elected as their king Duke Henry of Saxony (919–936), who had proven his abilities fighting the Danes and Magyars. Henry's son, Otto the Great (936–973), proved to be a strong ruler who subdued the other dukes and definitively crushed the Magyars. In 962 Otto was crowned emperor by Pope John XII (955–964), thus reviving the empire of Charlemagne, although only in its eastern half. However, the dukes of this eastern kingdom chafed constantly at the strong control the Ottonians attempted to exercise at their expense. Although the empire Otto reestablished endured until 1806, he and his successors never matched the political or cultural achievements of the Carolingians. By the tenth century, the early medieval kingdoms, based on inherited Roman notions of universal states and barbarian traditions of charismatic military leadership, had all ended in failure. After the demise of the Carolingian empire, the West began to find stability at a more local but also more permanent level.

Society and Culture in the High Middle Ages

The economic, social, and cultural transformations of Europe during the centures that followed the collapse of the Carolingian empire were as profound as the political transformations of that period. The demographic upsurge of the tenth and eleventh centuries, the revolution redirecting agriculture toward markets rather than subsistence, the rebirth of towns, and the development of complex commerical networks transformed the lives of Europeans everywhere. As peasants emerged from servitude and established autonomous social and cultural traditions, aristocrats wove together strands of Christianity and the warrior ethos to create an enduring social stratum whose values dominated elite ideology until the twentieth century. The increase in literacy and in the institutions of higher learning contributed to new visions of the relationship among people and between people and God.

The Countryside

From the tenth through the thirteenth centuries enormous transformations recreated the rural landscape of Europe. The most significant of these changes concerned the peasantry, but they are difficult to chronicle, since until the nineteenth century the majority of the common people left no record of their lives. What we know of them was written by a tiny literate elite whose interest in the masses was primarily either economic or judicial. With few exceptions, the only medieval peasants whose voices we hear are those who were forced to testify before the court of a secular lord or an ecclesiastical inquisitor.

By the tenth century the population of Europe was growing, and with this population growth came new forms of social organization and economic activity. Between the years 1000 and 1300 Europe's population almost doubled, from approximately 38 million to 74 million. Various reasons have been proposed for this growth. Perhaps the end of the Viking, Magyar, and Saracen raids left rural society in relative peace to live and reproduce. The decline of slavery meant that individual peasant families could grow and reproduce themselves without constraints imposed by masters. Gradually improving agricultural techniques and equipment lessened somewhat the constant danger of famine. Possibly, too, a slowly improving climate increased agricultural yields. None of these explanations are entirely satisfactory. Whatever the cause of the poulation growth, it changed the face of Europe.

During the tenth century the great forests that had covered most of Europe began to be cut back as population spread out from the islands of cultivation. In the north of Germany and in what is today Holland, from around 1100 enterprising peasants began to drain marshes, a slow process of creating new land that would continue into the present century. This progress was not everywhere linear. In England, for example, forests actually gained on plowland after the Norman Conquest of 1066.

The Peasantry: Serfs and Freemen.   The peasants who engaged in the opening of this internal frontier were the descendants of the slaves, unfree farmers, and petty free persons of the early Middle Ages. In the east along the frontier of the Germanic empire, in the Slavic world, in Scandinavia, in southern Gaul, in northern Italy, and in the reconquered portions of Christian Spain, they were free persons who owned land, entered into contracts with magnates, and remained responsible for their own fates. Across much of northwestern Europe and in particular in France in the course of the eleventh century, the various gradations in status disappeared, and the peasantry formed a homogeneous social category loosely described as serfs. While they were not slaves in a legal sense, their degraded status, their limited or nonexistent access to public courts of law, and their enormous dependency on their lords left them in a situation similar to that of those Carolingian slaves settled on individual farmsteads in the ninth century. Each year, peasants had to hand over to their lords certain fixed portions of their meager harvests. In addition, they were obligated to work a certain number of days the *demesne*, or reserve of the lord, the produce of which went directly to him for his use or sale. Finally, they were required to make ritual payments symbolizing their subordination.

Inadequately housed, clothed, and fed, subject to the constant scrutiny of their lords, and defenseless against natural or man-made disasters, most peasants led lives of constant insecurity. Their homes offered little protection from the elements. Most were small shacks constructed of mud and wood, with one or two rooms inhabited by the entire family and their most precious domestic animals. These huts usually had no windows and until the sixteenth century no chimneys.

Peasants' houses were clustered in villages on manors or large estates. In some parts of Europe this was the result of their lord's desire to keep a close eye on his labor supply. Beginning in the tenth century in central Italy and elsewhere, lords forced peasants to abandon isolated farmsteads and traditional villages and to move into small fortified settlements. In these new villages peasants were obligated to settle disputes in the lord's court, to grind their grain in the lord's mill, and to bake their bread in the lord's oven—all primary sources of revenue for the lord. The same sort of monopoly enforced on the lords' mills and ovens applied to the church. Villagers had to contribute a tenth of their revenues to the church and to make donations in order to receive the sacraments. In some villages these payments may have actually gone to the church; usually they too went to the lord.

Each morning men went out to their fields, which surrounded the village. In some villages each peasant householder held thin strips of widely scattered land, while pasturage and woodland were exploited in common. Such an open-field system allotted all peasant households a portion of all of the different sorts of land. In other villages, each household tended a unified parcel of land. Such closed fields generally corresponded with greater divergences in wealth within the village and encouraged more independence. While the men plowed and worked the fields, women took charge of the domestic tasks. These included wool carding, spinning, weaving, caring for the family's vegetable garden, bearing and raising children, and brewing the thick souplike beer that was a primary source of carbohydrates in the peasant diet. During harvest women worked in the fields alongside the men.

Beer, black bread, beans, cabbage, onions, and cheese made up the typical peasant fare. Meat was a rarity. Only in northern Europe, where inadequate winter fodder necessitated culling herds each winter, did peasants occasionally enjoy beef. Inadequate agricultural methods and inefficient storage systems left the peasantry in constant threat of famine.

The expansion of arable land offered new hope and opportunities to

*In this medieval farmstead newly cut from the for-
est, men beat acorns out of the trees for the pigs to
eat while horses wearing collars pull the plow. Note
the fenced-in vegetable garden at the right.*

peasants. As rapid as it was, between the tenth and twelfth centuries population growth did not keep up with the demand for laborers in newly settled
areas of Europe. Thus labor was increasingly in demand and lords were often
willing to make special arrangements with groups of peasants to encourage
them to bring new land under cultivation. From the beginning of the twelfth
century peasant villages acquired from their lord the privilege to deal with him
and his representatives collectively rather than individually. These good times
did not last forever. Gradually during the late twelfth and thirteenth centuries,
the labor market stagnated. Europe's population, particularly in France,
England, Italy, and western Germany, began to reach a saturation point. As a
result, lay and ecclesiastical lords found that they could profit more by hiring
cheap laborers than by demanding customary services and payments from
their serfs. They also found that their serfs were willing to pay for increasing
privileges.

Peasants could purchase the right to marry without the lord's consent, to
move to neighboring manors or to nearby towns, and to inherit. They acquired
personal freedom from their lord's jurisdiction, transformed their servile
payments into payments of rent for their manses, purchased their own land,

and commuted their labor services into annual or even onetime payments. In other words, they began to purchase their freedom. This free peasantry benefited the emerging states of western Europe, since kings and towns could extend their legal and fiscal jurisdictions over these persons and their lands at the expense of the nobility. Governments thus encouraged the extension of freedom and protected peasants from their former masters. By the fourteenth century, serfs were a rarity in many parts of western Europe. This is not to say that these freed serfs and their descendants necessarily gained prosperity. Freedom often meant freedom from the protection that lords had provided. It meant the freedom to fail and even to starve. Nevertheless, free peasants were increasingly able to involve themselves in the emerging world of cash crop farming and to tie into a growing trend toward agricultural specialization.

Even as western serfs were acquiring a precious though fragile freedom, the free peasantry in much of eastern Europe and Spain were losing it. In much of the Slavic world, through the eleventh century, peasants lived in large roughly territorial communes of free families. Gradually, however, princes, churches, and aristocrats began to build great landed estates. By the thirteenth century, under the influences of western and Byzantine models and of the Mongols, who dominated much of the Slavic world from 1240, lords began to acquire political and economic control over the peasantry. In Hungary during the twelfth century free peasants and unfree servants merged to form a stratum of serfs tied to the emerging landed aristocracy and the lesser nobility composed of free warriors. A similar process took place in parts of Spain. In all of these regions, the decline of the free peasantry accompanied the decline of public authority to the benefit of independent nobles. The aristocracy rose on the backs of the peasantry.

The Aristocracy: Fighters and Breeders. Beginning in the late tenth century, writers of legal documents began to employ an old term in a novel manner to designate certain powerful free persons who belonged neither to the old aristocracy nor to the peasantry. The term was *miles*. In classical Latin *miles* meant "soldier." As used in the Middle Ages, we would translate it as "knight."

The center of the knightly lifestyle was northern France. From there, the ideals of knighthood, or chivalry, spread out across Europe, influencing aristocrats as far east as Byzantium. The essence of this lifestyle was fighting. Through warfare this aristocracy had maintained or acquired its freedom and through warfare it justified its privileges. The origins of this small elite (probably nowhere more than 2 percent of the population) were diverse. Many were descended from the old aristocracy of the Carolingian age. In the region of Burgundy in eastern France, for example, by the twelfth century approximately forty-one families were considered "noble." These families, or "houses," had sprung from six great clans of the Carolingian period. They traced descent through the male line, inheritance was usually limited to the eldest sons, and daughters were given a dowry but did not share in inheritance. Younger sons had to find service with some great lord or live in the household of their older brothers.

Such noble families, proud of their independence and ancestry, maintained their position through complex kin networks, mutual defense pacts with other nobles, and control of castles, from which they could dominate the surrounding countryside. Safe behind the castle walls, they were by the twelfth century often independent even of the local counts, dukes, and kings. This lesser nobility absorbed control of such traditionally public powers as justice, peace, and taxation.

For the sons of such nobles preparation for a life of warfare began early, often in the entourage of a maternal uncle or a powerful lord. There boys learned to ride, to handle a heavy sword and shield, to manage a lance on horseback, to swing an ax with deadly accuracy. They also learned more subtle but equally important lessons about honor, pride, and family tradition. The feats of ancestors or heroes, sung by traveling minstrels at the banqueting table on long winter nights, provided models of knightly action. The culmination of this education for English and French nobles came in a ceremony of knighting. An adolescent of age 16 to 18 received a sword from an older, experienced warrior. No longer a "boy," he now became a "youth," ready to enter the world of fighting for which he had trained.

A youth was a noble who had been knighted but who had not married or acquired land either through inheritance or as a reward from a lord for service, and thus had not yet established his own "house." During this time the knight led the life of a warrior, joining in promising military expeditions and amusing himself with tournaments—mock battles that often proved as deadly as the real thing—in which one could win an opponent's horses and armor as well as renown. Drinking, gambling, and lechery were other common activities. This was an extraordinarily dangerous lifestyle, and many youths did not survive to the next stage in a knight's life, that of acquiring land, wife, honor, and his own following of youths.

The period between childhood and maturity was no less dangerous for noblewomen than for men. Marriages were the primary forms of alliances between noble houses, and the production of children was essential to the continued prosperity of the family. Thus daughters were raised as breeders, married at around age sixteen, and then expected to produce as many children as possible. Given the primitive knowledge of obstetrics, bearing children was even more dangerous than bearing a lance. Many noblewomen died in childbirth, often literally exhausted by frequent successive births. Although occasionally practiced, contraception was condemned both by the Church and by husbands eager for offspring.

In this martial society, the political and economic status of women declined considerably. Because they were considered unable to participate in warfare, in northern Europe women were also frequently excluded from inheritance, estate management, courts, and public deliberations. Although a growing tradition of "courtliness" glorified the status of aristocratic women in literature, women were actually losing ground in the real world. Some noblewomen did control property and manage estates, but usually such roles were possible only for widows who had borne sons and who could play a major part in raising them. For all their martial valor, medieval men feared women and female sexuality. They mistrusted this representative of another lineage who was essential to the continuance of their own. Both secular tradition and Christian teaching portrayed women as devious, sexually demanding tempt-resses often responsible for the corruption and downfall of men. Many men felt threatened by this aggressive sexual stereotype. They resented the power wielded by wealthy widows and abbesses.

To maintain a lifestyle of conspicuous consumption required wealth, and wealth meant land. The nobility was essentially a society of heirs who had inherited not only land but also the serfs who worked their manors. Lesser nobles acquired additional property from great nobles and from ecclesiastical institutions in return for binding contracts of mutual assistance. This tradition was at least as old as the Carolingians, who granted their followers land in return for military service. In later centuries, counts and lesser lords continued this tradition, exchanging land for support. Individual knights became *vassals* of lay or ecclesiastical magnates, swearing fealty or loyalty to the lord and promising to defend and aid him. In return the lord swore to protect his vassal and granted him a means of support by which the vassal could maintain himself while serving his lord. Usually this grant, termed a *fief*, was a parcel of productive land and the serfs and privileges attached to it.

Individual lords often had considerable numbers of vassals, who might also be the vassals of other lay and secular lords. The networks thus established formed vital social and political structures. In some unusual situations, such as in England immediately after the Norman Conquest and in the Latin Kingdom of Jerusalem founded following the First Crusade in 1099, these structures of lords and vassals constituted systems of hierarchical government. Elsewhere, individuals often held fiefs from and owed service to more than one lord, and not all of the individuals in a given county or duchy owed their primary obligation to the count or duke. Likewise, often most of a noble's land was owned outright rather than held in fief, thus making the feudal bond less central to his status. As a result these bonds, anachronistically called *feudalism* by French lawyers of the sixteenth and seventeenth centuries, constituted just one more element of a social system tied together by kinship, regional alliances, personal bonds of fealty, and the surviving elements of Carolingian administration inherited by counts and dukes.

The Church: Saints and Monks.   The religious needs of the peasantry remained those that their pre-Christian ancestors had known: fertility of land, animals, and women; protection from the ravages of climate and the warrior elite; supernatural cures for the ailments and disabilities of their harsh life. The cultural values of the nobility retained the essentials of the Germanic warrior ethos, including family honor, battle, and display of status. The rural Church of the High Middle Ages met the needs of both, although it subtly changed them in the process.

Most medieval people, whether peasants or lords, lived in a world of face-to-face encounters, a world in which abstract creeds counted for little and in which interior state and external appearance were rarely distinguished. In this world, religion meant primarily action, and the essential religious actions were the liturgical celebrations performed by the clergy, many of whom had received only rudimentary instruction from their predecessors and whose knowledge of Latin and theology was minimal. But these intellectual factors would become significant only centuries later. Ordinary laypeople wanted priests who would not extort them by selling the sacraments and would not seduce their wives and daughters. They wanted priests who would not leave the village for months or years at a time to seek clerical advancement elsewhere rather than remaining in the village performing the rituals necessary to keep the supernatural powers well disposed toward men and women in the community.

The most important of these supernatural powers was not some distant divinity but the saints—local, personal, even idiosyncratic persons. During their lives saintly men and women had shown that they enjoyed special favor with God. After their deaths, they continued to be the link between the divine and the earthly spheres. Through their bodies, preserved as relics in the monasteries of Europe, they continued to live among mortals even while

This gold-plated statue contains the skull of Saint Foy, a young girl who was martyred during the last Roman persecution of the Christians in 303. The image illustrates the medieval veneration of the physical relics of the saints.

participating in the heavenly court. Thus they could be approached just like local earthly lords and like them be won over through offerings, bribes, oaths, and rituals of supplication and submission. Saints were approached directly. Praying and fasting, petitioners pilgrimaged to a saint's tomb and kept vigil there, beseeching the saint's protection. These tombs were normally found in monasteries, which orchestrated and controlled the places and times by which the laity could have access to these patrons.

Monasteries did more than orchestrate the cult of the special category of the dead who were the saints. They were also responsible for the cult of the ordinary dead, for praying for the souls of ordinary mortals. In particular, monastic communities commemorated and prayed for those members of noble families who, through donations of land, had become especially associated with the monastic community. Association with such monasteries through gifts and exchanges of property, and particularly through burial in the monastic cemetery, provided the surest means of continuing noble families' honor and prestige into the next world. Across Europe noble families founded monasteries on their own lands or invited famous abbots to reorganize existing monasteries. These monasteries continued the ritual remembrance of the family, providing it with a history and forming an important part of its material as well as spiritual prestige.

Supported by both peasants and nobles, Benedictine monasteries reached their height in the eleventh and twelfth centuries. Within their walls developed a religious culture that was one of the greatest achievements of the Middle Ages. The essence of the monastic life was the passionate pursuit of God. The goal was not simply salvation but perfection, and this required discipline of the body through a life of voluntary chastity and poverty and discipline of the spirit through obedience and learning. The Benedictine's life moved to the rhythm of the divine office, the ancient series of eight hours each day when the monks put aside work, study, or rest and assembled in the monastic church for the communal chanting of prayers, psalms, and hymns. From matins, recited after midnight, until compline, the last evening prayer, the monks praised God and asked his aid and that of his saints on behalf of themselves, their secular patrons, their families, and all of society.

Monasteries were communities of professional prayers and therein found their social justification. They were also enormously rich and powerful social and political institutions. The monastery of Cluny, in saving souls through prayer, became the first international organization of monastic centers, with abbeys and dependent communities, called priories, throughout Europe. The abbots of Cluny were among the most powerful and influential people of the eleventh and twelfth centuries, dealing as equals with kings, popes, and emperors. In order to remain in form for the strenuous liturgical commemoration of living and dead patrons, Cluniac monks largely abandoned the tradition of manual work, leaving such mundane activities rather to their thousands of serfs and lay agents.

The Cluniac monks' comparative luxury and concentration on liturgy to the neglect of other spiritual activities led some monastic reformers to call for a return to simplicity, separation from the rest of society, and a deeper internal spirituality. Chief among these groups were the Cistercians, who, under the dynamic leadership of Bernard of Clairvaux (1090–1153), spread a rigorous ascetic form of monasticism from England to the Vienna Woods. The Cistercians built monasteries in the wilderness and discouraged the kinds of close ties with secular society established by the Cluniacs. Paradoxically, by establishing themselves in remote areas, organizing their estates in an efficient manner, and gaining a great reputation for asceticism, the Cistercians became enormously wealthy and successful leaders in the economic changes taking place in the twelfth and thirteenth centuries.

The rural Church not only served the lay population but worked to transform it. Although monks and bishops were spiritual warriors, most abhorred bloodshed among Christians and sought to limit the violence of aristocratic life. This attitude combined altruistic and selfish motives, since Church property was often the focus of aristocratic greed. The decline of public power and the rise of aristocratic autonomy and violence were particularly marked in southern France. There, beginning in the tenth century, churchmen organized the Peace of God and the Truce of God, movements that attempted to protect peasants, merchants, and clerics from aristocratic violence and to limit the times when warfare was allowed. During the eleventh century, the goals of warfare were shifted from attacks against other Christians to the defense of Christian society. This redirection produced the Crusades, those religious wars of conquest directed against Europe's non-Christian neighbors.

In order to direct noble violence away from Christendom, Pope Urban II (1088–1099) in 1095 urged Western knights to use their arms to free the Holy Land from Muslim occupation. In return he promised to absolve them from all of the punishment due for their sins in this life or the next. The First Crusade was remarkably successful. The crusaders took Jerusalem in 1099 and established the Latin Kingdom in Palestine. For over two centuries bands of Western warriors went on armed pilgrimage to defend this precarious kingdom and, after the reconquest of Jerusalem by the Muslim commander Saladin in 1187, to attempt to recapture it. Other such holy wars were directed against the Muslims in Spain, the Slavs in eastern Europe, and even against heretics and political opponents in France and Italy.

The Crusades, glorified in the nineteenth century by European imperialists who saw them as the model for Europe's expansion into the east, were brutal and vicious, and the crusaders were often motivated as much by greed as by piety. By the end of the thirteenth century the military failure of the Crusades, the immorality of many of the participants, and doubts about the spiritual significance of such wars contributed to their decline. So, too, did the rise of centralized monarchies, whose rulers usually viewed the Crusades as a wasteful and futile distraction.

Until the twelfth century, peasants, lords, and monks made up the great majority of Europe's population and lived together in mutual dependence, sharing involvement with the rhythm of the agrarian life. From the later part of the twelfth century, however, this rural world became increasingly aware of a different society, that of the growing cities and towns of Europe, whose citizens moved to a different rhythm, that of commerce and manufacture.

Medieval Towns

Monastic preachers liked to remind their listeners that according to the Bible, Cain had founded the first town after killing his brother Abel. Towns seemed somehow immoral and perverse but at the same time fascinating. Monks saw the city as the epitome of evil from which they had fled, and yet in the twelfth century new monasteries were being established in or near towns, while older monasteries established on the outskirts of towns found themselves being incorporated into growing urban areas. Nobles disdained urban society for its lack of respect for aristocracy and its disinterest in their cult of violence. Still, as rude warriors were transformed into courtly nobles, these nobles were drawn to the luxuries provided by urban merchants and became indebted to urban moneylenders in order to maintain their "gracious" lifestyles. For many peasants, towns were refuges from the hopelessness of their normal lives. "Town air makes one free," they believed, and many serfs fled the land to try their fortunes in the nearby towns. Clearly, something was very different about the urban communities that emerged, first in Italy, then in the Low Countries and across Europe in the later eleventh and twelfth centuries.

Italian Communes.   Urban life had never ceased to be an essential ingredient in Italy, which had maintained its urban traditions and ties with the Mediterranean world since antiquity. Although their populations had shrunk in late antiquity and they were dominated by their bishops, who exercised secular and ecclesiastical lordship, the towns of the peninsula had continued to play commercial and political roles and to attract not only runaway serfs but even nobles, who maintained fortified towers within the town walls.

The coastal cities of Amalfi, Bari, Genoa, and especially Venice had continued to play important roles in commerce both with the Byzantines and with the new Muslim societies. For Venice, this role was facilitated by its official status as a part of the Byzantine Empire, which gave it access to Byzantine markets. With nothing of their own to trade but perhaps salt and, in Venice, glass, these cities were forced to look to trade, serving as go-betweens for the transport of Eastern spices, silks, and ivories, which they exchanged for Western iron, slaves, timber, grain, and oil. In order to protect their merchant ships, Italian coastal cities developed their own fleets, and by the eleventh century they were major military forces in the Mediterranean. Venice's fleet became the primary protector of the Byzantine Empire and was thereby able to win more favorable commercial rights than those enjoyed by Greek merchants. As the merchants of the Italian towns penetrated the markets at the western end of the great overland spice routes connecting China, India, and central Asia with the Mediterranean, they established permanent merchant colonies in the East. They did not hesitate to use military force to win concessions.

The Crusades, armed pilgrimages for pious northern nobles, were primarily economic opportunities for the Italians, who had no scruples about trading with Muslims. Furthermore, only the Italians had the ships and the expertise to transport the crusaders by sea, the only option that offered hope of success, since every Crusade but the first that had followed an overland route had ended in failure. Moreover, the ships of the Italian cities were the only means of supplying the crusading armies once they were in Palestine. Crusaders paid the Italian merchants handsomely for their assistance and also granted them economic and political rights in the Palestinian port cities such as Tyre and Acre. The culmination of this relationship between northern crusaders and Italians was the Fourth Crusade. In 1204 a renegade Crusade short on funds was sidetracked by the Venetians into capturing and sacking Constantinople.

By the thirteenth century, Italian merchants had spread far beyond the Mediterranean. The great merchant banking houses of Venice, Florence, and Genoa had established offices around the Mediterranean and Black seas; south along the Atlantic coast of Morocco; east into Armenia and Persia; west to London, Bruges, and Ghent; and north to Scandinavia. Some individual

An illustration from a fourteenth-century manuscript. The Venetian merchant Marco Polo (1254–1324), with his father and uncle, is seen departing from Venice for points east in 1271. Marco traveled as far as China and did not return home to Venice until 24 years later.

merchants, the Venetian Marco Polo (1254–1324) for example, traded as far east as China.

These international commercial operations required more sophisticated systems of commercial law and credit than the West had ever known. Italian merchants developed the practices of double-entry bookkeeping, limited-liability partnership, commercial insurance, and international letters of exchange. Complex commercial affairs also required the development of a system of credit and interest-bearing loans, an idea abhorrent to traditional rural societies. Since usury, that is, borrowing and lending at credit, was regarded as making money by manipulating time, which belonged only to God, churchmen condemned the practice as a form of simony, the buying and selling of spiritual goods. In spite of ecclesiastical prohibitions, bankers found ways of hiding interest payments in contracts, thus allowing lender and seller to participate in the growing world of credit-based transactions.

Just as significant as the international trade networks established by these traders were the cultural and institutional infrastructures that made these far-flung operations possible. The most basic of these was a mentality that considered commerce an honorable occupation. Since antiquity, aristocratic culture had considered only warfare and agriculture as worthy pursuits. The strength of the Italian towns was that they were able to throw off such a rural, aristocratic value system. Already in the ninth century, even the doge, or duke, of Venice had invested much of his wealth in commercial operations. By the later tenth and eleventh centuries this passion for commerce had spread from the seacoasts to the towns throughout Italy and from there to cities such as Marseilles, Barcelona, and others in southern Europe. By the twelfth century wealthy citizens, whether descended from successful merchants or from landed aristocrats, were indifferently termed "magnates." The rest of the town's population were called "populars." The difference between the two was essentially economic. Since commercial activity offered a means of social mobility, the two could act in close accord, particularly when dealing with urban lords or outside powers. In the eleventh and early twelfth centuries, many Italian towns bought off or expelled their traditional lords such as counts and bishops, thus allowing the magnates and populars of these cities to create their own governing institutions or communes.

During the twelfth and thirteenth centuries Italy played host to a bewildering variety of experiments in self-government as urban populations banded together in communes of citizens who sought to govern themselves. These relatively small communities of citizens (the largest was approximately one hundred thousand adults) developed a keen sense of patriotism, local pride, and fierce independence reminiscent of the ancient Greek city-states. They manifested this pride in artistic and architectural competition as individual cities and their citizens sought to surpass each other in the construction of beautiful plazas, town halls, and sumptuous urban palaces.

The unity and patriotism the Italian cities showed the rest of the world was matched in intensity by the violence of their internal disputes. Every adult male was expected to participate in government, usually in his free time and at the expense of his private business activities. This involvement was intensely partisan as magnates disputed among themselves and with the ordinary populace for control of the town. These conflicts frequently turned violent as citizens took sides on wider issues of Italian and European politics.

Within many towns, the magnates formed their own corporation, the society of knights, to protect their privileged position. Families of nobles and magnates, whose cultural values were similar to those of the rural aristocracy, competed with each other for honor and power. Feuds fought out between noble families and their vassals in city streets were frequent events in Italian towns.

Opposing the magnates were popular corporations, the society of the people, which sought to rein in the violent and independent-minded nobles. These popular organizations could include anyone who was not a member of the society of knights, although in reality they were dominated by the prominent leaders of craft and trade associations, or guilds. To enforce its measures, the society had its own elected officers and its own military, headed by a "captain of the people," who might command as many as a thousand troops against the magnates.

In order to tip the scales in their favor, differing parties frequently invited outside powers into local affairs. The greatest outside contenders for power in the Italian cities were the Germanic empire and the papacy. Most towns had an imperial faction (named Ghibelline after Waiblingen castle, which belonged to the family of the emperor Frederick II), bitterly opposed by a papal faction (in time called Guelph after the Welf family, which opposed Frederick's family). In time, the issues separating Guelphs and Ghibellines changed, and the Guelphs became the party of the wealthy eager to preserve the status quo while those out of power rallied to the Ghibelline cause.

In order to maintain civic life in spite of these conflicts, cities established complex systems of government in which officers were selected by series of elections and lotteries designed to prevent any one faction from seizing control. Sovereignty lay with the *arengo*, or assembly, which comprised all adult male citizens. Except in very small communes this body was too large to function efficiently, so most communes selected a series of working councils. The great council might be as large as 400; an inner council had perhaps 24 to 40 members. Generally, executive authority was vested in consuls, whose numbers varied widely and who were chosen from various factions and classes. When these consuls proved unable to overcome the partisan politics of the factions, many towns turned to hiring *podestàs*, nonpolitical professional city managers from outside the community. These were normally magnates from other communes who had received legal educations and who served for relatively short periods. In Modena, for example, they served six months. They were required to bring with them 4 judges, 24 cavalrymen, and sergeants and grooms to help maintain order. They could not have any relatives in Modena, could not leave town without permission of the great council, and could not eat or drink with local citizens lest they be drawn into factional conflicts.

Northern "Towns." The Baltic and North seas and the English Channel tied together the peoples of Scandinavia, Lithuania, northern Germany, Flanders, and England. Scandinavian fish and timber, Baltic grain, English wool, and Flemish cloth circulated around the edges of these lands, linking them in a common economic network. Here, as in the south, there developed urban merchant and manufacturing communities linked by sea routes, distinguished from the surrounding countryside by the formation of a distinctly urban, commercial mentality.

The earliest of these interrelated communities were the cloth towns of Flanders, Brabant, and northern France. Chief among them were Ghent, Bruges, and Ypres, and the wool-exporting towns of England, particularly London. In the eleventh century, Flanders, lacking the land for large-scale sheep grazing and facing a growing population, began to specialize in the production of high-quality cloth made from English wool. At the same time, England, which experienced an economic and population decline following the Norman Conquest, began to export the greater part of its wool to Flanders to be worked. The production of wool cloth began to develop a cottage occupation into Europe's first major industry.

Woolen manufacture was a natural for such a transformation. The looms required to manufacture heavy wool cloth were large and expensive and the skills needed to produce the cloth were complex. The need for water both to power looms and to wash the cloth during production tended to concentrate cloth manufacture along waterways. Finally, as competition increased, only centralization and regulation of manufacture could ensure quality control and thus enhance marketability. Moreover, wool cloth was a necessity of life across Europe, and the growing population provided the first large-scale market for manufactured goods since the disintegration of the Roman Empire.

For all of these reasons, by the late eleventh century, the traditional image of medieval cloth production had been transformed. No longer did individual women sit in farmhouses spinning and weaving. Now manufacture was concentrated in towns, and men replaced women at the looms. Furthermore, production was closely regulated and controlled by a small group of extremely wealthy merchant-drapiers (cloth makers).

Concentration of capital, specialization of labor, and increase of urban population created vibrant, exciting cities essentially composed of three social orders. At the top were wealthy patricians, the merchant-drapiers. Their agents traveled to England and purchased raw wool, which they then distributed to weavers and other master craftsmen. These craftsmen, often using equipment rented from the patricians, carded, dyed, spun, and wove the wool into cloth. Finally, the finished cloth was returned to the patricians, whose agents then marketed it throughout Europe. Through their control of raw materials, equipment, capital, and distribution, the merchant-drapiers controlled the cloth trade and thus the economic and political life of the Flemish wool towns. Through their closed associations, or guilds, they controlled production and set standards, prices, and wages. They also controlled communal government by monopolizing urban councils.

At the bottom of urban society were the unskilled and semiskilled artisans, called "blue nails" because constant work with dye left their fingers permanently stained. These workers led an existence more precarious than that of most peasants. In the early fourteenth century, the temporary interruption of grain shipments from northern Germany to Ypres left thousands dead of starvation. Small wonder that from the thirteenth century on, blue nails were increasingly hostile to patricians. Sporadic rebellions and strikes spread across Flanders, Brabant, and northern France. Everywhere they were ruthlessly suppressed. The penalty for organizing a strike was death.

Between the patricians and the workers stood the masters—the skilled craftsmen who controlled the day-to-day production of cloth and lesser crafts. Masters organized into guilds with which they both regulated every aspect of their trades and protected them from competition. The masters often leased their looms or other equipment from the merchant-drapiers and from them received raw materials and wages to be distributed to their workers.

Tying together the northern and southern commercial worlds were the great fairs of Champagne. Six times during the year the towns of Champagne, particularly Troyes and Provins, swelled with exotic crowds of merchants from Flanders, England, Scandinavia, Germany, Brabant, Spain, and Italy. Rich and poor from the surrounding countryside also poured into the towns as merchants from north and south met to bargain and trade under the protection of the local counts.

Representing Flanders were agents of the merchant-drapiers of each town, whose carefully inspected and regulated products carried the prestige and financial prosperity of their communities. Cloth was known by the name of the town in which it was made, and thus quality control was a corporate rather than an individual issue. From Italy came merchants of great Italian trading companies to purchase northern cloth for resale throughout the Mediterranean.

Southern merchants brought silks, sugar, salt, alum (a chemical essential in cloth manufacture), and, most importantly, spices to trade at the fairs. Medieval cooks gloried in the use of spices, of which they knew over two hundred. The liberal use of exotic spices may have served as a preservative, and spices probably hid the taste of half-rotten food. But primarily the use of spices was a part of the conspicuous consumption by which the rich displayed their wealth and status.

In addition to the trade in cloth and spices, leather from Spain, iron from Germany, copper and tin from Bohemia, salted or smoked fish and furs from Scandinavia, and local wines, cheeses, and foodstuffs also changed hands under the watchful eyes of fair officials, who supervised weights, measures, and currency exchanges. The fair staff also provided courts to settle disagreements among merchants. These great international exchanges connected the financial and marketing centers of the south with the manufacturing and trading communities of the north, tying the northern world to the south more effectively than had any system since the political institutions of the Roman Empire.

Urban Culture

In the late eleventh and early twelfth centuries, the pace of urban intellectual life quickened. The combination of population growth, improved agricultural productivity, political stability, and educational interest culminated in what has been called the "renaissance of the twelfth century." Bologna and Paris became the undisputed centers of the new educational movements. Bologna specialized in the study of law. There from the eleventh century a number of important teachers began to make detailed, authoritative commentaries on the Justinian Code (*Corpus iuris civilis*), the sixth-century compilation of law prepared on the order of the Roman emperor Justinian. In the next century the same systematic study was applied to Church law, culminating in the *Decretum Gratiani*, or "Concord of Discordant Canons," prepared around 1140 in Bologna by the monk Gratian. The growing importance of legal knowledge in politics, international trade, and Church administration drew students from across Europe to Bologna, where they organized a *universitas*, or guild of students, the first true university. In Bologna, law students, many of them adults from wealthy backgrounds, controlled every aspect of the university from the selection of administrators to the exact length of professors' lectures. Professors and administrators were controlled by the guild and were fined if they broke any of the regulations.

North of the Alps, Paris became the center for study of the liberal arts and of theology during the twelfth century. The city's emergence as the leading educational center of Europe resulted from a convergence of factors. Paris was the center of an important cathedral school as well as of a monastic school. In the twelfth century it became the capital of the French kings, who needed educated clerics, or clerks, for their administration. Finally, in the early twelfth century, students from across Europe flocked to Paris to study with the greatest and most original intellect of the century, Peter Abelard (1079–1142).

Brilliant, supremely self-assured, and passionate, Abelard arrived in Paris in his early twenties and quickly took the intellectual community by storm. He ridiculed the established teachers, bested them in open debate, and established his own school, which drew the best minds of his day. Abelard's intellectual method combined the tools of legal analysis perfected in Bologna with Aristotelian logic and laid the foundation of what has been called the Scholastic method. Logical reasoning, Abelard believed, could be applied to all problems, even those concerning the mysteries of faith.

So great was Abelard's reputation that an ambitious local cleric engaged him to give private instruction to his brilliant niece, Heloise. Soon Abelard and

Heloise were having an affair. When Heloise became pregnant, the two were secretly married. Fearing to harm his clerical career, Abelard refused to make the marriage public, preferring to protect his career rather than Heloise's honor. Her outraged uncle hired thugs who broke into Abelard's room and castrated him. After Abelard recovered from his mutilation, he and Heloise each entered monasteries, and Abelard spent years as the abbot of a small monastery in Brittany. In 1136 he returned to teach in Paris, where he quickly drew new attacks, this time led by Bernard of Clairvaux, who accused him of heresy. Abelard was convicted by a local council and forced to burn some of his own works. He sought protection from his persecutors in the monastery of Cluny, where he died in 1142.

Although Abelard himself met tragedy in his personal and professional life, the intellectual ferment he had begun in Paris continued long after him. By 1200 education had become so important in the city that the universitas, or corporation of professors, was granted a charter by King Philip Augustus, who guaranteed its rights and immunities from the control of the city. Unlike that at Bologna, the University of Paris remained a corporation of masters rather than of students. It was organized like other guilds into masters; bachelors, who were similar to journeymen in other trades; and students, who were analogous to apprentices.

Students began their studies at around age fourteen or fifteen in the faculty of arts. After approximately six years, they received a bachelor of arts degree, which was a prerequisite to enter the higher faculties of theology, medicine, or law. After additional years of reading and commenting on specific texts under the supervision of a master, they received the title of master of arts, which gave them the license to teach anywhere within Christian Europe.

Though these years were filled with study, students also enjoyed a spirited life that revolved around the taverns and brothels that filled the student district, or Latin Quarter. Drunken brawls were frequent, and relationships between students and townspeople were often strained because students enjoyed legal immunity from city officials. In 1229 a fight between students and a tavern owner over their bill erupted into general rioting and street battles that left many students and citizens dead or injured. Furious at the government for having sent in soldiers to quell the riot, the masters dissolved the university for six years and threatened never to return to Paris. Masters and students migrated to Oxford, Reims, Orléans, and elsewhere, greatly aiding the development of these other intellectual centers. In 1231 most of the masters' demands were finally met and the teachers returned to Paris secure in their rights of self-governance.

The intellectual life of the universities was in its way as rough and tumble as any student brawl. Through the thirteenth and fourteenth centuries it was dominated by a pagan philosopher already dead for a thousand years. The introduction of the works of Aristotle into the West between 1150 and 1250 created an intellectual crisis every bit as profound as that of the Newtonian revolution of the seventeenth century or the Einsteinian revolution of the twentieth. For centuries, Western thinkers had depended on the Christianized

Neoplatonic philosophy of Origen and Augustine. Aristotle was known in the West only through his basic logical treatises, which in the twelfth century, thanks in large part to the work of Peter Abelard, had become the foundation of intellectual work. Logic, or dialectic, was seen as the universal key to knowledge, and the university system was based on its rigorous application to traditional texts of law, philosophy, and Scripture.

Beginning in the late twelfth century, Christian and Jewish scholars began translating Aristotle's treatises on natural philosophy, ethics, and metaphysics into Latin. Suddenly Christian intellectuals who had already accepted the Aristotelian method were brought face to face with Aristotle's conclusions: a world without an active, conscious God; a world in which everything from the functioning of the mind to the nature of matter could be understood without reference to a divine creator. Further complicating matters, the texts arrived not from the original Greek, but normally through Latin translations of Arabic translations accompanied by learned commentaries by Muslim and Jewish scholars, especially by Averroës, the greatest Aristotelian philosopher of the twelfth century.

As the full impact of Aristotelian philosophy began to reach churchmen and scholars, reactions varied from condemnation to wholehearted acceptance. At one extreme, in 1210 Church authorities forbade the teaching of Aristotle's philosophy in Paris, a prohibition the professors ignored. At the other extreme, Parisian scholars such as Siger de Brabant (ca. 1235–ca. 1281) eagerly embraced Aristotelian philosophy as interpreted by Averroës, even when these teachings varied from Christian tradition. To many, it appeared that there were two irreconcilable kinds of truth, one knowable through divine revelation, the other through human reason.

One Parisian scholar who refused to accept this dichotomy was Thomas Aquinas (1225–1274), a professor of theology and the most brilliant intellect of the High Middle Ages. Although an Aristotelian who recognized the genius of Averroës, Aquinas refused to accept the possibility that human reason, which was a gift from God, led necessarily to contradictions with divine revelation. Aquinas's great contribution, contained in his *Summa Against the Gentiles* (1259–1264) and in his incomplete *Summa of Theology* (1266–1273), was to defend the integrity of human reason and to reconcile it with divine revelation. Properly applied, the principles of Aristotelian philosophy could not lead to error, he argued. However, human reason unaided by revelation could not always lead to certain conclusions. Questions about such matters as the nature of God, creation, and the human soul could not be resolved by reason alone. In developing his thesis, Aquinas recast Christian doctrine and philosphy, replacing their Neoplatonic foundation with an Aristotelian base. Although not universally accepted in the thirteenth century (in 1277 the bishop of Paris condemned many of Aquinas's teachings as heretical), his synthesis came to dominate Christian intellectual life for centuries.

Aquinas was a member of a new religious order, the Dominicans, who along with the Franciscans appeared in response to the social and cultural needs of the new urbanized, monetized European culture. Benedictine monasticism was ideally suited to a rural, aristocratic world but had little place in the bustling cities of Italy, Flanders, and Germany. In these urban, commercial environments, Christians were more concerned with the problems of living in the world than escape from it. Laypersons and clerics alike were concerned with the growing wealth of ecclesiastical institutions, and across southern Europe especially, individual reformers attacked the wealthy lifestyles of monks and secular clergy as un-Christian. Torn between their own involvement in a commercial world and an inherited Christian-Roman tradition that looked upon commerce and capital as degrading, reformers called for a return to what they imagined to have been the life of the primitive Church, one that emphasized both individual and collective poverty. The poverty movement attracted great numbers of followers, many of whom added to their criticisms of traditional clergy a concern over clerical morality and challenges about the value of sacraments and the priesthood. Although many reformers were condemned as heretics and sporadically persecuted, the reform movement continued to grow and threatened to destroy the unity of Western Christendom.

The people who preserved the Church's unity were inspired by the same impulses, but they channeled their enthusiasm into reforming the Church from within. Francis of Assisi (1182–1226), the son of a prosperous Italian merchant, rejected his luxurious life in favor of one of radical poverty and service to others. He was a man of extraordinary simplicity, humility, and joy, and his piety was in keeping with his character. As he wandered about preaching repentance he drew great numbers of followers from all ranks, especially from the urban communities of Italy. Convinced of the importance of obedience, Francis asked Pope Innocent III to approve the way of life he had chosen for himself and his followers. The pope, recognizing that in Francis the impulses threatening the Church might be its salvation, granted his wish. The Order of Friars Minor, or Franciscans, grew by thousands, drawing members from as far away as England and Hungary.

Francis insisted that his followers observe strict poverty, both individually and collectively. The order could not own property, nor could its members even touch money. They were expected to beg food each day for their sustenance. They were to travel from town to town, preaching, performing manual labor, and serving the poor. In time the expansion of the order and its involvement in preaching against heresy and in education brought about compromises with Francis's original ideals. The Franciscans needed churches in which to preach, books with which to study, and protection from local bishops. Most of the friars accepted these changes. These, the so-called Conventuals, were bitterly opposed by the Spirituals, or rigorists, who sought to maintain the radical poverty of their founder. In the fourteenth century this conflict led to a major split in the order and ultimately to the condemnation of the Spirituals as heretics.

The order of friars founded by Dominic (1170–1221) also adopted a rule of strict poverty approved by Innocent III, but the primary focus of the Dominicans was on preaching to the society of the thirteenth century. This order, which emphasized intellectual activity, concentrated on preaching against heresies and on higher education. Thus the Dominicans, too, gravitated toward the cities of western Europe and especially toward its great universities. These new orders of preachers, highly educated, enthusiastic, and eloquent, began to formulate for the urban laity of Europe a new vision of Christian society, a society not only of peasants, lords, and monks, but also of merchants, craft workers, and professionals. Also, their central organizations and their lack of ties to the rural aristocracies made them the favorite religious orders of the increasingly powerful centralized monarchies.

The Romano-barbarian chieftains who inherited political power in the West experimented with a variety of ways to combine the political heritage of Rome and the military traditions of their peoples into enduring polities. The most successful were the Franks, whose early acceptance of orthodox Christianity made possible an amalgam of Roman and barbarian peoples. Under their kings, especially Charlemagne, they brought most of the old western empire under their control and introduced throughout it their synthesis of Frankish and Roman culture and institutions.

By 1300 Europe had achieved a level of population density, economic prosperity, cultural sophistication, and political organization greater than at any time since the Roman Empire. Across Europe, a largely free peasantry cultivated a wide variety of crops both for local consumption and for growing commercial markets, while landlords sought increasingly rational approaches to estate management and investment. In cities and ports, merchants, manufacturers, and bankers presided over an international commercial and manufacturing economy that connected Scandinavia to the Mediterranean Sea. In schools and universities, students learned the skills of logical thinking and disputation while absorbing the traditions of Greece and Rome to prepare themselves for careers in law, medicine, and government.

Although the political structure created by Charlemagne did not survive his grandsons, the Frankish model proved enduring in every other respect. The cultural renaissance laid the foundation of all subsequent European intellectual activities. The alliance between Church and monarch provided the formula for European kings for almost a thousand years. The administrative system with its central and local components, its counts and its missi, its diplomas and capitularies, provided the model for later medieval government in England and on the Continent. Finally, the idea of the Carolingian empire, the symbol of European unity, has never entirely disappeared from the West.

Suggestions for Further Reading

The Making of the Barbarian Kingdoms

James Campbell, ed., *The Anglo-Saxons* (Oxford, England: Phaidon, 1982). A collection of essays on Anglo-Saxon England by an outstanding group of archaeologists and historians.

Edward James, *The Origins of France: From Clovis to the Capetians, 500–1000* (London: Macmillan, 1982). A topical introduction to early French history.

Lucien Musset, *The Barbarian Invasions* (University Park: Penn State University Press, 1975). A survey of the barbarian peoples in late antiquity and the early Middle Ages.

*Timothy Reuter, *Germany in the Early Middle Ages 800–1056* (Longman: London and New York, 1991). An excellent introduction to early German history intended for an English reading public.

Living in the New Europe

*David Herlihy, *Medieval Households* (Cambridge, MA: Harvard University Press, 1985). An important survey of medieval peasant society.

Suzanne Fonay Wemple, *Women in Frankish Society: Marriage and the Cloister 500–900* (Philadelphia: University of Pennsylvania Press, 1981). A pioneering study of women in the early Middle Ages.

The Carolingian Achievement

*Rosamond McKitterick, *The Frankish Kingdoms Under the Carolingians, 751–987* (New York: Longman, 1983). A very detailed study of Carolingian history with an emphasis on intellectual developments.

A Tour of Europe in the Ninth Century

*Geoffrey Barraclough, ed., *Eastern and Western Europe in the Middle Ages* (New York: Harcourt Brace Jovanovich, 1970). Essays by specialists on eastern Europe and its relationship to the West.

*Peter Sawyer, *The Age of the Vikings* (New York: St. Martin's Press, 1971). A good introduction to Scandinavian history.

W. Montgomery Watt, *A History of Islamic Spain* (Edinburgh: Edinburgh University Press, 1965). An intelligent introduction to Spain under Islam for the nonspecialist.

After the Carolingians: From Empire to Lordships

Heinrich Fichtenau, *Living in the Tenth Century: Studies in Mentalities and Social Orders* (Chicago: University of Chicago Press, 1990). A brilliant evocation of the quest for order on the Continent following the dissolution of the Carolingian empire.

Society and Culture in the High Middle Ages

*Georges Duby, *Rural Economy and Country Life in the Medieval West* (Columbia: University of South Carolina Press, 1968). An authoritative survey of medieval agriculture and society.

Georges Duby, *The Kinght, the Lady, and the Priest: The Making of Modern Marriage in Medieval France* (New York: Pantheon, 1984). A short study of the conflict between lay and religious social values in medieval France.

---

*Indicates paperback edition available.

Ronald C. Finucane, *Soldiers of the Faith: Crusaders and Moslems at War* (New York: St. Martin's Press, 1984). A critical reappraisal of the Crusades for general readers.

*Robert S. Lopez, *The Commercial Revolution of the Middle Ages, 950–1350* (New York: Cambridge University Press, 1971). An excellent survey of medieval commercial history.

*R. W. Southern, *Western Society and the Church in the Middle Ages* (New York: Penguin, 1990). A well-written account of the medieval Church for a general public.

*Daniel Waley, *The Italian City-Republics* (New York: McGraw-Hill, 1969). A brief and highly readable account of Italian towns.

*Lynn White, Jr., *Medieval Technology and Social Change* (New York: Oxford University Press, 1966). Imaginative essays on the social impact of technology in the Middle Ages.

*Helene Wieruszowski, *The Medieval University* (Princeton, NJ: Van Nostrand, 1966). A short history of medieval universities.

8

Politics and Culture in the Later Middle Ages

Harold, King of the English

A few decades after William the Conqueror's victory at Hastings in 1066, his half brother, Bishop Odo of Bayeux (ca. 1036–1097), commissioned a great tapestry recording the Norman version of the conquest. An unknown Anglo-Saxon artist sketched the cartoon, drawing on models taken from Anglo-Saxon and Carolingian manuscript illumination. Anglo-Saxon women then embroidered the tapestry, a strip of linen 230 feet long and 20 inches high, a masterful piece of art.

Using such techniques familiar to modern moviemakers as jump cuts, flashbacks, close-ups, panoramas, and decomposing movement into freeze-frames, the artist and embroiderers vividly present life in eleventh-century warrior society. It is almost exclusively masculine. Of the 623 people represented, only 6 are women. We see peasants working the fields, craftsmen felling trees and building ships for William's Channel crossing. We see cities, palaces, and churches. We see cooking and banqueting, hunting, traveling, and of course we see fighting and dying. The artists accurately render clothing, armor, and even hairstyles. But the tapestry is not simply a naive piece of artistry, it is a masterpiece of propaganda.

When King Edward the Confessor (1042–1066) died, two major claimants disputed the succession. Anglo-Saxon sources insist that Edward and his nobles chose Earl Harold Godwinson (ca. 1022–1066). William insisted that Edward had designated him and that years before, when Harold had been shipwrecked on the Norman coast and befriended by the duke, he had sworn an oath to assist William in gaining the crown. Harold's death, [portrayed in the facing panel] suggests divine vengeance for his perjury. The message seems

clear. William was the rightful heir and Harold, by his perfidy, merited his tragic fate.

And yet the Anglo-Saxon artists who executed the tapestry for their Norman lord may have subtly introduced a different reading into the story of Harold. Nothing in the tapestry itself specifically labels him a perjurer or usurper. In the critical scene following his coronation, [shown above,] the legend declares him unambiguously the legitimate king: "Here sits Harold, King of the English." Moreover, in this scene he is acknowledged by representatives of the whole of society, that is, the workers, represented by the unarmed man at far left; the fighters, represented by the man holding the sword; and the prayers, present in the person of Stigand, the Archbishop of Canterbury.

In its vividness, its political subtlety, and its essential ambiguity, the Bayeux tapestry is a fitting introduction to the world of the High Middle Ages, that is, the period from about 1000 to 1300. It was a world of workers, fighters, and prayers, but also one of cities, merchants, and scholars. Its culture and religion combined, like the tapestry, the extremes of brutal warfare and subtle artistry.

*T*he Invention of the State

The disintegration of the Carolingian empire in the tenth century left political power fragmented among a wide variety of political entities. In general these were of two types. The first, the papacy and the empire, were elective traditional structures that claimed universal sovereignty over the Christian world, based on a sacred view of political power. The second, largely hereditary and less extravagant in their religious and political pretensions, were the limited kingdoms that arose within the old Carolingian world or on its borders.

The Universal States: Empire and Papacy

The Frankish world east of the Rhine had been less affected than the kingdom of the West Franks by the onslaught of Vikings, Magyars, and Saracens. The eastern Frankish kingdom, a loose confederacy of five duchies—Saxony, Lorraine, Franconia, Swabia, and Bavaria—had preserved much of the Carolingian religious, cultural, and institutional traditions. In 919 Duke Henry I of Saxony (919–936) was elected king, and his son Otto I (936–973) laid the foundation for the revival of the empire. Otto inflicted a devastating defeat on the Magyars in 955, subdued the other dukes, and tightened his control over the kingdom. He accomplished this largely through the extensive use of bishops and abbots, whom he appointed as his agents and sources of loyal support. In 951, in order to prevent a southern German prince from establishing himself in northern Italy, Otto invaded and conquered Lombardy. Eleven years later he entered Rome, where he was crowned emperor by the pope.

Otto, known to history as "the Great," had established the main features of German imperial policy for the next 300 years. These were conflict with the German aristocracy, reliance on bishops and abbots as imperial agents, and preoccupation with Italy. His successors, both in his own Saxon dynasty (919–1024) and in the succeeding dynasties, the Salians (1024–1125) and the Staufens (1138–1254), continued this tradition. Magnates elected the German kings who were then consecrated as emperors by the pope. Royal fathers generally were able to bring about the election of their sons, and in this manner they attempted to turn the kingship into a hereditary office. However, the royal families could not manage to produce male heirs in each generation, and thus the magnates continued to exercise real power in royal elections. Because of this elective tradition, German emperors were never able to establish effective control over the German magnates outside their own duchies.

The magnates' ability to expand their own power and autonomy at the expense of their Slavic neighbors to the east also contributed to the weakness of the German monarchy. In the 1150s for example, Henry the Lion (ca.

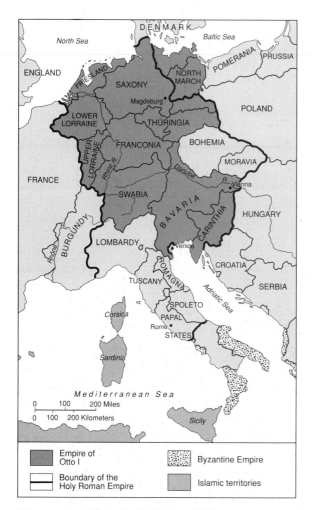

The empire of Otto the Great, ca. 963

1130–1195), Duke of Bavaria and Saxony, carved out an autonomous principality in the Slavic areas between the Elbe and the Vistula, founding the major
trading towns of Lübeck and Rostock. It was the goal of every great aristocratic family to extend its own independent lordship.

In order to counter such aristocratic power, emperors looked to the
Church both for the development of the religious cult of the emperor as "The
Anointed of the Lord" and as a source of reliable military and political support.
While the offices of count and duke had become hereditary within the great
aristocracy, the offices of bishop and abbot remained public charges to which
the emperor could appoint loyal supporters. Since these ecclesiastics had
taken vows of celibacy, the emperor did not fear that they would attempt to
pass their offices on to their children. Moreover, churchmen tended to be
experienced, educated administrators who could assist the emperor in the

THE SAXON, SALIAN, AND STAUFEN DYNASTIES

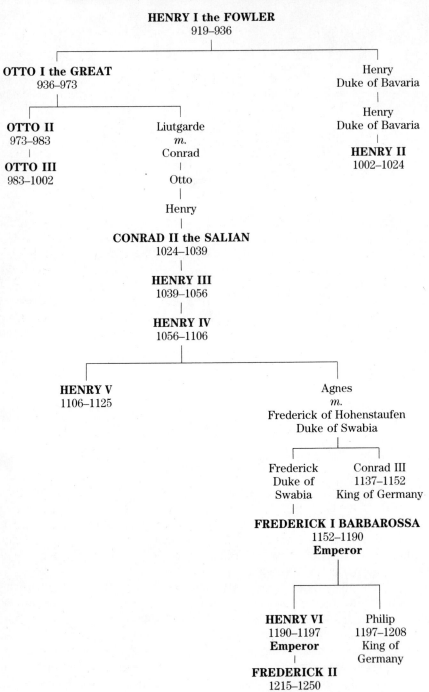

HENRY I the FOWLER
919–936

OTTO I the GREAT
936–973

Henry
Duke of Bavaria

OTTO II
973–983

Liutgarde
m.
Conrad

Henry
Duke of Bavaria

OTTO III
983–1002

Otto

HENRY II
1002–1024

Henry

CONRAD II the SALIAN
1024–1039

HENRY III
1039–1056

HENRY IV
1056–1106

HENRY V
1106–1125

Agnes
m.
Frederick of Hohenstaufen
Duke of Swabia

Frederick
Duke of
Swabia

Conrad III
1137–1152
King of Germany

FREDERICK I BARBAROSSA
1152–1190
Emperor

HENRY VI
1190–1197
Emperor

Philip
1197–1208
King of
Germany

FREDERICK II
1215–1250
Emperor

administration of the empire. Like the Carolingians, the Saxon and Salian emperors needed a purified, reformed Church free of local aristocratic control to serve the interests of the emperor. This imperial church system was the cornerstone of the empire.

Those laymen the emperor could count on, particularly from the eleventh century, were trusted household serfs whom the kings used as their agents. Although unfree, these ministerials were entrusted with important military commands and given strategic castles throughout the empire. Despised by the freeborn nobility, they tended at first to be loyal supporters of the emperor. In the twelfth century, they took on the chivalric ideals of their aristocratic neighbors and benefited from conflicts between emperor and pope to acquire autonomy. As old noble families died out, ministerial families replaced them as a new hereditary aristocracy.

Otto the Great had entered Italy to secure his southern flank. His successors became embroiled in Italian affairs until in the thirteenth century they abandoned Germany altogether. As emperors, they had to be crowned by the pope. This was possible only if they controlled Rome. Moreover, the growing wealth of northern Italian towns was an important source of financial support if Lombardy could be controlled. Finally, the preoccupation with Italy was a natural outcome of the nature of this empire. Imperial claims to universal sovereignty continued the Carolingian tradition of empire. An imperial office without Italy was unthinkable. Thus, the emperors found themselves drawn into papal and Italian politics, frequently with disastrous results. Germany became merely a source of men and material with which to fight the Lombard towns and the pope. From the eleventh through the thirteenth centuries emperors granted German princes autonomy in return for this support.

The early successes of this imperial program created the seeds of its own destruction. Imperial efforts to reform the Church resulted in a second, competing claimant to universal authority, the papacy. In the later tenth and early eleventh centuries, emperors had intervened in papal elections, deposed and replaced corrupt popes, and worked to ensure that bishops and abbots would be educated, competent churchmen. The most effective reformer was Emperor Henry III (1039–1056), who took seriously his role as the anointed of the Lord to reform the Church both in Germany and in Rome. When three rivals claimed the papacy, Henry called a synod, or meeting of bishops, which deposed all three and installed the first of a series of German popes. The most effective was Henry's own cousin who, as Leo IX (1049–1054), traveled widely in France, Germany, and Italy. He condemned simony, that is, the practice of buying Church offices, and fostered monastic reforms such as that of Cluny. He also encouraged the efforts of a group of young reformers drawn from across Europe.

In the next decades, these new, more radical reformers began to advocate a widespread renewal of the Christian world, led not by emperors but by popes. These reformers pursued an ambitious set of goals. They sought to reform the morals of the clergy and in particular to eliminate married priests.

They tried to free churches and monasteries from lay control both by forbidding laymen and women from owning churches and monasteries and by eliminating simony. They particularly condemned "lay investiture," that is, the practice by which kings and emperors appointed bishops and invested them with the symbols of their office. Finally, they insisted that the pope, not the emperor, was the supreme representative of God on earth and as such had the right to exercise a universal sovereignty.

Every aspect of the reform movement met with strong opposition throughout Europe. However, its effects were most dramatic in the empire because of the central importance there of the imperial church system. Henry III's son Henry IV (1056–1106) clashed head-on with the leading radical reformer and former protégé of Leo IX, Pope Gregory VII (1073–1085), over the emperor's right to appoint and to install or invest bishops in their offices. This investiture controversy changed the face of European political history. Legal scholars for both sides searched Roman and Church law for arguments to bolster their claims, thus encouraging the revival of legal studies at Bologna. For the first time, public opinion played a crucial role in politics, and both sides composed carefully worded propaganda tracts aimed at secular and religious audiences. Gradually, the idea of the separate spheres of church and state emerged for the first time in European political theory.

In the end, the conflict weakened both the empire and the papacy. In 1075 the emperor, supported by many German bishops, attempted to depose Gregory. Gregory excommunicated and deposed Henry, freed the German nobility from their obligations to him, and encouraged them to rebel. As anti-imperial strength grew, Henry took a desperate gamble. Crossing the Alps in the dead of winter in 1077, he arrived before the castle of Canossa in northern Italy, where Gregory was staying. Dressed as a humble penitent, Henry stood in the snow asking the pope for forgiveness and reconciliation. As a priest, the pope could not refuse, and he lifted the excommunication. Once more in power, Henry began again to appoint bishops. Again in 1080 Gregory excommunicated and deposed him. This time the majority of the German nobles and bishops remained loyal to the emperor and Henry marched on Rome. Deserted by most of his clergy, Gregory had to flee to the Normans in southern Italy. He died in Salerno in 1085.

Henry did not long enjoy his victory. Gregory's successors rekindled the opposition to Henry and even convinced his own son to join in the revolt. The conflict ended only in 1122, when Emperor Henry V (1106–1125) and Pope Calixtus II (1119–1124) reached an agreement known as the Concordat of Worms, which differentiated between the royal and the spiritual spheres of authority and allowed the emperors a limited role in episcopal election and investiture. This compromise changed the nature of royal rule in the empire, weakening the emperors and contributing to the long-term decline of royal government in Germany.

The decline that began with the investiture controversy continued as emperors abandoned political power north of the Alps in order to pursue their ambitions in Italy. Frederick I Barbarossa (1152–1190) spent much of his reign attempting to reimpose imperial authority and to collect imperial incomes from the rich towns of northern Italy. For this he needed the support of the German princes, and he granted them extraordinary privileges in return for their cooperation south of the Alps. In 1156, for example, he gave Henry Jasomirgott (ca. 1114–1177) virtual autonomy in the newly created duchy of Austria. Still, the combined efforts of the Lombard towns and the papacy were too much for Frederick and his armies to win a decisive victory. By the time of Frederick's death in 1190—he drowned crossing a river while on crusade—in Germany the emperor was more a feudal lord than a sovereign and in Italy his authority was disputed by the papacy and the towns. Frederick's successors continued his policy of focusing on Italy with no better success. In 1230 Frederick II (1215–1250) conceded to each German prince sovereign rights in his own territory. From the thirteenth to the nineteenth century these princes ruled their territories as independent states, leaving the office of emperor a hollow title.

The investiture controversy ultimately compromised the authority of the pope as well as that of the emperor. First, the series of compromises beginning with the Concordat of Worms established a novel and potent tradition in Western political thought: the definition of separate spheres of authority for secular and religious government. Secondly, while in the short run popes were able to exercise enormous political influence, from the thirteenth century they were increasingly unable to make good their claims to absolute authority.

Papal power was based on more than Scripture. Over the centuries, the popes had acquired large amounts of land in central Italy and in the Rhone Valley, which formed the nucleus of the Papal States. Moreover, in every corner of Europe, bishops and clergy were at least in theory agents of papal programs. The elaboration of systematic canon law encouraged by the papal reformers as a weapon in the investiture controversy created a system of courts and legal institutions more sophisticated than that of any secular monarch. Church courts claimed jurisdiction over all clerics regardless of the nature of the legal problem and over all baptized Christians in such fundamental issues as legitimacy of marriages, inheritances, and oaths. During the pontificate of Innocent III (1198–1216) the papacy reached the height of its powers. Innocent made and deposed emperors, excommunicated kings, summoned a crusade against heretics in the south of France, and placed whole countries such as England and France under interdict, that is, the suspension of all religious services, when rulers dared to contradict him. Still, he found time to support religious reformers, and in 1215 to call the Fourth Lateran Council, which culminated the reforms of the past century and had a lasting effect on the spiritual life of clergy and laity alike. At the council, more than twelve hundred assembled bishops and abbots, joined by great nobles from across Europe, defined fundamental doctrines such as the nature of the eucharist, ordered annual confession of sins, and detailed procedures for the election of bishops. They also mandated a strict lifestyle for clergy and forbade their participation in judicial procedures in which accused persons had to undergo painful ordeals, such as grasping a piece of red-hot iron and carrying it a prescribed distance, to prove their innocence. More ominously, the council also mandated that Jews wear special identifying markings on their clothing—a sign of the increasing hostility Christians felt toward the Jews in their midst.

During the thirteenth century the papacy continued to perfect its legal system and its control over clergy throughout Europe. However, politically the popes were unable to assert their claims to universal supremacy. This was true both in Italy, where the communes in the north and the kingdom of Naples in the south resisted direct papal control, and in the emerging kingdoms north of the Alps, where monarchs successfully intervened in Church affairs. The old claims of papal authority rang increasingly hollow. When Pope Boniface VIII (1294–1303) attempted to prevent the French king Philip IV (1285–1314) from taxing the French clergy, boasting that he could depose kings "like servants" if necessary, Philip proved him wrong. Philip's agents hired a gang of adventurers who kidnapped the pope, plundered his treasury, and released him a broken, humiliated wreck. The French king who had engineered Boniface's humiliation represented a new political tradition much more limited but ultimately more successful than either the empire or the papacy—the medieval nation-state.

The Nation-States: France and England

King was a less pretentious and more familiar office than that of emperor. As the Carolingian world disintegrated, a variety of kingdoms had appeared in France, Italy, Burgundy, and Provence. Beyond the confines of the old Carolingian world, kingship was well established in England and northern Spain. In Scandinavia, Poland, Bohemia, and Hungary powerful chieftains were consolidating royal power at the expense of their aristocracies. The claims of kings were much more modest than those of emperors or popes. Kings lay claim to a limited territory and, while the king was anointed, and thus a "Christus" (from the Greek word for sacred oil), kings were only one of many representatives of God on earth. Finally, kings were far from absolute rulers. During the tenth and eleventh centuries, the powers of justice, coinage, taxation, and military command, once considered public, had been usurped by aristocrats and nobles. Kings needed the support of these magnates and often—as in the case of France—these dukes and counts were wealthier and more powerful than the kings. Still, between the tenth and fourteenth centuries some monarchies, especially those of France and England, developed into powerful, centralized, and vigorous kingdoms. In the process they gave birth to what has become the modern state.

In 987, when Hugh Capet was elected king of the West Franks, no one suspected that his successors would become the most powerful rulers of Europe, for they were relatively weak magnates whose only real power lay in the region between Paris and Orléans. The dukes of Normandy, descendants of

Vikings whose settlement had been recognized by Frankish kings, ruled their duchy with an authority of which the kings could only dream. Less than a century later Duke William of Normandy expanded his power even more by conquering England. In the twelfth century, the English kings ruled a vast collection of hereditary lands on both sides of the English Channel termed the "Angevin Empire," territories much richer than those ruled by the French king. The counts of Flanders, too, ruled a prosperous region much better unified than the French king's small territory in the Parisian area. In the south, the counts of Poitou, who were also dukes of Aquitaine, were building up a powerful territorial principality in this most Romanized region of the kingdom, while in Anjou an ambitious aristocratic family was consolidating its territory as a virtually independent principality.

Biology and bureaucracy created the medieval French monarchy. Between 987 and 1314, every royal descendant of Hugh Capet (after whom the dynasty was called the Capetian) left a male heir—an extraordinary record for a medieval family. During the same period, by comparison, the office of emperor was occupied by men from no less than nine families. By simply outlasting the families of their great barons, the Capetian kings were able to absorb lands when other families became extinct. This success was not just the result of luck. Kings such as Robert the Pious (996–1031) and Louis VII (1137–1180) risked excommunication in order to divorce wives who had not produced male heirs. In 1152 Louis had his marriage with the richest heiress of the twelfth century, Eleanor of Aquitaine (1122–1204), annulled in part because she had given him no sons. With the annulment he also lost the chance to absorb her territories of Aquitaine and Poitou. A few months later Eleanor married Count Henry of Anjou (1133–1189), who two years later became King Henry II of England. Imagine Louis's chagrin when with Henry Eleanor produced four sons, in the process making the English kings the greatest magnates in France.

The Capetians' long run of biological luck, combined with the practice of having a son crowned during his father's lifetime and thus being firmly established before his father's death, was only part of the explanation for the Capetian success. The Capetians also wisely used their position as consecrated sovereign to build a power base in the Île de France (the region around Paris) and among the bishops and abbots of the kingdom, and then to insist on their feudal rights as the lords of the great dukes and counts of France. It was this foundation that Louis VII's son Philip II (1180–1223) used to create the French monarchy.

Philip II was known to posterity as Augustus, or the aggrandizer, because through his ruthless political intrigue and brilliant organizational sense he more than doubled the territory he controlled and more than quadrupled the revenue of the French crown. Through marriage he acquired Vermandois, the Amiénois, Artois, and Valois. He later absorbed Flanders and set the stage for the absorption of the great county of Toulouse by his son Louis VIII (1223–1226) in the aftermath of the crusade against the dualist Albigensian heretics launched by Pope Innocent III. Philip's greatest coup, however, was the

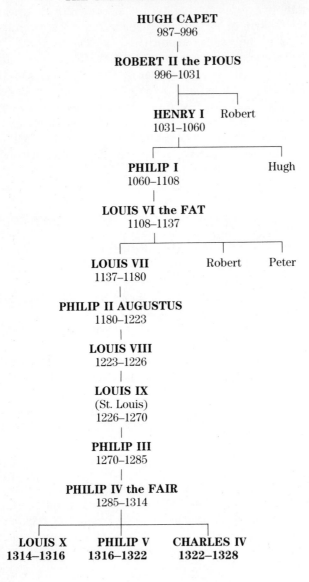

THE CAPETIAN DYNASTY OF FRANCE

HUGH CAPET
987–996

ROBERT II the PIOUS
996–1031

HENRY I　Robert
1031–1060

PHILIP I　　　　　　　　Hugh
1060–1108

LOUIS VI the FAT
1108–1137

LOUIS VII　　Robert　　Peter
1137–1180

PHILIP II AUGUSTUS
1180–1223

LOUIS VIII
1223–1226

LOUIS IX
(St. Louis)
1226–1270

PHILIP III
1270–1285

PHILIP IV the FAIR
1285–1314

LOUIS X　　**PHILIP V**　　**CHARLES IV**
1314–1316　**1316–1322**　**1322–1328**

confiscation of all the continental possessions of the English king John (1199–1216), the son of Henry II and Eleanor of Aquitaine. Although sovereign in England, as lord of Normandy, Anjou, Maine, and Touraine, John was technically a vassal of King Philip. When John married the fiancée of one of his continental vassals, the outraged vassal appealed to Philip in his capacity as John's lord. Philip summoned John to appear before the royal court, and when he refused to do so, Philip ordered him to surrender all of his continental fiefs. This meant war, and one by one John's continental possessions fell to the French king. Philip's victory over John's ally the emperor Otto IV (1198–1215)

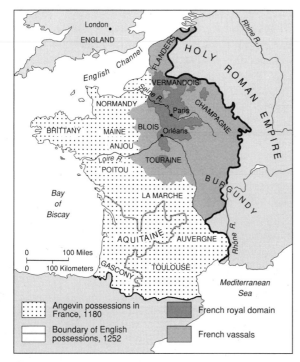

England and France in the mid-1200s

at Bouvines in 1214 sealed the English loss of Normandy, Maine, Anjou, Poitou, and Touraine.

As important as the absorption of these vast regions was the administrative system Philip organized to govern them. Using members of families from the old royal demesne, he set up administrative officials called *baillis* and *seneschals*, nonfeudal salaried agents who collected his revenues and represented his interests. The baillis in particular, who were drawn from non-noble families and who often had received their education at the University of Paris, were the foundation of the French bureaucracy, which grew in strength and importance through the thirteenth century. By governing the regions of France according to local traditions but always with an eye to the king's interest, these bureaucrats did more than anyone else to create a stable, enduring political system.

Philip's grandson Louis IX (1226–1270) fine-tuned this administrative machine and endowed it with the aura of sanctity. Louis was as perfect an embodiment of medieval Christian virtue as Saint Francis of Assisi, who died in the year of Louis's coronation. Generous and pious, but also brave and capable, Louis took seriously his obligation to provide justice for the poor and protection for the weak. A disastrous Crusade in 1248, which ended in his capture and ransom in Egypt, convinced Louis that his failure was punishment for his sins and those of his government. When he returned to France, he dispatched investigators to correct abuses by baillis and other royal officials and restored property unjustly confiscated by his father's agents during the

Albigensian Crusade. In addition he established a permanent central court in Paris to hear appeals from throughout the kingdom. Although much of the work was handled by a growing staff of professional jurists, Louis often became involved personally. In 1270, Louis attempted another crusade and died in an epidemic in Tunis. The goodwill and devotion Louis won from his subjects was a precious heritage that his successors were able to exploit for centuries. When his grandson Philip the Fair (1285–1314) faced the threat of Boniface VIII, he could rely on subjects and agents for whom the king of France and not the pope was sovereign.

The growth of royal power transformed the traditional role of the aristocracy. As the power and wealth of kings increased, the ability of the nobility to maintain their independence decreased. Royal judges undermined lords' control over the peasantry. Royal revenues enabled kings to hire warriors rather than relying on traditional feudal levies. At the same time, the increasing expenses of the noble lifestyle forced all but the wealthiest aristocrats to look for sources of income beyond their traditional estates. Increasingly they found this in royal service. Thus in the thirteenth century the nobility began to lose some of its independence to the state.

By a quite different path the English monarchy reached a level of power similar to that of the French kings by the end of the thirteenth century. France was made by a family and its bureaucracy. The kingdom originally forged by Alfred and his descendants was transformed by the successors of William the Conqueror, using its judges and its people, often in spite of themselves.

In 1066 the Norman conquerors of England acquired a small insular kingdom that had been united by Viking raids little more than a century before. Hostile Celtic societies bordered it to the north and west. Still, it had important strengths. First, the king of the English was not simply a feudal lord, a first among equals—he was a sovereign. Secondly, Anglo-Saxon government had been participatory, with the freemen of each shire taking part in court sessions and sharing the responsibilities of government. Finally, the king had agents, or *reeves*, in each shire (shire reeves, or sheriffs) who were responsible for representing the king's interests, presiding over the local court, and collecting royal taxes and incomes. This ability to raise money was the most important aspect of the English kingship for William the Conqueror and his immediate successors, who remained thoroughly continental in interest, culture, and language—the first English king to speak English fluently was probably King John. England was seen primarily as a source of revenue. To tap this wealth, the Norman kings transformed rather than abolished Anglo-Saxon governmental traditions, adding Norman feudal bonds and administrative control to Anglo-Saxon kingship.

William preserved English government while replacing Anglo-Saxon officers with his continental vassals, chiefly Normans and Flemings. He rewarded his supporters with land confiscated from the defeated Anglo-Saxons, but he was careful to give out land only in fief. In contrast to continental practice, where many lords owned vast estates outright, in England all land was held directly or indirectly of the king. Because he wanted to know the extent of his new kingdom and its wealth, William ordered a comprehensive survey of all royal rights. The recorded account, known as the Domesday Book, was the most extensive investigation of economic rights since the late Roman tax rolls had been abandoned by the Merovingians.

Since William and his successors concentrated on their continental possessions and spent little time in England, they needed an efficient system of controlling the kingdom in their absence. To this end they developed the royal court, an institution inherited from their Anglo-Saxon predecessors, into an efficient system of fiscal and administrative supervision. The most important innovation was the use of a large checkerboard, or exchequer, which functioned like a primitive computer to audit the returns of their sheriffs. Annual payments were recorded on long rolls of parchment called pipe rolls, the first continuous accounting system in Europe.

Almost two decades of warfare over the succession in the first half of the twelfth century greatly weakened royal authority, but Henry II (1154–1189), reestablished central power by reasserting his authority over the nobility and through his legal reforms. Using his continental wealth and armies, he brought the English barons into line, destroyed private castles, and reasserted his rights to traditional royal incomes. He strengthened royal courts by expanding royal jurisdiction at the expense of Church tribunals and of the courts of feudal lords.

Henry's efforts to control the clergy led to one of the epic clashes of the dispute between religious and secular powers. The archbishop of Canterbury, Thomas Becket (ca. 1118–1170), although a personal friend of Henry who had made him first chancellor and then archbishop, refused to accept the king's claim to jurisdiction over clergy. In spite of his friendship with the king, Becket, who had been educated at Paris, was deeply influenced by the papal reform movement and had a great sense of the dignity of his office. For six years Becket lived in exile on the Continent and infuriated Henry by his stubborn adherence to the letter of Church law. He was allowed to return to England in 1170, but that same year he was struck down in his own cathedral by four knights eager for royal favor. The king did panance but, unlike the German emperors, ultimately preserved royal authority over the English Church.

Henry's program to assert royal courts over local and feudal ones was even more successful, laying the foundation for a system of uniform judicial procedures through which royal justice reached throughout the kingdom—the common law. In France, royal agents observed local legal traditions but sought always to turn them to the king's advantage. In contrast, Henry's legal system simplified and cut through the complex tangle of local and feudal jurisdictions concerning land law. Any free person could purchase, for a modest price, a letter, or *writ*, from the king ordering the local sheriff to impanel a jury to determine if that person had been recently dispossessed of an estate, regardless of that person's legal right to the property. The procedure was swift and efficient. If the jury found for the plaintiff, the sheriff immediately restored the property, by force if necessary. While juries may not have meted out justice, they did resolve conflicts, and they did so in a way that protected landholders.

These writs became enormously successful and expanded the jurisdiction of royal courts into new legal areas.

Henry's son John may have made the greatest contribution to the development of the English state by losing Normandy and most of his other continental lands. Loss of these territories forced English kings to concentrate on ruling England, not on their continental territories. Moreover, John's financial difficulties, brought about by his unsuccessful wars to recover his continental holdings, led him to such extremes of fiscal extortion that his barons, prelates, and the townspeople of London revolted. In June 1215 he was forced to accept the "great charter of liberties," or *Magna Carta*, a conservative feudal document demanding that he respect the rights of his vassals and of the burghers of London. The great significance of the document was its acknowledgment that the king was not above the law.

John and his weak, ineffective son Henry III (1216–1272), although ably served by royal judges, were forced by their failures to cede considerable influence to the great barons of the realm. Henry's son Edward I (1272–1307), a strong and effective king who conquered Wales, defended the remaining continental possessions against France, and expanded the common law, found that he could turn baronial involvement in government to his own advantage. By summoning his barons, bishops, and representatives of the towns and shires to participate in a "parley," or "parliament," he could raise more funds for his wars. Like similar Spanish, Hungarian, and German assemblies of the thirteenth century, these assemblies were occasions to consult, to present royal programs, and to extract extraordinary taxes for specific projects. They were also opportunities for those summoned to petition the king for redress of grievances. Initially, representatives of the shires and towns attended only sporadically. However, since the growing wealth of the towns and countryside made their financial support essential, these groups came to anticipate that they had a right to be consulted and to consent to taxation. This forced self-government through a system of royal courts and justices employing local juries and through a tradition of representative parliaments, coupled with an exacting system of accounting, increased the power of the English monarchy. By 1300, France, with its powerful royal bureaucracy, and England, with its courts and accountants, were the most powerful states in the West.

*W*ar and Politics in the Later Middle Ages

Familial rivalries threatened to overwhelm the feudal monarchies of France and England in the fourteenth and fifteenth centuries. In both kingdoms, weakening economic climates and demographic catastrophe exacerbated dynastic crises and fierce competition. Three long-simmering disputes triggered the series of campaigns collectively termed the Hundred Years' War. The first issue was conflicting rights in Gascony in southern France. Since the mid thirteenth century, the kings of England had held Gascony as a fief of the French king. Neither monarchy was content with this arrangement, and for the next 75 years kings quarreled constantly over sovereignty in the region.

The second point of contention was the close relationship between England and the Flemish cloth towns, which were the primary customers for English wool. Early in the fourteenth century, Flemish artisans rose up in a series of bloody revolts against the aristocratic cloth dealers who had long monopolized power. The count of Flanders and the French king supported the wealthy merchants; the English sided with the artisans.

The final dispute concerned the royal succession in France. Charles IV (1322–1328), the son of Philip IV the Fair, died without an heir. The closest descendant of a French king was the grandson of Philip the Fair, King Edward III of England (1327–1377). However, Edward was the son of Philip's daughter Isabella. The French aristocracy, which did not want an English king to inherit the throne and unite the two kingdoms, pretended that according to ancient Frankish law, the crown could not pass through a woman. Instead, they preferred to give the crown to a cousin of the late king, Philip VI (1328–1350), who became the first of the Valois kings of France. At first, the English voiced no objection to Philip's accession, but in 1337, when the dispute over Gascony again flared up and Philip attempted to confiscate the region from his English "vassal" Edward III, the English king declared war on Philip. Edward's stated goal was not only to recover Gascony but also to claim the crown of his maternal grandfather.

A Hundred Years of War

Though territorial and dynastic rivalry were the triggers that set off the war, its deeper cause was chivalry. The elites of Europe were both inspired by and trapped in a code of conduct that required them not only to maintain their honor by violence but also to cultivate violence to increase that honor. This code had been appropriate in a period of weak kingship, but by the late thirteenth century the growth of courts and royal power in France and in England left little room for private vengeance and vendettas. Nobles were now more often royal retainers than knights errant traveling about the countryside righting wrongs. Government was increasingly an affair of lawyers and bureaucrats, war an affair of professionals. Yet kings and nobles alike still agreed with the sentiment expressed by a contemporary poet: "The glory of princes is in their pride and in undertaking great peril." By the fourteenth century only war provided sufficient peril.

Edward III of England and his rival Philip VI of France both epitomized the chivalrous knight. Both gloried in luxurious living and conspicuous consumption. Captivated by the romantic tales of King Arthur and the Round Table, in 1344 Edward organized a four-day-long round table celebration to which he invited the most outstanding nobles in England. A few years later Edward

THE FRENCH AND ENGLISH SUCCESSIONS

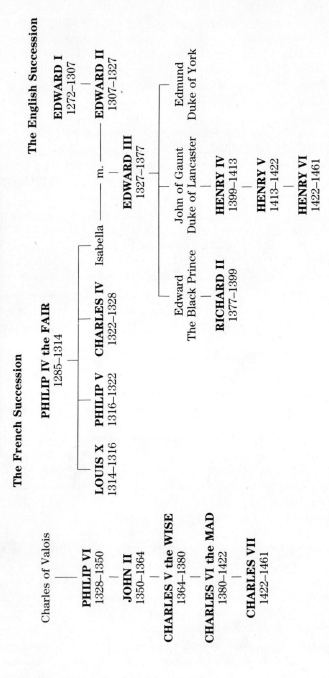

The French Succession

PHILIP IV the FAIR
1285–1314

LOUIS X
1314–1316

PHILIP V
1316–1322

CHARLES IV
1322–1328

Isabella

Charles of Valois

PHILIP VI
1328–1350

JOHN II
1350–1364

CHARLES V the WISE
1364–1380

CHARLES VI the MAD
1380–1422

CHARLES VII
1422–1461

The English Succession

EDWARD I
1272–1307

EDWARD II
1307–1327

m.

EDWARD III
1327–1377

Edward
The Black Prince

John of Gaunt
Duke of Lancaster

Edmund
Duke of York

RICHARD II
1377–1399

HENRY IV
1399–1413

HENRY V
1413–1422

HENRY VI
1422–1461

organized the Order of the Garter, a select group of nobles who were to embody the highest qualities of chivalry. For a ruler like Edward, obsessed with knightly glory, war with France was the ideal way to win honor and fame.

In spite of his chivalric ideals, Edward was practical when it came to organizing and financing his campaigns. Philip shared Edward's ideals but lacked his rival's practicality and self-assurance. Before his elevation to the throne, Philip had been a valiant and successful warrior, fond of jousting, tournaments, and lavish celebrations. After his coronation, he continued to act like a figure from a knightly romance, surrounding himself with aristocratic advisers who formed the most brilliant court of Europe, dispensing the royal treasure to his favorites, and dreaming of leading a great crusade to free the Holy Land. However, as the first French king in centuries elected rather than born into the right of succession, he treated the magnates from whose ranks he had come with excessive deference. He hesitated to press them for funds and deferred to them on matters of policy even while missing opportunities to raise other revenue from towns and merchants. Finally, although a competent warrior, Philip was no match in strategy or tactics for his English cousin.

Still, the sheer size and wealth of France should have made it the favorite in any war with England. Its population of roughly sixteen million made it by far the largest and most densely populated kingdom in Europe. The north of France was a major cereal producer. Vineyards around Bordeaux, Paris, Beaune, and Auxerre produced wines sold throughout the West. Paris, the largest city north of the Alps, was a center of commerce as well as an intellectual capital. The Flemish cloth towns, subdued by Philip in 1328, were the most industrialized area of Europe. England, by contrast, was a relatively small, sparsely populated kingdom. Its total population was under five million and its economy much less tied into international trade, with only the beginnings of a cloth industry and little to export except wool. At the start of the war Philip could rely on an income roughly three to five times greater than that of Edward. However, these inequalities mattered little because the French king had no means of harnessing the resources of his kingdom. His greater income was matched by greater expenses, and he had no easy way to raise extraordinary funds for war. In contrast, the English king could use Parliament as an efficient source of war subsidies. Edward could also extract great sums from taxes on wool exports. Even after the invasion of France, Philip had to rely on manipulation of the coinage, confiscation of Italian bankers' property, and a whole range of nuisance taxes to finance his campaigns.

War was expensive. In spite of chivalrous ideals, nobles no longer fought as vassals of the king but as highly paid mercenaries. The nature of this service differed greatly on the two sides of the Channel. In France, the tactics and personnel had changed little since the twelfth century. The core of any army was the body of heavily armored nobles who rode into battle with their lords, supported by lightly armored knights. Behind them marched infantrymen recruited from towns and armed with pikes. Although the French also hired mercenary Italian crossbowmen, the nobles despised them and never used them effectively.

In contrast, centuries of fighting against Welsh and Scottish enemies had transformed and modernized the English armies and their tactics. The great nobles continued to serve as heavily armored horsemen, but professional companies of foot soldiers raised by individual knights made up the bulk of the army. These professional companies consisted largely of pikemen and, most importantly, of longbowmen. Although it was not as accurate as the crossbow, the English longbow had a greater range. Moreover, when massed archers fired volleys of arrows into enemy ranks, they proved extremely effective against enemy pikemen and even lightly armored cavalry.

The first real test of the two armies came at the Battle of Crécy in 1346. There an overwhelmingly superior French force surrounded the English army. Massing their archers on a hill, the English rained arrows down on the French cavalry, which attacked in a glorious but suicidal manner. The English victory was total. By midnight they had repelled sixteen assaults, losing only a hundred men while killing over three thousand French. The survivors, including Philip VI, fled in disorder. Strangely enough, the French learned nothing from the debacle. In 1356 Philip's successor John II (1350–1364) rashly attacked an English army at Poitiers and was captured. In 1415 the French blundered in a different way at Agincourt. This time most of the heavily armored French knights dismounted and attempted to charge the elevated English position across a muddy field. Barely able to walk and unable to rise if

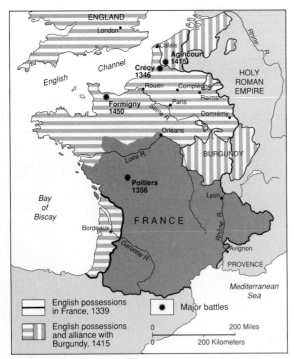

The Hundred Years' War

they fell, all were captured. Out of fear that his numerically inferior army would be overwhelmed if the French recovered their breath, the English king ordered over fifteen hundred French nobles and three thousand ordinary soldiers killed. English losses were less than one hundred.

Pitched battles were not the worst defeats for the French. More devastating was the constant raiding and systematic destruction of the French countryside by the English companies. The relief effort launched by Pope Benedict XII (1334–1342) in 1339 gives some idea of the scale of destruction. Papal agents, sent to aid victims of the English invasion, paid out over twelve thousand pounds, the equivalent of one-third of the English annual royal income, to peasants in just one region of northern France.

Raiding and pillaging continued for decades, even during long truces between the French and English kings. During periods of truce, unemployed free companies of French and English mercenaries roamed the countryside, supporting themselves by banditry while awaiting the renewal of more formal hostilities. Never had the ideals of chivalric conduct been so far distant from the brutal realities of warfare.

The French kings were powerless to prevent such destruction, just as they were unable to defeat the enemy in open battle. Since the kings were incapable of protecting their subjects or of leading their armies to victory, the "silken thread binding together the kingdom of France," as one observer put it, began to unravel, and the kingdom so painstakingly constructed by the Capetian monarchs began to fall apart. Not only did the English make significant territorial conquests, but the French nobles began behaving much as those in the Holy Roman Empire, carving out autonomous lordships. Private warfare and castle building, never entirely eradicated even by Louis IX and Philip IV, increased as royal government lost its ability to control the nobility. Whole regions of the kingdom slipped entirely from royal authority. Duke Philip the Good of Burgundy (1396–1467) allied himself with England against France and profited from the war to form a far-flung lordship that included Flanders, Brabant, Luxembourg, and Hainaut. By the time of his death, he was the most powerful ruler in Europe. Much of the so-called Hundred Years' War was actually a French civil war.

During this century of war the French economy suffered even more than the French state. Trade routes were broken and commerce declined as credit disappeared. French kings repeatedly seized the assets of Italian merchant bankers in order to finance the war. Such actions made the Italians, who had been the backbone of French commercial credit, extremely wary about extending loans in the kingdom. The kings then turned to French and Flemish merchants, extorting from them forced loans that dried up capital that might otherwise have been returned to commerce and industry. Politically and economically, France seemed doomed.

The flower of French chivalry did not save France. Instead, at the darkest moment of the long and bloody struggle, salvation came at the hands of a simple peasant girl from the county of Champagne. By 1429 the English and their Burgundian allies held virtually all of northern France including Paris.

Now they were besieging Orléans, the key to the south. The heir to the French throne, the dauphin, was the weak-willed and uncrowned Charles VII (1422–1461). To him came Joan of Arc (1412–1431), a simple, illiterate but deeply religious girl who bore an incredible message of hope. She claimed to have heard the voices of saints ordering her to save Orléans and have the dauphin crowned according to tradition at Reims.

Charles and his advisers were more than skeptical about this brash peasant girl who announced her divinely ordained mission to save France. Finally convinced of her sincerity if not of her ability, Charles allowed her to accompany a relief force to Orléans. The French army, its spirit buoyed by the belief that Joan's simple faith was the work of God, defeated the English and ended the siege. This victory led to others, and on 16 July 1429 Charles was crowned king at Reims.

After the coronation, Joan's luck began to fade. She failed to take Paris, and in 1431 she was captured by the Burgundians, who sold her to the English. Eager to get rid of this troublesome peasant girl, the English had her tried as a heretic. Charles did nothing to save his savior. After all, the code of chivalry did not demand that a king intervene on behalf of a mere peasant girl, even if she had saved his kingdom. She was burned at the stake in Rouen on 30 May 1431.

Despite Joan's inglorious end, the tide had turned. The French pushed the English back toward the coast. In the final major battle of the war, fought at Formigny in 1450, the French used a new and telling weapon to defeat the English—gunpowder. Rather than charging the English directly as they had done so often before, they mounted cannon and pounded the English to bits. Gunpowder completed the destruction of the chivalric traditions of warfare begun by archers and pikemen. By 1452 English continental holdings had been reduced to the town of Calais. The continental warfare of more than a century was over.

A fifteenth-century portrait of Joan of Arc. The Maid of Orléans was tried for heresy and executed in 1431. Later, in 1456, Pope Calixtus III pronounced her innocent. Pope Benedict XV formally declared her a saint in 1920.

Though war on the Continent had ended, warfare in England was just beginning. In some ways, the English monarchy had suffered even more from the Hundred Years' War than had the French. At the outset, English royal administration had been more advanced than the French. The system of royal agents, courts, and parliaments had created the expectation that the king could preserve peace and provide justice at home while waging successful and profitable wars abroad. As the decades dragged on without a decisive victory, the king came to rely on the aristocracy, enlisting its financial assistance by granting these magnates greater power at home. War created powerful and autonomous aristocratic families with their own armies. Under a series of weak kings these families fought among themselves. Ultimately they took sides in a civil war to determine the royal succession. For 30 years, from 1455 to 1485, supporters of the house of York, whose badge was the white rose, fought the rival house of Lancaster, whose symbol was the red rose, in the sort of dynastic struggle that would not have seemed out of place in the disintegrating German empire. The English Wars of the Roses, as the conflict came to be called, finally ended in 1485, when Henry Tudor of the Lancasterian faction defeated his opponents. He inaugurated a new era as Henry VII (1485–1509), the first king of the Tudor dynasty.

The Struggle for Central Europe

Fragmented and shifting territorial bases were typical of the great families of the fourteenth and fifteenth centuries. Everywhere, family politics threatened the fragile institutional developments of the thirteenth century, but this was especially true in the empire. Aristocrats competed for personal power and used public office, military command, and taxing power for private ends. What mattered was neither territorial boundaries nor political divisions but marriage alliances, kinship, and dynastic ambitions.

Between 1250 and 1350, the Luxembourg family greatly expanded its political and geographical powers by involving itself in the dynastic politics of the decaying Holy Roman Empire. During the fourteenth century, Charles of Luxembourg (later emperor Charles IV) controlled a patchwork of lands that included Luxembourg, Brabant, Lusatia, Silesia, Moravia, Meissen, and Brandenburg. His daughter married Richard II of England. A son succeeded him as king of Bohemia and another obtained the Hungarian crown.

In addition to the Luxembourgs, four other similarly ambitious families competed for dominance in the empire. First were the Wittelsbachs, the chief competitors of the Luxembourgs. The Wittelsbachs had originated in Bavaria but had since spread across Europe. In the west the Wittelsbachs had acquired Holland, Hainaut, and Frisia, while in the east they temporarily held Tyrol and Brandenburg. Next were the Habsburgs, allies of the Luxembourgs, who had begun as a minor comital family in the region of the Black Forest. They expanded east, acquiring Austria, Tyrol, Carinthia, and Carniola. When Rudolf

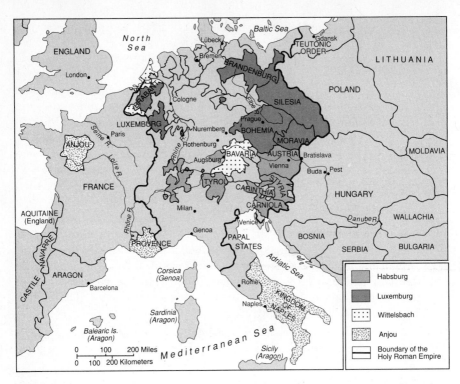

Central and Eastern Europe, ca. 1378

I of Habsburg (1273–1291) was elected emperor in 1273, Otakar II, king of Bohemia (1253–1278) and head of the powerful Premysl family, dismissed Rudolf as "poor." Compared with the Premysls perhaps he was. The Premysl family controlled at its height not only Bohemia but also Moravia, Austria, and a miscellany of lands stretching from Silesia in the north to the Adriatic Sea. Finally, the house of Anjou, descendants of Charles of Anjou, the younger brother of the French king Louis IX, who had become king of Naples, created a similar eastern network. Charles's son Charles Robert secured election as king of Hungary in 1310. His son Louis (1342–1382) added the crown of Poland (1370–1382) to the Hungarian crown of Saint Stephen. The protracted wars and maneuvers that these families conducted for dominance in the empire resembled nothing so much as the competition that had taken place three centuries earlier for dominance in feudal France.

For over a century, not only great princes but also monks, adventurers, and simple peasants streamed into the kingdoms and principalities of eastern Europe. Since the early thirteenth century the Teutonic orders had used the sword to spread Christianity along the Baltic coast. By the early fourteenth century these knight-monks had conquered Prussia and the coast as far east as the Narva River, now well within Russia, where they reached the borders of the Christian principality of Novgorod. The pagan inhabitants of these regions had to choose between conversion and expulsion. When they fled, their fields were turned over to land-hungry German peasants. Long wagon trains of pioneers snaked their way across Germany from the Rhineland, Westphalia, and Saxony to this new frontier. There they were able to negotiate advantageous contracts with their new lords, guaranteeing them greater freedom than they had known at home.

By the fifteenth century religious and secular German lords had established a new agrarian economy, modeled on western European estates, in regions previously unoccupied or sparsely settled by the indigenous Slavic peoples. This economy specialized in the cultivation of grain for export to the west. Each fall fleets of hundreds of ships sailed from Gdansk and Riga to the ports of the Netherlands, England, and France. Returning flotillas carried Flemish cloth and tons of salt for preserving food as far as Novgorod. The influx of Baltic grain into Europe caused a decline in domestic grain prices and a corresponding economic slump for landlords throughout the fourteenth and fifteenth centuries.

Farther south, the Christian kingdoms of Poland, Bohemia, and Hungary beckoned different sorts of westerners. Newly opened silver and copper mines in Bohemia, Silesia, southern Poland, and Hungarian Transylvania needed skilled miners, smelters, and artisans. Many were recruited from the overpopulated regions of western Germany. East-west trade routes developed to export these metals, giving new life to the Bohemian towns of Prague and Bruno, the Polish cities of Kraków and Lwów, and Hungarian Buda and Bratislava. Trade networks reached south to the Mediterranean via Vienna, the Brenner Pass, and Venice. To the north, trade routes extended to the Elbe River and the trading towns of Lübeck and Bremen. The Bavarian towns of Augsburg, Rothenburg, and Nuremberg flourished at the western end of this network. To the east, Lwów became a trading center connecting southern Russia with the west.

The wealth of eastern Europe, its abundant land, and its relative freedom attracted both peasants and merchants. The promise of profitable marriages with eastern royalty drew ambitious aristocrats. Continually menaced by one another and by the aggressive German aristocracy to the west, the royal families of Poland, Hungary, and Bohemia were eager to make marriage alliances with powerful aristocratic families from farther afield. Through such a marriage, for example, Charles Robert of Anjou became king of Hungary after the extinction of that realm's ancient royal dynasty. Similarly Charles Robert's son Louis inherited the Polish crown in 1370 after the death of Casimir III, the last king of the Polish Piast dynasty. Nobles of the eastern European kingdoms were pleased to confirm the election of such outsiders. The elections prevented powerful German nobles from claiming succession to the Bohemian, Hungarian, and Polish thrones. At the same time, the families of the western European aristocracy did not have sufficiently strong local power bases to challenge the autonomy of the eastern nobility.

Charles IV (1347–1378) was typical of these restless dynasts. His grandfather, Emperor Henry VII (1308–1313), had arranged for his son John of

Luxembourg to marry Elizabeth (d. 1330), the Premysl heiress of Bohemia, and thus acquire the Bohemian crown in 1310. John was king in name only. He spent most of his career fighting in the dynastic wars of the empire and of France. However, by mastering the intricate politics of the decaying Holy Roman Empire, he arranged the deposition of the Wittelsbach emperor Louis IV (1314–1347) and secured the election of Charles as king of the Romans, that is, heir of the empire, in 1346. The following year the Bohemian crown passed to Charles.

Although born in Prague, Charles had spent most of his youth in France, where he was deeply influenced by French culture. Upon his return to Prague in 1333, however, he rediscovered his Czech cultural roots. As king of Bohemia, he worked to make Prague a cultural center by combining French and Czech traditions. He imported craft workers, architects, and artists to transform and beautify his capital. In 1348 he founded a university in Prague, the first in the empire, modeled on the University of Paris. Keenly interested in history, Charles provided court historians with the sources necessary to write their histories of the Bohemian kingdom.

Charles took a more active role in this cultural renewal than perhaps any European king since Alfred of England, fostering a literary renaissance in both Latin and Czech. Although he had forgotten his native Czech during his long stay in France, he soon learned to read and write it as well as French, German, Italian, and Latin. He authored a number of religious texts, fostered the use of the Czech language in religious services, and initiated a Czech translation of the Bible.

The effects of Charles's cultural policies were far-reaching, but in directions he never anticipated. His interests in Czech culture and religious reform bore unexpected fruit during the reign of his son Sigismund, king of Germany (1410–1437), of Bohemia (1419–1437), of Hungary (1387–1437), and Holy Roman Emperor (1433–1437). During Sigismund's reign Czech religious and political reformers came into open confict with the powerful German-speaking minority in the University of Prague. Led by the theologian Jan Hus (ca. 1372–1415), this reform movement ultmately challenged the authority of the Roman Church and became the direct predecessor of the great Reformation of the sixteenth century.

Even while building up his beloved city of Prague, Charles was dismantling the Holy Roman Empire. By the fourteenth century, the title of emperor held little political importance, although as an honorific title it was still bitterly contested by the great families of the empire. Charles sought to end such disputes and at the same time to solidify the autonomy of the kingdoms such as Bohemia against the threats of future imperial candidates. In 1356 he issued the "Golden Bull," an edict that officially recognized what had long been the reality, namely that the various German princes and kings were autonomous rulers. The bull also established the procedure by which future emperors would be elected. Thereafter, the emperor was chosen by seven great princes of the empire without the consultation or interference of the pope, a tradition of interference that dated to the coronation of Charlemagne. The procedure made disputed elections less likely, but it acknowledged that the office itself was less significant.

The same process that sapped the power of the emperor also reduced the significance of the princes. The empire fragmented into a number of large kingdoms and duchies such as Bohemia, Hungary, Poland, Austria, and Bavaria in the east and over sixteen hundred autonomous principalities, free towns, and sovereign bishoprics in the west. The inhabitants of these territories, often ruled by foreigners who had inherited sovereign powers through marriage, organized themselves into estates—political units of knights, burghers, and clergy—to present a united front in dealing with their prince. The princes in turn did not enjoy any universally recognized right to rule and were forced to negotiate with their estates for any powers they actually enjoyed.

The disintegration of the empire left political power east of the Rhine widely disbursed for over five hundred years. While this meant that Germany did not become a nation-state until the nineteenth century, decentralization left late medieval Germany as a fertile region of cultural and constitutional creativity. In this creative process the office of emperor played no role. After the Habsburg family definitively acquired the imperial office in 1440, the office of emperor ceased to have any role in Germany. Rather the office became one of the building blocks of the great multinational Habsburg empire of central Europe, an empire that survived until 1918.

*L*ife and Death in the Later Middle Ages

By the end of the thirteenth century, population growth in the West had strained available resources to the breaking point. All arable land was under cultivation, and even marginal moorland, rocky mountainsides, and plains were being pressed into service to feed a growing population. At the same time, kings and nobles demanded ever higher taxes and rents to finance their wars and extravagant lifestyles. The result was a precarious balance in which a late frost, a bad harvest, or hungry mercenaries could mean disaster. Part of the problem could be alleviated by importing grain from the Baltic or from Sicily, but this solution carried risks of its own. Transportation systems were too fragile to ensure regular supplies, and their rupture could initiate a cycle of famine, disease, and demographic collapse. Population began to decline slowly around 1300 and the downturn became catastrophic within fifty years. Between 1300 and 1450 Europe's population fell by more than 30 percent. It did not recover until the seventeenth century.

Dancing with Death

Between 1315 and 1317 the first great famine of the fourteenth century, triggered by crop failures and war, struck Europe. People died by the thousands. Urban workers, because they were chronically undernourished, were particularly hard hit. In the Flemish cloth town of Ypres, whose total population was less than twenty thousand, the town ordered the burial of 2,794 paupers' corpses within a five-month period. Although this was the greatest famine in medieval memory, it was not the last. The relatively prosperous Italian city of Pistoria, for example, recorded 16 different famines and food shortages in the fourteenth and fifteenth centuries.

Disease accompanied famine. Crowded and filthy towns, opposing armies with their massed troops, and overpopulated countrysides provided fertile ground for the spread of infectious disease. Moreover, the greatly expanded trade routes of the thirteenth and fourteenth centuries that carried goods and grain between East and West also provided highways for deadly microbes. At Pistoia again, local chroniclers of the fourteenth and fifteenth centuries reported 14 years of sickness, fevers, epidemic, and plague.

Between 1347 and 1352 from one-half to one-third of Europe's population died from a virulent combination of bubonic, septicemic, and pneumonic plague known to history as the Black Death. The disease, carried by the fleas of infected rats, traveled the caravan routes from central Asia. It arrived in Messina, Sicily, aboard a merchant vessel in October 1347. From there the Black Death spread up the boot of Italy and then into southern France, England, and Spain. By 1349 it had reached northern Germany, Portugal, and Ireland. The following year the Low Countries, Scotland, Scandinavia, and Russia fell victim.

Plague victims died horribly. Soon after being bitten by an infected flea, they developed high fever, began coughing, and suffered excruciatingly painful swellings in the lymph nodes of the groin or armpits. These swellings were known as buboes, from which the disease took its name. In the final stages the victims began to vomit blood. The bubonic form of the disease usually killed within five days. The septicemic form, which attacked the blood, was more swift and deadly. Those infected by the airborne pneumonic form usually died in less than three days; in some cases, within a matter of hours.

Plague was all the more terrifying because its cause, its manner of transmission, and its cure were totally unknown until the end of the nineteenth century. Preachers saw the plague as divine punishment for sin. Ordinary people frequently accused Jews of causing it by poisoning drinking water. The medical faculty of Paris announced that it was the result of the conjunction of the planets Saturn, Jupiter, and Mars, which caused a corruption of the surrounding air.

Responses to the plague were equally varied. In many German towns terrified Christian citizens looked for outside scapegoats and slaughtered the Jewish community. Cities, aware of the risk of infection although ignorant of its process, closed their gates and turned away outsiders. Individuals with means fled to country houses or locked themselves in their homes to avoid contact with others. Nothing worked. As devastating as the first outbreak of the plague was, its aftershocks were even more catastrophic. Once established in Europe, the disease continued to return roughly once each generation. The last outbreak of the plague in Europe was the 1771 epidemic in Moscow that killed 60,000.

The Black Death, along with other epidemics, famines, and war-induced shortages, affected western much more than eastern Europe. The culminating effect of these disasters was a darker, more somber vision of life than that of the previous centuries. This vision found its expression in the Dance of Death, an increasingly popular image in art. Naked rotting corpses dance with great animation before the living. The latter, depicted in the dress of all social orders, are immobile, surprised by death, reluctant but resigned.

Although no solid statistics exist from the fourteenth century, the plague certainly killed more people than all of the wars and famines of the century. It was the greatest disaster ever to befall Europe. The Black Death touched every aspect of life, hastening a process of social, economic, and cultural transformation already under way. The initial outbreak shattered social and economic structures. Fields were abandoned, workplaces stood idle, international trade was suspended. Traditional bonds of kinship, village, and even religion were broken by the horrors of death, flight, and failed expectations. "People cared no more for dead men than we care for dead goats," wrote one survivor. Brothers abandoned brothers, wives deserted husbands, and terror-stricken parents refused to nurse their own children.

Nothing had prepared Europe for this catastrophe, no teaching of the Church or its leaders could adequately explain it, and in spite of desperate attempts to fix the blame on Jews or strangers, no one but God could be held responsible. Survivors stood alone and uncertain before a new world. Across Europe, moralists reported a general lapse in traditional ethics, a breakdown in the moral codes. The most troubling aspect of this breakdown was what one

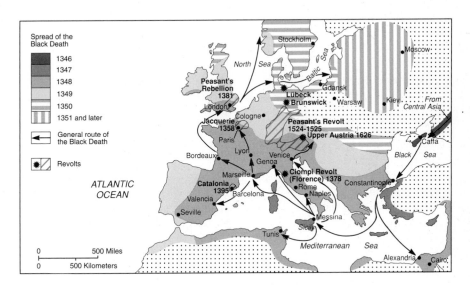

Spread of the Black Death

defender of the old order termed "the plague of insurrection" that spread across Europe. This plague was brought on by the dimming of the hopes held by the survivors of the Black Death.

The Plague of Insurrection

Initially, even this darkest cloud had a silver lining. Lucky survivors of the plague soon found other reasons to rejoice. Property owners, when they finished burying their dead, discovered that they were far richer in land and goods. At the other end of the social spectrum, the plague had eliminated the labor surplus. Peasants were suddenly in great demand. For a time at least, they were able to negotiate substantially higher wages and an improved relationship with landlords.

These hopes were short lived. The rise in expectations produced by the redistribution of wealth and the labor shortage created new tensions. Landlords sought laws forcing peasants to accept preplague wages and tightened their control over serfs in order to prevent them from fleeing to cities or other lords. At the same time governments attempted to benefit from laborers' greater prosperity by imposing new taxes. In cities, where the plague had been particularly devastating, the demographic decline sharply lowered demand for goods and thus lowered the need for manufacturing and production of all kinds. Like rural landowners, master craftsmen sought legislation to protect their incomes. New laws reduced production by restricting access to trades and increased masters' control over the surviving urban laborers. Social mobility, once a characteristic of urban life, slowed to a halt. Membership in guilds became hereditary, and young apprentices or journeymen had little hope of ever rising to the level of independent master craftsmen.

These new tensions led to violence when kings added their demands for new war taxes to the landlords' and masters' attempts to erase the peasants' and workers' recent gains. The first revolts took place in France, where peasants and townspeople, disgusted with the incompetence of the nobility in their conduct of the war against England, feared that their new wealth would be stolen from them by corrupt and incompetent aristocrats.

In 1358, in order to ransom King John II from the English, the French government attempted to increase taxes on the peasantry. At the same time, local nobles increased their rents and demands. Peasants in the area of Beauvais, north of Paris, fearing they would lose the modest level of prosperity they had gained over the previous ten years, rebelled against their landlords. The revolt, known as the Jacquerie for the archetypical French peasant, Jacques Bonnehomme, was a spontaneous outburst directed against the nobility, whom the peasants saw as responsible for all their ills. Without real leadership or program, peasants attacked as many nobles as they could find, killing them along with their wives and children and burning their homes and castles. The peasants' brutality deeply shocked the upper classes, whose own

Jacquerie rebellion, from a fifteenth-century manuscript. The well-armed soldiers have won the day, and the unarmed rebels are consigned to the river to sink or swim. Such rebellions were put down with great ruthlessness.

violence was constrained within the bounds of the chivalric code. Because the Church largely supported the power structure, the uprising was also strongly anticlerical. Churches were burned and priests killed. Success bred further attacks, and the disorganized army of peasants began to march south toward Paris, killing, looting, and burning everything associated with the despised nobility.

In the midst of this peasant revolt, Etienne Marcel (ca. 1316–1358), a wealthy Parisian cloth merchant, led an uprising of Parisian merchants, which sought to take control of royal finances and force fiscal reforms on the dauphin, the future Charles V. Although initially the rebels were primarily members of the merchant and guild elite, Marcel soon enlisted the support of the radical townspeople against the aristocracy. He even made overtures to the leaders of the Jacquerie to join forces. For a brief time it appeared that the aristocratic order in France might succumb. However, in the end peasant and merchant rebels were no match for professional armies. The Jacquerie met its end at Meaux, outside Paris, where an aristocratic force cut the peasants to pieces. Survivors were systematically hunted down and hung or burned alive. The Parisian revolt met a similar fate. Aristocratic armies surrounded the city and cut off its food supply. Marcel was assassinated and the dauphin Charles regained the city.

The French revolts set the pattern for similar uprisings across Europe. Rebels were usually relatively prosperous peasants or townspeople whose economic situations were threatened by aristocratic attempts to turn back the clock to the period before the Black Death. In 1381 English peasants, reacting to new and hated taxes, rose in a less violent but more coordinated revolt known as the Great Rebellion. Peasant revolts took place in the northern Spanish region of Catalonia in 1395 and in Germany throughout the fourteenth and fifteenth centuries. The largest was the great Peasant's Revolt of 1524. Although always ruthlessly suppressed, European peasant uprisings continued until the peasant rebellion of 1626 in upper Austria. These outbursts indicated not necessarily the desperation of Europe's peasantry, but the new belief that they could change their lives for the better through united action.

Urban artisans imitated the example of their rural cousins. Although there had been some uprisings in the Flemish towns before the Black Death, revolts of townspeople picked up momentum in the second half of the fourteenth century. In general the town rebels were not the destitute urban poor any more than the peasant rebels had been the landless rural poor. Instead they were generally independent artisans and small tradesmen who wanted to break the control of the powerful guilds. The one exception to this pattern was the Ciompi revolt of 1378 in Florence. There the wool workers rioted and forced recognition of two guilds of laborers alongside the powerful guilds of masters. The workers and artisans controlled city government until 1382, when mercenaries hired by the elite surrounded the workers' slums and crushed them in bloody house-to-house fighting. In spite of the brutal suppression and ultimate failure of popular revolts, they became permanent if intermittent features on the European social landscape. The line from the Jacquerie runs to the storming of the Bastille 431 years later, and beyond.

Living and Dying in Medieval Towns

Population decline, war, and class conflict in France and the Low Countries fatally weakened the vitality of the commercial and manufacturing system of northwestern Europe. These same events reduced the market for Italian goods and undermined the economic strength of the great Italian cities. The Hundred Years' War bankrupted many of Florence's greatest banking houses such as the Bardi and Peruzzi that lent to both French and English kings. Commercial activity declined as well. While in the 1330s Venice had sent between four and nine trading galleys to Flanders each year, by the 1390s the city was sending only three to five. Genoa, which earlier had led in the trade with the cloth towns of the north, saw the economic activity of its port decline by roughly one-third to one-half during the same period. While Italians did not disappear from northern cities, they no longer held a near monopoly on northern trade.

These setbacks for the Italians worked to the advantage of German towns in the disintegrating empire. Along the Baltic Sea, in Scandinavia, and in northern Germany, towns such as Lübeck, Lüneburg, Visby, Bremen, and Cologne formed a commercial and political alliance to control northern trade. During the second half of the fourteenth century, this Hanseatic League—the word *Hansa* means "company"—monopolized the northern grain trade and forced Denmark to grant its members exclusive rights to export Scandinavian fish throughout Europe. Hanseatic merchants established colonies from Novgorod to London to Bruges and even in Venice. They carried dried and salted fish to Prague and supplied grain from Riga to England and France.

English towns also profited from the decline of Flanders and France. The population decline of the fourteenth century led many English landowners to switch from traditional farming to sheep raising, since pasturing sheep required few workers and promised cash profits. While surviving peasants were driven off the land and forced to beg for a living, lords produced more wool than ever before. However, instead of exporting the wool to Flanders to be made into cloth, the English began to make cloth themselves. Protected by high tariffs on imports and low duties on exports, England had become a major exporter of finished cloth by the middle of the fifteenth century.

The new social and economic circumstances of European towns accentuated the gulf between rich and poor. The streets and markets of fifteenth-century towns bustled with the sights and sounds of rich Hanseatic merchants, Italian bankers, and prosperous local tradesmen. The back alleys and squatter settlements on the edges of these towns teemed with a growing mass of desperate and despairing workers and their families. The combination of economic depression, plague, and rural crisis deepened the misery of the growing population of urban poor. Driven both by mounting compassion for the urban poor and by a growing fear of the violent potential of this ever increasing population, medieval towns developed novel systems to deal with poverty. The first was public assistance, the second social control and repression.

Traditionally, charity had been a religious act that focused more on the soul of the giver than on the effect on the life of the recipient. The same had been true of charitable organizations such as confraternities and hospitals. Confraternities were pious religious organizations of laypeople and clergy who ministered to the poor and sick. Hospitals were all-purpose religious institutions providing lodging for pilgrims, the elderly, and the ill. By the fourteenth century, such pious institutions had become inadequate to deal with the growing numbers of poor and ill. Towns began to assume control over a centralized system of public assistance. Although men and women who had taken religious vows staffed these institutions, city governments contributed to their budgets and oversaw their finances. Cities also attempted to rationalize the distribution of charity according to need and merit. Antwerp, for example, established a centralized relief service, which distributed badges to those deemed worthy of public assistance. Only those who wore the badges could receive food.

One consequence of poverty was increased crime. Fear of the poor led to repressive measures and harsh punishments. Traditionally in much of Europe, crimes such as robbery, larceny, and even manslaughter had been punishable by fines and payments to the victim or the victim's heirs. Elsewhere, as in France and England, where corporal punishment had been the normal penalty for major crimes, hanging, blinding, and the loss of a hand or foot had been the

A page from the fourteenth-century psalter and prayer book of Bonne of Luxembourg, Duchess of Normandy. The three figures of the dead contrast with three living figures on the facing page to illustrate a moral fable.

most common punishments. During the later Middle Ages, gruesome forms of mutilation and execution became common for a long list of offenses. Petty larceny was punished with whipping, cutting off ears or thumbs, branding, or expulsion. In some towns, robbery of an amount over three pence was punished with death. Death by hanging might be replaced by more savage punishments such as breaking on the wheel. In this particularly burtal torture the prisoner's limbs and back were first broken with a wagon wheel. Then the criminal was tied to the wheel and left on a pole to die. Drowning, boiling, burning, and burial alive, a particularly common punishment for women, were other frequently used methods of execution.

The frequency of such punishments increased with their severity. In Augsburg until the middle of the thirteenth century executions were so rare that the city did not even have a public executioner before 1276. However, in the following two centuries, the city fathers increased executions in an attempt to control what they perceived as an ever rising crime rate, largely attributed to the growing masses of the poor. In 1452 the skulls of 250 hanged persons were found in pits on the gallows hill. At the same time the bodies of 32 thieves twisted in the wind above.

T he Spirit of the Later Middle Ages

The Dance of Death and the gallows were not the only images of later medieval life. The constant presence of death made life more precious. Europeans celebrated life with a vigor and creativity characterized by a growing sense of individuality, independence, and variety. During the four-teenth century, the Church failed to provide unified spiritual and cultural leadership to Europe. The institutional division of the Church was paralleled by divisions over how to lead the proper Christian life. Many devout Christians developed independent lifestyles intended to bring them closer to God without reliance on the Church hierarchy. Some elaborated beliefs branded by the Church as heresy. Others called into question the philosophical bases of theological speculation developed since the time of Abelard and Aquinas. Finally, the increasing pluralism of European culture gave rise to new literary traditions that both celebrated and criticized the medieval legacy of Christian-ity, chivalry, and social order.

Christendom Divided

The universal empire as well as its traditional competitor, the universal Church, declined in the later Middle Ages. The papacy never recovered from the humilitating defeat Pope Boniface VIII suffered at the hands of King Philip the Fair in 1303. The ecclesiastical edifice created by the thirteenth-century popes was shaken to its foundations, first by becoming a virtual appendage of the French monarchy, and then by a dispute that for over forty years gave European Christians a choice between two, and finally three, claimants to the chair of Saint Peter.

In 1305 the College of Cardinals elected as pope the bishop of Bordeaux. The new pope, who took the name Clement V (1305–1314), was close to Philip IV of France and had no desire to meet the fate of his predecessor, Pope Boniface VIII. Thus Clement took up residence not in Rome but in the papal city of Avignon on the east bank of the Rhone River. Technically, Avignon was a papal estate within the Holy Roman Empire. Actually, with France just across the river, the pope at Avignon was under French control.

For the next 70 years French popes and French cardinals ruled the Church. The traditional enemies of France as well as religious reformers who expected leadership from the papacy looked on this situation with disgust. Critics such as the Italian poet Petrarch accused the Avignon popes and their courtiers of every possible crime and sin, but they were no worse than any other great lords of the fourteenth century. In pursuit of political and financial rewards, they had simply lost sight of their roles as religious leaders.

The popes of Avignon were more successful in achieving their financial goals than in winning political power. Although they attempted to follow an independent course in international affairs, their French orientation eroded their influence in European politics, especially in the Holy Roman Empire. Pope John XXII (1316–1334), one of the most unpleasant and argumentative persons ever to hold the chair of Peter, tried to block the election of the Wittelsbach Louis of Bavaria as emperor. Louis ignored the pope, invaded Italy, and was proclaimed emperor by the people of Rome. In 1338 the German electors solemnly declared that the imperial office was held directly from God and did not require papal confirmation—a declaration later upheld in the Golden Bull. No longer could the popes exert any direct influence in the internal affairs of Europe's states. Frustrated politically, the Avignon popes concentrated on perfecting the legal and fiscal system of the Church and were enormously successful in concentrating the vast financial and legal power of the Church in the papal office. From the papal court, or curia, they created a vast and efficient central bureaucracy whose primary role was to increase papal revenues.

Revenues came from two main sources. The less lucrative but ultimately more critical source was the sale of indulgences. The Church had long taught that sinners who repented might be absolved of their sins and escape the fires of hell. However, they still had to suffer temporal punishment. This punishment, called penance, could take the form of fasting, prayer, or performance of some good deed. Failing to do penance on earth, absolved sinners would have to endure a period in purgatory before they could be admitted to heaven. However, since the saints had done more penance than was required to make up for the temporal punishments due them, they had established a treasury of merit, a sort of spiritual bank account. The pope was the "banker" and could transfer some of this positive balance to repentant sinners in return for some pious act such as contributing money to build a new church. These so-called indulgences could be purchased for one's own use or to assist the souls of family members already in purgatory. Papal "pardoners" working on commission used high-pressure sales pitches to sell indulgences across Europe.

The second and major source of papal income was the sale of Church offices, or benefices. Popes claimed the right to appoint bishops and abbots to all benefices and to collect a hefty tax for the appointment. Papal appointees often acquired numerous offices and viewed them merely as sources of income, leaving pastoral duties, when they were performed at all, to hired local clergy.

In 1377 Pope Gregory XI (1370–1378) returned from Avignon to Rome but died almost immediately upon arrival. Thousands of Italians, afraid that the cardinals would elect another Frenchman, surrounded the church where they were meeting and demanded an Italian pope. The terrified cardinals elected an Italian, who took the name of Urban VI (1378–1389). Once elected, Urban attempted to reform the curia, but he did so in a most undiplomatic way, insulting the cardinals and threatening to appoint sufficient non-French bishops to their number to end French control of the curia. The cardinals soon left Rome and announced that because the election had been made under duress it was invalid and Urban should resign. When he refused they held a second election and chose a Frenchman, Clement VII (1378–1394), who took up residence in Avignon. The Church now had two heads, both with reasonable claims to the office.

The chaos created by this so-called Great Schism divided Western Christendom. In every diocese, when a bishop died his successor had to be appointed by the pope. But by which pope? To whom did taxes go? Who

The Great Schism

Allegiance to Rome

Allegiance to Avignon

Eastern Orthodox

Islamic control

Shifting allegiances

received the income from the sale of indulgences or benefices? Did appeals in the Church courts go to Rome or to Avignon? More significantly, since each pope excommunicated the supporters of his opponent, everyone in the West was under a sentence of excommunication. Could anyone be saved?

Nothing in Church law or tradition offered a solution to this crisis. Nor did unilateral efforts to settle the crisis succeed. Twice France invaded Italy in an attempt to eliminate Urban but failed both times. The situation perpetuated itself. When Urban and Clement died, cardinals on both sides elected successors. By the end of the fourteenth century, France and the empire were exasperated with their popes and even the cardinals were determined to end the stalemate.

Church lawyers argued that a general council alone could end the schism. Both popes opposed this "conciliarist" argument because it suggested that an assembly of the Church rather than the pope held supreme authority. However, in 1408 cardinals from both sides summoned a council in the Italian city of Pisa. The council deposed both rivals and elected a new pope. But this solution only made matters worse, since neither pope accepted the decision of the council. Europe now had to contend with not two but three popes, each claiming to be the true successor of Saint Peter.

Six years later the Council of Constance managed a final solution. There under the patronage of the emperor-elect Sigismund (1410–1437), cardinals, bishops, abbots, and theologians from across Europe met to resolve the crisis.

Their goal was not only to settle the schism but also to reform the Church to prevent a recurrence of such a scandal. The participants at Constance hoped to restructure the Church as a limited monarchy in which the powers of the pope would be controlled through frequent councils. The Pisan and Avignon popes were deposed. The Roman pope, abandoned by all of his supporters, abdicated. Before doing so, however, he formally convoked the council in order to preserve the tradition that a general council had to be called by the pope. Finally, the council elected as pope an Italian cardinal not aligned with any of the claimants. The election of the cardinal, who took the name of Martin V (1417–1431), ended the schism.

The relief at the end of the Great Schism could not hide the very real problems left by over a century of papal weakness. The prestige of the papacy had been permanently compromised. Everywhere the Church had become more national in character. The conciliarist demand for control of the Church, which had ended the schism, lessened the power of the pope. Finally, during the century between Boniface VIII and Martin V, new religious movements had taken root across Europe, movements which the political creatures who had occupied the papal office could neither understand nor control. The Council of Constance, which brought an end to the schism, also condemned Jan Hus, the leader of the Czech reform movement and the spiritual founder of the Protestant reformation of the sixteenth century. The disintegration of the Church loomed ever closer as pious individuals turned away from the organized Church and sought divine help in personal piety, mysticism, or even magic.

Discerning the Spirit of God

When Joan of Arc first appeared before the dauphin in 1429, he feared that she was a witch. Only a physical examination by matrons, which determined that she was a virgin, persuaded him otherwise—witches were believed to have had intercourse with the devil. Everyone in the late Middle Ages was familiar with witches, saints, and heretics. Distinguishing among them was often a matter of perspective.

Accusations of witchcraft were relatively rare in the Middle Ages. The age of witch-hunts occurred in the sixteenth and seventeenth centuries. During the Middle Ages magic existed in a wide variety of forms, but its definition was fluid and its practitioners were not always considered evil. Alchemists and astrologers held honored places in society, while simple practitioners of folk religion, medicine, and superstition were condemned, particularly when they were poor women. Witches, believed to have made a contract with the devil, were condemned as one type of heretic and were persecuted like other heretics. Only at the end of the fifteenth century, with the publication of the *Witches' Hammer*, a great handbook for inquisitors, did the European witch craze begin in earnest. Earlier, authorities feared more those people who sought their own pacts not with the devil but with God.

Even as Europeans were losing respect for the institutional Church, people everywhere were seeking closer and more intimate relationships with God. Distrusting the formal institutions of the Church, laypersons and clerics turned to private devotions and to mysticism to achieve union with the divine. Most of these stayed within the Church. Others, among them many female mystics, maintained an ambiguous relationship with the traditional institutions of Christianity. A few, such as the Brethren of the Free Spirit, broke sharply with it.

In the fourteenth and fifteenth centuries, a great many pious laymen and women chose to live together to strive for spiritual perfection without entering established religious orders. The Brethren of the Common Life in the Rhineland and Low Countries dedicated themselves to preaching, charity, and a pious life. In the early fifteenth century an unknown member of the Brethren wrote the *Imitation of Christ*, a book of spiritual direction that remains today the most widely read religious text after the Bible.

Christians of the later Middle Ages sought to imitate Christ and venerated the Eucharist, or communion wafer, which the Church taught was the actual body of Jesus. Male mystics focused on imitating Jesus in his poverty, his suffering, and his humility. Women developed their own form of piety, which focused not on wealth and power but on spiritual nourishment, particularly as provided by the Eucharist. For women mystics, radical fasting became preparation for the reception of the Eucharist, often described in highly emotional and erotic terms. After a long period of fasting, Lukardis of Obverweimar (d. 1309) had a vision in which Jesus appeared to her as a handsome youth and blew into her mouth. In the words of her biographer, "She was infused with such sweetness and such inner fruition that she felt as if drunk." From the age of 23, Catherine of Sienna (d. 1380) subsisted entirely on the Eucharist, cold water, and bitter herbs that she sucked and then spat out. For those and other pious women, fasting and devotion to the Eucharist did not mean rejection of the body. Rather these were attempts to use their senses to approach perfect union with God, who was for them both food and drink.

Only a thin line separated the saint's heroic search for union with God from the heretic's identification with God. The radical Brethren of the Free Spirit believed that God was all things and that all things would return to God. Such pantheism denied the possibility of sin, punishment, and the need for salvation. Members of the sect were hunted down and many were burned as heretics. The specter of the Inquisition, the ecclesiastical court system charged with ferreting out heretics, hung over all such communities.

When unorthodox Christians were protected by secular lords, the ecclesiastical courts were powerless. This was the case with John Wycliffe (ca. 1330–1384), an Oxford theologian who attacked the doctrinal and political bases of the Church. He taught that the value of the sacraments depended on the worthiness of the priest adminstering them, that Jesus was present in the Eucharist only in spirit, that indulgences were useless, and that salvation depended on divine predestination rather than individual merit. Normally these teachings would have led him to the stake. But he had also attacked the

Church's right to wealth and luxury, an idea whose political implications pleased the English monarchy and nobility. Wycliffe's own exemplary manner of life and his teaching that the Church's role in temporal affairs should be severely limited made him an extremely popular figure in England. Thus he was allowed to live and teach in peace. Only under Henry V (1413–1422) were Wycliffe's followers, known as Lollards, vigorously suppressed by the state. Before this condemnation took place, however, Wycliffe's teachings reached the kingdom of Bohemia through the marriage of Charles IV's daughter Anne of Bohemia to the English king Richard II. Anne took with her to England a number of Bohemian clerics, some of whom studied at Oxford and absorbed the political and religious teachings of Wycliffe, which they then took back to Bohemia.

In Prague some of Wycliffe's less radical teachings took root among the theology faculty of the new university, where the leading proponent of Wycliffe's teachings was Jan Hus (1373–1415), an immensely popular young master and preacher. Although Hus rejected Wycliffe's ideas about the priesthood and the sacraments, he and other Czech preachers attacked indulgences and demanded a reform of Church liturgy and morals. They grafted these religious demands onto an attack on German dominance of the Bohemian kingdom. These attacks outraged both the Pisan pope John XXIII (1410–1415) and the Bohemian king Wenceslas IV (1378–1419), who favored the German faction. The pope excommunicated Hus, and the king expelled the Czech faculty from the university. Hus was convinced that he was no heretic and that a fair hearing would clear him. He therefore agreed to travel to the Council of Constance under promise of safe conduct from the emperor-elect

Illustration from the sixteenth-century Bohemian Gradual of Malá Strana. *Jan Hus, wearing the traditional heretic's cap adorned with devils, is burned at the stake.*

Sigismund to defend his position. There he was tried on a charge of heresy, convicted, and burned at the stake.

News of Hus's execution touched off a revolt in Bohemia. Unlike the peasant revolts of the past, however, this revolt had broad popular support throughout all levels of Czech society. Peasants, nobles, and townspeople saw the attack on Hus and his followers as an attack on Czech independence and national interest by a Church and an empire controlled by Germans. Soon a radical faction known as the Taborites was demanding the abolition of private property and the institution of a communal state. Although moderate Hussites and Bohemian Catholics combined to defeat the radicals in 1434, most of Bohemia remained Hussite through the fifteenth century. The sixteenth-century reformer Martin Luther declared himself a follower of Jan Hus.

William of Ockham and the Spirit of Truth

The critical and individualistic approach that characterized religion during the later Middle Ages was also typical of the philosophical thought of the period. The delicate balance between faith and reason taught by Aquinas and other intellectuals in the thirteenth century disintegrated in the fourteenth. As in other areas of life, intellectuals questioned the basic suppositions of their predecessors, directing intellectual activity away from general speculations and toward particular, observable reality.

The person primarily responsible for this new intellectual climate was the English Franciscan William of Ockham (ca. 1300–1349). Ockham developed a truly radical political philosophy. Imperial power, he argued, derived not from the pope but from the people. People are free to determine their own form of government and to elect rulers. They can make their choice directly, as in the election of the emperor by electors who represent the people, or implicitly, through continuing forms of government. In either case, government is entirely secular. Neither popes, nor bishops, nor priests have any role. Ockham went still further. He denied the absolute authority of the pope, even in spiritual matters. Rather, Ockham argued, parishes, religious orders, and monasteries should send representatives to regional synods, which in turn would elect representatives to general councils. Ockham's ideas on Church governance by a general council representing the whole Christian community offered the one hope for a solution to the Great Schism that erupted shortly after his death. Concilarists like Pierre d'Ailly (1350–1420) and Jean de Gerson (1363–1429) drew on Ockham's attack on papal absolutism to propose an alternative church. The Council of Constance, which ended the schism, was the fruit of Ockham's political theory.

As radical as Ockhams' political ideas were, his philosophical outlook was even more extreme and exerted a more direct and lasting influence. The Christian Aristotelianism that developed in the thirteenth century had depended on the validity of general concepts called universals, which could be

The Later Middle Ages, 1300–1500

1305–1377	Babylonian Captivity (Avignon papacy)
1337–1452	Hundred Years' War
1347–1352	Black Death spreads through Europe
1358	Jacquerie revolt of French peasants Étienne Marcel leads revolt of Parisian merchants
1378	Ciompi revolt in Florence
1378–1417	Great Schism divides Christianity
1381	Great Rebellion of English peasants
1409–1410	Council of Pisa
1414–1417	Council of Constance ends Great Schism
1415	Jan Hus executed
1455–1485	English Wars of the Roses

analyzed through the use of logic. Aquinas and others who studied the eternity of the world, the existence of God, the nature of the soul, and other philosophical questions believed that people could reach general truths by abstracting universals from particular, individual cases. Ockham argued that universals were merely names, no more than convenient tags for discussing individual things. Universals had no connection with reality and could not be used to reason from particular observations to general truths. This radical nominalism (from the Latin *nomen*, "name") thus denied that human reason could aspire to certain truth. For Ockham and his followers, philosophical speculation was essentially a logical, linguistic exercise, not a way to certain knowledge.

Just as Ockham's political theory dominated the later fourteenth century, his nominalist philosophy won over the philosophical faculties of Europe. Since he had discredited the value of Aristotelian logic to increase knowledge, the result was, on the one hand, a decline in abstract speculation and on the other, a greater interest in scientific observation of individual phenomena. In the next generation Parisian professors, trained in the tradition of Ockham, laid the foundation for scientific studies of motion and the universe that led to the scientific discoveries of the sixteenth and seventeenth centuries.

Vernacular Literature and the Individual

Just as the religious and philosophical concerns of the later Middle Ages developed within national frameworks and criticized accepted authority from the perspective of individual experience, so too did the vernacular (as opposed to Latin) literatures of the age begin to explore the place of the individual within an increasingly complex society. Across Europe, authors reviewed the traditional values of society with a critical eye, reworking and transforming traditional literary genres into statements both personal and profound.

From Prague to Paris, everywhere vernacular languages had come into their own. Poets used their native tongues to express a spectrum of sentiments and to describe a spectrum of emotions and values. The themes and ideas expressed ranged from the polished, traditional values of the aristocracy trying to maintain the ideals of chivalry in a new and changed world to the views of ordinary people, by turns reverent or sarcastic, joyful or despondent.

In Italy, a trio of Tuscan poets, Dante Alighieri (1265–1321), Petrarch (1304–1374), and Boccaccio (1313–1375), not only made Italian a literary language but composed in it some of the greatest literature of all time. Dante, the first and greatest of the three, was born into a modest but respectable Florentine family and after receiving an excellent education entered the public life of his city. In 1301 he fell victim to the viciousness of Florentine politics and was exiled from his beloved city for the remainder of his life. During his exile, he wrote philosophical treatises and literary works, which culminated in his *Divine Comedy*, written during the last years of his life.

The *Divine Comedy* is a view of the whole Christian universe, populated with people from antiquity and from Dante's own day. The poem is both a sophisticated summary of philosophical and theological thought at the beginning of the fourteenth century and an astute political commentary on his times. The poet sets this vision within a three-part poetic journey through hell (*Inferno*), purgatory (*Purgatorio*), and heaven (*Paradiso*). In each part Dante adopts a poetic style appropriate to the subject matter. His journey through hell to witness the sufferings of the damned is described in brutal, immediate language that makes one almost feel the agony of the condemned, each of whom receives an eternal punishment appropriate to his or her sins. In purgatory, Dante meets sinners whose punishments will someday end. These he describes in a language of dreams and imagination, of nostalgic recollections cast in a misty landscape of the memory. Dante describes paradise in a symbolic language that is nonphysical and nonrepresentational. In the face of transcendent perfection, human imagery and poetry fail. In his final vision, he sees the reflected light of a mystical rose in which the saints are ranked. The *Divine Comedy* is Dante's personal summary of all that is good and bad in medieval culture and politics.

English literature emerged from over two centuries of French cultural domination with the writings of William Langland (ca. 1330–1395) and Geoffrey Chaucer (ca. 1343–1400). Both presented images of contemporary society with a critical and often ironic view. In *Piers Plowman* Langland presents society from the perspective of the peasantry. Chaucer's work is much more sophisticated and wide ranging, weaving together the whole spectrum of late medieval literature and life.

Dante had set his great poem within a vision of the other world. Chaucer placed his tales in the mouths of a group of 30 pilgrims traveling to the tomb of

Thomas Becket at Canterbury. The pilgrims represent every walk of life and spectrum of society: a simple knight, a vulgar miller, a lawyer, a lusty widow, a merchant, a squire, a physician, a nun, her chaplain, and a monk, among others. Each pilgrim is at once strikingly individual and representative of his or her profession or station in life. The tales that they tell are drawn from folklore, Italian literature, the lives of the saints, courtly romance, and religious sermons. However, Chaucer plays with the tales and their genres in the retelling. He uses them to contrast or illuminate the persons and characters of their tellers as well as to comment in subtle and complex ways on the literary, religious, and cultural traditions of which they are part. In his mastery of the whole heritage of medieval culture and his independent use of this heritage, Chaucer proved himself the greatest English writer before Shakespeare.

Much of Italian and English literature drew material and inspiration from French, which continued into the fifteenth century to be the language of courtly romance. In France, literature continued to project an unreal world of allegory and nostalgia for a glorious if imaginary past. Popular literature, developed largely in the towns, often dealt with courtly themes, but with a critical and more realistic eye.

In this literary world appeared a new and extraordinary type of poet, a woman who earned her living with her pen, Christine de Pisan (1364–ca. 1430). As a professional woman of letters, Christine fought the stereotypical medieval image of women as weak, sexually aggressive temptresses. In her *Hymn to Joan of Arc*, she saluted her famous contemporary for her accomplishments, bringing dignity to women, striving for justice, and working for peace in France. Her life and writing epitomized the new possibilities and new interests of the fifteenth century. They included an acute sense of individuality, a willingness to look for truth not in the clichés of the past but in actual experience, and a readiness to defend one's views with tenacity. Although an heir of the medieval world, Christine, like her contemporaries, already embodied the attitudes of a new age.

That new age was reflected in a second tradition in fifteenth-century France, that of realist poetry. Around 1453, just as the English troops were enduring a final battering from the French artillery, Duke Charles of Orléans (1394–1465) organized a poetry contest. Each contestant was to write a ballad that began with the contradictory line, "I die of thirst beside the fountain." The duke, himself an outstanding poet, wrote an entry that embodied the traditional courtly themes of love and fortune:

> I die of thirst beside the fountain,
> Shaking from cold and the fire of love;
> I am blind and yet guide the others;
> I am weak of mind, a man of wisdom;
> Too negligent, often cautious in vain,
> I have been made a spirit,
> Led by fortune for better or for worse.

An unexpected and very different entry came from the duke's prison. The prisoner-poet, François Villon (1432–ca. 1464), was a child of the Paris streets, an impoverished student, a barroom brawler, a killer, and a thief who spent much of his life trying to escape the gallows. He was also the greatest realist poet of the Middle Ages. His entry read:

> I die of thirst beside the fountain,
> Hot as fire, my teeth clattering,
> At home I am in an alien land;
> I shudder beside a glowing brazier,
> Naked as a worm, gloriously dressed,
> I laugh and cry and wait without hope,
> I take comfort and sad despair,
> I rejoice and have no joy,
> Powerful, I have no force and no strength,
> Well received, I am expelled by all.

The duke focused on the sufferings of love; the thief on the physical sufferings of the downtrodden. The two poets represent the contradictory tendencies of literature in the later Middle Ages.

In the centuries that followed the disintegration of the Carolingian empire, the eastern half of the Carolingian world continued the imperial universalist tradition of the Carolingians until its conflicts with the other universalist tradition, that of the papacy, contributed to its disintegration into small autonomous principalities. In the west, public order was for a time largely replaced by numerous individual principalities. Gradually, however, first in France and in England, and then in the Iberian Peninsula, a new type of kingship emerged. Less ambitious than that in the east, it proved more enduring, surviving the centrifugal forces of the fourteenth and fifteenth centuries to emerge as the foundation of the nation-state.

The fourteenth and fifteenth centuries, with their demographic collapse, warfare, and dissension, placed enormous strains on these emerging forms of social and cultural organization. Individuals sought their own answers to the problems of life and death, using the legacy of the past, but using it in novel and creative ways. Mystics and heretics sought God without benefit of traditional religious hierarchies, and poets and philosophers sought personal expression outside the confines of inherited tradition.

The legacy of the Middle Ages was a complex and ambiguous one. The thousand-year synthesis of classical, barbarian, and Christian traditions did not disappear. The bonds holding this world together were not yet broken, but the last centuries of the Middle Ages bequeathed a critical detachment from this heritage, expressed in the revolts of peasants and workers, the preaching of radical religious reformers, and the poems of mystics and visionaries.

Suggestions for Further Reading

General Reading

*Johan Huizinga, *The Waning of the Middle Ages* (New York: St. Martin's Press, 1954). An old but still powerful interpretation of culture and society in the Burgundian court in the late Middle Ages.

Daniel Waley, *Later Medieval Europe* (London: Longman, 1975). A brief introduction with a focus on Italy.

The Invention of the State

John W. Baldwin, *The Government of Philip Augustus: Foundations of French Royal Power in the Middle Ages* (Berkeley: University of California Press, 1986). A detailed but important study of the crucial reign of Philip II.

M. T. Clanchy, *England and Its Rulers, 1066–1272* (New York: B & N Imports, 1983). A good survey of English political history.

*Horst Fuhrmann, *Germany in the High Middle Ages, c. 1050–1200* (New York: Cambridge University Press, 1986). A fresh synthesis of German history by a leading German historian.

*Joseph R. Strayer, *On the Medieval Origins of the Modern State* (Princeton, NJ: Princeton University Press, 1970). A very brief but imaginative account of medieval statecraft by a leading French institutional historian.

War and Politics in the Later Middle Ages

*C. T. Allmand, *The Hundred Years War: England and France at War c. 1300–c. 1450* (New York: Cambridge University Press, 1988). A brief introduction to the Hundred Years' War by a British historian.

Richard W. Kaeuper, *War, Justice and Public Order: England and France in the Later Middle Ages* (Oxford, England: Oxford University Press, 1988). A fine analysis of the effects of war in England and France.

*Joachim Leuschner, *Germany in the Late Middle Ages (Amsterdam: Elsevier, 1980). An introduction to late medieval German history.*

Life and Death in the Later Middle Ages

Georges Duby, ed., *A History of Private Life Volume 2: Revelations of the Medieval World* (Cambridge, MA: Harvard University Press, 1988). A series of provocative essays on the origins of privacy and the individual.

*Edith Ennen, *The Medieval Town* (New York: North Holland Publishing Company, 1979). A brief history of medieval cities by a German specialist.

Bronislaw Geremek, *Power or Pity: Europe and the Poor from the Middle Ages to the Present* (forthcoming). A history of the origins of public welfare, focusing on the late Middle Ages.

H. A. Miskimin, *The Economy of Early Renaissance Europe, 1300–1460* (New York: Cambridge University Press, 1975). An accessible introduction to the economic history of the later Middle Ages.

---

*Indicates paperback edition available.

*Michel Mollat and Philippe Wolff, *The Popular Revolutions of the Late Middle Ages* (London: Allen and Unwin, 1973). An accessible history of late medieval revolts, focusing on those of medieval cities.

*Philip Zieger, *The Black Death* (New York: Harper & Row, 1969). A reliable introduction to the plague in the fourteenth century.

The Spirit of the Later Middle Ages

*Geoffrey Barraclough, *The Medieval Papacy* (New York: W. W. Norton, 1968). A brief overview of the papacy.

H. S. Bennett, *Chaucer and the Fifteenth Century* (Oxford, England: Oxford University Press, 1961). An accessible historical introduction to Chaucer.

*Caroline Walker Bynum, *Holy Feast and Holy Fast: The Religious Significance of Food to Medieval Women* (Berkeley: University of California Press, 1987). An imaginative and scholarly examination of the role of food in the spirituality of medieval women.

E. F. Chaney, *François Villon in His Environment* (Oxford, England: Oxford University Press, 1946). An old but still valuable study of Villon and his world.

John Freccero, *Dante and the Poetics of Conversion* (Cambridge, MA: Harvard University Press, 1986). A serious and rewarding study of Dante by an acknowledged master.

Howard Kaminsky, *A History of the Hussite Revolution* (Berkeley: University of California Press, 1967). The best account of the Hussite movement.

Gordon Leff, *Heresy in the Later Middle Ages* (Manchester, England: Manchester University Press, 1967). A survey of heretical movements in the fourteenth and fifteenth centuries.

*Heiko A. Oberman, *The Harvest of Medieval Theology* (Cambridge, MA: Labyrinth Press, 1963). A technical but rewarding account of late medieval theology.

Yves Renouard, *The Avignon Papacy (1305–1403)* (Hamden, CT: Archon, 1970). A readable account of the Avignon popes.

9

The Italian Revival

A Civic Procession

It is 25 April 1444. On this day each year the city of Venice celebrates its patron, Saint Mark, with a procession around the square that bears his name. Processions are a common form of civic ritual through which a community defines itself. The special features that identify Venice for its citizens are all on display. Flags and emblems of the city are mounted on poles, and clothes bear the insignia of various orders and groups. The procession recreates all forms of communal life. Here are the religious orders (the white-clad brothers of the Confraternity of Saint John are passing before us now), and the civic leaders can be seen just behind them. Musicians entertain both marchers and onlookers. An entire band files by on the right. The procession is orderly, but it is by no means contrived. It is not staged, as would be a modern ceremony, and this difference is evident in the relaxed attitude of the ordinary citizens who stand in groups in the middle of the square. There is no apparent drama to observe, and they walk and talk quite naturally. So, too, do the participants. In the lower left-hand corner, some friars are reading music; at the lower right, members of the confraternity carry their candles negligently.

Yet the painting, *The Procession of the Relic of the Holy Cross* (1496) by Gentile Bellini (ca. 1429–1507), was commissioned to commemorate a miracle rather than a civic procession. On the evening before Saint Mark's day, a visiting merchant and his son were touring the square when the boy accidentally fell and cracked his skull. The doctors who were called to treat him regarded the case as hopeless and advised the father to prepare for his son's death. The next morning, the Brothers of the Confraternity of Saint John carried the relic of a piece of the true cross beneath an embroidered canopy.

320

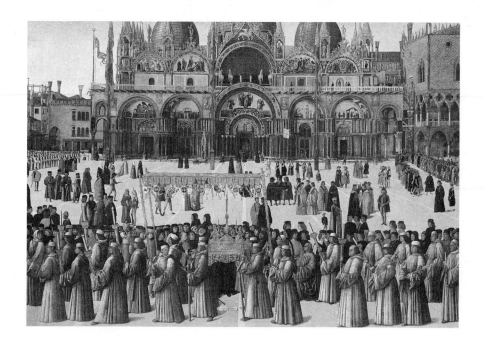

The merchant approached the golden altarpiece that contained the relic, dropped to his knees, and prayed that Saint Mark would miraculously cure his son. He is the red-clad figure kneeling just to the right of center where the line of brothers breaks. The next day, the boy revived and his injury healed.

The Brothers of Saint John commissioned Bellini to commemorate this event. Bellini came from the most distinguished family of painters in Venice. His father Jacopo had studied in Florence and had brought both of his sons into his workshop when they were young boys. Until the age of 30 Gentile and his younger and more famous brother, Giovanni, worked on their father's commissions, learning the difficult craft of painting. Art was very much a family business in fifteenth-century Italy. The large workshops with their master and hordes of apprentices turned out vast canvasses with almost assembly-line precision. The master created the composition and sketched it out; his skilled assistants, like the Bellini brothers, worked on the more complex parts; and young apprentices painted backgrounds and indistinct faces. The master was first and foremost a businessman, gaining commissions to sustain his family and his workers. The Bellinis were well connected to the Confraternity of Saint John, and it as only natural that Gentile would receive this lucrative contract.

Though *The Procession of the Relic of the Holy Cross* was designed to recreate a central moment in the history of the confraternity, it is not the confraternity that dominates the picture. Miracles were part of civic life, and each town took pride in the special manifestations of heavenly care that had taken place within it. And it is very much Venice that is the centerpiece of Bellini's canvas. Dominating the painting is the Basilica of San Marco, with its four great horses over the center portico and the winged lion, the city's symbol, on the canopy above the horses. The procession emanates from the duke's palace to the right of the church, and the great flags of the city are seen everywhere. By the end of the fifteenth century, Venice was one of the greatest powers on earth, the center for international trade and finance. Home to the largest concentration of wealthy families anywhere in Europe, it could well afford the pomp and splendor of its processions. The achievements of God and the achievements of humans blend together in this painting as they blended together in that era of remarkable accomplishments that historians call the Renaissance.

Renaissance Society

Perhaps the most surprising result of the Black Death was the way in which European society revived itself in the succeeding centuries. Even at the height of the plague a spirit of revitalization was evident in the works of artists and writers. Petrarch (1304–1374), the great humanist poet and scholar, was among the first to differentiate the new age in which he was living from two earlier ones: the classical world of Greece and Rome, which he admired, and the subsequent Dark Ages, which he detested. This spirit of self-awareness is one of the defining characteristics of the Renaissance. "It is but in our own day that men dare boast that they see the dawn of better things," wrote Matteo Palmieri (1406–1475). The Renaissance was a new age by self-assertion. In that self-assertion wave after wave of artistic celebration of the human spirit found its wellspring and created a legacy that is still vibrant 500 years later.

What was the Renaissance? A French word for an Italian phenomenon, *Renaissance* literally means "rebirth." The word captures both the emphasis on humanity that characterized Renaissance thinking and the renewed fascination with the classical world. But the Renaissance was an age rather than an event. There is no moment at which the Middle Ages ended. Late medieval society was artistically creative, socially well developed, and economically diverse. Yet eventually the pace of change accelerated, and it is best to think of the Renaissance as an era of rapid transitions. Encompassing the two centuries between 1350 and 1550, it passed through three distinct phases. The first, from 1350 to 1400, was characterized by a declining population, the uncovering of classical texts, and experimentation in a variety of art forms. The creation of a set of cultural values and artistic and literary achievements that defined Renaissance style distinguished the second phase, from 1400 to 1500. The large Italian city-states developed stable and coherent forms of government and the warfare between them gradually ended. In the final period, from 1500 to 1550, invasions from France and Spain transformed Italian political life, and the ideas and techniques of Italian writers and artists radiated to all points of the Continent. Though Renaissance ideas and achievements did spread through-

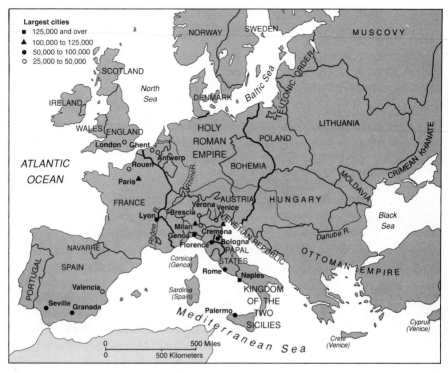

Europe, ca. 1500

out western Europe, they are best studied where they first developed, on the Italian peninsula.

The Environment

The Italian peninsula differed sharply from other areas of Europe in the extent to which it was urban. By the late Middle Ages nearly one in four Italians lived in a town, in contrast to one in ten elsewhere. Not even the plague did much to change this ratio. There were more Italian cities and more people in them. By 1500 seven of the ten largest cities in the West were in Italy. Naples, Venice, and Milan, each with a population of more than one hundred thousand, led the rest. But it was the numerous smaller towns, with populations nearer to one thousand, that gave the Italian peninsula its urban character. Cities were still the wonder of the world, dominating their regions economically, politically, and culturally. The diversified economic activities in which the inhabitants engaged created vast concentrations of wealth. Cities also served as convenient centers of judicial and ecclesiastical power.

Cities acted as central places around which a cluster of large and small villages was organized. Urban areas, especially the small towns, provided

markets for the agricultural produce of the countryside and for the manufactured goods of the urban craft workers. This allowed for the specialization in
agricultural and industrial life that increased both productivity and wages.
Cities also caught the runoff of rural population, especially the shower of
younger sons and daughters who could not be accommodated on the farms.
Cities grew by migration rather than by natural increase. Thus the areas
surrounding a city were critical to its prosperity and survival. The urban
system was a network of cities encompassed by towns encircled by rural
villages. Florence, the dominant city in the region of Tuscany, exemplifies this
relationship. Though it possessed two-thirds of its region's wealth, Florence
contained only 14 percent of the regional population. The surrounding countryside was agriculturally rich, for marketing costs were low and demand for
foodstuffs high. Smaller cities like Prato and Pistoia to the north and Pisa to the
west channeled their local produce and trade to Florence.

Though cities may have dominated Renaissance Italy, by present standards they were small in both area and population. A person could walk across
fifteenth-century Florence in less than half an hour. In 1427 its population was
37,000, only half its preplague size. Most Italian cities contained large fields for
agricultural production, and within the outer walls of Florence were gardens
and grain fields. Inside the inner city walls the people crowded together into
tightly packed quarters. The intensity of the stench from raw sewage, rotting
foodstuffs, and slaughtered animals was equaled only by the din made by hoofs
and wooden cartwheels on paving stones.

Urban populations were organized far differently from rural ones. On the
farms the central distinctions involved ownership of land. Some farmers
owned their estates outright and left them intact to their heirs. Others were
involved in a sharecropping system by which absentee owners of land supplied
working capital in return for half of the farm's produce. A great gulf in wealth
separated owners from sharecroppers. Those who owned their land normally
lived with surplus; those who sharecropped always lived on the margin of
subsistence. But within the groups the gaps were not as great. There were
gradations, but these were ordinarily temporary conditions that bad harvests,
generous dowries, or divided inheritances balanced out over time.

In the city, however, distinctions were based first on occupation, which
largely corresponded to social position and wealth. Cities began as markets
and it was the privilege to participate in the market that defined citizens. As the
trades and crafts expanded, city governments provided protection for consumers and producers by creating monopolies through which standards for
craftsmanship were maintained and profits for craft workers guaranteed.
These monopolies were called guilds or companies. Each large city had its own
hierarchy of guilds. At the top were the important manufacturing groups—
clothiers, metalworkers, and the like. Just below them were bankers, merchants, and the administrators of civic and church holdings. At the bottom
were grocers, masons, and other skilled workers. Roughly speaking, all of
those within the guild structure, from bottom to top, lived comfortably. Yet the
majority of urban inhabitants were not members of guilds. Many managed to

eke out a living as wage laborers; many more were simply destitute. As a group these poor constituted as much as half of the entire population. Most were dependent on civic and private charity for their very survival, but the continued migration of the destitute into cities suggests that opportunities were greater there than in the countryside.

The disparities between rich and poor were overwhelming. The concentration of wealth in the hands of an ever narrowing group of families and favored guilds characterized every large city. One reason for this was the extreme instability of economic life. Prices and wages fluctuated wildly in response to local circumstance. After an epidemic of plague, wages climbed and the prices of consumer goods tumbled. A bad harvest sent food prices skyrocketing. Only those able to even out these extreme swings by stockpiling goods in times of plenty and consuming them in times of want were safe. Capital, however initially accumulated, was the key to continued wealth. Monopolies ensured the profitability of trade and manufacturing, but only those with sufficient capital could engage in either. In Florence, for example, 10 percent of the families controlled 90 percent of the wealth, with an even more extreme concentration at the top.

Production and Consumption

This concentration of wealth and the way in which it was used defined the Renaissance economy. Economic life is bound up in the relationship between resources and desires, or, as economists would have it, supply and demand. The late medieval economy, despite the development of international banking and long-distance trade, was still an economy of primary producers: Between 70 and 90 percent of Europe's population was involved in subsistence agriculture. Even in Italy, which contained the greatest concentration of urban areas in the world, agriculture predominated. The manufacture of clothing was the only other significant economic activity, and it was dwarfed in comparison to farming. Moreover, most of what was produced was for local consumption rather than for the marketplace. The relationship between supply and demand was precisely measured by the full or empty stomach. Even in good times more than 80 percent of the population lived at subsistence level with food, clothing, and shelter their only expenses. Thus when we discuss the market economy of the Renaissance, we are discussing the circumstances of the few rather than the many.

The defining characteristic of the early Renaissance economy was change in population. Recurring waves of plague kept population levels low for more than a century. In the century between 1350 and 1450 one in every six years was characterized by an unusually high mortality rate. At the end of this period Florence's population was only a quarter of what it had been at the beginning. This dramatic reduction in population depressed economic growth. The general economy did not revive until the sustained population increase toward

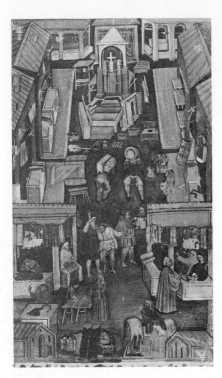

Cloth making was a major contributor to European economic growth during the Middle Ages. In this 1470 portrait of Cloth Merchants' Street, Bologna, a tailor (center) measures a prospective client.

the end of the fifteenth century. Until then, in both agriculture and manufacturing, supply outstripped demand. On the farms overabundance resulted from two related developments: the concentration of surviving farmers on the best land and the enlargement of their holdings. In the shops finished products outnumbered the consumers who survived the epidemics. Overproduction meant lower prices for basic commodities, and the decline in population meant higher wages for labor. At the lowest levels of society survivors found it easier to earn their living and even to create a surplus than had their parents. For a time the lot of the masses improved.

But for investors, such economic conditions meant that neither agriculture nor cloth making was particularly attractive. Expensive investments in land or equipment for sharecropping were paid off in inexpensive grain; high wages for the few surviving skilled workers brought a return in cheap cloth. In such circumstances, consumption was more attractive than investment and luxury became more alluring than ever. It was not merely the perceived shortage in profitable investments that brought on the increase in conspicuous consumption during the fifteenth century. In the psychological atmosphere created by unpredictable, swift, and deadly epidemics, people who were interested in life on earth became more concerned with the present than the future. Secondly, in order to pay for wars, both offensive and defensive, rates of taxation increased. Since both houses and personal property were normally exempt from the calculations of wealth upon which taxation was based, the richest members of the community could escape this additional burden by purchasing luxury goods.

For whatever reasons, the production and consumption of luxuries soared. By the middle of the fourteenth century Florence was known for its silks and jewelry as much as for its cloth. Venice became a European center for the glass industry, especially for the finely ground glass that was used in eyeglasses. Production of specialty crops like sugar, saffron, fruits, and high-quality wine expanded. International trade centered more than ever on bringing into western Europe the exotic goods of the East, resulting in the serious outflow of gold and silver that enriched first the Byzantine and then the Ottoman emperors. Both public and private building projects increased, spurring the demand for architects, sculptors, and painters. At the courts of the hereditary nobility and of the pope, the ceremonies of state were lavish beyond compare. The rise in the consumption of luxuries was everywhere apparent, taken by some as a sign of the vitality of the age, by others as an indication of its decay.

The Experience of Life

Luxury helped improve a life that for rich and poor alike was short and uncertain. Nature was still people's most potent enemy. Renaissance children who survived infancy found their lives governed by parentage and by gender. In parentage the great divide was between those who lived with surplus and those who lived at subsistence. The first category encompassed the wealthiest bankers and merchants down to those who owned their own farms or engaged in small urban crafts. The vast majority of urban and rural dwellers comprised the second category. About the children of the poor we know very little other than that their survival was unlikely. If they did not die at birth or shortly afterward, they might be abandoned—especially if female—to the growing number of orphanages in the cities, waste away from lack of nutrition, or fall prey to ordinary childhood diseases. Eldest sons were favored; younger daughters were disadvantaged. But in poor families this favoritism meant little more than early apprenticeship to day labor in the city or farm labor in the countryside. Girls were frequently sent out as domestic servants far from the family home.

Children of the wealthy had better chances for survival than children of the poor. For the better off, childhood might begin with "milk parents," life in the home of the family of a wet nurse who would breast-feed the baby through infancy. Only the very wealthy could afford a live-in wet nurse, which would increase the child's chances of survival. Again, daughters were more likely to be sent far from home and least likely to have their nursing supervised. The use of wet nurses not only emancipated parents from the daily care of infants, it also allowed them to resume sexual relations. Nursing women refrained from sex in the belief that it affected their milk.

During the period between weaning and apprenticeship Renaissance children lived with their families. There was no typical Renaissance family. Nuclear families—that is, parents and their children under one roof—were probably more common than extended families, which might include grandparents and other relatives. But the composition of the family changed over the course of the life cycle and included times in which married children or grandparents were present and others when a single parent and small children were the only members. Moreover, even nuclear families commonly contained stepparents and stepchildren as well as domestic servants or apprentices. Thus a child returning to the parental household was as likely to form emotional bonds with older siblings as with parents.

The family was an economic unit as well as a grouping of relatives. Decisions to abandon children, to send them away from the household when very young, or to take in domestic servants were based on economic calculations. In the competition for scarce resources, the way in which children were managed might determine the survival of the family unit. Sons could expect to be apprenticed to a trade probably between the ages of 10 and 13. Most, of course, learned the crafts of their fathers, but not necessarily in their father's shop. Sons inherited the family business and its most important possessions, tools of the trade or beasts of labor for the farm. Inheritance customs varied. In some places only the eldest son received the equipment of the family occupation; in others, like Tuscany, all the sons shared it. Still, in the first 15 years of life, these most favored children would have spent between one-third and one-half of their time outside the household in which they had been born.

Expectations for daughters centered on their chances of marriage. For a girl, dowry was everything. If a girl's father could provide a handsome one, her future was secure; if not, the alternatives were a convent, which would take a small bequest, or a match lower down the social scale, where the quality of life deteriorated rapidly. Daughters of poor families entered domestic service in order to have a dowry provided by their masters. The dowry was taken to the household of their husband. There the couple resided until they established their own separate family. If the husband died, it was to his parental household that the widow returned.

Women married in late adolescence, usually around the age of 20. Among the wealthy, marriages were perceived as familial alliances and business transactions rather than love matches. The dowry was an investment on which fathers expected a return, and while the bride might have some choice, it was severely limited. Compatibility was not a central feature in matchmaking. Husbands were, on average, ten years older than their wives and likely to leave them widows. In the early fifteenth century about one-fourth of all adult women in Florence were widows.

Married women lived in a state of nearly constant pregnancy. Alessandra Strozzi, whose father was one of the wealthiest citizens of Florence, married at age 16, gave birth to eight children in ten years, and was widowed at age 25. Not all pregnancies produced children. The rates of miscarriages and stillbirths were very high, and abortions and infanticide were not unknown. Only among the families who hovered between surplus and subsistence is there any evidence of attempts to control pregnancies. These efforts, which relied on techniques like the rhythm method and withdrawal, were not particularly effective. The rhythm method was especially futile because of the misunderstanding of the role of women in conception. It was not yet known that the woman contained an egg that was fertilized during conception. Without this knowledge it was impossible to understand the cycle of ovulation. Practically speaking, family size was limited on the one end by late marriages and on the other by early deaths.

Life experiences differed for males. Men married later, near the age of 25 on the farms, nearer 30 in the cities because of the cost of setting up in trade or on the land. Late marriage meant long supervision under the watchful eye of father or master, an extended period between adolescence and adulthood. The reputation that Renaissance cities gained for homosexuality and licentiousness must be viewed in light of the advanced age at which males married. The level of sexual frustration was high and its outlet in ritual violence and rape was also high.

The establishment of one's own household through marriage was a late rite of passage considering the expectations of early death. Many men, even with families, never succeeded in setting up separately from their fathers or elder brothers. Men came of age at 30 but were thought to be old by 50. Thus for men, marriage and parenthood took place in middle age rather than in youth. Valued all their lives more highly than their sisters, male heads of households were the source of all power in their domicile, in their shops, and in the state. They were responsible for overseeing every aspect of the upbringing of their children. But their wives were essential partners who governed domestic life. Women labored not only at the hearth, but in the fields and shops as well. Their economic contribution to the well-being of the family was critical, both in the dowry they brought at marriage and in the labor they contributed to the household. If their wives died, men with young children remarried quickly. While there were many bachelors in Renaissance society, there were few widowers.

In most cases death came suddenly. Epidemic diseases, of which plague was the most virulent, struck fifteenth-century Italians with fearful regularity. Even in the absence of a serious outbreak, there were always deaths in town and country attributable to the plague. Epidemics struck harder at the young—children and adolescents who were the majority of the population— and hardest in the summer months when other viruses and bacteria weakened the population. Medical treatment was more likely to hasten death than to prolong life. Lorenzo de Medici's physician prescribed powdered pearls for the Florentine ruler's gout. After that Lorenzo complained more of stomach pains than of gout. Such remedies revealed a belief in the harmony of nature and the healing power of rare substances. They were not silly or superstitious, but they were not effective either. Starvation was rare, less because of food shortage than because the seriously undernourished were more likely to succumb to disease than to famine. In urban areas, the government would intervene to provide grain from public storehouses at times of extreme shortage; in the countryside, large landholders commonly exercised the same function.

The Quality of Life

Though life may have been difficult during the Renaissance, it was not unfulfilling. Despite constant toil and frequent hardship, people of the Renaissance had reason to believe that their lives were better than those of their ancestors and that their children's lives would be better still. On the most basic level, health improved and, for those who survived plague, life expectancy increased. Better health was related to better diet. Improvement came from two sources, the relative surplus of grain throughout the fifteenth century and the wider variety of foods consumed. Bread remained the most widely consumed foodstuff, but there was more pork and lamb in the diet of ordinary people in the fifteenth century than there would be for the next 400 years. At the upper levels of society, sweet wine and citrus fruits helped offset the lack of vegetables. This diversification of diet resulted from improvements in transportation and communication, which brought more goods and services to a growing number of towns in the chain that linked the regional centers to the rural countryside.

But the towns and cities contributed more than consumer goods to Renaissance society. They also introduced a new sense of social and political cohesiveness. The city was something to which people belonged. In urban areas they could join social groups of their own choosing and develop networks of support not possible in rural environments. Blood relations remained the primary social group. Kin were the most likely source of aid in times of need, and charity began at home. Kin groups extended well beyond the immediate family, with both cousins and in-laws laying claim to the privileges of blood. The urban family could also depend on the connections of neighborhood. In some Italian cities, wealth or occupation determined housing patterns. In others, like Florence, rich and poor lived side by side and identified themselves with their small administrative unit and with their local church. Thus they could participate in relationships with others both above and below them in social scale. From their superiors they gained connections that helped their families; from their inferiors they gained devoted clients.

As in the Middle Ages, the Church remained the spatial, spiritual, and social center of people's lives. Though the Renaissance is singled out as a time when people became more worldly in their outlook, this worldliness took place within the context of an absorbing devotional life. There was not yet any separation between faith and reason. The Church provided explanations for both the mysterious and the mundane. In it were performed the rituals of baptism, marriage, and burial that measured the passage of life. The Church was also the source of the key symbols of urban society. The flags of militia troops, the emblems of guilds, the regalia of the city itself were all adorned by recognizably religious symbols. The Church preserved holy relics that were venerated for their power to protect the city or to endow it with particular skills and resources. Through its holy days, as much as through its rituals, the Church helped channel leisure activities into community celebrations.

A growing sense of civic pride and individual accomplishment were underlying characteristics of the Italian Renaissance, enhanced by the development of social cohesion and community solidarity that both Church and city-state fostered. It is commonly held that the Renaissance was both elitist and male dominated, that it was an experience separate from that of the society at large. There can be no question that it was the rich who commissioned works of art or that it was the highly skilled male craft workers who executed them. But neither lived in a social vacuum. The Renaissance was not an event whose causes were the result of the efforts of the few or whose consequences were limited to the privileged. In fact, the Renaissance was not an event at all. Family values that permitted early apprenticeships in surrogate households and emphasized the continuity of crafts from one generation to the next made possible the skilled artists of the Renaissance cities. The stress on the production of luxury goods placed higher value on individual skills and therefore on excellence in workmanship. Church and state sought to express social values through representational art. One of the chief purposes of wall murals was to instruct the unlettered in religion, to help them visualize the central episodes in Christian history. The grandiose architecture and statuary that adorned central places was designed to enhance civic pride and communicate the protective power of public institutions.

Renaissance Art

In every age, artistic achievement represents a combination of individual talent and predominant social ideals. Artists may be at the leading edge of the society in which they live, but it is the spirit of that society they capture in word or song or image. Artistic disciplines also have their own technical development. Individually, Renaissance artists were attempting to solve problems about perspective and three-dimensionality that had defeated their predecessors. But the particular techniques or experiments that interested them owed as much to the social context as they did to the artistic one. For example, the urban character of Italian government led to the need for civic architecture, public buildings on a grand scale. The celebration of individual achievement led to the explosive growth of portraiture. Not surprisingly, major technological breakthroughs were achieved in both areas.

This relationship between artist and social context was all the more important in the Renaissance, when artists were closely tied to the crafts and trades of urban society and to the demands of clients who commissioned their work. Although it was the elite who patronized art, it was skilled tradespeople who produced it. Artists normally followed the pattern of any craft worker, an apprenticeship begun as a teenager and a long period of training and work in a master's shop. This form of education gave the aspiring artist a practical rather than a theoretical bent and a keen appreciation for the business side of art. Studios were identified with particular styles and competed for commissions from clients, especially the Church. Wealthy individuals commissioned art as investments, as marks of personal distinction, and as displays of public piety. Isabella d'Este (1474–1539), one of the great patrons of Renaissance artists, wrote hundreds of letters specifying the details of the works she commissioned. She once sent an artist a thread of the exact dimensions of the pictures she had ordered. Demand for art was high. The vast public works projects needed buildings, the new piazzas (public squares) and palazzos (private houses) needed statuary, and the long walls of churches needed murals.

The survival of so many Renaissance masterpieces allows us to reconstruct the stages by which the remarkable artistic achievements of this era took place. Although advances were made in a variety of fields during the Renaissance, the three outstanding areas were architecture, sculpture, and painting. While modern artists would consider each a separate discipline, Renaissance artists crossed their boundaries without hesitation. Not only could these artists work with a variety of materials, their intensive and varied apprenticeships taught them to apply the technical solutions of one field to the problems of another. Few Renaissance artists confined themselves to one area of artistic expression, and many created works of enduring beauty in more than one medium. Was the greatest achievement of Michelangelo his sculpture of David, his paintings on the ceiling of the Sistine Chapel, or his design for the dome of Saint Peter's? Only a century of interdisciplinary cross-fertilization could have prepared the artistic world for such a feat.

Three Masters

That century began with the work of three Florentine masters who deeply influenced one another's development: Brunelleschi (1377–1446), Donatello (1386–1466), and Masaccio (1401–1428). In the Renaissance the dominant artistic discipline was architecture. Buildings were the most expensive investment patrons could make, and the technical knowledge necessary for their successful construction was immense. The architect not only designed a building, he served as its general contractor, its construction supervisor, and its inspector. Moreover, the architect's design determined the amount and the scale of the statuary and decorative paintings to be incorporated. By 1400 the Gothic style of building had dominated western Europe for over two centuries. Its characteristic pointed arches, vaulted ceilings, and slender spires had simplified building by removing the heavy walls formerly thought necessary to support great structures. Gothic construction permitted greater height, a

Florence Cathedral was begun by Arnolfo di Cambio in 1296. The nave was finished about 1350, and the dome, designed by Brunelleschi, was added in the 1420s. This view shows the dome and the apse end of the cathedral.

characteristic especially desirable in cathedrals, which stretched toward the heavens. But though the buildings themselves were simplified, the techniques for erecting them became more complex. By the fifteenth century architects had turned their techniques into an intricate style. They became obsessed by angular arches, elaborate vaultings and buttresses, and long pointed spires.

It was Brunelleschi who decisively challenged the principles of Gothic architecture by recombining its basic elements with those of classical structures. Basing his designs on geometric principles, Brunelleschi reintroduced planes and spheres as dominant motifs. His greatest work was the dome on the cathedral in Florence, begun in 1420. His design for the dome was simple but bold. The circular windows are set inside a square of panels, which in turn are set inside a rectangle. Brunelleschi is generally credited with having been the first Renaissance artist to have understood and made use of perspective, though it was immediately put to more dramatic effect in sculpture and painting.

The sculptor's study was the human form in all of its three-dimensional complexity. The survival of Roman and Hellenistic pieces, mostly bold and muscular torsos, meant that the influence of classical art was most direct in sculpture. Donatello translated these classical styles into more naturalistic forms. His technique is evident in the long flowing robes in most of his works, sculpted in the natural fashion in which cloth hung. Donatello revived the free-standing statue, which demanded greater attention to human anatomy because it was viewed from many angles. He also led the revival of the equestrian statue, sculpting the Venetian captain-general *Gattamelata* (1445–1450) for a public square in Padua. This enormous bronze horse and rider relied on the standpoint of the viewer to achieve its overpowering effect. This use of linear perspective is also seen in Donatello's breathtaking altar scenes of the miracles of Saint Anthony in Padua, which resemble nothing so much as a canvas cast in bronze.

These altar scenes clearly evince the unmistakable influence of the paintings of Masaccio. His frescoes in the Brancacci Chapel in Florence were studied and sketched by all of the great artists of the next generation, who unreservedly praised his naturalism. What most claims the attention of the modern viewer is Masaccio's shading of light and shadow and his brilliant use of linear perspective to create the illusion that a flat surface has three dimensions. Masaccio's work was on standard Christian themes, but he brought an entirely novel approach to them all. In an adoration scene he portrayed a middle-aged Madonna and a dwarfish baby Jesus; in a painting of Saint Peter paying tribute money, he used his own likeness as the face of one of the apostles. His two best known works are the *Holy Trinity* (1425) and the *Expulsion of Adam and Eve* (ca. 1427). In the *Holy Trinity* Masacchio provides the classic example of the use of linear perspective. In the painting, the ceiling of a Brunelleschi-designed temple recedes to a vanishing point beyond the head of God, creating the simultaneous illusion of height and depth.

In The Expulsion of Adam and Eve, *Masaccio's mastery of perspective helps create the illusion of movement. Eve's anguish is shown in her deep eyes and hollow mouth, which are accentuated by casting the source of light downward and shading what otherwise would be lit.*

Renaissance Style

By the middle of the fifteenth century a recognizable Renaissance style had triumphed. The outstanding architect of this period was Leon Battista Alberti (1404–1472), whose treatise *On Building* (1452) remained the most influential work on the subject until the eighteenth century. Alberti consecrated the geometric principles laid down by Brunelleschi and infused them with a humanist spirit. He revived the classical dictum that a building, like a body, should have an even number of supports and, like a head, an odd number of openings. This furthered precise geometric calculations in scale and design.

No sculptor challenged the preeminence of Donatello for another 50 years, but in painting there were many contenders for the garlands worn by Masaccio. The first was Piero della Francesca (ca. 1420–1492) who, though trained in the tradition of Masaccio, broke new ground in his concern for the visual unity of his paintings. From portraits to processions to his stunning fresco *The Resurrection* (ca. 1463), Piero concentrated on the most technical aspects of composition. Another challenger was Sandro Botticelli (1445–1510), whose classical themes, sensitive portraits, and bright colors set him apart from the line of Florentine painters with whom he studied. His mythologies of the *Birth of Venus* and *Spring* (ca. 1478) depart markedly from the naturalism inspired by Masaccio.

Boticelli's Primavera *(Spring) also called* Garden of Venus. *Venus, in the center, is attended by the three Graces and by Cupid, Flora, Chloris, and Zephyr.*

This concern with beauty and personality is also seen in the paintings of Leonardo da Vinci (1452–1519), whose creative genius embodied the Renaissance ideal of the "universal man." Leonardo's achievements in scientific, technical, and artistic endeavors read like a list of all of the subjects known during the Renaissance. His detailed anatomical drawings and the method he devised for rendering them, his botanical observations, and his engineering inventions (including models for a tank and an airplane) testify to his unrestrained curiosity. His paintings reveal a continuation of the scientific application of mathematics to matters of proportion and perspective. Leonardo's psychological portrait *La Gioconda* (1503–1506), popularly called the Mona Lisa, is quite possibly the best known picture in the Western world.

Michelangelo

The artistic achievements of the Renaissance culminated in the creative outpourings of Michelangelo Buonarroti (1475–1564). Poet, sculptor, painter, and architect, Michelangelo imparted his genius to everything he touched. Uncharacteristically, Michelangelo came from a family of standing in Florentine society. At the age of 14, over the opposition of his father, he was apprenticed to a leading painter and spent his spare time in Florentine churches copying the works of Masaccio among others.

In 1490 Michelangelo gained a place in the household of Lorenzo de Medici. During this two-year period he claimed to have taught himself sculpturing, a remarkable feat considering the skills required. In fact, what was unusual about Michelangelo's early development was that he avoided the long years of apprenticeship during which someone else's style was implanted

The Creation of Adam. *Detail from Michelangelo's frescoes on the ceiling of the Sistine Chapel. The Michelangelo frescoes had become obscured by dirt and layers of varnish and glue applied at various times over the years. In the 1980s they were cleaned to reveal their original colors.*

upon the young artist. In the Medici household he came into contact with leading Neoplatonists, who taught that humankind was on an ascending journey of perfectibility toward God. These ideas can be seen as one source of the heroic concept of humanity that Michelangelo brought to his work.

In 1496 Michelangelo moved to Rome. There his abilities as a sculptor quickly brought him to the attention of Jacopo Galli, a Roman banker who was interested in art and learning. Galli commissioned a classical work for himself and procured another for a French cardinal, which became the *Pietà*. Although this was his first attempt at sculpting a work of religious art, Michelangelo would never surpass it in beauty or composition. The *Pietà* created a sensation in Rome, and by the time Michelangelo returned to Florence in 1501, at the age of 26, he was already acknowledged as one of the great sculptors of his day. He was immediately commissioned to work on an enormous block of marble that had been quarried nearly a half century before and had defeated the talents of a series of carvers. He worked continuously for three years on his *David* (1501–1504), a piece that completed the union between classical and Renaissance styles.

Though Michelangelo always believed himself to be primarily a sculptor, his next outstanding work was in the field of painting. In 1508 Pope Julius II summoned Michelangelo to Rome and commissioned him to decorate the ceiling of the small ceremonial chapel that had been built next to the new papal residence. Michelangelo's plan was to portray, in an extended narrative, human creation and those Old Testament events that foreshadowed the birth of the Savior. First Michelangelo framed his scenes within the architecture of a massive classical temple. In this way he was able to give the impression of having flattened the rounded surface on which he worked. Within the center panels came his fresco scenes of the events of the creation and of human history from the Fall to the Flood. His representations were simple and compelling: The fingers of God and Adam nearly touching; Eve with one leg still emerging from Adam's side; the half-human snake in the temptation are all majestically evocative.

The *Pietà*, the *David*, and the paintings of the Sistine Chapel were the work of youth. Michelangelo's crowning achievement, the building of Saint Peter's basilica in Rome, was the work of age. The intervening years saw the production of masterpiece after masterpiece, enough completed and unfinished work to have established his genius. The base work of St. Peter's had already been laid and drawings for its completion had been made 30 years earlier by Bramante. Michelangelo altered these plans in an effort to bring more light within the church and provide a more majestic facade outside. His main contribution, however, was the design of the great dome, which centered the interior of the church on Saint Peter's grave. More than the height, it is the harmony of Michelangelo's design that creates the sense of the building thrusting upward like a Gothic cathedral of old. Michelangelo did not live to see the dome of Saint Peter's completed.

Renaissance art served Renaissance society. It reflected both its concrete achievements and its visionary ideals. It was a synthesis of old and new, building upon classical models, particularly in sculpture and architecture, but adding newly discovered techniques and skills. When Giorgio Vasari (1511–1574) came to write his *Lives of the Great Painters, Sculptors, and Architects* (1550) he found over two hundred artists worthy of distinction. But Renaissance artists did more than construct and adorn buildings or celebrate and beautify spiritual life. Inevitably their work expressed the ideals and aspirations of the society in which they lived, the new emphasis on learning and knowledge; on the here and now rather than the hereafter; and most importantly on humanity and its capacity for growth and perfection.

$\mathcal{R}$enaissance Ideals

Renaissance thought went hand in glove with Renaissance art. Scholars and philosophers searched the works of the ancients to find the principles on which to build a better life. They scoured monastic libraries for forgotten manuscripts, discovering, among other things, Greek poetry, history, the works of Homer and Plato, and Aristotle's *Poetics*. Their rigorous application of scholarly procedures for the collection and collation of these texts was one of the most important contributions of those Renaissance intellectuals who came to be known as humanists. Humanism developed in reaction to an intellectual world that was centered on the Church and dominated by otherworldly concerns. Humanism was secular in outlook, though by no means was it antireligious.

Humanists celebrated worldly achievements. Pico della Mirandola's *Oration on the Dignity of Man* (1486) is the best known of a multitude of Renaissance writings influenced by the discovery of the works of Plato. Pico believed that people could perfect their existence on earth because God had endowed humans with the capacity to determine their own fate. This emphasis on human potential found expression in the celebration of human achievement.

Humanism was neither a set of philosophical principles nor a program for social action. There were no antihumanists to give it form, and whatever coherence Italian humanism may have had, it was quickly diluted as it rapidly spread across Europe. Quite simply, humanists studied and taught the humanities, the skills of disciplines like philology, the art of language, and rhetoric, the art of expression. Though they were mostly laypeople, humanists applied their learning to both religious and secular studies. We must not think of humanists as antireligious. Although they reacted strongly against Scholasticism, they were heavily indebted to the work of medieval churchmen. Nor were they hostile to the Church. Petrarch, Bruni, and Alberti were all employed by the papal court at some time in their careers, as was Lorenzo Valla, the most influential of the humanists. Their interest in human achievement and human potential must be set beside their religious beliefs. As Petrarch stated quite succinctly, "Christ is my God; Cicero is the prince of the language I use."

The Humanists

The most important achievements of humanist scholars centered upon ancient texts. It was the humanists' goal to discover as much as had survived from the ancient world and to provide as full and accurate as possible texts of classical authors. Though much was already known of the Latin classics, few of the central works of ancient Greece had been uncovered. Humanists preserved this heritage by reviving the study of the Greek language and by translating Greek authors into Latin. After the fall of Constantinople in 1453, Italy became the center for Greek studies as scholars fled the Ottoman conquerors. Humanists also introduced historical methods in studying texts, establishing principles for determining which of many manuscript copies of an ancient text was the oldest and which had been least corrupted by their copyists. This was of immense importance in studying the writings of the ancient Fathers of the Church, many of whose manuscripts had not been examined for centuries. Their emphasis on the humanistic disciplines fostered new educational ideals. Along with the study of theology, logic, and natural philosophy, which had dominated the medieval university, humanist scholars stressed the importance of grammar, rhetoric, moral philosophy, and history. They believed that the study of these "liberal arts" should be undertaken for its own sake. This gave a powerful boost to the ideal of the perfectibility of the individual that appeared in so many other aspects of Renaissance culture.

Humanists furthered the secularization of Renaissance society through their emphasis on the study of the classical world. Philology became one of the most celebrated humanist skills and the study of ancient manuscripts one of the most common humanist activities. The rediscovery of Latin texts during the late Middle Ages spurred interest in all things ancient. Petrarch, who is rightly called the father of humanism, revered the great Roman rhetorician Cicero above all others. Leonardo Bruni (1370–1444) was reputed to be the greatest Greek scholar of his day. He translated Plato and Aristotle and did much to advance mastery of classical Greek and foster the ideas of Plato in the late fifteenth century.

The study of the origins of words, their meaning, and their proper grammatical usage may seem an unusual foundation for one of the most vital of all European intellectual movements. But philology was the humanists' chief concern. This can best be illustrated by the work of Lorenzo Valla (1407–1457). Valla was brought up in Rome, where he was largely self-educated, though according to the prescriptions of the Florentine humanists. Valla entered the service of Alfonso I, king of Naples, and applied his humanistic training to affairs of state. The kingdom of Naples bordered on the Papal States, and its kings were in continual conflict with the papacy. The pope asserted the right to withhold recognition of the king, a right that was based on the jurisdictional authority supposedly ceded to the papacy by the Emperor Constantine in the fourth century—the so-called Donation of Constantine. Valla settled the matter definitively. Applying historical and philological critiques to the text of the Donation, Valla proved that it could not have been written earlier than the eighth century, 400 years after Constantine's death. He mercilessly exposed words and terms that had not existed in Roman times, like *fief* and *satrap*, and thus proved beyond doubt that the Donation was a forgery and papal claims based on it were without merit.

Valla's career demonstrates the impact of humanist values on practical affairs. Although humanists were scholars, they made no distinction between an active and a contemplative life. A life of scholarship was a life of public service. This civic humanism is best expressed in the writings of Leon Battista Alberti (1404–1472), whose treatise *On the Family* (1443) is a classic study of the new urban values, especially prudence and thrift. Alberti extolled the virtues of "the fatherland, the public good, and the benefit of all citizens." An architect, a mathematician, a poet, a playwright, a musician, and an inventor, Alberti was one of the great virtuosi of the Renaissance.

Alberti's own life might have served as a model for the most influential of all Renaissance tracts, Castiglione's *The Courtier* (1528). Baldesar Castiglione (1478–1529) directed his lessons to the public life of the aspiring elite. It was his purpose to prescribe those characteristics that would make the ideal courtier, who was as much born as made. He prescribed every detail of the education necessary for the ideal state servant from table manners to artistic attainments. Castiglione's perfect courtier was an amalgam of all that the elite of Renaissance society held dear. He was to be educated as a scholar, he was to be occupied as a soldier, and he was to serve his state as an adviser.

Machiavelli

At the same time Castiglione was drafting a blueprint for the idealized courtier, Niccolò Machiavelli (1469–1527) was laying the foundation for the realistic sixteenth-century ruler. No Renaissance work has been more important or more controversial than Machiavelli's *The Prince* (1513). Its vivid prose, its epigrammatic advice—"men must either be pampered or crushed"—and its clinical dissection of power politics have attracted generation after generation of readers. With Machiavelli, for better or worse, begins the science of politics.

Machiavelli came from an established Florentine family. He entered state service as an assistant to one of his teachers and unexpectedly rode those coattails into the relatively important office of secretary to the Council of Ten, the organ of Florentine government that had responsibility for war and diplomacy. Here Machiavelli received his education in practical affairs. He was an emissary to Cesare Borgia during his consolidation of the Papal States at the turn of the century and carefully studied Borgia's methods. Machiavelli was a tireless correspondent, and he began to collect materials for various tracts on military matters.

But as suddenly as he rose to his position of power and influence, he fell from it. The militia he had advocated and in part organized was soundly defeated by the Spaniards, and the Florentine republic fell. Machiavelli was summarily dismissed from office in 1512 and was imprisoned and tortured the following year. Released and banished from the city, he retired to a small country estate. Immediately he began writing what became his two greatest works, *The Prince* (1513) and *The Discourses on Livy* (1519).

Machiavelli has left a haunting portrait of his life in exile, and it is important to understand how intertwined his studies of ancient and modern politics were.

> *On the coming of evening, I return to my house and enter my study; and at the door I take off the day's clothing covered with mud and dust, and put on garments regal and courtly; and reclothed appropriately, I enter the ancient courts of ancient men, where, received by them with affection, I feed on that food which only is mine and which I was born for.*

The Prince is a handbook for a ruler who would establish a lasting government. It attempts to set down principles culled from historical examples and contemporary events to aid the prince in attaining and maintaining power. By study of these precepts and by their swift and forceful application, Machiavelli believed that the prince might even control fortune itself. What made *The Prince* so remarkable in its day, and what continues to enliven debate over it, is that Machiavelli was able to separate all ethical considerations from his analysis. Whether this resulted from cynicism or from his own expressed desire for realism, Machiavelli uncompromisingly instructed the would-be ruler to be half human and half beast—to conquer neighbors, to murder enemies, and to deceive friends. Nothing better illlustrates the principle that humanists were not necessarily humanitarians.

Taken as a whole, Machiavelli's writings aspire to the restoration of the glory of Rome, the establishment of an empire that is a good in itself. A life bounded by a half century of destructive warfare might have taught no other lesson than the sweetness of peace. But Machiavelli's thought transcended the immediacy of his historical context. Steeped in the humanist ideals of fame and *virtù*—a combination of virtue and virtuosity, of valor, character, and ability—he sought to reestablish Italian rule and place government on a stable scientific basis that would end the perpetual conflict among the Italian city-states.

*T*he Politics of the Italian City-States

Like studs on a leather boot, city-states dotted the Italian peninsula. They differed in size, shape, and form. Some were large seaports, others small inland villages; some cut wide swaths across the plains, others were tiny islands. The absence of a unifying central authority in Italy, resulting from the collapse of the Holy Roman Empire and the papal schism, allowed ancient guilds and confraternities to transform themselves into self-governing societies. By the beginning of the fifteenth century the Italian city-states were the center of power, wealth, and culture in the Christian world.

This dominion rested on several conditions. First, their geographical position favored the exchange of resources and goods between East and West. Until the fifteenth century, and despite the crusading efforts of medieval popes, East and West fortified each other. A great circular trade had developed, encompassing the Byzantine Empire, the North African coastal states, and the Mediterranean nations of western Europe. The Italian peninsula dominated the circumference of that circle. Its port cities, Genoa and Venice especially, became great maritime powers through their trade in spices and minerals. Second, just beyond the peninsula to the north lay the vast and populous territories of the Holy Roman Empire. There the continuous need for manufactured goods, especially cloth and metals, was filled by long caravans that traveled from Italy through the Alps. Milan specialized in metal crafts. Florence was a financial capital as well as a center for the manufacture of fine luxury goods. Finally, the city-states and their surrounding areas were agriculturally self-sufficient.

Because of their accomplishments we tend to think of these Italian city-states as small nations. Even the term *city-state* implies national identity. Each city-state governed itself according to its own rules and customs and each defined itself in isolation from the larger regional or tribal associations that once prevailed. Italy was neither a nation nor a people.

The Five Powers

Although there were dozens of Italian city-states, by the early fifteenth century five had emerged to dominate the politics of the peninsula. In the south was the kingdom of Naples, the only city-state governed by a hereditary monarchy. Its politics were mired by conflicts over its succession. During the fourteenth century Naples was successively ruled by French and Hungarian princes. The fifteenth century began with civil warfare between rival claimants of both nations, and it was not until the Spaniard Alfonso I of Aragon (1442–1458) secured the throne in 1443 that peace was restored and Naples and Sicily were reunited. Bordering Naples were the Papal States, whose capital was Rome but whose territories stretched far to the north and lay on both sides of the spiny Apennine mountain chain that extends down the center of the peninsula. Throughout the fourteenth and early fifteenth centuries, the territories under the nominal control of the Church were largely independent and included such thriving city-states as Bologna, Ferrara, and Urbino. Even in Rome the weakened papacy had to contend with noble families for control of the city.

The three remaining dominant city-states were bunched together in the north. Florence, center of Renaissance culture, was one of the wealthiest cities of Europe before the devastations of the plague and the sustained economic downturn of the late fourteenth century. The city itself was inland, and its main waterway, the Arno, ran to the sea through Pisa, whose subjugation in 1406 was a turning point in Florentine history. Nominally Florence was a republic, but during the fifteenth century it was ruled in effect by its principal banking family, the Medici.

To the north of Florence was the duchy of Milan, the major city in Lombardy. It, too, was landlocked, cut off from the sea by Genoa. But Milan's economic life was oriented northward to the Swiss and German towns beyond the Alps, and its major concern was preventing foreign invasions. The most warlike of the Italian cities, Milan was a despotism, ruled for nearly two centuries by the Visconti family.

The last of the five powers was the republic of Venice. Ideally situated at the head of the Adriatic Sea, Venice became the leading maritime power of the age. Until the fifteenth century, Venice was less interested in securing a landed empire than in dominating a seaborne one. The republic was ruled by a hereditary elite, headed by an elected doge, who was the chief magistrate of Venice, and a variety of small elected councils.

The political history of the peninsula during the late fourteenth and early fifteenth centuries is one of unrelieved turmoil. Wherever we look, the governments of the city-states were threatened by foreign invaders, internal conspiracies, or popular revolts. In the 1370s the Genoese and Venetians fought their fourth war in little more than a century, this one so bitter that the Genoese risked much of their fleet in an unsuccessful effort to conquer Venice itself. At the turn of the century, the Hungarian occupant of the throne of Naples invaded both Rome and Florence. Florence and Milan were constantly at war with each other. Nor were foreign threats the only dangers. In Milan three Visconti brothers inherited power. Two murdered the third, and then the son of one murdered the other to reunite the inheritance. The Venetians executed one of their military leaders who was plotting treachery. One or another Florentine family usually faced exile when governments there changed hands. Popular revolts channeled social and economic discontent against the ruling elites in Rome, Milan, and Florence. The revolt of the "Ciompi" (the wooden shoes) in Florence in 1378 was an attempt by poorly paid wool workers to reform the city's exclusive guild system and give guild protection to the wage laborers lower down the social scale. In Milan an abortive republic was established in reaction against strong-arm Visconti rule.

By the middle of the fifteenth century, however, two trends were apparent amid this political chaos. The first was the consolidation of strong centralized governments within the large city-states. These took different forms but yielded a similar result—internal political stability. The return of the popes to Rome after the Great Schism restored the pope to the head of his temporal estates and began a long period of papal dominance over Rome and its satellite territories. In Milan one of the great military leaders of the day, Francesco Sforza (1401–1466), seized the reins of power after the failure of the Visconti line. The succession of King Alfonso I in Naples ended a half century of civil war. In both Florence and Venice the grip of the political elite over high offices was tightened by placing greater power in small advisory councils and, in Florence, by the ascent to power of the Medici family. In sum, this process is known as the rise of signorial rule. The rise of the signories made possible the second development of this period, the establishment of a balance of power within the peninsula.

It was the leaders of the Italian city-states who first perfected the art of diplomacy. Constant warfare necessitated continual alliances, and by the end of the fourteenth century the large city-states had begun the practice of keeping resident ambassadors at the major seats of power. This provided leaders with accurate information about the conditions of potential allies and enemies. Diplomacy was both an offensive and defensive weapon. This was especially so because the city-states hired their soldiers as contract labor. These mercenary armies, whose leaders were known as *condottieri* from the name of their contract, were both expensive and dangerous to maintain. If they did not bankrupt their employers, they might desert them or, even worse, turn on them. Thus Francesco Sforza, the greatest condottiere of the fifteenth century, gained power in Milan. Sforza's consolidation of power in Milan initially led to warfare, but ultimately it formed the basis of the Peace of Lodi (1454). This established two balanced alliances, one between Florence and Milan, the other between Venice and Naples. These states, along with the papacy, pledged mutual nonaggression, a policy that lasted for nearly forty years.

The Peace of Lodi did not bring peace. It only halted the long period in which the major city-states struggled against one another. Under cover of the peace, the large states continued the process of swallowing up their smaller neighbors and creating quasi empires. This was a policy of imperialism as aggressive as that of any in the modern era. Civilian populations were overrun, local leaders exiled or exterminated, tribute money taken, and taxes levied. Each of the five states either increased its mainland territories or strengthened its hold upon them. Venice and Florence especially prospered.

Venice

Water was the source of the prosperity of Venice. Located at the head of the Adriatic Sea, the city is formed by a web of lagoons. Through its center snakes the Grand Canal, whose banks were lined with large and small buildings that celebrated its civic and mercantile power. At the Piazza San Marco stood the vast palace of the doge, elected leader of the republic, and the Basilica of Saint Mark, a domed church built in the Byzantine style. At the Rialto were the stalls of bankers and moneylenders, less grand perhaps but no less important. Here, too, were the auction blocks for the profitable trade in European slaves, east European serfs, and battlefield captives who were sold into service to Egypt or Byzantium.

Its prosperity based on trade rather than conquest, Venice enjoyed many natural advantages. Its position at the head of the Adriatic permitted access to the raw materials of both East and West. The rich Alpine timberland behind the city provided the hardwoods necessary for shipbuilding. The hinterland population were steady consumers of grain, cloth, and the new manufactured goods—glass, silk, jewelry, and cottons—that came pouring onto the market in the late Middle Ages.

But the success of Venice owed more to its own achievements than to these rich inheritances. The triumph of the Venetian state was the triumph of dedicated efficiency. The heart of its success lay in the way in which it organized its trade and its government. The key to Venetian trade was its privileged position with the Byzantine Empire. Venice had exchanged with the Byzantines military support for tax concessions that gave Venetian traders a competitive edge in the spice trade with the East. The spice trade was so lucrative that special ships were built to accommodate it. These galleys were constructed at public expense and doubled as the Venetian navy in times of war. By controlling these ships, the government strictly regulated the spice trade. Rather than allow the wealthiest merchants to dominate it, as they did in other cities, Venice specified the number of annual voyages and sold shares in them at auction based on a fixed price. This practice allowed big and small merchants to gain from the trade and encouraged all merchants to find other trading outlets.

Like its trade, Venetian government was also designed to disperse power. Although it was known as the Most Serene Republic, Venice was not a republic in the sense that we use the word; it was rather an oligarchy—a government by a restricted group. Political power was vested in a Great Council whose membership had been fixed at the end of the thirteenth century. All males whose fathers enjoyed the privilege of membership in the Great Council were registered at birth in the Book of Gold and became members of the Great Council when adults. From the body of the Great Council, which numbered about twenty-five hundred at the end of the fifteenth century, was chosen the Senate, a council about one-tenth the size, whose members served a one-year term. It was from the Senate that the true officers of government were selected: the doge, who was chosen for life, and members of a number of small councils, who administered affairs and advised the doge. Members of these councils were chosen by secret ballot in an elaborate process by which nominators were selected at random. Terms of office on the councils were extremely short in order to limit factionalism and to prevent any individual from gaining too much power. Though small groups exercised more power in practice than they should have in theory, the Venetian oligarchy was never troubled by either civil war or popular rebellion.

With its mercantile families firmly in control of government and trade, Venice created a vast overseas empire in the East during the thirteenth and fourteenth centuries. Naval supremacy allowed the Venetians to offer protection to strategic outposts in return for either privileges or tribute. But in the fifteenth century Venice turned west. In a dramatic reversal of its centuries-old policy, it began a process of conquest in Italy itself. There were several reasons for this new policy. First, the Venetian navy was no longer the unsurpassed power that it once had been. The Genoese wars had drained resources, and the revival of the Ottoman Turks in the east posed a growing threat that ultimately resulted in the fall of Constantinople (1453) and the end of Venetian trading privileges. Outposts in Dalmatia and the Aegean came under assault from both the Turks and the king of Hungary, cutting heavily into the complicated system by which goods were circulated by Venetian merchants. It was not long before Portuguese competition affected the most lucrative of all the commodities traded by the Venetians—pepper. Perhaps most importantly, mainland expansion offered new opportunities for Venice. Not all Venetians were traders, and the new industries that were being developed in the city could readily benefit from control of mainland markets. Most decisively of all, opportunity was knocking. In Milan Visconti rule was weakening and the Milanese territories were ripe for picking.

Venice reaped a rich harvest. From the beginning of the fifteenth century to the Peace of Lodi, the Most Serene Republic engaged in unremitting warfare. Its successes were remarkable. It pushed out to the north to occupy all the lands between the city and the Habsburg territories; it pushed to the east until it straddled the entire head of the Adriatic; and it pushed to the west almost as far as Milan itself. The western conquests in particular brought large populations under Venetian control which, along with their potential as a market, provided a ready source of taxation. By the end of the fifteenth century the mainland dominions of Venice were contributing nearly 40 percent of the city's revenue at a cost far smaller than that of the naval empire a century earlier.

Florence

Florentine prosperity was built on two foundations: money and wool. Beginning in the thirteenth century, Florentine bankers were among the wealthiest and most powerful in the world. Initially their position was established through support of the papacy in its long struggle with the Holy Roman Empire. Florentine financiers established banks in all the capitals of Europe and the East. In the Middle Ages, bankers served more functions than simply handling and exchanging money. Most were also tied to mercantile adventures and underwrote industrial activity. So it was in Florence where international bankers purchased high-quality wool to be manufactured into the world's finest woven cloth.

The activities of both commerce and cloth manufacture depended on external conditions, and thus the wealth of Florence was potentially unstable. In the mid fourteenth century instability came with the plague that devastated the city. Nearly 40 percent of the entire population was lost in the single year 1348, and recurring outbreaks continued to ravage the already weakened survivors. Loss of workers and loss of markets seriously disrupted manufacturing. By 1380 cloth production had fallen to less than a quarter of preplague levels. On the heels of plague came wars. The property of Florentine bankers and merchants abroad was an easy target, and in this respect the wars with Naples at the end of the fourteenth century were particularly disastrous. Thirty years of warfare with Milan, interrupted by only a single decade of peace (1413–1423), resulted in total bankruptcy for many of the city's leading commercial families. More significantly, the costs of warfare, offensive and defensive, created a massive public debt. Every Florentine of means owned shares in this debt, and the republic was continually devising new methods for borrowing and staving off crises of repayment. Small wonder that the republic turned for aid to the wealthiest banking family in Europe, the Medici.

As befitted a city whose prosperity was based on manufacturing, Florence had a strong guild tradition. The most important guilds were associated with banking and cloth manufacture, but they included the crafts and food processing trades as well. Only guild members could participate in government, electing the nine *Signoria* who administered laws, set tax rates, and directed foreign and domestic policy. Like that of Venice, Florentine government was a republican oligarchy and like Venice, it depended on rotated short periods in office and selections by lot to avoid factionalism. But Florence had a history of factionalism longer than its history of republican government. Its formal structures were occasionally altered so that powerful families could gain control of the real centers of political power, the small councils and emergency assemblies through which the Signoria governed. Conservative leadership drawn from the upper ranks of Florentine society guided the city through the wars of the early fourteenth century. But soon afterward the leaders of its greatest families, the Albizzi, the Pazzi, and the Medici, again divided Florentine politics into factions.

The ability of the Medici to secure a century-long dynasty in a government that did not have a head of state is just one of the mysteries surrounding the history of this remarkable family. Cosimo de Medici (1389–1464) was one of the richest men in Christendom when he returned to the city in 1434 after a brief exile. His leading position in government rested on supporters who were able to gain a controlling influence on the *Signoria*. Cosimo built his party carefully, banishing his Albizzi enemies, recruiting followers among the craft workers he employed, and even paying delinquent taxes to maintain the eligibility of his voters. Most importantly, emergency powers were invoked to reduce the number of citizens qualified to vote for the Signoria until the majority were Medici backers.

Cosimo was a great patron of artists and intellectuals. He collected books and paintings, endowed libraries, and spent lavishly on his own palace, the Palazzo Medici. Cosimo's position as an international banker brought him into contact with the heads of other Italian city-states, and it was his personal relationship with Francesco Sforza that finally ended the Milanese wars and brought about the Peace of Lodi.

It was Cosimo's grandson, Lorenzo (1449–1492), who linked the family's name to that of the age. He held strong humanist values instilled in him by his mother, Lucrezia Tornabuoni, who organized his education. He brought Michelangelo and other leading artists to his garden; he brought Pico della Mirandola and other leading humanists to his table. Lorenzo's power was based on his personality and reputation. His diplomatic abilities were the key to his survival. Almost immediately after Lorenzo came to power, Naples and the papacy began a war with Florence, a war that was costly to the Florentines in both taxation and lost territory. In 1479 Lorenzo traveled to Naples and personally convinced the Neapolitan king to sign a separate treaty. This restored the Italian balance of power and ensured continued Medici rule in Florence.

There is some doubt whether Lorenzo should be remembered by the title "the Magnificent" that was bestowed on him. His absorption in politics came at the expense of the family's commercial enterprises, which were nearly ruined during his lifetime. Branch after branch of the Medici bank closed as conditions for international finance deteriorated, and the family fortune dwindled. Moreover, the emergency powers that Lorenzo invoked to restrict participation in government changed forever the character of Florentine republicanism, irredeemably corrupting it. There is no reason to accept the judgment of his enemies that Lorenzo was a tyrant, but the negative consequences of his rule cannot be ignored. In 1494, two years after Lorenzo's death, the peninsula was plunged into those wars that turned it from the center of European civilization into one of its lesser satellites.

Italy, 1494

The End of Italian Hegemony

In the course of the Renaissance, western Europe was Italianized. For a century the city-states dominated the trade routes that connected East and West. Italian manufactures, such as Milanese artillery, Florentine silk, and Venetian glass, were prized above all others. The ducat and the florin, two Italian coins, were universally accepted in an age when every petty prince minted his own. The peninsula exported culture in the same way that it exported goods. Humanism quickly spread across the Alps, aided by the recent invention of printing (which the Venetians soon dominated); Renaissance standards of artistic achievement were known worldwide and everywhere imitated. The city-states shared their technology as well. The compass and the navigational chart, projection maps, double-entry bookkeeping, eyeglasses, the telescope—all profoundly influenced what could be achieved and what could be hoped for. In this spirit Christopher Columbus, a Genoese seaman, successfully crossed the Atlantic under the Spanish flag, and Amerigo Vespucci, a Florentine merchant, gave his name to the newly discovered continents.

But it was not in Italy that the rewards of innovation or the satisfactions of achievement were enjoyed. There the seeds of political turmoil and military imperialism, combined with the rise of the Ottoman Turks, were to reap a not unexpected harvest. Under the cover of the Peace of Lodi, the major city-states had scrambled to enlarge their mainland empires. By the end of the fifteenth century they eyed one another greedily and warily. Each expected the others to begin a peninsula wide war for hegemony and took the steps that ultimately ensured the contest. Perhaps the most unusual aspect of the imperialism of the city-states was that it had been restricted to the peninsula itself. Each of the major powers shared the dream of recapturing the glory that was Rome. Long years of siege and occupation had militarized the Italian city-states. Venice and Florence balanced their budgets on the backs of their captured territories. Milan had been engaged in constant war for decades, and even the papacy was militarily aggressive.

And the Italians were no longer alone. The most remarkable military leader of the age was not a Renaissance condottiere but an Ottoman prince, Mehmed II (1451–1481), who conquered Constantinople and Athens and threatened Rome itself. The rise of the Ottomans, whose name is derived from Osman, their original tribal leader, is one of the most compelling stories in world history. Little more than a warrior tribe at the beginning of the fourteenth century, 150 years later the Ottomans had replaced stagnant Byzantine rule with a virile and potent empire. First they gobbled up the towns and cities in a wide arc around Constantinople. Then they fed on the Balkans and the eastern kingdoms of Hungary and Poland. By 1400 they were a presence in all the territory that stretched from the Black Sea to the Aegean. By 1450 they were its master.

Venice was most directly affected by the Ottoman advance. Not only was its favored position in eastern trade threatened, but during a prolonged war at the end of the fifteenth century the Venetians lost many of their most important commercial outposts. Ottoman might closed off the markets of eastern Europe, and by 1480 Venetian naval supremacy was a thing of the past.

The Italian city-states might have met this challenge from the east had they been able to unite in opposing it. Successive popes pleaded for holy wars to halt the advance of the Turks. The fall of Constantinople in 1453 was an event of epochal proportions for Europeans, many believing that it foreshadowed the end of the world. Yet it was Italians rather than Ottomans who plunged the peninsula into those wars from which it never recovered.

The Wars of Italy (1494–1529) began when Naples, Florence, and the Papal States united against Milan. At first this alliance seemed little more than another shift in the balance of power. But rather than call upon Venice to redress the situation, the Milanese leader, Ludovico Sforza, sought help from the French. An army of French cavalry and Swiss mercenaries, led by Charles VIII of France (1483–1498), invaded the peninsula in 1494. With Milanese support the French swept all before them. Florence was forced to surrender Pisa, a humiliation that led to the overthrow of the Medici and the establishment of French sovereignty. The Papal States were next to be occupied, and within a year Charles had conquered Naples without engaging the Italians in a single significant battle. Unfortunately, the Milanese were not the only ones who could play at the game of foreign alliances. Next it was the turn of the Venetians and the pope to unite and call upon the services of King Ferdinand of Aragon and the Holy Roman Emperor. Italy was now a battleground in what became a total European war for dynastic supremacy. The city-states used their foreign allies to settle old scores and to extend their own mainland empires. At the turn of the century Naples was dismembered. In 1509 the pope conspired to organize the most powerful combination of forces yet known against Venice. All of the mainland possessions of the Most Serene Republic were lost, but by a combination of good fortune and skilled diplomacy, Venice itself survived. Florence was less fortunate, becoming a pawn first of the French and then of the Spanish. The final blow to Italian hegemony was the sack of Rome in 1527.

The sense of living in a new age, the spirit of human achievement, and the curiosity and wonderment of writers and artists all characterized the Renaissance. The desire to recreate the glories of Rome was not Machiavelli's alone. It could be seen in the palaces of the Italian aristocracy, in the papal rebuilding of the Holy City, and in the military ambitions of princes. But the legacy of empire, of "ancient and heroic pride," had passed out of Italian hands.

Suggestions for Further Reading

General Reading

Ernst Breisach, *Renaissance Europe 1300–1517* (New York: Macmillan, 1973). A solid survey of the political history of the age.

*P. Burke, *Culture and Society in Renaissance Italy* (Princeton, NJ: Princeton University Press, 1987). A good introduction to social and intellectual developments.

J. R. Hale, ed., *A Concise Encyclopedia of the Italian Renaissance* (Oxford, England: Oxford University Press, 1981). A treasure trove of facts about the major figures and events of the era.

*Denys Hay, *The Italian Renaissance* (Cambridge, England: Cambridge University Press, 1977). An elegant interpretive essay. The best first book to read.

Renaissance Society

*M. Aston, *The Fifteenth Century: The Prospect of Europe* (London: Thames & Hudson, 1968). A concise survey of continental history; well written and illustrated.

*Carlo Cipolla, *Before the Industrial Revolution: European Society and Economy, 1000–1700* (New York: W. W. Norton, 1976). A sweeping survey of social and economic developments across the centuries.

*J. R. Hale, *Renaissance Europe: The Individual and Society* (Berkeley: University of California Press, 1978). A lively study that places the great figures of the Renaissance in their social context.

D. Herlihy and C. Klapiche-Zuber, *The Tuscans and Their Families* (New Haven, CT: Yale University Press, 1985). Difficult but rewarding study of the social and demographic history of Florence and its environs.

*Christiane Klapiche-Zuber, *Women, Family, and Ritual in Renaissance Italy* (Chicago: University of Chicago Press, 1985). A sparkling collection of essays on diverse topics in social history from wet nursing to family life.

*Harry Miskimin, *The Economy of Early Renaissance Europe 1300–1460* (Englewood Cliffs, NJ: Prentice-Hall, 1969). A detailed scholarly study of economic development.

---

*Indicates paperback edition available.

Renaissance Art

*Michael Baxandall, *Painting and Experience in Fifteenth Century Italy* (Oxford, England: Oxford University Press, 1972). A study of the relationship between painters and their patrons, of how and why art was produced.

Frederick Hartt, *History of Italian Renaissance Art* (Englewood Cliffs, NJ: Prentice-Hall, 1974). The most comprehensive survey, with hundreds of plates.

*Howard Hibbard, *Michelangelo* (New York: Harper & Row, 1974). A compelling biography of an obsessed genius.

*Michael Levey, *Early Renaissance* (London: Penguin, 1967). A concise survey of art; clearly written and authoritative.

*Linda Murray, *High Renaissance and Mannerism* (London: Thames & Hudson, 1985). The best introduction to late Renaissance art.

John Pope-Hennessy, *Introduction to Italian Sculpture* (New York: Phaidon, 1972). A thorough analysis of the development of sculpture; carefully illustrated.

*Rudolph Wittkower, *Architectural Principles in the Age of Humanism* (New York: W. W. Norton, 1971). A difficult but rewarding study of Renaissance architecture.

Renaissance Ideals

*Hans Baron, *The Crisis of the Early Italian Renaissance* (Princeton, NJ: Princeton University Press, 1966). One of the most influential intellectual histories of the period.

*Ernst Cassirer, ed., *The Renaissance Philosophy of Man* (Chicago: University of Chicago Press, 1948). Translations of the works of Petrarch, Valla, and Pico della Mirandola, among others, with excellent introductions.

George Holmes, *The Florentine Enlightment* (New York: Pegasus, 1969). The best work on the successive generations of Florentine humanists.

Albert Rabil, ed., *Renaissance Humanism* (Philadelphia: University of Pennsylvania Press, 1988). A multiauthored multivolume collection of essays on humanism, with all of the latest scholarship.

*Quentin Skinner, *Machiavelli* (Oxford, England: Oxford University Press, 1981). A brief but brilliant life.

The Politics of the Italian City-States

*Gene Brucker, *Renaissance Florence*, 2nd ed. (Berkeley: University of California Press, 1983). The best single-volume introduction to Florentine history.

*J. R. Hale, *Florence and the Medici* (London: Thames & Hudson, 1977). A compelling account of the relationship between a city and its most powerful citizens.

*Frederic C. Lane, *Venice: A Maritime Republic* (Baltimore, MD: Johns Hopkins University Press, 1973). A complete history of Venice that stresses its naval and mercantile developments.

*Lauro Martines, *Power and Imagination: City-States in Renaissance Italy* (New York: Knopf, 1979). An important interpretation of the politics of the Italian powers.

*Eugene E. Rice, Jr., *The Foundations of Early Modern Europe 1460–1559* (New York: W. W. Norton, 1970). The best short synthetic work.

10

The European Empires

Ptolemy's World

For over a thousand years, educated Europeans thought of the world as it had been described by Ptolemy in the second century. Most of their knowledge came from guesswork rather than observation. The world was a big place when you had to cross it on foot or by four-legged beast or in small rickety vessels that hugged the shoreline as they sailed. Those without education lived in a world bounded by their farm and their village and thought of neighboring cities as faraway places. There were few experiences to pass from generation to generation, and those that were handed down changed from fact to fancy in the retelling. The people of the Renaissance probably knew less for certain about the planet they inhabited than had the Greeks, and the Greeks knew precious little. But lack of knowledge did not cause confusion. People who lived at the end of the fifteenth century knew enough to conduct their affairs and to dream their dreams.

The map on the facing page depicts the image of the world that Ptolemy bequeathed, the world that the Renaissance inherited with his calculations and writings. The first thing to notice is that it is shaped as a sphere. Though popular myth, confirmed by common sense, held that the world was flat and that one could theoretically fall off its edges, educated Europeans understood that it was spherical. Ptolemy had shown the earth as an irregular semicircle divided into degrees of longitude, beginning with 0° in the west, where Europe was situated, and progressing to 180° in the east. His construction of latitude was less certain, for less was known (then as now) about the extreme north and south. But Ptolemy did locate an equator, somewhat off center, and he portrayed as accurately as he could what was known of the European

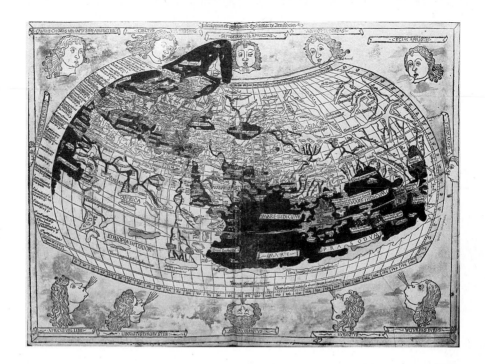

landmass. Scandinavia in the north and England and Ireland, set off from the Continent and from each other, are readily visible. The contours of Spain in the southwest are clear, though distorted. As the ancient world centered on the Mediterranean—literally "sea in the middle of the earth"—it was most accurately reconstructed. Italy, Greece and Asia Minor are easily recognizable, while France and Spain stretch out of shape like taffy. The size of the Mediterranean is grossly overestimated, its coastline occupying nearly a quarter of the map.

Africa, too, is swollen. It spans the too-wide Mediterranean and then balloons out to cover the entire Southern Hemisphere. Its eastern portions stretch into Asia, though so little is certain that they are labeled *terra incognita*—unknown lands. Europe, Africa and Asia are the only continents. They are watered by a single ocean whose name changes with the languages of its neighboring inhabitants. Most remarkable of all is the division of the earth's surface. Land covers three-quarters of it. This was the world as it was known in 1400, and this was why the ensuing century would be called the age of discovery.

*T*he European Discoveries

There were many reasons why this map of the world changed in the early sixteenth century. It was an age of discovery in many ways. Knowledge bequeathed from the past created curiosity about the present. Technological change made long sea voyages possible, and the demands of commerce

355

provided incentives. Ottoman expansion on the southern and eastern frontiers of the Continent threatened access to the goods of the East on which Europeans had come to rely. Spices were rare and expensive, but they were not merely luxuries. While nobles and rich merchants consumed them lavishly to enhance their reputations for wealth and generosity, spices had many practical uses. Some acted as preservatives, others as flavorings to make palatable the rotting foodstuffs that were the fare of even the wealthiest Europeans. Some spices were used as perfumes to battle the noxious gases that rose from urban streets and invaded homes and workplaces. The drugs of the East, the nature of which we can only guess at, helped soothe chronic ill health. The demand for all of these "spices" continued to rise at a greater rate than their supply.

Eastern spices were expensive. Most European manufactured goods had little utility in the East. Woven wool, which was the staple of western industry, was too heavy to be worn in eastern climes. Both silk and cotton came from the East and were more expertly spun there. Even western jewelry relied on imported stones. While metalwork was an attractive commodity for export, the dilemma of the arms trade was as acute then as it is now. Providing Ottomans or other Muslims with weapons to wage holy wars against Christian Europe posed problems of policy and morality. And once the Turks began to cast great bronze cannon of their own, European arms were less eagerly sought. Western gold and silver flowed steadily east. As supplies of precious metals dwindled, economic growth in Europe slowed. Throughout the fifteenth century ever larger amounts of western specie were necessary to purchase ever smaller amounts of eastern commodities. Europe faced a severe shortage of gold and silver, a shortage that threatened its standard of living and its prospects for economic growth. The search was on for new sources of gold.

A Passage to India

It was the Portuguese who made the first dramatic breakthroughs in exploration and colonization. Perched on the southwestern tip of Europe, Portugal was an agriculturally poor and sparsely populated nation. Among its few marketable commodities were fish and wine, which it traded with Genoese and Venetian galleys making their voyages to northern Europe. The Portuguese had long been sea explorers, especially in the Atlantic Ocean, where they had established bases in the Azores and Madeira islands. Their small ships, known as caravels, were ideal for ocean travel and their navigators among the most skillful in the world. Yet they were unable to participate in the lucrative Mediterranean trade in bullion and spices until the expanding power of the Ottomans threatened the traditional eastern sea routes.

In the early fifteenth century, the Portuguese gained a foothold in northern Africa and used it to stage voyages along the continent's unexplored western coast. Like most explorers, the Portuguese were motivated by an unselfconscious mixture of faith and greed. Establishing southern bases would enable them to surround their Muslim enemies while also giving them access to the African bullion trade. The Portuguese navigator Bartolomeu Dias (ca. 1450–1500) summarized these goals succinctly: "To give light to those who are in darkness and to grow rich." Under the energetic leadership of Prince Henry the Navigator (1394–1460), the Portuguese pushed steadily southward. Prince Henry studied navigational techniques, accumulated detailed accounts of voyages, and encouraged the creation of accurate maps of the African coastline. What was learned on one trip was applied to the next. Soon the Portuguese were a power in the West African trade in slaves and gold ore. Black slaves became a staple of the African voyages, with nearly 150,000 slaves imported in the first 50 years of exploration. Most slaves were used as domestics and laborers in Portugal; others were sent to work the lucrative sugar plantations established by Prince Henry on the island of Madeira.

Prince Henry's systematic program paid off in the next generation. By the 1480s Portuguese outposts had reached almost to the equator, and in 1487 Bartolomeu Dias rounded the tip of Africa and opened the eastern African shores to Portuguese traders. The aim of these enterprises was access to Asia rather than Africa. Dias might have reached India if his crew had not mutinied and forced him to return home. A decade later Vasco da Gama (ca. 1460–1524) rounded the Cape of Good Hope and crossed into the Indian Ocean. When he returned to Lisbon in 1499 laden with the most valuable spices of the East, Portuguese ambitions were achieved. Larger expeditions followed, one of which, blown off course, touched the South American coast of Brazil, which was soon subsumed within the Portuguese dominions.

The Portuguese came to the East as traders rather than as conquerors. Building on their experience in West Africa, they developed a policy of establishing military outposts to protect their investments and subduing native populations only when necessary. Their achievements resulted more from determination than from technological superiority. Throughout the East the Portuguese took advantage of local feuds to gain allies, and they established trading compounds that were easily defensible. The great Portuguese general Alfonso de Albuquerque (1453–1515) understood the need for strategically placed garrisons and conquered the vital ports of the Middle East and India. By the beginning of the sixteenth century the Portuguese were masters of a vast empire, which spanned both the eastern and western coasts of Africa and the western shores of India. Most importantly, the Portuguese controlled Ceylon and Indonesia, the precious Spice Islands from which came cloves, cinnamon, and pepper. Almost overnight, Lisbon became one of the trading capitals of the world, tripling in population between 1500 and 1550.

It was northern Europe that was to harvest what Portugal had sown. The long voyages around Africa were costly and dangerous. Portugal produced no valuable commodities and had to exchange bullion for spices. Moreover, the expense of maintaining a far-flung empire ate into the profits of trade at the same time that the increased volume necessary to make the voyages worthwhile drove down spice prices. Between 1501 and 1505 over eighty ships and seven thousand men sailed from Portugal to the East. This vast commitment was underwritten by Flemish, German, and Italian bankers. Soon Antwerp replaced Lisbon as the marketplace for Asian spices. Ironically, it was in the accidental discovery of Brazil rather than in Asia that the Portuguese were rewarded for the enterprise of their explorers.

Mundus Novus

While the bulk of Portuguese resources were devoted to the Asian trade, those of the Spanish kingdom came to be concentrated in the New World. Though larger and richer than its eastern neighbor, Spain had been segmented into a number of small kingdoms and principalities and divided between Christians and Muslims. Not until the end of the fifteenth century, when the crowns of Aragon and Castile were united and the Muslims expelled from Granada, could the Spanish concentrate their resources. By then they were far behind in establishing commercial enterprises. With Portugal dominating the African route to India, Queen Isabella of Castile was persuaded to take an interest in a western route by a Genoese adventurer, Christopher Columbus (ca. 1446–1506).

Like all well-informed people of his day, Columbus believed the world was round. By carefully calculating routes and distances, he concluded that a western track would be shorter and less expensive than the path that the Portuguese were breaking around Africa. Columbus's conclusions were based partly on conventional knowledge and partly on his own self-assurance. All were wholly erroneous. He misjudged the size of the globe by a quarter and the distance of the journey by 400 percent. Columbus sailed westward into the unknown in 1492, and on 12 October he landed in the Bahamas, on an island that he named San Salvador. He had discovered a Mundus Novus, a New World.

Initially, Columbus's discovery was a disappointment. He had gone in search of a western passage to the Indies and he had failed to return to Spain laden with eastern spices. Despite his own belief that the islands he had discovered lay just off the coast of Japan, it was soon apparent that he had found an altogether unknown landmass. Columbus's own explorations and those of his successors continued to focus on discovering a route to the Indies. This was all the more imperative once the Portuguese succeeded in finding the passage around Africa. Rivalry between the two nations intensified after 1500 when the Portuguese began exploring the coast of Brazil. In 1494 the Treaty of Tordesillas had confined Portugal's right to the eastern route to the Indies as well as to any undiscovered lands east of an imaginary line fixed west of the Cape Verde Islands. This entitled Portugal to Brazil. The Spanish received whatever lay west of the line. At the time few doubted that Portugal had the better of the bargain.

But Spanish-backed explorations soon proved the value of the newly discovered lands. In 1513 Vasco Núñez de Balboa (1475–1517) crossed the

Columbus made a total of four voyages to the New World, exploring the Caribbean and the coasts of Central and South America. For the rest of his life, he remained convinced that he had reached the East Indies by an Atlantic route.

Isthmus of Panama and became the first European to view the Pacific Ocean. The discovery of this ocean refueled Spanish ambitions to find a western passage to the Indies.

In 1519 Ferdinand Magellan (ca. 1480–1521), a Portuguese mariner in the service of Spain, set sail in pursuit of Columbus's goal of reaching the Spice Islands by sailing westward. His voyage, which he did not live to complete, remains the most astounding of the age. After making the Atlantic crossing, Magellan resupplied his fleet in Brazil. Then his ships began the long southerly run toward the tip of South America, though he had no idea of the length of the continent. Suppressing mutinies and overcoming shipwrecks and desertions, Magellan finally found the straits that still bear his name. By the time Magellan entered the Pacific, he had already lost two ships and much of his crew.

When Magellan finally reached land, first in the Marianas, and then in the Philippines, the crew fell prey to natives more aggressive than those they had met in South America. Magellan's foolhardy decision to become involved in a local war cost him his life. It was left to his navigator, Sebastián Elcano (ca.

1476–1526), to complete the journey. In 1522, three years and one month after setting out, Elcano returned to Spain with a single ship and 18 survivors of the crew of 280. But in his hold were spices of greater value than the cost of the expedition, and in his return was practical proof that the world was round.

The circumnavigation of Magellan and Elcano brought to an end the first stage of the Spanish exploration of the New World. Columbus's dreams were realized, but the vastness of the Pacific Ocean made a western passage to the Indies uneconomical. In 1529 the Spanish crown relinquished its claims to the Spice Islands to the Portuguese for a cash settlement. By then trading spices was less alluring than mining gold and silver.

The Spanish Conquests

At the same moment that Magellan's voyage closed one stage of Spanish discovery, the exploits of Hernando Cortés (1485–1547) opened another. The Spanish colonized the New World along the model of their reconquest of Spain. Individuals were given control over land and the people on it in return for military service. The interests of the crown were threefold: to convert the natives to Christianity, to extend sovereignty over new dominions, and to gain some measure of profit from the venture. The colonial entrepreneurs had a singular interest—to grow rich. By and large the colonizers came from the lower orders of Spanish society. Even the original captains and governors were drawn from groups, like younger sons of the nobility, that would have had little opportunity for rule in Castile.

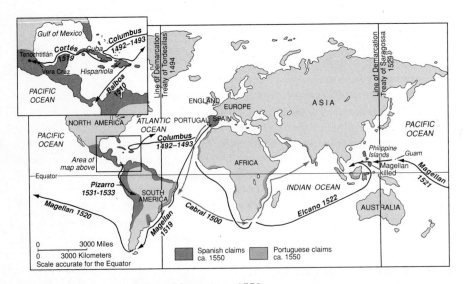

Voyages of discovery and world empires, 1550

Many of the protective measures taken by the crown to ensure orderly colonization and fair treatment of the natives were ineffective in practice. The *requiremiento* was a case in point. When conquering new lands, Spanish captains had to offer the natives the opportunity to live in peace and security if they would acknowledge the supremacy of the pope and the queen of Castile. Not surprisingly, few natives accepted this generous offer, read to them in Latin or Castilian. During the first decades of the sixteenth century, Spanish captains and their followers subdued the Indian populations of the Caribbean Islands and put them to work on the agricultural haciendas they had carved out for themselves. As early as 1498 Castilian women began arriving in the New World. Their presence helped change the character of the settlement towns from wild frontier garrisons to civilized settlements. Some of them ultimately inherited huge estates and participated fully in the forging of Spanish America.

Life on the hacienda, even in relative ease with a Castilian wife and family, did not always satisfy the ambitions of the Spanish colonizers. Hernando Cortés was one such *conquistador*. Having participated in the conquest of Cuba, Cortés sought an independent command to lead an expedition into the hinterland of Central America, where a fabulous empire was rumored to exist. Gathering a force of 600 men, Cortés sailed across the Gulf of Mexico in 1519, established a fort at Vera Cruz, where he garrisoned 200 men, and then sank his boats so that none of his company could turn back. With 400 soldiers, he began his quest. The company marched 250 miles through steamy jungles and over rugged mountains before glimpsing the first signs of the great Aztec civilization. The Aztec empire was a loose confederation of native tribes that the Aztecs had conquered during the previous century. They were ruled by the emperor Montezuma II (1502–1520) from his capital at Tenochtitlán, a marvelous city built of stone and baked clay in the middle of a lake. Invited to an audience with the Aztec emperor, Cortés and his men saw vast stores of gold and silver.

The conquest of the Aztecs took nearly a year and remains an overwhelming feat of arms. Nearly one hundred thousand natives from the tribes that the Aztecs had conquered supported the Spanish assault. Cortés's cavalry terrified the Aztecs. They had never seen either horses or iron armaments. Cortés also benefited from the Aztec practice of taking battlefield captives to be used in religious sacrifices. This allowed many Spanish soldiers who would otherwise have been killed to be rescued and to fight again.

By 1522 Cortés was master of an area larger than all of Spain. But the cost in native lives was staggering. In 30 years a population of approximately twenty-five million had been reduced to less than two million. Most of the loss was due to exposure to European diseases like smallpox, typhoid, and measles, against which the natives were helpless. Their labor intensive system of agriculture could not survive the rapid decrease in population, and famine followed pestilence.

This tragic sequence was repeated everywhere the Europeans appeared. In 1531 Francisco Pizarro (ca. 1475–1541) matched Cortés's feat when he conquered the Peruvian empire of the Incas. This conquest vastly extended the territory under Spanish control and became the true source of profit for the crown, when a huge silver mine was discovered in 1545 at Potosí in what is now southern Bolivia. The gold and silver that poured into Spain in the next quarter century helped support Spanish dynastic ambitions in Europe. During the course of the sixteenth century over two hundred thousand Spaniards migrated across the ocean. Perhaps one in ten were women, who married and set up families. In succeeding generations these settlers created huge haciendas built on the forced labor of black African slaves, who proved better able to endure the rigors of mining and farming than did the natives.

The Legacy of the Discoverers

By the seventeenth century, long-distance trade had begun to integrate the regions of the world into a single marketplace. Slaves bought in Africa mined silver in South America. The buillion was shipped to Spain, where it was distributed across Europe. Most went to Amsterdam to settle Spanish debts, Dutch bankers having replaced the Italians as the paymasters of Europe. From Holland the silver traveled east to the Baltic Sea, the Dutch lifeline where vital stores of grain and timber were purchased for home consumption. Even more of this African-mined Spanish silver, traded by the Dutch, was carried to Asia to buy spices in the Spice Islands, cottons in India, or silk in China. Millions of ounces flowed from America to Asia via the European trading routes. On the return voyage, Indian cottons were traded in Africa to purchase slaves for the South American silver mines.

Gold, God, and glory neatly summarized the motives of the European explorers. Perhaps it is not necessary to delve any further. The gold of Africa and the silver of South America enriched the western nations. Christian missions arose wherever the European empires touched down: among Africans, Asians, and Amerindians. And glory there was in plenty. The feats of the great discoverers were recounted in story and song.

They were worthy of celebration. In less than fifty years tenacious European seafarers found passages to the east and continents to the west. In doing so they overcame terrors both real and imagined. Hazardous journeys in uncharted waters took their toll in men and ships. The odds of surviving a voyage of discovery were no better than those of surviving the plague.

However harsh was reality, fantasy was more terrifying still. Sailors to the New World expected to find all manner of horrible creations. Cyclopes and headless one-legged torsos were popularized in drawings; cannibals and giants were described in realistic detail by the earliest voyagers. No wonder mutiny was a constant companion of discovery.

Yet all of these inhibitions were overcome. So, too, were those over which the discoverers had more control. The expansion of Europe was a feat of technology and a feat of arms. Advances in navigational skills, especially in dead reckoning and later in calculating latitude from the position of the sun, were essential preconditions for covering the distances that were to be traveled. So were the more sophisticated ship designs. The magnetic compass and the astrolabe were indispensable tools. New methods for the making of maps and charts, and the popular interest in them, fueled both ambitions and abilities. It was a mapmaker who named the newly found continents after Amerigo Vespucci (1451–1512), the Italian explorer who voyaged to Brazil for the Portuguese. It may have been an accident that Columbus found the New World, but it was no coincidence that he was able to land in the same place three more times.

Nor was it happenstance that European forces conquered the peoples they encountered in both east and west. Generations of warfare against Muslims had honed the skills of Christian warriors. European ships were sturdily built and armed with cannons that could be used on land or at sea. Soldiers were well equipped and battle-tested. Generals were trained and experienced in the arts of siege. Both Albuquerque and Cortés practiced the tactics of divide and conquer, cleverly building alliances and taking advantage of local warfare.

Riches and converts, power and glory—all came in the wake of discovery. But in the process of discovering new lands and new cultures, Europe also learned something of its own aspirations. Early Portuguese voyagers went in quest of the mythical Prester John, a saintly figure who was said to rule a heaven on earth in the middle of Africa. The first children born on Madeira were named Adam and Eve, though this slave plantation of sugar and wine was an unlikely Garden of Eden. The optimism of those who searched for the fountain of youth in the Florida swamps was not only that they would find it there, but that a long life was worth living. Contact with the cultures of the New World also forced a different kind of thinking about life in the old one. The supposed customs of strange lands provided the setting for one of the great works of English social criticism, Sir Thomas More's *Utopia* (1516).

Europe also discovered and revealed a darker side of itself in the age of exploration. Accompanying the boundless optimism and assertive self-confidence that made so much possible was a tragic arrogance and callous disregard toward native races. Portuguese travelers described Africans as "dog-faced, dog-toothed people, satyrs, wild men, and cannibals." Such attitudes helped justify enslavement. It is not the brutality of the European conquests that should give us pause—each age sets its own standards in that regard—but the wastefulness. The Dominican priest Bartolomé de Las Casas (1474–1566), in his *Apologetic History of the Indies* (1550), highlighted the complexity of native society even as he witnessed its destruction.

But few Europeans were so enlightened. Though they encountered heritages that were in some ways richer than their own, only the most farsighted westerners could see that there was more value in their preservation than in their demolition. The Portuguese spice trade did not depend on da Gama's indiscriminate bombardment of the port of Calicut. The obliteration of millions of Aztecs and Incas was not a necessary result of the fever for gold and silver. The destruction was wanton. It revealed the rapaciousness, greed, and cruelty of the Portuguese and Spanish conquerors. These were the impulses of the

Crusades rather than of the Renaissance. The Iberian *reconquista*, the holy war against the Muslims by which the peninsula was won back into Christian hands, was replayed throughout South America with tragic results.

"The discovery of America and that of a passage to the East Indies by the Cape of Good Hope are the two greatest and most important events in the history of mankind." So wrote the great Scottish economist Adam Smith (1723–1790) in *The Wealth of Nations* (1776). In the following centuries, under the watchful eye of the European states, a worldwide marketplace for the exchange of commodities was created. First the Dutch and then the English established monopoly companies to engage in exotic trades in the East. First the Spanish and Portuguese, then the English and French established colonial dependencies in the Atlantic, which they carefully nurtured in hope of economic gain. Protected trade flourished beyond the wildest dreams of its promoters. Luxury commodities became staples; new commodities became luxuries. Trade enhanced the material life of all European peoples, though it came at great cost to the Asians, Africans, and Latin Americans whose labor and raw materials were converted into the new crazes of consumption. The consequences of black slavery and the destruction of native populations have as much to do with the shape of the modern world as the discoveries themselves.

*E*urope in 1500

Just as the map of the world was changing as a result of the voyages of discovery, so the map of Europe was changing as a result of the activities of princes. The early sixteenth century was the age of the prince, the first great stage of nation building that would last for the next 300 years. The New Monarchies, as they are sometimes called, consolidated territories that were divided culturally, linguistically, and historically. The states of Europe are political units and they were forged by political means: by diplomacy, by marriage, and most commonly by war. The national system that we take for granted when thinking about Europe is a relatively recent development. Before we can observe its beginnings we must first have a picture of Europe as it existed in 1500. At that time it was composed of nearly five hundred distinct political units.

Europe is a concept, and like all concepts it is difficult to define. The vast plain that stretches from the Netherlands to the steppes of Russia presents few natural barriers to migration. Tribes had been wandering across this plain for thousands of years, slowly settling into the more fertile lands to practice their agriculture. Only in the south did geographical forces stem the flow of humanity. The Carpathian Mountains created a basin for the settlement of

Slavic peoples that ran down to the Black Sea. The Alps provided a boundary for French, Germanic, and Italian settlements. The Pyrenees defined the Iberian peninsula, with a mixture of African and European peoples.

Eastern Boundaries

In the East, three great empires had created the political geography that could be said to define a European boundary: the Mongol, the Ottoman, and the Russian. During the early Middle Ages, Mongol warriors had swept across the Asian steppes and conquered most of central and southern Ukraine. By the sixteenth century the Mongol empire was disintegrating, its lands divided into a number of separate states called *khanates*. The khanate of the Crimea, with lands around the northern shores of the Black Sea, created the southeastern border of Europe.

The Ottoman territories defined the southern boundary. By 1450 the Ottomans controlled all of Byzantium and Greece, dominating from the Black Sea to the Aegean. Fifty years later they had conquered nearly all the lands between the Aegean and the Adriatic seas. A perilous frontier was established on the Balkan peninsula. There the principalities of Moldavia, Wallachia, Transylvania, and Hungary held out against the Ottomans for another quarter century before being overrun.

The Russian state defined the eastern boundary of Europe. Russia, too, had been a great territorial unit of the Middle Ages, centered at Kiev in the west and stretching eastward into Asia. The advance of the Mongols in the thirteenth century had contracted the eastern part of Russia. Its western domains had disintegrated under the practice of dividing the ruling prince's inheritance among his sons. In 1500 Europe reached as far east as the principality of Muscovy. There the heritage of East and West mingled. In some periods of history Russia's ties with the West were most important; at other times Russia retreated into isolation from Europe.

The northern borders of eastern Europe centered on the Baltic Sea, one of the most important trading routes of the early modern era. On the northern coasts lay the Scandinavian nations of Sweden, Norway, and Denmark. These loosely confederated nations had a single king throughout the fifteenth century. Denmark, the southernmost of the three, was also the richest and most powerful. It enjoyed a favorable trading position on both the North and Baltic seas and social and economic integration with the Germanic states on its border. On the southern side of the Baltic lay the dominions of the Teutonic Knights, physically divided by the large state of Poland-Lithuania. The Teutonic territories, in the valuable Baltic region of Prussia, had been colonized by German crusaders in the thirteenth century.

Poland-Lithuania comprised an enormous territory that covered the length of Europe from the Baltic to the Black Sea. The crowns of these two nations had been joined at the end of the fourteenth century, and their dynastic history was tied up with the nations of Bohemia and Hungary to their west and south. While Bohemia was increasingly drawn into the affairs of central Europe, Hungary remained more eastern in orientation. This was partly because the Bohemians gave nominal allegiance to the Holy Roman Emperor and partly because the Ottoman conquests had engulfed a large part of the Hungarian territories. At the end of the fifteenth century Poland, Lithuania, Bohemia, and Hungary were all ruled by the same family, the Jagiellons.

Mongols and Ottomans to the south, Russians in the east, Scandinavia in the north, Poland-Lithuania in the center, and Hungary in the west: Such were the contours of the eastern portion of Europe. Its lands were, on the whole, less fertile than those farther west, and its climate was more severe. It was a sparsely populated region. Its wealth lay in the Baltic fisheries, in the Hungarian and Bohemian silver mines, and in the enormous Russian forests where wood and its by-products were plentiful. Except in the southern portions of Poland and central Bohemia, the region was agriculturally poor. The eastern territories had been resettled during the population crisis of the early fourteenth century. Then native Slavs were joined by German colonizers from the west and Asian conquerors from the east. This clash of races did much to define the political history of eastern Europe.

Central Europe

The middle of the continent was defined by the Holy Roman Empire and occupied almost entirely by Germanic peoples. In length the empire covered the territory from the North and Baltic seas to the Adriatic and the Mediterranean, where the Italian city-states were located. In width it stretched from Bohemia to Burgundy. Politically, central Europe comprised a bewildering array of principalities, church lands, and free towns. By the end of the fifteenth century, the Holy Roman Empire was an empire in name only. The large states of Brandenburg, Bohemia, and Bavaria resembled the political units of the east. In the south, the Alps provided an effective physical boundary, which allowed the Archduchy of Austria and the Swiss Confederation to follow their own separate paths. Stretching across the center of the empire, from the Elbe River to the North Sea, were a jumble of petty states. Great cities like Nuremberg and Ulm in the south, Bremen and Hamburg in the north, and Frankfurt and Cologne in the west were free municipalities. Large sections of the northwestern part of the empire were governed by the Church through resident bishops. Further to the west were the prosperous Low Countries, Holland and its port of Amsterdam, Brabant and its port of Antwerp. In the southwest, the empire extended in some places as far as the Rhone River and included the rich estates of Luxemborg, Lorraine, and Burgundy.

The riches of the empire made it the focal point of Europe. Nearly fifteen million people lived within its borders. Its agriculture varied from the olive- and wine-producing areas in the southwest to the great granaries in its center. Rich mineral deposits and large reserves of timber made the German lands industrially advanced. The European iron industry was centered here and the empire was the arms manufacturer for the Western world. The empire was also a great commercial center, heir to the Hanseatic League of the Middle Ages, and its merchants were replacing the Italians as the leading international bankers.

Like the empire, the Italian peninsula was divided into a diverse collection of small city-states. During the course of the fifteenth century five of these had emerged as most powerful (see Chapter 9). In the north were the Duchy of Milan, Florence, and Venice. In the south was Rome, spiritual center of Catholicism and residence of the pope. Though Roman and papal government were separate jurisdictions, in fact their fates were bound together. Papal lands stretched far to the north of Rome, and wars to defend or expand them were Roman as well as papal ventures. The kingdom of Naples, the breadbasket of the Mediterranean, occupied the southernmost part of Italy and included the agriculturally rich island of Sicily.

The West

The Iberian peninsula, the French territories, and the British Isles formed the westernmost borders of Europe. Separated from France in the north by the

Pyrenees, the Iberian peninsula is surrounded by the Atlantic Ocean and the Mediterranean Sea on the west and east. But neither its protective mountain barrier nor its ample coastlines was its most significant geographical feature during its formative period. Rather it was the fact that Iberia is separated from North Africa only by the easily navigable Strait of Gibraltar. During the Middle Ages the peninsula was overrun by North African Muslims, whom the Spanish called Moors. From the eighth to the fifteenth centuries, Iberian history was dominated by the reconquista, the recapture and re-Christianization of the conquered territories. This reconquest was finally completed in 1492, when the Moors were pushed out of Granada and the Jews were expelled from Spain. At the end of the fifteenth century, the Iberian peninsula contained several separate kingdoms. The most important were Portugal on the western coast, Aragon with its Mediterranean ports of Barcelona and Valencia, and Castile, the largest of the Iberian states. The marriage of King Ferdinand of Aragon and Queen Isabella of Castile in 1469 had joined the crowns of Aragon and Castile, but the two kingdoms remained separate.

The remnants of ancient Gaul were also favored by a maritime location. Like those of Iberia, French coasts let out onto the Mediterranean and the Atlantic. France's eastern boundaries touched the empire, its southern mountain border touched Spain. To the northwest, Britain was less than thirty miles from France across the English Channel. Toward the end of the fifteenth century, France was still divided into many smaller fiefs. The royal domain centered on Paris and extended to Champagne in the east and Normandy in the west. South of this area, however, from Orléans to Brittany, were principalities that had long been contested between England and France. Nor was the rich central plain yet integrated into the royal domain. Agriculturally, French lands were the richest in Europe. France enjoyed both Mediterranean and Atlantic climates, which suited the growing of the widest variety of foodstuffs. Its population of approximately thirteen million was second only to that of the empire.

Across the Channel lay Britain (comprising England, Scotland, and Wales) and Ireland. Britain had been settled by an array of European colonizers— Romans, Danes, Angles, and Saxons—before being conquered in the eleventh century by the French Normans. From that time, it was protected by the rough waters of the English Channel and the North Sea and allowed to develop a distinct cultural and political heritage. Wales to the west and Scotland to the north were still separate nations at the beginning of the sixteenth century. Both were mountaineous lands with harsh climates and few natural advantages. They were sparsely populated. Though Ireland, too, was sparsely populated, it contained several rich agricultural areas especially suited for dairying and grazing.

In 1500 Europe exhibited a remarkable diversity of political and geographical forms. Huge states in the east, tiny principalities in the center, and emerging nations in the west seemingly had little in common. There was as yet no state system and no clear group of dominant powers. The western migration of the Germanic peoples appeared to be over, but their consolidation was as yet unimagined. The Iberians struggled to expel the Moors, the Hungarians to hold back the Ottomans. Everywhere one looked there was fragmentation and disarray. Yet in less than half a century the largest empire yet known in the West would be formed. States would be consolidated and dynasties established all over the continent. And with the rise of the state would come the dream of dominion, an empire over all of Europe.

*T*he Formation of States

It was Machiavelli who identified the prince as the agent of change in the process of state formation. He believed that the successful prince could bring unity to his lands, security to his borders, and prosperity to his subjects. The unsuccessful prince brought nothing but ruin.

A process as long and as complex as the formation of nations is not subject to the will of individuals. Factors as diverse as geography, population, and natural resources are all decisive. So, too, are the structures through which human activity is channeled. The ways in which families are organized and wealth is transmitted from generation to generation can result in large estates with similar customs or small estates with varying ones. The manner in which social groups are formed and controlled can mean that power is centralized or dispersed. The beliefs of ordinary people and the way they practice them can define who is a part of a community and who is apart from it. All these elements and many others have much to do with the way in which European states began to take shape at the end of the fifteenth century. Despite these complexities, we should not lose sight of the simple truth of Machiavelli's observations. In the first stages of the consolidation of European nations the role of the prince was crucial.

Indeed, in the middle of the fifteenth century there were many factors working against the formation of large states in Europe. The most obvious involved simple things like transportation and communication. The distance that could be covered quickly was very small. In wet and cold seasons travel was nearly impossible. Similarly, directives from the center to the localities were slow to arrive and slower still to be adopted. Large areas were difficult to control and to defend. Communication was not only subject to the hazards of travel. Distinct languages or dialects were one of the principal features of small states. Separate languages contributed to separate cultures. Customary practices, common ancestry, and shared experiences helped define a sense of community through which small states defined themselves.

To these natural forces that acted to maintain the existence of small units of government were added invented ones. To succeed, a prince had to establish supremacy over a number of rivals. For the most part, states were inherited. In some places it was customary to follow the rule of primogeniture, inheritance by the eldest son. In others, estates were split among sons, or among children of both sexes. Some traditions, like the French, excluded inheritance through women; others, like the Castilian, treated women's claims as equal to men's. Short lives meant prolonged disputes about inheritance. Rulers had to defend their thrones from rivals with strong claims to legitimacy.

So, too, did rulers have to defend themselves from the ambitions of their mightiest subjects. The constant warfare of the European nobility was one of the central features of the later Middle Ages. To avoid resort to arms, princes and peers entered into all manner of alliances, using their children as pawns and the marriage bed as the chessboard. Rulers also faced independent institutions within their states, powerful organizations that had to be won over or crushed. By the end of the fifteenth century, the long process of taming the Church was about to enter a new stage. Fortified towns presented a different problem. They possessed both the labor and wealth necessary to raise and maintain armies. They also jealously guarded their privileges. Rulers who could not tax their towns could not rule their state. Finally, most kingdoms had assemblies representing the propertied classes, especially in matters of taxation. Some, like the English Parliament and the Spanish Cortes, were strong; others, like the Imperial Diet and the French Estates-General, were weak. But everywhere they posed an obstacle to the extension of the power of princes.

In combination, these factors slowed and shaped the process of state formation. But neither separately nor together were they powerful enough to overcome it. The fragmentation of Europe into so many small units of government made some consolidation inevitable. There were always stronger and weaker neighbors, always broken successions and failed lines. The practice of dynastic marriage meant that smaller states were continually being inherited by the rulers of larger ones. If the larger state was stable, it absorbed the smaller one. If not, the smaller state would split off again to await its next predator or protector. As the first large states took shape, the position of smaller neighbors grew ever more precarious.

This was especially true by the end of the fifteenth century because of the increase in the destructive power of warfare. Technological advances in cannonry and in the skills of gunners and engineers made medieval fortifications untenable. The fall of Constantinople was as much a military watershed as it was a political one. Gunpowder decisively changed battlefield tactics. It made heavy armor obsolete and allowed for the development of a different type of warfare. Lightly armored horses and riders could not only inflict more damage upon one another, but they were now mobile enough to be used against infantry. Infantry armed with long pikes or small muskets became the crucial components of armies that were growing ever larger. Systems of supply were better, sources of small arms were more available, and the rewards of conquest were more tangible. What could not be inherited, or married, could be conquered.

Eastern Configurations

The interplay of factors that encouraged and inhibited the formation of states is most easily observed in the eastern parts of Europe. There the different paths taken by Muscovy and Poland-Lithuania stand in contrast. At the beginning of the sixteenth century, the principality of Muscovy was the largest European political unit. Muscovy had established itself as the heir to the ancient state of Russia through conquest, shrewd political alliances, and the good fortune of its princes to be blessed with long reigns. Muscovy's growth was phenomenal. Under Ivan III, "the Great" (1462–1505), Muscovy expanded to the north and west. During a long series of wars it annexed Novgorod and large parts of Livonia and Lithuania. Its military successes were almost unbroken, but so, too, were its diplomatic triumphs. Ivan the Great preferred pacification to conquest, though when necessary he could conquer with great brutality. Between 1460 and 1530, Muscovy increased its territory by 1.5 million square miles.

A number of factors led to the rise of Muscovy. External threats had diminished. The deterioration of the Mongol empire which had dominated south central Russia allowed Ivan to escape the yoke of Mongol rule that the Russian princes had worn for centuries. Secondly, the fall of Constantinople made Muscovy the heir to eastern Christendom, successor to the Roman and Byzantine empires. Ivan's marriage to Sophia, niece of the last emperor of Byzantium, cemented this connection. Sophia brought both Italian craft workers and Byzantine customs to the Russian court, helping Ivan open his contacts with the wider world.

Territorial conquests and the decline of Byzantium were not the only important features of the consolidation of the Muscovite state. Ivan the Great was fortunate in having no competitors for his throne. He was able to use other social groups to help administer the new Muscovite territories without fear of setting up a rival to power. Ivan extended the privileges of his nobility and organized a military class who received land as a reward for their fidelity. He also developed a new theory of sovereignty that rested on divine rather than temporal power. Traditionally, Russian princes ruled their lands by patrimony. They owned both estates and occupants. Ivan the Great extended this principle to cover all lands to which there was an ancient Russian claim and combined it with the religious authority of the Orthodox church. Both he and his successors ruled with the aid of able church leaders who were normally part of the prince's council.

What made the expansion of Muscovy so impressive is that land once gained was never lost. The military and political achievements of Ivan the Great were furthered by his son Vasili and his more famous grandson Ivan IV, "the Terrible" (1533–1584). Ivan IV defeated the Mongols on his southeastern border and incorporated the entire Volga basin into Muscovy. But his greatest ambition was to gain a port on the Baltic Sea and establish a northern outlet for commerce. His objective was to conquer Livonia. Nearly three decades of warfare between Muscovy and Poland-Lithuania, with whom Livonia had allied itself, resulted in large territorial gains, but Muscovy always fell short of the real prize. And Ivan's northern campaigns seriously weakened the defense of the south. In 1571 the Crimean Tartars advanced from their territories on Muscovy's southwestern border and inflicted a powerful psychological blow when they burned the city of Moscow. Although the Tartars were eventually driven off Muscovite soil, expansion in both north and south was at an end for the next 75 years.

By the reign of Ivan IV, Muscovite society was divided roughly into three groups: the hereditary nobility known as the boyars, the military service class, and the peasantry who were bound to the land. There was no large mercantile presence in Muscovy, and its urban component remained small. The boyars, who were powerful landlords of great estates, owed little to the tsar. They inherited their lands and did not necessarily benefit from expansion and conquest. Members of the military service class, on the other hand, were bound to the success of the crown. Their military service was a requirement for the possession of their estates, which were granted out of lands gained through territorial expansion. Gradually the new military service class grew in power and prestige, largely at the expense of the older boyars. Ivan IV used members of the military service class as legislative advisers and elevated them in his parliamentary council (the Zemsky Sobor), which also contained representatives of the nobility, clergy, and towns.

Unlike his grandfather, Ivan IV had an abiding mistrust of the boyars. They had held power when he was a child, and it was rumored that his mother had been poisoned by them. It was in his treatment of the boyars that he earned the nickname "the Terrible." During his brutal suppression of supposed conspiracies, several thousand families were massacred by Ivan's own orders and thousands more by the violent excesses of his agents. He also forcibly relocated boyar families. This practice made the boyars' situation similar to that of the military service class, who owed their fortunes to the tsar. For the first time, the boyars were required to perform military service to the tsar.

All of these measures contributed to the breakdown of local networks of influence and power and to a disruption of local governance. But they also made possible a system of central administration, one of Ivan IV's most important achievements. He created departments of state to deal with the various tasks of administration, and this resulted in more efficient management of revenues and of the military. Ivan IV promoted the interests of the military service class over those of the boyars, but he did not destroy the nobility. New boyars were created, especially in conquered territories, and these new families owed their positions and loyalty to the prince. Both boyars and the military benefited from Ivan's policy of binding the great mass of people to the land. Russian peasants had few political or economic rights in comparison to Western peasants, but during the early sixteenth century even the meager rights of Russian peasants were curtailed. The right of peasants to move from the estate of one lord to that of another was suspended, all but binding the peasantry to the land. This serfdom made possible the prolonged absence of military leaders from their estates and contributed to the creation of the military service class. But it also made imperative the costly system of coercing agricultural and industrial labor. In the long term, serfdom retarded economic development by removing incentive from large landholders to make investments in commerce or to improve agricultural production.

The growth of an enlarged and centralized Muscovy stands in contrast to the experiences of Poland-Lithuania during the same period. At the end of the fifteenth century Casimir IV (1447–1492) ruled the kingdom of Poland and the grand duchy of Lithuania. His son Vladislav II ruled Bohemia (1471–1516) and Hungary (1490–1516).

Had the four states been permanently consolidated, they could have become an effective barrier to Ottoman expansion in the south and Russian expansion in the east. But the union of crowns had never been the union of states. The union of crowns had taken place over the previous century by political alliances, diplomatic marriages, and the consent of the nobility. Such arrangements kept peace among the four neighbors, but it kept any one of them from becoming a dominant partner.

While the Polish-Lithuanian monarchs enjoyed longevity similar to that of the Muscovites, those who ruled Hungary and Bohemia were not so fortunate. By the sixteenth century a number of claimants to both crowns existed and the competition was handled by diplomacy rather than war. The accession of Vladislav II, for example, was accompanied by large concessions first to the Bohemian towns and later to the Hungarian nobility. The formal union of the Polish and Lithuanian crowns in 1569 also involved the decentralization of power and the strengthening of the rights of the nobility in both countries. In the end, the states split apart. The Russians took much of Lithuania, the Ottomans much of Hungary. Bohemia, which in the fifteenth century had been ruled more by its nobles than its king, was absorbed into the Habsburg territories after 1526.

There were many reasons why a unified state did not appear in east central Europe. In the first place, external forces disrupted territorial and political arrangements. Wars with the Ottomans and the Russians absorbed resources. Second, the princes faced rivals to their crowns. Though Casimir IV was able to place his son on the thrones of both Bohemia and Hungary, he managed to do so against the powerful claims of the Habsburg princes, who continued to intrigue against the Jagiellons. These contests for power necessitated concessions to leading citizens, which decreased the ability of the princes to centralize their kingdoms or to effect real unification among them. The nobility of Hungary, Bohemia, and Poland-Lithuania all developed strong local interests that increased over time. In Bohemia, Vladislav II was king in name only, and even in Poland the nobility won confirmation of its rights and privileges from the monarchy. War, rivalries for power, and a strong nobility prevented any one prince from dominating this area as the princes of Muscovy dominated theirs.

The Western Powers

Just as in the East, there was no single pattern to the consolidation of the large western European states. They, too, were internally fragmented and externally imperiled. While England had to overcome the ruin of decades of civil war, France and Spain faced the challenges of invasion and occupation. Western European princes struggled against powerful institutions and individuals within their states. Some they conquered, others they absorbed. Each nation formed its state differently: England by administrative centralization, France by good fortune, and Spain by dynastic marriage. Yet in 1450 few imagined that any one of these states would succeed.

The Taming of England.   Alone among European states, England suffered no threat of foreign invasion during the fifteenth century. This island fortress might easily have become the first consolidated European state were it not for the ambitions of the nobility and the weakness of the crown. For 30 years the English aristocracy fought over the spoils of a helpless monarch. The Wars of the Roses (1455–1485), as they came to be called, were as much a free-for-all among the English peerage as they were a contest for the throne between the houses of Lancaster and York. At their center was an attempt by the dukes of York to wrest the crown from the mad and ineffective Lancastrian king Henry VI (1422–1461). All around the edges was the continuation of local and family feuds that had little connection to the dynastic struggle.

   Three decades of intermittent warfare had predictable results. The houses of Lancaster and York were both destroyed. Edward IV (1461–1483) succeeded in gaining the crown for the House of York, but he was never able to wear it securely. When he died, his children, including his heir, Edward V (1483), were placed in the protection of their uncle Richard III (1483–1485). It was protection that they did not survive. The two boys disappeared, reputedly murdered in the Tower of London, and Richard declared himself king. Richard's usurpation led to civil war, and he was killed by the forces of Henry Tudor at the battle of Bosworth Field in 1485. By the end of the Wars of the Roses the monarchy had lost both revenue and prestige, and the aristocracy had stored up bitter memories for the future.

   It was left to Henry Tudor to pick up the pieces of the kingdom as legend has it he picked up the crown off a bramble bush. The two chief obstacles to his determination to consolidate the English state were the power of the nobility and the poverty of the monarch. No English monarch had held secure title to the throne for over a century. Henry Tudor, as Henry VII (1485–1509), put an end to this dynastic instability at once. He married Elizabeth of York, in whose heirs would rest the legitimate claim to the throne. Their children were indisputable successors to the crown. He also began the long process of taming his overmighty subjects. Traitors were hung and turncoats rewarded. He and his son Henry VIII (1509–1547) adroitly created a new peerage, which soon was as numerous as the old feudal aristocracy. These new nobles owed

Holbein's last portrait of Henry VIII, 1542. Henry made England into one of the world's greatest naval powers, but embroiled the kingdom in a series of costly foreign wars. He married six times in an effort to produce a legitimate male heir.

their titles and loyalty to the Tudors. They were favored with offices and spoils and were relied on to suppress both popular and aristocratic rebellions.

The financial problems of the English monarchy were not so easily overcome. In theory and practice an English king was supposed to live "of his own," that is, off the revenues from his own estates. In normal circumstances, royal revenue did not come from the king's subjects. The English landed classes had established the principle that only on extraordinary occasions were they to be required to contribute to the maintenance of government. This principle was defended through their representative institution, the Parliament. When the kings of England wanted to tax their subjects, they had first to gain the assent of Parliament. Though Parliaments did grant requests for extraordinary revenue, especially for national defense, they did so grudgingly. The English landed elites were not exempt from taxation, but they were able to control the amount of taxes they paid.

The inability of the crown to extract its living from its subjects made it more dependent on the efficient management of its own estates. Thus English state building depended on the growth of centralized institutions that could oversee royal lands and collect royal customs. Gradually, medieval institutions like the Exchequer were supplanted by newer organs that were better able to adjust to modern methods of accounting, record keeping, and enforcement. Henry sent ministers to view and value royal lands. He ordered the cataloging and collection of feudal obligations. Whether Henry's reputation for greed and rapacity was warranted, it was undeniable that he squeezed as much as could be taken from a not very juicy inheritance. His financial problems limited both domestic and foreign policy.

It was not until the middle of the next reign that the English monarchy was again solvent. As a result of his dispute with the papacy, Henry VIII confiscated the enormous wealth of the Catholic church, and with one stroke solved the Crown's monetary problems (see Chapter 11). But the real contribution that Henry and his chief minister, Thomas Cromwell (ca. 1485–1540), made to forming an English state was the way in which this windfall was administered. Cromwell accelerated the process of centralizing government that had begun under Edward IV. He divided administration according to its functions by creating separate departments of state, modeled on courts. These new departments were responsible for record keeping, revenue collection, and law enforcement. Each had a distinct jurisdiction and a permanent trained staff. Cromwell coordinated the work of these distinct departments by expanding the power of the Privy Council, which included the heads of these administrative bodies. Through a long evolution, the Privy Council came to serve as the king's executive. Cromwell also saw the importance of Parliament as a legislative body. Through Parliament, royal policy could be turned into statutes that had the assent of the political nation. If Parliament was well managed, issues that were potentially controversial could be defused. Laws passed by Parliament were more easily enforced locally than were proclamations issued by the king.

The Unification of France. Perhaps the most remarkable thing about the unification of France is that it took place at all. The forces working against the consolidation of a French state were formidable. France was surrounded by aggressive and powerful neighbors with whom it was frequently at war. Its greatest nobles were semi-independent princes who were constant rivals for the throne and consistent opponents of the extension of royal power. French people were primarily loyal to their province. Great and small viewed the pretensions of the monarchy with deep suspicion. Provincialism was not simply a negative; it was a fierce pride and loyalty toward local customs and institutions that had deep roots within communities. And France was splintered by profound regional differences. The north and south were divided by culture and by language (the *langue d'oc* in the south and the *langue d'oïl* in the north).

The first obstacles that were overcome were the external threats to French security. For over a century the throne of France had been contested by the kings of England. The so-called Hundred Years' War, which was fought intermittently between 1337 and 1453, originated in a dispute over the inheritance of the French crown and English possessions in Gascony in southern France (see Chapter 7). The war was fought on French soil, and by the early fifteenth century English conquests in north central France extended from Normandy to the borders of the Holy Roman Empire.

The problems posed by the Hundred Years' War were not just in victory and defeat. The struggle between the kings of England and the kings of France allowed French princes and dukes, who were nominally vassals of the king, to enhance their autonomy by making their own alliances with the highest bidder. When the English were finally driven out of France in the middle of the fifteenth century, the kings of France came into a weakened and divided inheritance.

Nor was England the only threat to the security of the French monarchy. On France's eastern border, in a long arching semicircle, were the estates of the dukes of Burgundy. The dukes of Burgundy and the kings of France shared a common ancestry: Both were of the House of Valois. Still, the sons of brothers in one generation were only cousins in the next, and the two branches of the family grew apart. The original Burgundian inheritance was in the southeast, centered at Dijon. A good marriage and good fortune brought to the first duke the rich northern province of Flanders. For the next 100 years the aim of the dukes of Burgundy was to unite their divided estates. While England and France were locked in deadly embrace, Burgundy systematically grew. It absorbed territory from both the Holy Roman Empire and France. To little pieces gained through marriages were added little pieces taken through force. The conquest of Lorraine finally connected the ducal estates in one long unbroken string. But it was a string stretched taut. The power of Burgundy threatened its neighbors in all directions. Both France and the empire were too weak to resist its expansion, but the confederation of Swiss towns to the southwest of Burgundy was not. In a series of stunning military victories Swiss forces repelled the Burgundians from their lands and demolished their armies. Charles the Bold, the last Valois duke of Burgundy, fell at the Battle of Nancy in 1477. His estates were quickly dismembered. France recovered its ancestral territories, including Burgundy itself, and through no effort of its own was now secure on its eastern border.

The king most associated with the consolidation of France was Louis XI (1461–1483). He inherited an estate exhausted by warfare and civil strife. More by chance than by plan he vastly extended the territories under the dominion of the French crown and, more importantly, subdued the nobility. Louis XI was as cunning as he was peculiar. In an age in which royalty was expressed through magnificence, Louis sported an old felt hat and a well-worn coat. His enemies constantly underestimated his abilities, which earned him the nickname "the Spider." But gradually during the course of his reign, Louis XI won back what he had been forced to give away. Years of fighting both the English and each other left the ranks of the French aristocracy depleted. As blood spilled on the battlefields, the stocks of fathers and sons ran low. Estates to which no male heirs existed fell forfeit to the king. In this manner the crown absorbed Anjou and Maine in the northwest and Provence in the south. More importantly, Louis XI ultimately obtained control of the two greatest independent fiefs, Brittany and Orléans. He managed this feat by arranging the marriage of his son Charles to the heiress of Brittany and of his daughter Jeanne to the heir of Orléans. When in 1527 the lands of the duke of Bourbon fell to the crown, the French monarch ruled a unified state.

The consolidation of France was not simply the result of the incorporation of diverse pieces of territory into the domain of the king. More than in any other state the experience in France demonstrated how a state could be formed without the designs of a great leader. Neither Louis XI nor his son Charles VIII (1483–1498) was a nation builder. Louis's main objective was always to preserve his estate. His good fortune saved him from the consequences of many ill-conceived policies. But no amount of luck could make up for Louis's failure to obtain the Burgundian Low Countries for France after the death of Charles the Bold in 1477. The marriage of Mary of Burgundy to Maximilian of Habsburg was one of the great turning points in European history. It initiated the struggle for control of the Low Countries that endured for over two centuries.

These long years of war established the principle of royal taxation, which was so essential to the process of state building in France. This enabled the monarchy to raise money for defense and for consolidation. Because of the strength of the nobles, most taxation fell only on the commoners, the so-called third estate. The *taille* was a direct tax on property from which the nobility and clergy were exempt. The *gabelle* was a consumption tax on the purchase of salt in most parts of the kingdom, and the *aide* was a tax on a variety of commodities including meat and wine. These consumption taxes were paid by all members of the third estate no matter how poor they might be. Though there was much complaint about taxes, the French monarchy established a broad base for taxation and a high degree of compliance long before any other European nation.

Along with money went soldiers, fighting men necessary to repel the English and to defind the crown against rebels and traitors. Again the French monarchy was the first to establish the principle of a national army, raised and directed from the center but quartered and equipped regionally. From the nobility were recruited the cavalry, from the towns and countryside the massive infantry. Fortified towns received privileges in return for military service to the king. Originally towns were required to provide artillery, but constant troubles with the nobility had led the kings of France to establish their own store of heavy guns. The towns supplied small arms, pikes, and swords and later pistols and muskets. By the beginning of the sixteenth century the French monarch could raise and equip an army of his own.

Taxation and military obligation demanded the creation and expansion of centralized institutions of government. This was the most difficult development in the period of state formation in France. The powers of royal agents were constantly challenged by the powers of regional nobles. It is easy to exaggerate the extent of the growth of central control and to underestimate the enduring hold of regional and provincial loyalties. Even the crown's absorption of estates did not always end local privileges and customs. But despite continued regional autonomy, a beginning had been made.

The Marriages of Spain.   Before the sixteenth century there was little prospect of a single nation emerging on the Iberian peninsula. North African Muslims called Moors occupied the province of Granada in the south; the stable kingdom of Portugal dominated the western coast. The Spanish peoples were divided among a number of separate states. The two most important were Castile, the largest and wealthiest kingdom, and Aragon, which was composed of a number of quasi-independent regions, each of which maintained its own laws and institutions. Three religions and four languages (not including dialects) widened these political divisions. And the different states had different outlooks. Castile was, above all, determined to rid itself of the Moors in Granada and to convert to Christianity its large Jewish population. Aragon played in the high-stakes game for power in the Mediterranean. It claimed sovereignty over Sicily and Naples and exercised it whenever it could.

A happy teenage marriage brought together the unhappy kingdoms of Castile and Aragon. When Ferdinand of Aragon and Isabella of Castile secretly exchanged wedding vows in 1469, both their homelands were rent by civil war. In Castile, Isabella's brother Henry IV (1454–1474) struggled unsuccessfully against the powerful Castilian nobility. In Aragon, Ferdinand's father, John II (1458–1479), faced a revolt by the rich province of Catalonia on one side and the territorial ambitions of Louis XI of France on the other. Joining the heirs together increased the resources of both kingdoms. Ferdinand took an active role in the pacification of Castile, while Castilian riches allowed him to defend Aragon from invasion. In 1479 the two crowns were united and the Catholic monarchs, as they were called, ruled the two kingdoms jointly. But the unification of the crowns of Castile and Aragon was not the same as the formation of a single state. Local privileges were zealously guarded, especially in Aragon, where the representative institutions of the towns, the Cortes, were aggressively independent. The powerful Castilian nobility never accepted Ferdinand as their king and refused him the crown after Isabella's death.

But Ferdinand and Isabella (1479–1516) took the first steps toward forging a Spanish state. Their most notable achievement was the final recovery of the lands that had been conquered by the Moors. For centuries the Spanish kingdoms had fought against the North African Muslims who had conquered large areas of the southern peninsula. The reconquista was characterized by short bursts of warfare followed by long periods of wary coexistence. By the middle of the fifteenth century, the Moorish territory had been reduced to the province of Granada, but civil strife in Castile heightened the possibility of a new Moorish offensive. "We no longer mint gold, only steel," was how a Moorish ruler replied to Isabella's demand for the traditional payment of tribute money. The final stages of the reconquista began in 1482 and lasted for a decade. It was waged as a holy war and was financed in part by grants from the pope and the Christian princes of Europe. It was a bloody undertaking, but in 1492 Granada finally fell and the province was absorbed into Castile.

The reconquista played an important part in creating a national identity for the Christian peoples of Spain. In order to raise men and money for the war effort, Ferdinand and Isabella mobilized their nobility and town governments and created a central organization to oversee the invasion. The conquered territories were used to reward those who had aided the effort, though the crown maintained control and jurisdiction over most of the province. But the idea of the holy war also had a darker side and an unanticipated consequence. The Jewish population that had lived peacefully in both Castile and Aragon became another object of hostility. Many Jews had risen to prominence in government and in skilled professions. Others, who had accepted conversion to Christianity and were known as *conversos*, had become among the most powerful figures in church and state.

Both groups were now attacked. The conversos fell prey to a special church tribunal created to examine their sincere devotion to Catholicism. This was the Spanish Inquisition which, though it used traditional judicial prac-tices—torture to gain confessions, public humiliation to show contrition, and burnings at the stake to maintain purity—used them on a scale never before seen. Thousands of conversos were killed, and many more families had their wealth confiscated to be used for the reconquista. In 1492 the Jews themselves were expelled from Spain. Though the reconquista and the expulsion of the Jews inflicted great suffering on victims and incalculable loss to the Castilian economy, both events enhanced the prestige of the Catholic monarchs.

In many ways, Ferdinand and Isabella trod the paths of the medieval monarchy. They relied more on personal contact with their people than on the use of a centralized administration. They frequently dispensed justice person-ally, sitting in court and accepting petitions from their subjects. Queen Isabella was venerated in Castile, where women's rights to inheritance remained strong. Ferdinand's absences from Aragon were always a source of contention between him and the Cortes of the towns. Yet he was careful to provide regents to preside in his absence and regularly returned to visit his native kingdom.

The joint presence of Ferdinand and Isabella in the provinces of Spain was symbolic of the unity they wished to achieve. Despite the great obstacles, they were consciously interested in bringing about a more permanent blending. Ferdinand made Castilian the official language of government in Aragon and even appointed Castilians to Aragonese posts. He and Isabella actively encouraged the intermarriage of the two aristocracies and the expansion of the number of wealthy nobles who held land in both kingdoms. Nevertheless, these measures did not unify Spain or erase the centuries-long tradition of hostility among the diverse Iberian peoples.

It was left to the heirs of Ferdinand and Isabella to forge together the Spanish kingdoms, and the process was a painful one. The hostility to a foreign monarch that both the Castilian nobility and the Aragonese towns had shown to Ferdinand and Isabella increased dramatically at the accession of their grandson Charles V (1516–1556), who had been born and raised in the Low Countries, where he ruled over Burgundy and the Netherlands. Through a series of dynastic accidents, Charles was heir to the Spanish crown with its possessions in the New World and to the vast Habsburg estates that included Austria. Charles established his rule in Spain gradually. For a time he was forced to share power in Castile and to suppress a disorganized aristocratic rebellion.

Because of his foreign obligations, Charles was frequently absent from Spain. During those periods he governed through regents and royal councils that did much to centralize administration. Though Castile and Aragon had separate councils, they were organized similarly and had greater contact than before. Charles V realized the importance of Spain, especially of Castile, in his empire. He established a permanent bureaucratic court, modeled on that of Burgundy, and placed able Spaniards at the head of its departments. This smoothed over the long periods when Charles was abroad, especially the 13 years between 1543 and 1556.

Yet neither his personal efforts to rule as a Spanish monarch, nor those of his able administrators were the most important factor in uniting the Spanish kingdoms of Iberia. Rather it was the fact that Charles V brought Spain to the forefront of European affairs in the sixteenth century. Spanish prowess, whether in arms or in culture, became a source of national pride that helped erode regional identity. Gold and silver from the New World helped finance Charles's great empire. Whether or not he dreamed of uniting all of Europe under his rule, Charles V fulfilled nearly all of the ancient territorial ambitions of the Spanish kingdoms. In Italy he prosecuted Aragonese claims to Sicily and Naples; in the north he held on firmly to the kingdom of Navarre, which had been annexed by Ferdinand and secured Spain's border with France. In the south he blocked off Ottoman and Muslim expansion. The reign of Charles V ushered in the dawn of Spain's golden age.

*T*he Dynastic Struggles

The formation of large states throughout Europe led inevitably to conflicts among them. Long chains of marriages among the families of the European princes meant that sooner or later the larger powers would lay claim to the same inheritances and test the matter by force. Thus the sixteenth century was a period of almost unrelieved general warfare that took the whole of the Continent as its theater. Advances in technology made war more efficient and more expensive. They also made it more horrible. The use of artillery against infantry increased the number of deaths and maiming injuries, as did the replacement of the arrow by the bullet. As the size of armies increased, so did casualties. The slaughter of French nobility at Pavia in 1525 was the largest in a century; the Turkish sultan, Suleiman the Magnificent, recorded the burial of 24,000 Hungarian soldiers after the battle of Mohács in 1526.

Power and Glory

The frequency with which offensive war was waged in the sixteenth century raises a number of questions about the militaristic values of the age. Valor remained greatly prized—a Renaissance virtue inherited from the crusading zeal and chivalric ideals of the Middle Ages. Princes saw valor as a personal attribute and sought to do great deeds. Ferdinand of Aragon and Francis I (1515–1547) of France won fame for their exploits in war. Charles the Bold and Louis II of Hungary were less fortunate. Their battlefield deaths led to the breakup of their states. Wars were fought to further the interests of princes rather than the interests of national sovereignty or international Christianity. They were certainly not fought in the interests of their subjects. States were an extension of a prince's heritage; what rulers sought in battle was a part of their historical and familial rights, which defined themselves and their subjects. The wars of the sixteenth century were dynastic wars.

Along with desire came ability. The New Monarchs were capable of waging war. The very definition of their states involved the ability to accumulate territories and to defend them. Internal security depended on locally raised forces or hired mercenaries. Both required money, which was becoming available in unprecedented quantities as a result of the increasing prosperity of the early sixteenth century and the windfall of gold and silver from the New World. Professional soldiers, of whom the Swiss and Germans were the most noteworthy, sold their services to the highest bidders. Developments in transport and supply enabled campaigns to take place far from the center of a state. Finally, communications were improving. The need for knowledge about potential rivals or allies had the effect of expanding the European system of diplomacy. Resident agents were established in all the European capitals and they had a decisive impact on war and peace. Their dispatches formed the most reliable source of information about the strengths of armies or the weaknesses of governments, about the birth of heirs or the death of princes.

Personality also played a part in the international warfare of the early sixteenth century. The three most consistent protagonists, Charles V, Francis I, and Henry VIII, were of similar age and outlook. Each came unexpectedly to his throne in the full flush of youth, eager for combat and glory. The three were self-consciously rivals, each jealous of the others' successes, each triumphant in the others' failures. Henry VIII and Francis I held wrestling bouts when they met in 1520. Francis I challenged Charles V to single combat after the French king's humiliating imprisonment in Madrid in 1526. As the three monarchs aged together, their youthful wars of conquest matured into strategic warfare designed to maintain a continental balance of power.

The Italian Wars

The struggle for supremacy in Europe in the sixteenth century pitted the French House of Valois against the far-flung estates of the Habsburg empire. Yet the wars took place in Italy. The rivalries among the larger Italian city-states proved fertile ground for the newly consolidated European monarchies. Both French and Spanish monarchs had remote but legitimate claims to the kingdom of Naples in southern Italy. In 1494 the French king, Charles VIII, took up an invitation from the ruler of Milan to intervene in Italian affairs. His campaign was an unqualified, if fleeting, success. He marched the length of the peninsula, overthrew the Medici in Florence, forced the pope to open the gates of Rome, and finally seized the crown of Naples. The occupation was accomplished without a single great battle and lasted until the warring Italian city-states realized that they had more to fear from the French than from one another. Once that happened, Charles VIII beat a hasty retreat. But the French appetite for Italian territory was not sated. Soon a deal was struck with Ferdinand of Aragon to divide the kingdom of Naples in two. All went according to plan until these thieves fell out among themselves. In the end, Spain wound up with all of Naples, and France was left with nothing but debts and grievances.

Thus when Francis I came to the French throne and Charles V to the Spanish, Naples was just one of several potential sources of friction. Not only had Ferdinand betrayed the French in Naples, he had also broken a long-standing peace on the Franco-Spanish border by conquering the independent but French-speaking kingdom of Navarre. Francis could be expected to avenge both slights. Charles, on the other hand, was the direct heir of the dukes of Burgundy. From his childhood he longed for the restoration of his ancestral lands, including Burgundy itself, which had been gobbled up by Louis XI after the death of Charles the Bold. Competition between Francis and Charles became all the more ferocious when Charles's grandfather, the Holy Roman Emperor Maximilian I (1486–1519), died in 1519. Both monarchs launched a vigorous campaign for the honor of succeeding him.

For nearly a century the Holy Roman Emperor had come from the Austrian ruling family, and there was little reason to believe that Charles V, who now inherited the Habsburg lands in Austria and Germany, would not also succeed to this eminent but empty dignity. Nevertheless, the electors were willing to be bribed by French agents who supported Francis's candidacy and even English agents who supported Henry VIII. Charles spent the most of all, and his eventual election not only aggravated the personal animosity among the monarchs, but added another source of conflict in Italy. When Louis XII (1498–1515) succeeded Charles VIII as king of France, he had laid claim to the duchy of Milan through an interest of his wife's, though he was unable to enforce it. Francis I proved more capable. In 1515 he stunned all of Europe by crushing the vaunted Swiss mercenaries at the battle of Marignano. But the duchy of Milan was a territory under the protection of the Holy Roman Emperor and it soon appealed for imperial troops to help repel the French invaders. Milan was strategically important to Charles V because it was the vital link between his Austrian and Burgundian possessions. Almost as soon as he took up the imperial mantle, Charles V was determined to challenge Francis I in Italy.

The key to such a challenge was the construction of alliances among the various Italian city-states and most especially with England, whose aid both Charles and Francis sought to enlist in the early 1520s. Henry VII had found foreign alliances a ready source of cash, and he was always eager to enter into them as long as they did not involve raising armies and fighting wars. Henry VIII was made of sterner stuff. He longed to reconquer France and to cut a figure on the European scene. Despite the fact that his initial continental adventures had emptied his treasury without fulfilling his dreams, Henry remained eager for war. He was also flattered to find himself the object of attention by both Valois and Habsburg emissaries. Charles V made two separate trips to London, while Henry crossed the Channel in 1520 to meet Francis I in one of the gaudiest displays of conspicuous consumption that the century would witness, appropriately known as the Field of the Cloth of Gold.

The result of these diplomatic intrigues was an alliance between England and the Holy Roman Empire. English and Burgundian forces would stage an invasion of northern France while Spanish and German troops would again attempt to dislodge the French from Italy. The strategy worked better than anyone could have imagined. In 1523 Charles's forces gained a foothold in Milan by taking the heavily fortified town of Pavia. Two years later Francis was ready to strike back. At the head of his own royal guards, he massed Swiss mercenaries and French infantry outside Pavia and made ready for a swift assault. Instead, a large imperial army arrived to relieve the town, and in the subsequent battle the French suffered a shattering defeat. Francis I was captured.

The victory at Pavia, which occurred on Charles V's twenty-fifth birthday, seemingly made him master of all of Europe. His ally Henry VIII urged an immediate invasion and dismemberment of France and began raising an army to spearhead the attack. But Charles's position was much less secure than it appeared. The Ottomans threatened his Hungarian territories, and the Protestants threatened his German lands. He could not afford a war of conquest in France. His hope now was to reach an agreement with Francis I for a lasting European peace, and for this purpose the French king was brought in captivity to Madrid.

It is doubtful that there was ever any real chance for peace between Habsburg and Valois after the battle of Pavia. Francis's personal humiliation and Charles's military position were both too strong to allow for a permanent settlement in which Habsburgs ruled in Milan and Naples. But it was neither political nor personal considerations that were the source of another 30 years of continuous European warfare. Rather it was Charles's demand that Burgundy be returned to him. Though Francis was hardly in a position to bargain, he held out on this issue for as long as possible and secretly prepared a disavowal of the final agreement before it was made. By the Treaty of Madrid in 1526, Francis I yielded Burgundy and recognized the Spanish conquest of Navarre and Spanish rule in Naples. The agreement was sealed by the marriage of Francis to Charles's sister, Eleanor of Portugal. But marriage was not sufficient security for such a complete capitulation. To secure his release from Spain, Francis was required to leave behind as hostages his 7- and 8-year-old sons until the treaty was fulfilled. For three years the children languished in Spanish captivity.

No sooner had he set foot on French soil than Francis I renounced the Treaty of Madrid. Despite the threat that this posed to his children, Francis argued that the terms had been extracted against his will, and he even gained the sanction of the pope for violating his oath. Setting France on a war footing, he began seeking new allies. Henry VIII, disappointed with the meager spoils of his last venture, switched sides. So, too, did a number of Italian city-states, including Rome. Most importantly, Francis I entered into an alliance with the Ottoman sultan, Suleiman the Magnificent (1520–1566), whose armies were pressing against the southeastern borders of the Holy Roman Empire. In the year following Pavia, the Ottomans secured an equally decisive triumph at Mohács, which cut Hungary in two and threatened Vienna, the eastern capital of the Habsburg lands. Almost overnight Charles V had been turned from hunter into hunted. The Ottoman threat demanded immediate attention in Germany, the French and English were preparing to strike in the Low Countries, and the Italian wars continued. In 1527 Charles's unpaid German mercenaries stormed through Rome, sacked the papal capital, and captured the pope. Christian Europe was mortified.

The struggle for European mastery ground on for decades. The Treaty of Cateau-Cambrésis in 1559 brought to a close 60 years of conflict. In the end the French were no more capable of dislodging the Habsburgs from Italy than were the Habsburgs of forcing the Ottomans out of Hungary. The great stores of silver that poured into Castile from the New World were consumed in the fires of continental warfare. In 1557 both France and Spain declared bankruptcy to avoid foreclosures by their creditors. For the French, the Italian wars were disastrous. They seriously undermined the state's financial base, eroded confidence in the monarchy, and thinned the ranks of the ruling nobility. The adventure begun by Charles VIII in search of glory brought France nearly to ruin. It ended with fitting irony. After the death of Francis I, his son Henry II (1547–1559) continued the struggle. Henry never forgave his father for abandoning him in Spain, and he sought revenge on Charles V, who had been his jailer. He regarded the Treaty of Cateau-Cambrésis as a victory and celebrated it with great pomp and pageantry. Among the feasts and festivities were athletic competitions for the king's courtiers and attendants. Henry II entered the jousting tournament and there was killed.

Charles V died in his bed. The long years of war made clear that the dream to dominate Europe could only be a dream. He split apart his empire and granted to his brother, Ferdinand I (1558–1564), the Austrian and German lands and the mantle of the Holy Roman Empire. To his son, Philip II (1556–1598), he ceded the Low Countries, Spain and the New World, Naples, and his Italian conquests. In 1555 Charles abdicated all of his titles and retired to a monastery to live out his final days. The cares of an empire that once stretched from Peru to Vienna were lifted from his shoulders. Beginning with his voyage to Castile in 1517 he had made ten trips to the Netherlands, nine to Germany, seven to Italy, six to Spain, four to France, two to England, and two to Africa. "My life has been one long journey," he told those who witnessed him relinquish his crowns. On 21 September 1558, he rested forever.

Suggestions for Further Reading

General Reading

*Denys Hay, *Europe in the Fourteenth and Fifteenth Centuries* (London: Longman, 1966). A good first survey of political history.

*G. R. Potter, ed., *The New Cambridge Modern History Vol. I: The Renaissance 1493–1520* (Cambridge, England: Cambridge University Press, 1957). Comprehensive survey of political history written by renowned scholars.

*Eugene Rice, *The Foundations of Early Modern Europe 1460–1559* (New York: W.W. Norton, 1970). An outstanding synthesis.

The European Discoveries

C. R. Boxer, *The Portuguese Seaborne Empire 1415–1825* (London: Hutchinson, 1968). The best history of the first of the explorer nations.

*A. W. Crosby, *The Columbian Exchange: Biological and Cultural Consequences of 1492* (Westport, CT: Greenwood Press, 1972). An argument about the medical consequences of the transatlantic encounter.

*J. H. Elliot, *The Old World and the New 1492–1650* (Cambridge, England: Cambridge University Press, 1970). A brilliant look at the reception of knowledge about the New World by Europeans.

*Lyle McAlister, *Spain and Portugal in the New World 1492–1700* (Minneapolis: University of Minnesota Press, 1984). An up-to-date history of the great South American empires.

*Samuel Morrison, *Christopher Columbus, Mariner* (New York: New American Library, 1985). A biography by a historian who repeated the Columbian voyages.

*Dan O'Sullivan, *Age of Discovery 1400–1550* (London: Longman, 1984). A short synthetic work.

*J. H. Parry, *The Age of Reconnaissance* (New York: New American Library, 1963). A survey of technological and technical changes that made possible the European discovery of America.

Europe in 1500

N. J. G. Pounds, *An Historical Geography of Europe 1500–1800* (Cambridge, England: Cambridge University Press, 1979). A remarkable survey of the relationship between geography and history.

*Daniel Waley, *Later Medieval Europe* (London: Longman, 1985). A good brief account.

---

*Indicates paperback edition available.

The Formation of States

*S. B. Chrimes, *Henry VII* (Berkeley: University of California Press, 1972). A traditional biography of the first Tudor king.

Robert O. Crummey, *The Formation of Muscovy 1304–1613* London: Longman, 1987). The best one-volume history.

*Norman Davies, *God's Playground: A History of Poland Vol. I.: The Origins to 1795* (New York: Columbia University Press, 1982). The best treatment in English of a complex history.

*J. H. Elliot, *Imperial Spain 1469–1716* (New York: Mentor, 1963). Still worth reading for its insights and examples.

*G. R. Elton, *Reform and Reformation, England 1509–1558* (Cambridge, MA: Harvard University Press, 1977). An up-to-date survey by the dean of Tudor historians.

Bernard Guenée, *States and Rulers in Later Medieval Europe* (London: Basil Blackwell, 1985). An engaging argument about the forces that helped shape the state system in Europe.

*Henry Kamen, *Spain 1469–1714* (London: Longman, 1983). The most up-to-date survey.

*Paul M. Kendall, *Louis XI: The Universal Spider* (New York: W.W. Norton, 1971). A highly entertaining account of an unusual monarch.

*R. J. Knecht, *French Renaissance Monarchy* (London: Longman, 1984). A study of the nature of the French monarchy and the way it was transformed in the early sixteenth century.

*J. R. Lander, *Government and Community, England 1450–1509* (Cambridge, MA: Harvard University Press, 1980). A comprehensive survey of the late fifteenth century.

*Richard Pipes, *Russia Under the Old Regime* (London: Widenfeld and Nicolson, 1974). A majesterial account.

*C. D. Ross, *The Wars of the Roses* (London: Thames & Hudson, 1976). The best one-volume account.

J. H. Shennan, *The Origins of the Modern European State 1450–1725* (London: Hutchinson, 1974). An analytic account of the rise of the state.

Richard Vaughan, *Valois Burgundy* (Hampden, CT: Shoe String Press, 1975). An engaging history of a vanished state.

The Dynastic Struggles

M. E. Alvarez, *Charles V* (London: Thames & Hudson, 1975). An accessible biography of the most remarkable man of the age.

*J. R. Hale, *War and Society in Renaissance Europe* (Baltimore, MD: Johns Hopkins University Press, 1986). Assesses the impact of war on the political and social history of early modern Europe.

*R. J. Knecht, *Francis I* (Cambridge, England: Cambridge University Press, 1982). A compelling study by the leading scholar of sixteenth-century France.

*J. J. Scarisbrick, *Henry VIII* (Berkeley: University of California Press, 1968). The definitive biography.

11

The Reform of Religion

Sola Scriptura

"In the beginning was the Word, and the Word was with God, and the Word was God." In no other period of European history was this text of the apostle John so appropriate. Men and women shared a consuming desire to hear and to read the Word of God as set down in the Bible. In the early sixteenth century, Europeans developed an insatiable appetite for the Bible. Scriptures rolled off printing presses in every shape and form, from the great vellum tomes of Gutenberg, pictured here, to pocket Bibles that soldiers carried into battle. They came in every imaginable language. Before 1500 there were fourteen complete Bibles printed in German, four each in Italian, French, and Spanish, one in Czech, and even one in Flemish. There were hundreds more editions in Latin, the official Vulgate Bible first translated by Saint Jerome in the fourth century. Whole translations and editions of the Bible were only part of the story. Separate sections, especially the Psalms and the first books of the Old Testament, were printed by the thousands. There were 24 French editions of the Old Testament before an entirely new translation appeared in 1530. When Martin Luther began his own German translation of the Bible in 1522, it immediately became an international bestseller. In 25 years it went into 430 editions. It is estimated that one million German Bibles were printed in the first half of the sixteenth century—at a time when Europe had a German-speaking population of about fifteen million people, 90 percent of whom were illiterate.

Bible owning was no fad. It was but one element in a new devotional outlook that was sweeping the Continent and would have far-reaching consequences for European society during the next 150 years. A renewed spirituality was everywhere to be seen. It was expressed in a desire to change the

traditional practices and structures of the Roman church. It was expressed in a desire to have learned and responsible ministers to tend to the needs of their parishioners. It was expressed in a desire to establish godly families and godly cities and godly kingdoms. Sometimes it took the form of sarcasm and bitter denunciations; sometimes it took the form of quiet devotion and pious living. The need for reform was everywhere felt; the demand for reform was everywhere heard. It came from within the Roman church as much as from without.

The inspiration for reform was based on the Word of God. Scholars, following humanist principles, worked on biblical translations in an attempt to bring a purer text to light. Biblical commentary dominated the writings of churchmen as never before. Woodcut pictures, depicting scenes from the life of Jesus or from the Old Testament, were printed in untold quantities for the edification of the unlettered. For the first time common people could, in their own dwellings, contemplate representations of the lives of the saints. Many of the Bibles that were printed in vernacular—that is, in the languages spoken in the various European states rather than in Latin—were interleaved with illustrations of the central events of Christian history. Preachers spoke to newly aware audiences and relied on biblical texts to draw out their message. Study groups, especially in urban areas, proliferated so that the literate could read and learn together. Bible reading became a part of family life, one which mothers and fathers could share with their children and their servants. *Sola scriptura*—by the Word alone—became the battle cry of religious reform.

The Intellectual Reformation

There is nothing as powerful as an idea whose time has come. But the coming of ideas has a history as complex as the ideas themselves. In the early sixteenth century reformers throughout western Europe preached new ideas about religious doctrine and religious practice. At first these ideas took the form of a sustained critique of the Roman Catholic church, but soon they developed a momentum of their own. Some reformers remained within traditional Catholicism; others moved outside and founded new Protestant churches. Wherever this movement for religious reform, whether Catholic or Protestant, appeared, it was fed by new ideas. But if new ideas were to supplant old ones, they not only had to be heard and repeated but accurately recorded and understood. This was made possible by the development of printing, which appeared in Germany in the late fifteenth century and rapidly spread across Europe in the succeeding decades. Yet printing was as much a result as it was a cause of the spread of ideas. The humanist call for a return to the study of the classics and for the creation of accurate texts, first heard in Italy, aroused scholars and leaders in all of the European states. Their appetite for manuscripts exhausted the abilities of the scribes and booksellers who reproduced texts. Printing responded to that demand.

The Print Revolution

The development of printing did not cause religious reform, but it is difficult to see how reform would have progressed in its absence. The campaign to change the doctrine and practice of Catholicism was waged through the press, with millions of flyers and pamphlets distributed across Europe to spread the new ideas. A third of all books sold in Germany between 1518 and 1525 were written by Martin Luther. But the ways in which printing came to be used by religious reformers could hardly have been foreseen by the artisans, bankers, and booksellers who together created one of the true technological revolutions in Western history.

Printing was not invented. It developed as a result of progress made in a number of allied industries, of which papermaking and goldsmithing were the most important. Scholars and university students needed copies of manuscripts. Their need led to the development of a trade in bookselling that flourished in almost every university town. The process of reproduction was slowed by difficulties in obtaining the sheep- and calfskins on which the manuscripts were written. In the early fifteenth century, copyists began to substitute paper made from linen rags for the expensive vellum skins. A number of German craft workers experimented with using movable metal type to make exact reproductions of manuscripts on paper. In the 1450s in Mainz,

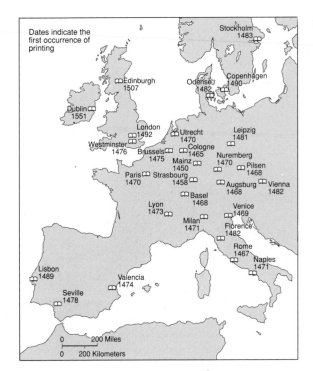

The spread of printing

Dates indicate the first occurrence of printing

Stockholm 1483

Edinburgh 1507

Odense 1482

Copenhagen 1490

Dublin 1551

London 1492

Westminster 1476

Utrecht 1470

Leipzig 1481

Brussels 1475

Cologne 1465

Mainz 1450

Nuremberg 1470

Pilsen 1468

Paris 1470

Strasbourg 1458

Augsburg 1468

Vienna 1482

Basel 1468

Lyon 1473

Venice 1469

Milan 1471

Florence 1482

Rome 1467

Naples 1471

Lisbon 1489

Valencia 1474

Seville 1478

0   200 Miles

0   200 Kilometers

Johannes Gutenberg (ca. 1400–1468) and his partners succeeded and published their famous Bibles.

The association of early printing with goldsmithing resulted from the high level of technical skill that was necessary to create the hard metal stamps from which the softer metal type was produced. Printing was an expensive business. The investment in type and in paper was considerable. Only the press itself was cheap. Any corn or wine press could be used to bring the long flat sheets of paper down upon a wooden frame filled with ink-coated metal type. Booksellers initially put up the capital needed to cast the stamps, mold the type, and buy the paper. They bound the printed pages and found the markets to distribute them. At first sales were slow. Printed books were considered inferior to handwritten manuscripts. Nor at first were printed books less expensive. Bibles, like those printed by Gutenberg, were major investments, equivalent to purchasing a house today. Many printing shops quickly went bankrupt as they misjudged their markets and were unable to pay back their loans.

Still, once it was begun, printing spread like wildfire. By 1480 over 110 towns had established presses, most in Italy and Germany. After that the pace quickened. By the beginning of the sixteenth century Venice and Paris were the centers of the industry, with the Paris presses producing over three hundred new titles annually. Most of the early printed works were either religious or classical. Bibles, church service books, and the commentaries of the Church Fathers were most common. Cicero topped the list of classical authors.

What is most amazing about the printing revolution is how rapidly printing came to be a basic part of life. In the first 40 years after the presses began, perhaps as many as 20 million books were produced and distributed. Printing changed the habits of teachers and students and therefore the possibilities of education. It altered the methods by which the state conducted its business. It affected both legal training and legal proceedings. Compilations of laws could now be widely distributed and more uniformly enforced. Printing had a similar effect on the development of scientific study. The printing press popularized the discoveries of the New World and contributed to the reproduction of more accurate charts and maps, which in turn facilitated further discovery. Printing also helped standardize language, both Latin and vernacular, by frequent repetition of preferred usage and spelling. Perhaps most importantly printing created an international intellectual community whose ideas could be dispersed the length and breadth of the Continent. The printing press enhanced the value of ideas and of thinking. Nothing could be more central to the reform of religion.

Christian Humanism

Many of the ideas that spread across Europe as the result of the printing revolution originated in Italian humanism (see Chapter 9). The revival of classical literature, with its concern for purity in language and eloquence in style, was one of the most admired achievements of the Renaissance. Students from all over Europe who descended upon Italian universities to study medicine and law came away with a strong dose of philology, rhetoric, moral philosophy, and the other liberal arts. By the beginning of the sixteenth century, the force of humanism was felt strongly in northern and western Europe, where it was grafted to the traditional theological teaching. The combination was a new and powerful intellectual movement known as Christian humanism.

Though the humanism of the north differed from that of the Italian city-states, this is not to say that northern humanists were Christians and Italian humanists were not. But Italian intellectual interests were in secular subjects, especially in mastering classical languages and in translating classical texts. Italian humanists had established techniques for the recovery of accurate texts and had developed principles for compiling the scholarly editions that now poured forth from the printing presses. Christian humanists applied these techniques to the study of the authorities and texts of the Church. Most of the new humanists had been trained in Italy, where they devoted themselves to the mastery of Greek and Latin. They had imbibed the idea that scholars, using their own critical faculties, could establish the authority of texts and the meaning of words. Building upon the patient work of their predecessors and the advantages offered by printing, this new generation of humanists brought learning to educated men and women throughout Europe.

Christian humanism was a program of reform rather than a philosophy. It aimed to make better Christians through better education. Humanists were especially interested in the education of women. Thomas More (1478–1535) raised his daughters to be among the educated elite of England. Renowned women scholars even held places at Italian universities. Humanist educational principles posed an implicit challenge to Roman Catholicism. Schools had once been the monopoly of the Church, which used them to train clergymen. Literacy itself had been preserved over the centuries so that the gospel could be propagated.

By the sixteenth century these purposes had been transformed. Schools now trained many who were not destined for careers in the Church, and literacy served the needs of the state, the aristocracy, and the merchant classes. More importantly, as the humanists perfected their techniques of scholarship, the Church continued to rely on traditional methods of training and traditional texts. The dominant manner of teaching at the schools and universities was known as Scholasticism. Passages of biblical texts were studied through the commentaries of generations of Church Fathers. Rote memorization of the opinions of others was more highly valued than critical thinking. Argument took place by formal disputation of questions on which the Fathers of the Church disagreed. The Vulgate Bible was used throughout Western Christendom. It was now a thousand years old.

The Humanist Movement

Many humanist criticisms of church teaching focused on its failure to inspire individuals to live a Christian life. Humanist writers were especially scathing about popular practices that bordered on superstition, like pilgrimages to holy places or the worship of relics from the early history of the Church. Such beliefs became the butt of popular humor: "If the fragments [of the Lord's Cross] were joined together they would seem a full load for a freighter. And yet the Lord carried his whole cross." Christian humanists wanted to inspire Christians. As the great Dutch humanist Desiderius Erasmus observed, "To be learned is the lot of only a few; but no one is unable to be a Christian, no one is unable to be pious."

Christian humanism was an international movement. The humanists formed the elite of the intellectual world of the sixteenth century, and their services were sought by princes and peers as well as by the most distinguished universities. In fact, the New Monarchs supported the humanists and protected them from their critics. Marguerite of Navarre, sister of Francis I, was an accomplished writer who frequently interceded on behalf of the leading French humanists. Ferdinand of Aragon, Henry VIII, and the Holy Roman Emperors Maximilian I and Charles V all brought humanists to their courts and aided their projects. Maria of Hungary and Mary and Elizabeth Tudor were trained in humanist principles and participated in humanist literary achievements. This support was especially important for educational reforms. Under the influence of the French humanist Jacques Lefèvre d'Étaples (ca. 1455–1536), Francis I established the Collège de France; under the direction of Cardinal Jiménez de Cisneros, the University of Alcalá was founded in Spain. Throughout northern Europe professorships in Greek and Latin were endowed at universities to help further the study of classical languages.

The centerpiece of humanist reforms was the translation of Christian texts. Armed with skills in Greek and Latin, informed by scholars of Hebrew and Aramaic, humanist writers prepared new editions of the books of the Bible and of the writings of the early Church Fathers. The Polyglot Bible—literally "many languages—that was produced in 1522 at the University of Alcalá took a team of scholars 15 years to complete. They rigorously compared texts of all known biblical manuscripts and established the principle that inconsistencies among Latin manuscripts were to be resolved by reference to Greek texts and difficulties in Greek texts by reference to Hebrew texts. The result was six volumes that allowed scholars to compare the texts. The Old Testament was printed in three parallel columns of Hebrew, Latin Vulgate, and Greek. The New Testament was printed in double columns of Greek and Vulgate. The Greek edition of the Bible and its establishment as a text superior to the Vulgate caused an immediate sensation throughout humanist and church circles.

The Wit of Erasmus

Though the Polyglot Bible contained the first completed Greek edition of the New Testament, it was not the first published one. That distinction belongs to the man whose name is most closely associated with the idea of Christian humanism, Desiderius Erasmus of Rotterdam (ca. 1466–1536). Orphaned at an early age, Erasmus was educated by the Brothers of the Common Life, a lay brotherhood that specialized in schooling children and preparing them for a monastic life. Marked out early by his extraordinary intellectual gifts, Erasmus entered a monastery and was then allowed to travel to pursue his studies, first in France and then in England.

In England Erasmus learned of new techniques for instructing children both in classical knowledge and in Christian morals, and he became particularly interested in the education of women. While in England, Erasmus decided to compose a short satire on the lines of his conversations with Thomas More, extolling what was silly and condemning what was wise. The result was *In Praise of Folly* (1509), a work that became one of the first bestsellers.

Before his visit to England, Erasmus had worked solely on Latin translations, but he came to realize the importance of recovering the texts of the early Church Fathers. At the age of 30 he began the arduous task of learning ancient Greek and devoted his energies to a study of the writings of Saint Jerome, the principal compiler of the Vulgate, and to preparing an edition of the Greek texts of the Bible. Erasmus's translation of the New Testament and his edition of the writings of Saint Jerome both appeared in 1516.

Erasmus devoted his life to restoring the direct connection between the individual Christian and the textual basis of Christian doctrine. Although he is called the father of biblical criticism, Erasmus was not a theologian. He was more interested in the practical impact of ideas than in the ideas themselves. His scathing attacks on the Scholastics, popular superstition, and the pretensions of the traditionalists in the Church and the universities all aimed at the same goal: to restore the experiences of Christ to the center of Christianity. Though his patrons were the rich and his language was Latin, Erasmus also hoped to reach men and women lower down the social order, those whom he believed the Church had failed to educate. "The doctrine of Christ casts aside no age, no sex, no fortune or position in life. It keeps no one at a distance."

*T*he Lutheran Reformation

On the surface the Roman Catholic church appeared as strong as ever at the end of the fifteenth century. The growth of universities and the spread of the new learning had helped create a better educated clergy. The printing press proved an even greater boon to the Church than it had to the humanists by making widely available both instructional manuals for priests and up-to-date service books for congregations. The prosperity of European societies enhanced the prosperity of the Church. In Rome successive late medieval popes had managed to protect church interests in the wake of the disintegration of the autonomous power of the Italian city-states. Popes had become first diplomats and then warriors in order to repel French and Spanish invaders. Rome was invaded, but never conquered. And it was more beautiful than ever as the great artists and craft workers of the Renaissance built and adorned its churches. On the surface all was calm.

Yet everywhere in Europe the cry was for reform. Reform the venal papacy and its money-sucking bishops. Reform the ignorant clergy and the sacrilegious priests. Raise up the fallen nuns and the wayward friars. Wherever one turned, one saw abuses. Parish livings were sold to the highest bidder to raise money. This was simony. Rich appointments were given to the kinsmen of powerful church leaders rather than to those most qualified. This was nepotism. Individual clergymen accumulated numerous positions whose responsibilities they could not fulfill. This was pluralism. Some priests who took the vow of chastity lived openly with their concubines. Some mendicants who took the vow of poverty dressed in silk and ate from golden plates.

The cry for reform at the beginning of the sixteenth century came at a moment when people from all walks of life demanded greater spiritual fulfillment and held those whose vocation it was to provide such fulfillment to higher standards. Expectation rather than experience powered the demands for reform.

The Spark of Reform

Europe was becoming more religious. The signs of religious fervor were everywhere. Cities hired preachers to expound the gospel. Pilgrims to the shrines of saints clogged the roadways every spring and summer. Rome remained the greatest attraction, but pilgrims covered the Continent. The shrine of the apostle Saint James at Compostela in Spain was believed to cure the ill. Endowments of masses for the dead increased. Henry VII of England provided money for 10,000 masses to be said for his soul. Even city merchants might bequeath funds for several hundred. In the chantries, where such services were performed, there were neither enough priests nor enough altars to supply the demand.

People wanted more from the Church than the Church could possibly give them. Humanists condemned visits to the shrines as superstitious; pilgrims demanded that the relics be made more accessible. Reformers complained of pluralism; the clergy complained that they could not live on the salary of a single office. Civic authorities demanded that the established Church take greater responsibility for good works; the pope demanded that civic authorities help pay for them.

Contradiction and paradox dominated the movements for reform. Though the most vocal critics of the Church complained that its discipline was too lax, for many ordinary people its demands were too rigorous. The obligations of penance and confession weighed heavily upon them. Church doctrine held that sins had to be washed away before the souls of the dead could enter heaven. Until then they suffered in purgatory. Sins were cleansed through penance, the performance of acts of contrition assigned after confession. But the ordeal of confession kept many people away. "Have you skipped mass? Have you dressed proudly? Have you thought of committing adultery? Have you insulted or cursed your parents?" These were just a few of the uncomfortable questions that priests were instructed to pose in confession. In towns merchants were asked about their trading practices, shopkeepers about the quality of their goods. Magistrates were questioned about their attitudes to the clergy, intellectuals about their attitudes to the pope.

Thus it is hardly surprising that the sale of indulgences became a popular substitute for penance and confession. An indulgence was a portion of the treasury of good works performed by righteous Christians throughout the ages. They could be granted to those who desired to atone for their sins. Strictly speaking, an indulgence supplemented penance rather than substituted for it. It was effective only for the contrite—for sinners who repented of their sins. But as the practice of granting indulgences spread, this subtle distinction largely disappeared. The living bought indulgences to cleanse the sins of the dead, and some even bought indulgences in anticipation of sins they had not yet committed.

By the sixteenth century, to limit abuses by local church authorities, only the pope, through his agents, could grant indulgences. Popes used special occasions to offer an indulgence for pilgrimages to Rome or for contributions to special papal projects. Other indulgences were licensed locally, usually at the shrines of saints or at churches that contained relics.

The indulgence controversy was a symptom rather than a cause of the explosion of feelings that erupted in the small German town of Wittenberg in the year 1517. In that year the pope was offering an indulgence to help finance the rebuilding of Saint Peter's Basilica in Rome. The pope chose Prince Albert of Brandenburg (1490–1545) to distribute the indulgence in Germany, and Albert hired the Dominican friar Johann Tetzel (ca. 1465–1519) to preach its benefits. Tetzel offered little warning about the theological niceties of indulgences to those who paid to mitigate their own sins or alleviate the suffering of their ancestors in purgatory.

Enthusiasm for the indulgence spread to the neighboring state of Saxony, where the ruler, Frederick III, the Wise (1463–1525), banned its sale. Frederick's great collection of relics carried their own indulgences, and Tetzel offered welcome competition. But Saxons flocked into Brandenburg to make their purchases, and by the end of October, Tetzel was not very far from Wittenberg Castle, where Frederick's relics were housed. On All Saints' Day the relics would be opened to view and, with the harvest done, one of the largest crowds of the year would gather to see them. On the night before, Martin Luther (1483–1546), a professor of theology at Wittenberg University, posted on the door of the castle church 95 theses attacking indulgences and their sale.

Other than the timing of Luther's action, there was nothing unusual about the posting of theses. In the Scholastic tradition of disputation, scholars presented propositions, or theses, for debate and challenged all comers to argue with them in a public forum. Luther's theses were controversial, but as that was the whole point of offering them for discussion, they were meant to be. Only circumstance moved Luther's theses from the academic to the public sphere. Already there was growing concern among clergy and theologians about Tetzel's blatant sale of indulgences. Hordes of purchasers believed that they were buying unconditional remission of sin. Individual priests and monks began to sound the alarm: An indulgence without contrition was worthless.

Luther's theses focused this concern and finally communnicated it beyond the walls of the Church and university. The theses were immediately translated into German and spread throughout the Holy Roman Empire by humanists who had long criticized practices such as the sale of indulgences as superstitious. Prospective buyers became wary; past purchasers became angry. They had been duped again by the Church and by the Italian pope who cared nothing for honest hard-working Germans. But Prince Albert and the pope needed the income. They could not stand by while sales collapsed and anticlerical and antipapal sentiment grew.

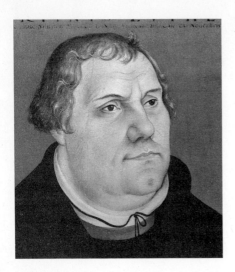

Martin Luther

The Faith of Martin Luther

Martin Luther was not a man to challenge lightly. Although he was only an obscure German professor, he had already marked himself out to all who knew him. In his youth Luther was an exceptionally able student whose father sent him to the best schools in preparation for a career in law. But against the wishes of his father he entered an Augustinian monastery, wholeheartedly followed the strict program of his order, and was ordained a priest in 1507. He received his doctorate at the university in Wittenberg and was appointed to the theology faculty in 1512.

Luther attracted powerful patrons in the university and gained a reputation as an outstanding teacher. He began to be picked for administrative posts and became overseer of 11 Augustinian monasteries. His skills in disputation were widely recognized and he was sent to Rome to argue a case on behalf of his order. He fulfilled each task beyond expectation. In all outward appearances Luther was successful and contented.

But beneath this tranquil exterior lay a soul in torment. As he rose in others' estimation, he sank in his own. Through beating and fasting he mortified his flesh. Through vigil and prayer he nourished his soul. Through study and contemplation he honed his intellect. Still he could find no peace. Despite his devotion, he could not erase his sense of sin; he could not convince himself that he could achieve the righteousness God demanded of him.

Salvation came to Luther through study. His internal agonies led him to ponder over and over again the biblical passages that described the righteousness of God. In the intellectual tradition in which he had been trained, that righteousness was equated with law. The righteous person either followed God's law or was punished by God's wrath. It was this understanding that tormented him. "I thought that I had to perform good works till at last through them Jesus would become a friend and gracious to me." But no amount of good works could overcome Luther's feelings of guilt for his sins. Almost from the moment he began lecturing in 1512 he searched for the key to the freedom of his own soul.

Even before he wrote his Ninety-five Theses, Luther had made the first breakthrough by a unique reading of the writings of Saint Paul.

> *"I pondered night and day until I understood the connection between the righteousness of God and the sentence 'The just shall live by faith.' Then I grasped that the justice of God is the righteousness by which through grace and pure mercy, God justifies us through faith. Immediately I felt that I had been reborn and that I had passed through wide open doors into paradise!"*

Finally he realized that the righteousness of God was a gift freely given to the faithful. To receive God's righteousness one only had to believe in God's infinite mercy. It was this belief that fortified Luther during his years of struggle with both civil and church powers.

Over the next several years, Luther refined his spiritual philosophy and drew out the implications of his newfound beliefs. His religion was shaped by three interconnected tenets. First came justification by faith alone—*sola fide*. An individual's everlasting salvation came from faith in God's goodness rather than from the performance of good works. Sin could not be washed away by penance, and it could not be forgiven by indulgence. Second, faith came only through the knowledge and contemplation of the Word of God—*sola scriptura*. All that was needed to understand the justice and mercy of God was contained in the Bible. Reading the Word, hearing the Word, expounding upon and studying the Word, this was the path to faith and through faith to salvation. Finally, all who believed in God's righteousness and had achieved their faith through the study of the Bible were equal in God's eyes. The priesthood was of all believers. Each followed his or her own calling and found his or her own faith through Scripture. Ministers and preachers could help others learn God's Word, but they could not confer faith.

Luther's spiritual rebirth and the theology that developed from it posed a fundamental challenge to the Roman Catholic church. Though for centuries the Church had met doctrinal challenges and had absorbed many seemingly unorthodox ideas, Luther's theology could not be among them. It struck too deeply at the roots of belief, practice, and structure. Yet for all of the transforming power of these apparently simple ideas, it was not Luther alone who initiated the reform of religion. His obsession with salvation was based on the same impulse that had made indulgences so popular. Justification by faith alone provided an alternative to the combination of works and faith that many Roman Catholics found too difficult to fulfill. Luther's insistence that faith comes only through the study of the Word of God was facilitated by the new learning and the invention of printing. The printing press prepared the ground for the dissemination of his thought as much as it disseminated it. This was a contribution of the Renaissance. Luther's hope for the creation of a spiritual elite, confirmed in their faith and confident of their salvation, readily appealed to the citizens of hundreds of German towns who had already made of themselves a social and economic elite. This was a contribution of the growth of towns. The idea of the equality of all believers meant that all were equally responsible for fulfilling God's commandments. This set secular rulers on an equal footing with the pope at a moment in Western history when they were already challenging papal power in matters of both church and state. This was a contribution of the formation of states. For all his painful soul-searching, Luther embodied the culmination of changes of which he was only dimly aware.

Lutheranism

The first to feel the seriousness of Luther's challenge to the established order was the reformer himself. The head of his order, a papal legate, and finally the Emperor Charles V all called for Luther to recant his views on indulgences. To all he gave the same infuriating reply that he made to the emperor at the Diet of Worms in 1521: If he could be shown the places in the Bible that contradicted his views he would gladly change them. In fact, during the three years between the posting of his theses and his appearance before the emperor, Luther came to conclusions much more radical than his initial attack on indulgences. He came to believe that the papacy was a human rather than a divine invention. Therefore he denounced both the papacy and the general councils of the Church. In his *Address to the Christian Nobility of the German Nation* (1520) he called upon the princes to take the reform of religion into their own hands. In 1521 the pope excommunicated him and Charles V declared him an enemy of the empire. In both church and state he was now an outlaw.

But Luther had attracted powerful supporters as well as powerful enemies. Prince Frederick III of Saxony consistently intervened on his behalf, and the delicate international situation forced Luther's chief antagonists to move more slowly than they might have wished. The pope hoped first to keep Charles V off the imperial throne and then to maintain a united front with the German princes against him. Charles V, already locked in his lifelong struggle with the French, needed German military support and peace in his German territories. These factors consistently played into Luther's hands.

While pope and emperor were otherwise occupied, Luther refined his ideas and thus was able to hold his own in the theological debates in which he won important converts. More importantly, as time passed Luther's reputation grew, not only in Germany, but all over Europe. Between 1517 and 1520 he published 30 works, all of which achieved massive sales. Yet Luther alone could not sustain what came to be called Lutheranism. The Roman Catholic church had met heresy before and knew how to deal with it. What turned Luther's theology into a movement, which after 1529 came to be known as Protestantism, was the support he received among German princes and within German cities.

There were many reasons why individual princes turned to Luther's theology. First and foremost was sincere religious conviction. Matters of the hereafter were a pressing concern in a world in which the average life span was 30 years and nearly all natural phenomena were inexplicable. And they were more pressing still among the educated elites infected by the new learning and self-confident of their power to reason critically. Yet there were secular reasons as well. The formation of large states had provided a model for civil government. On a smaller scale, German princes worked to centralize their administration, protect themselves from predatory neighbors, and increase their revenues. They had long suffered under the burden of papal exactions. Taxes and gifts flowed south to a papacy dominated by Italians. Luther's call for civil rulers to lead their own churches meant that civil rulers could keep their own revenues.

The Reformation spread particularly well in the German cities, especially those that the emperor had granted the status of freedom from the rule of any prince. Once Protestant ideas were established entire towns adopted them. The cities had long struggled with the tension of the separate jurisdictions of state and church. Much urban property was owned by the Church, and thus exempt from taxation and law enforcement, and the clergy constituted a significant proportion of urban populations. Reformed religion stressed the equality of clergy and laity and thus the indisputable power of civil authorities. Paradoxically, it was because the cities contained large numbers of priests that Luther's ideas reached them quickly. Many of his earliest students served urban congregations and began to develop doctrines and practices that, though based on Luther's ideas, were adapted to the circumstances of city life. The reform clergy became integrated into the life of the city in a way that the Catholic clergy had not. They married the daughters of citizens, became citizens themselves, and trained their children in the guilds. Moreover, the imperial free cities were also the center of the printing trade and home to many of the most noted humanists who were initially important in spreading Luther's ideas.

Luther's message held great appeal for the middle orders in the towns. While it was necessary for the leader of a state to support reform if it was to survive, in the cities it was the petty burghers, lesser merchants, tradespeople, and artisans who led the movements that ultimately gained the approval of city governments. These groups resented the privileges given to priests and members of religious orders who paid no taxes and were exempt from the obligations of citizenship. The level of anticlericalism, always high in Germany, was especially acute in cities that were suffering economic difficulties. Pressure from ordinary people and petty traders forced town leaders into action. The evangelism of reforming ministers created converts and an atmosphere of reform. Support from members of the ruling oligarchy both mobilized these pressures and capitalized on them. Town governments secured their own autonomy over the Church, tightening their grip on the institutions of social control and enhancing the social and economic authority of their members. Once Protestant, city governments took over many of the functions of the religious houses, often converting them into schools or hostels for the poor. Former monks were allowed to enter trades. Former nuns were encouraged to marry. Luther himself married an ex-nun after the dissolution of her convent.

Religious reform appealed to women as well as men, but it affected them differently. Noblewomen were among the most important defenders of Protestant reformers, especially in states in which the prince opposed it. Marguerite of Navarre (1492–1549), sister of Francis I, frequently intervened with her brother on behalf of individual Lutherans who fell afoul of church authorities. She created her own court in the south of France and stocked it with both humanists and Protestants. Her devotional poem, *Mirror of the Sinful Soul* (1533), inspired women reformers and was translated into English by Elizabeth I. Mary of Hungary (1505–1558) served a similar role in the Holy Roman Empire. Sister of both Charles V and Ferdinand I, queen of Hungary and later regent of the Netherlands, she acted as patron to Hungarian reformers. Though Mary was more humanist than Protestant, Luther dedicated an edition of Psalms to her, and she read a number of his works. Her independent religious views infuriated both of her brothers. Bona, wife of Sigismund I of Poland, was especially important in eastern reform. An Italian by birth, Bona (1493–1558) was a central figure in spreading both Renaissance art and humanist learning into Poland. She became one of the largest independent landowners in the state and initiated widespread agricultural and economic reforms. Her private confessor was one of Poland's leading Protestants.

Luther's reforms also offered much to women who were not so highly placed in society. The doctrine of the equality of all believers put men and

Marguerite of Navarre. She created her own court in the south of France and stocked it with both humanists and Protestants. Her devotional poem, Mirror of the Sinful Soul *(1533), inspired women reformers.*

women on an equal spiritual footing even if it did nothing to break the male monopoly of the ministry. But the most important difference that Protestantism made to ordinary women was in the private rather than the public sphere. Family life became the center of faith when salvation was removed from the control of the Church. Luther's marriage led him to a deeper appreciation of the importance of the wife and mother in the family's spirituality.

By following humanist teaching on the importance of educating women of the upper orders and by encouraging literacy, the reformers did much that was uplifting. Girls' schools were founded in a number of German cities and townswomen could use their newly acquired skills in their roles as shopkeepers, family accountants, and teachers of their children. But there were losses as well as gains. The attack on the worship of saints and especially of the Virgin Mary removed female images from religion. Protestantism was male dominated in a way that Catholicism was not. Moreover, the emphasis on reading the Bible tended to reinforce the image of women as weak and inherently sinful. The dissolution of the convents took away the one institution that valued their gender and allowed them to pursue a spiritual life outside marriage.

The Spread of Lutheranism

By the end of the 1520s the empire was divided between cities and states that accepted reformed religion and those that adhered to Roman Catholicism. Printing presses, traveling merchants, and hordes of students who claimed—not always accurately—to have attended Luther's lectures or sermons spread the message. Large German communities across northern Europe, mostly founded as trading outposts, became focal points for the penetration of reformist ideas. In Livonia the Teutonic Knights established a Lutheran form of worship that soon took hold all along the shores of the Baltic. Lutheran-inspired reformers seized control of the Polish port city of Gdańsk, which they held for a short time, while neighboring Prussia officially established a Lutheran church. Polish translations of Luther's writings were disseminated into Poland-Lithuania, and Protestant communities were established as far south as Kraków.

Merchants and students carried Luther's ideas into Scandinavia, but there the importance of political leaders was crucial. Christian III (1534–1559) of Denmark had been present at the Diet of Worms when Luther made his famous reply to Charles V. Christian was deeply impressed by the reformer, and after a ruinous civil war, he confiscated Catholic church property in Denmark and created a reformed religion under Luther's direct supervision.

Paradoxically, Lutheranism came to Sweden as part of an effort to throw off the yoke of Danish dominance. Here, too, direct connection with Luther provided the first impulses. Olaus Petri (1493–1552) had studied at Wittenberg and returned to preach Lutheran doctrine among the large German merchant community in Stockholm. He was a trained humanist who used both Erasmus's Greek New Testament and Luther's German one to prepare his Swedish translation (1526). When Gustav I Vasa (1523–1560) led a successful uprising against the Danes and became king of Sweden, he encouraged the spread of Protestant ideas and allowed Petri to continue his translations of the mass and the Lutheran service.

Luther's impact extended into central Europe. Bohemia had had a reforming tradition of its own that antedated Luther. Though the teachings of Jan Hus (1373–1415) had been condemned by the Catholic church, Hussitism was in fact the all but established religion in most parts of Bohemia. Ferdinand was bound by law to allow its moderate practice. Hussites had already initiated many of the reforms insisted upon by Luther: The mass was said in Czech, and the Bible had been translated into the vernacular. Hussites believed that communion in both forms was mandated by the Bible. This was the real issue that separated them from Roman Catholics, for the Hussites refused to accept the traditional view that the authority of either the pope or the general council of the Church could alter God's command. On all these issues, Hussites and Lutherans shared a common program. But the Hussites were conservative in almost everything else. While the German communities in Bohemia accepted the core of Lutheran doctrine, most Czechs rejected justification by faith alone and maintained their own practices.

As important as Protestant ideas were in northern and central Europe, it was in the Swiss towns of the empire that they proved most fertile. Here was planted the second generation of reformers, theologians who drew radical new conclusions from Luther's insights. In the east, Huldrych Zwingli (1484–1531) brought reformed religion to the town of Zurich. Educated at the University of Basel and deeply influenced by humanist thought early in his career, Zwingli was a preacher among the Swiss mercenary troops that fought for the empire. In 1516 he met Erasmus in Basel and under his influence began a study of the Greek writings of the Church Fathers and of the New Testament. Zwingli was also influenced by reports of Luther's defiance of the pope, for his own antipapal views were already developing. Perhaps most decisively for his early development, in 1519 Zwingli was stricken by plague. In his life-and-death struggle he came to a profoundly personal realization of the power of God's mercy.

These experiences became the basis for the reform theology Zwingli preached in Zurich. He believed that the Church had to recover its earlier purity and to reject the innovations in practices brought in by successive popes and general councils. He stressed the equality of believers, justification by faith alone, and the sufficiency of the gospel as authority for church practice. He attacked indulgences, penance, clerical celibacy, prayers to the Virgin, statues and images in churches, and a long list of other abuses. He also stressed that the mass was to be viewed as a cemmemorative event rather than one which involved the real presence of Christ. He preferred to call the service the Lord's Supper. His arguments were so effective that the town council adopted them as the basis for a reform of religion.

The principles Zwingli preached quickly spread to neighboring Swiss states. He participated in formal religious disputations in Bern and Basel. In both places his plea for a simple unadorned religious practice met widespread approval. Practical as well as theological, Zwingli's reforms were carried out by the civil government with which he allied himself. This was not the same as the protection that princes had given to Lutherans. Rather, in the places that came under Zwingli's influence, there was an important integration of church and state. He stressed the divine origins of civil government and the importance of the magistrate as an agent of Christian reform: "A church without the magistrate is mutilated and incomplete." This theocratic idea—that the leaders of the state and the leaders of the church were linked—became the basis for further social and political reform.

*T*he Protestant Reformation

By the middle of the 1530s Protestant reform had entered a new stage. Luther did not intend to form a new religion; his struggle had been with Rome. Before he could build he had to tear down—his religion was one of protest. Most of his energy was expended in attack and counterattack. The second generation of reformers faced a different task. The new reformers were the church builders who had to systematize doctrine for a generation that had already accepted religious reform. Their challenge was to draw out the logic of reformed ideas and to create enduring structures for reformed churches. The problems they faced were as much institutional as doctrinal. How was the new church to be governed in the absence of the traditional hierarchy? How could discipline be enforced when members of the reformed community went astray? What was the proper relationship between the community of believers and civil authority? Whatever the failings of the Roman Catholic church, it had ready answers to these critical questions.

Geneva and Calvin

The Reformation came late to Geneva. In the sixteenth century Geneva was under the dual government of the Duchy of Savoy and the Catholic bishop of the town, who was frequently a Savoy client. The Genevans also had their own town council, which traditionally struggled for power against the bishop. By the 1530s the council had gained the upper hand. The council confiscated church lands and institutions, secularized the Church's legal powers, and forced the bishop and most of his administrators to flee the city. War with Savoy inevitably followed and Geneva would certainly have been crushed into submission except for its alliance with neighboring Bern, a potent military power among the Swiss towns. Geneva was saved and was free to follow its own course in religious matters. In 1536 the adult male citizens of the city voted to become Protestant. But as yet there was no reformer in Geneva to establish a Protestant program and no clear definition of what that program might be.

Martin Luther had started out to become a lawyer and ended up a priest. John Calvin started out to become a priest and ended up a lawyer. The difference tells much about each man. Calvin (1509–1564) was born in France, the son of a bishop's secretary. His education was based on humanist principles, and he learned Greek and Hebrew, studied theology, and received a legal degree from the University of Orléans. Around the age of twenty he converted to Lutheranism. Francis I had determined to root Protestants out of France and Calvin fled Paris. Persecution of Protestants continued in France and one of Calvin's close friends was burned for heresy. These events left an indelible impression on him. In 1535 he left France for Basel, where he wrote and published the first edition of his *Institutes of the Christian Religion* (1536), a defense of French Protestants against persecution. Calvin returned briefly to France to wind up his personal affairs, and then decided to settle in Strasbourg, where he could retire from public affairs and live out his days as a scholar.

To Calvin, providence guided all human action. He could have no better evidence for this belief than what happened next. War between France and the empire clogged the major highways to Strasbourg. Soldiers constantly menaced travelers, and Protestants could expect the worst from both sides. Thus Calvin and his companions detoured through Geneva, where Guillaume Farel (1489–1565), one of Geneva's leading Protestant reformers, implored Calvin to remain in Geneva and lead its reformation. Calvin was not interested. Farel tried every means of persuasion he knew until, in exasperation, Farel declared "that God would curse my retirement if I should withdraw and refuse to help when the necessity was so urgent." For a quarter of a century, Calvin labored to bring order to the Genevan church.

Calvin's greatest contributions to religious reform came in church structure and discipline. He had studied the writings of the first generation of reformers and accepted without question justification by faith alone and the biblical foundation of religious authority. Like Luther and Zwingli he believed that salvation came from God's grace. But more strongly than his predecessors he believed that the gift of faith was granted only to some and that each individual's salvation or damnation was predestined before birth. The doctrine of predestination was a traditional one, but Calvin emphasized it differently and brought it to the center of the problem of faith. "Many are called but few are chosen," Calvin quoted from the Bible. Those who were predestined to salvation were obliged to govern; those who were predestined to damnation were obliged to be governed.

Calvin structured the institution of the Genevan church in four parts. First were the pastors who preached the Word to their congregations. While the pastors preached, the doctors, the second element in Calvin's church, studied

This painting shows a Calvinist service in Lyon, France, in 1564. The sexes are segregated and the worshipers are seated according to rank. An hourglass times the preacher's sermon.

and wrote. Deacons, the third element in Calvin's four-part structure, were laymen chosen by the congregation to oversee the institutions of social welfare, such as hospitals and schools, run by the church. The last element were the elders of the church, who were its governors in all moral matters. They were the most controversial part of Calvin's establishment and the most fundamental. They had the power to discipline. Chosen from among the elite of the city, the 12 elders enforced the strict Calvinist moral code that extended into all aspects of private life. Sexual offenses were the most common. Adultery and fornication were vigorously suppressed and prostitutes, who had nearly become a recognized guild in the early sixteenth century, were expelled from Geneva.

The structure that Calvin gave to the Genevan church soon became the basis for reforms throughout the Continent. The Calvinist church was self-governing, independent of the state, and therefore capable of surviving and even flourishing in a hostile environment. Expanded in several subsequent editions, *The Institutes of the Christian Religion* became the most influential work of Protestant theology. It had begun as an effort to extend Protestantism to Calvin's homeland, and waves of Calvinist-educated pastors returned to France in the mid sixteenth century and established churches along Calvinist lines. Calvinism spread north to the Low Countries, where it became the basis for Dutch Protestantism, and east, where it flourished in Lithuania. It reached places untouched by Luther and revitalized reform where Lutheranism had been suppressed. Perhaps its greatest impact was in Britain, where the reformation took place not once but twice.

The English Reformation

The king of England wanted a divorce. Henry VIII had been married to Catherine of Aragon (1485–1536) as long as he had been king and she had borne him no male heir to carry on his line. She had given birth to six children and endured several miscarriages, yet only one daughter, Mary, survived. Nothing so important as the lack of a male heir could happen by accident, and Henry came to believe that it was God's punishment for his marriage. Catherine had been married first to Henry's older brother, who had died as a teenager, and there was at least one scriptural prohibition against marrying a brother's wife. A papal dispensation had been provided for the marriage, and now Henry wanted a papal dispensation for an annulment. For three years his case ground its way through the papal courts. Catherine of Aragon was the aunt of the Emperor Charles V, and the emperor had taken her side in the controversy. With imperial power in Italy at its height, the pope was content to hear all of the complex legal and biblical precedents argued at leisure.

By 1533 Henry could wait no longer. He had already impregnated Anne Boleyn (ca. 1507–1536), one of the ladies-in-waiting at his court, and if the child—which Henry was certain would be a boy—was to be legitimate, a marriage would have to take place at once. Legislation was prepared in Parliament to prevent papal interference in the decisions of England's courts, and Thomas Cranmer (1489–1556), archbishop of Canterbury, England's highest ecclesiastical officer, agreed to annul Henry's first marriage and celebrate his second. This was the first step in a complete break with Rome. Under the guidance of Thomas Cromwell (ca. 1485–1540), the English Parliament passed statute after statute that made Henry supreme head of the church in England and owner of its vast wealth. Monasteries were dissolved and a Lutheran service was introduced. On 7 September 1533, Anne Boleyn gave birth not to the expected son, but to a daughter, the future Queen Elizabeth I.

Henry's reformation was an act of state, but the English Reformation was not. There was an English tradition of dissent from the Roman church that stretched back to the fourteenth century. Anticlericalism was especially virulent in the towns, where citizens refused to pay fees to priests for performing services like burial. And humanist ideas flourished in England, where Thomas More, John Colet, and a host of others supported both the new learning and its efforts to reform spiritual life. Luther's attack on ritual and the mass and his emphasis on Scripture and faith echoed the lost Lollard program and found many recruits in London and the northern port towns.

Protestantism grew slowly in England because it was vigorously repressed. Like Francis I and Charles V, Henry VIII viewed actual attacks on the established church as potential attacks on the established state. Henry had earned the title Defender of the Faith from the pope in 1521 for authoring an attack on Luther. The first published English translation of the New Testament, made by William Tyndale in 1525, had to be smuggled into England. As sensitivity to the abuses of the Church grew and Lutheran ideas spread, official persecution sharpened.

Henry's divorce unleashed a groundswell of support for religious change. The king's own religious beliefs remained a secret, but Anne Boleyn and Thomas Cromwell sponsored Lutheran reforms and Thomas Cranmer put them into practice. Religion was legislated through Parliament and the valuable estates of the Church were sold to the gentry. These practices found favor with both the legal profession and the landed elites and made Protestantism more palatable among these conservative groups. It was in the reign of Edward VI (1547–1553), Henry's son by his third wife, that the central doctrinal and devotional changes were made. Church service was now conducted in English and the first two English Prayer Books were created. The mass was reinterpreted along Zwinglian lines and became the Lord's Supper, the altar became the communion table, and the priest became the minister. Preaching became the center of the church service, and concern over the education of learned ministers resulted in commissions to examine and reform the clergy.

Beginning in the 1530s, state repression turned against Catholics. Those who would not swear the new oaths of allegiance or recognize the legality of Henry VIII's marriage suffered for their beliefs as the early Protestants had suffered for theirs. Thomas More and over forty others paid with their lives for their opposition. An uprising in the north in 1536, known as the Pilgrimage of Grace, posed the most serious threat to the English Crown since the Wars of the Roses. Henry's ability to suppress the Pilgrimage of Grace owed more to his political power than to the conversion of his governing classes to Protestantism. Catholicism continued to flourish in England, surviving underground during the reigns of Henry and Edward, and reemerging under Mary I (1553–1558).

Mary Tudor was her mother's child. The first woman to rule England, she held to the Catholic beliefs in which Catherine of Aragon had raised her, and she vowed to bring the nation back to her mother's church. She reestablished papal sovereignty, abolished Protestant worship, and introduced a crash program of education in the universities to train a new generation of priests. The one thing that Mary could not achieve was restoration of monastic properties and church lands. They had been scattered irretrievably and any attempt at confiscation from the landed elite would surely have been met with insurrection. Catholic retribution for the blood of their martyrs was not long in coming. Cranmer and three other bishops were burned for heresy.

Nearly eight hundred Protestants fled the country rather than suffer a similar fate. These Marian exiles, as they came to be called, settled in a number of reformed communities, Zurich, Frankfurt, and Geneva among them. There they imbibed the second generation of Protestant ideas, especially Calvinism, and from there they began a propaganda campaign to keep reformed religion alive in England. It was the Marian exiles who were chiefly responsible for the second English reformation, which began in 1558 when Mary died and her half sister, Elizabeth I (1558–1603), came to the throne.

Under Elizabeth, England returned to Protestantism, but what was reestablished was not what had come before. Even the most advanced reforms during Edward's reign now seemed too moderate for the returning exiles. Against Elizabeth's wishes the English church adopted the Calvinist doctrine of predestination and the simplification (but not wholesale reorganization) of the structure of the church. But it did not become a model of thoroughgoing reformation. The Thirty-nine Articles (1563) continued the English tradition of compromising points of disrupted doctrine and of maintaining traditional practices wherever possible.

The Reformation of the Radicals

Schism breeds schism. That was the stick with which Catholic church and civil authorities beat Luther from the beginning. By attacking the authority of the established church and flouting the authority of the established state he was fomenting social upheaval. But he insisted that his own ideas buttressed rather than subverted authority, especially civil authority under whose protection he had placed the Church. As early as 1525 peasants in Swabia appealed to Luther for support in their social rebellion. They based some of their most controversial demands, such as the abolition of tithes and labor service, on biblical authority. Luther instructed the rebels to lay down their arms and await their just rewards in heaven. But Luther's ideas had a life of their own. He clashed with Erasmus over free will and with Zwingli over the mass. Toward the end of his life he felt he was holding back the floodgates against the second generation of Protestant thinkers. Time and again serious reformers wanted to take one or another of his doctrines further than he was willing to go himself. The water was seeping in everywhere.

The most dangerous threat to the establishment of an orthodox Protestantism came from groups who were described, not very precisely, as Anabaptists. Though it identified people who practiced adult baptism—literally "baptism again"—the label was mainly used to tar religious opponents with the brush of extremism. Anabaptists appeared in a number of German and Swiss towns in the 1520s. Taking seriously the doctrine of justification by faith, Anabaptists argued that only believers could be members of the true church of God. Those who were not of God could not be members of his church. As baptism was the sacrament through which entry into the church took place, Anabaptists reasoned that it was a sacrament for adults rather than infants. But infant baptism was a core doctrine for both Catholics and Protestants. It symbolized the acceptance of Christ and without it eternal salvation was impossible. It was a practical doctrine. Unbaptized infants who died could not be accepted in heaven, and infant mortality was appallingly common.

Thus the doctrine of Anabaptism posed a psychological as well as a doctrinal threat to the reformers. But the practice of adult baptism paled in significance to many of the other conclusions that religious radicals derived from the principle of *sola scriptura*—by the Word alone. Some groups argued the case that since true Christians were only those who had faith, all others must be cast out of the church. These true Christians formed small separate sects. Many believed that their lives were guided by the Holy Spirit who directed them from within. Some went further and denied the power of civil authority over true believers. Some argued for the community of goods among believers and rejected private property. Others literally followed passages in the Old Testament that suggested polygamy and promiscuity.

Wherever they settled, these small bands of believers were persecuted to the brutal extent of the laws of heresy. Catholics burned them, Protestants drowned them, and they were stoned and clubbed out of their communities. There was enough substance in their ideas and enough sincerity in their patient sufferings that they continued to recruit followers as they were driven from town to town, from Germany into the Swiss cities, from Switzerland into Bohemia and Hungary.

There on the eastern edges of the empire the largest groups of Anabaptists finally settled. Though all practiced adult baptism, only some held goods in common or remained pacifist. Charismatic leaders such as Balthasar Hubmaier (1485–1528) and Jacob Hutter (d. 1536) spread Anabaptism to Moravia in southern Bohemia, where they converted a number of the nobility to their views. They procured land for their communities, which came to be known as the Moravian Brethren. Independent groups existed in England and throughout northwest Europe, where Menno Simons (1496–1561), a Dutch Anabaptist, spent his life organizing bands of followers who came to be known as Mennonites.

The Catholic Reformation

Like a rolling wave, Protestant reform slapped up across the face of Europe, but the rock of the Roman Catholic church endured. Though pieces of the universal church crumbled away, in northern Germany, Switzerland, Bohemia, Scandinavia, England, and Scotland, the dense mass remained in southern Germany, Italy, Poland-Lithuania, Spain, France, and Ireland. Catholics felt the same impulses toward a more fulfilling religious life as Protestants and complained of the same abuses of clerical, state, and papal powers. But the Catholic response was to reform the church from within. A new personal piety was stressed, which led to the founding of additional spiritual orders. The ecclesiastical hierarchy became more concerned with pastoral care and initiated reforms of the clergy at the parish level. The challenge of converting other races, Asians and Amerindians especially, led to the formation of missionary orders and to a new emphasis on preaching and education. Protestantism itself revitalized Catholicism.

The Catholic Revival

The quest for individual spiritual fulfillment dominated later medieval Roman Catholicism. Erasmus, Luther, and Zwingli were all influenced by a Catholic spiritual movement known as the New Piety. It was propagated in Germany by the Brethren of the Common Life, a lay organization that stressed the importance of personal meditation on the life of Christ. The *Imitation of Christ* (1427), the central text of the New Piety, commonly attributed to Thomas à Kempis (1379–1471), was among the most influential works of the later Middle Ages. The Brethren taught that a Christian life should be lived according to Christ's dictates as expressed in the Sermon on the Mount. They instructed their pupils to lead a simple ascetic life with personal devotion at its core. These were the lessons that the young Erasmus found so liberating and the young Luther so stifling.

The New Piety with its emphasis on a simple personal form of religious practice was a central influence on Christian humanism. It is important to realize that humanism developed within the context of Catholic education and that many churchmen embraced the new learning and supported educational reform or patronized works of humanist scholarship. The Polyglot Bible was organized by Cardinal Jiménez de Cisneros (1436–1517), Archbishop of Toledo and Primate of Spain. The greatest educational reformer in England, John Colet (1467–1519), was dean of Saint Paul's, London's cathedral church. Without any of his famed irony, Erasmus dedicated his Greek Bible to the pope. The leading Christian humanists remained within the Catholic church even after many of their criticisms formed the basis of Protestant reforms.

This combination of piety and humanism imbued the ecclesiastical reforms initiated by church leaders. Archbishop Jiménez de Cisneros, who also served as inquisitor-general of the Spanish Inquisition, undertook a wide-ranging reorganization of Spanish religious life in the late fifteenth century. Though not every project was successful, Jiménez de Cisneros's program took much of the sting out of Protestant attacks on clerical abuse, and there was never a serious Protestant movement in Spain.

The most influential reforming bishop was Gian Matteo Giberti (1495–1543) of Verona. Using his own frugal life as an example, Giberti rigorously enforced vows, residency, and the pastoral duties of the clergy. He founded almshouses to aid the poor and orphanages to house the homeless. In Verona Giberti established a printing press, which turned out editions of the central works of Roman Catholicism, especially the writings of Augustine.

The most important indication of the reforming spirit within the Roman church was the foundation of new religious orders in the early sixteenth century. Devotion to a spiritual life of sacrifice was the chief characteristic of the lay and clerical orders that had flourished throughout the Middle Ages. In one French diocese, the number of clergy quadrupled in the last half of the fifteenth century, and while entrants to the traditional orders of Franciscans and Dominicans did not rise as quickly, the growth of lay communities like the Brethren of the Common Life attested to the continuing appeal of Catholic devotionalism.

Devotionalism was particularly strong in Italy where a number of new orders received papal charters. The Capuchins were founded by the Italian peasant Matteo de Bascio (ca. 1495–1552). He sought to follow the strictest rule of the life of Saint Francis of Assisi, a path that even the so-called Observant Franciscans had found too arduous. In contrast, the Theatines were established by a group of well-to-do Italian priests who also wished to lead a more austere devotional existence than was to be found in the traditional orders. Like the Capuchins they accepted a life of extreme poverty, in which even begging was only a last resort.

This spiritual revival spread all over Catholic Europe and was not limited to male orders. In Spain, Saint Teresa of Avila (1515–1582) led the reform of the Carmelites. She believed that women had to withdraw totally from the world around them in order to achieve true devotion. Against the wishes of the male superiors of her order she founded a convent to put her beliefs into practice and began writing devotional tracts like *The Way of Perfection* (1583). In 1535 Angela Merici (ca. 1474–1540) established another female order. The Ursulines were one of the most original of the new foundations, composed of young unmarried girls who remained with their families but lived chaste lives devoted to the instruction of other women.

Loyola's Pilgrimage

At first sight Saint Ignatius Loyola (1491–1556) appears an unlikely candidate to lead one of the most vital movements for religious reform in the sixteenth century. The thirteenth child of a Spanish noble family, Loyola trained for a military life in the service of Castile. In 1521 he was one of the garrison defenders when the French besieged Pamplona. A cannonball shattered his leg and he was carried home for a long enforced convalescence. There he slowly and carefully read the only books in the castle, a life of Christ and a history of the saints. His reading inspired him. Before he had sought glory and renown in battle. But when he compared the truly heroic deeds of the saints to his own vainglorious exploits, he decided to give his life over to spirituality.

Loyola was not a man to do things by halves. He resolved to model his life on the sufferings of the saints about whom he had read. He renounced his worldly goods and endured a year-long regimen of physical abstinence and spiritual nourishment in the town of Manresa. He deprived himself of food and sleep for long periods and underwent a regimen of seven hours of daily prayer, supplemented by nearly continuous religious contemplation. "But when he went to bed great enlightenment, great spiritual consolations often came to him, so that he lost much of the time he had intended for sleeping." During this period of intense concentration he first began to have visions, which later culminated in a mystical experience in which Christ called him directly to his service.

Like Luther, Loyola was tormented by his inability to achieve grace through penance, but unlike Luther he redoubled his efforts. At Manresa Loyola encountered the *Imitation of Christ*, which profoundly influenced his conversion. He recorded the techniques he used during this vigil in *The Spiritual Exercises*, which became a handbook for Catholic devotion. In 1523, crippled and barefoot, he made a pilgrimage to Jerusalem. He returned to Spain intent on becoming a priest.

By this time Loyola had taken on a distinctive appearance that attracted both followers and suspicion. Twice the Spanish ecclesiastical authorities summoned him to be examined for heresy. In 1528 he decided to complete his studies in France. Education in France brought with it a broadening of horizons that was so important in the movement Loyola was to found. He entered the same college Calvin had just left, and it is more than likely that he came into contact with the Protestant and humanist ideas which were then in vogue. Given his own devotional experiences, Protestantism held little attraction. While in France, Loyola and a small group of his friends decided to form a brotherhood after they became priests. They devoted themselves to the cure of souls and took personal vows of poverty, chastity, and obedience to the pope. On a pilgrimage to Rome, Loyola and his followers again attracted the attention of ecclesiastical authorities. Loyola explained his mission to them and in 1540 won the approval of Pope Paul III to establish a new holy order, the Society of Jesus.

Loyola's Society was founded at a time when the spiritual needs of the Church were being extended beyond the confines of Europe. Loyola volunteered his followers, who came to be known as Jesuits, to serve in the remotest parts of the world. One disciple, Francis Xavier (1506–1552), made converts to Catholicism in the Portuguese port cities in the East and then in India and Japan. Other Jesuits became missionaries to the New World, where they offered Christian consolation to the Amerindian communities. By 1556 the Society of Jesus had grown from 10 to 1000 and Loyola had become a full-time administrator in Rome.

Loyola never abandoned the military images that had dominated his youth. He enlisted his followers in military terms. The Jesuits were "soldiers of God" who served "beneath the banner of the Cross." Loyola's most fundamental innovation in these years was the founding of schools to train recruits for his order. Jesuit training was rigorous. Since they were being prepared for an active rather than a contemplative life, Jesuits were not cloistered during their training. Jesuit schools were opened to the laity, and lay education became one of the Jesuits' most important functions. Loyola lived to see the establishment of nearly a hundred colleges and seminaries and the spread of his order throughout the world. He died while at prayer.

The Counter-Reformation

The Jesuits were both the culmination of one wave of Catholic reform and the advance guard of another. They combined the piety and devotion that stretched from medieval mysticism through humanism, diocesan reforms, and the foundations of new spiritual orders. But they also represented an aggressive Catholic response that was determined to meet Protestantism head on and repel it. This was the Church militant. Old instruments like the Inquisition were revived, and new weapons like the Index of prohibited books were forged. But the problems of fighting Protestantism were not only those of combating Protestant ideas. Like oil and water, politics and religion failed to combine. Emperor Charles V and the hierarchy of the German church, where Protestantism was strong, demanded thoroughgoing reform of the Catholic church; the pope and the hierarchy of the Italian church, where Protestantism was weak, resisted the call. As head of the Catholic church, the pope was distressed by the spread of heresy in the lands of the empire. As head of a large Italian city-state, the pope was consoled by the weakening of the power of his Spanish rival. Brothers in Christ, pope and emperor were mortal enemies in everything else. Throughout the Catholic states of Germany came the urgent cry for a reforming council of the Church. But the voices were muffled as they crossed the Alps and made their way down the Italian peninsula.

At the instigation of the emperor, the first serious preparations for a general council of the church were made in the 1530s. The papacy warded it off. The complexities of international diplomacy were one factor—the French king was even less anxious to bring peace to the empire than the pope—and the complexities of papal politics were another. The powers of a general council in relation to the powers of the papacy had never been clarified. After the advent and spread of Protestantism, successive popes had little reason to believe that in this gravest crisis of all a council would be mindful of papal prerogatives. In fact, Catholic reformers were as bitter in their denunciations of papal abuses as Protestants. The second attempt to arrange a general council of the Church occurred in the early 1540s. Again the papacy warded it off.

These factors ensured that when a general council of the church did finally meet, its task would not be an easy one. The northern churches, French and German alike, wanted reforms of the papacy; the papacy wanted a restatement of orthodox doctrine. Many princes whose states were divided among Catholics and Protestants wanted compromises that might accommodate both. Ferdinand I, King of Bohemia, saw the council as an opportunity to bring the Hussites back into the fold. Charles V and the German bishops wanted the leading Protestant church authorities to offer their own compromises on doctrine that might form a basis for reuniting the empire. The papacy wanted traditional church doctrine reasserted.

The general council of the Church that finally met in Trent from 1545 to 1563 thus had nearly unlimited potential for disaster. It began in compromise—Trent was an Italian town under the government of the emperor—but ended in total victory for the views of the papacy. For all of the papacy's seeming weaknesses—the defections of England and the rich north German territories cut into papal revenues and Italy was under Spanish occupation—an Italian pope always held the upper hand at the council. Fewer than a third of the delegates came from outside Italy. The French looked upon the council suspiciously and played only a minor role, and the emperor forbade his bishops to attend after the council moved to Bologna.

Yet for all of these difficulties, the councillors at Trent made some real progress. They corrected a number of abuses, of which the sale of indulgences was the most substantive. They formulated rules for the better regulation of parish priests and stressed the obligation of priests and bishops to preach to their congregations. They ordered seminaries to be founded in all dioceses where there was not already a university so that priests could receive sufficient education to perform their duties. They prepared a new modern and uniform Catholic service and centralized and updated the Index of prohibited books to include Protestant writings from all over the Continent.

The Council of Trent made no concessions to Protestants, moderate or radical. The councillors upheld justification by faith and works over justification by faith alone. They confirmed the truth of Scripture and the traditions of the Church against Scripture alone. They declared the Vulgate the only acceptable text of the Bible and encouraged vast bonfires of Greek and Hebrew Scriptures in an effort to undo the great scholarly achievements of the humanists. They reaffirmed the seven sacraments and the doctrine of the miracle of the Eucharist. They upheld clerical celibacy. The redefinition of traditional Roman Catholicism drew the doctrinal lines clearly and ended

The Reformation and the Counter-Reformation

1517	Luther writes his Ninety-five Theses
1521	Luther is excommunicated and declared an enemy of the empire; Henry VIII receives title Defender of the Faith
1523	Zwingli expounds his faith in formal disputation
1533	Henry VIII divorces Catherine of Aragon, marries Anne Boleyn, and breaks with the church of Rome
1536	Calvin publishes *Institutes of the Christian Religion*
1540	Loyola receives papal approval for Society of Jesus
1545–1563	Council of Trent
1553	Mary I restores Catholicism in England
1563	Elizabeth I enacts the Thirty-nine Articles, which restores Protestantism to England

decades of confusion. But it also meant that the differences between Catholics and Protestants could now be settled only by the sword.

The Empire Strikes Back

Warfare dominated the reform of religion almost from its beginning. The burnings, drownings, and executions by which both Catholics and Protestants attempted to maintain religious purity were but raindrops compared to the sea of blood that was shed in sieges and on battlefields beginning in the 1530s. The Catholic divisions were clear. The empire continued to be engaged in the west with its archenemy France, and in the south with the ever expanding Ottoman Empire. Charles V needed not only peace within his own German realms, but positive support for his offensive and defensive campaigns. He could never devote his full resources to suppressing Protestant dissent.

Yet there was never a united Protestant front to suppress. The north German towns and principalities that accepted Lutheranism in the 1520s had had a long history of warfare among themselves. Princes stored up gievances from past wars and contested inheritances; cities stored up jealousies from commercial rivalries and special privileges. Added to this was the division between Luther and Zwingli over doctrinal issues that effectively separated the German and Swiss components of the Reformation from each other.

Though both the Protestant and the Catholic sides were internally weak, it was the greater responsibilities of Charles V that allowed for the uneasy periods of peace. Each pause gave the Protestant reformers new life. Lutheranism continued to spread in the northern part of the empire, Zwinglian

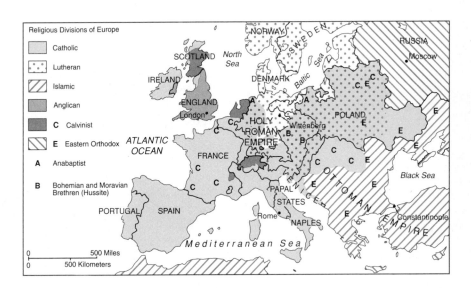

Religious divisions of Europe, ca. 1555

reform in the south. Charles V asked the papacy to convoke a general council and the Protestants to stop evangelizing in new territories. But Protestant leaders were no more capable of halting the spread of the Reformation than Catholics. Thus each violation of each uneasy truce seemed to prove treachery. In 1546, just after Luther's death, both sides raised armies in preparation for renewed fighting. In the first stage of war Charles V scored a decisive victory, capturing the two leading Protestant princes and conquering Saxony and Thuringia, the homeland of Lutheran reform.

Charles V's greatest victories were always preludes to his gravest defeats. The remaining Protestant princes were driven into the arms of the French, who placed dynastic interests above religious concerns. Again Europe was plunged into general conflict, with the French invading the German states from the west, the Turks from the south, and the Protestant princes from the north. Charles V, now an old and broken man, was forced to flee through the Alps in the dead of winter and was brought to the bargaining table soon after. By the Peace of Augsburg in 1555 the emperor agreed to allow the princes of Germany to establish the religion of their people. Protestant princes would govern Protestant states, and Catholic princes, Catholic states. The Peace of Augsburg ended 40 years of religious struggle in Germany.

In 1547 the then-victorious Charles V stood at the grave of Martin Luther. He had been buried in the shadow of the church in which he had been baptized, and now other shadows darkened his plot. Imperial troops were masters of all Saxony and were preparing to turn back the religious clock in Luther's homeland. The emperor was advised to have the body exhumed and burned, to carry out 25 years too late the Edict of Worms that had made Luther an outlaw from church and state. But Charles V was no longer the self-confident young emperor who had been faced down by the Saxon monk on that long-ago day. Popes had come and gone, and his warrior rivals Francis I and Henry VIII were both dead. He alone survived. He had little stomach for the petty revenge that he might now exact upon the man who more than any other had ruined whatever hope there might have been for a united empire dominant over all of Europe. "I do not make war on dead men," Charles declared as he turned away from the reformer's grave. But the ghosts of Luther and Zwingli, of Calvin and Ignatius of Loyola were not so easily laid. For another century they would haunt a Europe that could do nothing else but make war on dead men.

Suggestions for Further Reading

General Reading

*Owen Chadwick, *The Reformation* (London: Penguin, 1972). An elegant and disarmingly simple history of religious change.

*G. R. Elton, ed., *The New Cambridge Modern History Vol. II: The Reformation 1520–1559* (Cambridge, England: Cambridge University Press, 1958). A multiauthored study of the Protestant movement with sections on social and political life.

*Steven Ozment, *The Age of Reform 1250–1550* (New Haven, CT: Yale University Press, 1980). An important interpretation of an epoch of religious change.

*Lewis Spitz, *The Protestant Reformation 1517–1559* (New York: Harper & Row, 1985). A recent synthesis by a distinguished Reformation scholar.

The Intellectual Reformation

Roland Bainton, *Erasmus of Christendom* (New York: Scribner's, 1969). Still the best starting point and the most compelling biography.

Richard L. DeMolen, *Erasmus* (New York: St. Martin's Press, 1974). Selections from Erasmus's writings.

*E. Eisenstein, *The Printing Revolution in Early Modern Europe* (Cambridge, England: Cambridge University Press, 1983). An abridged edition of a larger work that examines the impact of printing on European society.

Lucien Febvre and Henri-Jean Martin, *The Coming of the Book* (Atlantic Highlands, NJ: Humanities Press, 1976). A study of the early history of bookmaking.

Richard Marius, *Thomas More* (New York: Knopf, 1984). A reinterpretation of the complex personality of England's greatest humanist.

R. W. Scribner, *For the Sake of Simple Folk* (Cambridge, England: Cambridge University Press, 1981). A study of the impact of the Reformation on common people. Especially good on the iconography of reform.

---

*Indicates paperback edition available.

The Lutheran Reformation

*Roland Bainton, *Here I Stand* (New York: New American Library, 1968). The single most absorbing biography of Luther.

*John Dillenberger, *Martin Luther: Selections from His Writings* (New York: Doubleday, 1961). A comprehensive selection from Luther's vast writings.

Mark U. Edwards, *Luther's Last Battles* (Ithaca, NY: Cornell University Press, 1983). A sophisticated study of Luther's later years.

Eric Erikson, *Young Man Luther* (New York: W.W. Norton, 1958). A classic psychoanalytic study of Luther's personality.

*Hajo Holborn, *A History of Modern Germany Vol. I: The Reformation* (New York: Knopf, 1964). A widely respected account in a multivolume history of Germany. Especially strong on politics.

R. Po-chia Hsia, ed., *The German People and the Reformation* (Ithaca, NY: Cornell University Press, 1988). A collection of essays exploring the social origins of the Reformation.

*Bernd Moeller, *Imperial Cities and the Reformation* (Durham, NC: Labyrinth Press, 1982). A central work that defines the connection between Protestantism and urban reform.

*Francis Oakley, *The Western Church in the Later Middle Ages* (Ithaca, NY: Cornell University Press, 1979). A study of the spiritual and intellectual state of the Roman Catholic church on the eve of the Reformation.

*Steven Ozment, *The Reformation in the Cities* (New Haven, CT: Yale University Press, 1975). A study of the social and intellectual basis of urban Protestantism.

G. R. Potter, *Huldrych Zwingli* (New York: St. Martin's Press, 1977). A difficult but important study of the great Swiss reformer.

The Protestant Reformation

William Bouwsma, *John Calvin* (Oxford, England: Oxford University Press, 1987). A study that places Calvin within the context of the social and intellectual movements of the sixteenth century.

Claus-Peter Clasen, *Anabaptism, A Social History 1525–1618* (Ithaca, NY: Cornell University Press, 1971). A study of the Anabaptist movement.

*A. G. Dickens, *The English Reformation* (New York: Schocken, 1964). An important interpretation of the underlying causes of the English Reformation.

*John Dillenberger, *John Calvin: Selections from His Writings* (New York: Doubleday, 1971). A comprehensive collection.

E. William Monter, *Calvin's Geneva* (London: Wiley, 1967). A social and political history of the birthplace of Calvinism.

*Rosemary O'Day, *The Debate on the English Reformation* (London: Methuen, 1986). A survey of conflicting views by eminent scholars.

T. H. L. Parker, *John Calvin: A Biography* (Philadelphia: Westminster Press, 1975). The classic study.

*J. J. Scarisbrick, *Henry VIII* (Berkeley: University of California Press, 1968). The classic biography of the larger-than-life monarch.

George H. Williams, *The Radical Reformation* (Philadelphia: Westminster Press, 1962). A comprehensive synthesis of the first generation of radical Protestants.

The Catholic Reformation

Jean Delumeau, *Catholicism Between Luther and Voltaire* (Philadelphia: Westminster Press, 1977). A reinterpretation of the Counter-Reformation.

*A. G. Dickens, *The Counter Reformation* (London: Thames & Hudson, 1968). An excellent introduction, handsomely illustrated.

*John C. Olin, *The Autobiography of St. Ignatius Loyola* (New York: Harper & Row, 1974). The best introduction to the founder of the Jesuits.

*A. D. Wright, *The Counter-Reformation* (New York: St. Martin's Press, 1984). A comprehensive survey.

12

The Experiences of Life in Sixteenth-Century Europe

Haymaking

It is summer in the Low Countries. The trees are full, the meadows green, flowers rise in clumps, and bushes hang heavy with fruit. The day has dawned brightly for haymaking. Yesterday the long meadow was mowed and today the hay will be gathered and the first fruits and vegetables of the season harvested. From throughout the village families come together in labor. Twice each summer the grass is cut, dried, and stacked. Some of it will be left in the fields for the animals until autumn, some will be carried into large lofts and stored for the winter.

This scene of communal farming is one that is repeated with little variation throughout Europe in the sixteenth century. The village we are viewing is fairly prosperous. We can see at least three horses and a large wheeled cart. Horses are still a luxury for farmers; they can be used for transportation as well as labor, making it possible to market goods at greater distances. But horses are weaker than oxen, prone to injury, and they must be fed on grain rather than grass. The houses of the village also suggest comfort. The one at the far right is typical. It contains one floor for living and a loft for storage. The chimney separates a kitchen in the back from the long hall where the family works, sleeps, and entertains itself. The bed—it is not uncommon for there to be only one for the whole family—would be located near the fireplace. It will be restuffed with straw after the harvest. The spinning wheel and whatever other machines the family possesses would be situated nearest the single window

that lets in light and air on good days and cold and rain on bad ones. It is covered by oiled animal skin, since glass is still much too expensive for use in rural housing. The long end of the hall, farthest from heat and light, will be home to the family's animals once winter sets in. But now, in summer, it is a luxurious space where children can play or parents claim a little privacy.

The church is easily distinguished by its steeple and arched doorway and is made of brick. The steeple has 16 windows, probably all set with expensive glass and some even stained. The church would have been built over several generations at considerable cost to the villagers. Even the most prosperous houses in the far meadow are all made of timber and thatch, and only the village well, in the middle of the picture, and the chimneys of the houses show any other sign of brick. The layout of the buildings shows us how the village must have grown. The original settlement was all on the rise above the church, where there appears to be another large meadow and, at the base of the craggy rocks, several planted fields. The houses nearer the center of the picture were undoubtedly added later, perhaps to allow the sons of the more prosperous village farmers to begin their own families before their parents' death. The larger setting of the community gives us an idea of the isolation of rural communities. A windmill, down the hill from the original settlement, marks the end of the village. Then as far as one can see there are no other habitations for miles until, in the upper right-hand quadrant, a town appears to be situated on the banks of the river.

In the center of the scene are a large number of laborers. Four men with pitchforks load the cart while two women sweep the hay that falls back into new piles. Throughout the field, men and women, distinguished only by their clothing, rake hay into large stacks for successive loadings of the cart. At least twenty-five individuals work at these tasks. Men perform the heaviest work of loading the haycart and hammering the scythes while men and women share all the other work. Though no children appear in the scene, some are undoubtedly at work picking berries and beans.

Perhaps the three women returning to work are of the same family, a young girl flanked by her grandmother and mother. The expression of the eldest woman tells a tale of lifelong exertion as she holds her rake loosely and balances it carefully on her shoulder to lessen its weight. The woman on the other end has a look of determination. She is holding her hat rather than wearing it, and her thick muscular shoulders suggest a regimen of heavy labor. She has made this journey many times before. The young girl seems almost serene, still invigorated rather than ground down by the day's exercise.

As a trio they remind us that the life of ordinary people in the sixteenth century was neither romantic nor despondent, neither quaint nor primitive. It had its own joys and sorrows, its own triumphs and failures, its own measures of progress and decay. Inevitably, we compare it to our experiences and contrast it to our comforts. By our standards, a sixteenth-century prince endured greater material hardships than a twentieth-century welfare recipient. There was no running water, no central heating, no lavatories, no electricity. There was no relief for toothache, headache, or numbing pain. Travel was dangerous and exhausting. There was no protection from the open air and many nights were spent on the bare ground. Waiting for winds to sail was more tedious than waiting for planes to fly. Entertainment was sparse and the court jester was no match for stereo and video. But though we cannot help but be struck by these differences, we will not understand very much about the experiences of life in sixteenth-century Europe if we judge it by our own standard of living. We must exercise our historical imagination if we are to appreciate the conditions of European society in the sixteenth century.

$\mathcal{E}$conomic Life

There was no typical sixteenth-century European. Language, custom, geography, and material conditions separated peoples in one place from those in another. Contrasts between social groups were more striking still. A Muscovite boyar had more in common with an English nobleman than either had with his country's peasants. A Spanish goldsmith and a German brass maker lived remarkably similar lives when compared to that of a shepherd anywhere in Europe. No matter how carefully historians attempt to distinguish between country and town life, between social or occupational groups, or between men and women, they are still smoothing out edges that are very rough, turning individuals into aggregates, and sacrificing the particular for the general.

But there were experiences that most Europeans shared and common structures through which their activities were channeled that separated them from their predecessors and their successors. There was a distinctive sixteenth-century experience that we can easily discern and they could dimly perceive. Much of it was a natural progression in which one generation improved upon the situation of another. Agriculture increased; more land was cleared, more crops were grown, and better tools were crafted. Some of the experience was natural regression. Irreplaceable resources were lost; more trees were felled, more soil was eroded, and more fresh water was polluted. But some of what was distinctive about sixteenth-century life resulted from dynamic changes in economic and social conditions. Change and reactions to change became dominant themes of everyday life.

Rural Life

In the sixteenth century as much as 90 percent of the European population lived on farms or in small towns in which farming was the principal occupation. Villages were small and relatively isolated. They might range in size from a hundred families, as was common in France and Spain, to less than twenty families, which was the average size of Hungarian villages. It was these

This picture, painted in 1530, shows farmworkers threshing grain. The figure at the door seems to be an overseer. He has just sold a sack of grain, indicating the transition from a system of self-sufficient manors to a market economy.

villages, large or small, prosperous or poor, that were the bedrock of the sixteenth-century state. Surplus peasant population fed the insatiable appetite of towns for laborers and crowns for soldiers. The manor, the parish, and the rural administrative district were the institutional infrastructures of Europe. Each organized the peasantry for its own purposes. Manorial rents supported the lifestyle of the nobility; parish tithes supported the works of the Church; local taxes supported the power of the state. Rents, tithes, and taxes easily absorbed more than half of the wealth produced by the land. From the remaining half the peasant had to make provision for the present and the future.

To survive, the village community had to be self-sufficient. In good times there was enough to eat and some to save for the future. Hard times meant hunger and starvation. One in every three harvests was bad, one in every five disastrous. Between one-fifth and one-half of the grain harvested had to be saved as seed for the next planting season. When hunger was worst, people faced the agonizing choice of eating or saving their "seed corn."

Hunger and cold were the constant companions of the average European. In Scandinavia and in Muscovy, winter posed as great a threat to survival as starvation. There the stove and garments made from animal fur were essential requirements as were the hearth and the woolen tunic in the south. Everywhere in Europe homes were inadequate shelter against the cold and damp. Most were built of wood and roofed in thatch. Inside walls were patched with dried mud, and windows were few and narrow. Piled leaves or straw that could be easily replaced covered the ground and acted as insulation. The typical house was one long room with a stone hearth at the end. The hearth provided both heat and light and belched forth soot and smoke through a brick chimney.

People had relatively few household possessions. The essential piece of furniture was the wooden chest, which was used for storage. A typical family could keep all of its belongings in the chest, which could then be buried or carried away in time of danger. The chest had other uses as well. Its flat top served as a table or bench or a raised surface on which food could be placed. Tables and stools were becoming more common during the sixteenth century, though chairs were still a great luxury. In areas in which spinnning, weaving, or other domestic skills were an important part of the family's economy, a long bench was propped against the wall, usually beneath a window. Bedsteads were also becoming more common as the century wore on. They raised the straw mattresses off the ground, keeping them warmer and drier. All other family possessions related to food production. Iron spits and pots, or at least metal rings and clamps for wooden ones, were treasured goods that were passed from generation to generation. Most other implements were wooden. Long-handled spoons, boards known as trenchers, which were used for cutting and eating, and one large cup and bowl were the basic stock of the kitchen. The family ate from the long trencher and passed the bowl and cup. Knives were essential farm tools that doubled for kitchen and mealtime duty, but forks were still a curiosity.

The scale of life was small and its pace was controlled by the limits that nature imposed. It was a civilization of daylight—up at dawn, asleep at dusk, long working hours in summer, short ones in winter. For most people, the world was bounded by the distance that could be traveled on foot. Those who stayed all their lives in their rural villages may never have seen more than a hundred other people at once. Their wisdom—hard won and carefully preserved—was of the practical experience necessary to survive the struggle with nature. This was the most important legacy that parents left their children.

Peasant life centered on agriculture. Technology and technique varied little across the Continent, but there were significant differences depending on climate and soil. Across the great plain, the breadbasket that stretched from the Low Countries to Poland-Lithuania, the most common form of crop growing was still the three-field rotation system. In this method, winter crops like wheat or rye were planted in one field, spring crops like barley, peas, or beans were planted in another, and the third field was left fallow. Over 80 percent of what was grown on the farm was consumed on the farm. In most parts of Europe, wheat was a luxury crop, sold at market rather than eaten at home. Wheat bread was prized for its taste, its texture, and its white color. Rye and barley were the staples for peasants. These grains were cheaper to grow, had higher yields, and could be brewed as well as baked. Most was baked into the coarse black bread that was the monotonous fare of the peasant diet. Two to three pounds a day for an adult male was an average allotment when grain was readily available. Beer and gruels of grain and skimmed milk or water flavored with fruit juice supplemented peasant fare. In one form or another grain provided over 75 percent of the calories in a typical diet.

The warm climate and dry weather of Mediterranean Europe favored a two-crop rotation system. With less water and stronger sunlight, half the land had to be left fallow each year to restore its nutrients. Here fruit, especially grapes and olives, was an essential supplement to diet. With smaller cereal crops, wine replaced beer as a beverage. The fermentation of grapes and grain into wine and beer also provided convenient ways of storing foodstuffs. Wine and olive oil were also luxury products and were most commonly exchanged for meat, which was less plentiful on southern European farms.

Animal husbandry was the main occupation in the third agricultural area of Europe—the mountainous and hilly regions. Sheep, the most common animal, provided the raw material for almost all clothing. Their skins were used for parchment and as window coverings, and they were a ready source of inexpensive meat. In western Europe, their wool was the main export of both England and Spain. Sheep could graze on land that was unsuitable for grain growing, and they could be sheared twice a year to provide a surplus of wool. Pigs were prevalent in woodland settlements. They foraged for food and were kept, like poultry, for slaughter. Oxen were essential as draft animals. In the dairying areas of Europe cattle produced milk, cheese, and butter; in Hungary and Bohemia, the great breeding center of the Continent, they were raised for export; and most everywhere else they were used as beasts of burden.

Because agriculture was the principal occupation of Europeans, land was the principal resource. Most land was owned not by those who worked it, but by lords who let it out in various ways. The land was still divided into manors, and the manor lord, or seigneur, was still responsible for maintaining order, administering justice, and arbitrating disputes. Lords were not necessarily individual members of the nobility; in fact, they were more commonly the church or the state. In western Europe peasants generally owned between a third and a half of the land they worked; eastern European peasants owned little if any land. But by the sixteenth century almost all peasants enjoyed security of tenure on the land they worked. In return for various forms of rents, they used the land as they saw fit and could hand it down to their children. Rents were only occasionally paid in coin, though money rents became more common as the century progressed. More frequently, the lord received a fixed proportion of the yield of the land or received labor from the peasant. Labor service was being replaced by monetary payments in northern and western Europe, but it continued in the east. German and Hungarian peasants normally owed two or three days' labor on the lord's estate each week, while Polish peasants might owe as much as four days. Labor service tied the peasants to the land they worked. Eastern European peasants were less mobile than peasants in the west, and, as a result, towns were fewer and smaller in the east.

Though the land in each village was set out in large fields so that crops could be rotated, families owned their own pieces within the field, usually in scattered strips. There were also large common fields used as pasture, as well as common woodlands where animals foraged, fuel was gathered, and game hunted. Villagers disputed frequently over rights to sticks and branches of trees and over the number of sheep or cows that could be grazed in the meadows, especially when resources were scarce.

Farm work was ceaseless toil. Six or seven times a year farmers tilled the fields to spread animal manure below the surface of the soil. While most villages possessed metal plows, the team of draft animals was the single essential component for farming. The births of foals and calves were more celebrated events than the births of children; the death of an ox or horse was a catastrophe that could drive a family into debt or from the land entirely. Calamities lurked everywhere, from rain and drought to locusts and crows. Most farms could support only one family at subsistence level, and excess sons and daughters had to fend for themselves, either through marriage in the village or by migration to a town.

Town Life

In the country men and women worked to the natural rhythm of the day, up at the cock's crow, at work in the cooler hours, at rest in the hotter ones. Rain and cold kept them idle, sunlight kept them busy. Each season brought its own activity. In the town the bell tolled every hour. In the summer the laborers gathered at the town gates at four in the morning, in the winter at seven. The bell signaled the time for morning and afternoon meals as well as the hour to lay down tools and return home. Wages were paid for hours worked, seven in winter, as many as sixteen in midsummer.

In all towns there was an official guild structure that organized and regulated labor. Rules laid down the requirements for training, the standards for quality, and the conditions for exchange. Only those officially sanctioned could work in trades, and each trade could perform only specified tasks.

While the life of the peasant community turned on self-sufficiency, that of the town turned on interdependence. Exchange was the medium that transformed labor and skill into food and shelter. The town was one large marketplace in which the circulation of goods dictated the survival of the residents. Men and women in towns worked as hard as people on farms, but town dwellers received a more varied and more comfortable life in return. This is not to suggest that hunger and hardship were unknown in towns. Urban poverty was endemic and grew worse as the century wore on. In most towns as much as a quarter of the entire population might be destitute, living from casual day labor, charity, or crime. But even for these people food was more readily available in greater varieties than in the countryside, and the institutional network of support for the poor and homeless was stronger. In Lyon the overseers of the poor distributed a daily ration of a pound and a half of bread, more than half of what a farm laborer would consume. The urban poor fell victim more often to disease than to starvation.

Towns were distinguished by the variety of occupations that existed within them. The preparation and exchange of food dominated small market towns. Peasants would bring in their finest produce for sale and exchange it for vital manufactured goods like iron spits or pots for cooking. In smaller towns there was as much barter as sale; in larger places money was exchanged for commodities. Women dominated the food trades in most market towns, trading, buying, and selling in the shop fronts that occupied the bottom story of their houses. In these small towns, men divided their time between traditional agricultural pursuits—there were always garden plots and even substantial fields attached to towns—and manufacturing. Almost every town made and distributed to the surrounding area some special product that drew to the town the wealth of the countryside.

In larger towns the specialization of labor was more intense and wage earning more essential. Large traders dominated the major occupations like baking, brewing, or cloth manufacture, leaving distribution in the hands of the family economy, where there might still be a significant element of bartering. Piecework handicrafts became the staple for less prosperous town families, who prepared raw materials for the large manufacturers or finished products before their sale. Metal- or glassworking normally took place in one quarter of the town, brewing or baking in another. Each craft required long years of technical training, which was handed down from parents to children.

In large towns there were also specialized trades performed by women. There were 55 midwives in Nuremberg in the middle of the sixteenth century, and a board of women chosen from among the leading families of the town supervised their work. Nursing the sick was a logical extension of these services and also appears to have been an exclusively female occupation. So, too, was prostitution, which was an officially sanctioned occupation in most large towns in the early sixteenth century. There were official brothels, which were subject to taxation and government control. Public bathhouses served as unofficial brothels for the upper ranks of urban society. They, too, were regulated, especially after the first great epidemic of venereal disease in the early sixteenth century.

Most town dwellers, however, lived by unskilled labor. The most lucrative occupations were strictly controlled, so those who flocked to towns in search of employment usually hired themselves out as day laborers, hauling and lifting goods onto carts or boats, or delivering water and food. After the first decades of the century the supply of laborers exceeded the amount of work to occupy them, and town authorities were constantly attempting to expel the throngs of casual workers. The most fortunate might succeed in becoming servants.

Domestic service was a critical source of household labor. Even families on the margins of subsistence employed servants to undertake the innumerable household tasks, which allowed parents to pursue their primary occupations. Domestics were not apprentices, though they might aspire to become apprentices to the trade followed in the family with whom they lived. If they had kinship bonds in the town, apprenticeship was a likely outcome. But more commonly, domestics remained household servants, frequently changing employers in hope of more comfortable housing and better food. Any number of circumstances, from the death of their employer to allegations of misconduct, could cost them their places. Male servants were scapegoats for missing household items; female servants were vulnerable to sexual assaults.

Just as towns grew by the influx of surplus rural population, they sustained themselves by the import of surplus agricultural production. Most towns owned vast tracts of land, which they leased to peasants or farmed by hired labor. The town of Nuremberg controlled 25 square miles of forest and farmlands; the region around Toledo was inhabited by thousands of peasants who paid taxes and rents to city landlords. All towns had municipal storehouses of grain to preserve their inhabitants from famine during harvest failures. The diet of even a casual laborer would have been envied by an average peasant. Male grape pickers in Stuttgart received meat, soup, vegetables, wine, and beer; females got soup, vegetables, milk, and bread. In addition they received their wages. It is hardly surprising that towns were enclosed by thick walls and defended by armed guards.

Economic Change

Over the course of the sixteenth century the European population increased by about a third, with much of the growth taking place in the first 50 years. Rough estimates suggest the rise to have been from about 80 to 105 million. Patterns of growth varied by region. The population of the eastern part of

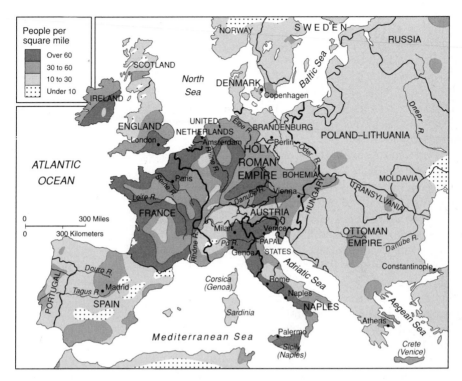

Population density in Europe, ca. 1600

Europe seems to have increased more steadily across the century, while in western Europe there was a population explosion in the early decades. The population of France may have doubled between 1450 and 1550, from 10 to 20 million, before the wars of religion reversed the trend at the end of the century. The population of England nearly doubled between 1500 and 1600 from over 2 million to over 4 million. Europe had finally recovered from the devastation of the Black Death and by 1600 its population was greater than it had ever been. Demographic growth was even more dramatic in the cities. In 1500 only four cities had populations greater than 100,000; in 1600 there were eight. Fifteen large cities more than doubled their populations, with London experiencing a phenomenal 400 percent increase.

The rise in population dramatically affected the lives of ordinary Europeans. In the early part of the century the first phase of growth brought prosperity. As there was uncultivated land that could be plowed and enough commons and woodlands to be shared, population increase was a welcome development. Even when rural communities began to reach their natural limits as people's needs pressed against resources, opportunity still existed in the burgeoning towns and cities. At first the cycle was beneficial. Surplus on the farms led to economic growth in the towns. Growth in the towns meant more opportunities for those on the farms. More food supported more workers, and more workers produced more goods and services, which were exchanged for more food.

The first waves of migrants to the towns found opportunity everywhere. Even the most lucrative textile and provisioning trades were recruiting new members, and apprenticeships were easy to find. A shortage of casual labor kept wages at a decent rate. For a short while, rural families did not have to make elaborate preparations to provide for their younger sons and daughters. They could be sent to the towns. Instead of saving every extra penny to give their children some start in life, farmers could purchase some luxury goods or expand their landholdings.

Such a window of opportunity could not remain open forever. With more mouths to feed, more crops had to be planted and new fields were carved from less fertile areas. In some villages land was taken from the wood- or scrublands that were used for animal forage and domestic fuel. This practice diminished other important resources. In Spain, for example, the land that was reclaimed came at the expense of land used for sheep grazing. This damaged both the domestic and the foreign wool trade. It also reduced the amount of fertilizer available for enriching the soil. In England and the Low Countries large drainage projects were undertaken to reclaim land for crops. In the east so-called forest colonies sprang up, clearing space in the midst of woodlands for new farms. Colonization of the eastern areas of Poland-Lithuania and Muscovy can be compared with the overseas ventures of Spain and Portugal.

By mid-century the window of opportunity shut more firmly on those who were attempting to enter the urban economy. There was a natural limit to the number of workers who could profitably engage in any given trade. Those safely in were eager to pull the ladder up behind them. Town governments came under pressure from the guilds to enforce apprenticeship requirements that had been relaxed during the period of growth. Guilds raised fees for new entrants and designated only a small number of places where their goods could be purchased. Most apprenticeships were limited to patrimony: one son for each full member. Such restrictions meant that newly arrived immigrants could enter only into the less profitable small crafts.

As workers continued to flood into the towns, real wages began to fall, not only among the unskilled but throughout the work force. A black market in labor developed to take advantage of the surplus population. In terms of purchasing power, the wages of a craft worker in the building trade in England fell by half during the sixteenth century. Peasants in the French region of Languedoc who hired out for farm labor lost 56 percent of their purchasing power during the century. Grape pickers, among the least skilled agricultural laborers, endured declines up to 300 to 400 percent.

The fall in real wages took place against a backdrop of inflation that has come to be called the Price Revolution. Over the course of the century, cereal prices increased between five- and sixfold, manufactured goods between two- and threefold. Most of the rapid increase came in the second half of the century, a result of both population growth and the import of precious metals from the New World. Sixteenth-century governments understood little about the relationship between money supply and prices. Gold and silver from America flooded the international economy, raising commodity prices. As prices rose so did the deficits of the state, which was the largest purchaser of both agricultural and manufactured goods. With huge deficits, states began to devalue their coins in the mistaken belief that this would lower their debt. But debased coinage resulted in still higher prices, and higher prices resulted in greater debt. The Price Revolution was felt throughout the Continent and played havoc with government finances, international trade, and the lives of ordinary people.

A 500 percent inflation in agricultural products over a century is not much by modern standards. Compounded, the rate averages less than 2 percent a year. But the Price Revolution did not take place in a modern society or within a modern market economy. In the sixteenth century this level of rising prices disrupted everything. In the Spanish town of Seville almost all buildings were rented on 99-year leases to the families who lived and worked in them. This was a fairly common practice throughout Europe. It meant that a landlord who rented a butcher shop and living quarters in 1501 could not raise the rent until 1600! Similarly, lords frequently held the right to purchase agricultural produce at specified prices. This system, similar to today's commodity market, helped both lords and peasants plan ahead, but it assumed steady prices.

The new money economy inspired this satirical portrait by Quentin Massys. It shows a money-lender counting his receipts while his wife is distracted from her Bible by the pile of coins. Many such merchants won fame and power and even titles.

Thus an enduring increase of prices created profound social dislocation and threw into turmoil all groups and sections of the European economy. Some people became destitute, others became rich beyond their dreams. The towns were particularly hard hit, for they exchanged manufactured goods for food and thus suffered when grain prices rose faster than other commodities. Landholders who derived their income from rents were squeezed; those who received payment in kind reaped a windfall of more valuable agricultural goods. As long as ordinary peasants consumed what they raised, the nominal value of commodities did not matter. But if some part of their subsistence was obtained by labor they were in grave peril.

There was now an enormous incentive to produce a surplus for market and to begin to specialize in particular grains that were in high demand. Every small scrap of land that individual peasant families could bring under cultivation would now yield foodstuffs which could be exchanged for manufactured goods that had been unimaginable luxuries a generation earlier. The tendency for all peasants to hold roughly equivalent amounts of land abruptly ceased. The fortunate could now become prosperous by selling their surplus. The unfortunate found ready purchasers for their strips and common rights.

The beneficial cycle now turned vicious. Those who had sold out and left the land looking for prosperity in the towns were forced to return to the land as agrarian laborers. In western Europe they became the landless poor, seasonal migrants without the safety net of rooted communal life. In eastern Europe, labor service enriched the landed nobility, who were able to sell vast stores of grain in the export market. Poland-Lithuania became a major supplier of cereals to northern Europe. But agricultural surplus from the east could not make up for the great shortfall in the west. By the end of the sixteenth century the western European states faced a crisis of subsistence.

Social Life

Social organization combines elements of tradition, belief, and function, but these elements are so fused together that it is impossible to determine where one ends and the other begins. The basic assumption of sixteenth-century European society was inequality. The group, rather than the individual, was the predominant unit in society. The first level of the social order was the family and the household, then came the village or town community, and finally the gradations of ranks and orders of society at large. Elaborate rituals helped define membership in all of these groups, from the marriage ceremony to the initiation rites of citizens, to the processions and ceremonial displays of the nobility. All stressed the rights and obligations of different levels of society. Each group had its own place in the social order and each performed its own essential function. Society was the sum of its parts.

This traditional social organization was severely tested over the course of the sixteenth century. Economic change reshaped ideas of mobility and drew sharper distinctions between rural and urban life. The growth of towns challenged beliefs about the primacy of agricultural production and the subordinate nature of trade and commerce. The rise to new wealth and prominence of some social groups challenged traditional elites' hold on power and prestige. The transformation of landholding patterns in the villages challenged the stability of rural communities. The rising numbers of poor challenged the institutions of charitable relief and posed the threat of crime and disorder. Eventually these developments led to bloody confrontations between social groups.

Social Constructs

Hierarchy was the dominant principle of social organization in the sixteenth century. The hierarchy of masters, journeymen, and apprentices dominated trades; trades themselves existed in a hierarchy. In the hierarchy of civic government, each official held a place in an ascending order up to the elite of councillors and mayors. On the land was the hierarchy of freeholder, laborer, and leaseholder among the peasants, as well as the more flexible social hierarchy among the ancient and prosperous families and the newer and struggling ones. The family itself was hierarchically organized, with the wife subordinate to her husband, the children to their parents, and the apprentices and servants to their master and mistress.

Hierarchy was a principle of orderliness that helped govern social relations. It is tempting to approach hierarchy through wealth, to divide groups and individuals into rich and poor. Many gradations in the sixteenth-century social hierarchy corresponded to levels of wealth, but they were threshold levels rather than absolute levels. Lords, by definition, did not engage in manual labor. They were wealthier than peasants. The governing elites of towns needed sufficient wealth to neglect their own affairs while occupied in public service. They were wealthier than wage earners. But the ranks of the nobility cannot be explained by gradations of wealth among nobles, and there were many rich town dwellers who were not members of the governing elite.

Status rather than wealth determined the social hierarchy of the sixteenth century. It conferred privileges and exacted responsibilities according to rank. Status was everywhere apparent. It was confirmed in social conventions like bowing and hat doffing. In towns and cities the clothing people were allowed to wear, even the foods they were allowed to eat reflected status. It was signified in titles, not just in the ranks of the nobility, but even in ordinary communities of masters and mistresses, goodmen and goodwives, squires and ladies, to adopt the English equivalents of a wide variety of European titles. The acceptance of status was an everyday, uncomplicated, unreflective act. Inequality was a fact of European social life that was as unquestioned as it was unquestionable.

Images that people used to describe both the natural world and their social world reinforced the functional nature of hierarchy. The first, and most elaborate image, was that of the Great Chain of Being. The Great Chain was a description of the universe in which everything had a place, from God at the top of the chain to inanimate objects like rocks and stones at the bottom. Complex accounts of the Chain listed the nine orders of angels, the multiple ranks of humans, even the degrees of animals and plants, from which lions emerged as kings of the jungle. For ordinary people, the Great Chain of Being expressed the belief that all life was interconnected, that every link was a part of a divinely ordered universe and was as necessary as every other.

The second metaphor used to describe society stressed this notion of interdependency even more strongly. This was the image of the Body Politic. In the Body Politic, the head ruled, the arms protected, the stomach nourished, and the feet labored. In the state the king was the head, the church the soul, the nobles the arms, the artisans the hands, and the peasants the feet. Each performed its own function and each function was essential to the health of the body. Like the Chain of Being, it was a profoundly conservative concept of social organization. Taken literally, it precluded the idea of social mobility, of people rising or falling from one group to another.

Social Structure

The Great Chain of Being and the Body Politic were static concepts of social organization. But in the sixteenth century, European society was in a state of dynamic change. Fundamentally, all European societies were divided between nobles and commoners. This was a basic distinction that existed throughout the Continent, though relationships between the two orders differed from place to place. Nobility was a legal status that conferred certain privileges on its holders. The first was rank and title, a well-defined place at the top of the social order that was passed from one generation to the next. Each rank had its own privileges and each was clearly demarcated from the next. The coat of arms was a universally recognized symbol of rank and family connection. Though there were various systems of title in use across the Continent, the hierarchy of prince, duke, earl, count, and baron was roughly standard.

Because rulers conferred these titles on individuals, elevating some to higher ranks and others from commoner to noble, the nobility was a political order as well as a social one. Political privileges were among the nobility's most important attributes. In many countries, the highest offices of the state and the military were reserved for members of the nobility. This was a privilege that could work both ways, either restricting officeholders to those already ennobled or, as in town councils in France and Spain, ennobling those who achieved certain offices. The nobility was also granted rights of political participation in the deliberative bodies of the state. In England, the peerage was defined as all those who were summoned to the House of Lords. In most parts of central Europe the nobility alone composed the diets that advised the monarch.

Finally, members of the nobility held economic privileges, a result both of their rank and of their role as lords on the lands they owned. In almost every state, the nobility was exempt from most kinds of taxation. The interests of the nobles conflicted directly with those of the ruler, and the larger the number of tax exemptions for the nobility, the stronger was its power in relation to the monarch. Tax exemptions of the nobility were most extensive in eastern and central Europe. There the crowns were elective rather than hereditary, allowing the nobles to bargain their support. As Polish agriculture developed into an export industry, exemption from internal tolls and customs gave the nobility a competitive advantage over merchants in the marketing of goods. The nobility in western Europe enjoyed fewer immunities but not necessarily less valuable ones. French nobles were exempt from the taille, Spanish nobles from the hearth tax. As French nobles had vast incomes and Spanish nobles' houses had many hearths, both were important exclusions. The English nobility enjoyed no exemptions from direct taxation, but then there was little direct taxation from which to be exempted. The most important English taxes were on exports of wool and cloth and thus fell on merchants rather than landholders.

Privileges implied obligations. Initially the nobility was the warrior caste of the state and its primary obligations were to raise, equip, and lead troops into battle. Much of the great wealth that nobles possessed was at the service of the ruler during times of war, and war was a perpetual activity. By the sixteenth century, the military needs of the state had far surpassed the military power of its nobility. Warfare had become a national enterprise that required central coordination. Nobles became administrators as much as warriors, though it is fair to say that many did both. The French nobility came to be divided into the nobility of the sword and the nobility of the robe—that is, warriors and officeholders.

Nobles also had the obligation of governing at both the national and the local level. At the discretion of the ruler, they could be called to engage in any necessary occupation, no matter how disruptive to their economic or family affairs. They administered their estates and settled the disputes of their tenants. In times of want they were expected to provide for the needy. The obligation of good lordship was implicitly understood, if not always explicitly carried out, between lord and peasant.

The principal distinction in sixteenth-century society was between lord and commoners, but it was not the only one. A new social group was emerging that had neither the legal nor the social privileges of nobility but performed many of the same functions. Over the course of the century this group carved out a place that was clearly distinct from the commoners even if it was not clearly identical to the lords. It is easiest to describe in the towns, which remained a separate unit of social organization in most states. Towns enjoyed many of the same political and economic privileges as the nobility. Representatives of the towns met with the nobles and the king and were the most important part of the national deliberative assemblies, like the English Parliament or the French estates. Towns were granted legal rights to govern their own citizens, to engage in trade, and to defend themselves by raising and storing arms. Though they paid a large share of most taxes, towns also received large tax concessions.

Yet as individuals, members of the town elite held no special status in society at large. Some were among the richest people in the state, great bankers and merchants wealthier than dukes, but they had to devise their own systems of honor and prestige. In Venice the Book of Gold distinguished the local elite from the ranks of ordinary citizens. In France and Spain, some of the highest officers of leading towns were granted noble status. In England wealthy guild members could become knights, a rank just below noble status. German burghers, as prosperous townsmen were called, remained caught between noble and common, despised from above because they worked with their hands, envied from below for their wealth and comfort. In Wurtenberg the nobility withdrew from the towns and sought the status of free knights.

In the rural society the transformation of agricultural holdings in many places also created a group that fit uncomfortably between lords and commoners. The accumulation of larger and larger estates, by purchase from the nobility, the state, or the church, made lords—in the sense of landowners with tenants—out of many who were not lords in rank. They received rents and dues from their tenants, administered their estates, and preserved the so-called moral economy that sustained the peasants during hard times. In England this group came to be known as the gentry, and there were parallel groups in Spain, France, and the empire. The gentry aspired to the privileges of the nobility. In England members of the gentry had the right to have a coat of arms and could be knighted. But knighthoods were not hereditary and did not confer membership in the House of Lords. In Spain, the caballeros and hidalgos gained noble privileges but were still of lower status than the grandees. The gentry aped the habits of the nobility, often outdoing nobles in lavish displays of wealth.

Social stratification did not only apply to the wealthy groups within European societies. Though it is more difficult to reconstruct the principles on which rural communities based their complicated systems of status and order, there can be no doubt that orders existed and that they helped create the bonds which tied communities together. In many German villages a principal distinction was between those who held land in the ancient part of the settlement—the *Esch*—and those who held land in those areas into which the village had expanded. The Esch was normally the best land. But interestingly, the holders of the Esch were tied to the lord of the estate while holders of the less desirable lands were free peasants. Here freedom to move from place to place was less valued than the right to live in the heart of the village.

Just the opposite set of values prevailed in English villages, where freeholders were in the most enviable position. They led the movements to break up the common fields for planting and were able to initiate legal actions against their lord. Whenever village land was converted to freehold, unfree tenants would go into debt to buy it. Increasingly, French peasants came to own the land they farmed. They protested against the very title of *villein*, claiming that its older association with serfdom discouraged others from trading with those so labeled. The relationship of free and unfree went even further in Muscovy, where thousands of starving laborers sold themselves into slavery.

In towns, the order of rank below the elite pertained as much to the kind of work that one performed as it did to the level at which it was undertaken. The critical division in town life was between those who had the freedom of the city—citizens—and those who did not. Citizenship was restricted to membership in certain occupations and was closely regulated. It could be purchased, especially by members of learned professions whose services were becoming vital in the sixteenth century. But most citizenship was earned by becoming a master in one of the guilds after a long period of apprenticeship and training. Only males could be citizens. In Germany, the feminine equivalent for the word used to denote a male citizen meant prostitute! But women who were married to citizens enjoyed their privileges, and widows of citizens could pass the privileges to their new husbands when they remarried.

Social Change

In the sixteenth century, social commentators believed that change was transforming the world in which they lived. In 1600 a Spanish observer blamed the rise of the rich commoners for the ills of the world. An Englishman commenting on the rise of the gentry could give no better definition of its status than to say that a gentleman was one who lived like a gentleman. The challenge that the new nobility of the robe posed to the old nobility of the sword poisoned relations between these two segments of the French ruling elite. The military service class in Muscovy, who were of more use to the Muscovite princes than the traditional landed nobility, posed an even greater threat to the privileges of the boyars.

Pressures on the ruling elites of European society came from above as well as below. The expansion of the state and the power of the prince frequently came as a result of direct conflict with the nobility. Only in east central Europe did the consolidation of the state actually enhance the privileges of the traditional noble orders, and these were areas in which towns were small and urban elites weak.

There were many reasons why the traditional European social hierarchy was transformed during the course of the sixteenth century. In the first place, population increase necessitated an expansion of the ruling orders. With more people to govern there had to be more governors who could perform the military, political, and social functions of the state. The traditional nobility grew slowly as titles could be passed to only one son and intermarriage within the group was very high. Secondly, opportunities to accumulate wealth expanded dramatically with the Price Revolution. Traditionally wealth was calculated in land and tenants rather than in the possession of liquid assets like gold and silver. But with the increase in commodity prices, surplus producers could rapidly improve their economic position. Moreover, state service became a source of unlimited riches. The profits to be made from tax collecting, officeholding, or the law could easily surpass those to be made from landholding. The newly rich clamored for privileges, and many were in a position to lobby rulers effectively for them. Across European society the nobility grew, fed from fortunes made on the land, in trade, and in office.

Social change was equally apparent at the bottom of the social scale, but here it could not be so easily absorbed. The continuous growth of population created a group of landless poor who squatted in villages and clogged the streets of towns and cities. Rough estimates suggest that as many as a quarter of all Europeans were destitute. This was a staggering figure in great cities, amounting to tens of thousands in London or Paris.

Traditionally, local communities cared for their poor. Widows, orphans, and the handicapped, who would normally constitute over half of the poor in a village or town, were viewed as the "deserving poor," worthy of the care of the community through the Church or through private almsgiving. Catholic communities like Venice created a system of private charity that paralleled the institutions of the Church. Though Protestant communities took charity out of the control of the Church, they were no less concerned about the plight of the deserving poor. In England a special tax, the poor rate, supported the poor. Perhaps the most elaborate system of all existed in the French town of Lyon. There all the poor were registered and given identity cards. Each Sunday they

Feeding the Hungry, *by Cornelius Buys, 1504. A maidservant is doling out small loaves to the poor and the lame at the door of a wealthy person's home. The poor who flocked to the towns were often forced to rely on charity to survive.*

would receive a week's worth of food and money. Young girls were provided with dowries, young boys were taught crafts. But this enlightened system was for the deserving poor only, and as the century progressed it was over-whelmed.

Charity was an obligation of the community, but as the sixteenth century wore on, the number of destitute people grew beyond the ability of the local community to care for them. Perhaps more importantly, many of those who now begged for alms fell outside the traditional categories of the deserving poor. They were men and women capable of working but incapable of finding more than occasional labor. They left their native communities in search of employment and thus forfeited their claims on local charity. Most wound up in the towns and cities, where they slept and begged in the streets. As strangers they had no claim on local charity, as able-bodied workers they had no claim on sympathy. Poor mothers abandoned their newborn infants on the steps of foundling hospitals or the houses of the rich.

The problem of crime complicated the problems of poverty and vagrancy. Increasing population and increasing wealth equaled increasing crime; the addition of the poor to the equation aggravated the situation. The poor, outsiders to the community without visible means of support, were the easiest targets of official retribution. Throughout the century numerous European states passed vagrancy laws. In England the poor were whipped from village to village until they were returned home. Both Venetian and Dutch vagrants were regularly rounded up for galley service, while vagrants in Hungary were sold into slavery. Physical mutilation was used in an ineffective effort at deterrence; thieves had fingers chopped off which, of course, made it impossible for them to perform manual labor and thus likely to steal again. Sexual offenses were criminalized, especially bastardy, since the birth of illegitimate children placed an immediate burden on the community. Prostitutes, who had long been tolerated and regulated in towns, were now persecuted. Rape increased. Capital punishment was reserved for the worst crimes—murder, incest, and grand larceny being most common—but not surprisingly, executions were carried out mostly on outsiders to the community.

Peasant Revolts

The economic and social changes of the sixteenth century bore serious consequences. Most telling was the upswing of violent confrontations between peasants and their lords. Across Europe and with alarming regularity peasants took up arms to defend themselves from what they saw as violations of traditional rights and obligations. Peasant revolts were not hunger riots. Though they frequently occurred in periods of want, after bad harvests or marauding armies had impoverished villages, peasant revolts were not desper-ate attacks against warehouses or grain silos. Nor did those who took part in them form an undisciplined mob. Most revolts chose leaders, drew up petitions of grievances, and organized the rank and file into a semblance of military order. Leaders were literate—drawn more commonly from among the lower clergy or minor gentry than from the peasantry—political demands were moderate, and tactics were sophisticated. But peasant revolts so profoundly threatened the social order that they were met with the severest repression.

It is essential to realize that while peasants revolted against their lords, at bottom their anger and frustration were products of agrarian changes that could be neither controlled nor understood. As population increased and market production expanded, many of the traditional rights and obligations of lords and peasants became oppressive. One example is that of forest rights. On most estates, the forests surrounding a village belonged to the lord. Commonly the village had its own woodlands in which animals foraged and fuel and building material were available. As population increased, more farms came into existence. New land was put under the plow and grain fields pressed up against the forest. There were more animals in the village and some of them were let loose to consume the young sprouts and saplings. Soon there was not enough food for the wild game that was among the lord's most valuable property. So the game began to feed on the peasants' crops, which were now placed so appetizingly close to the forests. It was a capital crime for a peasant to kill wild game, but neither could the peasants allow the game to consume their crops.

A similar conflict arose over enclosing crop fields. An enclosure was a device—normally a fence or hedge that surrounded an area—to keep a parcel of land separate from the planted strips of land owned by the villagers. It could be used for grazing animals or raising a specialty crop for the market. But an enclosure destroyed the traditional form of village agriculture whereby decisions on which crops to plant were made communally. It became one of the chief grievances of the English peasants. But while enclosures broke up the old field system in many villages, they were a logical response to the transformation of land ownership that had already taken place. As more and more land was accumulated by fewer and fewer families, it made less and less sense for them to work widely scattered strips all over the village. If a family could consolidate its holdings by swaps and sales, it could gain an estate large enough to be used for both crops and grazing. An enclosed estate allowed wealthy farmers to grow more luxury crops for market or to raise only sheep on a field that had once been used for grain.

Enclosure was a process that both lord and rich peasant undertook, but it was a process that drove the smallholders from the land and was thus a source of bitter resentment for the poorer peasants. It was easy to protest the greed of the lords who, owning the most land, were the most successful enclosers. But enclosures resulted more from the process whereby villages came to be characterized by a very small elite of large landholders and a very large mass of smallholders and landless poor. It was an effect rather than a cause.

From Hungary to England peasant revolts brought social and economic change into sharp relief. A call for a crusade against Ottoman advances in 1514 provided the opportunity for Hungarian peasants to revolt against their noble landlords. Thousands dropped their plowshares and grasped the sword of a holy war. But, in fact, war against the Ottomans did not materialize. Instead the mobilized peasants, under the leadership of disaffected army officers and clergymen, issued grievances against the labor service that they owed to their lords as well as numerous violations of customary agricultural practices. Their revolt turned into a civil war and was crushed with great brutality. In eastern England Ket's Rebellion centered on peasant opposition to enclosure. The rebels occupied Norwich, the second largest city in the realm, but their aspirations were for reform rather than revolution. They, too, were crushed by well-trained forces.

The complexity of these problems is perhaps best revealed in the series of uprisings that are known collectively as the German Peasants' War. It involved tens of thousands of peasants, and it combined a whole series of agrarian grievances with an awareness of the new religious spirit preached by Martin Luther. Luther condemned both lords and peasants, the lords for their rapaciousness, the peasants for their rebelliousness. Though he had a large following among the peasants, his advice that earthly oppressions be passively accepted was not followed. The Peasants' War was directed against secular and ecclesiastical lords, and the rebels attacked both economic and religious abuses. The combination of demands, such as the community's right to select its own minister and the community's right to cut wood freely, attracted a wide following in the villages and small towns of southern and central Germany. The printed demands of the peasantry, the most famous of which was the Twelve Articles of the Peasants of Swabia (1525), helped spread the movement far beyond its original bounds. The peasants organized themselves into large armies led by experienced soldiers, but ultimately, those movements that refused compromise were ruthlessly crushed.

At base the demands of the peasantry addressed the agrarian changes that were transforming German villages. Population growth was creating more poor villagers who could only hire out as laborers but who demanded a share of common grazing and woodlands. Because the presence of these poor increased the taxable wealth of the village, they were advantageous to the lord. But the strain they placed on resources was felt by both the subsistence and the surplus farmers. Tensions within the village were all the greater in that the landless members were the kin of the landed. If they were properly to be settled on the land, then the lord would have to let the village expand. If they were to be kept on the margins of subsistence, then the more prosperous villagers would have to be able to control their numbers and their conduct. In either case, the peasants needed more direct responsibility for governing the village than existed in their traditional relationship with their lord. Thus the grievances of the peasants of Swabia demanded release of the village peasantry from the status of serfs. They wanted to be allowed to move off the land, to marry out of the village without penalty, and to be free of the death taxes that further impoverished their children. They also wanted stable rents fixed at fair rates, a limit placed on labor service, and a return to the ancient customs that governed relations between lords and peasants. All of these proposals were backed by an appeal to Christian principles of love and charity. They were profoundly conservative.

The demands of the German peasants reflected a traditional order that no longer existed. In many places the rents and tithes that the peasants wanted to control no longer belonged to the lords of the estates. They had been sold to town corporations or wealthy individuals who purchased them as an investment and expected to realize a fair return. Most tenants did enjoy stable and fixed rents, but only on their traditional lands. As they increased their holdings, perhaps to keep another son in the village or to expand production for the market, they were faced with the fact that rents were higher and land more expensive than it had been before. Marriage fines, death duties, and labor service were oppressive, but then they balanced the fact that traditional rents were very low. In many east German villages, peasants willingly increased their labor service for a reduction in their money rents. It was hardly likely that they could have both. If the peasants were being squeezed, and there can be little doubt that they were, it was not only the lords who were doing the squeezing. The church took its tenth, the state increased its exactions, and the competition for survival and prosperity among the peasants themselves was ferocious. Peasants were caught between the jaws of an expanding state and a changing economy. When they rebelled, the jaws snapped shut.

𝒫rivate Life

The great events of the sixteenth century—the discovery of the New World, the consolidation of states, the increasing incidence and ferocity of war, the reform of religion—all had a profound impact on the lives of ordinary people. There could be no private life separate from these developments. However slowly they penetrated to isolated village communities, however intermittent their effect, they were inextricably bound up with the experiences and the worldview of all Europeans. The states offered more protection and demanded more resources. Taxes increased and tax collecting became more efficient. Wars took village boys and made them soldiers. Armies brought devastation to thousands of communities. The New World offered new opportunities, brought new products, and increased the wealth of the Continent. Religious reform, both Protestant and Catholic, penetrated into popular beliefs and personal piety. All these sweeping changes blurred the distinction between public and private life.

The Family

Sixteenth-century life centered on the family. The family was a crucial organizing principle for Europeans of all social ranks and it served a variety of functions. In the most obvious sense, the family was the primary kin group. European families were predominantly nuclear, composed of a married couple and their children. In western Europe, a small number of families contained the adult siblings of the family head, uncles and aunts who had not yet established their own families. This pattern was more common in the east, especially in Hungary and Muscovy, where taxation was based on households and thus encouraged extended families. Yet however families were composed, kinship had a wider orbit than just parents and children. In-laws, step relations, and cousins were considered part of the kin group and could be called on for support in a variety of contexts from charity to employment and business partnerships. In towns, such family connections created large and powerful clans.

In a different sense, family was lineage, the connections between preceding and succeeding generations. This was an important concept among the upper ranks of society where ancient lineage, genuine or fabricated, was a valued component of nobility. This concept of family imparted a sense of stability and longevity in a world in which individual life was short. Even in peasant communities, however, lineage existed in the form of the strips in the field that were passed from generation to generation and named for the family that owned them.

The family was also an economic unit. Here family overlapped with the household, that is, all those members who lived under the same roof, including servants and apprentices. In its economic functions, the family was the basic unit for the production, accumulation, and transmission of wealth. Occupation determined the organization of the economic family. Every member of the household had his or her own functions that were essential to the survival of the unit. Tasks were divided by gender and by age, but there was far more intermixture than is traditionally assumed. On farms, women worked at nearly every occupation with the exception of mowing and plowing. In towns they were vital to the success of shops and trades, though they were denied training in the skilled crafts. As laborers, they worked in the town fields—for little more than half the wages of men performing the same tasks—and in carrying and delivering goods and materials. Children contributed to the economic vitality of the household from an early age.

Finally, the family was the primary unit of social organization. It was in the family that children were educated and the social values of hierarchy and discipline were taught. Authority in the family was strictly organized in a set of three overlapping categories. At the top was the husband, head of the household, who ruled over his wife, children, and servants. All members of the family owed obedience to the head. But two other categories of relationships in the family dispersed this authority. Children owed obedience to their parents, male or female. In this role the wife and mother was governor as well as governed. Similarly, servants owed obedience to both master and mistress. Male apprentices were under the authority of the wife, mother, and mistress of the household. The importance of the family as a social unit was underscored by the fact that people unattached to families attracted suspicion in sixteenth-century society. Single men were often viewed as potential criminals, single women as potential prostitutes.

Though the population of Europe was increasing in the sixteenth century, families were not large. Throughout northern and western Europe, the size of the typical family was two adults and three or four children. Late marriages and breast feeding helped control family size. The first restricted the number of childbearing years, the second increased the space between pregnancies. Women married around age twenty-five, men slightly later. Most women could expect about fifteen fertile years and seven or eight pregnancies if neither they nor their husband died in the interim. Only three or four children were likely to survive beyond the age of 10. In her fertile years, a woman was constantly occupied with infants. If she used a wet nurse, as many women in the upper ranks of society did, then she was likely to have 10 or 12 pregnancies during her fertile years and correspondingly more surviving children.

Constant pregnancy and child care may help explain some of the gender roles that men and women assumed in the sixteenth century. Biblical injunctions and traditional stereotypes help explain others. Pregnant or not, women's labor was a vital part of the domestic economy, especially until the first surviving children were strong enough to assume their share. The woman's sphere was the household. On the farm she was in charge of the preparation of food, the care of domestic animals, the care and education of children, and the manufacture and cleaning of the family's clothing. In towns, women supervised the shop that was part of the household. They sold goods, kept accounts, and directed the work of domestics or apprentices.

The man's sphere was the public one, the fields in rural areas, the streets in towns. Men plowed, planted, and did the heavy reaping work of farming. They made and maintained essential farm equipment and had charge of the large farm animals. They marketed surplus produce and made the few purchases of equipment or luxury goods. Men performed the labor service that was normally due the lord of the estate, attended the local courts in various capacities, and organized the affairs of the village. In towns, men engaged in heavy labor, procured materials for craft work, and marketed their product if it was not sold in the household shop. Only men could be citizens of the towns or full members of most craft guilds, and only men were involved in civic government.

This separation of men and women into the public and the domestic spheres meant that marriage was a blending of complementary skills. Each partner brought to the marriage essential knowledge and abilities that were fundamental to the economic success of the union. Except in the largest towns, nearly everyone was married for at least a part of his or her life. Remarriage was more common for men than women, however, because men continued to control the family's property after the death of their wife, whereas a widow might have only a share of it after bequests to children or provisions for apprentices.

While male roles were constant throughout the life cycle, as men trained for and performed the same occupations from childhood to death, female roles varied greatly depending on the situation. While under the care of fathers, masters, or husbands, women worked in the domestic sphere; once widowed, they assumed the public functions of head of household. Many women inherited shops or farmland; most became responsible for the placement and training of their children. But because of the division of labor on which the family depended and because of the inherent social and economic prejudices that segregated public and domestic roles, widows were particularly disadvantaged.

Community

Despite its central place in all aspects of sixteenth-century life, the family was a fragile and impermanent institution. The early death of one of the partners abbreviated the life of the natural family. New marriage partners or social welfare to aid the indigent were sought from within the wider community of which families were a part. On the farm this community was the rural village; in the town it was the ward, quarter, or parish in which the family lived. Community life must not be romanticized. Interpersonal violence, lawsuits, and feuds were extraordinarily common in both rural and urban communities. Like every other aspect of society, the community was socially and economically stratified, gender roles were segregated, and resources were inequitably divided. But the community was the place where people found their social identity. It provided marriage partners for its families, charity for its poor, and a local culture for all of its inhabitants.

The two basic forces that tied the rural community together were the lord and the priest. The lord set conditions for work and property ownership that necessitated common decision making on the part of the village farmers. The lord's presence, commonly in the form of an agent, could be both a positive and a negative force for community solidarity. Use of the common lands, the rotation of labor service, and the form in which rents in kind were paid were all decisions that had to be made collectively. Village leadership remained informal, though in some villages headmen or elders bargained with the lord's agent or resolved petty disputes among the villagers. Communal agreement was also expressed in communal resistance to violations of custom or threats to the moral economy. All these forms of negotiation fused individual families into a community. So, too, in a different way did the presence of the parish priest or minister, who attended all the pivotal events of life—birth, marriage, and death. The church was the only common building of the community; it was the only space that was not owned outright by the lord or an individual family. The scene of village meetings and ceremonies, it was the center of both spiritual and social life. The parish priest served as a conduit for all the news of the community and the focal point for the village's festive life.

Communities were bound together by the authorities that ruled them and by their common activities. But they were also bound together by their own social customs. In rural parishes there was the annual perambulation, a walk around the village fields that usually occurred before planting began. It was led by the priest, and behind him followed the village farmers. The perambulation had many purposes. The priest blessed the fields and prayed for a bountiful crop; the farmers surveyed their own strips and any damage that had been done to the fields during the winter; the community defined its geographical space in distinction to the space of others.

In towns, ceremonial processions were far more elaborate. Processions might take place on saints' days in Catholic communities or on anniversaries of town liberties. The order of the march, the clothing worn by the participants, and the objects displayed reflected the strict hierarchies of the town's local organizations. In Catholic towns the religious orders led the town governors in their robes of office. Following the governors were the members of guilds, each guild placed according to its rank of importance and each organized by masters, journeymen, and apprentices.

Not all ceremonial occasions were so formal. The most common ceremony was the wedding, a rite of passage that was simultaneously significant to the individual, the family, and the community. The wedding was a public event that combined a religious ceremony and a community procession with feasting and festivity. It took different forms in different parts of Europe and in different social groups. But whether eastern or western, noble or common, the wedding was celebrated as the moment when the couple entered fully into the community. Parents were a central feature in the event, both in arranging the economic aspects of the union—dowry and inheritance—and in approving the occasion. Many couples were engaged long before they were married, and in many places it was the engagement that was most important to the individuals and the wedding that was most important to the community.

Traditional weddings involved the formal transfer of property, an important event in rural communities where the ownership of strips of land or common rights concerned everyone. The bridal dowry and the groom's inheritance were formally exchanged during the wedding, even if both were small. The public procession, "the marriage in the streets" as it was sometimes called in towns, proclaimed the union throughout the community and was considered to be as important as the religious ceremony. It was followed by a feast as abundant as the families of bride and groom could afford. Weddings also legitimated sexual relations. Many of the dances and ceremonies that followed the feast symbolized the sexual congress. Among the nobility, the consummation of the marriage was a vital part of the wedding, for without it the union could be annulled. Finally, the marriage inaugurated both bride and groom into new roles in the community. Their place at the wedding table next to their parents elevated them to the status of adults.

Other ceremonies were equally important in creating a shared sense of identity within the community. In both town and countryside the year was divided by a number of festivals that defined the rhythm of toil and rest. They coincided with both the seasonal divisions of agricultural life and with the central events of the Christian calendar. There was no essential difference between the popular and Christian elements in festivals, however hard the

Carnivals were occasions for games and feasting. A Carnival on the Feast Day of Saint George in a Village Near Antwerp, *painted around 1605 by Abel Grimmer, shows the revels of the villagers presided over by the religious figure on the banner at the right.*

official church insisted upon one. Christmas and Easter were probably the most widely observed Christian holidays, but Carnival, which preceded Lent, was a frenzied round of feasts and parties that resulted in a disproportionate number of births nine months later. The 12 days of Christmas were only loosely attached to the birth of Jesus and were even abolished by some Protestant churches. The rites of May, which celebrated the rebirth of spring, were filled with sexual play among the young adults of the community. All Hallows' Eve was a celebration for the community's dead. Their spirits wandered the village on that night, visiting kin and neighbors.

Festivals helped maintain the sense of community that might be weakened during the long months of increased work or enforced indoor activity. They were first and foremost celebrations in which feasting, dancing, and play were central. But they also served as safety valves for the pressures and conflicts that built up over the year. There were frequently group and individual sports, like soccer or wrestling, which served to channel aggressions. Village elders would arbitrate disputes, and marriage alliances or property transactions would be arranged.

Festivals further cemented the political cohesion of the community. Seating arrangements signaled the hierarchy of the community, and public punishment of offenders reinforced deference and social and sexual mores. Youth groups, or even the village women, might band together to shame a promiscuous woman or to place horns on the head of a cuckolded husband. These forms of community ritual worked not only to punish offenders but also to reinforce the social and sexual values of the village as a whole.

Popular Beliefs

Ceremony and festival are reminders that sixteenth-century Europe was still a preliterate society. Despite the introduction of printing and the millions of books that were produced during the period, the vast majority of Europeans conducted their affairs without the benefit of literacy. Their culture was oral and visual. They had need of an exact memory and they developed a shorthand of adages, charms, and spells that helped them organize their activities and pass down their knowledge. It is difficult for us to recreate this mental world in which almost all natural events were unpredictable and where there was little certainty. Outside a small circle of intellectuals, there was little effective knowledge about either human or celestial bodies. The mysteries of the sun, moon, and stars were as deep as those of health and sickness. But this does not mean that ordinary people lived in a constant state of terror and anxiety. They used the knowledge they did have to form a view of the universe that conformed to their experiences and responded to their hopes.

These beliefs blended Christian teaching and folk wisdom with a strong strain of magic. Popular belief in magic could be found everywhere in Europe, and it operated in much the same way as science does today. Only skilled practitioners could perform magic. It was a technical subject that combined expertise in the properties of plants and animals with theories about the composition of human and heavenly bodies. It had its own language, a mixture of ancient words and sounds with significant numbers and catch phrases. Magicians specialized. Alchemists worked with rocks and minerals, astrologers with the movement of the stars. Witches were thought to understand the properties of animals especially well.

Magical practices appealed to people at all levels of society. The wealthy favored astrology and paid handsomely to discover which days and months were the most auspicious for marriages and investments. The poorest villagers sought the aid of herbalists to help control the constant aches and pains of daily life. Sorcerers and wizards were called upon in more extreme circumstances, such as a threatened harvest or matters of life and death. These magicians competed with the remedies offered by the Church. Special prayers and visits to the shrines of particular saints were believed to have similar curative value. Magical and Christian beliefs did not oppose each other; they existed on a spectrum and were practiced simultaneously. In some French villages, for example, four-leaf clovers were considered especially powerful if they were found on a particular saint's day. It was not until the end of the century when Protestant and Catholic leaders condemned magical practices and began a campaign to root them out that magic and religion came into conflict.

Magical practices served a variety of purposes. Healing was the most common and many "magical" brews were effective remedies to the minor ailments for which they were prescribed. Most village magicians were women because it was believed that women had unique knowledge and understanding of the body. Magic was also used for predictive purposes. Certain charms and rituals were believed to have the power to affect the weather, the crops, and even human events. As always, affairs of the heart were as important as those of the stomach. Magicians advised the lovesick on potions and spells that would gain them the object of their desires. Finally, it was believed that magic had the power to alter the course of nature and could be used for both good and evil purposes.

Magic for evil was black magic, or witchcraft, which utilized beliefs in the presence of spiritual forces in nature. Witches were believed to possess special powers that put them into contact with the devil and the forces of evil which they could then use for their own purposes. Belief in the prevalence of good and evil spirits was Christian as well as magical. But the Church had gradually consigned the operation of the devil to the afterlife and removed his direct agency from earthly affairs. Beginning in the late fifteenth century, church authorities began to prosecute large numbers of suspected witches. By the end of the sixteenth century there was a Continent-wide witch craze. Unexplained misfortune or simple malice could set off accusations that might include dozens or even hundreds of suspected witches. Confessions were obtained under torture as were further accusations.

Witches were usually women, most often those unmarried or widowed. In

A reluctant witch rides off to hell with the devil while indifferent peasants go about their business. This woodcut is from the Historia de gentibus septentrionalibus *(History of the Northern Folk), by Olaus Magnus, published at Rome in 1555.*

Children's Games, by Pieter Bruegel, 1560. In this picture, the whole town becomes a playground. Most of the games—more than eighty have been identified—are still popular today.

a sample of more than seven thousand cases of witchcraft prosecuted in early modern Europe, over 80 percent of the defendants were women. There is no clear explanation for why women fulfilled this important and powerful role. Belief in women's special powers over the body through their singular ability to give birth is certainly one part of the explanation, for many stories about the origins of witches suggest that they were children fathered by the devil and left to be raised by women. This sexual element of union with the devil and the common belief that older women were sexually aggressive combined to threaten male sexual dominance. Witches were also believed to have peculiar physical characteristics. A group of Italian witches, male and female, were distinguished by having been born with a caul, that is, a membrane around their heads that was removed after birth. Accused witches were strip searched to find the devil's mark, which might be any bodily blemish. Another strand of explanation lies in the fact that single women existed on the fringes of society, isolated and exploited by the community at large. Their occult abilities thus became a protective mechanism that gave them a function within the community while they remained outside it.

It is difficult to know how important black magical beliefs were in ordinary communities. Most of the daily magic that was practiced was a mixture of charms, potions, and prayers that mingled magical, medical, and Christian beliefs. Misfortunes that befell particular families or social groups were blamed on the activities of witches. The campaign of the established churches to root out magic was largely directed against witches. The churches transposed witches' supposed abilities to communicate with the devil into the charge that they worshiped the devil. Because there was such widespread belief in the presence of diabolical spirits and in the capabilities of witches to control them, Protestant and Catholic church courts could easily find witnesses to testify in support of the charges against individual witches. Yet wherever sufficient evidence exists to understand the circumstances of witchcraft prosecutions, it is clear the community itself was under some form of social or economic stress rather than that there was any increase in the presence or use of witches. Sacrificing a marginal member of the community might be the means to restore village solidarity.

Population growth, economic diversification, and social change characterized life in sixteenth-century Europe. It was a century of extremes. The poor were getting poorer and the rich were getting richer. The early part of the century has been called the golden age of the peasantry; the later part has been called the crisis of subsistence. At all levels of the social scale the lives of grandparents and grandchildren were dramatically different. For surplus producers, the quality of life improved throughout the century. The market economy expanded. Agricultural surplus was exchanged for more land and a wider variety of consumer goods. Children could be provided with an education, and domestic and agricultural labor was cheap and plentiful. For subsistence producers, the quality of life eroded. In the first half of the century their diet contained more meat than it would for the next 300 years. Their children could be absorbed on new farms or sent to towns where there was a shortage of both skilled and unskilled labor. But gradually the outlook turned bleak. The land could support no more new families, and the towns needed no more labor. As wages fell and prices rose, peasants in western Europe were caught between the crushing burdens of taxation from lord, state, and church, and the all too frequent catastrophes of poor harvests, epidemic disease, and warfare. In eastern Europe the peasantry was tied to the land in a new serfdom, which provided minimum subsistence in return for the loss of freedom and opportunity. When peasants anywhere rose up against these conditions, they were cut down and swept away like new-mown hay.

Suggestions for Further Reading

General Reading

George Huppert, *After the Black Death* (Bloomington: Indiana University Press, 1986). An up-to-date and detailed study of social history in all parts of the Continent.

Henry Kamen, *European Society 1500–1700* (London: Hutchinson, 1984). A general survey of European social history.

*Peter Laslett, *The World We Have Lost: Further Explored* (New York: Scribner's, 1984). One of the pioneering works in the family and population history of England.

*Robert Mandrou, *Introduction to Modern France* (New York: Harper & Row, 1977). Explores a variety of subjects in French social history from the mental to the material world.

Economic Life

*Fernand Braudel, *Civilization and Capitalism: The Structures of Everyday Life* (New York: Harper & Row, 1981). Part of a larger work filled with fascinating detail about people's social behavior during the early modern period.

*Carlo Cipolla, ed., *Fontana Economic History of Europe Vol. II: The Sixteenth and Seventeenth Centuries* (London: Harvester Press, 1977). A multiauthored compendium of information and analysis on all aspects of European economic life.

*Natalie Z. Davis, *Society and Culture in Early Modern France* (Stanford, CA: Stanford University Press, 1975). A collection of compelling essays drawn from the author's research on the French town of Lyon.

Hermann Kellenbenz, *The Rise of the European Economy* (London: Weidenfeld and Nicolson, 1976). A general survey of economic life with good material from Scandinavian and German sources.

*Peter Kriedte, *Peasants, Landlords and Merchant Capitalists* (Cambridge, England: Cambridge University Press, 1983). A Marxist interpretation of the transformations of the European economy.

Gerald Strauss, *Nuremberg in the Sixteenth Century* (New York: Wiley, 1966). A political and social history of a typical German town.

Social Life

Yves-Marie Bercé, *Revolt and Revolution in Early Modern Europe* (New York: St. Martin's Press, 1987). A study of the structure of uprisings throughout Europe by a leading French historian.

*Peter Blickle, *The Revolution of 1525* (Baltimore, MD: Johns Hopkins University Press, 1981). A provocative interpretation of the causes and meaning of the German Peasants' War.

Michael Bush, *Noble Privilege* (New York: Holmes & Meier, 1983). An analytic account of the types of privileges enjoyed by the European nobility, based on wide reading.

*Arthur Lovejoy, *The Great Chain of Being* (New York: Random House, 1959). An intellectual history of an idea through its centuries of development.

Antoni Maczak, Henryk Samsonowicz, and Peter Burke, eds., *East Central Europe in Transition* (Cambridge, England: Cambridge University Press, 1985). Essays by leading historians of eastern Europe, most of which focus on economic development.

Margaret Spufford, *Contrasting Communities* (Cambridge, England: Cambridge University Press, 1974). A detailed reconstruction of three English villages that explores social, economic, and religious life in the late sixteenth and early seventeenth centuries.

---

*Indicates paperback edition available.

*E. M. W. Tillyard, *The Elizabethan World Picture* (New York: Harper & Row, 1960). The classic account of the social constructs of English society.

Private Life

*Peter Burke, *Popular Culture in Early Modern Europe* (New York: Harper & Row, 1978). A lively survey of cultural activities among the European populace.

*Jean-Louis Flandrin, *Families in Former Times* (Cambridge, England: Cambridge University Press, 1976). Studies of kinship, household, and sexuality by one of the leading French family historians.

*Ralph Houlbrooke, *The English Family 1450–1700* (London: Longman, 1984). A thorough survey of family history for the society that has been most carefully studied.

*Brian Levack, *The Witch-Hunt in Early Modern Europe* (London: Longman, 1987). A study of the causes and meaning of the persecution of European witches in the sixteenth and seventeenth centuries.

R. Muchembled, *Popular Culture and Elite Culture in France 1400–1750* (Baton Rouge: Louisiana State University Press, 1985). A detailed treatment of the practices of two conflicting cultures.

*Keith Thomas, *Religion and the Decline of Magic* (New York: Scribner's, 1971). A gargantuan descriptive and anecdotal account of the forms of religious and magical practice in England.

Merry Wiesner, *Working Women in Renaissance Germany* (New Brunswick, NJ: Rutgers University Press, 1986) A survey of women's work in Germany and the ways in which it changed during the sixteenth century.

13

Centuries of Warfare: Europe 1555–1763

The Massacre of the Innocents

"War is one of the scourges with which it has pleased God to afflict men," wrote Cardinal Richelieu (1585–1642), the French minister who played no small part in spreading the scourge. War was a constant of European society and penetrated to its very core. It dominated all aspects of life. It enhanced the power of the state, it defined gender roles, it consumed lives and treasure and commodities ravenously. War affected every member of society from combatants to civilians. There were no innocent bystanders. Grain in the fields was destroyed because it was food for soldiers; houses were burned because they provided shelter for soldiers. Civilians were killed for aiding the enemy or holding out against demands for their treasure and supplies. Able-bodied men were taken forcibly to serve as conscripts, leaving women to plant and harvest as best they could.

Neither the ancient temple nor the Roman costume can conceal the immediacy of the picture on the facing page. It is as painful to look at now as it was when it was created over 350 years ago. Painted by Nicolas Poussin (1594–1665) at the height of the Thirty Years' War, the *Massacre of the Innocents* remains a horrifying composition of power, terror, and despair. The cruel and senseless slaughter of the innocent baby that is about to take place is echoed throughout the canvas. Between the executioner's legs can be seen a mother clasping her own child tightly and anticipating the fall of the sword. In the background on the right another mother turns away from the scene and carries her infant to safety. In the foreground strides a mother holding her dead child. She tears at her hair and cries in anguish. To a culture in which the image of mother and child—of Mary and Jesus—was one of sublime peacefulness and inexpressible joy, the contrast could hardly be more shocking.

456

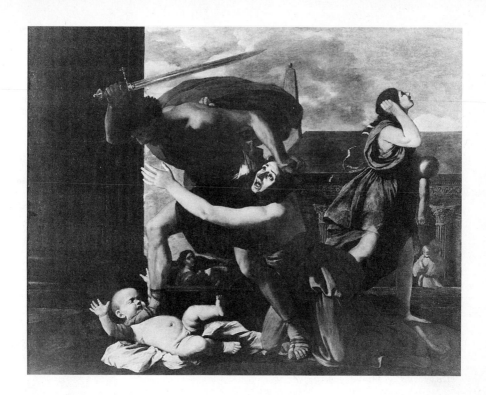

The picture graphically displays the cruelty of the soldier, the helplessness of the child, and the horror of the mother. By his grip on the mother's hair and his foot on the baby's throat, the warrior shows his brute power. The mother's futile effort to stop the sword illustrates her powerlessness. She scratches uselessly at the soldier's back. Naked, the baby boy raises his hands as if to surrender to the inevitable, as if to reinforce his innocence.

To study Europe at war, we must enter into a world of politics and diplomacy, of issues and principles, of judgment and error. There can be no doubt that the future of Europe was decisively shaped by the centuries of wholesale slaughter from 1555 to 1763, during which dynastic and religious fervor finally ran its course. The survival of Protestantism, the disintegration of the Spanish empire, the rise of Holland and Sweden, the collapse of Poland and Muscovy, the fragmentation of Germany—these were all vital transformations whose consequences would be felt for centuries. We cannot avoid telling this story, untangling its causes, narrating its course, revealing its outcome. But neither should we avoid facing its reality. Look again at the painting by Poussin.

$\mathcal{E}$urope at War, 1555–1648

There was nothing new about war in the middle of the sixteenth century. The early part of the century had witnessed the dynastic struggle between the Habsburgs and the House of Valois as well as the beginnings of the religious struggle between Catholics and Protestants. But the wars that dominated Europe from 1555 to 1648 brought together the worst of both of these conflicts. War was fought on a larger scale, it was more brutal and more expensive, and it claimed more victims, civilians and combatants alike. During this century war extended throughout the Continent. Dynastic strife, rebellion, and international rivalries joined together with the ongoing struggle over religion. Ambition and faith were an explosive mixture. The French endured 40 years of civil war; the Spanish, 80 years of fighting with the Dutch. The battle for hegemony in the East led to dynastic strife for decades on end, as Poles, Russians, and Swedes pressed their rival claims to each other's crowns. Finally, in 1618, these separate theaters of war came together in one of the most brutal and terrifying episodes of destruction in European history, the Thirty Years' War.

The Crises of the Western States

In the sixteenth century, society was an integrated whole, equally dependent on monarchical, ecclesiastical, and civil authority for its effective survival. A European state could no more tolerate the presence of two churches than it could the presence of two kings. But the Reformation had created two churches. The coexistence of both Catholics and Protestants in a single realm posed a stark challenge to accepted theory and traditional practice.

The problem proved intractable because it admitted only one solution: total victory. There could be no compromise for several reasons. Religious beliefs were profoundly held. Religious controversy was a life-and-death struggle, but it was a struggle between everlasting life and eternal damnation. Doomed, too, was the practical solution of toleration. To the modern mind, toleration seems so logical that it is difficult to understand why it took over a century of bloodshed before it came to be grudgingly accepted by those countries most bitterly divided. But toleration was not a practical solution in a society that admitted no principle of organization other than one king, one faith.

The French Wars of Religion. Protestantism came late to France. It was not until after Calvin reformed the Church in Geneva and began to export his brand of Protestantism that French society began to divide along religious lines. By 1560 there were over two thousand Protestant congregations in France, whose membership totaled nearly 10 percent of the French popula-

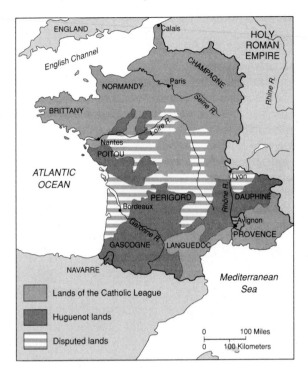

Religious divisions in France

tion. Calvin and his successors had their greatest success among the middle ranks of urban society, merchants, traders, and craft workers. They also found a receptive audience among aristocratic women, who eventually converted their husbands and their sons.

The wars of religion, however, were brought on by more than the rapid spread of Calvinism. Equally important was the vacuum of power that had been created when Henry II (1547–1559) died in a jousting tournament. Surviving Henry were his extraordinary widow, Catherine de Médicis, three daughters, and four sons, the oldest of whom, Francis II (1559–1560), was only 15. Under the influence of his beautiful young wife, Mary, Queen of Scots, Francis allowed the Guise family to dominate the great offices of state and to exclude their rivals from power. The Guises controlled the two most powerful institutions of the state—the army and the Church.

The Guises were staunchly Catholic and among their enemies were the Bourbons, princes of the blood with a direct claim to the French throne but also a family with powerful Protestant members. The revelation of a Protestant plot to remove the king from Paris provided the Guises with an opportunity to eliminate their most potent rivals. The Bourbon Duc de Condé, the leading Protestant peer of the realm, was sentenced to death. But five days before Condé's execution, Francis II died and Guise power evaporated. The new king

Kings of France, 1547–1610

Henry II	1547–1559
Francis II	1559–1560
Charles IX	1560–1574
Henry III	1574–1589
Henry IV	1589–1610

Charles IX (1560–1574) was only 10 years old and firmly under the grip of his mother, Catherine de Médicis, who now declared herself regent of France.

Condé's death sentence convinced him that the Guises would stop at nothing to gain their ambitions. Force would have to be met with force. Protestants and Catholics alike raised armies and in 1562 civil war ensued. Because of the tangle of motives among the participants, each side in the struggles had different objectives. Catherine wanted peace and was willing to accept almost any strategy for securing it. At first she negotiated with the Bourbons, but she was ultimately forced to accept the fact that the Guises were more powerful. The Guises wanted to suppress Protestantism and eliminate Protestant influence at court. They were willing to undertake the task with or without the king's express support. Once the wars began, the leading Protestant peers fled the court, but the position of the Guises was not altogether secure. Henry Bourbon, king of Navarre, was the next in line to the throne should Charles IX and his two brothers die without male heirs. Henry had been raised in the Protestant faith by his mother, Jeanne d'Albret, whose own mother, Marguerite of Navarre, was among the earliest protectors of the Huguenots, as the French Calvinists came to be called.

The inconclusive nature of the early battles might have allowed for the pragmatic solution by Catherine de Médicis had it not been for the assassination of the Duc de Guise in 1563 by a Protestant fanatic. This act added a personal vendetta to the religious passions of the Catholic leaders. They encouraged the slaughter of Huguenot congregations and openly planned the murder of Huguenot leaders. Protestants gave as good as they got. In open defiance of Valois dynastic interests, the Guises courted support from Spain, while the Huguenots imported Swiss and German mercenaries to fight in France. Noble factions and irreconcilable religious differences were together pulling the government apart.

By 1570 Catherine was ready to attempt another reconciliation. She announced her plans for a marriage between her daughter Margaret and Henry of Navarre, a marriage that would symbolize the spirit of conciliation between the crown and the Huguenots. The marriage was to take place in Paris during August 1572. The arrival of Huguenot leaders from all over France to attend the marriage ceremony presented an opportunity of a different kind to the Guises and their supporters. If leading Huguenots could be assassinated in Paris, the Protestant cause might collapse and the truce that the wedding signified might be turned instead into a Catholic triumph.

Saint Bartholomew was the apostle that Jesus described as a man without guile. Ironically it was on his feast day that the Huguenots who had innocently come to celebrate Henry's marriage was led like lambs to the slaughter. On 24 August 1572 the streets of Paris ran red with Huguenot blood. Though frenzied, the slaughter was inefficient. Henry of Navarre and a number of other important Huguenots escaped the carnage and returned to their urban strongholds. In the following weeks the violence spread from Paris to the countryside, and thousands of Protestants paid for their beliefs with their lives.

After Saint Bartholomew's Day, a genuine revulsion against the massacres swept the nation. A number of Catholic peers now joined with the Huguenots to protest the excesses of the crown and the Guises. These Catholics came to be called the *politiques* from their desire for a practical settlement of the wars. They were led by the duc d'Anjou, next in line to the throne when Charles IX died in 1574 and Henry III (1574–1589) became king. Against them, in Paris and a number of other towns, the Catholic League was formed, a society that pledged its first allegiance to religion. The League took up where the Saint Bartholomew's Day massacre left off, and the slaughter of ordinary people who unluckily professed the wrong religion continued. Matters grew worse in 1584 when Anjou died. With each passing year it was becoming apparent that Henry III would produce no male heir. After Anjou's death, the Huguenot

The French Wars of Religion

1559 Death of Henry II

1560 Protestant Duc de Condé sentenced to death

1562 First battle of wars of religion

1563 Catholic Duc de Guise assassinated; Edict of Amboise grants limited Protestant worship

1572 Saint Bartholomew's Day massacre

1574 Accession of Henry III

1576 Formation of Catholic League

1584 Death of Duc d'Anjou makes Henry of Navarre heir to throne

1585 War of the three Henrys

1588 Henry Guise murdered by order of Henry III

1589 Catherine de Médicis dies; Henry III assassinated

1594 Henry IV crowned

1598 Edict of Nantes

Henry of Navarre was the next in line for the throne. Catholic Leaguers talked openly of altering the royal succession and began to develop theories of lawful resistance to monarchical power. By 1585, when the final civil war began—the war of the three Henrys, named for Henry III, Henry Guise, and Henry of Navarre—the crown was in the weakest possible position. Paris and the Catholic towns were controlled by the League, the Protestant strongholds by Henry of Navarre. King Henry III could not abandon his capital or his religion, but neither could he gain control of the Catholic party. The extremism of the Leaguers kept the politiques away from court, and without the politiques, there could be no settlement.

In December 1588 Henry III summoned Henry Guise and Guise's brother to a meeting in the royal bedchamber. There they were murdered by the king's order. The politiques were blamed for the murders—revenge was taken on a number of them—and Henry III was forced to flee his capital. He made a pact with Henry of Navarre and together royalist and Huguenot forces besieged Paris. All supplies were cut off from the city and only the arrival of a Spanish army prevented its fall. In 1589 Catherine de Médicis died, her ambition to reestablish the authority of the monarchy in shambles, and in the same year a fanatic priest gained revenge for the murder of the Guises by assassinating Henry III.

Now Henry of Navarre came into his inheritance. But after nearly thirty years of continuous civil war it was certain that a Huguenot could never rule France. If Henry was to become king of all France, he would have to become a Catholic king. It is not clear when Henry made the decision to accept the Catholic faith—"Paris is worth a mass," he reportedly declared—but he did not announce his decision at once. Rather he strengthened his forces, tightened his bonds with the politiques, and urged his countrymen to expel the Spanish invaders. He finally made his conversion public and in 1594 was crowned Henry IV (1589–1610). In 1598 Henry proclaimed the Edict of Nantes, which granted limited toleration to the Huguenots. It was the culmination of decades of attempts to find a solution to the existence of two religions in one state.

The World of Philip II.   By the middle of the sixteenth century Spain was the greatest power in Europe. The dominions of Philip II (1556–1598) of Spain stretched from the Atlantic to the Pacific: His continental territories included the Netherlands in the north and Milan and Naples in Italy. In 1580 Philip became king of Portugal, uniting all the states of the Iberian peninsula. With the addition of Portugal's Atlantic ports and its sizable fleet, Spanish maritime power was now unsurpassed. Philip saw himself as a Catholic monarch fending off the spread of heresy. He came to the throne at just the moment that Calvinism began its rapid growth in northern Europe and provided the impetus for the greatest crisis of his reign: the revolt of the Netherlands.

Though Philip's father, Charles V, amassed a great empire, he had begun only as the Duke of Burgundy. Charles's Burgundian inheritance encompassed a diverse territory in the northwestern corner of Europe. The 17 separate provinces of this territory were called the Netherlands or the Low Countries

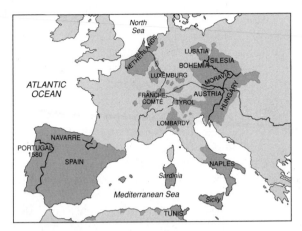

Habsburg Empire under Philip II

because of the flooding that kept large portions of them under water. The Netherlands was one of the richest and most populous regions of Europe, an international leader in manufacturing, banking, and commerce. In the southern provinces French was the background and language of the inhabitants; in the northern ones Germans had settled and Dutch was spoken.

The Low Countries had accepted the Peace of Augsburg in a spirit of conciliation in which it was never intended. Here Catholics, Lutherans, Anabaptists, and Calvinists peaceably coexisted. As in France, this situation changed dramatically with the spread of Calvinism. The heavy concentration of urban populations in the Low Countries provided the natural habitat for Calvinist preachers, who made converts across the entire social spectrum. As Holy Roman Emperor, Charles V may have made his peace with Protestants, but as king of Spain he had not. Charles V had maintained the purity of the Spanish Catholic church through a sensible combination of reform and repression.

Philip II intended to pursue a similar policy in the Low Countries. With papal approval he initiated a scheme to reform the hierarchy of the Church by expanding the numbers of bishops, and he invited the Jesuits to establish schools for orthodox learning. Simultaneously, he strengthened the power of the Inquisition and ordered the enforcement of the decrees of the Council of Trent. The Protestants sought the protection of their local nobility who, Catholic or Protestant, had their own reasons for opposing the strict enforcement of heresy laws. Provincial nobility and magistrates resented both the policies that were being pursued and the fact that they disregarded local autonomy. Town governors and noblemen refused to cooperate in implementing the new laws.

The Revolt of the Netherlands. The passive resistance of nobles and magistrates was soon matched by the active resistance of the Calvinists. Unable to enforce Philip's policy, Margaret of Parma, his half sister, whom Philip had made regent, agreed to a limited toleration. But in the summer of 1566, before it could be put into effect, bands of Calvinists unleashed a storm of iconoclasm in the provinces, breaking stained glass windows and statues of the Virgin and the saints, which they claimed were idolatrous. Local authorities were helpless in the face of determined Calvinists and apathetic Catholics; they could not protect church property. Iconoclasm gave way to open revolt. Fearing social rebellion, even the leading Protestant noblemen took part in suppressing these riots.

In Spain, the events in the Netherlands were treated for what they were: open rebellion. Despite the fact that Margaret had already restored order, Philip II was determined to punish the rebels and enforce the heresy laws. A large military force under the command of the Duke of Alba (1507–1582) was sent from Spain as an army of occupation. Alba lured leading Protestant noblemen to Brussels, where he publicly executed them in 1568. He also established a military court to punish participants in the rebellion, a court that came to be called the Council of Blood. The Council handed down over nine thousand convictions, a thousand of which carried the death penalty, and as many as sixty thousand Protestants fled beyond Alba's jurisdiction. Alba next made an example of several small towns that had been implicated in the iconoclasm. He allowed his soldiers to pillage the towns at will before slaughtering their entire populations and razing them to the ground. By the end of 1568 royal policy had gained a sullen acceptance in the Netherlands, but for the next 80 years, with only occasional truces, Spain and the Netherlands were at war.

Alba's policies had driven Protestants into rebellion, and this forced the Spanish government to maintain its army by raising taxes from those provinces that had remained loyal. Soon the loyal provinces were also in revolt, not over religion, but over taxation and local autonomy. Tax resistance and fear of an invasion from France left Alba unprepared for the series of successful assaults Protestants launched in the northern provinces during 1572. The Protestant generals established a permanent base in the northwestern provinces of Holland and Zeeland. By 1575 they had gained a stronghold that they would never relinquish. Prince William of Orange assumed the leadership of the two provinces, which were now united against the tyranny of Philip's rule.

Spanish government was collapsing all over the Netherlands. William ruled in the north, and the States-General, a parliamentary body composed of representatives from the separate provinces, ruled in the south. Margaret of Parma had resigned in disgust at Alba's tactics, and Alba had been relieved of his command when his tactics had failed. No one was in control of the Spanish army. The soldiers, who had gone years with only partial pay, now roamed the southern provinces looking for plunder. Brussels and Ghent both had been targets, and in 1576 the worst atrocities of all occurred when mutinous Spanish troops sacked Antwerp. Over seven thousand people were slaughtered and nearly a third of the city burned to the ground.

The "Spanish fury" in Antwerp effectively ended Philip's rule over his Burgundian inheritance. The Protestants had established a permanent home in the north. The States-General had established its ability to rule in the south, and Spanish policy had been totally discredited. To achieve a settlement, the

Revolt of the Netherlands

1559 Margaret of Parma named regent of the Netherlands

1566 Calvinist iconoclasm begins revolt

1567 Duke of Alba arrives in Netherlands and establishes Council of Blood

1572 Protestants capture Holland and Zeeland

1573 Alba relieved of his command

1576 Sack of Antwerp
      Pacification of Ghent

1581 Catholic and Protestant provinces split

1585 Spanish forces under Alexander Farnese take Brussels and Antwerp

1609 Twelve Years' Truce

Pacification of Ghent of 1576, the Spanish government conceded local autonomy in taxation, the central role of the States-General in legislation, and the immediate withdrawal of all Spanish troops from the Low Countries. This rift among the provinces was soon followed by a permanent split. In 1581 one group of provinces voted to depose Philip II while a second group decided to remain loyal to him. Philip II refused to accept the dismemberment of his inheritance or to recognize the independent Dutch state that now existed in Holland. Throughout the 1580s and 1590s military expeditions attempted to reunite the southern provinces and to conquer the northern ones. But Spanish military successes in the south were outweighed by the long-term failure of their objectives in the north. In 1609 Spain and the Netherlands concluded the Twelve Years' Truce, which tacitly recognized the existence of the state of Holland. By the beginning of the seventeenth century Holland was not only an independent state, it was one of the greatest rivals of Spain and Portugal.

The Reorganization of Northeastern Europe

Until the end of the sixteenth century, Poland-Lithuania was the dominant power in the eastern part of Europe. It was economically healthy and militarily strong. Through its Baltic ports, especially Gdańsk, Poland played a central role in international commerce and a dominant role in the northern grain trade. The vast size of the Polish state made defense difficult, and during the course of the sixteenth century it had lost lands to Muscovy in the east and to the Crimean Tartars in the south. But the permanent union with Lithuania in 1569 and the gradual absorption of the Baltic region of Livonia more than compen-

THE JAGIELLON MONARCHY OF POLAND

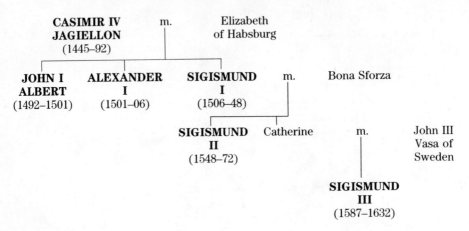

sated for these losses. Matters of war and peace, of taxation, and of reform were placed under the strict supervision of the Polish Diet, a parliamentary body that represented the Polish landed elite. The Diet also carefully controlled religious policy. Roman Catholicism was the principal religion in Poland, but the state tolerated numerous Protestant and Eastern creeds. In the Warsaw Confederation of 1573 the Polish gentry vowed "that we who differ in matters of religion will keep the peace among ourselves."

The biological failure of the Jagiellon monarchy in Poland ended that nation's most successful line of kings. Without a natural heir, the Polish nobility and gentry, who officially elected the monarch, had to peddle their throne among the princes of Europe. When Sigismund III (1587–1632) was elected to the Polish throne in 1587, he was also heir to the crown of Sweden. Sigismund accepted the prohibitions against religious repression outlined in the Warsaw Confederation, but he actively encouraged the establishment of Jesuit schools, the expansion of monastic orders, and the strengthening of the Roman Catholic church.

All of these policies enjoyed the approval of the Polish ruling classes. But the Diet would not support Sigismund's efforts to gain control of the Swedish crown, which he inherited in 1592 but from which he was deposed three years later. If Sigismund triumphed in Sweden, all Poland would get was a part-time monarch. The Polish Diet consistently refused to give the king the funds necessary to invade Sweden successfully. Nevertheless, Sigismund mounted several unsuccessful campaigns against the Swedes that sapped Polish money and manpower.

Muscovy's Time of Troubles.   The wars of Ivan the Great and Ivan the Terrible in the fifteenth and sixteenth centuries were waged to secure agricultural territory in the west and a Baltic port in the north. Both objectives came at the expense of Poland-Lithuania. But following the death of Ivan the Terrible in

---

Tsars of Russia, 1440–1645

Ivan III	1440–1505
Vasily III	1505–1533
Ivan IV	1533–1584
Feodor I	1584–1598
(Time of Troubles)	1598–1613
Michael Romanov	1613–1645

1584, the Muscovite state began to disintegrate. For years it had been held together only by conquest and fear. Ivan's conflicts with the boyars, the hereditary nobility, created an aristocracy unwilling and unable to come to the aid of his successors. By 1601 the crown was plunged into a crisis of legitimacy known as the Time of Troubles. Ivan had murdered his heir in a fit of anger and left his half-witted son to inherit the throne. This led to a vacuum of power at the center as well as a struggle for the spoils of government. Private armies ruled great swaths of the state and pretenders to the crown—all claiming to be Dimitri, the lost brother of the last legitimate tsar—appeared everywhere. Ambitious groups of boyars backed their own claimants to the throne. So, too, did ambitious foreigners who eagerly sought to carve up Muscovite possessions.

Muscovy's Time of Troubles was Poland's moment of opportunity. While anarchy and civil war raged, Poland looked to regain the territory that it had lost to Muscovy over the previous century. Sigismund abandoned war with Sweden in order to intervene in the struggle for the Russian crown. Polish forces crossed into Muscovy and Sigismund's generals backed one of the strongest of the false Dimitris, but their plan to put him on the throne failed when he was assassinated. Sigismund used the death of the last false Dimitri as a pretext to assert his own claim to the Muscovite crown. More Polish forces poured across the frontier. In 1610 they took Moscow and Sigismund proclaimed himself tsar, intending to unite the two massive states.

The Russian boyars, so long divided, now rose against the Polish enemy. The Polish garrison in Moscow was starved into submission and a native Russian, Michael Romanov (1613–1645), was chosen tsar by an assembly of landholders, the Zemsky Sobor. He made a humiliating peace with the Swedes—who had also taken advantage of the Time of Troubles to invade Muscovy's Baltic provinces—in return for Swedish assistance against the Poles. Intermittent fighting continued for another 20 years. In the end, Poland agreed to peace and a separate Muscovite state, but only in exchange for large territorial concessions.

The rise of Russia

The Rise of Sweden. Until the Reformation, Sweden had been part of the Scandinavian confederation ruled by the Danes. Although the Swedes had a measure of autonomy, they were very much a junior partner in Baltic affairs. Denmark controlled the narrow sound that linked the Baltic with the North Sea, and its prosperity derived from the tolls it collected on imports and exports. When, in 1523, Gustav I Vasa led the uprising of the Swedish aristocracy that ended Danish domination, he won the right to rule over a poor, sparsely populated state with few towns or developed seaports. The Vasas ruled Sweden in conjunction with the aristocracy. Although the throne was hereditary, the part played by the nobility in elevating Gustav I Vasa (1523–1560) gave the nobles a powerful voice in Swedish affairs. Through the council of state, known as the Rad, the Swedish nobility exerted a strong check on the monarch.

Sweden's aggressive foreign policy began accidentally. When in the 1550s the Teutonic Knights found themselves no longer capable of ruling in Livonia, the Baltic seaports that had been under their dominion scrambled for new alliances. Muscovy and Poland-Lithuania were the logical choices, but the town of Reval, an important outlet for Russian trade near the mouth of the Gulf of Finland, asked Sweden for protection. After some hesitation, since the occupation of territory on the southern shores of the Baltic would involve great expense, Sweden fortified Reval in 1560. A decade later, Swedish forces captured Narva, farther to the east, and consolidated their hold on the Livonian

The rise of Sweden

coast. By occupying the most important ports on the Gulf of Finland, Sweden could control a sizable portion of the Muscovite trade.

Now only two obstacles prevented the Swedes from dominating trade with Muscovy: Archangel in the north and Riga in the south. In the 1580s, the Muscovites established a port at Archangel on the White Sea. With this new port they opened a trading route to the west, around northern Scandinavia. Sweden benefited from the White Sea trade by claiming the northern portions of the Scandinavian peninsula necessary to make the trade secure. In all of their dealings with Muscovy the Swedes sought further privileges at Archangel while laying plans for its conquest. Riga was a problem of a different sort. As the Swedes secured the northern Livonian ports, more of the Muscovy trade moved to the south and passed through Riga, which would have to be captured or blockaded if the Swedes were to control commerce in the eastern Baltic.

Sigismund's aggressive alliance with the Polish Jesuits had persuaded the Swedish nobility that he would undermine their Lutheran church, and Sigismund was deposed in favor of his uncle Charles IX (1604–1611). War between Sweden and Poland resulted from Sigismund's efforts to regain the Swedish crown, and the Swedes used the opportunity to blockade Riga and to occupy more Livonian territory. The Swedish navy was far superior to any force that the Poles could assemble, but on land Polish forces were masters. The Swedish invasion force suffered a crushing defeat and had to retreat to its coastal enclaves. The Poles now had an opportunity to retake all of Livonia but, as

Rulers of Sweden, 1523–1654

Gustav I Vasa	1523–1560
Eric XIV	1560–1568
John III	1568–1592
Sigismund	1592–1600
Charles IX	1604–1611
Gustavus Adolphus	1611–1632
Christina	1632–1654

always, the Polish Diet was reluctant to finance Sigismund's wars. Furthermore, Sigismund had his eyes on a bigger prize. Rather than follow up its Swedish victory, Poland invaded Muscovy.

Meanwhile, the blockade of Riga and the assembly of a large Swedish fleet in the Baltic threatened Denmark. The Danes continued to claim sovereignty over Sweden and took the opportunity of the Polish-Swedish conflict to reassert it. In 1611, under the energetic leadership of the Danish king Christian IV (1588–1648), Denmark invaded Sweden from both the east and the west. The Danes captured the towns of Kalmar and Alvsborg and threatened to take Stockholm. To end the Danish war, Sweden accepted humiliating terms in 1613. Sweden renounced all claims to the northern coasts and recognized Danish control of the Arctic trading route.

Paradoxically, these setbacks became the springboard for Swedish success. Fear of the Danes led both the English and the Dutch into alliances with Sweden. These countries all shared Protestant interests, and the English were heavily committed to the Muscovy trade, which was still an important part of Swedish commerce. Fear of the Poles had a similar effect on Muscovy. In 1609 the Swedes agreed to send 5000 troops to Muscovy to help repel the Polish invasion. In return, Muscovy agreed to cede to Sweden its Baltic possessions. This was accomplished in 1617 and gave Sweden complete control of the Gulf of Finland.

In 1611, during the middle of the Danish war, Charles IX died and was succeeded by his son Gustavus Adolphus (1611–1632). Gustavus's greatest skills were military, and the calamitous wars inherited from his father occupied him during the early years of his reign. He was forced to conclude the humiliating peace with the Danes in 1613 and to go to war with the Russians in 1614 to secure the Baltic coastal estates that had been promised in 1609. Gustavus's first military initiative was to resume war with Poland in order to force Sigismund to renounce his claim to the Swedish throne. In 1621 Gustavus landed in Livonia and in two weeks captured Riga, the capstone of Sweden's Baltic ambitions. Occupation of Riga increased Swedish control of the Mus-

Gustavus Adolphus of Sweden, shown at the Battle of
Breitenfield in 1631. The battle was the first important
Protestant victory of the Thirty Years' War. Gustavus died
on the battlefield at Lutzen in the following year.

covy trade and it deprived Denmark of a significant portion of its customs
duties. Gustavus now claimed Riga as a Swedish port and successfully
demanded that ships sailing from there pay tolls to Sweden rather than
Denmark.

The Thirty Years' War

In 1609 Spain and the Dutch Republic had signed a truce that was to last until
1621. In over forty years of nearly continuous fighting the Dutch had carved out
a state in the northern Netherlands. They used the truce to consolidate their
position and increase their prosperity. Spain had reluctantly accepted Dutch
independence, but Philip III (1598–1621), like his father before him, never
abandoned the objective of recovering his Burgundian inheritance. By the
opening of the seventeenth century Philip had good reasons for hope. Beginning in the 1580s, Spanish forces had reconquered the southern provinces of
the Netherlands. The prosperous towns of Brussels, Antwerp, and Ghent were
again under Spanish control, and they provided a springboard for another
invasion.

The Twelve Years' Truce gave Spain time to prepare for the final assault.
During this time Philip III attempted to resolve all of Spain's other European
conflicts so that he could then give full attention to a resumption of the Dutch
war. Circumstance smiled on his efforts. In 1603 the pacific James I (1603–
1625) came to the English throne. Secure in his island state, James I desired
peace among all Christian princes. He quickly concluded the war with Spain

that had begun with the invasion of the Spanish Armada, and he entered into negotiations to marry his heir to a Spanish princess. In 1610 the bellicose Henry IV of France was felled by an assassin's knife. French plans to renew war with Spain were abandoned with the accession of the 8-year-old Louis XIII (1610–1643).

The Bohemian Revolt. The Peace of Augsburg had served the German states well. The principle that the religion of the ruler was the religion of the state complicated the political life of the Holy Roman Empire, but it also pacified it. Though rulers had the right to enforce uniformity on their subjects, in practice many of the larger states tolerated more than one religion. By the beginning of the seventeenth century Catholicism and Protestantism had achieved a rough equality within the German states, symbolized by the fact that of the seven electors who chose the Holy Roman Emperor, three were Catholic, three Protestant, and the seventh was the emperor himself, acting as king of Bohemia. This situation was not unwelcome to the leaders of the Austrian Habsburg family who succeeded Emperor Charles V. By necessity, the eastern Habsburgs were more tolerant than their Spanish kinfolk. The head of their house was elected king of Bohemia and king of Hungary, both states with large Protestant populations.

In 1617 Mathias, the childless Holy Roman Emperor, began making plans for his cousin, Ferdinand Habsburg, to succeed him. Ferdinand was Catholic, very devout and very committed. In order to ensure a Catholic majority among the electors, the emperor relinquished his Bohemian title and pressed for Ferdinand's election as the new king of Bohemia. The Protestant nobles of Bohemia forced the new king to accept the strictest limitations on his political and religious powers, but once elected Ferdinand had not the slightest intention of honoring the provisions that had been thrust upon him. His opponents were equally strong willed. When Ferdinand violated Protestant religious liberties, a group of noblemen marched to the royal palace in Prague in May 1618, found two of the king's chief advisers, and hurled them out of an upper-story window.

Austrian Habsburg Emperors, 1519–1657

Charles V	1519–1556
Ferdinand I	1556–1564
Maximilian II	1564–1576
Rudolph II	1576–1612
Matthias	1612–1619
Ferdinand II	1619–1637
Ferdinand III	1637–1657

The Defenestration of Prague, as this incident came to be known, initiated a Protestant counteroffensive throughout the Habsburg lands. Fear of Ferdinand's policies led to Protestant uprisings in Hungary as well as Bohemia. Those who seized control of the government declared Ferdinand deposed and the throne vacant. But they had no candidate to accept their crown. Whatever their religion, princes were always uneasy about the overthrow of a lawful ruler. Whoever came to be called king of Bohemia in place of Ferdinand would have to face the combined might of the Habsburgs. When Emperor Mathias died in 1619, Ferdinand succeeded to the imperial title as Ferdinand II (1619–1637) and Frederick V, one of the Protestant electors, accepted the Bohemian crown.

Frederick was a sincere but weak Calvinist whose credentials were much stronger than his abilities. His mother was a daughter of Prince William of Orange and his wife, Elizabeth, a daughter of James I of England. It was widely believed it was Elizabeth's resolution she would "rather eat sauerkraut with a king than roast meat with an elector" that decided the issue. No decision could have been more disastrous for the fate of Europe. Frederick ruled a geographically divided German state known as the Palatinate. One hundred miles separated the two segments of his lands, but both were strategically important. The Lower Palatinate bordered on the Catholic Spanish Netherlands and the Upper Palatinate on Catholic Bavaria.

Once Frederick accepted the Bohemian crown, he was faced with a war on three fronts. Ferdinand II had no difficulty enlisting allies to recover the Bohemian crown, since he could pay them with the spoils of Frederick's lands. Spanish troops from the Netherlands occupied the Lower Palatinate, and Bavarian troops occupied the Upper Palatinate. Frederick, on the other hand, met rejection wherever he turned. Neither the Dutch nor the English would send more than token aid—both had advised him against breaking the imperial peace. The Lutheran princes of Germany would not enter into a war between Calvinists and Catholics, especially after Ferdinand II promised to protect the Bohemian Lutherans.

At the Battle of the White Mountain in 1620, Ferdinand's Catholic forces annihilated Frederick's army. Frederick and Elizabeth fled to Denmark, and Bohemia was left to face the wrath of Ferdinand, the victorious king and emperor. The retribution was horrible. Mercenaries who had fought for Ferdinand II were allowed to sack Prague for a week. Elective monarchy was abolished and Bohemia became part of the hereditary Habsburg lands. Free peasants were enserfed and subjected to imperial law. Those nobles who had supported Frederick lost their lands and their privileges. Calvinism was repressed and thoroughly rooted out, consolidating forever the Catholic character of Bohemia. Frederick's estates were carved up and his rights as elector transferred to the Catholic duke of Bavaria. The Battle of the White Mountain was a turning point in the history of central Europe.

The War Widens.   For the Habsburgs, religious and dynastic interests were inseparable. Ferdinand II and Philip III of Spain fought for their beliefs and for their patrimony. Their victory gave them more than they could have expected. Ferdinand swallowed up Bohemia and strengthened his position in the empire. Philip gained possession of a vital link in his supply route between Italy and the Netherlands. Spanish expansion threatened France. The occupation of the Lower Palatinate placed a ring of Spanish armies around France from the Pyrenees to the Low Countries.

Frederick, now in Holland, refused to accept the judgment of battle. He lobbied for a grand alliance to repel the Spaniards from the Lower Palatinate and to restore the religious balance in the empire. Though his personal cause met with little sympathy, his political logic was impeccable, especially after Spain again declared war on the Dutch. A grand Protestant alliance—secretly supported by the French—brought together England, Holland, a number of German states, and Denmark. It was the Danes who led this potentially powerful coalition. In 1626 a large Danish army under the command of King Christian IV engaged imperial forces on German soil. But Danish forces could not match the superior numbers and the superior leadership of the Catholic mercenary forces under the command of the ruthless and brilliant Count Albrecht von Wallenstein (1583–1634). In 1629 the Danes withdrew from the empire and sued for peace.

If the Catholic victory at the White Mountain in 1620 threatened the well-being of German Protestantism, the Catholic triumph over the Danes threatened its survival. More powerful than ever, Ferdinand II determined to turn the religious clock back to the state of affairs that had existed when the Peace of Augsburg was concluded in 1555. He demanded that all lands which had then been Catholic but had since become Protestant must now be returned to the fold. He also proclaimed that as the Peace of Augsburg made no provision for the toleration of Calvinists, they would no longer be tolerated in the empire. These policies together constituted a virtual revolution in the religious affairs of the German states, and they proved impossible to impose. Ferdinand succeeded in only one thing—he united Lutherans and Calvinists against him.

The costs of the war were heavy even for the victors. Wallenstein, who had over 130,000 men in arms, would no longer take orders from anyone, and Ferdinand II was forced to dismiss him from service. Then in 1630 King Gustavus Adolphus of Sweden decided to enter the German conflict to protect Swedish interests. While Gustavus Adolphus struggled to construct his alliance, imperial forces continued their triumphant progress. In 1631 they besieged, captured, and put to the torch the town of Magdeburg. The sack of Magdeburg marked a turning point in Protestant fortunes. Brandenburg and Saxony joined Gustavus Adolphus, not only enlarging his forces, but allowing him to open a second front in Bohemia. In the autumn of 1631 this combination overwhelmed the imperial armies. Gustavus won a decisive triumph at Breitenfeld, while the Saxons occupied Prague.

Gustavus Adolphus lost no time in pressing his advantage. While Ferdinand II pleaded with Wallenstein to again lead the imperial forces, the Swedes marched west to the Rhine, easily conquering the richest of the Catholic cities and retaking the Lower Palatinate. In early 1632 Protestant forces plundered Bavaria, but Wallenstein resumed his command and chose to chase the Saxons from Bohemia rather than the Swedes from Bavaria. Not until the winter of 1632 did the armies of Gustavus and Wallenstein finally meet. At the Battle of Lutzen the Swedes won the field but lost their beloved king. Wounded in the leg, the back, and the head, Gustavus Adolphus died. In less than two years he had decisively transformed the course of the war and the course of Europe's future. Protestant forces now occupied most of central and northern Germany.

The final stages of the war involved the resumption of the century-old struggle between France and Spain. When the Twelve Years' Truce expired in 1621, Spain again declared war on the Dutch. Dutch naval power was considerable, and the Dutch took the war to the far reaches of the globe, attacking Portuguese settlements in Brazil and in the East and harassing Spanish shipping on the high seas. In 1628 the Dutch captured the entire Spanish treasure fleet as it sailed from the New World. Spain had declared bankruptcy in 1627, and the loss of the whole of the next year's treasure from America exacerbated an already catastrophic situation.

These reversals, combined with the continued successes of Habsburg forces in central Europe, convinced Louis XIII and his chief minister, Cardinal Richelieu, that the time for active involvement in European affairs was now at hand. Throughout the early stages of the war, France had secretly aided anti-Habsburg forces. Gustavus Adolphus's unexpected success dramatically altered French calculations. Now it was evident that the Habsburgs could no longer combine their might, and Spanish energies would be drained off in the Netherlands and in central Europe. The time had come to take an open stand. In 1635 France declared war on Spain.

France took the offensive first, invading the Spanish Netherlands. In 1636 a Spanish army struck back, pushing to within twenty-five miles of Paris before it was repelled. Both sides soon began to search for a settlement, but pride prevented them from laying down their arms. Spain toppled first. Its economy in shambles and its citizens in revolt over high prices and higher taxes, it could no longer maintain its many-fronted war. The Swedes again defeated imperial forces in Germany. The Dutch destroyed much of Spain's Atlantic fleet in 1639, and the Portuguese rose up against the union of crowns that had brought them nothing but expense and the loss of crucial portions of their empire. In 1640 the Portuguese regained their independence. In 1643 Spain gambled once more on a knockout blow against the French. But at the Battle of Rocroi, exhausted French troops held out and the Spanish invasion failed.

By now the desire for peace was universal. Most of the main combatants had long since perished: Philip III, ever optimistic, in 1621; Frederick V, an exile to the end, in 1632; Gustavus Adolphus, killed at Lutzen in the same year; Wallenstein, murdered by order of Ferdinand II in 1634; Ferdinand himself in 1637; and Louis XIII in 1643, five days before the French triumph at Rocroi. Those who succeeded them had not the same passions, and after so many decades the longing for peace was the strongest emotion on the Continent.

In 1648 a series of agreements, collectively known as the Peace of

Westphalia, established the outlines of the political geography of Europe for the next century. Its focus was on the Holy Roman Empire and it reflected Protestant successes in the final two decades of war. Sweden gained further territories on the Baltic, making it master of the north German ports. France, too, gained in territory and prestige. It kept the vital towns in the Lower Palatinate through which Spanish men and matériel had moved and, though it did not agree to come to terms with Spain immediately, France's fear of encirclement was at an end. The Dutch gained statehood through official recognition by Spain and through the power they had displayed in building and maintaining an overseas empire.

Territorial boundaries were reestablished as they had existed in 1624, giving the Habsburgs control of both Bohemia and Hungary. The independence of the Swiss cantons was now officially recognized as were the rights of Calvinists to the protection of the Peace of Augsburg, which again was to govern the religious affairs of the empire. Two of the larger German states were strengthened as a counterweight to the emperor's power. Bavaria was allowed to retain the Upper Palatinate, and Brandenburg, which ceded some of its coastal territory to Sweden, gained extensive territories in the east. The emperor's political control over the German states was also weakened. German rulers were given independent authority over their states and the imperial diet, rather than the emperor, was empowered to settle disputes. Thus weakened, future emperors ruled in the Habsburg territorial lands with little

The Thirty Years' War

1618 Defenestration of Prague

1619 Ferdinand Habsburg elected Holy Roman Emperor; Frederick of the Palatinate accepts the crown of Bohemia

1620 Catholic victory at battle of White Mountain

1621 End of Twelve Years' Truce; war between Spain and Netherlands

1626 Danes form Protestant alliance under Christian IV

1627 Spain declares bankruptcy

1630 Gustavus Adolphus leads Swedish forces into Germany

1631 Sack of Magdeburg; Protestant victory at Breitenfield

1632 Protestant victory at Lutzen; death of Gustavus Adolphus

1635 France declares war on Spain

1640 Portugal secedes from Spain

1643 Battle of Rocroi; French forces repel Spaniards

1648 Peace of Westphalia

The Peace of Westphalia, Europe 1648

ability to control, or influence, or even arbitrate German affairs. The judgment that the Holy Roman Empire was neither holy, Roman, nor an empire was now irrevocably true.

The Rise of the Royal State

The religious and dynastic wars that dominated the early part of the seventeenth century had a profound impact on the western European states. Not only did they cause terrible suffering and deprivation, but they also demanded efficient and better centralized states to conduct them. More and more power was absorbed by the monarch and his chief advisers. More and more of the traditional privileges of aristocracy and of towns were eroded. At the center of these rising states, particularly in western Europe, were the king and his court. In the provinces were tax collectors and military recruiters.

Divine Kings

In the early sixteenth century, monarchs treated their states and their subjects as personal property. Correspondingly, rulers were praised in personal terms, for their virtue, their wisdom, or their strength. By the early seventeenth century, the monarchy had been transformed into an office of state. Now rulers embodied their nation and, no matter what their personal characteristics, they were held in awe because they were monarchs. They had permanent seats of government attended by vast courts of officials, place seekers, and servants. The idea of the capital city emerged, with Madrid, London, and Paris as the models. Artistic enterprise glorifying the monarchy flourished across the Continent. Portraits of rulers in action and repose conveyed the central message—the grandeur and pomp, the power and self-assurance of seventeenth-century monarchs. National history, particularly of recent events, enjoyed wide popularity. Its avowed purpose was to draw the connection between the past and the present glories of the state. One of the most popular French histories of the period was entitled *On the Excellence of the Kings and the Kingdom of France.* In England it was a period of renaissance. Poets, playwrights, historians, and philosophers by the dozens gravitated to the English court. Writers such as Ben Jonson (1572–1637) and William Shakespeare (1564–1616) took the grandeur of England and its rulers for their themes.

The political theory of the divine right of kings further enhanced the importance of monarchs. This theory held that the institution of monarchy had been created by God, and the monarch functioned as God's representative on earth. In *The True Law of Free Monarchies* (1598) King James I of England reasoned that God had placed kings on earth to rule, and he would judge them in heaven for their transgressions. This sentiment echoed the commonplace view of French political theorists.

Though at first glance the theory of the divine right of kings appears to be a blueprint for arbitrary rule, in fact it was yoked together with a number of principles that restrained the conduct of the monarch. Kings were bound by the law of nature and the law of nations. They could not deprive their subjects of their lives, their liberties, or their property without due cause established by law. Wherever they turned, kings were instructed in the duties of kingship. In tracts, in letters, and in literature they were lectured on the obligations of their office.

The Court and the Courtiers

For all of the bravura of divine right theory, far more was expected of kings than they could possibly deliver. The day-to-day affairs of government had grown beyond the capacity of any monarch to handle them. The expansion in the powers of the western states absorbed more officials than ever. At the beginning of the sixteenth century the court of Francis I employed 622 officers;

at the beginning of the seventeenth century the court of Henry IV employed over 1,500. Yet the difference was not only in size. Members of the seventeenth-century court were becoming servants of the state as well as of the monarch.

Expanding the court was one of the ways in which monarchs coopted potential rivals within the aristocracy. In return, those who were favored enhanced their power by royal grants of titles, lands, and income. As the court expanded so did the political power of courtiers. Royal councils—a small group of leading officeholders who advised the monarch on state business—grew in significance. Yet, like everything else in seventeenth-century government, the court revolved around the monarch. The monarch appointed, promoted, and dismissed officeholders at will. Ministers acted as a safety valve for the monarchy. When royal policy succeeded it was the king's success; when royal policy failed it was the minister's failure. As befit this type of personal government, most monarchs chose a single individual to act as a funnel for private and public business. This was the "favorite," whose role combined varying proportions of best friend, right-hand man, and hired gun.

Some favorites, like the French Cardinal Richelieu (1585–1642) and the Spanish Count-Duke Olivares (1587–1645), were able to transform themselves into chief ministers with a political philosophy and a vision of government. Cardinal Richelieu was given a court post through the patronage of Queen Marie de Médicis, mother of Louis XIII. The two men made a good match. Louis XIII hated the work of ruling and Richelieu loved little else. Though Richelieu received great favor from the king—he became a duke and amassed the largest private fortune in France—his position rested on his managerial abilities. Richelieu never enjoyed a close personal relationship with his monarch or felt his position was secure. In 1630, Marie de Médicis turned against him, and he was very nearly ousted from office.

This portrait of Richelieu by Philippe de Champaigne shows the cardinal's intellectual power and controlled determination.

The Count-Duke Olivares, a younger son of a lesser branch of a great Spanish noble family, became the favorite of King Philip IV (1621–1665). Like Richelieu, Olivares attempted to further the process of centralizing royal power. And like his French counterpart, he was unable to overcome entrenched opposition. Olivares's plans for a nationally recruited and financed army ended in disaster. He advocated the aggressive foreign policy that mired Spain in the Thirty Years' War in Europe and the 80 years of war in the Netherlands. As domestic and foreign crises mounted, Philip IV could not resist the pressure to dismiss his chief minister. In 1643 Olivares was removed from office, and two years later, physically exhausted and mentally deranged, he died. Richelieu and Olivares met different ends, yet in their own ways they shared a common goal: to extend the authority and control of the monarch over his state.

The Drive to Govern

One of the chief means by which kings and councillors attempted to expand the authority of the state was through the legal system. Administering justice was one of the sacred duties of the monarchy. The complexities of ecclesiastical, civil, and customary law gave trained lawyers an essential role in government. As legal experts and the demands for legal services increased, royal law courts multiplied and expanded. In France the Parlement of Paris, the main law court of the state, became a powerful institution that contested with courtiers for the right to advise the monarch. The number of regional parlements increased, bringing royal justice to the farthest reaches of the realm. In Spain the *letrados*—university-trained lawyers who were normally members of the nobility—were the backbone of royal government. Formal legal training was a requirement for many of the administrative posts in the state.

In England the legal system expanded differently. Central courts situated in the royal palace of Westminster grew and the lawyers and judges who practiced in them became a powerful profession. They were especially active in the House of Commons of the English Parliament, which along with the House of Lords had extensive advisory and legislative powers. More important than the rise of the central courts, however, was the rise of the local ones. The English crown extended royal justice to the counties by granting legal authority to members of the local social elite. These justices of the peace, as they were known, became agents of the crown in their own localities. Justices were given power to hear and settle minor cases and to imprison those who had committed serious offenses until the assizes, the semiannual sessions of the county court.

Assizes combined the ceremony of rule with its process. Royal authority was displayed in a great procession to the courthouse that was led by the judge and the county justices, followed by the grand and petty juries of local citizens who would hear the cases, and finally by the carts carrying the prisoners to trial. Along with the legal business that was performed, assizes were occasions for edifying sermons, typically on the theme of obedience.

Efforts to integrate center and locality extended to more than the exercise of justice. The monarch also needed officials who could enforce royal policy in those localities where the special privileges of groups and individuals remained strong. The best strategy was to appoint local leaders to royal office. But with so much of the aristocracy resident at court, this was not always an effective course. By the beginning of the seventeenth century, the French monarchy began to rely on new central officials known as *intendants* to perform many of the tasks of the provincial governors. The Lords Lieutenant were a parallel institution created in England. Unlike every other European state, England had no national army. Every English county was required to raise, equip, and train its own militia. Lords Lieutenant chosen from the greatest nobles of the realm were in charge of these trained bands, but they delegated their work to members of the gentry, large local landholders who took on their tasks as a matter of prestige rather than profit.

Efforts to centralize the affairs of the Spanish monarchy could not proceed so easily. The separate regions over which the king ruled maintained their own laws and privileges. Attempts to apply Castilian rules or implant Castilian officials always drew opposition from other regions. In 1625 Olivares proposed a way to solve the dual problems of military manpower and military finance. He launched a plan for a Union of Arms to which all the separate regions of the empire, including Mexico and Peru in the west, Italy in the east, and the separate regions in Iberia would contribute. Catalonia stood upon its ancient privileges and refused to grant either troops or funds, but Olivares was able to establish at least the principle of unified cooperation.

More than anything else, war propelled the consolidation of the state. Perhaps half of all revenue of the western states went to finance war. To maintain the armies and navies, old taxes had to be collected more efficiently and new taxes had to be introduced and enforced. But the unprecedented demands for money on the part of the state were always resisted. The privileged challenged the legality of levying taxes; the unprivileged did whatever they could to avoid paying them. In Spain and France, the principal problem was that so much of the wealth of the nation was beyond the reach of traditional royal taxation. The nobility and many of the most important towns had long achieved exemption from basic taxes on consumption and wealth. European taxation was regressive, falling most heavily on those least able to pay. Though rulers and subjects alike recognized the inequities of the European system of taxation, the fiscal crisis that the European wars provoked did result in an expansion of state taxation.

New taxes and increased rates of traditional taxation created suffering and a sense of grievance throughout the western European states. Opposition to taxation was not based on greed. The state's right to tax was not yet an established principle. Monarchs received certain forms of revenue in return for grants of immunities and privileges to powerful groups in their state. The state's efforts to go beyond these restricted grants was reviewed as theft of private property.

*T*he Crises of the Royal State

The expansion of the functions, duties, and powers of the state in the early seventeenth century was not universally welcomed in European societies. The growth of central government came at the expense of local rights and privileges held by corporate bodies like the Church and the towns or by individuals like provincial officials and aristocrats. State exactions burdened all segments of society. Peasants lost the small benefit that rising prices had conferred on producers. Larger landholders, whose prosperity depended on rents and services from an increasingly impoverished peasantry, suffered along with their tenants.

By the middle of the seventeenth century, a Europe-wide crisis was taking shape. Rural protests, like grain riots and mob assaults on local institutions, had a long history in all of the European states. Popular revolt was not the product of mindless despair, but rather the natural form of political action for those who fell outside the institutionalized political process. Bread riots and tax revolts became increasingly common in the early seventeenth century. More importantly, as the focus of discontent moved from local institutions to the state, the forms of revolt changed. So, too, did the participants. Members of the political elite began to formulate their own grievances against the expansion of state power. A theory of resistance, first developed in the French wars of religion, came to be applied to political tyranny and posed a direct challenge to the idea of the divine right of kings. By the 1640s all of these forces converged and rebellion exploded across the Continent. In Spain the ancient kingdoms of Catalonia and Portugal asserted their independence from Castilian rule; in France members of the aristocracy rose against a child monarch and his regent. In Italy, revolts rocked Naples and Sicily. In England, a constitutional crisis gave way to civil war and then to the first political revolution in European history.

The Right to Resist

Europeans lived more precariously in the seventeenth century than in any period since the Black Death. One benchmark of crisis was population decline. In the Mediterranean, Spanish population fell from 8.5 to 7 million and Italian population from 13 to 11 million. The ravages of the Thirty Years' War were most clearly felt in central Europe. Germany lost nearly a third of its people, Bohemia nearly half. Northwestern Europe—that is, England, the Netherlands,

The Plague in Milan, *a painting by Caspar Crayer of the seventeenth-century Flemish school. The victims of the epidemic are shown being consoled by a priest.*

and France—was hardest hit in the first half of the century and only gradually recovered by 1700. Population decline had many causes and, rather remarkably, direct casualties from warfare were a very small component. The indirect effects of war, the disruption of agriculture, and the spread of disease were far more devastating. All sectors of the European economy from agriculture to trade stagnated or declined in the early seventeenth century. Not surprisingly, peasants were hardest hit. The surplus from good harvests did not remain in rural communities to act as a buffer for bad ones.

The most spectacular popular uprisings occurred in Spanish-occupied Italy—at Palermo and Naples. The Neapolitan revolt began in 1647 after the Spanish placed a tax on fruit. A crowd gathered to protest the new imposition, burned the customs house, and murdered several local officials. But neither of the Italian urban revolts could attract support from the local governors or the nobility, and both uprisings were eventually crushed.

Rural and urban revolts by members of the lower orders of European society were doomed to failure. Not only did the state control vast military resources, but it could count on the loyalty of the governing classes to suppress local disorder. It was only when local elites rebelled and joined their social and political discontent to the economic grievances of the peasants that the state faced a genuine crisis. Traditionally, aristocratic rebellion, such as the French Fronde, which began in 1648, centered on the legitimacy rather than the power of the state.

Luther and Calvin had preached a doctrine of passive obedience. Magistrates ruled by divine will and must be obeyed in all things, they argued. Both left a tiny crack in the door of absolute submission, however, by recognizing the right of lesser magistrates to resist their superiors if divine law was violated. It was during the French civil wars that a broader theory of resistance began to develop. In attempting to defend themselves from accusations that they were rebels, a number of Huguenot writers responded with an argument which accepted the divine right of kings but limited royal power. They claimed that kings were placed on earth by God to uphold piety and justice. When they failed to do so, lesser magistrates were obliged to resist. But in the writings of both Huguenot and Dutch Protestants there remained strict limits to this right to resist. These authors accepted all the premises of divine right theory and restricted resistance to other divinely ordained magistrates.

Obedience tied society together at all levels. Loosening any of the knots might unravel everything. In fact, one crucial binding had already come loose when the arguments used to justify resistance in matters of religion came to be applied to matters of state. Logic soon drove the argument further. In *The King and the Education of the King* (1598), a Jesuit professor, Juan de Mariana (1536–1624), declared that magistrates were nothing other than the people's representatives, and if it was the duty of magistrates to resist the tyranny of monarchs, then it must also be the duty of every individual citizen. Such theories of resistance were to have their greatest application in England.

Civil War and Revolution in England

James I was not a lovable monarch but he was capable, astute, and generous. In the eyes of his critics he had two great faults: He succeeded a legend and he was Scottish. There was little he could do about either. Elizabeth I had ruled England successfully for over forty years. As the economy soured and the state tilted toward bankruptcy in the 1590s, the queen remained above criticism. She sold off royal lands worth thousands of pounds and ran up huge debts at the turn of the century. Yet the gleaming myth of the glorious virgin queen tarnished not the least bit. When she died, the general population wept openly and the governing elite breathed a collective sigh of relief. There was so much to be done to set things right. But if Elizabeth could do no wrong, James could do little right. Though he relied on Elizabeth's most trusted ministers to guide state business, James was soon plunged into financial and political difficulties. He never escaped from either.

The financial problems of James I resulted directly from the fact that the tax base of the English monarchy was undervalued. For decades the monarchy had staved off a crisis by selling lands that had been confiscated from the Church in the mid sixteenth century. But this solution reduced the crown's long-term revenues and made it dependent on extraordinary grants of taxation from Parliament. Royal demands for money were met by parliamentary demands for political reform, and these differing objectives provoked unintentional political controversies in the 1620s. The most significant, in 1628, during the reign of Charles I (1625–1649), led to the formulation of the Petition of Right, which restated the traditional English freedoms from arbitrary arrest and imprisonment (habeas corpus), from nonparliamentary taxation, and from the confiscation of property by martial law.

Religious problems mounted on top of economic and political difficulties. Demands were made for thoroughgoing church reforms by groups and individuals who had little in common other than the name given to them by their detractors: Puritans. One of the most contentious issues raised by some Puritans was the survival in the Anglican church of the Catholic hierarchy of archbishops and bishops. They demanded the abolition of this episcopal form of government and its replacement with a presbyterial system similar to that in Scotland, in which congregations nominated their own representatives to a national assembly. As the king was the supreme head of the English church, an attack on church structure was an attack on the monarchy. "No bishop, no king," James I declared.

Neither James I nor his son, Charles I, opposed religious reform, but to achieve their reforms they strengthened episcopal power. In the 1620s Archbishop William Laud (1573–1645) rose to power in the English church by espousing a Calvinism so moderate that many denied it was Calvinism at all. One of Laud's first projects after he was appointed archbishop of Canterbury was to establish a consistent divine service in England and Scotland by creating new prayer books. In Scotland, the new prayer books were met with strong resistance. To Charles I the opposition was rebellion and he began to raise forces to suppress it. But Scottish soldiers were far more determined to preserve their religious practice than were English soldiers to impose the king's. By the end of 1640 a Scottish army had successfully invaded England.

For 11 years Charles I had managed to do what he was in theory supposed to do: live from his own revenues. He had accomplished this by a combination of economy and the revival of ancient feudal rights that struck hard at the governing classes. He levied fines for unheard-of offenses, expanded traditional taxes, and added a brutal efficiency to the collection of revenue. While these expedients sufficed during peacetime, now that an army had to be raised and a war fought, Charles I was again dependent on grants from Parliament, which he reluctantly summoned in 1640. The Long Parliament, which met in November 1640 and sat for 13 years, saw little urgency in levying taxes to repel the Scots. Members of Parliament had a host of political grievances to be redressed before they granted the king his money. They proposed a number of constitutional reforms that Charles I reluctantly accepted: The Long Parliament would not be dismissed without its own consent. In the future Parliaments would be summoned once every three years. Due process in common law would be observed and the ancient taxes that the crown had revived would be abolished.

At first Charles I could do nothing but bide his time and accept these assaults on his power and authority. Once he had crushed the Scots he would be able to bargain from a position of strength. But as the months passed it became clear that Parliament had no intention of providing him with money or forces. Rather, the members sought to negotiate with the Scots themselves and to continue to demand concessions from the king as long as the Scottish threat remained. By the end of 1641 Charles's patience had worn thin. He bungled an attempt to arrest the leaders of the House of Commons, but he successfully spirited his wife and children out of London. Then he, too, left the capital and headed north where, in the summer of 1642, he raised the royal standard and declared the leaders of Parliament rebels and traitors. England was plunged into civil war.

There were strong passions on both sides. Parliamentarians believed that they were fighting to defend their religion, their liberties, and the rule of law. Royalists believed they were fighting to defend their monarch, their church, and social stability. After nearly three years of inconclusive fighting, in June 1645 Parliament won a decisive victory at Naseby and brought the war to an end the following summer. The king was in captivity, bishops had been abolished, a Presbyterian church had been established, and limitations were placed on royal power. All that remained necessary to end three years of civil war was the king's agreement to abide by the judgment of battle.

But Charles I had no intention of surrendering either his religion or his authority. Despite the rebels' successes, they could not rule without him, and he would concede nothing as long as opportunities to maneuver remained. In 1647 there were opportunities galore. The war had proved ruinously expensive to Parliament. It owed enormous sums to the Scots, to its own soldiers, and to the governors of London. Each of these elements had its own objectives in a final settlement of the war, and they were not altogether compatible. London feared the parliamentary army, unpaid and camped dangerously close to the capital. The Scots and the English Presbyterians in Parliament feared that the religious settlement already made would be sacrificed by those known as Independents, who desired a more decentralized church. The Independents feared that they would be persecuted just as harshly by the Presbyterians as they had been by the king. In fact, the war had settled nothing.

The civil war, which had come so close to resolution in 1647, now became a military revolution. New fighting broke out in 1648 as Charles encouraged his supporters to resume the war. But forces under the command of Sir Thomas Fairfax (1612–1671) and Oliver Cromwell (1599–1658) easily crushed the royalist uprisings in England and Scotland. The army now demanded that Charles I be brought to justice for his treacherous conduct both before and during the war. When the majority in Parliament refused, still hoping against hope to reach an accommodation with the king, the soldiers again acted decisively. In December 1648 army regiments were sent to London to purge the two houses of Parliament of those who opposed the army's demands. The remaining members, contemptuously called the Rump Parliament, voted to bring the king to trial for his crimes against the liberties of his subjects. On 30 January 1649, Charles I was executed and England was declared a commonwealth. The monarchy and the House of Lords were abolished. The nation was to be governed by the Rump Parliament.

For four years the members of the Rump Parliament struggled with proposals for a new constitution while balancing the demands of moderate and radical reformers and an increasingly hostile army. In 1653 Oliver Cromwell, with the support of the army's senior officers, forcibly dissolved the Rump and became the leader of the revolutionary government. At first he ruled along with a Parliament handpicked from among the supporters of the commonwealth. But when Cromwell's Parliament proved no more capable of governing than the Rump, a written constitution, The Instrument of Government (1653), established a new polity. Cromwell was given the title Lord Protector. He was to rule along with a freely elected Parliament and an administrative body known as the council of state. Though many urged him to accept the crown of England and begin a new monarchy, Cromwell steadfastly held out for a government in which fundamental authority resided in Parliament.

But a sense that only a single person could effectively rule a state remained too strong for the reforms of the revolutionary regimes to have much chance of success. When Cromwell died in 1658 his eldest son Richard was proposed as the new Lord Protector, but Richard had very little experience in either military or civil affairs. In 1659 the army again intervened in civil affairs, dismissing the recently elected Parliament and calling for the restoration of the monarchy to provide stability to the state. After the king agreed to a general

Rulers of England, 1603–1714

James I	1603–1625
Charles I	1625–1649
Cromwell	1649–1658
Charles II	1649–1685
James II	1685–1688
William III and Mary	1689–1702
Anne	1702–1714

amnesty with only a few exceptions, the Stuarts were restored when Charles II (1649–1685) took the throne in 1660.

Twenty years of civil war and revolution had their effect. Parliament became a permanent part of civil government and now had to be managed rather than ignored. Royal power over taxation and religion was curtailed, though in fact Parliament proved more vigorous in suppressing religious dissent than the monarchy ever had. England was to be a reformed Protestant state though there remained much dispute about what constituted reform. Absolute monarchy had become constitutional monarchy with the threat of revolution behind the power of Parliament and the threat of anarchy behind the power of the crown.

Both threats proved potent in 1685 when James II (1685–1688) came to the throne. An avowed Catholic, James attempted to use his power of appointment to foil the constraints that Parliament imposed on him. He elevated Catholics to leading posts in the military and in the central government and began a campaign to pack a new Parliament with his supporters. This proved too much for the governing classes, who entered into negotiations with William, Prince of Orange, husband of Mary Stuart, James's eldest daughter. In 1688 William landed in England with a small force. Without support, James II fled to France, the English throne was declared vacant, and William and Mary were proclaimed king and queen of England. There was little bloodshed in England and little threat of social disorder, and the event soon came to be called the Glorious Revolution. Its achievements were set down in the Declaration of Rights (1689), which was presented to William and Mary before they took the throne. The Declaration reasserted the fundamental principles of constitutional monarchy as they had developed over the previous half century. Security of property and the regularity of Parliaments were guaranteed. The Toleration Act (1689) granted religious freedom to nearly all groups of Protestants. The liberties of the subject and the rights of the sovereign were to be in balance.

The events of 1688 in England reversed a trend toward increasing power on the part of the Stuarts. This second episode of resistance resulted in the development of a unique form of government which, a century later, would spawn dozens of imitators. John Locke (1632–1704) was the theorist of the Revolution of 1688. He was heir to the century-old debate on resistance and he carried the doctrine to a new plateau. In *Two Treatises on Civil Government* (1690), Locke developed the contract theory of government. Political society was a compact that individuals entered into freely for their own well-being. It was designed to maintain each person's natural rights—life, liberty, and property. Natural rights were inherent in individuals; they could not be given away. The contract between rulers and subjects was an agreement for the protection of natural rights. When rulers acted arbitrarily, they were to be deposed by their subjects, preferably in the relatively peaceful manner in which James II had been replaced by William III.

$\mathcal{T}$ he Zenith of the Royal State

Opposition to the rising royal states made clear the universal desire for stable government, which was seen as the responsibility of both subjects and rulers. The natural advantages of monarchy had to be merged with the interests of the citizens of the state and their desires for wealth, safety, and honor. After so much chaos and instability, the monarchy had to be elevated above the fray of day-to-day politics, elevated to become a symbol of the power and glory of the nation.

By the second half of the seventeenth century, effective government was the byword of the royal state. In England, Holland, and Sweden a form of constitutional monarchy developed in which rulers shared power, in varying degrees, with other institutions of state. In England it was Parliament, in Holland the town oligarchies, and in Sweden the nobility. But in most other states in Europe there developed a pure form of royal government known as absolutism. Absolute monarchy revived the divine right theories of kingship and added to them a cult of the personality of the ruler.

Absolute Monarchy

The English philosopher Thomas Hobbes (1588–1679), in his greatest work *Leviathan* (1651), argued that before civil society had been formed, humans lived in a savage state of nature, "in a war of every man against every man." People came together to form a government for the most basic of all purposes: for self-preservation. Without government they were condemned to a life that was "solitary, poor, nasty, brutish, and short." To escape the state of nature, individuals pooled their power and granted it to a ruler. The terms of the Hobbesian contract were simple. Rulers agreed to rule; subjects agreed to obey. When the contract was intact, people ceased to live in a state of nature. When it was broken, they returned to it. With revolts, rebellions, and revolutions erupting in all parts of Europe, Hobbes's state of nature never seemed very far away, and for most states of Europe in the later seventeenth century, the consolidation of power in the hands of the divinely ordained monarch who, nevertheless, ruled according to principles of law and justice, was seen as the perfect form of government.

The main features of absolute monarchy were all designed to extend royal control. As in the early seventeenth century, the person of the monarch was revered. Courts grew larger and more lavish in an effort to enhance the glory of the monarchy and thereby of the state. *L'état, c'est moi*—"I am the state"— Louis XIV was supposed to have said. No idea better expresses absolutism's connection between governor and governed. As the king grew in stature, his competitors for power all shrank. Large numbers of nobles were herded together at court under the watchful eye of monarchs who now ruled rather than reigned. Representative institutions, especially those that laid claim to control over taxation, were weakened or cast aside for obstructing efficient government and endangering the welfare of the state. Monarchs needed standing armies, permanent forces that could be drilled and trained in the increasingly sophisticated arts of war. Thus the military was expanded and made an integral part of the machinery of government.

Frederick William, the great elector of Brandenburg-Prussia (1640–1688), was one of the European princes who made the most effective use of the techniques of absolutism. In 1640 he inherited a scattered and ungovernable collection of territories. The nobility, known as *die Junker*, enjoyed immunity from almost all forms of direct taxation, and the towns had no obligation to furnish either men or supplies for military operations beyond their walls. By the 1650s Frederick William had established the excise—a commodity tax on consumption—in the towns.

With the excise as a steady source of revenue, the great elector could now create one of the most capable standing armies of the age. The strictest discipline was maintained in the new Prussian army, and it developed into a feared and efficient fighting machine. Frederick William organized one of the first departments of war to oversee all of the details of the creation of his army, from housing and supplies to the training of young officer candidates. This department was also responsible for the collection of taxes. By integrating military and civilian government, Frederick William was able to create an efficient state bureaucracy that was particularly responsive in times of crisis. The creation of the Prussian army was the force that led to the creation of the Prussian state.

Louis le Grand

Nowhere was absolutism as successfully implanted as in France, and nowhere was it less likely to have grown. Louis XIII (1610–1643) was only 8 years old when he came to the throne, and he grew slowly into his role under the tutelage of Cardinal Richelieu. It was Richelieu's vision that stabilized French government. As chief minister, he saw clearly that the prosperity and even the survival of France depended on strengthening royal power. He preached a doctrine of *raison d'état*—reason of state—in which he placed the needs of the nation above the privileges of its most important groups.

Richelieu's program was a vital prelude to the development of absolute monarchy in France. Seeing the power of local officials as a threat to stable royal government, he used intendants to examine their conduct and to reform their administration. He made careful appointments of local governors and brought more regions under direct royal control. Against the Huguenots,

Richelieu's policy was more subtle. He was less interested in challenging their religion than their autonomy. In 1627 when the English sent a force to aid the Huguenots against the government, Richelieu and Louis XIII abolished the Huguenots' privileges altogether. They were allowed to maintain their religion but not their special status. Finally, in 1685 Louis XIV (1643–1715) revoked the Edict of Nantes. All forms of Protestant worship were outlawed and the ministers who were not killed were forced into exile.

Louis XIV (1643–1715) was four years old when he inherited the French throne. His mother, Anne of Austria (1601–1666), ruled as regent with the help

This Hyacinthe Rigaud portrait of Louis XIV in his corona-
tion robes shows the splendor of the Roi Soleil (Sun King)
who believed himself to be the center of France as the sun is
the center of the solar system.

of her Italian adviser, Cardinal Mazarin (1602–1661). In the circumstances of war, agricultural crises, and financial stringency, no regency government was going to be popular, but Anne and Mazarin made the worst of a bad situation. They initiated new taxes on officeholders, Parisian landowners, and the nobility. Soon all three united against them, led by the Parlement of Paris, the highest court in the land, in which new decrees of taxation had to be registered. In 1648 the Parlement refused to register a number of the new taxes proposed by the government and soon insisted on the right to control the crown's financial policy. When Anne and Mazarin struck back by arresting a number of leading members of the Parlement, barricades went up in Paris, and the court, along with the 9-year-old king, fled the capital. Quickly the Fronde—which took its name from the slingshots that children used to hurl stones at carriages—became an aristocratic revolt aimed not at the king, but at his advisers. Demands for Mazarin's resignation, the removal of the new taxes, and greater participation in government by nobles and Parlement were coupled with profuse statements of loyalty to the king.

The Duc de Condé, leader of the Parisian insurgents, courted Spanish aid against Mazarin's forces, and the cardinal was forced to make concessions to prevent another Spanish invasion of France. The leaders of the Fronde agreed that the crown must overhaul its finances and recognize the rights of the administrative nobility to participate in formulating royal policy. But they had no concrete proposals to accomplish either aim. Nor could they control the deteriorating political situation in Paris and a number of provincial capitals where urban and rural riots followed the upper-class attack on the state. The catastrophic winter of 1652, with its combination of harvest failure, intense cold, and epidemic disease, brought the crisis to a head. Louis XIV, now aged 13, was declared old enough to rule and his forces recaptured Paris, where he was welcomed as a savior.

It was not until Mazarin died in 1661 that the king began to rule. The greatest achievements of his reign were built on the backs of fiscal and military reforms, which were themselves a product of the continuing sophistication of French administration. Louis was blessed with able and energetic ministers. The two central props of his state—money and might—were in the hands of dynamic men, Jean-Baptiste Colbert (1619–1683) and the Marquis de Louvois (1639–1691). Colbert, to whom credit belongs for the building of the French navy, the reform of French legal codes, and the establishment of national academies of culture, was Louis's chief minister for finance. Colbert's fiscal reforms were so successful that in less than six years a debt of 22 million French pounds had become a surplus of 29 million. To Louvois, Louis's minister of war, fell the task of reforming the French army. During the Fronde, royal troops were barely capable of defeating the makeshift forces of the nobility. By the end of the reign, the army had grown to 400,000 and its organization had been thoroughly reformed. Louis XIV built on the institution of the intendant that Richelieu had developed with so much success. Intendants were now a permanent part of government, and their duties expanded from their early responsibilities as coordinators and mediators into areas of policing and tax collection.

Though Louis XIV was well served, it was the king himself who set the tone for French absolutism. "If he was not the greatest king he was the best actor of majesty that ever filled the throne," wrote an English observer. The acting of majesty was central to Louis's rule. His residence at Versailles was the most glittering court of Europe, renowned for its beauty and splendor. During his reign, France replaced Spain as the greatest nation in Europe. Massive royal patronage of art, science, and thought brought French culture to new heights. The French language replaced Latin as the universal European tongue. France was the richest and most populous European state, and Louis's absolute rule finally harnessed these resources to a single purpose.

The Wars of Commerce

For the nearly eighty years between 1565 and 1648 that the Dutch were at war they grew ever more prosperous. Unlike most other Europeans they regarded precious metal as a commodity like any other and took no interest in accumulating it for its own sake. This attitude enabled them to pioneer triangular trading and develop the crucial financial institutions necessary to expand their overseas commerce. The Dutch saw the practical value in Italian accounting and banking methods and raised them to new levels of efficiency.

Elsewhere in Europe, trade was the king's business. The wealth of the nation was part of the prestige of the monarch and its rise or fall part of the crown's power. The competition for trade was seen as a competition between states rather than individual merchants. Trading privileges involved special arrangements with foreign powers, arrangements that recognized the sovereign power of European monarchs.

The competition for power and glory derived from the theory of mercantilism, a set of assumptions about economic activity that were commonly held throughout Europe and guided the policies of almost every government. There were two interrelated ideas. One was that the wealth of a nation resided in its stock of precious metal, and the other was that economic activity was a zero-sum game. There was thought to be a fixed amount of money, a fixed amount of commodities, and a fixed amount of consumption. Thus what one country gained, another lost. If England bought wine from France and paid £ 100,000 in precious metal for it, then England was £ 100,000 poorer and France £ 100,000 richer. If one was to trade profitably, it was absolutely necessary to wind up with a surplus of precious metal. Therefore it was imperative that governments regulate trade so that the stocks of precious metal were protected from the greed of the merchants. The first and most obvious measure of protection, then, was to prohibit the export of coin except by license, a prohibition that was absolutely unenforceable and was violated more often by government officials than by merchants.

These ideas about economic activity led to a variety of forms of economic regulation. The most common was the monopoly, a grant of special privileges in return for both financial considerations and an agreement to abide by the rules set out by the state. Two monopoly companies, the English and the Dutch East India companies, dominated the Asian trade. For those states with Atlantic colonies, regulation took the form of restricting markets rather than traders. In the 1660s the English government, alarmed at the growth of Dutch mercantile activity in the New World, passed a series of Navigation Acts designed to protect English shipping. Colonial goods—primarily tobacco and sugar—could be shipped to and from England only in English boats. In the 1670s Louis XIV's finance minister, Jean-Baptiste Colbert (1619–1683), developed a plan to bolster the French economy by protecting it against European imports. He used tariffs to make imported goods unattractive in France. To protect the investments in French manufacturing, enormous duties were placed on the import of similar goods manufactured elsewhere. The English Navigation Acts and the French tariffs cut heavily into the Dutch trade, but protectionism had its price. Just as the dynastic wars were succeeded by the wars of religion, so were the wars of religion succeeded by the wars of commerce.

The Mercantile Wars.   The belief that there was a fixed amount of trade in the world was still strong in the late seventeenth century. One country's gains in trade were another's losses. There was not more than enough to go around, and it could not be easily understood how the expansion of one country's trade could benefit all countries. Competition for trade was the same as competition for territory or subjects, part of the struggle by which the state grew powerful. It was not inevitable that economic competition would lead to warfare, only that restrictive competition would. This was the lesson that Adam Smith attempted to teach in *The Wealth of Nations* (1776). He argued in economic affairs that government governs best that governs least. Monopolies, special trading privileges, tariffs—all were equally destructive of commerce, wealth, and political stability. Smith advocated a policy of laissez-faire toward all commercial enterprise. Governments should leave commerce to follow its natural path without any legislative interference. This freedom would allow nations to grow, wealth to accumulate, and goods to circulate freely. But Smith's ideas were built on a century of commercial warfare, which had sapped the strength of even the strongest European states.

Commercial warfare in Europe began between the English and the Dutch in the middle of the seventeenth century. Both had established aggressive overseas trading companies in the Atlantic and in Asia. In the early seventeenth century the Dutch were the undisputed leaders, their carrying capacity and trade monopolies the greatest in the world. But the English were rising quickly. Their Atlantic colonies began to produce valuable new commodities like tobacco and sugar and their Asian trade was expanding decade after

Painter Jan Peter depicts an incident in the naval warfare caused by trade rivalry between the Dutch and the English. The Dutch fleet sailed up the Medway River and destroyed many English vessels, towing away a battleship.

decade. Conflict was inevitable, and the result was a series of three naval wars fought between 1652 and 1674.

The Dutch had little choice but to strike out against English policy, but they also had little chance of overall success. Their spectacular naval victory in 1667, when the Dutch fleet surprised many English warships at port and burned both ships and docks at Chatham, obscured the fact that Dutch commercial superiority was slipping. In 1664 the English conquered New Netherland on the North American mainland and renamed it New York. With this defeat, the Dutch lost their largest colonial possession. The wars were costly to both states, nearly bankrupting the English crown in 1672. Anglo-Dutch rivalry was finally laid to rest after 1688, when William of Orange, stadtholder of Holland, became William III (1689–1702), king of England.

The Anglo-Dutch commercial wars were just one part of a larger European conflict. Dutch commerce was as threatening to France as it was to England, though in a different way. Under Colbert, France pursued a policy of economic independence. The state supported internal industrial activity through the financing of large workshops and the encouragement of new manufacturing techniques. To protect French products, Colbert levied a series of punitive tariffs on Dutch imports, which severely depressed both trade and manufacture in Holland. Though the Dutch retaliated with restrictive tariffs of their own—in 1672 they banned the import of all French goods for an entire year—the Dutch economy depended on free trade. The Dutch had much more to lose than France in a battle of protective tariffs.

But the battle that Louis XIV had in mind was to be more deadly than one of tariffs. Greedily he eyed the Spanish Netherlands—to which he had a weak claim through his Habsburg wife—and believed that the Dutch stood in the way of his plans. The Dutch had entered into an alliance with the English and Swedes in 1668 to counter French policy, and Louis was determined to crush them in retaliation. He successfully bought off both of Holland's supposed allies, providing cash pensions to the kings of England and Sweden in return for England's active participation and Sweden's passive neutrality in the impending war. In 1672 Louis's army, over one hundred thousand strong, invaded the Low Countries and swept all before them. Only the opening of the dikes prevented the French from entering the province of Holland itself.

The French invasion coincided with the third Anglo-Dutch war, and the United Provinces found themselves besieged on land and sea. Their international trade was disrupted, their manufacturing industries were in ruins, and their military budget skyrocketed. Only able diplomacy and skillful military leadership prevented total Dutch demise. A separate peace was made with England, and Spain, whose sovereign territory had been invaded, entered the war on the side of the Dutch as did a number of German states. Louis's hope for a lightning victory faded, and the war settled into a series of interminable sieges and reliefs of fortified towns. The Dutch finally persuaded France to come to terms in the Treaty of Nijmegen (1678–1679). While Louis XIV retained a number of the territories he had taken from Spain, his armies withdrew from the United Provinces and he agreed to lift most of the commercial sanctions against Dutch goods. The first phase of mercantile warfare was over.

The Wars of Louis XIV.   It was Louis XIV's ambition to restore the ancient Burgundian territories to the French crown and to provide secure northern and eastern borders for his state. Pursuit of these aims involved him in conflicts with nearly every other European state. Spain had fought for 80 years to preserve the Burgundian inheritance in the Low Countries. By the Peace of Westphalia (1648), the northern portion of this territory became the United Provinces while the southern portion remained loyal to the crown and became the Spanish Netherlands. This territory provided a barrier between Holland and France that both states attempted to strengthen by establishing fortresses and bridgeheads at strategic places. In the east, Louis eyed the duchies of Lorraine and Alsace and the large swath of territory further south known as Franche-Comté. The Peace of Westphalia had granted France control of a number of imperial cities in these duchies, and Louis aimed to link them together. All of these territories were ruled by Habsburgs: Alsace and Lorraine by the Austrian Holy Roman Emperor, Franche-Comté by the Spanish king.

In the late seventeenth century, ambassadors and ministers of state began to develop the theory of a balance of power in Europe. This was a belief that no state or combination of states should be allowed to become so powerful that its existence threatened the peace of the others. Behind this purely political idea of the balance of power lay a theory of collective security that knit together the European state system. French expansion in either direction not

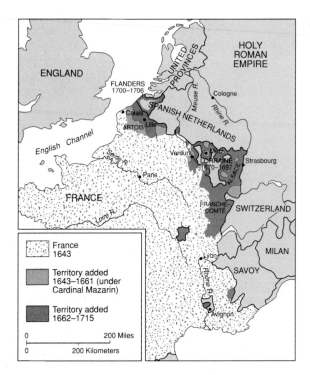

France under Louis XIV

only threatened the other states directly involved but also posed a threat to European security in general.

Louis showed his hand clearly enough in the Franco-Dutch war that had ended in 1679. Though he withdrew his forces from the United Provinces and evacuated most of the territories he had conquered, by the Treaty of Nijmegen France absorbed Franche-Comté as well as portions of the Spanish Netherlands. Louis began plotting his next adventure almost as soon as the treaty was signed. Over the next several years, French troops advanced steadily into Alsace, ultimately forcing the city of Strasbourg, a vital bridgehead on the Rhine, to recognize French sovereignty. Expansion into northern Italy was similarly calculated. Everywhere Louis looked, French engineers rushed to construct fortresses and magazines in preparation for another war.

It finally came in 1688 when French troops poured across the Rhine to seize Cologne. A united German empire led by Leopold I, Archduke of Austria, combined with the maritime powers of England and Holland, led by William III, to form the Grand Alliance, the first of the great balance of power coalitions. In fact, the two sides proved so evenly matched that the Nine Years' War (1688–1697) settled very little, but it demonstrated that a successful European coalition could be formed against France. It also signified the permanent shift in alliances that resulted from the Revolution of 1688 in England. Although the English had allied with France against the Dutch in 1672, after William became king he persuaded the English Parliament that the real enemy was France.

THE SPANISH SUCCESSION

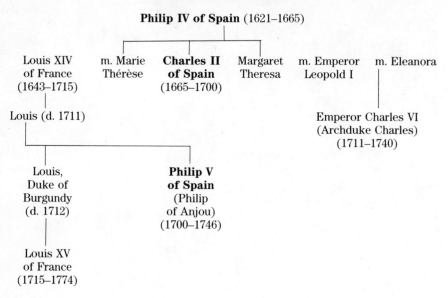

Philip IV of Spain (1621–1665)

Louis XIV
of France
(1643–1715)

m. Marie
Thérèse

**Charles II
of Spain**
(1665–1700)

Margaret
Theresa

m. Emperor
Leopold I

m. Eleanora

Louis (d. 1711)

Emperor Charles VI
(Archduke Charles)
(1711–1740)

Louis,
Duke of
Burgundy
(d. 1712)

**Philip V
of Spain**
(Philip
of Anjou)
(1700–1746)

Louis XV
of France
(1715–1774)

Louis's greatest objective, to secure the borders of his state, had withstood its greatest test. He might have rested satisfied but for the vagaries of births, marriages, and deaths.

Like his father, Louis XIV had married a daughter of the king of Spain. Philip IV had married his eldest daughter to Louis XIV and a younger one to Leopold I of Austria, who subsequently became the Holy Roman Emperor (1658–1705). Before he died, Philip finally fathered a son, Charles II (1665–1700), who attained the Spanish crown at the age of 4 but was mentally and physically incapable of ruling his vast empire. For decades it was apparent that there would be no direct Habsburg successor to an empire which, despite its recent losses, still contained Spain, South America, the Spanish Netherlands, and most of Italy. Louis XIV and Leopold I both had legitimate claims to an inheritance that would have irreversibly tipped the European balance of power.

As Charles II grew increasingly feeble, efforts to find a suitable compromise to the problem of the Spanish succession were led by William III who, as stadtholder of Holland, was vitally interested in the fate of the Spanish Netherlands and, as king of England, in the fate of the Spanish-American colonies. In the 1690s two treaties of partition were drawn up. The first achieved near universal agreement but was nullified by the death of the German prince who was to inherit the Spanish crown. The second, which would have given Italy to Louis's son and everything else to Leopold's son, was opposed by Leopold, who had neither naval nor commercial interests and who claimed most of the Italian territories as imperial fiefs.

All of these plans had been made without consulting the Spanish. If it was the aim of the European powers to partition the Spanish empire in order to prevent any one state from inheriting too much of it, it was the aim of the Spanish to maintain their empire intact. To this end, they devised a brilliant plan. Charles II bequeathed his entire empire to Philip of Anjou, the younger grandson of Louis XIV, with two stipulations: first that Philip renounce his claim to the French throne, and second that he accept the empire intact, without partition. If he—or more to the point, if his grandfather Louis XIV—did not accept these conditions then the empire would pass to Archduke Charles, the younger son of Leopold I. Such provisions virtually assured war between France and the empire unless compromise between the two powers could be reached. But before terms could even be suggested, Charles II died and Philip V (1700–1746) was proclaimed king of Spain and its empire.

Thus the eighteenth century opened with the War of the Spanish Succession (1702–1714). Emperor Leopold rejected the provisions of Charles's will and sent his troops to occupy Italy. Louis XIV confirmed the worst fears of William III when he provided his grandson with French troops to "defend" the Spanish Netherlands. William III revived the Grand Alliance and initiated a massive land war against the combined might of France and Spain. The allied objectives were twofold: to prevent the unification of the French and Spanish thrones and to partition the Spanish empire so that both Italy and the Netherlands were ceded to Austria. The objective of Louis XIV was simply to preserve as much as possible of the Spanish inheritance for the house of Bourbon.

William III died in 1702 and was succeeded by Anne (1702–1714). John Churchill (1650–1722), Duke of Marlborough and commander in chief of the army, continued William's policy. England and Holland again provided most of the finance and sea power, but in addition the English also provided a land army nearly seventy thousand strong. Prussia joined the Grand Alliance, and disciplined Prussian troops helped offset the addition of the Spanish army to Louis's forces. In 1704 Churchill defeated French forces at Blenheim in Germany and in 1706 at Ramillies in the Spanish Netherlands. France's military ascendancy was over.

Efforts to negotiate a peace settlement took longer than the war itself. The Austrians had taken control of Italy, the English and Dutch had secured the Spanish Netherlands, and the French had been driven back beyond the Rhine. The Allies believed that they could now enforce any treaty they pleased on Louis XIV and along with concessions from France attempted to oust his grandson, Philip V, from the Spanish throne. This proved impossible to achieve though it took more than five years to learn the lesson. By then the European situation had taken another strange twist. Both the Emperor Leopold and his eldest son had died. Now Leopold's younger son, Archduke Charles, inherited the empire as Charles VI (1711–1740) and raised the prospect of an equally dangerous combined Austrian-Spanish state. Between 1713 and 1714 a series of treaties at Utrecht settled the War of the Spanish Succession. Spanish possessions in Italy and the Netherlands were ceded to Austria; France

War and Peace, 1648–1763

1648	Peace of Westphalia
1652–1654	First Anglo-Dutch War
1665–1667	Second Anglo-Dutch War
1672	Franco-Dutch war
1672–1674	Third Anglo-Dutch war
1678–1679	Treaty of Nijmegen
1688	Revolution of 1688; William of Orange becomes William III of England Grand Alliance formed
1688–1697	Nine Years' War (France vs. Grand Alliance)
1697	Peace of Ryswick
1702–1714	War of the Spanish Succession
1713–1714	Treaty of Utrecht
1756–1763	Seven Years' War
1763	Peace of Paris

abandoned all its territorial gains east of the Rhine and ceded its North American territories of Nova Scotia and Newfoundland to England. England also acquired Gibraltar on the southern coast of Spain and the island of Minorca in the Mediterranean from Spain. Both were strategically important to English commercial interests. English intervention in the Nine Years' War and the War of the Spanish Succession did not net large territorial gains, but it did result in an enormous increase in English power and prestige. Over the next 30 years England would assert its own imperial claims.

The Colonial Wars.   The Treaty of Utrecht (1713–1714) ushered in almost a quarter century of peace in western Europe. Austrian rule in the Netherlands and Italy remained a major irritant to the Spanish, but Spain was too weak to do more than sulk and snarl. The death of Louis XIV in 1715 quelled French ambitions for a time and even led to an Anglo-French accord, which guaranteed the preservation of the settlement reached at Utrecht. Peace allowed Europe to rebuild its shattered economy and resume the international trade that had been so severely disrupted over the last 40 years. The Treaty of Utrecht had resolved a number of important trading issues, all in favor of Great Britain, as England was known after its union with Scotland in 1707. In addition to receiving Gibraltar and Minorca from Spain, Britain was also granted the monopoly to provide slaves to the Spanish-American colonies and the right to

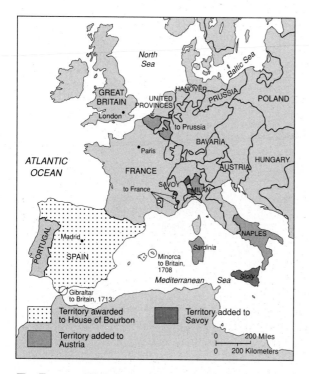

The Treaty of Utrecht, Europe 1714

send one trading ship a year to them. In east and west, Britain was becoming the dominant commercial power in the world.

At least some of the reason for Britain's preeminence was the remarkable growth of the Atlantic colonies. The colonial economy was booming and consumer goods that were in demand in London, Paris, and Amsterdam were also in demand in Boston, Philadelphia, and New York. Like every other colonial power, the British held a monopoly on their colonial trade. They were far less successful than the Spanish and French in enforcing the notion that colonies existed only for the benefit of the parent country, but the English Parliament continued to pass legislation aimed at restricting colonial trade with other nations and other nations' colonies. Like almost all other mercantile restrictions, these efforts were stronger in theory than in practice. Tariffs on imports and customs duties on British goods provided a double incentive for smuggling.

France emerged as Britain's true colonial rival. In the Caribbean, the French had the largest and most profitable of the West Indian sugar islands, Saint Domingue (modern-day Haiti). In North America France held not only Canada but laid claim to the entire continent west of the Ohio River. The French did not so much settle their colonial territory as occupy it. They surveyed the land, established trading relations with the Native Americans, and built forts at strategic locations. The English, in contrast, had developed fixed communities, which grew larger and more prosperous by the decade. France determined to defend its colonies by establishing an overseas military presence. Regular French troops were shipped to Canada and installed in Louisburg, Montreal, and Quebec. The British responded with troopers of their own and sent an expeditionary force to clear the French from the Ohio River Valley. This action was the immediate cause of the Seven Years' War (1756–1763).

Although the Seven Years' War had a bitter continental phase, it was essentially a war for empire between the English and the French. There were three main theaters: the North American mainland, the West Indian sugar plantations, and the eastern coast of India. All over the globe, the British won smashing victories. The British navy blockaded the water route to Canada, inflicting severe hardship on French settlers in Montreal and Quebec. British forces ultimately captured both towns. After some initial successes, the French were driven back west across the Mississippi River and their line of fortresses in the Ohio Valley fell into English hands. The English also succeeded in taking all the French sugar islands except Saint Domingue. British success in India was equally complete. The French were chased from their major trading zone and English dominance was secured.

By the end of the Seven Years' War, Britain had become a global imperial power. In the Peace of Paris (1763) France ceded all of Canada in exchange for the return of its West Indian islands. British dominion in the East Indian trade was recognized and led ultimately to British dominion of India itself. In less than a century the ascendancy of France was broken and Europe's first modern imperial power had been created.

The Treaty of Paris ended nearly two centuries of European warfare. The devastation of humanity in the name of God with which the reform of religion had begun was now exhausted. So, too, were the dynastic struggles of the Habsburgs and Bourbons. Protestantism and Catholicism now coexisted, and there was to be little further change in the geography of religion. Monarchs now ruled as well as reigned by incorporating vital elements of the state into the process of government. In England the importance of the land-holding classes was recognized in the constitutional powers of Parliament. In Prussia the military power of die Junker was asserted through command in the army. In France Louis XIV coopted many nobles at his court, while he made use of a talented pool of lawyers, clergymen, and administrators in his government. A delicate balance existed between the will of the king and the will of the state.

Suggestions for Further Reading

General Reading

*Jan de Vries, *The European Economy in an Age of Crisis* (Cambridge, England: Cambridge University Press, 1976). A comprehensive study of economic development, including long-distance trade and commercial change.

*William Doyle, *The Old European Order* (Oxford, England: Oxford University Press, 1978). An important synthetic essay bristling with ideas.

*J. H. Elliott, *Europe Divided 1559–1598* (New York: Harper & Row, 1968). An outstanding synthesis of European politics in the second half of the sixteenth century.

*K. H. D. Haley, *The Dutch in the Seventeenth Century* (London: Thames & Hudson, 1972). A well-written and illustrated history of the golden age of Holland.

*Derek McKay and H. M. Scott, *The Rise of the Great Powers 1648–1815* (London: Longman, 1983). An outstanding survey of diplomacy and warfare.

*Geoffrey Parker, *Europe in Crisis 1598–1648* (London: William Collins and Sons, 1979). The best introduction to the period.

Europe at War, 1555–1648

J. H. Elliott, *Richelieu and Olivares* (Cambridge, England: Cambridge University Press, 1984). A comparison of statesmen and statesmanship in the early seventeenth century.

*Mark Greengrass, *France in the Age of Henri IV* (London: Longman, 1984). An important synthesis of French history in the early seventeenth century.

*Henry Kamen, *Spain 1469–1714* (London: Longman, 1983). A recent survey with up-to-date interpretations.

Robert Kingdon, *Myths About the St. Bartholomew's Day Massacres 1572–76* (Cambridge, MA: Harvard University Press, 1988). A study of the impact of a central event in the history of France.

---

*Indicates paperback edition available.

*Peter Limm, *The Thirty Years' War* (London: Longman, 1984). An excellent brief survey with documents.

*Garrett Mattingly, *The Armada* (Boston: Houghton Mifflin, 1959). Still the classic account despite recent reinterpretations.

*Geoffrey Parker, *The Dutch Revolt* (London: Penguin, 1977). An outstanding account of the tangle of events that comprised the revolts of the Netherlands.

Geoffrey Parker, *Philip II* (Boston: Little, Brown, 1978). The best introduction.

W. E. Reddaway, et al., eds., *The Cambridge History of Poland to 1696* (Cambridge, England: Cambridge University Press, 1950). A difficult but thorough narrative of Polish history.

Michael Roberts, *Gustavus Adolphus and the Rise of Sweden* (London: English Universities Press, 1973). A highly readable account of Sweden's rise to power.

J. H. M. Salmon, *Society in Crisis* (New York: St. Martin's Press, 1975). The best single-volume account of the French civil wars; difficult but rewarding.

*C. V. Wedgwood, *The Thrity Years' War* (New York: Doubleday, 1961). A heroic account; the best narrative history.

The Rise of the Royal State

*J. H. Elliott, *The Count-Duke of Olivares* (New Haven, CT: Yale University Press, 1986). A massive and massively important study of the leading statesman of Spain.

The Crises of the Royal State

*J. S. Morrill, *The Revolt of the Provinces* (London: Longman, 1980). An outstanding essay on the importance of the localities in the English civil war.

G. Parker and L. Smith, eds., *The General Crisis of the Seventeenth Century* (London: Routledge & Kegan Paul, 1978). A collection of essays on the problem of the general crisis.

*Quentin Skinner, *The Foundations of Modern Political Thought*, 2 vols. (Cambridge, England: Cambridge University Press, 1978). A seminal work on the history of ideas from Machiavelli to Calvin.

*Lawrence Stone, *The Causes of the English Revolution* (New York: Harper & Row, 1972). A vigorously argued explanation of why England experienced a revolution in the mid seventeenth century.

The Zenith of the Royal State

*William Beik, *Absolutism and Society in Seventeenth Century France* (Cambridge, England: Cambridge University Press, 1985). The single best study of the government of a French province in the seventeenth century.

*Paul Dukes, *The Making of Russian Absolutism* (London: Longman, 1982). A thorough survey of Russian history in the seventeenth and eighteenth centuries.

Ragnhild Hatton, ed., *Louis XIV and Europe* (London: Macmillan, 1976). An important collection of essays on French foreign policy in its most aggressive posture.

*Vasili Klyuchevsky, *Peter the Great* (Boston: Beacon Press, 1984). A classic work; still the best study of Peter.

*H. W. Koch, *A History of Prussia* (London: Longman, 1978). A comprehensive study of Prussian history with an excellent chapter on the great elector.

Paul Langford, *The Eighteenth Century 1688–1815* (New York: St. Martin's Press, 1976). A reliable guide to the growth of British power.

John Wolf, *Louis XIV* (New York: W.W. Norton, 1968). An outstanding biography of the Sun King.

14

The New European Powers

Calling the Tune

Frederick the Great loved music. During his youth it was one of his private passions that so infuriated his father. Mathematics, political economy, modern languages, even dreaded French, were the subjects that a future king of Prussia should learn. But music, never. Rather the boy should be at the hunt watching the dogs tear apart a stag, or on maneuvers with the Potsdam guards, a troop of soldiers all nearly seven feet tall. This was the regimen King Frederick William I prescribed for his son. But Frederick the Great loved music. He secretly collected all the books and manuscripts he could find on the subject, outspending his tiny allowance in the process. He had Johann Quantz (1697–1773), the greatest flutist of the day, placed on his staff to teach him and to conspire with him against his father. At night, while the old king drank himself into a stupor—an activity he warmly recommended to his son—Frederick would powder his hair, put on a jacket of the latest French style, and regale his friends with his newest compositions. He and Quantz would take turns playing the flute, and the young spectators would do their best to imitate what they believed to be the essence of courtly manners. A lookout guarded the door in case the king wandered by unexpectedly. Once the musicians were almost discovered and Frederick's fine new jacket was tossed on the fire, but the flutes and musical scores remained safely hidden.

After he became king, Frederick the Great could indulge his passion more openly. Yet he preferred to hold his concerts, usually small gatherings, at the palace of Sans Souci, which he built in Potsdam. A special music room was designed for the king's use and he lavished attention on it. The great chandelier, lit by a circle of candles, illuminated the center of the room and

highlighted the soloist. The entire palace reflected Frederick's personal taste. Unlike most great palaces of state, it was small, functional, and beautiful. Here Frederick could escape the mounting cares of governing one of the most powerful states in Europe by reading, corresponding with eminent French intellectuals, and playing the flute. In this picture, *Das Flötenkonzert* (The Flute Concert), Frederick is portrayed performing in his great music room. Before a small audience of courtiers and intimates, he plays to the accompaniment of cello, violins, and piano.

Frederick's talent was real enough. A British visitor to Sans Souci, who had little reason to flatter the king, reported: "I was much pleased and surprised with the neatness of his execution. His performance surpassed anything I had ever heard among the dilettanti or even professors." This judgment is reinforced when one studies the expressions of the three men in the left-hand corner of the painting. They are taking genuine pleasure in the music they are hearing, all the more genuine in that the king's back is to them. So, too, are the musicians who are accompanying the king. There is as much joy as concentration on their faces.

Frederick's musical accomplishment was not unique among eighteenth-century monarchs. Joseph II of Austria was also a skilled flutist. But it was not so much music as accomplishment that was coming to be valued among the monarchs of the new European powers. Catherine the Great of Russia corresponded with philosophers; Frederick the Great brought the great French intellectual Voltaire (1698–1778) to his court—though they quickly took a dislike to each other. The acquisition of culture seemed to matter more and more as the century wore on. Museums, opera houses, great art collections were established all over the Continent. The Hermitage in Saint Petersburg was stocked with the works of Dutch and English masters. The British Museum was founded in London with the support of King George II, who deposited his great library there. Whether this veneer of culture did anything to lessen the brutality of warfare and power politics is a matter of opinion. But as a veneer it was as highly polished as the flute that Frederick the Great is so delicately pressing to his mouth.

*E*urope in 1714

The Peace of Utrecht (1713–1714) brought about a considerable reorganization of the political geography of Europe. Utrecht created a new Europe in the west; the Treaty of Nystad (1721) created a new Europe in the east. Both agreements reflected the dynamics of change that had taken place over the previous century. The rise of France on the Continent and of Britain's

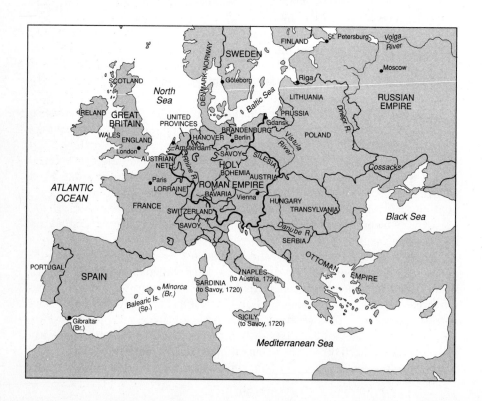

colonial empire around the globe were facts that could no longer be ignored. The decline of Sweden and Poland and the emergence of Russia as a great power were the beginning of a long-term process that would continue to dominate European history.

All of this could be seen on a map of Europe in the early eighteenth century. France's absorption of Alsace and encroachments into Lorraine would be a bone of contention between the French and Germans for two centuries and ultimately contributed to the outbreak of World Wars I and II. The political footballs of the Spanish Netherlands and Spanish Italy, now temporarily Austrian, continued to be kicked about until the nationalist movements of the nineteenth century gave birth to Belgium, Luxembourg, and a united Italy. The emergence of Brandenburg-Prussia on the north German coast and the gradual decline in the power of the Holy Roman Emperor were both vital to the process that created a unified Germany and a separate Austria. In the southeast, the slow but steady reconquest of the Balkans from Ottoman dominion restored the historic southern border of the Continent. The inexorable expansion of Russia was also already apparent.

The West

Perhaps the most obvious transformation in the political geography of western Europe was the expansion of European power around the globe. In the Atlantic, Spain remained the largest colonial power. Through its vice-royalty system it controlled all of central America, the largest and most numerous of the Caribbean islands, North America from Colorado to California (as well as Florida), and most of South America. The other major colonial power in the region was Portugal, which shared dominion over the South American continent. In the Portuguese colony of Brazil, production of sugar, dyestuffs, timbers, and exotic commodities amply repaid the meager investment the Portuguese had made.

In North America the French and British shared the eastern half of the continent. The French controlled most of it. They had landed first in Canada and then slowly made their way down the Saint Lawrence River. New France, as their colonial empire was called, was a trading territory and it expanded along the greatest of the waterways, the Great Lakes, and the Ohio, Missouri, and Mississippi rivers. French settlements had sprung up as far south as the Gulf of Mexico. France also claimed the territory of Louisiana, named for Louis XIV, which stretched from New Orleans to Montana. The British settlements were all coastal, stretching from Maine to Georgia on the Atlantic seaboard. Unlike the French, the British settled their territory and were only interested in expansion when their population, which was doubling every 25 years, outgrew its resources. By the early eighteenth century the ports of Boston, New York, Philadelphia, and Charleston were thriving commercial centers.

Europeans managed their eastern colonial territories differently than they did those in the west. Initially the Portuguese and the Dutch had been satisfied with establishing trading factories—coastal fortresses that could be used as warehouses and defended against attack. But in the seventeenth century, the European states began to take control of vital ports and lucrative islands. Here the Dutch were the acknowledged leaders, replacing the Portuguese who had begun the process at the end of the sixteenth century. Holland held by force or in conjunction with local leaders all the Spice Islands in the Pacific. The Dutch also occupied both sides of the Malay Peninsula and nearly all the coastal areas of the islands in the Java Sea. Dutch control of Ceylon was strategically important for its Indian trade. Compared to the Dutch Republic, all other European states had only a minor territorial presence in the East, with the exception of Spain, which still controlled the Philippines. The British had limited their eastern outposts to trading establishments. Through these they maintained a significant presence in India. During the eighteenth century the British began to colonize the Indian subcontinent directly.

Imperial expansion was the most obvious change in the geopolitical boundaries of Europe, but it was not the only one. A brief tour of the western states after the Treaty of Utrecht reveals some others. In 1707 England and Scotland formally joined together to form Great Britain. In addition to its eastern and western colonies, Britain had also gained control of Gibraltar at the foot of Spain and the island of Minorca in the Mediterranean. Both territories were strategically important to British commerce. But the greatest changes in Britain's geopolitical makeup had to do with its sovereigns. After the Revolution of 1688, Britain had shared a ruler with Holland, but there had never been any attempt to integrate the two states. After William III died in 1702 the two countries went their separate ways. In 1714 the British throne passed to George of Hanover, a German prince whose rich territories on the North Sea brought Britain into continental affairs in a new and unforeseen way.

Across the English Channel were the Low Countries, now permanently divided between the United Provinces in the north, led by Holland, and those provinces in the south that had remained loyal to the Spanish crown in the sixteenth century. By 1714 the golden age of the Dutch was over. Though the Dutch continued as a colonial and maritime power, their small numbers and meager natural resources eventually outweighed their abilities as innovators and managers. They lost their eastern empire to Britain, their predominance in European trade to France. What the Dutch gained at Utrecht was the right to maintain their forces in the towns along the border between France and the old Spanish Netherlands. The Spanish Netherlands, the original Burgundian inheritance, were now being slowly dismembered. Since the accession of Louis XIV, France had plucked small pieces from the territories that had been contested between Habsburg and Valois since the fifteenth century. Between French aggression and the Dutch occupation of such important places as Ghent and Ypres, the ability of the southern provinces to maintain a separate identity suffered a grave blow. But not as grave as that formalized at Utrecht, when sovereignty over this territory was assigned to Austria, ostensibly because the emperor was a Habsburg, but really because the balance of power in western Europe demanded it.

To the south lay France, still the most powerful nation in Europe despite its losses in the War of the Spanish Succession. By 1714 Louis XIV had broken forever the danger of Spanish encirclement that had been the worry of every French king since Francis I in the early sixteenth century. Louis had methodically set out to occupy those territories that were strategically necessary to defend his state from invasion by the Dutch, the Spanish, the British, or the emperor. In the northeast he absorbed the Duchy of Bar. In the north he absorbed a healthy portion of Flanders including Dunkirk on the English Channel and the prosperous clothing town of Lille. He pushed the eastern boundary of his state to the Rhine by overrunning Alsace and parts of Lorraine. Strasbourg remained French under the settlement of 1714, testimony to the fact that it was possible to hold France only at the western banks of the Rhine. Finally, farther to the south Louis had won and held Franche-Comté, once the center of Burgundy. In 1714 France was larger, stronger, and better able to defend its borders than ever before. It was also exhausted.

As France expanded, so Spain contracted. Less than two centuries earlier a Spanish king had dreamed of being monarch over all of Europe. Now a Bourbon sat on the great Habsburg throne and Spain was slowly being sliced to pieces. By 1714 the European territories of the Spanish empire had been reduced to Iberia itself. But the loss of its European empire was to prove a blessing in disguise for Spain, which now entered upon a new and unexpected phase of growth and influence.

The center of Europe remained occupied by the agglomeration of cities, bishoprics, principalities, and small states known collectively as the Holy Roman Empire, but now more accurately called the German empire. There were still over three hundred separate jurisdictions, most of them vulnerable to preying neighbors such as Louis XIV. Bavaria in the south, and Saxony, Brandenburg, and Hanover in the north were among the most important of the large states with the added twist that Hanover was now ruled by the king of Great Britain. The emperor, now officially prohibited from interference in the internal administration of the large states, was less dominant in German affairs than he had been before the Thirty Years' War.

Increasingly, Habsburg power centered on Austria, Bohemia, and Hungary. This was especially true during the reign of Leopold I (1655–1705). Withstanding threats on all sides, Leopold was able to expand his state both to the west and to the south and to bring Austria into the ranks of the great European powers. Such an outcome could hardly have been foreseen in the middle of the seventeenth century, when the Ottomans made their last great thrust into the interior of Europe. In 1683 the Ottomans besieged Vienna itself, and only the arrival of 70,000 Polish-led troops saved it from falling. But from that time forward, Austrian forces scored stunning victories. By 1699 almost all of Hungary had been retaken by Austria; at the Treaty of Passarowitz in 1718 Austria gained the rest of Hungary and Serbia. When the Treaty of Utrecht granted Austria control of the Netherlands, Lombardy, and Naples, the Austrian Habsburgs took the place of their Spanish cousins as rulers of a European empire.

Austria's Italian possessions included the vast southern territories of Naples (including Sicily after 1720) and the rich industrial area surrounding Milan in the north. Alongside the Austrian territories a number of independent city-states continued to flourish on the Italian peninsula. Both Venice on the Adriatic and Genoa on the Mediterranean remained prosperous and independent. The Grand Duchy of Tuscany, with its great city of Florence, and the Papal States had expanded over the course of the seventeenth century, absorbing their smaller neighbors until both were large consolidated territories. To the west of the Italian states was the Duchy of Savoy. Savoy had pursued a flexible foreign policy, pleasing whichever of its powerful neighbors was most dangerous and accepting the patronage of whichever seemed most friendly. Client of the Spanish, French, and Austrians, Savoy grew and prospered. After the War of the Spanish Succession, Savoy was counted among the victors, though it fought on both sides. Duke Victor Amadeus II became a king when he received the island of Sicily, which he exchanged with Austria for Sardinia in 1720.

The East

This was western Europe in 1714. In the east, it was the Treaty of Nystad (1721) ending the Great Northern War (1700–1721) that fixed the political geography. Here the emerging powers were Russia and Prussia, those in decline were Sweden and Poland. The critical factor in eastern European politics remained access to the sea. Outlets to the Baltic Sea in the north and the Black Sea in the south were the vital lifeline for this part of the Continent, and control of these outlets was the central motivation for the long years of war fought among the eastern states.

The expansion of Russia is one of the central events in European history, and the early eighteenth century is its pivotal period. During the long years of social and economic recovery after the death of Ivan the Terrible in 1584, Russia had been easy prey for its powerful neighbors Sweden and Poland. Through a series of wars and political pacts, Russia had ceded most of its Baltic territories to Sweden while it had relinquished land and population in the west to Poland. Peter the Great (1682–1725) set out to reclaim what had been lost. As a result of the Great Northern War, Russia regained the eastern Baltic coastline from the southeastern end of Finland to Riga in the west. Russia now controlled all of the vital Baltic ports in the east. Peter built a new capital on the Gulf of Finland. In this new city, named Saint Petersburg, he laid the foundation for the Russian navy.

What Russia gained, Sweden lost. At the height of its power in the middle of the seventeenth century, Sweden had dominated the Baltic. It occupied all

This portrait of Peter the Great by his court painter Louis Caravague pays homage to Peter's intense interest in naval matters. Ships flying English, Dutch, Danish, and Russian flags prepare for maneuvers under his command.

of Finland, controlled the important eastern coast of Norway, and had gained a foothold in Germany. Most importantly, Sweden had captured the southern tip of its own peninsula from the Danes, making the mainland portion of its state whole. But Sweden's century-long rise to power was followed by a rapid period of decline. The small and relatively poor population could not long succeed in governing an empire. The Great Northern War ended whatever pretensions Sweden had left. It lost all of its German territories: Those on the North Sea went to Hanover, those on the Baltic to Prussia. Livonia, Estonia, and the eastern provinces were returned to Russia, but Sweden was able to hold on to its vital gains from the Danes. Sweden had built its own window to the west at Göteborg on the North Sea, and from there it could carry on a direct trade with Britain and the Netherlands.

The acquisition of Pomerania from Sweden was just one of the territorial gains made by Brandenburg-Prussia. Since the end of the Thirty Years' War, this strange configuration of a state had been steadily growing. Its geographical heart was in Brandenburg, one of the domains of the Holy Roman Empire. From the capital at Berlin the princes of Brandenburg directed the accumulation of small neighboring German lands: Magdeburg and Halle to the southwest, a piece of Pomerania to the northeast. But while Brandenburg expanded in every direction, it could do little to join itself to the kingdom of Prussia. A huge swath of Poland, cutting between the two, stood in the way. This division of Brandenburg-Prussia was its most important geopolitical feature. In the eighteenth century, the determination to expand to the east dominated Prussian history.

This aim meant, of course, eventual conflict with Poland. Despite its political weakness, Poland was one of the largest landmasses in Europe. On its southern border it held back Ottoman expansion; on its eastern border it held back the Russians. Its great port of Gdańsk on the Baltic dominated the grain and timber trade with northern Europe as well as local Baltic commerce between Scandinavia and the mainland. Sweden and Russia, the eastern powers, controlled Poland politically, helping nominate its elected kings and ensuring that its decentralized form of aristocratic government kept Poland weak. Poland served as a useful counterweight in the balance of power in eastern Europe. Except for its Baltic territories, Poland was not yet seen as a great prize to be fought over. But by the beginning of the eighteenth century it was a helpless giant ready to be toppled.

*T*he Rise of Russia

In 1721 Peter I, the Great, who had been tsar in Russia since 1682, assumed the title of Emperor of All Russias. The Treaty of Nystad had confirmed the magnitude of his victory over the Swedes in the Great Northern War, both in territory and prestige. The change created consternation in the courts of Europe. Just a quarter century before, no one had cared very much what the king of Russia called himself. In fact, little was known for sure about the Russian ruler or his state. What little mercantile contact there was between Russia and the West was conducted entirely by westerners. Foreign merchants were allowed to live in Moscow in a separate ghetto called "Germantown." Their letters were the main source of western knowledge about the vast Muscovite empire.

Peter the Great changed all of this. Twice he visited Europe to discover the secrets of western prosperity and might. He arranged marriages between the closest heirs to his throne, including his son Alexis, and the sons and daughters of German princes and dukes. By 1721 he had established 21 separate foreign embassies. The sons of the Russian gentry and nobility were sent to the

West—sometimes forcibly—to further their education and to learn to adapt to western outlooks. Peter recruited Europeans to fill the most important skilled positions in the state: foreign engineers and gunners to serve in the army; foreign architects to build the new capital at Saint Petersburg; foreign scholars to head the new state schools; foreign administrators to oversee the new departments of state. Peter borrowed freely and adapted sensibly. If necessary, he would drag his compatriots kicking and screaming into the modern world.

By 1721 Russia was recognized all over Europe as an emerging power. The military defeat of the seemingly invincible Swedes had made monarchs from Louis XIV to William III sit up and take notice. And the great Russian victory at Poltava in 1709 was no fluke. Peter's forces followed it up with several strong campaigns which proved that Russia could organize, equip, finance, and train an up-to-date military force. Moreover, Peter's absorption of Sweden's Baltic territories made Russia a power in the north. A navy, built mostly by foreigners, was now capable of protecting Russian interests and defending important ports such as Riga and Saint Petersburg. Even the Dutch, who had long plotted the decline of Swedish might, now became nervous. Thus it was unsettling that Peter wished to be recognized as emperor. There was only one emperor in Europe—the Holy Roman Emperor—and those who aspired to that title did so in the traditional way, by attempting to bribe the German electors.

Russia Turns West

Peter the Great was not the first Russian tsar to attempt to borrow from western developments. The process had been underway for decades. The opening of the northern port of Archangel led to direct contact with British and Dutch traders, who brought with them new ideas and useful products, which were adapted to Russian needs and conditions. Russia was a vast state and Europe was only one of its neighbors. Its religion had come from Byzantium rather than Rome, thus giving Russian Christianity an eastern flavor. Its Asian territories mixed the influence of Mongols and Ottomans; its southern borders met Tartars and Cossacks. While most European states were racially and ethnically homogeneous, Russia was a loose confederation of diverse peoples. Yet it was the western states that posed the greatest threat to Russia in the seventeenth century, and it was to the West that Tsar Alexis I (1645–1676) and his son Peter turned their attention.

It would be wrong to see Peter's westernizing innovation as a systematic program. More to the point, nearly all of what he did was done to enhance military efficiency rather than civil progress. In his 30 years of active rule there was only one year—1724—during which he was not at war. Vital reforms like the poll tax (1724), which changed the basis of taxation from the household to the individual adult male, had enormous social consequences. The new policy of taxing individuals officially erased whole social classes. A strict census taken (and retaken) to inhibit tax evasion became the basis for further governmental encroachments on the tsar's subjects. Yet the poll tax was not designed for any of these purposes. It was instituted to increase tax revenue for war. Similarly, the establishment of compulsory lifetime military service required of the landowning classes (the nobility and gentry) was undertaken to provide officers and state servants for an expanding military machine.

Yet if Peter's reforms were not systematic and developed from little other than military necessity, nevertheless they constituted a fundamental transformation in the life of all Russian people. The creation of a gigantic standing army and an entirely new navy meant conscription of the Russian peasantry on a grand scale. In a ten-year period of the Great Northern War the army absorbed 330,000 conscripts, most of whom never returned to their homes. Military service was not confined to the peasantry. Traditionally, the rural gentry raised and equipped the local conscript forces and gave them what training they could. Most gentry lived on estates that had been granted to them along with the resident peasants as a reward for their military contributions. Peter the Great intensified the obligations of the gentry. Not only were they to serve the state for life, but they were to accompany their regiments to the field and lead them in battle. When too old for active military service, they were to perform administrative service in the new departments of state.

The expansion of military forces necessitated an expansion of military administration as well. Peter's first innovation was the creation of the Senate, a group of nine senior administrators who were to oversee all aspects of military and civil government. The Senate became a permanent institution of government led by an entirely new official, the Procurator-General, who presided over its sessions and could propose legislation as well as oversee administration. From the Senate emanated 500 officials known as the fiscals, who traveled throughout the state looking for irregularities in tax assessment and collection. They quickly developed into a hated and feared internal police force.

Peter's efforts to reorganize his government went a step further in 1722, when he promulgated the Table of Ranks. This was an official hierarchy of the state divided into three categories—military service, civil service, and those who owned landed estates. Each category contained 14 ranks and it was decreed that every person who entered the hierarchy did so at the bottom and worked his way up. The creation of the Table of Ranks was significant in a number of ways. It demonstrated Peter's continued commitment to merit as a criterion for advancement. This standard had been shown in the military, where officers were promoted on the basis of service and experience rather than birth or background. Equally important was Peter's decision to make the military service the highest of the three categories. This reversed the centuries-old position of the landed aristocracy and the military service class. Though the old nobility also served in the military and continued to dominate state service, the Table of Ranks opened the way for the infusion of new elements into the Russian elite.

Many of those who were able to advance in the Table of Ranks did so through attendance at the new institutions of higher learning that Peter founded. His initial educational establishments were created to further the military might of the state. The colleges of mathematics, engineering, and artillery, which became the training grounds for his army officers, were all founded during the Great Northern War. But Peter was interested in liberal education as well. He had scores of western books translated into Russian. He had a press established in Moscow to print original works, including the first Russian newspaper. He decreed that a new, more westernized alphabet replace that used by the Russian Orthodox Church and that books be written in the language the people spoke rather than in the formal literary language of religious writers. He also introduced Arabic numerals into official accounting records.

Peter's reforms of government and society were matched by his efforts to energize the economy. No state in Europe had as many natural resources as did Russia, yet manufacturing barely existed there. As with everything else he did, Peter took a direct hand in establishing factories for the production of textiles, glass, leather, and most importantly, iron and copper. The state directly owned about half of these establishments, most of them on a larger scale than any known in the West. By 1726 more than half of all Russian exports were manufactured goods and Russia had become the largest producer of iron and copper in the world.

In all of these ways and more Peter the Great transformed Russia. But the changes Peter wrought did not come without cost. The traditions of centuries were not easily broken. Intrigue against Peter led first to confrontation with the old military elite and later to conflict with his only son, Alexis. It remains unclear if the plot with which Alexis was connected existed anywhere other than in Peter's mind, but it is abundantly clear that Alexis's death from torture plunged the state into a succession crisis in 1725. Finally, the great costs of westernization were paid by the masses of people who benefited little from the improvement in Russia's international standing or from the social and economic changes that affected the elites.

Life in Rural Russia

Nearly 97 percent of the Russian people lived on the land and practiced agriculture. Farming techniques and agrarian lifestyles had changed little for centuries. Most of the country's soil was poor. Harsh climate and low yields characterized Russian agriculture. Thirty-four of the 100 Russian harvests during the eighteenth century can be termed poor or disastrous, yet throughout the century state taxation was making larger and larger demands on the peasantry. During Peter's reign alone, direct taxation increased by 500 percent.

The theory of the Russian state was one of service, and the role of Russian peasants was to serve their master. Beginning in the mid seventeenth century, the peasantry had undergone a change in status. The law code of 1649 formalized a process that had been underway for over a century whereby peasants were turned into the property of their landlords. During the next century laws curtailed the ability of peasants to move freely from one place to another, eliminated their right to hold private property, and abolished their freedom to petition the tsar against their masters. At the same that landlords increased their hold over peasants, the state increased its hold over landlords. They were made responsible for the payment of taxes owed by their peasants and for the military service due from them. By the middle of the eighteenth century over half of all peasants—6.7 million adult males by 1782—had thus become serfs, the property of their masters, without any significant rights or legal protection.

Private landlords reckoned their wealth in the number of serfs they owned. But in fact most owned only a small number, fewer than fifty in the middle of the eighteenth century. This resulted from the common practice whereby a father divided his estate among all of his surviving sons. Most gentry were small landholders, constantly in debt and rarely able to meet their financial and service obligations to the state. This life of poverty at the top was, of course, magnified at the bottom. The vast majority of serfs lived in small villages where they divided up their meager surplus to pay their taxes and drew lots to see who would be sent for military service. When the debts of their lords became too heavy, it was the serfs who were foreclosed upon. Serf families or particularly desirable individuals would be sold at auction, some to be resettled in new villages, others to be deployed at the whim of their purchasers.

If serfs made up the bottom half of the Russian peasantry, there were few advantages to being in the top half among the state peasants. State peasants lived on lands owned by the monarchy itself. Like the serfs, they were subject to the needs of the state for soldiers and workers. The use of forced labor was a feature of each of Peter's grandiose projects. Saint Petersburg was built on the backs of peasant conscripts. From 1709, when the project began, perhaps as many as forty thousand laborers a year were forced to work on the various sites. The unhealthy conditions of the swampy environment from which the new capital rose claimed the lives of thousands of these workers, as did the appalling conditions of overwork and undernourishment in which they lived.

Many Russian peasants developed a philosophy of submission and a rich folk culture that valued a stubborn determination to endure. For those who would no longer bend to the knout—the heavy leather whip that was the omnipresent enforcer of obedience—there was only flight or rebellion. Hundreds of thousands of serfs fled to state-owned lands in hope of escaping the cruelties of individual landlords. Although severe penalties were imposed for aiding runaway serfs, in fact most state overseers and many private landlords encouraged runaways to settle on their lands.

The Enlightened Empress

Of all the legacies of Peter the Great, perhaps the most important was that government could go on without him. During the next 37 years six tsars ruled

Russia, "three women, a boy of twelve, an infant, and a mental weakling," as one commentator acidly observed. More to the point, each succession was contested because there were no direct male heirs to the throne in this period. Peter's wife, his two grandsons, his daughter, and a niece all served a turn. Nevertheless, despite turmoil at the top, government continued to function smoothly and Peter's territorial conquests were largely maintained. Russia also experienced a remarkable increase in numbers during this period. Between 1725 and 1762 population increased from 13 to 19 million, a jump of nearly one-third in a single generation. This explosion of people dramatically increased the wealth of the land-holding class, who reckoned their status by the number of serfs they owned.

The expansion of the economic resources of the nobility was matched by a rise in legal status and political power. This was the period sarcastically dubbed "the emancipation of the nobility," a phrase that captures not only the irony of the growing gap between rich and poor but also the contrast between the social structures of Russia and those of western Europe. In return for their privileges and status, Peter the Great extended the duties the landowning classes owed to the state. By granting unique rights, like the ownership of serfs, to the descendants of the old military service class, Peter had forged a Russian nobility. Lifetime service, however, was the price of nobility.

In order to gain and hold the throne, each succeeding tsar had to make concessions to the nobility. At first it was a few simple adjustments. The sons of wealthy landowners who completed a course of education at one of the state academies were allowed to enter the Table of Ranks in the middle of the hierarchy rather than at the bottom. Then life service was commuted to a term of 25 years, still a long term in a world of short lives and sudden deaths. But these concessions were not enough. Twenty-five years of service did not solve the problem of estate management, especially as the tasks of management grew along with the population of serfs. Thus the next capitulation was that a single son could remain on the estate and escape service altogether. This decree opened the door more than a crack. The births of younger sons were concealed; owners of multiple estates claimed the exemption of one son for each. Most decisively, the talented remained at home to serve the family while the wastrels were sent to serve the state. Finally in 1762, the obligation for state service by the nobility was abolished entirely. If nothing else, Russia had westernized its aristocracy. The abolition of compulsory service was not the same as the abolition of service itself. In fact the end of compulsory service enabled Catherine II, the Great (1762–1796), to enact some of the most important reforms of her reign.

Catherine began life as Sophie of Anhalt-Zerbst, the daughter of a petty German prince. She was brought to Russia in 1744 as the bride of the future Tsar Peter III, and took the name Catherine on converting to the Russian Orthodox faith. She came to the throne as a result of a coup against her feeble-minded husband. At first, Catherine's accession seemed nothing more than a continuation of monarchical instability—her first two acts were to have Peter murdered and to lower the salt tax. Each bought her a measure of security.

Catherine was a dynamic personality who alternately captivated and terrified those with whom she came into contact. Her policies were as complex as her personality, influenced alike by the new French ideas of social justice and the nobility of the human race and the traditional Russian ones of absolute rule over an enserfed and subhuman population. Catherine handled these contrasting dimensions of her rule masterfully, which gained her abroad the reputation as the most enlightened of European monarchs and at home the sincere devotion of her people.

The most important event in the early years of Catherine's reign was the establishment of a legislative commission to review the laws of Russia. Catherine herself wrote the *Instruction* (1767) by which the elected commissioners were to operate. She borrowed her theory of law from the French jurist Baron de Montesquieu (1689–1755) and her theory of punishment from the Italian reformer Cesare Beccaria (1738–1794). Among other things, Catherine advocated the abolition of capital punishment, torture, serf auctions, and the breakup of serf families by sale. Few of these radical reforms were ever put into practice. But one of the most important aspects of the legislative commission was that it drew upon the service of elected noblemen, who came to Saint Petersburg with lists of local grievances. Catherine and her advisers were able to learn firsthand about the failures of rural administration and to take steps to correct them.

With this knowledge Catherine set about, in 1775, the restructuring of local government. Russia was divided into 50 provincial districts, each with a population of between 300,000 and 400,000 inhabitants. Each district was to be governed by both a central official and elected local noblemen. This reform was modeled on the English system of justices of the peace. The failure of all previous local reforms had stemmed from the absence of a resident local nobility. The abolition of compulsory service finally made possible the establishment of local institutions. In 1785 Catherine issued the Charter of the Nobility, a formal statement of the rights and privileges of the noble class. The Charter incorporated all the gains the nobility had made since the death of Peter the Great, but it also instituted the requirements for local service that had been the basis of Catherine's reforms. District councils with the right to petition directly to the tsar became the centerpiece of Russian provincial government.

In order to train the local nobility for government service, Catherine introduced educational reforms. Peter had established military schools for the nobility and had staffed them with foreigners. The University of Moscow had been founded in 1755, and its faculty, too, was dominated by European emigrants. Catherine saw the need to broaden the educational system. Borrowing from the Austrian system, she established provincial elementary schools to train the sons and daughters of the local nobility. To staff these, Catherine created teachers' colleges so that the state would have its own educators. Though the program called for the equal education of women, except in Saint Petersburg and Moscow few women attended either elementary or high schools.

Catherine's reforms did little to enhance the lives of the vast majority of her people. Though she often spoke in the terms of the French philosophers who saw the enserfment of fellow humans as a blot on civilization, Catherine effectively took no action either to end serfdom or to soften its rigors. In fact, by grants of state land Catherine gave away 800,000 state peasants, who became serfs. So, too, did millions of Poles who became her subjects after the partition of Poland in 1793 and 1795.

Indeed, the most significant uprising of the century, Pugachev's revolt (1773–1775), took place during her reign. Emelyan Pugachev (1726–1775) was a Cossack who in his youth had been a military adventurer. Disappointed in his career, he made his way to the Ural mountains, where he recruited Asian tribe members and laborers forced to work in the mines. By promising freedom and land ownership, he drew peasants to his cause. Pugachev declared himself to be Tsar Peter III, the murdered husband of Catherine II. He began with small raiding parties against local landlords and military outposts and soon had gained the allegiance of tens of thousands of peasants. In 1774, with an army of nearly twenty thousand, Pugachev took the city of Kazan and threatened to advance on Moscow. It was another year before state forces could effectively control the rebellion. Finally, Pugachev was betrayed by his own followers and sent to Moscow to be executed.

*T*he Two Germanies

The Thirty Years' War initiated a profound transformation of the Holy Roman Empire. Warfare had devastated imperial territory. It was decades before the rich imperial lands recovered, and then the political consequences of the war had taken effect. There were now two empires, a German and an Austrian, though both were ruled by the same person. In the German territories, whether Catholic or Protestant, the Holy Roman Emperor was more of a constitutional than an absolute ruler. The larger states like Saxony, Bavaria, and Hanover made their own political alliances despite the jurisdictional control that the emperor claimed to exercise. Most decisively, so did Brandenburg-Prussia. By the beginning of the eighteenth century, the electors of Brandenburg had become the kings of Prussia, and Prussia's military power and efficient administrative structure became the envy of its German neighbors.

The Austrian empire was composed of Austria and Bohemia, the Habsburg hereditary lands, and as much of Hungary as could be controlled. In Austria, the Habsburgs clung tightly to their power. Victories over the Turks had expanded their control in Hungary. For decades Austria was the center of the still-flourishing Counter-Reformation, and the power and influence of the Jesuits was as strong here as it was in Spain. The War of the Spanish Succession, which gave the Habsburgs control of the southern Netherlands and parts of Italy, brought Austria an enhanced role in European affairs. Austria remained one of the great powers of Europe and the leading power in the Holy Roman Empire despite the rise of Prussia. Indeed from the middle of the eighteenth century the conflict between Prussia and Austria was the defining characteristic of central European politics.

The Prussian Miracle

The transformation of Brandenburg-Prussia from a petty German principality to a great European power was one of the least expected developments of the eighteenth century. Frederick William, the great elector (1640–1688), had begun the process of forging Brandenburg-Prussia into a power in its own right by building a large and efficient military machine. At the beginning of the eighteenth century Prussia was on the winning side in both the War of the Spanish Succession and the Great Northern War. When the battlefield dust had cleared, Prussia found itself in possession of Pomerania and the Baltic port of Stettin. It was now a recognized power in eastern Europe.

Frederick William I (1713–1740) and his son Frederick II, the Great (1740–1786), turned this promising beginning into an astounding success. A devout Calvinist, Frederick William I deplored waste and display as much on moral as on fiscal grounds. The reforms he initiated were intended to subordinate both aristocracy and peasantry to the needs of the state and to subordinate the needs of the state to the demands of the military.

Because of its geographical position, Prussia's major problem was to maintain an efficient and well-trained army during peacetime. Defense of its exposed territories required a constant state of military preparedness, yet the

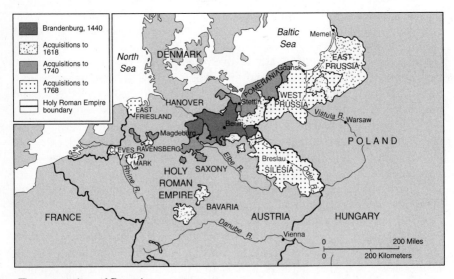

The expansion of Prussia

relaxation of military discipline and the desertion of troops to their homes inevitably followed the cessation of hostilities. Frederick William I solved this problem by integrating the economic and military structures of his state. First he appointed only German officers to command his troops, eliminating the mercenaries who sold their services to the highest bidders. Then he placed these noblemen at the head of locally recruited regiments. Each adult male in every district was required to register for military service in the regiment of the local landlord.

These reforms dramatically increased the effectiveness of the army by shifting the burden of recruitment and training to the localities. But the system also had a serious drawback. It threatened to impoverish the nobles by forcing them to take their own laborers off the land for military service. Frederick William I overcame this problem by instituting the seasonal call-up. Except in times of actual warfare, troops were called up and trained for specific periods of time and then returned to their agricultural pursuits.

Yet despite all the attention that Frederick William I lavished on the military—by the end of his reign nearly 70 percent of state expenditures went to the army—his foreign policy was largely pacific. In fact, his greatest achievements were in civil affairs, reforming the bureaucracy, establishing a sound economy, and raising state revenues. Through generous settlement schemes and by welcoming Protestant and Jewish refugees, Frederick William was able to expand the economic potential of these eastern territories. Frederick William I pursued an aggressive policy of land purchase to expand the royal domain, and the addition of so many new inhabitants in Prussia further increased his wealth. While the major western European powers were discovering deficit financing and the national debt, Prussia was running a surplus.

Financial security was vital to the success of Frederick II, the Great (1740–1786). Father and son had quarreled bitterly throughout Frederick's youth, and most observers expected that out of spite Frederick would tear down all that his father had built up. In fact, father and son were cast in the same mold, with the unexpected difference that the son was the more ruthless and ambitious. With his throne, Frederick II inherited the fourth largest army in Europe and the richest treasury. He wasted no time in putting both to use. His two objectives were to acquire the Polish corridor of West Prussia that separated his German and Prussian territories and the agriculturally and industrially rich Austrian province of Silesia to the southeast of Berlin. Just months after his coronation, Frederick conquered Silesia, increasing the size of Prussia by nearly a quarter. Within a decade the province dominated the Prussian economy, outproducing and outconsuming all other areas of Frederick's state.

It was Frederick's military prowess that earned him the title "the Great." But this was only a part of his achievement. More than his father, Frederick II forged an alliance with the Prussian nobility, integrating them into a unified state. A tightly organized central administration, which depended on the cooperation of the local nobility, directed both military and bureaucratic affairs. At the center, Frederick worked tirelessly to oversee his government. Where Louis XIV had proclaimed, "I am the state," Frederick the Great announced, "I am the first servant of the state." He codified the laws of Prussia, abolished torture and capital punishment, and instituted agricultural techniques imported from the states of western Europe. By the end of Frederick's reign, Prussia had become a model for bureaucratic organization, military reform, and enlightened rule.

Austria Survives

Austria was the great territorial victor in the War of the Spanish Succession, acquiring both the Netherlands and parts of Italy. Austrian forces recaptured a large part of Hungary from the Turks, thereby expanding their territory to the south and the east. Hereditary ruler of Austria and Bohemia, king of Hungary, and Holy Roman Emperor of the German nation, Charles VI (1711–1740) was recognized as one of Europe's most potent rulers. But appearances were deceptive. The apex of Austrian power and prestige had already passed. Austria had benefited from balance-of-power politics not so much from its own strength as from the leverage it could give to others. With the rise of Russia and Prussia there was now more than one fulcrum to power in eastern Europe.

The difficulties facing Austria ran deep. The Thirty Years' War had made the emperor more an Austrian monarch than an imperial German ruler. On the Austrian hereditary estates, the Catholic Counter-Reformation continued unabated, bringing with it the benefits of Jesuit education, cultural revival, and the religious unity necessary to motivate warfare against the Ottomans. But these benefits came at a price. Perhaps as many as two hundred thousand Protestants fled Austria and Bohemia, many resettling in Prussia and bringing with them their skills and capital. For centuries the vision of empire had dominated Habsburg rule. This meant that the Austrian monarchy was a multiethnic confederation of lands loosely tied together by loyalty to a single head. The components preserved a high degree of autonomy: Hungary elected the Habsburg emperor its king in a separate ceremony. Local autonomy continually restricted the imposition of central policy, and never were the localities more autonomous than in the matter of taxation.

A predominantly rural land, Austria was also predominantly agricultural. Less than 5 percent of the population lived in towns of ten thousand or more; less than 15 percent lived in towns at all. On the land the local aristocracy, whether nobility or gentry, exploited serfs to the maximum. Not only were serfs required to give labor service three days a week (and up to six during planting and harvest times), but the nobility maintained a full array of feudal privileges including the right to mill all grain and brew all beer. When they married, when they transferred property, even when they died, serfs paid taxes to their lord. As a result they had little left to give the state. In consequence, the

Austrian army was among the smallest and the poorest of the major powers despite the fact that it had the most active enemies along its borders.

Lack of finance, lack of human resources, and lack of governmental control were the underlying problems of Austria, but they were not the most immediate difficulties facing Charles VI. With no sons to succeed him, Charles feared that his hereditary and elective states would go their separate ways after his death and that the great Habsburg monarchy would end. For 20 years his abiding ambition was to gain recognition for the principle that his empire would pass intact to his daughter, Maria Theresa. He expressed the principle in a document known as the Pragmatic Sanction, which stated that all Habsburg lands would pass intact to the eldest heir, male or female. Charles VI made concession after concession to gain acceptance of the Pragmatic Sanction. At every turn Austria demonstrated its inherent weakness, losing territory in Italy and Hungary during a series of bungled wars. Despite the Pragmatic Sanction, the leaders of Europe licked their lips at the prospect of a dismembered Austrian empire.

Maria Theresa (1740–1780) quickly discovered what it was like to be a pregnant woman in a man's world. In 1740 Frederick of Prussia invaded the rich Austrian province of Silesia and attracted allies for an assault on Vienna. Faced with Bavarian, Saxon, and Prussian armies, Maria Theresa might well

Maria Theresa and her family. Eleven of Maria Theresa's 16 children are posed with the empress and her husband, Francis of Lorraine. Standing next to his mother is the future emperor Joseph II.

have lost her inheritance had she not shown her remarkable capacities so early in her reign. She appeared before the Hungarian estates, accepted their crown, and persuaded them to provide her with an army capable of halting the allied advance. Though she was unable to reconquer Silesia, Hungarian aid helped her hold the line against her enemies.

The loss of Silesia, the most prosperous part of the Austrian domains, signaled the need for fundamental reform. The new eighteenth-century idea of building a state replaced the traditional Habsburg concern with maintaining an empire. Maria Theresa and her son Joseph II (1780–1790) began the process of transformation. For Austria, state-building meant first the reorganization of the military and civil bureaucracy to clear the way for fiscal reform. As in Prussia, a central directory was created to oversee the collection of taxes and the disbursement of funds. Maria Theresa personally persuaded her provincial estates both to increase taxation and to extend it to the nobles and the clergy. While her success was limited, she finally established royal control over the raising and collection of taxes.

The second element in Maria Theresa's reform program involved the condition of the Austrian peasantry. Maria Theresa established the doctrine that the "peasant must be able to support himself and his family and pay his taxes in time of peace and war." She limited labor service to two days per week and abolished the most burdensome feudal dues. Joseph II ended serfdom altogether. The new Austrian law codes guaranteed peasants' legal rights and established their ability to seek redress through the law. Joseph II hoped to extend reform even further. In the last years of his life he abolished obligatory labor service and ensured that all peasants kept one-half of their income before paying local and state taxes. Such a radical reform met a storm of opposition and with ultimately abandoned at the end of the reign.

The reorganization of the bureaucracy, the increase in taxation, and the social reforms that created a more productive peasantry revitalized the Austrian state. The efforts of Maria Theresa and Joseph II to overcome provincial autonomy worked better in Austria and Bohemia than in Hungary. The Hungarians declined to contribute at all to state revenues, and Joseph II took the unusual step of refusing to be crowned king of Hungary so that he would not have to make any concessions to Hungarian autonomy. He even imposed a tariff on Hungarian goods sold in Austria. More seriously, parts of the empire already had been lost before the process of reform could begin. Prussia's seizure of Silesia was the hardest blow of all. Yet in 1740 when Frederick the Great and his allies swept down from the north few would have predicted that Austria would survive.

The Politics of Power

Frederick the Great's invasion of Silesia in 1740 was callous and cynical. Since the Pragmatic Sanction bound him to recognize Maria Theresa's succession,

Frederick cynically offered her a defensive alliance in return for which she would simply hand over Silesia. It was an offer she should not have refused. Though Frederick's action initiated the War of the Austrian Succession, he was not alone in his desire to shake loose parts of Austria's territory. Soon nearly the entire Continent became embroiled in the conflict.

The War of the Austrian Succession (1740–1748) resembled nothing so much as a pack of wolves stalking its injured prey. Spain joined the fighting to recover its Italian possessions, Saxony claimed Moravia, France entered Bohemia, and the Bavarians moved into Austria from the south. With France and Prussia allied, it was vital that Britain join with Austria to maintain the balance of power. Initially the British did little more than subsidize Maria Theresa's forces, but once France renewed its efforts to conquer the Netherlands, both Britain and the Dutch Republic joined in the fray. That the British cared little about the fate of the Habsburg empire was clear from the terms of the treaty they dictated at Aix-la-Chapelle (Aachen) in 1748. Austria was to recognize Frederick's conquest of Silesia, as well as the loss of parts of its Italian territories to Spain. France, which the British had always regarded as the real enemy, withdrew from the Netherlands in return for the restoration of a number of colonial possessions. The War of the Austrian Succession made Austria and Prussia permanent enemies and gave Maria Theresa a crash course in international diplomacy. One of the things she learned was that it is not always easy to distinguish friend from foe. This lesson was reinforced in 1756 when Britain and Prussia entered into a military accord at the beginning of the Seven Years' War (1756–1763). Prussian expansion and duplicity had already alarmed both Russia and France, and Frederick II feared he would be squeezed from east and west. He could hardly expect help from Maria Theresa, so he extended overtures to Britain, whose interests in protecting Hanover, the hereditary estates of their German-born king, outweighed their prior commitments to Austria. Frederick's actions drove France into the arms of both the Austrians and the Russians, and an alliance that included the German state of Saxony was formed in defense. Thus was initiated a diplomatic revolution in which France and Austria became allies after 300 years as enemies.

Once again, Frederick the Great took the offensive and once again, he won his risk against the odds. His attack on Saxony and Austria in 1756 brought a vigorous response from the Russians, who interceded on Austria's behalf with a massive army. Three years later, at the battle of Kunersdorf, Frederick suffered the worst military defeat of his career when the Russians shattered his armies. In 1760 his forces were barely a third of the size of those massed by his opponents, and it was only a matter of time before he was fighting defensively from within Prussia.

In 1762 Tsarina Elizabeth died. Her successor was the childlike Peter III, a German by birth who worshiped Frederick the Great. When Peter came to the throne, he immediately negotiated peace with Frederick, abandoning not only his allies but also the substantial territorial gains that the Russian forces had made within Prussia. It was small wonder that the Russian military leadership joined in the coup d'état that brought Peter's wife, Catherine, to the throne in

1762. With Russia out of the war, Frederick was able to fend off further Austrian offensives and to emerge with his state, including Silesia, intact.

The Seven Years' War did little to change the boundaries of the German states, but it had two important political results. The first was to establish beyond doubt the status of Prussia as a major power and a counterbalance to Austria in central Europe. The existence of the dual Germanies, one led by Prussia and the other by Austria, was to have serious consequences for German unification in the nineteenth century and for the two world wars in the twentieth. The second result of the Seven Years' War was to initiate a long period of peace in eastern Europe. Both Prussia and Austria found themselves financially exhausted from two decades of fighting. Both states needed a breathing spell to initiate administrative and economic improvements, and the period following the Seven Years' War witnessed the sustained programs of internal reforms for which Frederick the Great, Maria Theresa, and Joseph II were famous.

Peace among the eastern European powers did not mean that they abandoned their territorial ambitions. All over Europe absolute rulers re-formed their bureaucracies, streamlined their administrations, increased their sources of revenue, and built enormous standing armies. All over Europe except in Poland. There the autonomous power of the nobility remained as strong as ever. No monarchical dynasty was ever established, and each elected ruler not only confirmed the privileges of the nobility but usually was forced to extend them. In the Diet, the Polish representative assembly, small special interest groups could bring legislative business to a halt by exercising their veto power. Given the size of Poland's borders its army was pathetically inadequate for the task it had to face. The Polish monarchy was helpless to defend its subjects from the destruction on all sides.

In 1764 Catherine the Great and Frederick the Great combined to place one of Catherine's former lovers on the Polish throne and to turn Poland into a weak dependent. Russia and Prussia had different interests in Poland's fate. For Russia, Poland represented a vast buffer state that kept the German powers at a distance from Russia's borders. It was more in Russia's interest to dominate Polish foreign policy than to conquer its territory. For Prussia, Poland looked like another helpless flower, "to be picked off leaf by leaf," as Frederick observed. Poland seemed especially appealing because Polish territory, including the Baltic port of Gdańsk, separated the Prussian and Brandenburg portions of Frederick's state.

By the 1770s the idea of carving up Poland was being actively discussed in Berlin, Saint Petersburg, and Vienna. Austria, too, had an interest in a Polish partition, especially to maintain its power and status with the other two states, and perhaps to use Polish territory as a potential bargaining chip for the return of Silesia. Finally, in 1772, the three great eastern powers struck a deal. Russia would take a large swath of the grain fields of northeast Poland, which included over one million people, while Frederick would unite his lands by seizing West Prussia. Austria gained both the largest territories, including Galicia, and the greatest number of people, nearly two million Polish subjects.

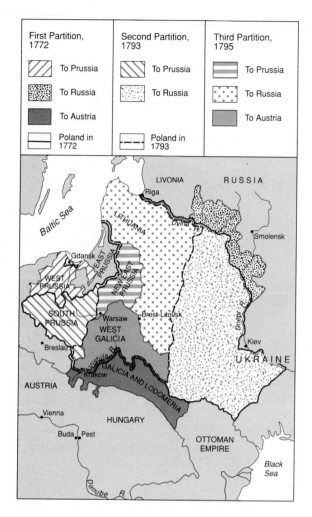

The partition of Poland

First Partition, 1772	Second Partition, 1793	Third Partition, 1795
To Prussia	To Prussia	To Prussia
To Russia	To Russia	To Russia
To Austria		To Austria
Poland in 1772	Poland in 1793	

LIVONIA   RUSSIA
Riga
Baltic Sea
LITHUANIA   Dvina R.
Smolensk
Gdansk   EAST PRUSSIA   NEW EAST PRUSSIA
WEST PRUSSIA
Brest-Litovsk
SOUTH PRUSSIA   Warsaw   WEST GALICIA
Breslau   Kiev
Dnepr R.
UKRAINE
Vistula R.   GALICIA AND LODOMERIA
Krakow
AUSTRIA
Vienna   HUNGARY
Buda Pest   OTTOMAN EMPIRE
Danube R.   Black Sea

*T*he Greatness of Britain

By the middle of the eighteenth century, Great Britain had become the leading power of Europe. It had won its spurs in continental and colonial wars. Britain was unsurpassed as a naval power, able to protect its far-flung trading empire and to make a show of force in almost any part of the world. Perhaps more impressively for a nation that did not support a large standing army, British soldiers had won decisive victories in the European land wars. Until the American Revolution, Britain came up a winner in every military venture it undertook. But might was only one part of British success. Economic preeminence was every bit as important. British colonial possessions in the Atlantic and Indian oceans poured consumer products into Britain for export to the European marketplaces. Growth in overseas trade was matched by growth in home production. British advances in agricultural technique had transformed Britain from an importer to an exporter of grain. The manufacturing industries that other European states attempted to create with huge government subsidies flourished in Britain through private enterprise.

British military and economic power was supported by a unique system of government. In Britain the nobility served the state through government. The British constitutional system, devised in the seventeenth century and refined in the eighteenth, shared power between the monarchy and the ruling elite through the institution of Parliament. Central government integrated monarch and ministers with chosen representatives from the localities. Such integration not only provided the crown with the vital information necessary to formulate national policy, but it eased acceptance and enforcement of government decisions. Government was seen as the rule of law which, however imperfect, was believed to operate for the benefit of all.

The parliamentary system gave Britain some of its particular strengths, but they came at a cost. Politics was a national pastime rather than the business of an elite of administrators and state servants. Decentralization of decision making led to half measures designed to placate competing interests. Appeals to public opinion, especially by candidates for Parliament, often played upon fears and prejudices that divided rather than united the nation. Moreover, the relative openness of the British system hindered diplomatic and colonial affairs, in which secrecy and rapid changes of direction were often the monarch's most potent weapons. These weaknesses came to light most dramatically during the struggle for independence waged by Britain's North American colonists. There the clash of principle and power was most extreme and the strengths and weaknesses of parliamentary rule were ruthlessly exposed.

The British Constitution

The British Constitution was a patchwork of laws and customs that was only gradually sewn together to form a workable system of government. Many of its greatest innovations came about through circumstance rather than design, and circumstance continued to play an essential role in its development in the eighteenth century. At the apex of the government stood the king, not an absolute monarch like his European counterparts, but not necessarily less powerful for having less arbitrary power. The British people revered monarchy and the monarch. The theory of mixed government depended on the balance of interests represented by the monarch in the crown, the aristocracy in the House of Lords, and the people in the House of Commons. Less abstractly, the monarch was still regarded as divinely ordained and a special gift to the nation.

The monarch was the actual and symbolic leader of the nation as well as the "Supreme Governor" of the Church of England. Allegiance to the Anglican church, whether as a political creed among the elite or as a simple matter of devotion among the populace, intensified allegiance to the king.

The political power of the British monarch was limited by law. A series of statutes enacted after the Revolution of 1688 clearly defined the king's prerogatives and the subjects' rights. The king could no longer suspend or dispense with the laws of the land, nor could he dismiss royal judges at his pleasure. The Act of Succession (1701) established that only Protestants could wear the crown, thus bypassing the Catholic heirs of James II in favor of the princes of Hanover. More important than these general constraints were those designed to bring the crown into partnership with Parliament. No army could be raised without the consent of Parliament, just as no tax could be established or collected. At first, it was legislated that a new parliament had to be called every three years, but the Septennial Act (1716) extended the period to seven. In reality, Parliament sat in continuous session, since most of the vital bills to fund the government and the military were passed for one year only.

The partnership between crown and representative body was best expressed in the idea that the British government was composed of King-in-Parliament. Parliament consisted of three separate organs: monarch, lords, and commons. Though each existed separately as a check on the potential excesses of the others, it was only when the three functioned together that parliamentary government could operate. The king was charged with selecting ministers, initiating policy, and supervising administration. The two houses of Parliament were charged with raising revenue, making laws, and presenting the grievances of subjects to the crown.

There were 558 members of the House of Commons after the union with Scotland in 1707. Most members of the lower house were nominated to their seats. The largest number of seats were located in small towns where a local oligarchy, or neighboring patron, had a customary right to make nominations that were invariably accepted by the electorate. Even in the largest cities influential citizens made arrangements for nominating members in order to avoid the cost and confusion of an actual election. Campaigns were ruinously expensive for the candidates—an election in 1754 cost the losing candidates £ 40,000—and potentially dangerous to the local community, where bitter social and political divisions boiled just below the surface.

The British gentry dominated the Commons, occupying over 80 percent of the seats in any session. Most of these members also served as unpaid local officials in the counties, as justices of the peace, captains of the local militias, or collectors of local taxes. They came to Parliament not only as representatives of the interests of their class, but as experienced local governors who understood the needs of both crown and subject. Most had direct connections with those who sat in the House of Lords. The peerage and the gentry together formed the class that in most other European societies was labeled the nobility. Their division into the two houses of Parliament obscured similarities in background, outlook, and interest. Dozens of members of the House of

Commons were the sons of members of the House of Lords. Such ties enabled the two houses of Parliament to work together in enacting legislation.

Nevertheless, the crown had to develop methods to coordinate the work of the two houses of Parliament and facilitate the passage of governmental programs. The king and his ministers began to use the deep royal pockets of offices and favors to bolster their friends in Parliament. Not only were those employed by the crown encouraged to find a place in the House of Commons, but those who had a place in Parliament were encouraged to take employment from the crown. Despite its potential for abuse, this was a political process that integrated center and locality, and at first it worked rather well. Those with local standing were brought into central offices. There they could influence central policy-making while protecting their local constituents. These office-holders, who came to be called *placemen*, never constituted a majority of the members of Parliament. They formed the core around which eighteenth-century governments operated, but it was a core that needed direction and cohesion. It was such leadership and organization that was the essential contribution of eighteenth-century politics to the British Constitution.

Parties and Ministers

Though parliamentary management was vital to the crown, it was not the crown that developed the basic tools of management. Rather these techniques originated within the political community itself and their usefulness was only slowly grasped by the monarchy. The first and, in the long term, most important tool was the party system. Political parties initially developed in the late seventeenth century around the issue of the Protestant succession. Those who opposed James II because he was a Catholic attempted to exclude him from inheriting the crown. They came to be called by their opponents Whigs, which meant "Scottish horse thieves." Those who supported James's hereditary rights but who also supported the Anglican church came to be called by their opponents Tories, which meant "Irish cattle rustlers." The Tories cooperated in the Revolution of 1688 that placed William and Mary on the throne because James had threatened the Anglican church by tolerating Catholics and because Mary had a legitimate hereditary right to be queen. After the death of Queen Anne in 1714, the Tories supported the succession of James III, James II's Catholic son who had been raised in France, rather than of George I (1714–1727), prince of Hanover and Protestant great-grandson of James I. An unsuccessful rebellion to place James III on the throne in 1715 discredited the leadership of the Tory party, but did not weaken its importance in both local and parliamentary politics.

The Whigs supported the Protestant succession and a broad-based Protestantism. They attracted the allegiance of large numbers of dissenters, those—heirs to the Puritans of the seventeenth century—who practiced forms of Protestantism different from the Anglican church. The struggle between

Whigs and Tories was less a struggle for power than it was for loyalty to their opposing viewpoints. As the Tories opposed the Hanoverian succession and the Whigs supported it, it was no mystery which party would find favor with George I. Moreover, as long as there was a pretender to the British throne— another rebellion took place in Scotland in 1745 led by the grandson of James II—the Tories continued to be tarred with the brush of disloyalty.

The division of political sympathies between Whigs and Tories helped create a set of groupings to which parliamentary leadership could be applied. A national, rather than a local or regional outlook, could be used to organize support for royal policy as long as royal policy conformed to that national outlook. The ascendancy of the Whigs enabled George I and his son George II (1727–1760) effectively to govern through Parliament, but at the price of dependence on the Whig leaders. Though the monarch had the constitutional freedom to choose his ministers, realistically he could choose only Whigs, and practically none but the Whig leaders of the House of Commons. Happily for the first two Georges, they found a man who was able to manage Parliament but desired only to serve the crown.

Sir Robert Walpole (1676–1745) came from a long-established gentry family in Norfolk. Walpole was an early supporter of the Hanoverian succession and an early victim of party warfare. But once George I was securely on the throne, Walpole became an indispensable leader of the House of Commons. His success rested upon his extraordinary abilities: He was an excellent public speaker; he relished long working days and the details of government; and he understood better than anyone else the intricacies of state finance. Walpole became first lord of the treasury, a post that he transformed into first minister of state. From his treasury post, Walpole assiduously built a Whig parliamentary party. He carefully dispensed jobs and offices, using them as bait to lure parliamentary supporters. Walpole's organization paid off both in the passage of legislation desired by the crown and at the polls, where Whigs were returned to Parliament time and again.

From 1721 to 1742 Walpole was the most powerful man in the British government. He refused an offer of a peerage so that he could continue to lead the House of Commons. Walpole's long tenure in office was as much a result of his policies as of his methods of governing. He brought a measure of fiscal responsibility to government by establishing a fund to pay off the national debt. In foreign policy he pursued peace with the same fervor that both his predecessors and successors pursued war. The long years of peace brought prosperity to both the landed and merchant classes, but they also brought criticism of Walpole's methods. The way in which he used government patronage to build his parliamentary party was attacked as corruption. So, too, were the ways in which the pockets of Whig officeholders were lined. During his last decade in office Walpole struggled to survive. His attempt to extend the excise tax on colonial goods nearly led to his loss of office in 1733. His refusal to respond to the clamor for continued war with Spain in 1741 finally led to his downfall.

Walpole's 20-year rule established the pattern of parliamentary government. The crown needed a "prime" minister who was able to steer legislation through the House of Commons. It also needed a patronage broker who could take control of the treasury and dispense its largess in return for parliamentary backing. Walpole's personality and talents had combined these two roles. Hereafter they were divided. Those who had grown up under Walpole had learned their lessons well. The Whig monopoly of power continued unchallenged for nearly another twenty years. The patronage network Walpole had created was vastly extended by his Whig successors. Even minor posts in the customs or the excise offices were now exchanged for political favor, and only those approved by the Whig leadership could claim them. The cries of corruption grew louder not only in the country houses of the long disenfranchised Tories, but in the streets of London, where a popular radicalism developed in opposition to the Whig oligarchy. They were taken up as well in the North American colonies, where two million British subjects champed at the bit of imperial rule.

America Revolts

Britain's triumph in the Seven Years' War (1756–1763) had come at great financial cost to the nation. At the beginning of the eighteenth century, the national debt stood at £ 14 million; in 1763 it had risen to £ 130 million despite the fact that Walpole's government had been paying off some of it. Then, as now, the cost of world domination was staggering. George III (1760–1820) came to the throne with a desire to break the Whig stranglehold on government and a taste for reform. He was to have limited success on both counts, though not for want of trying. In 1763 the king and his ministers agreed that reform of colonial administration was long overdue. Such reform would have the twin benefit of shifting part of the burden of taxation from Britain to North America and of making the commercial side of colonization pay.

This was sound thinking all around, and in due course Parliament passed a series of duties on goods imported into the colonies, including glass, wine, coffee, tea, and most notably sugar. The so-called Sugar Act (1764) was followed by the Stamp Act (1765), a tax on printed papers such as newspapers, deeds, and court documents. Both acts imposed taxes in the colonies similar to those that already existed in Britain. Accompanying the acts were administrative orders designed to cut into the lucrative black market trade. The government instituted new rules for searching ships and transferred authority over smuggling from the local colonial courts to Britain's Admiralty courts. Though British officials could only guess at the value of the new duties imposed, it was believed that with effective enforcement £ 150,000 would be raised. All this would go to pay the vastly greater costs of colonial administration and security.

British officials were more than perplexed when these mild measures met with a ferocious response. Assemblies of nearly every colony officially protested the Sugar Act. They sent petitions to Parliament begging for repeal and warning of dire economic and political consequences. Riots followed passage of the Stamp Act. Tax collectors were hounded out of office, their resignations precipitated by threats and acts of physical violence. In Massachusetts mobs that included political leaders in the colony razed the homes of the collector and the lieutenant-governor. However much the colonists might have regretted the violence that was done, they believed an essential political principle was at stake. It was a principle of the freedom of an Englishman.

At their core, the protests of the American colonists underscored the vitality of the British political system. The Americans argued they could not be taxed without their consent and that their consent could come only through representation in Parliament. Since there were no colonists in Parliament, Parliament had no jurisdiction over the property of the colonists. Taxation without representation was tyranny. There were a number of subtleties to this argument that were quickly lost as political rhetoric and political action heated up. In the first place, the colonists did tax themselves through their own legislatures and much of that money paid the costs of administration and defense. Secondly, as a number of pamphleteers pointed out, no one in the colonies had asked the British government to send regiments of the army into North America. The colonists had little reason to put their faith in British protection. Hard-fought colonial victories were tossed away at European negotiating tables, while the British policy of defending Indian rights in the Ohio Valley ran counter to the interests of the settlers. When defense was necessary, the colonists had proven themselves both able and cooperative in providing it. A permanent tax meant a permanent army, and a standing army was as loathed in Britain as it was in the colonies.

Colonists also tried to draw a distinction between internal and external taxation in opposing the Stamp Act. They deemed regulation of overseas commerce a legitimate power of Parliament but argued that the regulation of internal exchange was not. But this distinction was lost once the issue of parliamentary representation was raised. If the colonists had not consented to British taxation, then it made no difference whether taxation was internal or external. The passion generated in the colonies was probably no greater than that generated in Britain. The British government also saw the confrontation as a matter of principle, but for Britain the principle was parliamentary sovereignty. This, above all, was the rock on which the British Constitution had been built over the last century. Parliament had entered into a partnership with the crown. The crown had surrendered—willingly or not—many of its prerogatives. In return, Parliament had bound the people to obedience. There were well-established means by which British subjects could petition Parliament for redress of grievances against the monarch, but there were no channels by which they could question the sovereignty of Parliament.

Once the terms of debate had been so defined, it was difficult for either side to find a middle ground. Parliamentary moderates managed repeal of the Stamp Act and most of the clauses of the Sugar Act, but they also joined in passing the Declaratory Act (1766), which stated unequivocally that Parliament held sovereign jurisdiction over the colonies "in all cases whatsoever." This was a claim that became more and more difficult to sustain as colonial leaders began to cite the elements of resistance theory that had justified the Revolution of 1688. Then the protest had been against the tyranny of the king; now it was against the tyranny of Parliament. American propagandists claimed that a conspiracy existed to deprive the colonists of their property and rights, to enslave for the benefit of special interests and corrupt politicians.

The techniques of London radicals who opposed parliamentary policy were imported into the colonies. Newspapers were used to whip up public support; boycotts brought ordinary people into the political arena; public demonstrations like the Boston Tea Party (1774) were carefully designed to intimidate; mobs were occasionally given free rein. Though the government had faced down these tactics when they were used in London to support John Wilkes (1725–1797), an ardent critic of royal policy, they were less successful when the crisis lay an ocean away. When, in 1770, British troops fired upon a Boston mob, American propagandists were provided with empirical evidence that Britain intended to enslave the colonies. Violence was met by violence, passion by passion. In 1775 full-scale fighting was under way. Eight years later Britain withdrew from a war it could not win, and the American colonies were left to govern themselves.

The New European Powers

1707	England and Scotland unite to form Great Britain
1713–1714	Peace of Utrecht ends war of the Spanish Succession (1702–1714)
1714	British crown passes to House of Hanover
1721	Treaty of Nystad ends Great Northern War (1700–1721)
1721–1742	Sir Robert Walpole leads British House of Commons
1722	Peter the Great of Russia creates Table of Ranks
1740	Frederick the Great of Prussia invades Austrian province of Silesia
1748	Treaty of Aix-la-Chapelle ends War of the Austrian Succession (1740–1748)
1756–1763	Seven Years' War pits Prussia and Britain against Austria, France, and Russia
1773–1775	Pugachev's Revolt in Russia
1774	Boston Tea Party
1775	American Revolution begins
1785	Catherine the Great of Russia issues Charter of the Nobility

By the end of the third quarter of the eighteenth century, Europe had a new political configuration. A continent once dominated by a single power—Spain in the sixteenth century and France in the seventeenth—was now dominated by a states system in which alliances among several great powers held the balance. Despite the loss of its American colonies, Great Britain had proved the most potent of the states. Its victories over the French in the Seven Years' War and over France and Prussia in the War of the Austrian Succession secured its position. But it was a position that could only be maintained through alliances with the German states, either with Prussia or Austria. The rise of Prussia provided a counterweight to French domination of the Continent. Though these two states found themselves allies in the middle of the century, the ambitions of their rulers made them natural enemies, and it would not be long before French and Prussian armies were again pitted against each other. France, still the wealthiest and most populous of European states, had slumbered through the eighteenth-century reorganization. The legacies of Louis XIV took a long time to reach fruition. He had claimed glory for his state, giving the French people a sense of national identity and national destiny, but making them pay an enormous price in social and economic dislocation. Thus the mid eighteenth century was to be an age of the greatest literary and philosophical achievement for France, but the late eighteenth century was to be an age of the greatest social upheaval that Europe had ever known.

Suggestions for Further Reading

General Reading

*M. S. Anderson, *Europe in the Eighteenth Century 1713–1783* (London: Longman, 1976). A country-by-country survey of political developments.

*Olwen Hufton, *Europe: Privilege and Protest 1730–1789* (Ithaca, NY: Cornell University Press, 1980). An excellent survey of the political and social history of the mid eighteenth century.

*Leonard Krieger, *Kings and Philosophers 1689–1789* (New York: W.W. Norton, 1970). A brilliant depiction of the personalities and ideas of eighteenth-century Europe.

Nicholas Riasanovksy, *A History of Russia* (New York: Oxford University Press, 1984). The best one-volume history of Russia.

Europe in 1714

*Derek McKay and H. M. Scott, *The Rise of the Great Powers* (London: Longman, 1983). An outstanding survey of diplomacy and warfare.

*Indicates paperback edition available.

The Rise of Russia

John T. Alexander, *Catherine the Great: Life and Legend* (Oxford, England: Oxford University Press, 1989). The most up-to-date and enjoyable of many biographies.

*M. S. Anderson, *Peter the Great* (London: Thames & Hudson, 1978). A well-constructed, comprehensive biography.

*Jerome Blum, *Lord and Peasant in Russia* (New York: Columbia University Press, 1961). The best work on the social life of Russians.

*Paul Dukes, *The Making of Russian Absolutism 1613–1801* (London: Longman, 1982). An extensive survey of the Russian monarchy in its greatest period.

*B. H. Sumner, *Peter the Great and the Emergence of Russia* (New York: Collier, 1962). A short and readable study; the best introduction.

The Two Germanies

*T. C. W. Blanning, *Joseph II and Enlightened Despotism* (London: Longman, 1970). Displays the relationship between new ideas, reform policies, and the practical necessities of government.

*Walther Hubatsch, *Frederick the Great of Prussia* (London: Thames & Hudson, 1975). A full account of the reign of Prussia's greatest leader.

*H. W. Koch, *A History of Prussia* (London: Longman, 1978). An up-to-date study of the factors that led to Prussian dominance of Germany.

C. A. Macartney, *Maria Theresa and the House of Austria* (Mystic, CT: Verry, 1969). Still the best introductory study.

*Gerhard Ritter, *Frederick the Great* (Berkeley: University of California Press, 1974). A classic biography; short and readable.

*Ernst Wangermann, *The Austrian Achievement* (New York: Harcourt Brace Jovanovich, 1973). The most readable study of Austrian politics, culture, and society in the eighteenth century.

The Greatness of Britain

*Bernard Bailyn, *The Ideological Origins of the American Revolution* (Cambridge, MA: Harvard University Press, 1967). A brilliant interpretation of the underlying causes of the break between Britain and the North American colonies.

*John Brewer, *Party Ideology and Popular Politics at the Accession of George III* (Cambridge, England: Cambridge University Press, 1976). Examines the pressures on the political system in the late eighteenth century.

*Ian Christie and Benjamin W. Labaree, *Empire or Independence 1760–1777* (New York: W.W. Norton, 1977). Surveys the American troubles from the British point of view.

*J. C. D. Clark, *English Society 1688–1832* (Cambridge, England: Cambridge University Press, 1985). A bold reinterpretation of the most important features of English society.

*Edward Countryman, *The American Revolution* (New York: Hill & Wang, 1985). A readable up-to-date narrative of the events of the American Revolution.

Ragnhild Hatton, *George I Elector and King* (Cambridge, MA: Harvard University Press, 1978). An outstanding biography that shows the German side of a British monarch.

*J. H. Plumb, *The Origins of Political Stability, England 1675–1725* (Boston: Houghton Mifflin, 1967). A comprehensive account of the contributions of Walpole to the establishment of the British Constitution.

15

Culture and Society in Early Modern Europe

Rembrandt's Lessons

By the early seventeenth century interest in scientific investigation had spread out from narrow circles of specialists to embrace educated men and women. One of the more spectacular demonstrations of new knowledge was public dissection, by law performed only on the corpses of criminals. Here the secrets of the human body were revealed both for those who were in training as physicians and for those who had the requisite fee and strong stomach. Curiosity about the human body was becoming a mark of education. New publications, both scientific and popular, spread ancient wisdom as well as the controversial findings of the moderns. Pictures drawn on the basis of dissections filled the new medical texts like the one on the stand at the feet of the corpse in *The Anatomy Lesson of Dr. Nicolaes Tulp* (1632) by Rembrandt van Rijn (1606–1669).

Dr. Tulp's anatomy lesson was not meant for the public. In fact, those gathered around him in various poses of concentration were not students at all. They were members of the Amsterdam company of surgeons, the physicians' guild of the early seventeenth century. The sitters had commissioned the picture, which was a celebration of themselves as well as of the noted Professor Tulp. They hired the young Rembrandt to compose the picture with the assurance that each of the sitters (whose names are written on the paper one of them holds in his hand) would appear as if he alone were the subject of a portrait. Rembrandt succeeded beyond expectation. Each individual was given his due. The expressions on their faces as much as their physical characteristics mark each one out from the group. Yet the portraits were only one part of the painting. The scene that Rembrandt depicted unified them.

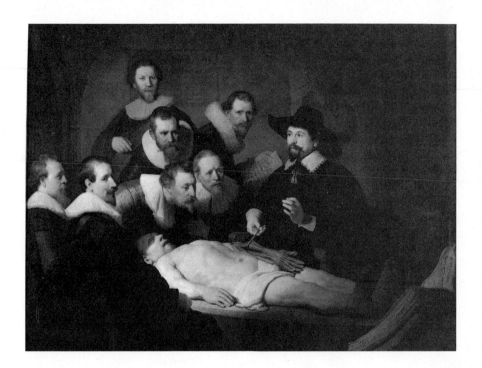

They became a group of their participation in the anatomy lesson. Rembrandt has chosen a moment of drama to stop the action. Dr. Tulp is demonstrating how the gesture he is making with his left hand looks in the dissected arm of the gruesome cadaver. The central figures of the group are rapt in attention though only one of them is actually observing the procedure of the anatomy. Each listens to Tulp, comparing his own experience and knowledge to that of the professor and the text that stands open.

The Anatomy Lesson established the 25-year-old Rembrandt as one of the most gifted and fashionable painters in Amsterdam. If any people could be said to be consumers of art in seventeenth-century Europe, it was the Dutch. Artists flourished and pictures abounded. Travelers were struck by the presence of artwork in both public and private places and in the homes of even moderately prosperous people. The group portrait, which Rembrandt brought to new levels of expression, was becoming a favorite genre. It was used to celebrate the leaders of Dutch society who, unlike the leaders of most other European states, were not princes and aristocrats, but rather merchants, guild officials, and professionals. Rembrandt captured a spirit of civic pride in his group portraits. Here it was the surgeons' guild; later it would be the leaders of the cloth merchants' guild, another time a militia company.

Like the leaders of the surgeons' guild who commissioned their own portrait, which hung in their company's hall, the Dutch Republic swelled with pride in the seventeenth century. Its long war with Spain was finally drawing to a close and it was time to celebrate the birth of a new state. The Dutch were a trading people and their trade flourished as much in times of war as in times of peace. Their ships traveled to all parts of the globe and they dominated the great luxury trades of the age. Bankers and merchants were the backbone of the Dutch Republic. Yet this republic of merchants was also one of the great cultural centers of the Continent. Intellectual creativity was cultivated in the same manner as was a trading partner. In the burgeoning port of Amsterdam, the fastest growing city in Europe, artists, philosophers, and mathematicians lived cheek by jowl. The free exchange of ideas made Amsterdam home to those exiled for their beliefs. The Dutch practiced religious toleration as did no one else. Catholics, Protestants, and Jews all were welcomed to the Republic and found that they could pursue their own paths without persecution. Freedom of thought and freedom of expression helped develop a new spirit of scientific inquiry, like that portrayed in *The Anatomy Lesson of Dr. Nicolaes Tulp.*

C onquering the Material World

"And new Philosophy calls all in doubt,/ The element of fire is quite put out;/ The sun is lost and the earth, and no man's wit/ Can well direct him where to look for it." So wrote the English poet John Donne (1572–1631) about one of the most astonishing yet perplexing moments in the history of Western thought: the emergence of the new science. It was astonishing because it seemed truly new. The discoveries of the stargazers, like those of the sea explorers, challenged people's most basic assumptions and beliefs. Men dropping balls from towers or peering at the skies through a glass claimed that they had disproved thousands of years of certainty about the nature of the universe. "And new Philosophy calls all in doubt." But it was perplexing because it seemed to loosen the moorings of everything that educated people thought they knew about their world. Nothing could be more disorienting than to challenge common sense. One needed to do little more than wake up in the morning to know that the sun moved from east to west while the earth stood still. But mathematics, experimentation, and deduction were needed to understand that the earth was in constant motion and that it revolved around the sun. "And no man's wit/ Can well direct him where to look for it."

The New Science

The scientific revolution was the opening of a new era in European history. After two centuries of classical revival, European thinkers had finally come against the limits of ancient knowledge. Ancient wisdom had served Europeans well, and it was not to be discarded lightly. But one by one, the certainties of the past were being called into question. The explanations of the universe and the natural world that had been advanced by Aristotle and codified by his followers no longer seemed adequate. There were too many contradictions between theory and observation, too many things that did not fit. Yet breaking the hold of Aristotelianism was no easy task. A full century was to pass before even learned people would accept the proofs that the earth revolved around the sun. Even then, the most famous of them—Galileo—had to recant these views or be condemned as a heretic.

The two essential characteristics of the new science were that it was materialistic and mathematical. Its materialism was contained in the realization that the universe is composed of matter in motion. This meant that the stars and planets were not made of some perfect ethereal substance but of the same matter that was found on earth. They were thus subject to the same rules of motion as earthly objects. The mathematics of the new science was contained in the realization that calculation had to replace common sense as the basis for understanding the universe. Mathematics itself was transformed with the invention of logarithms, analytic geometry, and calculus. More importantly, scientific experimentation took the form of measuring repeatable phenomena. When Galileo attempted to develop a theory of acceleration, he rolled a brass ball down an inclined plane and recorded the time and distance of its descent 100 times before he was satisfied with his results.

The new science was also a Europe-wide movement. The spirit of scientific inquiry flourished everywhere. The main contributors to astronomy were a Pole, a Dane, a German, and an Italian. The founder of medical chemistry was Swiss; the best anatomist was Belgian. England contributed most of all—the founders of modern chemistry, biology, and physics. By and large, these scientists operated outside the traditional seats of learning at the universities. Though most were university trained and not a few taught the traditional Aristotelian subjects, theirs was not an academic movement. Rather it was a public one made possible by the printing press. Once published, findings became building blocks for scientists throughout the Continent and from one generation to the next. Many discoveries were made in the search for practical solutions to ordinary problems, and what was learned fueled advances in technology and the natural sciences. The new science gave seventeenth-century Europeans a sense that they might finally master the forces of nature.

Heavenly Revolutions

There was much to be said for Aristotle's understanding of the world, for his cosmology. For one thing, it was harmonious. It incorporated a view of the physical world that coincided with a view of the spiritual and moral one. The

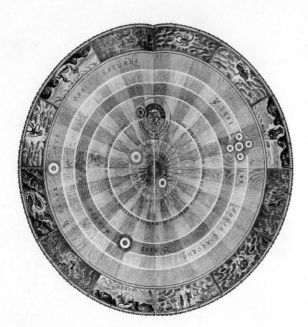

This chart of the heavens was engraved by Andreas Cellarius in 1660. It portrays the heliocentric universe described by Nicolaus Copernicus and accepted by Galileo. Earth and Jupiter are shown with moons orbiting them.

heavens were unchangeable and therefore they were better than the earth. The sun, moon, and planets were all faultless spheres, unblemished and immune from decay. Their motion was circular because the circle was the perfect form of motion. The earth was at the center of the universe because it was the heaviest planet and because it was at the center of the Great Chain of Being, between the underworld of spirits and the upperworld of gods. The second advantage to the Aristotelian worldview was that it was easily incorporated into Christianity. Aristotle's description of the heavens as being composed of a closed system of crystalline rings that held the sun, moon, and planets in their circular orbits around the earth left room for God and the angels to reside just beyond the last ring.

There were, of course, problems with Aristotle's explanation of the universe as it was preserved in the work of Ptolemy, the greatest of the Greek astronomers. For one thing, if the sun revolved in a perfect circle around the earth, then why were the seasons not perfectly equal? If the planets all revolved around the earth in circles, then why did they look nearer or farther, brighter or darker at different times of year? To solve these problems, a host of ingenious hypotheses were advanced. Perhaps the sun revolved around the earth in an eccentric circle, that is, a circle not centered on the earth. This would account for the differing lengths of seasons. Perhaps the planets revolved in circles that rested on a circle around the earth. Then when the planet revolved within the larger circle, it would seem nearer and brighter, and when it revolved outside it, it would seem farther away and darker. This was the theory of epicycles.

In the 1490s, Nicolaus Copernicus (1473–1543) came to the Polish University of Kraków, which had one of the leading mathematical faculties in Europe. There they taught the latest astronomical theories and vigorously debated the existence of eccentric circles and epicycles. Copernicus came to Kraków for a liberal arts education before pursuing a degree in church law. He became fascinated by astronomy and puzzled by the debate over planetary motion. Copernicus believed, like Aristotle, that the simplest explanations were the best. If the sun was at the center of the universe and the earth simply another planet in orbit, then many of the most elaborate explanations of planetary motion were unnecessary. "At rest, in the middle of everything is the sun," Copernicus wrote in *On the Revolutions of the Heavenly Spheres* (1543). "For in this most beautiful temple who would place this lamp in another or better position than that from which it can light up the whole thing at the same time?" Because Copernicus accepted most of the rest of the traditional Aristotelian explanation, especially the belief that the planets moved in circles, his sun-centered universe was only slightly better at predicting the position of the planets than the traditional earth-centered one, but Copernicus's idea stimulated other astronomers to make new calculations.

Under the patronage of the king of Denmark, Tycho Brahe (1546–1601) built a large observatory to study planetary motion. In 1572 Brahe discovered a nova, a brightly burning star that was previously unknown. This discovery challenged the idea of an immutable universe composed of crystalline rings. In 1577 the appearance of a comet cutting through the supposedly impenetrable rings punched another hole into the old cosmology. Brahe's own views were a hybrid of old and new. He believed that all planets but the earth revolved around the sun and that the sun and the planets revolved around a fixed earth. To demonstrate this theory, Brahe and his students compiled the largest and most accurate mathematical tables of planetary motion yet known. From this research, Brahe's pupil, Johannes Kepler (1571–1630), one of the great mathematicians of the age, formulated laws of planetary motion. Kepler discovered that planets orbited the sun in an elliptical rather than a circular path. This accounted for their movements nearer and farther from the earth. More importantly, he demonstrated that there was a precise mathematical relationship between the speed with which a planet revolved and its distance from the sun. Kepler's findings supported the view that the galaxy was heliocentric and that the heavens, like the earth, were made of matter that was subject to physical laws.

What Kepler demonstrated mathematically, the Italian astronomer Galileo (1564–1642) confirmed by observation. Creating a telescope by using magnifying lenses and a long tube, Galileo saw parts of the heavens that had never been dreamt of before. In 1610 he discovered four moons of Jupiter, proving conclusively that not all heavenly bodies revolved around the earth. He observed the landscape of the earth's moon and described it as full of mountains, valleys, and rivers. It was of the same imperfect form as the earth itself. He even found spots on the sun, which suggested that it, too, was composed of ordinary matter. Many of Galileo's scientific discoveries had to do with motion—he was the first to posit a law of inertia—but his greatest contribution to the new science was his popularization of the Copernican theory.

As news of his experiments and discoveries spread, Galileo became famous throughout the Continent, and his support for heliocentrism became a celebrated cause. In 1616 the Roman Catholic church cautioned him against promoting his views. In 1633, a year after publishing his *A Dialogue Between the Two Great Systems of the World*, Galileo was tried by the Inquisition and forced specifically to recant the idea that the earth moves. He spent the rest of his life under house arrest. But Galileo insisted there was nothing in the new science that was anti-Christian. He rejected the view that his discoveries refuted the Bible, arguing that the Bible was often difficult to interpret and that nature was another way in which God revealed himself.

The Natural World

The new science originated from a number of traditions that were anything but scientific. Inquiry into nature and the environment grew out of the discipline of natural philosophy and was nurtured by spiritual and mystical traditions. Much of the most useful medical knowledge had come from the studies of herbalists; the most reliable calculations of planetary motion had come from astrologers. Though the first laboratories and observatories were developed in aid of the new science, practice in them was as much magical as experimental. For those attempting to unlock the mysteries of the universe, there was no separation between magic and science. Some of the most characteristic features of modern science, such as the stress on experimentation and empirical observation, developed only gradually. What was new about the new science was the determination to develop systems of thought that could help humans understand and control their environment. Thus there was a greater openness and spirit of cooperation about discoveries than in the past, when experiments were conducted secretly and results were kept hidden away.

Aristotelianism was not the only philosophical system to explain the nature and composition of the universe. During the Renaissance the writings of Plato attracted a number of Italian humanists, most notably Marsilio Ficino (1433–1499) and Pico della Mirandola (1463–1494). They taught Plato's theory that the world was composed of ideas and forms, which were hidden by the physical properties of objects. These Neoplatonic humanists believed the architect of the universe possessed the spirit of a geometrician and that the perfect disciplines were music and mathematics. These elements of Neoplatonism created an impetus for the mathematically based studies of the new scientists. They were especially important among the astronomers, who used both calculation and geometry in exploring the heavens. But they served as well to bolster the sciences of alchemy and astrology. Alchemy was the use of fire in the study of metals, an effort to find the essence of things through their purification. While medieval alchemists mostly attempted to find gold and silver as the essence of lead and iron, the new experimentation focused on the properties of metals in general. Astrology was the study of the influence of the stars on human behavior, calculated by planetary motion and the harmony of the heavenly spheres. Astrologers made careful calculations based on the movement of the planets and were deeply involved in the new astronomy. The Neoplatonic emphasis on mathematics also accorded support for a variety of mystical sciences based on numerology. These were efforts to predict events from the combination of particular numbers.

The most influential of these mystical traditions was that associated with Hermes Trismegistus (Thrice Greatest), an Egyptian who was reputed to have lived in the second century A.D. and to have known the secrets of the universe. A body of writings mistakenly attributed to Hermes was discovered during the Renaissance and formed the basis of a Hermetic tradition. The core of Hermetic thinking centered on the idea of a universal spirit that was present in all objects and that spontaneously revealed itself. Kepler was one of many of the new scientists influenced by Hermeticism. His efforts to understand planetary motion derived from his search for a unifying spirit.

A combination of Neoplatonic and Hermetic traditions was central to the work of one of the most curious of the new scientists, the Swiss alchemist Paracelsus (1493–1541). Paracelsus studied with a leading German alchemist before following in his father's footsteps by becoming a physician. Though he worked as a doctor, his true vocation was alchemy, and he conducted innumerable experiments designed to extract the essence of particular metals. Paracelsus taught that all matter was composed of combinations of three principles: salt, sulfur, and mercury. This view replaced the traditional belief in the four elements of earth, water, fire, and air.

The Paracelsian system transformed ideas about chemistry and medicine. Paracelsus rejected the theory that disease was caused by an imbalance in the humors of the body, the standard view of Galen, the great Greek physician of the second century A.D. Instead, Paracelsus argued that each disease had its own cause, which could be diagnosed and remedied. Where traditional doctors treated disease by bloodletting or sweating to correct the imbalance of humors, Paracelsus prescribed the ingestion of particular chemicals, especially distilled metals like mercury, arsenic, and antimony, and he favored administering them at propitious astrological moments.

Although established physicians and medical faculties rejected Paracelsian cures and methods, his influence spread among ordinary practitioners. It ultimately had a profound impact on the studies of Robert Boyle (1627–1691), an Englishman who helped establish the basis of the science of chemistry. Boyle devoted his energies to raising the study of medical chemistry above that of merely providing recipes for the cure of disease. He worked carefully and recorded each step in his experiments. Boyle's first important work, *The Sceptical Chymist* (1661), attacked both the Aristotelian and Paracelsian views of the basic components of the natural world. Boyle rejected both the four humors and the three principles. Instead he favored an atomic explanation in which matter "consisted of little particles of all sizes and shapes." Changes in these particles, which would later be identified as the chemical elements, resulted in changes in matter. Boyle's most important experiments were.with gases—a word invented by Paracelsus. He formulated the relationship between the volume and pressure of a gas (Boyle's law) and invented the air pump.

The new spirit of scientific inquiry also affected medical studies. The study of anatomy through dissection had helped the new scientists reject many of the descriptive errors in Galen's texts. The Belgian doctor Andreas Vesalius (1514–1564) published the first modern set of anatomical drawings in 1543. But accurate knowledge of the composition of the body did not also mean better understanding of its operation. Dead bodies didn't easily yield the secrets of life. Much of what was known about matters as common as reproduction was an inadequate combination of ancient wisdom and the practical experiences of midwives and doctors.

One of the greatest mysteries was the method by which blood moved through the vital organs. It was generally believed that the blood originated in the liver, traveled to the right side of the heart, and then passed to the left side through invisible pores. William Harvey (1578–1657), an Englishman who had received his medical education in Italy, offered an entirely different explanation. Harvey's main interest was in studying the anatomy of the heart. He examined hearts in more than forty species before concluding that the heart worked like a pump or, as he put it, a water bellows. Harvey observed that the valves of the heart chambers allowed the blood to flow in only one direction. He thus concluded that the blood was pumped by the heart and circulated throughout the entire body.

The greatest of all English scientists was the mathematician and physicist Sir Issac Newton (1642–1727). It was Newton who brought together the various strands of the new science. He made a great study of Hermetic writings and from them revived the mystical notions of attraction and repulsion. He merged the materialists and Hermeticists, the astronomers and astrologers, the chemists and alchemists. Newton was the first to understand the composition of light, the first to develop a calculus, the first to build a reflecting telescope. He made stunning contributions to the sciences of optics, physics, astronomy, and mathematics, and his magnum opus, *Mathematical Principles of Natural Philosophy* (1687), is one of a handful of the most important scientific works ever composed. Most importantly, Newton solved the single most perplexing problem: If the world was composed of matter in motion, what was motion?

Though Galileo had first developed a theory of inertia, the idea that a body at rest stays at rest, most materialists believed that motion was inherent in objects. In contrast, Newton believed that motion was the result of the interaction of objects and that it could be calculated mathematically. From his experiments he formulated the concept of force and his famous laws of motion: (1) objects at rest or of uniform linear motion remain in such a state unless acted upon by an external force; (2) changes in motion are proportional to force; and (3) for every action there is an equal and opposite reaction. From these laws of motion, Newton advanced one step further. If the world was no more than matter in motion and if all motion was subject to the same laws, then the movement of the planets could be explained in the same way as the movement of an apple falling from a tree. There was a mathematical relationship between attraction and repulsion, a universal gravitation as Newton called it, that governed the movement of all objects. Newton's theory of gravity joined Kepler's astronomy and Galileo's physics. The mathematical, materialistic world of the new science was now complete.

Science Enthroned

By the middle of the seventeenth century, the new science was firmly established throughout Europe. Royal and noble patrons supported the enterprise by paying some of the costs of equipment and experimentation. Royal observatories were created for the astronomers, colleges of physicians for the doctors, laboratories for the chemists. Both England and France established royal societies of learned scientists to meet together and discuss their discoveries. The French Académie des Sciences (1666) was composed of 20 salaried scientists and an equal number of students, divided among the different branches of scientific learning. The English Royal Society (1662) boasted some of the greatest minds of the age. It was there that Newton first made public his most important discoveries. Scientific bodies were also formed outside the traditional universities. These were the so-called mechanics colleges, like Gresham College in London, where the practical applications of mathematics and physics were taught.

The establishment of learned scientific societies and practical colleges fulfilled part of the program advocated by Sir Francis Bacon (1561–1626), one of the leading supporters of scientific research in England. In *The Advancement of Learning* (1605) Bacon proposed a scientific method through inductive, empirical experimentation. Bacon believed that experiments should be carefully recorded so that results were both reliable and repeatable, and in his numerous writings he stressed the practical impact of scientific discovery.

Bacon's support for the new science contrasts markedly with the stance taken by the Roman Catholic church. Embattled by the Reformation and the wars of religion, the Church had taken the offensive in preserving the core of its heritage. By the early seventeenth century the missionary work of the Jesuits had won many reconversions and had halted the advance of Protestantism. Now the new science appeared to be another heresy. Not only did it confound ancient wisdom and contradict church teachings, but it was also a lay movement that was neither directed nor controlled from Rome. The trial of Galileo slowed the momentum of scientific investigation in Catholic countries and starkly posed the conflict between authority and knowledge. But the stand taken by the Church was based on more than narrow self-interest. Ever since Copernicus had published his views, a new skepticism had emerged among European intellectuals. Every year new theories competed with old ones, and dozens of contradictory explanations for the most common phenomena were advanced and debated. The skeptics concluded that nothing was known and nothing was knowable. Their position led inevitably to the most shocking of all possible views: atheism. But there was no necessary link between the new science and an attack on established religion. So Galileo had argued all along. Few of the leading scientists saw a contradiction between their studies and their faith. Still, by the middle of the century attacks on the Church were increasing and some blamed the new science for them. Thus it was altogether fitting that one of the leading mathematicians of the day should provide the method for harmonizing faith and reason.

René Descartes (1596–1650) was trained in one of the best Jesuit schools in France before taking a law degree in 1616. He entered military service in the Dutch Republic and after the outbreak of the Thirty Years' War, in the Duke of Bavaria's army. Descartes was keenly interested in mathematics, and during his military travels he met and was tutored by a leading Dutch mathematician. For the first time he learned of the new scientific discoveries and of the advances made in mathematics. In 1619 he dreamt of discovering the scientific principles of universal knowledge. After this dream, Descartes returned to Holland and began to develop his system. He was on the verge of publishing his views when he learned of Galileo's condemnation. Reading Galileo's *Dialogue Between the Two Great Systems of the World* (1632), Descartes discovered that he shared many of the same opinions and had worked out mathematical proofs for them, but he refrained from publishing until 1637, when he brought out the *Discourse on Method.*

In the *Discourse on Method*, Descartes demonstrated how skepticism could be used to produce certainty. He began by declaring he would reject everything that could not be clearly proven beyond doubt. Thus he rejected the material world, the testimony of his senses, all known or imagined opinions. He was left only with doubt. But what was doubt, if not thought, and what was thought, if not the workings of his mind? The only thing of which he could be certain, then, was that he had a mind. Thus his famous formulation: "I think, therefore I am." From this first certainty came another, the knowledge of perfectibility. He knew that he was imperfect and that a perfect being had to have placed that knowledge within him. Therefore, a perfect being—God—existed.

Descartes's philosophy, known as Cartesianism, rested on the dual existence of matter and mind. Matter was the material world subject to the incontrovertible laws of mathematics. Mind was the spirit of the creator. Descartes was one of the leading mechanistic philosophers, believing that all objects operated in accord with natural laws. He invented analytic geometry and made important contributions to the sciences of optics and physics on which Newton would later build. Yet it was in his proof that the new science could be harmonized with the old religion that Descartes made his greatest contribution.

Descartes was one of many new scientists who saw the practical import of what they had learned and who hoped to bring that knowledge to the aid of the material well-being of their contemporaries. John Dee (1527–1608) translated the Greek geometrician Euclid into English so that ordinary people might "find out and devise new works, strange engines and instruments for sundry purposes in the commonwealth." Though many of the breakthrough discoveries of the new scientists would not find practical use for centuries, the spirit of discovery was to have great impact in an age of commerce and capital. The quest for mathematical certainty and prime movers led directly to improvements in agriculture, mining, navigation, and industrial activity. The new sense of control over the material world provided a new optimism for generations of Europeans.

The Enlightenment

The Enlightenment was less a set of ideas than it was a set of attitudes. At its core was criticism, a questioning of traditional institutions, customs, and morals. In 1762 the French philosopher Jean-Jacques Rousseau (1712–1778) published one of the most important works on social theory, *The Social Contract*, which opened with the gripping maxim "Man is born free and everywhere he is in chains." But most of the great thinkers of the Enlightenment were not so much philosophers as savants, knowledgeable popularizers whose skills were in simplifying and publicizing a hodgepodge of new views.

In France Enlightenment intellectuals were called *philosophes* and claimed all the arts and sciences as their purview. The *Encyclopedia* (35 volumes, 1751–1780), edited by Denis Diderot (1713–1784), was one of the greatest achievements of the age. Entitled the *Systematic Dictionary of the Sciences, Arts, and Crafts*, it attempted to summarize all acquired knowledge and to dispel all imposed superstitions. There was no better definition of a philosophe than that given them by one of their enemies. "Just what is a philosophe? A kind of monster in society who feels under no obligation towards its manners and morals, its proprieties, its politics, or its religion. One may expect anything from men of their ilk."

The influence of French counterculture on enlightened thought was great, but the Enlightenment was by no means a strictly French phenomenon. Its greatest figures included the Scottish economist Adam Smith (1723–1790), the Italian legal reformer Cesare Beccaria (1738–1794), and the German philosopher Immanuel Kant (1724–1804). While in France it was first composed of antiestablishment critics, in Scotland and the German states it flourished in the

Jean-Jacques Rousseau

universities, and in Prussia, Austria, and Russia it was propagated by the monarchy. The Enlightenment began in the 1730s and was still going strong a half century later when its attitudes had been absorbed into the mainstream of European thought.

No brief summary can do justice to the diversity of enlightened thought in eighteenth-century Europe. Because it was an attitude of mind rather than a set of shared beliefs, there are many contradictory strains to follow. In his famous essay *What is Enlightenment?* (1784) Immanuel Kant described it simply as freedom to use one's own intelligence. "I hear people clamor on all sides: Don't argue! The officer says: Don't argue, drill! The tax collector says: Don't argue, pay. The pastor says: Don't argue, believe." To all of them Kant replied: "Dare to know! Have the courage to use your own intelligence."

The Spirit of the Enlightenment

In 1734 a small book appeared in France entitled *Philosophical Letters Concerning the English Nation*. Its author, Voltaire (1694–1778), had spent two years in Britain and while there he made it his business to study the differences between the peoples of the two nations. In a simple but forceful style Voltaire demonstrated time and again the superiority of the British. They practiced religious toleration and were not held under the sway of a venal clergy. They valued people for their merits rather than their birth. Their political constitution was a marvel—"The English nation is the only one on earth that has succeeded in controlling the power of kings by resisting them." They made national heroes of their scientists, their poets, and their philosophers. In all of this Voltaire contrasted British virtue with French vice. He attacked the French clergy and nobility directly, the French monarchy implicitly. Not only did he praise the genius and accomplishments of Sir Isaac Newton above those of René Descartes, but he also graphically contrasted the Catholic church's persecution of Descartes with the British state's celebration of Newton. "England, where men think free and noble thoughts," Voltaire enthused.

It is difficult now to recapture the psychological impact of the *Philosophical Letters* on the generation of educated French who first read them. The book was officially banned and publicly burned, and a warrant was issued for Voltaire's arrest. The *Letters* dropped like a bombshell on the moribund intellectual culture of the Church and the universities and burst open the complacent, self-satisfied Cartesian worldview. The book ignited in France a movement that would soon be found in nearly every corner of Europe.

Born in Paris in 1694 into a bourgeois family with court office, François-Marie Arouet, who later took the pen name Voltaire, was educated by the Jesuits, who encouraged his poetic talents and instilled in him an enduring love of literature. He was a difficult student, especially as he had already rejected the core of the Jesuits' religious doctrine. He was no less difficult as he grew and began a career as a poet and playwright. It was not long before he was imprisoned in the Bastille for penning verses that maligned the honor of the regent of France. Released from prison, he insulted a nobleman, who retaliated by having his servants publicly beat Voltaire. Voltaire issued a challenge for a duel, a greater insult than the first, given his low birth. Again he was sent to the Bastille and was only released on the promise that he would leave the country immediately.

Thus Voltaire found himself in Britain, where he spent two years learning English, writing plays, and enjoying his celebrity free from the dangers that celebrity entailed in France. When he returned to Paris in 1728, it was with the intention of popularizing Britain to the French people. He wrote and produced a number of plays and began writing the *Philosophical Letters* (1734), a work

Voltaire

that not only secured his reputation but also forced him into exile at the village of Cirey, where he moved in with the Marquise du Châtelet (1706–1749).

The Marquise de Châtelet, though only 27 at the time of her liaison with Voltaire, was one of the leading advocates of Newtonian science in France. She built a laboratory in her home and introduced Voltaire to experimental science. While she undertook the immense challenge of translating Newton into French, Voltaire worked on innumerable projects: poems, plays, philosophical and antireligious tracts (which the marquise wisely kept him from publishing), and histories. It was one of the most productive periods of his life, and when the Marquise due Châtelet died in 1749, Voltaire was crushed.

Now past fifty years old, Voltaire began his travels. He was invited to Berlin by Frederick the Great, who admired him most of all the intellectuals of the age. The relationship between these two great egotists was predictably stormy and resulted in Voltaire's arrest in Frankfurt. Finally allowed to leave Prussia, Voltaire eventually settled in Geneva, where he quickly became embroiled in local politics and was none too politely asked to leave. He was tired of wandering and tired of being chased. His youthful gaiety and high spirits, which remained in Voltaire long past youth, were dealt a serious blow by the tragic earthquake in Lisbon in 1755, when thousands of people, attending church services, were killed. Optimism in the face of such a senseless tragedy was no longer possible. His black mood was revealed in *Candide* (1759), which was to become his enduring legacy. *Candide* introduced the ivory tower intellectual Dr. Pangloss, the overly optimistic Candide, and the very practical philosophy, "everyone must cultivate their own garden." It was Voltaire's capacity to challenge all authority that was probably his greatest contribution to Enlightenment attitudes. He held nothing sacred. He questioned his own paternity and the morals of his mother; he lived openly with the Marquise du Châtelet and her husband; and he spoke as slightingly of kings and aristocrats as he did of his numerous critics.

Some enlightened thinkers based their critical outlook on skepticism, the belief that nothing could be known for certain. When the Scottish philosopher David Hume (1711–1776) was accused of being an atheist, he countered the charge by saying he was too skeptical to be certain that God did not exist. Hume's first major philosophical work, *A Treatise of Human Nature* (1739), made absolutely no impression on his contemporaries. For a time he took a post as a merchant's clerk; then he served as a tutor; and finally he found a position as a private secretary. During the course of these various employments he continued to write, publishing a series of essays on the subject of morality and rewriting his treatise into *An Enquiry Concerning Human Understanding* (1748), his greatest philosophical work.

Hume made two seminal contributions to Enlightenment thought. In the first place, he argued that neither matter nor mind could be proved to exist with any certainty. Only perceptions existed, either as impressions of material objects or as ideas. This argument exploded the classic Cartesian synthesis of mind and matter, which dominated teaching in the schools. If human understanding was based on sensory perception rather than on reason, then there

David Hume

could be no certainty in the universe. Hume's second point launched a frontal attack on established religion. If there could be no certainty, then the revealed truths of Christian religion could have no basis. In his historical analysis of the origins of religion Hume argued that "religion grows out of hope or fear." He attacked the core of Christian explanations based on either Providence or miracles by arguing that to anyone who understood the basis of human perception it would take a miracle to believe in miracles.

In 1749 Hume received in the mail a work from an admiring Frenchman, entitled *The Spirit of the Laws*. Charles-Louis de Secondat, Baron Montesquieu (1689–1755), was born in Bordeaux. He ultimately inherited both a large landed estate and the office of president of the Parlement of Bordeaux. His novel *Persian Letters* (1721) was a brilliant satire of Parisian morals, French society, and European religion all bound together by the story of a Persian despot who leaves his harem to learn about the ways of the world. The use of the Persian outsider allowed Montesquieu to comment on the absurdity of European customs in general and French practices in particular. The device of the harem allowed him to titillate his audience with exotic sexuality.

After this success, Montesquieu decided to sell his office and make the grand tour. He spent nearly two years in England for which, like Voltaire, he came to have the greatest admiration. Back in Bordeaux, Montesquieu began to assemble his thoughts for what he believed would be a great work of political theory. The two societies that he most admired were ancient Rome and present-day Britain, and he studied the forms of their government and the principles that animated them. *The Spirit of the Laws* was published in 1748, and despite its gargantuan size and densely packed examples, it was immediately recognized as a masterpiece. Catherine the Great of Russia kept it at her bedside, and it was the single most influential work for the framers of the U.S. Constitution.

In both the *Persian Letters* and *The Spirit of the Laws* Montesquieu explored how liberty could be achieved and despotism avoided. He divided all forms of government into republics, monarchies, and despotisms. Each form had its own peculiar spirit: virtue and moderation in republics, honor in monarchies, and fear in despotisms. Like each form, each spirit was prone to abuse and had to be restrained if republics were not to give way to vice and excess, monarchies to corruption, and despotisms to repression. Montesquieu classified regimes as either moderate or immoderate, and through the use of extensive historical examples attempted to demonstrate how moderation could be maintained through rules and restraints, through the spirit of the law.

For Montesquieu, a successful government was one in which powers were separated and checks and balances existed within the institutions of the state. As befit a provincial magistrate, he insisted on the absolute separation of the judiciary from all other branches of government. The law needed to be independent and impartial and it needed to be just. Montesquieu advocated that law codes be reformed and reduced mainly to regulate crimes against persons and property. Punishment should fit the crime but should be humane. He was one of the first to advocate the abolition of torture. Like most Europeans of his age, he saw monarchy as the only realistic form of government, but he argued that for a monarchy to be successful, it needed a strong and independent aristocracy to restrain its tendency toward corruption and despotism. He based his arguments on what he believed was the case in Britain, which he praised as the only state in Europe in which liberty resided.

Enlightened thinkers attacked established institutions, above all the Church. Most were deists who believed in the existence of God on rational grounds only. Following the materialistic ideas of the new science, deists believed that nature conformed to its own material laws and operated without divine intervention. God, in a popular Enlightenment image, was like a clockmaker who constructed the elaborate mechanism, wound it, and gave the pendulum its first swing. After that the clock worked by itself. Deists were accused of being anti-Christian, and they certainly opposed the ritual forms of both Catholic and Protestant worship. They also opposed the role of the Church in education, for education was the key to an enlightened view of the future. This meant, above all, conflict with the Jesuits. "Let's eat a Jesuit," was Voltaire's half-facetious comment.

Jean-Jacques Rousseau authored one of the most important Enlightenment tracts on education, disguised as the romantic novel *Émile* (1762), in which he argued that children should be taught by appealing to their interests rather than with strict discipline. Education was crucial because the Enlightenment was dominated by the idea of the British philosopher John Locke

(1632–1704) that the mind was blank at birth, a *tabula rasa*—"white paper void of all characters"—and that it was filled up by experience. Contrary to the arguments of Descartes, Locke wrote in *An Essay Concerning Human Understanding* (1690) that there were no innate ideas and no good or evil that was not conditioned by experience. For Locke, as for a host of thinkers after him, good and evil were defined as pleasure and pain. We do good because it is pleasurable and we avoid evil because it is painful. Morality was a sense experience rather than a theological one. It was also relative rather than absolute. This was an observation that derived from increased interest in non-European cultures. The *Persian Letters* of Baron Montesquieu was the most popular of a genre that described non-European societies that knew nothing of Christian morality.

By the middle of the eighteenth century the pleasure/pain principle enunciated by Locke had come to be applied to the foundations of social organization. If personal good was pleasure, then social good was happiness. The object of government, in the words of the Scottish moral philosopher Francis Hutcheson (1694–1746), "was the greatest happiness of the greatest number." This principle was at the core of *Crimes and Punishments* (1764), Cesare Beccaria's pioneering work of legal reform. Laws were instituted to promote happiness within society. They had to be formulated equitably for both criminal and victim. Punishment was to act as a deterrent to crime rather than as retribution. Therefore Beccaria advocated the abolition of torture to gain confessions, the end of capital punishment, and the rehabilitation of criminals through the improvement of penal institutions. By 1776 happiness

Major Works of the Enlightenment

1690	*An Essay Concerning Human Understanding* (Locke)
1721	*Persian Letters* (Baron Montesquieu)
1734	*Philosophical Letters Concerning the English Nation* (Voltaire)
1739	*A Treatise of Human Nature* (Hume)
1740	*Pamela* (Richardson)
1748	*An Enquiry Concerning Human Understanding* (Hume) *The Spirit of the Laws* (Baron Montesquieu)
1751–1780	*Encyclopedia* (Diderot)
1759	*Candide* (Voltaire)
1762	*Émile; The Social Contract* (Rousseau)
1764	*Crimes and Punishments* (Beccaria)
1748	*What Is Enlightenment?* (Kant)
1795	*The Progress of the Human Mind* (Marquis de Condorcet)
1798	*An Essay on the Principles of Population* (Malthus)

was established as one of the basic rights of man, enshrined in the American Declaration of Independence as "life, liberty, and the pursuit of happiness."

It was in refashioning the world through education and social reform that the Enlightenment revealed its orientation toward the future. *Optimism* was a word invented in the eighteenth century to express this feeling of liberation from the weight of centuries of traditions. "This is the best of all possible worlds and all things turn out for the best," was the satirical slogan of Voltaire's Candide. But if Voltaire believed that enlightened thinkers had taken optimism too far, others believed that it had to be taken further still.

Progress, an idea that not all enlightened thinkers shared, was another invention of the age. It was expressed most cogently by the French philosopher the Marquis de Condorcet (1743–1794) in *The Progress of the Human Mind* (1795), in which he developed an almost evolutionary view of human development from a savage state of nature to a future of harmony and international peace.

The Impact of the Enlightenment

As there was no single set of Enlightenment beliefs, so there was no single impact of the Enlightenment. Its general influence was felt everywhere, even seeping to the lowest strata of society. Its specific influence is harder to gauge. Paradoxically, enlightened political reform took firmer root in the East where the ideas were imported than in the West where they originated. It was absolute rulers who were most successful in borrowing Enlightenment reforms.

It is impossible to determine what part enlightened ideas and what part practical necessities played in the eastern European reform movement that began around mid-century. In at least three areas the coincidence between ideas and actions was especially strong: law, education, and the extension of religious toleration. Law was the basis of Enlightenment views of social interaction, and the influence of Montesquieu and Beccaria spread quickly. In Prussia and Russia the movement to codify and simplify the legal system did not reach fruition in the eighteenth century, but in both places it was well under way. The Prussian jurist Samuel von Cocceji (1679–1755) initiated the reform of Prussian law and legal administration. Cocceji's project was to make the enforcement of law uniform throughout the realm, to prevent judicial corruption, and to produce a single code of Prussian law. The code, finally completed in the 1790s, reflected the principles of criminal justice articulated by Beccaria. In Russia, the Law Commission summoned by Catherine the Great in 1767 never did complete its work. Nevertheless, profoundly influenced by Montesquieu, Catherine attempted to abolish torture and to introduce the Beccarian principle that the accused was innocent until proven guilty. In Austria, Joseph II presided over a wholesale reorganization of the legal system. Courts were centralized, laws codified, and torture and capital punishment abolished.

Enlightenment ideas also underlay the efforts to improve education in eastern Europe. The religious orders, especially the Jesuits, were the most influential educators of the age, and the Enlightenment attack on them created a void that had to be filled by the state. Efforts at compulsory education were first undertaken in Russia under Peter the Great, but these were aimed at the compulsory education of the nobility. It was Catherine who extended the effort to the provinces, attempting to educate a generation of Russian teachers. She was especially eager that women receive primary schooling, although the prejudice against educating women was too strong to overcome. Austrian and Prussian reforms were more successful in extending the reach of primary education, even if its content remained weak.

Religious toleration was the area in which the Enlightenment had its greatest impact in Europe, though again it was in the East that this was most visible. Freedom of worship for Catholics was barely whispered about in Britain, while neither France nor Spain were moved to tolerate Protestants. Nevertheless, within these parameters there were some important changes in the religious makeup of the western European states. In Britain, Protestant dissenters were no longer persecuted for their beliefs. By the end of the eighteenth century the number of Protestants outside the Church of England was growing, and by the early nineteenth century discrimination against Protestants was all but eliminated. In France and Spain relations between the national church and the papacy were undergoing a reorientation. But states were asserting more independence—both theologically and financially—from Rome. The shift was symbolized by disputes over the role of the Jesuits, who were finally expelled from France in 1764 and from Spain in 1767.

In the East, enlightened ideas about religious toleration did take effect. Catherine the Great abandoned persecution of a Russian Orthodox sect known as the Old Believers. Prussia had always tolerated various Protestant groups, and with the conquest of Silesia it acquired a large Catholic population. Catholics were guaranteed freedom of worship, and Frederick the Great even built a Catholic church in Berlin to symbolize this policy. Austria extended furthest enlightened ideas about toleration. Maria Theresa was a devout Catholic and actually increased religious persecution in her realm. But Joseph II rejected his mother's dogmatic position. In 1781 he issued a Patent of Toleration, which granted freedom of worship to Protestants and members of the Eastern Orthodox church. The following year he extended this toleration to Jews. Joseph's attitude toward toleration was as practical as it was enlightened. He believed that the revocation of the Edict of Nantes at the end of the seventeenth century had been an economic disaster for France, and he encouraged religious toleration as a means to economic progress.

A science of economics was first articulated during the Enlightenment. A group of French thinkers known as the *physiocrats* subscribed to the view that land was wealth and thus argued that agricultural activity, especially improved means of farming and livestock breeding, should take first priority in state reforms. As wealth came from land, taxation should be based only on land ownership, a principle that was coming into increased prominence, despite the opposition of the landowning class. Physiocratic ideas combined a belief in the sanctity of private property with the need for the state to increase agricultural output. Ultimately the physiocrats, like the great Scottish economic theorist Adam Smith, came to believe that government should cease to interfere with private economic activity. They articulated the doctrine *laissez faire, laissez passer*—"let it be, let it go." The ideas of Adam Smith and the physiocrats ultimately formed the basis for nineteenth-century economic reform.

If the Enlightenment did not initiate a new era, it did offer a new vision, whether in Hume's psychology, Montesquieu's political science, Rousseau's sociology, or Smith's economic theory. All of these subjects, which have such a powerful impact on contemporary life, had their modern origins in the Enlightenment. As the British poet Alexander Pope (1688–1744) put it: "Know then thyself, presume not God to scan/ The proper study of mankind is man." A new emphasis on self and on pleasure led to a new emphasis on happiness. All three fed into the distinctively Enlightenment idea of self-interest. Happiness and self-interest were values that would inevitably corrode the old social order, which was based on principles of self-sacrifice and corporate identity. It was only a matter of time.

*H*igh and Low in the Eighteenth Century

Eighteenth-century society was a hybrid of old and new. It remained highly stratified. Birth and occupation determined wealth, privilege, and quality of life as much as they had in the past. There were now more paths toward the middle and upper classes, more wealth to be distributed among those above the level of subsistence, but at the top of society the nobility remained the privileged order in every European state.

The Nobility

Nobles were defined by their legal rights. They had the right to bear arms, the right to special judicial treatment, the right to tax exemptions. In Russia only nobles could own serfs; in Poland only nobles could hold government office. In France and Britain the highest court positions were always reserved for noblemen. Nobles dominated the Prussian army. The Spanish nobility, rich or poor, shunned all labor as a right of their heritage. Swedish and Hungarian noblemen had their own legislative chambers, just as the British had the House of Lords.

Though all who enjoyed these special rights were noble, not all nobles were equal. In many states the noble order was subdivided into easily identifiable groups. The Spanish grandees, the upper nobility, were numbered in the thousands; the Spanish *hidalgos*, the lower nobility, in the hundreds of thousands. In Hungary out of 400,000 noblemen only about 15,000 belonged to the "landed" nobility who held titles and were exempt from taxes. In England the elite class was divided between the peerage and the gentry. The peerage held titles, were members of the House of Lords, and had a limited range of judicial and fiscal privileges. In the mid eighteenth century there were only 190 British peers. The gentry, which numbered over twenty thousand, dominated the House of Commons and local legal offices but were not strictly members of the nobility. The French nobility was informally distinguished among the small group of peers known as the *Grandes*, whose ancient lineage, wealth, and power set them apart from all others; a rather larger service nobility whose privileges derived in one way or another from municipal or judicial service; and what might be called the country nobility, whose small estates and local outlook made their fiscal immunities vital to their survival.

These distinctions among the nobilities of the European states masked a more important one: wealth. As the saying went, "All who were truly noble were not wealthy, but all who were truly wealthy were noble." In the eighteenth century, despite the phenomenal increase in mercantile activity, wealth was still calculated in profits from the ownership of land, and it was the wealthy landed nobility who set the tone of elite life in Europe.

For the wealthy, aristocracy was becoming an international status. The influence of Louis XIV and the court of Versailles lasted for well over a century and spread to town and country life. Most nobles maintained multiple residences. Here the British elite led all others. Over 150 British country houses were built in the early eighteenth century alone. To the expense of architecture was added the expense of decoration. The high-quality woodwork and plastering made fashionable by the English Adam brothers was quickly imitated on the Continent.

The building of country houses was only one part of the conspicuous consumption of the privileged orders. Improvements in travel, both in transport and roads, permitted increased contact between members of the national elites. The stagecoach linked towns, and canals linked waterways. Both made travel quicker and more enjoyable. The grand tour of historical sites continued to be used as a substitute for formal education. The grand tour was a means of introducing the European aristocracies to each other and also a means of communicating taste and fashion among them. Whether it was a Russian noble in Germany, or a Briton in Prussia, all spoke French and shared a common cultural outlook.

Decorative architecture, especially interior design, reflected the increasing sociability of the aristocracy. Entertainment became a central part of aristocratic life, losing its previous formality. In this atmosphere music became one of the passions of noble culture. The string quartet made its first appearance in the eighteenth century and chamber music enjoyed unparalleled popularity.

Musical entertainments in European country houses were matched by the literary and philosophical entertainments of the urban salons. The salons, especially in Paris, blended the aristocracy and bourgeoisie with the leading intellectuals of the age. At formal meetings, papers on scientific or philosophical topics were read and discussed. At informal gatherings, new ideas were examined and exchanged. There were to be found the most influential thinkers of the day presenting the ideas of the Enlightenment. The Enlightenment was not an aristocratic movement; indeed, many Enlightenment ideas were profoundly antiaristocratic. But it was the nobility who had the leisure to read, write, and discuss, and many of the nobility were actively engaged in the intellectual and social changes that the Enlightenment brought in its wake. Though enlightened thinkers sought the improvement of life for the many, they pitched their appeal to the few. "Taste is thus like philosophy," Voltaire opined. "It belongs to a very small number of privileged souls."

The Bourgeoisie

Bourgeois is a French word, and it carried the same tone of derision in the eighteenth century that it does today. The bourgeois was a person on the make, scrambling after money or office or title—neither well born nor well bred, or so said the nobility. Yet the bourgeoisie served vital functions in all European societies. They dominated trade, both nationally and internationally. They made their homes in cities and did much to improve the quality of urban life. They were the civilizing influence in urban culture, for unlike the nobility they were permanent denizens of the city. Perhaps most importantly, the bourgeoisie provided the safety valve between the nobility and those who were acquiring wealth and power but who lacked the advantages of birth and position. By developing their own culture and class identity, the bourgeoisie provided successful individuals with their own sense of pride and achievement and eased the explosive buildup of social resentments.

The new bourgeois values centered on the family and the home. A new interest in domestic affairs touched both men and women of the European bourgeoisie. Their homes became a social center for kin and neighbors and their outlook on family life reflected new personal relationships. Marriages were made for companionship as much as for economic advantage. Romantic love between husbands and wives was newly valued. So were children, whose futures came to dominate familial concern. Childhood was recognized as a separate stage of life and the education of children as one of the most important of parental concerns. The image of the affectionate father replaced that of the hard-bitten businessman; the image of the doting mother replaced that of the domestic drudge.

Urban Elites

In the society of orders, nobility was the acid test. The world was divided into the small number of those who had it and the large number of those who did not. At the apex of the non-noble pyramid was the bourgeoisie, the elites of urban Europe whose place in the society of orders was ambiguous. Bourgeois, or burgher, simply meant "town dweller," but as a social group it had come to mean "wealthy town dweller." The bourgeoisie was strongest where towns were strongest: in western rather than in eastern Europe, in northern rather than southern Europe, with the notable exception of Italy. Holland was the exemplar of a bourgeois republic. More than half of the Dutch population lived in towns and there was no significant aristocratic class to compete for power. The regents of Amsterdam were the equivalent of a European court nobility in wealth, power, and prestige, though not in the way in which they had accumulated their fortunes. The size of the bourgeoisie in various European states cannot be absolutely determined. At the end of the eighteenth century the British middle classes probably constituted around 15 percent of the population, the French bourgeoisie less than 10 percent. By contrast, the Russian or Hungarian urban elites were less than 2 percent of the population in those states.

Like the nobility, the bourgeoisie constituted a diverse group. At the top were great commercial families engaged in the expanding international marketplace and reaping the profits of trade. In wealth and power they were barely distinguishable from the nobility. At the bottom were the so-called petit bourgeois: shopkeepers, craft workers, and industrial employers. The solid core of the bourgeoisie was employed in trade, exchange, and service. Most were engaged in local or national commerce. Trade was the lifeblood of the city, for by itself the city could neither feed nor clothe its inhabitants. Most bourgeois fortunes were first acquired in trade. Finance was the natural outgrowth of commerce, and another segment of the bourgeoisie accumulated or preserved their capital through the sophisticated financial instruments of the eighteenth century. While the very wealthy loaned directly to the central government or bought shares in overseas trading companies, most bourgeois participated in government credit markets. They purchased state bonds or lifetime annuities and lived on the interest. The costs of war flooded the urban credit markets with high-yielding and generally stable financial instruments. Finally, the bourgeoisie were members of the burgeoning professions that provided services for the rich. Medicine, law, education, and the bureaucracy were all bourgeois professions, for the cost of acquiring the necessary skills could be borne only by those already wealthy.

During the course of the eighteenth century, this combination of occupational groups was expanding both in numbers and in importance all over Europe. So was the bourgeois habitat. The urbanization of Europe continued steadily throughout the eighteenth century. A greater percentage of the European population were living in towns and a greater percentage were living in large towns of over ten thousand inhabitants which, of necessity, were developing complex socioeconomic structures. In France alone there were probably over a hundred such towns, each requiring the services of the bourgeoisie and providing opportunities for their expansion. And the larger the metropolis the greater the need. In 1600 only 20 European cities contained as many as 50,000 people; in 1700 that number had risen to 32; and by 1800 to 48. London, the largest city, had grown to 865,000, a remarkable feat considering that in 1665 over a quarter of the London population died in the Great Plague. In such cities the demand for lawyers and doctors, for merchants and shopkeepers was almost insatiable.

Besides wealth, the urban bourgeoisie shared another characteristic: mobility. The aspiration of the bourgeoisie was to become noble, either through office or by acquiring rural estates. In Britain, a gentlemen was still defined by lifestyle. "All are accounted gentlemen in England who maintain themselves without manual labor." Many trading families left their wharves and countinghouses to acquire rural estates, live off rents, and practice the openhanded hospitality of a gentlemen. In France and Spain, nobility could still be purchased, though the price was constantly going up. For the greater bourgeoisie, the transition was easy; for the lesser, the failure to move up was all the more frustrating for being just beyond their grasp. The bourgeoisie did not only imagine their discomfort, they were made to feel it at every turn. They were the butt of jokes, of theater, and of popular songs. They were the first victims in the shady financial dealings of the crown and court, the first casualties in urban riots. Despised from above, envied from below, the bourgeoisie were uncomfortable with the present yet profoundly conservative about the future. The one consolation to their perpetual misery was that as a group they got richer and richer.

The leisure that wealth bestowed on the bourgeoisie quickly became, in good bourgeois fashion, commercialized. Theater and music halls for both light and serious productions proliferated. Voltaire's plays were performed before packed houses in Paris, with the author himself frequently in attendance to bask in the adulation of the largely bourgeois audiences who attended them. In Venice it was estimated that over twelve hundred operas were produced in the eighteenth century. Public concerts were a mark of bourgeois culture, for the court nobility was entertained at the royal palaces or at great country houses.

Theater and concert going were part of the new attitude toward socializing that was one of the greatest contributions of the Enlightenment. Enlightened thinkers spread their views in the salons, and the salons soon spawned the academies, local scientific societies which, though led and patronized by provincial nobles, included large numbers of bourgeois members. The academies sponsored essay competitions, built up libraries, and became the local center for intellectual interchange. A less structured form of sociability took place in the coffeehouses and tearooms that came to be a feature of even small provincial towns. In the early eighteenth century there were over two thousand London coffee shops were men—for the coffeehouse was largely a male preserve—could talk politics, read the latest newspapers and magazines, and indulge their taste for this still-exotic beverage. Parisian clubs, called *sociétés*, covered a multitude of diverse interests. Literary *sociétés* were the most popular, maintaining their purpose by forbidding drinking, eating, and gambling on their premises.

Above all, bourgeois culture was literate culture. Wealth and leisure led to mental pursuits—if not always to intellectual ones. The proliferation of relatively cheap printed material had an enormous impact on the lives of those who were able to afford it. This was the first great period of the newspaper and the magazine. News reports tended to be bland, avoiding controversy and concentrating on general national and international events. For entertainment and serious political commentary, the reading public turned to magazines, of which there were over 150 separate titles in Britain alone by the 1780s. The longest lived of all British magazines was *The Ladies Diary* (1704 to 1871), which doled out self-improvement, practical advice, and fictional romances in equal proportion.

The Ladies Diary was not the only literature aimed at the growing number of leisured and lettered bourgeois women. Though enlightened thinkers could be ambivalent about the place of women in the new social order, they generally stressed the importance of female education and welcomed women's partici-pation in intellectual pursuits. Whether it was new ideas about women or simply the fact that more women had leisure, a growing body of both domestic literature and light entertainment was available to them. This included a vast number of teach-yourself books aimed at instructing women how best to organize domestic life or how to navigate the perils of polite society. Moral instruction, particularly on the themes of obedience and sexual fidelity, was also popular. But the greatest output directed toward women was in the form of fanciful romances, from which a new genre emerged. The novel first appeared in its modern form in the 1740s. Samuel Richardson (1689–1761) wrote *Pamela* (1740), the story of a maidservant who successfully resisted the advances of her master until he finally married her. It was composed in long episodes, or chapters, that developed Pamela's character and told her story at the expense of the overt moral message that was Richardson's original intention.

Family Life

In the eighteenth century a remarkable transformation in home life was under way, one that the bourgeoisie shared with the nobility. In the pursuit of happiness encouraged by the Enlightenment, one of the newest joys was domesticity. The image—and sometimes the reality—of the happy home, where love was the bond between husband and wife and care between parents and children, came to dominate both the literary and visual arts. Only those wealthy enough to afford to dispense with women's work could partake of the new domesticity; only those touched by Enlightenment ideas could attempt to make the change. But where it occurred, the transformation in the nature of family life was one of the most profound alterations in eighteenth-century culture.

The first step toward the transformation of family relationships was in centering the conjugal family in the home. In the past, the family was a less

The Snatched Kiss, *or* The Stolen Kiss *(1750s) by Jean-Honoré Fragonard, was one of the "series paintings" popular in the late eighteenth century. A later canvas entitled* The Marriage Contract *shows the next step in the lives of the lovers.*

important structure for most people than the social groups to which they belonged or the neighborhood in which they lived. Marriage was an economic partnership at one end and a means to carry on lineage at the other; individual fulfillment was not an object.

Patriarchy was the dominant value within the family. Husbands ruled over wives and children, making all of the crucial decisions that affected both the quality of their lives and their futures. As late as the middle of the eighteenth century a British judge established the "rule of thumb," which asserted that a husband had a legal right to beat his wife with a stick, but the stick should be no thicker than a man's thumb. It was believed children were stained with the sin of Adam at birth and that only the severest upbringing could clean some of it away. Children were sent out first for wet nursing, then at around the age of seven for boarding, either at school or in a trade, and finally into their own marriages.

There can be no doubt that this profile of family life began to change, especially in western Europe, during the second half of the eighteenth century. Though the economic elements of marriage remained strong—newspapers actually advertised the availability of partners and the dowries or annual income that they would bring to the marriage—other elements now appeared. Fed by an unending stream of stories and novels and a new desire for individual happiness, romantic and sexual attraction developed into a factor in marriage. Potential marriage partners were no longer kept away from each other or smothered by chaperons. Perhaps more importantly, the role of potential spouses in choosing a partner appears to have increased. Even in earlier centuries parents did not simply assign a spouse to their children, but by the eighteenth century adolescents themselves searched for their own marriage partners and exercised a strong negative voice in identifying unsuitable ones.

The quest for compatibility, no less than the quest for romantic love, led to a change in personal relationships between spouses. The extreme formality of the past was gradually breaking down. Husbands and wives began spending more time with each other, developing common interests and pastimes. Their personal life began to change. For the first time houses were built to afford the couple privacy from their children, their servants, and their guests. Rooms were designed for specific functions and were set off by hallways. This new design allowed for an intimate life that earlier generations did not find necessary and which they could not, in any case, put into practice.

Couples had more time for each other because they were beginning to limit the size of their families. There were a number of reasons for this development, which again pertained only to the upper classes. For one thing, child mortality rates were declining among wealthy social groups. Virulent epidemic diseases like the plague, which knew no class lines, were gradually disappearing. Moreover, though there were few medical breakthroughs in this period, sanitation was improving. Bearing fewer children had an enormous impact on the lives of women, reducing the danger of death and disablement in childbirth and giving them leisure time to pursue domestic tasks. This is not to say that the early part of a woman's marriage was not dominated by children; in fact, because of new attitudes toward child rearing it may have been so dominated more than ever.

The transformation in the quality of relationships between spouses was mirrored by an even greater transformation in attitudes toward children. There were many reasons why childhood now took on a new importance. Decline in mortality rates had a profound psychological impact. Parents could feel that their emotional investment in their children had a greater chance of fulfillment. But equally important were the new ideas about education, especially Locke's belief that the child enters into the world a blank slate whose personality is created through early education. This view not only placed a new responsibility upon parents but also gave them the concept of childhood as a stage through which individuals passed. This idea could be seen in the commercial sphere as well as in any other. In 1700 there was not a single shop in London that sold children's toys exclusively; by the 1780s there were toyshops everywhere. There were also shops that sold clothes specifically designed for children, no longer simply adult clothes in miniature. Most important of all was the development of materials for the education of children. This took place in two stages. At first so-called children's books were books whose purpose was to help adults teach children. Later came books directed at children themselves with large print, entertaining illustrations, and nonsensical characters, usually animals who taught moral lessons.

The commercialization of childhood was, of course, directed at adults. The new books and games that were designed to enhance a child's education not only had to be purchased by parents but had to be used by them as well. More and more mothers were devoting their time to their children. Among the upper classes the practice of wet nursing began to decline. Mothers wanted to nurture their infants both literally by breast feeding and figuratively by teaching them. Children became companions to be taken on outings to the increasing number of museums or shows of curiosities.

The preconditions of this transformation of family life could not be shared by the population at large. Working women could afford neither the cost of instructional materials for their children nor the time to use them. Ironically, they now began using wet nurses, once the privilege of the wealthy, for increasingly a working woman's labor was the margin of survival for her family. Working women enjoyed no privacy in the hovels in which they lived with large families in single rooms. Wives and children were still beaten by husbands and fathers and were unacquainted with enlightened ideas of the worth of the individual and the innocence of the child. By the end of the eighteenth century two distinct family cultures coexisted in Europe, one based on companionate marriage and the affective bonds of parents and children, the other based on patriarchal dominance and the family as an economic unit.

The Masses

The paradox of the eighteenth century was that for the masses life was getting better by getting worse. More Europeans were surviving than ever before, more food was available to feed them; there was more housing, better sanitation, even better charities. Yet for all of this, there was more misery. Those who would have succumbed to disease or starvation a century before now survived from day to day, beneficiaries—or victims—of increased farm production and improved agricultural marketing. The market economy organized a more effective use of land, but it created a widespread social problem. The landless agrarian laborer of the eighteenth century was the counterpart of the sixteenth-century wandering beggar. In the cities, the plight of the poor was as desperate as ever. Even the most openhearted charitable institutions were unable to cope with the massive increase in the poor. Thousands of mothers abandoned their children to the foundling hospitals, hoping they would have a better chance of survival, even though hospital death rates were near 80 percent.

Not all members of the lower orders succumbed to poverty or despair. In fact, many were able to benefit from existing conditions to lead a more fulfilling life than ever before. The richness of popular culture, signified by a spread of literacy into the lower reaches of European society, was one indication of this change. So, too, were the reforms urged by enlightened thinkers to improve basic education and to improve the quality of life in the cities. For that segment of the lower orders that could keep its head above water, the eighteenth century offered new opportunities and new challenges.

Breaking the Cycle

Of all the legacies of the eighteenth century, none was more fundamental than the steady increase in European population that began around 1740. This was not the first time Europe had experienced sustained population growth, but it was the first time that such growth was not checked by a demographic crisis. Breaking the cycle of population growth and crisis was a momentous event in European history despite the fact that it went unrecorded at the time and unappreciated for centuries after.

The figures tell one part of the story. In 1700 European population is estimated to have been 120 million. By 1800 it had grown 50 percent to over 180 million. And the aggregate hides significant regional variations. While France, Spain, and Italy expanded between 30 and 40 percent, Prussia doubled and Russia and Hungary may have tripled in number. Britain increased by 80 percent from about 5 to 9 million, but the rate of growth was accelerating. In 1695 the English population stood at 5 million. It took 62 years to add the next million and 24 years to add the million after that. In 1781 the population was 7 million, but it took only 13 years to reach 8 million and only 10 more years to reach 9 million. Steady population growth had continued without significant checks for well over half a century.

Ironically, the traditional pattern of European population found its theorist at the very moment that it was about to disappear. In 1798 Thomas Malthus (1766–1834) published *An Essay on the Principles of Population*. Reflecting on the history of European population, Malthus observed the cyclical pattern by which growth over one or two generations was checked by a crisis that significantly reduced population. From these lower levels new growth began until it was checked and the cycle repeated itself. Because people increased more quickly than food supplies, the land could only sustain a certain level of population. When that level was near, population became prone to a demographic check. Malthus divided population checks into two categories, positive and preventive. Positive checks were war, disease, and famine, all of which Malthus believed were natural, although brutal, means of population control. Famine was the obvious result of the failure of food supplies to keep pace with demand; war was the competition for scarce resources; and disease often accompanied both. It was preventive checks that most interested Malthus. These were the means by which societies could limit their growth to avoid the devastating consequences of positive checks. Celibacy, late marriages, and sexual abstinence were among the choices of which Malthus approved, though abortion, infanticide, and contraception were also common.

In the sixteenth and seventeenth centuries, the dominant pattern of the life cycle was high infant and child mortality, late marriages, and early death. All controlled population growth. On average, the childbearing period for most women was between 10 and 12 years, long enough to endure six pregnancies, which would result in three surviving children. Three surviving children for every two adults would, of course, have resulted in a 50 percent rise in population in every generation. Celibacy was one limiting factor; cities were another. Perhaps as much as 15 percent of the population in western Europe remained celibate either by entering religious orders that imposed celibacy or by lacking the personal or financial attributes necessary to make a match. Rural migrants accounted for the appallingly high urban death rates in cities. When we remember that the largest European cities were continuously growing—London from 200,000 in 1600 to 675,000 in 1750; Paris from 220,000 to 576,000; Rome from 105,000 to 156,000; Madrid from 49,000 to 109,000; Vienna from 50,000 to 175,000—then we can appreciate how many countless thousands of immigrants perished from disease, famine, and exposure before marriage. If urban perils were not enough, there were still the positive checks. Plagues carried away hundreds of thousands, wars halved populations of places in their path, and famine overwhelmed the weak and the poor.

The late seventeenth and early eighteenth centuries was a period of population stagnation if not actual decline. It was not until the third or fourth decade of the eighteenth century that another growth cycle began. It rapidly gained momentum throughout the Continent and showed no signs of abating after two full generations. More importantly, this upward cycle revealed unusual characteristics. In the first place fertility was increasing. This had several causes. In a few areas, most notably in Britain, women were marrying younger, thereby increasing their childbearing years. This pattern was also true in eastern Europe where women traditionally married younger. Sexual activity outside marriage was also rising. Illegitimacy rates, especially in the last decades of the century, were spurting everywhere.

But increasing fertility was only part of the picture. More significant was decreasing mortality. The positive checks of the past were no longer as potent. European warfare not only diminished in scale after the middle of the century, it changed location as well. Rivalry for colonial empires removed the theater of conflict from European communities. So did the increase in naval warfare. The damage caused by war had always been more by aftershock than by actual fighting. The destruction and pillage of crops and the wholesale slaughter of livestock created food shortages that weakened local populations for the diseases that came in train with the armies. As the virulence of warfare abated, so did that of epidemic disease. The plague had all but disappeared from western Europe by the middle of the eighteenth century. The widespread practice of quarantine, especially in Hungary, which had been the crucial bridge between eastern and western epidemics, went far to eradicate the scourge of centuries.

Without severe demographic crises to maintain the cyclical pattern, the European population began a gentle but continuous rise. Urban sanitation, at least for permanent city dwellers, was becoming more effective. Clean water supplies, organized waste and sewage disposal, and strict quarantines were increasingly part of urban regulations. The use of doctors and trained midwives helped lower the incidence of stillbirth and decreased the number of women who died in childbirth. Almost everywhere levels of infant and child mortality were decreasing. More people were being born, more were surviving the first ten dangerous years, and thus more were marrying and reproducing. Increased fertility and decreased mortality could have only one result: renewed population growth. No wonder Malthus was worried.

Daily Bread

In the past, if warfare or epidemic diseases failed to check population growth, famine would have done the job. How the European economy conquered famine in the eighteenth century is a complicated story. There was no single breakthrough that accounts for the ability to feed the tens of millions of additional people who now inhabited the Continent. Holland and Britain, at the cutting edge of agricultural improvement, employed dynamic new techniques that would ultimately provide the means to support continued growth, but most European agriculture was still mired in the time-honored practices that had endured for centuries. Still, not everyone could be fed or fed adequately. Widespread famine might have disappeared, but slow starvation and chronic undernourishment had not. It is certainly the case that hunger was more common at the end of the eighteenth century than at the beginning and that the nutritional content of a typical diet may have reached its lowest point in European history.

Nevertheless, the capacity to sustain rising levels of population can only be explained in terms of agricultural improvement. Quite simply, European farmers were now producing more food and marketing it better. The three-field crop rotation system left a significant proportion of land fallow each year, while the concentration on subsistence cereal crops progressively eroded the land that was in production. Livestock was a crucial variable in agricultural improvement. As long as there was only enough food for humans to eat, only essential livestock could be kept alive over the winter. Oxen, which were still the ordinary beasts of burden, and pigs and poultry, which required only minimal feed, were the most common. But few animals meant little manure and without manure the soil could not easily be regenerated.

It was not until the middle of the seventeenth century that solutions to these problems began to appear. The first change was consolidation of land-holdings so that traditional crop rotations could be abandoned. A second innovation was the introduction of fodder crops, some of which—like clover— added nutrients to the soil, while others—like turnips—were used to feed livestock. Better grazing and better winter feed increased the size of herds, while new techniques of animal husbandry, particularly crossbreeding, produced hardier strains. It was quite clear that the key to increased production lay in better fertilization, and by the eighteenth century some European farmers had broken through the "manure barrier." Larger herds, the introduction of clover crops, the use of human waste from towns, and even the first experiments with lime as an artificial fertilizer were all part of the new agricultural methods.

Along with the new crops that helped nourish both soil and animals came new crops that helped nourish people. Indian corn, or maize, was a staple crop for Native Americans and gradually came to be grown in most parts of western Europe. Maize not only had higher nutritional value than most other cereals, it also yielded more food per acre than traditional grains. So, too, did the potato, which also entered the European diet from the New World. The potato grew in poor soil, required less labor, and yielded an abundant and nutritious harvest. It rapidly took hold in Ireland and parts of Prussia, from which it spread into eastern Europe. The potato allowed families to subsist on smaller amounts of land and with less capital outlay.

It must be stressed, however, that these new developments involved only a very narrow range of producers. The new techniques were expensive, and knowledge of the new crops spread slowly. Change had to overcome both inertia and intransigence. With more mouths to feed, profits from agriculture soared without landowners having to lift a finger. Only the most ambitious were interested in improvement. At the other end, peasant farmers were more concerned with failure than success. An experiment that did not work could devastate a community; one that did only meant higher taxes. Thus the most important improvements in agricultural production were more traditional ones. Basically, there was an increase in the amount of land that was utilized for growing. In Russia, Prussia, and Hungary hundreds of thousands of new acres came under the plow; in the west, drainage schemes and forest clearance expanded productive capacity.

There was also an upswing in the efficiency with which agricultural products were marketed. From the seventeenth century onward, market agriculture was gradually replacing subsistence agriculture in most parts of Europe. Market agriculture had the advantage of allowing specialization on farms. Single-crop farming enabled farmers to benefit from the peculiarities of their own soil and climate. They could then exchange their surplus for the range of crops they needed to subsist. Market exchange was facilitated by improved transportation and communication and above all by the increase in the population of towns, which provided demand. The new national and international trade in large quantities of grain evened out regional variations in harvests and went a long way toward reducing local grain shortages. The upkeep of roads, the building of canals, and the clearing of waterways created a national lifeline for the movement of grain.

Finally, it is believed the increase in agricultural productivity owed something to a change in climate that took place in the late eighteenth century.

The European climate is thought to have been unusually cold and wet during the seventeenth century—some have even called it a little ice age—and it seems to have gradually warmed during the eighteenth century. Even moderate climatic change, when combined with new techniques, new crops, expanded cultivation, and improved marketing, would go a long way toward explaining how so many more people were being fed at the end of the eighteenth century.

The Plight of the Poor

There can be no doubt that the most serious social problem of the eighteenth century centered on the population explosion of poor people throughout Europe. There was grim irony in the fact that advances in the production and distribution of food and the retreat of war and plague allowed more people to survive from hand to mouth than ever before. Where their ancestors had succumbed to quick death from disease or starvation, they eked out a miserable existence of constant hunger and chronic pain with death at the end of a seemingly endless corridor.

It is impossible to gauge the number of European poor or to separate them into categories of greater and greatest misery. The truly indigent, the starving poor, probably composed 10 to 15 percent of most societies, perhaps as many as twenty million people throughout the Continent. They were most prevalent in towns but were an increasing burden on the countryside, where they wandered in search of agricultural employment. The wandering poor had no counterpart in the east, where serfdom kept everyone tied to the land, but the hungry and unsheltered certainly did. Yet the problem of poverty was not only to be seen among the destitute. In fact, the uniqueness of the poor in the eighteenth century is that they were drawn from social groups that even in the hungry times of the early seventeenth century had been successful subsistence producers.

It was easy to see why poverty was increasing. The relentless advance of population drove up the price of food and drove down the price of wages. In the second half of the eighteenth century, the cost of living in France rose by over 60 percent while wages rose only by 25 percent. In Spain the cost of living increased by 100 percent while wages rose only 20 percent. Only in Britain did wages nearly keep pace with prices. Rising prices made land more valuable. At the beginning of the eighteenth century, as the first wave of population expansion hit western Europe, smallholdings began to decrease in size. The custom of partible inheritance, by which each son received a share of land, shrank the average size of a peasant holding below that necessary to sustain an average-size family, let alone one that was growing larger. In one part of France it was estimated that 30 acres was a survival plot of land in good times. At the end of the seventeenth century 80 percent of the peasants there owned less than 25 acres.

Beggar Feeding a Child, *by Giacomo Ceruti. Every eighteenth-century European city had its legion of beggars. This man has done well enough to be able to feed himself and his little daughter for one more day.*

As holdings contracted, the portion of the family income derived from wage labor expanded. In such circumstances males were more valuable than females, either as farmers or laborers, and there is incontrovertible evidence that European rural communities practiced female infanticide. In the end, however, it became increasingly difficult for the peasant family to remain on the land. Small freeholders were forced to borrow against future crops until a bad harvest led to foreclosure. Many were allowed to lease back their own lands, on short terms and at high rents, but most swelled the ranks of agricultural laborers, migrating during the planting and harvest seasons, suffering cruelly during winter and summer.

Emigration was the first logical consequence of poverty. In places where rural misery was greatest, like Ireland, whole communities pulled up stakes and moved to America. Frederick the Great attracted hundreds of thousands of emigrants to Prussia by offering them land. But most rural migrants did not move to new rural environments. Rather they followed the well-trodden paths to the cities. Many traditional domestic crafts were evolving into industrial activities. In the past, peasants supplemented their family income by processing raw materials in the home. Spinning, weaving, and sewing were common cottage industries in which the workers took in the work, supplied their own equipment, and were paid by the piece. Now, especially in the cloth trades, a new form of industrial activity was being organized. Factories, usually located in towns or larger villages, assembled workers together, set them at larger and more efficient machines, and paid them for their time rather than for their output. Families unable to support themselves from the land had no choice but to follow the movement of jobs.

Neither state nor private charities could cope with the flood of poor immigrants. Hospitals, workhouses, and more ominously, prisons were established or expanded to deal with them. Hospitals were residential asylums rather than places for health care. They took in the old, the incapacitated, and increasingly, the orphaned young. Workhouses existed for those who were capable of work but incapable of finding it. They were supposed to improve the values of the idle by keeping them busy, though in most places they served only to improve the profits of the industrialists, who rented out workhouse inmates at below-market wages. Prisons grew with crime. There were spectacular increases in crimes against property in all eighteenth-century cities, and despite severe penalties that could include hanging for petty theft, more criminals were incarcerated than executed. Enlightened arguments for the reform of prisons and punishment tacitly acknowledged the social basis of most crime. As always, the victims of crime were mostly drawn from the same social backgrounds as the perpetrators. Along with all of their other troubles, it was the poor who were most commonly robbed, beaten, and abused.

Popular Culture

However depressing is this story of the unrelieved misery of the poor, we should not think of the masses of eighteenth-century society only as the downtrodden victims of social and economic forces beyond their control. For the peasant farmer about to lose his land or the urban artisan without a job, security was an overwhelming concern. While many were to endure such fates, many others lived comfortably by the standards of the age, and almost everyone believed that things were better now than they had ever been before. Popular culture was a rich mixture of family and community activities that provided outlets from the pressures of work and the vagaries of fortune. It was no less sustaining to the population at large than was the purely literate culture

The Cockpit *(ca. 1759), by William Hogarth. The central figure is a blind noble-man who was said never to have missed an important cockfight. The steel spurs on the birds' legs enabled them to inflict serious damage in the heat of the battle.*

of the elite, no less vital as a means of explanation for everyday events than the theories of the philosophers or the programs of the philosophes.

In fact, the line between elite and popular culture in the eighteenth century was a thin one. For one thing, there was still much mixing of social classes in both rural and urban environments. Occasions of display, like festivals, village fairs, or religious holidays, brought entire communities together and rein-forced their collective identities. Moreover, there were many shared elements between the two cultures. All over Europe, literacy was increasing, the result of primary education, of new business techniques, and of the millions of books that were available in editions tailored to even the most modest purse. Nearly half of the inhabitants of France were literate by the end of the eighteenth century, perhaps 60 percent of those in Britain. Men were more likely to have learned to read than women, as were those who lived in urban areas. More than a quarter of French women could read, a number that had doubled over the century. As the rates of female literacy rose, so did overall rates, for women took the lead in teaching children.

Nevertheless, literate culture was not the dominant form of popular culture. Traditional social activities continued to reflect the violent and even brutal nature of day-to-day existence. Village festivals were still the safety valve of youth gangs who enforced sexual morals by shaming husbands whose wives were unfaithful or women whose reputations were sullied. Many holidays were celebrated by sporting events that pitted inhabitants of one village against those of another. These almost always turned into free-for-alls in which broken bones were common and deaths not unknown.

Even more popular were the so-called blood sports, which continued to be the most common form of popular recreation. These were brutal competitions in which, in one way or another, animals were maimed or slaughtered. Dog- and cockfighting were among those that still survive today. Less attractive to the modern mind were bearbaiting or bull running, in which the object was the slaughter of a large beast over a prolonged period of time. Blood sports were certainly not confined to the masses—fox hunting and bullfighting were pastimes for the very rich—but they formed a significant part of local social activity.

So, too, did the tavern or alehouse, which in town or country was the site for local communication and recreation, where staggering amounts of alcohol were consumed. The increased use of spirits—gin, brandy, rum, and vodka—changed the nature of alcohol consumption in Europe. Wine and beer had always been drunk in quantities that we would find astounding, but these beverages were also an important part of diet. The nutritional content of spirits was negligible. People drank spirits to get drunk. The level to which drunkenness rose in the eighteenth century speaks volumes about the changes in social and economic life that the masses of European society were now experiencing.

Eighteenth-century Europe was a society of orders gradually transforming itself into a society of classes. At the top, as vigorous as ever, was the nobility. But the bourgeoisie was growing in both numbers and importance. An active commercial and urban life gave many members of this group new social and political opportunities and many of them passed into the nobility through the purchase of land or office. Opulence and poverty increased in step as the fruits of commerce and land enriched the upper orders while rising population impoverished the lower ones. The rise of the new science and of Enlighten-ment ideas highlighted the contradictions. The attack on traditional authority, especially the Roman Catholic church, was an attack on a conservative, static worldview. Enlightenment thinkers looked to the future, to a new world shaped by reason and knowledge, a world ruled benevolently for the benefit of all human beings. Government, society, the individual—all could be improved if only the rubble of the past was cleared away. They could hardly imagine how potent their vision would become.

Suggestions for Further Reading

General Reading

*William Doyle, *The Old European Order 1660–1800* (Oxford, England: Oxford University Press, 1978). An important essay on the structure of European societies and the way in which they held together.

*A. Rupert Hall, *The Revolution in Science 1500–1750* (London: Longman, 1983). The best introduction to the varieties of scientific thought in the early modern period. Detailed and complex.

*Olwen Hufton, *Europe: Privilege and Protest 1730–1789* (Ithaca, NY: Cornell University Press, 1980). An excellent survey of the political and social history of the mid eighteenth century.

*Leonard Krieger, *Kings and Philosophers 1689–1789* (New York: W. W. Norton, 1970). A brilliant depiction of the personalties and ideas of eighteenth-century Europe.

Conquering the Material World

*Allen Debus, *Man and Nature in the Renaissance* (Cambridge, England: Cambridge University Press, 1978). An especially good account of the intellectual roots of scientific thought.

*Stillman Drake, *Galileo* (New York: Hill and Wang, 1980). A short but engaging study of the great Italian scientist.

*Margaret C. Jacob, *The Cultural Meaning of the Scientific Revolution* (New York: Knopf, 1988). Scientific thought portrayed in its social context.

*Frank E. Manuel, *Sir Isaac Newton: A Portrait* (Cambridge, MA: Harvard University Press, 1968). A readable account of one of the most complex intellects in European history.

The Enlightenment

Theodore Besterman, *Voltaire* (Chicago: University of Chicago Press, 1976). The best of many biographies of an all-too-full life.

*John G. Gagliardo, *Enlightened Despotism* (New York: Thomas Y. Crowell, 1967). A sound exploration of the impact of the Enlightenment ideas on the rulers of Europe, with most emphasis on the East.

*Peter Gay, *The Enlightenment: An Interpretation*, 2 vols. (New York: Knopf, 1966–1969). A difficult but rewarding study by one of the leading historians of the subject.

*Norman Hampson, *The Enlightenment* (London: Penguin, 1982). The best one-volume survey.

Carolyn Lougee, *Le Paradis des Femmes: Women, Salons, and Social Stratification* (Princeton, NJ: Princeton University Press, 1976). A study of the foundation of the French salons and the role of women in it.

*Judith Sklar, *Montesquieu* (Oxford; England: Oxford University Press, 1987). A concise readable study of the man and his work.

---

*Indicates paperback edition available

High and Low in the Eighteenth Century

*Peter Burke, *Popular Culture in the Early Modern Europe* (New York: Harper & Row, 1978). A wide survey of practices throughout the Continent.

Michael Bush, *Noble Privilege* (New York: Holmes & Meier, 1983). A good analytic survey of the rights of European nobles.

Jan de Vries, *European Urbanization 1500–1800* (Cambridge, MA: Harvard University Press, 1984) An important, though difficult study of the transformation of towns into cities with the most reliable estimates of size and rates of growth.

*Michael W. Flinn, *The European Demographic System* (Baltimore, MD: Johns Hopkins University Press, 1981). The best single-volume study, especially for the nonspecialist reader.

*Albert Goodwin, ed., *The European Nobility in the Eighteenth Century* (New York: Harper & Row, 1967). Separate essays on the national nobilities, including those of Sweden, Poland, and Spain.

Olwen Hufton, *The Poor in Eighteenth Century France* (Oxford; England: Oxford University Press, 1974). A compelling study of the life of the poor.

Robert Muchembled, *Popular Culture and Elite Culture in France, 1400–1750* (Baton Rouge: Louisiana State University Press, 1985). A complex but richly textured argument about the relationship between two cultures.

*Roy Porter, *English Society in the Eighteenth Century* (London: Penguin, 1982). A breezy, entertaining survey of English social life.

*Simon Shama, *The Embarrassment of Riches* (Berkeley: University of California Press, 1987). The social life of Dutch burghers richly portrayed.

Samia Spencer, *French Women and the Age of Enlightenment* (Bloomington: Indiana University Press, 1984). A survey of the role of women in French high culture.

*Lawrence Stone, *The Family, Sex and Marriage in England 1500–1800* (New York: Harper & Row, 1979). A controversial but extremely important argument about the changing nature of family life.

George Sussman, *Selling Mothers' Milk: The Wet-Nursing Business* (Bloomington: Indiana University Press, 1982). A study of buyers and sellers in this important social marketplace.

16

The French Revolution and the Napoleonic Era, 1789–1815

"Let Them Eat Cake"

The Queen of France was bored. Try as she might, Marie Antoinette (1755–1793) found insufficient diversion in her life at the great court of Versailles. When she was 14, she had married the heir to the French throne, the future Louis XVI. By the age of 19, she was queen of the most prosperous state in continental Europe. Still, she was bored. Her life, she complained to her mother, Empress Maria Theresa of Austria, was futile and meaningless. Maria Theresa advised the unhappy queen to suffer in silence or risk unpleasant consequences.

Sometimes mothers know best. As head of the Habsburg Empire, Maria Theresa understood more about politics than her youngest child. She understood that people have little sympathy with the boredom of a monarch, especially a foreign-born queen. But Marie Antoinette chose to ignore maternal advice and pursued amusements and intrigues that had unpleasant consequences indeed.

Unpopular as a foreigner from the time she arrived in France, Marie Antoinette suffered a further decline in her reputation as gossip spread about her gambling and affairs at court. The public heard exaggerated accounts of the fortunes she spent on clothing and jewelry. In 1785 she was linked to a cardinal in a nasty scandal over a gift of a diamond necklace. In spite of her innocence, rumors of corruption and infidelity surrounded her name. Dubbed

"Madame Deficit," she came to represent all that was considered decadent in royal rule.

She continued to insist, "I am afraid of being bored." To amuse herself, she ordered a life-size play village built on the grounds of Versailles, complete with cottages, a chapel, a mill, and a running stream. Then, dressed in the silks and muslins intended as the royal approximation of a milkmaid's garb, she whiled away whole days with her friends and children, all pretending they were inhabitants of this picturesque "Hamlet." Her romantic view of country life helped pass the time, but it did little to bring her closer to the struggling peasants who made up the majority of French subjects.

Marie Antoinette's problems need not have mattered much. Monarchs before her had been considered weak and extravagant. The difference was that her foibles became public in an age when the opinion of the people affected political life. Rulers, even those believed to be divinely appointed, were subjected to a public scrutiny all the more powerful because of the growth of the popular press. Kings, their ministers, and their spouses were held accountable—a dangerous phenomenon for an absolute monarchy.

This Austrian-born queen may not have been more shallow or spendthrift than other queens, but it mattered that people came to see her that way. The queen's reputation sank to its nadir when it was reported that she dismissed the suffering of her starving subjects with the haughty retort: "Let them eat cake." What better evidence could there be of the queen's insensitivity than this heartless remark?

Marie Antoinette never said, "Let them eat cake," but everyone thought she did. This was the kind of callousness that people expected from the monarchy in 1789. Marie Antoinette understood the plight of her starving subjects, as her correspondence indicates. Probably a courtier at Versailles was the real source of the brutal retort, but the truth didn't matter. Marie Antoinette and her husband were being indicted by the public for all the political, social, and fiscal crises that plagued France.

In October 1793 Marie Antoinette was put on trial by the Revolutionary Tribunal and found guilty of treason. She was stripped of all the trappings of monarchy and forced to don another costume. Dressed as a poor working woman, her hair shorn, the former queen mounted the guillotine, following in the footsteps of her husband, who had been executed earlier that year. The monarchy did not fall because of a spendthrift queen with too much time on her hands. Nor did it fall because of the mistakes of the well-meaning but inept king. The monarchy had ceased to be responsive to the profound changes that shook France. It fell because of a new concern in the land for royal accountability in words and deeds. A rising democratic tide carried with it ideas about political representation, participation, and equality. If a queen could change places with a milkmaid, why should not a milkmaid be able to change places with a queen?

*T*he Crisis of the Old Regime in France, 1715–1788

France in the eighteenth century, the age of the Enlightenment, was a state invigorated by new ideas. It was also a world dominated by tradition. The traditional institutions of monarchy, church, and aristocracy defined power and status. Talk of reform, progress, and perfectibility coexisted with the social realities of privileges and obligations determined by birth. The eighteenth century was a time when old ways prevailed even as a new view of the world was taking shape.

At the end of the eighteenth century, a number of foreign visitors to France commented on the disparities that characterized French social and political life. One English visitor in particular, Arthur Young (1741–1820), an agronomist writing on his travels in France in the 1780s, observed that although a prosperous land, France was pocked with extreme poverty; although a land of high culture and great art, it was riddled with ignorance, illiteracy, and superstition; although a land with a centralized bureaucracy, it was also saddled with local interests and obsolete practices.

The tensions generated by the clash of continuity and change made this an exciting and complex period in both Britain and France. In France, reformers talked of progress while peasants still used wooden plows. The *philosophes* glorified reason in a world of violence, superstition, and fear. The great crisis of eighteenth-century France, the French Revolution, destroyed what we now know as the *ancien régime* (old regime). But the Revolution was as much a product of continuities and traditions as it was a product of change and the challenge of new ideas.

Louis XV's France

When Louis XV (1715–1774) died, he was a hated man. In his 59-year reign, he managed to turn the public against him. He was denounced as a tyrant who was trying to starve his people, a slave to the mistresses who ruled his court, and an indecisive sybarite dominated by evil ministers. Louis XV's apathy and ineptitude contributed to his poor image. The declining fortunes and the damaged prestige of the monarchy, however, reflected more than the personality traits of an ineffectual king: They reflected structural challenges to fiscal solvency and absolutist rule that the monarchy was unable to meet.

Louis XV, like his great-grandfather Louis XIV, laid claim to rule as an absolute monarch. He insisted, "The rights and interests of the nation . . . are of necessity one with my own, and lie in my hands only." Such claims failed to mask the weaknesses of royal rule. Louis XV lacked a sufficiently developed bureaucracy to administer and tax the nation in an evenhanded fashion. By the beginning of the eighteenth century, the absolute monarchy had extended royal influence into the new areas of policing, administration, lawmaking, and taxation. But none of this proved sufficient to meet the growing needs of the state.

The growing tensions between the monarch and the aristocracy found expression in various institutions, especially the *parlements*, the 13 sovereign courts in the French judicial system with their seats in Paris and a dozen provincial centers. The magistrates of each parlement were members of the nobility, some of them nobles of recent origin and others of long standing, depending on the locale. The king needed the parlements to record royal decrees before they could become law. This recording process conferred real political power on the parlements, which could withhold approval for the king's policies by refusing to register his decrees. When the king attempted to make new laws, the magistrates could refuse to endorse them. When decrees involved taxation, they often did. Because magistrates purchased their offices in the parlements, the king found it difficult to control the courts. His fiscal difficulties prevented him from buying up the increasingly valuable offices in order to appoint his own men. Stripping magistrates of their positions was considered tantamount to the theft of property. By successfully challenging the king, the parlements became a battleground between the elite, who claimed they represented the nation, and the king, who said the nation was himself.

The king repeatedly attempted to neutralize the power of the parlements by relying instead on his own state bureaucracy. His agents in the provinces, called *intendants*, were accountable directly to the central government. The intendants, as the king's men, and the magistrates who presided in the parlements represented contradictory claims to power. As the king's needs increased in the second half of the eighteenth century, the situation was becoming intolerable for those exercising power and those aspiring to rule in the name and for the good of the nation.

The nadir of Louis XV's reign came in 1763 with the French defeat in the Seven Years' War both on the Continent and in the colonies. In the Treaty of Paris, France ceded territory, including its Canadian holdings, to Great Britain. France lost more than lands; it lost its footing in the competition with its chief rival Great Britain, which had been pulling ahead of France in international affairs since the early eighteenth century. The war was also a financial debacle, paid for by loans secured against the guarantee of victory. The defeat not only left France barren of funds; it also promoted further expenditures for strengthening the French navy against the superior British fleet. New taxation was the way out of the financial trap in which the king now found himself.

Louis XV's revenue problem was not easily solved. In order to raise taxes, the king had to turn to the recording function of the parlements. Following the costly Seven Years' War, the parlements chose to exercise the power of refusal by blocking a proportional tax to be imposed on nobles and commoners alike. The magistrates resisted taxation with an argument that confused liberty with privilege: The king, the magistrates asserted, was attacking the liberty of his subjects by attempting to tax those who were exempt by virtue of their privileged status.

René Nicolas Charles Augustin de Maupeou (1714–1792), Louis XV's chancellor from 1768 to 1774, decided that the political power of the parlements had to be curbed. In 1770, in an attempt to coerce the magistrates into compliance with the king's wishes, he engineered the overthrow of the Parlement of Paris, the most important of the high courts. Those magistrates who remained obdurate were sent into exile. New courts whose membership was based on appointment instead of the sale of offices took their place amid much public criticism. Ultimately, Maupeou's attempt did nothing to improve the monarch's image and it did less to solve the fiscal problems of the regime.

The dignity and prestige of the monarchy were seriously damaged in the course of Louis XV's long reign. His legacy was well captured in the expression erroneously attributed to him, *après moi, le déluge*—"after me, the flood." Continuing to live the good life at the court, he failed dismally to offset rising state expenditures—caused primarily by military needs—with new sources of revenue. In 1774 Louis XV died suddenly of smallpox. His unprepared 20-year-old grandson, Louis XVI (1774–1792), a young man who amused himself by hunting and pursuing his hobby as an amateur locksmith, was left to try to stanch the flood.

The End of the Old Regime

Louis XV left to his heir Louis XVI the legacy of a disastrous deficit. From the beginning of his reign, Louis XVI was caught in the vicious circle of excessive state spending—above all, military spending—followed by bouts of heavy borrowing. Borrowing at high rates required the government to pay out huge sums in interest and service fees on the loans that were keeping it afloat. These outlays in turn piled the state's indebtedness even higher, requiring more loans, and threatening to topple the whole financial structure and the regime itself.

In inheriting this trouble-ridden fiscal structure, Louis XVI made his own contribution to it. Following in the footsteps of his grandfather, Louis XVI involved France in a costly war, the War of American Independence (1775–1783), by supporting the 13 colonies in their revolt against Great Britain. The involvement brought the French monarchy to the brink of bankruptcy. Contrary to public opinion, most of the state's expenditures did not go toward lavishing luxuries on the royal court and the royal family at Versailles. They went to pay off loans. More than half of the state budget in the 1780s represented interest on loans taken to pay for foreign military ventures.

The king needed money and he needed it fast. To those who could afford to purchase them, the king continued to sell offices that carried with them titles, revenues, and privileges. He also relied on the sale of annuities that paid high interest rates and attracted speculators, large and small. The crown had leased out its rights to collect the salt tax in return for large lump-sum advances from the Royal General Farms, a syndicate of about one hundred wealthy financier families. But the combined revenues collected by the king through these various stratagems were little more than a drop compared to the vast ocean of debt that threatened to engulf the state.

The existing tax structure proved hopelessly inadequate to meet the state's needs. The *taille*, a direct tax, was levied, either on persons or on land, according to region. Except for those locales where the taille was attached to land, the nobility was always exempt from direct taxation. Members of the bourgeoisie could also avoid the direct tax as citizens of towns enjoying exemption. That meant the wealthy, those best able to pay, were often exempt.

Indirect taxes, like those on salt (the *gabelle*) and on food and drink (the *aide*), and internal and external customs taxes were regressive taxes that hit hardest those least able to pay. The peasantry bore the brunt of the nation's tax burden, and Louis XVI knew all too well that he could not squeeze blood from a stone by increasing indirect taxes. A peasantry too weighted down would collapse—or rebel. The privileged elite persisted in rejecting the crown's attempts to tax them. As one of the first acts of his reign, in 1775 Louis XVI had restored the magistrates to their posts in the parlements, treating their offices as a form of property of which they had been deprived. By 1776 the Parlement of Paris was again obstructing royal decrees.

Louis XVI appointed Anne-Robert-Jacques Turgot (1727–1781) as his first controller-general. Turgot's reformist economic ideas were influenced by Enlightenment philosophes. In order to generate revenues, Turgot reasoned, France needed to prosper economically. The government was in a position to stimulate economic growth by eliminating regulations, by economizing at court, and by improving the network of roads through a tax on landowners. Each of Turgot's reforms offended established interests, thereby ensuring his early defeat. Emphasis on a laissez-faire economy outraged the guilds; doing away with the forced labor of peasants on the roads (the *corvée*) threatened privileged groups that had never before been taxed. As the king was discovering, divine right did not bring with it absolute authority or fiscal solvency.

As he floundered about for a solution to his economic difficulties, the king turned to a new adviser, Jacques Necker (1732–1804), a Swiss-born Protestant banker. The king and the public expected great things from Necker, whose international business experience was counted on to save the day. Necker, a prudent man, applied his accounting skills to measuring—for the first time—the total income and expenditures of the French state. The budget he produced and widely circulated allayed everyone's fears of certain doom and assured the nation that no new taxes were necessary—an assurance based on disastrous miscalculations. Instead of raising taxes, Necker commmitted his ministry to eliminating costly inefficiencies. He promised to abolish venal offices that drained revenues from the crown. He next set his sights on contracts of the farmers-general, collectors of the indirect salt taxes.

Necker and those who preceded him in controlling and directing the finances of the state under Louis XV and Louis XVI were committed to reforming the system. All the advisers recognized that the state's fiscal problems were structural and required enlightened solutions, but no two of them agreed on the same program of reforms. Necker had somehow captivated popular opinion and there was widespread regret expressed when he was forced to resign in 1781.

Charles Alexandre de Calonne (1734–1802), appointed controller-general in 1783, had his own ideas of how to bail out the ship of state. He authored a program of reforms that would have shifted the tax burden off those least able to pay and onto those best able to support the state. He proposed a tax on land proportional to land values, a measure that would have most seriously affected the land-rich nobility. In addition, taxes that affected the peasantry were to be lightened or eliminated. Finally, Calonne proposed the sale of church lands for revenues. In an attempt to bypass the recalcitrant parlements, Calonne advised the crown in 1787 to convene an Assembly of Notables made up of 150 individuals from the magistracy, the church hierarchy, the titled nobility, and municipal bodies, for the purpose of enlisting their support for reforms. Louis listened to Calonne, who was denounced by the Assembly of Notables for attacking the rights of the privileged. He, too, was forced to resign.

All of Louis XVI's attempts to persuade the nobility to agree to tax reforms had failed. Louis was incapable of the effort required either to inspire or to manipulate the privileged classes to support his plans. Aristocratic magistrates insisted on a constitution, in which their own right to govern would be safeguarded and the accountability of the king would be defined. In opposing the royal reforms, nobles spoke of the "rights of man" and used the term *citizen*. The nobility had no sympathy for tax programs that would have resulted in a loss of privilege and that some nobles were beginning to consider an attack on individual freedom. Louis XVI met with passivity from the Assembly of Notables and resistance from the Parlement of Paris and the provincial parlements. In the 1780s almost 50 percent of annual expenditures went to servicing the accumulated national debt of four billion livres and paying interest. The new controller-general, Archbishop Loménie de Brienne (1727–1794), recommended emergency loans. The crown once again disbanded the Paris Parlement, which was now threatening to block loans as well as taxes.

Louis XVI was a desperate man in 1788, so desperate that he yielded to the condition placed on him by the Paris Parlement: He agreed to convene the Estates-General, a medieval body that had not met since 1614 and had been considered obsolete with the rise of a centralized bureaucratic government. The Estates-General included representatives from the three "estates" of the clergy, nobility, and commoners. About two hundred thousand subjects belonged to the first two estates. The Third Estate was composed of all those members of the realm who enjoyed a common identity only in their lack of privilege—over twenty-three million French people. In the 1614 voting of the Estates-General, each of the three orders was equally weighted. This arrangement favored the nobility, who controlled the first two estates and thus were not worried by the prospect of the Estates-General deciding the tax reform program. Many were sure that a new age of liberty was at hand.

The Three Estates

French society was divided by law and custom into a pyramid of three tiers called orders or estates. At the top were those who prayed—the clergy, followed by those who fought—the nobility. The base of the pyramid was formed by the largest of the three orders, those who worked—the bourgeoisie, the peasantry, and urban and rural workers. In the second half of the eighteenth century, these traditional groups no longer reflected social realities—a situation that proved to be a source of serious problems for the Estates-General. The piety of the first order had been called into doubt as religious leaders were criticized for using the vast wealth of the Church for personal benefit instead of public worship. The protective military function of the second order had ceased to exist with the rise of the state and the changing nature of war. The bourgeoisie, those who worked with their heads, not their hands, shared privileges with the nobility and aspired to a noble lifestyle, in spite of their legal and customary presence in the ranks of the Third Estate.

The vast majority of French subjects who constituted the Third Estate certainly were identified by work, but the wide array of mental and physical labor—and lack of work—splintered the estate into a myriad of occupations, aspirations, and identities. All power flowed upward in this arrangement, with the First and Second estates dominating the social and political universe. Women and men accepted this hierarchy as the natural organization of society in eighteenth-century France.

The king continued to stand at the pinnacle of the eighteenth-century social pyramid. Traditionally revered as the "father" of his subjects, he claimed to be divinely appointed by God. Kingship in this era had a dual nature. The king was both supreme overlord from feudal times and absolute monarch. As supreme overlord he stood dominant over the aristocracy and the court. As absolute monarch he stood at the head of the state and society. Absolutism required a weakened nobility and a bureaucracy strong enough to help the monarchy to adjust to changes. After the death of Louis XIV in 1715, Louis XV and Louis XVI faced a resurgent aristocracy without the support of a state bureaucracy capable of successfully challenging aristocratic privilege or of solving fiscal problems.

While the system of orders set clear boundaries of social status, distinctions within estates created new hierarchies. The clergy, a privileged order, contained both commoners and nobles, but leadership in the Church depended on social rank. The aristocracy retained control of the bishoprics, even as an activist element among the lower clergy agitated for reforms and better salaries. In a state in which the king claimed to rule by God's will, Catholicism, virtually the state religion, was important in legitimizing the divine claims of the monarchy.

The nobility experienced its own internal tensions, generated by two groups: the older nobility of the sword, who claimed descent from medieval times, and the more recent nobility of the robe, who had acquired their position through the purchase of offices that conferred noble status. By increasing the numbers of the nobility of the robe, Louis XIV hoped to undermine the power of the aristocracy as a whole and to decrease its political influence. But aristocrats rallied and closed ranks against the dilution of their power. As a result, both Louis XV and Louis XVI faced a reviving rather than declining aristocracy. One in four nobles had moved from the bourgeoisie to the aristocratic ranks in the eighteenth century; two out of every three had been ennobled during the seventeenth and eighteenth centuries. Nobles had succeeded in restoring their economic and social power. A growing segment of the aristocracy, influenced by Enlightenment ideas and the example of English institutions, was intent on increasing the political dominance of the aristocracy, too.

The nobility strengthened their powers in two ways. First, they monopolized high offices and closed access to non-nobles. They took over posts in ministries, the Church, and the army. Second, the nobility benefited greatly from the doubling in land values brought on by the increase in the value of crops. Seeking ever higher returns from the land, some members of the aristocracy adopted new agricultural techniques to achieve greater crop yields. Those aristocrats who controlled sizable holdings profited greatly from higher dues paid to them, as they reaped increased incomes from crops. In addition, many aristocrats revived feudal claims to ancient seigneurial, or lordly, privileges. They hired lawyers to unearth old claims and hired agents to collect dues.

A spirit of innovation characterized the values of certain members of the nobility. Although technically prevented from participating in trade by virtue of their titles and privileges, an active group among the nobility succeeded in making fortunes in metallurgy, glassmaking, and mining. These nobles were an economically dynamic and innovative segment of the aristocracy. In spite of the obsolete aspect of their privileges, aristocrats were often responsible for the introduction of modern ideas and techniques in the management of estates and in the bookkeeping involved with collection of rents. These nobles formed an elite partnership with forward-looking members of the bourgeoisie.

Common people, that is, those who did not enjoy the privileges of the nobility, embraced a broad range of the French populace. The peasantry was by far the largest group, joined in the designation as "commoners" by the middle class, or bourgeoisie, and by workers in both cities and rural areas. Most French peasants were free, no longer attached to the soil as serfs were in a feudal system. Yet all peasants endured common obligations placed on them by the crown and the privileged classes. Peasants owed the tithe to the Church, land taxes to the state, and seigneurial dues and rents to the landlord. A bewildering array of taxes afflicted peasants. In some areas peasants repaired roads and drew lots for military service. Dues affected almost every aspect of rural life, including harvests and the sale of property. In addition, indirect taxes like that on salt (the hated gabelle) were a serious burden for the peasantry. As if all this were not enough, peasants who were forced to take loans to survive from one harvest to another paid exorbitant interest rates.

The precariousness of rural life and the increase in population in the countryside contributed to the permanent displacement and destitution of a growing sector of rural society. Without savings and destroyed by poor harvests, impoverished rural inhabitants wandered the countryside looking for odd jobs and eventually begging to survive. Many peasants with small plots were able to work for wages. Peasant women sought employment in towns and cities as seamstresses and servants in order to send money back home. Children, too, added their earnings to the family pot. In spite of various strategies for survival, more and more families were disrupted by the end of the eighteenth century.

The bourgeoisie—as the term was used in the eighteenth century—meant those members of the middle class who lived on income from investments. Yet the term really embraced within it a whole hierarchy of professions from bankers and financiers to businesspeople, merchants, entrepreneurs, lawyers, shopkeepers, and craft workers. Along with the nobility, wealthy bourgeois formed the urban elites that administered cities and towns. Prestigious service to the state or the french purchase of offices that carried with them noble status enabled the wealthiest members of the bourgeoisie to move into the ranks of the nobility. Many bourgeois served as middlemen for the nobility by running estates and collecting dues.

Like the rest of the social universe, the world of artisans and workers was shaded with various gradations of wealth and status. Those who owned their own shops and perhaps employed other workers stood as an elite among the working class. In spite of their physical proximity, there was a vast difference between those who owned their own shops and those who earned wages or were paid by the piece. Wage earners represented about 30 percent of the population of cities and towns. And their numbers were swelling, as craft workers were pushed out of their guilds and peasants were pushed off their land.

In 1775 the king temporarily abolished the guilds in an attempt to promote free trade. Those who worked in crafts were a labor elite, and guilds were intended to protect the corporations of masters, journeymen, and apprentices through monopolistic measures. Guilds insisted that they were best able to ensure the quality of goods. But the emphasis on free trade and the expansion of markets in the eighteenth century weakened the hold of the guilds. Merchants often took them over and paid workers by the piece. The effect was a reduction in the wages of skilled workers. By the 1780s most journeymen who hoped to be masters knew that their dream would never be realized. Frustration and discontent touched workers in towns and cities who may not have shared a common work experience. But they did share a common anger about the high cost of food—especially bread.

In August 1788 Louis XVI announced that the Estates-General would meet at Versailles in May 1789. He directed each of the three estates—clergy, nobility, and commoners—to elect their representatives, who would come together to discuss the fiscal and political problems plaguing the nation. Every social group, from the nobles to the poorest laborers, had its own grievances and concerns, but all greeted the news with fireworks, parades, and toasts to the best of all kings.

The French Revolution and the End of the Old Regime

Those who lived through it were sure there had never been a time like it before. The French Revolution, or the Great Revolution, as it was known to contemporaries, was a time of creation and discovery. The ten years from

1789 to 1799 were punctuated by genuine euphoria and democratic transformations. From the privileged elites who initiated the overthrow of the existing order to peasants and workers, women and men, who united against tyranny, the Revolution touched every segment of society.

The Revolution achieved most in the area of politics. The overthrow of absolutist monarchy brought with it new social theories, new symbols, and new behavior. The excitement of anarchy was matched by the terror of repression. Revolutionary France had to contend with a Europe-wide war. The Revolution had its dark side of violence and instability. In the Revolution's wake came internal discord, civil war, and violent repression. In the search for a new order, political forms followed one upon the other in rapid succession: constitutional monarchy, republic, oligarchy. The creation of Napoleon's dictatorship at the end of the century was the act that signified the Revolution had come to an end.

Revolutionary incidents flared up throughout Europe in the second half of the eighteenth century—in the Netherlands, Belgium, and Ireland. Absolute authority was challenged and sometimes modified. Across the Atlantic, American colonists concerned with the principle of self-rule had thrown off the yoke of the British in the War of Independence. But none of these events, including the American Revolution, was so violent in breaking with the old order, so extensive in involving millions of men and women in political action, and so consequential for the political futures of other European states, as was the French Revolution. The triumphs and contradictions of the revolutionary experiment in democracy mark the end of the old order and the beginning of modern history. Politics would never be the same.

Taking Politics to the People

Choosing representatives for the Estates-General in March and April 1789 stirred up hope and excitement in every corner of France. From the very beginning, there were warning signs that a more astute monarch might have noticed. The call for national elections set in motion a politicizing process the king could not control. Members of the Third Estate, traditionally excluded from political and social power, were presented with the opportunity of expressing their opinions on the state of government and society. In an increasingly literate age, pamphlets, broadsides, and political tracts representing every political persuasion blanketed France. Farmhands and urban laborers realized they were participating in the same process as their social betters. And they believed they had a right to speak and be heard.

This was a time of great hope, especially for people who had been buffeted by the rise in prices, decline in real wages, and the hunger that followed crop failures and poor harvests. Now there was the promise of a respite and a solution. Taxes could be discussed and changed, the state bureaucracy could be reformed—or better, abolished.

Intellectuals discussed political alternatives in the salons of the wealthy. Nobles and bourgeois met in philosophical societies dedicated to enlightened thought. Commoners gathered in cafés to drink and debate. The poor fell outside of this network of communication, but they were not immune to the ideas that emerged. In the end, people of all classes had opinions and they were more certain than ever of their right to express their ideas. Absolutism was in trouble, although Louis XVI did not know it, as people began to forge a collectively shared idea of politics. People now had a forum—the Estates-General—and a focus—the politics of taxation. But most important, they had the elections. The message of the elections and the representative principle on which they were based was that one could compete for power.

In competing for power, some members of the Third Estate were well aware of their vast numerical superiority over the nobility. Because of it, they demanded greater representation than the 300 members per estate defined according to the practices of 1614. At the very least, they argued, the number of representatives of the Third Estate should be doubled to 600 members giving commoners equality in numbers with nobles and priests together. Necker, recalled as director-general of finance in August 1788, agreed to the doubling in the size of the Third Estate as a compromise but left unresolved the additional demand of vote by head rather than by order. If voting was to be left as it was, in accordance with the procedures of 1614, the nobility who controlled the First and Second Estates would determine all outcomes. With a voting procedure by head instead of by order, however, the deputies of the Third Estate could easily dominate the Estates-General, confident that they could count on liberal nobles like the Marquis de Lafayette and parish priests to defect from the First and Second Estates and join their cause.

In conjunction with this political activity and in scheduled meetings, members of all three estates drew up statements of their problems. This took place in a variety of forums, including guilds and village and town meetings. The people of France set down their grievances in notebooks—known as *cahiers de doléances*—that were then carried to Versailles by the deputies elected to the Estates-General. This was the first national poll of opinion commissioned by the crown, and it involved every level of society. It was a tool of political education as the mass of French people were given the impression for the first time that they were part of the policy-making process.

"If only the king knew!" In this phrase, French men and women expressed their belief in the inevitability of their fate and the benevolence of their king. They saw the king as a loving and wise father who would not tolerate the injustices visited upon his subjects, if only he knew what was really happening. In 1789 peasants and workers were questioning why their lives could not be better, but they continued to express their trust in the king.

The cahiers expressed the particular grievances of each estate. These notebooks contained a collective outpouring of problems and are important for two major reasons. First, they made clear the similarity of grievances shared throughout France. Second, they indicated the extent to which a common political culture, based on a concern with political reform, had permeated different levels of French society. Both the privileged and the nonprivileged identified a common enemy in the system of state bureaucracy to which the monarch was so strongly tied. Although the king was still addressed with respect, new concerns with liberty, equality, property, and the rule of law were voiced.

Those who opposed the Revolution later alleged that these notebooks proved the existence of a highly coordinated plot on the part of secret societies out to destroy the regime. They were wrong. Similarities in complaints, similarities in demands, similarities in language proved, not a conspiracy, but the forging of a new political consciousness. Societies and clubs circulated "model" cahiers among themselves, resulting in the use of similar forms and vocabulary. People were questioning their traditional roles and now had elected deputies who would represent them before the king. In the spring of 1789 a severe economic crisis that heightened political uncertainty swept through France. For a king expected to save the situation, time was running out.

Convening the Estates-General

The elected deputies arrived at Versailles at the beginning of May 1789, carrying in their valises and trunks the grievances of their estates. The opening session of the Estates-General took place in a great hall especially constructed for the event. The 1248 deputies presented a grand spectacle as they filed to their assigned places to hear speeches by the king and his ministers. Contrasts among the participants were immediately apparent. Seated on a raised throne under a canopy at one end of the hall, Louis XVI was vested in full kingly regalia. On his right sat the archbishops and cardinals of the First Estate, dramatically clad in the pinks and purples of their offices. On his left were the richly and decorously attired nobility. Facing the stage sat the 648 deputies of the Third Estate, dressed in plain black suits, stark against the colorful and costly costumes of the privileged. It was clear, in the most visual terms, that "clothes make the man." Members of the Third Estate had announced beforehand that they would not follow the ancient custom for commoners of kneeling at the king's entrance. Fired by the hope of equal treatment and an equal share of power, they had come to Versailles to make a constitution.

The tension between commoners and privileged was further aggravated by the unresolved issue of how the voting was to proceed. The Third Estate was adamant in its demand for vote by head. The privileged orders were equally adamant in insisting on vote by order. Paralysis set in, as days dragged into weeks and the estates were unable to act. The body that was to save France from fiscal collapse was hopelessly deadlocked.

Two men in particular whose backgrounds made them unlikely heroes emerged as leaders of the Third Estate. One, the Abbé Emmanuel Joseph Sieyès (1748–1836), was a member of the clergy who frequented Parisian salons. The other, the comte Honoré Gabriel Victor de Mirabeau (1749–1791), a black sheep among the nobility, had spent time in prison because of his father's charges that he was a defiant son who led a misspent, debauched, and profligate youth. In spite of his nobility, Mirabeau appeared at Versailles as a deputy for Aix and Marseilles to the Third Estate. His oratory and presence commanded attention from the start. As a consummate politician, Mirabeau combined forces with Sieyès, who had already established his reputation as a firebrand reformer with his eloquent pamphlet, "What Is the Third Estate?" published in January 1789. To the question posed in the title, Sieyès answered, "What is the Third Estate? Everything! What has it been in the political order up to the present? Nothing!"

Sieyès and Mirabeau reminded members of the Third Estate of the reformist consensus that characterized their ranks. Under their influence, the Third Estate decided to proceed with its own meetings. On 17 June 1789, the Third Estate, joined by some sympathetic clergy, changed its name to the National Assembly as an assertion of its true representation of the French nation. Three days later, members of the new National Assembly found themselves locked out of their regular meeting room by the king's guard. Outraged by this insult, they moved to a nearby indoor tennis court, where they vowed to stay together for the purpose of writing a constitution. This event, known as the Oath of the Tennis Court, marked the end of the absolutist monarchy and the beginning of a new concept of the state that power resided in the people. The Revolution had begun.

This painting of the Oath of the Tennis Court is by the Revolution's leading artist, Jacques-Louis David. Sieyès sits at a table on which Bailly stands reading the oath. Robespierre is seen clutching his breast in the group behind Sieyès.

The drama of Versailles, a staged play of gestures, manners, oaths, and attire, also marked the beginning of a far-reaching political revolution. Although it was a drama that took place behind closed doors, it was not one unknown to the general public. Throughout May and June 1789, Parisians trekked to Versailles to watch the deliberations. Then they brought news back to the capital. Deputies wrote home to their constituents to keep them abreast of events. Newspapers that reported daily on these wranglings and pamphleteers who analyzed them spread the news throughout the nation. Information, often conflicting, stirred up anxiety; news of conflict encouraged action.

The frustration and the stalemate of the Estates-General threatened to put the spark to the kindling of urban unrest. The people of Paris had suffered through a harsh winter and spring under the burdens of high prices (especially of bread), limited supplies, and relentless tax demands. The rioting of the spring had for the moment ceased, as people waited for their problems to be solved by the deputies of the Estates-General. The suffering of the urban poor was not new, but their ability to connect economic hardships with the politics at Versailles and to blame the government was. As hopes began to dim with the news of political stalemate, news broke of the creation of the National Assembly. It was greeted with new anticipation.

The Storming of the Bastille

The king, who had temporarily withdrawn from sight following the death of his son at the beginning of June, reemerged to meet with the representatives of each of the three estates and propose reforms, including a constitutional monarchy. But Louis XVI refused to accept the now popularly supported National Assembly as a legitimate body, choosing instead to rely on the three estates for advice. He simply did not understand that the choice was no longer his to make. He summoned troops to Versailles and began concentrating soldiers in Paris. Civilians constantly clashed with members of the military, whom they jostled and jeered. The urban crowds recognized the threat of repression that the troops represented. People decided to meet force with force. To do so, they needed arms themselves and they knew where to get them.

On 14 July 1789, the irate citizens of Paris stormed the Bastille, a royal armory that also served as a prison for a handful of debtors. The storming of the Bastille has become the great symbol in the revolutionary legend of the overthrow of the tyranny and oppression of the old regime. But it is significant for another reason. It was an expression of the power of the people to take politics into their own hands. Parisians were following the lead of their deputies in Versailles. They had formed a citizen militia, known as the National Guard, and were prepared to defend their concept of justice and law.

The people who stormed the Bastille were not the poor, the unemployed, the criminals, or the urban rabble, as they were portrayed by their detractors.

This lively amateur painting of the fall of the Bastille is by Claude Cholat, one of the attackers. Tradition has it that Cholat is manning the cannon in the background along with those he calls "Conquerors of the Bastille."

They were bourgeois and petit bourgeois, shopkeepers, guild members, family men and women, who considered it their right to seize arms to protect their interests. The Marquis de Lafayette (1757–1834), a noble beloved of the people because of his participation in the American Revolution, helped organize the National Guard. Under his direction, the militia adopted the tricolor flag as their standard. The tricolor combined the red and blue colors of the city of Paris with the white of the Bourbon royal family. It became the flag of the Revolution, replacing the fleur-de-lis of the Bourbons. It is the national flag of France today.

The king could no longer dictate the terms of the constitution. By their actions, the people in arms had ratified the National Assembly. Louis XVI was forced to yield. The events in Paris set off similar uprisings in cities and towns throughout France. National guards in provincial cities modeled themselves after the Parisian militia. Government officials fled their posts and abandoned their responsibilities. Commoners stood ready to fill the power vacuum that now existed. But the Revolution was not just an urban phenomenon. The peasantry had their own grievances and their own way of making a revolution.

The Revolution of the Peasantry

In the spring and early summer of 1789, food shortages drove bands of armed peasants to attack manor houses throughout France. In the areas surrounding

Paris and Versailles, peasants destroyed game and devastated the forests where the king and his nobles hunted. The anger reflected in these seemingly isolated events was suspended as the hope grew that the proceedings at Versailles would produce results. Remote as peasant involvement in the drawing up of the cahiers might have been, peasants everywhere expected that aid was at hand.

News of the events of Versailles and then of the revolutionary action in Paris did not reassure rural inhabitants. By the end of June the hope of deliverance from crippling taxes and dues was rapidly fading. The news of the Oath of the Tennis Court and the storming of the Bastille terrified country folk, who saw the actions as evidence of an aristocratic plot that threatened sorely needed reforms. As information moved along postal routes in letters from delegates to their supporters, or news was repeated in the Sunday market gatherings, distortions and exaggerations crept in. It seemed to rural inhabitants that their world was falling apart. Some peasants believed that Paris was in the hands of brigands and that the king and the Estates-General were victims of an aristocratic plot. Rural vision, fueled by empty stomachs, was apocalyptic.

This state of affairs was aggravated as increasing numbers of peasants were pushed off the land to seek employment as transient farm laborers, moving from one area to another with the cycles of sowing and harvesting. Throughout the 1780s the number of peasants without land was increasing steadily. Filthy, poorly dressed, and starving men, women, and children were frightening figures to villagers who feared that the same fate would befall them with the next bad harvest. As one landowner lamented, "We cannot lie down without fear, the nighttime paupers have tormented us greatly, to say nothing of the daytime ones, whose numbers are considerable."

Hope gave way to fear. Beginning on 20 July 1789, peasants in different areas of France reacted with a kind of collective hysteria, spreading false rumors of a great conspiracy. Fear gripped whole villages, and in some areas spawned revolt. Just as urban workers had connected their economic hardships to politics, so, too, did desperate peasants see their plight in political terms. They banded together and marched to the residences of the local nobility, breaking into the chateaus with a single mission in mind: to destroy all legal documents by which nobles claimed payments, dues, and services from local peasants. They drove out the lords and in some cases burned their chateaus, putting an end to the tyranny of the privileged over the countryside.

The overthrow of privileges rooted in a feudal past was not as easy as that. Members of the National Assembly were aghast at the eruption of rural violence. They knew that to stay in power they had to maintain peace. They also knew that to be credible they had to protect property. Peasant destruction of seigneurial claims posed a real dilemma for the bourgeois deputies directing the Revolution. If they gave in to peasant demands, they risked losing aristocratic support and undermining their own ability to control events. If they gave in to the aristocracy, they risked a social revolution in the country-

side, which they could not police or repress. Liberal members of the aristocracy cooperated with the bourgeois leaders in finding a solution.

In a dramatic meeting that lasted through the night of 4–5 August 1789, the
National Assembly agreed to abolish the principle of privilege. The peasants
had won—or thought they had. In the weeks and months ahead, rural people
learned they had lost their own prerogatives—the rights to common grazing
and gathering—and were expected to buy their way out of their feudal
services. In the meantime, parliamentary action had saved the day, as the
deputies stabilized the situation by legislating compromise.

Women's Actions

Women participated with men in both urban and rural revolutionary actions.
Acting on their own, women were responsible for the most dramatic event of
the early years of the Revolution: In October 1789 they forced the king and the
royal family to leave Versailles for Paris to deal in person with the problems of
bread supply, high prices, and starvation. Women milling about in the marketplaces of Paris on the morning of 5 October were complaining bitterly about
the high cost and shortages of bread. The National Assembly was in session
and the National Guards were patrolling the streets of Paris. But these
trappings of political change had no impact on the brutal realities of the
marketplace.

Women were in charge of buying the food for their families. Every morning
they stood in lines with their neighbors reenacting the familiar ritual. Some

*A contemporary print of the women of Paris advancing on Versailles. The deter-
mined marchers are shown waving pikes and dragging an artillery piece. The
women were hailed as heroines of the Revolution.*

mornings they were turned away, told by the baker or his assistants that there was no bread. On other days they did not have enough coins in their purses to buy this staple of their diet. Women, who were responsible for managing the consumption of the household, were most directly in touch with the state of provisioning the capital. When they were unable to feed their families, the situation became intolerable.

So it was on the morning of 5 October 1789, that 6000 Parisian women marched out of the city and toward Versailles. They were taking their problem to the king with the demand that he solve it. Later in the day, Lafayette, sympathetic to the women's cause, led the Parisian National Guard to Versailles to mediate events. The women were armed with pikes, the simple weapon available to the poorest defender of the Revolution, and they were prepared to use them. The battle came early the next morning, when the women, tired and cold from waiting all night at the gates of the palace, invaded the royal apartments and chased Marie Antoinette from her bedroom. Several members of the royal guards, hated by the people of Paris for alleged insults against the tricolor cockade, were killed by the angry women, who decapitated them and mounted their heads on pikes. A shocked Louis XVI agreed to return with the crown to Paris. The crowd cheered Louis's decision, which briefly reestablished his personal popularity. But as monarch, he had been humiliated at the hands of women of the capital. "The baker, the baker's wife, and the baker's son" were forced to return to Paris that very day. Louis XVI was now captive to the Revolution, whose efforts to form a constitutional monarchy he purported to support.

The Revolution Threatened

The disciplined deliberations of committees intent on fashioning a constitutional monarchy replaced the passion and fervor of revolutionary oratory. The National, or Constituent, Assembly divided France into new administrative units—*départements*—for the purpose of establishing better control over municipal governments. Along with new administrative trappings, the government promoted its own rituals. On 14 July 1790, militias from each of the newly created 83 départements of France came together in Paris to celebrate the first anniversary of the storming of the Bastille. A new national holiday was born and with it a sense of devotion and patriotism for the new France liberated by the Revolution. In spite of these unifying elements, however, the newly achieved revolutionary consensus showed signs of breaking down.

In February 1790 legislation dissolved all monasteries and convents, except for those that provided aid to the poor or that served as educational institutions. As the French church was stripped of its lands, Pope Pius VI (1775–1799) denounced the principles of the Revolution. In July 1790 the government approved the Civil Constitution of the Clergy: Priests now became the equivalent of paid agents of the state. By requiring an oath of loyalty to the state from all practicing priests, the National Assembly created a new arena for dissent: Catholics were forced to choose to embrace or reject the Revolution. Many "nonjuring" priests who refused to take the oath went into hiding. The wedge driven between the Catholic church and revolutionary France allowed a mass-based counterrevolution to emerge. Aristocratic émigrés who had fled the country because of their opposition to the Revolution were languishing because of lack of a popular base. From his headquarters in Turin, the king's younger brother, the comte d'Artois, was attempting to incite a civil war in France. When the revolutionaries decided to attack the Church not just as a landed and privileged institution but also as a religious one, the counterrevolution rapidly expanded.

The Constitution of 1791, completed after over two years of deliberations, established a constitutional monarchy with a ministerial executive power answerable to a legislative assembly. Louis XVI, formerly the divinely anointed ruler of France, was now "Louis, by the grace of God and the constitutional law of the state, King of the French." In proclaiming his acceptance of the constitution, Louis expressed the sentiments of many when he said, "The end of the revolution is come. It is time that order be reestablished so that the constitution may receive the support now most necessary to it; it is time to settle the opinion of Europe concerning the destiny of France, and to show that French men are worthy of being free." Louis, who had been wrong often enough in the past, could not have been more mistaken when he declared that the end of the Revolution was at hand.

The Constitution of 1791 marked the triumph of the principles of the Revolution. But months before the ink was dry on the final document, the actions of the king doomed the new constitution to failure. To be successful, constitutional monarchy required a king worthy of honor and respect. Louis XVI seemed to be giving the revolutionaries what they wanted by cooperating with the framers of the constitution. Yet late one night in June 1791, Louis XVI, Marie Antoinette, and their children disguised themselves as commoners, crept out of the royal apartments in the Tuileries Palace, and fled Paris. Louis intended to leave France to join foreign forces opposing the Revolution at Metz. He got as far as Varennes, where he was captured by soldiers of the National Guards and brought back to a shocked Paris. The king had abandoned the Revolution. Although he was not put to death for another year and a half, he was more than ever a prisoner of the Revolution. The monarchy was effectively finished as part of a political solution, and with its demise went liberal hopes for a constitutional settlement. The defection of the king was certainly serious, but other problems plagued the revolutionary government, notably the fiscal crisis coupled with inflation, and foreign war.

In order to establish its seriousness and legitimacy, the National Assembly had been willing in 1789 to absorb the debts of the old regime. The new government could not sell titles and offices, as the king had done to deal with financial problems, but it did confiscate church property. In addition, it issued treasury bonds in the form of *assignats* in order to raise money. The assignats soon assumed the status of banknotes, and by spring 1790 they became compulsory legal tender. Initially they were to be backed by land confiscated from the Church and now being sold by the state. But the need for money soon outran the value of the land available and the government continued to print assignats according to its needs. Depreciation of French currency in international markets and inflation at home resulted. The revolutionary government found itself in a situation which in certain respects was worse than that experienced by Louis XVI before the calling of the Estates-General. Assignat-induced inflation produced a sharp decline in the fortunes of bourgeois investors living on fixed incomes. Rising prices meant increased misery for workers and peasants.

New counterrevolutionary groups were becoming frustrated with revolutionary policies. Throughout the winter and spring of 1791–1792, people rioted and demanded that prices be fixed, as the assignat dropped to less than half of its face value. Peasants refused to sell their crops for the worthless paper. Hoarding further drove up prices. Angry crowds turned to pillaging, rioting, and murders, which became more frequent as the value of the currency declined and prices rose.

Foreign war beginning in the fall of 1791 also challenged stability. Some moderate political leaders welcomed war as a blessing in disguise, since it could divert the attention of the masses away from problems at home and could promote loyalty to the Revolution. Others envisioned war as a great crusade to bring revolutionary principles to oppressed peoples throughout Europe. The king and queen, trapped by the Revolution, saw war as their only hope of liberation. Louis XVI could be rightfully restored as the leader of a France defeated by the sovereigns of Europe. Others opposed the war, believing it would destabilize the Revolution. France must solve its problems at home, they argued, before fighting a foreign enemy. Louis, however, encouraged those ministers and advisers eager for battle. In April 1792 France declared war against Austria.

Individuals, events, economic realities, and the nature of politics conspired against the success of the first constitutional experiment. The king's attempt to flee France and the Revolution in the summer of 1791 seriously wounded the attempt at compromise. Many feared that the goals of the Revolution could not be preserved in a country at war and with a king of dubious loyalties.

$\mathcal{E}$xperimenting with Democracy

A political universe populated by individual citizens replaced the eighteenth-century world of subjects loyal to their king. This new construction of politics in which all individuals were equal ran counter to prevailing ideas about collective identities defined in guilds and orders. Before the Revolution, public opinion was being voiced outside of traditional institutions—in cafés, salons, and philosophical societies. French provincial academies sponsored a dynamic intellectual life as centers for debate over capital punishment, civic virtue, and the best form of government. Nobles and bourgeois met in these provincial academies to talk about government, power, and the means of social improvement.

New forms of social intercourse fostered the growth of democratic ideas and the emergence of a new political culture that was both progressive and democratic and considered individuals as perfectible. Political documents, like the Constitution of 1791, reflected these changes to some extent. But the revolutionaries intended to do more than reallocate political power: They aimed to change the ways people thought, talked, and lived. People needed new symbols to replace those that had been repudiated. They needed new words to talk about new political realities. The Revolution created its own calendar, setting the beginning of accounted time in the revolutionary era. The first day of the first year of the rest of history was 22 September 1792—the beginning of the Year I. People now addressed each other familiarly as *tu* instead of the more formal *vous* as the vague concepts of liberty, equality, and fraternity took root.

The French Revolution was a school for the French nation. People on all levels of society learned politics by doing it. In the beginning, experience helped. The elites, both noble and bourgeois, had served in government and administration. But the rules of the game under the old regime had been very different, with birth determining power. After 1789 all men were declared free and equal, in opportunity if not in rights. Men of ability and talent, who had served as middlemen for the privileged elite under the old regime, now claimed power as their due. Many of them were lawyers, educated in the rules and regulations of the society of orders. They experienced firsthand the problems of the exercise of power in the old regime and had their own ideas about reform. But the school of the Revolution did not remain the domain of a special class. Women demanded their places. Workers seized their rights. And because of the inherent contradictions of representation and participation, experimenting with democracy led to outcomes that did not look very democratic at all.

Declaring Political Rights

Sounding a refrain similar to that of the American Declaration of Independence, the *Declaration of the Rights of Man and Citizen* was adopted by the National Assembly on 26 August 1789. The document amalgamated a variety of Enlightenment ideas drawn from the works of political philosophy, including those of Locke and Montesquieu. "Men are born and remain free and equal in rights. Social distinctions may be based only on common utility." Perhaps most significant of all was the attention given to property, which was declared a "sacred and inviolable," "natural," and "imprescriptable" right of man.

In the year of tranquility that followed the violent summer of 1789, the new politicians set themselves the task of creating institutions based on the principle of liberty and others embodied in the *Declaration of the Rights of Man and Citizen*. The result was the Constitution of 1791, a documentary monument to the belief in a progressive constitutional monarchy. A king accountable to an elected parliamentary body would lead France into a prosperous and just age. The constitution acknowledged the people's sovereignty as the source of political power. It also enshrined the principle of property by making voting rights dependent on property ownership. All men might be equal before the law, but by the Constitution of 1791 only wealthy men had the right to vote for representatives and hold office.

All titles of nobility were abolished. In the early period of the Revolution, civil liberties were extended to Protestants and Jews, who had been persecuted under the old regime. Previously excluded groups were granted freedom of thought and worship and full civil liberties. More reluctantly, slavery in the colonies was outlawed in 1794. Slave unrest in Saint Domingue (modern-day Haiti) had coincided with the political conflicts of the Revolution and exploded in rebellion in 1791, driving the revolutionaries in Paris to support black independence although it was at odds with French colonial interests. Led by Toussaint L'Ouverture (1743–1803), black rebels worked to found an independent Haitian state, which was declared in 1804. But the concept of equality with regard to race remained incompletely integrated with revolutionary principles, and Napoleon reestablished slavery in the French colonies in 1802.

Men were the subject of these newly defined rights. No references to women or their rights appear in the constitutions or the official Declarations of Rights. Women's organizations agitated for an equitable divorce law, and divorce was legalized in September 1792. Women were critical actors in the Revolution from its very inception and their presence shaped and directed the outcome of events, as the women's march to Versailles in 1789 made clear. The Marquis de Condorcet (1743–1794), elected to the Legislative Assembly in 1791, was one of the first to chastise the revolutionaries for overlooking the political rights of women who, he pointedly observed, were half of the human race. "Either no individual of the human race has genuine rights, or else all have the same; and he who votes against the right of another, whatever the religion, color, or sex of that other, has henceforth abjured his own." Condorcet argued forcefully but unsuccessfully for the right of women to be educated. Women's talents, he warned, were slumbering under the ignorance of neglect.

"Woman, wake up!" In such a manner did Olympe de Gouges (d. 1793), a self-educated playwright and the daughter of a butcher, address French women in 1791. Aware that women were being denied the new rights of liberty and property extended to all men by the *Declaration of the Rights of Man and Citizen*, Gouges composed a *Declaration of the Rights of Woman and Citizen*, modeled on the 1789 document. "Article One. Woman is born free and remains equal in rights to man." Women are equal to men before the law in citizenship, duties, and property rights. "The right of property is inviolable and sacred to both sexes, jointly or separately." Gouges spoke out for the freedom of slaves and for women's political rights. She foreshadowed her own demise for her political beliefs at the mercy of revolutionary justice when she wrote, "Woman has the right to mount the scaffold; she must equally have the right to mount the rostrum."

The Second Revolution: The Revolution of the People

The first revolution of 1789 through the beginning of 1792 was based on liberty—the liberty to compete, to own, and to succeed. The second revolution that began in 1792 took equality as its rallying cry. This was the revolution of the working people of French cities. The popular movement that spearheaded political action in 1792 was committed to equality of rights in a way not characteristic of the leaders of the Revolution of 1789. Urban workers were not benefiting from the Revolution, but they had come to believe in their own power as political beings. Organized on the local level into sections, craft workers in cities identified themselves as *sans-culottes*, literally those who did not wear knee breeches, to distinguish themselves from the privileged elite.

On 10 August 1792, the people of Paris stormed the Tuileries, chanting their demands for "Equality!" and "Nation!" The people tramped across the silk sheets of the king's bed and broke his fine furniture, reveling in the private chambers of the royal family. Love and respect for the king had vanished. What the people of Paris demanded now was universal manhood suffrage and participation in a popular democracy. Working people were now acting independently of other factions, and the bourgeois political leadership became quickly aware of the need to scramble.

Who constituted the popular movement? The self-designated sans-culottes were the working men and women of Paris. Some were wealthier than others, some were wage earners, but all shared a common identity as consumers in the marketplace. They hated the privileged (*les gros*), who appeared to be profiting at the expense of the people. The sans-culottes wanted government power to be decentralized, with neighborhoods ruling themselves through sectional organizations. When they invaded the Tuileries Palace on the morning of 10 August, the sans-culottes did so in the name of the people. They saw themselves as patriots whose duty it was to brush the monarchy aside. The people were now a force to be reckoned with and feared.

"Terror Is the Order of the Day"

Political factions characterized revolutionary politics from the start. The terms *Left* and *Right*, which came to represent opposite ends of the political spectrum, originated in a description of where people sat in the Assembly in relation to the podium. The arrest and trial of Louis XVI for treason, followed by his execution on the guillotine in January 1793, irrevocably polarized politics. As the royalist Right was weakened and eliminated, political factions within the new legislative body, the National Convention, were described in terms borrowed from geography. The Mountain, sitting in the upper benches on the left, was made up of members of the Jacobin Club (named for its meeting place in an abandoned monastery). The Jacobins were the most radical element in the National Convention, supporting democratic solutions and speaking in favor of the cause of people in the streets. The Plain held the moderates, who were concerned with maintaining public order against popular unrest. Many members of the Plain came to be called Girondins in the mistaken belief that they originated in the Gironde département of France.

Both Girondins and Jacobins were from the middle ranks of the bourgeoisie and both groups were dedicated to the principles of the Revolution. At first the two groups were more similar than different. Although controlling the ministries, the Girondins began to lose their hold on the Revolution and the war. The renewed European war fragmented the democratic movement, and the Girondins, unable to control violence at home, saw political control slipping away. They became prisoners of the Revolution when 80,000 armed Parisians surrounded the National Convention in June 1793.

Girondin power had been eroding in the critical months between August 1792 and June 1793. A new leader was working quietly and effectively behind the scenes to weld a partnership between the popular movement of sans-culottes and the Jacobins. He was Maximilien Robespierre (1758–1794), leader of the Mountain and the Jacobin Club. Robespierre was typical of the new breed of revolutionary politician. Only 31 years old in 1789, he wrote mediocre poems and attended the local provincial academy to discuss the new ideas, when he was not practicing law in his hometown of Arras. Elected to the Estates-General, he joined the Jacobin Club and quickly rose to become its leader. He was willing to take controversial stands on issues: Unlike most of his fellow members of the Mountain, he opposed the war in 1792. Although neither an original thinker nor a compelling orator, Robespierre discovered with the Revolution that he was a stunning political tactician. He gained a following and learned how to manipulate it. It was he who engineered the Jacobin replacement of the Girondins as leaders of the government.

Robespierre's chance for real power came when he assumed leadership of the Committee of Public Safety in July 1793. Due to the threat of internal anarchy and external war, the elected body, the National Convention, yielded political control to the 12-man Committee of Public Safety that ruled dictatorially under Robespierre's direction. The Great Committee, as it was known at the time, orchestrated the Reign of Terror (1793–1794), a period of systematic state repression that meted out justice in the people's name. Summary trials by specially created revolutionary tribunals were followed by the swift execution of the guilty under the blade of the guillotine.

Influenced by the *Social Contract* (1762) and other writings of Jean-

Jacques Rousseau, Robespierre believed that sovereignty resided with the people. For him individual wills and even individual rights did not matter when faced with the will of the nation. As head of the Great Committee, Robespierre oversaw a revolutionary machinery dedicated to economic regulation, massive military mobilization, and a punitive system of revolutionary justice characterized by the slogan, "Terror is the order of the day." Militant revolutionary committees and revolutionary tribunals were established in the départements to identify traitors and to mete out the harsh justice that struck hardest against those members of the bourgeoisie who were perceived as opponents of the government. The civil war, which raged most violently in the Vendée in the west of France, consisted often of primitive massacres that sent probably a quarter of a million people to their deaths. The bureaucratized Reign of Terror was responsible for about forty thousand executions in a nine-month period.

The Cult of the Supreme Being, a civic religion influenced by Rousseau's ideas about nature, followed de-Christianization. The cathedral of Notre Dame de Paris was turned into the Temple of Reason, and the new religion established its own festivals to undermine the persistence of Catholicism. The cult was one indication of the Reign of Terror's attempt to create a new moral universe of revolutionary values.

Conspicuously absent from the summit of political power were women. After 1793 Jacobin revolutionaries, who were willing to empower the popular movement of workers, turned against women's participation and denounced it. Women's associations were outlawed and the Society of Revolutionary Republican Women was disbanded. Olympe de Gouges was guillotined. Women were made unfit for political participation, the Jacobins declared, by their biological functions of reproduction and child rearing. Rousseau's ideas about family policy were probably more influential than his political doctrines. His best-selling books, *La Nouvelle Héloïse* (1761) and *Émile* (1762), were moral works that transformed people's ideas about family life. Under his influence, the reading public came to value a separate and private sphere of domestic and conjugal values. Following Rousseau's lead, Robespierre and the Jacobins insisted that the role of women as mothers was incompatible with women's participation in the political realm.

Robespierre attacked his critics to the Left and to the Right, thereby undermining the support he needed to stay in power. He abandoned the alliance with the popular movement that had been so important in bringing him to power. Robespierre's enemies—and he had many—were able to break the identification between political power and the will of the people that Robespierre had established. As a result, he was branded a traitor by the same process that he had enforced against many of his own enemies and friends. He saved France from foreign occupation and internal collapse but he could not save democracy through terror. In the summer of 1794, Robespierre was guillotined. The Reign of Terror ceased with his death.

The Revolution did not end with the fall of Robespierre, but his execution initiated a new phase. For some, democracy lost its legitimacy. The popular

The French Revolution

August 1788	Louis XVI announces meeting of Estates-General to be held May 1789
5 May 1789	Estates-General convenes
17 June 1789	Third Estate declares itself the National Assembly
20 June 1789	Oath of the Tennis Court
14 July 1789	Storming of the Bastille
20 July 1789	Revolution of peasantry begins
26 August 1789	*Declaration of the Rights of Man and Citizen*
5 October 1789	Parisian women march to Versailles; force Louis XVI to return to Paris
February 1790	Monasteries, convents dissolved
July 1790	Civil Constitution of the Clergy
June 1791	Louis XVI and family attempt to flee Paris; are captured and returned
April 1792	France declares war on Austria
10 August 1792	Storming of the Tuileries
22 September 1792	Revolutionary calendar implemented
January 1793	Louis XVI executed
July 1793	Robespierre assumes leadership of Committee of Public Safety
1793–1794	Reign of Terror
1794	Robespierre guillotined
1799	Napoleon overthrows the Directory and seizes power

movement was reviled and sans-culotte became a term of derision. Jacobins were forced underground. Price controls were abolished, resulting in extreme hardship for most urban residents. Out of desperation in April 1795, the Jacobins and the sans-culottes renewed their alliance and united to demand "Bread and the Constitution of 1793." The politics of bread had never been more accurately captured in slogan. But their demands went unheeded and the popular revolution was suppressed.

The End of the Revolution

The Revolution that had begun with a bang ended with a whimper. In the four years after Robespierre's fall, a new government by committee called the Directory appeared to offer mediocrity, caution, and opportunism, in place of the idealism and action of the early years of the Revolution. No successor to Robespierre stepped forward to command center stage; there were no heroes like Lafayette or the great Jacobin orator Georges-Jacques Danton (1759–1794) to inspire patriotic fervor. Nor were there women like Olympe de Gouges to demand in the public arena equal rights for women. Most people, numbed after years of change, barely noticed that the Revolution was over. Ordinary men in parliamentary institutions effectively did the day-to-day job of running the government. They tried to steer a middle path between royalist resurgence and popular insurrection. Ironically, this nearly forgotten period in the history of the French Revolution was the fulfillment of the liberal hopes of 1789 for a stable constitutional rule.

The Directory, however, continued to be dogged by European war. A mass army of conscripts and volunteers had successfully extended France's power and frontiers. France expelled foreign invaders and annexed territories, including Belgium, while increasing its control in Holland, Switzerland, and Italy. But the expansion of revolutionary France was expensive and increasingly unpopular. Military defeats and the corruption of the Directory undermined government control. The Directory might have succeeded in the slow accretion of a parliamentary tradition. But reinstatement of conscription in 1798 met with widespread protest and resistance. No matter what their political leanings, people were weary. The people turned to those who promised stability and peace. Ironically, the savior they found was a military man who plunged France into 16 more years of intermittent war.

$\mathcal{T}$he Reign of Napoleon, 1799–1815

Napoleon is one of those individuals about whom one can say that if he had not lived, history would have been different. He left his mark on an age and on a continent. The great debate that rages to this day about Napoleon revolves around the question of whether he fulfilled the aims of the Revolution or perverted them. In his return to a monarchical model, Napoleon resembled the enlightened despots of eighteenth-century Europe. In a modern sense, he was also a dictator, manipulating the French people through a highly centralized administrative apparatus. He locked French society into a program of military expansionism that depleted its human and material resources. Yet, in spite of destruction and war, he dedicated his reign to building a French state according to the principles of the Revolution.

Bonaparte Seizes Power

In Paris in 1795 a young, penniless, and unknown military officer moved among the wealthy and the beautiful of Parisian society and longed for fame. Already

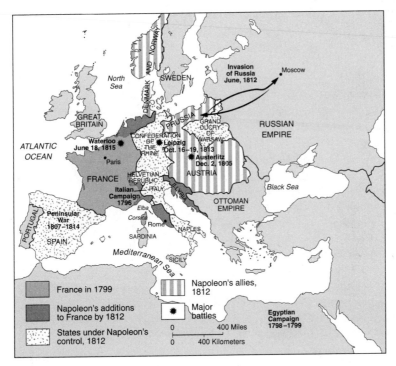

Napoleon's Empire

nicknamed at school "the Little Corporal" on account of his short stature, he was snubbed because of his background and ridiculed for his foreign accent. His story is typical of all stories of thwarted ambition. Yet the outcome of this story is unique. Within four years this young man had become ruler of France.

Napoleon Bonaparte (1769–1821) was a true child of the eighteenth century. He shared the philosophes' belief in a rational and progressive world. Napoleon was born into an Italian noble family in Corsica, which until a few months before his birth was part of the Republic of Genoa. He secured a scholarship to the French military school at Brienne, graduating in 1784. He then spent a year at the Military Academy in Paris, and received a commission as a second lieutenant of artillery in January 1786.

The Revolution changed everything for him. First, it opened up careers previously restricted by birth, including those in the military, to talent. Second, the Revolution made new posts available when aristocratic generals defected and crossed over to the enemy side both before and after the execution of the king. Finally, the Revolution created great opportunities for military men to test their mettle. Foreign war and civil war required military leaders devoted to the Revolution.

Bonaparte's early career seemed a web of contradictions. Forced to flee Corsica because he had sided with the Jacobins, he coolly crushed Parisian protesters who rioted against the Directory in 1795. His highly publicized campaigns in Egypt and Syria made him a hero at home as a defender of the government. Above all, his victories in the Italian campaign in 1796–1797 launched his political career. As he extended French rule into central Italy, he became the embodiment of revolutionary values and energy. In 1799 he readily joined a conspiracy that pulled down the Directory, the government he had earlier preserved, and became the First Consul of a triumvirate of consuls.

Napoleon set out to secure his position of power by eliminating his enemies on the Left and weakening those on the Right. He guaranteed the security of property acquired in the Revolution, a move that undercut the royalists, who wanted to return property to its original owners. Through policing forces and special criminal courts, law and order prevailed and civil war subsided. The First Consul promised a balanced budget and appeared to deliver it. Bonaparte spoke of healing the nation's wounds, especially those opened by religious grievances caused by de-Christianization during the Revolution. Realizing the importance of religion in maintaining domestic peace, Napoleon reestablished relations with the pope in 1801 in the Concordat, which recognized Catholicism as the religion of the French and restored the Roman Catholic hierarchy.

Napoleon's popularity as First Consul flowed from his military and political successes and his religious reconciliation. He had come to power in 1799 by appealing for the support of the army. In 1802 Napoleon decided to extend his power by calling for a plebiscite in which he asked the electorate to

The 1804 coronation of Napoleon by Jacques-Louis David. Pope Pius VII is seated behind the emperor, who is about to place a crown on the head of Josephine. Napoleon later ordered David to alter the painting to show the pope's hand raised in blessing.

vote him First Consul for life. Public support was overwhelming. An electoral landslide gave Napoleon greater political power than any of his Bourbon predecessors. Using revolutionary mechanisms, Napoleon laid the foundation for a new dynasty.

War and More War

Napoleon was at war or preparing for war during his entire reign. His military successes, real and apparent, before 1799 had been crucial in his bid for political power. By 1802 he had signed favorable treaties with both Austria and Great Britain. He appeared to deliver a lasting peace and to establish France as the dominant power in Europe. But the peace was short lived. In 1803 France embarked on an 11-year period of continuous war. Under Napoleon's command, the French army delivered defeat after defeat to the European powers. Austria fell in 1805, Prussia in 1806, and the Russian armies of Alexander I were defeated at Friedland in 1807. In 1808 Napoleon invaded Spain in order to drive out British expeditionary forces intent on invading France. Spain became a satellite kingdom in the French Empire, although the conflict continued.

Britain was the one exception to the string of Napoleonic victories. Napoleon initially considered sending a French fleet to invade the island nation. Lacking the strength necessary to achieve this, he turned to economic warfare and blockaded European ports against British trade. Beginning in 1806 the Continental System, as the blockade was known, erected a structure of protection for French manufactures in all continental European markets. The British responded to the tariff walls and boycotts with a naval blockade that succeeded in cutting French commerce off from its Atlantic markets. The Continental System did not prove to be the decisive policy that Napoleon had planned: The British economy was not broken and the French economy did not flourish when faced with restricted resources and the persistence of a black market in smuggled goods.

Still, by 1810 the French leader was master of the Continent. French armies had extended revolutionary reforms and legal codes outside France and brought with them civil equality and religious toleration. They had also drained defeated countries of their resources and had inflicted the horrors of war with armies of occupation, forced billeting, and pillage. Napoleon's empire extended across Europe, with only a diminished Austria, Prussia, and Russia remaining independent. He placed his relatives and friends on the thrones of the new satellite kingdoms of Italy, Naples, Westphalia, Holland, and Spain.

Peace at Home

Napoleon measured domestic prosperity in terms of the stability of his reign. Through the 1802 plebiscite that voted him first consul for life, he maintained the charade of constitutional rule while he ruled as virtual dictator. In 1804 he abandoned all pretense and had himself proclaimed emperor of the French. Mimicking the rituals of kingship, he staged his own coronation and that of his wife Josephine at the cathedral of Notre Dame de Paris. Breaking the tradition set by Charlemagne, Napoleon took the crown from the hands of Pope Pius VII (1800–1823) and placed it on his own head.

Secure in his regime, surrounded by a new nobility he created based on military achievement and talent, and that he rewarded with honors, Napoleon set about implementing sweeping reforms in every area of government. He recognized the importance of science for both industry and war. The Revolution had removed an impediment to the development of a national market by creating a uniform system of weights and measures—the metric system, which was established in 1799. But Napoleon felt the need to go further. To assure French predominance in scientific research and application, Napoleon became a patron of science, supporting important work in the areas of physics and chemistry. Building for the future, Napoleon made science a pillar in the new structure of higher education.

The Directory had restored French prosperity through stabilization of the currency, fiscal reform, and support of industry. Napoleon's contribution to the French economy was the much needed reform of the tax system. He authorized the creation of a central banking system. French industries flourished under the protection of the state. The blockade forced the development of new domestic crops like beet sugar and indigo, which became substitutes for colonial products. Napoleon extended the infrastructure of roads so necessary for the expansion of national and European markets.

Perhaps his greatest achievement was the codification of law, a task begun under the Revolution. Combined with economic reforms, the new Napoleonic Code facilitated trade and the development of commerce by regularizing contractual relations and protecting property rights and equality before the law. The civil laws of the new code carved out a family policy characterized by hierarchy and subordination. Married women were neither independent nor equal to men in ownership of property, custody of children, and access to divorce. Women also lacked political rights. In the Napoleonic Code, women, like children, were subjected to paternal authority. The Napoleonic philosophy of woman's place is well captured in an anecdote told by Madame Germaine de Staël (1766–1817), a leading intellectual of her day. As the daughter of Jacques Necker, the Swiss financier and adviser to Louis XVI at the time of the Revolution, she had been educated in Enlightenment ideas from an early age. On finding herself seated next to Napoleon at a dinner party, she asked him what was very likely a self-interested question: Whom did he consider the greatest woman, alive or dead? Napoleon had no name to give her, but he responded without pausing, "The one who has had the most children."

Napoleon turned his prodigious energies to every aspect of French life. He encouraged the arts while creating a police force. He had monuments built but did not forget about sewers. He organized French administrative life in a fashion that has endured. In place of the popular democratic movement, he offered his own singular authority. In place of elections, clubs, and free associations, he gave France plebiscites and army service. To be sure, Napoleon believed in constitutions, but he thought they should be "short and obscure." For Napoleon the great problem of democracy was its unpredictability. His regime solved that problem by eliminating choices.

Decline and Fall

Militarily, Napoleon went too far. The first cracks in the French facade began to show in the Peninsular War (1808–1814) with Spain, as Spanish guerrilla tactics proved costly for French troops. But Napoleon's biggest mistake, the one that shattered the myth of his invincibility, occurred when he decided to invade Russia in June 1812. Having decisively defeated Russian forces in 1807, Napoleon entered into a peace treaty with Tsar Alexander I that guaranteed Russian allegiance to French policies. But Alexander repudiated the Continental System in 1810 and appeared to be preparing for his own war against France. Napoleon seized the initiative, sure that he could defeat Russian forces once again. With an army of 500,000 men, Napoleon moved deep into Russia in

This 1835 painting by De Boisdenier depicts the suffering of Napoleon's Grand Army on the retreat from Moscow. The Germans were to meet a similar fate over one hundred years later when they invaded Russia without adequate winter clothing.

the summer of 1812. The tsar's troops fell back in retreat. It was a strange war, one that pulled the French army to Moscow like a bird following bread crumbs. When Napoleon and his men entered Moscow in September, they found a city in flames. The people of Moscow had destroyed their own city to deprive the French troops of winter quarters.

Napoleon's men found themselves facing a severe Russian winter without overcoats, without supplies, and without food. The Russian strategy has become legendary. The Russians destroyed grain and shelter that might be of use to the French. Napoleon and his starving and frostbitten troops were forced into retreat. Fewer than one hundred thousand men made it back to France.

The empire began to crumble. Britain, unbowed by the Continental System, remained Napoleon's sworn enemy. Prussia joined Great Britain, Sweden, Russia, and Austria in opposing France anew. In the Battle of Nations at Leipzig in October 1813, France was forced to retreat. Napoleon refused a negotiated peace and fought on until the following March, when the victorious allies marched down the streets of Paris and occupied the French capital. Deserted by his allies, Napoleon abdicated in April 1814, in favor of his young son, the titular king of Rome (1811–1832). When the allies refused to accept the young "Napoleon II," the French called on the Bourbon Louis XVIII and crowned him king. Napoleon was then exiled to the Mediterranean island of Elba.

Still, it was not quite the end for Napoleon. While the European heads of state sat in Vienna trying to determine the future of Europe and France's place in it, Napoleon returned from his exile on Elba. On 15 June 1815, Napoleon once again and for the final time confronted the European powers in one of the most famous battles in history—Waterloo. With 125,000 loyal French forces, Napoleon seemed within hours of reestablishing the French Empire in Europe, but the defeat of his forces was decisive. Napoleon's return proved brief—it lasted only 100 days. He was exiled to the island of Saint Helena in the South Atlantic. For the next six years, Napoleon wrote his memoirs under the watchful eyes of his British jailers. He died on 5 May 1821.

The period of revolution and empire from 1789 to 1815 radically changed the face of France. A new, more cohesive elite of bourgeois and nobles emerged, sharing power based on wealth and status. Ownership of land remained a defining characteristic of both old and new elites. A new state bureaucracy, built on the foundations of the old, expanded and centralized state power.

The people as sovereign now legitimated political power. Napoleon at his most imperial never doubted that he owed his existence to the people. In this sense, Napoleon was the king of the Revolution—an apparently contradictory fusion of old forms and new ideology. Napoleon channeled democratic forces into enthusiasm for empire. He learned his lessons from the failure of the Bourbon monarchy and the politicians of the Revolution. For 16 years Napoleon successfully reconciled the old regime with the new France. Yet he could not resolve the essential problem of democracy: the relationship

The Reign of Napoleon

1799	Napoleon establishes consulate, becomes First Consul
1800	Plebiscite recognizes Napoleon First Consul
1801	Napoleon reestablishes relations with pope, restores Roman Catholic hierarchy
1802	Plebiscite approves Napoleon's consulship for life
1804	Napoleon proclaims himself emperor of the French
1806	Continental System implemented
1808–1814	France engaged in Peninsular War with Spain
June 1812	Napoleon invades Russia
September 1812	French army reaches Moscow, is trapped by Russian winter
1813	Napoleon defeated at Battle of Nations at Leipzig
March 1814	Napoleon abdicates and goes into exile on island of Elba
March 1815	Napoleon escapes Elba and attempts to reclaim power
15 June 1815	Napoleon is defeated at Waterloo and exiled to island of Saint Helena

between the will of the people and the exercise of political power. The picture in 1815 was not dramatically different from the situation in 1789. The Revolution might be over, but changes fueled by the revolutionary tradition were just beginning. The struggle for a workable democratic culture recurred in France for another century and elsewhere in Europe through the twentieth century.

Suggestions for Further Reading

The Crisis of the Old Regime in France, 1715–1788

C. B. A. Behrens, *Society, Government, and the Enlightenment* (New York: Harper & Row, 1985). A comparative study of eighteenth-century France and Prussia, focusing on the relationship between government and the ruling classes, that explains how pressures for change in both countries led to different outcomes: revolution in France, and reform in Prussia.

Olwen Hufton, *The Poor in Eighteenth-Century France, 1750–1789* (Oxford, England: Clarendon, 1974). Examines the lives of the poor before the Revolution and the institutions that attempted to deal with the problem of poverty.

---

*Indicates paperback edition available.

Olwen Hufton, *Europe: Privilege and Protest, 1730–1789* (Sussex, England: The Harvester Press, 1980). An overview of the impact of rapid social, ideological, and economic changes on the concept and exercise of privilege.

*Daniel Roche, *The People of Paris* (Berkeley: University of California Press, 1987). An essay on popular culture in the eighteenth century, in which the author surveys the lives of the Parisian popular classes—servants, laborers, and artisans—and examines their housing, furnishing, dress, and leisure activities.

Isser Woloch, *Eighteenth-Century Europe: Tradition and Progress, 1715–1789* (New York: W.W. Norton, 1982). A discussion of eighteenth-century Europe, comparing social, economic, political, and intellectual developments elsewhere in Europe to the French experience, with special attention to cultural aspects, such as popular beliefs and religion.

The French Revolution and the End of the Old Regime

François Furet and Denis Richet, *The French Revolution* (New York: Macmillan, 1970). Two experts on the French Revolution present a detailed overview of the period from 1789 to 1798, when Bonaparte returned to Paris.

*Georges Lefebvre, *The Great Fear of 1789* (New York: Pantheon, 1973). This classic study analyzes the rural panic that swept through parts of France in the summer of 1789. The Great Fear is presented as a distinct episode in the opening months of the Revolution, with its own internal logic.

*Michel Vovelle, *The Fall of the French Monarchy* (Cambridge, England: Cambridge University Press, 1984). A social history of the origins and early years of the Revolution beginning with a brief examination of the old regime and paying special attention to social and economic changes initiated by the Revolution, the role of the popular classes, and the creation of revolutionary culture.

Experimenting with Democracy

*François Furet, *Interpreting the French Revolution* (Cambridge, England: Cambridge University Press, 1981). A series of essays challenging many of the assumptions concerning the causes and outcome of the Revolution and reviewing the historiography of the Revolution. The author argues that political crisis, not class conflict, was the Revolution's primary cause and that revolutionary ideas concerning democracy are central to an understanding of the Terror.

*Lynn Hunt, *Politics, Culture, and Class in the French Revolution* (Berkeley: University of California Press, 1984). A study of the Revolution as the locus of the creation of modern political culture. The second half of the book examines the social composition and cultural experiences of the new political class that merged in the Revolution.

*Joan R. Landes, *Women and the Public Sphere* (Ithaca, NY: Cornell University Press, 1988). Landes examines the genesis of the modern notion of the public sphere from a feminist perspective and argues that within the revolutionary process women were relegated to the private sphere of the domestic world.

*Albert Soboul, *The Sans-Culottes* (New York: Anchor, 1972). An exhaustive study of the artisans who composed the core of popular political activism in revolutionary Paris. The political demands and ideology of the sans-culottes are examined with the composition, culture, and actions of the popular movement during the Revolution.

The Reign of Napoleon, 1799–1815

*Louis Bergeron, *France Under Napoleon* (Princeton, NJ: Princeton University Press, 1981). An analysis of the structure of Napoleon's regime, its social bases of support, and its opponents.

Isser Woloch, *The French Veteran from the Revolution to the Restoration* (Chapel Hill: University of North Carolina Press, 1979). Examines the social impact of revolutionary and Napoleonic policies by concentrating on the changing fortunes of war veterans.

17

Industrial Europe

Portrait of an Age

The Normandy train has reached Paris. The coast and the capital are once again connected. Passengers in their city finery disembark and are greeted by others who have awaited their scheduled arrival. Workers stand ready to unload freight, porters to carry luggage. Steam billows forth from the resting engine, which is the object of all human activity. The engine stares at us as enigmatically as any character in a Renaissance portrait. We hardly think to ask what lies behind the round black face with its headlight for an eye and chimney for a snout. Yet the train that has arrived in *La Gare Saint-Lazarre* by Claude Monet (1840–1926) is as much the central character in this portrait of the industrial age as was any individual in portraits of ages past.

The train's iron bulk dwarfs the people around it. Indeed, iron dominates our attention. Tons of it are in view. The rails, the lampposts, the massive frame of the station, no less than the train itself, are all formed from iron—pliable, durable, inexpensive iron, the miracle product of industrialization. The iron station with its glass panels became as central a feature of nineteenth-century cities as were stone cathedrals in the Middle Ages. Railway stations changed the shape of urban settings just as railway travel changed the lives of millions of people.

There had never been anything like it before. Ancient Romans had hitched four horses to their chariots; nineteenth-century Europeans hitched four horses to their stagecoaches. The technology of overland transportation had hardly changed in 2000 years. Coach journeys were long, uncomfortable, and expensive. They were governed by the elements and the muddy rutted roads, which caused injuries to humans and horses with alarming regularity. First-

class passengers rode inside, where they were jostled against one another and breathed the dust that the horses kicked up in front of them. Second-class passengers rode on top, braving the elements and risking life and limb in an accident.

Railway travel was a quantum leap forward. It was faster, cheaper, and safer. Overnight it changed conceptions of time, space, and, above all, of speed. People could journey to what once were distant places in a single day. Voyages became trips, and the travel holiday was born. Commerce was transformed, as was the way in which it was conducted. Large quantities of goods could be shipped quickly from place to place; orders could be instantly filled. The whole notion of locality changed, as salesmen could board a morning train for what only recently had been an unreachable market. Branch offices could be overseen by regional directors, services and products could be standardized, and the gap between great and small cities and between town and countryside could be narrowed. Wherever they went, the railroads created links that had never been forged before. In Britain the railroad schedule became the source of the creation of official time. Trains that left London were scheduled to arrive at their destinations according to London time which came to be kept at the royal observatory in Greenwich. Trains carried fresh fish inland from the coasts and fresh vegetables from rural farms to city tables. Mail moved farther and more quickly; news spread more evenly. Fashionable ideas from the capital cities of Europe circulated everywhere, as did new knowledge and discoveries. The railroads brought both diversity and uniformity.

They also brought wonderment. The engine seemed to propel itself with unimaginable power and at breathtaking speed. The English actress Fanny Kemble (1809–1893) captured the sensation memorably: "You can't imagine how strange it seemed to be journeying on thus, without any visible cause of progress other than the magical machine, with its flying white breath and rhythmical, unvarying pace. I felt no fairy tale was ever half so wonderful as what I saw." For many the railroad symbolized the genius of the age in which they were living, an age in which invention, novelty, and progress were everywhere to be seen. It combined the great innovations of steam, coal, and iron that were transforming nearly every aspect of ordinary life. But for others, the railway was just as centrally a symbol of disquiet, of the passing of a way of life that was easier to understand and to control. "Seated in the old mail-coach we needed no evidence out of ourselves to indicate the velocity," wrote the English author Thomas De Quincey (1785–1859) in his obituary for the passing of horse travel. "We heard our speed, we saw it, we felt it. This speed was not the product of blind, insensate agencies, that had no sympathy to give, but was incarnated in the fiery eyeballs of the noblest among brutes."

The fruits of the railways, like the fruits of industrialization, were not all sweet. As the nineteenth century progressed, there could be no doubt that year by year one way of life was being replaced by another. More and more laborers were leaving the farms for the factories, and more and more products were being made by machines. Everywhere there was change, but it was not always or everywhere for the better. Millions of people poured into cities that mushroomed up without plan or intention. Population growth, factory labor, and ultimately the grinding poverty that they produced overwhelmed traditional means of social control. Families and communities split apart; the expectations of ordinary people were no longer predictable. Life was spinning out of control for individuals, for groups, for whole societies, an engine racing down a track that only occasionally ended as placidly as did the Normandy train at the Gare Saint-Lazarre.

*T*he Traditional Economy

For generation after generation, age after age, economic life was dominated by toil. Every activity was labor intensive. Wood for shelter or fuel was chopped with thick blunt axes. Water was drawn from deep wells by the long slow turn of a crank or dragged in buckets from the nearest stream. Everything that was consumed was pulled or pushed or lifted. French women carried soil and water up steep terraces in journeys that could take as long as seven hours. The capital that was invested in the traditional economy was human capital, and by the middle of the eighteenth century nearly eight out of ten Europeans still tilled the soil.

Though the traditional economy was dominated by agriculture, an increasing amount of labor was devoted to manufacture. The development of a secure and expanding overseas trade created a worldwide demand for consumer goods. In the countryside, small domestic textile industries grew up. Families would take in wool for spinning and weaving to supplement their income from agriculture. When times were good they would expend proportionately less effort in manufacturing; when times were bad, they would expend more. Their tasks were set by an entrepreneur who provided raw materials and paid the workers by the piece. Wages paid to rural workers were lower than those paid to urban laborers because they were not subject to guild restrictions and because they supplemented farm income. Though domestic industry increased the supply of manufactures, it demanded even more labor from an already overworked sector of the traditional economy.

By the eighteenth century the process that would ultimately transform the traditional economy was already under way. It began with the Agricultural Revolution, one of the great turning points in human history. Before it occurred, the life of every community and of every citizen was always held hostage to nature. The struggle to secure an adequate food supply was the dominant fact of life to which nearly all productive labor was dedicated. After the Agricultural Revolution, an inadequate food supply was a political rather than an economic fact of life. Fewer and fewer farmers were required to feed more and more people. In Britain, where nearly 70 percent of the population was engaged in agriculture at the end of the seventeenth century, less than 2 percent worked on farms at the end of the twentieth century. By the middle of the nineteenth century, the most advanced economies were capable of producing vast surpluses of basic commodities. The Agricultural Revolution was not an event, and it did not happen suddenly. It would not deserve the label *revolution* at all were it not for its momentous consequences: Europe's escape from the shackles of the traditional economy.

Rural Manufacture

By the end of the eighteenth century the European population was reaching the point at which another check on its growth might be expected. Between 1700 and 1800 total European population had increased by nearly 50 percent, and the rate of growth was continuing to accelerate. This vast expansion of rural population placed a grave strain on agricultural production. Decade by decade more families attempted to eke out an existence from the same amount of land. The gains made by intensive cultivation were now lost to overpopulation.

The crisis of overpopulation meant that not only were there more mouths to feed, there were more bodies to clothe. This increased the need for spun and

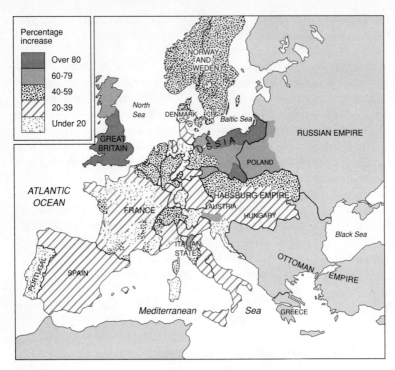

Population growth in Europe, 1800–1850

woven cloth, and thus for spinners and weavers. Traditionally, commercial cloth production was the work of urban artisans, but the expansion of the marketplace and the introduction of new fabrics, especially cotton and silk, had eroded the monopoly of most of the clothing guilds. Merchants could sell as much finished product as they could find, and the teeming rural population provided a tempting pool of inexpensive labor for anyone willing to risk the capital to purchase raw materials. Initially, farming families took manufacturing work into their homes to supplement their income. Spinning and weaving were the most common occupations, and they were treated as occasional work, reserved for the slow times in the agricultural cycle. This was known as cottage industry. It was by-employment, less important and less valuable than the vital agricultural labor that all members of the family undertook.

But by the middle of the eighteenth century, cottage industry was developing in a new direction. As land-holdings grew smaller, even good harvests did not promise subsistence to many families. This oversupply of labor was soon organized into the putting-out system, which mobilized the resources of the rural labor force for commercial production of large quantities of manufactured goods. The characteristics of the putting-out system were similar throughout Europe, whether it was undertaken by individual entrepreneurs or lords of the manor, or even sponsored by the state. The process began with the capital of the entrepreneur, which was used to purchase raw materials. These materials were "put out" to the homes of workers where the manufacture took place, most commonly spinning or weaving. The finished goods were returned to entrepreneurs, who sold them at a profit, with which they bought raw materials to begin the process anew.

Putting-out required only a low level of skill and inexpensive common tools. Rural families did their own spinning and rural villages their own weaving. Thus putting-out demanded little investment, either in plant, equipment, or education. Nor did it inevitably disrupt traditional gender-based tasks in the family economy. Spinning was women's work, weaving was done by men, and children helped at whichever task was under way.

As long as rural manufacture supplemented agricultural income, it was seen as a benefit for everyone involved—the entrepreneur, the individual worker, and the village community. But gradually the putting-out system came to dominate the lives of many rural families. Spinning and weaving became full-time occupations for families that kept no more than a small garden. But without agricultural earnings, piecework rates became starvation wages, and families unable to purchase their subsistence were forced to rely on loans from the entrepreneurs who set them at work. Long hours in dank cottages performing endlessly repetitive tasks became the lot of millions of rural inhabitants. And their numbers increased annually. While the sons of farmers waited to inherit land before they formed their families, the sons of cottage

Eighteenth-century cottage industry. The entire family participates in the preparation of the flax. Another cottager will weave the thread into cloth.

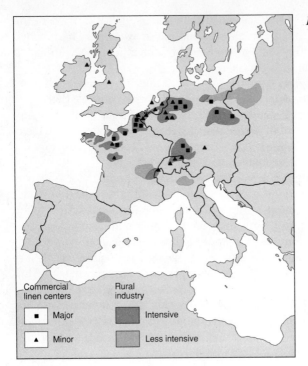

European linen industry

Commercial
linen centers

■ Major

▲ Minor

Rural
industry

Intensive

Less intensive

weavers needed only a loom to begin theirs. They could afford to marry younger and to have more children, for children could contribute to manufacturing from an early age. Consequently, the expansion of the putting-out system, like the expansion of traditional agriculture, contributed to overpopulation. The putting-out system was labor rather than capital intensive, and as long as there were ready hands to employ, there was little incentive to seek better methods or more efficient techniques.

The Agricultural Revolution

The continued growth of Europe's population necessitated an expansion of agricultural output. In most places this was achieved by intensifying traditional practices, bringing more land into production and more labor to work the land. But in the most advanced European economies, first in Holland and then in England, traditional agriculture underwent a long but dynamic transformation, an agricultural revolution. It was a revolution of technique rather than technology. Humans were not replaced by machines nor were new forms of energy substituted for human and animal muscle. Indeed, many of the methods that were to increase crop yields had been known for centuries and practiced during periods of population pressure. But they had never been practiced as systematically as they came to be from the seventeenth century onward, and they were never combined with a commercial attitude toward farming. It was the willingness and ability of owners to invest capital in their land that transformed subsistence farming into commercial agriculture.

As long as farming was practiced in open fields, there was little incentive for individual landowners to invest in improvements to their scattered strips. While the community as a whole could enclose a small field or plant some fodder crops for the animals, its ability to change traditional practice was limited. In farming villages even the smallest landholder had rights in common lands, which were jealously guarded. Rights in commons meant a place in the community itself. Commercial agriculture was more suited to large rather than small estates and was more successful when the land could be utilized in response to market conditions rather than the necessities of subsistence.

The consolidation of estates and the enclosure of fields was thus the initial step toward change. This was a long-term process that took many forms. In England, where it was to become most advanced, enclosure was already under way in the sixteenth century. Prosperous families had long been consolidating their strips in the open fields, and at some point the lord of the manor and the members of the community agreed to carve up the common fields and make the necessary exchanges to consolidate everyone's lands. Perhaps as much as three-quarters of the arable land in England was enclosed by agreement before 1760. Enclosure by agreement did not mean that the breakup of the open-field community was necessarily a harmonious process. Riots preceding or following agreed enclosures were not uncommon.

Opposition to enclosure by agreement led, in the eighteenth century, to enclosure by act of Parliament. Parliamentary enclosure was legislated by government, a government composed for the most part of large landowners. A commission would view the community's lands and divide them, usually by a prescribed formula. Between 1760 and 1815 over one and a half million acres of farmland were enclosed by act of Parliament. During the late eighteenth century the Prussian and French governments emulated this practice by ordering large tracts of land enclosed.

The enclosure of millions of acres of land was one of the largest expenses of the new commercial agriculture. Hedging or fencing off the land and plowing up the commons required extra labor beyond that necessary for basic agrarian activities. Thus many who sold the small estates that they received on the breakup of the commons remained in villages as agricultural laborers or leaseholders. But now they practiced a different form of farming. More and more agricultural activity become market oriented. Single crops were sown in large enclosed fields and exchanged at market for the mixture of goods that previously had been grown in the village. Market production turned attention from producing a balance of commodities to increasing the yield of a single one.

The first innovation was the widespread cultivation of fodder crops such as clover and turnips. Crops like clover restore nutrients to the soil as they grow, shortening the period in which land has to lie fallow. Moreover, farm animals grazing on clover or feeding on turnips return more manure to the land, further increasing its productivity. Turnip cultivation had begun in Holland and was brought to England in the sixteenth century. But it was not until the late seventeenth century that Viscount Charles "Turnip" Townshend (1675–1738) made turnip cultivation popular. Townshend and other large Norfolk landowners developed a new system of planting known as the four-course rotation, in which wheat, turnips, barley, and clover succeeded one another. This method kept the land in productive use, and both the turnip and clover crops were used to feed larger herds of animals.

The ability of farmers to increase their livestock was as important as their ability to grow more grain. Not only were horses and oxen more productive than humans—a horse could perform seven times the labor of a man while consuming only five times the food—but the animals also refertilized the land as they worked. Light fertilization of a single acre of arable land required an average of 25,000 pounds of manure. But animals competed with humans for food, especially during the winter months when little grazing was possible. To conserve grain for human consumption, lambs were led to the slaughter and the fatted calf was killed in the autumn. Thus the development of the technique of meadow floating was a remarkable breakthrough. By flooding low-lying land near streams in the winter, English and Dutch farmers could prevent the ground from freezing during their generally mild winters. When the water was drained, the land beneath it would produce an early grass crop on which the beasts could graze. This meant that more animals could be kept alive during the winter.

The relationship between animal husbandry and grain growing became another feature of commercial agriculture. In many areas farmers could choose between growing grain and pasturing animals. When prices for wool or meat were relatively higher than those for grain, fields could be left in grass for grazing. When grain prices rose, the same fields could be plowed. Consolidated enclosed estates made this convertible husbandry possible. The decision to hire field-workers or shepherds could be taken only by large agricultural employers. Whatever the relative price of grain, the open-field village continued to produce grain as its primary crop. Farmers who could convert their production in tune to the market could not only maximize their profits, they could also prevent shortages of raw materials for domestic manufactures or of foodstuffs for urban and rural workers.

Convertible husbandry was but the first step in the development of a true system of regional specialization in agriculture. Different soils and climates favored different use of the land. In southern and eastern England the soil was thin and easily depleted by grain growing. Traditionally, these light soil areas had been used almost exclusively for sheep rearing. On the other hand, the clay soils of central England, though poorly drained and hard to work, were more suited to grain growing. The new agricultural techniques reversed the pattern. The introduction of fodder crops and increased fertilization rejuvenated thin soils, and southeastern England became the nation's breadbasket. Large enclosed estates provided a surplus of grain throughout the eighteenth century. By the 1760s England was exporting enough grain to feed over half a million people. Similarly, the midland clays became the location of great sheep runs and cattle herds. Experiments in herd management, crossbreeding, and fattening all resulted in increased production of wool, milk, meat, leather, soap, and tallow for candles.

There can be no doubt about the benefits of the transformation of agricultural practices that began in Holland and England in the seventeenth century and spread slowly to all corners of the Continent over the next 200 years. Millions more mouths were fed at lower cost than ever before. In 1700 each person engaged in farming in England produced enough food for 1.7 people; in 1800 enough for 2.5. Cheaper food allowed more discretionary spending, which fueled the demand for consumer goods, which in turn employed more rural manufacturers. But there are no benefits without costs. The transformation of agriculture was also a transformation in a way of life. The open-field village was a community; the enclosed estate was a business. The plight of the rural poor was tragic enough in villages of kin and neighbors, where face-to-face charity might be returned from one generation to the next. With their scrap of land and their common rights, even the poorest villagers laid claim to a place of their own. But as landless laborers, either on farms or in rural manufacturing, they could no longer make that claim. They would soon be fodder for the factories, the "dark satanic mills" that came to disfigure the land once tilled in open-field villages. For the destitute, charity was now visited upon them in anonymous parish workhouses or in the good works of the comfortable middle class. In all of these ways the Agricultural Revolution changed the face of Europe.

$\mathcal{T}$he Industrial Revolution in Britain

Like the changes in agriculture, the changes in manufacturing that began in Britain during the eighteenth century were more revolutionary in consequence than in development. A work force that was predominantly agricultural in 1750 had become predominantly industrial a century later. A population that for centuries had centered on the south and east was now concentrated in the north and west. Liverpool, Manchester, Glasgow, and Birmingham mushroomed into giant cities. While the population of England grew by 100 percent between 1801 and 1851, from about 8.5 million to over 17 million, the populations of Liverpool and Manchester grew by over 1000 percent.

It was the replacement of animal muscle by hydraulic and mineral energy that made this continued population growth possible. Water and coal drove machinery that dramatically increased human productivity. In 1812 one woman could spin as much thread as had 200 women in 1770. What was most revolutionary about the Industrial Revolution was the wave after wave of technological innovation, a constant tinkering and improving of how things were made, which could have the simultaneous effects of cutting costs and improving quality. It was not just the great breakthrough inventions like the steam engine, the smelting of iron with coke, and the spinning jenny that were important, but also the hundreds of adjustments in technique that applied new ideas in one industry to another, that opened bottlenecks and solved problems.

The Industrial Revolution was a sustained period of economic growth and change brought about by the application of mineral energy and technological innovations to the process of manufacturing. It took place during the century between 1750 and 1850, though different industries moved at different paces, and sustained economic growth continued in Britain until the First World War. It is difficult to define the timing of the Industrial Revolution with any great precision because, unlike a political event, an economic transformation does not happen all at once. Nor are new systems and inventions ever really new. Coal miners had been using rails and wheeled carriages to move ore since the seventeenth century; in the sixteenth century "Jack of Newbury" had housed his cloth workers in a large shed. The one was the precursor of the railroad and the other precursor of the factory, but each preceded the Industrial Revolution by more than a century. Before 1750 innovations made their way slowly into general use, and after 1850 the pace of growth slowed appreciably. By then, Britain had a manufacturing economy, less than a quarter of its labor force engaged in agriculture and nearly 60 percent involved in industry, trade, and transport.

Britain First

The Industrial Revolution occurred first in Britain, but even in Britain industrialization was a regional rather than a national phenomenon. There were many areas of Britain that remained untouched by innovations in manufacturing methods and agricultural techniques, though no one remained unaffected by the prosperity that industrialization brought. This was the result of both national conditions and historical developments. When industrialization spread to the Continent it took hold—as it had in Britain—in regions where mineral resources were abundant or where domestic manufacturing was a traditional activity. There was no single model for European industrialization, however much contemporaries looked toward Britain for the key to unlock the power of economic growth. There was as much technological innovation in France, as much capital for investment in Holland. Belgium was rich in coal, while eastern Europe enjoyed an agricultural surplus that sustained an increase in population. The finest cotton in the world was made in India, the best iron was made in Sweden. Each of these factors was in some way a precondition for industrialization, but none by itself proved sufficient. Only in Britain did these circumstances meld together.

Among Britain's blessings, water was foremost. Water was its best defense, protecting the island from foreign invasion and making it unnecessary to invest in a costly standing army. Rather Britain invested heavily in its navy to maintain its commercial preeminence around the globe. The navy protected British interests in times of war and transported British wares in times of peace. Britain's position in the Asian trade made it the leading importer of cottons, ceramics, and teas. Its colonies, especially in North America, not only provided sugar and tobacco, but also formed a rich market for British manufacturing.

But the commercial advantages that water brought were not confined to oceanic trade. Britain was favored by an internal water system that tied inland communities together. In the eighteenth century, no place in Britain was more than 70 miles from the sea or more than 30 miles from a navigable river. Water transport was far cheaper than hauling goods overland; a packhorse could carry 250 pounds of goods on its back or move 100,000 pounds by walking alongside a river pulling a barge. Small wonder that river transport was one of the principal interests of merchants and traders. Beginning in the 1760s private concerns began to invest in the construction of canals, first to move coal from inland locations to major arteries and then to connect the great rivers themselves. Over the next 50 years several hundred miles of canals were built by authority of Navigation Acts, which allowed for the sale of shares to raise capital. In 1760 the Duke of Bridgewater (1736–1803) lived up to his name by completing the first great canal. It brought coal to Manchester and ultimately to Liverpool. The canal cost more than £ 250,000 and took 14 years of labor to build, but it repaid the duke and his investors many times over as an uneconomical coal field was brought into production. Not the least of the beneficiaries were the people of Manchester, where the price of coal was halved.

Coal was the second of Britain's natural blessings on which it improved. Britain's reserves of wood were nearly depleted by the eighteenth century, especially those near centers of population. Coal had been in use as a fuel for several centuries, and the coal trade between London and the northern coal pits had been essential to the growth of the capital. Coal was abundant, much of it almost at surface level along the northeastern coast, and easily trans-ported on water. The location of large coalfields along waterways was a vital condition of its early use. As canals and roadways improved, more inland coal was brought into production for domestic use. Yet it was in industry rather than in the home that coal was put to its greatest use. Here again Britain was favored, for large seams of coal were also located near large seams of iron. At first this coincidence was of little consequence, since iron was smelted by charcoal made from wood and iron foundries were located deep in forests. But ultimately ironmakers learned to use coal for fuel, and then the natural economies of having mineral, fuel, and transport in the same vicinity were given full play.

The factors that contributed to Britain's early industrialization were not only those of natural advantage. Over the course of years, Britain had developed an infrastructure for economic advancement. The transformation of domestic handicrafts to industrial production depended as much on the abilities of merchants as on those of manufacturers. The markets for domestic manufacturing had largely been overseas, where British merchants built up relationships over generations. Export markets were vital to the success of industrialization as production grew dynamically, and most ventures needed a quick turnaround of sales to reinvest their profits in continued growth. The flexibility of English trading houses would be seen in their ability to shift from reexporting eastern and North American goods to exporting British manufactures. Equally important, increased production meant increased demand for raw materials: Swedish bar iron for casting, Egyptian and American cotton for textiles, Oriental silk for luxuries. The expansion of shipping mirrored the expansion of the economy, tripling during the eighteenth century to over one million tons of cargo capacity.

The expansion of shipping, of agriculture, of investment in machines, plant, and raw material all required capital. Not only did capital have to exist, but it had to be made productive. Profits in agriculture, especially in the south and east, had somehow to be shifted to investment in industry in the north and west. The wealth of merchants, which flowed into London, had to be redistributed throughout the economy. More importantly, short-term investments had to give way to long-term financing. At the end of the seventeenth century, the creation of the Bank of England had begun the process of constructing a reliable banking system. The Bank of England dealt almost entirely with government securities, but it also served as a bill broker. It bought the debts of reputable merchants at a discount in exchange for Bank of England notes. Bank of England notes could then be exchanged between merchants, and this increased the liquidity of the English economy, especially in London. It also became the model for provincial banking by the middle of the eighteenth century.

Private family banks also grew in importance in London, handling the accounts of merchants and buying shares in profitable enterprises, of which the canals were a favorite. Regional banks, smaller and less well capitalized, began to use these private London banks as correspondents, that is, as extensions of their own banks in the city. This allowed local manufacturers and city merchants to do business with one another. The connections between the regional banks and London facilitated the flow of capital from one section of the nation to the other. In 1700 there were just 12 provincial banks; by 1790 there were nearly 300. Banks remained reluctant to invest for the long term, preferring to discount bills for a few months, but after they developed a relationship with a particular firm, they were usually willing to continue to roll the debt over. Though the banking system was vital to large enterprises, in fact the capital for most industry was raised locally, from kin and neighbors, and grew by plowing back profits into the business. At least at the beginning, manufacturers were willing to take risks and to work for small returns to ensure the survival and growth of their business.

Minerals and Metals

There could have been no Industrial Revolution without coal. It was the black gold of the eighteenth century, the fuel that fed the furnaces and turned the engines of industrial expansion. The coal produced by one miner generated as much energy as twenty horses. Coal was the first capital-intensive industry in Britain, already well developed by the seventeenth century. Owners paid the costs of sinking shafts, building roads, and erecting winding machines. Miners were brought to a pit and paid piecework for their labor. Only the very wealthy could afford to invest in coal mining, and it was by chance that British law vested mineral rights in owners rather than users of the land, as was the case on the Continent. This meant that the largest English coalfields were owned by landed families of means who were able to invest agricultural profits in mining. Britain's traditional elites thus played a crucial role in the industrial transformation of the agrarian economy from which their wealth and social standing had derived.

By far the most difficult mining problem was water. As pits were sunk deeper they reached pools of groundwater, which enlarged as the coal was stripped away from the earth. The pit acted like a riverbed and was quickly filled. Water drainage presented the greatest obstacle to deep-shaft mining. Women and children could carry the water out in large skin-lined baskets, which were attached to a winding wheel and pulled up by horses. Primitive pumps, also horse powered, had been devised for the same purpose. Neither method was efficient or effective when shafts sank deeper. In 1709 Thomas Newcomen (1663–1729) introduced a steam-driven pump, which enabled water to be sucked through a pipe directly from the pit bottom to the surface. Though the engine was expensive to build and needed tons of coal to create the steam, it could raise the same amount of water in a day as 2500 humans. Such economies of labor were enormous, and within twenty years of its introduction there were 78 engines draining coal and metal mines in England.

Innovations like Newcomen's engine helped increase output of coal at just the time that it became needed as an industrial fuel. Between 1700 and 1830 coal production increased tenfold despite the fact that deeper and more difficult seams were being worked. Eventually, the largest demand for coal came from the iron industry. In 1793 just two ironworks consumed as much coal as the entire population of Edinburgh. Like mining coal, making iron was both capital and labor intensive, requiring expensive furnaces, water-powered bellows, and mills in which forged iron could be slit into rods or rolled into sheets. Ironmaking depended on an abundance of wood, for it took the charcoal derived from ten acres of trees to refine one ton of iron ore. After the ore was mined, it was smelted into pig iron, a low-grade brittle metal. Pig iron was converted to higher quality bar iron in charcoal-powered forges that burned off some of its impurities. From bar iron came the rods and sheets used in casting household items like pots and nails or in making finer wrought-iron products like plows and armaments. Because each process in the making of iron was separate, furnaces, forges, and mills were located near their own supplies of wood. The shipping of the bulky ore, pig iron, and bar iron added substantially to its cost, and it was cheaper to import bars from Sweden than to carry them 20 miles overland.

The great innovations in the production of iron came with the development of techniques that allowed for the use of coal rather than wood charcoal in smelting and forging. As early as 1709 Abraham Darby (1678?–1717), a Quaker nailmaker, experimented with smelting iron ore with coke, coal from which most of the gas has been burned off. Iron coking greatly reduced the cost of fuel in the first stages of production, but because most ironworks were located in woodlands rather than near coal pits, the method was not widely adopted. Moreover, although coke made from coal was cheaper than charcoal made from wood, coke added its own impurities to the iron ore. Nor could it provide the intense heat needed for smelting without a large bellows. The cost of the bellows offset the savings from the coke until James Watt (1736–1819) invented a new form of steam engine in 1775.

Like most innovations of the Industrial Revolution, Watt's steam engine was an adaptation of existing technology made possible by the sophistication of techniques in a variety of fields. Although James Watt is credited with the invention of the condensing steam engine, one of the seminal creations in human history, the success of his work depended on the achievements of numerous others. Watt's introduction to the steam engine was accidental. An instrument maker in Glasgow, he was asked to repair a model of a Newcomen engine and immediately realized that it would work more efficiently if there were a separate chamber for the condensation of the steam. Though his idea was sound, Watt spent years attempting to implement it. He was continually frustrated that poor quality valves and cylinders never fit well enough together to prevent steam escaping from the engine. Watt was unable to translate his idea into a practical invention until he became partners with the Birmingham ironmaker and manufacturer Matthew Boulton (1728–1809). At Boulton's works, Watt found craft workers who could make precision engine valves, and at the foundries of John Wilkinson (1728–1808) he found workers who could bore the cylinders of his engine to exact specifications. Watt later designed the mechanism to convert the traditional up-and-down motion of the pumping engine into rotary motion, which could be used for machines and ultimately for locomotion.

Watt's engine received its first practical application in the iron industry. Wilkinson became one of the largest customers for steam engines, using them for pumping, moving wheels, and ultimately increasing the power of the blast of air in the forge. Increasing the heat provided by coke in the smelting and forging of iron led to the transformation of the industry. In the 1780s Henry Cort (1740–1800), a naval contractor, experimented with a technique for using coke as fuel in removing the impurities from pig iron. The iron was melted into puddles and stirred with rods. The gaseous carbon that was brought to the surface burned off, leaving a purer and more malleable iron than even charcoal could produce. Because the iron had been purified in a molten state, Cort reasoned that it could be rolled directly into sheets rather than first made into bars. He erected a rolling mill adjacent to his forge and combined two separate processes into one.

Puddling and rolling had an immediate impact on iron production. There was no longer any need to use charcoal in the stages of forging and rolling. From mineral to workable sheets, iron could be made entirely with coke. Ironworks moved to the coalfields, where the economies of transporting fuel and finished product were great. Moreover, the distinct stages of production were eliminated. Rather than separate smelting, forging, and finishing industries, one consolidated manufacturing process had been created. Forges, furnaces, and rolling machines were brought together and powered by steam engines. By 1808 output of pig iron had grown from 68,000 to 250,000 tons and of bar iron from 32,000 to 100,000 tons.

Cotton Is King

Traditionally British commerce was dominated by the woolen cloth trade, in which techniques of production had not changed for hundreds of years. Running water was used for cleaning and separating fleece; crude wooden wheels spun the thread; simple hand looms wove together the long warp threads and the short weft ones. It took nearly four female spinners to provide the materials for one male weaver, the tasks having long been gender-specific. During the course of the seventeenth century new fabrics appeared on the domestic market, particularly linen, silk, and cotton. It was cotton that captured the imagination of the eighteenth-century consumer, especially brightly colored, finely spun Indian cotton.

Spinning and weaving were organized as domestic industries. Work was done in the home on small inexpensive machines to supplement the income from farming. Putters-out were especially frustrated by the difficulty in obtaining yarn for weaving in the autumn when female laborers were needed for the harvest. Even the widespread development of full-time domestic manufacturers did not satisfy the increased demand for cloth. Limited output and variable quality characterized British textile production throughout the early part of the eighteenth century. The breakthrough came with technological innovation. Beginning in the mid-eighteenth century a series of new machines dramatically increased output and, for the first time, allowed English textiles to compete with Indian imports.

The first innovation was the flying shuttle, invented by John Kay (1704–1764) in the 1730s. A series of hammers drove the shuttle, which held the weft, through the stretched warp on the loom. The flying shuttle allowed weavers to work alone rather than in pairs, but it was adopted slowly for it increased the demand for spun thread, which was already in short supply. The spinning bottleneck was opened by James Hargreaves (17?–1778), who devised a machine known as the jenny. The jenny was a wooden frame containing a number of spindles around which thread was drawn by means of a hand-

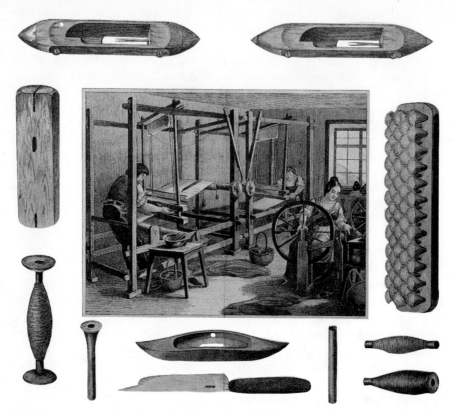

This hand-colored engraving shows the interior of a German weaver's shop around 1850. Two men are weaving at looms and two women are winding bobbins. The scene is bordered with details of tools such as shuttles and quills.

turned wheel. The first jennies allowed for the spinning of eight threads at once, and improvements brought the number to over a hundred. Jennies replaced spinning wheels by the tens of thousands. The jenny was a crucial breakthrough in redressing the balance between spinning and weaving though it did not solve all problems. Jenny-spun thread was not strong enough to be used as warp, which continued to be wheel spun. But the jenny could spin cotton in unimaginable quantities.

As is often the case with technological change, one innovation followed another. The problem set by improvements in weaving gave rise to solutions for increasing the output of spinners. The need to provide stronger warp threads posed by the introduction of the jenny was ultimately solved by the development of the water frame. It was created in 1769 by Richard Arkwright (1732–1792), whose name was also to be associated with the founding of the modern factory system. Arkwright's frame consisted of a series of water-power-driven rollers, which stretched the cotton before spinning. These stronger fibers could be spun into threads suitable for warp, and English manufacturers could finally produce an all-cotton fabric. It was not long before another innovator realized that the water frame and the jenny could be combined into a single machine, one that would produce an even finer cotton yarn than that made in India. The mule, so named because it was a cross between a frame and a jenny, was invented by Samuel Crompton (1753–1827). It was the decisive innovation in cotton production. By 1811 ten times as many threads were being spun on mules than on water frames and jennies combined.

The original mules were small machines that, like the jennies, could be used for domestic manufactures. But increasingly, the mule followed the water frame into purposely built factories, where it became larger and more expensive. The need for large rooms to house the equipment and for a ready source of running water to power it provided an incentive for the creation of factories, but secrecy provided a greater one. The original factories were called "safe-boxes," and whether they were established for the manufacture of silk or cotton, their purpose was to protect trade secrets. Innovators took out patents to prevent their inventions from being copied and fought long lawsuits to prevent their machines from being used. Though the factory was designed to protect secrets, its other benefits were quickly realized. Manufacturers could maintain control over the quality of products through strict supervision of the work force.

Richard Arkwright constructed the first cotton factories in Britain, all of which were designed to house water frames. The first was established in 1769 at Cromford near Nottingham, which was the center of stocking manufacture. The Cromford mill was a four-story building that ultimately employed over eight hundred workers.

The organization of the cotton industry into factories was one of the pivotal transformations in economic life. Domestic spinning and weaving took place in agricultural villages; factory production took place in mill towns. The location of the factory determined movements of population, and from the first quarter of the eighteenth century onward a great shift toward the northeast of England was under way. Moreover, the character of the work itself changed. The operation of heavy machinery reversed the traditional gender-based tasks. Mule spinning became men's work; hand-loom weaving was taken over by women. The mechanization of weaving took longer than that of spinning, both because of difficulties in perfecting a power loom and because of opposition to its introduction by workers known as Luddites, who organized machine-breaking riots in the 1810s. The Luddites attempted to maintain the traditional organization of their industry and the independence of their labor. For a time, hand-loom weavers managed to survive by accepting lower and lower piece rates. But their competition was like that of a horse against an automobile. In 1820 there were over 250,000 hand-loom weavers in Britain; by 1850 the number was less than 50,000.

The transformation of cotton manufacture had a profound effect on the overall growth of the British economy. It increased shipping because the raw material had to be imported, first from the Mediterranean and then from America. American cotton, especially after 1794 when American inventor Eli

Whitney (1765–1825) patented his cotton gin, fed a nearly insatiable demand. In 1750 Britain imported less than 5 million pounds of raw cotton; a century later the volume had grown to 588 million pounds. And to each pound of raw cotton, British manufacturers added the value of their technology and of their labor. By the mid nineteenth century nearly half a million people earned their living from cotton, which alone accounted for over 40 percent of the value of all British exports.

The Iron Horse

The first stage of the Industrial Revolution in Britain was driven by the production of consumer goods. Pottery, cast-iron tools, clocks, toys, and textiles, especially cottons, all were manufactured in quantities unknown in the early eighteenth century. These products fed a ravenous market at home and abroad. The greatest complaint of industrialists was that they could not get enough raw materials or fuel, nor could they ship their finished products fast enough to keep up with demand. Transportation was becoming a serious stumbling block to continued economic growth. Even with the completion of the canal network that linked the major rivers and improvement in highways and tollways, raw materials and finished goods moved slowly and uncertainly.

It was the need to ship increasing amounts of coal to foundries and factories that provided the spur for the development of a new form of transportation. Ever since the seventeenth century, coal had been moved from the seam to the pit on rails, first constructed of wood and later of iron. Broad-wheeled carts hitched to horses were as much dragged as rolled, but this still represented the most efficient form of hauling and these railways ultimately ran from the seam to the dock. By 1800 there was perhaps as much as three hundred miles of iron rail in British mines. In the same year, Watt's patent on the steam engine expired, and inventors began to apply the engine to a variety of mechanical tasks.

Richard Trevithick (1771–1833) was the first to experiment with a steam-driven carriage. George Stephenson (1781–1848), who is generally recognized as the father of the modern railroad, made two crucial improvements. In mine railways the wheels of the cart were smooth and the rail was grooved. Stephenson reversed this construction to provide better traction and less wear. Perhaps more importantly, Stephenson made the vital improvement in engine power by increasing the steam pressure in the boiler and exhausting the smoke through a chimney. In 1829 he won a £500 prize with his engine "The Rocket," which pulled a load three times its own weight at a speed of 30 miles per hour and could actually outrun a horse.

In 1830 the first modern railway, the Manchester to Liverpool line, was opened. Like the Duke of Bridgewater's canal, it was designed to move coal and bulk goods, but surprisingly its most important function came to be moving people. In its first year the Manchester-Liverpool line carried over four hundred thousand passengers, which generated double the revenue derived from freight. The railway was quicker, more comfortable, and ultimately cheaper than the coach. Investors in the Manchester-Liverpool line, who pocketed a comfortable 9.5 percent when government securities were paying 3.5 percent, learned quickly that links between population centers were as important as those between industrial sites. The London to Birmingham and London to Bristol lines were both designed with passenger traffic in mind. Railway building was one of the great boom activities of British industrialization. By 1835 Parliament had passed 54 separate acts establishing over 750 miles of railways. In 1845 over 6000 miles had been sanctioned and over 2500 miles built; by 1852 over 7500 miles of track were in use.

By the 1850s the original purpose of the railways was being realized as freight revenues finally surpassed passenger revenues. Coal was the dominant cargo shipped by rail, and the speedy efficient service continued to drive down prices. The iron and steel industries were modernized on the back of demand for rails, engines, and cast-iron seats and fittings. In peak periods—and railway building was a boom-and-bust affair—as much as quarter of the output of the rolling mills went into domestic railroads and much more into continental systems. The railways were also a massive consumer of bricks for beddings, sidings, and especially bridges, tunnels, and stations. Finally, the railways were a leading employer of labor, surpassing the textile mills in peak periods. Hundreds of thousands worked in tasks as varied as engineering and ditchdigging, for even in this most advanced industry sophisticated mechanized production went hand in hand with traditional drudgery.

Most of all, the railroads changed the nature of people's lives. Whole new concepts of time, space, and speed emerged to govern daily activities. As Henry Booth, an early railroad official, observed, "Notions which we have received from our ancestors and verified by our own experience are overthrown in a day. What was quick is now slow; what was distant is now near." The cheap railway excursion was born to provide short holidays or even daily returns. Over six million people visited London by train to view the Crystal Palace exhibition in 1851, a number equivalent to a third of the population of England and Wales. The railways did more than link places; they brought people together and helped develop a sense of national identity by speeding all forms of communication.

Entrepreneurs and Managers

The Industrial Revolution in Britain was not simply invented. Too much credit is given to a few breakthroughs and too little to the ways in which they were improved and dispersed. The Industrial Revolution was an age of gadgets when people believed that new was better than old and that there was always room for improvement. "The age is running mad after innovation," the English moralist Dr. Johnson wrote. "All the business of the world is done in a new way;

men are hanged in a new way." Societies for the advancement of knowledge sprang up all over Britain. Journals and magazines promoted new ideas and techniques. Competitions were held for the best invention of the year; prizes were awarded for agricultural achievements. Practical rather than pure science was the hallmark of industrial development.

Yet technological innovation was not the same as industrialization. A vital change in economic activity took place in the organization of industry. Putters-out with their circulating capital and hired laborers could never make the economies necessary to increase output and quality while simultaneously lowering costs. This was the achievement of industrialists, producers who owned workplace, machinery, and raw materials and who invested fixed capital by plowing back their profits. Industrial enterprises came in all sizes and shapes. A cotton mill could be started with as little as £300, or as much as £10,000. As late as 1840 less than 10 percent of the mills employed over 500 workers. Most were family concerns with under 100 employees, and many of them failed. For every story with a happy ending there was another with a sad one. When Major Edmund Cartwright (1740–1824) erected a cotton mill, he was offered a Watt steam engine built for a distiller who had gone bankrupt. He acquired his machinery at the auction of another bankrupt. Cartwright's mill, engine, and machinery ended on the auction block less than three years later. There were over thirty thousand bankruptcies in the eighteenth century, testimony both to the risks of business and the willingness of entrepreneurs to take them.

To survive against these odds, successful industrialists had to be both entrepreneur and manager. As entrepreneurs they raised capital, almost always locally from relatives, friends, or members of their church. Quakers were especially active in financing each other's enterprises. The industrial entrepreneur also had to understand the latest methods for building and powering machinery and the most up-to-date techniques for performing the work. One early manufacturer claimed "a practical knowledge of every process from the cotton-bag to the piece of cloth." Finally, entrepreneurs had to know how to market their goods. In these functions, industrial entrepreneurs developed logically from putters-out.

But industrialists also had to be managers. The most difficult task was organization of the workplace. Most gains in productivity were achieved through the specialization of function. The processes of production were divided and subdivided until workers performed a basic task over and over. The education of the work force was the industrial manager's greatest challenge. Workers had to be taught how to use and maintain their machines and disciplined to apply themselves continuously. At least at the beginning, it was difficult to staff the factories. Many employed children as young as age 7 from workhouses or orphanages who, though cheap to pay, were difficult to train and discipline. It was the task of the manager to break old habits of intermittent work, indifference to quality, and petty theft of materials. Families were preferred to individuals, for then parents could instruct and supervise their children. There is no reason to believe that industrial managers were more brutal masters than farmers or that children were treated better in workhouses than in mills. Labor was a business asset, what was sometimes called "living machinery," and its control with carrots and sticks was the chief concern of the industrial manager.

Who were the industrialists who transformed the traditional economy? Because British society was relatively open, they came from every conceivable background: dukes and orphans, merchants and salespeople, inventors and improvers. Though some went from rags to riches, like Richard Arkwright, who was the thirteenth child of a poor barber, it was extremely difficult for a laborer to acquire the capital necessary to set up a business. Wealthy landowners were prominent in capital-intensive aspects of industries, for example, owning ironworks and mines, but few established factories. Most industrialists came from the middle classes, which while comprising a third of the British population, provided as much as two-thirds of the first generation of industrialists. These included lawyers, bankers, merchants, and those already engaged in manufacturing, as well as tradespeople, shopkeepers, and self-employed craft workers. The career of every industrialist was different, as a look at two, Josiah Wedgwood and Robert Owen, will show.

Josiah Wedgwood (1730–1795) was the thirteenth child of a long-established English potting family. He worked in the potteries from childhood, but a deformed leg made it difficult for him to turn the wheel. Instead he studied the structure of the business. His head teemed with ideas for improving ceramic manufacturing, but it was not until he was 30 that he could set up on his own and introduce his innovations. These encompassed both technique and organization, the entrepreneurial and managerial sides of his business.

Wedgwood developed new mixtures of clays that took brilliant colors in the kiln and new glazes for both "useful" and "ornamental" ware. His technical innovations were all the more remarkable in that he had little education in mineral chemistry and made his discoveries by simple trial and error. But there was nothing of either luck or good fortune in Wedgwood's managerial innovations. He was repelled by the disorder of the traditional pottery with its waste of materials, uneven quality, and slow output. When he began his first works he divided the making of pottery into distinct tasks and separated his workers among them. One group did nothing but throw the pots on the wheel, another painted designs, a third glazed. To achieve this division of function, Wedgwood had to train his own workers almost from childhood. Traditional potters performed every task from molding to glazing and prized the fact that no two pieces were ever alike. Wedgwood wanted each piece to replicate another, and he stalked the works breaking defective wares on his wooden leg. He invested in schools to help train young artists, in canals to transport his products, and in London shops to sell them. Wedgwood was a marketing genius. He named his famed cream-colored pottery Queen's ware and made special coffee and tea services for leading aristocratic families. He would then sell replicas by the thousands. In less than twenty years Wedgwood pottery was prized all over Europe, and Wedgwood's potting works were the standard of the industry.

Robert Owen (1771–1858) did not have a family business to develop. The son of a small tradesman, he was apprenticed to a clothier at the age of 10. As a teenager he worked as a shop assistant in Manchester, where he audaciously applied for a job as a manager of a cotton mill. At 19 he was supervising 500 workers and learning the cotton trade. Owen was immediately successful, increasing the output of his workers and introducing new materials to the mill. In 1816 he entered a partnership to purchase the New Lanark mill in Scotland. Owen found conditions in Scotland much worse than those in Manchester. Over five hundred workhouse children were employed at New Lanark, where drunkenness and theft were endemic. Owen believed that to improve the quality of work one had to improve the quality of the workplace. He replaced old machinery with new, reduced working hours, and instituted a monitoring system to check theft. To enhance life outside the factory, he established a high-quality company-run store, which plowed its profits into a school for village children.

Owen was struck by the irony that in the mills machines were better cared for than humans. He thought that with the same attention to detail which had so improved the quality of commodities he could make even greater improvements in the quality of life. He prohibited children under ten from mill work and instituted a ten-hour day for child labor. His local school took infants from a year old, freeing women to work and ensuring each child an education. Owen instituted old-age and disability pensions, funded by mandatory contributions from workers' wages. Taverns were closed and workers were fined for drunkenness and sexual offenses. In the factory and the village Owen established a principle of communal regulation to improve both the work and the character of his employees. New Lanark became the model of the world of the future, and each year thousands made an industrial pilgrimage to visit it.

The Wages of Progress

Robert Owen ended his life as a social reformer. His efforts to improve the lot of his workers at New Lanark led to experiments to create ideal industrial communities throughout the world. He founded cooperative societies, in which all members shared in the profits of the business, and supported trade unions in which workers could better their lives. His followers planted colonies where goods were held in common and the fruits of labor belonged to the laborers. Owen's agitation for social reform was part of a movement that produced results of lasting consequence. The Factory Act (1833) prohibited factory work by children under nine, provided two hours of daily education, and effectively created a 12-hour day in the mills until the Ten Hours Act (1847). The Mines Act (1842) prohibited women and children from working underground.

Nor was Owen alone in dedicating time and money to the improvement of workers' lives. The rapid growth of unplanned cities exacerbated the plight of those too poor and overworked to help themselves. Conditions of housing and sanitation were appalling even by nineteenth-century standards. *The Report on the Sanitary Condition of the Laboring Population in Britain* (1842), written by Edwin Chadwick (1800–1890), so shocked Parliament and the nation that it helped to shift the burden of social reform to government. The Public Health Act (1848) established boards of health and the office of medical examiner; the Vaccination Act (1853) and the Contagious Diseases Act (1864) attempted to control epidemics.

The movement for social reform began almost as soon as industrialization. The Industrial Revolution initiated profound changes in the organization of British society. Cities sprang up from grain fields almost overnight. The lure of steady work and high wages prompted an exodus from rural Britain and spurred an unremitting boom in population. In 1750 about 15 percent of the population lived in urban areas; by 1850 about 60 percent did. Industrial workers married younger and produced more children than their agricultural counterparts. For centuries women had married in their middle twenties, but by 1800 age at first marriage had dropped to 23 for the female population as a whole and to nearly 20 in the industrial areas. This was in part because factory hands did not have to wait until they inherited land or money, and in part because they did not have to serve an apprenticeship. But early marriage and large families were also a bet on the future, a belief that things were better now and would be even better soon, that the new mouths would be fed and the new bodies clothed.

It is difficult to calculate the benefits of the Industrial Revolution or to weigh them against the costs. What is certain is that there was a vast expansion of wealth as well as a vast expansion of people to share it. Agricultural and industrial change made it possible to support comfortably a population over three times that of the seventeenth century, when it was widely believed that England had reached the limits of expansion. Despite the fact that population doubled between 1801 and 1851, per capita income rose by 75 percent, which means that had the population remained stable, per capita income would have increased by a staggering 350 percent. At the same time, untold millions of pounds had been sunk into canals, roads, railways, factories, mines, and mills.

But the expansion of wealth is not the same as the improvement in the quality of life, for wealth is not equally distributed. An increase in the level of wealth may mean only that the rich are getting richer more quickly than the poor are getting poorer. Similarly, economic growth over a century involved the lives of several generations, which experienced different standards of living. One set of parents may have sacrificed for the future of their children, another may have mortgaged it. Moreover, economic activity is cyclical. Trade depressions, like those induced by the War of 1812 and the American Civil War, which interrupted cotton supplies, could have disastrous short-term effects. The "Great Hunger" of the 1840s was a time of agrarian crisis and industrial slump. The downturn of 1842 threw 60 percent of the factory workers in the town of Bolton out of work at a time when there was neither unemployment insurance nor a welfare system. Finally, quality of life cannot simply be measured in economic terms. People with more money to spend may still be worse off than their ancestors, who may have preferred leisure to wealth or independence to the discipline of the clock.

Thus there are no easy answers to the quality-of-life question. In the first stages of industrialization it seems clear that only the wealthy benefited economically, though much of their increased wealth was reinvested in expansion. Under the impact of population growth, the Napoleonic wars, and regional harvest failure, real wages seem to have fallen from the levels reached in the 1730s. Industrial workers were not substantially better off than agricultural laborers when the high cost of food and rent is considered. But beginning around 1820 there is convincing evidence that the real wages of industrial workers were rising despite the fact that more and more work was semi- and unskilled machine-minding, and more of it was being done by women, who were generally paid only two-thirds the wages of men. Thus in the second half of the Industrial Revolution, both employers and workers saw a bettering of their economic situation. This was one reason why rural workers flocked to the cities to work the lowest paid and least desirable jobs in the factories.

But economic gain had social costs. The first was the decline of the family as a labor unit. In both agricultural and early industrial activity families labored together. Workers would not move to mill towns without the guarantee of a job for all members of their family and initially they could drive a hard bargain. The early factories preferred family labor to workhouse conscripts, and it was traditional for children to work beside their parents, cleaning, fetching, or assisting in minding the machines. Children provided an essential part of family income, and youngest children were the agency of care for infirm parents. Paradoxically, it was the agitation for improvement in the conditions of child labor that spelled the end of the family work unit. At first young children were barred from the factories and older ones allowed to work only a partial adult shift. Though reformers intended that schooling and leisure be substituted for work, the separation of children from parents in the workplace ultimately made possible the substitution of teenagers for adults, especially as machines replaced skilled human labor. The individual worker now became the unit of labor, and during economic downturns it was adult males with their higher salaries who were laid off first.

The decline of the family as a labor unit was matched by other changes in living conditions when rural dwellers migrated to cities. Many rural habits were unsuited to both factory work and urban living. The tradition of "Saint Monday," for example, was one that was deeply rooted in the pattern of agricultural life. Little effort was expended at the beginning of the work week and progressively more at the end. Sunday leisure was followed by Monday recovery, a slow start to renewed labor. The factory demanded constant application six days a week. Strict rules were enforced to keep workers at their stations and their minds on their jobs. More than efficiency was at stake. Early machines were not only crude, they were dangerous, with no safety features to cover moving parts. Maiming accidents were common in the early factories, the fault of both workers and machines. Similarly, industrial workers entered the world of the cash economy. Most agricultural workers were used to being paid in kind and to barter exchange. Money was an unusual luxury that was associated with binges of food, drink, and frivolities. This made adjustment to the wage packet as difficult as adjustment to the clock. Cash had to be set aside for provisions, rent, and clothing. On the farm the time of a bountiful harvest was the time to buy durable goods; in the factory "harvesttime" was always the same.

Such adjustments were not easy, and during the course of the nineteenth century a way of life passed forever from England. For some its departure caused profound sorrow; for others it was an occasion of good riddance. A vertically integrated society in which lord of the manor, village worthies, independent farmers, workers, and servants lived together interdependently was replaced by a society of segregated social classes. By the middle decades of the nineteenth century a class of capitalists and a class of workers had begun to form and had begun to clash. The middle classes abandoned the city centers, building exclusive suburban communities in which to raise their children and insulate their families. Conditions in the cities deteriorated under the pressure of overcrowding, lack of sanitation, and the absence of private investment. The loss of interaction between these different segments of society had profound consequences for the struggle to improve the quality of life for everyone. Leaders of labor saw themselves fighting against profits, greed, and apathy; leaders of capital against drunkenness, sloth, and ignorance. Between these two stereotypes there was little middle ground.

*T*he Industrialization of the Continent

Though Britain took the first steps along the road to an industrial economy, it was not long before other European nations followed. There was intense interest in the British miracle, as it was dubbed by contemporaries. European ministers, entrepreneurs, even heads of state, visited British factories and mines in hope of learning the key industrial secrets that would unlock the prosperity of a new age. The Crystal Palace exhibition of manufacturing and industry held in London in 1851 was the occasion for a Continentwide celebration of the benefits of technology and a chance for ambitious Europeans to measure themselves against the mighty British. By then many European nations had begun the transformation of their own economies and had entered a period of sustained growth.

There was no single model for the industrialization of the continental states. Contemporaries continually made comparisons with Britain, but in truth the process of British industrialization was not well suited to any but the coal-rich regions in Belgium and the Rhineland. Nevertheless, all of Europe benefited from the British experience. No one else had to invent the jenny, the mule, or the steam engine. Although the British government banned the export of technology, none of these path-breaking inventions remained a secret for long. Britain had demonstrated a way to make cheap durable goods in factories, and every other state in Europe was able to skip the long stages of discovery and improvement. Thus while industrialization began later on the Continent, it could progress more quickly. France and Germany were building a railroad system within years of Britain despite the fact that they had to import most of the technology, raw materials, and engineers.

Britain shaped European industrialization in another way. Its head start made it very difficult for follower nations to compete against British commodities in the world market. This meant that European industrialization would be directed first and foremost to home markets where tariffs and import quotas could protect fledgling industries. Though European states were willing to import vital British products, they placed high duties on British-made consumer goods and encouraged higher cost domestic production. Britain's competitive advantage demanded that European governments become involved in the industrialization of their countries, financing capital-intensive industries, backing the railroads, and favoring the establishment of factories.

European industrialization was therefore not the thunderclap that occurred in Britain. In France it was a slow accretive development that took advantage of traditional skills and occupations and gradually modernized the marketplace. In Germany industrialization had to overcome the political divisions of the empire, the economic isolation of the petty states, and the wide dispersion of vital resources. Regions rather than states industrialized in the early nineteenth century, and parts of Austria, Italy, and Spain imported machinery and techniques and modernized their traditional crafts. But most of these states and most of the eastern part of Europe remained tied to a traditional agrarian-based economy that provided neither labor for industrial production nor purchasing power for industrial goods. These areas quickly became sources for raw materials and primary products for their industrial neighbors.

Industrialization Without Revolution

The experience of France in the nineteenth century demonstrates that there was no single path in industrialization. Each state blended together its natural resources, historical experiences, and forms of economic organization in unique combinations. While some mixtures resulted in explosive growth, as in Britain, others made for steady development, as in France.

French industrialization was keyed to domestic rather than export markets and to the application of new technology to a vast array of traditional crafts. The French profited, as did all of the continental states, from British inventions, but they also benefited from the distinct features of their own economy. France possessed a pool of highly skilled and highly productive labor, a manufacturing tradition oriented toward the creation of high-quality

A French steelworks, Manufacture Nationale, in Paris, 1800. At that time this was the only French steelworks that compared with those in Sheffield, England.

goods, and consumers who valued taste and fashion over cost and function. Thus while the British dominated the new mass market for inexpensive cottons and cast-iron goods, a market with high sales but low profit margins, the French were producing luxury items whose scarcity kept both prices and profits high.

Two decisive factors determined the nature of French industrialization: population growth and the French Revolution. From the early eighteenth to the mid nineteenth centuries, France grew slowly. In 1700 French population stood at just under 20 million; in 1850 it was under 36 million, a growth rate of 80 percent. In contrast, Germany grew 135 percent, from 15 to 34 million, and England 300 percent, from 5 to 20 million, during the same period. Nevertheless, France remained the most populous nation in western Europe, second on the Continent only to Russia. There is no simple explanation for France's relatively sluggish population growth. The French had been hit particularly hard by subsistence crises in the seventeenth century, and there is reliable evidence that the rural population consciously attempted to limit family size by methods of birth control as well as by delaying marriages. Moreover, France urbanized slowly at a time when city dwellers were marrying younger and producing larger families. As late as the 1860s a majority of French workers were farmers. Whatever the cause of this moderate population growth, its consequences were clear. France was not pressured by the force of numbers to abandon its traditional agricultural methods, nor did it face a shortage of traditional supplies of energy. Except during crop failures, French agriculture could produce to meet French needs, and there remained more than enough wood for domestic and industrial use.

The consequences of the French Revolution are less clear. Throughout the eighteenth century, the French economy performed at least as well as had the British and in many areas better. French overseas trade had grown spectacularly until checked by military defeat in the Seven Years' War (1756–1763).

French agriculture steadily increased output while French rural manufactures flourished. A strong guild tradition still dominated urban industries, and although it restricted competition and limited growth, it also helped maintain the standards for the production of high-quality goods that made French commodities so highly prized throughout the world. The Revolution disrupted every aspect of economic life. Some of its outcomes were unforeseen and unwelcome. For example, Napoleon's Continental System, which attempted to close European markets to Britain, resulted in a shipping war, which the British won decisively and which eliminated France as a competitor for overseas trade in the mid nineteenth century. But other outcomes were the result of direct policies, even if their impact could not have been entirely predicted. Urban guilds and corporations were abolished, opening trades to newcomers but destroying the close-knit groups that trained skilled artisans and introduced innovative products. Similarly, the breakup of both feudal and common lands to satisfy the hunger of the peasantry had the effect of maintaining a large rural population for decades. .

Despite the efforts of the central government, there had been little change in the techniques used by French farmers over the course of the eighteenth century. French peasants clung tenaciously to traditional rights that gave even the smallest landholder a vital say in community agriculture. Landlords were predominantly absentees, less interested in the organization of their estates than in the dues and taxes that could be extracted from them. Thus the policies of successive revolutionary governments strengthened the hold of small peasants on the land. With the abolition of many feudal dues and with careful family planning, smallholders could survive and pass a meager inheritance on to their children. French agriculture was able to supply the nation's need for food, but it could not release large numbers of workers for purely industrial activity.

Thus French industrial growth was constrained on the one hand by the relatively small numbers of workers who could engage in manufacturing and on the other by the fact that a large portion of the population remained subsistence producers, cash poor and linked only to small rural markets. Throughout the eighteenth century the French economy continued to be regionally segregated rather than nationally integrated. The size of the state inhibited a highly organized internal trade, and there was little improvement of the infrastructure of transportation. Though some British-style canals were built, it must be remembered that canals in Britain were built to move coal rather than staple goods, and France did not have much coal to move. Manufacturing concerns were still predominantly family businesses whose primary markets were regional rather than international. Roads that connected the short distances between producers and consumers were of greater importance to these producers than arterial routes that served the markets of others. Similarly, there was no national capital market until the mid nineteenth century and precious few regional ones. Though French producers were as thrifty and profit oriented as any others, they found it more difficult to raise the large amounts of capital necessary to purchase the most expensive new machinery and build the most up-to-date factories. Ironworks, coal mines, and railroads, the three capital-intensive ventures of industrialization, were financed either by government subsidy or by foreign investment.

It was not until mid-century that sustained industrial growth became evident in France. This was largely the result of the construction of railroads on a national plan, financed in large part by the central government. Whereas in Britain the railways took advantage of a national market, in France they created one. They also gave the essential stimulation to the modernization of the iron industry, in which much refining was still done with charcoal rather than coke; of machine making; and of the capital markets.

The disadvantages of being on the trailing edge of economic change were mitigated for a time by conventional practices of protectionism. Except in specialty goods, agricultural produce, and luxury products, French manufacturers could not compete with either British or German commodities. Had France maintained its position as a world trader, this comparative disadvantage would have been devastating. But defeat in the wars of commerce had led to a drawing inward of French economic effort. Marseilles and Bordeaux, once bustling centers of European trade, became provincial backwaters in the nineteenth century. But the internal market was still strong enough to support industrial growth, and domestic commodities could be protected by prohibitive tariffs, especially against British textiles, iron, and ironically, coal.

While France achieved industrialization without an industrial revolution, it also achieved economic growth within the context of its traditional values. Agriculture may not have modernized, but the ancient village communities escaped the devastation modernization would bring. The orderly progression of generations of farming families characterized rural France until the shattering experiences of the Franco-Prussian War (1870) and the First World War (1914–1918). Nor did France experience the mushroom growth of new cities with all of their problems of poverty, squalor, and homelessness. Slow population growth ameliorated the worst of the social diseases of industrialization while traditional rural manufacturing softened the transformation of a way of life.

Industrialization and Union

The process of industrialization in Germany was dominated by the historic divisions of the empire of the German peoples. Before 1815 there were over three hundred separate jurisdictional units within the empire, and after 1815 there were still more than thirty. These included large advanced states like Prussia, Austria, and Saxony as well as small free cities and the personal enclaves of petty nobles who had guessed right during the Napoleonic wars. Political divisions had more than political impact. Each state clung tenaciously to its local laws and customs, which favored its citizens over outsiders. Merchants who lived near the intersection of separate jurisdictions could find themselves liable for several sets of tolls to move their goods and several sets of customs duties for importing and exporting them. These would have to be paid in different currencies at different rates of exchange according to the different regulations of each state. Small wonder that German merchants exhibited an intense localism, preferring to trade with members of their own state and supporting trade barriers against others. Such obstacles had a depressing effect on the economies of all German states, but pushed with greatest weight against the manufacturing regions of Saxony, Silesia, and the Rhineland.

Most of imperial Germany was agricultural land suited to a diversity of uses. The mountainous regions of Bavaria and the Austrian alpine communities practiced animal husbandry; there was a grain belt in Prussia, where the soil was poor but the land plentiful, and one in central Germany in which the soil was fertile and the land densely occupied. The Rhine Valley was one of the richest in all of Europe and was the center of German wine production. While English farmers were turning farms into commercial estates, German peasants were learning how to make do with less land.

Agricultural estates were organized differently in different parts of Germany. In the east, serfdom still prevailed. Peasants were tied to the land and its lord and were responsible for labor service during much of the week. Methods of cultivation were traditional, and neither peasants nor lords had much incentive to adopt new techniques. In central Germany, the long process of commuting labor service into rents was nearly completed by the end of the eighteenth century. The peasantry was not yet free, as a series of manorial relationships still tied them to the land, but they were no longer mere serfs. Finally, western Germany was dominated by free farmers who either owned or leased their lands and who had a purely economic relationship with their landlords. The restriction of peasant mobility in much of Germany posed difficulties for the creation of an industrial work force. As late as 1800 over 80 percent of the German population was engaged in agriculture, a proportion that would drop slowly over the next half century.

Though Germany was well endowed with natural resources and skilled labor in a number of trades, it had not taken part in the expansion of world trade during the seventeenth century, and the once bustling Hanseatic ports had been far outdistanced by the rise of the Atlantic economies. The principal exported manufacture was linen, which was expertly spun and woven in Saxony and the Prussian province of Silesia. The linen industry was organized traditionally, with a mixture of domestic production managed on the putting-out system and some factory spinning, especially after the introduction of British mechanical innovations. But even the most advanced factories were still being powered by water, and thus they were located in mountainous regions where rapidly running streams could turn the wheels. Neither linens nor traditional German metal crafts could compete on the international markets, but they could find a wider market within Germany if only the problems of political division could be resolved.

These were especially acute for Prussia after the reorganization of

European boundaries in 1815 (see Chapter 18). Prussian territory now included the coal- and iron-rich Rhineland provinces, but a number of smaller states separated these areas from Prussia's eastern domain. Each small state exacted its own tolls and customs duties whenever Prussian merchants wanted to move goods from one part of Prussia to the other. Such movement became more common in the nineteenth century as German manufacturing began to grow in step with its rising population. Between 1815 and 1865 the population of Germany grew by 60 percent to over thirty-six million. This was an enormous internal market, nearly as large as France, and the Prussians resolved to make it a unified trading zone by creating a series of alliances with smaller states known as the Zollverein (1834). The Zollverein was not a free-trade zone, like the British Empire, but rather a customs union in which member states adopted the liberal Prussian customs regulations. Every state was paid an annual portion of receipts based on its population, and every state—except Prussia—increased its revenues as a result. The crucial advantage the Prussians received was the ability to move goods and materials from east to west, but Prussia reaped political profits as well. It forced Hanover and Saxony into the Zollverein and kept its powerful rival Austria out. Prussia's economic union soon proved to be the basis for the union of the German states.

The creation of the Zollverein was vital to German industrialization. It permitted the exploitation of natural advantages, like plentiful supplies of coal and iron, and it provided a basis for the building of railroads. Germany was a follower nation in the process of industrialization. It started late and it self-consciously modeled its success on the British experience. British equipment and engineers were brought to Germany in an attempt to plant the seeds of an industrial economy. German manufacturers sent their children to England to learn the latest techniques in industrial management. Friedrich Engels (1820–1895) worked in a Manchester cotton factory, where he observed the appalling conditions of the industrial labor force and wrote *The Condition of the Working Class in England* (1845). Steam engines were installed in coal mines, if not in factories, and the process of puddling revolutionized iron making, though most iron was still smelted with charcoal rather than coke. Though coal was plentiful in Prussia, it was to be found at the eastern and western extremities of Germany. Even with the lowering of tolls and duties, it was still too expensive to move over rudimentary roads and an uncompleted system of canals. Thus the railroads were the key to tapping the industrial potential of Germany. Here they were a cause rather than a result of industrialization. The agreements hammered out in the creation of the Zollverein made possible the planning necessary to build single lines across the boundaries of numerous states.

Germany imported most of its engines directly from Britain and thus adopted standard British gauge for its system. As early as 1850 there were over 3500 miles of rail in Germany, with important roads linking the manufacturing districts of Saxony and the coal and iron deposits of the Ruhr. Twenty years later Germany was second only to Britain in the amount of track that had been laid and opened. By then it was no longer simply a follower. German engineers

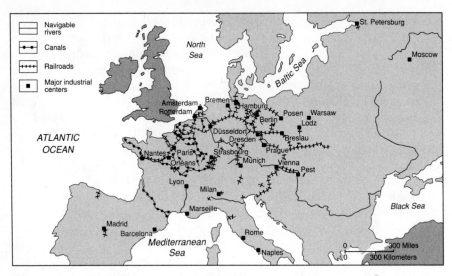

The Industrial Revolution on the Continent

and machinists, trained in Europe's best schools of technology, were turning out engines and rolling stock second to none. And the railroads transported a host of high-quality manufactures, especially durable metal goods that came to carry the most prestigious trademark of the late nineteenth century: made in Germany.

The Lands That Time Forgot

Nothing better demonstrates the point that industrialization was a regional rather than a national process than a survey of those states that did not develop industrial economies by the middle of the nineteenth century. These states ranged from the Netherlands, which was still one of the richest areas in Europe, to Spain and Russia, which were the poorest. Also included were Austria-Hungary, the states of the Italian peninsula, and Poland. In all of these nations there was some industrial progress. The Bohemian lands of Austria contained a highly developed spinning industry; the Spanish province of Catalonia produced more cotton than Belgium, and the Basque region was rich in iron and coal. Northern Italy mechanized its textile production, particularly silk spinning, while in the regions around both Moscow and Saint Petersburg factories were run on serf labor. Nevertheless, the economies of all these states remained nonindustrial and, with the exception of the Netherlands, dominated by subsistence agriculture.

There were many reasons why these states were unable to develop their industrial potential. Some, like Naples and Poland, were simply underendowed with resources; others, like Austria-Hungary and Spain, faced difficulties of transport and communications that could not easily be overcome. Spain's modest resources were located on its northern and eastern edges while a vast arid plain dominated the center. To move raw materials and finished products from one end of the country to the other was a daunting task, made more difficult by lack of waterways and the rudimentary condition of Spanish roads. Two-thirds of Austria-Hungary is either mountains or hills, a geographic feature presenting obstacles that not even the railroads could easily solve. But there was far more than natural disadvantage behind the failure of these parts of Europe to move in step with the industrializing states. Their social structure, agricultural organization, and commercial policies all hindered the adoption of new methods, machines, and modes of production.

The leaders of traditional economies maintained tariff systems that insulated their own producers from competition. But protection was sensible only when it protected rather than isolated. Inefficiently produced goods of inferior quality were the chief results of the protectionist policies of the follower nations. Failure to adopt steam-powered machines made traditionally produced linens and silks so expensive that smuggling occurred on an international scale. Though these goods might find buyers in domestic markets, they could not compete in international trade, and one by one the industries of the follower nations atrophied. Those economies that remained traditionally organized came to be exploited for their resources by those that had industrialized. Traditional agriculture could not produce the necessary surplus of either labor or capital to support industry, and industry could not economize sufficiently to make manufactured goods cheap enough for a poor peasantry.

There was more than irony in the fact that one of the first railroads built on the Continent was built in Austria but designed to be powered by horses rather than engines. The first railways in Italy linked royal palaces to capital cities;

A Russian peasant tills a field with a primitive horse-drawn wooden plow. Russian fields produced low yields partly because of the use of such crude farming methods.

The railroads changed the whole pattern of living during the industrial Revolution. On this circular track, Richard Trevithick displayed his high-pressure steam locomotive, the "Catch-me-who-can," to a marvelling London public in 1808.

those in Spain radiated from Madrid and bypassed most centers of natural resources. In these states the railroads were built to move the military rather than passengers or goods. They were state financed, occasionally state owned, and almost always lost money. They were symbols of the industrial age, but in these states they were symbols without substance.

The industrialization of Europe in the eighteenth century was an epochal event in human history. The constraints on daily life imposed by nature were loosened for the first time. No longer did population growth in one generation mean famine in the next; no longer was it necessary for the great majority of people to toil in the fields to earn their daily bread. Manufacture replaced agriculture as humanity's primary activity, though the change was longer and slower than the burst of industrialization that took place in the first half of the nineteenth century. For the leaders, Britain especially, industrialization brought international eminence. British achievements were envied, British inventors celebrated, Britain's constitutional and social organization lauded. A comparatively small island nation had become the greatest economic power in Europe. Industrialization had profound consequences for economic life, but its effects ran deeper than that. The search for new markets would result in the conquest of continents; the power of productivity unleashed by coal and iron would result in the first great arms race. Both would reach fruition in World War I, the first industrial war. For better or worse we still live in the industrial era that began in Britain in the middle of the eighteenth century.

Suggestions for Further Reading

General Reading

*T. S. Ashton, *The Industrial Revolution* (Oxford, England: Oxford University Press, 1969). A brief but compelling account of the traditional view of industrialization.

*Carlo Cipolla, ed., *The Fontana Economic History of Europe: The Emergence of Industrial Societies*, 2 vols. (London: Fontana, 1973). Country-by-country survey of continental European industrialization.

*E. L. Jones, *The European Miracle*, 2nd ed. (Cambridge, England: Cambridge University Press, 1987). A comparative study of the acquisition of technology in Europe and Asia and the impact of industrialization on the two continents.

*David Landes, *The Unbound Prometheus* (Cambridge, England: Cambridge University Press, 1969). Vigorously argued study of the impact of technology on British and European society from the eighteenth to the twentieth century.

The Traditional Economy

J. D. Chambers and G. E. Mingay, *The Agricultural Revolution* (London: Batsford, 1966). The classic survey of the changes in British agriculture.

*L. A. Clarkson, *Proto-Industrialization: The First Phase of Industrialization?* (London: Macmillan, 1985). Study of domestic manufacturing and its connection to the process of industrialization.

E. L. Jones, *Agriculture and the Industrial Revolution* (New York: Wiley, 1974). Detailed study of the relationship between agricultural innovations and the coming of industrialization in Britain.

*E. A. Wrigley, *Continuity, Chance and Change* (Cambridge, England: Cambridge University Press, 1988). Explores the nature of the traditional economy and the way in which Britain escaped from it.

---

*Indiciates paperback edition available.

The Industrial Revolution in Britain

T. S. Ashton, *Iron and Steel in the Industrial Revolution* (Manchester, England: Manchester University Press, 1963). Lucid account of the transformation of iron making, including the story of James Watt.

Philip Bagwell, *The Transport Revolution from 1770* (London: Batsford, 1974). Thorough survey of the development of canals, highways, and railroads in Britain.

N. F. R. Crafts, *British Economic Growth During the Industrial Revolution* (Oxford, England: Oxford University Press, 1985). Study by a new economic historian arguing the case for slow economic growth in the early nineteenth century. Highly quantitative.

*Francois Crouzet, *The First Industrialists* (Cambridge, England: Cambridge University Press, 1985). Analysis of the social background of the first generation of British entrepreneurs.

*Phyllis Deane, *The First Industrial Revolution*, 2nd ed. (Cambridge, England: Cambridge University Press, 1979). The best introduction to the technological changes in Britain.

Friedrich Engels, *The Condition of the Working Class in England in 1844* (London: Allen and Unwin, 1952). The classic eyewitness account of the horrors of the industrial city.

*Peter Mathias, *The First Industrial Nation*, 2nd ed. (London: Methuen, 1983). Up-to-date general survey of British industrialization.

*D. N. McCloskey and R. Floud, *The Economic History of Britain, Since 1700* (Cambridge, England: Cambridge University Press, 1981). Collection of essays by new economic historians. Quantitative in presentation and econometric in argument.

A. E. Musson, *The Growth of British Industry* (New York: Holmes & Meier, 1978), In-depth survey of British industrialization that is especially strong on technology.

*Harold Perkin, *The Origins of Modern English Society 1780–1880* (London: Routledge & Kegan Paul, 1969). Outstanding survey of British social history in the industrial era.

*E. P. Thompson, *The Making of the English Working Class* (New York: Random House, 1966). Brilliant and passionate study of the ways in which laborers responded to the changes brought about by the industrial economy.

The Industrialization of the Continent

W. O. Henderson, *The Rise of German Industrial Power* (Berkeley: University of California Press, 1975). Chronological study of German industrialization that centers on Prussia.

*Tom Kemp, *Industrialization in Nineteenth-Century Europe*, 2nd ed. (London: Longman, 1985). Survey of the process of industrialization in the major European states.

Sidney Pollard, *Peaceful Conquest* (Oxford, England: Oxford University Press, 1981). Argues for the regional nature of industrialization throughout western Europe.

Roger Price, *The Economic Transformation of France* (London: Croom Helm, 1975). Study of French society before and during the process of industrialization.

*Wolfgang Schivelbusch, *The Railway Journey* (Berkeley: University of California Press, 1986). Social history of the impact of railways, drawn from French and German sources.

*Clive Trebilcock, *The Industrialization of the Continental Powers 1780–1914* (London: Longman, 1981). Complex study of Germany, France, and Russia.

18

Revolutions and Reforms, 1815–1871

Potato Politics

Vegetables have histories too. But none has a more interesting history in the West than the humble potato. First introduced to northern Europe from the Andean highlands in South America at the end of the sixteenth century, it rapidly became a staple of peasant diets from Ireland to Russia. Frederick the Great encouraged its adoption in Prussia in the eighteenth century, well aware of its ability to contribute to the well-being of his people.

The potato's vitamins, minerals, and high carbohydrate content provided a rich source of energy to Europe's rural poor. By the nineteenth century attitudes toward the potato had been transformed from the seventeenth-century view that it caused leprosy to its canonization as "the miracle vegetable." It was simple to plant, it required little or no cultivation, and it did well in damp, cool climates. Best of all, it could be grown successfully on the smallest plots of land. One acre could support a peasant family of four for a year. Potato peelings helped sustain the family cow and pig, further supplementing family income.

The French painter Jean-Francois Millet (1814–1875) provides a view of the peasant labor involved in *Planting Potatoes*. Millet, the son of a wealthy peasant family, understood well the importance of the potato crop in the peasant family diet. The man and woman in this canvas plant their potatoes as a reverent act, bowing as field laborers might in prayer (as they do in Millet's more sentimental work, *The Angelus*). The primitive nature of the process is striking: The man uses a short hoe to scrape at what seems to be most unyielding soil. The peasants seem part of the nature surrounding them,

patient as the beast that waits in the shade, bent and gnarled and lovely as the tree that arches in the background.

French, Belgian, Scottish, German, and Polish peasants included the potato as a staple in their diets, but only the Irish relied on it exclusively. An all-potato diet may have been bland and dull, but it was not a nutritional hardship. The cooked potato was a substitute for wheat. As the sole item of diet, it provided life-sustaining nutrients and a significant amount of the protein so necessary for heavy labor. The Irish adult ate an average of 12 to 14 pounds of potatoes a day—a figure that may seem preposterous to us today. The British economist Adam Smith, marveling at the strength, height, and health of the Irish at the end of the eighteenth century, attributed it all to the economy of the potato.

The fleshy root not only guaranteed health, it also affected social life. Peasants had traditionally delayed marriage and starting their families because of the unavailability of land. The potato changed that behavior. Now the potato allowed peasants with only a little land to marry and have children earlier. Millet's depiction of the man and woman working together in the field resonates with the simple fact that potato cultivation aided in the formation of the couple. Millet's couple are parents whose baby sleeps swaddled in a basket and shaded by the tree. In those peasant homes where family members did putting-out work for local entrepreneurs, potato cultivation drew little labor away from the spinning wheel and loom. It permitted prosperous farmers to devote more land to cash crops, since only a small portion was required to feed a family. Most commonly, however, the potato was the single crop grown by most Irish farm workers.

Proverbs warned peasants against putting all their eggs in one basket, but no folk wisdom prepared the Irish for the potato disaster that struck them. In 1845 a fungus from America destroyed the new potato crop. Although they were certainly accustomed to bad harvests and crop failures, the peasants had no precedent for the years of blight that followed. From 1846 to 1850, famine and the diseases resulting from it—scurvy, dysentery, cholera, and typhus fever—killed over a million people in what became known as the Great Hunger. Another million people emigrated, many to the United States. Only the lucky survived the voyage across the ocean on the disease-infested death ships. Total dependence on the potato reaped its grim harvest, devastating all levels of Irish society. Within five years the Irish population was reduced by almost 25 percent.

The Irish potato famine has been called the "last great European *natural* disaster," to distinguish it from the social horrors of war and revolution. But the famine was as much a social disaster as a natural one. Food was the most political of issues. Many argued that the disaster could have been averted. The United Kingdom of Great Britain and Ireland had been created in 1801, and this political unit, which also included England, Scotland, and Wales, constituted one of the world's most prosperous states. The British government expected that the free market would solve the problems caused by famine once trade barriers had been removed. The British Corn Laws, which had been enacted to protect domestic growers from foreign competition, were repealed in 1846. But the famine hit the Irish so hard, they simply did not have the money available to buy what grains might be available. Emergency work relief was established and soup kitchens were opened in the spring of 1847, but even this meager assistance was withdrawn because the famine coincided with a banking crisis in England. There is little to indicate that the continuation of work relief and soup kitchens could have reversed the death rates. In 1847 the problem was handed over to the Irish Poor Law system, a system Britain had imposed on Ireland in 1838. The workhouses created by the recent law were not intended to deal with disasters. Poor and starving Irish peasants were expected to support themselves. Mass deaths and mass graves were the inevitable result.

The Irish Great Hunger was the most striking example of the problem that plagued all Western societies in the first half of the nineteenth century: what to do with the poor. The Irish famine was an extreme case of crisis that Great Britain was unable to handle. In this context of poverty and the politics of food, Millet's melancholy painting of *Planting Potatoes* was a political statement. In its reverence for humble work, it presents the dignity and worthiness of the poor. It also confronts us with their isolation.

$\mathcal{E}$urope after 1815

The primary goal of the European leaders who met at the Congress of Vienna in 1815 was to devise the most stable territorial arrangement possible. The settlement that emerged from their meeting was not simply a reaction to the ideological challenges of the French Revolution, nor was it a restoration of the European state system that had existed before Napoleon. During the negotiations traditional claims of the right to rule came head to head with new ideas about stabilization. The three principles of legitimacy, compensation, and balance of power dominated the 1815 settlement of negotiation and set the terms of international relations for succeeding generations.

The Congress of Vienna

Because of the concern with establishing harmony at the time of Napoleon's defeat, the peace enforced against France was not a punitive one. After

Europe in 1815

Napoleon's abdication in 1814, the Four Powers decided that leniency was the best way to support the restored Bourbon monarchy. After 1793 royalist émigrés referred to the young son of the executed Louis XVI as Louis XVII, although the child died in captivity and never reigned. In 1814 the Great Powers designated the elder of the two surviving brothers of Louis XVI as the appropriate candidate for the restored monarchy. Because of the circumstances of his restoration, the new king, Louis XVIII (1814–1815; 1815–1824), bore the ignominious image of returning "in the baggage car of the Allies." Every effort was made not to weigh Louis XVIII down with a harsh settlement. The First Peace of Paris, signed by the Allies with France in May 1814, had cut French frontiers back to the 1792 boundaries, which included Avignon, Venaissin, parts of Savoy, and German and Flemish territories, none of which had belonged to France in 1789.

After the 100-day return of Napoleon, the "usurper," the Second Peace of Paris of November 1815 somewhat less generously declared French frontiers restricted to the boundaries of 1790 and exacted from France an indemnity of 700 million francs. An army of occupation consisting of 150,000 troops was also placed on French soil at French expense, but was removed ahead of schedule in 1818. As part of the first peace treaty, representatives of the victorious Allies agreed to convene in the Austrian capital of Vienna in September 1814 to mop up the mess created in Europe by French rule and to restore order to European monarchies.

The central actors whose personalities dominated the Congress of Vienna were the Austrian minister of foreign affairs Prince Klemens von Metternich, British foreign secretary Viscount Castlereagh, French minister of foreign affairs Charles Maurice de Talleyrand, the Russian tsar Alexander I, and the Prussian king Frederick William III. In spite of personal eccentricities and occasionally outright hostilities among Europe's leaders, all shared a common concern with reestablishing harmony in Europe.

The dominant partnership of Austria and Britain at the Congress of Vienna resulted in treaty arrangements that served to restrain the ambitions of Russia and Prussia. No country was to receive territory without giving up something in return, and no one country was to receive enough territory to make it a present or future threat to the peace of Europe. To contain France, some steps taken prior to the Congress were ratified or expanded. In June 1814 the Low Countries had been set up as a unitary state, a buffer against future French expansion on the Continent and a block to the revival of French sea power. The new Kingdom of the Netherlands had been created out of the former Dutch Republic and the Austrian Netherlands and placed under the rule of William I of Orange (1815–1840). The Catholic southern provinces were thus uneasily reunited with the Protestant northern provinces, regions that had been separated since the Peace of Westphalia in 1648. Lest there be any doubt about the intended purpose of this new kingdom, Great Britain gave William I of the Netherlands two million pounds to fortify his frontier against France. The reestablishment of a monarchy that united the island kingdom of Sardinia with Piedmont and included Savoy, Nice, and part of Genoa contained France on its southeast border. To the east, Prussia was given control of the left bank of the Rhine. Switzerland was reestablished as an independent confederation of cantons. Bourbon rule was restored in Spain on France's southwestern border.

Austria's power was firmly established in Italy, either through outright territorial control or influence over independent states. The Papal States were returned to Pope Pius VII (1800–1823), along with territories that had been Napoleon's Cisalpine Republic and the Kingdom of Italy. The Republic of Venice was absorbed into the Austrian Empire. Lombardy and the Illyrian provinces on the Dalmatian coast were likewise restored to Austria. The Italian duchies of Tuscany, Parma, and Modena were placed under the rule of Habsburg princes.

After the fall of Napoleon, the Allies made no attempt to restore the Holy Roman Empire. Napoleon's Confederation of the Rhine, which organized the majority of German territory under French auspices in 1806, was dissolved. In its place the German Confederation was created by reorganizing the 300 petty states into 38. The German Confederation was intended as a bulwark against France and not to serve any nationalist or parliamentary function. The 38 states, along with Austria as the 39th, were represented in a new Federal Diet at Frankfurt, dominated by Austrian influence.

All of these changes were the result of carefully discussed but fairly noncontroversial negotiations. The question of Poland was another matter indeed. Successive partitions by Russia, Austria, and Prussia in 1772, 1793, and 1795 had completely dismembered the land that had been Poland. Napoleon had reconstituted a small portion of Poland as the Grand Duchy of Warsaw. The dilemma of the Congress was what to do with this Napoleonic creation and with Polish territory in general. Fierce debate over Poland threatened to shatter congressional harmony.

Tsar Alexander I (1801–1825) of Russia argued for a large Poland that he intended to be fully under his influence. It would extend Russian-controlled territories to the banks of the Oder. He also envisioned extending Russian dominance farther into central and eastern Europe. He based his claim on the significant contribution the Russian army had made to Napoleon's defeat. But such thinking conflicted with Austrian minister Metternich's pursuit of equilibrium.

Frederick William III (1797–1840) of Prussia contended that if a large Poland was to be created, Prussia would expect compensation by absorbing Saxony. Both Great Britain and France distrusted Russian and Prussian territorial aims. Talleyrand (1754–1838), the wily and brilliant French negotiator, was able to take advantage of his position of nothing to lose to work out a compromise. As a bishop under the old regime, a revolutionary who managed to keep his head, an exile in America during the Terror, Napoleon's chief minister, and now the representative of a Bourbon monarchy at the Congress, Talleyrand knew something about survival and taking advantage of opportunities. Talleyrand was also a shrewd and experienced diplomat who managed to convince the Allies to accept France, their defeated enemy, as an equal partner in negotiations. In the midst of the crisis over Poland, he persuaded

Britain and Austria to sign a secret treaty with France to preserve an independent Polish territory. He then deliberately leaked news of the secret agreement of these powers to go to war, if necessary, to block Russian and Prussian aims. Alexander I and Frederick William III immediately backed down.

In the final arrangement, Prussia retained the Polish territory of Posen, and Austria kept the Polish province of Galicia. Kraków, with its population of 95,000, was declared a free city. Finally, a kingdom of Poland, nominally independent but in fact under the tutelage of Russia, emerged from what remained of the Grand Duchy of Warsaw.

In addition to receiving Polish territories, Prussia gained two-fifths of the kingdom of Saxony. Prussia also received territory on the left bank of the Rhine, the Duchy of Westphalia, and Swedish Pomerania. With these acquisitions Prussia doubled its population to around eleven million people. The Junkers, the landed class of east Prussia, reversed many of the reforms of the Napoleonic period. The new territories that Prussia gained were rich in waterways and resources but geographically fragmented. The dispersal of holdings that was intended to contain Prussian power in central Europe spurred Prussia to find new ways of uniting its markets. In this endeavor, Prussia constituted a future threat to Austrian power over the German Confederation.

In Scandinavia, Russia's conquest of Finland was acknowledged by the members of the Congress and, in return, Sweden acquired Norway from Denmark. Unlike Austria, Prussia, and Russia, Great Britain made no claim to territories at the Congress. Having achieved its aim of containing France, its greatest rival for dominance on the seas, Britain returned the French colonies it had seized in war. The redrawing of the territorial map of Europe had achieved its pragmatic aim of guaranteeing the peace. It was now left to a system of alliances to preserve that peace.

The Alliance System

Only by joining forces had the European powers been able to defeat Napoleon, and the necessity of a system of alliances was recognized even after the battles were over. Two alliance pacts dominated the post-Napoleonic era: the renewed Quadruple Alliance and the Holy Alliance. The Quadruple Alliance, signed by the victorious powers of Great Britain, Austria, Russia, and Prussia in November 1815, was intended to protect Europe against future French aggression and to preserve the status quo. In 1818 France, having completed its payment of war indemnities, joined the pact, which now became the Quintuple Alliance. The five powers promised to meet periodically over the next 20 years to discuss common problems and to ensure the peace.

The Holy Alliance, very different in tone and intent, was the brainchild of Alexander I and was heavily influenced by his mystical view of international politics. In this pact the monarchs of Prussia, Austria, and Russia agreed to renounce war and to protect the Christian religion. The Holy Alliance spoke of "the bonds of a true and indissoluble brotherhood . . . to protect religion, peace, and justice." Russia was able to give some credibility to the alliance with the sheer size of its army. Career diplomats were aware of the hollowness of the Holy Alliance as a treaty arrangement, but it did indicate the willingness of Europe's three eastern autocracies to intervene in the affairs of other states.

The concept of Europe acting as a whole, through a system of periodic conferences, marked the emergence of a new diplomatic era. Conflict, however, was inherent in the commitment of parliamentary governments to open consultation and the need for secrecy in diplomacy. Dynastic regimes sought to intervene in smaller states to buoy up despots. That certainly seemed to be the case in 1822, when European powers met to consider restoring the Bourbon monarchy in Spain. The British, acting as a counterbalance to revolutionary tendencies, refused to cooperate and blocked united action by the Alliance. France took military action on its own in 1823, restored King Ferdinand VII, and abolished the Spanish constitution.

Social Transformations

The peace that emerged from the Congress of Vienna did not restore the old order, although it did preserve principles of rule that a property-owning elite held dear. The search for stability, restoration, and the reaction to change characterized national and international affairs after 1815. Social structure and the world of production were undergoing dramatic transformations, and the daily lives of growing numbers of Europeans were transformed between 1815 and 1850.

In 1800 two out of every one hundred Europeans lived in a city. By 1850 the number of urban dwellers per hundred had jumped to five and was rising rapidly. Urban workers were poorly paid and women workers were more poorly paid than men. When working women were cut free of the support of home and family, uncounted numbers were forced into part-time prostitution to supplement meager incomes. Urban crime grew astronomically, with thefts accounting for the greatest number of crimes.

Social reformers identified poverty and urban crowding as causes of the increase in criminal behavior. In 1892 both Paris and London began to create modern urban police forces to deal with the challenges to law and order. Crime assumed the character of disease in the minds of middle-class reformers. Statisticians and social scientists, themselves a new urban phenomenon, produced massive theses on social hygiene, lower class immorality, and the unworthiness of the poor. Always at the center of the issue was the "social question": the growing problem of the poor.

State-sponsored work relief expanded after 1830 for the deserving poor: the old, the sick, and children. Able-bodied workers who were idle were regarded as undeserving and dangerous, regardless of the causes of their unemployment. Performance of work became an indicator of moral worth, as urban and rural workers succumbed to downturns in the economic cycle. Those unable to work sought relief, as a last resort, from the state. What has been called "a revolution in government" took place in the 1830s and 1840s, as legislative bodies increased regulation of everything from factories and mines to prisons and schools.

Industrialization profoundly altered the structure of daily life within the family during the first half of the nineteenth century. By mid-century population growth was beginning to slow down throughout Europe. The hope of a better life for one's progeny required that existing resources be concentrated on fewer children. With the rise of the state and a growing emphasis on education, the socialization role of the family was gradually taken over by public institutions. Changes affected both middle-class and working-class families, although to varying degrees.

The privacy of family life intensified with the transfer of paid work to a public workplace. Middle-class Europeans filled their homes with knick-knacks, curios, and mass-produced art. By accumulating these objects, the middle class asserted its right as an arbiter of its own style. But a vast gulf separated working-class families from these middle-class consumers. Factory owner and social critic Friedrich Engels (1820–1895) left a bleak but accurate account of working-class life in Manchester in *The Condition of the Working Class in England in 1844*. Working women, unsupervised children, and unemployed husbands figured prominently in his brutal tale of misery and immorality.

Reformers confronted the disparities in family life and placed the blame squarely on women's absence from the home. Women had made industrialization possible, as they poured into the British and continental textile factories and became the primary work force. The solution to the perceived decline in the working-class family was found in legislation to restrict women from the workplace and return them to the home to care for their husbands and children.

Women's rights, little affected by industrialization, were increasingly disputed in public forums after 1815. In France, the equality of citizens before the law did not extend to women. In English law, men could terminate their marriages but their wives had no such access to divorce. Critics blamed the decline in sexual mores on women's refusal to "know their place." By the mid nineteenth century women were organizing to demand equal political rights, political representation, assistance in caring for children, and better living conditions.

In 1837 in Great Britain, an 18-year-old young woman became queen. Reigning until her death in 1901, Victoria gave her name to an age and its morals. Girls became queens of Portugal and Spain. But they, like the young Victoria, were little more than political figureheads, protecting the survival of dynastic claims and contributing little to the growing debate about women's proper place in society.

Family portrait of Queen Victoria, the Prince Consort, and their eldest children, painted by Franz Xavier Winterhalter in 1846. Their first daughter, Victoria, would become the mother of Kaiser Wilhelm II of Germany.

The New Ideologies

The political and economic upheavals of the first half of the nineteenth century encouraged a new breed of thinkers to search for ways to explain the transformations of the period. Before mid-century Europeans witnessed one of the most intellectually fertile periods in the history of the West. The search for understanding during this era gave birth to new ideologies—liberalism, nationalism, romanticism, conservatism, and socialism—that came to shape the ideas and institutions of the present day.

The two main tenets of belief that underlay liberalism were the freedom of the individual and the corruptibility of authority. As a political doctrine, liberalism built on Enlightenment rationalism and embraced the right to vote, civil liberties, legal equality, constitutional government, parliamentary sovereignty, and a free-market economy. Liberals believed that human beings were basically good and reasonable and needed freedom in which to flourish. The sole end of government should be to promote that freedom.

Jeremy Bentham (1748–1832) founded utilitarianism, a fundamentally liberal doctrine that argued for "the greatest happiness of the greatest number" in such works as *Introduction to the Principles of Morals and Legislation*.

Bentham believed that government could achieve positive ends through limited and "scientific" intervention. John Stuart Mill (1806–1873) forged his own brand of classical liberalism in his treatise *On Liberty* (1859). Mill went beyond existing political analyses to apply economic doctrines to social conditions in *Principles of Political Economy* (1848). He espoused social reform for the poor and championed the equality of women and the necessity of birth control. David Ricardo (1772–1823), in *Principles of Political Economy and Taxation* (1817), outlined his opposition to government intervention in foreign trade and elaborated his "iron law of wages," which contended that wages would stabilize at the subsistence level. Increased wages would cause the working classes to increase, and the resulting competition in the labor market would drive wages down to the subsistence level.

In its most basic sense, nationalism before 1850 was the political doctrine that glorified the people united against the absolutism of kings and the tyranny of foreign oppressors. The success of the French Revolution and the spread of Napoleonic reforms boosted nationalist doctrines, which were most fully articulated on the Continent. In the period between 1830 and 1850, many nationalists were liberals and many liberals were nationalists. The nationalist yearning for liberation meshed with the liberal political program of overthrowing tyrannical rule. Beyond ideology and political practices, nationalism began to capture the imagination of groups who resented foreign domination. Expanding state bureaucracies did little to tame the centrifugal forces of nationalist feeling and probably exacerbated a desire for independence in eastern and central Europe, especially in the Habsburg-ruled lands.

Unlike liberalism and nationalism, which were fundamentally political ideologies, romanticism designated a variety of literary and artistic movements throughout Europe that spanned the period from the late eighteenth century to the mid nineteenth century. Among the first romantics were the English poets William Wordsworth (1770–1850) and Samuel Taylor Coleridge (1772–1834), whose collaborative *Lyrical Ballads* (1798) exemplified the iconoclastic romantic idea that poetry was the result of "the spontaneous overflow of powerful feelings," rather than a formal and highly disciplined intellectual exercise.

Romantics in general rebelled against the confinement of classical forms and refused to accept the supremacy of reason over emotions. By rooting artistic vision in spontaneity, romantics endorsed a concept of creativity based on the supremacy of human freedom. The artist was valued in a new way as a genius through whose insight and intuition great art was created. Building on the work of the eighteenth-century philosopher Immanuel Kant (1724–1804), romanticism embraced subjective knowledge. Inspiration and intuition took the place of reason and science in the romantic pantheon of values.

Conservatism was not a rejection of political, economic, and social change. Like liberalism, conservatism represented a dynamic adaptation to a social system in transition. In place of individualism, conservatives stressed the corporate nature of European society; in place of reason and progress, conservatives saw organic growth and tradition. Liberty, argued British statesman Edmund Burke (1729–1797) in *Reflections on the Revolution in France* (1790), must emerge out of the gradual development of the old order and not its destruction.

Socialism, like other ideologies of the first half of the nineteenth century, grew out of the changes in the structure of daily life and the structure of power. There were as many stripes of socialists as there were liberals, nationalists, and conservatives. Socialists as a group shared a concern with "alienation," although they may not all have used the term. Socialist thinkers in France theorized about alternative societies in which wealth would be more equitably distributed.

To Henri de Saint-Simon (1760–1825) the accomplishments and potential of industrial development represented the highest stage in history. In a perfect and just society, productive work would be the basis of all prestige and power. The elite of society would be organized according to the hierarchy of its productive members with industrial leaders at the top. Like Saint-Simon, the French social theorist Pierre Joseph Proudhon (1809–1865) recognized the social value of work. But unlike Saint-Simon, Proudhon refused to accept the dominance of industrial society. Proudhon gained national prominence with his ideas about a just society, free credit, and equitable exchange. In his famous pamphlet, *What Is Property?* (1840), Proudhon answered, "Property is theft." This statement was not, however, an argument for the abolition of private ownership. Proudhon reasoned that industrialization had destroyed workers' rights, which included the right to the profits of their own labor. In attacking "property" in its meaning of profits amassed from the labor of others, Proudhon was arguing for a socialist concept of limited possession: People had the right to own only what they had earned from their own labor.

The emancipation of women had been an issue acknowledged and then silenced by French revolutionary leaders at the end of the eighteenth century. The question of women's emancipation, tied as it often was to talk of freeing the slaves, reemerged again in the nineteenth century as a moral question. After 1815 it became a political question as well. Individual critiques coalesced into action by reform groups. Some social reformers put the issue of women's freedom at the center of their plans to redesign society.

*R*evolution and Unification

Few Europeans alive in 1830 remembered the age of revolution from 1789 to 1799. Yet the legends were kept alive from one generation to the next. Secret political organizations perpetuated Jacobin republicanism. Mutual aid societies and artisan associations preserved the rituals of democratic culture. A revolutionary culture seemed to be budding in the student riots in Germany and in the revolutionary waves that swept across southern and central Europe in the early 1820s. Outside Manchester, England, in August

A savage satire of the Peterloo massacre by cartoonist George Cruikshank. One soldier urges the others on by telling them that the more poor people they kill, the less taxes they will have to pay for poor relief.

1819, a crowd of 80,000 people gathered in St. Peter's Field to hear speeches for parliamentary reform and universal male suffrage. The cavalry swept down on them in a bloody slaughter that came to be known as the "Peterloo" massacre, a bitter reference to the Waterloo victory four years before.

Conservatism took a reactionary turn in the hands of the Austrian statesman Prince Klemens von Metternich ((1773–1859). The Carlsbad decrees of 1819 are a good example of the "Metternich system" of espionage, censorship, and university repression in central Europe, which sought to eliminate any constitutional or nationalist sentiments that had arisen during the Napoleonic period. The German Confederation approved the decrees against free speech and civil liberties and set up mechanisms to root out "subversive" university students. Metternich set out to crush liberalism, constitutionalism, and parliamentarianism in central Europe. For most of the 1820s, Metternich, sitting comfortably in Vienna, was reassured that all was well. The diplomatic settlements of the Congress of Vienna and subsequent international conferences were working to maintain the status quo. Few understood—least of all Metternich—that the fabric of stability and order was beginning to unravel at the end of the decade.

The Revolutions of 1830

In France the late 1820s was a period of increasing political friction. Charles X (1824–1830), the former comte d'Artois, had never resigned himself to the constitutional monarchy accepted by his brother and predecessor, Louis XVIII. When Charles assumed the throne in 1824, he dedicated himself to a true restoration of kingship as it existed before the Revolution. To this end, he realigned the monarchy with the Catholic church and undertook several unpopular measures, including approval of the death penalty for those found guilty of sacrilege. The king's bourgeois critics, heavily influenced by liberal ideas about political economy and constitutional rights, sought increased political power through their activities in secret organizations and in public elections. The king responded to his critics by relying on his ultraroyalist supporters to run the government. In May 1830 the king dissolved the Chamber of Deputies and ordered new elections. The elections returned a liberal majority unfavorable to the king. Charles X retaliated with what proved to be his last political act, the Four Ordinances, in which he censored the press, changed the electoral law to favor his own candidates, dissolved the newly elected Chamber, and ordered new elections.

Opposition to Charles X might have remained at the level of political wrangling and journalistic protest, if it had not been for the problems plaguing the people of Paris. A severe winter in France had driven up food prices by 75 percent. The king underestimated the extent of hardship and the political volatility of the population. Throughout the spring of 1830 prices continued to rise and Charles continued to blunder. In a spontaneous uprising in the last days of July 1830, workers took to the streets of Paris. The revolution they initiated spread rapidly to towns and the countryside, as people throughout France protested the cost of living, hoarding by grain merchants, tax collection, and wage cuts. In "three glorious days" the restored Bourbon regime was pulled down and Charles X fled to England.

The people fighting in the streets demanded a republic, but they lacked organization and political experience. Liberal bourgeois politicians quickly filled the power vacuum. They presented Charles' cousin, the duc d'Orléans, as the savior of France and the new constitutional monarch. This July Monarchy, born of a revolution, put an end to the Bourbon Restoration. Louis-Philippe, the former duc do'Orléans, became "king of the French." The Charter that he brought with him was, like its predecessor, based on restricted suffrage, with property ownership a requisite for voting.

Popular disturbances did not always result in revolution. In Britain rural and town riots erupted over grain prices and distribution, but no revolution followed. German workers broke their machines to protest low wages and loss of control of the workplace, but princes were not displaced. In Switzerland reformers found strength in the French revolutionary example. Ten Swiss cantons granted liberal constitutions and established universal manhood suffrage, freedom of expression, and legal equality.

In southern Europe, Turkish overlords ruled Greece as part of the Ottoman Empire. The longing for independence smoldered in Greece throughout the 1820s as public pressure to support the Greeks mounted in Europe. Greek insurrections were answered by Turkish retaliations throughout the Ottoman Empire. The sultan of Turkey had been able to call on his vassal, the pasha of Egypt, to subdue Greece. In response, Great Britain, France, and Russia signed the Treaty of London in 1827, pledging intervention on behalf of Greece. In a joint effort, the three powers defeated the Egyptian fleet.

Russia declared war on Turkey the following year, seeking territorial concessions from the Ottoman Empire. Following the Russian victory, Great Britain and France joined Russia in declaring Greek independence. The concerted action of the three powers in favor of Greek independence was neither an endorsement of liberal ideals nor a support of Greek nationalism. The British, French, and Russians were reasserting their commitment made at the Congress of Vienna to territorial stability.

The overthrow of the Bourbon monarch in France served as a model for revolution in other parts of Europe. Following the French lead in the midst of the Greek crisis, the Belgian provinces revolted against the Netherlands. The Belgian uprising struck at the heart of the Vienna settlement. The Belgians wanted their own nation. Provoked by a food crisis similar to that in France, Belgian revolutionaries took to the streets in August 1830. Belgians protested the deterioration of their economic situation and made demands for their own Catholic religion, their own language, and constitutional rights. Bitter fighting on the barricades in Brussels ensued, and the movement for freedom and independence spread to the countryside.

The Great Powers disagreed on what to do. Russia, Austria, and Prussia were all eager to see the revolution crushed. France, having just established the new regime of the July Monarchy, and Great Britain, fearing the involvement of the central and eastern European powers in an area where Britain had traditionally had interests, were reluctant to intervene. A provisional government in Belgium set about the task of writing a constitution. All five great powers recognized Belgian independence, with the proviso that Belgium was to maintain the status of a neutral state.

Russia, Prussia, and Austria were convinced to accept Belgian independence because they were having their own problems in eastern and southern Europe. Revolution erupted to the east in Warsaw, Poland. Filled with a longing for national independence and driven by a desire for a true constitution, Polish army cadets and university students revolted in November 1830. Landed aristocrats and gentry helped establish a provisional government but soon split over how radical reforms should be. Polish peasants refused to support either landowning group. Within the year, Russia brought in 180,000 men to crush the revolution and reassert its rule over Poland.

In February 1831 the Italian states of Modena and Parma rose up to throw off Austrian domination of northern Italy. The revolutionaries were ineffective against Austrian troops. Revolution in the Papal States resulted in French occupation that lasted until 1838 without serious reforms. Nationalist and republican yearnings were driven underground, kept alive there in the Young Italy movement under the leadership of Giuseppe Mazzini.

Although the revolutions of 1830 are called "the forgotten revolutions" of the nineteenth century, they are important for several reasons. First, they made clear to European states their dependence on one another. The events of 1830 were a test of the Great Powers' commitment to stability and a balance of power in Europe. True to the principles of the Vienna settlements of 1815, European leaders preserved the status quo. Revolutions in Poland and Italy were contained by Russia and Austria without interference from the other powers. Where adaptation was necessary, as in Greece and Belgium, the Great Powers were able to compromise on settlements, although the solutions ran counter to previous policies. Heads of state were willing to use the forces of repression to stamp out protest. The international significance of the revolutions reveals a second important aspect of the events of 1830: the vulnerability of international politics to domestic instability.

Finally, the 1830 revolutions exposed a growing awareness of politics at all levels of European society. If policies in 1830 revealed a shared consciousness of events and shared values among ruling elites, the revolutions disclosed a growing awareness among the lower classes of the importance of politics in their daily lives. The impact of the French revolution of 1830 throughout Europe demonstrated the degree to which peoples of different countries identified with international events.

Reform in Great Britain

The right to vote had been an issue of contention in the revolutions of 1830 in western Europe. Only the Swiss cantons enforced the principle of one man, one vote. The July Revolution in France had doubled the electorate, but still only a tiny minority of the population (less than 1 percent) enjoyed the vote. Universal male suffrage had been mandated in 1793 during the Great Revolution but not implemented. This exclusion of the mass of the population from participation in electoral politics was no oversight. Those in power believed that the wealthiest property owners were best qualified to govern, in part because they had the greatest stake in politics and society. One also needed to own property in order to hold office because those who served in parliaments received no salary.

The propertied ruled Britain, too. There the dominance of a wealthy elite was strengthened by the geographic redistribution resulting from industrialization. Migration to cities had depleted the population of rural areas. Yet the electoral system did not adjust to these changes: Large towns had no parliamentary representation, while dwindling county electorates maintained their parliamentary strength. Areas that continued to enjoy representation greater than that justified by their population were dubbed *rotten* or *pocket* boroughs to indicate a corrupt and antiquated electoral system. In general, urban areas were grossly underrepresented as the wealthy few controlled county seats. Liberal reformers attempted to rectify the electoral inequalities by reassigning parliamentary seats on the basis of density of population.

Vested interests balked at attempted reforms and members of Parliament wrangled bitterly. Popular agitation by the lower classes provoked the fear of civil war and helped break the parliamentary deadlock. The Great Reform Bill of 1832 proposed a compromise. Although the vast majority of the population still did not have the vote, the new legislation strengthened the industrial and commercial elite in the towns, enfranchised most of the middle class, opened the way to social reforms, and encouraged the formation of political parties.

In the 1830s new radical reformers, disillusioned with the 1832 Reform Bill because it strengthened the power of a wealthy capitalist class, argued that democracy was the only answer to the problems plaguing British society. In 1838 a small group of labor leaders, including representatives of the London Working Men's Association, an organization of craft workers, drew up a document known as the People's Charter. The single most important demand of the Charter was that all men must have the vote. In addition, Chartists petitioned for a secret ballot, salaries for parliamentary service, elimination of property qualifications to run for office, equal electoral districts, and annual elections.

Chartism blossomed as a communal phenomenon in working-class towns and appeared to involve all members of the family. Women organized Chartist schools and Sunday schools in radical defiance of local church organizations. Many middle-class observers were sure that the moment for class war and revolutionary upheaval had arrived. The government responded with force to the perceived threat of armed rebellion and imprisoned a number of Chartist leaders. The final moment for Chartism occurred in April 1848 when 25,000 Chartist workers, inspired by revolutionary events on the Continent, assembled in London to march on the House of Commons. They carried with them a newly signed petition demanding the enactment of the terms of the Charter. In response, the government deputized nearly two hundred thousand "special" constables in the streets. These deputized private citizens were London property owners and skilled workers intent on holding back a revolutionary rabble. Tired, cold, and rain-soaked, the Chartist demonstrators disbanded. No social revolution took place in Great Britain, and the dilemma of democratic representation was deferred.

Workers Unite

The word *proletariat* entered European languages before the mid nineteenth century to describe those workers afloat in the labor pool who owned nothing, not even the tools of their labor, and who were becoming "appendages" to the new machines that dominated production. From the 1820s to the 1850s sporadic but intense outbursts of machine breaking occurred in continental

Europe, and skilled workers, fearing that they would be pulled down into the new proletariat because of mechanization and the increased scale of production, began organizing in new ways after 1830.

Uprisings and strikes in France increased dramatically from 1831 to 1834 and favored the destruction of the monarchy and the creation of a democratic republic. Many French craft workers grew conscious of themselves as a class and embraced a socialism heavily influenced by their own traditions and contemporary socialist writings. Republican socialism spread throughout France by means of a network of traveling journeymen and tapped into growing economic hardship and political discontent with the July Monarchy. Government repression drove worker organizations underground in the late 1830s, but secret societies proliferated.

Women were an important part of the work force in the industrializing societies. Nevertheless, the French historian and social observer Jules Michelet (1798–1874) exclaimed, "The working woman, what a blasphemous term!" Working men were keenly aware of the competition with cheaper female labor in the factories. Women formed a salaried work force in the home, too. In order to produce cheaply and in large quantities, some manufacturers turned to subcontractors for the simpler tasks in the work process. These new middlemen contracted out work like cutting and sewing to needy women, who were often responsible for caring for family members in their homes.

Cheap female labor paid by the piece allowed employers to profit by keeping overhead costs low and by driving down the wages of skilled workers. Trade unions opposed women's work both in the home and in the factories. Women's talents, union leaders explained, were more properly devoted to domestic chores; their accomplishments as paid workers were consistently regarded as inferior in skill and strength. Unions argued that their members should earn a family wage "sufficient to support a wife and children." Unions consistently excluded women workers from their ranks.

In some cases, working women formed their own organizations like that of the Parisian seamstresses who joined together to demand improved working conditions. On the whole, however, domestic workers in the home remained isolated from other working women, and many women in factories feared the loss of their jobs if they engaged in political activism. The wages of Europe's working women remained low, often below the level of subsistence.

The Revolutions of 1848

Europeans had never experienced a year like 1848. Beginning soon after the ringing in of the new year, revolutionary fervor swept through nearly every European country. By year's end, regimes had been created and destroyed. France, Italy, the German states, Austria, Hungary, and Bohemia were shaken to their foundations. Switzerland, Denmark, and Romania experienced lesser upheavals. Great Britain had survived reformist agitation, and famine-crippled

Ireland had endured a failed insurrection. No one was sure what had happened. Each country's conflict was based on a unique mix of issues, but all were connected in their conscious emulation of a revolutionary tradition.

Hindsight reveals warning signs in the two years before the 1848 cataclysm. Beginning in 1846 a severe famine—the last serious food crisis Europe would experience—racked Europe. Lack of grain drove up prices. An increasing percentage of disposable income was spent on food for survival. Lack of spending power severely damaged markets and forced thousands of industrial workers out of their jobs. The famine hurt everyone—the poor, workers, employers, and investors—as recession paralyzed the economy.

The food crisis took place in a heavily charged political atmosphere. Throughout Europe during the 1840s middle and lower classes had intensified their agitation for democracy. Chartists in Great Britain argued for a wider electorate. Bourgeois reformers in France campaigned for universal manhood suffrage. The movement was known as the "banquet" campaign because its leaders attempted to raise money by giving speeches at subscribed dinners. In making demands for political participation, those agitating for the vote necessarily criticized those in power. Freedom of speech and freedom of assembly were demanded as inalienable rights. The food crisis combined with political activism were the ingredients of an incendiary situation.

In addition to a burgeoning democratic culture, growing demands for national autonomy based on linguistic and cultural claims spread through central, southern, and eastern Europe. The revolts in Poland in 1846, although failures, encouraged similar movements for national liberation among Italians and Germans. Even in the relatively homogeneous nation of France, concerns with national mission and national glory grew among the regime's critics. National unity was primarily a middle-class ideal. Liberal lawyers, teachers, and businessmen from Dublin to Budapest to Prague agitated for separation from foreign rule. Austria, with an empire formed of numerous ethnic minorities, had the most to lose. Since 1815 Metternich had been ruthless in stamping out nationalist dissent. By the 1840s national claims were assuming a cultural legitimacy that was difficult to dismiss or ignore.

The events in France in the cold February of 1848 ignited the conflagration that swept Europe. On 22 February bourgeois reformers had staged their largest banquet to date in Paris in support of extension of the vote. City officials became nervous at the prospect of thousands of workers assembling for political purposes and canceled the scheduled banquet. This was the spark that touched off the powder keg. In a spontaneous uprising Parisians demonstrated against the government's repressive measures. Skilled workers took to the streets not only in favor of the banned banquet but also with the hope that the government would recognize the importance of labor to the social order. Shots were fired; a demonstrator was killed. The French Revolution of 1848 had begun.

Events moved quickly. The National Guard, a citizen militia of bourgeois Parisians, defected from Louis-Philippe. Many army troops garrisoned in Paris crossed the barricades to join revolutionary workers. The king attempted

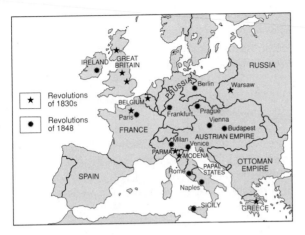

Revolutions of 1830–1848

some reform, but it was too little and too late. Louis-Philippe fled. The Second Republic was proclaimed at the insistence of the revolutionary crowds on the barricades. The Provisional Government, led by the poet Alphonse de Lamartine (1790–1869), included members of both factions of political reformers of the July Monarchy: moderates who sought constitutional reforms and an extension of the suffrage, and radicals who favored universal manhood suffrage and social programs to deal with poverty and work. Only the threat of popular violence held together this uneasy alliance.

The people fighting in the streets had little in common with the bourgeois reformers who assumed power on 24 February. Workers made a social revolution out of a commitment to their "right to work," which would replace the right to property as the organizing principle of the new society. Only one member of the new Provisional Government was a worker, and he was included as a token symbol of the intentions of the new government. He was known as "Albert, the worker," and was not addressed by his surname, Martin. The government acknowledged the demand of the "right to work" and set up two mechanisms to guarantee workers' relief. First, a commission of workers and employers was created to act as a grievance and bargaining board and settle questions of common concern in the workplace. Headed by the socialist Louis Blanc (1811–1882) and known as the Luxembourg Commission, the worker-employer parliament was an important innovation but accomplished little other than deflecting workers' attention away from the problems of the Provisional Government. The second measure was the creation of "national workshops" to deal with the problems of unemployment in Paris. Workers from all over France poured into Paris with the hope of finding jobs. The workshops, however, had a residency requirement that even Parisians had difficulty meeting. As a result, unemployment skyrocketed. Furthermore, the government was going bankrupt trying to support the program. The need to raise taxes upset peasants in the provinces. National pressure mounted to repudiate the programs of the revolution.

French workers were too weak to dominate the revolution. In May the government dissolved the workshops, and recalled General Louis Cavaignac (1802–1857) from service in Algeria to maintain order. In a wave of armed insurrection, Parisian workers rebelled in June. Using troops from the provinces who had no identification with the urban population and employing guerrilla techniques he had mastered in Algeria, Cavaignac put down the uprising. The Second Republic was placed under the military dictatorship of Cavaignac until December, when presidential elections were scheduled.

France was not alone in undergoing revolution in 1848. Long-suppressed desires for civil liberties and constitutional reforms erupted in widespread popular disturbances in Prussia and the German states. Fearing a war with France and unable to count on Austria or Russia for support, the princes who ruled Baden, Württemberg, Hesse-Darmstadt, Bavaria, Saxony, and Hanover followed the advice of moderate liberals and acceded quickly to revolutionary demands. In Prussia, King Friedrich Wilhelm IV (1840–1861) preferred to use military force to respond to popular demonstrations. Only in mid-March 1848 did the Prussian king yield to the force of the revolutionary crowds building barricades in Berlin by ordering his troops to leave the city and by promising to create a national Prussian assembly. The king was now a prisoner of the revolution.

Meanwhile, the collapse of absolute monarchy in Prussia gave further impetus to a constitutional movement among the liberal leaders of the German states. The governments of all the German states were invited to elect delegates to a national parliament in Frankfurt. The Frankfurt parliament, which was convened in May 1848, had as its dual charge the framing of a constitution and the unification of Germany. It was composed for the most part of members of the middle class, with civil servants, lawyers, and intellectuals predominating. In spite of the principle of universal manhood suffrage, there was not a single worker among the 800 men elected. To most parliamentarians, who were trained in universities and shared a social and cultural identity, nationalism and constitutionalism were inextricably related. Germans consistently linked national identity with political goals of independence and self-expression.

As straightforward as the desire for a German nation appeared to be, it was complicated by two important facts. First, there were non-German minorities living in German states. What was to be done with the Poles, Czechs, Slovenes, Italians, and Dutch in a newly constituted and autonomous German nation? Second, there were Germans living outside the German states under Habsburg rule in Austria, in Danish Schlewsig and Holstein, in Posen (Poznan), in Russian Poland, and in European Russia. How were they to be included within the linguistically and ethnically constituted German nation? After much wrangling over a "small" Germany that excluded Austrian Germans and a "large" Germany that included them, the Frankfurt Parliament opted for the small Germany solution in March 1849. The crown of the new nation was offered to the unpredictable Friedrich Wilhelm IV of Prussia, head of the largest and most powerful of the German states. Unhappy with his capitulation to the revolutionary crowd in March 1848, the Prussian king refused to accept a "crown from the gutter." He had his own plans to rule over a middle European bloc but not at the behest of liberal parliamentary rule. The attempt to create a German nation crumbled with his unwillingness to lead.

Revolution in Austrian-dominated central Europe was concentrated in three places: Vienna, where German students, workers, and middle-class liberals were agitating for constitutional reform and political participation; Budapest, where the Magyars, the dominant ethnic group in Hungary, led a movement for national autonomy; and Prague, where Czechs were attempting

In this incident from the revolutionary year of 1848, imperial Austrian troops fire on a Viennese crowd assembled at the convening of the Estates-General to petition for their right to a voice in the new social order.

self-rule. By April 1848 Metternich had fallen from power and the Viennese revolutionaries had set up a constituent assembly. In Budapest the initial steps of the patriot Lajos Kossuth (1802–1894) toward establishing a separate Hungarian state seemed equally solid, as the Magyars defeated Habsburg troops. Habsburg armies were more successful in Prague, where they crushed the revolution in June 1848.

The Habsburg Empire was also under siege in Italy, where the Kingdom of the Two Sicilies, Tuscany, and Piedmont declared new constitutions in March 1848. Championed by Charles Albert of Piedmont, Venice and Lombardy rose up against Austria. Nationalist sentiments had percolated underground in the Young Italy movement, founded in 1831 by Giuseppe Mazzini. Mazzini (1805–1872), a tireless and idealistic patriot, favored a democratic revolution. In spite of a reputation for liberal politics, Pope Pius IX (1846–1878) lost control of Rome and was forced to flee the city. Mazzini became head of the Republic of Rome, created in February 1849.

The French government decided to intervene to protect the pope's interests and sent in troops to defeat the republicans. One of Mazzini's disciples, Giuseppe Garibaldi (1807–1882), returned from exile in South America to undertake the defense of Rome. Garibaldi was a capable soldier who had learned the tactics of guerrilla warfare by joining independence struggles in Brazil and Argentina. Although his legion of poorly armed patriots and soldiers of fortune, known from their attire as the Red Shirts, waged a valiant effort to defend the city from April to June 1849, they were no match for the highly trained French army. French troops restored Pius IX as ruler of the Papal States.

Meanwhile, from August 1848 to the following spring, the Habsburg armies fought and finally defeated each of the revolutions. Austrian success can be explained in part because the various Italian groups of Piedmontese, Tuscans, Venetians, Romans, and Neapolitans continued to identify with their local concerns and lacked coordination and central organization. Both Mazzini and Pius IX had failed to provide the focal point of leadership necessary for a successful national movement.

By the fall of 1849, Austria had solved the problems in its own capital and with Italy and Hungary by military dominance. Emperor Ferdinand I (1835–1848), whose authority had been weakened irreparably by the overthrow of Metternich, abdicated in favor of his 18-year-old nephew, Franz Josef I (1848–1916). Austria understood that a Germany united under Friedrich Wilhelm IV of Prussia would undermine Austrian dominance in central Europe. In 1850 Austrians threatened the Prussians with war if they did not give up their plans for a unified Germany. In November of that year Prussian ministers signed an agreement with their Austrian counterparts in the Moravian city of Olmutz. The convention became known as "the humiliation of Olmutz" because Prussia was forced to accept Austrian dominance or go to war. In every case, military force and diplomatic measures prevailed to defeat the national and liberal movements within the German states and the Austrian Empire.

The Politics of Unification

The revolutions of 1848 had occurred in a period of experimentation from below. Radicals enlisting popular support had tried and failed to reshape European states for their own nationalist, liberal, and socialist ends. Governments in Paris, Vienna, Berlin, and a number of lesser states had been swept away. The revolutions had created a power vacuum but no durable solutions. To fill that vacuum, a new breed of politicians emerged in the 1850s and 1860s, men who did not speak of restorations or concerted European efforts. These were men who understood the importance of the centralized nation-state and saw the need of reforms from above. They also had a new appreciation of the importance of foreign policy successes as a means of furthering domestic programs. Cavour of Italy, Bismarck of Germany, and Louis Napoleon of France shared a new realism about means and ends.

Between 1815 and 1850 those who experimented with political power had worked from below or outside the traditional political system. In the 1850s and 1860s those committed to radical transformations worked from within the existing system. When revolutionary goals were achieved, direction came from above. National unification had escaped the grasp of liberals and radicals between 1848 and 1850. After 1850 liberal nationalism was subordinated to conservative state-building. Military force validated what intellectuals and revolutionaries had not been able to legitimate through ideological claims.

The Crimean War. After 1815 Russia had flexed its muscles as the greatest military power in Europe. With the containment of France in 1815, Russia was committed to preserving the status quo in the West. It had fulfilled its role as policeman of Europe by supporting Austria against Hungary and Prussia in 1849 and 1850. But Russia sought greater power to the south in the Balkans. The narrow straits connecting the Black Sea with the Aegean Sea were controlled by the Ottoman Empire. Russia hoped to benefit from Ottoman weakness caused by internal conflicts and gain control of the straits, which were the only outlet for the Russian fleet to the warm waters of the Mediterranean, Russia's southern outlet to the world.

At the center of the hope for Ottoman disintegration lay the "Eastern Question," the term used to designate the problems surrounding the European territories controlled by the Ottoman Empire. Each of the Great Powers—including Russia, Great Britain, Austria, Prussia, and France—hoped to benefit territorially from the collapse of Ottoman control. In 1853 Great Power rivalry over the Eastern Question created an international situation that led to war.

In 1853 the Russian government demanded that the Turkish government recognize Russia's right to protect Greek Orthodox believers in the Ottoman Empire. The Turkish government refused Russian demands and the Russians, feeling that their prestige had been damaged, ordered troops to enter the Danubian Principalities held by the Turks. In October 1853 the Turkish government, counting on support from Great Britain and France, declared war on Russia.

Russia easily prevailed over its weaker neighbor to the south. In a four-hour battle, a Russian squadron destroyed the Turkish fleet off the coast of Sinope. Tsar Nicholas I (1825–1855) drew up the terms of a settlement with the Ottoman Empire and submitted them to Great Britain and France for review. The two western European powers, fearing Russian aggrandizement at Turkish expense, responded by declaring war on Russia on 28 March 1854, the date that marked a new phase in the Crimean War. Both Great Britain and France, like Russia, had ambitions in the Balkans and the eastern Mediterranean. The Austrian Empire, frightened by Russia's seizure of the Danubian Principalities of Moldavia and Walachia, remained neutral but threatened to enter the war with Britain and France on the side of Turkey. The Italian kingdom of Piedmont-Sardinia joined the war on the side of the western European powers in January 1855, hoping to make its name militarily and win recognition for its aim to unite Italy into a single nation. Without explicit economic interests, the Great Powers and the lesser Italian state of Piedmont-Sardinia were motivated by ambition, prestige, and rivalry in the Balkans.

British and French troops landed in the Crimea, the Russian peninsula extending into the Black Sea, in September 1854, with the intention of capturing Sevastopol, Russia's heavily fortified chief naval base on the Black Sea. The allies laid siege to the fortress at Sevastopol, which fell only after 322 days of battle on 11 September 1855. The defeated Russians abandoned Sevastopol, blew up their forts, and sank their own ships. Russia, now facing the threat of Austrian entry into the war, agreed to preliminary peace terms.

In the Peace of Paris of 1856, Russia relinquished its claim as protector of Christians in Turkey. The British gained the neutralization of the Black Sea. The mouth of the Danube was returned to Turkish control, and an international commission was created to oversee safe navigation on the Danube. The Danubian Principalities were placed under joint guarantee of the powers, and Russia gave up a small portion of Bessarabia. In 1861 the Principalities were united in the independent nation of Romania. The war had dramatic and enduring consequences. Russia ceased playing an active role in European affairs and turned toward expansion in central Asia. Its withdrawal opened up the possibility for a move by Prussia in central Europe. The concert of Europe so carefully crafted by European statesmen in 1815 came to an end with the Crimean War.

Unifying Italy.   The movement to reunite Italy culturally and politically was known as the *Risorgimento*, literally, "resurgence." Both Giuseppe Mazzini's Young Italy movement and Giuseppe Garibaldi's Red Shirts had as their goal in 1848 a united republican Italy achieved through direct popular action. But they had failed. It took a politician of aristocratic birth to recognize that Mazzini's and Garibaldi's model of revolutionary action was doomed against the powerful Austrian military machine. Mazzini was a moralist. Garibaldi was a fighter. But Camillo Benso di Cavour (1810–1861), the opportunistic politician, was a realist.

As premier of Sardinia from 1852 to 1859 and again in 1860–1861, Cavour was well placed to launch his campaign for Italian unity. The kingdom of Sardinia, whose principal state was Piedmont, had made itself a focal point for unification efforts. Its king, Carlo-Alberto (1831–1849), had stood alone among Italian rulers in opposing Austrian domination of the Italian peninsula in 1848 and 1849. Severely defeated by the Austrians, he was forced to abdicate. He was succeeded by his son Victor Emmanuel II (1849–1861), who had the good sense to appoint Cavour as his first minister. From the start, Cavour undertook liberal administrative reforms that included tax reform, stabilization of the currency, improvement of the railway system, the creation of a transatlantic steamship system, and the support of private enterprise. With these programs Cavour created for Sardinia the dynamic image of progressive change. He involved Sardinia in the Crimean War, thereby securing its status among the European powers.

Most important, however, was his successful pursuit of an alliance with France against Austria in the Treaty of Plombières, signed by Napoleon III in 1858. The treaty was quickly followed by an arranged provocation against the Habsburg monarchy. Austria declared war in 1859 and was easily defeated by French forces in the battles of Magenta and Solferino. The peace, signed in November 1859 at Zurich, joined Lombardy to the Piedmontese state. Cavour wielded the electoral weapon of the plebiscite, a method of direct voting that gives to electors the choice of voting for or against some important public question, in order to unite Tuscany, Parma, and Modena under Sardinia's king.

Cavour's approach was not without its costs. His partnership with a stronger power meant sometimes following France's lead, and the need to cajole French support meant enriching France with territorial gain in the form of Nice and Savoy. Sardinia, however, got more than it gave up. In the summer of 1859 revolutionary assemblies in Tuscany, Modena, Parma, and the Romagna, wanting to eject their Austrian rulers, voted in favor of union with the Piedmontese. By April 1860 these four areas of central Italy were under Victor Emmanuel's rule. Sardinia had doubled in size to become the dominant power on the Italian peninsula.

Southern Italians took their lead from events in central Italy and in the spring of 1860 initiated disorders against the rule of King Francis II (1859–1861) of Naples. Uprisings in Sicily inspired Giuseppe Garibaldi to return from his self-imposed exile to organize his own army of Red Shirts, known as the Thousand, who liberated Sicily and then crossed to the Italian mainland to expel Francis II from Naples. Garibaldi next turned his attention to the liberation of the Holy City, where a French garrison protected the pope.

As Garibaldi's popularity as a national hero grew, Cavour became alarmed at the competition in uniting Italy and took secret steps to block the advance of the Red Shirts and their leader. To seize the initiative, Cavour directed the Piedmontese army into the Papal States. After defeating the pope's troops, Cavour's men crossed into the Neapolitan state and scored important victories against forces loyal to the king of Naples. Cavour proceeded to annex southern Italy for Victor Emmanuel, using plebiscites to seal the procedure. At this point, in 1860, Garibaldi yielded his own conquered territories to the Piedmon-

Unification of Italy

tese ruler, making possible the declaration of a united Italy under Victor Emmanuel II, who reigned as king of Italy from 1861 to 1878.

The new king of Italy was now poised to acquire Venetia, still under Austrian rule, and Rome, still ruled by Pope Pius IX, and he devoted much of his foreign policy in the 1860s to these ends. In 1866, when Austria lost a war with Prussia, Italy struck a deal with the victor and gained control of Venetia. When Prussia prevailed against France in 1870, Victor Emmanuel II took over Rome. The boot of Italy, from top to toe, was not a single nation. The pope remained in the Vatican, opposed to an Italy united under King Victor Emmanuel II.

Unifying Germany. In an age of realistic politicians, Otto von Bismarck (1815–1898) emerged as the supreme practitioner of *Realpolitik*, the ruthless pursuit by any means, including illegal and violent ones, to advance the interests of his country. Bismarck was a Junker, an aristocratic estate owner from east of the Elbe River, who entered politics in 1847. In the 1850s he became aware of Prussia's future in the center of Europe: He saw that the old elites must be allied with the national movement in order to survive.

In 1850 Prussia had been forced to accept Austrian dominance in central Europe or go to war. Throughout the following decade, however, Prussia systematically undermined Austrian power by wielding the trade agreements of the Zollverein as a tool to exclude Austria from German economic affairs. In

1862, at the moment of a crisis provoked by the king over military reorganization, Bismarck became minister-president of the Prussian cabinet and foreign minister. He overrode the parliamentary body, the Diet, by reorganizing the army without a formally approved budget. In 1864 he constructed an alliance between Austria and Prussia for the purpose of invading Schleswig, a predominantly German-speaking territory controlled by the king of Denmark, whose population hoped to become part of the German Confederation. Within five days of invasion, Denmark yielded the duchies of Schleswig and Holstein, now to be ruled jointly by Austria and Prussia.

Ascertaining that he had a free hand in central Europe, Bismarck skillfully promoted a crisis between Austria and Prussia over management of the territories. Counting on the neutrality of France and Great Britain, the support of Piedmont-Sardinia, and good relations with Russia, Bismarck led his country into war with Austria in June 1866. The war took its name from its short duration. In this Seven Weeks' War Austrian forces proved to be no match for the better equipped and better trained Prussian army. Bismarck dictated the terms of the peace, which demonstrated that he had no desire to cripple Austria, only to exclude it from a united Germany in which Prussia would be the dominant force. Austria's exclusion from Germany forced the Austrian government to deal with its own internal problems of imperial organization. In 1867, in response to pressures from the subject nationalities, the Habsburg Empire transformed itself into a dual monarchy of two independent and equal states under one ruler, who would be both the emperor of Austria and the king of Hungary. In spite of the reorganization, the nationalities problem persisted, and ethnic groups began to agitate for total independence from imperial rule.

Bismarck's biggest obstacle to German unification was laid to rest with Austria's defeat. The south German states continued to resist the idea of Prussian dominance, but growing numbers of people in Baden, Württemberg, Bavaria, and the southern parts of Hesse-Darmstadt recognized the necessity of uniting under Prussian leadership.

Many French observers were troubled by the Prussian victory over Austria and were apprehensive over what a united Germany might portend for the future of French dominance in Europe. Napoleon III made clear his opposition to further Prussian growth and attempted unsuccessfully to contain Prussian ambitions through diplomatic maneuverings. Instead, France found itself stranded without important European allies. In the spring of 1870 Bismarck decided to seize the initiative and provoke a crisis with France. The issue of succession to the Spanish throne gave him the opportunity he sought. On 13 July 1870, the Prussian king (later Emperor William I) sent a message to Napoleon III reporting a meeting with the French ambassador. Bismarck skillfully edited this "Ems Dispatch" to suggest that the French ambassador had insulted the Prussian king, then leaked news of the incident to the press in both countries.

As a direct result of this misunderstanding deliberately manufactured by Bismarck, France declared war on Prussia in July 1870. The southern German princes, as Bismarck hoped, immediately sided with the Prussian king. For years before hostilities broke out, the Prussians had been preparing for war. Unlike the Germans, the French had not coordinated deployment with the new technology of the railroad. Although French troops had the latest equipment, they were sent into battle without instructions on how to use it. Finally, the Prussian-led German army was superior, outnumbering French troops 450,000 to 260,000. All these factors combined to spell disaster for the French. Within a matter of weeks, it was clear that France had lost this Franco-Prussian War. The path was now clear for the declaration of the German Empire in January 1871.

In unifying Germany, Bismarck built on the constitution of the North German Confederation formed in 1867, which guaranteed Prussian dominance. Bismarck used the bureaucracy as a mainstay of the emperor. The new Reichstag—the national legislative assembly—was to be elected by means of universal male suffrage, a concession to the liberals. Yet the constitution was not a liberal one, since the Reichstag was not sovereign and the chancellor was accountable only to the emperor.

The unification of Germany was not achieved by democratic means. Bismarck understood the new age. As he explained in a speech to the Prussian Diet, "The great questions of the time are not decided by speeches and majority decisions—that was the error of 1848 and 1849—but by iron and blood."

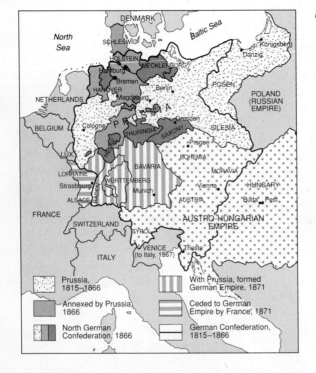

Unification of Germany

Reforming European Society

Three different models for social and political reform developed in Europe after 1850. One model is that of France, where the French emperor worked through a highly centralized administrative structure and with a highly valued elite of specialists in order to achieve social and economic transformation.

Great Britain provides another model, in which reform was fostered through liberal parliamentary democracy. In government by "amateurs," with local rather than a highly centralized administration, British legislation alternated between a philosophy of freedom and one of protection. But reforms were always hammered out by parliamentary means with the support of a gradually expanding electorate.

Finally, Russia offers a model for reform. Like Britain, Russia had avoided revolution at mid-century. Like Britain, it hoped to preserve social peace. Yet the Russian model for reform stands in dramatic contrast to Britain's. Russia was still a semifeudal society in the 1850s. Beginning in the late 1850s, Russia embarked on a radical restructuring of society by autocratic means. Reforms in the three societies had little in common ideologically, but all reflected a commitment to progress and an awareness of the state's role and responsibility in achieving it.

The Second Empire in France, 1852–1870

Louis Napoleon (1808–1873) was a nephew of the emperor Napoleon I, and with the death of Napoleon's son in 1832, Louis was aware that the mantle of future power and the family destiny fell to him. Nobody took Louis Napoleon very seriously, even when as the dark horse candidate he was elected president of the Second Republic in December 1848. The politicians were sure that he could be managed, so insignificant did he seem. They and the rest of France were literally caught sleeping before dawn on 2 December 1851, when the nephew of the great Napoleon seized power in a coup d'état and became dictator of France. Exactly one year later, he proclaimed himself Emperor Napoleon III and set about the tasks of establishing his dynasty and reclaiming French imperial glory.

The Second Empire achieved significant successes in a variety of areas. Napoleon III supported economic expansion and industrial development. During his reign the French economy prospered and flourished. A new private banking system, founded in 1852 by financiers and key political figures, enabled the pooling of investors' resources, small and large, to finance industrial expansion. Napoleon III surrounded himself with advisers who saw in prosperity the answer to all social problems. Between 1852 and 1860 the government supported a massive program of railroad construction. Jobs multiplied and investment increased. Agriculture expanded as railroad lines opened new markets. The rich got richer, but the extreme poverty of the first half of the nineteenth century was shrinking.

The best single example of the energy and commitment of the imperial regime was the rebuilding of the French capital. Before mid-century Paris was one of the most unsanitary, crime-ridden, and politically volatile capitals in Europe. Within fifteen years it had been transformed into a city of lights, wide boulevards and avenues, monumental vistas, parks, and gardens. Poor districts were turned into rubble to make way for the elegant apartment buildings of the Parisian bourgeoisie. The new housing was too expensive for workers, who were pushed out of Paris to the suburbs. Paris as the radical capital of France was being physically dismantled, and a new, more conservative political entity rose in its place as the middle classes took over the heart of the city.

Napoleon wanted Paris to be the center of Western culture and the envy of the world. Its wide, straight avenues served as the model for other French cities. The new Paris became an international model copied in Mexico City, Brussels, Madrid, Rome, Stockholm, and Barcelona between 1870 and 1900.

Workers demolish buildings to make way for the new Rue des Écoles during the rebuilding of the city of Paris. By 1870 few traces of the medieval walled city could be found.

Just as a new Paris would make France the center of culture, Napoleon III intended his blueprint for foreign policy to restore France to its pre-1815 status as the greatest European power. French governments after 1815 had been forced to abandon adventurous foreign policies. By involving France in both the Crimean War and the war for Italian unification, Napoleon III reversed this pattern. The accession of Nice and Savoy from Piedmont-Sardinia increased French territory and reversed the settlements of 1815.

The Italian campaign complicated relations with Great Britain, which feared a resurgent French militarism. French construction of the Suez Canal between the Red Sea and the Mediterranean also created tensions with Great Britain, protective of its own dominance in the Mediterranean and the Near East. Nevertheless, the free trade agreement between the British and the French in 1860—the Chevalier-Cobden Treaty—was a landmark in overseas policy and a commitment to liberal economic policies.

The Second Empire's involvement in Mexico was another matter. It was simply a fiasco. The Mexican government had been chronically unable to pay its foreign debts and France was Mexico's largest creditor. Napoleon III hoped that by intervening in Mexican affairs he could strengthen ties with Great Britain and Spain, to whom the Mexicans also owed money. With the backing of Mexican conservatives who opposed Mexican president Benito Juárez (1806–1872), Napoleon III supported the Austrian archduke Maximilian (1832–1867) as emperor of Mexico. After he was crowned in 1863, the new Mexican emperor struggled to rule in an enlightened manner, but he was stymied from the beginning by the lack of popular support. Napoleon III recalled the 34,000 French troops that, at considerable expense, were keeping Maximilian's troubled regime in place. Abandoned, Maximilian was captured and executed by a firing squad in the summer of 1867.

The Prussian victory over Austria in the Seven Weeks' War had dramatically changed the situation on the Continent. Pundits in Paris were fond of saying that the Austrian loss really marked the defeat of France. France's position within Europe was threatened and Napoleon III knew it. The Mexican disaster had damaged the prestige of Napoleon III's regime in the international arena, and in 1870 the humiliatingly rapid defeat of French imperial forces in the Franco-Prussian War brought to an end the experiment in liberal empire.

The Paris Commune.   Soundly defeated on 2 September 1870, Napoleon III and his fighting force of 100,000 men became Prussia's prisoners of war. With the emperor's defeat, the Second Empire collapsed. But even with the capture of Napoleon III, the French capital city of Paris refused to capitulate. The regime's liberal critics in Paris seized the initiative to proclaim France a republic. If a corrupt and decadent empire could not save the nation, then France's Third Republic could. In mid-September 1870 two German armies surrounded Paris and began a siege that lasted for over four months. Bismarck's troops were intent on bringing the city to its knees not by fighting but by cutting off its vital supply lines. By November, food and fuel were dwindling and Parisians were facing starvation.

Yet the population was committed to fighting on. Men and women became part of the city's citizen militia, the National Guard, and trained for combat. The Germans began a steady bombardment of the city at the beginning of January 1871. The shells fell for three weeks but Parisian resistance prevailed. But the rest of France wanted an end to the war. The Germans agreed to an armistice at the end of January 1871 in order that French national elections could be held to elect representatives to the new government. In the elections, French citizens outside Paris repudiated the war and returned an overwhelmingly conservative majority to seek peace. Thus the siege came to an end.

Parisians felt they had been betrayed by the rest of France. Through four months as a besieged city, they had sacrificed, suffered, and died. The war was over but Paris was not at peace. The new national government, safely installed outside Paris at Versailles, attempted to reestablish normal life. The volatility of the city motivated the government's attempt in March 1871 to disarm the Parisian citizenry by using army troops. In the hilly neighborhood of northern Paris, men, women, and children poured into the streets to protect their cannons and to defend their right to bear arms. In the fighting that followed the Versailles troops were driven from the city.

The spontaneity of the March uprising was soon succeeded by organization. Citizens rallied to the idea of the city's self-government and established the Paris Commune, as other French cities followed the capital's lead. Parisians were still at war. It was not war against a foreign enemy, nor was it a class war. It was a civil war against the rest of France.

The social experiment of self-defense in the Commune lasted for 72 days, as armed women formed their own fighting units, the city council regulated labor relations, and neighborhoods ruled themselves. In May 1871 government troops reentered the city and brutally crushed the Paris Commune. In one "Bloody Week" 25,000 Parisians were massacred and 40,000 others were arrested and tried. Such reprisals inflamed radicals and workers all over Europe. The myth of the Commune became a rallying cry for revolutionary movements throughout the world and inspired the future leaders of the Russian revolutionary state.

The Victorian Compromise

Contemporaries were aware of two facts of life about Great Britain in 1850: first, that Britain had an enormously productive capitalist economy of sustained growth; and second, that Britain enjoyed apparent social harmony without revolution and without civil war. As revolutions ravaged continental Europe in 1848, the British took pride in a parliamentary system that valued a tradition of freedom.

The political rhetoric of stability and calm was undoubtedly exaggerated. Great Britain at mid-century had its share of serious social problems. British slums rivaled any in Europe. Poverty, disease, and famine ravaged the kingdom. Many feared that British social protests of the 1840s would result in upheavals similar to those in continental Europe. Yet Great Britain avoided a revolution. One explanation for Britain's relative calm lay in the shared political tradition that emphasized liberty as the birthright of English citizens. Building on an established political culture, the British Parliament was able to adapt to the demands of an industrializing society. Adaptation was gradual, but as slow as it seemed, a compromise was achieved among competing social interests. The great compromise of Victorian society was the reconciliation of industrialists' commitment to unimpeded growth with the workers' need for the protection of the state.

The British political system was democratized slowly after 1832. The Reform Bill of that year gave increased political power to the industrial and manufacturing bourgeoisie, who joined a landed aristocracy and merchant class. But the property qualification meant that only 20 percent of the population was able to vote. In 1867, under conservative leadership, a second Reform Bill was introduced. Approval of this bill doubled the electorate, giving the vote to a new urban population of shopkeepers, clerks, and workers. In 1884 farm laborers were enfranchised. Women, however, remained disenfranchised; they were granted the vote only after World War I.

William Ewart Gladstone (1809–1898) was a classical liberal who believed in free enterprise and was opposed to state intervention. Good government, according to Gladstone, should remove obstacles to talent, competition, and individual initiative but should interfere as little as possible in economy and society. Many of the significant advances of the British liberal state were achieved during Gladstone's first term as prime minister (1868–1874). Taking advantage of British prosperity, Gladstone abolished tariffs, cut defense expenditures, lowered taxes, and sponsored sound budgets. He furthered the liberal agenda by disestablishing the Anglican church in Ireland in 1869. The Church had been the source of great resentment to the vast majority of Irish Catholics, who had been forced to pay taxes to support the Protestant state church.

Gladstone reformed the army, in disrepute after its poor performance in the Crimea, so that one could no longer purchase a commission. Training and merit would justify all future advancements. Similarly, Gladstone reformed the civil service system by separating it from political influence and seniority. Merit and examinations were intended to ensure the most efficient and effective system of government administration. The secret ballot was introduced to prevent coercion in voting. Finally, the Liberals stressed the importance of education for an informed electorate and passed an Education Act that aimed to make elementary schooling available to everyone. These reforms added up to a Liberal philosophy of government. Liberal government was, above all, an attack on privilege. It sought to remove restraints on individual freedom and to foster opportunity and talent.

During these years another political philosophy also left its mark on British government. This was conservatism. Under the flamboyant leadership of Benjamin Disraeli (1804–1881), the Conservative party supported state

This female above-ground coal mine worker was photographed in 1864 by Arthur J. Munby. Such women, who sorted the coal, had low status and no prospects. They were regarded as "unsexed, immoral Amazons."

intervention and regulation on behalf of the weak and disadvantaged. Disraeli sponsored the Factory Act of 1875, which set a maximum of 56 hours on the factory work week. The Public Health Act established a sanitary code. The Artisans Dwelling Act defined minimum housing standards. Probably the most important conservative legislation was the Trade Union Act, which permitted picketing and other peaceful labor tactics.

The split between Disraeli and Gladstone was clearly apparent in 1846 when they disagreed over the issue of free trade versus tariffs. Disraeli moved on to champion protection and through the early 1860s consistently opposed Gladstone's financial system. Unlike the Liberals, Disraeli insisted on the importance of traditional institutions like the monarchy, the House of Lords, and the Church of England. Disraeli placed value in the ability of the state to correct and protect. His work in organizing a national party machinery facilitated the adaptation of the parliamentary system to mass politics. His methods of campaigning and building a mass base of support were used by successful politicians regardless of political persuasion.

In spite of Liberal hopes, Great Britain never had a purely laissez-faire economy. As the intersecting careers of Gladstone and Disraeli demonstrate, the British model combined free enterprise with intervention and regulation. The clear issues and the clear choices of the two great parties—Liberal and Conservative—dominated parliamentary life after mid-century. In polarizing parliamentary politics, they also invigorated it.

The terms *liberal* and *conservative* hold none of the meaning today that they did for men and women in the nineteenth century. Classical liberalism has little in common with its twentieth-century counterpart, which favors an active interventionist state. Disraeli is a far more likely candidate for the twentieth-century liberal label than Gladstone, Britain's leading nineteenth-century liberal statesman.

Reform in Russia

In 1850 Russia was an unreformed autocracy, a form of government in which the tsar held absolute power. Without a parliament, without a constitution, and without civil liberties for his subjects, the Russian ruler governed through a bureaucracy and a police force. Economically, Russia was a semifeudal agrarian state with a class of privileged aristocrats supported by serf labor on their estates.

For decades—since the reign of Alexander I (1801–1825)—the tsars and their advisers realized that they were out of step with developments in western Europe. An awareness was growing that serfdom was uncivilized and morally wrong. The remnants of feudalism had been swept away in France in the Great Revolution at the end of the eighteenth century. Prussia had abolished hereditary serfdom beginning in 1806. Among the European powers, only Russia remained a serf-holding nation. Russian serfs were tied to the land and owed dues and labor services in return for the lands they held. Peasant protests mounted, attracting public attention to the plight of the serfs. But in spite of growing moral concern, there were many reasons to resist the abolition of serfdom. Granting freedom to all serfs was a vastly complicated affair. How were serf-holders to be compensated for the loss of labor power? What was to be the freed serf's relationship to the land?

Hesitation about abolition evaporated with the Russian defeat in the Crimean War. The new tsar, Alexander II (1855–1881), viewed Russia's inability to repel an invasion force on its own soil as proof of its backwardness. Russia had no railroads and was forced to transport military supplies by carts to the Crimea. It took Moscow three months to provision troops, while the enemy could do so in three weeks. Alexander II believed in taking matters into his own hands. Russia must be reformed. Abolition of serfdom would permit a well-trained reserve army to exist without fear of rebellion. Liberating the serfs would also create a system of free labor so necessary for industrial development.

In March 1861 the tsar signed the emancipation edict that liberated 52 million serfs. Serfdom was eliminated in Poland three years later. Alexander II, who came to be known as the "Tsar-Liberator," compromised between landlord and serf by allotting land to freed peasants, while requiring from the former serfs redemption payments that were spread out over a period of 49 years. The peasant paid the state in installments; the state reimbursed the landowner in lump sums. To guarantee repayment, the land was not granted directly to individual peasants but to the village commune *(mir)*, which was responsible for collecting redemption payments. In 1864 Alexander introduced *zemstvos*, local elected assemblies, on the provincial and county levels, to govern local affairs.

The tsar introduced a vast array of "Great Reforms"—emancipating the serfs, creating local parliamentary bodies, reorganizing the judiciary, modernizing the army—yet Russia was not sufficiently liberalized or democratized to satisfy the critics of autocracy. Between 1860 and 1870 a young generation of intelligentsia, radical intellectuals who benefited from democratization in education and were influenced by the rhetoric of revolution in the West, assumed a critical stance in protest against the existing order. Many young intellectuals in Russia decided to "go to the people," traveling from village to village to educate and in some cases to attempt to radicalize the peasants. They paid dearly for what proved to be a fruitless commitment to populism in the mass trials and repression of the late 1870s.

Some of the tsarist regime's critics fled into exile to reemerge as revolutionaries in western Europe, where they continued to oppose the tsarist regime and helped shape the tradition of revolution and dissent in Western countries. Other educated men and women who remained in Russia chose violence as the only effective weapon against absolute rule. Terrorists who called themselves "Will of the People" decided on assassination as the best strategy and condemned the tsar to death. In the "emperor hunt" that followed, numerous attempts were made on the tsar's life. In the end, the Will of the People movement succeeded in its mission. A terrorist bomb killed Alexander II, the "Tsar-Liberator," in St. Petersburg in 1881.

The Force of New Ideas

In any age, changes in material life find their way into literature, philosophy, science, and art. Changes in the environment affect the way people look at the world. In turn, intellectuals can have a profound effect on values and behavior. Truly great thinkers not only reflect their times; they also shape them. The third quarter of the nineteenth century was especially rich in both the creativity and critical stance that shaped modern consciousness. Amid the tumult of new ideas in the period after 1850, two titans stand out. Not artists, but scientists—one of biology, the other of society—they sought regularity and predictability in the world they observed and measured. The ideas of Charles Darwin and Karl Marx both reflected and changed the world they lived in.

Charles Darwin (1809–1882), the preeminent scientist of the age, was a great synthesizer. Darwin began his scientific career as a naturalist with a background in geology. As a young man, he sailed around the world on the *Beagle* (1831–1836). He collected specimens and fossils as the ship's naturalist, with his greatest finds in South America and especially the Galápagos Islands. He spent the next 20 years of his life taking notes of his observations of the natural world. In chronically poor health, Darwin produced 500 pages of what he called "one long argument." *On the Origin of Species by Means of Natural Selection* (1859) was a book that changed the world.

Darwin's argument was a simple one: Life forms originated in and perpetuated themselves through struggle. The outcome of this struggle was determined by "natural selection," or what came to be known as "survival of the fittest." Better adapted individuals survived; others died out. Competition between species and within species produced a dynamic model of organic evolution.

Darwin did not use the word *evolution* in the original edition, but a positivist belief in an evolutionary process permeated the 1859 text. In the world of biology, Darwin's ideas embodied a new belief in progress based on struggle. Force explained the past and would guarantee the future, as the fittest survived. These were ideas that a general public found applicable to a whole range of human endeavors.

Karl Marx (1818–1883) in his masterwork, *Das Kapital*, viewed himself as the theorist of the socialism he called "scientific" and as an evolutionist who demonstrated that history is the dialectical struggle of classes. Friedrich Engels was a wealthy German businessman whose father owned factories in Manchester, England. He first encountered Marx in Paris. It was a meeting of kindred spirits. Engels had just written *Condition of the Working Class in England in 1844*. Marx was an iconoclast. The son of a Prussian lawyer who had converted from Judaism to Christianity, he rejected the study of the law and belief in a deity. In exile because of his political writings, Marx was the most brilliant of the German young Hegelians, philosophers heavily influenced by the ideas of Georg Friedrich Hegel (1770–1831), which held sway over the German intellectual world of the 1830s and 1840s. But by the mid-1840s, Marx had rebelled against Hegel's idealism and was developing his own materially grounded view of society.

The philosophy of Marx and Engels recognized that human beings were not defined by their souls but by their labor. Labor was a struggle to transform nature by producing commodities useful for survival. Building on this funda-mental concept of labor, Marx and Engels saw society as divided into two camps: those who own property and those who do not. Nineteenth-century capitalist society was divided into two classes: the bourgeoisie, those who owned the means of production as its private property, and the proletariat, the propertyless working class.

This materialist perspective on society was the engine driving Marx's theory of history. For Marx, every social system based on a division into classes carries within it the seeds of its own destruction. The different stages of history are determined by different forms of the ownership of production. In a feudal-agrarian society, the aristocracy controlled and exploited the unfree labor of serfs. In a world of commerce and manufacturing, the capitalist bourgeoisie are the new aristocracy exploiting free labor for wages.

Marx was more than an observer: He was a critic of capitalism. His labor theory of value was the wedge he drove into the self-congratulatory rhetoric of the capitalist age. Labor is the source of all value, he argued, and yet the bourgeois employer denies workers the profit of their work by refusing to pay them a decent wage. Instead, he pockets the profits. Workers are separated, or *alienated*, from the product of their labor. But more profoundly, in a capitalist system all workers are alienated from the creation that makes them human; they are alienated from their labor.

In the second half of the nineteenth century, political parties throughout Europe coalesced around Marxist beliefs and programs. Marxists were beginning to be heard in associations of workers, and they helped found the International Working Men's Association in London in 1864, an organization of French, German, and Italian workers dedicated to "the end of all class rule." The promise of a common association of workers transcending national boundaries became a compelling idea to those who envisioned the end of capitalism.

In *The Communist Manifesto* (1848) Marx and Engels promised that the growing poverty and alienation of the proletariat would bring to industrialized Europe a class war against the capitalists. Exploited workers must prepare themselves for the moment of revolution by joining with each other across national boundaries: "Workers of the world, unite. You have nothing to lose but your chains." Marx predicted that capitalism would produce more and more goods but would continue to pay workers the lowest wages possible. By driving out smaller producers, the bourgeoisie will increase the size of the proletariat. Yet Marx was optimistic. As workers are slowly pauperized, they will become conscious of their exploitation and they will revolt.

The force of these ideas mobilized thousands of contemporaries aware of the injustices of capitalism. Few thinkers in the history of the West have left a more lasting legacy than Karl Marx. The legacy survived the fact that much of his analysis rested on incorrect predictions about the increasing misery of workers and the inflexibility of the capitalist system.

The 1848 revolutions have been called a turning point at which modern history failed to turn. Contemporaries wondered how so much action could have produced so few lasting results. Yet the perception that nothing had changed was wrong. Conservatives and radicals alike turned toward a new realism in

This illustration by Gustave Doré appeared in Condition of the Working Class in England in 1844 *by Friedrich Engels. Small and cramped industrial working-class houses with their tiny walled backyards are framed by railway lines.*

politics. Everywhere governments were forced to adapt to new social realities. No longer could the state ignore economic upheavals and social dislocations, if it wanted to survive.

State-building in Western societies went hand in hand with the growth in the social responsibilities of government. The national powers that would dominate world politics and economy in the twentieth century all underwent modernizing transitions in the 1860s. These included the United States, France, Great Britain, and Germany. New nations came into existence in this period through the limited use of armed force. With the establishment of the German Empire, Otto von Bismarck was intent on preserving the peace in Europe by balancing the power of the great European states. Reform, not revolution, many were sure, was the key to the future progress of European societies.

Suggestions for Further Reading

Europe After 1815

*Jonathan Beecher, *Charles Fourier: The Visionary and His World* (Berkeley: University of California Press, 1986). An intellectual biography that traces the development of Fourier's theoretical perspective and roots it firmly in the social context of nineteenth-century France.

*Robert Gildea, *Barricades and Borders, Europe 1800–1914* (Oxford, England: Oxford University Press, 1987). A synthetic overview of economic, demographic, political, and international trends in European society.

*William H. Sewell, Jr., *Work and Revolution in France: The Language of Labor from the Old Regime to 1848* (Cambridge, England: Cambridge University Press, 1980). Traces nineteenth-century working-class socialism to the corporate culture of Old Regime guilds through traditional values, norms, language, and artisan organizations.

*Alan Sked, *The Decline and Fall of the Habsburg Empire, 1815–1918* (London: Longman, 1989). A revisionist interpretation that demonstrates the strength and viability of Europe's greatest dynasty throughout the nineteenth century.

*Edward P. Thompson, *The Making of the English Working Class* (New York: Pantheon, 1963). Spans the late eighteenth to mid nineteenth centuries in examining the social, political, and cultural contexts in which workers created their own identity and put forward their own demands.

*Louise A. Tilly and Joan W. Scott, *Women, Work and Family* (New York: Holt, Rinehart and Winston, 1978). An overview of the impact of a wage economy on the family and on women's work.

Revolution and Unification

*Maurice Agulhon, *The Republican Experiment, 1848–1852* (Cambridge, England: Cambridge University Press, 1983). Traces the Revolution of 1848 from its roots to its ultimate failure in 1852 through an analysis of the ideologies of the republicanism of workers, peasants, and the bourgeoisie.

Derek Beales, *The Risorgimento and the Unification of Italy* (London: George Allen & Unwin, 1982). Drawing a distinction between unification and national revival, Beales situates the period of unification within the larger process of the cultural and political revival.

Clive Church, *Europe in 1830: Revolution and Political Change* (London: George Allen & Unwin, 1983). Considers the origins of the 1830 revolutions within a wider European crisis through a comparative analysis of European regions.

*Gordon A. Craig, *Germany, 1866–1945* (New York: Oxford University Press, 1978). This synthetic view of German history provides a thorough examination of German unification. Craig analyzes all aspects of imperial development with special attention to the institutional framework, its politics, economy, and diplomacy.

James J. Sheehan, *German Liberalism in the Nineteenth Century* (Chicago: University of Chicago Press, 1978). Explores the problems of transferring Western liberalism to Germany by examining the origins of German liberalism, the revolutions of 1848, and the politics of the Bismarckian state.

---

*Indicates paperback edition available.

*Dorothy Thompson, *The Chartists: Popular Politics in the Industrial Revolution* (New York: Pantheon,1984). Thompson demonstrates that Chartism was an extraordinary coalition of women, laborers, artisans, and alehouse keepers whose goals were transforming public life and forging a new political culture.

Reforming European Society

Jenni Calder, *The Victorian Home* (London: R. T. Batsford, 1977). A cultural and social history of Victorian domestic life in which the author describes both bourgeois and working-class domestic environments.

*David Pinkney, *Napoleon III and the Rebuilding of Paris* (Princeton, NJ: Princeton University Press, 1972). Describes how Paris was transformed into the monumental city that became not only a manifestation of French culture, but also a symbol of European culture as a whole. The planning, financing, and building of Napoleon III's Paris are analyzed, as is the impact of the rebuilding on the city's residents.

*Alain Plessis, *The Rise and Fall of the Second Empire, 1852–1871*, translated by Jonathan Mandelbaum (Cambridge, England: Cambridge University Press, 1985). Discusses the Second Empire as an important transitional period in French history, when the conflict was between traditional and modern values in political, economic, and social transformations.

*Bonnie G. Smith, *Ladies of the Leisure Class: The Bourgeoisie of Northern France in the Nineteenth Century* (Princeton, NJ: Princeton University Press, 1981). Explores the impact of industrialization on the lives of bourgeois women in northern France and demonstrates how the cult of domesticity emerged in a particular community.

*Martha Vicinus, *Independent Women: Work and Community for Single Women, 1850–1920* (Chicago: University of Chicago Press, 1985). Chronicles the choice that Victorian women made to live outside the norms of marriage and domesticity in various communities of women, including sisterhoods, nursing communities, colleges, boarding schools, and settlement houses.

H. Seton Watson, *The Russian Empire, 1801–1917* (Oxford, England: Clarendon Press, 1967). This narrative history describes the social and economic background of late imperial Russia with attention to intellectual trends and political ideologies.

19

Mass Society and the New Imperialism, 1871–1914

Speeding to the Future

"We want to demolish museums and libraries." These are not the words of an anarchist or a terrorist but of a poet. The Italian writer Emilio Marinetti (1876–1944) endeavored, symbolically at least through the power of his pen, to destroy the citadels of Western culture at the beginning of the twentieth century. Marinetti was not alone in wanting to pull down all that preserved art and learning in the West. Joined by other artists and writers who called themselves futurists, Marinetti represented a desire to break free of the past. By shocking complacent bourgeois society with their art, futurists hoped to fashion a new and dynamic civilization. Although they were a small group with limited influence, their concerns were shared by a growing number of intellectuals who judged European culture to be in the throes of a serious moral and cultural crisis. Futurist ideas also reflected the growing perception among European men and women who spurned the value of tradition for dealing with the challenges of the future.

The futurist painter Umberto Boccioni (1882–1916) captures an aspect of the dynamic intensity of this changing world in his *Riot in the Galleria* (1910). Look at the painting. The setting is a galleria, the equivalent of a modern shopping mall, in front of a respectable *caffé*, an Italian coffee shop, this one frequented by well-dressed men and women, clearly members of the middle class. Here is a modern urban scene, a public space in every way characteristic of the new age of enjoyment and consumption.

There is a story here. In a flurry of light and shadow, a rush of figures moves toward the middle ground of the canvas. At the center of this movement

are two women engaged in a brawl that seems to pull the figures of shoppers and strollers toward it. The fact that the brawlers are female is intended to underscore the irrationality of the incident. Yet the brawl itself is not compelling our attention. It is rather the movement of the crowd, like moths to a flame, that Boccioni intends us to see. The objects in motion are little more than vibrations in space, faceless and indistinguishable as individuals. The crowd does not walk or run. It appears instead to be in flight. In his studies for the canvas Boccioni reduces movement to a series of lines both swirling and directed.

The riot Boccioni depicts here is an irrational event. This is not ordinary rabble; it is a well-dressed mob, as the blurred but sumptuously flowered hats and the occasional straw boaters make clear. Movement is taking place without forethought, fueled by the attraction of the violence and the possibility of participating in it. There are those on the periphery who have not joined the frenzy, but we as spectators are confident they will be swept up into the action as the energy of the brawl sucks everything into its center like the vortex of a tornado. European society seemed to many contemporaries to be moving into an abyss, a world of tumultuous change but one without values.

In the violence of the riot we are shown the beauty of movement which surpasses that of an orderly waltz. Boccioni uses the warm glow of the electric lights, symbol of the modern age, to illuminate a "new reality." The beauty of the mosaic is strangely at odds with the theme of the two brawling figures who activate the crowd. There is no meaning beyond the movement.

Riot in the Galleria reflects the preoccupation with change in the early twentieth century. Life was moving so fast that European society seemed to have outrun its own heritage by 1900. Technology was transforming Europe with a breakneck speed unmatched in human history. Science undermined the way people thought about themselves by challenging moral and religious values as hollow and meaningless. The natural sciences threw into doubt the existence of a creator. New forms of communication and transportation—the telephone, the wireless telegraph, the bicycle, the automobile, the airplane— were obliterating traditional understandings of time and space. The cinema and the X ray altered visual perception and redefined the ways people saw the world around them. This was a period of intense excitement and vitality in the history of the West, one which traditional values did not always explain.

Like the political revolutionaries of an earlier age, futurist artists issued "manifestoes." They sought the liberation of the human spirit from a world that could no longer be understood or controlled. Liberation could only be achieved through immersion in mass society and rapid change. Boccioni's goal was a revolutionary one: "Let's turn everything upside down. . . . Let's split open our figures and place the environment inside them."

Futurists were not alone in their confusion over what to keep and what to reject in Western culture or in their inability to break entirely with the past. But they were single-minded in their rebellion against constraints. Before 1914 a new generation of Europeans rushing forward abandoned the lessons of the past for the promise of the future.

*E*uropean Economy and the Politics of Mass Society

Between 1871 and 1914 the scale of European life was radically altered. Industrial society had promoted largeness as the norm, as growing numbers of people worked under the same roof. Large-scale heavy industries fueled by new energy sources dominated the economic landscape. With every passing year fewer people remained on the land. Those who did stay in the agricultural sector were linked to cities and tied into national cultures by new transportation and communications networks.

Changes in the scale of political life paralleled the rise of heavy industry and the increasing urbanization of European populations. Great Britain experienced the transformation in political organization and social structure before other European nations. But after 1870 changes in politics influenced by the scale of the new industrial society spread to every European country. Mass democracy was on the rise and was pushing aside the liberal emphasis on individual rights valued by parliamentary governments everywhere.

In spite of dramatic changes in politics and society, the old order still persisted. Throughout Europe monarchy remained the dominant form of government, whether in the small German dynasties or the great Habsburg holdings. Women were excluded from national political participation, although the right to vote was gradually being extended to all men in western Europe, regardless of property or social rank. Extraparliamentary groups— lobbies, trade unions, and cartels—grew in influence and power and exerted pressure on the political process. The politics of mass society made clear the contradictions inherent in democracy.

Regulating Boom and Bust

Between 1873 and 1895 an epidemic of slumps battered the economics of European nations. These slumps, characterized by falling prices, downturns in productivity, and declining profits, did not strike European nations simultaneously, nor did they affect all countries with the same degree of severity. But the slumps of the late nineteenth century and the boom period of intense economic expansion from 1895 to 1914 did teach industrialists, financiers, and politicians one important lesson: Alternative booms and busts in the business cycle were dangerous and had to be regulated.

Too much of a good thing brought on the steady deflation of the last quarter of the nineteenth century. In the world economy, there was an overproduction of agricultural products—a sharp contrast to the famines that had ravaged Europe only 50 years earlier. Overproduction resulted from two new factors in the world economy: technological advances in crop cultivation and the low cost of shipping and transport, which had opened up European markets to cheap agricultural goods from the United States, Canada, and Argentina. The drop in food prices affected purchasing power in other sectors and resulted in long-term deflation and unemployment.

Financiers, politicians, and businesspeople dedicated themselves to eliminating the boom-and-bust phenomenon, which they considered dangerous. The application of science and technology to industrial production required huge amounts of capital. The two new sources of power after 1880, petroleum and electricity, could only be developed with heavy capital investment. Large mechanized steel plants were costly and out of reach for small family firms of the scale that had industrialized so successfully earlier in the century in textiles. Heavy machinery, smelting furnaces, buildings, and transport were all beyond the abilities of the small entrepreneur.

In order to raise the capital necessary for the new heavy industry at the end of the nineteenth century, firms had to look outside themselves to the stock market, banks, or the state to find adequate capital resources. But investors and especially banks refused to invest without guarantees on their capital. Because investment in heavy industry meant tying up capital for extended periods of time, banks insisted on safeguards against falling prices. The solution they demanded was the elimination of uncertainty through the regulation of markets.

Regulation was achieved through the establishment of *cartels*, combinations of firms in a given industry united to fix prices and to establish production quotas. Cartels were agreements among big firms intent on controlling markets and guaranteeing profits. Trusts were another form of collaboration that resulted in the elimination of unprofitable businesses. Firms joined together horizontally within the same industry—for example, all steel producers agreed to fix prices and set quotas. Or they combined vertically by controlling all levels of the production process from raw materials to the finished product and all other ancillary products necessary to or resulting from the production process.

Firms in Great Britain, falling behind in heavy industry, failed to form cartels and for the most part remained in private hands. But heavy industry in Germany, France, and Austria, to varying degrees, sought regulation of markets through cartels. International cartels appeared that regulated markets and prices across national borders within Europe.

Banks, which had been the initial impetus behind the transformation to a regulated economy, in turn formed consortia to meet the need for greater amounts of capital. A *consortium*, paralleling a cartel, was a partnership among banks, often international in character, in which interest rates and the movement of capital were regulated by mutual agreement. The state, too, played an important role in directing the economy. In capital-poor Russia, the state used indirect taxes on the peasantry to finance industrialization and railway construction at the end of the nineteenth century. Russia also needed to import capital, primarily from France after 1887.

Throughout Europe nation-states protected domestic industries by erecting tariff barriers that made foreign goods noncompetitive in domestic markets. Only Great Britain among the major powers stood by a policy of free trade. Europe was split into two tiers—the haves and have-nots: those countries with a solid industrial core and those that had remained unindustrialized. This division had a geographic character, with the north and west of Europe heavily developed and capitalized and the southern and eastern parts of Europe remaining heavily agricultural. For both the haves and have-nots, tariff policies were an attractive form of regulation by the state to protect established industries and to nurture those industries struggling for existence.

Challenging Liberal England

Great Britain had avoided revolution and social upheaval in the nineteenth century. It prided itself on the progress achieved by a strong parliamentary tradition. Parliamentary government was based on a homogeneous ruling elite. Aristocrats, businesspeople, and financial leaders shared a common educational background in England's elitist educational system of the public schools and the universities of Oxford or Cambridge. Schooling produced a common outlook and common attitudes toward parliamentary rule, whether in Conservative or Liberal parties, and guaranteed a certain stability in policies and legislation.

In the 1880s issues of unemployment, public health, housing, and education challenged the attitudes of Britain's ruling elite and fostered the advent of an independent working-class politics. Between 1867 and 1885 extension of the suffrage increased the electorate fourfold. Protected by the markets of its empire, the British economy did not experience the roller-coaster effect of recurrent booms and busts after 1873. But after 1900 wages stagnated as prices continued to rise, and workers responded to their distress by supporting militant trade unions.

Trade unions, drawing on a long tradition of working-class associations, were all that stood between workers and the economic dislocation caused by unemployment, sickness, or old age. In addition, new unions of unskilled and semiskilled workers flourished, beginning in the 1880s and 1890s. A Scottish miner, James Keir Hardie (1856–1915), attracted national attention as the spokesman for a new political movement, the Labour party, whose goal was to represent workers in Parliament. In 1892 Hardie was the first independent working man to sit in the House of Commons. Hardie and his party convinced trade unions that it was in their best interests to support Labour candidates instead of Liberals in parliamentary elections after 1900. By 1906 the new Labour party had 29 seats in Parliament. Intellectuals now joined with trade unionists in demanding public housing, better public sanitation, municipal reforms, and improved pay and benefits for workers.

After 1906, under threat of losing votes to the Labour party, the Liberal party heeded the pressures for reform. The "new" Liberals supported legislation to strengthen the right of unions to picket peacefully. Led by David Lloyd George (1863–1945), who was chancellor of the exchequer, Liberals sponsored the National Insurance Act of 1911. The act provided compulsory payments to workers for sickness and unemployment benefits.

In order to gain approval to pay for this new legislation, Lloyd George recognized that Parliament itself had to be renovated. The Parliament Bill of 1911 reduced the House of Lords, dominated by Conservatives resistant to proposed welfare reforms, from its status as equal partner with the House of Commons. Commons could and now did raise taxes without the consent of the House of Lords to pay for new programs that benefited workers and the poor. But social legislation did not silence unions and worker organizations. Be-

A union leader addresses striking British coal miners in 1912. Labor unions became increasingly militant after the turn of the century, as rising unemployment and declining real wages cut into the gains of the working class.

tween 1910 and 1914 strike waves broke over England. Coal miners, seamen, railroad workers, and dockers protested against stagnant wages and rising prices.

The high incidence of strikes was a consequence of growing distrust of Parliament and distrust, too, of a regulatory state bureaucracy responsible for the social welfare reforms. Labour's voice grew more strident. The Trade Unions Act of 1913 granted unions legal rights to settle their grievances with management directly. Only the outbreak of war in 1914 ended the possibility of a general strike by miners, railwaymen, and transport workers. The question of Irish home rule also plagued Parliament. In Ulster in northern Ireland army officers of Protestant Irish background threatened to mutiny. In addition, women agitating for the vote shattered parliamentary complacence. The most advanced industrial nation with its tradition of peaceful parliamentary rule had entered the age of mass politics.

Political Struggles in Germany and Austria

During his reign as chancellor of the German Empire (1871–1890), Otto von Bismarck repeatedly and successfully blocked the emergence of fully democratic participation in government. Bismarck's objective remained always the successful unification of Germany, and he promoted cooperation with democratic institutions and parties only to enhance that goal.

Throughout the 1870s the German chancellor collaborated with the German liberal parties in constructing the legal codes, the monetary and banking system, the judicial apparatus, and the railroad network that pulled the new Germany together. Bismarck backed German liberals in their anti-papal campaign in which the Catholic church was declared the enemy of the German state. He suspected the identification of Catholics with Rome, which the liberals depicted as an authority in competition with the nation-state. The antichurch campaign, launched in 1872, was dubbed *Kulturkampf*, "struggle for civilization," because its supporters contended that it was a battle waged in the interests of humanity.

The legislation of the Kulturkampf expelled Jesuits from Germany, removed priests from state service, attacked religious education, and instituted civil marriage. Many Germans grew concerned over the social costs of such widespread religious repression, and the Catholic Center party increased its parliamentary representation by rallying Catholics as a voting bloc in the face of state repression. With the succession of a new pontiff, Leo XIII (1878–1903), Bismarck took the opportunity of negotiating a settlement with the Catholic church, cutting his losses and bringing the Kulturkampf to a halt.

Bismarck's repressive policies also targeted the Social Democratic party. The Social Democrats were committed to a Marxist critique of capitalism and to international cooperation with other socialist parties. Seeing them as a threat to stability in Germany and in Europe as a whole, he set out to smash them. In 1878, using the opportunity for repression presented by two attempts on the emperor's life, Bismarck outlawed the fledgling Socialist party. The Anti-Socialist Law forbade meetings among socialists, fund-raising, and distribution of printed matter. Nevertheless, individual Social Democratic candidates stood for election in this period and learned quickly how to work with middle-class parties in order to achieve electoral successes. By 1890 Social Democrats had captured 20 percent of the electorate and controlled 35 Reichstag seats in spite of Bismarck's antisocialist legislation.

Throughout the 1880s as his ability to manage Reichstag majorities declined and as socialist strength steadily mounted, Bismarck grew disenchanted with universal manhood suffrage. Beginning in 1888 the chancellor found himself at odds with the new emperor William II (1888–1918) over his foreign and domestic policies. The young emperor dismissed Bismarck in March 1890 and abandoned the chancellor's antisocialist legislation. The Social Democratic party became the largest Marxist party in the world, and by 1914 the largest single party in Germany. During the period when the Social Democratic movement had been outlawed, Bismarck and William II used social welfare legislation to win mass support, including accident insurance, sick benefits, and old age and disability benefits. But such legislation did not undermine the popularity of socialism nor did it attract workers away from Marxist programs, as the mounting electoral returns demonstrated.

Unable to defeat social democracy by force or by state-sponsored welfare policies, Bismarck's successors set out to organize mass support. Agrarian and industrial interests united strongly behind state policies. An aggressive foreign policy was judged as the surest way to win over the masses.

In the end the Reichstag failed to defy the absolute authority of Emperor William II, who was served after 1890 by a string of ineffectual chancellors. Despite its constitutional forms, Germany was ruled by a state authoritarianism in which the bureaucracy, the military, and various interest groups exercised influence over the emperor. A high-risk foreign policy that had a mass appeal was one way to circumvent a parliamentary system incapable of decision making.

In the 1870s the liberal values of the bourgeoisie dominated the Austro-Hungarian Empire. The Habsburg monarchy had adjusted to constitutional government, which was introduced throughout Austria in 1860. Faith in parliamentary government based on a restricted suffrage had established a tenuous foothold. After setbacks of 1848 and the troublesome decade of the 1860s, when Prussia had trounced Austria and Bismarck had routed the hope of an Austrian-dominated German Empire, the Austrian bourgeoisie counted on a peaceful future with a centralized multinational state dedicated to order and progress.

But by 1900 the urban and capitalist middle class that ruled Austria by virtue of a limited suffrage based on property had lost ground to new groups which were essentially anticapitalist and antiliberal in their outlook. The new groups were peasants, workers, urban artisans and shopkeepers, and the colonized Slavic peoples of the empire. Bourgeois politics and laissez-faire economics had offered little or nothing to these varied groups, who were now claiming the right of participation. Mass parties were formed based on radical pan-Germanic feeling, anticapitalism that appealed to peasants and artisans, hatred of the Jews shared by students and artisans, and nationalist aspirations that attracted the lower middle classes.

The political experiences of Great Britain, Germany, France, and Austria between 1871 and 1914 make clear the common challenges confronting Western parliamentary systems in a changing era of democratic politics. In spite of variations, each nation experienced its own challenge to liberal parliamentary institutions and each shaped its own responses to a new international phenomenon—the rise of the masses as a political force.

Political Scandals and Mass Politics in France

The Third Republic in France had an aura of the accidental about its origins and of the precarious about its existence. Yet appearances were misleading. Founded in 1870 with the defeat of Napoleon III's empire by the Germans, the

Third Republic claimed legitimacy by placing itself squarely within the revolutionary democratic tradition. The Third Republic successfully worked toward the creation of a national community based on a common identity of citizens. Compulsory schooling, one of the great institutional transformations of French government in 1885, socialized French children in common values, patriotism, and identification with the nation-state. Old ways, local dialects, superstitious practices, and peasant insularity dropped away or were modified under the persistent pressure of a centralized curriculum of reading, writing, arithmetic, and civics. Compulsory service in the army for the generation of young men of draft age served the same end of communicating national values to a predominantly peasant population. Technology also accelerated the process of shaping a national citizenry, as railroad lines tied people together and new and better roads made distances shrink.

A truly national and mass culture emerged in the period between 1880 and 1914. Two events, in particular, that occurred in the three decades before World War I indicate the extent of the transformation of French political life. The first, the Boulanger Affair, involved the attempt of a French general to seize power. The second, the Dreyfus Affair, involved all of French society in the treason conviction of a Jewish army captain.

As minister of war, General Georges Boulanger (1837–1891) became a hero to French soldiers when he undertook needed reforms of army life. He won over businesspeople by leading troops against strikers. Above all, he cultivated the image of a patriot ready to defend France's honor at any cost. But Boulanger was a shallow man whose success was created by a carefully orchestrated publicity campaign that made him the most popular man in France by 1886.

Boulanger's potential in the political arena attracted the attention of right-wing backers, including monarchists who hoped eventually to restore kingship to France. Supported by big money interests that favored a strengthened executive and a weaker parliamentary system, Boulanger undertook a nationwide political campaign, hoping to appeal to those unhappy with the Third Republic and promising vague constitutional reforms. Boulangists hoped that through universal suffrage an authoritarian government could be established. By 1889 Boulanger was able to amass enough national support to frighten the defenders of parliamentary institutions. The charismatic general ultimately failed in his bid for power and fled the country because of allegations of treason. But he left in his wake an embryonic mass movement on the Right that operated outside the channels of parliamentary institutions.

A very different type of crisis began to take shape in 1894 with the controversy surrounding the trial of Captain Alfred Dreyfus (1859–1935) that came to be known simply as "the Affair." Dreyfus was an Alsatian Jewish army officer accused of selling military secrets to the Germans. His trial for treason served as a lightning rod for xenophobia—the hatred of foreigners, especially Germans—and anti-Semitism, the hatred of Jews. Dreyfus was stripped of his commission and honors and sentenced to solitary confinement for life on Devil's Island, a convict colony off French Guiana in South America.

Illegal activities and outright falsifications by Dreyfus's superiors in order

Captain Dreyfus, accused of treason, marches with a "guard of dishonor." After Dreyfus was declared innocent, he became a lieutenant colonel in the French army and was enrolled in the Legion of Honor.

to secure a conviction came to light in the mass press. The nation was soon divided. Those who supported Dreyfus's innocence, the pro-Dreyfusards, were for the most part on the left of the political spectrum and spoke of the Republic's duty to uphold justice and freedom. The anti-Dreyfusards were associated with the traditional institutions of the Catholic church and the army and considered themselves to be defending the honor of France.

The Affair represented the ability of an individual to seek redress against injustice. On the national level, the Affair represented an important transformation in the nature of French political life. Existing parliamentary institutions had been found wanting and unable to cope with the mass politics stirred up by Dreyfus's conviction. New groups entered public life after 1894, coalescing around the question of the guilt or innocence of an individual man. The newspaper press vied with parliament and the courts as a forum for investigation and decision making. The crises provoked by Boulanger's attempt at power and the Dreyfus Affair demonstrated the major role of the press and the importance of public opinion in exerting pressure on the system of government. The press emerged as a mythmaker in shaping and channeling public opinion. Émile Zola (1840–1902), the great French novelist, spearheaded the pro-Dreyfusard movement with his damning article *"J'accuse!"* (*"I Accuse!"*) in which he pointed to the military and the judiciary as the "spirits of social evil" for persecuting an innocent man. The article appeared in a leading French newspaper and was influential in securing Dreyfus's eventual exoneration and the discovery of the real culprit, one of Dreyfus's colleagues in the General Staff. The Third Republic was never in danger of collapsing, but it was transformed. The locus of power in parliament was challenged by pressure groups outside of it.

Mass Politics and the New Consciousness

By the end of the nineteenth century, a faceless, nameless elector-ate had become the basis of new political strategies and a new political rhetoric. A concept of class identification of workers was devalued in favor of interest-group politics in which lobbies formed around single issues to pressure European governments. But the apparently all-inclusive concept of mass society continued to exclude some groups—women, ethnic minorities, and Jews. Women and ethnic minorities learned to incorporate strategies and techniques of politics and organization that permitted them to challenge the existing political system. Others, including anarchists, rejected both the organizational techniques of mass society and the values of the nation-state.

Feminists and the State

Women's emancipation had been a recurrent motif of European political culture throughout the nineteenth century. In the areas of civil liberties, legal equality with men, and economic autonomy, only the most limited reforms had been enacted. The cult of domesticity, important throughout the nineteenth century, assigned women to a separate sphere, that of the home. Glorifying domesticity was a recognition of women's unique contribution to society in the home, but it may itself have been a means of controlling women who protested the separation between public and private space.

European women were paid at best one-third to one-half of what men earned for the same work. In Great Britain women did not enjoy equal divorce rights until the twentieth century. In France married women had no control over their own incomes: All their earnings were considered their husband's private property. From the Atlantic to the Urals, women were excluded from economic and educational opportunities.

Growing numbers of women, primarily from the middle classes, began calling themselves *feminist*, a term coined in France in the 1830s. The new feminists throughout western Europe differed from earlier generations in their willingness to organize mass movements and to appropriate the techniques of interest-group politics. The first international congress of women's rights, held in Paris in 1878, initiated an era of international cooperation and exchange among women's organizations. Women's groups now positioned themselves for sustained political action.

On the whole, feminist organizations were divided into two camps. In the first group were those who agitated for the vote; the second included those who thought the vote was beside the point and that the central issues were economic, social, and legal reforms of women's status. The lessons of the new electoral politics were not lost on feminists seeking women's emancipation through the vote. Leaders like Hubertine Auclert (1848–1914) in France and Emmeline Pankhurst (1858–1928) in Great Britain recognized the need for a mass base of support. If women's organizations were to survive as competing interest groups, they needed to form political alliances, control their own newspapers and magazines, and keep their cause before the public eye.

There was a growing willingness to use mass demonstrations, rallies, and violent tactics by a variety of women's organizations. No movement operated more effectively in this regard than the British suffrage movement. In 1903 the Women's Social and Political Union (WSPU) was formed by a group of eminently respectable middle-class and aristocratic British women. At the center of the movement was Emmeline Pankhurst, a middle-aged woman of frail and attractive appearance, with a will of iron and a gift for oratory. Joined

Emmeline Pankhurst (third from right) at a rally to turn out the vote against a government that was unresponsive to women's issues.

by her two daughters Christabel (1880–1958), a lawyer by training, and Sylvia (1882–1960), an artist, these three women succeeded in keeping women's suffrage before the British public and brought the plight of British women to international attention.

Women's demands for political power were the basis of an unheralded revolution in Western culture. In Great Britain the decade before the Great War of 1914 was a period of profound political education for women seeking the vote. An unprecedented 250,000 women gathered in Hyde Park in 1908 to hear more about female suffrage. Laughed at by men, ridiculed in the press, taunted in public demonstrations, women activists refused to be quiet and to know their place.

Mrs. Pankhurst and others advocated violence against personal property to highlight the violence done to women by denying them their rights. Militant women set mailboxes on fire or poured glue and jam over their contents, threw bombs into country houses, and slashed paintings in the National Gallery. These tactics seemed to accomplish little before the war, although they certainly kept the issue of women's suffrage in the public eye until the outbreak of war in 1914.

European women did not gain the right to vote easily. In France and Germany moderate and left-wing politicians opposed extension of the vote to women because they feared that women would strengthen conservative candidates. Many politicians felt women were not "ready" for the vote and that they should receive it only as a reward—an unusual concept in democratic societies. It was not until 1918 that British women were granted limited suffrage and not until 1928 that women gained voting rights equal to those of men. Only after war and revolution was the vote extended to other women in the West: Germany in 1918, the United States in 1920, and France at the end of World War II.

Not all activist women saw the right to vote as the solution to women's oppression. Those who agitated for social reforms for poor and working-class women parted ways with the miltant suffragettes. Sylvia Pankhurst, for example, left her mother and sister to their political battles in order to work for social reform in London's poverty-stricken East End. Differing from those who focused on women's right to vote as a primary goal, women socialists were concerned with working-class women's "double oppression" in the home and in the workplace. Working-class women, most notably in Germany, united feminism with socialism in search of a better life.

In the late nineteenth century, scientific ideas had a formative impact on prevailing views of gender relations and female sexuality. The natural sciences were employed to prove the inferiority of women in the species. In *The Descent of Man* (1871), Charles Darwin concluded that the mental power of man was higher than that of woman. The female's need for male protection, the father of evolution reasoned, had increased her dependence over time while at the same time increasing the competition of natural selection among men. The result, Darwin argued, was inequality between the sexes. Others made a dubious case for brain size as an index of superiority.

The French physiologist Paul Broca (1824–1880), a contemporary of Darwin's, countered in 1873 that the skull capacity of the two sexes was very similar and a case for inferiority could not be based on measurement. But Broca was atypical. Most scientific opinion argued in favor of female frailty and outright inferiority. These "scientific" arguments justified the exclusion of women from educational opportunities and from professions like medicine and law. Biology became destiny as women's attempts at equal education came up against closed doors.

In this age of scientific justification of female inferiority, the "new woman" emerged. All over Europe the feminist movement had demanded social, economic, and political progress for women. But the new-woman phenomenon exceeded the bounds of the feminist movement and can be described as a general cultural phenomenon. Victorian stereotypes of the angel at the hearth were crumbling. The new woman was a woman characterized by intelligence, strength, and sexual desire, in every way man's equal. The Norwegian playwright Henrik Ibsen (1828–1906) created a fictional embodiment of the phenomenon in Nora, the protagonist of *A Doll's House* (1879), who was typical of the restive spirit for independence among wives and mothers confined to suffocating households and relegated to the status of children.

The women's movements of the period from 1871 to 1914 differed socially and culturally from nation to nation. Yet there is a sense in which the women's movements constituted an international phenomenon. The rise in the level of political consciousness of women occurred in the most advanced Western countries almost simultaneously and had a predominantly middle-class character. By 1900 sexuality and reproduction were openly connected to discussions of women's rights. In spite of concerted efforts, women remained on the outside of societies that excluded them from political participation, access to education, and social and economic equality.

The Jewish Question and the Zionist Solution

The word *anti-Semitism*, meaning hostility to Jews, was first used in 1879 to give a pseudoscientific legitimacy to bigotry and hatred. Persecution was a harsh reality for Jews in eastern Europe at the end of the nineteenth century. In Russia, Jews could not own property and were restricted to living in certain territories. Organized massacres, or pogroms, in Kiev, Odessa, and Warsaw followed the assassination of Tsar Alexander II in 1881 and occurred again after the failed Russian revolution of 1905. Russian authorities blamed the Jews, perceived as perennial outsiders, for the assassination and revolution and the social instability that followed them. Pogroms resulted in the death and displacement of tens of thousands of eastern European Jews.

Two million eastern European Jews migrated westward between 1868 and 1914 in search of peace and refuge. Seventy thousand settled in Germany. Others continued westward, stopping in the United States. Another kind of Jewish migration took place in the nineteenth century—the movement of Jews from rural to urban areas within nations. In eastern Europe Jewish migrations coincided with downturns in the economic cycle, and Jews became scapegoats for the high rates of unemployment and high prices that seemed to follow in their wake. Most migrants were peddlers, artisans, or small shopkeepers who were seen as threatening to small businesses. Differing in language, culture, and dress, they were viewed as alien in every way.

In western Europe Jews considered themselves as "assimilated" into their national cultures, identifying with their nationality as much as with their religion. Austrian and German Jews were granted full civil rights in 1867 on the principle that citizens of all religions enjoyed full equality. In France Jews had been legally emancipated since the end of the eighteenth century. But the western and central European politics of the 1890s had a strong dose of anti-Semitism. Demagogues like Georg von Schönerer (1842–1921) of Austria were capable of whipping up a frenzy of riots and violence against Jews. They did not distinguish between assimilated and immigrant Jewish populations in their irrational denunciations. Western and central European anti-Semitism assumed a new level of virulence at the end of the nineteenth century. Fear of an economic depression united aristocrat and worker alike in blaming a Jewish conspiracy. German anti-Semitism proliferated in the 1880s. "It is like a horrible epidemic," the scholar Theodor Mommsen (1817–1903) observed.

Fear of the Jews was connected with hatred of capitalism. In France and Germany, Jews controlled powerful banking and commercial firms that became the targets of blame in hard times. Upwardly mobile sons of Jewish immigrants entered the professions of banking, trading, and journalism. They were also growing in numbers as teachers and academics. In the 1880s more than half of Vienna's physicians (61 percent in 1881) and lawyers (58 percent of barristers in 1888) were Jewish. Their professional success only heightened tensions and condemnations of Jews as an "alien race." Anti-Semitism served as a violent means of mobilizing mass support, especially among those groups who felt threatened by capitalist concentration and large-scale industrialization. For anti-Semitic Europeans, Jews embodied the democratic, liberal, and cosmopolitan tendencies of the culture that they were consciously rejecting in their new political affiliations.

A Jewish leadership emerged in central and western Europe that treated anti-Semitism as a problem that could be solved by political means. For their generation at the end of the nineteenth century, the assimilation of their fathers and mothers was not the answer. Jews needed their own nation, it was argued, since they were a people without a nation. Zionism was the solution to what Jewish intellectuals called "the Jewish problem." Zion, the ancient homeland of biblical times, would provide a national territory, and a choice, to persecuted Jews. Zionism became a Jewish nationalist movement dedicated to the establishment of a Jewish state. Although Zionism did not develop mass support in western Europe among assimilated Jews, its program for national identity and social reforms appealed to a large following of eastern European Jews in Galicia (Poland), Russia, and the eastern lands of the Habsburg Empire, those directly subjected to the extremes of persecution.

Theodor Herzl (1860–1904), an Austrian Jew born in Budapest, was the founder of Zionism in its political form. As a student in Vienna, he encountered discrimination, but his commitment to Zionism developed as a result of his years as a journalist in Paris. Observing the anti-Semitic attacks in republican France provoked by the scandals surrounding the misappropriation of funds by leading French politicians and businesspeople during the failed French attempt to build a Panama canal and the divisive conflict over the Dreyfus Affair in the 1890s, Herzl came to appreciate how deeply imbedded anti-Semitism was in European society. He despaired of the ability of corrupt parliamentary governments to solve the problem of anti-Semitism. In *The Jewish State* (1896), Herzl concluded that Jews must have a state of their own. Under his direction, Zionism developed a world organization with the aim of establishing a Jewish homeland in Palestine.

Jews began emigrating to Palestine. With the financial backing of Jewish donors like the French banker Baron de Rothschild, nearly ninety thousand Jews had established settlements there by 1914. Calculated to tap a common Jewish identification with an ancient heritage, from the beginning the choice of Palestine as a homeland was controversial, and the problems arising from the choice have persisted through the twentieth century.

The promised land of the Old Testament, Zion is a holy place in Judaism. The Austrian psychoanalyst Sigmund Freud (1815–1939), who described himself as "a Jew from Moravia," was sympathetic to the Zionist cause but critical of the idea of Palestine as a Jewish state. He considered the idea unworkable and one bound to arouse Christian and Islamic opposition. Freud feared that Palestine would arouse the suspicions of the Arab world and challenge "the feelings of the local natives." He would have preferred a "new, historically unencumbered soil."

Some Jewish critics of Zionism felt a separate Jewish state would prove that Jews were not good citizens of their respective nation-states and would exacerbate hostilities toward Jews as outsiders. Yet Zionism had much in common with the European liberal tradition because it sought in the creation of a nation-state for Jews the solution to social injustice. Zion, the Jewish nation in the Middle East, was a liberal utopia for the Jewish people. Zionism learned from other mass movements of the period the importance of a broad base of support. By the time of the First Zionist Congress, held in Basel, Switzerland, in 1897, it had become a truly international movement. Zionism did not achieve its goals before World War I, and the Jewish state of Israel was not recognized by the world community until 1948.

Workers and Minorities on the Margins

In 1892 the Parisian trial of a bomb-throwing anarchist named Ravachol attracted great public attention. He and other French anarchists had threatened to destroy bourgeois society by bombing private residences, public buildings, and restaurants. Ravachol opposed the state and the capitalist economy as the dual enemy that could only be destroyed through individual acts of random physical violence. Not all anarchists were terrorists intent on destruction, but all shared a desire for a revolutionary restructuring of society. They spurned the Marxist willingness to organize and to participate in parliamentary politics.

Mikhail Bakunin (1814–1876), a member of the Russian nobility, became Europe's leading anarchist spokesperson. He broke with Marx, whom he considered a "scientific bourgeois socialist" out of touch with the mass of workers. Bakunin's successor in international anarchist doctrine was also a Russian of aristocratic lineage—Prince Petr Kropotkin (1842–1921). Kropotkin joined together communism and anarchism, arguing that goods should be communally distributed, "from each according to his ability, to each according to his needs." Anarchism had special appeal to workers in trades staggering under the blows of industrial capitalism. Calling themselves anarcho-syndicalists, artisans, especially in France, were able to combine local trade union organization with anarchist principles.

The problems of disaffected groups in general intensified before 1914. Anarchists and anarcho-syndicalist workers deplored the centralization and organization of mass society. Yet anarchism posed no serious threat to social stability because of the effectiveness of policing in most European states. The politics of mass society excluded diverse groups, including women, Jews, and ethnic minorities from participation. Yet the techniques, values, and organization of the world of politics remained available to all these groups. It was the outbreak of war in 1914 that silenced, temporarily at least, the challenge of these outsiders.

The Authority of Science

Imagine a world that discovered how to eliminate the difference between night and day. Imagine further a civilization that could obliterate distance or shrink it. Imagine a people who could see for the first time into solid mass, into their own bodies, and send images through space. These are the imaginings of fable and fantasy that can be traced back to prehistory. But what had always been the stuff of magic became reality between 1880 and 1914. The people of the West used science and technology to reshape the world and their understanding of it.

The discoveries of science had ramifications that extended beyond the laboratory, the hospital, and the classroom. Science changed the way people thought and the way they lived. It improved the quality of life by defeating diseases, improving nutrition, and lengthening life span. But scientific knowledge was not without its negative costs. Scientific discoveries led to new forces of destruction. Scientific ideas challenged morals and religious beliefs. Science was invoked to justify racial and sexual discrimination. Traditional values and religious belief also did combat with the new god of science, as philosophers proclaimed that God was dead. New disciplines claimed to study society scientifically with methods similar to those applied to the study of bacilli and the atom. A traditional world of order and hierarchy gave way to a new reality in which the center was no longer holding and the limits were constantly expanding.

What may seem commonplace at the end of the twentieth century was no less than spectacular at the end of the nineteenth. Scientific discoveries in the last quarter of the century pushed out the frontiers of knowledge. In physics, James Clerk Maxwell (1831–1879) discovered the relation between electricity and magnetism. Maxwell showed mathematically that an oscillating electric charge produces an electromagnetic field and that such a field radiates outward from its source at a constant speed—the speed of light. His theories led to the discovery of the electromagnetic spectrum, comprising radiation of different wavelengths, including X rays, visible light, and radio waves. This discovery had important practical applications for the development of the electrical industry and led to the invention of radio and television. Within a generation, the names of Edison, Westinghouse, Marconi, Siemens, and Bell entered the public realm.

Discoveries in the physical sciences succeeded one another with great rapidity. The periodic table of chemical elements was formulated in 1869. Radioactivity was discovered in 1896. Two years later Marie Curie (1867–1934) and her husband Pierre (1859–1906) discovered the elements radium and polonium. At the end of the century, Ernest Rutherford (1871–1937) identified alpha and beta rays in radioactive atoms. Building on the new discoveries, Max Planck (1858–1947), Albert Einstein (1879–1955), and Niels Bohr (1885–1962) dismantled the classical physics of absolute and determined principles and left in its place modern physics based on relativity and uncertainty. In 1900 Planck propounded a theory that renounced the emphasis in classical physics on energy as a wave phenomenon in favor of a new "quantum theory" of energy as emitted and absorbed in minute, discrete amounts.

The name *Einstein* has become synonymous with genius in the twentieth century. In 1905 Albert Einstein formulated his special theory of relativity in which he established the relationship of mass and energy in the famous equation $E = mc^2$. In 1916 he published his general theory of relativity, a mathematical formulation that created new concepts of space and time. Einstein disproved the Newtonian view of gravitation as a force and instead saw it as a curved field in the time-space continuum created by the presence of mass. No one at the time foresaw that applying Einstein's theory that a particle of matter could be converted into a great quantity of energy would unleash the greatest destructive power in history—the atomic and hydrogen bombs—something that Einstein, a pacifist, lived to see developed in his lifetime.

Though the discoveries in the physical sciences were the most dramatic, the biological sciences, too, witnessed great breakthroughs. Research biologists dedicated themselves to the study of disease-causing microbes and to the chemical bases of physiology. French chemist Louis Pasteur (1822–1895) studied microorganisms to find methods of preventing the spread of diseases in humans, animals, and plants. He developed methods of inoculation to provide protection against anthrax in sheep, cholera in chickens, and rabies in animals and humans.

The pace of breakthroughs in biological knowledge and medical treatment was staggering. The malaria parasite was isolated in 1880. The control of diseases such as yellow fever contributed toward improvement in the quality of life. Knowledge burst the bounds of disciplines and new fields developed to accommodate new concerns. Research in human genetics, a field that was only starting to be understood, was begun in the first decade of the twentieth century. The studies of Austrian botanist Gregor Mendel (1822–1884) in the crossbreeding of peas in the 1860s led to the Mendelian laws of inheritance.

Biological discoveries resulted in new state policies. Public health benefited from new methods of prevention and detection of diseases caused by germs. A professor at the University of Berlin, Rudolf Virchow (1821–1902) discovered the relationship between microbes, sewage, and disease that led to the development of modern sewer systems and pure water for urban populations. Biochemistry, bacteriology, and physiology promoted a belief in social progress through state programs. After 1900 health programs to educate the general public spread throughout Europe.

Discoveries that changed the face of the twentieth century proliferated in a variety of fields. This was a time of firsts in all directions: Airplane flights and deep-sea expeditions, based on technological applications of new discoveries, pushed out boundaries of exploration above the land and below the sea. In 1909, the same year that work began in human genetics, American explorer Robert E. Peary (1856–1920) reached the North Pole. In that year, too, plastic was first manufactured, under the trade name Bakelite. Irish-born British astronomer Agnes Mary Clerke (1842–1907) did pioneering work in the new field of astrophysics. Rutherford proposed a new spatial reality in his theory of the nuclear structure of the atom, which stated that the atom can be divided and consists of a nucleus surrounded by electrons revolving around it.

Establishing the Social Sciences

Innovations in the social sciences paralleled the drama of discovery in the biological and physical sciences. The "scientific" study of society purported to apply the same methods of observation and experimentation to human interactions. After 1870 sociology, economics, history, psychology, anthropology, and archaeology took shape at the core of new social scientific endeavors. But just as scientific advances could be applied to destructive ends, so, too, did the social sciences promote inequities and prejudices in the Western world.

Archaeology uncovered lost civilizations. Heinrich Schliemann (1822–1890), who discovered Troy, and Sir Arthur Evans (1851–1941), who began excavations in Crete in 1900, used scientific procedures to reconstruct ancient cultures. Historians, too, applied new techniques to the study of the past. German historian Leopold von Ranke (1795–1886) eschewed a literary form of historical writing that relied on legend and tradition in favor of objective, "scientific" history based on documentation and other forms of material evidence.

The social scientific study of economics came to the aid of business-people. The neoclassical economic theory of Alfred Marshall (1842–1924) and others recognized the centrality of individual choice in the marketplace, while dealing with the problem of overproduction: How can businesses know they have produced enough to maximize profits? Economists concerned with how individuals responded to prices devised a theory of marginal utility, by which producers could calculate costs and project profits based on a pattern of response of consumers to price changes.

"Scientific" psychology developed in a variety of directions. Wilhelm Wundt (1832–1920) established the first laboratory devoted to psychological research in Leipzig in 1879. From his experiments he concluded that thought is grounded in physical reality. The Russian physiologist Ivan Pavlov (1849–1936) won fame with a series of experiments demonstrating the conditioned reflex in dogs. Sigmund Freud (1859–1939) greatly influenced the direction of psychology with his theory of personality development and the creation of psychoanalysis, the science of the unconscious. Freudian probing of the unconscious was a model greatly at odds with the behavioral perspective of conditioned responses based on Pavlov's work.

Émile Durkheim (1858–1917) is regarded as the founder of modern sociology. In his famous study of suicide as a social phenomenon, Durkheim pitted sociological theory against psychology and argued that deviance was the result not of psychic disturbances but of environmental factors and hereditary forces. Heredity became a general explanation for behavior of all sorts. Everything from poverty, drunkenness, crime, and a declining birthrate could be attributed to biologically determined causes. For some theorists, this reasoning teetered on the edge of racism and ideas about "better blood." Intelligence was now measured for the first time "scientifically" with IQ tests developed at the Sorbonne by the psychologist Alfred Binet (1857–1911) in the 1890s. But the tests did not acknowledge the importance of cultural factors in the development of intelligence, and they scientifically legitimated a belief in natural elites.

*T*he European Search for Territory and Markets

The concept of empire was certainly not invented by Europeans in the last third of the nineteenth century. Before 1870 European states had controlled empires. The influence of Great Britain stretched beyond the limits of its formal holdings in India and South Africa. Russia held Siberia and central Asia, and France ruled Algeria and Indochina. Older empires, Spain for example, had survived from the sixteenth century but as hollow shells. What, then, was new about the "new imperialism" practiced by England, France, and Germany after 1870? In part, the new imperialism was the acquisition of territories on an intense and unprecedented scale. Industrialization created the tools of transportation, communication, and domination that permitted the rapid pace of global empire-building. Above all, what distinguished the new imperialism was the domination by the industrial powers over the nonindustrial world.

Only nation-states commanded the technology and resources necessary for the new scale of imperialist expansion. Rivalry among a few European nation-states—notably, Great Britain, France, and Germany—was a common denominator that set the standards by which these nations and other European states gained control of the globe by 1900. Why did the Europeans create vast empires? Were empires built for economic gain, military protection, or national glory? Questions about motives may obscure common features of the new imperialism. Industrial powers sought to take over nonindustrial regions, not in isolated areas but all over the globe. In the attempt they necessarily competed with one another, successfully adapting the resources of industrialism to the needs of conquest.

The New Imperialism

For Europeans at the end of the nineteenth century, the world had definitely become a smaller place. Steam, iron, and electricity—the great forces of Western industrialization—were responsible for shrinking the globe. Technology not only allowed Europeans to accomplish tasks and to mass-produce goods efficiently, but it also altered previous understandings of time and space.

Steam, which powered factories, proved equally efficient as an energy source in transportation. Great iron steamships fueled by coal replaced the smaller, slower, wind-powered wooden sailing vessels that had ruled the sea for centuries. For most of the nineteenth century British trading ships and the British navy dominated the seas, but after 1880 other nations, especially Germany, challenged England by building versatile and efficient iron steamers. In a society in which time was money, steamships were important because, for the first time, oceangoing vessels could meet schedules as precisely and as predictably as railroads.

While technology improved European mobility on water, it also literally moved the land. Harbors were deepened to accommodate the new iron- and then steel-hulled ships. One of the greatest engineering feats of the century was the construction of a 100-mile-long canal across the Isthmus of Suez in Egypt. Completed in 1869, the Suez Canal joined the Mediterranean and Red seas and created a new, safer trade route to the East. The Panama Canal, completed by the United States in 1914, connected the world's two largest bodies of water, the Atlantic and Pacific oceans, across the Isthmus of Panama by a waterway containing a series of locks. Both the Suez and Panama canals were built in pursuit of speed. Shorter distances meant quicker travel, which in turn meant higher profits.

Technology also altered time by increasing the speed with which Westerners communicated with other parts of the world. Thousands of miles of copper telegraph wire laced countries together; insulated underwater cables linked continents to each other. By the late nineteenth century a vast telegraph network connected Europe to every area of the world. Now Europeans could communicate immediately with their distant colonies, dispatching troops, orders, and supplies.

Technological advances in other areas helped foster European imperialism in the nineteenth century. Advances in medicine permitted European men and women to penetrate disease-laden swamps and jungles. David Livingstone (1813–1873) and Henry M. Stanley (1841–1904) were just two of the many explorers who crossed vast terrains and explored the waterways of Africa, after malaria, the number one killer of Europeans, had been controlled by quinine.

Europeans also carried the technologies of destruction with them into less developed areas of the world. New types of firearms produced in the second half of the nineteenth century included breech-loading rifles, repeating rifles, and machine guns. The new weapons offered the advantages of both accurate aim and rapid fire. The spears of African warriors and the primitive weaponry of Chinese rebels were no match for sophisticated European arms. The new technology did not cause the new imperialism. The Western powers used technological advances as a tool for establishing their control of the world. Viewed as a tool, however, the new technology does explain how vast areas of land and millions of people were conquered so rapidly.

If technology was not the cause but only a tool, what explains the new imperialism of the late nineteenth century? There are no easy or simple explanations. Individuals made their fortunes overseas, and heavy industries like the Krupp firm in Germany prospered with the expansion of state-protected colonies. Yet many colonies were economically worthless. Each imperial power held one or more colonies whose costs outweighed the return.

Economics.   The test for economic motivation cannot simply be reduced to a balance sheet of debits and credits because, in the end, an account of state revenues and state expenditures provides only a static picture of the business of empire. Even losses cannot be counted as proof against the profit motive in expansion. In modern capitalism, profits, especially great profits, are often predicated on risks. Portugal and Italy took great risks and failed as players in the game in which the great industrial powers called the shots. Prestige through the acquisition of empire was one way of keeping alive in the game. Imperialism was influenced by business interests, market considerations, and the pursuit of individual and national fortunes. Not by accident did the great industrial powers control the scramble and dictate the terms of expansion. Nor was it merely fortuitous that Great Britain, the nation that provided the model for European expansion, dedicated itself to the establishment of a profitable worldwide network of trade and investment. Above all, the search for investment opportunities, whether railroads in China or diamond mines in South Africa, lured Europeans into a world system that challenged capitalist ingenuity and imagination. Acquiring territory was only one means of protecting investments. But there were other benefits associated with the acquisition of territory that cannot be reduced to economic terms, and those, too, must be considered.

Geopolitics.   Geopolitics, or the politics of geography, is based on the recognition that certain areas of the world are valuable for political reasons. The term, first used at the end of the nineteenth century, described a process well under way in international relations. Statesmen influenced by geopolitical concerns recognized the strategic value of land. Some territory was considered important because of its proximity to acquired colonies or to territory targeted for takeover. France, for example, occupied thousands of square miles of the Sahara Desert to protect its interests in Algeria. Other territory was important because of its proximity to sea routes. Egypt had significance for Great Britain not because of its inherent economic potential but because it permitted the British to protect access to lucrative markets in India through the Suez Canal. Beginning in 1875, the British purchased shares in the canal.

A third geopolitical motive for annexation was the necessity of fueling bases throughout the world. Faster and more reliable than wind-powered vessels, coal-powered ships were, nonetheless, dependent on guaranteed fueling bases in friendly ports of call. Islands in the South Pacific and the Indian Ocean were acquired primarily to serve as coaling stations for the great steamers carrying manufactured goods to colonial ports and returning with foodstuffs and raw materials.

In turn, the acquisition of territories justified the increase in naval budgets and the size of fleets. Britain still had the world's largest navy, but by the beginning of the twentieth century, the United States and Germany had entered the competition for dominance of sea-lanes. Japan joined the contest by expanding its navy as a vehicle for its own claims to empire in the Pacific. The politics of geography was land- as well as sea-based. As navies grew to protect sea-lanes, armies expanded to police new lands. A side effect of the growing importance of geopolitics was the increased influence of military and naval leaders in foreign and domestic policy-making.

Nationalism.   Many European statesmen in the last quarter of the nineteenth century gave stirring speeches about the importance of empire as a means of enhancing national prestige. Nation-states could, through the acquisition of overseas territories, gain bargaining chips to be played at the international conference table. In this way, smaller nations hoped to be taken seriously in the system of alliances that preserved "the balance of power" in Europe.

Western newspapers deliberately fostered the desire for the advancement of national interests. Newspapers competed for readers, and their circulations often depended on the passions they aroused. Newspapers forged a national consciousness whereby individuals identified with collective causes they did not fully comprehend. Government elites, who formerly operated behind closed doors far removed from public scrutiny, were now accountable in new ways to faceless masses. Even in autocratic states like Austria-Hungary, the opinion of the masses was a powerful political force that could destroy individual careers and dissolve governments.

Information conveyed in newspapers shaped opinion, and opinion, in turn, could influence policy. Leaders had to reckon with this new creation of "public opinion." In a typical instance, French newspaper editors promoted feverish public outcry for conquest of the Congo by pointing out the need to revenge British advances in Egypt. "Colonial fever" in France was so high in the summer of 1882 that French policymakers were pressured to pursue claims in the Congo Basin without adequate assessment or reflection.

Public opinion was certainly influential, but it could be manipulated. In Germany the government often promoted colonial hysteria through the press in order to advance its own political ends. Chancellor Otto von Bismarck used his power over the press to support imperialism and to influence electoral outcomes in 1884. His successors were deft at promoting the "bread and circuses" atmosphere that surrounded colonial expansion in order to direct attention away from social problems at home and to maintain domestic stability.

To varying degrees, all of these factors—economics, geopolitics, and nationalism—motivated the actions of the three great imperialist powers— Britain, France, and Germany—and their less powerful European neighbors. The same reasons account for the global aspirations of non-European nations like the United States and Japan. None of these powers acted independently— each was aware of what the others were doing and tailored its actions accordingly. Imperialism followed a variety of patterns but always with a built-in component of emulation and acceleration. It was both a cause and a proof of a world system of states in which the actions of one nation affected the others.

Scrambling for Africa

Among the nonindustrialized regions of the world that were the targets of Western imperialism, societies were organized in two vastly different ways. Tribal societies predominated in sub-Saharan Africa. Built on the concept of community, tribal societies had no provision for the individual. In China, India, and other parts of Asia, hierarchies were the rule. Hierarchies, based on social divisions like the caste system in India, had individual leaders and mechanisms to regulate the inheritance of power and land. Though they were more difficult to conquer, hierarchical societies were also more likely to cooperate with Western powers because clearly identifiable ruling elites were willing to work with Westerners for their own ends.

For these reasons, European empire builders favored informal empires (as in China) or formal but indirect rule over hierarchical societies (as in India). Tribes, in contrast, had to be conquered outright and ruled both directly and formally. Formal empires required occupation of territory and the introduction of European institutions and European administrators, as was the case, for example, in the Belgian Congo.

European involvement in Africa in the last two decades of the nineteenth century is the clearest example of how Europeans established formal empires among widely dispersed tribal societies. Europeans were not new in Africa. For most of the nineteenth century Europeans controlled about 10 percent of the African continent. The situation changed at the end of the century: By 1914 nine European states had taken over 90 percent of the continent. Only Ethiopia, ruled by a strong emperor, and Liberia, under the protection of the United States, maintained their independence.

The abolition of the slave trade by Great Britain in 1807 sparked the first burst of colonization. The abolitionists provided passage to missionaries to set up hospitals and way stations in order to care for freed slaves, who were

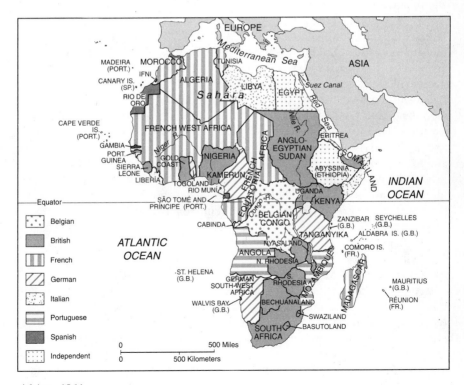

Africa, 1914

separated from their tribes, weak, and often sick, in the coastal towns of Africa. These temporary facilities became permanent when missionaries recognized that the freed slaves presented opportunities for conversion and Christianization. In the process of carrying out their mission, they sent accounts back home of Africa's natural wealth. The information they recorded about tribes and indigenous languages and customs provided invaluable tools for later explorers.

Religious and philanthropic societies needed permanent bases for their activities and so they began to acquire land. As Europeans began to acquire land, they began to need protection. Missions needed to be safeguarded against natives as well as from competing Europeans. Policing European holdings could be most efficiently achieved by converting territories into colonies.

Until the 1870s individual efforts defined the new European presence in Africa. Private backing financed the efforts of missionaries, explorers, adventurers, and merchants, and their holdings dotted the African landscape. In the last quarter of the nineteenth century, imperialism took on a new character with the large-scale involvement of European states and their representatives in the formal acquisition of land occupied and claimed by their citizens. Rather than creating the scramble, state intervention brought new features to the intense competition already under way: national rivalries, military conflict, and opportunities for war.

In the case of Great Britain, the reasons for territorial acquisition can be found in its nineteenth-century trading history. With a world empire that by the mid-1850s included holdings in India, Hong King, the South Pacific, Mauritius, Seychelles, Malta, Gibraltar, and the Cape of Good Hope, the British confidently ruled the seas. Through free trade, British manufacturers dominated European markets. Seeing the British accumulate both wealth and power, merchants and bankers from other Western nations began to develop their own world markets. They eventually sought state protection for their actions and promoted resistance against further British incursions in European, Asian, and African markets. They demanded that their governments impose tariffs to protect these new markets. Britain responded by rapidly developing new markets in areas not yet strangled by European protectionism.

German and French traders could circumvent British industrial advantage only by operating in areas free of the British presence. German merchants from Hamburg and Bremen, for example, sought overseas markets in West Africa in the first half of the nineteenth century. German trade prospered and expanded in West Africa after 1850, and German interests became firmly entrenched in key trading ports and surrounding territories. By the mid-1880s, the German state had annexed Togo, Cameroons, South-West Africa, and the territory of German East Africa. The pattern of economic interests demanding state protection and forcing intervention proved a general one for European annexation in Africa.

The formal seizure of territories accelerated in the early 1880s. State-supported colonizers stampeded for territory, often with no better motive than the fear that others would beat them to it. In the competition for land, the three great imperial nations, France, Germany, and Britain, began butting into one another in central and western Africa. In 1879 France decided to use military force to expand into the sub-Sahara, nurturing the dream of a trans-Saharan railway to connect its holdings in North and West Africa. The British Foreign Office judged such activity as "antagonistic" to British interests in Egypt and the Sudan. In 1881 France annexed Tunisia, and the following year Britain occupied Egypt. The French also antagonized the Belgians in the Congo. Hoping to protect their trade interests in Africa, the British negotiated with the Portuguese for control of the mouth of the Congo River. Both the French and the Germans opposed British and Portuguese claims as threatening to their own interests. The chaotic situation was becoming dangerous.

Conflict over the Congo made clear the necessity of drawing up the rules of the imperialist game. At the instigation of German chancellor Otto von Bismarck and French president Jules Ferry, representatives of 14 nations, including the United States, met at Berlin in late fall 1884 to establish procedures for fair and orderly annexations in Africa. The conference acknowledged that the scramble for territory was well under way and sought to control it. The Berlin Act of 1885 set new rules for the game of empire building. Control of an area was to be the prerequisite for its annexation. Planting a flag was simply not enough.

Although regulation was the goal, intensified competition was the result. Conflicting British and French claims to the Nile Valley threatened to escalate into armed conflict and war in 1898. A French expedition led by Captain J. P. Marchand (1863–1934) set up camp near the banks of the Nile and planted a French flag at Fashoda in southeastern Sudan. British General Horatio H. Kitchener (1850–1916), leading an Anglo-Egyptian army through the Sudan, met Marchand on 18 September 1898 at Fashoda and demanded his withdrawal. This volatile situation endured until 3 November 1898, when the French government, crippled by serious problems at home and unwilling to risk war with Britain, ordered Marchand to withdraw.

The incident at Fashoda marked the end of one era and the beginning of another. Fashoda initiated an era of friction, war hysteria, and the readiness to accept armed conflict as an appropriate response to colonial disagreements. It opened a new era of posturing and showdowns based on the concept of self-aggrandizement at the expense of one's enemies. The scramble for Africa was drawing to a close, as the vast majority of the continent had been partitioned. When the scramble was over, the French had carved out the largest African empire, mainly in the north and west, consisting of 4 million of Africa's 11.7 million square miles. In actual square miles taken, the British placed second, but they were arguably superior in the strategic and economic value of their territories in western, southern, and eastern Africa. Germany came to the scramble late, but by 1884 it stood as the third competitor for domination of Africa.

Imperialism in Asia

The British Parliament proclaimed that on New Year's Day, 1877, Queen Victoria (1837–1901) would add the title Empress of India to her many honors. The title was more than merely a symbolic assertion of dominance over a country long controlled by the British. India was the starting point of all British expansion and it stood at the center of British foreign policy. To protect its sea routes to India and to secure its Indian markets, Britain acquired territories and carved out concessions all over the world. Devised by Prime Minister Benjamin Disraeli to flatter an aging monarch, the new title of empress was really a calculated warning to Russia, operating on India's northern frontier in Afghanistan, and to France, busily pursuing its own interests in Egypt.

Formal British rule in India began in 1861 with the appointment of a viceroy, who was assisted by legislative and executive councils. Both of these bodies included some Indian representatives. British rule encountered the four main divisions of the highly stratified Hindu society. At the top were Brahmans, the learned and priestly class, followed by the warriors and rulers, then by farmers and merchants, and finally by the peasants and laborers. On the outside existed the "untouchables," a fifth division intended to perform society's most menial tasks. Rather than disrupt this divisive caste system, the British found it to their advantage to maintain the status quo.

Queen Victoria was proclaimed Empress of India in 1877, after most of the subcontinent became part of the British Empire. Here the queen is seen at her writing table, attended by an Indian servant in national dress.

The special imperial relationship, rung in with the new year in 1877, originated in the seventeenth century, when the British East India Company, a joint-stock venture free of government control, began limited trading in Indian markets. The need for regulation and protection firmly established British rule by the end of the eighteenth century. Conquest of the Punjab in 1849 brought the last independent areas under British control. Throughout this period Britain invested considerable overseas capital in India, and in turn India absorbed one-fifth of total British exports. The market for Indian cotton, for centuries exported to markets in Asia and Europe, collapsed under British tariffs and India became a ready market for cheap Lancashire cotton. The British also exploited India's agriculture, salt, and opium production for profit.

At the end of the eighteenth century, the British traded English wool and Indian cotton for Chinese tea and textiles. But Britain's thirst for Chinese tea grew, while Chinese demand for English and Indian textiles slackened. Britain discovered that Indian opium could be used to balance the trade deficit created by tea. British merchants and local Chinese officials, especially in the entry port of Canton, began to expand their profitable involvement in a contraband trade in opium. The East India Company held a monopoly over opium cultivation in Bengal. Opium exports to China mounted phenomenally: from 200 chests in 1729 to 40,000 chests in 1838. By the 1830s opium was probably Britain's most important crop in world markets. The British prospered as opium was pumped into China at rates faster than tea was flowing out. Chinese buyers began paying for the drug with silver.

Concerned with the sharp rise in addiction, the accompanying social problems, and the massive outflow of silver, the Chinese government reacted. As Chinese officials saw it, they were exchanging their precious metal for British poison. Addicts were threatened with the death penalty. In 1839 the Chinese government destroyed British opium in the port of Canton, touching off the so-called Opium War (1839–1842). British expeditionary forces blockaded Chinese ports, besieged Canton, and occupied Shanghai. In protecting the rights of British merchants engaged in illegal trading, Great Britain became the first Western nation to use force to impose its economic interests on China. The Treaty of Nanking (1842) initiated a series of unequal treaties between Europeans and the Chinese and set the pattern for exacting large indemnities.

Between 1842 and 1895 China fought five wars with foreigners and lost all of them. Defeat was expensive because China had to pay costs to the winners. Before the end of the century, Britain, France, Germany, and Japan had managed to establish major territorial advantages in their "spheres of influence," sometimes through negotiation and sometimes through force. By 1912 over fifty major Chinese ports had been handed over to foreign control as "treaty ports." British spheres included Shanghai, the lower Yangtze, and Hong Kong. France maintained special interests in South China. Germany controlled the Shantung peninsula. Japan laid claim to the northeast.

Treaty ports were centers of foreign residence and trade, where rules of extraterritoriality applied. This meant that foreigners were exempt from Chinese law enforcement and that, although present on Chinese territory, they could be judged only by officials of their own countries. Extraterritoriality, a privilege not just for diplomats but one shared by every foreign national, implied both a distrust of Chinese legal procedures and a cultural arrogance about the superiority of Western institutions. These arrangements stirred Chinese resentment and contributed considerably to growing antiforeignism.

The rise of Western influence in China coincided with and benefited from Chinese domestic problems, including dynastic decline, famine, and successive rebellions. The European powers were willing, however, to prop up the crumbling structure for their own ends. The Boxer Rebellion of 1900 made clear to the Western powers their limited ability to control social unrest in China. The Boxers, peasants so named by Westerners because of the martial rites practiced by their secret society, the Harmonious Fists, rose up against the foreign and Christian exploitation in north China. At the beginning of the summer of 1900, the Boxers—with the concealed encouragement of the

The claims of the Boxer troops to invulnerability were believed by millions of Chinese. In this Chinese print, the Boxer forces use cannon, bayonets, dynamite, and sabers to drive the Western "barbarians" from the Middle Kingdom.

Chinese government—killed Europeans and seized the foreign legations in Beijing. An international expeditionary force of 16,000 well-armed Japanese, Russian, British, American, German, French, Austrian, and Italian troops entered Beijing in August to defend the treaty interests of their respective countries. Led by a German general, the international force followed Emperor William II's urgings to remember the Huns: "Show no mercy! Take no prisoners!" Systematic plunder and slaughter followed. Beijing was sacked.

Abandoning earlier discussions of partitioning China, the international powers accepted the need for a central Chinese government—even one that had betrayed their interests—which would police a populace plagued by demographic pressures, famine, discrimination against minorities, excessive taxation, exorbitant land rents, and social and economic dislocations created by foreign trade. During the previous year (1899), the United States had asserted its claims in China in the "Open Door" policy. This policy, formulated by U.S. Secretary of State John Hay, was as much concerned with preserving Chinese sovereignty as it was with establishing equal economic opportunity for foreign competition in Chinese markets. Europeans and Americans wanted to send bankers to China, not gunboats. A stable central government facilitated their preferences. By operating within delineated spheres of influence and using established elites to further their own programs, Westerners protected their financial interests without incurring the costs and responsibilities of direct rule.

European nations pursued imperialist endeavors elsewhere in Asia, acquired territories on China's frontiers, and took over states that had formerly paid tribute to the Chinese empire. The British acquired Hong Kong (1842), Burma (1886), and Kowloon (1898). The Russians took over the Maritime Provinces in 1858. The French made gains in Indochina (Annan and Tonkin) in 1884 and in 1893 and extended control over Laos and Cambodia.

New Imperial Contenders

The new imperialism was a European phenomenon, with two important exceptions: Japan and the United States. In the mid nineteenth century Japan was a rural and feudal island kingdom isolated from the rest of the world. It seemed destined for the same fate of Western control that was befalling China. Yet within two generations, Japan had become an industrial and imperial power with global aspirations. The spark for the change was lit in 1854 when Commodore Matthew C. Perry (1794–1858) sailed a U.S. squadron to Japan for the purpose of opening up Japanese ports to U.S. trading. Japan, like China, was forced to accept a series of unequal treaties, prompting Japanese attacks on foreigners and the collapse of the ruling shogunate.

The Meiji restoration that followed in 1868 responded to the foreign threat neither by resistance nor by collaboration but by emulation. Meiji rulers sent young men to Europe to learn Western administration, technology, and military strategy. Feudalism was abolished and a Prussianlike constitution was adopted. Preserving traditional values of family life and paternal authority and employing the new knowledge from the West, by the 1880s Japan had industrialized in textiles and ten years later had moved into heavy industry. Japan telescoped into two decades changes that had taken western Europe centuries to accomplish. Foreign trade increased steadily with Japanese silk eventually surpassing its Chinese counterpart in world markets. The transformation, although breathtaking, was not without its cost: the pressures of population growth and the threat of exhaustion of resources.

Japan, once again taking its lead from the West, saw overseas expansion as the solution to its problems. In the Sino-Japanese War of 1894–1895 and the Russo-Japanese War of 1904–1905, Japan established an empire on the Asian mainland and extended its holdings to the north and the south in the Pacific. The wars also gave notice to the world that, although small, Japan intended to take its place among the great imperial powers.

The United States provided another variation on imperial expansion. Its westward drive across the North American continent, beginning at the end of the eighteenth century, established the United States as an imperial power in the Western Hemisphere. At the end of the nineteenth century, the United States, possessing both the people and the resources for rapid industrial development, turned to the Caribbean and the Pacific in pursuit of markets and investment opportunities.

By acquiring stepping-stones of islands across the Pacific in the Hawaiian Islands and Samoa, the United States secured fueling bases and access to lucrative east Asian ports. And by intervening repeatedly in Central America and building the Panama Canal, it established its hegemony in the Caribbean by 1914. Growing in economic power and hegemonic influence, both Japan and the United States had joined the club of imperial powers and were making serious claims against European expansion.

Conflicts in Empires

Colonies easy to acquire were often difficult to maintain. Few understood the demands of colonial rule when the new imperialism began to intensify in the 1870s. German chancellor Otto von Bismarck, for example, looked on the pursuit of empire as a useful diversion that preserved peace in continental Europe by keeping France and Britain busy overseas and draining their resources. By 1885 Germany had entered into the race for empire, and the race no longer promised to be diversionary. Imperial rivalry intensified the competition among Western powers and created another arena for conflict.

South Africa.   The British took the Cape of Good Hope from the Dutch in 1795. The south African region had been settled by the Boers, descendants of Dutch farmers, who spoke only Afrikaans, a Dutch dialect, and lived apart in a culture that was Calvinist, traditional, and patriarchal. The Boer farming economy relied heavily on African slave labor. When the British outlawed slavery in the colonies in 1834, the Boers refused to continue to live in Cape Colony under British rule, packed up their belongings, and headed eastward into Natal on what has become known as the Great Trek (1837–1844). Overcoming fierce Zulu resistance, they established the Natal Republic, which the British took over in 1843. Trekking northward, the Boers established the Transvaal Republic and the Orange Free State. These two independent states, built by enslaving native Africans, became especially attractive to the British when diamonds and gold were discovered in South Africa in the 1870s and 1880s. Thousands of English citizens streamed into the region in search of their fortunes. Among them was a 17-year-old named Cecil Rhodes (1853–1902).

Rhodes used shrewd investments, political maneuvering, unscrupulous business practices, and exploitation of cheap African labor to build a fortune from Africa's fabulous natural wealth. By the time he was 35, Rhodes controlled the entire diamond industry, and his company, De Beers Consolidated Mining, produced 90 percent of the world's diamonds.

Rhodes viewed the Boer states as impediments to British control of the continent. He aimed to harness the long tradition of conflict between the Boers and the British for British aggrandizement. In 1896 Rhodes backed a raid into the Transvaal led by his friend Dr. Jameson. Working behind the scenes with other South African millionaires, known popularly as the "gold bugs," Rhodes hoped in vain that the thousands of British, who had rushed into the Boer state when gold was discovered, would rise up and pull down the government in Johannesburg, the capital. The Jameson Raid failed, but it did draw the British further into hostilities with the Boers.

Disputes provoked over the denial of voting rights to Uitlanders (British immigrants in Boer states) led to the Boers' declaration of war on Great Britain in 1899. The advantages of guerrilla tactics and knowledge of the terrain accounted for initial Boer successes. But superior numbers proved to be the deciding factor. Under the brutal command of General Kitchener, the British threw 350,000 troops against 60,000 Boer farmers. The international press condemned the British for their ruthless tactics of burning the farms in their path and interning Boer women and children in concentration camps. Thousands of those interned died. By the time the peace treaty was signed in 1902, 22,000 British, 25,000 Boers, and 12,000 Africans had died. Following the war, the British annexed the Boer states, which eventually became part of the newly formed Union of South Africa, established in 1910.

The Boer War indicated to the world the extent to which Britain would go to protect and increase its holdings. It also made Britain vulnerable to widespread criticism for its naked aggrandizement. Emperor Wilhelm's expression of sympathy for the beleaguered Boers brought into the open the rivalry between Germany and Britain. The war not only foreshadowed other African conflicts, it also dramatically illustrated the potential for hostility in European empires throughout the world.

The New Imperialism in Africa and Asia

1834	Great Britain abolishes slavery in all its colonies
1837–1844	Great Trek
1839–1842	Opium War
1869	Suez Canal completed
1885	Berlin Act attempts to regulate imperialism in Africa
1894–1895	Sino-Japanese War
1898	Fashoda incident
1899–1902	Boer War
1900	Boxer Rebellion
1904–1905	Russo-Japanese War
1905	First Moroccan Crisis
1911	Second Moroccan Crisis

Crises in Morocco.   In 1904, after two years of negotiations, Britain and France struck a series of colonial bargains over North Africa. The French agreed to cease obstructing British administration in Egypt, and the British accepted French influence in Morocco. This cooperation between Britain and France advanced further in 1905 when the Germans challenged French interests in Morocco. Under pressure, the French agreed to an international conference to deal with German complaints.

At the international conference held in the Spanish city of Algeciras in 1906, Russia, Great Britain, Italy, and the United States stood with France against Germany. Austria alone sided with Germany. The resulting Act of Algeciras affirmed an "open door" in Morocco, although France was granted control over Moroccan finances and de facto dominance over the North African country. This first Moroccan crisis marked the polarization of European states into two antagonistic and irreconcilable camps struggling over world hegemony.

Five years later internal struggles in Morocco precipitated a second Moroccan crisis. When the French responded to Moroccan instability by occupying the country, Germans, regarding this action as a violation of the 1906 agreement, sent a gunboat to Agadir, a harbor on Morocco's Atlantic coast. The British supported the French action and guaranteed French claims to Morocco, which became a French protectorate the following year. Germany received some territory in the Congo as poor compensation. Divisions between Germany and Austria-Hungary, supported now by Italy on the one side and France, Great Britain, and Russia on the other side, had become more rigid. Although the conflict was peaceably settled, Germany's apparent willingness to use armed force to assert its claims marked a turning point in international relations.

Wars in Asia. The Sino-Japanese War of 1894–1895 revealed Japan's intentions to compete as an imperialist power in Asia. The modernized and westernized Japanese army easily defeated the ill-equipped and poorly led Chinese forces. As a result, Japan gained the island of Taiwan. Pressing its ambitions on the continent, Japan locked horns with Russia over claims to the Liaotung peninsula, Korea, and South Manchuria. Following its victory in the Russo-Japanese War of 1904–1905, Japan expanded into all of these areas, annexing Korea outright in 1910. The war sent a strong message to the West about the ease with which the small Asian nation had defeated the Russian giant and contributed to the heightening of anti-imperialist sentiments in China.

*R*esults of a European-Dominated World

The nineteenth-century liberal belief in progress encouraged Europeans to impose their beliefs and institutions on captive millions. After all, industrial society had given the West the technology, the wealth, and the power to tame nature and dominate the world. Imperialists moralized that they had not only the right but also the duty to develop the nonindustrialized world for their own purposes.

A World Economy

Imperialism produced an interdependent world economic system with Europe at its center. Industrial and commercial capitalism linked together the world's continents in a communications and transportation network unimaginable in earlier ages. As a result, foreign trade increased from 3 percent of world output in 1800 to 33 percent by 1913. The greatest growth in trade occurred in the period from 1870 to 1914, as raw materials, manufactured products, capital, and men and women were transported across seas and continents by those seeking profits.

Most trading in the age of imperialism still took place among European nations and North America. But entrepreneurs in search of new markets and new resources saw in Africa and Asia opportunities for protected exploitation. Opportunities were not seized but created in nonindustrialized areas of the world, as new markets were shaped to meet the needs of Western producers and consumers. European landlords and managers trained Kenyan farmers to put aside their traditional agricultural methods and to grow more "useful" crops like coffee, tea, and sugar. The availability of cheaper British textiles of inferior quality drove Indian weavers away from their hand looms. Chinese silk producers changed centuries-old techniques to produce silk thread and cloth that was suited to the machinery and mass production requirements of the French. Non-European producers undoubtedly derived benefits from this new international trading partnership, but those benefits were often scarce. Trade permitted specialization but at the choice of the colonizer, not the colonized. World production and consumption were being shaped to suit the needs of the West.

The City of London had become the world's banker, serving as the clearinghouse for foreign investment on a global scale. The adoption of gold as the standard of exchange for most European currencies by 1874 further facilitated the operation of a single, interdependent trading and investment system. Britain remained the world's biggest trading nation with half of its exports going to Asia, Africa, and South America, and the other half to Europe and the United States. But Germany was Britain's fastest growing competitor with twice as many exports to Europe and expanding overseas trade by 1914. The United States had recently joined the league of the world's great trading nations and was running a strong third in shares of total trade.

Foreign investments often took the form of loans to governments or to enterprises guaranteed by governments. Investors might be willing to take risks, but they also expected protection, no less so than merchants and industrialists trading in overseas territories. The vast amounts of money involved help explain the expectations of state involvement and the reasons why international competition, rivalry, and instability threatened to lead to conflict and to war.

Race and Culture

The West's ability to kill and conquer as well as to cure was, as one Victorian social observer argued, proof of its cultural superiority. Every colonizing nation had its spokespeople for the "civilizing mission" to educate and to convert African and Asian "heathens." Cultural superiority was only a short step from arguments for racial superiority.

Some European women participated directly in the colonizing experience. As missionaries and nurses, they supported the civilizing mission. As wives of officials and managers, they were expected to embody the gentility and values of Western culture. Most men who traded and served overseas did so unaccompanied by women. But when women were present in any numbers, as they were in India before 1914, they were expected to preserve the exclusivity of Western communities and to maintain class and status differentiations as a proof of cultural superiority.

Views of cultural superiority received support from evolutionary theories, based on the scientific work of Herbert Spencer (1820–1903) and Charles Darwin (1809–1882). In the 1880s popularizers applied evolutionary ideas about animal and plant life to the development of human society. These "social Darwinists" argued that just as animals could be hierarchically organized according to observable differences, so, too, could the different races of human beings. Race and culture were collapsed into each other. If Westerners were culturally superior, as they claimed, they must be racially superior as well. The "survival of the fittest" came to justify conquest and subjugation as "laws" of human interaction and, by extension, of relations among nations.

Early explorers had disrupted little as they arrived, observed, and then moved on. The missionaries, merchants, soldiers, and businesspeople who came later required those with whom they came into contact to change their thought and behavior. In some cases, dislocation resulted in material improvements, better medical care, and the introduction of modern technology. For the most part, however, the initial impact of the imperialist was negative. Western men and women carried diseases to people who did not share their immunity. Traditional village life was destroyed in rural India, and African tribal societies disintegrated under the European onslaught.

When Asian and African laborers started producing for the Western market, they became dependent on its fluctuations. Victimized for centuries by the vagaries of weather, they now had to contend with the instability and cutthroat competition of cash crops in world markets. Individuals migrated from place to place in the countryside and from the countryside to newly formed cities. The fabric of tribal life unraveled. Such migrations necessarily affected family life, with individuals marrying later because they lacked the resources to set up households. In the most extreme example of the colonizer's disdain for the colonized, some European countries used their overseas territories as dumping grounds for hardened and incorrigible convicted criminals.

In 1914 Europe stood confidently at the center of the world. Covering only 7 percent of the earth's surface, it dominated the world's trade and was actively exporting both European goods and European culture all over the globe. Proud of the progress and prosperity of urban industrial society, Europeans had harnessed nature to transform their environment. They extended their influence beyond the confines of their continent, sure that their achievements marked the pinnacle of civilization.

From the very beginning of the competition for territories and concessions, no European state could act in Africa or Asia without affecting the interests and actions of its rivals at home. The scramble for Africa made clear how interlocking the system of European states was after 1870. Europeans fashioned the world in their own image, but in doing so, Western values and Western institutions underwent profound and unintended transformations. The discovery of new lands, new cultures, and new peoples altered the ways in which European women and men regarded themselves and viewed their place in the world. With the rise of new contenders for power, the United States and Japan, the Western world was not as predictable in 1914 as it had appeared in 1870.

Suggestions for Further Reading

European Economy and the Politics of Mass Society

Michael Burns, *Rural Society and French Politics: Boulangism and the Dreyfus Affair, 1886–1900* (Princeton, NJ: Princeton University Press, 1984). Examines the impact on rural France of two political watersheds of the Third Republic in order to gauge the importance of national politics in nonurban settings.

*Carl E. Schorske, *Fin-de-Siècle Vienna: Politics and Culture* (New York: Knopf, 1980). A series of essays describing the break with nineteenth-century liberal culture in one of Europe's great cities, as artists, intellectuals, and politicians responded to the disintegration of the Habsburg Empire.

*Eugen Weber, *Peasants into Frenchmen: The Modernization of Rural France* (Stanford, CA: Stanford University Press, 1976). Views the integration of the French peasantry into national political life through agents of change, including the railroads, schools, and the army. The author contends that a national political culture took the place of traditional beliefs and practices between 1870 and 1914 in France.

*Hans-Ulrich Wehler, *The German Empire, 1871–1918* (Leamington Spa, England: Berg, 1985). Stresses the institutional continuities of German society and links pre–World War I Germany to the rise of Nazism.

Mass Politics and the New Consciousness

*Steven C. Hause and Anne R. Kenney, *Women's Suffrage and Social Politics in the French Third Republic* (Princeton, NJ: Princeton University Press, 1984). Examines the women's suffrage movement from its origins through its defeat after World War I in the Senate. Aims, tactics, and leadership of the women's movement receive special attention.

*Stephen Kern, *The Culture of Time and Space, 1880–1918* (Cambridge, MA: Harvard University Press, 1983). Describes how late nineteenth-century technological advances created new modes of thinking about and experiencing time and space.

*Michael R. Miller, *The Bon Marché: Bourgeois Culture and the Department Store, 1869–1920* (Princeton, NJ: Princeton University Press, 1981). A social and cultural history of the department store as the creation and reflection of bourgeois culture.

*Richard Stites, *The Women's Liberation Movement in Russia: Feminism, Nihilism, and Bolshevism, 1860–1930* (Princeton, NJ: Princeton University Press, 1978). Situates the Russian women's movement within the contexts of both nineteenth-century European feminism and twentieth-century communist ideology and traces its development from the early feminists through the rise of the Bolsheviks to power. Includes a discussion of the Russian Revolution's impact on the status of women.

*Martin Wiener, *English Culture and the Decline of the Industrial Spirit, 1850–1980* (Cambridge, England: Cambridge University Press, 1981). A cultural history of growth and decline from Victoria to Thatcher. By drawing on literature, art, architecture, politics, and economics, the author describes the ambiguous attitude of the elite toward industry and argues that English culture was never conducive to sustained industrial growth.

---

*Indicates paperback edition available.

The European Search for Territory and Markets

*Winfried Baumgart, *Imperialism: The Idea and Reality of British and French Colonial Expansion, 1880–1914* (New York: Oxford University Press, 1982). Principally concerned with the motives leading to imperial expansion, the author argues that motives were numerous and each action must be studied within its specific social, political, and economic context.

*Michael W. Doyle, *Empires* (Ithaca, NY: Cornell University Press, 1986). Nineteenth-century imperialism is placed in a broad historical context, which emphasizes a comparative perspective of the European imperial experience.

*Daniel R. Headrick, *The Tools of Empire: Technology and European Imperialism in the Nineteenth Century* (New York: Oxford University Press, 1981). By focusing on technological innovations in the nineteenth century, the author demonstrates how Europeans were able to establish control over Asia, Africa, and Oceania rapidly at little cost.

*Eric Hobsbawm, *The Age of Empire, 1875–1914* (New York: Pantheon, 1987). A wide-ranging interpretive history of the late nineteenth century, which spans economic, social, political, and cultural developments.

Results of a European-Dominated World

Anna Davin, "Imperialism and Motherhood," *History Workshop*, 5 (Spring 1978): 9–65. Davin's article links imperialism and economic expansion with the increasing intervention of the state into family life. The author offers an analysis of an ideology that focused on the need to increase population in support of imperial aims and led to the social construction of motherhood, domesticity, and individualism.

*Paul R. Rich, *Race and Empire in British Politics* (Cambridge, England: Cambridge University Press, 1986). An intellectual history of ideas about race in the imperial tradition. Focusing on the years between 1890 and 1970, the author examines the political dimensions of race and race ideology in British society.

20

War and Revolution, 1914–1920

Selling the Great War

Advertising is a powerful influence in modern life. Some feel that it makes us buy goods we do not need. Others insist that advertising is an efficient way of conveying information on the basis of which people make choices. The leaders of Western nations discovered the power of advertising in the years of world war from 1914 to 1918. Advertising did not create the Europe-wide conflict that became known as the Great War. Nor did it produce the enthusiasm that excited millions of Europeans when war was declared in 1914. But when death counts mounted, prices skyrocketed, and food supplies dwindled, the frenzy and fervor for the war flagged. Then governments came to rely more heavily on the art of persuasion. Survival and victory required the support and coordination of the whole society. For the first time in history, war had to advertise.

By the early decades of the twentieth century businesspeople had learned that it was not enough to develop efficient technologies and to mass-produce everything from hair oil to corsets—they had to sell their goods to the public. People would not buy goods they did not know about and whose merits they did not understand. Modern advertising pioneered sales techniques that convinced people to buy. Now political leaders came to realize that the advertising techniques of the marketplace could be useful. Governments took up the "science" of selling—not products, but the idea of war. It was not enough to have a well-trained and well-equipped army to ensure victory. Citizens had to be persuaded to join, to fight, to work, to save, and to believe in the national war effort. Warring nations learned how to organize enthusiasm and how to mobilize the masses in support of what proved to be a long and bloody conflict.

Much poster art from the Great War represented the centrality of women's work to the waging of a new kind of war in the twentieth century. The battlefront had to be backed up by a *home front*—the term used for the first time in the Great War—of working men, women, and even children. The poster communicates the dignity and worth that lay in the concerted partnership of soldiers and civilians to defeat the enemy.

Early war posters stressed justice and national glory. Later, as weariness with the war spread, the need for personal sacrifice became the dominant theme. Look at the sad female figure rising from a sea of suffering and death on the facing page. The woman, both goddesslike and vulnerable, symbolizes Great Britain. She is making a strong visual plea for action, seeking soldiers for her cause. This appeal for volunteers for the armed forces was unique to Great Britain, where conscription was not established until 1916. Yet the image is typical of every nation's reliance on a noble female symbol to emphasize the justice of its cause. The dark suffering and death in the water lapping at her robes are reflected in her eyes. She evinces a fierce determination as she exhorts, "Take up the sword of justice." In February 1915 Germany declared the waters around the British Isles to be a war zone. All British shipping was subject to attack as well as neutral merchant vessels, which were attacked without warning. In May 1915 the *Lusitania* was sunk, taking with it over a thousand lives, including 128 Americans. The poster frames an illuminated horizon where the ship that is probably the *Lusitania* goes down. We need not read a word to understand the call to arms against the perfidy of an enemy who has killed innocent civilians. The female figure's determined jaw, clenched fist, and outstretched arms communicate the nobility of the cause and the certainty of success.

Civilians had to be mobilized for two reasons. First, it became evident early in the fighting that the costs of the war were high in human lives. Soldiers at the front had to be constantly replenished from civilian reserves. Second, the costs of the war in food, equipment, and productive materials were so high that civilian populations had to be willing to endure great hardships and to sacrifice their own well-being to produce supplies for soldiers at the front. Advertising was used by nations at war to coordinate civilian and military contributions to a common cause. More than communicating information, advertising inspired belief in the justice of the national cause in every warring country and a commitment to total victory, no matter how high the price.

The European Balance of Power

In addition to mounting conflicts in colonized areas, European states were locked in a competition within Europe for dominance and control. The politics of geography combined with rising nationalist movements in southern Europe and the Ottoman Empire to create a mood of increasing confrontation among Europe's Great Powers. The European balance of power so carefully crafted by Bismarck began to disintegrate with his departure from office in 1890. By 1914 a Europe divided into two camps was no longer the sure guarantee of peace that it had been a generation earlier.

The Geopolitics of Europe

The map of Europe had been redrawn in the two decades after 1850. By 1871 Europe consisted of five Great Powers, known as the Big Five—Britain,

France, Germany, Austria-Hungary, and Russia—and a handful of lesser states. Although not always corresponding to linguistic and cultural differences among Europe's peoples, national boundaries appeared fixed, with no country aspiring to territorial expansion at the expense of its neighbors. But the creation of the two new national units of Germany and Italy had legitimized nationalist aspirations and the militarism necessary to enforce them.

Under the chancellorship of Otto von Bismarck, Germany led the way in forging a new alliance system based on the realistic assessment of power politics within Europe. In 1873 Bismarck joined together the three most conservative powers of the Big Five—Germany, Austria-Hungary, and Russia—into the Three Emperors' League. Consultation over mutual interests and friendly neutrality were the cornerstones of this alliance. Identifying one's enemies and choosing one's friends in this new configuration of power came in large part to depend on geographic weaknesses. The Three Emperors' League was one example of the geographic imperatives driving diplomacy. Bismarck was determined to banish the specter of a two-front war by isolating France on the Continent.

Each of the Great Powers had a vulnerability, a geographic Achilles's heel. Germany's vulnerability lay in its North Sea ports. German shipping along its only coast could be easily bottlenecked by a powerful naval force. Such an event, the Germans knew, could destroy their rapidly growing international trade. As Germany surged forward to seize its share of world markets, it was acutely aware that it was hemmed in on the Continent. Germany could not extend its frontiers the way Russia had to the east. German gains in the Franco-Prussian war in Alsace and Lorraine could not be repeated without risking greater enmity. German leaders saw the threat of encirclement as a second geographic weakness. Bismarck's awareness of these geographic facts of life prompted his engineering of the Three Emperors' League in 1873, two years after the founding of the German Empire.

Austria-Hungary was Europe's second largest landed nation and the third largest in population. The same factors that had made it a great European power—its size and its diversity—now threatened to destroy it. The ramshackle empire of Europe, it had no geographical unity. Its vulnerability came from within, from the centrifugal forces of linguistic and cultural diversity. Weakened by nationalities clamoring for independence and self-rule and by an unresponsive political system, Austria-Hungary remained backward agriculturally and unable to respond to the Western industrial challenge. It seemed most likely to collapse from social and political pressures.

Another feature must be added to the picture of Europe in the late nineteenth century. To the southeast on the map stood the Ottoman Empire, a great decaying conglomeration that bridged Europe and Asia. Politically feeble and on the verge of bankruptcy, the Ottoman Empire with Turkey at its core comprised a vast array of ethnically, linguistically, and culturally diverse peoples. In the hundred years before 1914, increasing social unrest and nationalist bids for independence had plagued the Ottoman Empire. As was the case with the Habsburgs in Austria-Hungary, the Ottomans maintained power with increasing difficulty over these myriad ethnic groups struggling to be free. Fortunately for the Ottoman Empire, its enemies were willing to preserve it in its weakened state rather than see one of the other rival European powers benefit from its collapse.

The Ottomans had already seen parts of their holdings lopped off in the nineteenth century. Britain, ever conscious of its interests in India, had acquired Cyprus, Egypt, Aden, and Sudan from the Ottomans. Germany insinuated itself into Turkish internal affairs and financed the Baghdad Railway in the attempt to link the Mediterranean to the Persian Gulf. Russia acquired territories on the banks of the Caspian Sea and had plans to take Constantinople. But it was the volatile Balkan Peninsula that threatened to upset the European power balance. The Balkans appeared to be a territory that begged for dismemberment. Internally, the Slavs sought independence from their Habsburg and Turkish oppressors. External pressures were equally great with each of the major powers following its own geopolitical agenda.

The Instability of the Alliance System

The system of alliances formed between and among European states was guided by two realities of geopolitics. The first was the recognition of tension between France and Germany. France had lost its dominance on the Continent in 1870–1871, when it was easily defeated by Prussia at the head of a nascent German Empire. It had suffered the humiliation of losing territory to Germany—Alsace and Lorraine in 1871—and was well aware of its continued vulnerability. Geopolitically France felt trapped and isolated and in need of powerful friends as a counterweight to German power.

The second reality guiding alliances was Russia's preoccupation with maintaining free access to the Mediterranean Sea. Russia was obsessed with protecting its warm water ports on the Black Sea. Whoever controlled the strait of the Bosporus controlled Russia's grain export trade, on which its economic prosperity depended. All diplomatic arrangements, especially after 1900, took into account these two geopolitical realities.

Ostensibly, Russia had the most to gain from the extension of its frontiers and the creation of pro-Russian satellites. It saw that by championing Pan-Slavic nationalist groups in southeastern Europe, it could greatly strengthen its own position at the expense of the two great declining empires, Ottoman Turkey and Austria-Hungary. Russia hoped to draw the Slavs into its orbit by fostering the creation of independent states in the Balkans. A Serbian revolt began in two Ottoman provinces, Bosnia and Herzegovina, in 1874. International opinion pressured Turkey to initiate reforms. Serbia declared war on Turkey on 30 June 1876; Montenegro did the same the next day. Britain, supporting the Ottoman Empire because of its trading interests in the Mediterranean, found itself in a delicate position of perhaps condemning an ally when it received news of Turkish atrocities against Christians in Bulgaria. Prime

Minister Disraeli insisted that Britain was bound to defend Constantinople because of British interests in the Suez Canal and India. While Britain stood on the sidelines, Russia, with Romania as an ally, declared war against the Ottoman Empire. The war was quickly over, with Russia capturing all of Armenia, forcing the Ottoman sultan, Abdul Hamid II (1842–1918), to sue for peace on 31 January 1878.

Bismarck, a seemingly disinterested party acting as an "honest broker," hosted the peace conference that met at Berlin. The British succeeded in blocking Russia's intentions for a Bulgarian satellite and keeping the Russians from taking Constantinople. Russia abandoned its support of Serbian nationalism, and Austria-Hungary occupied Bosnia and Herzegovina. The peace concluded at the 1878 Congress of Berlin disregarded Serbian claims, thereby promising continuing conflict over the nationalities question.

The Berlin Congress also marked the emergence of a new estrangement among the Great Powers. Russia felt betrayed by Bismarck and abandoned in its alliance with Germany. Bismarck in turn cemented a Dual Alliance between Austria-Hungary and Germany in 1879 that survived until the collapse of the two imperial regimes in 1918. The Three Emperors' League was renewed in 1881, now with stipulations regarding the division of the spoils in case of a war against Turkey.

In 1882 Italy was asked to join the Dual Alliance with Germany and Austria-Hungary, thus converting it into the Triple Alliance, which prevailed until the Great War of 1914. Germany, under Bismarck's tutelage, signed treaties with Italy, Russia, and Austria-Hungary, and established friendly terms with Great Britain. A new Balkan crisis in 1885, however, shattered the illusion of stable relations.

Hostilities erupted between Bulgaria and Serbia. Russia threatened to occupy Bulgaria, but Austria stepped in to prevent Russian domination of the Balkans, thus threatening the alliance of the Three Emperors' League. Russia was further angered by German unwillingness to support its interests against Austrian actions in the Balkans. Germany maintained relations with Russia in a new Reinsurance Treaty drawn up in 1887, which stipulated that each power would maintain neutrality should the other find itself at war. Bismarck now walked a fine line, balancing off alliances and selectively disclosing the terms of secret treaties to nonsignatory countries with the goal of preserving the peace.

After Bismarck's dismissal in 1890, Germany allowed the arrangement with Russia to lapse. Russia, in turn, allied itself in 1894 with France. Also allied with Great Britain, France had broken out of the isolation that Bismarck had intended for it two decades earlier. The Triple Entente came into existence following the Anglo-Russian understanding of 1907. Now it was the Triple Entente of Great Britain, France, and Russia against the Triple Alliance of Germany, Austria-Hungary, and Italy.

There was still every confidence that these two camps could balance each other and preserve the peace. But in 1908–1909 the unresolved Balkan problem threatened to topple Europe's precarious peace. Against Russia's objections,

Austria-Hungary annexed Bosnia and Herzegovina, the provinces it had occupied since 1878. Russia supported Serbia's discontent over Austrian acquisition of these predominantly Slavic territories that Serbia felt should be united with its own lands. Unwilling to risk a European war at this point, Russia was ultimately forced to back down under German pressure. Germany had to contend with its great geopolitical fear—hostile neighbors, France and Russia, on its western and eastern frontiers.

A third Balkan crisis erupted in 1912 when Italy and Turkey fought over the possession of Tripoli in North Africa. The Balkan states took advantage of this opportunity to increase their holdings at Turkey's expense. This action quickly involved Great Power interests once again. A second war broke out in 1913 over Serbian interests in Bulgaria. Russia backed Serbia against Austro-Hungarian support of Bulgaria. The Russians and Austrians prepared for war while the British and Germans urged peaceful resolution. Although hostilities ceased, Serbian resentment toward Austria-Hungary over its frustrated nationalism was greater than ever. Britain, in its backing of Russia, and Germany, in its support of Austria-Hungary, were enmeshed in alliances that could involve them in a military confrontation.

Great Britain did not share Germany's and Russia's fears of strangulation by blockade. And although the question of Irish home rule was a nationalities

European Crises and the Balance of Power

1871 German Empire created

1873 Three Emperors' League: Germany, Austria-Hungary, Russia

1874 First Balkan Crisis: Serbian revolt in Bosnia and Herzegovina

1875 Russo-Turkish War

1876 Serbia declares war on Turkey; Montenegro declares war on Turkey

1878 Congress of Berlin

1879 Dual Alliance: Germany and Austria-Hungary

1881 Three Emperors' League renewed

1882 Triple Alliance: Germany, Austria-Hungary, Italy

1885 Second Balkan Crisis: Bulgaria versus Serbia

1887 Reinsurance Treaty between Germany and Russia

1894 Russia concludes alliance with France

1907 Triple Entente: Great Britain, France, Russia

1908 Austria-Hungary annexes Bosnia and Herzegovina

1912 Third Balkan Crisis: Italy versus Turkey

1913 War erupts between Serbia and Bulgaria

problem for Britain, it paled in comparison with Austria-Hungary's internal challenge. As an island kingdom, however, Great Britain relied on imports for its survival. The first of the European nations to become an urban and industrial power, Britain was forced to do so at the expense of its agricultural sector. It could not feed its own people without importing foodstuffs. Britain's geographic vulnerability was its dependence on access to its empire and the maintenance of open sea-lanes. Britain saw its greatest menace coming from the rise of other sea powers—notably Germany.

*T*he War Europe Expected

The values of nineteenth-century liberalism permeated the self-confident worldview of European men and women in 1914. Westerners took stability and harmony for granted as preconditions for progress. Yet they also recognized the utility of war. Local confrontations between European states in Africa had been successfully contained in recent times in bids for increased territory. While warfare was accepted as an instrument of policy, no one expected or wanted a general war. Liberal values served the goals of limited war, just as they had justified imperial conquest. Statesmen decided there were rules to the game of war that could be employed in the interests of statecraft. Science and technology also served war makers. Modern weapons, statesmen and generals were sure, would prevent a long war. Superiority in armed force became a priority for European states seeking to protect the peace.

European alliances on the eve of World War I

"Armed peace" was the result of the beginning of the modern arms race as a defense against war. Leaders nevertheless expected and planned for a war, short and limited, in which the fittest and most advanced nation would win. Previous confrontations among European states had been limited in duration and destruction, as in the case of Prussia and France in 1870, or confined to peripheries, as squabbles among the Great Powers in Africa indicated. The alliance system was expected to defend the peace.

As international tensions mounted, the hot summer days of 1914 were a time of hope and glory. The hope was that war, when it came, would be "over by Christmas." The glory was the promise of ultimate victory in the "crusade for civilization" that each nation's leaders held out to their people. When war did come in 1914, it was not an accident, it was a choice. Yet it was a choice that Europeans did not understand, one whose limits they could not control. Their unquestioned pride in reason and progress that had ironically led them to this war did not survive the four years of barbaric slaughter that followed.

Military Timetables

As Europe soon discovered, military timetables restricted the choices of leaders at times of conflict. The crisis of the summer of 1914 revealed the extent to which politicians and statesmen had come to rely on military expertise and strategic considerations for decisions. Military general staffs assumed increasing importance in state policy-making. War planners became powerful, as war was accepted as an alternative to the negotiation of differences. Germany's military preparations are a good example of how war strategy exacerbated crises and prevented peaceful solutions.

Alfred von Schlieffen (1833–1913), the Prussian general and chief of the German General Staff from 1891 to 1905, who developed the war plan, understood little about politics but spent his life studying the strategic challenges of warfare. His war plan was designed to make Germany the greatest power on the Continent. The Schlieffen Plan, which he set before his fellow officers in 1905, was a bold and daring one: In the likely event of war with Russia, Germany would launch a devastating offensive against France. Schlieffen reasoned that France was a strong military presence which would come to the aid of its ally, Russia. Russia, lacking a modern transportation system, could not mobilize as rapidly as France.

Russia also had the inestimable advantage of the ability to retreat into its vast interior. If Germany was pulled into a war with Russia, its western frontier would be vulnerable to France, Russia's powerful ally. The Schlieffen Plan recognized that France must first be defeated in the west before Germany could turn its forces to the task of defeating Russia. The Schlieffen Plan thus committed Germany to a war with France regardless of particular circumstances. Furthermore, the plan, with its strategy of invading the neutral countries of Belgium, Holland, and Luxembourg in order to defeat France in six weeks, ignored the rights of the neutral countries.

Germany was not alone in being driven by military timetables when conflicts arose. Russian military strategists planned full mobilization if war broke out with Austria-Hungary, which was menacing the interests of Russia's ally Serbia. Russia foresaw the likelihood that Germany would come to the aid of Austria-Hungary. Russia knew, too, that because of its primitive railway network it would be unable to mobilize troops rapidly. In order to compensate for this weakness, Russian leaders planned to mobilize *before* war was declared. German military leaders had no choice in the event of full Russian mobilization but to mobilize their own troops immediately and to urge the declaration of war. There was no chance of containing the conflict once a general mobilization on both sides was under way. Mobilization would mean war.

Like the Schlieffen Plan, the French Plan XVII called for the concentration of troops in a single area with the intention of decisively defeating the enemy. The French command, not well informed about German strengths and strategies, designated Alsace and Lorraine for the immediate offensive against Germany in the event of war. Plan XVII left Paris exposed to the German drive through Belgium called for in the Schlieffen Plan.

Military leaders throughout Europe argued that if their plans were to succeed, speed was essential. Delays to consider peaceful solutions would cripple military responses. Diplomacy bowed to military strategy. When orders to mobilize went out, armies would be set on the march. Like a row of dominoes falling with the initial push, the two alliance systems would be at war.

Assassination at Sarajevo

A teenager with a handgun started the First World War. On 28 June 1914, Gavrilo Princip (1895–1918), a 19-year-old Bosnian Serb, pulled the trigger of his Browning revolver repeatedly, killing the designated heir of the Habsburg throne, Archduke Franz Ferdinand and his wife, Sophie, in Sarajevo, the sleepy capital of the Austro-Hungarian province of Bosnia. Princip belonged to the Young Bosnian Society, a group of students, workers, a few peasants, Croats, Muslims, and intellectuals, who wanted to free Slavic populations from Habsburg control. Princip was part of a growing movement of South Slavs struggling for national liberation who considered themselves to be held in colonial servitude by Austria-Hungary.

Struggle over control of the Balkans had been a long-standing issue that had involved all the major European powers for decades. As Austria-Hungary's ally since 1879, Germany was willing to support Vienna's showdown in the Balkans as a way of stopping Russian advances in the area. The alliance with Germany gave Austria-Hungary a sense of security and confidence to pursue its Balkan aims. Germany had its own plans for domination of the Continent and feared a weakened Austria-Hungary would undermine its own position in central Europe. Independent Balkan states to the south and east were also a

Austrian Archduke Franz Ferdinand and his wife Sophie leave the Senate House in Sarajevo on 28 June 1914. Five minutes later, Serbian terrorist Gavrilo Princip assassinated the couple.

threat to Germany's plans. German leaders hoped that an Austro-Serbian war would remain localized and strengthen their ally, Austria-Hungary. While Austria-Hungary had Germany's support, Serbia was backed by a sympathetic Russia that favored nationalist movements in the Balkans. Russia had, in turn, been encouraged by France, its ally by military pact since 1894, to take a firm stand in its struggle with Austria-Hungary for dominance among Balkan nationalities.

The five weeks between the assassination of the Archduke Ferdinand and the outbreak of the war were a period of intense diplomatic activity. The assassination gave Austria-Hungary the excuse it needed to bring a troublesome Serbia into line. Austria-Hungary held Serbia responsible for the shootings. Leaders in Vienna had no evidence at the time to justify their allegations of a Serbian conspiracy, but they saw in this event the perfect pretext for military action. On 23 July 1914, Austria-Hungary issued an ultimatum to the small Balkan nation and secretly decided to declare war regardless of Serbia's response. The demands were so severe that, if met, they would have stripped Serbia of its independence. Austria's aim was to destroy Serbia. In spite of a conciliatory, although not capitulatory, reply from Serbia to its ultimatum, Austria-Hungary declared war on the Balkan nation on 28 July 1914. Russia mobilized two days after the Austro-Hungarian declaration of war against Serbia. Germany mobilized in response to the Russian action and declared war on Russia on 1 August and on France on 3 August. France had begun mobilizing on 30 July, when its ally, Russia, entered the war.

Great Britain stood briefly outside the fray in the futile attempt to mediate a settlement in the Austro-Serbian conflict. Britain's dependence on its alliance with France as a means of protecting British sea routes in the Mediterranean meant that Great Britain could not remain neutral once France declared war. On 4 August, after Germany had violated Belgian neutrality in its march to France, Great Britain honored its treaty obligations and declared war on Germany. Great Britain entered the war because it judged that a powerful Germany could use ports on the English Channel to invade the British Isles. Italy alone of the major powers remained for the moment outside the conflict. Although allied with Germany and Austria-Hungary, its own aspirations in the Balkans kept it from fighting for the Austrian cause in 1914.

Self-interest, fear, and ambition motivated the Great Powers in different ways in the pursuit of war. The international diplomatic system that had worked so well to prevent war in the preceding decades now enmeshed European states in interlocking alliances and created a chain reaction. The Austro-Serbian war of July 1914 became a Europe-wide war within a month.

*T*he War Europe Got

Early in the war, the best laid plans of political and military leaders collapsed. First, Europe got a war that was not limited but one which quickly spread throughout Europe and became global. Switzerland, Spain, the Netherlands, and all of Scandinavia remained neutral, but every other European nation was pulled into the war. In August 1914 Japan cast its lot with the Allies, as the Entente came to be known, and in November the Ottoman Empire joined the Central Powers of Germany and Austria-Hungary. In the following year Italy joined the war, not on the side of its long-term treaty partners, Germany and Austria-Hungary, but on the side of the Allies, with the expectation of benefiting in the Balkans from Austrian defeat. Bulgaria joined Germany and Austria-Hungary in 1915, seeking territory at Serbia's expense. By the time of the U.S. entry in 1917, the war had become a world war.

The second surprise for the European powers was that they did not get a preventive war of movement, nor one of short duration. Within weeks, that pattern had given way to what promised to be a long and costly war of attrition. All started as Schlieffen's successors had planned, with German victory in battle after battle. The end seemed near. But in the space of less than a month the war changed in ways that no one had predicted. Technology was the key to understanding the change and to explaining the surprises.

Technology and the Trenches

In the history of nineteenth-century European warfare, armies had relied on mobile cavalry and infantry units whose greatest asset was speed. Rapid advance had been decisive in the Prussian victory over the French in 1870, which had resulted in the formation of the German Empire. Soldiers of the twentieth century were also trained for a moving war, high maneuverability, and maximum territorial conquest. Yet after the first six weeks of battle, soldiers were ordered to do something unimaginable to strategists of European warfare: They were ordered to dig ditches and fight from fixed positions. Soldiers on both sides shoveled out trenches 4 feet deep, piled up sandbags, mounted their machine guns, and began to fight an unplanned defensive war.

The front lines of Europe's armies in the west wallowed within the 400 miles of trenches that ran from the English Channel to the Swiss frontier. The British and French on one side and the Germans on the other fought each other with machine guns and mortars, backed up by heavy artillery to the rear.

A typical World War I trench. Millions of soldiers lived amid mud, disease, and vermin, awaiting death from enemy shells. After the French army mutiny in 1916, the troops wrung this concession from their commanders: They did not have to charge German machine guns while armed only with rifles.

Strategists on both sides believed they could break through enemy lines. As a result, the monotony of trench warfare was punctuated periodically by infantry offensives in which immense concentrations of artillery caused great bloodshed. Ten million men were killed in this bizarre and deadly combination of old and new warfare. The glamour of battle that attracted many young men disappeared quickly in the daily reality of living in mud with rats and constantly facing death. The British poet Wilfred Owen (1893–1918) wrote shortly before his own death in battle about how the soldier next to him had been shot in the head, soaking Owen in blood: "I shall feel again as soon as I dare, but now I must not."

The invention of new weaponry and heavy equipment had transformed war into an industry of increasing complexity. Military and naval staffs expanded to meet new needs of warfare. Old ways persisted. In their bright blue coats and red trousers, French and Belgian infantrymen made easy targets. Outmoded cavalry units survived despite more efficient mechanization. The railroad made the mobilization, organization, and deployment of mass armies possible. Specialists were needed to control the new war machines that heavy industry had created.

It has been observed that the spade and the machine gun transformed war. The machine gun was not new in 1914, but its strategic value was not fully appreciated before then. The Maxim machine gun had been used by the British in the Matabele War in 1893 against African warriors. Fifty infantrymen with only four machine guns killed 3000 charging natives in less than ninety minutes. Strategists regarded this carnage as a stunning achievement but failed to ask how a weapon of such phenomenal destructive power would work against an enemy equally armed with machine guns instead of spears. Military strategists drew all the wrong conclusions. They continued to plan an offensive strategy when the weaponry developed for massive destruction had pushed them into fighting a defensive war from the trenches. Both sides resorted to concentration of artillery, increased use of poison gas, and unrestricted submarine warfare, in desperate attempts to break the deadlock caused by meeting armed force with force.

The necessity of total victory drove the Central Powers and the Allies to grisly new inventions. Late in the war, the need to break the deadlock of trench warfare ushered in the airplane and the tank. Neither was decisive in altering the course of the war, although the airplane was useful for reconnaissance and for limited bombing and the tank promised the means of breaking through defensive lines. Chlorine gas was first used in warfare by the Germans in 1915. "Mustard" gas, which was named for its distinctive smell and caused severe blistering, was introduced two years later. The Germans were the first to use flamethrowers, especially effective against mechanized vehicles with vulnerable fuel tanks. Barbed wire, invented in the U.S. Midwest to contain farm animals, became an essential aspect of trench warfare as it marked off the no-man's-land between combatants and prevented surprise attacks.

The technology that had been viewed as a proof of progress was now channeled toward engineering new instruments of death. Yet technology itself

Gassed, by the American painter John Singer Sargent. A line of walking wounded, blinded by German poison gas attack, threads its way past fallen comrades, hanging on to each other behind a sighted leader. Poison gas was later thought to be self-defeating, and it was not used in World War II.

produced a stalemate. New weapons sometimes produced their antidotes, for example, the invention of deadly gas was followed soon after by gas masks. Each side was capable of matching the other's ability to devise new armaments. Deadlocks caused by technological parity forced both sides to resort to desperate concentrations of men and weaponry that resulted not in decisive battles but in ever escalating casualty rates. Improving their efficiency at killing, the European powers were not finding a way to end the war.

The Battle of the Marne

German forces seized the offensive in the west and invaded neutral Belgium at the beginning of August 1914. The Belgians resisted stubbornly but unsuccessfully. Belgian forts were systematically captured and the capital of Brussels fell under the German advance on August 20. After the fall of Belgium, German military might swept into northern France with the intention of defeating the French in six weeks.

In the years preceding the war, the German General Staff, unwilling to concentrate all of their troops in the west, had modified the Schlieffen Plan by committing divisions to its eastern frontier. The absence of the full German fighting force in the west did not appreciably slow the German advance through Belgium. Yet the Germans had underestimated both the cost of holding back the French in Alsace-Lorraine and the difficulty of maneuvering German forces and transporting supplies in an offensive war. Eventually, unexpected Russian advances in the east also siphoned off troops from the west. German forces in the west were so weakened by the offensive that they were unable to swing west of Paris, as planned, and instead chose to enter the French capital from the northeast by crossing the Marne River. This shift exposed the German First Army on its western flank and opened up a gap on its eastern flank.

Despite an initial pattern of retreat and a lack of coordination of forces, Allied French and British troops were ready to take advantage of the vulnerabilities in the German advance. In a series of battles between 6 and 10 September 1914 that came to be known as the First Battle of the Marne, the Allies counterattacked and advanced into the gap. The German army was forced to drop back. In the following months each army tried to outflank the other in what has been called "the race to the sea." By late fall it was clear that the battles from the Marne north to the border town of Ypres in northwest Belgium near the English Channel ended an open war of movement on the western front. Soldiers now dug in along a line of battle that changed little in the long three and a half years until March 1918.

The Allies gained a strategic victory in the First Battle of the Marne by resisting the German advance in the fighting that quickly became known as the "miracle" of the Marne. The legend was further enhanced by true stories of French troops being rushed from Paris to the front in taxicabs. Yet the real significance of the Marne lay in the severe miscalculations of military leaders and statesmen on both sides, who had expected a different kind of war. They did not understand the new technology that made a short war unlikely. Nor did they understand the demands that this new kind of warfare would make on civilian populations. Those Parisian taxi drivers foreshadowed how other European civilians would be called upon again and again to support the war in the next four years. The Schlieffen Plan was dead. But it was no more a failure than any of the other military timetables of the Great Powers.

"I don't know what is to be done—this isn't war." So spoke Lord Horatio Kitchener (1850–1916), one of the most decorated British generals of his time. He was not alone in his bafflement over the stalemate of trench warfare at the end of 1914. By that time, Germany's greatest fear, a simultaneous war on two fronts, had become a grim reality. The Central Powers were under a state of siege, cut off from the world by the great battlefront in the west and by the Allied blockade at sea. The rules of the game had changed, and the European powers settled in for a long war.

War on the Eastern Front

War on Germany's eastern front was a mobile war, unlike its western counterpart, because there were relatively fewer men and guns in relation to the vast distances. The Russian army was the largest in the world. Yet it was crippled from the outbreak of the war by inadequate supplies and poor leadership. At the end of August 1914 the smaller German army, supported by divisions drawn from the west, delivered a devastating defeat to the Russians in the one great battle on the eastern front. At Tannenberg, the entire Russian Second Army was destroyed, and about one hundred thousand Russian soldiers were taken prisoner. Faced with this humiliation, general Aleksandr Vasilievich Samsonov (1859–1914), head of the Russian forces, committed suicide on the field of battle.

The German general Paul von Hindenburg (1847–1934), a veteran of the Franco-Prussian war of 1870, had been recalled from retirement to direct the campaign against the Russians because of his intimate knowledge of the area. Assisted by Quartermaster General Erich Ludendorff (1865–1937), Hindenburg followed the stunning victory of Tannenberg with another devastating blow in September 1914 to Russian forces at the Masurian Lakes.

The Russians were holding up their end of the bargain in the Allied war effort, but at great cost. They kept the Germans busy and forced them to divert troops to the eastern front, weakening the German effort to knock France out of the war. In the south the tsar's troops defeated the Austro-Hungarian army at Lemberg in Galicia in September. This Russian victory gave Serbia a temporary reprieve. But by mid-1915 Germany had thrown the Russians back and was keeping Austria-Hungary propped up in the war. By fall Russia had lost most of Galicia, the Polish lands of the Russian Empire, Lithuania, and parts of Latvia and Belorussia to the advancing enemy. These losses amounted to 15 percent of its territory and 20 percent of its population. The Russian army staggered, with over one million soldiers taken as prisoners of war and at least as many killed and wounded.

The Russian army, as one of its own officers described it, was being bled to death. Russian soldiers were poorly led into battle or not led at all because of the shortage of officers. Munitions shortages meant that soldiers often went into battle without rifles, armed only with the hope of scavenging arms from their fallen comrades. Despite these difficulties the Russians, under the direction of General Aleksei Brusilov (1853–1926), commander of the Russian armies in the southern part of the eastern front, remarkably managed to throw back the Austro-Hungarian forces in 1916 and almost eliminated Austria as a military power. But this was the last great campaign on the eastern front and Russia's last show of strength in the Great War.

Russia's near destruction of the Austrian army tremendously benefited Russia's allies. In order to protect its partner, Germany was forced to withdraw eight divisions from Italy, alleviating the Allied situation in the Tyrol, and twelve divisions from the western front, providing relief for the French at Verdun and the British at the Somme. In addition, Russia sent troops to the aid of a new member of the Allied camp, Romania, an act that probably further weakened Brusilov's efforts. In response to Brusilov's challenge, the Germans established control over the Austrian army, assigning military command of the coalition to General Ludendorff.

By the summer of 1917, the tsardom had been overthrown and a provisional government ruled Russia. Tens of thousands of Russian soldiers were walking away from the war. Russia withdrew from the war and in March 1918 signed a separate peace by which Germany gained extensive territorial advantages and important supply bases for carrying on the war in the west. To

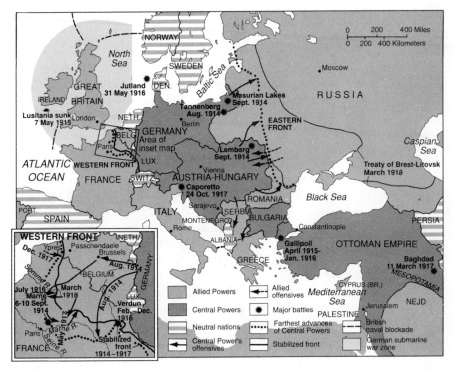

World War I

protect these territories and their resources, the Germans had to maintain an army on this front. No longer fighting in the east, however, Germany could release the bulk of its forces to fight in the west.

War on the Western Front

Along hundreds of miles of trenches, the French and British tried repeatedly to expel the Germans from Belgium. Long periods of inactivity were punctuated by orgies of heavy bloodletting. The German phrase, "All quiet on the western front," used in military communiques to describe those periods of silence between massive shellings and infantry attacks, reported only the uneasy calm before the next violent storm.

Military leaders on both sides cherished the dream of a decisive offensive, the breakthrough that would win the war. In 1916 the Allies planned a joint strike at the Somme, a river in northern France flowing west into the English Channel, but the Germans struck first at Verdun, a small fortress city in northeast France. By concentrating great numbers of troops, the Germans outnumbered the French five to two. As General Erich von Falkenhayn (1861–1922), chief of the General Staff of the German army from 1914 to 1916, explained it, the German purpose in attacking Verdun was "to bleed the French white by virtue of our superiority in guns."

On the first day of battle one million shells were fired. The battlefield was a living hell as soldiers stumbled across corpse after corpse. Against the German onslaught, French troops were instructed to hold out although they lacked adequate artillery and reinforcements. General Joseph Joffre (1852–1931), commander-in-chief of the French army, was unwilling to divert reinforcements to Verdun.

The German troops advanced easily through the first line of defense. But the French held their position for ten long horrifying months of continuous mass slaughter from February to December 1916. General Henri Philippe Pétain (1856–1951), a local commander planning an early retirement before the war, bolstered morale by constantly rotating his troops to the point that most of the French army—259 of 330 infantry battalions—saw action at Verdun. Nearly starving and poorly armed, the French stood alone in the bloodiest offensive of the war. Attack strategy backfired on the Germans as their own death tolls mounted.

Pétain and his flamboyant general Robert Georges Nivelle (1856–1924) were both hailed as heroes for fulfilling the instruction to their troops: "They shall not pass." Falkenhayn fared less well and was dismissed from his post. Yet no real winners emerged from the scorched earth of Verdun, where observers could see the nearest thing to desert created in Europe. Verdun was a disaster. The French and the Germans each suffered about six hundred thousand casualties. A few square miles of territory had changed hands back and forth. In the end, no military advantage was gained. Almost seven hundred thousand lives were lost. The legends of brilliant leadership of Pétain and Nivelle, who both went on to greater positions of authority, and the failed command of Falkenhayn, who retired in disgrace, obscured the real lesson of the battle: An offensive war under these conditions was impossible.

Still, new offensives were devised. The British went ahead with their planned offensive on the Somme in July 1916. For an advance of 7 miles, 400,000 British and 200,000 French soldiers were killed or wounded. The American writer F. Scott Fitzgerald (1896–1940), who had served as an army officer in World War I, wrote of the battle of the Somme in his novel *Tender Is the Night* (1934). One of his characters is describing a visit to the Somme Valley after the war: "See that little stream. We could walk to it in two minutes. It took the British a whole month to walk to it—a whole empire walking very slowly, dying in front and pushing forward behind. And another empire walked very slowly backward a few inches a day, leaving the dead like a million bloody rugs." German losses brought the total casualties of this offensive to one million men. Despite his experience at Verdun, French general Robert Nivelle planned his own offensive in the Champagne region in spring 1917, sure that he could succeed where others had failed in "breaking the crust." The Nivelle offensive resulted in 40,000 deaths. Nivelle was dismissed. The French army was falling apart, with mutiny and insubordination everywhere.

The British believed they could succeed where the French had fallen.

Under General Douglas Haig (1861–1928), the commander-in-chief of British expeditionary forces on the Continent, the British launched an attack in Flanders through the summer and fall of 1917. Known as the Passchendaele offensive, named for the village and ridge in whose "porridge of mud" much of the fighting took place, this campaign resulted in almost four hundred thousand British soldiers slaughtered for insignificant territorial gain. The Allies and the Germans finally recognized that "going over the top" in offensives was not working and could not work. The war must be won by other means.

War on the Periphery

Recognizing the stalemate in the west, the Allies attempted to open up other fronts where the Central Powers might be vulnerable. In the spring of 1915 the Allies were successful in convincing Italy to enter the war on their side by promising that it would receive at the time of the peace the South Tyrol and the southern part of Dalmatia and key Dalmatian islands, which would assure Italy's dominance over the Adriatic Sea. By thus capitalizing on Italian antagonism toward Austria-Hungary over control of this territory, the Allies gained 875,000 Italian soldiers for their cause. Although these Italian troops were in no way decisive in the fighting that followed, Great Britain, France, and Russia saw the need to build up Allied support in southern Europe in order to reinforce Serbian attempts to keep Austrian troops beyond its borders. The Allies also hoped that by pulling Germans into this southern front, some relief might be provided for British and French soldiers on the western front.

Germany, in turn, was well aware of the need to expand its alliances beyond Austria-Hungary if it was to compete successfully against superior Allied forces. Trapped as they were to the east and west, the Central Powers established control over a broad corridor stretching from the North Sea through central Europe and down through the Ottoman Empire to the Suez Canal so vital to British interests. In the Balkans, where the war had begun, the Serbs were consistently bested by the Austrians. By late 1915 the Serbs had been knocked out of the war, in spite of Allied attempts to assist them. Serbia paid a heavy price in the Great War: It lost one-sixth of its population through war, famine, and disease. The promise of booty persuaded Bulgaria to join Germany and Austria-Hungary. Over the next year and a half, the Allies responded by convincing Romania and then Greece to join them.

The theater of war continued to expand. Although the Ottoman Empire had joined the war in late 1914 on the side of the Central Powers, its own internal difficulties attenuated its fighting ability. As a multinational empire consisting of Turks, Arabs, Armenians, Greeks, Kurds, and other ethnic minorities, it was plagued by Turkish misrule and Arab nationalism. Hence the Ottoman Empire was the weakest link in the chain of German alliances. Yet it held a crucial position. The Turks could block shipping of vital supplies to Russia through the Mediterranean and the Black seas. Coming to the aid of their Russian ally, a combined British and French fleet attacked Turkish forces at the Straits of the Dardanelles in April 1915. In the face of political and military opposition, First Lord of the Admiralty Winston Churchill (1874–1965) supported the idea of opening a new front by sea. Poorly planned and mismanaged, the expedition was a disaster. When the naval effort in the German-mined straits failed, the British foolishly decided to land troops on the Gallipoli Peninsula, which extends from the southern coast of European Turkey. There British soldiers were trapped on the rocky terrain, unable to advance against the Turks, unable to fall back. Gallipoli was the first large-scale attempt at amphibious warfare. The Australian and New Zealand forces (ANZACs) showed great bravery in some of the most brutal fighting of the war. Critics in Britain argued that the only success of the nine-month campaign was its evacuation completed in January 1916.

Britain sought to protect its interests in the Suez Canal. Turkish troops menaced the canal effectively enough to terrify the British into maintaining an elaborate system of defense in the area and concentrating large troop reinforcements in Egypt. War with the Ottoman Empire also extended battle into the oil fields of Mesopotamia and Persia. This attempt at a new front was initially a fiasco for the British and Russian forces that threatened Baghdad. The Allies proceeded not only without plans but also without maps. They literally did not know where they were going. Eventually, British forces recovered and took Baghdad on 11 March 1917, while Australian and New Zealand troops captured Jerusalem. The tentacles of war spread out, following the path of Western economic and imperial interests throughout the world.

Most surprising of all was the indecisive nature of the war at sea. The great battleships of the British and German navies avoided confrontation on the high seas. The only major naval battle of the Great War, the Battle of Jutland in the North Sea, took place on 31 May 1916. Each side inflicted damage on the other but, through careful maneuvering, avoided a decisive outcome to the battle. Probably the enormous cost of replacing battleships deterred both the British and the Germans from risking their fleets in engagements on the high seas. With the demands for munitions and equipment on the two great land fronts of the war, neither side could afford to lose a traditional war at sea. Instead, the British used their sea power as a policing force to blockade German trade and strangle the German economy.

The German navy, much weaker than the British, relied on a new weapon, the submarine, which threatened to become decisive in the war at sea. Submarines were initially used in the first months of the war for reconnaissance. Their potential for inflicting heavy losses on commercial shipping became apparent in 1915. Undergoing technological improvements throughout the war, U-boats, or *Unterseebooten* as German submarines were called, torpedoed 6 million tons of Allied shipping in 1917. With cruising ranges as high as 3600 miles, German submarines attacked Allied and neutral shipping as far away as off the shore of the United States and the Arctic supply line to Russia. German insistence on unrestricted use outraged neutral powers, who considered the Germans in violation of international law. The Germans rejected the requirements of warning an enemy ship and boarding it for investigation as too dangerous for submarines, which were no match for battleships above water. The Allies invented depth charges and mines that were capable of blowing German submarines out of the water. These weapons, combined with the use of the convoy system in the Atlantic and the Mediterranean, produced a successful blockade and antisubmarine campaign that put an end to the German advantage.

Adjusting to the Unexpected: Total War

The period from 1914 to 1918 marked the first time in history that the productive activities of entire populations were directed toward a single goal: military victory. The Great War became a war of peoples, not just of armies. Wars throughout history have involved noncombatants caught in the cross fire or standing in the wrong place at the wrong time. But this unexpected war of attrition required civilian populations to adjust to a situation in which what went on at the battlefront transformed life on the home front. For this reason, the Great War became known as history's first *total* war.

Adjusting to the unexpected war of 1914, governments intervened to centralize and control every aspect of economic life. Technology and industrial capacity made possible a war of unimaginable destruction. The scale of production and distribution of war-related materials required for victory was unprecedented. To persuade civilians to suffer at home for the sake of the war, leaders pictured the enemy as an evil villain who must be defeated at any cost. The sacrifice required for a total war made total victory necessary. And total victory required an economy totally geared to fighting the war.

Mobilizing the Home Front

While soldiers were fighting on the eastern and western fronts, businesspeople and politicians at home were creating bureaucratic administrations to control wages and prices, distribute supplies, establish production quotas, and, in general, mobilize human and material resources. Just as governments had conscripted the active male population for military service, the Allies and the Central Powers now mobilized civilians of all ages and both sexes to work for the war.

Women played an essential role in the mobilization of the home front. They had never been isolated from the experiences and hardships of war, but they now found new ways to support the war effort. In cities women went to work in munitions factories and war-related industries that had previously employed only men. Women filled service jobs, from fire fighters to trolley car

During World War I, women workers flocked to the munitions plants to take the place of men who had marched off to war. The women shown here are operating cranes in a shell-filling factory.

conductors, jobs that were essential to the smooth running of industrial society and that had been left vacant by men. On farms women literally took up the plow, as both men and horses were requisitioned for the war effort.

By 1918, 650,000 French women were working in war-related industries and in clerical positions in the army. And they had counterparts all over Europe. In Germany two out of every five munitions workers were women. Women became more prominent in the work force as a whole, as the case of Great Britain makes clear: There the number of women workers jumped from 250,000 at the beginning of the war to 5 million by the war's end. Women also served in the auxiliary units of the armed services in the clerical and medical corps in order to free men for fighting at the front. In eastern European nations, women entered combat as soldiers. Although most women were displaced from their wartime jobs with the return of men after the armistice, they were as important to the war effort as men fighting at the front.

In the first months of the war the private sector had been left to its own devices with nearly disastrous results. Shortages, especially of shells, and bottlenecks in production threatened military efforts. Governments were forced to establish controls and to set up state monopolies in order to guarantee the supplies necessary to wage war. In Germany industrialists Walter Rathenau (1867–1922) and Alfred Hugenberg (1865–1951) worked with the government. By the spring of 1915, they had eliminated the German problem of munitions scarcity. France was in trouble six weeks after the outbreak of the war: It had used up half of its accumulated munitions supplies in the First Battle of the Marne. German occupation of France's northern industrial basin further crippled munitions production. Through government intervention, France improvised and relocated its war industries. The British government got involved in production, too, by establishing in 1915 the first Ministry of Munitions under the direction of David Lloyd George (1863–1945). Distinct from the Ministry of War, the Ministry of Munitions was to coordinate military needs with the armaments industry.

In a war that leaders soon realized would be a long one, food supplies assumed paramount importance. Germany, dependent on food imports to feed its people and isolated from the world market by the Allied blockade, introduced rationing five months after the outbreak of the war. Other continental nations followed suit. Government agents set quotas for agricultural producers. Armies were fed and supplied at the expense of domestic populations. Great Britain, which enjoyed a more reliable food supply by virtue of its sea power, did not impose food rationing until 1917.

Three factors put food supplies at risk. First, the need for large numbers of soldiers at the front pulled farmers and peasants off the land. The resultant drop in the agricultural work force meant that land was taken out of production and what remained was less efficiently cultivated. Productivity declined. A second factor was fear of requisitioning and the general uncertainties of war that caused agricultural producers to hoard supplies. What little was available was traded on black markets. Finally, because all European countries depended to some extent on imports of food and fertilizers, enemies successfully targeted trade routes for attack.

War Governments

The strains of total war were becoming apparent. Two years of sacrificing, scrimping, and, in some areas, starving began to take their toll among soldiers and civilians on both sides. With the lack of decisive victories, war weariness was spreading. Work stoppages and strikes, which had virtually ceased with the outbreak of war in 1914, began to climb rapidly in 1916. Between 1915 and 1916 in France, the number of strikes by dissatisfied workers increased by 400 percent. Underpaid and tired workers went on strike, staged demonstrations, and protested exploitation. Labor militancy also intensified in the British Isles and Germany. Women, breadwinners for their families, were often in the forefront of these protests throughout Europe. Social peace between unions and governments was no longer held together by patriotic enthusiasm for war.

Politicians, too, began to rethink their suspension of opposition to government policies as the war dragged on. Dissidents among European Socialist parties regained their prewar commitment to peace. Most socialists had enthusiastically supported the declarations of war in 1914. By 1916 the united front that political opponents had presented against the enemy was crumbling under growing demands for peace.

In a total war, unrest at home guaranteed defeat. Governments knew that all opposition to war policies had to be eliminated. In a dramatic extension of the police powers of the state, whether among the Allies or the Central Powers, criticism of the government became treason. Censorship was enforced. Propaganda became more virulent. Those who spoke for peace were no better than the enemy. The governments of every warring nation resorted to harsh measures. Parliamentary bodies were stripped of power, civil liberties were suspended, democratic procedures were ignored. The civilian governments of Premier Georges Clemenceau (1841–1929) in France and Prime Minister Lloyd George in Great Britain resorted to rule by emergency police power to repress criticism. Under Generals von Hindenburg and Ludendorff in Germany, military rule became the order of the day. Nowhere was government as usual possible in total war.

Every warring nation sought to promote dissension from within the societies of its enemies. Germany provided some aid for the Easter Rebellion in Ireland in 1916 in the hope that the Irish demand for independence that predated the war would deflect British attention and undermine fighting strength and morale. Germany also supported separatist movements among minority nationalities in the Russian Empire and was responsible for returning Lenin under escort to Russia in April 1917. The British engaged in similar tactics. The British foreign secretary Arthur Balfour (1848–1930) worked with Zionist leaders in 1917 in drawing up the Balfour Declaration, which promised to "look with favor" on the creation of Jewish homeland in Palestine. The British thereby encouraged Zionist hopes among central European Jews, with the intent of creating difficulties for German and Austrian rulers. Similarly, the British encouraged Arabs to rebel against Turks with the same promise of Palestine. Undermining the loyalties of colonized peoples and minorities would be at minimum a nuisance to the enemy. Beyond that, it could erode war efforts from within.

The Turning Point and Victory, 1917–1918

For the Allies, 1917 began with a series of crises. Under the hammering of one costly offensive after another, French morale had collapsed and military discipline was deteriorating. A combined German-Austrian force had eliminated the Allied states of Serbia and Romania. The Italians experienced a military debacle at Caporetto beginning on 24 October 1917 and were effectively out of the war.

The year 1917 was "the blackest year of the war" for the Allies. At the beginning of the year, the peril on the sea had increased with the opening of unrestricted U-boat warfare against Allied and neutral shipping. The greatest blow came when Russia, now in the throes of domestic revolution, withdrew. Germany was able to concentrate more of its resources in the west and fight a one-front war. Perhaps more significantly, it was able to utilize the foodstuffs and raw materials of its newly acquired Russian territories to buoy its home front.

Yet in spite of Allied reversals, it was not at all the case that the war was turning in favor of the Central Powers. Both Austria-Hungary and the Ottoman Empire teetered on the verge of collapse, with internal difficulties increasing as the war dragged on. Germany suffered from labor and supply shortages and economic hardship, resulting from the blockade and an economy totally dedicated to waging war.

The war had gone from a stalemate to a state of crisis for both sides. Every belligerent state was experiencing war weariness that undermined civilian and military morale. Pressure to end the war increased everywhere. Attrition was not working. Attacks were not working. Every country suffered on the home front and battlefront from strikes, food riots, military desertions, and mutinies. Defeatism was everywhere on the rise.

The Allies longed for the entry of the United States into the war. Although the United States was a neutral country, it had become an important supplier to the Allies from early in the war. Trade with the Allies had jumped from $825 million in 1914 to $3.2 billion in 1916. American bankers also made loans and extended credit to the Allies to the amount of $2.2 billion. The United States had made a sizable investment in the Allied war effort, and its economy was prospering.

Beginning with the sinking of the *Lusitania* in 1915, German policy on the high seas had incensed the American public. Increased U-boat activity in 1916 led U.S. President Woodrow Wilson (1856–1924) to issue a severe warning to the Germans to cease submarine warfare. The Germans, however, were driven to desperate measures. The great advantage of submarines was in sneak attacks, a procedure against the international rules that required warning. Germany initiated a new phase of unrestricted submarine warfare on 1 February 1917, when the German ambassador informed the U.S. government that U-boats would sink on sight all ships, including passenger ships, even those neutral and unarmed.

German machinations in Mexico were also revealed on 25 February 1917, with the interception of a telegram from Arthur Zimmermann (1864–1940), the German foreign minister. The telegram communicated Germany's willingness to support Mexico's recovery of "lost territory" in New Mexico, Arizona, and Texas in return for Mexican support of Germany in the event of U.S. entry into the war. U.S. citizens were outraged. On 2 April 1917, Wilson, who had won the presidential election of 1916 on the promise of peace, asked the U.S. Congress for a declaration of war against Germany.

U.S. entry was the turning point in the war, tipping the scales dramatically in favor of the Allies. The United States contributed its naval power to the large Allied convoys formed to protect shipping against German attacks. In a total war, control and shipment of resources had become crucial issues, and it was in these areas that the U.S. entry gave the Allies indisputable superiority. The United States was also able to send "over there" tens of thousands of conscripts fighting with the American Expeditionary Forces under the leadership of General John "Black Jack" Pershing (1860–1948). They reinforced British and French troops and gave a vital boost to morale.

For such a rich nation, however, the help that the United States was able to give was at first very little. The U.S. government was new to the business of coordinating a war effort, but it displayed great ingenuity in creating a wartime bureaucracy that increased a small military establishment of 210,000 soldiers to 9.5 million young men registered before the beginning of summer 1917. By July 1918 the Americans were sending a phenomenal 300,000 soldiers a month to Europe. By the end of the war 2 million young American men had traveled to Europe to fight in the war.

The U.S. entry is significant not just because it provided reinforcements, fresh troops, and fresh supplies to the beleaguered Allies. From a broader perspective, it marked a shift in the nature of international politics: Europe was no longer able to handle its own affairs and settle its own differences without outside help.

U.S. troops, although numerous, were not well trained, and they relied on France and Great Britain for their arms and equipment. But the Germans correctly understood that they could not hold out indefinitely against this superior Allied force. Austria-Hungary was effectively out of the war. Germany had no replacements for its fallen soldiers, but it was able to transfer troops from Russia, Romania, and Macedonia to the west. It realized its only chance of victory lay in swift action. The German high command decided on a bold measure: one great, final offensive that would knock the combined forces of Great Britain, France, and the United States out of the war once and for all by striking at a weak point and smashing through enemy lines. The great surprise was that it almost worked.

Known as the Ludendorff offensive, after the general who devised it, the final German push began in March 1918. Secretly amassing tired troops from the eastern front pulled back after the Russian withdrawal, the Germans counted on the element of surprise to enable them to break through a weak sector in the west. On the first day of spring Ludendorff struck. The larger German force gained initial success against weakened British and French forces. Yet in spite of breaches in defense, the Allied line held. Allied Supreme Commander, General Ferdinand Foch (1851–1929), coordinated the war effort that withstood German offensives throughout the spring and early summer of 1918.

The final drive came in mid-July. More than one million German soldiers had already been killed, wounded, or captured in the months between March and July. German prisoners of war gave the French details of Ludendorff's plan. The Germans, now exposed and vulnerable, were placed on the defensive. The German army was rapidly disintegrating. On the other side, tanks, plentiful munitions, and U.S. reinforcements fueled an Allied offensive that began in late September. The Germany army retreated, destroying property and equipment as it went. With weak political leadership and indecision in Berlin, the Germans held on until early November. The end came finally after four years of war. On 11 November 1918, an armistice signed by representatives of the German and Allied forces took effect. As the victors danced in the streets, and the defeated allowed themselves to feel relief, the task of settling the peace loomed.

Reshaping Europe: After War and Revolution

In the aftermath of war, the task of the victors was to define the terms of a settlement that would guarantee peace and stabilize Europe. Russia was the ghost at the conference table, excluded from the negotiations because of its withdrawal from the Allied camp in 1917 and its separate peace with Germany in March 1918. The Bolsheviks were dealing with problems of their own following the revolution, including a great civil war lasting through 1920. Much of what happened in the peace settlements reflected the unspoken concern with the challenge of revolution that the new Soviet Russia represented. Meanwhile, the new Russian leaders carefully watched events in the west, looking for opportunities that might permit them to extend their revolution to central Europe.

Settling the Peace

From January to June 1919, an assembly of nations convened in Paris to draw up the new European peace. Although the primary task of settling the peace fell to the Council of Four—Premier Georges Clemenceau of France, Prime Minister David Lloyd George of Great Britain, Prime Minister Vittorio Emanuele Orlando of Italy, and President Woodrow Wilson of the United States—small states, newly formed states, and non-European states, Japan in particular, joined in the task of forging the peace. The states of Germany, Austria-Hungary, and Soviet Russia were excluded from the negotiating tables where the future of Europe was to be determined.

President Wilson, who captured international attention with his liberal views on the peace, was the central figure of the conference. He was firmly

Europe after World War I

committed to the task of shaping a better world: Before the end of the war he had proclaimed the "Fourteen Points" as a guideline to the future peace and as an appeal to the people of Europe to support his policies. Believing that secret diplomacy and the alliance system were responsible for the events leading up to the declaration of war in 1914, he put forward as a basic principle, "open covenants of peace, openly arrived at." Other points included the reduction of armaments, freedom of commerce and trade, self-determination of peoples, and a general association of nations to guarantee the peace that became the League of Nations. The Fourteen Points were, above all, an idealistic statement of the principles for a good and lasting peace. Point 14, which stipulated "mutual guarantees of independence and territorial integrity" through the establishment of the League of Nations, was endorsed by the Peace Conference. The League, which the United States refused to join in spite of Wilson's advocacy, was intended to arbitrate all future disputes among states and to keep the peace.

Georges Clemenceau of France represented a different approach to the challenge of the peace, one motivated primarily by a concern for his nation's security. France had suffered the greatest losses of the war in both human lives and property destroyed. In order to prevent a resurgent Germany, Clemenceau supported a variety of measures to cripple it as a military force on the Continent. Germany was disarmed. The territory west of the Rhine River was demilitarized, with occupation by Allied troops to last for a period of 15 years. With Russia unavailable as a partner to contain Germany, France supported the creation of a series of states in eastern Europe carved out of former Russian, Austrian, and German territory. Wilson supported these new states out of a concern for self-determination of peoples. Clemenceau's main concern was self-defense.

Much time and energy were devoted to redrawing the map of Europe. New states were created out of the lands of three failed empires. Based on self-determination, Finland, Latvia, Estonia, Lithuania, Poland, Czechoslovakia, Austria, Hungary, and Yugoslavia were all granted status as nation-states. However, the right of ethnic and cultural minorities were violated in some cases because of the impossibility of redrawing the map of Europe strictly according to the principle of self-determination. In spite of good intentions, every new nation had its own national minority, a situation that held the promise of future troubles.

The Peace Conference produced five separate treaties with each of the defeated nations: Austria, Hungary, Turkey, Bulgaria, and Germany. The treaty signed with Germany on 28 June 1919, known as the Treaty of Versailles because it was signed in the great Bourbon palace, preceded the others in timing and importance. In that treaty, the Allies imposed blame for the war on Germany and its expansionist aims in the famous War Guilt Clause. If the war was Germany's fault, then Germany must be made to pay. Reparations, once the price of defeat, were now exacted as compensation for damages inflicted by a guilty aggressor.

The principle of punitive reparations was included in the German settlement. By 1920 the German people knew that Germany had to make a down payment of $5 billion against a future bill; had to hand over a significant portion of merchant ships, including all vessels of more than 1600 tons; had to lose all German colonies; and had to deliver coal to neighboring countries. These harsh clauses, more than any other aspect of the peace settlement, came to haunt the Allies in the succeeding decades.

In the end, no nation got what it wanted from the peace settlement. The defeated nations felt they had been badly abused. The victorious nations were aware of the compromises they had reluctantly accepted. Cooperation among nations was essential if the treaty was to work successfully. It had taken the combined resources of not only France and the British Empire but also Russia with its vast population and the United States with its great industrial and financial might to defeat the power of Germany and the militarily ineffective Austro-Hungarian Empire. A new and stable balance of power depended on the participation of Russia, the United States, and the British Empire. But Russia was excluded from and hostile to the peace settlement, the United States was uncommitted to it, and the British Empire declined to guarantee it. All three Great Powers backed off their European responsibilities at the end of the war. By 1920 all aspects of the treaty, but especially the reparations clause, had been questioned and criticized by the very governments that had written them and had accepted them. The search for a lasting peace had just begun.

Revolution in Russia, 1917–1920

Every country has its prophets. So, too, did Russia in 1914 when a now-forgotten former government minister advised Tsar Nicholas II (1894–1917) to avoid war or else face a social revolution. Other advisers prevailed: They said that Russia must go to war because it was a great power with interests beyond its borders. But within its empire, the process of modernization was widening social divisions. Nicholas preferred to listen to those who promised that a short successful war would strengthen his monarchy against the domestic forces of change.

The Last Tsar.   The Romanov dynasty surely needed strengthening. In 1914 Russia was considered backward by the standards of Western industrial society. Russia still recalled a recent feudal past. The serfs had been freed in the 1860s, but the nature of the emancipation exacerbated tensions in the countryside and peasant hunger for land. Russia's limited, rapid industrialization in the 1880s and 1890s was an attempt to catch up with Great Britain, France, and Germany as a world industrial power. But the speed of such change brought with it severe dislocations, especially in the industrial city of Moscow and the capital, St. Petersburg.

Twelve years earlier, in 1905, the workers of St. Petersburg protested hardships due to cyclical downturns in the economy. On a Sunday in January 1905 the tsar's troops fired on a peaceful mass demonstration in front of the Winter Palace. A thousand people were killed, including many women and children, who were appealing to the tsar for relief. The event, which came to be known as Bloody Sunday, set off a revolution that spread to Moscow and the countryside. In October 1905 the regime responded to the disruptions with a series of reforms that legalized political parties and established the Duma, or national parliament. Peasants, oppressed with their own burdens of taxation and endemic poverty, launched mass attacks on big landowners throughout 1905 and 1906. The government met workers' and peasants' demands with a return to repression in 1907. In the half decade before the Great War, the Russian state stood as an autocracy of parliamentary concessions blended with severe police controls.

What workers had learned in 1905 was the power and the means of independent organization. Factory committees, trade unions, and "soviets," or workers' councils, proliferated. Despite winning a grant of legal status after 1906, unions gained little in terms of ability to act on behalf of their members. Unrest among factory workers revived on the eve of the Great War, a period of rapid economic growth and renewed trade union activity. Between January and July 1914 Russia experienced 3500 strikes in a six-month period. Although economic strikes were considered legal, strikes deemed political were not. With the outbreak of war, all collective action was banned. Protest stopped, but only momentarily. The tsar certainly weighed the workers' actions in his decision to view war as a possible diversion from domestic problems.

Russia was less prepared for war than any of the other belligerents.

Russian imperial troops fire on demonstrators outside the Winter Palace in St. Petersburg. The people were asking for better working conditions and a more responsive government. This day, 22 January 1905, is known in Russian history as Bloody Sunday.

Undoubtedly, it had more soldiers than other countries, but it lacked arms and equipment. Problems of provisioning such a huge fighting force placed great strains on the domestic economy and on the work force. Under government coercion to meet the needs of war, industrial output doubled between 1914 and 1917, while agricultural production plummeted. The tsar, who unwisely insisted on commanding his own troops, left the government in the hands of his wife, the Tsarina Alexandra, a German princess by birth, and her eccentric peasant adviser, Rasputin. Scandal, sexual innuendo, and charges of treason surrounded the royal court. The incompetence of a series of unpopular ministers further eroded confidence in the regime.

In the end, the war sharpened long-standing divisions within Russian society. Led by exhausted and starving working women, poorly paid and underfed workers toppled the regime in the bitter winter of March 1917. This event was the beginning of a violent process of revolution and civil war. The tsar abdicated, and all public symbols of the tsardom were destroyed. The banner bearing the Romanov two-headed eagle was torn down and in its place the Red Flag flew over the Winter Palace.

Dual Power. With the tsar's abdication, two centers of authority replaced autocracy. One was the Provisional Government, appointed by the Duma and made up of bourgeois liberals attempting to rule from the center; the other was the "soviets," committees or councils elected by workers and soldiers, who were supported by radical lawyers, journalists, and intellectuals in favor of socialist self-rule. The Petrograd Soviet was the most prominent among the councils. This duality of power was matched by duality in policies and objectives and guaranteed a short-lived and unstable regime.

The problems facing the new regime soon became apparent as revolution spread to the provinces and to the battlefront. Peasants, who made up 80 percent of the Russian population, accepted the revolution and demanded land and peace. Without waiting for government directives peasants began seizing the land. Peasants tried to alleviate some of their suffering by hoarding what little they had. The food crisis of winter persisted throughout the spring and summer, as breadlines lengthened and prices rose. Workers in cities gained better working conditions and higher wages. But wage increases were invariably followed by higher prices that robbed workers of their gains. Real wages declined.

In addition to the problems of land and bread, the war itself presented the new government with other insurmountable difficulties. Hundreds of thousands of Russian soldiers at the front deserted the war, having heard news from home of peasant land grabs and rumors of a new offensive planned for July. The Provisional Government, concerned with Russia's territorial integrity and its position in the international system, continued to honor the tsar's commitments to the Allies by participating in the war. By spring 1917 six to eight million Russian soldiers had been killed, wounded, or captured. The Russian army was incapable of fighting.

The Provisional Government tried everything to convince its people to carry on with the war. In the summer of 1917, the Women's Battalion of Death, composed exclusively of female recruits, was enlisted into the army. Its real purpose, officials admitted, was to "shame the men" into fighting. The all-female unit, like its male counterparts, experienced high losses: 80 percent of the force suffered casualties. The Provisional Government was caught in an impossible situation: It could not withdraw from the war but neither could it fight. Continued involvement in the lost cause of the war blocked any consideration of social reforms.

While the Provisional Government was trying to deal with the calamities, many members of the intelligentsia, Russia's educated class, who had been exiled by the tsar for their political beliefs, now rushed back from western Europe to take part in the great revolutionary experiment. Theorists of all stripes put their cases before the people. Those in favor of gradual reform debated with those who favored violent revolution about the relative merits of various government policies. The months between February and July 1917 were a period of great intellectual ferment. It was the Marxists, or Social Democrats, who had the greatest impact on the direction of the revolution.

The Social Democrats believed there were objective laws of historical development that could be discovered. Russia's future could only be understood in terms of the present situation in western Europe. Like Marxists in the West, the Russian Social Democrats split over how best to achieve a socialist state. The more moderate Mensheviks (the term means "minority") wanted to work through parliamentary institutions and were willing to cooperate with the Provisional Government. A *smaller* faction—despite its name—calling themselves Bolsheviks (meaning "majority") dedicated themselves to preparation for a revolutionary upheaval. After April 1917 the Bolsheviks refused to work with the Provisional Government and organized themselves to take control of the Petrograd Soviet.

The leader of the Bolsheviks was Vladimir Ilich Ulyanov (1870–1924), best known by his revolutionary name, Lenin. Forty-seven years old at the time of the revolution, Lenin had spent most of his life in exile or in prison. More a pragmatist than a theoretician, he argued for a disciplined party of professional revolutionaries, a vanguard that would lead the peasants and workers in a socialist revolution against capitalism. In contrast to the Mensheviks, he argued that the time was now ripe for a successful revolution, and that it could be achieved through the soviets.

Immediately upon arrival in Petrograd from Switzerland, Lenin threw down the gauntlet to the Provisional Government. In his April Theses, he promised the Russian people peace, land, and bread. The war must be ended immediately, he argued, because it represented an imperialist struggle that was benefiting capitalists. Russia's duty was to withdraw and wait for a world revolution. This was more than rhetoric on Lenin's part. His years in exile in the West and news of mutinies and worker protests convinced him that revolution was imminent. His revolutionary policies on land were little more than endorsements of the seizures already taking place all over Russia. Even his promises of bread had little substance. But on the whole, the April Theses constituted a clear critique of the policies of the Provisional Government.

Dissatisfaction with the Provisional Government increased as the war dragged on hopelessly and breadlines lengthened. In the midst of these calamities, a massive popular demonstration erupted in July 1917 against the Provisional Government and in favor of the soviets, which excluded the upper classes from voting. The Provisional Government responded with repressive force reminiscent of the tsardom. The July Days were proof of the growing influence of the Bolsheviks among the Russian people. Although the Bolshevik leadership had withdrawn support for the demonstrations at the last moment, Bolshevik rank-and-file party members strongly endorsed the protest. Indisputably, Bolshevik influence was growing in the soviets despite repression and persecution of its leaders. Lenin was forced to flee to Finland.

As a result of the July Days, a socialist, Aleksandr Kerenski (1881–1970), was named prime minister and continued the Provisional Government's moderate policies. In order to protect the government from a coup on the right, Kerenski permitted the arming of the Red Guards, the workers' militia units of the Petrograd Soviet. The traditional chasm between the upper and the lower classes was widening: The days of dual power were numbered.

Lenin and the Bolsheviks Seize Power. The second revolution came in November (October in the Russian calendar). This time it was not a spontaneous street demonstration by thousands of working women that triggered the revolution, but rather the seizure of the Russian capital by the Red Guards of the Petrograd Soviet. The revolution was carefully planned and orchestrated by Lenin and his vanguard of Bolsheviks, who now possessed majorities in the soviets in Moscow and Petrograd and other industrial centers. Returning surreptitiously from Finland, Lenin moved through the streets of Petrograd disguised in a curly wig and head bandages, watching the Red Guard seize centers of communication and public buildings. The military action was directed by Lev Bronstein, better known by his revolutionary name, Leon Trotsky (1879–1940). The Bolshevik chairman of the Petrograd Soviet, Trotsky used the Red Guard to seize political control and arrest the members of the Provisional Government. Kerenski escaped and fled the city.

The takeover was achieved with almost no bloodshed and was immediately endorsed by an All-Russian Congress of Soviets, which consisted of representatives of local soviets from throughout the nation who were in session amid the takeover of the capital. A Bolshevik regime under Lenin now ruled Russia. Tsar Nicholas II and the royal family were executed by the revolutionaries in July 1918.

The Russian Civil War, 1917–1920. Lenin immediately set to work to end the war for Russia. After months of negotiation, Russia signed a separate peace with the Germans in March 1918 in the Treaty of Brest-Litovsk. By every measure, the treaty was a bitter humiliation for the new Soviet regime. The territorial losses were phenomenal. In a vast amputation, Russia was reduced to the size of its Muscovite period: It recognized the independence of Ukraine, Georgia, and Finland; it relinquished its Polish territories, the Baltic states, and part of Belorussia to Germany and Austria-Hungary; and it handed over other territories on the Black Sea to Turkey. Lenin felt he had no choice: He needed to buy time to consolidate the revolution at home.

The Treaty of Brest-Litovsk was judged a betrayal not only outside Russia among the Allied powers but also inside Russia among some army officers who had sacrificed much for the tsar's war. To these military men, the Bolsheviks were no more than German agents who held the country in their sway. Combining forces with Cossacks, who feared the loss of their lands and privileges under a Bolshevik state, army officers formed the White Armies to engage in war against Trotsky's Red fighting force. Lacking sufficient organization, unable to coordinate their movements because the Bolsheviks dominated the country's center, and torn apart by different political goals, the White Armies ultimately failed to challenge successfully the Bolshevik hold on the reins of state. But in the three years of civil war between Whites and Reds, the Whites posed a serious threat to Bolshevik policies.

Anti-Bolshevik forces were assisted with materials by the Allies, who intended to keep the eastern front viable. The Allies sent over one hundred thousand troops and supplies for the purpose of overthrowing the Bolshevik regime by supporting its enemies. Allied support for the White Armies came primarily from the United States, Great Britain, France, and Japan and continued beyond the armistice that ended the Great War in 1918. Although Allied support was not crucial to the outcome of the civil war, it played a significant role in shaping Soviet perceptions of the outside world. For generations of Soviet citizens, anti-Bolshevik assistance has been viewed as the indication of a hostile and predatory capitalist world intent on destroying the fledgling Soviet state for its own ends.

The civil war had another legacy for the future of the Soviet state. To deal with the anarchy caused by the fratricidal struggle, Lenin had to strengthen the government's dictatorial elements at the expense of its democratic ones. The new Soviet state used state police to suppress all opposition. The dictatorship of the proletariat yielded to the dictatorship of the repressive forces.

In the course of the civil war, Lenin was no more successful than Kerenski and the Provisional Government in solving the problems of food supplies. Human costs of the civil war were high, with over eight hundred thousand soldiers dead on both sides, and two million civilian deaths from dysentery and diseases caused by poor nutrition. Industrial production ceased and people fled towns to return to the countryside. In 1920 it seemed Russia could drop no lower. Millions had been killed in war or died from famine. Stripped of territories and sapped of its industrial strength, Russia was a defeated nation. Yet Bolshevik idealism about the success of the proletarian revolution prevailed. No longer sure that a world socialist revolution would come to their aid, Bolshevik leaders set out to build the future.

By every measure, the Great War was disastrously expensive. Some European nations suffered more than others, but all endured significant losses of life, property, and productive capacity. The cost in human lives was enormous. In western Europe 8.5 million were dead; total casualties amounted to 37.5 million. France lost 20 percent of its men between the ages of 20 and 44, Germany lost 15 percent, and Great Britain 10 percent. The war also resulted in huge losses in productive capacity. National economies buckled under the weight of foreign debts and resorted to a variety of methods to bail themselves out, including taxes, loans, and inflations. The people of Europe continued to pay for the war long after the fighting had ended.

The big winner in the war was the United States, now a creditor nation holding billions of dollars of loans to the Allies and operating in new markets established during the war. The shift was not a temporary move but a structural change. The United States now took its place as a Great Power in the international system. The world of 1914 was gone. What was to replace it was still very much in flux. To the east, Russia was engaged in a vast experiment of building a new society. In the west, the absence of war was not peace.

Suggestions for Further Reading

The European Balance of Power

*George E. Kennan, *The Decline of Bismarck's European Order: Franco-Russian Relations, 1875–1890* (Princeton, NJ: Princeton University Press, 1979). A diplomatic history of the origins of the 1894 military alliance between Russia and France, which views the alliance as a critical factor in the breakdown of the European balance of power established by Bismarck's diplomacy.

*Alan Sked, *The Decline and Fall of the Habsburg Empire, 1815–1918* (London: Longman, 1989). An overview of the Habsburg Empire's history from Metternich to World War I. The author interprets the various historiographical debates over the collapse of Habsburg rule. Rather than treating the late empire as a case of inevitable decline, the book examines the monarchy as a viable institution within a multinational state.

The War Europe Expected

Marc Ferro, *The Great War, 1914–1918* (London: Routledge & Kegan Paul, 1973). The origins of World War I within a broad social and cultural context. Stressing the importance of an imagined war and patriotism as two factors that precipitated actual conflict, Ferro shows how the gulf between imagination and reality led to domestic conflict and social unrest once war broke out.

*James Joll, *The Origins of the First World War* (New York: Longman, 1984). In an examination of the decisions that brought about war in 1914, importance is placed on the limited options available to decision makers. The July crisis, the international system, the arms race, domestic politics, the international economy, imperial rivalries, and cultural and psychological factors are considered in terms of their contributions to the outbreak of war.

*Keith Robbins, *The First World War* (Oxford, England: Oxford University Press, 1984). The major cultural, political, military, and social developments between 1914 and 1918. Includes discussion of the course of the land war and modes of warfare.

The War Europe Got

*Gerd Hardach, *The First World War, 1914–1918* (Berkeley: University of California Press, 1977). Describes the changes in the world economy leading up to the war, the war's impact on trade, wartime monetary and fiscal policies, and the war's impact on labor. Each major power is included in an analysis of wartime economic history.

R. E. Schmitt and H. C. Vedeler, *The World in a Crucible, 1914–1919* (New York: Harper & Row, 1984). A broad survey of the military and political history of World War I; the war is viewed here as a period of revolution in both warfare and politics. Includes considerable discussion of the Russian Revolution and a section on the entry of the United States into European affairs.

*Denis Winter, *Death's Men: Soldiers of the Great War* (London: Penguin, 1979). Not an account of military strategy and battlefield tactics, *Death's Men* goes inside the infantrymen's war to convey the experience of war in the trenches.

---

*Indicates paperback edition available.

Adjusting to the Unexpected: Total War

John Williams, *The Homefronts: Britain, France and Germany, 1914–1918* (London: Constable, 1972). A comparative study of the home fronts, their impact on the course of the war, and the war's impact on civilian life.

Reshaping Europe: After War and Revolution

*Sheila Fitzpatrick, *The Russian Revolution, 1917–1932* (Oxford, England: Oxford University Press, 1982). An analysis of the October Revolution of 1917 from the perspective of Stalinist society. The February and October revolutions of 1917, the civil war, and the economic policies of the 1920s are treated as various aspects of a unitary revolutionary movement.

Tsuyoshi Hasegawa, *The February Revolution: Petrograd, 1917* (Seattle: University of Washington Press, 1981). A thorough examination of the effects of World War I on Russian workers, liberals, and revolutionary parties leads to an interpretation of the February Revolution as the outcome of a conflict between the state and civil society. Particular attention is given to events leading to the abdication of the tsar, the establishment of the Provisional Government, and the early stages of the Russian Revolution.

Arno J. Mayer, *The Politics and Diplomacy of Peacemaking* (New York: Knopf, 1967). A comprehensive examination of the role of internal political concerns and the foreign policy of the warring nations as well as a thorough analysis of the struggle between Bolshevism, Wilsonian liberalism, and counterrevolution.

*David Stevenson, *The First World War and International Politics* (Oxford, England: Oxford University Press, 1988). A study of the global ramifications of World War I, this work traces the development of war aims on both sides, the reasons peace negotiations failed, and why compromise proved elusive.

21

Searching for Stability: Europe, 1920–1932

Buildings for the Future

Buildings tell tales. Archaeologists trying to understand other civilizations excavate ancient dwellings in order to reconstruct past lives. Family life, social values, the nature of work, technology, and progress are all embodied in the structures in which people live and work. If future generations had only traces of the buildings of the twentieth century, they would nonetheless hold a key to understanding our civilization and values.

The twentieth-century architecture that we call "modern" was the child born from the union of technology and art in the aftermath of the Great War of 1914–1918. In reaction to the horrors of the battlefront, a new generation of architects, many of them ex-soldiers, committed themselves to the creation of buildings as works of art that answered the needs of modern society. Those who followed the lead of the prewar avant-garde disdained imitating past masters. They saw their task as "starting from zero"—that is, striking out in a new direction unencumbered by the cultural baggage of a past that had proven itself to be morally bankrupt. In building for the future, the postwar generation felt that the present must create a new style of its own.

The battle cry for a new architectural style arose from defeated Germany and in particular from a single man, Walter Gropius (1883–1969). In 1919, only a few months after the Treaty of Versailles ended World War I, Gropius, a recent veteran of the front, founded the Bauhaus, a school based on the collaborative efforts of architects, sculptors, artists, and craft workers. The untranslatable term *Bauhaus*, resulting from joining the German words "building" and "house," soon characterized a new movement in the arts and architecture. As director of the Bauhaus until 1928, Gropius attracted some of

Project for a Glass Skyscraper *(1921)*, *by Ludwig Mies van der Rohe*

Europe's artists to the school, including the architects Marcel Breuer (1902–1981) and Ludwig Mies van der Rohe (1886–1969). Russian abstract artist Vasili Kandinski (1866–1944) and his Swiss colleague Paul Klee (1879–1940) were also members of the teaching staff at the Bauhaus. Characterized by intense activity, exciting experimentation, and enthusiastic collaboration, the men and women who assembled at the Bauhaus pioneered new designs in everything from kitchen utensils and furniture to lighting fixtures and skyscrapers.

Gropius was a utopian dreamer who saw in buildings and in the humble objects of daily life the means of creating human happiness. Beauty in design was defined by the fit between form and function. Rather than rejecting industrial society, Gropius sought a new way of uniting art with it. Unlike other arts and crafts movements, the Bauhaus was willing to make use of the machine to produce for the masses, whether the production was of prefabricated houses or teacups. Gropius knew well that architecture does not move faster than the society it seeks to serve. But he also knew that it must keep pace with the world around it. The school's motto, one that Gropius considered realistic and responsible, proclaimed: "Art and technology—a new unity!"

Pictured here is one of the first Bauhaus models of a skyscraper. Modest by subsequent standards, its 32 stories dwarf the traditional building at its base. Steel and glass were expressly used to liberate the structure from supporting walls. With new engineering knowledge about support, loads, stress, and mass, sheer facades of glass opened up inside space to the outside world. Interior walls were eliminated. Gropius admired the new functional factory structures and early skyscrapers in the United States and Canada for their starkness and simplicity and sought to introduce their "majesty" to residential architecture.

The architects of the Bauhaus were in the right place at the right time. Germany needed new buildings, and in the period from 1924 to 1929 the return of economic prosperity allowed them to be built. Under Gropius's direction, working-class apartment blocks with open floor plans, unadorned facades, clean lines, and a stark simplicity spread across the German landscape. Office buildings of reinforced concrete with little to distinguish them from the new residential housing also mushroomed. By the end of the decade Bauhaus architects had left their mark on German towns and cities. Then, seeking refuge from Hitler (eventually in the United States), Gropius and some of his associates transformed the skylines of America's great cities within a decade. In the second half of the twentieth century, the Bauhaus style of architecture spread throughout the world.

The architects of the Bauhaus changed the appearance of the modern world and with it the twentiety-century experience. Critics who longed for a traditional architecture of decoration and classical emulation judged the Bauhaus style to be barren and ugly. Yet its emphasis on design and function prevailed. The skyscrapers of the twentieth century are products of the lessons of war and technology and the idealistic pursuit of a better world that took shape very visibly in the 1920s.

*I*nternational Politics and Economic Nationalism

Europe in 1918 differed vastly from the prewar world of 1914. The changes that took place between 1918 and 1921 in the three years after the armistice made the European world different yet again. In 1918 parts of war-torn Europe faced the possibility of revolution. Russia, where revolution had destroyed tsardom, expectantly watched revolutionary developments in countries from the British Isles to eastern Europe. The Bolshevik leaders of Russia's revolution counted on the capitalist system to destroy itself. That did not happen. By 1921 revolutions had been brutally crushed in Berlin, Munich, and Budapest. The Soviets, meanwhile, had won the civil war against the Whites and survived the intervention of the British, French, Japanese, and Americans and the blockade with which they had surrounded Russia. But the new Russian regime was diplomatically isolated and in a state of almost total economic collapse.

In 1917–1918 the United States had played a significant and central role in

Europe in the 1920s

the waging of war and in the pursuit of peace. Under U.S. president Woodrow Wilson, who urged his country to guarantee European security and guide Europe's future, the American nation seemed promising as an active and positive force in international politics. By 1921, however, the United States had retreated to a position, not of isolation, but of selective involvement. For America, the period of wartime sacrifice was over; its participation in European international affairs would be unilateral, ad hoc, and based on America's own self-interest. With one giant, Russia, devastated and isolated, and the other, the United States, reluctant, Europeans faced an uncertain future.

The future of Europe was embedded in its geography. Germany, despite some territorial losses after World War I, continued to sit as a large landed nation at the center of the European continent. It exceeded all western European states in territory and population. A picket fence of newly created states separated Germany from Russia, the only country in Europe with greater land, population, and natural resources. On its western frontier, Germany shared a stretch of border with France. France considered itself unprotected in western Europe, with weak neighbors and with former allies uncommitted to France's security. Across the English Channel, the island nation of Great Britain maintained its detachment. But there was one major fact of international power that a map of Europe could not show. The United States, not a European power at all, was in a position to dominate and determine the future of the West.

East Central Europe

Before World War I, east central Europe was a region divided among four great empires—the Ottoman, the Habsburg, the Russian, and the German. Under the pressure of defeat those empires collapsed into their component national parts, and when the dust of the peace treaties had settled, the region had been molded into a dozen sovereign states. The victorious Allies hoped that independent states newly created from fragments of empire would buffer Europe from the spread of communism westward and the expansion of German power eastward.

A swath of new independent states cut through the center of Europe. Finland had acquired its independence from Russia in 1917. Estonia, Latvia, and Lithuania, also formerly under Russian rule, comprised the now independent Baltic states. After more than a century of dismemberment among three empires, Poland became a single nation again. Czechoslovakia was carved out of former Habsburg lands. Austria and Hungary shriveled to small independent states. Yugoslavia was pieced together from a patchwork of territories. Romania swelled, fed on a diet of settlement concessions. These new nations assured the victorious powers and especially France that the new political geography of east central Europe, wedged between Russian and German ambitions, would guarantee the peace.

World War I victor nations hoped that these new states would stabilize

European affairs; they could not have been more wrong. They erred in three important ways in their calculations. First, many of the new states were internally unstable precisely because of the principle of national self-determination, the idea that nationalities had the right to rule themselves. Honoring the rights of nationalities was simple in the abstract, but application of the principle proved complicated and at times impossible. Religious, linguistic, and ethnic diversity abounded, and recognizing nationality often meant ignoring the rights of minorities. In Czechoslovakia, for example, the Czechs dominated the Slovaks and the Germans even though the Czechs were fewer in number. Ethnic unrest plagued all of eastern Europe. Minority tensions weakened and destabilized the fragile governments.

Second, the struggle for economic prosperity further destabilized the new governments. East central Europe was primarily agricultural and the existence of the great empires had created guaranteed markets. The war disrupted the economy and generated social unrest. The peace settlements only compounded the economic problems of the region. When the Habsburg Empire disintegrated, the Danube River basin ceased to be a cohesive economic unit. New governments were saddled with borders that made little economic sense.

Creating cohesive economic units proved an insurmountable task for newly formed governments and administrations that lacked both resources and experience. Low productivity, unemployment, and overpopulation characterized most of east central Europe. Attempts to industrialize and to develop new markets confronted many obstacles. Much of the land was farmed on a subsistence basis. What agricultural surplus was created was difficult to sell abroad. East central Europeans, including Poles, Czechs, Yugoslavs, and Romanians, all tied to France through military and political commitments, were excluded from western European markets and were isolated economically from their treaty allies. Economic ties with Germany endured in ways that perpetuated economic dependence and threatened future survival.

Finally, common borders produced tensions over territories. The peace settlements made no one happy. Poland quarreled with Lithuania, and Czechoslovakia vied with Poland over territorial claims. Poland actually went to war with Russia for six months in 1920 in an effort to reclaim the Ukraine and expand its borders to what they had been more than a century earlier. The Bolsheviks counterattacked and tried to turn the conflict into a revolutionary war to spread communism to central Europe. French military advisers came to the aid of the Poles and turned the Russians back. The Treaty of Riga, signed in March 1921, gave Poland much but not all of the territory it claimed.

Hungary, having lost the most territory in World War I, held the distinction of having the greatest number of territorial grievances against its neighbors—Czechoslovakia, Romania, and Yugoslavia. Yugoslavia made claims against Austria. Bulgaria sought territories controlled by Greece and Romania. Ethnicity, strategic considerations, and economic needs motivated claims for territory. Disputes festered, fed by the intense nationalism that prevented the cooperation necessary for survival.

Germany, the Soviet Union, and Italy had their own territorial claims against their east central European neighbors. The new German government refused to accept the loss of the "corridor" controlled by Poland that severed East Prussia from the rest of Germany. Nor was Germany resigned to the loss of part of Silesia to Poland. Russia refused to forget its losses to Romania, Poland, Finland, and the Baltic states. Italy, too weak to act on its own, nevertheless dreamed of expansion into Yugoslavia, Austria, and Albania. Despite the old saying that good fences make good neighbors, the redefined borders of eastern and central Europe produced only animosity.

Germany

From defeat, the German nation emerged strong. Its population of 60 million exceeded France's 40 million. Because World War I had not been fought in Germany, German transportation networks and industrial plant had escaped serious damage. Its industry was fed by raw materials and energy resources unsurpassed anywhere in Europe outside Russia. In east central Europe, Germany had actually benefited from the dismantling of the Habsburg Empire and the removal of Poland and the Baltic states from Russian control. Replacing its formerly large neighbor to the east were weak states potentially susceptible to Germany's influence. Because the governments of east central Europe feared communism, they were not likely to ally with the Soviet state. The existence of the small buffer states left open the possibility of German collaboration with Russia, since the two large nations might be able to negotiate their interests in the area. Germany stood as the dominant nation in central Europe.

On its western frontier, Germany's prospects were not so bright. Alsace and Lorraine had been returned to France. From German territory, a demilitarized zone had been created in the Rhineland. Allied troops were settled there for 15 years, a period of occupation that could be extended—at Germany's expense. The Saar district was under the protection of League of Nations commissioners, and the Saar coal mines were transferred to French ownership. A plebiscite in 1935 finally returned the region to Germany. Humiliated and betrayed by the geographic consequences of its defeat, Germany looked to recover its status.

Germany's primary foreign policy goal was revision of the treaty settlements of World War I. German politicians and military leaders perceived disarmament, loss of territory, and payment of reparations as serious obstacles in restoring Germany's position as a great power. In the mid-1920s statesmen spelled out the territorial aims of Germany's foreign policy: liberation of the Rhineland from foreign military occupation; return of the Saar basin; and recovery of the Corridor and Upper Silesia from Poland.

German leaders set economic recovery as the basis of their new foreign policy. In 1922 Germany signed the Treaty of Rapallo with Russia, a peacetime agreement that shocked the western powers. Economics motivated the new Russo-German partnership: German industry needed markets and the Russians needed loans to reconstruct their economy. Both states wanted to break out of the isolation imposed on them by the victors of World War I. However, Germany quickly learned that markets in Russia were limited and hopes for recovery depended on financial cooperation with western Europe and the United States. At the end of 1923 Gustav Stresemann (1878–1929) assumed direction of the German Foreign Ministry and began to implement a conciliatory policy toward France and Britain. By displaying peaceful intentions he hoped to secure American capital for German industry and win the support of the West for the revision of the peace settlement.

Stresemann joined his French and British counterparts, Aristide Briand (1862–1932) and Austen Chamberlain (1863–1937), in fashioning a series of treaties at Locarno, Switzerland, in 1925. In a spirit of cooperation, Germany, France, and Belgium promised never again to go to war against each other and to respect the demilitarized zone that separated them. Britain and Italy "guaranteed" the borders of all three countries and assured the integrity of the demilitarized zone. The treaties initiated an atmosphere of goodwill, a "spirit of Locarno," that heralded a new age of security and nonaggression.

Under Stresemann's direction, Germany did not renounce its ambitions in eastern Europe. Stresemann expected Germany to recover the territory lost to Poland. He also knew that Germany must rearm and expand to the east. From the early 1920s until 1933, Germany secretly rearmed in violation of Versailles. Undercover, it rebuilt its army and trained its soldiers and airmen on Russian territory. Germany planned to be once again a great power with the same rights as other European countries.

Western Europe

Having learned the harsh lessons of 1870–1871 and 1914–1918, France understood well the threat posed by a united, industrialized, and well-armed Germany. During the years immediately following World War I, France deeply distrusted Germany. How was France to defend itself and Europe? France had a smaller population than Germany, and its industrial production was not as great. France was devastated by the war and Germany was not. But France did have certain advantages in 1921. It had the best manned and best equipped army in the world. Germany was disarmed. The Rhineland was demilitarized and occupied. But these military advantages would last only as long as the Treaty of Versailles was enforced. France knew that alone it could not enforce the treaty and keep Germany militarily weak. The wartime alliance of France, Britain, and the United States against Germany must be carried over into peacetime.

The Americans and the British refused to conclude a long-term peacetime alliance with the French. In place of an alliance in the west with Britain and the United States, therefore, France committed itself to an alliance in the east with Poland, and the Little Entente nations of Czechoslovakia, Romania, and

Yugoslavia. Treaties with these four states of east central Europe gave France some security in the event of an attack. But the treaties were also liabilities because France would have to fight to defend east central Europe.

To keep Germany militarily and economically weak, the French attempted to enforce the Treaty of Versailles fully and completely in 1921–1923. They were willing to do so alone if necessary. In 1923 the French army invaded the Ruhr district of Germany and occupied it with the intention of collecting reparations payments. But the Ruhr invasion only served to isolate France further from its wartime allies. France depended on loans from American banks to balance its budget, and the Americans disapproved of the French use of military might to enforce the treaty.

In 1924–1925 France decided to cooperate with the United States and Great Britain rather than continue a policy of enforcing the treaty alone and keeping Germany weak. France withdrew its army from the Ruhr and some troops from the Rhineland. It agreed to lower German reparations payments. In addition, by signing the Locarno treaties, France went along with the Anglo-American policy that rejected the use of military force against Germany and promoted German economic recovery.

French anxiety about security continued. Nothing indicated the nature of this anxiety more clearly than the construction, beginning in the late 1920s, of the Maginot Line, a system of defensive fortifications between Germany and France. Behind this wall France hoped to repel what many of its military leaders considered the inevitable German advance.

Throughout the 1920s French political leaders tried to engage Great Britain in guaranteeing the security of France and Europe. The British agreed to defend France and Belgium against possible German aggression. They stopped short, however, of promising to defend Poland and Czechoslovakia. After settling this matter at Locarno, Britain largely reverted to its prewar pattern of withdrawing from continental Europe and concentrating its attention on the demands of its global empire.

The United States in Europe

The Treaty of Versailles marked the demise of European autonomy. In World War I, Germany had conquered large areas of eastern Europe, defeated Russia, dominated the Balkans, brought the French army to the point of mutiny, and threatened Great Britain with submarine strangulation. It had done so with only a little help from the other Central Powers. In the end, the defeat of Germany required the combined forces of France, Russia, the British Empire, and the United States. American intervention had boosted French and British morale during the crucial months of 1917. In providing financial help, ships, troops, and supplies, the United States had rescued the Allied powers. A balance of power in Europe could no longer be maintained without outside help. Germany had been defeated, but if it recovered, France and Britain alone would probably not be able to protect Europe again. Security and peace now depended on the presence of an outside force to guarantee a stable balance of power in Europe and to defend Western hegemony in the world. That outside force was the United States.

The United States was unwilling, however, to assume a new role as political leader of Europe and mediator of European conflict. It refused to sign a joint peace, arranging instead a separate peace with Germany. It also refused to join the League of Nations. Following the war, the League had been devised as an international body of nations committed, according to Article 10 of its covenant, to "respect and preserve as against external aggression the territorial integrity and existing political independence" of others. Germany was excluded from membership until 1926, and the USSR (Union of Soviet Socialist Republics) was denied entry until 1934. Otherwise, the League of Nations claimed a global membership. But the absence of U.S. support and the lack of any machinery to enforce its decisions undermined the possibility of the League's long-term effectiveness. The hopes that the international body could serve as a peacekeeper collapsed in 1931 with the League's failure to deal with the crisis of Japanese aggression against Manchuria.

The United States persisted in avoiding political and military obligations in Europe with the idea of protecting its own freedom and autonomy. Instead, it sought to promote German economic recovery and reasoned that a peaceful and stable Europe would be reestablished without a real balance of power in Europe and without a commitment from the United States.

Many feared that territorial settlements of the peace held the promise of another war. Even efforts at comprehensive international cooperation like the League of Nations did not overcome the problem of competitive nations, nor did the Kellogg-Briand Pact signed by 23 nations in 1928. Named for U.S. Secretary of State Frank B. Kellogg (1856–1937) and French foreign minister Aristide Briand, who devised the plan, the pact renounced war. In the atmosphere of the 1920s, a time of hope and caution, the agreement carried all the weight of an empty gesture.

Economic Nationalism in the 1920s

When the Great War ended in 1918, the European nations set out to rebuild their shattered economies. Except in northeastern France, Belgium, and parts of Russia, productive capacity had not been significantly destroyed, but former markets and trade patterns had been devastated. Restoration of trade became a primary goal for nations trying to reestablish economic prosperity in the 1920s.

In 1918 the belligerent nations—winners and losers alike—had big bills on their hands. Although nations at war had borrowed from their own populations through the sale of war bonds, private citizens could not provide all the money needed to finance four years of war. France borrowed from Great Britain. Both

Great Britain and France took loans from the United States. When all else failed, belligerent nations could and did print money not backed by productive wealth. Because more money had claims on the same amount of national wealth, the money in circulation was worth less. When the people who had purchased war bonds were then paid off with depreciated currency, they lost real wealth. Inflation had the same effect as taxation. The people had less wealth and the government had less debt. In the end, those who had purchased war bonds absorbed the costs of war through payoffs in depreciated currency. Not surprisingly, those countries that had loaned out money during the war wanted to be repaid. The United States, for the first time in history the leading creditor nation in the world, had no intention of forgiving war debts. Nor did it intend to accept repayment in less valuable postwar currencies: Loans were tied to gold.

Britain, France, and Belgium counted on reparations from Germany to pay their war debts and to rebuild their economies. As for Germany, the postwar Reparations Commission determined that Germany owed the victors 132 billion gold marks ($33 billion) to be paid in annual installments of 2 billion gold marks ($500 million) plus 26 percent of the value of German exports. Reparations were calculated on the basis of the damages Germany had inflicted on the Allies.

The Allies never really expected Germany to pay the full amount, and most Germans believed it could not be paid. Germany, too, wanted to recover from the years of privation of the war. Substantial reparations payments would have transferred real wealth from Germany to the Allies. Transferring wealth would have cut into any increase in the German standard of living in the 1920s, and it would have diminished the investment needed to make the German economy grow. For the German people and for German leaders, reparations were an unacceptable punitive levy that mortgaged the prosperity of future generations.

France was caught in the middle. Germany was not paying reparations and America was demanding from France war debt payment. Britain was taking a lenient attitude toward Germany. Raymond Poincaré (1860–1934), who had served as president of the Third Republic throughout the war and was prime minister of France from 1922 to 1924, insisted that Germany must pay reparations to enable France to recover and pay the United States. In January 1923 French and Belgian troops entered the Ruhr district of Germany, an area rich in coal and the center of the most important industrial complex in Europe. Their purpose was to collect reparations directly—by digging up coal and shipping it back to France. They intended to remain in the Ruhr until Germany was able and willing to pay reparations on its own.

The German government recommended that German miners, trainmen, and civic officials respond to the military presence with passive resistance. To pay idle employees and employers, the German government printed huge amounts of currency. The mark collapsed, and world currencies were endangered. The French occupation of the Ruhr, called an invasion by France's critics, was denounced throughout the world. With financial disaster looming,

French soldiers and engineers guard a German railroad locomotive during the French occupation of the Ruhr industrial district in 1923.

the British and Americans decided to intervene. A plan must be devised that would permit Germany to prosper while funneling payments to France, so dependent on reparations for its own recovery and for its war debt payments to the United States.

In 1924 the American banker Charles G. Dawes (1865–1951), along with a group of international financial experts appointed by the Allied governments, sought a solution to the reparations problem. The Dawes Plan aimed to end inflation and restore economic prosperity in Germany. Germany was given a more modest and realistic schedule of payments and a loan from American banks to get payments started.

The protection of the German economy rather than the defense of French treaty rights commanded the attention and the concern of the United States. American bankers threatened not to renew their loan unless France agreed never again to enforce the Treaty of Versailles by military means without the consent of the British and Americans. Because the French treasury depended on the American loan to balance its national budget, France accepted the Dawes Plan and promised to undertake no more Ruhr invasions. France lost its independence in foreign policy, and its status as a great power was permanently undermined.

As important as reparations and war debts are in any understanding of the Western world in the 1920s, they cannot be considered in isolation. Debtor nations, whether Allies paying back loans to the United States or defeated nations paying reparations to the victors, needed to be able to sell their goods in world markets. They saw trade as the principal way to accumulate enough national income to pay back what they owed and to prosper domestically without burying their citizens under a mountain of new taxes. Profits from exports would both fuel domestic recovery and generate the capital necessary to pay reparations and repay loans.

If trade was to be the stepladder out of the financial hole of indebtedness, open markets and stable currencies were absolutely necessary. The United States recognized that its own best interests lay in promoting economic recovery in Europe. A stable Europe would give the United States a market for its own agricultural and industrial products and provide a guarantee for recovery of its loans and investments. The proverbial monkey wrench in a smoothly functioning international economy was the trade policy of the United States. Republican political leaders in the United States insisted on high tariffs to protect domestic goods against imports. But high tariffs prevented Europeans from selling in the United States and earning the dollars they needed to repay war debts.

While blocking imports, the United States planned to expand its own exports to world markets, especially in Europe. American government officials, businesspeople, farmers, and bankers all agreed on the importance of European markets for a prosperous American economy. The problem for American exporters, however, was the instability of European currencies in the first half of the 1920s. All over Europe governments allowed inflation to rise with the expectation that depreciating currencies would make their goods cheaper in world markets.

Depreciating European currencies on the one hand meant an appreciating dollar on the other. For the "grand design" of U.S. trade expansion, a strong dollar was no virtue. More and more German marks, British pounds, and French francs had to be spent to purchase American goods. The result was that fewer American exports were sold in European markets. But instead of changing a tariff policy that seriously hampered the chances for recovery of European economies, and instead of canceling or forgiving war debts that threatened to soak up Europe's meager capital, the United States subscribed to another policy, one based on what was considered to be in the best interests of Europe and the United States. American banks were authorized to extend private loans to European governments.

New private loans to Germany were possible only after 1924 when the Dawes Plan redesigned reparations payments and inflation was controlled. Germany's capacity to pay was a central feature of the Dawes Plan, and thus for the first few years German payments were to be lowered and Germany was to be assisted by loans from the United States. The need to maintain a stable German currency received special attention. The Dawes Plan was based on the combined lessons of the hyperinflation of the preceding two years and the international disaster of the French occupation of the Ruhr. German leaders reminded the world that both these crippling events were consequences of reparations.

As a result of the Dawes Plan and the American loans, Germany was linked directly to the international economy after 1924. Germany's economic fate could now be determined by events occurring elsewhere. Two-thirds of Germany's long-term credits came from the United States. Conversely, the soundness of American banks depended on a solvent Germany, which now absorbed 18 percent of U.S. capital exports. Wages and salaries in Germany increased significantly and German state welfare programs expanded. The United States recognized in German economic recovery the necessary prerequisite for stable European markets. By 1932 government leaders in Washington also supported revision of the Versailles Treaty with German interests in mind. Republican leaders minimized French concerns for security and ignored British channels for moving funds and resources. They supported instead increased and direct contact with Germany.

Growing U.S. involvement in European affairs flowed from its recently assumed role as a creditor nation. The international economy did not exist in isolation from political realities. To the contrary, economic and financial imperatives drove American foreign policy in Europe. Economic decisions were in turn influenced by strategic considerations. Germany was recognized and supported as a bulwark against bolshevism, and for that reason Germany had to be prosperous. France's cry for protection against a strong Germany was silenced by the American need to export and by America's fear of communism.

Despite the scaled-down schedule of the Dawes Plan, reparations remained a bitter pill for German leaders and the German public to swallow. In 1929 American bankers devised a new plan under the leadership of the American businessman Owen D. Young (1874–1962), chairman of the board of General Electric. Although the Young Plan initially transferred $100 million to Germany, Germans saw the twentieth century stretching before them as year after year of nothing but humiliating reparations payments. To make matters worse, after 1928 American private loans shriveled in Germany, as American investors sought the higher yields of a booming stock market at home. In this atmosphere, reparations continued to undermine Weimar politics.

Until the economic collapse of 1929, problems over reparations, trade, stable currencies, and international security had seemed on the way to being settled. The Locarno treaties augured well for French and German relations, and the Dawes Plan had scaled down and rescheduled reparations. With high employment, high profits, and high consumption, the United States set the pace for other industrial producers. Europe as a whole made rapid progress in manufacturing production during the second half of the decade, and by 1929 had surpassed its prewar (1913) per capita income.

Yet structural weaknesses were present, although they went almost unnoticed. The false security of a new gold standard masked the instability and interdependence of currencies. Low prices prevailed in the agricultural sector, keeping incomes of a significant segment of the population low. The low rate of long-term capital investment was obscured in the flurry of short-term loans, whose disappearance in 1928 spelled the beginning of the end for European recovery. The protectionist trade policy of the United States conflicted with its insistence on repayment of war debts. Germany's resentment over reparations was in no way alleviated by the Dawes and Young repayment plans. The irresponsibility of American speculation in the stock market pricked the bubble of prosperity. None of these factors operated in isolation to cause the collapse that began in 1929. Taken together, however, they spelled a collapse of previously unimagined severity of the international economic system.

The Great Depression

In the history of the Western world the year 1929 has assumed mythic proportions. During one week in October of that year, the stock market in the United States collapsed. This crash set off the Great Depression in an international economic system already plagued with structural problems. It also marked the beginning of a long period of worldwide economic stagnation and depression.

A confluence of factors made Europe and the rest of the world vulnerable to reversals in the American economy. Heavy borrowing and reliance on American investment throughout the 1920s contributed to the inherent instability of European economies. Even Great Britain, itself a creditor, relied on short-term loans; "borrowing short and lending long" proved to be disastrous when loans were recalled. Excessive lending and leniency were fatal mistakes of creditor nations, especially the United States. When in the summer of 1929 American investors turned off the tap of the flow of capital to search for higher profits at home, a precarious situation began to get worse.

A depression is a severe downturn marked by sharp declines in income and production, as buying and selling slow down to a crawl. Depressions were not new in the business cycles of modern economies, but what happened in October 1929 was more serious in its extent and duration than any depression before or since. The bottom was not reached until three years after it began. In 1932 one in four American workers was without a job. One in three banks had closed its doors. People lost their homes, unable to pay their mortgages; farmers lost their land, unable to earn enough to survive. The great prosperity of the 1920s had vanished.

The plight of the United States rippled through world markets. Americans stopped buying foreign goods. The Smoot-Hawley Tariff Act, passed by the U.S. Congress in 1930, created an impenetrable tariff fortress against agricultural and manufactured imports and hampered foreign producers. The major trading nations of the world, including Great Britain, enacted similar protectionist measures. American investment abroad dried up, as the lifelines of American capital to Europe were cut.

European nations tried to staunch the outward flow of capital and gold by restricting the transfer of capital abroad. Large amounts of foreign-owned gold ($6.6 billion from 1931 to 1938) nevertheless were deposited in American banks. In 1931 President Herbert Hoover supported a moratorium on the payment of reparations and war debts. The moratorium, combined with the pooling of gold in the United States, led to a run on the British pound sterling in 1931 and the collapse of Great Britain as one of the world's great financial centers. Britain was forced to repudiate both the gold standard and its preeminent position as a world financial power.

The gold standard disappeared from the international economy, never to return. So, too, did reparations payments and war debts when the major nations of Europe met without the United States at a special conference held in Lausanne, Switzerland, in 1932. Something else died as the 1920s ended: confidence in a self-adjusting economy, an "invisible hand" by which the business cycle would be righted, was attacked at its liberal foundations. In 1932–1933 the Depression, showing no signs of disappearing, reached its nadir and became a global phenomenon. Economic hardship transformed political realities. The Labour cabinet in Great Britain was forced to resign, and a new national government composed of Conservative, Liberal, and Labour leaders was formed to deal with the world economic emergency. Republican government was torn by bitter divisions in France. In the United States the Republican party, which had been in power since 1920, was defeated in 1932. Franklin D. Roosevelt, a Democrat, was elected president in a landslide victory and with a mandate to transform the American economy. But in no place did the Depression have more dramatic political consequences than in Germany, where democratic institutions were pulled down in favor of fascist dictatorship.

The Soviet Union's Separate Path

In Russia in the 1920s, industrialization had barely begun. In the decade following war, revolution, and civil war, the Soviet state committed its people to a program of rapid industrial growth in order to ensure its survival as a great power. The costs of Russia's rapid industrialization were wasted resources, enormous human suffering, and millions of lost lives. Lenin's successor, Joseph Stalin (1879–1953), committed the Soviet people to the achievement in a single generation of what it had taken the West a century and a half to accomplish.

The Soviet Regime at the End of the Civil War

The revolution had been made and the civil war had been won in the name of "the dictatorship of the proletariat," as Lenin echoed Marx. The people were in control—or they were supposed to be. Representing the united rule of workers and peasants, the hammer and sickle on the Soviet flag were symbolic reminders of the commitment to rule from below. But at the end of the civil war in 1921, the Bolsheviks, not the people, were in charge. Having come to power in November 1917, the revolutionaries had struggled for survival for over three years against internal and external opposition. Although the revolutionaries had succeeded, serious problems remained.

The industrial sector, small as it was, was in total disarray by 1921. Famine and epidemics in 1921–1922 killed and weakened more people than the Great War and the civil war combined. The countryside had been plundered to feed the Red and White armies. The combination of empty promises and a declining standard of living left workers and peasants frustrated and discontented. Urban strikes and rural uprisings defied short-term solutions. The proletarian revolutionary heroes of 1917 were rejecting the new Soviet regime. The

Leon Trotsky, a loser in the Soviet power struggle that followed the death of Lenin. Trotsky was exiled from Russia in 1929 and in 1940 was assassinated on Stalin's orders.

Bolshevik party now faced the task of restoring a country exhausted by war and revolution, its resources depleted, its economy destroyed.

At the head of the Soviet state was Lenin, the first among equals in the seven-man Politburo. The Central Committee of the Communist party decided "fundamental questions of policy, international and domestic," but in reality the Politburo, the inner committee of the Central Committee, held the reins of power. The men of the Politburo were relatively young and extremely ambitious. United in ideology and outlook as Bolsheviks, the members of the Politburo differed over policies in everything from education to industrial production.

Among the Politburo seven, three men in particular attempted to leave their mark on the direction of Soviet policy: Leon Trotsky (1879–1940), Nikolai Bukharin (1888–1938), and Joseph Stalin (1879–1953). The great drama of Soviet leadership in the 1920s revolved around how the most brilliant (Trotsky) and the most popular (Bukharin) failed at the hands of the most shrewdly political (Stalin).

The two poles in the debate over the direction of economic development were on one end a planned economy totally directed from above, and on the other an economy controlled from below. In 1920–1921 Leon Trotsky, at that time people's commissar of war, favored a planned economy based on the militarization of labor. Trade unions opposed such a proposal and argued for a share of control over production. Lenin, however, favored a proletarian democracy and supported unions organized independently of state control.

The controversy was resolved in the short run at the Tenth Party Congress in 1921, when Lenin chose to steer a middle course between trade union autonomy and militarization by preserving the unions and at the same time insisting on the state's responsibility for economic development. His primary goal was to stabilize Bolshevik rule in its progress toward socialism. He recognized that nothing could be achieved without the peasants. As a result, Lenin found himself embracing a new economic policy that he termed a "temporary retreat" from communist goals.

The New Economic Policy

In 1921 Lenin ended the forced requisitioning of peasant produce, which had been in effect during the civil war. In its place, peasants were to pay a tax in kind, that is, a fixed portion of their yield, to the state. Peasants in turn were permitted to reinstate private trade on their own terms. Party leaders accepted this dramatic shift in economic policy because it held the promise of prosperity, so necessary for political stability. The actions of Lenin to return the benefits of productivity to the economy, combined with those of the peasants to reestablish markets, created the New Economic Policy, or NEP, that emerged in the spring and summer of 1921.

It remained for Nikolai Bukharin to give shape and substance to the economic policy that permitted Russian producers to engage in some capitalist practices. Along with Lenin and Trotsky, Bukharin was one of the founding fathers of the Soviet state and the youngest of the top Bolshevik leaders. With the success of the Bolshevik revolution, Bukharin took his place on the Central Committee of the Communist party and on the Politburo as well.

Bukharin set about solving the task of Russia's single greatest problem: How could Russia, crippled by poverty, find enough capital to industrialize? Insisting on the need for long-term economic planning, Bukharin counted on a prosperous and contented peasantry as the mainstay of his policy. Retail prices must be lowered, overhead must be reduced, and productivity must be improved to accelerate commodity turnover. Bukharin was strongly interested in attracting foreign investment to Soviet endeavors as a way of ensuring future productivity.

Bukharin planned to keep the Russian peasants happy. At base he appreciated the importance of land-holding to Russian peasants and defended a system of individual farms and private accumulation. Agriculture would operate through a market system, and the peasants would have the right to control their own surpluses. Because agriculture was such an overwhelmingly important sector of the economy, rural prosperity would generate profits that could be used for gradual industrial development. Bukharin's policy stood in stark contrast to Stalin's later plan to feed industry by starving agriculture. To later generations the NEP marked the golden age of the Soviet state. The Bolshevik party monopolized political power, while a pluralistic approach was tolerated in the society and the economy. Peace, stability, and recovery all seemed possible.

Yet the period of the NEP from 1921 to 1928 was a time filled with contradictions and uncertainties. The Soviet Union had returned to some capitalist practices and a limited market economy in the hopes of reestablishing a functioning and eventually prosperous economy. This policy was profoundly at odds with the programs of a communist state, whose ultimate goal was to pull down the capitalist system and establish socialism. Collective and large-scale farming had to be deferred indefinitely in order to reconcile the peasantry to the state. In 1924 the tax in kind was replaced with a tax in cash. With this shift the state now procured grain through commercial agencies and cooperative organizations instead of directly from the peasants. The move toward Western capitalist models seemed more pronounced than ever to critics of the NEP.

Lenin had reasoned in the early days of the NEP that it was a temporary and strategic measure. Beginning in 1922 Lenin suffered a series of strokes, which virtually removed him from power by March 1923. When he died on 21 January 1924, the communist leadership split over the ambiguities of the NEP and the future of socialism in Russia. Many communist revolutionaries believed that the revolution had been sold out for bourgeois liberalism. With Lenin's death the struggle for political dominance intensified.

The backward nature of agriculture did not permit the kind of productivity that the NEP policymakers anticipated. Cities demanded more food as their populations swelled with the influx of unskilled workers from rural areas. In

1927 peasants held back their grain. The Soviet Union was then experiencing a series of foreign policy setbacks in the West and in China, and Bolshevik leaders spoke of an active anti-Soviet conspiracy, led by Great Britain, which could lead to an attack by the capitalist powers. The Soviet state lowered the price of grain, squeezing the peasantry. The war scare, combined with the drop in food prices, soon led to an economic crisis.

By 1928 the NEP was in trouble. Stalin, general secretary of the Communist party of the Soviet Union, saw his chance. Under his supervision, the state intervened to prevent peasants from disposing of their own grain surpluses. The peasants responded violently to requisitioning. Rioting erupted in the countryside as peasants continued to hoard their produce. Bukharin and his policy were in danger. Stalin manipulated the political machinery that allowed him to exploit the internal crisis and external dangers with the aim of eliminating his political rivals. Trotsky was expelled from the Communist party in November 1927 on Stalin's charges that he had engaged in antiparty activities. Banished from Russia in 1929, he eventually found refuge in Mexico, where he was assassinated in 1940 at Stalin's command.

Bukharin's popularity in the party also threatened Stalin's aspirations. Bukharin was dropped from the Politburo in 1929. Tolerated through the early 1930s, he was arrested in 1937, and tried and executed for alleged treasonous activities the following year. The fate that befell Trotsky and Bukharin was typical of that which afflicted those who stood in the way of Stalin's pursuit of dictatorial control. Stalin was, in a colleague's words, "a gray blur." Beneath his apparently colorless personality, however, was a dangerous man of great political acumen, a ruthless behind-the-scenes politician who controlled the machinery of the party to his own ends and was not averse to employing violence in order to achieve them.

Stalin's Rise to Power

Joseph Stalin was born Iosif Vissarionovich Dzhugashvili in 1879. His self-chosen revolutionary name, Stalin, means "steel" in Russian and is as good an indication as any of his opinion of his own personality and will. Stalin, the man who ruled Russia as a dictator from 1928 until his death in 1953, was not a Russian. He was from Georgia, an area between the Black and Caspian seas, and spoke Russian with an accent. Georgia, with its land occupied and its people subjugated by invading armies for centuries, was annexed to the expanding Russian empire in 1801.

As the youngest of four and the only surviving child of Vissarion and Ekaterina Dzhugashvili, Stalin endured a childhood of brutal misery. Vissarion was a poor and often unemployed shoemaker who intended his son be apprenticed in the same trade. Under his mother's protection, young Iosif received an education and entered a seminary against his father's wishes. Iosif's schooling, extraordinary for someone of his poverty-stricken back-

Joseph Stalin

ground, gave him the opportunity to learn about revolutionary socialist politics. At the turn of the century, Georgia had a strong Marxist revolutionary movement that opposed Russian exploitation. Iosif dropped out of the seminary in 1899 to engage in underground Marxist activities, and he soon became a follower of Lenin.

Stalin's association with Lenin kept him close to the center of power after the October Revolution of 1917. First as people's commissar for nationalities (1920–1923) and then as general secretary of the Central Committee of the Communist party (1922–1953), Stalin showed natural talent as a political strategist. His familiarity with non-Russian nationalities was a great asset in his dealings with the ethnic diversity and unrest in the vast Soviet state. Unlike other party leaders who had lived in exile in western Europe before the revolution, Stalin had little knowledge of the West. Stalin also lacked Lenin's image as the legitimate and charismatic leader. After Lenin's death in 1924, Stalin shrewdly promoted such an image for himself and bolstered his own reputation by orchestrating a cult of worship for Lenin.

In 1929 Stalin used the occasion of his fiftieth birthday to fashion for himself a reputation as the living hero of the Soviet state. Icons, statues, busts, and images of all sorts of both Lenin and Stalin appeared everywhere in public buildings, schoolrooms, and homes. He systematically began eliminating his rivals, so that he alone stood unchallenged as Lenin's true successor. The Stalin cult consolidated his personal power and prepared the way for his plan of rapid industrialization.

The First Five-Year Plan.   The cult of Stalin coincided with the first Five-Year Plan, which initiated an economic revolution. Between 1929 and 1936, the period covered by the first two five-year plans, truncated because of their proclaimed success, Stalin laid the foundation for an urban industrial society in the Soviet Union. By brutally squeezing profits out of the agricultural sector, Stalin managed to increase heavy industrial production between 300 and 600 percent. A simple slogan summarized the political philosophy that justified Stalin's economic plans: "Socialism in one country!"

"Socialism in one country" committed the Soviet Union to rapid industrialization as the only way to preserve socialism in the Soviet Union. The failure of revolutionary movements in the West was now used as the stick with which to beat the supporters of the NEP. Socialism meant machines and technology and economic power for Stalin, not just a system of political rule. The NEP guaranteed Russian backwardness and communist failure, Stalin argued. The revolution was in danger and must be saved. Stalin insisted that only he, as a dynamic leader interpreting the will of the great Lenin, could move the revolution ahead. "Those who fall behind get beaten." Thus spoke Stalin of the Soviet Union's compelling need to industrialize.

Stalin made steel the idol of the new age. The Soviet Union needed heavy machinery to build the future. An industrial labor force was created virtually overnight as peasant men and women were placed at workbenches and before the vast furnaces of modern metallurgical plants. The number of women in the industrial work force tripled in the decade after 1929. The reliability of official indices varied, but there is little doubt that heavy industrial production soared in the first Five-Year Plan (1929–1932). The Russian people were constantly reminded that no sacrifice could be too great in producing steel and iron.

When he first began to deal with the grain crisis of 1928, Stalin did not intend collective agriculture as a solution. But by the end of 1929 the increasingly repressive measures instituted by the state against the peasants had led both to collectivization and to the deportation of *kulaks*, the derisive term for wealthy peasants that literally means "the tight-fisted ones." Stalin achieved forced collectivization by confiscating land and establishing collective farms run by the state. Within a few months, half of all peasant farms were collectivized. By 1938 private land was virtually eliminated. The state set prices, controlled distribution, and selected crops with the intention of ensuring a steady food supply and freeing a rural labor force for heavy industry. More as a publicity ploy than a statement of fact, the Five-Year Plan was declared a success after only three years. It was a success in one important sense: It did lay the foundations of the Soviet planned economy, in which the state made all decisions about production, distribution, and prices. The leap forward toward urban industrial society had been taken.

Enormous human cost was the price of the rapid changes that occurred under the first Five-Year Plan. Collectivization meant misery for the 25 million peasant families who suffered under it. At least five million peasants died between 1929 and 1932. Peasants who resisted collectivization retaliated by destroying their own crops and livestock. Collectivization ripped apart the fabric of village life, destroyed families, and sent homeless peasants into exile. Rapid industrial development shattered the delicate shells of the lives of millions of people. Stalin considered collectivization of agriculture the only way to develop an industrial sector overnight. He, as tsars before him, saw that Russia could be carried into the future only on the backs of its peasants.

The Comintern and World Politics. In addition to promoting its internal economic development, the Soviet Union had to worry about survival in a world political system composed entirely of capitalist countries. After the Bolshevik revolution in 1917, Lenin had fully expected that other socialist revolutions would follow throughout the world, especially in central and western Europe. These revolutions would destroy capitalism and secure Russia's place in a new world order. But as the prospects for world proletarian revolution evaporated, Soviet leaders sought to protect their revolutionary country from what they saw as a hostile capitalist world. They used diplomacy for this purpose. The end of the Allied intervention and blockade of Russia allowed the Bolshevik state to initiate diplomatic relations with the West, beginning with the Treaty of Rapallo signed with Germany in 1921. By 1924 all the major countries of the world—with the exception of the United States— had established diplomatic relations with the Soviet Union. In 1928 the USSR cooperated in the preparation of a world disarmament conference to be held in Geneva and joined western European powers in a commitment to peace. The United States and the Soviet Union exchanged ambassadors for the first time in 1933.

In addition to diplomatic relations, the Soviet state in 1919 encouraged various national Communist parties to form an association for the purpose of promoting and coordinating the coming world revolution. This Communist International, or Comintern, was based in Moscow and included representatives from 37 countries by 1920. As it became clear that a world revolution was not imminent, the Comintern concerned itself with the ideological purity of its member parties. Under Lenin's direction, the Soviet Communist party determined policy for all the member parties.

Bukharin and Stalin shared a view of the Comintern that prevailed from 1924 to 1929: The Comintern must take as its starting point the fact that Western capitalist societies were, for the moment at least, stable. Since the collapse of capitalism was not imminent, the Comintern should work to promote the unity of working classes everywhere and should cooperate with existing worker organizations.

In 1929, however, Stalin argued that advanced capitalist societies were teetering on the brink of new wars and revolutions. As a result, the Comintern must seek to sever the ties between foreign Communist parties and social democratic parties in the West in order to prepare for the revolutionary struggle. Stalin purged the Comintern of dissenters, and he decreed a policy of noncooperation in Europe from 1929 to 1933. As a result, socialism in Europe was badly split between communists and democratic socialists precisely at the moment when new right-wing and fascist groups were making their bid for power.

Women and the Family in the New Soviet State

The building of the new Soviet state exacted high costs from the Russian people, in particular from women. Russian women had been active in the revolution from the beginning. Lenin and the Bolshevik leaders were committed to the liberation of women, who, like workers, were considered to be oppressed under capitalism. Lenin denounced housework as "barbarously unproductive, petty, nerve-wracking, stultifying, and crushing drudgery." In its early days the Soviet state pledged to protect the rights of mothers without narrowing women's opportunities or restricting women's role in the family.

After the October revolution of 1917, the Bolsheviks passed a new law establishing equality for women within marriage. In 1920 abortion was legalized. New legislation established the right to divorce and removed the stigma from illegitimacy. Communes, calling themselves "laboratories of revolution," experimented with sexual equality. Russian women were enfranchised in 1917, the first women in the major countries to win this right in national elections. The Russian revolution went further than any revolution in history toward the legal liberation of women within such a short span of time.

These advances, as utopian as they appeared to women in the West, did not deal with the problems faced by the majority of Russian women. Bolshevik legislation did little to address the special economic hardships of peasant and factory women. Paid maternity leaves and nursing breaks were required by law. But these guarantees became a source of discrimination against women workers who, under the NEP, were the last hired and first fired by employers trying to limit expenses. Divorce legislation was hardly a blessing for women with children, since men incurred no financial responsibility toward their offspring in terminating a marriage. Even as legislation was being passed in the early days of the new Soviet state, women were losing ground in the struggle for equal rights and independent economic survival.

By the early 1930s, reforms affecting women were in trouble due in large part to a plummeting birthrate. This decline created special worries for Soviet planners, who forecast doom if the rate was not reversed. In 1936 women's right to choose to end a first pregnancy was revoked. In the following decade all abortions were made illegal. Sexuality was a state concern and homosexuality was declared a criminal offense. The family was glorified as the mainstay of the socialist order and the independence of women was challenged as a threat to Soviet productivity. While motherhood was idealized, the Stalinist drive to industrialize could not dispense with full-time women workers. The "new woman" of the revolutionary period gave way to the post-1936 woman, who was depicted as the perfect mother who equaled her husband's productivity in the workplace, ran the household, and raised a large family.

Women's double burden in the home and workplace became heavier during Stalin's reign. Most Russian women held full-time jobs in the factories or on the farms. They also worked what they called a "second shift" in running a household and taking care of children. In the West, the growth of a consumer economy lightened women's labor in the home to some extent. In Russia procuring the simplest necessities was women's work that required waiting in long lines for hours. Lack of indoor plumbing meant that women spent more hours hauling water for their families at the end of a working day. In such ways, rapid industrialization exacted its special price from Soviet women.

$\mathcal{T}$he Promise of Fascism

The experiences of the war and postwar conditions were the catalysts for the emergence of the new mass movement of fascism in Europe. The Great War had created a political vacuum caused by the crisis in liberal values. In condemning the war and its costs, new fascist leaders, who tended to start their political careers as social reformers and even socialists, proposed a radical reformation of the status quo.

In the Soviet Union, Bolshevik leaders reassured their people that socialism was the only way of dealing with the weaknesses and inequities of the world capitalist system laid bare in the world war. In its initial condemnations of the capitalist economy and liberal political institutions and values, fascism sounded very like socialism. Fascists employed revolutionary language similar to that of the Left, while manipulating the political symbols of the Right—the nation, the flag, and the army—in radically new ways. Fascism promised to steer a course between the uncertainties and exploitation of a liberal capitalist system and the revolutionary upheaval and expropriation of a socialist system. Fascism was ultranationalist, and the use of force was central to its appeal.

The word *fascism* is derived from the Latin *fasces*, the name for the bundle of rods with ax head carried by the magistrates of the Roman Empire. Fascism was rooted in the mass political movements of the late nineteenth century, which emphasized nationalism, antiliberal values, and a politics of the irrational. The electoral successes of the German variant, National Socialism, or nazism, were just beginning in the late 1920s. In the same period, fascist movements were making their appearance in England, Hungary, Spain, and France. But none was more successful and none demanded more attention than the fascist experiment in Italy that inspired observers throughout the West to consider emulation.

Mussolini's Italy

Being on the side of the victors in World War I did not alter the fact that Italy was a poor nation. The peace settlement of 1919 had resulted in a sense of disillusionment and betrayal for many Italians, who felt they had not received what they were promised for entering the war. A recently created electoral system based on universal manhood suffrage had produced parliamentary chaos and ministerial instability. The lack of coherent political programs only heightened the general disapproval with government that accompanied the peace negotiations. People were beginning to doubt the parliamentary regime's hold on the future. It was under these circumstances that the Fascist party, led by Benito Mussolini (1883–1945), entered politics in 1920 by attacking the large Socialist and Popular (Catholic) parties.

Named after the Mexican revolutionary Benito Juárez, Mussolini was

Benito Mussolini (center foreground) at the time of the march on Rome. Il Duce himself did not participate in the march, but after his fascist followers had taken over the capital, King Victor Emmanuel asked Mussolini to form a government.

instructed by his blacksmith father in the tenets of radical socialist politics and had begun his political career before the war as a socialist. The young Mussolini earned certification as an elementary school teacher but did not pursue education as a career. Instead, he left school to engage in socialist political activities for which he was arrested numerous times and placed under state surveillance. An ardent nationalist, Mussolini volunteered for combat in World War I and was promoted to the rank of corporal. Injured in early 1917 by an exploding shell detonated during firing practice, he returned to Milan to continue his work as editor of *Il Populo d'Italia* (The People of Italy), the newspaper he founded in 1914 to promote Italian participation in the war.

Mussolini yearned to be the leader of a revolution in Italy comparable to that directed by Lenin in Russia. Although his doctrinal allegiance to socialism was beginning to flag, Mussolini recognized, like Lenin, the power of the printed word to stir political passions. Emphasizing nationalist goals and vague measures of socioeconomic transformation, Mussolini identified a new enemy for Italy: bolshevism. He organized his followers into the Fascist party, a political movement that by utilizing strict party discipline quickly developed its own national network.

Many fascists were former socialists and war veterans like Mussolini who were disillusioned with postwar government. They dreamed of Italy as a great world power, as it had been in the days of ancient Rome. Their enemies were not only communists with their international outlook but also the big businesses, which they felt drained Italy's resources and kept its people poor and powerless. Panicky members of the lower middle classes sought security against the economic uncertainties of inflation and were willing to endorse violence to achieve it. Unions were to be feared because they used strikes to further their demands for higher salaries and better working conditions for their members while other social groups languished. Near civil war erupted as Italian communists and fascists clashed violently in street battles in the early 1920s. The fascists succeeded in overthrowing city governments and began entering national politics. In spite of its visibility on the national political scene, the Fascist party was still very much a minority party when Mussolini refused to serve as a junior minister in the new government in 1922.

His refusal to serve as representative of a minority party reflected Mussolini's belief that the fascists must be in charge. On 28 October 1922, the fascists undertook their famous March on Rome, which followed similar fascist takeovers in Milan and Bologna. Mussolini's followers now occupied the capital. This event marked the beginning of the end of parliamentary government in Italy and the gradual emergence of fascist dictatorship and institutionalized violence. Rising unemployment and severe inflation contributed to the politically deteriorating situation that helped bring Mussolini to power.

Destruction and violence, not the ballot box, became fascism's most successful tools for securing political power. *Squadristi*, armed bands of fascist thugs, attacked their political enemies, both Catholic and socialist, destroyed private property, dismantled the printing presses of adversary groups, and generally terrorized both rural and urban populations. By the end of 1922, fascists could claim a following of 300,000 members, who endorsed the new politics of intimidation.

The fascists achieved their first majority in the Chamber of Deputies by using violent tactics of intimidation to secure votes. One outspoken socialist critic of fascist violence, Giacomo Matteotti (1885–1924), was murdered by Mussolini's subordinates. The deed threatened the survival of Mussolini's government as 150 Socialist, Liberal, and Popular party deputies resigned in protest. Mussolini chose this moment to consolidate his position by arresting and silencing his enemies to preserve order. Within two years, fascists were firmly in control, monopolizing politics, suppressing a free press, creating a secret police force, and transforming social and economic policies. Mussolini destroyed political parties and made Italy into a one-party dictatorship.

In 1925 the Fascist party entered into an agreement with Italian industrialists that gave industry a position of privilege protected by the state in return for its support. Mussolini presented this partnership as the end to class conflict, but in fact it ensured the dominance of capital and the control of labor and professional groups. A corrupt bureaucracy filled with Mussolini's cronies and run on bribes took shape to organize the new relationship between big business and the state. With the Fascist party, Mussolini spoke of creating a "corporativist" economy, that is, one that eliminated the free market, and through planning and management, reallocated economic activities for maximum efficiency. Corporativism was used for rhetorical effect, while big business controlled economic organization on its own terms. Workers gained little from corporativist rhetoric and in fact lost representation with the weakening of trade unions.

Mussolini, himself an atheist, recognized the importance of the Catholic church in securing his regime. In 1870 when Italy had been unified, the pope was deprived of his territories in Rome. This event, which quickly became known as the "Roman Question," proved to be the source of ongoing problems for Italian governments. In February 1929 Mussolini settled matters with Pope Pius XI in the Lateran Treaty and the accompanying Concordat, which granted to the pope sovereignty over the territory around St. Peter's Basilica and the Vatican. The treaty also protected the role of the Catholic church in education and guaranteed that Italian marriage laws would conform to Catholic dogma. Tensions resurfaced in the 1930s, when the pope condemned the "pagan intentions" of fascism. For the most part, however, the Lateran Treaty laid to rest an important problem plaguing Italian rule.

By 1929 *Il Duce*, or the leader, as Mussolini preferred to be called, was at the height of his popularity and his power. Apparent political harmony had been achieved by ruthlessly crushing fascism's opponents. The agreement with the pope, which restored harmony with the Church, was matched by a new sense of order and accomplishment in Italian society and the economy. But as Europe and the world were to learn, fascism did not stop in Italy and did not depend on the person of Benito Mussolini for its success. Fascism appealed to frightened middle classes outside Italy who were losing their footing in a world they no longer comprehended.

The Failure of Democracy in Germany

In September 1918 the leaders of the German High Command, Erich Ludendorff (1865–1937) and Paul von Hindenburg (1847–1934), knowing that the
German war effort was a lost cause, decided that a constitutional monarchy
must be introduced in Germany. Their intention was to save the throne of
Emperor Wilhelm II and to save themselves by handing the responsibility for
the government over to the socialist and liberal politicians who were dedicated
to ending the war, getting German soldiers home, and demobilizing the army.
Popular uprisings in the navy and in urban areas followed, forcing the emperor
to abdicate. In spring 1919 a national assembly meeting in the city of Weimar
produced Germany's first democratic constitution. The Weimar Republic
was born.

The Weimar Republic was in trouble from the start. Germany's first
democracy came into existence saddled with a harsh peace. Many Germans
identified the new government with defeat and humiliation. Rumors spread
that the German military had never really been defeated and that communists
and Jews now associated with the new government had "stabbed the German
army in the back" on the home front. The harsh terms of the Treaty of
Versailles compounded the negative image of the Weimar Republic. Lost
territory and people, destroyed markets, a vastly reduced military force, and
reparations payments were the legacy of the new democratic experiment.

Born of political revolution and social upheaval, the Weimar Republic
faced the challenges of establishing its legitimacy and maintaining social
peace. Yet it lacked a democratic tradition on which to draw. Traditional ruling
groups—the Prussian military, and agrarian and bureaucratic elites—preserved their power and privileges even as democratic institutions struggled for
existence. Political as well as economic power continued to be concentrated in
the hands of the privileged elite that had ruled the Second Reich.

Repeated economic, political, and diplomatic crises of the 1920s buffeted
Germany's internal stability. Most Germans considered reparations to be an
unfair burden, so onerous that payment should be evaded and resisted in every
way possible. The German government did not actually promote inflation in
order to avoid paying reparations but it did do so to avoid a postwar recession,
revive industrial production, and maintain high employment. But the moderate
inflation that stimulated the economy spun out of control into destructive
hyperinflation. Weimar bore a burden of blame for that disaster, too.

The fiscal problems of Weimar obscure the fact that, in the postwar period,
Germany experienced real economic growth. German industry advanced,
productivity was high, and German workers flexed their union muscles to
secure better wages. Weimar committed itself to large expenditures for social
welfare programs, including unemployment insurance. By 1930 social welfare
was responsible for 40 percent of all public expenditures, compared to 19
percent before the war. All these changes, apparently fostering the well-being
of the German people, aggravated the fears of German big businesspeople,
who resented the trade unions and the perceived trend toward socialism. The

*The runaway inflation of the 1920s is dramatized
by this photo of a German housewife who is lighting
the cooking fire with millions of marks. She
declared that it was cheaper to use the worthless
currency for kindling than to buy wood with it.*

lower middle classes felt cheated and economically threatened by inflation.
They were a politically volatile group, susceptible to the antidemocratic
appeals of some of Weimar's critics.

Constitutional provisions that allowed for the constant wrangling of a
multiparty system divided the Weimar Republic. Political parties formed and
destroyed cabinet after cabinet while Germany's real problems remained—the
humiliating peace treaty, reparations, and a weak economic structure. As a
result, growing numbers of Germans expressed disgust with parliamentary
democracy. The Depression dealt a staggering blow to the Weimar Republic in

1929 as American loans were withdrawn and German unemployment skyrocketed. The government could not fulfill its commitment to supporting the unemployed in hard times. By 1930 the antagonisms among the parties was so great that the parliament was no longer effective in ruling Germany. As chancellor from 1930 to 1932, Centrist leader Heinrich Brüning (1885–1970) attempted to break this impasse by overriding the Weimar constitution. This move opened the door to enemies of the republic, and Brüning was forced to resign.

Everyone with a grievance now blamed the Weimar Republic. German industrialists denounced the high costs of social welfare and reparations. Other Germans saw their savings and their income dwindling, first in the inflation and then in the Depression. Germany's first experiment in democracy was collapsing. The Depression and the harsh Versailles Treaty gave ammunition to Wiemar's enemies. One man in particular knew how to exploit Weimar's weaknesses for his own political ends. That man was Adolf Hitler.

The Beginnings of the Nazi Movement

Just as Stalin was born a Georgian and not an ethnic Russian, Adolf Hitler (1889–1945) was born an Austrian outside the German fatherland he came to rule. Hitler, the son of a customs agent who worked on the Austrian side of the border with Germany, came from a middle-class family with social pretensions. Aimlessness and failure marked Hitler's early life. Denied admission to architecture school, he took odd jobs to survive. Hitler welcomed the outbreak of war in 1914 that put an end to his self-described sleepwalking. He volunteered immediately for service in the German army. Wounded and gassed at the front, he was twice awarded the Iron Cross for bravery in action.

Hitler's war experiences were not unique. He later described what he had learned from war in terms of the solidarity of struggle against a common enemy and the purity of heroism. The army provided him with a sense of security and direction. What he learned from the peace that followed was an equally powerful lesson and determined his commitment to a career in politics. Hitler profoundly believed in the stab-in-the-back legend: Germany had not lost the war, it had been defeated from within. The army had been on the verge of victory when a revolution took place, led, Hitler believed, by Jews and communists, people he called "the November Criminals." It was they who asked the Allies for an armistice and signed the humiliating Treaty of Versailles. The Weimar Republic that resulted from their revolution continued to betray the German people by taxing wages to pay reparations. His highly distorted and false view of the origins of the Republic and its policies was the basis for his demand that the "Weimar System" must be abolished and replaced by a Nazi regime.

Hitler had become the chief of the National Socialist German Workers' party and surrounded himself with men who shared his hatred of Weimar and his political programs—Joseph Goebbels (1897–1945), a master of mass

This photograph of Hitler miming to a recording of his speeches was one of a series he commissioned to help him improve his hold over an audience. His remarkable oratorical skills contributed greatly to his success with a disillusioned public.

propaganda; Hermann Göring (1893–1946), an air force squadron commander during World War I; and Ernst Röhm (1887–1934), who formed the private army known as the SA (*Sturmabteilung*), Hitler's Brown Shirts.

Prominent among Hitler's followers were army veterans who felt frustration over German military defeat and the postwar economic hardships of inflation and unemployment. Soldiers brought their battlefront experiences home with them. Some of these young ex-servicemen committed themselves to idealism and peace, but others did not readjust to the civilian life of Weimar and were eager to hear Hitler's promises.

Hitler believed that Weimar was ready to be overthrown in 1923, as Germany was buffeted by French occupation and hyperinflation. Hitler's willingness to use violence for political ends surfaced when he and General Erich Ludendorff, German Quartermaster General in World War I, carried out the Beer Hall Putsch in Munich in 1923. Hitler's plan was to seize control of local government in Munich, take over the leadership of all right-wing nationalist, racist organizations in Bavaria, march on Berlin, and do away with the Weimar Republic. Hitler tried to signal the beginning of "the national revolution" by firing a revolver into the ceiling of a Munich beer hall. He and his small band of followers then marched toward the center of the city but were stopped by the rifles of the army.

For his activities Hitler served nine months of a five-year sentence. In jail he began writing the first volume of his autobiography, *Mein Kampf* (My Struggle). In this turgid work, he condemned the decadence of Western society and singled out for special contempt Jews, Bolsheviks, and middle-class

During the years of the Weimar Republic, thousands of middle-class people were ruined by inflation and the continuing depression. The humiliating experience of standing in line for bread made such people susceptible to the message of Adolf Hitler, who promised a return to prosperity.

liberals, who he believed had betrayed Germany and were preventing it from becoming strong again. Hitler learned one important lesson from his failed attempt. He learned that he could succeed against the German republic only from within, by coming to power legally. By 1928 he had a small party of about one hundred thousand Nazis. Hitler had modified his anticapitalist message, appealed to the discontented small farmers, and tailored his nationalist sentiments to a frightened middle class.

The commitment to electoral gains guided the organization of the Nazi party in its bid for parliamentary power in the late 1920s. Although the Nazi party never controlled a majority of parliamentary seats, it had become the single largest party by 1932. It appeared to be the only mass party that could form a government to engineer a way out of the crisis of the Great Depression. The great irony of fascism in Germany was that as an antidemocratic and antiparliamentary movement, it successfully manipulated democracy and parliamentary politics for its own ends to ensure the destruction of the Weimar Republic between 1930 and 1933.

The period from 1921 to 1932 is one of the most difficult decades in the history of the West to characterize. Many today look on these years as a period of holding one's breath, part of an interlude between two world wars, a time-out in the 30 years of war (1914–1945) in the first half of the twentieth century. It is undoubtedly true that the problems which brought about the war in 1914 were still in place throughout the 1920s. Nationalist feelings intensified and nationalist conflicts proliferated as new borders delineated new animosities, especially in central and eastern Europe.

Yet the 1920s was also a time of great idealism and greater hope that the horrors of war might teach a lasting commitment to peace and that technology could be used to create a better and brighter future. Economic productivity in the late 1920s created a new and deceptively secure prosperity.

Those who probed beneath the surface could find the signs that existing political and economic structures were inadequate to deal with new problems of inflation, depression, and economic collapse. Old problems were demanding new solutions—often violent ones. Empty statements about commitments to peace were matched by secret plans for rearmament. Fascism proposed a third way, not liberalism's way and not communism's way, to address the challenges of power and stability in the modern state.

Suggestions for Further Reading

International Politics and Economic Nationalism

*Derek H. Aldcroft, *From Versailles to Wall Street, 1919–1929* (Berkeley: University of California Press, 1977). Traces the recovery of the international economy and the systemic forces of its disintegration in the 1920s, with special attention to such areas as war debts, reparations, the gold standard, the agricultural sector, and patterns of international lending.

Marshall M. Lee and Wolfgang Michalka, *German Foreign Policy, 1917–1933: Continuity or Break?* (Leamington Spa, England: Berg, 1987). A solid and synthetic treatment of Weimar diplomacy that takes into account the historiographical debates over revisionism and expansion.

*Melvyn P. Leffler, *The Elusive Quest: America's Pursuit of European Stability and French Security, 1919–1933* (Chapel Hill: University of North Carolina Press, 1979). Examines the economic and financial imperatives guiding U.S. foreign policy after World War I and identifies a particular Republican party approach labeled "economic diplomacy." Special attention is paid to European stabilization, French security, and Germany's rehabilitation.

*Joseph Rothschild, *East Central Europe Between the Two World Wars* (Seattle: University of Washington Press, 1983). A balanced survey of interwar developments in Poland, Czechoslovakia, Hungary, Yugoslavia, Romania, Bulgaria, Albania, and the Baltic states, highlighting internal weaknesses and external vulnerabilities. A concluding chapter covers cultural contributions.

*Stephen A. Schuker, *The End of French Predominance in Europe: The Financial Crisis of 1924 and the Adoption of the Dawes Plan* (Chapel Hill: University of North Carolina Press, 1976). Locates the decline of France as a great power in the financial crisis of 1924 and the diplomacy of reparations and examines the domestic bases for French powerlessness.

The Soviet Union's Separate Path

*Stephen E. Cohen, *Bukharin and the Bolshevik Revolution: A Political Biography, 1888–1938* (Oxford, England: Oxford University Press, 1980). This milestone work is a general history of the period as well as a political and intellectual biography of Bukharin, "the last Bolshevik," who supported an evolutionary road to modernization and socialism and whose policies were an alternative to Stalinism.

*Sheila Fitzpatrick, *The Russian Revolution, 1917–1932* (Oxford, England: Oxford University Press, 1985). Arguing from the premise that the revolutionary upheaval did not end with the Bolshevik seizure of power in November 1917, Fitzpatrick interprets the developments of the 1920s and early 1930s, including the NEP and the first Five-Year Plan, as stages in a single revolutionary process.

*Robert C. Tucker, *Stalin as Revolutionary, 1879–1929: A Study in History and Personality* (New York: W.W. Norton, 1973). Traces Stalin's development from his Georgian childhood to his fiftieth year, when he established himself as the new hero of the Soviet state. Tucker uses Freudian terms of analysis in considering Stalin's hero identification with Lenin.

The Promise of Fascism

*Volker R. Berghahn, *Modern Germany: Society, Economy and Politics in the Twentieth Century* (Cambridge, England: Cambridge University Press, 1987). Considers the particular challenges of rapid industrialization faced by Germany and how they interacted with social tensions and political conflict.

Eberhard Kolb, *The Weimar Republic*, translated from the German by P. S. Falla (London: Unwin Hyman, 1988). An introduction to the history of Germany's first republic both as a historic survey and as an examination of the basic problems and trends in research.

*Adrian Lyttelton, *The Seizure of Power: Fascism in Italy, 1919–1929* (New York: Scribner's, 1973). Addresses the question of why fascism first took root in Italy.

22

Crisis and Global Conflict, 1933–1945

The Screams from Guernica

Rarely does a piece of art scream out. The mural *Guernica* is different. Listen to the painting shown here. It is a painting whose images convey sounds, the shrieks of terror, fear, suffering, and death. There is a chaos of noise here that seems at odds with the drab grays, black, and white, the monochromatic colorlessness of the artist's palette. But no, the lack of color only heightens the noise and allows us to focus on the sound, the screams that come from open mouths of human and beast on the canvas. Death and brutality reverberate throughout the painting. The open mouths of the dead baby's mother, the bull standing behind her, the small bird to the right of the bull, and the wounded horse at the center of the canvas emit fear like projectiles, beak and tongues thrusting forth in pointed daggers.

Pablo Picasso (1881–1973) painted this great mural in May and June 1937 for the Spanish Pavilion of the International Exhibition to be held in Paris. He called it *Guernica* in commemoration of the bombing of the small Basque town in Spain by German and Italian planes at the end of April 1937. The destruction of Guernica was an event that shocked the world and devastated the Spanish artist, then living in France. Working in collaboration with the insurgent forces of Francisco Franco (1892–1975), German planes dropped bomb after bomb on the ancient city, destroying it in three and a half hours. Their purpose was to cut off the retreat of opposing troops and to terrorize civilians through saturation bombing. Noncombatants were no longer just hapless bystanders but were, in fact, the very targets of indiscriminate killing. Picasso demonstrates this well in the women and children depicted in his painting.

Guernica is a huge canvas, measuring over eleven feet high and twenty-five feet long. It dwarfs spectators who stand before it, enveloping them in a modern-day apocalypse of contorted bodies. Picasso was well aware of Poussin's *Massacre of the Innocents* (see introduction to Chapter 13) and deliberately used the traditional religious symbols of the Madonna and Child and the Pietà as models for his terrifying image of maternity.

We do not look at war directly in the mural but at the terror it creates in this modern-day version of needless slaughter. The lips of the baby, who hangs like a limp rag doll in the arms of its despairing mother on the far left of the canvas, are sealed in the silence of death. The mother finds her counterpoint in the figure of the limping woman in the right foreground, who drags behind her a wounded arm and a swollen knee. Above her a woman, gaping in disbelief and clutching her breasts in anguish, raises a lamp over the scene. On the far right is a fourth woman, trapped in the flames of a burning building. She appears to be exploding upward in terrified petition. On the ground under the horse lies a dead man with his head and arm severed from his body, clutching a broken sword and flower whose petals wait to be picked in his right hand. The presentation of his head as a piece of statuary fallen from its pedestal reinforces the bloodless horror of his death. His left palm is crisscrossed with the lines of fate or perhaps marked with the toil of heavy labor. Suspended over the scene like a huge eye is a naked light bulb, symbol of technology, illuminating the timelessness of the theme of the horror of war.

In one of his rare moments of self-interpretation, Picasso explained to a public eager to grasp the mural's symbolism that the horse whose side is opened by a terrible gash is "the people," victimized by incomprehensible cruelty. The bull is an enigmatic figure symbolizing, Picasso tells us, darkness and brutality. The horned beast appears as a powerful and vulnerable witness to this scene of needless destruction.

No matter how you read the individual symbols in the painting, *Guernica* is above all a condemnation of war. In its classic simplicity, Picasso's drama is cartoonlike in stripping images down to their essences of suffering and grief. *Guernica* has been hailed as the most significant painting of the twentieth century. His greatness as an artist, Picasso claimed, derived from his ability to understand his time. In *Guernica* he presents us with a picture of Western civilization that is brutal and horrible. Subsequent events made Germany's actions in the Spanish Civil War seem like a dress rehearsal for atrocities and destruction, when Germany bombed the population centers of Warsaw, Rotterdam, and London. Some years later, during the Second World War, a Nazi official challenged Picasso with a photograph of the great mural, "So it was you who did this." The artist answered, "No, you did."

*P*olitical Polarization in the 1930s

The fragile postwar stability of the 1920s crumbled under the pressures of economic depression, ongoing national antagonisms, and insecurity in the international arena. Europe after 1932 was plagued by the consequences of economic collapse, fascist success, and the growing threat of armed conflict. Parliamentary institutions were fighting—and losing—a tug-of-war with authoritarian movements. A fascist regime was in place in Italy. Political and electoral defeats eroded democratic and liberal principles in Germany's Weimar Republic. Dictatorships triumphed in Spain and in much of eastern and central Europe. Liberal parliamentary governments were failing to solve the economic and social challenges of the postwar years. In the democratic nations of France, Great Britain, and, during the brief period from 1931 to 1936, Spain, parliamentary institutions appeared to be persevering. But even here, polarization and increasing intransigence on both the Left and the Right threatened the future of democratic politics.

The exclusion of the Soviet Union from Western internationalism both reflected the crisis and exacerbated it. The Bolshevik revolution had served as a political catalyst among workers in the West, attracting them to the possibility of radical solutions. That potential radicalization aggravated class antagonisms where mass politics prevailed and drove political leaders to seek conservative solutions as a means of stabilizing class politics.

Dictatorships in Control

Dictatorships were the most prevalent form of government in interwar Europe. The values of nineteenth-century liberalism that had produced parliamentary institutions, constitutions, and representative government based on elections offered no quick solution to the problems of economic depression

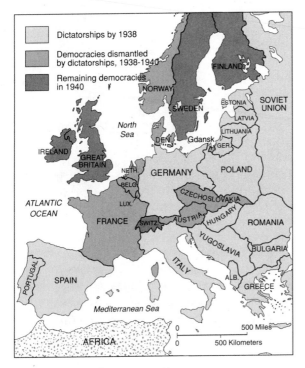

Europe: Types of government

and the violence of political extremism. Men who ruled by virtue of charismatic appeal and armed force promised an escape from parliamentary chaos, party wranglings, and the threat of communism. Dictatorships appealed to middle classes who feared loss of their property to socialists and loss of their money to the vagaries of international markets.

The move toward dictatorship appeared relentless in the interwar period. In 1920, of the 28 states in Europe, 26 were parliamentary democracies. By the end of 1940, only five democracies remained: the United Kingdom, Ireland, Sweden, Finland, and Switzerland. The rest of Europe was under dictatorial rule. The European dictatorships of the 1930s displayed a variety of forms. On the Left, the "dictatorship of the proletariat" in the Soviet Union was in fact a regime driven by the ruthless brutality of Joseph Stalin toward the goal of building socialism. Other dictatorships were on the Right. Italy and Germany each constructed fascist dictatorships that regarded Soviet communism as their mortal enemy. The Soviet Union, in turn, saw fascism as a serious threat.

Stalin's Plans and Purges. In 1933 Joseph Stalin announced the second Five-Year Plan, which lasted until 1937. The success of this plan—especially in the areas of heavy industry, machinery, and metalworks—reduced considerably the Soviet Union's dependence on foreign imports. The basic physical plant for armaments production was in place by 1937, and resources continued to be shifted away from consumer goods to heavy industrial development. This industrial development, and the collectivization of agriculture, brought growing urbanization. By 1939 one in three people were living in cities, compared to one in six in 1926. In his commitment to increased production, Stalin introduced incentives and differential wage scales into the workplace at odds with the principles and programs of the original Bolshevik revolution. Stricter discipline was enforced; absenteeism was punished with severe fines or loss of employment. Workers who exceeded their quotas were rewarded and honored.

The purges dealt a severe blow to the command of the army and resulted in a shortage of qualified industrial personnel, slowing industrial growth. As scapegoats, the victims of the purges, however, contributed to the state's ability to sustain economic expansion. These "class enemies" helped Stalin channel discontent away from the Soviet state and helped him maintain absolute power. If the Soviet people did not have eggs it was because of the evil plotting of these "spies," "traitors," and "wreckers," who smashed eggs and exploited worker discontent. The Great Purge coerced the Soviet people at a time when they were being asked to make great sacrifices in the drive for industrialization. It prevented any possible dissension or opposition within the USSR at a time when the "foreign threat" posed by Nazi Germany was becoming increasingly serious. Stalin was able to maintain loyalty to his personal authority. His personal dictatorship was assured.

The human suffering associated with the dislocation and heavy workloads of rapid, coerced industrialization cannot be measured. Planned growth brought with it a top-heavy and often inefficient bureaucracy, and that bureaucracy ensured that the Soviet Union was the most highly centralized of the European states. The growing threat of foreign war meant an even greater diversion of resources from consumer goods to war industries, beginning with the third Five-Year Plan in 1938. Stalin was well aware of the Soviet Union's backwardness in preparations for war. He was also aware that time was running out.

Mussolini's Plans for Empire.   In spite of official claims, fascist Italy had not done well in riding out the Depression. A large rural sector masked the problems of high unemployment by absorbing an urban work force without jobs. Corporatism, a system of economic self-rule by interest groups, was a sham promoted on paper by Benito Mussolini that had little to do with the dominance of the Italian economy by big business. By lending money to Italian businesses on the verge of bankruptcy, the government acquired a controlling interest in key industries, including steel, shipping heavy machinery, and electricity.

As fascism failed to initiate effective social programs, Mussolini's popularity plummeted. In the hope of boosting his sagging image, Il Duce committed Italy to a foreign policy of imperial conquest. Italy had conquered Ottoman-controlled Libya in North Africa in 1911. Now in the 1930s Mussolini targeted Ethiopia for his expansionist aims and ordered Italian troops to invade that east African kingdom in October 1935. Using poison gas and aerial bombing, the Italian army defeated the native troops of Ethiopian emperor Haile Selassie (1930–1974). Western democracies, under the pressure of public opinion, cried out against the wanton and unwarranted attack, but Mussolini succeeded in proclaiming Ethiopia an Italian territory.

The invasion of Ethiopia exposed the ineffectiveness of the League of Nations to stop such flagrant violations. Great Britain and France took no action other than to express their disapproval of Italy's conquest. Yet a rift opened up between these two western European nations and Italy. Mussolini had distanced himself from the Nazi state in the first years of the German regime's existence and he was critical of Hitler's plans for rearmament. Now, in light of the disapproval of Britain and France, Mussolini turned to Germany for support. In the summer of 1936, Mussolini supplied military assistance to Francisco Franco and his insurgents in Spain, an act that Hitler seconded. A few months later, in October 1936, Italy aligned itself with Germany in what Mussolini called the "Rome-Berlin Axis." Germany and Italy agreed to offer support in any offensive or defensive war; the agreement, known as the Pact of Steel, in fact bound Italy militarily to Germany.

Mussolini pursued other imperialist goals within Europe. The small Balkan nation of Albania entered into a series of agreements with Mussolini beginning in the mid-1920s that made it dependent financially and militarily on Italian aid. By 1933 Albanian independence had been undermined by this "friendship" with its stronger neighbor. In order not to be outdone by Hitler, who was at the time dismantling Czechoslovakia, Mussolini invaded and annexed Albania in April 1939, ending the fiction that Albania was an Italian protectorate.

Hitler and the Third Reich

Hitler's rise to power in the 1930s attracted admirers as well as critics in western Europe and the United States. For many, the supposed efficiency and organization of Hitler's regime outweighed the suspension of civil liberties and the high social costs, the extent of which few understood at the time. With his magnetic appeal, Hitler inspired and manipulated the devotion of nearly all who heard him speak. Leni Riefenstahl, a young filmmaker working for Hitler, made a documentary of a National Socialist, or Nazi, party rally at Nuremberg. In scenes of swooning women and cheering men, the film, called *Triumph of the Will*, recorded the dramatic force of Hitler's rhetoric and his ability to move the German people. Hitler's public charisma masked a profoundly troubled and incomplete individual capable of irrational rage and sick hatred of his fellow human beings. His warped views of the world were responsible for the greatest outrages committed in the name of legitimate power.

Adolf Hitler became chancellor of Germany in January 1933 by legal, constitutional, and democratic means. The Nazi party was supported by farmers, small businesspeople, civil servants, and young people. In the elections of 1930 and 1932, the voters made the Nazi party the largest party in the country—although not the majority. A few conservative nationalist politicians believed that Germany needed a stronger, more stable political system than the one offered by the Weimar Republic. They convinced President Paul von Hindenburg to invite Hitler to form a government. Once Hitler was in office, they expected to be able to control Hitler and use him for their own purposes.

They were mistaken. Hitler claimed that Germany was on the verge of a communist revolution, and he persuaded Hindenburg and the Reichstag to consent to a series of emergency laws, which the Nazis used to establish themselves firmly in power. These laws outlawed freedom of the press and public meetings, and approved the use of violence against Hitler's political enemies, particularly the socialists and the communists. Within two months after Hitler came to office, Germany was a police state and Hitler was a "legal" dictator who could issue his own laws without having to gain the consent of either the Reichstag or the president. After carrying out this "legal revolution" incapacitating representative institutions and ending civil liberties, the Nazis worked to consolidate their position and their power. They abolished all other political parties, established single-party rule, dissolved trade unions, and put their own people into state governments and the bureaucracy.

Many observers at the time considered the new Nazi state to be a monolithic structure, ruled and coordinated from the center. This was not, however, an accurate observation. Hitler actually issued few directives. Policy was set by an often chaotic jockeying for power among rival Nazi factions. Moreover, Hitler was careful not to alienate the non-Nazi conservative and nationalist politicians, landowners, industrialists, and military men who supported the Nazi regime and continued to hold positions of power in it until 1936–1937. His political alliance with these right-wingers helped give the state created by Adolf Hitler, which he called the Third Reich, an element of continuity with the past and make it seem less alarming and more normal to both the German people and to foreigners. (The first Reich was the medieval German empire; the second Reich was the German Empire created by Bismarck.) Hitler ruled by eliminating his enemies. Key to his success was his ability to marshal the use of violence to achieve his ends. For this purpose, paramilitary forces were the right arm of the Nazi party.

The first of the paramilitary groups was the SA *(Sturmabteilung)*, or the storm troopers, under Ernst Röhm (1877–1934), who helped Hitler achieve electoral victories by beating up political opponents on the streets and using other thuglike tactics. The group was organized in 1921 as the gymnast and sports division of the Nazi party, and its membership consisted of a large number of army veterans. Adopting a military appearance for their terrorist operations, SA members were also known as Brown Shirts. By the beginning of 1934, there were 2.5 million members, vastly outnumbering the regular army of 100,000 soldiers.

Heinrich Himmler (1900–1945) headed an elite force of the Nazi party within the SA called the SS *(Schutzstaffel,* or protection squad), a group whose members wore black uniforms and menacing skull-and-crossbones insignia on their caps. Himmler seized control of political policing and now stood as Röhm's chief rival. The SS became indispensable to the success of the Nazi party. In 1934 with the assistance of the army, Hitler and the SS purged the SA and executed Röhm. The leaders of the army feared Röhm's demands that the SA become the core of a new, enlarged army of the Third Reich. Hitler saw Röhm's demands for a "second revolution" and a more radical Nazi regime as a threat to his leadership of the Nazi movement. The SS rid itself of its rival organization and became Hitler's exclusive elite corps, responsible for carrying out his extreme programs and responsible later for the greatest atrocities of the Second World War.

Nazi Goals.   Hitler identified three organizing goals for the Nazi state: *Lebensraum*, or living space; rearmament; and economic recovery. These goals were the basis of the new foreign policy Hitler forged for Germany. And they served to fuse that foreign policy with the domestic politics of the Third Reich.

Key to Hitler's worldview was the concept of Lebensraum, which he considered the right and the duty of the German master race. The term *Lebensraum* embodied the concept that the Third Reich would be the world's greatest empire, one that would endure for a thousand years. Hitler first stated his ideals about living space in *Mein Kampf*, where he argued that superior nations had the right to expand into the territories of inferior states. Living space meant for him German domination of central and eastern Europe at the expense of Slavic peoples. The Aryan master race would dominate inferior peoples. In order for the German population to expand, Germany needed more land. Colonies were unacceptable because they weakened rather than strengthened national security. Germany must expand within continental Europe. Hitler's primary target was what he called "Russia and her vassal border states." But his aspirations stretched beyond the European continent to include German domination of the entire world.

Hitler also committed the Nazi state to the rearmament of Germany. He withdrew Germany from the world arena to prepare the German nation for war. By postponing his rearmament plans for the first year of his rule and then by using devious bookkeeping practices to bury his budgetary expenditures, he managed to obscure from the world his massive commitment to rearmament. In 1933 the German state was illicitly spending a billion reichsmarks on arms. In 1939 annual expenditures to prepare Germany for war had climbed to 30 billion.

Hitler knew that preparation for war meant more than amassing weapons. One of Germany's great weaknesses in World War I had been its dependence on imports of raw materials and foodstuffs. To avoid this problem again, Hitler instituted a program of *autarky*, or economic self-sufficiency, by which Germany aimed to produce everything that it consumed. He encouraged the efforts of German industry to develop synthetics, including petroleum, rubber, metals, and fats.

Autarky, as a rearmament measure, contributed to Hitler's third goal for the Nazi state: economic recovery from the Great Depression. The state pumped money into the private economy, creating new jobs and achieving full employment after 1936, an accomplishment unmatched by any other Western nation. Recovery was built on armaments as well as consumer products. The Nazi state's concentration of economic power in the hands of a few strengthened big businesses. The victims of corporate consolidation were the small firms that could no longer compete with government-sponsored corporations like the chemical firm of I. G. Farben.

Some of the non-Nazi conservative and nationalist leaders who supported the Nazi regime thought that the emphasis on rearmament was potentially dangerous. Economists feared it would cause serious inflation. Even some generals thought Hitler was rearming Germany in a too rapid and disorderly manner. Hitler prevailed in 1936–1937, when he introduced his Four-Year Plan dedicated to the goals of full-scale rearmament and economic self-sufficiency. Before the third year of the Four-Year Plan, however, Hitler was aware of the failure to develop synthetic products sufficient to meet Germany's needs. But if Germany could not create substitutes, it could control the territories that provided fuel, metals, and foodstuffs. Germany had been importing raw materials from southeastern Europe and wielding increasing economic influence over the Balkan countries. Hitler now realized that economic self-sufficiency could be directly linked to the main goal of the Nazi state: Lebensraum. Acquiring new lands would solve Germany's supply needs.

Hitler was thus committed to territorial expansion from the time he came to power. He rearmed Germany for that purpose. When economists and generals cautioned him, he refused to listen. Instead he informed them of his commitment to Lebensraum and of his intention to use aggressive war to acquire it. He removed his critics from their positions of power and replaced them with Nazis loyal to him. Massive and rapid rearmament continued after 1937, now based on a drive for economic self-sufficiency.

Organizing Loyalty.   For Hitler to pursue successfully the goals of the Nazi state, he had to have the loyalty and obedience of the German people. To realize his desire for the *total state*, a term he used to describe the absolute regulation of the German people, he set about destroying the rights of the individual: "We must develop organizations in which an individual's entire life can take place." The Nazi party was the preeminent organization. It coordinated the activities of approved groups of all sorts whose chief purpose was to inspire adherence to Nazi ideology. The organized terror of the SS and the Gestapo, the secret state police, silenced opposition.

To reinforce his personal power, Hitler created a Ministry of Propaganda to be headed by Joseph Goebbels (1897–1945), a former journalist and Nazi party district leader in Berlin. Goebbels was a master of manipulating emotions in mass demonstrations held to organize enthusiasm for Nazi policies. Flying the flag and wearing the swastika signified identification with the Nazi state. Family, too, was carefully regulated. Loyalty only to the state meant less loyalty to the family. Special youth organizations indoctrinated boys with

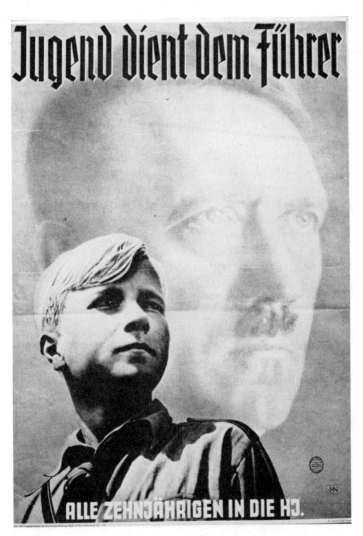

A recruiting poster bearing the slogan "Youth serves the Fuhrer" and "All ten-year-olds in the Hitler Youth" urges young boys to join the paramilitary youth organization.

nationalistic and military values. Hitler Youth comprised 82 percent of all young people in 1939. Children all over Germany recited the slogans of the organization: "Führer, command—we follow!" "We are born to die for Germany."

Organizations for girls were intended to mold them into worthy wives and mothers. Teenage girls were required to join a Nazi organization called Faith and Beauty, which taught them etiquette, dancing, fashion consciousness, and beauty care. Woman's natural function, Hitler argued, was to serve in the home. Education for women beyond the care of home and family was a waste. Adult women had their own organizations to serve the Nazi state. The German Women's Bureau under Gertrud Scholtz-Klink instructed women in their "proper" female duties. In an effort to promote large families, the state paid allowances to couples for getting married, subsidized families according to their size, and gave tax breaks to large families. Abortion and birth control were outlawed and women who sought such measures risked severe penalties and imprisonment.

By 1937 the need for women workers conflicted with the goals of Nazi propaganda. With the outbreak of war in 1939, women were urged to work, especially in jobs like munitions manufacture, formerly held by men. For working women with families, the double burden was a heavy one, as women were required to work long shifts—60-hour work weeks were not unusual— for low wages. Many women resisted entering the work force if they had other income or could live on the cash payments they received as the wives of soldiers. At the beginning of 1943, the German people were ordered to make sacrifices for a new era of "total war." Female labor became compulsory and women were drafted into working for the war.

Racism and Culture.   Nazi propaganda was directed toward excluding out- siders because they were deemed a threat to Hitler's New Order. Purging foreign influences meant purging political opponents, especially members of the Communist party, who were rounded up and sent to concentration camps in Germany. Communism was identified as an international Jewish conspiracy to destroy the German *Volk*, or people. Nazi literature also identified "asocials," those who were considered deviant in any way, including homosexuals, who were likewise to be expelled. Euthanasia was used against the mentally ill and the mentally disabled in the 1930s. Concentration camps were expanded to contain enemies of the state. Later, when concentration camps became sites of extermination and forced labor, gypsies, homosexuals, criminals, and religious offenders had to wear triangles of different colors to indicate their basis for persecution. But no group received greater attention for exclusion from Nazi Germany, and then from Europe, than the Jews.

Racism was nothing new in European culture. Nor was its particular variant, anti-Semitism—hatred of the Jews—the creation of the Third Reich. The link the Nazis cultivated between racism and politics was built on cultural precedents. In the 1890s in France and Austria and elsewhere in Europe, anti-Semitism was espoused by political and professional groups that formed themselves around issues of militant nationalism, authoritarianism, and mass politics. Hitler himself was both a racist and an anti-Semite and he placed theories of race at the core of his fascist ideology. Racist theories came to justify more than displacement and exclusion. "Experts" decided sterilization was the surest way to protect "German blood." In 1933 one of the early laws of Hitler's new Reich decreed compulsory sterilization of "undesirables" in order to "eliminate inferior genes." The Nazi state identified these "undesirables" and forced the sterilization of 400,000 men and women.

Democracies in Crisis

Democracies in the 1930s turned in on themselves in order to survive. In contrast to the fascist mobilization of society and the Soviet restructuring of the economy, Western democracies took small steps to respond to the challenges of the Great Depression. Democratic leaders lacked creative vision or even clear policy. Both France and Great Britain were less successful than Germany in responding to the challenges of the Depression. France paid a high price for parliamentary stalemate and was still severely depressed on the eve of war in 1938–1939. Great Britain maintained a stagnant economy and stable politics under Conservative leadership. Internal dissension, however, ripped Spain apart. Its civil war assumed broader dimensions as the Soviet Union, Italy, and Germany struggled over Spain's future, while Europe's democratic nations stood by and accepted defeat.

The Failure of the Left in France.   France's Third Republic, like most European parliamentary democracies in the 1930s, was characterized by a multiparty system. Genuine political differences often separated one party from another. The spectrum of political views in the Third Republic commonly meant stalemate. This situation was aggravated by the Depression and by the increasingly extremist politics on both the Left and the Right in response to developments in the Soviet Union and Germany.

The belief of the French people in a private enterprise economy was shaken by the Great Depression, but no new unifying belief replaced it. Some felt that state planning was the answer; others were sure that state intervention had caused the problem. Distrusting both the New Deal model of the United States and the Nazi response to Depression politics, the Third Republic followed a haphazard wait-and-see policy of insulating the economy, discouraging competition, and protecting favored interests in both industry and agriculture. Stimulating the economy by deficit spending was considered anathema. Devaluation of the franc, which might have helped French exports, was regarded by policymakers as an unpatriotic act. France stood fast as a bastion of liberal belief in the self-adjusting mechanism of the market, and it suffered greatly for it. Party politics worked to reinforce the defensive rather than offensive response to the challenges of depression and a sluggish economy.

In 1936 an electoral mandate for change swept the Left into power. The new premier, Léon Blum (1872–1950), was a socialist. Lacking the votes to rule with an exclusively socialist government, Blum formed a Popular Front of Left and Center parties intent on economic reforms. Before the new government could take power, a wave of strikes swept France. Though reluctant to intervene in the economy, the Popular Front nevertheless was pushed into some action. It promised wage increases, paid vacations, and collective bargaining to French workers.

Problems plagued Blum's Popular Front. German rearmament, now publicly known, forced France into rearmament, which France could ill afford.

The economic policies of the Left aggravated the problems they set out to solve. The reduced work week of 40 hours caused a drop in productivity, as did the short-lived one-month vacation policy, which was eventually suspended until after World War II. The government did nothing to prevent the outflow of investment capital from France. Higher wages failed to generate increased consumer demand because employers raised prices to cover their higher operating costs. Blum's government failed in 1937, with France still bogged down in a sluggish and depressed economy. The last peacetime government of the 1930s represented a conservative swing back to laissez-faire policies that put the needs of business above those of workers and brought a measure of revival to the French economy.

The radical Right drew strength from the Left's failures. Right-wing leagues and organizations multiplied, appealing to a frightened middle class. The failure of the socialists, in turn, drove many sympathizers further to the Left to join the Communist party. A divided France could not stand up to the foreign policy challenges of the 1930s posed by Hitler's provocations. Just as economic policy had no direction, foreign policy, too, lacked the sharp focus necessary to deal with the growing German threat.

Muddling Through in Great Britain.   Great Britain was hard hit by the Great Depression of the 1930s; only Germany and the United States experienced comparable economic devastation. The socialist Labour government of the years 1929 to 1931 under Prime Minister Ramsay MacDonald (1866–1937) was unprepared to deal with the 1929 collapse and lacked the vision and the planning to devise a way out of the morass. It took a coalition of moderate groups from the three parties—Liberal, Conservative, and Labour—to address the issues of high unemployment, a growing government deficit, a banking crisis, and the flight of capital. The National Government (1931–1935) was a nonparty, centrist coalition whose members included Ramsay MacDonald, retained as prime minister, and Stanley Baldwin (1867–1947), a Conservative with a background in iron and steel manufacturing.

The National Government undertook measures that had been unpopular only a decade earlier. In response to the endemic crisis, the government took Britain off the international gold standard and devalued the pound. In order to protect domestic production, tariffs were established. The British economy showed signs of slow recovery, probably due less to these government measures than to a gradual improvement in the business cycle. The government had survived the crisis without resorting to the kind of creative alternatives devised in the Scandinavian countries where, for example, consumer and producer cooperatives provided widespread economic relief. Moderates and classical liberals in Great Britain persisted in defending the nonintervention of the government in the economy, despite new economic theories, such as that of John Maynard Keynes (1883–1946), who urged government spending to stimulate consumer demand as the best way to shorten the duration of the Depression.

In 1932 Sir Oswald Mosley (1896–1980) founded the British Union of

Fascists (BUF), a group with its own goon squads of bodyguards. BUF was opposed to free trade liberalism and communism alike. Mosley developed a corporate model for economic and political life in which interest groups rather than an electorate would be represented in a new kind of parliament. He favored, above all, national solutions by relying on imperial development; he rejected the world of international finance as corrupt.

The BUF shared similarities with European fascist organizations. Its members adopted a uniformed military look and identified themselves as the Blackshirts. Like fascists on the Continent, BUF squads beat up their political opponents and began attacking Jews, especially the eastern European émigrés living in London. The British fascists struck a responsive chord among the poorest working classes of London's East End; at its peak the group claimed a membership of 20,000. Public alarm over increasingly inflammatory and anti-Semitic rhetoric converged with parliamentary denunciation. Popular support for the group was already beginning to erode when the BUF was outlawed in 1936. By this time, anti-Hitler feeling was spreading in Great Britain.

Mosley's response to harsh economic times had proven to be no match for the steady and reassuring strength of Stanley Baldwin's National Government, which seemed to be in control of an improving economic situation. The traditional party system prevailed not because of its brilliant solutions to difficult economic problems but because of the willingness of moderate parliamentarians to cooperate and to adapt, however slowly, to the new need for economic transformation.

The Spanish Republic as Battleground. In 1931 Spain became a democratic republic after centuries of Bourbon monarchy and almost a decade of military dictatorship. Within five years, the voters of Spain had elected a Popular Front government. The Popular Front in Spain was more radical than the one in France: It unleashed a social revolution. The property of aristocratic landlords was seized; revolutionary workers went on strike; the Catholic church and its clergy were attacked. Three years of civil war followed. On one side were the Republicans, the Popular Front defenders of the Spanish Republic and of social revolution in Spain. On the other side were the Nationalists, those who sought to overthrow the Republic—aristocratic landowners, supporters of the monarchy and the Catholic church, and much of the Spanish army. In this civil war foreign powers—Italy, Germany, and the Soviet Union—intervened in what became a dress rehearsal for World War II.

The Spanish Civil War began in July 1936 with a revolt against the Republic from within the Spanish army. It was led by General Francisco Franco, a tough, shrewd, and stubborn man, a conservative nationalist allied with the Falange, the Fascist party in Spain. The conflict soon became a bloody military stalemate, with the Nationalists controlling the more rural and conservative south and west of Spain and the Republicans holding out in the cities of the north and east—Madrid, Valenica, and Barcelona.

Almost from the beginning, the Spanish Civil War was an international event. Mussolini sent ground troops, "volunteers," to fight alongside Franco's forces. Hitler dispatched technical specialists, tanks, and the Condor Legion, an aviation unit. The Germans treated Spain as a testing ground for new equipment and new methods of warfare, including aerial bombardment. The Soviet Union intervened on the side of the Republic, sending armaments, supplies, and technical and political advisers. No democratic nation came to the aid of the Spanish Republic. Because the people of Britain and France were deeply divided in their attitudes toward the war in Spain, the British government stayed neutral, and the government of France was unable to aid its fellow Popular Front government in Spain. The American government did not prevent the Texas Oil Company from selling 1.9 million tons of oil to Franco's insurgents, nor did it block the Ford Motor Company, General Motors, and Studebaker from supplying the rebels with trucks.

The Spanish government pleaded, "Men and women of all lands! Come to our aid!" In response, 2800 American volunteers, among them college students, professors, intellectuals, and trade unionists, joined the loyalist army and European volunteers in defense of the Spanish Republic. The American battalion was called the Abraham Lincoln Brigade, a name that reflected its idealism and commitment to the defense of democratic ideals. Britons and antifascist émigrés from Italy and Germany also joined international brigades, which were vital in helping the city of Madrid hold out against the Nationalist generals. The Russians withdrew from the war in 1938, disillusioned by the failure of the French, British, and Americans to come to the aid of the Republicans. Madrid fell to the Nationalists in March 1939. The government

Spanish refugees stream into France after the Republican defeat and the fall of Barcelona. More than two hundred thousand refugees and troops were interned in France.

established by Franco sent one million of its enemies to prison or concentration camps.

*T*he Coming of World War II

The years between 1933 and 1939 marked a bleak period in international affairs when the British, the French, and the Americans were unwilling or unable to recognize the dire threat of Hitler and his Nazi state to world peace. The leaders of these countries took no action against Hitler's initial acts of aggression. When war began in Europe in 1939 it eventually became a great global conflict that pitted Germany, Italy, and Japan—the Axis Powers—against the British Empire, the Soviet Union, and the United States—the Grand Alliance.

Even before war broke out in Europe, there was armed conflict in Asia. The rapidly expanding Japanese economy depended on Manchuria for raw materials and on China for markets. Chinese boycotts against Japanese goods and threats to Japanese economic interests in Manchuria led to a Japanese military occupation of Manchuria and the establishment of a Japanese puppet state there in 1931–1932. When the powers of the League of Nations, led by Great Britain, refused to recognize this state, Japan withdrew from the League. Fearing that the Chinese government was becoming strong enough to exclude Japanese trade from China, Japanese troops and naval units began an undeclared war in China in 1937. Many important Chinese cities—Beijing, Shanghai, Nanking, Canton, and Hankow—fell to Japanese forces. Relentless aerial bombardment of Chinese cities and atrocities committed by Japanese troops against Chinese civilians outraged Europeans and Americans. The governments of the Soviet Union, Great Britain, and the United States, seeking to protect their own ideological, economic, and security interests in China, gave economic, diplomatic, and moral support to the Chinese government of Chiang Kai-shek. The stage was set for a major military conflict in Asia and in Europe.

Hitler's Foreign Policy and Appeasement

For Hitler a war against the Soviet Union for living space was inevitable. It would come, he told some of his close associates, in the years 1943 to 1945. However, he wanted to avoid refighting the war that had led to Germany's defeat in 1914–1918. World War I was a war fought on two fronts—in the east and in the west. It was a war in which Germany had to face many enemies at the same time, and a war that lasted until German soldiers, civilians, and resources were exhausted. In the next war, Hitler wanted, above all, to avoid fighting Great Britain while battling Russia for living space. He convinced himself that the British would remain neutral if Germany agreed not to attack the British Empire. Would they not appreciate his willingness to abolish forever the menace of communism? Where they not Aryans also?

From the time he assumed power in 1933, Hitler began to prepare the German nation for war. He continued the secret rearmament of Germany begun by his Weimar predecessors in violation of the restrictions of the Treaty of Versailles. He withdrew Germany from the League of Nations and from the World Disarmament Conference, signaling a new direction for German foreign policy. Hitler vastly expanded the rearmament program. In 1935 he publicly renounced the Treaty of Versailles and announced that Germany was rearming. The following year he openly defied the French and moved German troops into the Rhineland, the demilitarized security zone that separated the armed forces of the two countries. Hitler also reversed the cooperative relationship his nation had established with the Soviet Union in the 1920s. He maintained a consistently anti-Soviet stance until just before war began in 1939.

Beginning in 1938, with the non-Nazi conservatives removed from positions of power in Germany, Hitler alone determined foreign policy. He became increasingly impatient. He considered time his greatest enemy: Germany could fail by waiting too long to act. And he became more aggressive and willing to use military force as he set out to remove the obstacles to German domination of central Europe—Austria, Czechoslovakia, and Poland. In March he annexed Austria to the German Reich. Many Austrians wished to be united with Germany; others had no desire to be led by Nazis. Using the threat of invasion, he intimidated the Austrian government into legalizing the Nazi party, bringing pro-Nazis into the Cabinet, and finally inviting German troops into their country. Encouraged by his success, Hitler provoked a crisis in Czechoslovakia in the summer of the same year. He demanded "freedom" for the German-speaking people of the Sudetenland area of Czechoslovakia. His main objective, however, was not to protect the Germans of Czechoslovakia but to smash the Czech state, the major obstacle in central Europe to the launching of an attack on living space farther east.

Western statesmen did not understand Hitler's commitment to destroying Czechoslovakia or his willingness to fight a limited war against the Czechs to do so. Hitler did everything possible to isolate Czechoslovakia from its neighbors and its allies. France, an ally of Czechoslovakia, appeared distinctly unwilling to defend it against Germany's menaces. Britain, seeking to avoid a war that the government did not think was necessary and for which the British were not prepared, sent Prime Minister Neville Chamberlain (1869–1940) to reason with Hitler. Believing that transferring the Sudetenland, the German-speaking area of Czechoslovakia, to Germany was the only solution—and one that would redress some of the wrongs done to Germany after World War I—Chamberlain convinced France and Czechoslovakia to yield to Hitler's demands.

Chamberlain's actions were the result of British self-interest. British leaders agreed their country could not afford another war like the Great War of 1914–1918. Defense expenditures had been dramatically reduced in order to devote national resources to improving domestic social services, protecting world trade, and fortifying Britain's global interests. Britain understood well its weakened position in its dominions. In the British hierarchy of priorities, defense of the British Empire ranked first, above defense of Europe; and Britain's commitment to western Europe ranked above the defense of eastern and central Europe.

Hitler's response to being granted everything he requested was to renege and issue new demands. His desire for war could not have been more transparent, nor could his unwillingness to play by the rules of diplomacy have been clearer. One final meeting was held at Munich to avert war. On 29 September 1938, one day before German troops were scheduled to invade Czechoslovakia, Mussolini and the French prime minister, Edouard Daladier (1884–1970), joined Hitler and Chamberlain at Munich to discuss a peaceful resolution to the crisis.

At Munich, Chamberlain and Daladier again yielded before Hitler. The Sudetenland was ceded to Germany and German troops occupied the area. The policy of the British and French was dubbed *appeasement* to indicate the willingness to concede to demands in order to preserve peace. Appeasement has become a dirty word in twentieth-century European history, taken to mean weakness and cowardice. Yet Chamberlain was neither weak nor cowardly. His great mistake was in assuming that Hitler was a reasonable man, who like all reasonable persons wanted to avoid another war.

Chamberlain thought his mediation at Munich had won for Europe a lasting peace—"peace for our time," he reported. The people of Europe received Chamberlain's assessment with a sense of relief and shame—relief over what had been avoided, shame at having deserted Czechoslovakia. In fact, the policy of appeasement further destabilized Europe and accelerated Hitler's plans for European domination. Within months, Hitler cast aside the Munich agreement by annihilating Czechoslovakia. German troops occupied the western Czech part of the state including the capital of Prague. The Slovak eastern part became independent and a German satellite. At the same time, Lithuania was pressured into surrendering Memel to Germany, and Hitler demanded that Germany control Gdańsk and the Polish Corridor. No longer could Hitler be ignored or appeased. No longer could his goals be misunderstood.

Hitler's War, 1939–1941

In the tense months that followed the Munich meeting and the occupation of Prague, Hitler readied himself for war in western Europe. In order to strengthen his position, in May 1939 he formed a military alliance with Mussolini's Italy, the Pact of Steel. Then, Hitler and Stalin shocked the West by uniting their two nations in a pact of mutual neutrality, the Non-Aggression

Pact of 1939. Opportunism lay behind Hitler's willingness to ally with the communist state that he had denounced throughout the 1930s. A German alliance with the Soviet Union would, Hitler believed, force the British and the French to back down and to remain neutral while Germany conquered Poland—the last obstacle to a drive for living space—in a short, limited war. Stalin recognized the failure of the West to stand up to Hitler. There was little possibility, he thought, of an alliance against Germany with the virulently anticommunist Neville Chamberlain. The best Stalin could hope for was that the Germans and the Western powers would fight it out while the Soviet Union waited to enter the war at the most opportune moment. As an added bonus, Germany promised not to interfere if the Soviet Union annexed eastern Poland, Bessarabia, and the Baltic republics of Latvia and Estonia.

Finally recognizing Hitler's intent, the British and the French also signed a pact in the spring of 1939, promising assistance to Poland in the event of aggression. Tensions mounted throughout the summer. On 1 September 1939 Germany attacked Poland. By the end of the month, in spite of valiant resistance, the vastly outnumbered Poles surrendered. Although the German army needed no assistance, the Russians invaded Poland ten days before its collapse, and Germany and Russia divided the spoils. Almost immediately, Stalin took measures to defend Russia against a possible German attack. The Soviet Union assumed military control in the Baltic states and demanded of Finland territory and military bases from which the city of Leningrad could be defended. When Finland refused, Russia invaded. In the snows of the "Winter War" of 1939–1940, the Finns initially fought the Russian army to a standstill, much to the encouragement of the democratic West. The Finns, however, were eventually defeated in March 1940.

Hitler's war, the war for German domination of Europe, had begun. But it had not begun the way he intended. Great Britain and France, true to their alliance with Poland, and contrary to Hitler's expectations, declared war on Germany on 3 September 1939, even though they were unable to give any help to Poland. In the six months after the fall of Poland, no military action took place between Germany and the Allies, because Hitler postponed offensives in northern and western Europe due to poor weather conditions. This strange interlude that became known as "the phony war" was a period of suspended reality in which France and Great Britain waited for Hitler to make his next move. Civilian morale in France deteriorated among a population that still remembered the death and destruction France had endured in the Great War. An attitude of defeatism germinated and grew before the first French soldier fell in battle.

With the arrival of spring, Germany attacked Denmark and Norway in April 1940. Then on 10 May 1940, Hitler's armies invaded the Netherlands, Belgium, and Luxembourg. By the third week of May, German mechanized forces were racing through northern France toward the English Channel, cutting off the British and Belgian troops and 120,000 French forces from the rest of the French army. With the rapid defeat of Belgium, these forces were crowded against the Channel and had to be withdrawn from the beaches of

Dunkirk. France, with a large and well-equipped army, was in a desperate situation with the loss of Allied support.

In France the German army fought a new kind of war called *Blitzkrieg*, or lightning war, so named because of its speed. The British and the French had expected the German army to behave much as it had in World War I, concentrating its striking forces in a swing through coastal Belgium and Holland in order to capture Paris. With stunning speed, Germany drove its tanks—*Panzers*—through the French defenses at Sedan in eastern France. French strategists believed that France was safe because of the hilly and forested terrain they thought was impassable. They also counted on the protection of the fortress wall known as the Maginot Line that France had built in the interwar period. The Maginot Line stretched for hundreds of miles but was useless against mobile tank divisions that outflanked it.

The French could have pinched off the advance of the overextended Panzers, but the French army, suffering from severe morale problems, collapsed and was in retreat. On 17 June 1940, only weeks after German soldiers had stepped on French soil, Marshal Henri-Philippe Pétain, the great hero of the Battle of Verdun in World War I, petitioned the Germans for an armistice. Three-fifths of France, including the entire Atlantic seaboard, was occupied by the German army and placed under direct German rule. In what remained, Pétain created a collaborationist government that resided at Vichy, a spa city in central France, and worked in partnership with the Germans for the rest of the war. General Charles de Gaulle (1890–1970) withdrew to London, where he set up a Free French government in exile.

French capitulation in June 1940 followed Italian entry into the war on the side of Germany in the same month. The British were now alone in a war against the two Axis powers as Germany made plans for an invasion of the British Isles from across the English Channel. To prepare the way, the German air force under Reichsmarshal Hermann Göring (1893–1946) launched a series of air attacks against England—the Battle of Britain from July to October 1940. The German air force first attacked British aircraft, airfields, and munitions centers and then shifted targets to major population centers like London and industrial cities like Coventry. The Blitz of London consisted of 19 air attacks on the city between September 1940 and May 1941. Civilians suffered with 15,000 dead and the heavy destruction of residential areas.

The British resisted these attacks under the leadership of Winston Churchill, who had succeeded Chamberlain as prime minister in 1940. Churchill was a master public speaker who, in a series of radio broadcasts, inspired the people of Britain with the historic greatness of the task confronting them—holding out against nazism until the forces of the overseas British Empire and the United States could be marshaled to liberate Europe. The British Royal Air Force inflicted serious losses on German aircraft while British industry was able to maintain steady production of planes, bombs, and armaments. Civilians endured the nightly destruction and air raids in what Churchill termed Britain's "finest hour." Recognizing his lack of success in establishing air superiority over the Channel or in breaking the will of the

British people, Hitler abandoned the Battle of Britain and canceled the invasion.

By the middle of 1941 Hitler controlled a vast continental empire that stretched from the Baltic to the Black Sea and from the Atlantic Ocean to the Russian border. In addition to occupied territories and satellites, he had the support of collaborationist governments. Some collaborators served in puppet governments out of an ideological commitment to fascism. They were hostile to communism and believed that Hitler's nazism was far preferable to Stalin's communism. They saw in the German victory the chance to put their beliefs into practice. Some governments collaborated with the Germans out of national self-interest. The government of Hungary allied with Germany in the hope of winning back territory lost at the end of World War I. Romania hoped to gain territory from Russia. The government of Slovakia was loyal to the

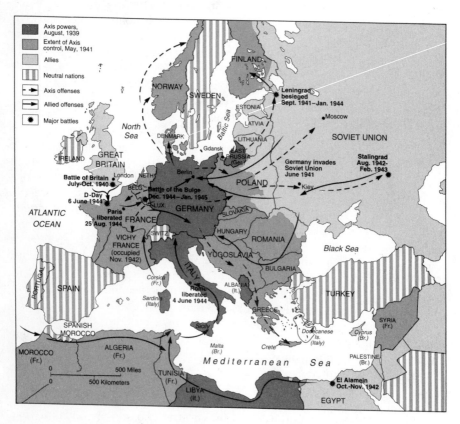

World War II in Europe

Third Reich because Hitler had given it independence from the Czechs. A German puppet state was set up in the Yugoslav province of Croatia. Other collaborators were pragmatists who believed that by taking political office they could negotiate with the German conquerors and soften the effects of the Nazi conquest on their people.

Resistance against German occupation and collaborationist regimes took many forms. Resisters wrote subversive tracts or distributed them, gathered intelligence information for the Allies, sheltered Jews or other enemies of the Nazis, committed acts of sabotage or assassination or other violent acts, and carried on guerrilla warfare against the German army. Resisters ran the risk of endangering themselves and their families, who, if discovered, would be tortured and killed. Resistance movements developed most strongly after the German attack on the Soviet Union in 1941, when the Communist parties of occupied Europe formed the core of the violent resistance against the Nazi regime.

The greatest resistance fighter of the Second World War, or perhaps of any war, was Josip Broz (1892–1980), alias Tito. He was a Croatian communist and a Yugoslav nationalist. Instead of waiting to be liberated by the Allies, his partisans fought against Italian and German troops. Ten or more German divisions that might otherwise have fought elsewhere were tied up combating Tito's forces. He gained the admiration and the support of Churchill, Roosevelt, and Stalin. After liberation, Tito's organization won 90 percent of the vote in the Yugoslav elections, and he became the leader of the country in the postwar era. Resistance entailed enormous risks and required secrecy, moral courage, and great bravery. But, on the whole, the actions of resistance fighters were militarily insignificant in changing the course of the war.

Racism and Destruction

War, as the saying goes, is hell. But the horrors perpetrated in World War II exceeded anything ever experienced in Western civilization. Claims of racial superiority were invoked to justify inhuman atrocities. The Germans and Japanese used spurious arguments of racial superiority to fuel their war efforts in both the European and Asian theaters of battle. In Asia the subjugation of inferior peoples became a rallying cry for conquest. But the Germans and the Japanese were not alone in using racist propaganda. The United States employed racial stereotypes to depict the inferiority of the enemy and interned Japanese Americans living on the West Coast to camps and seized their property.

Nowhere, however, was the use of racism by the state more virulent than in Germany. German racist ideology distorted pseudoscientific theories for the purpose of separating the racially superior from the racially inferior. Those human beings worthy of living were the master race; those not worthy were deemed "subhuman." Hatred of certain groups fueled both politics and war. Hitler promised the German people a purified Reich of Aryans "free of the Jews" and the racially and mentally inferior. Slavic peoples—Poles and Russians—were designated as subhumans who could be displaced in the search for Lebensraum and German destiny. With the war in eastern Europe, anti-Semitism changed from a policy of persecution and expropriation in the 1930s into a program of systematic extermination beginning in 1941.

The Destruction of Europe's Jews

Although anti-Semitism was an integral part of Hitler's view of the world, he did not think the peoples of Germany or of Europe were ready for harsh measures against the Jews. The Nazis did not have a blueprint for the destruction of Europe's Jews when they came to power in 1933; the anti-Semitic policies of the Third Reich evolved incrementally in the 1930s and 1940s. The first measures against the German Jews, such as their exclusion from public employment and higher education, began almost immediately in 1933. In 1935 the Nuremberg Laws were enacted to identify Jews, to deprive them of their citizenship, and to forbid marriage and extramarital sexual relations between Jews and non-Jews.

Massive public violence against Jews took place five years after the Nazis came to power. On the night of 9 November 1938, synagogues were set afire and books and valuables owned by Jews were confiscated throughout Germany. Jews were beaten, about ninety-one were killed, and twenty to thirty thousand were imprisoned in concentration camps. The night came to be called *Kristallnacht*, meaning "night of broken glass," which referred to the Jewish shop windows smashed by the Brown Shirts under orders from Goebbels. The government claimed that Kristallnacht was an outpouring of the German people's will. An atmosphere of state-sanctioned hate prevailed. German citizens acquiesced, sometimes silently and in many cases vociferously. In the aftermath of Kristallnacht civil servants expropriated Jewish property as the rightful property of the state. When the war began, Jews were rounded up and herded into urban ghettos in Germany and in the large cities of Poland.

The "Final Solution." Confinement in urban ghettos was the beginning of a policy of concentration that ended in annihilation. After having identified Jews, seized their property, and then confined them to ghettos, German authorities began to implement a step-by-step plan for extermination. There appears to have been no single order from Hitler that decreed what became known to German officials as the "Final Solution"—the total extermination of European Jews. But Hitler's recorded remarks make it clear that he knew and approved of what was being done to the Jews. A spirit of shared purpose permeated the entire administrative system from the civil service through the judiciary. Administrative agencies competed to interpret the Führer's will. Those involved in carrying out the plan for extermination understood what was meant by the Final Solution and what their responsibilities were for enforcing it. To assure that the whole process operated smoothly, a planning conference for the Final Solution was conducted by Reinhard Heydrich (1904–1942), leader of the *Sicherheitsdienst* (SD), or Security Service of the SS, for the benefit of state and party officials at Wannsee, a Berlin suburb, in January 1942.

Mass racial extermination began with the German conquest of Poland, where both Jews and non-Jews were systematically killed. It continued when Hitler's army invaded the Soviet Union in 1941. This campaign, known as Operation Barbarossa, initiated the mass execution of eastern Europeans declared to be enemies of the Reich. Its tactics pointed the way to the Final Solution. To the Nazi leadership, Slavs were "subhuman." Russian Jews were, by extension, the lowest of the low, even more despised than German Jews. Nazi propaganda had equated Jews with communists, and Hitler had used the single word *Judeocommunist* to describe the most dangerous criminal and enemy of the Third Reich, the enemy who must be annihilated at any cost.

The executions were the work of the SS, the elite military arm of the Nazi party. Special mobile murder squads of the SD under Heydrich were organized behind the German lines in Poland and Russia. Members of the army were aware of what the SS squads were doing and participated in some of the extermination measures. In the spring of 1941 Hitler ordered a massive propaganda campaign to be conducted among the armed forces. The army was indoctrinated to believe that the invasion of the Soviet Union was more than a military campaign; it was a "holy war," a crusade that Germany was waging for civilization. SS chief Heinrich Himmler, probably responding to oral orders from Hitler, set about to enforce the Führer's threats with concrete extermination policies. Fearful that the SS would be outstripped by the regular army in the Führer's favor, Himmler exhorted his men to commit the worst atrocities.

Firing squads shot Russian victims en masse, then piled their bodies on top of one another in open graves. Reviewing these procedures for mass killings, Himmler—ever competitive with other Nazi agencies—suggested a more efficient means of extermination that would require less manpower and would enhance the prestige of the SS. As a result, extermination by gas was introduced, using vans whose exhaust fumes were piped into the enclosed cargo areas that served as portable gas chambers. In Poland, Himmler replaced the vans with permanent buildings housing gas chambers using Zyklon B, a gas developed by the chemical firm I.G. Farben for the purpose. The chambers could annihilate thousands at a time.

The Third Reich began erecting its vast network of death in 1941. The first extermination camp was created in Chelmno, Poland, where 150,000 people were killed between 1941 and 1944. The camps practiced systematic extermination for the savage destruction of those groups deemed racially inferior, sexually deviant, and politically dangerous. The terms *genocide*, *judeocide*, and *holocaust* have been used to describe the mass slaughter of the Jewish people, most of which took place in the five major killing centers in what is now Polish territory—Chelmno, Belzec, Sobibor, Treblinka, and Auschwitz.

Many victims died before ever reaching the camps, transported for days in sealed railroad cars, without food, water, or sanitation facilities. Others died within months as forced laborers for the Reich. People of all ages were starved, beaten, and systematically humiliated. Guards taunted their victims verbally, degraded them physically, and tortured them with false hope. Promised clean clothes and nourishment, camp internees were herded into "showers," which dispensed gas rather than water. Descriptions of life in the camps reveal a systematized brutality and inhumanity on the part of the German, Ukrainian, and Polish guards toward their victims. In all, 11 million people died by the extermination process—6 million Jews and almost as many non-Jews, including Slavic slave laborers, Soviet prisoners of war, communists, members of the Polish and Soviet leadership, various resistance elements, gypsies, Jehovah's Witnesses, and homosexuals.

Work Makes Free.   The words *Arbeit Macht Frei* ("Work Makes Free") were emblazoned over the main gate at Auschwitz, the largest of the concentration camps. It was at Auschwitz that the greatest number of persons died in a single place, including more than one million Jews. The healthy and the young were kept barely alive to work. Hard labor, starvation, and disease—especially typhus, tuberculosis, and other diseases that spread rapidly because of the lack of sanitation—claimed many victims.

On entering the camps, the sick and the aged were automatically designated for extermination because of their uselessness as a labor force. Many children were put to work, but some were designated for extermination. Many mothers chose to accompany their children to their deaths to comfort them in their final moments. Pregnant women, too, were considered useless in the forced labor camps and were sent immediately to the "showers." The number of German Jewish women who died in the camps was 50 percent higher than the number of German Jewish men. Starvation diets meant that women stopped menstruating. Women who showed signs of menstruation were killed immediately. The Nazis worried that women of childbearing age would continue to reproduce. Women who were discovered to have given birth undetected in the camp were killed, as were their infants. Family relations were completely destroyed, as inmates were segregated by sex. It soon became clear that even those allowed to live were only intended to serve the short-term needs of the Nazis.

Resisting Destruction.   Could the victims of extermination have resisted? The answer is no. The impossibility of any effective resistance was based on two essential characteristics of the process of extermination. First, the entire

These women and children, many wearing the yellow star that identified them as Jews, were photographed minutes before they entered the gas chambers at Auschwitz.

German state and its bureaucratic apparatus were involved in the policies, laws, and decrees of the 1930s that singled out victims, and most Germans stood silently by. There was no course of appeal and no place to hide. Those who understood early what was happening and who had enough money to buy their way out emigrated to safer places, including Palestine and the United States. But most countries blocked the entry of German and eastern European refugees with immigration quotas. Neither Britain nor the United States was willing to deal with the mass influx of European Jews. Jews in the occupied countries and the Axis nations had virtually no chance to escape. They were trapped in a society where all forces of law and administration worked against them.

A second reason for the impossibility of resistance was the step-by-step nature of the process of extermination, which meant that few understood the final outcome until it was too late. Initially in the 1930s, many German Jews believed that things could get no worse and obeyed the German state as good citizens. Even the policy of removing groups from the ghetto militated against resistance because the hope was that sending 1000 Jews to "resettlement" would allow 10,000 Jews remaining behind to be saved. The German authorities deliberately controlled information to cultivate this misunderstanding of what was happening.

Isolated instances of resistance in the camps—rioting at Treblinka, for example—only highlight how impossible rebellion was for physically debilitated people in these heavily guarded centers. In the Warsaw ghetto, a

838

Chapter 22   Crisis and Global Conflict, 1933–1945

resistance movement was organized with a few firearms and some grenades and homemade Molotov cocktails in April 1943. Starvation, overcrowding, and epidemics made Warsaw, the largest of the ghettos, into an extermination camp. As news reached the ghetto that "resettlement" was the death warrant of tens of thousands of Polish Jews, armed rebellion erupted. It did not succeed in blocking the completion of the Final Solution against the Warsaw ghetto the following year when the SS commandant proclaimed, "The Jewish Quarter of Warsaw is no more!" Polish and Russian Jews account for 70 percent of the total Jewish deaths.

Who Knew?

It is impossible that killing on such a scale could have been kept secret. Along with those who ordered extermination operations, the guards and camp personnel involved in carrying out the directives were aware of what was happening. Those who brought the Jews to the camps, returning always with empty railroad cars, knew it too. Neighbors who saw Jews disappearing for a time believed that they were being resettled in the east. But as news got back to central and western Europe, it was harder to sustain belief in this ruse. People who lived near the camps could not ignore the screams and smells of gas and burning bodies emitted from the camps.

Although never publicly announcing its extermination program, the German government convinced its citizens that the policies of the Nazi state could not be judged by ordinary moral standards. The benefits to the German state were justification enough for the annihilation of 11 million people. Official propaganda successfully convinced millions that the Reich was the supreme good. Admitting the existence of the extermination program carried with it a responsibility on which few acted, perhaps out of fear of reprisals. There were some heroes like Raoul Wallenberg of Sweden, who interceded for Hungarian Jews and provided Jews in the Budapest ghetto with food and protection. The king of Denmark, when informed that the Nazis had ordered Danish Jews to wear the yellow star, stated that he and his family would also wear the yellow star as a "badge of honor." Heroic acts, however, were isolated and rare.

Collaborationist governments and occupied nations often cooperated with Nazi extermination policies. The French government at Vichy introduced and implemented a variety of anti-Jewish measures. All of this was done without German orders and without German pressure. By voluntarily identifying and deporting Jews, the Vichy government sent 75,000 men, women, and children to their deaths.

As the war dragged on for years, internees of the camps hoped and prayed for rescue by the Allies. But such help did not come. The U.S. State Department and the British Foreign office had early and reliable information on the nature and extent of the atrocities. But they did not act. American Jews were unable to convince President Franklin D. Roosevelt to intercede to prevent the slaughter. Appeals to bomb the gas chambers at Auschwitz and the railroad lines leading to them were rejected by the United States on strategic grounds. Those trying to survive in the camps and the ghettos despaired at their abandonment.

The handful of survivors found by Allied soldiers who entered the camps after Germany's defeat presented a haunting picture of humanity. The sight of corpses piled on top of one another lining the roads, the piles of shoes, clothing, underwear, and gold teeth extracted from the dead shocked those who came to liberate the camps. One of the two survivors of Chelmno summed it all up: "No one can understand what happened here."

The Final Solution was a perversion of every value of civilization. The achievements of twentieth-century industry, technology, state, and bureaucracy in the West were turned against millions to create, as one German official called it, murder by assembly line. Mass killing was not prompted by military or security concerns. Nor was the elimination of vital labor power consistent with the needs of the Nazi state. The international tribunal for war crimes that met in 1945 in the German city of Nuremberg attempted to mete out justice to the criminals against humanity responsible for the destruction of 11 million Europeans labeled as demons and racial inferiors. History in the end must record, if it cannot explain, such inhumanity.

Allied Victory

The situation at the end of 1941 appeared grim for the British and their dominions and the Americans who were assisting them with munitions, money, and food. Hitler commanded the greatest fighting force in the world, one that had knocked France out of the war in a matter of weeks, brought destruction to British cities, and conquered Yugoslavia in 12 days. Much of the world was coming to fear German invincibility. Then in June 1941 Hitler's troops invaded the Soviet Union, providing the British with an ally. In December the naval and air forces of Japan attacked American bases in the Pacific, providing the British and the Russians with still another ally. What was a European war became a world war. This was the war Hitler did not want and which Germany could not win—a long total war to the finish against three powers with inexhaustible resources—the British Empire, the Soviet Union, and the United States.

The Soviet Union's Great Patriotic War

Hitler had always considered the Soviet Union to be Germany's primary enemy. His hatred of communism was all-encompassing: Bolshevism was an evil invention of the Jewish people and a dangerous ideological threat to the

Third Reich. The 1939 Non-Aggression Pact with Stalin was no more than an expedient for him. "Everything I undertake is directed against Russia," Hitler told a Swiss diplomat in 1939.

When German armies marched into Russia on 22 June 1941, they found the Soviet army larger but totally unprepared for war. In contrast to German soldiers, who had fought in Spain, Poland, and France, Soviet troops had no firsthand battle experience. Nor were they well led. Stalin's purges of the officer corps in the late 1930s removed 35,000 officers from their posts by dismissal, imprisonment, or execution. Many of the men who replaced them were unseasoned in the responsibilities of leadership.

Russian military leaders were sure they would be ready for a European war against the capitalist nations by 1942, and Stalin had refused to believe that Hitler would attack the Soviet Union before then. When the Germans attacked, Stalin accepted offers of support from the United States and Great Britain, the two nations that had worked consistently to exclude the Soviet Union from European power politics since the Bolshevik Revolution in 1917. With France defeated and Great Britain crippled, the future of the war depended on Soviet fighting power and American supplies.

Hitler's invasion of Russia involved three million soldiers from Germany and Germany's satellites, the largest invasion force in history. It stretched along an immense battlefront from the Baltic to the Black Sea. Instead of exclusively targeting Moscow, the capital, the German army concentrated first on destroying Soviet armed forces and capturing Leningrad in the north and the oil-rich Caucasus in the south. In the beginning the German forces advanced rapidly in a Blitzkrieg across western Russia, where they were greeted as liberators in Ukraine. The Germans took 290,000 prisoners of war and massacred tens of thousands of others in their path through the Jewish settlements of western Russia.

Within four months, the German army had advanced to the gates of Moscow, but they concentrated their forces too late. The Red Army rallied to defend Moscow, as thousands of civilian women set to work digging trenches and antitank ditches around the city. The Soviet people answered Stalin's call for a scorched-earth policy by burning everything that might be useful to the advancing German troops. German troops had also burned much in their path, depriving themselves of essential supplies for the winter months ahead. The German advance was stopped, as the best ally of the Red Army—the Russian winter—settled in. The first snow fell at the beginning of October. By early November German troops were beginning to suffer the harsh effects of an early and exceptionally bitter Russian winter.

Hitler promised the German people that "final victory" was at hand. So confident was Hitler of a speedy and decisive victory that he sent his soldiers into Russia wearing only light summer uniforms. Hitler's generals knew better and tried repeatedly to explain military realities to the Führer. General Heinz Guderian (1888–1954), commander of the tank units, reported that his men were suffering frostbite, tanks could not be started, and automatic weapons were jamming in the subzero temperatures. Back in Germany, the civilian population received little accurate news of the campaign. They began to suspect the worst when the government sent out a plea for woolen blankets and clothing for the troops.

By early December the German military situation was desperate. The Soviets, benefiting from intelligence information about German plans and an awareness that Japan was about to declare war on the United States, recalled fresh troops from the Siberian frontier and the border with China and Manchuria and launched a powerful counterattack against the poorly outfitted German army outside Moscow. Under the command of General Gyorgi Zhukov (1896–1974), Russian troops, dressed and trained for winter warfare, pushed the Germans back in retreat across the snow-covered expanses. By February the campaign had cost the German army over a million casualties. It probably cost the Soviets twice that number of wounded, missing, captured, and dead soldiers. At the end of the Soviet counterattack in March, the German army and its satellite forces were in a shambles reminiscent of Napoleon's troops, who 130 years earlier had been decimated in the campaign to capture Moscow. An enraged Hitler dismissed his generals for retreating without his permission, and he himself assumed the position of commander-in-chief of the armed forces.

Hitler was not daunted by the devastating costs of his invasion of Russia. In the summer of 1942 he initiated a second major offensive, this time to take the city of Stalingrad. Constant bombardment gutted the city, and the Soviet army was forced into hand-to-hand combat with the German soldiers. But the German troops, once again inadequately supplied and unprepared for the Russian winter, failed to capture the city. The Battle of Stalingrad was over in the first days of February 1943.

The Soviets succeeded by exploiting two great advantages in their war against Germany: the large Soviet population and their knowledge of Russian weather and terrain. There was a third advantage that Hitler ignored: the Soviet people's determination to sacrifice everything for the war effort. In the summer of 1941, as Hitler's troops threatened Moscow, Stalin appealed to his Soviet "brothers and sisters" to join him in waging "the Great Patriotic War." The Russian people shared a sense of common purpose, sacrifice, and moral commitment in their loyalty to the nation.

The advancing Germans themselves intensified Soviet patriotism by torturing and killing tens of thousands of peasants who might have willingly cooperated against the Stalinist regime. Millions of Soviet peasants joined the Red Army. Young men of high school age were drafted into the armed forces. Three million women became wage earners for the first time as they replaced men in war industries. Women who remained on the land worked to feed the townspeople and the soldiers. Tens of thousands of Russians left their homes in western Russia to work for relocated Soviet industries in the Urals, the Volga region, Siberia, and Central Asia. More than twenty million Soviet people, soldiers and civilians, died in the course of World War II. In addition to those

Men and women on a Ukrainian collective farm labor to erect huge antitank traps during the German invasion of the Soviet Union. The steadfast courage of the civilian population contributed greatly to the defeat of Hitler's quest for Lebensraum *in the east.*

killed in battle, millions starved as a direct result of the hardships of war. In 1943 food was so scarce that seed for the next year's crops was eaten. One in every three men born in 1906 died in the war. But Soviet resistance did not flag.

The Soviet Union sacrificed 10 percent of its population to the war effort, incurring well over 50 percent of all the deaths and casualties of the war. Few families escaped the death of members in the defense of the nation. Soviet citizens correctly considered that they had given more than any other country to defeat Hitler. For the Soviet people, their suffering in battle made World War II the Soviet Union's war and their sacrifice made possible the Allied victory.

The United States Enters the War

Although a neutral power, the United States began extending aid to the Allies after the fall of France in 1940. Since neither Britain nor the Soviet Union could afford to pay the entire costs of defending Europe against Hitler, the U.S. Congress passed the Lend-Lease Act in 1941. This act authorized President Roosevelt to provide armaments to Great Britain and the Soviet Union without payment. America became "the arsenal of democracy." The United States and Britain sent 4100 airplanes and 138,000 motor vehicles as well as steel and machinery to the Soviet Union for the campaign of 1943. In all, America pumped $11 billion worth of equipment into the Soviet war effort between 1941 and 1945.

President Roosevelt and his advisers considered Germany, not Japan, to be America's primary target for a future war. Japan nevertheless had been threatening American trade interest in Asia and had embroiled the United States in disputes over Japanese imperialist expansion in the late 1930s. In the summer of 1941 Japanese-American relations appeared to be deteriorating following the Japanese invasion of Indochina and Thailand. The United States insisted that Japan vacate China and Indochina and reestablish the open door for trade in Asia. But Japan held fast and in September 1940 joined forces with the Axis Powers of Germany and Italy in the Tripartite Pact, in which the signatories promised mutual support against aggression. The United States knew that it was only a matter of time until Japan attacked but was uncertain about where that attack would take place.

On Sunday morning, 7 December 1941, Japan struck at the heart of the American Pacific Fleet stationed at Pearl Harbor, Hawaii. The fleet was literally caught asleep at the switch: 2300 people were killed, and eight battleships and numerous cruisers and destroyers were sunk or severely damaged. The attack crippled American naval power in the Pacific as the American navy suffered its worst loss in history in a single engagement. The attack on Pearl Harbor led to the immediate U.S. declaration of war against Japan. In the next three months, Japan captured Hong Kong, Malaya, and the important naval base at Singapore from the British, taking 60,000 prisoners. They drove the Dutch from all of Indonesia but New Guinea, pushed American forces in the Philippines into the Bataan Peninsula, occupied Burma, and inflected severe defeats on British, Dutch, and American naval power in East Asia. With the armies of Germany deep in Russian territory, Australia now faced the threat of a Japanese invasion.

Hitler praised the Japanese government for its action against the British Empire and against the United States and its "millionaire and Jewish backers." Germany, with its armies retreating from Moscow, nevertheless declared war against the United States on 11 December 1941. Hitler, in fact, considered that the United States was already at war with Germany because of its policy of supplying the Allies. Within days the United States, a nation with an army smaller than Belgium's, had gone from neutrality to a war in two theaters. Although militarily weak, the United States was an economic giant, commanding a vast industrial capacity and access to resources. America grew even stronger under the stimulus of war, increasing its production by 400 percent in two years. It now devoted itself to the demands of a total war and the unconditional surrender of Germany and then Japan.

The Allies, however, did not always share the same strategies or concerns. President Roosevelt and Prime Minister Churchill had already discussed common goals in the summer of 1941 before U.S. entry into the war. The United States embraced the priority of the European war and the postponement of war in the Pacific. Stalin pleaded for the Anglo Americans to open up a second front against Germany in western Europe in order to give his troops some relief and save Soviet lives. Anglo-American resources were committed to the

Pacific in order to stop the Japanese advance, and the Americans and the British disagreed as to where a second front in Europe might be opened.

Because of British interests in the Mediterranean, Churchill insisted on a move from North Africa into Sicily and Italy. This strategy was put into effect in 1942. In North Africa, German and Italian troops under German Field Marshal Erwin Rommel (1891–1944) were defeated by the British Eighth Army led by Field Marshal Bernard Montgomery (1887–1976) at the decisive battle of El Alamein in November 1942. The Italian government withdrew from the war in September, but German troops carried on the fight in Italy. The Anglo-American invasion of Italy did little to alleviate Russian losses, and the Soviet Union absorbed almost the entire force of German military power until 1944. Stalin's distrust of his allies increased. Churchill, Roosevelt, and Stalin met for the first time in late November 1943 at Teheran, Iran. Roosevelt and Churchill made a commitment to Stalin to open a second front in France within six months. Stalin, in turn, promised to attack Japan in order to aid the United States in the Pacific. The great showdown of the global war was at hand.

On 6 June 1944, Allied troops under the command of the American general Dwight D. Eisenhower (1890–1969) came ashore on the beaches of Normandy in the largest amphibious landing in history. In a daring operation identified by the code name Operation Overlord, and known as D-Day, 2.2 million American, British, and Free French forces, 450,000 vehicles, and 4 million tons of supplies poured into northern France. Allied forces broke through German lines to liberate Paris in late August. The Germans launched a last ditch counterattack in late December 1944 in Luxembourg and Belgium. This Battle of the Bulge only slowed the Allied advance; in March 1945 American forces crossed the Rhine into Germany. Hitler, meanwhile, refused to surrender and insisted on a fight to the death of the last German soldier. Members of his own High Command had attempted unsuccessfully to assassinate Hitler in July 1944. The final German defeat came in April 1945, when the Russians stormed the German capital of Berlin. Hitler, living in an underground bunker near the Chancellery building, committed suicide on 30 April 1945.

In the Pacific, the planned Japanese invasion of Australia was thwarted. Fighting in the jungles of New Guinea, Australian and American troops under the command of General Douglas MacArthur (1880–1964) turned back the Japanese army. U.S. Marines did likewise with a bold landing at Guadalcanal and months of bloody fighting in the Solomon Islands. In June 1942, within six months of the attack at Pearl Harbor, American naval forces commanded by Admiral Chester Nimitz (1885–1966) inflicted a defeat on the Japanese navy from which it could not recover. In the Battle of Midway Japan lost four aircraft carriers, a heavy cruiser, over three hundred airplanes, and 5000 men. Midway was the Pacific equivalent of the Battle of Stalingrad.

In the summer of 1943, as the Soviet Union launched the offensive that was to defeat Germany, America began to move across the Pacific toward Japan. Nimitz and MacArthur conceived a brilliant plan in which American land, sea, and air forces fought in a coordinated effort. With a series of amphibious landings, they hopped from island to island. Some Japanese island fortresses like Tarawa were taken; others like Truk were bypassed and cut off from Japanese home bases. With the conquest of Saipan in November 1944 and Iwo Jima in March 1945, the U.S. air force acquired bases from which B-29 bombers could strike at the Japanese home islands. In the summer of 1945, in the greatest air offensive in history, American planes destroyed what remained of the Japanese navy, crippled Japanese industry, and mercilessly firebombed major population centers. The attack ended with the dropping of atomic bombs on the cities of Hiroshima and Nagasaki. The Japanese government accepted American terms for peace and surrendered unconditionally on 2 September 1945. Four months after the defeat of Germany the war in Asia was over.

The Fate of Allied Cooperation: 1945

The costs of World War II in terms of death and destruction were the highest in history. Fifty million lives were lost. Most of the dead were Europeans, and most of them were Russians and Poles. The high incidence of civilian deaths distinguished the Second World War from previous wars—well over 50 percent of the dead were noncombatants. Deliberate military targeting of cities explains this phenomenon only in part. The majority of civilian deaths were the result of starvation, enslavement, massacre, and deliberate extermination. The psychological devastation of continual violence, loss, injury, and rape of survivors cannot be measured.

Material destruction was also great. Axis and Allied cities, centers of civilization and culture, were turned into wastelands by aerial bombing. The Germans bombed Rotterdam and Coventry. The British engineered the firebombing of Dresden. Warsaw and Stalingrad were destroyed by the German army. Hiroshima and Nagasaki were leveled by the United States. The nations of Europe were weakened after World War I; after World War II, they were crippled. Europe was completely displaced from the position of world dominance it had held for centuries. The United States alone was undamaged and stronger after the war than before, its industrial capacity and production greatly improved by the war.

The leaders of the United States, Great Britain, and the Soviet Union—the Big Three as they were called—met three times between 1943 and 1945: first at Teheran; then in February 1945 at Yalta, a Russian Black Sea resort; and finally in July and August 1945 at Potsdam, a suburb of Berlin. They coordinated their attack on Germany and Japan and discussed their plans for postwar Europe. After Allied victory, the governments of both Germany and Japan would be totally abolished and completely reconstructed. No deals would be made with Hitler or his successors; no peace would be negotiated with the enemy; surrender would be unconditional. Germany would be disarmed and denazified and its leaders tried as war criminals. The armies of the Big Three would occupy Germany, each with a separate zone, but the country would be governed as a single economic unit. The Soviet Union, it was agreed, could collect reparations from Germany. With Germany and Japan defeated, a United Nations organization would provide the structure for a lasting peace in the world.

Stalin expected the Soviet Union would decide the future of the territories of eastern Europe that the Soviet army had liberated from Germany. This area was vital to the security of the war-devastated Soviet Union; Stalin saw it as a protective barrier against another attack from the west. Romania, Bulgaria, Hungary, Czechoslovakia, and Poland, the Big Three decided, would have pro-Soviet governments. Since Soviet troops occupied these countries in 1945, there was little that the Anglo Americans could do to prevent Russian control unless they wanted to go to war against the USSR. Churchill realistically accepted this. But for Americans who took seriously the proclamations of President Roosevelt that their country had fought to restore freedom and self-determination to peoples oppressed by tyranny, Soviet power in eastern Europe proved to be a bitter disappointment.

The presence of Soviet armies in eastern Europe guaranteed that communism would prevail there after 1945. In western Europe the American and British presence fostered the existence of parliamentary democracies. Germany was divided. A similar pattern emerged in Asia. The U.S. forces of occupation in Japan oversaw the introduction of democratic institutions. The USSR controlled Manchuria. Korea was divided. The celebration of victory after a war in which 50 million people died did not last long. Nor did the Anglo-American cooperation with the Soviet Union endure. With the defeat of Germany and Japan, two ideological systems stood facing each other suspiciously across a divided Europe and a divided Asia.

Suggestions for Further Reading

Political Polarization in the 1930s

Ian Kershaw, *The "Hitler Myth": Image and Reality in the Third Reich* (New York: Oxford University Press, 1987). Examines the power of the "Hitler" myth created by the German Propaganda Ministry, the German people, and Hitler. The myth accounted for the stability of the Third Reich throughout the 1930s and in the first years of the war.

*MacGregor Knox, *Mussolini Unleashed, 1939–1941: Politics and Strategy in Fascist Italy's Last War* (Cambridge, England: Cambridge University Press, 1982). Argues that Mussolini had a consistent and planned foreign policy in the Mediterranean and a genuine program for living space in the Mediterranean and the Middle East. In his bid for power and prestige, Mussolini was willing to risk war and short-term instability at home.

Maurice Larkin, *France Since the Popular Front: Government and People, 1936–1986* (Oxford, England: Clarendon Press, 1988). A work of total history that

---

*Indicates paperback edition available.

situates French political developments in the history, traditions, social structure, and economy of France. Separates the legend from the legacy of the Popular Front.

*Detlev Peukert, *Inside Nazi Germany: Conformity, Opposition, and Racism in Everyday Life* (New Haven, CT: Yale University Press, 1987). Discusses the informal modes of resistance among the German people.

The Coming of World War II

*Paul Kennedy, *The Realities Behind Diplomacy: Background Influences on British External Policy, 1865–1980* (London: Allen & Unwin, 1981). Essay dealing with the continuity of appeasement in British foreign policy across two centuries.

*Ian Kershaw, *The Nazi Dictatorship* (London: Edward Arnold, 1985). A fine synthesis of key problems of interpretation regarding the Third Reich. Special attention is paid to the interdependence of domestic and foreign policy and the inevitability of war in Hitler's ideology.

*Donald Cameron Watt, *How War Came: The Immediate Origins of the Second World War* (London: Heinemann, 1989). An international historian chronicles the events leading to the outbreak of the war.

Racism and Destruction

*Renate Bridenthal, Atina Grossmann, and Marion Kaplan, eds., *When Biology Became Destiny: Women in Weimar and Nazi Germany* (New York: Monthly Review Press, 1984). A volume of essays pursuing common themes on the relation between sexism and racism in interwar and wartime Germany.

*Raul Hilberg, *The Destruction of the European Jews* (New York: Holmes and Meier, 1985), 3 vols. An exhaustive study of the annihilation of European Jews beginning with cultural precedents and antecedents. Examines step-by-step developments that led to extermination policies and contains valuable appendices on statistics and a discussion of sources.

*Charles S. Maier, *The Unmasterable Past: History, Holocaust, and German National Identity* (Cambridge, MA: Harvard University Press, 1988). A thoughtful discussion of the historical debate over the Holocaust and the comparative dimensions of the event. Especially valuable in placing the Holocaust within German history.

*Michael R. Marrus, *The Holocaust in History* (New York: New American Library, 1987). A comprehensive survey of all aspects of the Holocaust, including the policies of the Third Reich, the living conditions in the camps, and the prospects for resistance and opposition.

Allied Victory

John Campbell, ed., *The Experience of World War II* (New York: Oxford University Press, 1989). This richly illustrated work provides an overview of the Second World War in both the Asian and European theaters, in terms of origins, events, and consequences.

*Akira Iriye, *The Origins of the Second World War in Asia and the Pacific* (London: Longman, 1987). Examines the events of the 1930s leading up to hostilities in the Pacific theaters with a special focus on Japanese isolation and aggression.

*John Keegan, *The Second World War* (New York: Viking, 1990). Provides a panoramic sweep of "the largest single event in human history," with special attention to warfare in all its forms and the importance of leadership.

23

Postwar Recovery and Crisis: From the Cold War to the New Europe, 1945–1968

Sex and Drugs and Rock 'n' Roll

"I Wanna Hold Your Hand" seems an unlikely anthem for a generation. Yet this song performed by the British rock group the Beatles was known around the world in the early 1960s by an entire generation of the young. Youth screamed and swooned and danced to it. Parents and educators screamed, too, but out of fear that "Beatlemania" signaled the decline of the younger generation in Western societies. Adults worried that young people were being caught up in hedonism, sexual pleasure, and mind-numbing drugs, all because of this loud, cacophonous music.

Young people of the 1950s and 1960s saw the advent of rock 'n' roll differently. Rock 'n' roll emerged as a national phenomenon in the United States in the mid-1950s, firmly rooted in the black music of rhythm and blues. White country and western music was also influential in shaping the new sound. Titles like "Rock Around the Clock," "Shake, Rattle, and Roll," "Keep A-Knockin'," and "Blue Suede Shoes" captured the attention of a generation. The experiences of teenagers were at the center of the new rhythms, confronted in the lyrics and amplified with electric guitars. Rock 'n' roll appealed to the young because it dealt openly with the issues of sex and young love and

was aimed at the hypocrisy of the adult white world. Even the sound was revolutionary. It became "the music of the young," something that accentuated their differences from the adult world and their commonalities with each other.

Babies born after World War II began entering adolescence near the end of the 1950s, constituting a new audience for mass entertainment. They were also an important international mass market for music, as popular recordings began selling in the millions for the first time in history on such a scale. Music was now a consumer product. Elvis Presley, a white country blues singer from Memphis, Tennessee, emerged as the greatest figure on the rock 'n' roll scene in the late 1950s. His overt and androgynous sexuality, gyrating hips, and explicit lyrics made him an object of adult fears about loss of control of their children. He quickly developed a worldwide following of devoted fans, who hailed him "the King" and who continue to honor his memory years after his death.

In the 1960s British groups such as the Beatles from Liverpool entered the international rock scene. Dubbed "the mop tops" because of their long hair, they were condemned for transgressing sex roles in their appearance. Millions of boys copied their idols as hair became a political issue, a symbol of rebellion. Billboards appeared across the United States that proclaimed, "Beautify America—Get a Haircut!" With the new music came a new style of dressing, what adults saw as a uniform of disrespect for traditional values and parental authority. The British group Rolling Stones, who introduced electronic innovations to rock music, was considered more outrageously sexual, vulgar, and lewd than their countrymen the Beatles. Antirock movements cited "specialists" who warned that the new amplified music caused deafness, drug addiction, and excessive sexual activity.

The gap between the generations yawned into a gulf as rock music became political in the mid-1960s. Bob Dylan, an American rock performer, introduced folk music to the genre with songs of social protest like "Blowin' in the Wind" and "Only a Pawn in Their Game." Rock music was denounced as a communist plot, as performers urged their audiences to "Make Love, Not War." Dylan's "Subterranean Homesick Blues" targeted the hypocrisy of his society:

Ah get born, keep warm
Short pants, romance, learn to dance
Get dressed, get blessed
Try to be a success
Please her, please him, buy gifts
Don't steal, don't lift
Twenty years of schoolin'
And they put you on the day shift
Look out kid
they keep it all hid

Although rock music served as a rallying cry for a generation that opposed war and exploitation, its frankness about sexuality did not result in a reformulation of gender roles. Woman's place in rock music was usually as an object of desire. Few of the major rock stars were women. The American artist Janis Joplin was a striking exception. What was known in the rock world as "girl groups"—the Ronettes and the Shangri-Las are two examples—reinforced predominantly male views of sexuality both by their dress and by the lyrics of their songs. The female body was treated as a commodity itself in the fashions associated with the new youth culture, such as the miniskirt and the bikini. Girls and young women were important consumers of the new music and the values it communicated.

Rock music quickly became an international phenomenon, spreading from the United States and Great Britain to appeal to the young throughout the world. Rock stars were the new self-made millionaires, often from working-class backgrounds, who were able to benefit from advertising innovations and mass marketing techniques in a new age of consumption. The postwar generation that grew into adulthood beginning in the late 1960s shared a common musical culture. Student protest movements spread throughout Europe and the United States, and in the same period rock music gained acceptance as a legitimate and important musical genre. Through radio, television, and the international distribution of recordings, an international youth culture linked European and American youth together with common symbols and a common language of protest.

Regulating the Cold War

With the cessation of the "hot" war that had ripped Europe apart from 1939 to 1945, the armies of the United States and the Soviet Union met on the banks of the Elbe River in 1945. Greeting each other as victors and allies, the occupying armies waited for direction on how to conduct the peace. Europe and Japan were destroyed, leaving the United States and the Soviet Union as indisputably the two richest and strongest nations in the world. The Soviets understood that they ran a sorry second to American military superiority—the United States was alone in possessing the atomic bomb—and to American wealth, which, measured in GNP, was 400 percent greater than that of the Soviet Union. War had made these two superpowers allies; now the peace promised to make them once again into wary foes. In the three years that followed the war, a new kind of conflict emerged between the two superpower victors, a war deemed "cold" because of its lack of military violence, but a bitter war nonetheless.

The Cold War emerged as an ideological opposition between communism and capitalist democracies, dominated by the two superpowers, the Soviet Union and the United States, and affecting the entire globe. Drawing on three decades of distrust between the East and the West, the Cold War was related to the economic and foreign policy goals of both superpowers.

Cold War conflict initially developed because of differing Russian and American notions regarding the economic reconstruction of Europe. The Soviet Union realized that American aid to Europe was not a primarily humanitarian program. It was part of an economic offensive in Europe that would contribute to the dominance of American capital in world markets. The United States recognized that the Soviet Union hoped to achieve its own recovery through outright control of eastern Europe. Needing the stability of peace, the Soviets saw in eastern Europe, hostile as the area may have been to forced integration, a necessary buffer against Western competition. The Soviet Union feared U.S. intentions to establish liberal governments and capitalist markets in these states bordering its own frontiers and viewed such attempts as inimical to Soviet interests. For these reasons, Stalin refused to allow free elections in Poland and by force of occupying armies annexed neighboring territories that included eastern Finland, the Baltic states, East Prussia, eastern Poland, Subcarpathian Ukraine (Ruthenia), and Bessarabia. With the exception of East Prussia, these annexations were all limited to territories that had once been part of tsarist Russia.

Winston Churchill captured the drama of the new international order in a speech he delivered in Missouri in 1946: "From Stettin in the Baltic to Trieste in the Adriatic an iron curtain has descended across the continent." The term *iron curtain* described graphically for many the new fate of Europe, rigidly divided between East and West, a pawn in the struggle of the superpowers.

Atomic Politics

The nuclear arms race began in earnest during World War II, well before the first atomic bomb was dropped in August 1945. The Germans, the Russians, and the British all had teams exploring the destructive possibilities of nuclear fission during the war. But the Americans had the edge in the development of the bomb. Stalin understood the political significance of the weapon and committed the Soviet Union to a breakneck program of development following the war. The result was that the USSR ended the American monopoly and tested its first atomic bomb in 1949. Both countries developed the hydrogen bomb almost simultaneously in 1953. Space exploration by satellite was also deemed important in terms of detection and deployment of bombs, and the Soviets pulled ahead in this area with the launching of the first satellite, *Sputnik I*, in 1957. Intercontinental ballistic missiles (ICBMs) followed, further accelerating the pace of nuclear armament.

The atomic bomb and thermonuclear weapons contributed greatly to the shape of Cold War politics. The incineration of Hiroshima and Nagasaki sent a clear message to the world about the power of total annihilation available to those who controlled the bombs. The threat of such total destruction made full and direct confrontation with an equally armed enemy impossible. Both the United States and the Soviet Union, the first two members of the nuclear "club," knew that they had the capability of obliterating their enemy but not before the enemy could respond in retaliation. They also knew that the technology necessary for nuclear arms was available to any industrial power. By 1974 the "nuclear club" included Great Britain, France, the People's Republic of China, and India. These countries joined the United States and the Soviet Union in spending billions every year to expand nuclear arsenals and to develop more sophisticated weaponry and delivery systems.

A new vocabulary transformed popular attitudes and values. *Missile gaps, deterrence, first strike, second strike, radioactive fallout,* and *containment* were all terms that colored popular fears. Citizens in the Soviet Union learned of American weapons stockpiling and American deployment of military forces throughout the world. Americans learned that the Russians had the ability to deliver bombs that could wipe out major U.S. cities. Paranoia on both sides was encouraged by heads of state in their public addresses throughout the 1950s. Traitors were publicly tried, while espionage was sponsored by the state.

The first nuclear test-ban treaty, signed in 1963, banned tests in the atmosphere. Arms limitation and nonproliferation were the subjects of a series of conferences between the United States and the Soviet Union in the late 1960s and pointed the way to limitations eventually agreed on in the next decade. The United Nations, created by the Allies immediately following World War II to take the place of the defunct League of Nations, established international agencies for the purpose of harnessing nuclear power for peaceful uses. On the whole, however, the arms race persisted as a key continuity in Cold War politics. The race required the dedication of huge national resources to maintain a competitive stance. Conventional forces, too, were expanded to protect Eastern and Western bloc interests. With the aim of containing the USSR, the United States entered into a series of military alliances around the world. In order to provide mutual assistance should any member be attacked, the United States joined with Belgium, Britain, Canada, Denmark, France, Iceland, Italy, the Netherlands, Norway, and Portugal in 1949 to form the North Atlantic Treaty Organization (NATO). Greece and Turkey became members in 1952, West Germany in 1955, and Spain in 1982. The potential military threat of the Soviet Union in western Europe prompted this peacetime military alliance. The Southeast Asia Treaty Organization (SEATO) in 1954 and the Baghdad Pact of 1955 (known as CENTO in 1959) followed.

The United States strengthened its military presence throughout the period by acquiring 1400 military bases in foreign countries for its own forces. The Soviet Union countered developments in the West with its own alliances and organizations. In 1949 the USSR established the Council for Mutual Economic Assistance, or Comecon, with bilateral agreements between the Soviet Union and eastern European states. Comecon was Stalin's response to the U.S. Marshall Plan in western Europe. Rather than providing aid, however, Comecon benefited the Soviet Union at the expense of its partners and sought to integrate and control the economies of eastern Europe for Soviet gain. In 1955 Albania, Bulgaria, Romania, Czechoslovakia, Hungary, Poland, and East Germany—all Comecon members—joined with the Soviet Union to form a defensive alliance organization known as the Warsaw Pact. The USSR intended its eastern European allies to serve as a strategic buffer zone against the NATO forces.

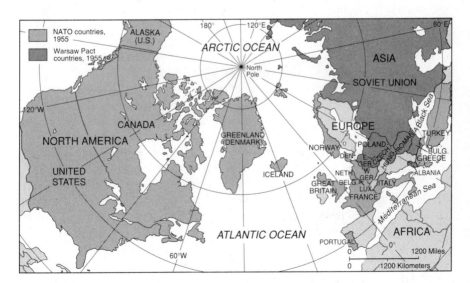

The Cold War: U.S. and Soviet alliances

Atomic politics encouraged *brinksmanship,* a term coined by John Foster Dulles (1888–1959), U.S. secretary of state from 1953 to 1959. Brinksmanship referred to a confrontationist foreign policy that brought the superpowers repeatedly to the edge of armed conflict. It encouraged a new kind of global politics in which the superpowers vied with each other to find new partners, especially in formerly colonized areas, to join their camps.

Decolonization

By the end of the Second World War, European colonial empires had been weakened or destroyed by the ravages of battle, by occupation, and by neglect. The United States, committed to free and open markets, pushed its advantage at the conclusion of the peace by insisting on the dismantling of the empires of its allies as well as those of its enemies. The Soviets, preoccupied with their own recovery, were in no position to assert a global policy at the end of the war.

Nationalist movements had been growing in power in the 1930s, and many nationalist leaders saw the war as a catalyst for independence, especially in Asia. Great Britain knew that it no longer commanded the resources to control India, historically its richest colony, which under the leadership of Mohandas Gandhi (1869–1948) had been agitating for independence since 1920. Given the title of "Mahatma" or "great-souled" by his people, Gandhi advocated passive resistance to achieve independence. He campaigned by means of civil disobedience, boycotts, and public fasts instead of violence to bring pressure on the colonizers. The British granted self-government to India in 1946 with the proviso that if the bitter conflict between Hindus and Muslims was not settled by mutual agreement, Great Britain would decide on the division of power. As a result, Muslim and Hindu representatives agreed to the division of British India into the independent states of India and Pakistan in 1947. Ceylon (now Sri Lanka) and Burma (now Myanmar) achieved full independence in 1948.

In its march through Asia during the war, Japan had smashed colonial empires. Japan's defeat created a power vacuum that nationalist leaders were eager to fill. Civil wars erupted in China, Burma, Korea, and Indochina. Anticolonial resistance opened the way to communist insurgence. Indochina declared its independence in 1945 and waged war with France until 1954. South Vietnam was declared a republic, and the United States sponsored a regime that was considered favorable to Western interests. The North Vietnamese state was established under the French-educated leader Ho Chi Minh. The civil war continued, with the North Vietnamese backing the National Liberation Front in the South. After almost two decades of escalating involvement, in 1973 American troops were finally withdrawn from a war they could not win. Cold War politics had enmeshed the United States in Southeast Asia and Cold War imperatives had kept it there.

The first wave of decolonization after 1945 had been in Asia. A second wave crested and crashed in the late 1950s and early 1960s in Africa, another ready battleground for Cold War dominance. Wartime experiences and rapid economic development fed existing nationalist aspirations and encouraged the emergence of mass political demands for liberation. A new generation of leaders, many of them educated in European institutions, moved from cooperation with home rule to demands for independence by the early 1960s. British prime minister Harold Macmillan (1894–1986) spoke of "the winds of change" in 1960, the year that proved to be a turning point in African politics. Britain and Belgium yielded their colonies. In 1960 Patrice Lumumba (1925–1961) became the first prime minister of the Republic of the Congo (present-day Zaire). White European rule continued in Rhodesia (now Zimbabwe) and South Africa, despite continued world pressure.

The French, having faced what its officer corps considered a humiliating defeat in Indochina, held on against the winds of change in North Africa. France's problems in Algeria began in earnest in 1954 when Muslims seeking independence and self-rule revolted. Although the Algerian rebels successfully employed terrorist and guerrilla tactics, European settlers and the French army in Algeria refused to accept defeat. The Fourth Republic was on the verge of collapse when General Charles de Gaulle (1890–1970), leader of the Free French resistance in World War II, stepped in to establish the Fifth Republic with a strong executive. He ended the war and agreed to Algeria's independence, which was achieved in 1962. One supporter of the Algerian revolution, Frantz Fanon (1925–1961), was working as a French-trained psychiatrist in Algeria when the revolution began. In his writings, especially his book *The Wretched of the Earth* (1961), he argued in favor of national liberation movements and for the necessity of violence.

Decolonization meant continued dependence for many third-world countries, as they were now known. First-world nations were identified as the advanced industrial countries; second-world countries were those whose lower level of prosperity indicated a transition from agricultural to industrial production. Third-world nations were suppliers of raw materials and food to the countries of the first world. These countries were no longer directly controlled as colonies but continued to be dominated by the Western capitalist powers and Japan, on which they relied for their markets and trade. As Frantz Fanon had described it, these newly independent countries had to continue doing what they had done as colonies: supplying raw materials to their former masters. African leader Kwame Nkrumah (1909–1972) of Ghana denounced this situation of dependence as "neocolonialism" and called for a united Africa as the only means of resistance. He led Ghana in a policy of nonalignment in the Cold War. With Jomo Kenyatta (1894–1978) of Kenya, he founded the Pan-African Federation, which promoted African nationalism.

Soviet leader Joseph Stalin limited the Soviet Union's foreign involvement following the Second World War to communist regimes that shared borders with the USSR in eastern Europe and Asia. After Stalin's death in 1953, the Soviet Union turned to the third world. Former colonies played an important new role in the Cold War strategies with the accession to power of Nikita Khrushchev (1894–1971) in the mid-1950s. The Soviet Union abandoned its previous caution and assumed a global role in offering "friendship treaties," military advice, trade credits, and general support for attempts at national liberation in Asia, Africa, and Latin America. Cold warriors took advantage of tribalism and regionalism, which mitigated against the establishment of strong central governments. Military rule and fragmentation often resulted. Instability and acute poverty continued to characterize former colonies after emancipation, regardless of which camp the new leaders joined.

The Two Germanies and the World in Two Blocs

In central Europe Cold War tensions first surfaced over the question of how to treat Germany. The United States and the Soviet Union had very different ideas about the future of their former enemy. In fostering economic reconstruction in Europe, the United States counted on a German economy transfused with American funds that would be self-supporting and stable. To the contrary, the Soviet Union, blaming Germany for its extreme destruction, demanded that German resources be siphoned off for Soviet reconstruction. Stricken as the Soviets were with 20 million dead, millions of homeless refugees surviving in dire poverty, and many cities in ruins, commandeering German labor and stripping Germany of its industrial plant seemed to them only fair.

With Germany's defeat, its territory had been divided into four zones, occupied by American, Soviet, British, and French troops. An Allied Control Commission consisting of representatives of the four powers was to govern Germany as a whole in keeping with the decisions made at Yalta before the end of the war. As Soviet and American antagonisms over Germany's future deepened, however, Allied rule polarized between East and West, with the internal politics of each area determined by the ideological conflicts between communism and capitalist free enterprise.

Allied attempts to administer Germany as a whole faltered and failed in 1948 over a question of economic policy. The zones of the Western occupying forces (the United States, Great Britain, and France), now administered as a single unit, issued a uniform and stable currency that the Russians accurately saw as a threat to their own economic policies in Germany. The Soviets blockaded the city of Berlin which, although behind the frontier of the Russian sector, was being administered in sectors by the four powers and whose western sector promised to become a successful enclave of Western capitalism. With the support of the people of West Berlin the Allies responded by airlifting food and supplies into West Berlin for a period of almost a year, defending it as an outpost that must be preserved from the advance of communism. The Russians were forced to withdraw the blockade in the spring of 1949. The Berlin blockade hardened the commitment on both sides to two Germanies.

The two new states came into existence in 1949, their origins separated by less than a month. The Federal Republic of Germany, within the American

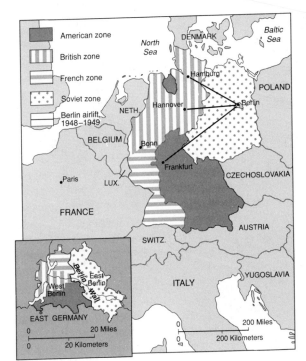

The division of Germany

orbit, was established as a democratic, parliamentary regime. Free elections brought the Christian Democrat Konrad Adenauer to power as chancellor. The German Democratic Republic was ruled as a single-party state under Walter Ulbricht, who took his direction from the Soviet Union.

The division of Germany became a microcosm of the division of the world into two armed camps. With the support of local Communist parties, Soviet-dominated governments were established in Poland, Hungary, Bulgaria, and Romania in 1947. The following year Czechoslovakia was pulled into the Soviet orbit.

In 1953 the man who had ruled the Soviet Union in his own image for almost three decades died. The death of Joseph Stalin unleashed a struggle for power among the Communist party leadership. It also initiated almost immediately a process of de-Stalinization and the beginnings of a thaw in censorship and repression. A growing urban and professional class expected improvements in the quality of life and greater freedoms after years of war and hardship. In 1956, at the Twentieth Party Congress, Nikita Khrushchev, as head of the Communist party, denounced Stalin as incompetent and cruel. After five years of jockeying for power among Stalin's former lieutenants, Khrushchev emerged victorious and assumed the office of premier in 1958.

De-Stalinization also blossomed in eastern Europe. Discontent over collectivization, low wages, and the lack of consumer goods fueled a latent nationalism among eastern European populations resentful of Soviet control and influence. Violence erupted in 1953 in East Berlin as workers revolted over conditions in the workplace, but it was quickly and effectively suppressed. Demands for reforms and liberalization in Poland also produced riots and changes in Communist party leadership. Wladislaw Gomulka (1905–1982), a communist with a nationalist point of view who had survived Stalin's purges, aimed to take advantage of the power vacuum created by the departure of Stalinist leaders. Gomulka refused to back down in the face of severe Soviet pressure and the threat of a Soviet invasion to keep him from power. Elected as the first secretary of the Communist party in Poland, Gomulka sought to steer his nation on a more liberal course.

Hungarians followed suit with their demands for diversity and for the withdrawal of Hungary from the Warsaw Pact. On 23 October 1956, inspired by the events in Poland, Hungarians rose up in anger against their old-guard Stalinist rulers. Imre Nagy (1896–1958), a liberal communist, took control of the government, attempted to introduce democratic reforms, and relaxed economic controls. The Soviets, however, were unwilling to lose control of their sphere of influence in Eastern bloc nations and to jeopardize their system of defense in the Warsaw Pact. Moscow responded to liberal experimentation in Hungary by sending tanks and troops into Budapest. Brutal repression and purges followed. The Hungarian experience in 1956 made clear that too much change too quickly would not be tolerated by the Soviet rulers. The violent crushing of the Hungarian revolution reminded everyone of the realities of Soviet control and the Soviet Union's defense priorities in eastern Europe.

East Berlin in the late 1950s and early 1960s posed a particular problem for communist rule. Unable to compete successfully in wages and standard of living with the western, capitalist sector of the city, East Berlin saw increasing numbers of its population, especially the educated and professional classes, crossing the line to a more prosperous life. In 1961 the Soviet Union responded to this problem by building a wall that cordoned off the part of the city it controlled. The Berlin Wall eventually stretched for 103 miles, with heavily policed crossing points, turrets, and troops and tanks facing each other across the divide that came to symbolize the Cold War.

In 1968 the policy of de-Stalinization reached a critical juncture in Czechoslovakia. Early in 1968 Alexander Dubček, Czech party secretary and a member of the younger, educated generation of technocrats, supported liberal reforms in Czechoslovakia. He acted on popular desires for nationalism, the end of censorship, and better working conditions. Above all, he led the way to democratic reforms in the political process that would restore rule to the people. Dubček spoke of "socialism with a human face," although, unlike the Hungarians in 1956, he made no move to withdraw his country from the Warsaw Pact or to defy Soviet leadership. Moscow nevertheless feared the erosion of obedience within the Eastern bloc and the collapse of one-party rule in the Czech state, and sent in thousands of tanks and hundreds of thousands of Warsaw Pact troops to Prague and other Czech cities to reestablish control. The Czechs responded with passive resistance. The Soviet invasion made clear that popular nationalism was intolerable in an Eastern bloc nation.

Soviet tanks rumbled through Prague as troops from the Warsaw Pact countries invaded the Czechoslovakian capital in 1968, bringing an end to Alexander Dubček's reform movement. Dubček was rehabilitated in the liberalization of 1989 and elected chairman of the parliament.

Alone among eastern European leaders, Josip Broz, better known as Marshal Tito, of Yugoslavia resisted Soviet encroachment. As a partisan leader of communist resistance during World War II, Tito had heroically battled the Germans. Ruling Yugoslavia as a dictator after 1945, he refused to accede to Soviet directives to collectivize agriculture and to participate in joint economic ventures.

Asia was the next arena for the development of Cold War antagonisms. In 1950 the United States and the United Nations intervened when North Korea attacked South Korea. Korea, formerly controlled by Japan, had been divided following the war as a result of the presence of Russian and American troops. Communist-dominated North Korea refused to accept the artificial boundary between it and Western-dominated South Korea. China, a communist state following the victory of Mao Ze-dong (1893–1976) in 1949, intervened in the Korean conflict when American troops advanced on Chinese frontiers in October 1950. After three years of military stalemate, Korea was partitioned on the 38th parallel in 1953. The Soviet Union was not party to the conflict in Korea, but the United States considered China to be in the Soviet camp rather than an independent contender for power.

The Middle East was another theater of confrontation between the superpowers. The United States and the Soviet Union used aid to win support of "client" states. The withdrawal, sometimes under duress, of British and

French rule in the Middle East and North Africa, and the creation of the new state of Israel in 1948 destabilized the area and created the opportunities for new power alliances. Egypt and Syria, for example, sought Soviet support against the new Israeli state, which had been formed out of the part of Palestine under British mandate from 1920 and was dependent on U.S. aid.

Oil, an essential resource for rapid industrialization, was the object of Soviet politicking in Iran after the war. Western oil companies, long active in the area, had won oil concessions in Iran in 1946, but such rights eluded the Soviets. In 1951 a nationalist Iranian government sought to evict Westerners by nationalizing the oil fields. The British blockaded Iranian trade in the Persian Gulf, and the newly formed American espionage organization, the Central Intelligence Agency (CIA), subverted the nationalist government and placed in power the shah of Iran, a leader favorable to American interests.

A crisis came in 1956 in Egypt. Egyptian president Gamal Abdel Nasser (1918–1970), a nationalist in power by virtue of a military coup d'état in 1952, oversaw the nationalization of the Suez Canal. British and French military forces attacked and were forced to withdraw by pressure from both the Soviet Union and the United States, which cooperated in seeking to avert a disaster. The Middle East, however, remained a Cold War powder keg, with Israeli and Arab nationalist interests and Soviet and American aid running on a collision course. The expansion of the Israeli state at the expense of its Arab neighbors further exacerbated tensions.

The United States was heavily committed as a military presence in Southeast Asia after the French withdrawal from Indochina caused by its defeat at Dien Bien Phu in 1954. Arguing the domino theory—that one Southeast Asian country after another would fall like a row of dominoes to communist takeover—the United States also intervened in Laos and Cambodia. Between 1961 and 1973, the United States committed American troops to a full-scale war—though officially termed only a military action—against communist guerrilla forces throughout the region.

The United States was also experiencing Cold War problems closer to home. In 1954 the CIA plotted the overthrow of Guatemala's leftist regime in order to keep Soviet influence out of the Western Hemisphere. In 1959 a revolution in Cuba, an island nation only 90 miles off the American coast, resulted in the ejection of U.S. interests and the establishment of a communist regime under the leadership of a young middle-class lawyer, Fidel Castro. In 1962 a direct and frightening confrontation occurred between the United States and the USSR over Soviet missile installations in Cuba. Following the Russian withdrawal from the island, both U.S. president John F. Kennedy and Soviet leader Nikita Khrushchev pursued policies of "peaceful coexistence," intent on averting nuclear confrontation.

Another kind of challenge to Cold War power politics came from within the NATO alliance. General Charles de Gaulle, as president of the French Fifth Republic, rejected the straitjacket of American dominance in Western Europe and asserted his country's independent status by exploding the first French atomic bomb in 1960. Refusing to place the French military under an American general who served as supreme Allied Commander for NATO, de Gaulle completely withdrew France from participation in NATO by 1966. He forged an independent French foreign policy, taking advantage of the loosening of bloc politics around the mid-1960s.

In May 1965 U.S. secretary of state Dean Rusk observed, "This has become a very small planet. We have to be concerned with all of it—with all of its land, waters, atmosphere, and with surrounding space." In the mid-1960s leaders of the two great blocs of East and West began to realize that peaceful coexistence was the only reasonable outcome of the atomic age and that alternatives to the arms race must be found.

Reconstructing Europe

When the dust from the last bombs settled over Europe's cities, the balance sheets of destruction were tallied. Millions of survivors found themselves homeless. Millions returned home to rubble from battlefronts and concentration camps with wounds beyond healing. There were no jobs; there was nothing to eat. What was not measured in the statistics on physical and human destruction, at least immediately, was the psychological devastation that succeeded such loss. There could be no returning to life as normal. For many the war was far gentler than the peace. For these peacetime combatants, often women and children, digging out and surviving were the greatest battles of all.

The Problem: Europe in Ruins

An American observer wrote back to his government in 1947, "Europe is steadily deteriorating. The political position reflects the economic. One political crisis after another merely denotes the existence of economic distress. Millions of people in the cities are slowly starving." Even the winners were losers as survivors experienced a level of human and material destruction unknown in the history of warfare. Economists judged that Europe would need at least twenty-five years to regain its prewar economic capacity. The worst was also feared: that Europe would never recover as a world economic power.

Large-scale population movements made matters worse. Displaced persons by the millions moved across Europe. The release of prisoners of war and slave workers imprisoned during the Third Reich strained already weak economies. Germans were expelled from territories that Germany had controlled before the war. Soviet expansionist policies forced others to flee Estonia, Latvia, and Lithuania. Jews who survived the concentration camps resettled outside Europe, primarily in Palestine and the United States.

Industrial production in 1945 was a third of its level in 1938. Housing shortages existed everywhere. France had lost one-fifth of its housing during the war years; Germany's 50 largest cities had seen two-fifths of their buildings reduced to rubble. Frankfurt, Düsseldorf, Dresden, Warsaw, and Berlin were virtually destroyed. The transportation infrastructure was severely damaged: Railways, roads, and bridges were in shambles all over Europe. Communications networks were in disarray. In some cases, industrial plants had not been as adversely affected as urban centers. Yet machinery everywhere had been worn out in wartime production and replacement parts were nonexistent. German equipment was dismantled and seized by Soviet soldiers to be used in Russia in place of what the Germans had destroyed.

Agriculture, too, suffered severe reversals in wartime economies and was unable to resume prewar production in 1945. In general, European agriculture was producing at 50 percent of its prewar capacity. Italy suffered greatly, with one-third of its overall assets destroyed. The scarcity of goods converged with ballooning inflation. Black markets with astronomical prices for necessities flourished, as currency rates plummeted. Everywhere the outlook was bleak. Yet in less than a decade, the situation had been reversed. The solution came from outside Europe.

The Solution: The Marshall Plan

The Soviet Union implemented an expansion of its territorial boundaries as a way of reversing some of its drastic losses in the war. Above all, it wanted a protective ring of satellite states as security from attack from the West. Picking up territory from Finland and Poland, parts of East Prussia and eastern Czechoslovakia, forcibly reincorporating the Baltic states of Estonia, Latvia, and Lithuania, and recovering Bessarabia, the Soviet Union succeeded in acquiring sizable territories. In addition, the Soviet state dedicated itself to economic reconstruction behind a protective buffer of satellite states— Poland, East Germany, Czechoslovakia, Hungary, Romania, Bulgaria—over which Soviet leaders exercised strong control. Yugoslavia and Albania chose to follow a more independent communist path. Lacking the capital necessary to finance recovery, the Soviets sought compensation from eastern and central European territories.

In contrast to the Soviet Union, the United States had incurred relatively light casualties in World War II. Because the fighting had not taken place on the North American continent, U.S. cities, farmlands, and factories were intact. The United States had benefited economically from the conflict in Europe and actually expanded its productivity during the war. In 1945 the United States was producing a full 50 percent of the world's gross national product—a staggering fact to a displaced Great Britain, whose former trade networks were permanently destroyed. Furthermore, the United States held two-thirds of the world's gold. A United States bursting with energy and prosperity was a real threat to the Soviet Union viewing the rubble of its destroyed cities and counting the bodies of its dead.

The United States knew that it lacked one important guarantee to secure its growth and its future prosperity: adequate international markets for its goods. In the 1920s the United States had exported capital to Europe in the form of private loans with the hope that trade would flourish as a result. The decade following the Great Depression of 1929 witnessed the search for a policy to expand U.S. markets. Both Europe and Japan were recognized as potential buyers for American goods, but both areas parried with protectionism to foster their own post-depression recovery. World War II facilitated the success of an international economic policy consistent with U.S. economic goals since 1920. In both Europe and Japan, the United States intervened to aid reconstruction and recovery of war-torn nations. These economies, hungry for capital, no longer opposed U.S. intervention or erected trade barriers against American goods.

By the spring of 1947 it was clear to American policymakers that initial postwar attempts to stabilize European economies and promote world recovery were simply not working. The United States had, earlier in the same year, engineered emergency aid to Turkey and Greece, both objects of Soviet aspirations for control. The aid emerged in an atmosphere of opposition between the United States and the Soviet Union over issues of territorial control in eastern and southern Europe. The Cold War coincided with and reinforced the U.S. need to reconstruct Western Europe.

On 5 June 1947, Secretary of State George C. Marshall (1880–1959) delivered the commencement address at Harvard University. In his speech Marshall introduced the European Recovery Act, popularly known as the Marshall Plan, through which billions of dollars in aid would be made available to European states, both in the East and in the West, provided that two conditions were met: (1) the recipient states must cooperate with one another in aligning national economic policies and improving the international monetary system; (2) they must work toward breaking down trade barriers.

Participating countries included Austria, Belgium, Denmark, France, West Germany, Great Britain, Greece, Iceland, Italy, Luxembourg, the Netherlands, Norway, Sweden, Switzerland, and Turkey. Russia and eastern European countries were also eligible for aid under the original formulation. But Russia opposed the plan from the first, wary of U.S. intentions to extend the influence of Western capitalism. Soviet opposition encouraged members of the U.S. Congress, afraid of a communist takeover in Europe, to support the plan.

Like the United States, the Soviet Union had its own economic imperatives that dictated its attitudes toward European economic development. Under Stalin's direction, the Soviet Union concentrated all its efforts on reconstructing its devastated economy and, to this end, sought integration with eastern European states, whose technology and resources were needed for the rebuilding of the Soviet state. U.S. dominance threatened the vital connection with eastern Europe that the Soviet Union was determinedly solidifying in the postwar years.

The amount of U.S. aid to Europe was massive. Over $23 billion was pumped into western Europe between 1947 and 1952. American foreign aid restored western European trade and production, while at the same time controlling inflation. Dean Acheson (1893–1971), Marshall's successor as secretary of state, described the plan in terms of "our duty as human beings" but nevertheless considered it "chiefly as a matter of national self-interest."

Administering the Plan

As significant as the gift of funds to European states undoubtedly was, no less important was the whole administrative apparatus that American money brought in its wake. In order to expend available monies most effectively and comply with stipulations for cooperation and regulation, the states of western Europe resorted to intensified planning and limited nationalization. Regulation and state intervention dominated the formulation of economic policy. Special attention was given to workers' welfare through unemployment insurance, retirement benefits, public health, and housing policies. European states recognized the need to provide a safety net for their citizens in order to avoid the disastrous depression and stagnation of the 1930s, while attempting to rebuild their shattered economies.

The economic theory of John Maynard Keynes, applied successfully by neutral Sweden to its economic policies during the war, came into vogue throughout Europe in 1945, and the postwar era saw the triumph of Keynesian economics. Keynes favored macroeconomic policies to increase productivity and argued for an active role for government in "priming the pump" of economic growth. The government should be responsible, according to Keynes, for the control and regulation of the economy with the goal of ensuring full employment for its people. Governments could and should check inflation and eliminate boom-and-bust cycles, incurring deficits by spending beyond revenues if necessary.

U.S. foreign aid contributed mightily to the extension of central planning and the growth of the welfare state throughout western Europe. But money alone could not have accomplished the recovery that took place. The chief mechanism for administering Marshall Plan aid was the Office of European Economic Cooperation (OEEC). This master coordinating agency made the requirements for recovery clear. European states had to stabilize their own economies. Cooperation between the public and private sectors was intended to free market forces, modernize production, and raise productivity. Planning mechanisms, including transnational organizations and networks, resulted in the modernization of production and the assimilation of new techniques, new styles of management, and innovative business practices from the United States.

The major exception to the establishment of central planning agencies and the nationalization of key industries was West Germany. Deciding against the British and French models of planned growth, the West Germans endorsed a free-market policy that encouraged private enterprise while providing state insurance for all workers. What has been described as "a free enterprise economy with a social conscience" produced the richest economy in western Europe by the mid-1950s. Some West German industries had been dismantled, but much of West Germany's productive capacity remained intact in the late 1940s. The wealth of great industrialists like Krupp, serving prison sentences as war criminals, was not expropriated, and their commercial empires stood ready to direct the economic revival. The Krupp and I.G. Farben empires were successfully broken up into smaller units. Industries forced to start afresh benefited from the latest technology.

Japanese economic challenges in the postwar era were similar to those of western Europe. As a defeated and occupied nation in 1945, Japan faced a grim future. U.S. aims for Asia were similar to those for Europe: American policymakers sought to create a multilateral system of world trade and preserve America's sphere of influence against communist encroachment. The American general Douglas MacArthur was appointed the Supreme Commander for the Allied Powers and the head of occupation forces in Japan. His mission in Japan was to impose rapid economic change from above. The occupation government set out to erect institutions to promote political democratization and to eliminate militaristic institutions, official patronage, and censorship. Planning, both formal and informal, reshaped the economy as U.S. aid flowed into Japan during the late 1940s and early 1950s. These changes in Japan, as in western Europe, took place alongside growing American fears of communism in the region.

Japan turned its wartime devastation into an advantage by replacing destroyed obsolete factories with the latest technology obtained by license from foreign firms. Through a combination of bureaucracy and patronage devoted to planned growth, Japan's GNP reached prewar levels by 1956. By 1968 Japan had turned defeat into triumph and stood as the third largest industrial nation in the world. The abolition of the army and navy was a boon for the Japanese economy, since 16 percent of prewar GNP had been devoted to support of the military. Postwar demilitarization freed Japan from the financial exigencies of the arms race. Funds formerly used for arms now flowed into investment and new technology. Slowed population growth after 1948 and increased volume in foreign trade contributed to Japanese prosperity. The United States had succeeded in exporting aspects of its own economy abroad. Through management and planning, recipients of American aid surpassed U.S. goals. A multilateral system of world trade emerged out of the ashes of war.

Western European Economic Integration

European integration, discussed before and during the war, received added impetus in the postwar period. The Marshall Plan reconciled western Europe with West Germany through economic cooperation, although that was by no means its original purpose. Realizing that Europe as a region needed the cooperation of its member states if it was to contend in world markets, associations dedicated to integration began to emerge alongside economic planning mechanisms. The Council of Europe dealt with the "discussion of questions of common concern and by agreements and common action in economic, social, cultural, scientific, legal, and administrative matters and in the maintenance and further realization of human rights and fundamental freedoms." Although not itself a supranational institution with its own authority, the Council of Europe urged a federation among European states. Britain alone rejected all attempts to develop structures of loose intergovernmental cooperation.

Belgium, the Netherlands, and Luxembourg were the first European states to establish themselves as an economic unit—the Benelux. Internal customs duties were removed among the three states and a common external tariff barrier was erected. The Schuman Plan joined France and West Germany in economic cooperation by pooling all coal and steel resources beginning in 1950. Creators of the plan, Jean Monnet (1888–1979) and Robert Schuman (1886–1963) of France, saw it as the first step toward the removal of all economic barriers among European states and as a move toward eventual political integration. In 1951 the Netherlands, Belgium, Luxembourg, France, Italy, and West Germany formed the European Coal and Steel Community (ECSC). While constantly confronting domestic opposition on nationalist grounds, the ECSC succeeded in establishing a "common market" in coal and steel among its member states. In 1957 the same six members created the European Economic Community (EEC) and committed themselves to broadening the integration of markets. This was the beginning of what became known as the Common Market.

The Common Market aimed to establish among its member states a free movement of labor and capital, the elimination of restrictions on trade, common investment practices, and coordinated social welfare programs. National agricultural interests were to be protected. Great Britain was initially a vocal opponent of the Common Market and continued to defend its own trading relationship with its Commonwealth countries. In 1973 Great Britain became a member of the Common Market and joined with other European nations in defining common economic policies. The EEC meanwhile achieved the support of the United States in its transitional period, in which it had 15 years to accomplish its aims.

European union was a phenomenon of exclusion as much as inclusion. It sharpened antagonisms between the West and the East by its very success. While promoting prosperity, European economic unification favored concentration and the emergence of large corporations. Vast individual fortunes flourished under state sponsorship and the rule of the experts. National parliaments were sometimes eclipsed by superfluous new economic decision-making organizations that aimed to make Western Europe into a single free-trade area. The Soviet Union, too, relied on state planning to foster rapid economic growth, but it was central planning emanating from Moscow, based on different assumptions and directed toward different ends.

*C*reating the Welfare State

The welfare state, a creation of the post–World War II era throughout Europe, grew out of the social welfare policies of the interwar period and out of the war itself. Welfare programs aimed to protect citizens through the establishment of a decent standard of living available for everyone. The experiences of the Great Depression had done much to foster concern for economic security. In France, the primary concern of the welfare state was the protection of children and the issue of family allowances. In Great Britain, as in Germany, emphasis was placed on unemployment insurance and health-care benefits. Everywhere, however, the welfare state developed a related set of social programs and policies whereby the state intervened in the cycles of individual lives to provide economic support for the challenges of birth, sickness, old age, and unemployment.

Protection of citizenry took varied forms according to Cold War politics. In the Warsaw Pact countries, the need to industrialize rapidly and to dedicate productive wealth to armament and military protection resulted in a nonexistent consumer economy in which the issues of quality of life and protection took a very different direction. Based on a concept of equal access to a minimum standard of living, welfare states did not treat all its members equally. Women were often disadvantaged in social welfare programs, as family needs, men's rights, and the protection of children led to different national configurations.

Prosperity and Consumption in the West

Despite the different paths toward reconstruction following World War II, every western European nation experienced dramatic increases in total wealth. Per capita income was clearly on the rise through the mid-1960s, and there was more disposable wealth than ever before. Prosperity encouraged new patterns of spending based on confidence in the economy. This new consumerism, in turn, was essential to economic growth and future productivity.

The social programs of the welfare state played an important role in promoting postwar consumption. People began to relax about their economic futures, more secure because of the provisions of unemployment insurance, old-age pensions, and health and accident insurance. In the mid-1950s all over western Europe people began to spend their earnings, knowing that accidents, disasters, and sicknesses would be taken care of by the state. In addition, western Europeans began to buy on credit, spending money they had not yet earned. This, too, was an innovation in postwar markets.

Welfare programs could be sustained only in an era of prosperity and economic growth, since they depended on taxation of income for their funds. Such taxation did not, however, result in a redistribution of wealth. Wealth remained in the hands of a few and became even more concentrated as a result of phenomenal postwar economic growth. In West Germany, for example, 1.7 percent of the population owned 35 percent of the society's total wealth.

Just as the welfare state did not redistribute wealth, neither did it provide equal pay for equal work. In France women who performed the same jobs as men in typesetting, for example, and who on average set 15,000 keystrokes per hour at the keyboards compared to 10,000 by men, earned 50 percent of men's salaries and held different titles for their jobs. Separate wage scales for women drawn up during the Nazi period remained in effect in West Germany until 1956. The skills associated with occupations performed by women were downgraded, as were their salaries. Women earned two-thirds or less of what men earned throughout western Europe. Welfare state revenues were a direct result of pay scale inequalities. Lower salaries for women meant higher profits and helped make economic recovery possible.

The Eastern Bloc and Recovery

In the years before his death in 1953, Joseph Stalin succeeded in making the Soviet Union a vital industrial giant second only to the United States. The Soviet economy experienced dramatic recovery after 1945, in spite of the severe damage inflicted on it during the war. The production of steel, coal, and crude oil skyrocketed under state planning. Heavy industry was the top priority of Soviet recovery, in keeping with prewar commitments to rapid modernization. In addition, the postwar Soviet economy assumed the new burdens of the development of a nuclear arsenal and an expensive program for the exploration of space. Stalin maintained the Soviet Union on the footing of a war economy, restricted occupational mobility, and continued to rely on forced labor camps.

The Soviet Union's standard of living remained relatively low in these years when western Europe was undergoing a consumer revolution. In the Soviet Union and throughout the Eastern bloc countries, women's full partic-ipation in the labor force was essential for recovery. In spite of their presence in large numbers in highly skilled sectors like medicine, Soviet and Eastern bloc women remained poorly paid, as did women in the West. Soviet men received higher salaries for the same work on the grounds that they had to support families.

With Stalin's death, new leaders recognized the need for change, especially with regard to the neglected sectors of agricultural production and consumer

Women worked alongside men in heavy industrial jobs to implement the Soviet Five-Year plans. This woman welder is working on the construction of a giant tractor factory in Byelorussia.

products. The Soviet population was growing rapidly, from 170 million in 1939 to 234 million in 1967. Khrushchev promised the Russian people lower prices and a shorter work week but in 1964, when he fell from power, Russians were paying higher prices for their food than before. With a declining rate of development, the Soviet economy lacked the necessary capital to advance the plans for growth in all sectors. Defense spending nearly doubled in the short period between 1960 and 1968.

The nature of planned Soviet growth exacted heavy costs in the Eastern bloc countries. Adhering to the Soviet pattern of heavy industrial expansion at the expense of agriculture and consumer goods, East Germany nearly doubled its industrial output by 1955, despite having been stripped of its industrial plant by the Soviet Union before 1948. Czechoslovakia, Bulgaria, Romania, and Yugoslavia all reported significant industrial growth in this period. Yet dislocations caused by collectivization and heavy defense expenditures stirred up social unrest in East Germany, Czechoslovakia, Poland, and Hungary. The

Soviet Union responded with some economic concessions but on the whole stressed common industrial and defense pursuits, employing ideological persuasion and military pressure to keep its reluctant partners in line. The slowed growth of the 1960s, the delay in development of consumer durables, and the inadequacy of basic foodstuffs, housing, and clothing were the costs that Eastern bloc citizens paid for their inefficient and rigid planned economies dedicated to the development of heavy industry. In eastern Europe and the Soviet Union, poverty was virtually eliminated, however, as the state subsidized housing, health care, and higher education, which were available to all.

Family Strategies

Prewar concerns with a declining birthrate intensified after World War II. In some European countries the birthrate climbed in the years immediately following the war, an encouraging sign to observers who saw in this trend an optimistic commitment to the future after the cessation of the horrors of war. The situation was more complicated in France and the United States, where the birthrates began to climb even before the war was over. Nearly everywhere throughout Europe, however, the rise in the birthrate was momentary, with the United States standing alone in experiencing a genuine and sustained "baby boom" that lasted until about 1960. In Germany and in eastern Europe (Poland and Yugoslavia, for example) the costs of the war exacted heavy tolls on families long after the hostilities ended. On average, women everywhere were having fewer children by choice.

Technology had expanded the range of choices in family planning. In the early 1960s the birth control pill became available on the European and American markets, primarily to middle-class women. Europeans were choosing to have smaller families. The drop in the birthrate had clearly preceded the new technological interventions that included intrauterine devices (IUDs), improved diaphragms, sponges, and more effective spermicidal creams and jellies. The condom, invented a century earlier, was now sold to a mass market. Controversies surrounded the unhealthy side effects of the pill and the dangerious Dalkon Shield, an IUD that had not been adequately tested before marketing and resulted in the death or sterilization of thousands of women. Religious leaders spoke out on the moral issues surrounding sexuality without reproduction. Information about their reproductive lives became more accessible to young women. Illegal abortions continued to be an alternative for women. In France and Italy birth control information was often withheld from the public. Abortion was probably the primary form of birth control in the Soviet Union in the years following the war.

The Family and Welfare.   Concurrent with a low birthrate was a return to family life and family values in the years after the war. Those who had lived through the previous 20 years were haunted by the memories of the Great Depression, severe economic hardships, destructive war, and the loss of loved ones. Women and men throughout western Europe and the United States embraced family values and a return to normal life, even if they did not opt for large families. Expectations for improved family life placed new demands on welfare state programs. They also placed increased demands on mothers, whose presence in the home was now seen as all-important for the proper development of the child.

European states implemented official programs to encourage women to have more children and to be better mothers. *Pronatalism*, as this policy was known, resulted from an official concern over low birthrates and a decline in family size. Considerations about racial dominance and woman's proper role seem to have affected the development of these policies. In 1945 Lord Beveridge (1879–1960), the architect of the British welfare state, emphasized the importance of women's role "in ensuring the adequate continuance of the British race" and argued that women's place was in the home.

Welfare state programs differed from country to country as the result of a series of different expectations of women as workers and women as mothers. Konrad Adenauer, chancellor of West Germany, spoke of "a will to children" as essential for his country's continued economic growth and prosperity. In Great Britain the welfare system was built on the ideal of the mother at home with her children. With the emphasis on the need for larger families—four children was considered "desirable" in England—English society focused on the importance of the role of the mother. Family allowances determined by the number of children were tied to men's participation in the work force; women were defined according to their husband's status. The state welfare system strengthened the financial dependence of English wives on their husbands.

In Great Britain anxiety over the low birthrate was also tied to the debate over equal pay for women. Opponents of the measure argued that equal pay would cause women to forego marriage and motherhood and should, therefore, be avoided. There was a consensus about keeping women out of the work force and paying them less in order to achieve that end.

The French system of *sécurité sociale* defined all women, whether married or single, as equal to men; unlike the British system, all French women had the same rights of access to welfare programs as men. This may well have reflected the different work history of women in France and the recognition of the importance of women's labor for reconstruction of the economy. As a result, family allowances, pre- and postnatal care, maternity benefits, and child care were provided on the assumption that working mothers were a fact of life. French payments were intended to encourage large families and focused primarily on the needs of children. More and more women entered the paid labor force after 1945, and they were less financially dependent on their husbands than their British counterparts.

Both forms of welfare state, the British that emphasized women's role as mothers and the French that accepted women's role as workers, were based on different attitudes about the nature of gender difference and equality. Women's political consciousness developed in both societies. The women's liberation movements of the late 1960s and early 1970s found their roots in the contradictions of differing welfare policies.

The Beginnings of Women's Protest. The 1960s was a period of protest in Western countries as people demonstrated for civil rights and free expression. The movement againt U.S. involvement in Vietnam was fueled by the activism of the black civil rights movement. Pacifist and antinuclear groups united to "Ban the Bomb." Women participated in all of these movements, and by the end of the 1960s had begun to question their own place in organizations that did not acknowledge their claims to equal rights, equal pay, and liberation from the oppression of male society. A new critique began to form within the welfare state that indicated there were cracks in the facade.

One book in particular, written after World War II, captured the imagination of many women who were aware of the contradictions and limitations placed on them by state and society. *The Second Sex* (1949), written by Simone de Beauvoir (1908–1986), a leading French intellectual, analyzed women in the context of Western culture. By examining the assumptions of political theories, including Marxism, in the light of philosophy, biology, history, and psychoanalysis, de Beauvoir uncovered the myths governing the creation of the female self. By showing how the male is the center of culture and the female is "other," de Beauvoir urged women to be independent and to resist male definitions. *The Second Sex* became the handbook of the women's movement in the 1960s.

A very different work appeared in 1963, *The Feminine Mystique.* In this work author Betty Friedan voiced the grievances of a previously politically quiescent group of women. Friedan was an American suburban homemaker and the mother of three children when she wrote about what she saw as the schizophrenic split in her own middle-class world between the reality of women's lives and the idealized image of the perfect homemaker. After World War II women were expected to find personal fulfillment in the domestic sphere. Instead, Friedan found women suffering from "the sickness with no name" and "the nameless desperation" of a profound crisis in identity.

A new politics centered on women's needs and women's rights slowly took root. The feminist critique did not emerge as a mass movement until the 1970s. Youth culture and dissent among the young further informed growing feminist discontent. But the agenda of protest in the 1960s accepted gender differences reinforced by social policies as normal and natural.

Youth Culture and the Generation Gap

Youth culture was created by outside forces as much as it was a self-creation. Socialized together in an expanding educational system from primary school through high school, the young came to see themselves as a social force. They were also socialized by marketing efforts that appealed to their particular needs as a group.

The prosperity that characterized the period from the mid-1950s to the mid-1960s throughout the West provided a secure base from which radical dissenters could launch their protests. The young people of the 1960s were the first generation to come of age after World War II. Though they had no memory themselves of the destruction of that war, they were reminded daily of the imminence of nuclear destruction in their own lives. The combination of the security of affluence and the insecurity of Cold War politics created a widening gap between the world of decision-making adults and the idealistic universe of the young. To the criticisms of parents, politicians, and teachers, the new generation responded that no one over 30 could be trusted.

New styles of dress and grooming were a rejection of middle-class culture in Europe and the United States. Anthropologists and sociologists in the 1960s began studying youth as if they were a foreign tribe. The "generation gap" appeared as the subject of hundreds of specialized studies. Adolescent behavior was examined across cultures. Sexual freedom and the use of drugs were subjected to special scrutiny. But it was above all the politics of the young that baffled and enraged many observers. When the stable base of economic prosperity began to erode as a result of slowed growth and inflation in the second half of the 1960s, first in western Europe and then in the United States, frustrated expectations and shrinking opportunities for the young served as a further impetus for political action.

Sex and Drugs and Protest

Increased emphasis on fulfillment through sexual pleasure was one consequence of the technological revolution in birth control devices, and it led to what has been called a revolution in sexual values in Western societies in the 1960s. The sexual revolution drew attention to sexual fulfillment as an end in itself. Women's bodies were displayed more explicitly than ever before in mass advertising to sell products from automobiles to soap. Sex magazines, sex shops, and movies were part of an explosion in the marketing of male sexual fantasies in the 1960s.

Technology allowed women and men to separate pleasure from reproduction but did nothing to alter men's and women's domestic roles. Pleasure was also separated from familial responsibilities, yet the domestic ideal of the woman in the home remained. Some women were beginning to question their exploitation in the sexual revolution. In the early 1970s this issue became the basis of mass feminist protest.

Just as sexuality was invested with new meaning within the context of protest, so was the use of drugs. Drugs began to pervade Western cultures in apparently harmless ways. At the end of the nineteenth century in the United States, the newly created Coca-Cola was actually made with cocaine, a drug derived from the coca shrub. Another ingredient in the soft drink formula was the kola nut, which contains the stimulant caffeine. In the 1950s and 1960s, chemical technology made possible the manufacture of synthetic drugs.

Pharmaceutical industries in Europe and the United States expanded by leaps and bounds with the mass marketing of amphetamines, barbiturates, and tranquilizers. Doctors prescribed these new drugs for a variety of problems from obesity to depression to sleeplessness. People discovered that these drugs had additional mood-altering effects.

Marijuana grew in popularity as a safe "recreational" drug, especially among college and university students in the 1960s. In fact, young people were the primary users of drugs of all sorts, including synthetic drugs like the hallucinogen LSD (lysergic acid diethylamide). Hallucinogens were considered by their proponents to be mind-expanding drugs that permitted the achievement of new levels of consciousness. Drugs used by young people affluent enough to afford them served to widen the gap between the generations still further.

The Protests of 1968

Student protest, which began at the University of California at Berkeley in 1964 as the Free Speech movement, by the spring of 1968 had become an international phenomenon that had spread to other American campuses and throughout Europe and Japan. A common denominator of protest, whether in New York, London, or Tokyo, was opposition to the war in Vietnam. Growing numbers of intellectuals and students throughout the world condemned the U.S. presence in Vietnam as an immoral violation of the rights of the Vietnamese people and a violent proof of U.S. imperialism.

Student protesters shared other concerns in addition to opposition to the war in southeast Asia. The growing activism on American campuses was aimed at social reform, student self-governance, and the responsibilities of the university in the wider community. In West Germany highly politicized radical activists, a conspicuous minority among the students at the Free University of Berlin, directed protest out into the wider society. Student demonstrations met with brutal police repression and violence, and rioting was common.

European students, more than their American counterparts, were also experiencing frustration in the classroom. European universities were unprepared to absorb the huge influx of students in the 1960s. The student-teacher ratio at the University of Rome, for example, was 200 to 1. In Italian universities in general, the majority of over half a million students had no contact with their professors. The University of Paris was similarly overcrowded.

For the most part, student protest was primarily a middle-class phenomenon. In France, for example, only 4 percent of university students came from below the middle class. Higher education had been developed after World War II to serve the increased needs of a technocratic society. Instead of altering the social structure, as politically committed student protesters had hoped, mass education served as a certifying mechanism for bureaucratic and technical institutions. Many of the occupations that students could look forward to were in dead-end service jobs or in bureaucratic posts.

Students riot in Paris in 1968. The student protests of the late 1960s were sparked in part by the war in Vietnam and by disillusionment with the present and uncertainty about the future.

Student dissent reflected the changing economy of the late 1960s. Inflation, which earlier in the decade had spurred prosperity, was spiraling out of control. In the advanced industrial countries of western Europe and later in the United States, the growth of the postwar period was slowing down. Economic opportunity was evaporating and jobs were being eliminated. One survey estimated that only one in three Italian university graduates in 1967 was able to find a job. The dawning awareness of shrinking opportunities in the workplace, once students had attained their degrees and been properly certified, further aggravated student frustration and dissent.

By the late 1960s universities and colleges provided the forum for expressing their discontent in advanced industrial societies. In their protests, student activists rejected the values of consumer society. The programs and politics of the student protesters aimed to transform the world in which they lived. Student protesters in France chanted, "Métro—Boulot—Dodo," a slang condemnation of the treadmill-like existence of those who spent their lives in a repetitive cycle of subway riding (Métro), mindless work (Boulot), and sleep (Dodo).

In May 1968 in France, protest spread beyond the university when workers and managers joined students in paralyzing the French economy and threatening to topple the Fifth Republic. Between seven and ten million people went on strike in support of worker and student demands. White-collar employees and technicians joined blue-collar factory workers in the strike. Student

A train carrying iron ore crosses the Franco-Luxembourg bor-
der; celebrating the joint community in coal and steel that be-
came effective in 1953. The Euopean Coal and Steel Community
was the first step in the economic integration of Europe.

demands, based on a thoroughgoing critique of the whole society, proved to be
incompatible with the wage and consumption issues of workers. But the
unusual if short-lived alliance of students and workers shocked those in power
and induced reforms.

The division of the world into two camps framed the recovery of combatant
nations dealing with the losses of World War II. The Cold War instilled fear and
terror in the populations who lived on both sides of the divide. Yet the Cold War
also created the terms for stability following the upheaval of war. It promoted

prosperity that preserved the long-term policies of both the United States and the Soviet Union in the twentieth century. The belief that the USSR had won the war for the Allies and the sense of betrayal that followed the war determined the outlook of grim distrust shared by postwar Soviet leaders who had survived the years from 1939 to 1945.

The United States, on the other hand, found itself playing the role of rich uncle in bankrolling the European recovery. Its long-term commitment to promote its own economic interests by helping future trading partners led it also into playing the role of policeman throughout the world. The escalating war in Vietnam made America vulnerable to growing world criticism and to growing domestic discontent. But the gains of economic recovery began to unravel in the mid-1960s. In the West, rising expectations of consumer societies came up against the harsh realities of slowed growth. In the East, frustrated nationalism, the lack of consumer goods, and repressive conditions resulted in low morale, demonstrations, and outright conflict. The nations of Europe and the United States sensed that they stood at a crossroads in 1968. Whether the future inspired confidence or fear remained to be seen. The threat of nuclear annihilation had considerably diminished. If the rivalry between East and West no longer dominated the international arena, what lay ahead?

Suggestions for Further Reading

Regulating the Cold War

*Franz Ansprenger, *The Dissolution of the Colonial Empires* (London: Routledge, 1989). An analysis of Europe's withdrawal from Asia and Africa following the Second World War, beginning with an examination of post–World War I imperialism.

*William Roger Louis and Roger Owen, eds., *Suez 1956: The Crisis and Its Consequences* (New York: Oxford University Press, 1989). A series of essays resulting from new research into the origins and consequences of the Suez crisis.

Charles S. Maier, ed., *The Origins of the Cold War and Contemporary Europe* (New York: Franklin Watts, 1978). A series of essays considering the origins of the Cold War and its impact on the political economy of Europe.

*Charles S. Maier, *In Search of Stability: Explorations in Historical Political Economy* (Cambridgeshire, England: Cambridge University Press, 1987). Covers a wide variety of issues affecting twentieth-century Europe, including the foundation of American international economic policy after World War II and the conditions for stability in western Europe after 1945.

---

*Indicates paperback edition available.

*Bruce D. Porter, *The USSR in Third World Conflicts: Soviet Arms and Diplomacy in Local Wars, 1945–1980* (Cambridgeshire, England: Cambridge University Press, 1984). A case study approach to the Soviet Union's changing postwar policies toward the third world that centers on local wars in Africa and the Middle East.

*Tony Smith, ed., *The End of the European Empire: Decolonization After World War II* (Lexington, MA: Heath, 1975). A collection of articles dealing with the rapid decolonization of the overseas holdings of Great Britain, France, the Netherlands, and Belgium, and the growing agitation and organization of nationalist movements.

Reconstructing Europe

*Stanley Hoffman and Charles Maier, *The Marshall Plan: A Retrospective* (Boulder, CO: Westview Press, 1984). Based on a commemorative conference held at Harvard University, 35 years after George C. Marshall's address at that university, this collection assembles the work of specialists and actual participants in the plan's implementation.

*Michael J. Hogan, *The Marshall Plan: America, Britain, and the Reconstruction of Western Europe* (Cambridgeshire, England: Cambridge University Press, 1987). A thoroughly researched argument on the continuities of U.S. economic policy in the twentieth century. Hogan counters the interpretation that the Marshall Plan was merely a response to the Cold War.

Creating the Welfare State

*Simone de Beauvoir, *The Second Sex* (New York: Knopf, 1963). The author, one of France's leading intellectuals in the twentieth century, describes the situation of women's lives in the postwar West by placing them within the context of the history and myths governing Western culture.

*Jane Jenson, "Both Friend and Foe: Women and State Welfare," in Renate Bridenthal, Claudia Koonz, and Susan Stuard, eds., *Becoming Visible: Women in European History* (Boston: Houghton Mifflin, 1987). This essay illuminates the mixed blessing of the welfare state for women after 1945 by focusing on the experiences of women in Great Britain and France.

Denise Riley, *War in the Nursery: Theories of the Child and Mother* (London: Virago Press, 1983). Treats social policies of postwar pronatalism within the context of the popularization of developmental and child psychologies in Europe, with special attention to Britain and the United States, and emphasis on the postwar period as a turning point in attitudes toward women and the family.

*Mary Ruggie, *The State and Working Women: A Comparative Study of Britain and Sweden* (Princeton, NJ: Princeton University Press, 1984). A sociological study comparing the economic status of women in two European welfare states.

Youth Culture and the Generation Gap

*David Caute, *The Year of the Barricades: A Journey Through 1968* (New York: Harper & Row, 1988). More than its title suggests, this work is an overview of postwar youth culture on three continents. The politics of 1968 is featured, although other topics regarding the counterculture, lifestyles, and cultural ramifications are considered.

John R. Gillis, *Youth and History: Tradition and Change in European Age Relations, 1770–Present* (New York: Academic Press, 1981). Connects the history of European youth to broad trends in economic and demographic modernization over the last 200 years.

*Margaret Mead, *Culture and Commitment: The New Relationships Between the Generations in the 1970s* (New York: Columbia University Press, 1978). This series of essays, written by one of America's premier anthropologists, explores the origins and the consequences of the generation gap with special attention to Cold War politics, historical conditions, and technological transformations.

24

Europe Faces the Future: Hope and Uncertainty, 1968 to the Present

Toppling Communism

"Nothing lasts forever." Such was the wisdom of Western women and men at the end of the twentieth century as they faced cataclysmic changes in their world. After over forty years of relative stability, the year 1989 marked a period of rapid political transformations. In February the Soviet Union withdrew its troops from an increasingly unpopular war in Afghanistan. In the spring of 1989 the Soviet people participated in elections that indicated a new democratic process, and popular debate was challenging Communist party rule. Reformers ousted by party leaders appealed directly to the electorate; one such reformer, Boris Yeltsin, dismissed as the head of the Moscow party in 1987, garnered 89 percent of the popular vote in the elections for the Congress of People's Deputies. Soviet citizens looked forward to democratic reforms. Soviet leader Mikhail Gorbachev took the measure of popular opinion and appeared to champion free enterprise, individual initiative, open markets, and self-determination of peoples. The apparent democratization of Soviet political life in 1989 was matched by dramatic transformations in central and eastern Europe among the Warsaw Pact nations that had been allied with the Soviet Union since 1955. In April Hungarians disinterred the body of Imre Nagy, leader of the 1956 anti-Soviet uprising. He was declared a state hero and reburied with full funeral honors. The Western world was stunned. In June, after a number of political reversals in the 1980s, Poland established democratic rule.

Symbols of freedom and democratic cooperation appeared everywhere in 1989. One million people joined hands to form a 370-mile-long human chain that stretched across the Soviet Baltic republics of Estonia, Latvia, and

Lithuania in protest against Soviet annexation in 1940. In September 1989 East German citizens flooded into Hungary at the rate of 300 people an hour with the hope of escaping to West Germany and political and economic freedom. Soon thereafter the German borders were opened to the free movement of people. The 35-year reign of Todor Zhivkov, dictator of Bulgaria, was ended as Bulgarians, too, endorsed parliamentary government.

Throughout central and eastern Europe people were successfully rejecting communist values in favor of democratic free institutions. In November 1989 Czechoslovakia embraced pluralist politics and democratic rule. Tens of thousands of Czech demonstrators in the capital city of Prague sang songs about freedom and cheered their new heroes, dissidents persecuted and jailed under the former communist regime.

In the illustration here, a nicked and battered bust of the long-reigning Soviet dictator, Joseph Stalin (1928–1953) is being carried through the streets of Prague. The placard around the neck of the bust is a reminder of the impermanence of all things: translated, it reads, "Nothing lasts forever." Stalinism had been long dead by 1989 even within the Soviet Union, where it was criticized and buried by Stalin's successors. Yet the bust of Stalin continued to be an easily recognizable symbol of the worst aspects of communist rule: dictatorship, repression, and denial of individual liberties and civil rights. To the Czech people, the bust stood for communism controlled from the center by a bureaucratic elite they were intent on overthrowing.

For many, the most dramatic moment in the collapse of communism came in November 1989 as bulldozers moved against the Berlin Wall, the tangible symbol of Cold War politics that had been erected through the center of Berlin in 1961. As the barrier came down, so, too, did the 18-year-old government of communist leader Erich Honecker, who was forced to resign. The East German Communist party, confronted with popular discontent and charges of corruption, decided to change both its tune and its name.

Poland, Hungary, Bulgaria, Czechoslovakia, and East Germany all underwent what were considered to be "velvet revolutions," characterized by a lack of violence and smooth passage to a new order. The year 1989 did not end, however, without bloody upheaval. In December 1989 Nicolae Ceaucescu, communist dictator of Romania, ordered his troops to fire on demonstrators. Thousands of men, women, and children were killed and buried unceremoniously in mass graves. The slaughter set off a revolution in which Ceaucescu and his wife and co-ruler Elena were captured, tried, and executed by a firing squad. The charges against them were genocide—the slaughter of 64,000 people—and the mismanagement of the economy. In the days that followed, Romanians interviewed by the international media spoke of their newly won freedom, as videotaped images of the slain leaders were broadcast to the world.

Any one of these events by itself could have commanded world attention and shocked international opinion. Combined, they spelled the end of an era. The Eastern bloc under Soviet control was disintegrating, and communism as an ideology was crumbling. No one was sure what the future held, as changes brought instability and cut eastern and central European states free of their Soviet protector. "Nothing lasts forever" was a sign of the times. It reflected the optimism of hundreds of thousands of people who saw democracy, nationalism, and free markets as guarantees of a better future. Few recognized that the aphorism was a double-edged one which also contained the cynical recognition, perhaps forgotten in the euphoria of the moment, that change, even the toppling of communism, did not guarantee stability.

$\mathcal{E}$nding the Cold War

In the 1960s dissent in eastern Europe and the Soviet Union was handled very differently. In 1968 the Soviet action against Czechoslovakia and other expressions of dissent in eastern Europe seemed to affirm the power of communist unity in the Eastern bloc. The use of military intervention to resolve the Czech crisis opened an era governed by what came to be known as the Brezhnev Doctrine. Leonid Brezhnev (1906–1982), general secretary of the

Communist party and head of the Soviet Union from 1966 to 1982, established a policy whereby the Soviet Union claimed the right to interfere in the internal affairs of its allies in order to prevent counterrevolution. Brezhnev was responsible for the decision to intervene in Czechoslovakia, arguing that a socialist state was obliged to take action in another socialist state if the survival of socialism was at stake. The Brezhnev Doctrine influenced developments in eastern Europe through the next decade. After 1968 rigidity and stagnation characterized the Soviet, East German, and Czechoslovak governments, as well as rule in other east European states.

Within the Soviet Union dissent appeared to be growing, and Soviet dissidents were commanding international attention. Criticism of the Soviet Union by its own citizens was at first strongly repressed, as was the case for other Eastern bloc nations. Discontent over domestic issues converged with growing criticisms of foreign policy aims to form a trenchant critique of communism and Cold War politics.

Soviet Dissent

In December 1989 Andrei Sakharov was buried with full state honors in the Soviet Union. Soviet president Gorbachev hailed him as a hero, "a man of conviction and sincerity." In terms of Sakharov's early career, such a description would hardly have been surprising. Much decorated for his research as the father of the Soviet hydrogen bomb, Sakharov was a Russian scientist of great eminence. But he was also one of the leading dissidents of the Soviet Union.

During the Brezhnev years, dissidence took on new forms in response to state repression. Growing numbers of Soviet Jews sought to emigrate to Israel, in an attempt to escape anti-Semitism within the Soviet Union and to embrace their own cultural heritage. Some of the 178,000 who were allowed to emigrate found their way to western Europe and the United States.

In May 1976 a number of Soviet dissidents, many of them Jewish, declared themselves united for the purpose of securing human rights. Some of the leading organizers were charged with anti-Soviet propaganda and given harsh prison sentences, which attracted international attention.

Samizdat, the Russian word for self-published, privately circulated manuscripts, became the chief vehicle of dissident information. For the most part, dissidents came from an educated elite with professional and university training. Sakharov was joined by other figures of stature, including novelist Alexander Solzhenitsyn and historian Roy Medvedev. In his novels, such as *Gulag Archipelago* and *One Day in the Life of Ivan Denisovich*, Solzhenitsyn showed the abuses of Soviet bureaucracy. For his writings he was forced into exile in the West. Medvedev criticized Stalinism and continued to speak out in favor of peace and democratic principles in the Gorbachev years.

For three decades Andrei Sakharov and other dissidents waged a lonely battle within the Soviet Union for civil liberties, democratic rights, and the end of the nuclear arms race. For his efforts, Sakharov endured internal exile for six years in the closed city of Gorki. But in the few years before his death, he was reinstated as a public figure, taking a seat as a member of the Soviet Parliament. The changing fate of dissidents like Sakharov was one of the best barometers of the social revolution that was transforming Soviet politics in the late 1980s.

Détente: The Soviets and the West

The Nuclear Test Ban Treaty of 1963 inaugurated a period of lessening tension between the Eastern and Western blocs. By the early 1970s both the United States and the Soviet Union recognized the importance of a rapprochement between the superpowers. The USSR and the United States had achieved nuclear parity: From positions of equality, both sides expressed a willingness to negotiate. The 1970s became a decade of détente, a period of cooperation between the two superpowers. The Strategic Arms Limitation Treaty, known as SALT I, signed in Moscow in 1972, limited defensive antiballistic missile systems.

The refusal in 1979 of the United States to sign SALT II to limit strategic nuclear weapons ushered in "the dangerous decade" of the 1980s, when the possibility of peaceful coexistence seemed crushed. U.S. president Ronald Reagan, during his first term in office, revived traditional Cold War posturing. Nuclear strategists on both sides were once again talking about nuclear war as possible and winnable. Popular concern over the nuclear arms race intensified in the United States, the Soviet Union, and throughout Europe. U.S. plans for the Strategic Defense Initiative (SDI), popularly called the "Star Wars" defense system, promised an escalation in nuclear defense spending in an attempt to end the parity between the United States and the Soviet Union.

On balance, however, East-West relations after 1983 were characterized by less confrontation and more attempts at cooperation between the Soviet Union and the United States. The world political system itself appeared to have stabilized with a diminution of conflict in the three main arenas of superpower competition—the third world, China, and western Europe. By the end of 1989, leaders in the East and the West declared that the Cold War was over. A new and permanent détente was now possible.

New Leadership and New Values in the Soviet State

By the mid-1980s, Soviet leaders faced the costs of increasing internal dissent and the promise of benefits from improved relations with the West. During the 40 years following World War II a new leadership was being forged in the ranks of the Communist party among a generation that favored more open political values and dynamic economic growth. Typical of the new generation of political leaders was Mikhail Gorbachev, who was above all a technocrat, someone who could apply specialized knowledge to the problems of the Soviet economy.

Gorbachev was born in 1931 on a collective farm near Stavropol, on the plains north of the Caucasus Mountains. At age 19 he traversed the great social distance from the collective farm to Moscow and entered Moscow University to study law. At the unusually young age of 39, he was elected to the central committee; he achieved the status of the central committee's secretary in charge of agriculture and then, in 1980, he became a voting member of the Politburo.

When Yuri Andropov (1914–1984), head of the KGB, the Soviet secret police controlled by the Communist party and responsible for internal intelligence gathering and surveillance, succeeded Brezhnev as general secretary in 1983, he recognized Gorbachev's abilities as a problem solver. Gorbachev became Andropov's principal deputy and, following the brief regimes of Andropov and then Konstantin Chernenko (1911–1985), Gorbachev assumed party leadership in 1985.

Gorbachev's story is, however, more than simply a tale of an individual man of exceptional ability and ambition making it to the top. His rise to political power was part of a general phenomenon in which social changes— urbanization, education, and increased communication—fostered the emergence of a generation of leaders committed to finding new and better ways of building Soviet prosperity. Gorbachev's life also reflects the changing outlook and experiences of an educated urban elite. Highly educated groups of professionals and managers constituted a significant 22 percent of the population by the 1980s.

In 1985, when Gorbachev came to power as Communist party general secretary and the youngest Soviet leader since Stalin, he set in motion bold plans for increased openness, which he called *glasnost*, and a program of political and economic restructuring, which he dubbed *perestroika*. Appointing men who shared his vision to key posts, especially in the foreign ministry, Gorbachev extended the olive branch to the West and met in Geneva for his first superpower summit with President Ronald Reagan. By 1989 many observers inside and outside the Soviet Union felt that a new age was at hand, as the Soviet leader loosened censorship, denounced Stalin, and held the first free elections in the Soviet Union since 1917.

The Changing Soviet Economy. The Soviet Union had undergone dramatic changes after Stalin's death in 1953, and many Stalinist policies were repudiated. The 1960s was a period of increasing prosperity, as the population became more urban (180 million people lived in cities by mid-1970) and more literate (the majority of the population stays in school until age 17 or 18).

Soviet citizens of the 1960s and 1970s were better fed, better educated, and in better health than their parents and grandparents had been. When people grumbled over food shortages and long lines, the Soviet state reminded its citizens of how far they had come and told them that Soviet economic planning was not a failure. Yet while growth continued throughout the postwar years, the rate of growth was slowing down in the 1970s. Some planners feared that the Soviet Union would never catch up to the economies of the United States, Japan, and West Germany. Soviet citizens were increasingly aware of the sacrifices and suffering that economic development had cost them in the twentieth century and of the disparities in the standards of living between the capitalist and communist worlds. Due to outmoded technology, declining older industries, pollution, labor imbalances, critical shortages of foodstuffs and certain raw materials, and a significant amount of hidden unemployment in unproductive industries, discontent mounted.

Consumer products were either of poor quality or unavailable. People queued on the average of two hours every day to purchase food and basic supplies. Housing, when it was available, was inadequate, and there were long waiting lists for vacancies. The black market flourished, with high prices on everything from Western blue jeans to Soviet automobiles. People could look around them and see corruption in their ruling elite, who wore Western clothes, had access to material goods not available to the general population, and lived in luxury.

Workers were well paid, with more disposable income than ever before and that was, ironically, a key to the problem. People had money to spend. In fact, purchasing power far outstripped supplies. The state system of production, which emphasized quantity over quality, resulted in overproduction of some goods and underproduction of others. The state kept prices low in order to control the cost of living, but low prices did not provide incentives for the production of better quality goods.

Programs between 1985 and 1988 promised more than they delivered. Modest increases in output were achieved, but people's expectations regarding food and consumer goods were rising faster than they could be met. The Soviet Union did not increase imports of consumer durables or food to meet demand, nor did quality improve appreciably. Rising wages only gave workers more money that they could not or would not spend on Soviet products. The black market was a symbol both of the economic failures of the state and of the growing consumerism of Soviet citizens. Rather than purchase poor quality goods, Soviets purchased foreign products at vastly inflated prices.

Although his economic reforms broke sharply with the centralized economy established by Stalin in the 1930s, Gorbachev candidly warned that there would be no consumption revolution in the near future. Many critics, including Boris Yeltsin, felt that he did not go far or fast enough. In place of a controlled economy, Gorbachev proposed a limited open market free of state controls for manufacturing enterprises organized on a cooperative basis and for light industry. He loosened restrictions on foreign trade, encouraged the development of a private service sector, and decentralized economic decision making for agriculture and the service sector.

Price increases and the importation of foreign goods, the two essential measures necessary for progress in the Soviet consumer economy, had been resisted by Gorbachev's predecessors as politically explosive. The state kept

The Big Mac comes to Moscow. McDonald's opened its first Soviet fast-food outlet in 1990, just a few blocks from the Kremlin. Muscovites stood in long lines for milkshakes, fries, and the "Bolshoi Mak."

prices down in order to maintain the low cost of living. But prices of raw materials and energy were kept so low that they discouraged increased productivity, efficiency, and quality. In both the economy and in politics Gorbachev wanted to usher in a period of change and greater freedom. In contrast to the ingrained conservatism of his predecessors, Gorbachev represented experimentation, innovation, and vitality. For him, economic and political reforms had to be accomplished in concert; the economy could only be restructured by "a democratization of our society at all levels."

Gorbachev's foreign policy also served his economic goals. Military participation in decision making declined, as state expenditures on defense were decreased. Moscow had always borne larger military costs than Washington. Gorbachev recognized that Cold War defense spending must decline if the Soviet Union was to prosper. Consumer durables had to take the place of weapons on the production lines.

Changing Soviet Politics.   From the beginning of the twentieth century, Soviet leaders had dealt with a vast array of crises from civil war, world war, collectivization, rapid industrialization, purges, and massive social dislocations. Stalin's planning had created a rigidly centralized bureaucracy that had proven itself incapable of meeting the consumer needs of the Soviet people in the late twentieth century. By the time Gorbachev came to power, Soviet citizens had enjoyed 40 years of peace and were demanding a change from the decades of sacrifice for defense.

The Communist party, set in place as a disciplined body of cadres by Lenin, operated on the principle that power must flow from the top in order to preserve and advance the revolution. In the late 1980s, grass-roots movements responding to Gorbachev's rhetoric of reform and democracy asserted that they should have a political voice. On coming to power, Gorbachev could blame his predecessors for the Soviet Union's problems, but this defense had its limits, as people began demanding results. Tensions became most apparent over how Communist party rule and centralization could be coordinated with the demands for freedom and autonomy that Gorbachev's own reforms fostered.

To gain credibility and backing, Gorbachev supported the formation of new parliamentary bodies, including a 2250-member Congress of People's Deputies in 1988. The new Congress soon became the forum for attacks on the Communist party and the KGB. In the first free elections held in the Soviet Union since 1917, Communist party officials suffered further reversals in March 1989. Early in 1990 Gorbachev ended the party's constitutional monopoly of power; the party now no longer played a "leading role" in Soviet political life.

New parties proliferated, some defending the old order but many demanding a total break with the past and with communist ideology and programs. Among Gorbachev's harshest critics was his former ally and supporter, Boris N. Yeltsin, the former Moscow party leader, who began in 1987 to criticize Gorbachev's caution in implementing reforms. Later, as the popularly elected president of the Russian republic in 1990, Yeltsin called for a true democracy and decisive economic action.

Aware of his precarious political position, Gorbachev appeared to retrench by increasing control over the media and by attempting to consolidate his own political position. Many felt that the regime was becoming authoritarian. Gorbachev was clearly walking a fine line attempting to maintain stability, yet neither Communist party hard-liners nor Western-oriented supporters of capitalism and democracy were happy.

In August 1991 the world watched in shock as a quasi-military council of hard-liners usurped power in order to restore communist rule and reverse democratic reforms. Soviet citizens from the Baltic republics to Siberia protested the takeover, and tens of thousands of Muscovites poured into the streets to defy the tanks and troops of the rebel government. Three people were killed outside Russia's parliament building, which had become a rallying point for the protesters. Meanwhile, Gorbachev was held prisoner in his vacation home in the Crimea. The timing of the coup was probably determined by the fact that Gorbachev was scheduled to sign a new union treaty with nine of the republics the day following his house arrest.

Boris Yeltsin publicly defied the plotters, rallying popular support behind him and helping convince Soviet army troops to disobey orders to attack the White House, as the parliament building is called. After only two days, the coup d'état had failed; Gorbachev returned to Moscow and banned the Communist party. Although Gorbachev retained his title of Soviet president, his prestige was seriously damaged by the coup and by the challenge of Yeltsin's new dominance as a popular hero.

As the Soviet Union came to an end, the popularity and prominence of Boris Yeltsin, the first popularly elected president of the Russian Republic, eclipsed that of former Soviet president Mikhail Gorbachev. Yeltsin is shown here taking the oath of office during his inauguration ceremony at the Kremlin.

The End of the Soviet Union

In 1979 the Soviet Union listed 102 nationalities in its census. Twenty-two of those nationalities had populations of a million or more people. Some Western observers predicted that this diversity would destroy the Soviet Union, that the Soviet empire was crumbling from within. Others wondered how Gorbachev could support the demands for self-determination in eastern European states and deny it in the Soviet republics. For many, the nationalities problem posed the single greatest threat to Gorbachev's regime, even more challenging than the establishment of a free-market economy.

The nationalities problem in the Soviet Union was in fact shaped by the very social forces that brought Gorbachev to power. The three major areas of nationalist conflict—Central Asia, Armenia, and the Baltic states—had had grievances against the Soviet state since the 1920s. What was different about the protests of the 1980s was the emergence of a new and educated urban elite, formed after World War II, as the driving force behind nationalist reform. Moscow relied on these groups of university-educated and upwardly mobile professionals to further economic reforms. Gorbachev's challenge was to harness nationalist protest without undermining the Party's authority in favor of local organizations. The challenge before him was to make the Party responsible to these new social groups and to local needs.

Ethnic minorities, especially in the Soviet Baltic republics of Latvia, Lithuania, and Estonia, threatened the dominance of Party rule in favor of immediate self-determination. Large-scale riots erupted in Lithuania over demands for nationalist rights. Nationalist awareness was not unprecedented in the Baltic states in the 1980s—but the context of perestroika in which nationalist demands were now being voiced posed a serious challenge to Gorbachev's democratic reforms. In 1988 Estonians demanded the right of veto over any law passed in Moscow. Russians, who were a minority in Estonia, protested attacks and prejudicial treatment at the hands of Estonians.

Endorsing diversity of opinion, individual rights, and freedom as the bases of good government, Gorbachev now had to deal with vocal nationalist awareness in the Baltic states and the republic of Georgia and with outright violence in Azerbaijan. In 1988 tens of thousands of Armenians took to the streets to demand the return of the Armenian enclave of Nagorno-Karabakh, incorporated into Azerbaijan in 1921. In the Azerbaijan capital of Baku, the center of Russia's oil-producing region, demonstrators demanded greater autonomy for their republic and the accountability of their deputies in Moscow. Violence between Azerbaijanis and Armenians resulted in 32 deaths and the displacement of tens of thousands. The situation of upheaval climaxed in December 1988 when an earthquake in Armenia killed 25,000 people. Soviet troops were placed in the area, ostensibly to deal with the aftermath of the natural disaster.

In 1986 university students in the central Asian republic of Kazakhstan incited two days of demonstrations and rioting over the removal of a corrupt local leader who was replaced with a Russian. The Soviet government's attempt to clean up politics in the area betrayed a clumsy disregard for ethnic issues and seemed at odds with Gorbachev's commitment to decentralization. Crimean Tatars, who had been exiled in Islamic fundamentalist Kazakhstan since World War II, agitated for return home.

One by one, all 15 of the Soviet republics proclaimed their independence, following the lead of the breakaway Baltic republics of Estonia, Lithuania, and Latvia. Having failed to agree on a new plan for union, Gorbachev and the leaders of ten republics transferred authority to an emergency State Council in September 1991 until a plan could be devised. By the end of the year the Soviet Union was faced with serious food shortages and was bankrupt, unable to pay its employees and dependent on the financial backing provided by Yeltsin. Rejecting all Soviet authority, Russia, Belarus, and Ukraine joined together in December 1991 to form the Commonwealth of Independent States (CIS). Eight other republics followed their lead. The Soviet Union came to an end on 25

December 1991, with the resignation of Mikhail Gorbachev, who had become a man without a country to rule. Russian president Yeltsin moved into Gorbachev's presidential offices at the Kremlin.

Many issues remained unresolved. The new political organization did not address the endemic problems of economic hardship, and left unanswered the question of who would control the former Soviet Union's vast military machine, including its nuclear arsenal. How would the strong nationalist demands for autonomy accord with the need for cooperation to establish a stable monetary policy, market economies, and effective trade networks? The Soviet Union, which ruled as a world power for over seven decades, no longer existed. Communism had been totally discredited, but the new nations of the former Soviet Union faced an uncertain future.

$\mathcal{E}$ astern and Central Europe Since 1968

The dramatic upheavals in eastern Europe in the late 1980s had been in the making for over two decades. Czechoslovakia's attempt in 1968 to strike out on a more independent path to socialism only strengthened the Soviet Union's hold on Warsaw Pact nations. The Soviet Union's use of troops had sent a clear message that it would not tolerate deviation. When the dust of tens of thousands of Soviet-led troops settled in the Czech capital of Prague, one-party rule was reestablished and a more democratic socialism based on freer markets and individual initiative had failed.

The demands for consumer goods and national autonomy behind the protests of 1968 were effectively quelled in the 1970s by the memory of Soviet invasion, but they did not disappear. The recurrent crises over oil prices and the greater hardships inflicted on eastern European consumers fanned the embers of unsettled issues in the 1980s. Incidents of protest and resistance began to mount.

Solidarity in Poland

Poland was especially important to the Soviet bloc both because it was eastern Europe's most populous country and because of its strategic location. Poland provided a corridor for supplies to the Soviet Union's 380,000 troops in East Germany. In Poland, as in Czechoslovakia, demonstrations against Soviet dominance and one-party rule by the communists had been brutally repressed. Poland entered the 1970s economically handicapped. In December 1970 the Polish government instituted major price increases for food. Workers spontaneously struck in protest, with demonstrations beginning in the shipyards of Gdańsk, the Baltic seaport in northern Poland, and spreading to other cities.

The Polish government responded by sending the militia to teargas the workers. People were killed and injured but protest was not silenced.

Wladislaw Gomulka, who had been head of the Polish government since 1956, was replaced by Edward Gierek in hopes of improving the economic situation. More protests followed before prices were rolled back and the Soviet Union provided economic aid. Throughout the 1970s one-party rule prevailed, as workers attempted to maintain forms of permanent organization. The Polish government drew loans from abroad for investment in technology and industrial expansion. Resisting raising prices at home, Poland increased its indebtedness to the West from $2.5 billion in 1973 to $17 billion in 1980. Poland was sinking into the mire of ever higher interest payments that absorbed the country's export earnings. In 1976, however, Gierek could no longer avoid price increases. A new wave of spontaneous strikes erupted, forcing the government to rescind the increases.

At the beginning of July 1980 the government was forced once again to raise food prices. Shipyard workers in Gdańsk were ready, solidly organized in a new noncommunist labor union called Solidarity (Solidarnosc), under the leadership of a politically astute electrician named Lech Walesa. The union staged a sit-down strike that paralyzed the shipyards. Union committees coordinated their activities from one factory to the next and succeeded in shutting down the entire economy. The government agreed to a series of union-backed reforms known as the Gdańsk Accords, which, among other measures, increased civil liberties and acknowledged Solidarity's right to exist.

Within a year Solidarity had an astounding 8 million members out of a population of 35 million. The Catholic church lent important support to those who opposed communist rule. Dissident intellectuals also cast their lot with the organized workers in demanding reforms. General Wojciech Jaruzelski, who became prime minister in February 1981, was unable to change the situation of shortages appreciably. Jaruzelski attempted to curb the union's demands for democratic government and participation in management by harsh measures: He declared martial law on 13 December 1981. Jaruzelski was trying to save the Polish Communist party by using the Polish military to crack down on the dissidents. The Soviet response was to do nothing. Poland was left to Polish rule.

Martial law in Poland produced military repression. Solidarity was outlawed and Walesa was jailed. The West did not lose sight of him: In 1983 the union leader was awarded the Nobel Peace Prize for his efforts. After years of negotiations and intermittent strikes, Solidarity was legalized once again in 1989. Jaruzelski knew he needed Solidarity's cooperation in order to address dire economic conditions: He agreed to open elections. At the polls, Solidarity candidates soundly defeated the Communist party. Poland was the first country anywhere to turn a communist regime out of office peacefully.

The great challenge before the new Solidarity government, as for the communist regime that preceded it, was economic recovery. Inflation drove food prices up at the rate of 50 percent a month. Poland faced the task of earning enough foreign trade credits to alleviate its indebtedness and to justify foreign investment. This was the challenge that Lech Walesa took up when he was elected president of Poland in 1990.

Emancipation in Eastern Europe

In the 1970s Hungarians began to experiment cautiously with free markets and private control. Romania under Nicolae Ceaucescu appeared to be successful in evading its military responsibilities in the Warsaw Pact. It alone of the member states had refused to participate in the Czechoslovak intervention of 1968. The East German government tolerated the Lutheran church's criticism of the Soviet military presence in East Germany in the 1970s. Deviation was not punished by Soviet repression but quietly and carefully pursued in an age colored by Soviet attempts at détente with the West.

The Soviet example and Gorbachev's calls for reforms and openness gave the lead to eastern Europe. In 1988 Gorbachev, speaking before the United Nations, assured the West that he would not prevent eastern European satellites from going their own way: "Freedom of choice is a universal principle," the Soviet head of state declared. Poland's first free elections in 40 years were part of a vast mosaic of protest from which a pattern began to emerge in the spring of 1989. Hungary dismantled the barbed-wire fences on its Austrian border; and it opened all of its borders to the West in September 1989. East German vacationers in Hungary poured across the frontiers, creating an international crisis. People wanted freedom of movement and freedom of

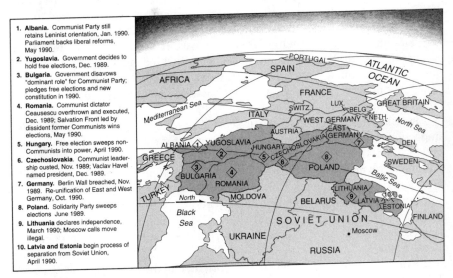

1. **Albania.** Communist Party still retains Leninist orientation, Jan. 1990. Parliament backs liberal reforms, May 1990.
2. **Yugoslavia.** Government decides to hold free elections, Dec. 1989.
3. **Bulgaria.** Government disavows "dominant role" for Communist Party; pledges free elections and new constitution in 1990.
4. **Romania.** Communist dictator Ceaucescu overthrown and executed, Dec. 1989; Salvation Front led by dissident former Communists wins elections, May 1990.
5. **Hungary.** Free election sweeps non-Communists into power, April 1990.
6. **Czechoslovakia.** Communist leadership ousted, Nov. 1989; Vaclav Havel named president, Dec. 1989.
7. **Germany.** Berlin Wall breached, Nov. 1989. Re-unification of East and West Germany, Oct. 1990.
8. **Poland.** Solidarity Party sweeps elections June 1990.
9. **Lithuania** declares independence, March 1990; Moscow calls move illegal.
10. **Latvia and Estonia** begin process of separation from Soviet Union, April 1990.

Events in eastern Europe, 1989–1990

expression. Everywhere east Europeans demanded democratic institutions modeled on those of Western nations. In Czechoslovakia the dissident playwright Vaclav Havel emerged as the leader of the democratic opposition and was elected president of the new government. "People power" swept away communist leaders and ousted the Communist party, many felt for good.

The iceberg of communism was melting. But as dictators were replaced by democrats, some observers wondered if counterrevolution was waiting in the wings, should the new capitalist experiments fail. Proto-fascist and anti-Semitic groups became more vocal in the early 1990s amidst the economic chaos. Festering ethnic differences erupted in civil war beginning in 1991 in Yugoslavia between the Serbs and secessionist Slovenes and Croats. Other eastern European states were riddled with ethnic troubles, including the Czechs and Slovaks in Czechoslovakia, the Hungarians and Romanians over the border region of Transylvania, and the Bulgarians and Turks in Bulgaria.

The Two Germanies Since 1968

The German Democratic Republic (East Germany) and the German Federal Republic (West Germany) continued to develop after 1968 as two separate countries with different social, economic, and political institutions. On the surface, their differences seemed insurmountable. The Berlin Wall, erected in 1961, divided the former German capital and served its intended purpose of keeping East Germans confined behind it. German leaders in the West continued to voice their long-term commitment to reunification; East German leaders insisted on the independence and autonomy of their state.

From the 1960s through the 1980s East Germany underwent a series of economic transformations. Under the leadership of Walter Ulbricht (1893–1973), East Germans achieved their own version of recovery, the "other economic miracle." Ulbricht committed the German Democratic Republic to an economic policy in which performance was measured in terms of profits rather than quotas. Individual initiative and market incentives replaced Soviet-style central planning and bureaucratic decision making. By 1969 East Germany's economy was the strongest among Eastern bloc nations, with the highest per capita output.

In spite of his economic successes, Ulbricht fell from power in 1971. An important factor in his removal was his support for rule by government bodies rather than Communist party control. Party members eagerly seized on economic reversals in 1970 to promote Moscow's disfavor with Ulbricht. In addition to his arrogance toward Soviet leaders, Ulbricht's opposition to improved relations between the Soviet Union and West Germany after 1969 gave Soviet leaders cause for complaint. Ulbricht felt that such a Soviet course of détente would only retard East Germany's chance for full recognition in the West.

Erich Honecker, who succeeded Ulbricht, had the mission of bringing the German Democratic Republic back into the fold of Soviet economic policy.

Honecker's policies were not a return to Stalinism but were built on an awareness of the consumer expectations of the East German population. Honecker's "consumer socialism" gave top priority to consumer goods and housing. But the oil crises of the 1970s undermined this orientation by driving up the costs of production, so dependent on foreign fuel, and thereby driving up consumer prices. Trade deficits soared and consumer industries slowed.

In West Germany politics took a new direction in 1969. For the first time since 1930, the Social Democrats were back in power, displacing the more conservative Christian Democrats. An era of social-liberal cooperation between the leftist Social Democrats and the centrist Free Democrats began. Under the chancellorship of Social Democrat Willy Brandt, the new government promised to make the welfare state more responsive to social needs, to involve labor more directly in economic decision making, and to attend to feminist demands regarding abortion, divorce, and pornography.

Brandt was equally committed to changes in foreign policy. From the first, he set out to improve relations with eastern Europe and the Soviet Union. While maintaining West Germany's commitment to NATO and western European integration, Brandt pursued a new cooperation with the Soviet Union through a nonaggression pact. Negotiated in 1970, the pact renounced territorial claims and the use of force. A treaty with Poland accepted the status quo of existing borders in return for Polish exit visas for ethnic Germans. Still without the official recognition of East Germany, West Germany agreed to normalized relations in 1972 in the Basic Treaty, which permitted West German citizens easier movement to visit relatives in East Germany. In 1973 both Germanies joined the United Nations.

Willy Brandt captured international acclaim with his bold foreign policy of *Ostpolitik*, the establishment of cooperative politics with the East, for which he was awarded the Nobel Peace Prize in 1971. Ostpolitik was a clear break with superpower hegemony, as Brandt, in his own version of détente, seized the initiative without waiting for directions from the United States. At home, however, he was not always a hero, as his domestic policies underwent reversals and the fabric of the social-liberal coalition began to fray. The 1973 oil crisis brought about rising unemployment and a decline in consumer demand. Shrinking tax revenues undermined Brandt's plans to expand the welfare state.

Added to these challenges at home was an espionage scandal in which a close aide of Chancellor Brandt's was discovered to be an East German spy. Cold War paranoia flared. Brandt resigned in 1974 and was succeeded by Social Democrat Helmut Schmidt, who continued Brandt's policies of rapprochement with the East. In 1981 Honecker, head of the East German state, and Schmidt, head of the West German state, sat down to discuss common concerns. Bonn and East Berlin were engaging in their own détente.

When he came to power in 1974, Schmidt found he had inherited a recession that became more severe over the next year. Necessary compromises with the Free Democrats in the 1970s produced growing dissension within the Social Democratic party and eroded Schmidt's support as chancellor. Taking advantage of the split between the Free Democrats and the Social Democrats and growing concern over the economic situation, the Christian Democrats displaced the Social Democrats with their candidate, Helmut Kohl, in 1982. Kohl stressed the importance of individual enterprise and competition and ran a winning campaign with the slogan, "Less State, More Market."

Germany Reunited

The two Germanies were linked economically, if not politically, throughout most of the postwar period. When the Federal Republic of Germany entered the European Community in 1957, it insisted that in matters related to trade the two Germanies were to be treated as one country. As a result, the German Democratic Republic benefited from its free trade relationship with West Germany. This advantage provided an important part of East Germany's prosperity since the 1960s. West Germany, in turn, achieved much of its prosperity through export-led growth, and it found markets in the German Democratic Republic.

West Germany stood in the 1980s as an economic giant, second only in foreign trade to the United States and far ahead of Japan. With its economic opportunities and advanced social welfare programs, West Germany exerted considerable attraction for East Germans. East Germany, too, established itself as an important trading nation—fifteenth in the world in 1975. East Germany's number one problem in the 1950s was the exodus of skilled workers and professionals in search of a better life in the West. The flow of emigration throughout the 1950s turned into a torrent in the first eight months of 1961 when the number of refugees fleeing from East to West Germany reached 160,000 people. The Berlin Wall was, more than anything else, an effort to keep the labor force, so expensive to train and so necessary for economic recovery, in the German Democratic Republic.

Applications for authorized immigration increased in the 1980s, and in 1984 East Germany allowed 30,000 citizens to emigrate to the West. Throughout the late 1980s the emigration rate remained high, with an average exodus of 20,000 a year. With Hungary's refusal to continue to block the passage of East Germans into West Germany, the floodgates were opened: 57,000 East Germans migrated within a matter of weeks. In the face of angry demonstrations, Honecker was forced to resign. The new government opened the Berlin Wall on 9 November 1989, ending all restrictions on travel between East and West. An East Germany with open borders could no longer survive as its citizens poured into the promised land of the West in record numbers. The Federal Republic intervened to assist East Germany in shoring up its badly faltering economy; the West German deutsche mark was substituted for East German currency. Monetary union prefigured political unification. In October 1990 Germany became a single, united nation once again.

Germans represent the largest nationality in Europe west of Russia. Other Europeans, particularly the French, feared the prospect of a united German,

More than any other event, the dismantling of the Berlin Wall in November 1989 has come to symbolize the end of the Cold War.

although publicly they endorsed the principle of the self-determination of peoples. In addition, western Europeans were troubled by the impact a united Germany might have on plans for European unification in the European Community. Not least of all, Germans themselves feared their new identity as citizens of a single nation. Former East Germans were wary about marginalization and second-class citizenship, while those of the west worried that their poor cousins from the east would be a brake on the sustained economic expansion which had made West Germany one of the world's leading export economies.

Unity and Diversity in Western Europe

The events of 1968 in eastern Europe sent a negative message to western European communists, who were intent on adopting a more liberal and cooperative stance with both parliamentary institutions and capitalism.

United Germany, 1990

By the end of the 1960s the fate of Communist parties in the West appeared uncertain. The events of 1968 in Prague catalyzed a new kind of communism, dubbed Eurocommunism, among western European Communist parties in the 1970s.

Western European nations had met the challenges of wartime devastation with miraculous economic recoveries in the 1950s and 1960s. Their economies were able to grow despite labor shortages thanks to an available pool of workers from southern Europe and from former colonies in Asia and Africa. After the phenomenal growth and prosperity of the postwar years, western Europe experienced a new set of harsh realities in the 1970s with skyrocketing oil prices, inflation, and recession. The permanent presence of foreign workers, many of them unemployed or erratically employed in the economic downturns of the 1970s and 1980s, came to be seen as a problem by welfare state leaders and politicians of the new Right.

With the goal of reviving the economy, in the 1980s the 12 member states of the European Economic Community devoted themselves to making western Europe competitive as a bloc in world markets. At the same time that Russian satellites in eastern Europe were breaking free of Soviet control and attempting to strike out on their own, the nations of western Europe were negotiating a new unity based on a single market and centralized policy-making.

Eurocommunism

Divisions among the Left excluded the western European communists from wielding political power in the early 1970s. Then in 1973 the international politics of oil prices provoked an economic crisis, followed by a recession. The Organization of Petroleum Exporting Countries (OPEC) raised prices and cut back production. Western European countries depended heavily on imported oil, which they used to fuel their prosperity through the early 1970s. Poor Soviet economic performance in the postwar era offered no model for action, especially for dealing with Western economies after 1973. European communists decided to cooperate with other leftists and moderates in a new electoral politics.

The Italian Communist party, the largest in Europe, led the way under the leadership of Enrico Berlinguer, who became the spearhead for Eurocommunism in western Europe. Eurocommunism, a designation resisted by its practitioners, was a response to the dual influences of democratic institutions and Western economies that combined free enterprise and state control. It was above all a recognition that revolution was not likely—at least in the near future—in western Europe. Eurocommunists accepted the European Community and membership in NATO. After 1973 communists, first in Italy and then in Spain and France, moved from a position of opposition to partnership with liberal and left-wing reformers. With the move, communists became Eurocommunists, rejecting unquestioned allegiance to Soviet policies and trying to become a mainstream electoral party.

In Spain the death of Generalissimo Francisco Franco in November 1975 ended the authoritarian regime set in place in the 1930s. The Spanish Communist party was granted legal status in 1977 and its leader, Santiago Carrillo, returned from exile in France to establish a Spanish version of Eurocommunism under a constitutional monarchy headed by King Juan Carlos. Moderates prevailed, with reformist socialists coming to power in 1982.

Eurocommunism also helped to bring a socialist president to power in France in 1981. The French Communist party had maintained its loyalty to Moscow longer than had its counterparts in Italy and Spain. Conservatives had controlled French politics since 1958 when Charles de Gaulle became president of the Fifth Republic. De Gaulle's successors, Georges Pompidou and Valéry Giscard d'Estaing, made it clear to the Left that they needed to cooperate with each other if they were to wrest power from the conservatives. In the late 1970s the Communist party threw in its lot with the French socialists, and their coalition resulted in the election of socialist François Mitterrand as president. Yet at the moment of victory, the Communist party was in decline, and a reformist Left was taking its place in electoral politics.

Eurocommunism's influence diminished in the 1980s as moderate politics maintained its appeal to voters. Eurocommunism had been a creative attempt to meet the challenge of preserving socialist goals in capitalist democracies. It paralleled attempts at democratic reforms in Czechoslovakia and Poland in the 1960s, except that the Eastern bloc revisionists were met with repression and control rather than with electoral failures. Eurocommunism's attempt at adaptation actually marked the demise of communism's appeal in western Europe. By criticizing Soviet actions, Western communists had abandoned their self-imposed isolation within Western democracies.

A New Working Class: Foreign Workers

Foreign workers played an important role in the industrial expansion of western Europe beginning in the 1950s. Western European nations needed cheap unskilled laborers. Great Britain, France, and West Germany were the chief labor importing countries, whose economic growth in the 1950s and 1960s was made possible by readily available pools of cheap foreign labor. The chief labor-exporting countries included Portugal, Turkey, Algeria, Italy, and Spain, whose sluggish economic performance spurred workers to seek employment opportunities beyond national borders. Great Britain imported workers from the West Indies, Ireland, India, Pakistan, Africa, and southern Europe. Migrant employment was by definition poorly paid, unskilled or semiskilled manual work. The lot of foreign workers was difficult and

Indian immigrants in France sewing in a "sweat shop." Immigrant workers in European countries took low-paying menial jobs. They faced resentment from xenophobic native Europeans.

sometimes dangerous. Onerous and demanding labor was common. Foreign workers were often herded together in crowded living quarters, socially marginalized, and identified with the degrading work they performed.

Commonly, married men migrated without their families with the goal of earning cash to send home to those left behind. The inability to put down roots hampered assimilation among this sizable percentage of foreign workers. Third and fourth generations of foreign workers born on West German soil, for example, were ineligible for citizenship and naturalization. In economic downturns foreign workers were the first to be laid off. Yet their obligations to send money back home to aged parents, spouses, children, and siblings persisted.

Women endured special problems within the foreign work force. Between 1964 and 1974 the majority of Portuguese immigrants to France came with families, but there was little in the way of social services to support them on their arrival. Dependable child care was either too expensive or unavailable to female workers with children. Increasing numbers of single women began migrating to western Europe independently of households and male migrants. Like men, they worked in order to send money back home.

Before 1973 most countries in western Europe, including Great Britain, actively encouraged foreign labor. After that date restrictions became the order of the day. Western governments enforced new conservative policies throughout the 1970s and 1980s aimed at keeping out third-world refugees. Opposition to the presence of foreign workers was often expressed in an ultranationalist rhetoric and usually flared up in periods of economic reversals.

In 1986 in France the xenophobic National Front campaigned on a platform of "France for the French" and captured 10 percent of the vote in national elections. In 1992 the same party garnered 16 percent of the vote in regional elections. Racism was out in the open in Western countries that had depended on a foreign labor force for their prosperity. Riots in Great Britain in 1980 and 1981, particularly in the London ghetto of Brixton, were motivated by racial discrimination against blacks, severe cuts in social welfare spending, and deteriorating working conditions.

On the whole, restrictions failed to achieve what they set out to do— remove foreign workers from Western countries by repatriation. Foreign workers in West Germany learned to get around the restrictions and sent for their families to join them. British laws also had the effect of converting temporary migration by single men into permanent family migrations. In 1977 foreign workers in France were offered cash incentives to encourage them to return to their home countries, but all to little avail.

By the end of the 1970s there were ten million foreign workers settled in Europe. Their presence heightened racism and overt antagonism from a resurgent extreme Right. At the moment in the late 1980s when movements for democratic freedom and human rights were being endorsed in eastern Europe, the problem of permanent resident "aliens" was without a solution in western Europe.

Women's Changing Lives

During the last quarter of the twentieth century, the lives of Western women reflected dramatic social changes. Women were more educated than ever before. Access to institutions of higher learning and professional schools allowed women to participate in the work force in the areas of education, law, medicine, and business throughout the world, whether it was in France, the United States, or the Soviet Union. Women had been active in the politics of liberation of peoples in the 1960s. These activities served to heighten their collective awareness of the disparities between their own situations and the role of men in Western societies: Women worked at home without pay; in the workplace women received less than men for the same work.

In this period of increased educational and work opportunities, an international women's movement emerged. International conferences about issues related to women were media events in the 1970s. In 1975 the United Nations Conference on the Decade for Women was convened in Mexico City. On 8 March 1976—International Women's Day—the International Tribunal of Crimes Against Women was convened in Brussels. Modeling the Brussels conference on tribunals like the Nuremberg Commission, which dealt with Nazi atrocities in World War II, feminists from all over the world concentrated on crimes against women for the purpose of promoting greater political awareness and action. Fertility and sexuality were at the center of the new politics of the women's movement, justified in the slogan "The personal is political." Rape and abortion were problems of international concern. "Sisterhood is powerful!" gave way to a new organizing cry that "International sisterhood is more powerful!"

In Italy women's political action resulted in a new law in 1970 that allowed divorce under very restricted circumstances. Italian feminists used the legal system as a public forum. In France the sale of contraceptives was legalized in 1968. French feminists, like their Italian counterparts, worked through the courts to make abortion legal: They achieved their goal in 1975.

The feminist movement also created a new feminist scholarship that incorporated women's experiences and perspectives into the disciplines of history, humanities, and the social sciences. Women's studies courses, which emphasized the history of women and their contributions to civilization, became part of university and college curricula throughout Europe and the United States. Reformers also attempted to transform language, which, they argued, had served as a tool of oppression.

Issues of domestic violence, incest, and heterosexuality entered the political arena. In 1970 Western feminism was discovering that "socialism was not enough," and that women had to address problems of discrimination in terms of gender as much as class. Debates over sexual oppression radicalized the movement, as lesbian separatists rejected men as the enemy. Separatism provoked a rift in the women's movement. Feminists continued to be politically active in the 1970s and 1980s in the peace movement, antinuclear protests, and in ecological groups concerned with protecting the environment.

The women's movement recognized that women in socialist and capitalist countries alike shared similar problems. An awakening concern among Soviet women resulted in reforms and the creation of a women's protest literature in the 1970s. Most Soviet women, however, rejected feminism as a political movement. In spite of greater professional and political participation, women enjoyed little real authority in the higher echelons of political life. Soviet women enjoyed more representation in parliamentary bodies than women in the West. More than half of the 2.3 million deputies to the local soviets in the 1980s were women. One-third of the 1500 members of the Supreme Soviet were women. Gorbachev appointed a woman as one of the twelve Central Committee secretaries—the most politically influential people in the USSR.

The same pattern held true for Soviet women in the work force. Over 85 percent of Soviet women worked, compared to about 60 percent of women in the West. Seventy percent of doctors and 73 percent of teachers were women, but women held few positions of authority. Both their pay and status were lower than men's as the example of primary school teaching reveals: 80 percent of primary school teachers were women but two out of three head teachers were men. Unlike Western women, many Soviet women—two out of three on average, according to censuses in the 1970s—performed heavy manual labor. In her doctoral dissertation on the sociology of the rural village of Stavropol, Raisa Gorbachev, wife of the Soviet leader, argued that while men were trained to run machines and tractors, women were expected more and more to perform the heavy physical labor associated with farm work.

Birthrates fell in the Soviet Union as in Western countries. Technology had made controlled fertility possible in safer, more dependable ways. Reliable birth control devices, however, remained unavailable to Soviet women. Abortion continued to be a common form of birth control in the Soviet Union, with two abortions for every live birth. Women were also choosing to have their children later, often because of work and financial considerations, with a growing percentage delaying childbearing until their thirties.

In the late 1980s, Soviet president Gorbachev made direct appeals for women's support by promising preschool nurseries and kindergartens for every child. Gorbachev also committed himself to support increased sick leave for mothers of sick children, paid maternity leave for a period of 18 months, increased child-care allowances, and shorter workdays for women who work at home. In support of women's voice in the workplace, women's councils were to be revived.

Women's work experience in the East and the West varied in degree, but a startlingly similar pattern of home and work life prevailed in the late twentieth century. Neither state institutions nor the law met the needs of women.

Terrorism and Contemporary Society

Terrorism persisted as a force of political violence in the second half of the twentieth century. The Middle East, Latin America, Africa, and Asia all witnessed growing terrorist opposition to enemies described as imperialists and colonizers. The creation of Israel in 1948 affected the territory of four Middle Eastern nations—Palestine, Jordan, Egypt, and Syria. Israel became the target of terrorist opposition among the Palestinian dispossessed. Having lost all of their territory by 1967, Palestinian guerrillas decided that the best way to attack Israel and its protectors was with a global strategy of terrorist violence.

The first Palestinian highjacking took place in the summer of 1968. Ejected from Jordan, Palestinian guerrillas set up their headquarters in Syria and Lebanon in order to continue their terrorist activities. By the late 1970s terrorism appealed to European revolutionaries, and terrorist activity intensified with political killings in western Europe. A small group of left-wing radicals known as the Red Army Faction executed key industrial, financial, and judicial leaders in West Germany. The Red Army Faction was also responsible for a number of bombings, including that of the West German embassy in Stockholm. In Italy a small group known as the Red Brigades was responsible for violent incidents, including the "kneecapping"—permanently crippling people by shooting them in the knees—of leading Italian businessmen and the kidnapping and murder of the former Italian prime minister Aldo Moro. In 1981 the Red Brigades targeted the United States for their terrorist reprisals when they abducted an American general, James Dozier.

Terrorism was politically motivated violence performed by groups claiming to represent some greater political cause. Victims were targeted by terrorists not because they merited any punishment themselves but as a means of attracting international attention to the terrorists' cause. Although motivated by different political agendas, terrorist groups often formed cooperative networks on an international basis, sharing training, weapons, and information.

Western Europe served as an important arena for terrorist acts. In order to succeed—that is, to terrify—terrorism had to be publicized: Terrorists relied on media exposure and claimed responsibility for their acts after they had been successfully completed. In September 1972 members of the Palestinian Black September movement kidnapped 11 Israeli athletes at the Olympic Games in Munich. An estimated five hundred million people watched in horror as all 11 were slaughtered during an American sports broadcast. In a dramatic televised shoot-out five of the terrorists also died. Later in the decade OPEC oil ministers were held hostage in Vienna.

A recurrent pattern of terrorism prevailed throughout the 1980s, highlighted by international media coverage. In 1981 a Turkish fascist attempted to kill the pope. In 1983 a Lebanese Shi'ite guerrilla blew up the American marine garrison in Beirut, taking hundreds of American lives along with his own. In October 1985 the cruise ship *Achille Lauro* was highjacked by a Palestinian ultranationalist group. One aged American passenger, confined to a wheelchair, was killed. In 1985 Palestinian terrorists bombed the airports in Vienna and Rome.

The Provisional Wing of the Irish Republican Army justified its bombing of

A hooded Arab terrorist stands on a balcony during the attack on the Israeli Olympic team headquarters at the Munich Olympics in 1972.

Christmas crowds in London with the need to unite Northern Ireland with the independent Irish Republic. Resistance fighters in World War II had used bombs and assassinations as their means of fighting a more powerful enemy. Seeing themselves engaged in wars of liberation, revolution, and resistance, terrorists argued that they used the only weapons at their disposal against the great imperialist powers: Plastic explosives in suitcases, nearly impossible to detect by available technology in the 1980s, became the weapon of choice. If all was fair in war—and World War II demonstrated that both sides bombed innocent civilian victims in pursuit of victory—then, terrorists countered, they were fighting the war with the only weapons and in the only arena at their disposal.

By the 1990s terrorism was challenging the tranquility of Western capitalist nations in effective ways. One reason for terrorism's success was the vulnerability of advanced industrial societies to random terror. Modern terrorists were able to evade policing and detection. Surveillance has not prevented terrorists from striking at airplanes and cruise ships. In December 1988 hundreds of people died when a Pan American flight was bombed over Lockerbie, Scotland, probably in retaliation for the downing of an Iranian passenger airliner by the U.S. Navy in the Persian Gulf. Yet terrorism accomplished little by way of bringing about political change or solutions to problems like the question of a Palestinian homeland in the Middle East.

West European governments often refused to bargain with terrorists. Yet at times European nations have been willing to negotiate for the release of kidnapped citizens. They have also been willing to use violence themselves against terrorists. Israel led the way in creating antiterror squads. In 1976 Israeli commandos succeeded in freeing captives in Entebbe in Uganda. The following year specially trained West German troops freed Lufthansa passengers and crew held hostage at Mogadishu in Somalia on the east coast of Africa. The Arab kidnappers had hoped to bargain for the release of the imprisoned leaders of the Red Army Faction; the West German government refused. In 1986 the United States bombed Libya, long recognized as a training ground for international terrorist recruits, in retaliation for the bombing of a discotheque frequented by American service personnel in West Germany. Israel bombed refugee camps to retaliate against Palestinian nationalists. The goal of this "counterterrorism" was the undermining of support for terrorists among their own people, which made it very similar in tactics and ends to the terrorism it was opposing.

Toward a United Europe

In 1957 the founders of the European Economic Community, Robert Schuman and Jean Monnet, envisioned the idea of a United States of Europe. Both men perceived that Europe's only hope of competing in a new world system was through unity. The European Community was created in 1967 by merging the three transnational European bodies—the European Coal and Steel Community, the European Economic Community or Common Market, and Euratom. It operated with its own commission, parliament, and council of ministers, although it had little real power over the operations of member states. In 1974 a "European Council" was created within the European Community, made up of heads of government who met three times a year for the purpose of furthering European integration.

The oil crisis of the 1970s encouraged isolationism among the members of the EEC and eroded foreign markets, with growing dependence on national suppliers. As the crisis abated, competition and efficiency reemerged as priorities within the European Community. Europeans were well aware that the United States and Japan had surged ahead after the 1973 crisis. They also recognized that the Common Market had been successful in promoting European growth and integration since 1958. They now realized that integration was the only defense against the permanent loss of markets and dwindling profits. In unity there was strength, as the aggregate economic indicators for 1987 made clear.

In 1985 the European Community negotiated the Single European Act, which was ratified by the parliamentary bodies of the member nations by 1987. Final steps were initiated to establish a fully integrated market beginning at midnight on 31 December 1992. The 12 members of the European Community intended to eliminate internal barriers and to create a huge open market among the member states with common external tariff policies. In addition, the elimination of internal frontier controls, with a single-format European

Community passport was intended to make travel easier and to avoid shipping delays at frontiers, thereby lowering costs. An international labor market based on standardized requirements for certification and interchangeable job qualifications would result. The easier movement of capital was encouraged to areas where profitability was greatest. All aspects of trade and communication, down to electrical plugs and sockets, had to be standardized. The goal behind the planning for 1992 was to make the European Community think and act as a single country. Supporters compared it to the 50 individual American states participating in the single U.S. nation.

In 1989 there were 320 million European citizens of the 12 countries of the European Community: The original Common Market six of France, West Germany, Belgium, the Netherlands, Luxembourg, and Italy were joined by Britain, Denmark, and Ireland in 1973, Greece in 1981, and Portugal and Spain in 1986. Plans for European economic integration moved dramatically forward in October 1991 when the 12-nation European Community and the 7 nations of the European Free Trade Association (EFTA) joined forces to form a new common market to be known as the European Economic Area. The EFTA countries that joined forces with the EC include Austria, Finland, Iceland, Liechtenstein, Norway, Sweden, and Switzerland. Several of the EFTA nations announced plans to join the EC as well. The European Economic Area constituted the world's largest trading bloc, stretching from the Arctic Circle to the Mediterranean and consisting of around 380 million consumers. The nations of the EFTA agreed to abide by the EC's plans for economic integration and adopted the vast array of laws and regulations that governed the European Community.

The European Community plan has had at its core the adoption of a single currency (based on the European Currency Unit, or ECU) by the member nations. Meeting in Maastricht, the Netherlands, in December 1991, the heads of the 12 EC countries agreed that a common currency, the ECU, would replace the national currencies of eligible nations as early as 1997 and no later than 1999. A single central banking system, known as the European Monetary Institute, would begin operations on 1 January 1994, for the purpose of guiding member nations in reducing inflation rates and budget deficits. Economic union would be reinforced by political union, as members states agreed to a common European defense system and common social policies regulating immigration and labor practices. At the end of 1988 President François Mitterrand of France endorsed the goals of the 1992 integration: "One currency, one culture, one social area, one environment." Many worried, however, that the long histories, traditions, and national identifications of the individual member states would stand in the way of a fully integrated Europe.

Britain was the most reluctant of the member states at the prospect of European integration. British negotiators strongly resisted plans for monetary union because of fear of losing national sovereignty rights. Nonetheless, Prime Minister Margaret Thatcher and her successor John Major solidly committed Great Britain to the European Community. As Thatcher explained it, "Britain does not dream of an alternative to the European Community, of some cozy isolated existence on its fringes. Our destiny is in Europe, as part of the Community." In addition to resisting monetary union, the British also expressed cynicism at the 1991 Maastricht negotiations over a Europe-wide social policy affecting working hours, minimum wages, and conditions of employment.

Some planners were wary about the prospect of including all of eastern Europe, whose troubled economies, they feared, would dilute the economic strength of the European Community. Others predicted a fully integrated Europe, including the eastern European nations, by the year 2014. Three of the new regimes—Poland, Czechoslovakia, and Hungary—were admitted with the status of associate members.

The plan for a single European market affected more than just economics. Education, too, faced standardization of curricula and requirements for degrees. There were proposals for a common European history textbook that, in place of national perspectives, would emphasize the values of a single political entity in its discussion of battles, wars, social change, and culture.

Export-producing nations, including Japan and the United States, expressed concerns over "Fortress Europe," that is, Europe as a global trading bloc with a common external tariff policy that would exclude them. A united Europe would constitute a formidable presence in the world arena with the world's largest volume of trade and highest productivity. The move might easily place Europe at the center of world politics, as the Cold War thawed and

Europe Community, 1992

the bloc politics of East versus West no longer dominated the international system.

Nationalist feelings were intensifying within eastern Europe at the very moment integration accelerated in the West. Demand for autonomy lay behind the revolutionary events in Poland, the Baltic Soviet states, Hungary, Bulgaria, and Romania. Meanwhile in western Europe, planners spoke of a European Community in which national differences would be muted for the common good. Europeans were assured that the federal solution would preserve national identities, culture, and language, and that the new federal government would make only those decisions not better made on the local and regional levels.

At the end of the twentieth century Western women and men faced the future filled with uncertainty. Jacques Delors, president of the European Community's Executive Commission, stated simply, "I don't want to live in a Europe that is like it was in 1914." Commentators warned of new nationalist conflicts on the horizon. Social change threatened to wither without producing fruit, as governments cut free of the security of old ways grappled with new political challenges and economic chaos. Yet there was hope, too, as Europe's leaders spoke of a common European destiny for communist and democratic nations who had once been enemies. On Christmas morning 1989, an international orchestra led by the American conductor Leonard Bernstein gathered at the Berlin Wall to celebrate the new era that seemed to be dawning in Europe. For the event, Bernstein chose Beethoven's Ninth Symphony, "Ode to Joy," which he took the liberty of recasting as "Ode to Freedom." The symphony rang out as an anthem for the aspirations of Europeans facing the twenty-first century.

Suggestions for Further Reading

Ending the Cold War

*Patrick Cockburn, *Getting Russia Wrong: The End of Kremlinology* (London: Verso, 1989). A Moscow correspondent takes the measure of the politics of the Gorbachev era, while attempting to uncover the shortcomings of Western misconceptions about the Soviet Union.

*Stephen E. Cohen, *Rethinking the Soviet Experience: Politics and History Since 1917* (New York: Oxford University Press, 1985). Offers a revisionist analysis of the historiographical debates in Soviet studies with the intention of casting light on contemporary Soviet politics.

Geoffrey Hosking, *The Awakening of the Soviet Union* (Cambridge, MA: Harvard University Press, 1990). Published in the midst of the dramatic changes taking place in

*Indicates paperback edition available.

the Soviet Union, this study emphasizes the social bases of reform and the challenges to Soviet leadership.

*Brian McNair, *Images of the Enemy: Reporting the New Cold War* (London: Routledge, 1988). Focuses on the importance of television in conveying the East-West debate to a mass audience in the 1980s. McNair demonstrates that the Soviets learned in the 1980s to manage communication techniques to their own advantage.

*Adam B. Ulam, *Dangerous Relations: The Soviet Union in World Politics, 1970–1982* (New York: Oxford University Press, 1983). Discusses the making of détente and the relationship between internal developments in the Soviet Union and their impact on foreign policy.

Eastern and Central Europe Since 1968

*Teresa Rakowska-Harmstone and Andrew Gyorgy, eds., *Communism in Eastern Europe* (Manchester, England: Manchester University Press, 1984). Provides a comprehensive country-by-country approach with consideration of nationalism and shared regional problems.

*Joseph Rothschild, *Return to Diversity: A Political History of East Central Europe* (New York: Oxford University Press, 1989). A historical and analytical survey of Poland, Czechoslovakia, Hungary, Yugoslavia, Romania, Bulgaria, and Albania that appeared just before the great changes which swept eastern Europe in 1989. Rothschild highlights the tensions between nationalist aspirations and communist rule.

Henry Ashby Turner, Jr., *The Two Germanies Since 1945* (New Haven, CT: Yale University Press, 1987). A political history from the postwar division of Germany until 1987, which bridges a period that the author contends was one of increasing involvement and underlying mutual interests between the two nations.

Unity and Diversity in Western Europe

*J. Bowyer Bell, *Transnational Terror* (Washington, DC: American Enterprise Institute, 1975). Presents a compelling argument about the social revolutionary origins of terror and its threat to Western democracies.

*Richard Clutterbuck, *Guerrillas and Terrorists* (London: Faber and Faber, 1977). Clutterbuck considers terrorism as a kind of war rooted in historical experience and global in nature. His purpose is to consider protection against terrorists by examining the roles of the media, the police, and the public.

*Michael Emerson, et al., *The Economics of 1992: The E.C. Commission's Assessment of the Economic Effects of Completing the Internal Market* (Oxford, England: Oxford University Press, 1988). A work replete with empirical data that gives a comprehensive assessment of the potential impact of establishing a single internal market in the European Economic Community.

Wolfgang Mommsen and Gerhard Hirschfeld, eds., *Social Protest, Violence and Terror in Nineteenth- and Twentieth-Century Europe* (London: MacMillan Press, 1982). Places terrorism within a historical context in Europe over the last century and a half in a series of articles that proceed with a national case history approach.

Richard E. Rubinstein, *Alchemists of Revolution: Terrorism in the Modern World* (New York: Basic, 1987). Examines the local root causes of terrorism in historical perspective and argues that it is a social and moral crisis of a disaffected intelligentsia.

Photo Credits

Unless otherwise acknowledged, all photographs are the property of ScottForesman.

CHAPTER 1
3 Europe photographed from space. European Space Agency 6 © Kazuyoshi Nomachi/Pacific Press Service 8 Kathleen M. Kenyon/Jericho Excavations 13 Hirmer Fotoarchiv, Munich 16 Hirmer Fotoarchiv, Munich 21 Hirmer Fotoarchiv, Munich 24 The Metropolitan Museum of Art, Rogers Fund, 1931 (31.3.157) 29 Erich Lessing/Art Resource, NY

CHAPTER 2
37 *Achilles Dragging the Body of Hector around the Walls of Troy.* Attic black-figured water jar, c. 510 B.C. William Francis Warden Fund. Courtesy, Museum of Fine Arts, Boston 40 The Metropolitan Museum of Art, Rogers Fund, 1947 (47.100.1) 41 Hirmer Fotoarchiv, Munich 47 Reproduced by Courtesy of the Trustees of the British Museum 54 Scala/Art Resource, NY 55 (top left, bottom) Hirmer Fotoarchiv, Munich; (top right) The Metropolitan Museum of Art, Fletcher Fund, 1932 (32.11.1) 63 Wadsworth Atheneum, Hartford. J. P. Morgan Collection. © Wadsworth Atheneum

CHAPTER 3
69 *Battle of Issus.* Mosaic copy of a Hellenistic painting. Alinari/Art Resource, NY 72 American School of Classical Studies at Athens: Agora Excavations 86 The Metropolitan Museum of Art, Rogers Fund, 1952 (52.11.4) 87 Robert Frerck/Odyssey Productions, Chicago

CHAPTER 4
103 The Roman Forum. Istituto Geografico de Agostini, Milan. Photo: A. De Gregorio 110 Hirmer Fotoarchiv, Munich 118 Alinari/Art Resource, NY 126 Alinari/Art Resource, NY 127 The Metropolitan Museum of Art 132 Römisch-Germanisches Zentralmuseum, Mainz 140 Roger-Viollet

CHAPTER 5
147 Barbarian medallion (front and back) of Valentinian I and Valens. (both) Hirmer Fotoarchiv, Munich 148 Scala/Art Resource, NY 157 Alinari/Art Resource, NY 167 Bibliothèque Nationale, Paris 171 Alinari/Art Resource, NY 179 Vatican Museums 186 © Photo R.M.N.

CHAPTER 6
191 Courtyard, the Great Mosque, Damascus. Hubertus Kanus/SuperStock 194 Hirmer Fotoarchiv, Munich 196 Reproduced by Courtesy of the Trustees of the British Museum 204 Courtesy of the Freer Gallery of Art, Smithsonian Institution, Washington, D. C. (30.60) 206 Bibliothèque Nationale, Paris 215 The Metropolitan Museum of Art, Bequest of Edward C. Moore, 1891 (91.1.535)

CHAPTER 7
225 Interior of the Palatine Chapel, Aachen. Domkapitel Aachen. Photo: Ann Münchow 231 The British Library 234 Österreichische Nationalbibliothek, Vienna 243 The Board of Trinity College Dublin 254 Bridgeman/Art Resource, NY 258 Giraudon/Art Resource, NY 262 Bodleian Library, University of Oxford. MS. Bodley 264, fol. 218r

CHAPTER 8
275 Details of the *Bayeux Tapestry,* c. 1073–1083. (both) Giraudon/Art Resource, NY 294 Giraudon/Art Resource, NY 303 Bibliothèque Nationale, Paris 306 The Metropolitan Museum of Art, The Cloisters Collection, 1969 (69.86) 312 University Library, Prague

CHAPTER 9
321 *The Procession of the Relic of the Holy Cross* by Gentile Bellini, 1496. Alinari/Art Resource, NY 326 Alinari/Art Resource, NY 333 Alinari/Art Resource, NY 334 Alinari/Art Resource, NY 335 Alinari/Art Resource, NY 336 Alinari/Art Resource, NY

CHAPTER 10

355 Map of the world from Ptolemy's *Geography*, Ulm, 1486. Michael Holford 359 Library of Congress 375 Thyssen-Bornemisza Collection

CHAPTER 11

389 The Gutenberg Bible. Library of Congress 398 Courtesy of the Fogg Art Museum, Harvard University, Cambridge, Massachusetts, Gift of Meta and Paul J. Sachs 402 Giraudon/Art Resource, NY 407 Photo François Martin, Genève. Document BPU

CHAPTER 12

423 *Haymaking* by Pieter Bruegel the Elder, 1565. National Gallery, Prague 425 Scala/Art Resource, NY 433 © Photo R.M.N. 440 Rijksmuseum Amsterdam 449 Bridgeman/Art Resource, NY 452 Kunsthistorisches Museum, Vienna

CHAPTER 13

457 *Massacre of the Innocents* by Nicolas Poussin. Musée Condé, Chantilly/Giraudon/Art Resource, NY 471 Musée de Strasbourg 479 Reproduced by courtesy of the Trustees, The National Gallery, London 483 The Bettmann Archive 491 © Photo R.M.N. 495 National Maritime Museum London

CHAPTER 14

507 *Das Flötenkonzert* by Adolph von Menzel, 1850–1852. Staatliche Museen Preussischer Kulturbesitz, Nationalgalerie, Berlin. Photo: Jörg P. Anders 513 Central Naval Museum, St. Petersburg 525 Kunsthistorisches Museum, Vienna

CHAPTER 15

541 *The Anatomy Lesson of Dr. Nicolaes Tulp* by Rembrandt van Rijn, 1632. © Mauritshuis, The Hague 544 The British Library 552 Brown Brothers 553 Giraudon/Art Resource, NY 555 Scottish National Portrait Gallery 566 Scala/Art Resource, NY 574 Alinari/Art Resource, NY 576 The Metropolitan Museum of Art, Harris Brisbane Dick Fund, 1932 (32.35(129))

CHAPTER 16

581 *Marie Antoinette à la Rose* by Elisabeth Vigée-Lebrun. Bulloz 594 Bulloz 596 Bulloz 598 Bulloz 610 Bulloz 613 Musée des Beaux-Arts, Rouen

CHAPTER 17

619 *Saint-Lazare Train Station, the Normandy Train (La Gare Saint-Lazare, le train de Normandie)* by Claude Monet, 1877, oil on canvas, 59.6 x 80.2 cm. Mr. and Mrs. Martin A. Ryerson Collection, 1933.1158. Photograph © 1992, The Art Institute of Chicago. All Rights Reserved. 623 Reproduced by Courtesy of the Trustees of the British Museum 634 Museum of American Textile History 645 Bulloz 651 Free Library of Philadelphia 652 Bridgeman/Art Resource, NY

CHAPTER 18

657 *Potato Planters* by Jean François Millet. Gift of Quincy Adams Shaw through Quincy A. Shaw, Jr. and Mrs. Marian Shaw Haughton. Courtesy, Museum of Fine Arts, Boston 665 The Royal Collection. Copyright Reserved to Her Majesty Queen Elizabeth II 668 Reproduced by Courtesy of the Trustees of the British Museum 677 Historisches Museum der Stadt Wien 690 The Master and Fellows of Trinity College, Cambridge

CHAPTER 19

699 *Riot in the Galleria* by Umberto Boccioni, 1910. Bridgeman/Art Resource, NY 708 Bibliothèque Nationale, Paris 710 Museum of London 726 National Portrait Gallery, London 728 Reproduced by Courtesy of the Trustees of the British Museum

CHAPTER 20

739 *Take Up the Sword of Justice* by Sir Bernard J. Partridge, England, 1915. From copy in Bowman Gray Collection, Rare Book Collection, UNC Library, Chapel Hill, North Carolina 748 UPI/Bettmann 750 Imperial War Museum, London 752 Imperial War Museum, London 760 Imperial War Museum, London 769 Novosti

Index